FROMMER'S

ENGLAND & SCOTLAND ON $25 A DAY

by Darwin Porter

1984-85 Edition

Published by Frommer/Pasmantier Publishers
A Division of Simon & Schuster, Inc.
1230 Avenue of the Americas
New York, New York 10020

ISBN 0-671-46789-1

Manufactured in the United States of America

CONTENTS

MAPS

To Stanley Haggart

Acknowledgment

We gratefully acknowledge the field research of Peter and Caryl Barnes and the editorial assistance of Margaret Foresman. We are also indebted to Danforth Prince for his help.

A Disclaimer

Although every effort was made to ensure the accuracy of the prices and travel information appearing in this book, it should be kept in mind that prices do fluctuate in the course of time, and that information does change under the impact of the varied and volatile factors that affect the travel industry.

Readers should also note that the establishments described under Readers' Selections or Suggestions have not in many cases been inspected by the author and that the opinions expressed there are those of the individual reader(s) only. They do not in any way represent the opinions of the publisher or author of this guide.

Britain's VAT

On June 18, 1979, Great Britain raised its standard Value Added Tax (called VAT for short) from 8% to 15%. Most Common Market countries already have a tax similar to VAT (France, for example, a paralyzing 23%). In Britain, hotel rates and meals in restaurants are now taxed 15%. This extra VAT charge will show up on your bill unless otherwise stated. It is in addition to the service charge. Should the service charge be 15%, you will, in effect, be paying 30% higher than the prices quoted. The service charges, if included as part of the bill, are also taxable!

As part of an energy-saving scheme, the British government has also added a special 25% tax on gasoline ("petrol")!

Introduction

ENGLAND AND SCOTLAND ON $25 A DAY

The Reason Why

THE AIM OF THIS BOOK is to bring you closer to the heart of England and Scotland.

In the pages that follow, I'll invite you to live—among other places—in a timbered, 17th-century home one hour from London; to sleep in a four-poster wooden bed; to enjoy festive, multicourse meals while seated at a polished black oak refectory table before a 15-foot-wide fireplace in which cherry logs burn brightly.

I'll take you to the cottage of a Scottish sea captain where you can experience genial country hospitality and hear tales of the deep—or to a hillside farm, perched on a wild moor, where you'll be served a four o'clock tea accompanied by home-churned butter and crusty bread, warm from the oven, and thick cream piled high on a bowl of tiny strawberries that you yourself have just picked in a nearby field.

Such experiences as these have two characteristics in common: they represent the best way to live in England and Scotland—and they are inexpensive. For the inns, guest houses, and restaurants recommended in this book are those designed for and primarily patronized by Britishers, whose average wage is far below the North American standard. Prices at the establishments recommended in this guide are therefore low to moderate in terms of the U.S. dollar.

You'll be taken to pubs dating back to the days of Shakespeare and Queen Elizabeth I that offer complete luncheons for £5 ($8.75). You'll be guided deep into the English countryside to a stone manor house which stands proudly at the end of an avenue of old trees. Here, for only £12 ($21) daily, you'll receive bed, breakfast, and a four-course evening dinner.

The budget details start in just a few pages. First, I'll outline the order of our discussion, then tell you a bit about the $25-a-day limit I've placed on basic expenditures.

THE ORGANIZATION OF THIS BOOK: Here's how *England and Scotland on $25 a Day* sets forth its information:

Chapter I, directly ahead, deals with getting to England and Scotland—mainly by air—and then with the various modes of transportation within these countries. Naturally, our focus is on the least expensive means of transport—on such items as excursion fares and off-season discounts. The chapter also includes some vital data on the ABCs of life in Britain that will help ease your adjustment into that country.

Chapters II through IV turn the spotlight on London, documenting first the budget hotels, then the restaurants, pubs, and wine bars, concluding with data on the major sights (including my personal list of the Top Ten), shopping bargains, inexpensive nightlife, and one-day trips within Greater London.

Chapter V explores some of the most history-rich sights within easy reach of London: Windsor Castle, Woburn Abbey, and the university city of Oxford.

Chapters VI through IX move away from London to the south of England: Kent, Surrey, Sussex, then Hampshire and Dorset (Thomas Hardy country), followed by "The West"—Cornwall, Devon, Wiltshire, Somerset, and Avon. Here you'll find my descriptions of inexpensive thatched cottages, hillside farms, and Elizabethan manor houses, which you can use for exploring this varied English countryside.

Chapters X and XI do the same with respect to the most tourist-trodden district of England, the Shakespeare Country, and the sleepy hamlets of the Cotswolds.

Chapter XII focuses on some less-visited, magnificent, points for exploration—East Anglia (Cambridge, of course, but also Ely, Norwich, the fen and broads country), and the pink villages of Suffolk.

Chapter XIII cuts through unknown England, ferreting out the attractions of the East Midlands, including the cathedral city of Lincoln.

Chapters XIV and XV travel across the entire northern sweep of England, from the wilds of Northumbria to the cathedral city of York, to Liverpool and Cheshire, all the way to the beautiful Lake District, immortalized by the poets.

Chapters XVI through XIX journey to Britain's second half, Scotland, visiting the gentle Lowlands, the rugged Highlands, and such historic islands as Skye, Mull, and Iona of the Inner Hebrides. You'll find budget accommodations described and also tips on sightseeing and some of the best pubs to visit from Edinburgh to Inverness and Aviemore to Glasgow.

$25 A DAY—WHAT THAT MEANS: You can live in England and Scotland on a number of price levels. The unknowing can lavish huge sums on sterile holidays, but comfort and charm are not necessarily priced so high at all. I aim to establish that fact by showing you exactly what you can get for $25 a day.

The specific aim of this book—as it is in all its companion books—is to show you clearly how to keep *basic living costs* (room and three meals a day) down to $25 per person per day. There is nothing gimmicky about this goal, as readers of my other books have found. Since the cost of entertainment, sightseeing, shopping, and transportation is all *in addition* to that basic $25-a-day figure, I prescribe reasonable standards for the budget-minded.

Half of this book is devoted to recommendations for comfortable rooms and well-prepared meals—within a $25-a-day budget. You'll find comfortable rooms in London and in the country, usually with innerspring mattresses and almost always with hot and cold running water. None of the rooms in this price bracket, unless otherwise stated, has a private bath.

The $25-a-day budget roughly breaks down this way—$15 per person (based on double occupancy) for a room and breakfast, $4 for lunch, and $6 for dinner.

You'll note also that I do include in these pages recommendations above our allowances—to enable you a wider range of choices where few budget establishments are available and also to give you opportunities for a good old-fashioned splurge.

Many of the accommodations recommended were chosen because of a unique historical, cultural, or architectural feature that gives them special value. This is truer for the country than it is for London, where the $25-a-day hotels were selected more for their facilities, comfort, and conveniences than for any spectacular charm. Almost no London hotels can compare favorably with their countryside counterparts.

THE SOUL OF BRITAIN: A word, now, about the nonmonetary standards I've followed in seeking hotel, restaurant, and pub selections.

This book has *not* been written for the North American who likes only the expensive and the gaudy, who goes through Europe rudely demanding "a room, a private bath, and a good cuppa coffee." It is, rather, for those who want to experience the land's true charm, traditions, and food, and who hope to make new friends.

In my search for people and places to share with you, I am more interested in the goodness of the human spirit than in bathrooms. Of course, I like modern plumbing, steam heat, and elevators, but I have never made these things my gods. I value charm, the artful touch of creative people who have dared assert their individuality, who scorn the ordinary and show a respect for the good things of life. I am attracted by personal gestures, such as a proudly made deep-dish apple pie or wood surfaces scrubbed clean with years of loving care or the smile of a hostess who is sincerely concerned with her guests' welfare.

SOME DISCLAIMERS: No restaurant, inn, hotel, guest house, or shop paid to be mentioned in this book. What you read are entirely personal recommendations—in many cases, proprietors never knew that their establishments were being visited or investigated for inclusion in a travel guide.

A word of warning: Unfortunately, prices change, and they rarely go downward. England and Scotland have no governmental control of hotel prices, as is the practice in countries such as Spain. "Mine host" can charge a guest anything he or she "bloody well chooses." Competition is what keeps the rate down. Always, when checking into a hotel or guest house, inquire about the price and agree on it. This can save much embarrassment and disappointment when it comes time to settle the tab.

Hotel owners sometimes complain that $25-a-day'ers have arrived at their establishments and demanded to be charged prices quoted in an earlier edition of this guide. Your chances of pulling off this stunt are about as good as they would be in the United States. *England and Scotland on $25 a Day* is revised every other year at considerable expense, involving not only travel research but heavy typesetting and printing costs. It is foolish economy to travel with a copy that your brother-in-law and his wife used on their trip abroad some years ago. That cozy little family dining room of a year ago can change colors, blossoming out with cut-velvet walls and dining tabs that include the decorator's fee and the owner's new Bentley.

Finally, even in a book revised frequently, it may develop that some of the people, animals, or settings I've described are no longer there. Viennese chefs have nervous breakdowns, red-cheeked English maids elope with charming Italians, overstuffed sofas are junked in favor of streamlined modern ones, and 19-year-old dogs go to heaven—so any and all of these things may be different. But while people, dogs, and sofas come and go, many of the old inns and pubs recommended have weathered the centuries intact, and barring war, fire, or flood, should be standing proudly to greet you on your visit.

The $25-a-Day Travel Club—How to Save Money on All Your Travels

In this book we'll be looking at how to get your money's worth in England and Scotland, but there is a "device" for saving money and determining value on *all* your trips. It's the popular, international $25-a-Day Travel Club, now in its 21st successful year of operation. The Club was formed at the urging of numerous readers of the $$$-a-Day and Dollarwise Guides, who felt that such an organization could provide continuing travel information and a sense of community to value-minded travelers in all parts of the world. And so it does!

In keeping with the budget concept, the membership fee is low and is immediately exceeded by the value of your benefits. Upon receipt of $14 (U.S. residents), or $16 (Canadian, Mexican, and other foreign residents), by check drawn on a U.S. bank or via international postal money order in U.S. funds to cover one year's membership, we will send all new members, by return mail (book rate), the following items:

(1) The latest edition of *any two* of the following books (please designate in your letter which two you wish to receive):

Europe on $25 a Day
Australia on $25 a Day
England and Scotland on $25 a Day
Greece on $25 a Day
Hawaii on $35 a Day
Ireland on $25 a Day
Israel on $30 & $35 a Day
Mexico on $20 a Day
New Zealand on $20 & $25 a Day
Scandinavia on $25 a Day
South America on $25 a Day
Spain and Morocco (plus the Canary Is.) on $25 a Day
Washington, D.C. on $35 a Day

Dollarwise Guide to Canada
Dollarwise Guide to the Caribbean (including Bermuda and the Bahamas)
Dollarwise Guide to Egypt
Dollarwise Guide to England and Scotland
Dollarwise Guide to France
Dollarwise Guide to Germany
Dollarwise Guide to Italy
Dollarwise Guide to Portugal (plus Madeira and the Azores)
Dollarwise Guide to Switzerland (to be published March 1984)
Dollarwise Guide to California and Las Vegas
Dollarwise Guide to Florida

Dollarwise Guide to New England
Dollarwise Guide to the Southeast and New Orleans
(Dollarwise Guides discuss accommodations and facilities in all price ranges, with emphasis on the medium-priced.)

How to Beat the High Cost of Travel
(This practical guide details how to save money on absolutely all travel items—accommodations, transportation, dining, sightseeing, shopping, taxes, and more. Includes special budget information for seniors, students, singles, and families.)

The New York Urban Athlete
(The ultimate guide to all the sports facilities in New York City for jocks and novices.)

Museums in New York
(A complete guide to all the museums, historic houses, gardens, zoos, and more in the five boroughs. Illustrated with over 200 photographs.)

The Fast 'n' Easy Phrase Book
(The four most useful languages—French, German, Spanish, and Italian—all in one convenient, easy-to-use phrase guide.)

The Adventure Book
(From the Alps to the Arctic, from the Sahara to the southwest, this stunning four-color showcase features over 200 of the world's finest adventure travel trips.)

Where to Stay USA
(By the Council on International Educational Exchange, this extraordinary guide is the first to list accommodations in all 50 states that cost anywhere from $3 to $25 per night.)

A Guide for the Disabled Traveler
(A guide to the best destinations for wheelchair travelers and other disabled vacationers in Europe, the United States, and Canada by an experienced wheelchair traveler. Includes detailed information about accommodations, restaurants, sights, transportation, and their accessibility. [To be published March 1984.])

The Weekend Book
(This very selective guide covers the best mini-vacation destinations within a 175-mile radius of New York City. It describes special country inns and other accommodations, restaurants, picnic spots, sights, and activities—all the information needed for a two- or three-day stay. [To be published May 1984.])

(2) A one-year subscription to the quarterly eight-page tabloid newspaper—**The Wonderful World of Budget Travel**—which keeps you up to date on fast-breaking developments in low-cost travel in all parts of the world bringing you the latest money-saving information—the kind of information you'd have to pay $25 a year to obtain elsewhere. This consumer-conscious publication also provides special services to readers: **The Traveler's Directory** (a list of members all over the world who are willing to provide hospitality to other

members as they pass through their home cities); **Share-a-Trip** (offers and requests from members for travel companions who can share costs and help avoid the burdensome single supplement); and **Readers Ask. . . .Readers Reply** (travel questions from members to which other members reply with authentic firsthand information).

(3) A copy of **Arthur Frommer's Guide to New York,** a newly revised pocket-size guide to hotels, restaurants, nightspots, and sightseeing attractions in all price ranges throughout the New York area. (4) Your personal membership card which, once received, entitles you to purchase through the Club all Arthur Frommer publications *(including* the *Adventure Book* which is available to members at $7.50), for a third to a half off their regular retail prices during the term of your membership.

So why not join this hardy band of international budgeteers and participate in its exchange of travel information and hospitality? Simply send your name and address, together with your membership fee of $14 (U.S. residents) or $16 (Canadian, Mexican, and other foreign residents), by check drawn on a U.S. bank or via international postal money order in U.S. funds to: $25-A-Day Travel Club, Inc., Frommer/Pasmantier Publishers, 1230 Avenue of the Americas, New York, NY 10020. And please remember to specify which *two* of the books in section (1) above you wish to receive in your initial package of members' benefits. Or, if you prefer, use the last page of this book, simply checking off the two books you select and enclosing $14 or $16 in U.S. currency.

THE FUTURE OF THIS BOOK: Like all the books in this series, *England and Scotland on $25 a Day* hopes to maintain a continuing dialogue between its author and its readers. All of us share a common aim—to travel as widely and as well as possible, at the lowest possible cost. In achieving that goal, your comments and suggestions can be of aid to other readers. Therefore, if you come across a particularly appealing hotel, restaurant, shop, or bargain, please don't keep it to yourself. And this applies to any comments you may have about the existing listings. The fact that a hotel or restaurant is recommended in this edition doesn't mean that it will necessarily appear in future editions if readers report that its service has slipped or that its prices have risen too drastically. You have my word that each and every letter will be read by me personally, although I find it well-nigh impossible to *answer* each and every one. Be assured, however-I'm listening. Send your comments or finds to Darwin Porter, c/o Frommer/Pasmantier Publishers, 1230 Avenue of the Americas, New York, NY 10020.

Chapter I

GETTING THERE

1. Plane Economics
2. By Ship
3. The ABC's of Britain

PRESIDENT CARTER'S deregulation of the airline industry made world headlines in 1979, and ever since then any vestiges of simplicity and uniformity in price structures for transatlantic flights have disappeared.

Airlines now compete fiercely with one another, offering a confusing barrage of pricing systems and package deals, changing some of the public's preconceived ideas about the best available prices.

Travel agents laughingly refer to the masses of documentation they have received as "chaos." However, that can mean beneficial chaos to the alert traveler willing to study and consider all the choices available. The key to bargain airfares is to shop around.

1. Plane Economics

Latter-day pilgrims making the return trip to Britain will find the voyage a lot easier than their ancestors did, yet they will still have to overcome the hurdles of a complicated series of flight options. In what follows, I'll try to unravel the red tape of some attractive possibilities of air travel to Britain.

Please note that all fares appearing on these pages are those available at press time, and are subject to change and/or government approval. *Double-check all fares with the airline of your choice or your travel agent.*

Many charter flights exist to London with organizations which profit from group discounts. They are too numerous to describe here, and difficult to recommend because of the low capitalization of many of these companies and the changing legalities of the airline industry. Check with your travel agent for legitimate plans.

BRITISH AIRWAYS: The premier airline of the United Kingdom, British Airways has more flights into Britain than any other airline. It also offers a wide variety of domestic flights within the British isles, including connecting flights from London to most major destinations within the country. From North America, British Airways flies to London from such gateways as New York, Boston, Washington, D.C., Miami, Chicago, Detroit, Seattle, Los Angeles, San Francisco, Anchorage, Toronto, Vancouver, and Montréal.

British Airways offices and their staffs are unusually well qualified to discuss touring in Britain and to make whatever arrangements—hotels, sightseeing, escorted bus trips, and the like—you need.

LEAST EXPENSIVE "REGULAR" FARES: Currently, your cheapest option with regular airlines falls into two categories: Super Apex and Standby.

Super Apex Fares

This is now the most heavily used fare to London from North America. On most airlines, Apex tickets are valid for a stay abroad of from seven days to six months, and must be purchased at least 21 days in advance. Travel dates in both directions must be reserved at the time of purchase, with a $50 penalty assessed for alterations or cancellations

For the purpose of Apex travelers, **British Airways** divides its year into three tariff schedules. Round-trip fares from New York to London are $599 in peak season (April 1 to September 14), $579 in shoulder season (September 15 to October 31 and December 10 to December 24), and $549 in low season (November 1 to December 9 and December 25 to March 31). These fares carry a surcharge of $25 each way for travel on weekends. Children less than 12 years old pay two-thirds of the adult rate, and infants (under 2 years of age) travel for 10% of the adult rate.

Note to readers planning an extended stay in Britain: With several kinds of round-trip air packages, including the Apex fares of British Airways, eastbound passengers (i.e., those beginning their round-trip journey to Britain from North America) pay a slightly higher tariff than westbound passengers. If you're committed to sojourning in Britain for an extended stay, and if an unforeseen emergency should require a temporary return to North America, you should probably purchase your Britain/America/Britain ticket in England for the slight savings this will give you.

A growing number of airlines now fly from North America directly to London.

Delta Airlines offers Super Apex fares from Atlanta nonstop to London. The low-season round-trip fare from Atlanta is $702; in shoulder season it's $777, and in peak season $779, only a $2 increase. Please note that Delta divides its calendar year slightly differently from British Airways, but its Apex ticketing system is basically the same.

Air Florida offers a Super Apex round-trip fare from Miami to London for $770 between late spring and early autumn, and for $690 the rest of the year. The airline also offers an unusual form of a nonrefundable ticket from Miami to London for $315 one way during high season (June 1 to August 14) and $299 during low season (August 15 to May 31). This ticket must be paid for and a seat must be reserved 60 days in advance, with no changes permitted in scheduling. Name changes on the ticket are permitted, however, up to four hours before departure time at airport ticket windows of Air Florida.

Northwest Orient Airlines' newly inaugurated services from Minneapolis through Boston fly to London's Gatwick Airport (directly connected to the heart of London by a "tube" to Victoria Station). Round-trip Apex fares from Minneapolis to London are $762 during low and shoulder seasons, rising to $827 in high season. Northwest Orient's scheduled flights from Boston and Minneapolis land not only at Gatwick but at Prestwick in Scotland for those wishing to explore that country before wending their way down to London.

Standby Fares

Many airlines flying to London offer standby fares sold at the airport on the day of departure, and subject to availability. You'll have to risk waiting hours at the airport to find out whether you're confirmed, and you'll also risk being stranded at the airport for anywhere from one to several days on either leg of your trip if no seats become available. If you're emotionally prepared to hazard those risks, and your travel plans are flexible enough, then read on.

Although the price structure is less attractive than in earlier years, **British Airways** offers standby seats between New York and London for $350 one way. No stopovers are permitted on any standby flight offered by BA, and while with other packages at BA there is a discount for children, that is not available to standby passengers.

Please note an interesting quirk in the transatlantic price structures to London. Finding that the last-minute rush of standby ticketing was causing unnecessary strain at ticket counters, the policy of British Airways has been to phase out gradually the standby system. Consequently, a quick review of the earlier section on the Super Apex fares might reveal that the standby system is no longer the most attractive way to fly to Britain.

As told to me by a BA representative, the significant drawback for most passengers is the necessary advance reservations of a return flight from Britain. Payment of $50 penalty ensures the ability to change return flight dates once a traveler is in Britain. Even if such a penalty should be paid, the round-trip price on Apex at peak season, the highest priced time, would still be cheaper than a round-trip standby ticket.

Northwest Orient Airlines also offers standby one-way fares to London from Boston (low season, $245; shoulder season, $258; and peak season, $325), and from Minneapolis.

Going "Economy" or First Class

To show how inexpensive the Super Apex fares can be within the morass of international ticketing, I'll record here some economy and first-class fares quoted by several major carriers.

The economy one-way fares on **Delta Airlines** from Atlanta to London nonstop and with no restrictions are $543 in low season, $603 in shoulder season, and $664 in peak season.

Economy-class fares on **British Airways,** for one-way travel from New York to London, are $355 in low season, $395 in shoulder, and $440 in high. Also from New York, British Airways flies an unrestricted business class to London, at a one-way, year-round fare costing $956, rising to $1929 in first class.

The relatively inexpensive **Northwest Orient Airlines** flies first class to London from Minneapolis for a one-way, year-round fare of $818. In an unrestricted one-way coach class, the charge is only $381 during low and shoulder seasons, going up to $448 at peak.

For the ultimate answer to Charles Lindbergh's 29-hour crossing of the Atlantic, British Airways has made the Concorde available to passengers who want the acme in commercial space-age technology. For a $165 surcharge (each way) over first-class passage, this supersonic bird will fly you from New York to London for $2090 eastbound, and, for $2258 westbound, will return you to your native shores in a style—and at a price—that the Pilgrims would never have thought possible.

PEOPLE EXPRESS: As we go to press, People Express, the U.S. cut-rate airline, has inaugurated a no-frills flight from Newark, New Jersey, to London's Gatwick Airport. The service is designed to fill the void in cheap transatlantic service left by the bankruptcy of Sir Freddie Laker's now-defunct Skytrain service. Obviously any information reported here is likely to be vastly out of date by the time of your actual flight, so all prices and scheduling should be verified with a travel agent or else People Express (if you can ever get them on the phone!).

People Express will collect $149 per passenger in coach class, $439 in premium class, for a one-way Boeing 747 flight, as of this writing. Service is five times weekly from Newark to London.

The no-frills is no joke. For example, there's a $3 charge for each piece of luggage checked in the baggage compartment, and meals cost $6 apiece ($14 in premium class). The fare is collected by airline personnel once passengers are in flight. They take British or American currency, travelers checks, personal checks (with two forms of identification), or major credit cards. Don't think, however, that you'll get away with showing up on the plane without funds and bluffing your way free to England. A People Express spokesman said such passengers are arrested on felony charges at Gatwick.

Passengers should reserve space, *way, way in advance* through a travel agent or with the phone number listed in your local area. For New York, reservations are made by calling 212/772-0344, and in Newark, 201/596-6000.

2. By Ship

Traveling by air sometimes brings cultures jarringly close to one another, allowing only a few hours to elapse before total immersion in a different lifestyle. Because of that, you might find sea travel in either direction a distinctive and restful way to collect your thoughts and feelings before or after the onslaught of your British experience.

The **Cunard Line,** 555 Fifth Ave., New York, NY 10017 (tel. 212/880-7500), boasts the *Queen Elizabeth 2* as its flagship—self-styled, quite accurately, as "the most advanced ship of the age." It is the only ocean-going liner providing regular transatlantic service—24 sailings from April to November—between New York and Cherbourg, France, and Southampton, England.

Designed for extended cruises, the *QE-2* is reaching a younger market, those leery of the traditional liner-type crossing. Hence you'll find four swimming pools, a sauna, nightclubs, a balconied theater, an art gallery, cinemas, chic boutiques, and an exercise and weight-loss spa designed after the Golden Door in California.

The vessel is a two-class ship, with both first and transatlantic classes. Each class has a number of public rooms for its exclusive use; however, most public rooms, such as the Casino, are used in common.

Throughout the year, lively entertainment is provided aboard. Called "Festival of Life," a series of lectures introduces you to such public personalities as Meryl Streep, Norman Vincent Peale, Jason Robards, William F. Buckley, Rex Reed, and Carroll O'Connor.

The Cunard Line divides its sailing year into thrift, intermediate, and high season. The prices quoted by Cunard are per person, based on double occupancy. Fares are complicated, and if you don't live in New York, it's suggested you call a travel agent or a Cunard representative on a toll-free number: 800/221-4700.

One of the most popular packages offered is the **air/sea trip.** On it, you cross in one direction by air and sail the other direction. The round-trip fares for this air/sea passage depend on the time of year and the size and opulence of your cabin. They range from a minimum of $1185 per person to a maximum of $6185 per person. For a supplement of $499 you can fly the Concorde on one of the legs of your trip. Part of your air passage will always be with British Airways to or from one of 45 gateways in the United States and Canada.

Another form of passage is known as **"One-Way Free Sailing."** That is, you pay for a one-way ticket by ship, but you get your return by ship included free. Passage in both directions is reserved with sailing dates determined in advance by Cunard.

The time spent abroad with such a "matched sailing" can range from two days to six months. Reserve early for the widest choice of sailing dates in both directions. Round-trip prices per person for double occupancy range from $1505 to $2800; for single occupancy, from $1580 to $2800 per person, depending on the season and type of accommodations. Port taxes in transatlantic class are $50, rising to $60 for first class.

Cunard offers a one-way **Youth Fare** for passengers who haven't reached their 26th birthday. That fare is $495 for quadruple accommodations, which are mostly standby although a few such passages are reserved in advance.

To allow business travelers to bring their spouses with them to Britain, Cunard will upgrade the accommodations of anyone reserving a first-class single cabin to a first-class double cabin at no extra charge. If this is part of an air/sea package, the spouse pays her or his air passage home. Such an arrangement requires a stay abroad (including time spent sailing) of less than 12 days.

Passengers on the *QE-2* are entitled to discounts at Cunard hotels in London, including the Ritz, the Cunard Bristol, and the Cunard International.

3. The ABC's of Britain

AIRPORTS: London has two main airports, **Heathrow** and **Gatwick.** Both of them are connected to the heart of London by subway, a far cheaper choice than a taxi which would cost about $22.50 plus tip from Heathrow into London. By subway it will cost £2.50 ($3.85) and take 35 minutes to get to Piccadilly Circus.

For a ride with a view, try a **London Transport Airbus,** which leaves each of Heathrow's terminals at 20-minute intervals from 6:40 a.m. to 8:40 p.m. The 45-minute ride (longer at rush hour) costs £2.50 ($4.38) to either Victoria Station or Paddington Station. Double-decker buses—so good for your first glimpse of the metropolis—have been specially adapted with plenty of luggage space. Route A1 from Victoria, Grosvenor Gardens, calls at Cromwell Road (by the Penta Hotel and convenient for many others), and Route A2 from Paddington Station, Eastbourne Terrace, calls at Bayswater (again useful for many hotels in the area) on the way to Heathrow. Another route, A3, calls at Russell Square and goes through Kensington. There are two buses leaving every hour from Paddington and three from Victoria. The buses will accept U.S. or Canadian currency. Up-to-date information can be obtained by phoning 222-1234. Slower bus service, the Green Line, leaves Heathrow every half hour until 7:30 p.m., and then every hour until 10:30 p.m., making local stops on its way to Victoria Station. For more information, refer to "Buses in Britain."

Gatwick Airport is 30 miles south of London. Trains leave from there every 15 minutes until midnight, and every hour after midnight. Also from Gatwick, there's an express bus that runs to Victoria Station every half hour

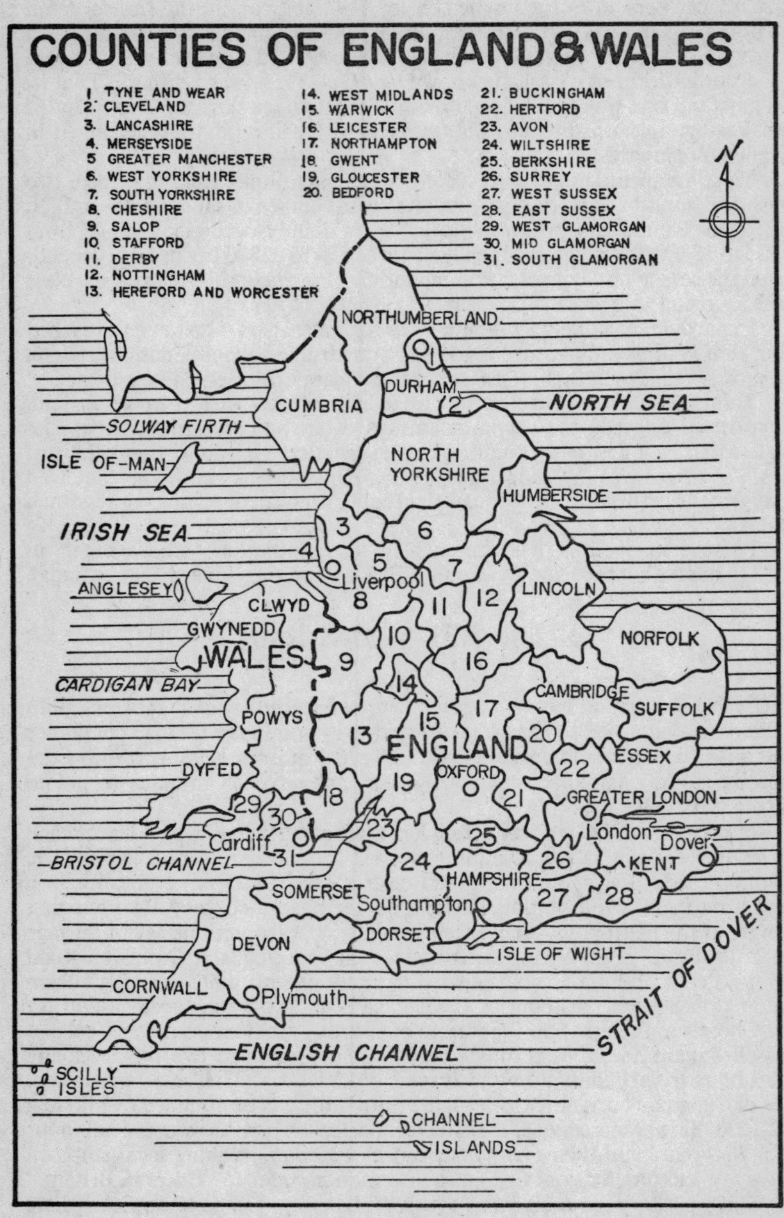
COUNTIES OF ENGLAND & WALES
1. TYNE AND WEAR
2. CLEVELAND
3. LANCASHIRE
4. MERSEYSIDE
5 GREATER MANCHESTER
6. WEST YORKSHIRE
7. SOUTH YORKSHIRE
8. CHESHIRE
9. SALOP
10. STAFFORD
11. DERBY
12. NOTTINGHAM
13. HEREFORD AND WORCESTER
14. WEST MIDLANDS
15. WARWICK
16. LEICESTER
17. NORTHAMPTON
18. GWENT
19. GLOUCESTER
20. BEDFORD
21. BUCKINGHAM
22. HERTFORD
23. AVON
24. WILTSHIRE
25. BERKSHIRE
26. SURREY
27. WEST SUSSEX
28. EAST SUSSEX
29. WEST GLAMORGAN
30. MID GLAMORGAN
31. SOUTH GLAMORGAN
N
NORTHUMBERLAND
DURHAM
CUMBRIA
NORTH SEA
SOLWAY FIRTH
NORTH YORKSHIRE
ISLE OF-MAN
HUMBERSIDE
IRISH SEA
Liverpool
ANGLESEY
CLWYD
LINCOLN
GWYNEDD
WALES
NORFOLK
CARDIGAN BAY
CAMBRIDGE
SUFFOLK
POWYS
ENGLAND
ESSEX
DYFED
OXFORD
GREATER LONDON
Cardiff
London
Dover
BRISTOL CHANNEL
KENT
HAMPSHIRE
SOMERSET
Southampton
DORSET
DEVON
ISLE OF WIGHT
STRAIT OF DOVER
CORNWALL
Plymouth
ENGLISH CHANNEL
SCILLY ISLES
CHANNEL ISLANDS

from 6:30 a.m. until 8 p.m., and every hour from 8 p.m. to 11 p.m. The fare is $3.20. Children ride for half price. Taxis from Gatwick charge a set fee, which should be confirmed before departure.

There is a bus service between the two airports, leaving every hour, the trip taking about 70 minutes and costing £3.50 ($6.13). There is also an expensive helicopter service that takes only 15 minutes between the airports. For flight information, telephone Heathrow at 01/759-4321. For Gatwick, telephone Crawley 31299. Airline phone numbers are listed in the London directory.

Scotland has one international airport, **Prestwick,** near Ayr. It has bus connections to Central Glasgow (about an hour) and to Edinburgh (about two hours).

In addition, most of Britain's major cities have domestic airports fairly close by.

AMERICAN EXPRESS: The main office in London is at 6 Haymarket, S.W.1 (tel. 930-4411). There are about ten other London locations.

BABYSITTERS: These are very hard to find, and the only safe way would be to get your hotel to recommend someone—possibly a staff member. Expect to pay the cost of travel to and from your hotel.

A number of organizations advertised in the Yellow Pages provide sitters using registered nurses and carefully screened mothers as trained "nannies." In London, **Childminders,** 67A Marylebone High St., W.1 (tel. 935-9763), is your best bet. "Minders" are provided to sit for an evening or to act as a day nanny. You pay a membership fee of £12 ($21), then a day charge of £1.50 ($2.63) per hour, plus meals. A minimum of four hours is required. The evening charge is £1.25 ($2.19) per hour, plus meals and transport to and from your address. Again, a minimum of four hours is required.

Another London outfit is **Babysitters Unlimited,** 313 Brompton Rd., S.W.3 (tel. 730-7777). **Universal Aunts,** 36 Walpole St., S.W.3 (tel. 730-9834), runs a comprehensive service, acting as substitute parents for children.

BACKPACKING: For those who prefer to rely on their own two legs and savor the countryside at close quarters, the **Countryside Commission,** John Dower House, Crescent Place, Cheltenham, Gloucestershire GL50 3RA, will provide maps for interesting walking tours, and give details of places to stay en route. They offer a good deal of very relevant advice to make your journey safe—clothes to wear, equipment to take.

The **Backpackers' Club,** 20 St. Michael's Rd., Tilehurst, Reading, Berkshire RG3 4RP (tel. 0734/28754), has other information concerning the main routes—along Offa's Dyke, the border between England and Wales; the North and South Downs Ways, and the Pennine Way through the Yorkshire Dales and across Hadrian's Wall, to name only a few.

BANKS: Hours, generally, are from 9:30 a.m. to 3:30 p.m., Monday to Friday. There are also Bureaux de Change, which charge for cashing travelers checks or personal checks (limited to checks drawn on United Kingdom banks only). They also change dollars into sterling. Bureaux are often open 18 hours a day, seven days a week. There are also branches of the main banks at the international airports which offer a 24-hour service to travelers.

BICYCLES: If you choose this form of transportation, you may want to join the **Cyclists' Touring Club,** Cotterell House, 69 Meadrow, Godalming, Surrey (tel. 04868/7217). It costs £10 ($17.50) to join (less if you're under 21) and the membership is good for one year. The club helps members not only with information, but provides maps, insurance, touring routes, and a list of low-cost accommodations—farmhouses, inns, guest houses, even private homes which cater especially to cyclists.

A popular place to rent a bike in London is **Savile's Stores,** 97 Battersea Rise, Battersea (tel. 228-4279), which charges £8.50 ($14.88) per week. After the first week, tariffs are reduced £1 ($1.75) per day. A deposit of £10 ($17.50) is required with a passport, £20 ($35) without. Padlocks are provided free, and insurance costs £1.50 ($2.63) for any one period of rental. The shop is closed all day Wednesday.

The **London Bicycle Company** at 41–42 Floral St., Covent Garden, W.C.2 (tel. 836-2969), and at 55 Pimlico Rd., S.W.1 (tel. 730-6898) offers three-speeds for £2 ($3.50) a day or £10 ($17.50) a week, ten-speed touring bikes for £4 ($7) a day or £20 ($35) a week. A deposit of £10 ($17.50) is required, but it'll be refunded if you return the bike in good order.

BOATING: Cruising the Thames aboard a slipper-stern river launch equipped with awnings in case of rain will reveal aspects of England that you might not otherwise see.

Passengers are collected from their London hotel in the morning by car and driven to Runnymede, where they embark for a cruise downstream through Runnymede Fields past Magna Carta Island, where King John is reputed to have signed the famous document and then upstream through Windsor, under the shadow of the castle, Eton College, and Bray, to Maidenhead, frequented in Edwardian times by young sportsmen and their ladies.

Lunch is taken either as a picnic, while moored in some quiet backwater, or in a riverside hotel or pub. At Maidenhead, the Skindles Hotel grounds run down to the river, making it a popular stopping-off place. Passengers then turn downstream again during the afternoon, disembarking at Windsor Town Quay, within yards of the railway station. From there, the journey back to London is quick, cheap, and easy.

The cost for up to six people is £100 ($175). A picnic lunch is provided at an extra cost of £8 ($14).

Extended cruises can be arranged to suit the time available and the passengers' inclination.

Overnight accommodations must be arranged in advance and are not included in the price (neither are meals).

Passengers are transferred from and to London at the start and finish of the cruise.

Advance booking is essential. Write to **Peter J. E. Barnes,** Willow Point, Friary Island, Wraysbury, near Staines, Middlesex TW19 5 JR (tel. Wraysbury 2259).

Another form of viewing Britain by boat, would be to rent a **live-in houseboat.** The English call them "river cruisers," and despite the unfamiliar rituals of looking for moorings and negotiating river traffic, some travelers consider this a unique form of sightseeing.

The facilities on these boats vary, but you can usually expect to find a gas cooker with an oven, hot and cold water, cooking utensils, cutlery, a refrigerator, blankets and pillows, along with flush toilets. The larger boats are also equipped with showers. Navigational aids, other than a map of the river, aren't needed.

Houseboats are also available on the Norfolk Broads and on much of the networks of canals covering the country.

The bulk of the self-drive cruisers on the Thames, and on the canal network throughout the country, are available through central booking agencies. A leading one is **Hoseasons Holidays,** Sunway House, Lowestoft NR32 3LT. Hoseasons has various telephone numbers for whichever part of the system you want to hire a boat in. Try Lowestoft 0502/62211. A four-berth cruiser on the Thames costs from £135 ($236.25) weekly in low season to £350 ($612.50) weekly in high season, but do inquire around, as there are many large and small boats available, and at varying prices, depending on the season.

BULLETIN: One of the most current, innovative, and provocative travel newsletters in the business, *Travel Bulletin,* a four-page, information-packed letter intended for travel agents only, has now been made available to the general public. The newsletter is mailed first class to its subscribers every month; and in addition, it includes a two-page travel supplement on a timely subject every season.

It's a useful service that should appeal especially to readers of the $$$-a-Day books. Subscription cost is $35 a year ($12 extra for Canada and overseas). Write to *Travel Bulletin,* c/o Pinder Lane, Dept. ENG, 159 West 53rd St., New York, NY 10019.

BUSES IN BRITAIN: Covering the greater part of Britain, the **Express Motorcoach Network** links villages with towns and cities with frequent schedules, convenient timetables, and efficient operation in all seasons. Most places not on the direct line of route can be reached readily from a stopoff point by local buses. Fares are relatively cheap, making travel on Express Motorcoach Network economical. For example, to show price advantage, a midweek round-trip ("return") ticket from London to Cardiff (Wales) is £6.50 ($11.38) by bus. On the other hand, the second-class round-trip fare by rail is £25 ($43.75).

Most of the bus lines depart from Victoria Coach Station, a block up from Victoria Railroad Station. You'd be well advised to have reservations for the express buses; the locals can usually be boarded on the spot.

Other departure points are Kings Cross Coach Station and Gloucester Road, beside the Forum Hotel.

A **British Express Pass** gives bus travel to most major cities in England, Scotland, and Wales. The cost for five days is £28 ($49) for adults and £15 ($26.25) for children. For ten days, the price goes up to £45 ($78.75) for adults and £22 ($38.50) for children. This pass can be used on separate, individual days within any calendar month; they need not be consecutive. The pass may be obtained with a passport from Victoria Coach Station information desk, 164 Buckingham Palace Rd., S.W.1 in London (tel. 730-0202).

Most suburban spots are serviced by **Green Line Coaches,** which you can board throughout the city wherever you see green bus signs. These buses go as far as Dorking, Guildford, Horsham, or Tunbridge Wells, all 25 to 40 miles south from the center of London. To the north, they go as far as Aylesbury, Luton, Hitchin, and St. Albans, all around 20 to 25 miles from Victoria. To the west, they reach Slough, High Wycombe, or Windsor, within a range of 20 to 40 miles from London. And to the east, they go to Grays or Gravesend, approximately 15 to 26 miles from the center of London. Personal callers can go to the Green Line Information Office on Eccleston Bridge, Victoria, in London, S.W.1 (tel. 834-6563).

Day Explorer tickets are available for both families and individuals. These run to chosen parts of the countryside, to stately homes, the seaside, museums, and zoos. They almost halve the cost of travel, and with a family of two adults and two children this can amount to quite a savings.

London Country Bus Services provide the green "London Country" buses around London and also the fast "Green Line" services which run from the heart of London to the surrounding countryside, or around the edge of London linking several major towns with Heathrow Airport. Although the country buses don't go into the heart of London itself, they do link up with the Green Line coaches and also the red buses of London Transport.

Jetlink 747 is the nonstop Green Line link between London and Heathrow, taking just over one hour and costing £3.50 ($6.13) per person. The ticket increases to £7 ($12.25) between midnight and 5 a.m. Children under 5 years of age travel free.

Flightline is the name given to special Green Line express routes from Central London to its surrounding airports. Flightline 767 runs nonstop between Victoria Station in London and Heathrow, the trip taking about 40 minutes and costing £1.50 ($2.63) for a one-way journey. Flightline 777 leaves London's Victoria Station, heading for Gatwick Airport; the trip takes 70 minutes and costs £2 ($3.50) for a one-way fare.

Golden Rover Tickets cost £2.95 ($5.16) for adults and £1.48 ($2.59) for children, and are available for one day's travel on most London Country and Green Line routes (but not the Jetlink and Flightlines). It is possible for a very small cost to cover quite a large area around London and into the countryside.

For more precise information on routes, fares, and schedules, write to **London Country Bus Services Ltd.,** Lesbourne Road, Reigate, Surrey RH2 7LE (tel. 07372/42411).

BUS TERMINALS: **Victoria Coach Station,** Victoria, S.W.1 (Tube: Victoria), in London is that capital's main bus terminal. Other buses leave from **Kings Cross Station,** 250 Pentonville Rd., London, N.1 (Tube: Kings Cross). For departure times and general information, call 01/750-0202.

CAR RENTALS: There are many car-rental services available in Britain, including **National, Kemwel,** and **Avis.** In addition, there are dozens of British-owned car-rental firms, most of them charging rates to match their American competitors.

Hertz is particularly well represented, with major branches at Heathrow (tel. 01/897-3349) and Gatwick Airports (tel. 0293/30555) and at such strategic locations throughout the country as Cambridge, Brighton, and Edinburgh in Scotland. When making a reservation, inquire if the unlimited-mileage rates of three days or more are still available. All Hertz cars are fitted with radios, and you can rent both manual and automatic transmission.

Godfrey Davis Europcar Ltd., Bushey House, High Street, Bushey, Watford, Hertfordshire, WD2 IRE (tel. 01/950-5050), has a wide network of offices throughout the United Kingdom and additional depots at most major railway stations, so you can take a train out of London and pick up your car with very little trouble. The firm offers very competitive rates as well as holiday specials for rentals of more than three days. Godfrey Davis is now part of Europcar and is represented in the U.S. by National Car Rental.

Another excellent auto-rental establishment is **Two Horse Hire,** whose office and reception is at 4 Farnham Royal, Kennington Lane, Vauxhall, S.E.11 (tel. 735-6079) in London. The location is near the Oval Cricket Ground. The firm exclusively rents Citroëns 2CVs which are in good condition. These cars, while not in the luxury class, have the power and accessories necessary for a safe and reasonably comfortable journey. Readers Terrence W. Dunlop and Joanne B. Kaufman report that they recently drove about 1500 miles in nine days and experienced no trouble whatsoever. The rental personnel are cordial and helpful, and best of all, the tariff is about 30% below those quoted at most London car-rental agencies—that is, about £59 ($103.25) weekly on the unlimited-mileage rate (Royal Automobile Club membership is included as well).

And finally, **Woods of Reigate,** Sidlow Bridge, Reigate in Surrey (tel. Reigate 40291), offers a good deal on car rentals. Its service is good, and about 13 different models are available. They even have their own Ford dealership. A small family-run company, Woods is a one-hour drive from Central London, a one-hour drive from Heathrow Airport, and a ten-minute trek from Gatwick Airport. A free transfer service to Gatwick and its rail station is operated. For an extra charge, they will collect or deliver you anywhere in the country. Weekly rates with unlimited mileage begin at £77 ($134.75).

CLIMATE: British temperatures can range from 30° to 110°F. It is, however, a temperate country with no real extremes, and even in summer evenings are cool. No Britisher will ever really advise you about the weather—it's far too uncertain. However, if you come from a hot area, bring some warm clothes. If you come from the cooler climes, you should be all right.

CLOTHING SIZES: Women will find the size of stockings the same in Britain as in America. Likewise, men will find suits and shirts the same size. However, there are some exceptions.

For Women

Dresses, Coats, and Skirts

American	7	8	9	10	11	12	13	14	15	16	17	18
British	9	10	11	12	13	14	15	16	17	18	19	20

Blouses and Sweaters

American	10	12	14	16	18	20
British	32	34	36	38	40	42

Shoes

American	4½	5	5½	6	6½	7	7½	8	8½	9	9½	10
British	3	3½	4	4½	5	5½	6	6½	7	7½	8	8½

For Men

Shoes

American	7	8	9	10	11	12	13
British	6	7	8	9	10	11	12

CRIME: Theft is not as bad, perhaps, as in the U.S. In the main, mugging is limited to the poor areas. Use discretion and a little common sense.

CURRENCY EXCHANGE: As a general guideline, the price conversions in this book have been computed at the rate of £1 (one pound sterling) for each $1.75 U.S. Bear in mind, however, that international exchange rates are far from stable, and this ratio might be hopelessly outdated by the time you actually arrive in Britain.

CUSTOMS: Overseas visitors may import 400 cigarettes and one quart of liquor. But if you come from the Common Market (EEC) area, you're allowed 300 cigarettes and one quart of liquor, provided you bought them and paid tax in that EEC country. If you have obtained your allowance on a ship or plane, then you may only import 200 cigarettes and one liter of liquor. There is no limit on money, film, or other items which are for your own use. Obviously commercial goods, such as video films and nonpersonal items, will require payment of a bond and will take a number of hours to clear and deal with. Do not try to import live birds or animals. You may be subjected to heavy fines, and the pet will be destroyed.

Upon leaving Britain, citizens of the United States who have been outside the country for 48 hours or more are allowed to bring back to their home country $400 worth of merchandise duty free—that is, if they haven't claimed such an exemption within the past 30 days. Beyond that free allowance, you'll be charged a flat rate of 10% duty on the next $1000 worth of purchases. If you make purchases in Britain, it is most important to keep your receipts. On gifts, the duty-free limit has been increased to $50.

DENTIST: In London, telephone 01/584-1008 for the name of the dentist nearest to you. Expect to pay about £15 ($26.25) for treatment unless it is a genuine emergency. Or else get in touch with the **Royal Dental Hospital,** 32 Leicester Square, London, W.C. 2 (tel. 930-8831). Inquire about the likely cost when you telephone. Also call 01/229-4335 and 01/834-8345 in London for 24-hour private emergency dental treatment. Outside London, ask the nearest sympathetic local resident, a hotelier, for example.

DOCUMENTS FOR ENTRY: While every U.S. citizen needs a valid passport to enter Great Britain, no entry visa is required.

DOCTORS: Hotels have their own list of local practitioners, for whom you'll have to pay. (Look under "Hospitals" for 24-hour emergency service.) If out of town, dial "0" and ask the operator for the local police, who will give you the name, address, and phone number of a doctor in your area. Emergency treatment is free, but if you're admitted to a hospital, referred to an outpatient clinic, or treated for an already-existing condition, you will be required to pay. You will also pay if you visit a doctor in his or her office or if the doctor makes a "house call" to your hotel. Be safe. Take out adequate medical/accident insurance or extend your existing insurance to cover you while you're abroad.

DRIVING REQUIREMENTS: To drive a car in Britain, your passport and your own driver's license must be presented along with your deposit; no special

British license is needed. The prudent driver will secure a copy of the *Highway Code,* available from almost any stationer or news agent. It is now compulsory to wear a seatbelt if you're in the front seat of a car or minibus, either as a driver or passenger.

Although not mandatory, a membership in one of the two major auto clubs in England can be helpful: the **Automobile Association** and the **Royal Automobile Club.** The headquarters of the AA are at Fanum House, Basingstoke, Hampshire (tel. Basingstoke 20123); the RAC offices are at 83 Pall Mall, London, S.W. 1 5HW (tel. 01/839-7050). Membership in one of these clubs is usually handled by the agent from whom you rent your car. Upon joining, you'll be given a key to the many telephone boxes you see along the road, so that you can phone for help in an emergency.

DRUGSTORES: In Britain they're called "chemist" shops. Every police station in the country has a list of emergency chemists. Dial "0" and ask the operator for the local police. The only 24-hour druggist I could find in the whole of London is called, bless them, **Bliss the Chemist,** 50–56 Willesden Lane, N.W.6 (tel. 624-8000). It lies a 20-minute taxi ride heading north from Piccadilly Circus. Check by phone first to see if they have your requirements. Other druggists open almost 24 hours are: **V. J. Hall,** 85 Shaftesbury Ave., London, W.1 (tel. 01/437-3174), which is open until 11 p.m. Monday through Saturday and until 10 p.m. on Sunday (take the tube to Piccadilly Circus); another is **W. W. Brunton,** 240 Earls Court Rd., London, S.W.5 (tel. 01/373-5078) (Tube: Earls Court), which is open until 10:30 p.m. Monday through Saturday, and till 10 p.m. on Sunday.

Emergency drugs are normally available at most hospitals, but you'll be examined to see that the drugs you request are really necessary.

ELECTRICAL APPLIANCES: The electrical current is 240 volts, AC (50 Hz). Some international hotels are specially wired to allow North Americans to plug in their appliances, but you'll usually need a transformer plus an adapter for your electric razor, hairdryer, or soft contact lens sterilizer. Ask at the electrical department of a large hardware store for the size converter you'll need.

EMBASSY AND HIGH COMMISSION: The **U.S. Embassy** is at 24 Grosvenor Square, London W.1 (tel. 499-9000), and the **Canadian High Commission** is at Canada House, Trafalgar Square, London, S.W.1 (tel. 629-9492).

EMERGENCY: In London, for police, fire, or ambulance, dial 999. Give your name and address, plus your telephone number, and state the nature of the emergency. Misuse of the 999 service will result in a heavy fine (cardiac arrest, yes; dented fender, no).

In London, the following numbers might prove useful: **Alcoholics Anonymous** (tel. 834-8202); **Gamblers Anonymous** (tel. 352-3060); **Rape Crisis Centre** (tel. 340-6145); **Gay Switchboard** (tel. 837-7324); **Consumer Association** (tel. 839-1222); **Law Society** (tel. 969-7473); and **Help Advisory Centre** (tel. 937-6445). Call the last number when you don't know where to get the sort of help you need. Suicidal or very depressed? Telephone **The Samaritans,** 39 Walbrook, E.C.4 (tel. 283-3400).

ETIQUETTE: In short, be normal, be quiet. The British do not like hearing other people's conversations. In pubs, you are not expected to buy a round of drinks unless someone has bought you a drink. Don't talk religion or politics in pubs.

GAS: It's called "petrol." Prices are rising, and as of this writing it sells for £1.65 ($2.89) a gallon. Be aware that prices quoted to you will be for liters per pound. Luckily, gas stations will sometimes have a comparative list of prices.

GLASSES: Lost or broken? Try **Selfridge's Optical,** in Selfridges Department Store, 400 Oxford St., London W.1 (tel. 629-1234, ext. 3889). If the prescription is straightforward you can be fitted and "back in vision," as the British say, in one or two hours. Cost, including examination, will be around £45 ($78.75). But you'll pay more for elaborate frames.

HAIRDRESSING: Ask at your hotel. You should tip the "hairwasher" 20p (39¢) and the stylist 50p (88¢), more if you have a tint or permanent. Hairdressing services are available in most department stores, and for men, at the main railway stations in London.

HITCHHIKING: It is not illegal and is normally quite safe and practical. It is, however, illegal for pedestrians to be on motorways. The cleaner and tidier you look, the better your chance. Have a sign with your destination written on it.

HOLIDAYS AND FESTIVALS: Christmas Day, Boxing Day (December 26), New Year's Day, Good Friday and Easter Monday, May Day, spring and summer bank holiday. Scotland also takes January 2 as a holiday, but does not recognize the summer bank holiday, taking the first Monday in August instead of the last for a holiday. Scotland does not take Easter Monday as a bank holiday.

HOSPITALS: The following offer emergency treatment in London 24 hours a day, and it's free under the National Health Service (if you have an existing condition, chances are it will not be treated free): **Royal Free Hospital,** Pont Street, N.W.3 (tel. 794-0500); **Middlesex Hospital,** Mortimer Street, W.1 (tel. 636-8333); **New Charing Cross Hospital,** Fulham Palace Road (tel. 748-2040); **St. Bartholomew's Hospital,** West Smithfield, E.C.1 (tel. 600-9000); **St. Stephen's Hospital,** 369 Fulham Rd., S.W.10 (tel. 352-8161); **St. Thomas's Hospital,** Lambeth Palace Road, S.E.1 (tel. 928-9292); and **University College Hospital,** Gower Street, W.C.1 (tel. 387-9300). Only emergency treatment or the first visit is free—any subsequent referrals will have to be paid for. Take along your insurance coverage, if available.

HOSPITALITY SERVICE: The **International Friendship League** is a highly commendable, nonpolitical organization with members in 54 countries throughout the world. Since this organization does not have headquarters in the United States, Americans can join through the British organization. For full details, please get in touch with (and enclose three international reply coupons): Miss Kathleen Suter, IFL Hospitality Service Organizer, 4 Wilton

Close, Taunton, Somerset TA1 4EZ, England. There are 155 cities and towns in England, Scotland, and Wales that have IFL hospitality service. The IFL offers an excellent opportunity for Americans (and others) to meet the British, to visit with them in their homes, perhaps to have a meal with them, and sometimes to be accommodated with overnight lodging.

INFORMATION: There are more than 650 tourist information offices in England and Wales, and 160 in Scotland. All are well signposted in their cities, and some are closed in winter.

The **British Tourist Authority,** Queens House, 64 St. James's St., London, S.W.1 (tel. 629-9191), will answer most questions about the country. You might also consult the **English Tourist Board,** 4 Grosvenor Gardens, London, S.W.1 (tel. 730-3400); the **Scottish Tourist Board,** 23 Ravalston Terrace, Edinburgh EH4 3EU (tel. 031/332-2433); and the **Welsh Tourist Board,** Brunci House, 2 Fitzalan Rd., Cardiff CF2 1UY (tel. 0222/49-99-09). The regional boards will answer questions of a more detailed nature, providing data on accommodations and local sights. They'll also give you the addresses of the tourist offices in the local towns.

In London, the **National Tourist Information Centre** at Victoria Station is operated by the London Tourist Board. It is in the forecourt of Victoria Station (S.W.1) and is open regularly from 9 a.m. to 8:30 p.m., Monday to Saturday, and from 9 a.m. to 5 p.m. on Sunday (there are extended hours during the summer). Services include tourist information on London as well as England in general. Hotel bookings can be made in London as well as at selected centers throughout England. Theater and tour bookings can also be made and tourist tickets purchased.

Other tourist information centers include branches of the London Tourist Board at Selfridges Department Store on the ground floor, at Harrods Department Store on the fourth floor, and at Heathrow Central Station at Heathrow Airport.

To telephone for information, call 730-0791 in London Monday to Friday from 9 a.m. to 5:30 p.m.

Also in London, telephone 246-8041 for a recording of the day's events. For children's London, telephone 246-8007.

Written inquiries should be directed to the **London Tourist Board,** Central Information Unit, 26 Grosvenor Gardens, London, S.W1W ODU.

INSOMNIACS: Late-night and all-night movies are shown in London at the **Gate Cinema,** 87 Notting Hill Gate, W.11 (tel. 727-5750); **Paris Pullman,** 65 Drayton Gardens, S.W.1 (tel. 373-5898); or **The Classic,** Leicester Square, W.C.2 (tel. 930-6915).

ITINERARIES: If you plan to drive yourself around the countryside, you can save the cost in gas by having Peter Barnes prepare a route, including road numbers, the places you want to see, and suggestions for overnight accommodations and places to eat. His vast experience touring the country on behalf of the British Tourist Authority and leading his own tours enables him to produce a driveable itinerary.

Just send your check for $25 (U.S.) for the first seven days, plus another $3.75 per day thereafter, with a brief description of what you hope to see and do, and the itinerary will be mailed to you. If payment is by personal check, add another $4 to cover bank charges. Of course, it helps him to know what you've already seen and don't want to do, too. You must submit your request at least eight weeks before your departure from home.

Mr. Barnes also provides a London orientation tour—a nonstop trip by car around the places of major interest, as well as some others which visitors rarely see, along with personal commentary. The cost is $160 for the seven-hour tour, and as many as four passengers can go along for the ride. Lunch in a pub or restaurant is extra. The charge for four hours for up to three persons is $100.

Mr. Barnes will also meet you at the airport on your arrival and take you to your London hotel. The rate for up to three persons is $60 from Heathrow, $20 from Gatwick. Even if your plane is delayed, he will be there to meet you but you may have to pay a little more for his waiting time.

A day's guided tour to Oxford, Windsor, Hampton Court, Cambridge, Stratford-upon-Avon, or Salisbury and Stonehenge costs around $160 for up to four passengers.

For small parties, Mr. Barnes will plan an itinerary, book accommodations, and personally escort two-or-more-day tours by private car or minibus throughout the island. You must make up your own group, however. The cost of six or seven passengers is around $325 per person weekly for transportation and Mr. Barnes's services. Accommodations, meals, and admission charges are extra, but for this figure you get 1400 miles of touring.

For those who need to stretch their golfing muscles, there are several courses around London, including Wentworth, Royal Ascot, and Moor Park, along with the less formal Datchet. Club rental and caddy can be arranged, and Peter Barnes will collect you from your London hotel, smooth your way at the clubhouse, and return you to London after half a day's exercise. The cost is £30 ($52.50), plus greens fee and club and caddy rental. For the buff, complete tours of the courses of England and Scotland can be arranged.

For more information, write to **Peter J. E. Barnes,** Willow Point, Friary Island, Wraysbury, near Staines, Middlesex TW19 5JR (tel. Wraysbury 2259).

LAUNDRY AND DRY CLEANING: Most places take two days to complete the job. In London, the **Brunswick Launderette,** 1 Brunswick Centre, Bernard Street, W.C.1, opposite the Russell Square tube station, is a good bet right in an area of tourist hotels. The launderette is open daily from 7 a.m. til 8 p.m., including weekends, and there is always someone in attendance. If you wish, you can drop off your wash, go shopping or on a day tour, then pick it up that afternoon.

There are plenty of establishments around, and the **Association of British Launderers and Cleaners,** 319 Pinner Rd., Harrow, Middlesex (tel. 01/863-7755), will give you a list of companies in your area.

LIBRARIES: Every town has a public library, and as a visitor you can use the reference sections. The lending of volumes, however, is restricted to local citizens.

LIQUOR LAWS: No alcohol is served to anyone under the age of 18. Children under 16 aren't allowed in pubs, except in special rooms. Hours vary, but as a general guide pubs are open from 11:30 a.m. to 2:30 p.m. and from 6 to 10:30 p.m., Monday to Saturday. Sunday hours are from noon to 2:30 p.m. and from 7 to 10 p.m.

Many general stores have "off licence" departments where you can buy liquor for home consumption, and hours are generally from 9 a.m. to 5 p.m., depending on the store. There are also "off licence" shops which are usually open from 11 a.m. to 3 p.m. and from 5 to 9 p.m. (or later).

LITERATURE: If you're really dedicated in your exploring, I'd suggest Churchill's *History of the English-Speaking Peoples* (four volumes) and Trevelyan's *History of England.* These tomes will help you understand a lot more about what you'll be seeing. Otherwise, just read this guidebook and use a good map if you're touring.

LOST PROPERTY: Don't give up hope if you leave your prize possession on the tube or in a taxi—or elsewhere. Report the loss to the police first, and they will advise you where to apply for its return. Taxi drivers are required to hand lost property to the nearest police station. London Transport's Lost Property Office will try to assist personal callers only at their office at the Baker Street underground station.

For lost passports, credit cards, or money, report the loss and circumstances immediately to the nearest police station. For lost passports, you should then go immediately to your embassy. The address will be in the telephone book (and see "Embassy and High Commission," above). For lost credit cards, report to the appropriate organization; the same holds true for lost travelers checks.

LUGGAGE STORAGE: You may want to make excursions throughout Britain, taking only your essentials along. Very few B&B hotels in London have space to store lots of luggage, and you might want to return to a different hotel. It's possible to store suitcases at most railway stations, but there is a place in central London where it's even cheaper and the service much friendlier.

Michael Gibbons & Co., Ltd., 25 Great Windmill St., W.1, off Shaftesbury Avenue (tel. 437-2866), will store personal effects on its premises at the rate of 25p (44¢) per case per day. Maximum weight per case is 88 pounds, and monthly terms are by negotiation. The office is open Monday to Friday from 8:45 a.m. to 5 p.m. Most important, clients have free access to their stored effects during those hours.

MAIL DELIVERY: Any letter sent *Post Restante,* London, is available for collection at the Head Post Office, St. Martin-le-Grand, London, E.C.1 (personal callers only; near St. Paul's Cathedral). Otherwise, have your mail addressed Poste Restante at any of the big towns or give your hotel address. A letter generally takes about seven to ten days to arrive in the U.S. When claiming personal mail, always carry along identification.

MEASURES: For the measurement of distance, Britain uses miles and inches, but probably soon will switch to the metric system. The conversion ratios follow:

1 inch	=2.54 centimeters		
1 foot	=0.30 meters	1 meter	= 3.3 feet (about 39 inches)
1 mile	=1.61 kilometers	1 kilometer	= 0.62 miles (roughly, 1 kilometer is 2/3 mile)
1 yard	= 0.91 meters		

Weights and measures, for the most part, are already metric.

1 ounce	= 28.35 grams	1 gram = 0.035 ounces
1 pound	= 0.45 kilograms	1 kilogram = 2.2 pounds
1 imperial pint	= 1.2 U.S. liquid pint	= 0.56 liters
1 imperial quart	= 1.2 U.S. liquid quarts	= 0.946 liters
1 imperial gallon	= 1.2 U.S. liquid gallons	= 4.5 liters
1 British ton	= 1 U.S. long ton	= 2240 pounds
(In America, the more commonly used short ton = 2000 lbs.)		
1 metric ton	= 1000 kilograms	= 1.102 U.S. short tons

MEDICAL SERVICES: Medical treatment is free only for unforeseen emergency conditions which arise during your stay in the United Kingdom. You'll need to consult a physician privately for any other medical treatment you require. The larger hotels will get in touch with their house doctor should you need him or her. In cases of extreme urgency, you can attend one of the several Accident and Emergency Departments in Central London. The same holds true for dental emergencies. However, you'll normally pay a small charge of £3 ($5.25) for any treatment. See also: "Doctors," "Dentists," "Drugstores," "Emergency," "Glasses," and "Hospitals," above.

MOTORCYCLES: These are real money-savers in this land of steep petrol (gas) prices. If you don't mind getting drenched occasionally, **Scootabout Limited,** 17–19 Tachbrook St. S.W.1 (tel. 821-5177), just a two-minute walk from Victoria Station, is the only motorcycle rental company in London insured to rent to North Americans. Under certain circumstances they can also arrange for European travel on their motorcycles. You can pick up a Moped by the day, week, or month. They are two-stroke, fully automatic motors with a kick-start and a twist throttle grip. They get 150 miles to the gallon, and prices are inclusive of VAT, insurance, helmet rental, carrier, as well as unlimited mileage and RAC membership. A single-seater Moped costs £7.50 ($13.13) for the day, increasing to £10 ($17.50) for a two-seater. For vehicles over 125cc, the renter must be 21 years or older and possess a valid licence in his or her own country. A £50 ($87.50) deposit is required and is refunded on a no-damage-done return of the vehicle.

NEWSPAPERS: *The Times* is the top, then the *Telegraph,* the *Daily Mail,* and the *Guardian,* all papers carrying the latest news. Others have some news, but rely on gimmicks to sell. The *International Herald Tribune,* published in Paris, is available daily. *What's On* and similar publications appear weekly and are sold at all bookstores and newsstands in London.

OFFBEAT HOLIDAYS: Have you ever thought of spending a week pony-trekking across Dartmoor's wild heather-covered country, staying overnight in youth hostels?

Britain is an ideal choice for those who want to put some action in their holidays. The activities are widely varied, ranging from underwater swimming off the coast of Devon, to canoeing on the River Wye, climbing in Scotland, walking, and gliding.

One way to find out information about these adventure holidays is to go to the London office of the **Youth Hostels Association,** 14 Southampton St., W.C.2 (tel. 836-8541). The yearly membership fee is £6 ($10.50) for adults and £3 ($5.25) for children. Pony-trekking tours costs around £105 ($183.75) for seven nights, these terms fully inclusive.

For a full list, write to YHA National, Trevelyan House, St. Stephens, St. Albans, Herts., England (tel. 0727/55215).

OFFICE HOURS: Business hours are from 9 a.m. to 5 p.m., Monday to Friday. The lunch break lasts an hour, but most places stay open all day.

PETS: See "Customs." It is illegal to bring in pets, except with veterinary documents, and even then they are subject to a quarantine of six months. Hotels have their own rules, but generally do not allow dogs in restaurants or public rooms and often not in the bedrooms either.

POLICE: The best source of help and advice in emergencies is the police (dial 999). If the local police can't assist, they will have the address of a person who can. Losses, theft, and other crimes should be reported immediately to the police.

POST OFFICE: Post offices and sub post offices are centrally situated, and are open from 9 a.m. to 5 p.m., Monday to Friday. On Saturday, the hours are from 9 a.m. to noon. The **Trafalgar Square Post Office** in London is open from 8 a.m. to 8 p.m., Monday to Friday, and from 10 a.m. to 5 p.m. on Saturday.

RAILROAD INFORMATION: In London, personal callers are welcome at **British Rail/Sealink,** Lower Regent Street, S.W.1, or at the **British Rail Travel Centres** in the main London railway stations, where they deal mainly with their own regions (there are five). For general information, call 01/246-8030) or "ring" the appropriate station—all numbers are listed in the phone book. Elsewhere, get in touch with the local station or a travel agent who holds a British Rail licence.

RELIGIOUS SERVICES: Times of services are posted outside the various places of worship. Almost every form of worship is catered to in London and other large cities. But in the smaller towns and villages you are likely to find only Anglican (Episcopalian), Roman Catholic, Baptist, and Nonconformist forms of worship. The **Interdenominational American Church** is on Tottenham Court Road, W.1, in London.

REST ROOMS: These are usually found at signs saying "Public Toilets." Expect to pay from 2p (4¢) to 5p (9¢) tip for women; men are free. Hotels can be used, but they discourage nonresidents. Garages (filling stations) also have facilities for use of customers only, and the key is often kept by the cash register. There's no need to tip except in hotels where there is an attendant.

SENIOR DISCOUNTS: These are only available to holders of a British pension book.

SHOE REPAIRS: Many of the large department stores of Britain have "Shoe Bars" where repairs are done while you wait.

SHOP HOURS: In general, stores are open from 9 a.m. to 5:30 p.m., Monday to Saturday. Late shopping in London is on Thursday, when stores close at 7 p.m. There are very few all-night stores, and those are mostly in the Bayswater section of London.

In the East End of London, around Aldgate and Whitechapel, many shops are open on Sunday morning from 9 a.m. to 2 p.m. Try **Houndsditch Warehouse,** 123 Houndsditch, London, E.C.3 (tel. 283-3131), an Aladdin's cave of bargains, clothes, household goods, cameras, stereo, and videos. It is open Sunday from 10 a.m. to 2 p.m., and on Monday to Friday from 9 a.m. to 5 p.m.; closed Saturday.

A 24-hour-a-day supermarket for food and household goods is at **68 Westbourne Grove,** London, W.2 (near Paddington Station). It never closes, serving the public seven days a week.

SUBWAYS: In London, this is called the "underground." If you ask for a "subway," you may end up in a tunnel for pedestrians beneath a road. In the underground, you pay according to the distance you travel. Posted by the ticket office is a list of fares, showing the cost to most stations. There are also ticket machines for certain fares to destinations shown on the machines.

TAXES: There is no local sales tax. However, Great Britain imposes a standard Value Added Tax (called VAT for short) of 15%. Most Common Market countries already have a tax similar to VAT. In Britain, hotel rates and meals in restaurants are now taxed this 15%. The extra VAT charge will show up on your bill unless otherwise stated. It is in addition to the service charge. Should the service charge be 15%, you will, in effect, be paying 30% higher than the prices quoted. The service charges, if included as part of the bill, are also taxable!

As part of an energy-saving scheme, the British government has also added a special 25% tax on gasoline ("petrol").

TELEGRAMS: Inland telegrams have now been replaced by **Telemessages** at £3 ($5.25) for 50 words. If your message is sent on Monday to Saturday before 8 p.m., the message will be delivered by the first mail delivery the next morning or you get your money back. Overseas cables can still be sent from main (not sub) post offices or by telephone.

TELEPHONES: To make a phone call from a call box, you'll need 5p (9¢) and 10p (18¢) coins. Phone numbers in Britain don't have any consistency or pattern. It's what the British call a "real hotch-potch." Next-door neighbors may have a six-figure number and an eight-figure number. In some cases you have an exchange name, in others a set of figures. You'll need all the figures, which can vary from six up to ten figures.

Consider Directory Enquiries to aid you. Dial 192, give the operator the town where you want the number, the subscriber's name, and then the address. A guide to telephone costs—a call at noon from London to Reading, 40 miles away, lasting three minutes, goes for 84p ($1.47). A local call within a radius of one mile can cost 21p (37¢) for three minutes. These costs are roughly halved between 6 p.m. and 8 a.m. You will have to pay far more if you use a hotel operator at any time.

Telephone Services: In addition to being able to reach anywhere in the world, the telephone service offers the weather forecast (dial 246-8091 in London); the time (dial 123 in London); motoring conditions (dial 246-8021 in London); daily information about main events in and around London (tel. 246-8007); and the Financial Times Share Index and business news summaries (tel. 246-8026 in London).

To operate a telephone in London, pick up the receiver and dial your number. Have your money ready. When the person on the other end answers, insert 5p (9¢) for local calls. If you don't insert the coin, the party you are calling cannot hear your voice. You are granted two minutes per 5p coin. Long distance is known as a "trunk call." Coinboxes take only 5p and 10p coins, although a number of 50p (88¢) coinboxes are being installed experimentally in some places. Dialing codes are shown in the notice frame in the telephone kiosks. After you dial your number, or code and number, you will either hear a regularly interrupted single tone, which means the line is busy, or a repeated brr-brr sound which means the exchange is trying to connect you. When the call is answered, you will hear rapid pips. Immediately put a coin into the slot and speak. If you hear the pips again and wish to continue speaking, put another coin in the slot at once. Long-distance calls are cheaper between 6 p.m. and 8 a.m. Monday to Friday, and all day Saturday and Sunday.

Note: Calls through a hotel switchboard will have a surcharge added to the normal post office cost of the call. Pay telephones are available in most hotel foyers.

The **Westminster International Telephone Bureau,** 1 Broadway, S.W.1, is open daily from 9 a.m. to 5:30 p.m., including Sunday. The bureau allows you to call all countries not available through call boxes (that is, outside Europe). There is a receptionist to help and take your money once you've finished your call. You can also send Telexes from here.

For more telephone numbers, refer to the section on "Emergency." See also "Useful Telephone Numbers," below.

TELEX: Telexes are more common in Europe than in the U.S., but are still mostly restricted to business premises and hotels. If your hotel has a Telex, they will send it for you. You may need to arrange the receipt of an expected message in advance.

TIME: England and Scotland are based on Greenwich Mean Time with BST—British Standard Time (GMT + 1 hour)—during the summer (roughly April to October). When London is 12 noon, New York is 7 a.m., Chicago is 6 a.m., Denver is 5 a.m., and Los Angeles an early 4 a.m.

TIPPING: Many establishments add a service charge. If service has been good, it is usual to add an additional 5% to that. If no service is added to the bill, give 10% for poor service; otherwise, 15%. If service is bad, tell them and don't tip!

TRANSPORTATION IN LONDON: If you know the ropes, transportation within London can be unusually easy and inexpensive, because London enjoys one of the best underground (subway) and bus systems in the world.

The **Underground:** The electric subways are, to begin with, comfortable—the trains have cushioned seats, no less. You purchase your ticket in advance either at a ticket booth or from an automatic ticket machine. The fare usually ranges from 40p (70¢) for one zone to 70p ($1.23) for two zones. There are higher fares as well. Be sure to keep your ticket—it must be presented when you get off. If you owe extra, you'll be billed by an attendant.

Each subway has its own distinctive color, and all you need follow are the clearly painted arrows. On every stairway, at every corridor turning, on every platform, are additional diagrams in color, giving the routes of the various trains. Most diagrams are inside the trains.

Note: If you're out on the town and are dependent on the underground, watch your time carefully—*many of the trains stop running at midnight* (11:30 p.m. on Sunday).

On Sunday you can travel anywhere on the network for £1 ($1.75). This is not a rover ticket and only covers a single journey.

The new Jubilee Line runs from Stanmore in the north to Baker Street, then Bond Street, Green Park, and Charing Cross.

Buses: The comparably priced bus system is almost as good. To learn about available routes, pick up a free bus map at the **British Tourist Authority,** 64 St. James's St., S.W.1, off Piccadilly, or at any **London Transport Enquiry Office.** The map is available to personal callers only, not by mail.

After you've queued up for the bus and selected a seat downstairs or on the upper deck (the best seats are on top, where you'll see more of the city), a conductor will come by to whom you tell your destination. He or she then collects the fare and gives you a ticket. As with the underground, the fare varies according to the distance you travel. If you want to be warned when to get off, simply ask the conductor.

Bargain Travel Passes: A London Explorer ticket is available for unlimited bus and underground travel for one, three, four, or seven days within central London and the inner suburbs. London Explorer costs £3.50 ($6.13) for adults, £1.30 ($2.28) for children for one day; £10 ($17.50) for adults and £3 ($5.25) for children for three days; £13 ($22.75) for adults and £4 ($7) for children for four days; and £19 ($33.25) for adults and £6 ($10.50) for children for seven days.

With this pass you don't have to queue up at the ticket counter leading to the underground: just flash your pass at the end of the run, or when the bus conductor comes around. To buy the London Explorer ticket, apply at the London Transport Travel Information Centres or at underground stations.

For shorter stays in London, or for special excursions, you may want to consider the **Red Bus Rover,** valid for one day and unlimited bus travel. The cost is £2.10 ($3.68) for adults and 60p ($1.05) for children. The pass is good on any of the central red buses. Red Bus Rover tickets are sold at most underground stations, bus garages, and the Travel Information Centres.

Taxis: You can pick up a taxicab in London either by heading for a cab stand, hailing one in the streets, or by telephoning 286-6010, 286-6128, or 272-3030. The minimum fare is 60p ($1.05). On weekends and at night, a surcharge of 40p (70¢) is added. All these tariffs include VAT. It's recommendable that you tip about 20% of the fare, and never less than 20p (35¢). *Be Warned:* If you telephone for a cab, the meter starts when a taxi receives instructions from the dispatcher, so you could find 60p ($1.05) or more on the meter when you get into the taxi for your trip.

TRAVEL BY RAIL: You should, of course, be warned that *your Eurailpass is not valid on trains in Great Britain.* But the cost of rail travel in England, Scotland, Northern Ireland, and Wales can be quite low—particularly if you take advantage of certain cost-saving travel plans.

BritRail Pass

This pass gives unlimited rail travel in England, Scotland, and Wales, and is valid on all British Rail routes, on Lake Windermere steamers, and on Sealink ferry services to the Isle of Wight. It is *not* valid on ships between Great Britain and the continent, the Channel Islands, or Ireland. An economy pass costs $107 for seven days, $162 for two weeks, $205 for 21 days, and $243 for one month. Children under 5 travel free; children from 5 to 14 pay approximately half fare. BritRail also offers a **Youth Pass** to people aged 16 through 25. A seven-day economy Youth Pass is $93, rising to $144 for two weeks, $183 for 21 days, and $215 for one month. Seats are in the economy section.

In addition, a **Senior Citizen Pass** (first-class seats) is offered those aged 65 or more. A seven-day pass costs $107, going up to $162 for two weeks, $205 for three weeks, and $243 for one month.

BritRail Passes cannot be obtained in Britain, but should be secured before leaving North America, either through travel agents or by writing or visiting BritRail Travel International, 630 Third Ave., New York, NY 10017; 510 West Sixth St., Los Angeles, CA 90014; or 333 North Michigan Ave., Chicago, IL 60601. Canadians can write to BritRail Travel International, 94 Cumberland St. East, Suite 601, Toronto M5R 1A3, ON; or 409 Granville St., Vancouver V6C 1T2, BC.

BritRail Passes do not have to be predated. Validate your pass at any British Rail station when you start your first rail journey.

BritRail's other products include the Seapass which combines unlimited rail travel in Britain with a one-way or a round-trip journey by sea between the continent or Ireland and mainland Britain.

Special Bargain Fares

British Rail from time to time offers special round-trip fares for optional travel and weekend travel, which may only be purchased in Great Britain. Because of the changing nature of these fares and facilities, it is not possible to give information about them to travelers from abroad. Information may be obtained from travel agents and British Rail stations in Great Britain.

If you're in London, and want more information on transportation rates, schedules, or facilities, go to the **British Rail Travel Centre,** 4–12 Lower Regent St., S.W.1 (tel. 839-4343), only a few minutes' walk from Piccadilly Circus. You can also make reservations and purchase rail tickets there and at the British Rail Travel Centres at Oxford Street, Victoria Station, the Strand, King William Street, Heathrow Airport, and the main London stations.

Travelpass for Scotland

BritRail passes, valid on all lines of the British Rail system, are not valid for many of the Scottish railway lines. To fill in the gap in your travel excursions around the United Kingdom, a Travelpass for Scotland is available from BritRail International, 630 Third Ave., New York, NY 10017 (tel. 212/599-5400). Travelpass may be used on all direct trains from Edinburgh and Glasgow, to the Highlands and the Scottish islands, on ferries between the mainland and the Outer Hebrides, the Firth of Clyde, the Orkneys and the Shetlands, and on scheduled buses throughout Scotland. They are issued for five- or ten-day blocks of time between March 1 and October 31, costing $68 and $113, respectively. *This Travelpass must be purchased in the United States.*

InterCity Saver Tickets

Britain's government-sponsored InterCity Rail network offers special discounts on train rides between many destinations in Britain. The conditions attached vary and you'll need to check on the spot, but as an example, let's take travel between London and Edinburgh.

Passengers must prebook their passage at either Kings Cross or Paddington Station at least two hours before departure time. You can also book your passage with a travel agent, but in such a case you must reserve before 4 p.m. on the day prior to taking your trip. If booking for travel on a Monday, you must reserve before 4 p.m. on Saturday.

You are limited to travel at certain times of the day. Departing London for Edinburgh, you can take any train going there from Kings Cross or Paddington Station between 10 a.m. and 2 p.m. On Saturday you can travel from either station on any train at any time. On Sunday you're limited to trains leaving Kings Cross between midnight and 2 p.m., although you can take any train from Paddington to Edinburgh on Sunday regardless of the departure time.

On the return from Edinburgh to London, there are no restrictions as to hours of departure. Children under 5 travel free, and children from 5 to 16 travel for half fare. Travel is by second class only, and you can't break your journey before arriving at your final destination. Because of these restrictions, savings can be considerable.

The regular unrestricted second-class rail fare from London to Edinburgh round trip is about £60 ($105), as opposed to £32 ($56) for an InterCity Saver Ticket.

WEATHER INFORMATION: There is continually updated information available by telephone. In London, dial 246-8091.

Part One

ENGLAND

Chapter II

LONDON: HOTELS

1. What to Expect
2. Hotels by Area
3. London Airport Hotels
4. Flats, Services, and Hostels

LONDON IS A HYBRID, a gathering place of people from the far corners of a once-great empire. The country gentleman and the blue-collar worker from the provinces visit London somewhat in the mood of going abroad.

The true Londoner, usually from the East End, is called a Cockney. He or she is a person born within the sound of "Bow Bells," the chimes of a church in Cheapside. But the city is also the home of the well-bred English lady who has had to sell her family estate of 400 years and take meager lodging in Earl's Court; of the expatriate Hollywood actress living in elegance in a Georgian town house; of the islander from Jamaica who comes seeking a new life and ends up collecting fares on one of London's red double-decker buses; and of the farmer's son who shuns his family's sheep pastures in the austere Lake District in favor of singing rock in a coffeehouse in the West End.

Cosmopolitan or not, Europe's largest city is still like a great wheel of village communities, with flippantly named Piccadilly Circus as the hub. Since London is such a conglomeration of sections—each having its own life (hotels, restaurants, favorite pubs)—the visitor may be intimidated until he or she gets the hang of it.

In this chapter I'll concentrate on what is called the West End (although nobody has been able to come up with a satisfactory explanation as to what that includes). For the most part, foreign visitors will live and eat in the West End, except when they venture into the historic part of London known as "The City," or go on a tour to the Tower of London, or seek rooms in remote "villages" such as Hampstead Heath.

The East End—the docks, the homes of the Cockney working class, the commercial and industrial districts—is rarely visited by tourists, except the more experienced and adventurous travelers bent on discovering offbeat London.

1. What to Expect

Since London is one of the gateway cities to Europe, some basic points about low-budget accommodations should be covered to avoid disappointing the first-timer abroad.

The majority of budget hotels aren't hotels at all (in the sense of having elevators, porters, private baths). Rather, they are old (averaging between 75 and 200 years), family-type guest houses masquerading under the name hotel. When the street pump ceased to supply the water, many of these homes for Victorian families were hastily, often badly, converted.

London still contains hundreds of these four- and five-story hotels, even though many blocks are being razed to make way for skyscrapers and commercial buildings. Some of the former town houses are attached in rows in the Georgian style and open onto a pleasant square. At first glance, most of them look the same, but, once inside, you'll find widely varying degrees of cleanliness, service, and friendliness. In some cases the personality of the hotel manager or proprietor can be a distinct advantage, particularly if he or she shows a personal concern for guests. Many of the hotel owners have been known to take guests to their private clubs or pubs, and to shower them with useful tips about survival in London.

Most bed-and-breakfast hotels **(B&B)** serve a proper English breakfast or at least a continental one, usually in a converted servants' room in the basement (rarely any other meal). The rooms on higher floors tend to be smaller. The rooms have sinks (except in the most rock bottom of establishments), innerspring mattresses (occasionally), adequate closet and dresser space (hopefully), and a desk and armchair (maybe). The bathroom may be half a flight down, two flights down, or (miracle of miracles) on the same floor.

It can even be in your bedroom. There is no longer the shortage of baths and showers as in days of yore. Most good B&B establishments now have adequate baths. Expect to pay around £2 ($3.50) to £3 ($5.25) extra on a room rate for a unit with private bath and toilet. Ask first what is included in the room rate, and in the case of a B&B, ask to see the room before accepting. You'll probably be asked to pay in advance in most B&B establishments. Incidentally, the designation of a private shower (or bath) on the tariff sheet presented to you doesn't always include a toilet in smaller places or in made-over old hotels.

Reservations by Mail: Most hotels require at least a day's deposit before they will reserve a room for you. This can be accomplished either by an international money order or a personal check. Usually you can cancel a room reservation one week ahead of time and get a full refund. A few hotelkeepers will return your money three days before the reservation date. It's no trouble if you reserve well in advance, but if you send off several deposits at the last minute, you may lose money. Many hotel owners operate on such a narrow margin of profit they find just buying stamps for airmail replies too expensive by their standards. Therefore it's most important that you enclose a prepaid International Reply Coupon.

If you're stuck, you can go to London Tourist Board's Public Information Office, named the **National Tourist Information Centre** in the Victoria Railway Station Forecourt, S.W.1 (tel. 730-0791), open from 9 a.m. to 8:30 p.m. seven days a week. The staff there will find you an accommodation. Beds are available from £4.50 ($7.88) in shared accommodations. Single rooms start at £6 ($10.50) and up. They also operate a book-a-bed-ahead service for the intending traveler. For all reservations, the charge is £2 ($3.50) and a £4 ($7) deposit. Bookings can be made by mail at the above address (include the zip code of SW1W 0DU), but the reservation is provisional only. You must confirm it and send the required deposit directly to the hotel.

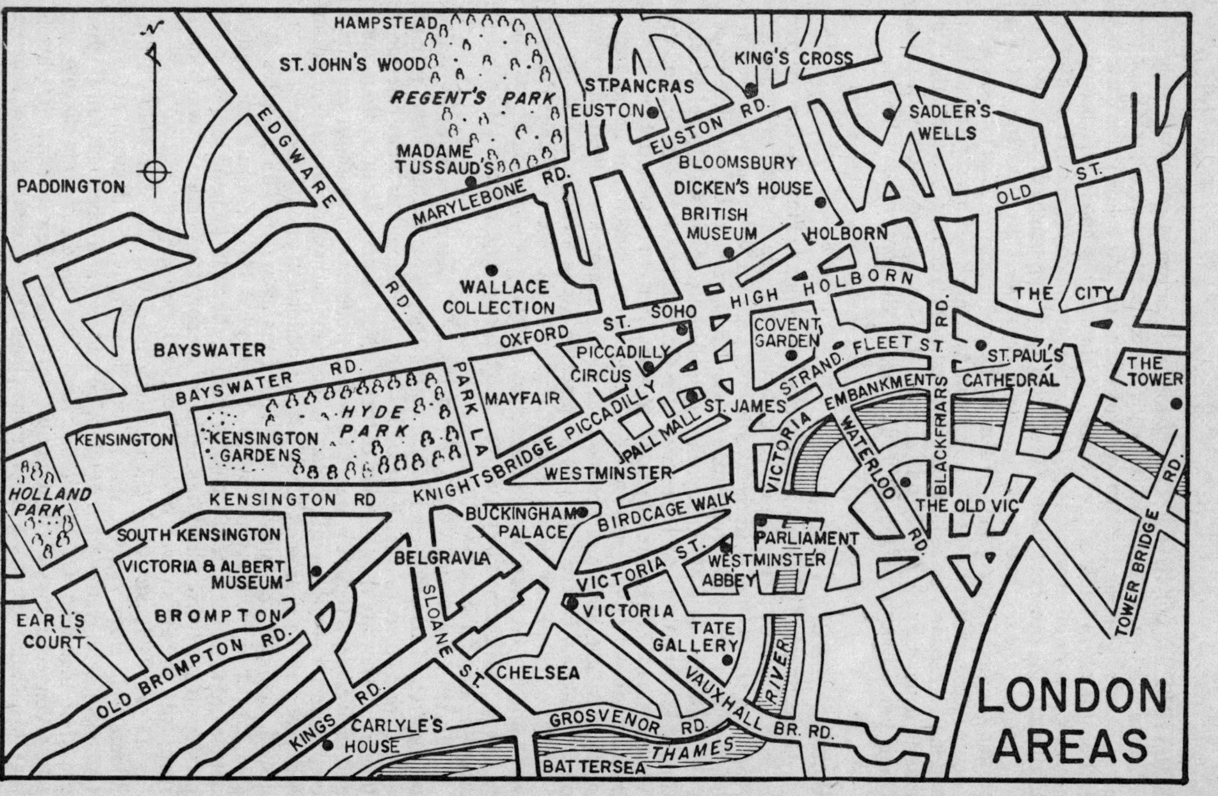
LONDON AREAS
PADDINGTON
N
HAMPSTEAD
ST. JOHN'S WOOD
REGENT'S PARK
MADAME TUSSAUD'S
ST. PANCRAS
EUSTON
KING'S CROSS
EUSTON RD.
SADLER'S WELLS
OLD ST.
EDGWARE RD.
MARYLEBONE RD.
BLOOMSBURY
DICKEN'S HOUSE
BRITISH MUSEUM
HOLBORN
HIGH HOLBORN
THE CITY
WALLACE COLLECTION
OXFORD ST.
SOHO
COVENT GARDEN
FLEET ST.
RD.
ST. PAUL'S CATHEDRAL
THE TOWER
BAYSWATER
BAYSWATER RD.
PARK LA
PICCADILLY CIRCUS
MAYFAIR
PICCADILLY
ST. JAMES
STRAND
EMBANKMENT
BLACKFRIARS RD.
HYDE PARK
KENSINGTON
KENSINGTON GARDENS
PALL MALL
VICTORIA
WATERLOO RD.
KNIGHTSBRIDGE
WESTMINSTER
HOLLAND PARK
KENSINGTON RD
BUCKINGHAM PALACE
BIRDCAGE WALK
THE OLD VIC
TOWER BRIDGE RD.
SOUTH KENSINGTON
PARLIAMENT
VICTORIA & ALBERT MUSEUM
BELGRAVIA
VICTORIA ST.
WESTMINSTER ABBEY
SLOANE ST.
EARL'S COURT
BROMPTON
VICTORIA
TATE GALLERY
BROMPTON RD.
OLD BROMPTON RD.
RIVER
CHELSEA
VAUXHALL BR. RD.
KINGS RD.
CARLYLE'S HOUSE
GROSVENOR RD.
THAMES
BATTERSEA

2. Hotels by Area

SOUTHWEST LONDON: During the most crowded periods already referred to, the wise budget visitor heads for the southwestern portion of the city—by which I mean the area south of Piccadilly and below Hyde Park, but still on the north bank of the Thames. Although the hotels here are not as numerous as in other sections of town, they are plentiful enough, and more likely than the others to have vacancies, even at the height of the season.

Most of the southwestern hotels are in the moderately expensive **Victoria** section (around Victoria Station) and in the less expensive **Earl's Court** area (where large numbers of the Canadian and Australian visitors stay). Scattered, and most reasonably priced, hotels and guest houses are also to be found in the museumland of **South Kensington** and the neighboring middle-class district of **Brompton.** I'll begin where you'll find most of the southwestern hotels.

Victoria—B&B

Directly south of Buckingham Palace is a section in Pimlico often referred to as Victoria, with its namesake, sprawling Victoria Station, as its center. Known as the "Gateway to the Continent," Victoria Station is where you get boat trains to Dover and Folkestone for that trip across the Channel to France.

The section also has many other advantages from the standpoint of location, as the British Airways Terminal, the Green Line Coach Station, and the Victoria Coach Station are all just five minutes from Victoria Station. From the bus stations, you can hop aboard many a Green Line Coach fanning out to the suburbs. In addition, an inexpensive bus tour of London departs from a point on Buckingham Palace Road, just behind the Victoria Railroad Station.

As you gaze down Belgrave Road, looking at the hotels that line the street, you'll find few recommendable choices, as many are now occupied by welfare recipients. With some exceptions, you'll find the pickings better on the satellite streets jutting off Belgrave Road.

Enrico, 79 Warwick Way, S.W. 1 (tel. 834-9538), is owned by an attractive couple from Tunis, Mr. and Mrs. Desira. They have brought their love of bright, fresh colors to this simple B&B house, trimming their white exterior in tangerine. They are rightly proud of their central heating, clean corridor baths and showers, and their TV lounge as well as double rooms with private showers. There are phones in all rooms. The corridor baths and showers are within easy reach of the bedrooms. Each accommodation is prettily and freshly furnished, and each contains hot and cold running water. The charge is £11 ($19.25) per night in a single room. Couples can stay here in a unit with a double bed at a charge of £8 ($14) per person, the tariff going up to £9 ($15.75) per person in a twin-bedded room. The most expensive doubles, a twin-bedded room with private shower, costs £10 ($17.50) per person.

Leyward House Hotel, 37 Denbigh St., S.W.1 (tel. 828-2440), a five-minute walk from Victoria Station, is a small hotel run by John and Joyce Callaghan, who charge from £9 ($15.75) per person for bed and full English breakfast, including VAT but not service. The Callaghans enjoy the give and take of conversations with their guests from abroad (often advising on sightseeing). Mr. Callaghan was a major in the cavalry for more than three decades. They prepare good breakfasts in an enlarged dining room. The bedrooms have hot and cold running water, and some have radios. And as a further incentive to staying here, the Callaghans offer reduced rates for children in one of their family rooms. Arrangements can be made for babysitting. The Leyward is at the corner of Denbigh Street and Denbigh Place.

Kerwin Hotel, 20 St. George's Dr. (tel. 834-1595), stands at the corner of Warwick Way, near the Victoria Railway Station, and the B.A., B.U.A., and B.E.A. Air Terminals. The daily rate for a single room with a full English breakfast ranges from £11 ($19.25) to £13 ($22.75), increasing to anywhere from £15 ($26.25) to £18 ($31.50) in a double, including VAT and service. Try for a corner room, as they are more spacious. Units come with a dresser, wardrobe, bedside tables, and chairs; and the hotel is fully centrally heated, with hot and cold running water in all the rooms. Mr. and Mrs. Patel, the owners, provide a warm welcome for travelers on a budget, as they are world travelers themselves, having visited many countries and continents. Tube: Victoria Station.

READER'S HOTEL SELECTION: "I would like to recommend the best of our many B&B experiences—**Ceil Court,** 122 Belgrave Rd., S.W.1 (tel. 834-4077), a beautifully decorated older building near Victoria Station. For an immaculate double room, unlimited free coffee and tea, and the use of a charming sunroom, you pay £20 ($35) nightly. Family rooms for three and four persons are also available. All services and reasonably priced restaurants are nearby in the colorful Pimlico district. Bus and underground stops are less than a block away to take you to the Houses of Parliament or the British Museum within five to ten minutes. James McGoldrick is a jovial host, and Juanita is immensely helpful with general advice and suggestions as to securing discounts on various items, including theater tickets" (Mrs. Keith Lummis, San Francisco, Calif.).

In and Around Earl's Court—B&B

Another popular hotel and rooming-house district is the area in and around Earl's Court, below Kensington, bordering the western half of Chelsea. A 15-minute subway ride from the Earl's Court Station will take you into the heart of Piccadilly, via either the District or Piccadilly lines. It is convenient to both the West End Air Terminal and the Exhibition Halls.

Incidentally, Earl's Court was for years a staid residential district, drawing genteel ladies who wore pince-nez, but I haven't seen one for a long time. Now a new young crowd is attracted to the district at night, principally to a number of pubs, wine bars, and coffeehouses.

The bulletin boards at 214 Earl's Court Rd. and the news agents next to the Earl's Court underground station are still the best place to go for those seeking either a single overnight accommodation or a shared apartment (three women, for example, will advertise for a fourth to help meet expenses). At this type of do-it-yourself operation, rates and accommodations vary widely, according to availability. A B&B can often be found for as little as £5 ($8.75) per night in a single. Doubles can be rented for £7.50 ($13.13) per night and up. But remember, you get what you pay for.

The **Beaver Hotel,** 57–58 Philbeach Gardens, S.W.5 (tel. 373-4553), is run by the genial Jan Lis, who shows a concern for his guests. The Beaver comprises 55 rooms on four floors. Built in the typical townhouse fashion, the hotel offers handsome doubles starting at £10.50 ($18.38) per person nightly (double occupancy) for a bed and a full English breakfast, including service and tax. A few rooms have three or four beds, and these are ideal for families with children. Several of the rooms possess private baths and rent for £13 ($22.75) per person, based on double occupancy. But all the rooms are centrally heated, and contain water basins, radios, and telephones. An attractive bar serves drinks and snacks in the evenings. The parents of Mr. Lis own the well-recommended **Garden Court Hotel,** 30–31 Kensington Gardens Square in Bayswater, W.2.

Coronet Hotel, 59 Nevern Square (tel. 373-6396), stands on a quiet square, just a five-minute walk from the tube station of Earl's Court. The accommodations provided by the resident owners, the James family, are quite good, and the bedrooms are warm and clean, with an endless supply of hot running water. In a single, the charge is £11.50 ($20.13) nightly, increasing to £16 ($28) in a double or twin-bedded room. Some twins or doubles are rented with private baths or showers, costing from £21 ($36.75) nightly, these tariffs including a cooked English breakfast. Three-bedded rooms are also rented, going for £21 ($36.75) nightly, and a family room costs £26 ($45.50). All units have phones and radios. The staff is friendly and most helpful. The cosmopolitan life of Earl's Court Road is just a two-minute walk from the hotel. The nearest underground is Earl's Court.

Terstan Hotel, 29–31 Nevern Square, S.W.5 (tel. 373-5368), accommodates up to 90 guests in rooms that are centrally heated with radio and phone. An elevator runs to all floors, and 27 of the bedrooms, which are comfortably furnished, contain private baths. Depending on the plumbing, singles range in price from £12.50 ($21.88) to £15.50 ($27.13), with doubles or twins renting for £19.50 ($34.13) to £23 ($40.25). Ask about one of the family rooms with bath, costing from £30 ($52.50). All these tariffs include an English breakfast, VAT, and service charge. Rooms with private baths also contain color TV sets. In addition to a public lounge, there is a licensed bar and separate TV room. London buses 74 and 31 pass within 100 yards of Nevern Square, and the Earl's Court underground station is adjacent. The hotel is family owned and personally managed.

Brompton and South Kensington—B&B

Brompton and South Kensington (S.W.7), south of Kensington Gardens and Hyde Park, are essentially residential areas, not as elegant as bordering Belgravia and Knightsbridge. The section is, however, rich in museums—in fact, is often dubbed museumland—and it has a number of colleges and institutes, which draw large numbers of students.

Staying in this section of London has much to recommend it. In addition to the nearby Kensington museums, such as the Victoria and Albert, Albert Hall is within the district, and Kensington Gardens and Harrods department store are within walking distance. At the South Kensington Station, you can catch trains for Kew Gardens and Richmond in Surrey.

Sumner Place Hotel, 14 Sumner Place, S.W.7 (tel. 589-2005), is directed by the steady hand of Mrs. Helgi Czerwinski, who has completely redecorated the place in a chic white and gold decor. If you can reserve one of the handsomely furnished units in front, complete with private balconies, you'll have the feeling of living luxuriously in one of the better sections of London. Most of the rooms contain small refrigerators for storing those cold drinks. You can also pick up already prepared food in some of the nearby shops, bringing it back. Expect to pay from £13.50 ($23.63) per person for B&B, a splurge but worth it to many readers. The location is just a block from the underground station and within walking distance of Hyde Park and the Victoria and Albert Museum. Tube: South Kensington.

Sydney Place Hotel, 6 Sydney Pl., S.W.7 (tel. 584-5637), is a spotlessly clean hotel under the supervision of Mr. and Mrs. C. J. Bygraves. It is centrally situated near the museumland of London, as well as the best shopping areas of Knightsbridge, King's Road, and Chelsea. It is also close to the home of the prime minister, Margaret Thatcher. The tariffs are from £10.50 ($18.38) in a single, from £18 ($31.50) in a double, and from £8.50 ($14.88) per person in a triple. Special terms are quoted for children under 12. Units contain hot and cold running water, a gas or electric heater, and TV. Tube: South Kensington.

Snow's Hotel, 139–141 Cromwell Rd., S.W.7 (tel. 370-1222), consists of two of the fine old houses on Cromwell Road, near the Gloucester Road underground station. At a bus stop outside, the A1 stops to pick up passengers on its way to and from Heathrow Airport. There is a comfortable lounge with TV, along with a bar and restaurant where simple meals are served in the evening, including fried plaice and french fries or grilled chops. Some of the bedrooms have private baths. Rates are from £11.50 ($20.13) per person in a twin or double without bath, going up to £13.50 ($23.63) per person in a twin or double with bath, including service, VAT, and a continental breakfast. Snow's is pleasant and convenient for the South Kensington museums and for transport to the West End. They also have three- and five-bedded rooms for families and students, renting for £5 ($8.75) per person nightly, including service, VAT, and a continental breakfast.

Leicester Court Hotel, 41 Queens Gate Gardens, S.W.7 (tel. 584-0512), is a good conversion of an old London mansion, once the home of the Earls of Strathmore. Rooms, reached by elevator, come with or without bath. There is a residents' lounge, plus a simple restaurant. The front desk will give you what information you need about tours and the theater, and there's also a night porter in case you return late from revelry in the West End. Singles rent for £16 ($28) without bath, £23 ($40.25) with bath. Doubles cost from £13 ($22.75) per person without bath, rising to £19.50 ($34.13) per person with bath. An extra bed is another £7 ($12.25) per adult. All rates include an English breakfast, service, and VAT. Tube: Gloucester Road.

In the same group and reached by going to the same tube station (Gloucester Road), is the **Tudor Court,** 58–66 Cromwell Rd., S.W.7 (tel. 584-8273), with singles going for £16 ($28) to £23 ($40.25), depending on the plumbing, and doubles costing from £13 ($22.75) per person without bath, going up to £19.50 ($34.13) per person with bath. These tariffs include an English breakfast, service, and VAT.

And quieter and more comfortable if you're anticipating a longer stay, the **Onslow Court Hotel,** 109–113 Queens Gate, S.W.7 (tel. 589-6300), and the **Stanhope Court Hotel,** 46-52 Stanhope Gardens, S.W.7 (tel. 370-2161), are excellent choices. Both charge from £19 ($33.25) to £26 ($45.50) in a single, from £14.50 ($25.38) to £20 ($35) per person in a double. The higher tariffs have private baths, and rates include an English breakfast, service, and VAT. There is color TV in most bedrooms, and it's useful to know that the Stanhope Court has some ground-floor rooms, with easy access once you have negotiated the steps to the hotel lobby from the street.

READER'S HOTEL SELECTION: "The **Imperial College,** Southside Prince's Gardens and Exhibition Road (tel. 589-9994), offers single rooms, each four rooms sharing a bath, to travelers from July to September (when the residences are not being occupied by students of the college). The rate per night, including full breakfast, is £10.50 ($18.38), with discounts available to those with a student I.D. Reservations are necessary. Not only is this the best accommodation for the price, but it is an excellent choice for those traveling alone. The bar and large TV room offer a meeting place for single travelers" (Lynn Wasserman, Brighton, Mass.).

Off the Strand—B&B

Royal Adelphi Hotel, 21 Villiers St., W.C.2 (tel. 930-8764), is clean and comfortable. Under new ownership, it has been redecorated and improved, although its prices still remain reasonable for the area. Single rooms rent for

£14 ($24.50), increasing to £16 ($28) with private bath. Depending on the plumbing, doubles or twins range from £21 ($36.75) to £24 ($42). A continental breakfast and VAT are included in the tariffs. All rooms have telephones and radios.

Belgravia—B&B

Alison House, 82 Ebury St., S.W.1 (tel. 730-9529), offers the seemingly impossible, a relatively inexpensive place to stay in exclusive Belgravia. You'll get the flavor when you walk in and are handed a glass of sherry by the resident English proprietors, Frank and Alison Haggis, who have had a lifetime of experience in hotel management. They may even walk you around the corner to Chester Square to point out the homes of famous neighbors such as Julie Andrews, Rex Harrison, and Vincent Price. The charge for staying here (close to Victoria Station and all major air terminals) is from £10 ($17.50) per person, plus VAT. This includes a "burster" of an English breakfast. Guards march past the door regularly on the way to Buckingham Palace nearby for the Changing of the Guard ceremony. Wolfgang Mozart composed his First Symphony just along the street, at 180 Ebury St. Because of the high increase in postal charges, prospective guests writing for reservations are requested to enclose an International Postal Coupon for a prompt reply.

Collin House, 104 Ebury St., S.W.1 (tel. 730-8031), provides a good, clean, and friendly B&B, under the watchful eye of its resident proprietors, Mr. and Mrs. D. L. Thomas. Everything is kept in top shape here, and all bedrooms have fitted carpets, hot and cold running water, built-in wardrobes, and comfortable divan beds. In a single room the charge is £14 ($24.50) a night, including a full English breakfast and use of the baths and showers. In a double-bedded room the charge is £22 ($38.50), rising to a high of £27 ($47.25) if you want your own private shower and toilet. The main bus, coach, and rail termini are just a three-minute walk from the hotel. Mr. and Mrs. Thomas extend a warm, personal welcome.

Chelsea—B&B

This most fashionable district stretches along the Thames, south of Hyde Park, Brompton, and South Kensington. Beginning at Sloane Square, it runs westward toward the periphery of Earl's Court and West Brompton. Its spinal cord is King's Road. The little streets and squares on either side of the King's Road artery have hundreds of tiny cottages used formerly by the toiling underprivileged of the 18th and 19th centuries. By now, except maybe for Mayfair or Belgravia, Chelsea couldn't be more chic. Hence, the tourist seeking reasonably priced accommodations should follow Greeley's sage advice to go west. For those who can afford the super-splurge prices, I have the following recommendations:

Sloane Hall, 6 Sloane Gardens, S.W.1 (tel. 730-9206), is an authentic Victorian mansion from 1888. Derek R. Jones converted it to accommodate visitors, especially families. Some rooms have private baths and all have hot and cold running water. A few rooms house as many as five persons in two doubles and one single. The chambers are pleasantly furnished, renting for £15 ($26.25) in a single. Doubles without bath go for £21 ($36.75), £23 ($40.25) with bath. Rates include breakfast and VAT. Breakfast is served in a paneled room which doubles as a lounge with color TV. Courtesy tea and coffee are available at all times in all bedrooms. Tube: Sloane Square.

Willett Hotel, 32 Sloane Gardens, S.W.1 (tel. 730-0634), opening onto the gardens, is a 19th-century town house with many architectural curiosities, including a Dutch-style roof and varying styles of bay windows. It's an intimate hotel with many luxurious and stylish features. Each of the pleasantly decorated bedrooms has a radio, TV, dressing table, and facilities for making coffee or tea. Best of all is the full English breakfast served in a club-style room with black leather chairs. Most of the accommodations contain private baths. Including breakfast, singles rent for £22 ($38.50); doubles and twins, £26 ($45.50) to £32 ($56). An extra single bed in a family room costs an additional £10 ($17.50). Tube: Sloane Square.

Culford Hall, 7 Culford Gardens, off Sloane Square (tel. 581-2211), is a small, well-run hotel in one of the most fashionable parts of Chelsea. It's quiet, comfortable, and attractively furnished with contemporary pieces. Singles without bath cost from £14 ($24.50) nightly, and bathless doubles go from £20 ($35). However, the double rate in a unit with private bath and TV begins at £23 ($40.25). Breakfast, at no extra charge, is served in the rooms (which, incidentally, contain phones and radios). However, VAT is added. The units have won the approval of many a visiting American, who cited the shaving outlets, intercom, good beds, central heating, and cleanliness. The hotel attracts people connected with embassies, universities, airlines, and foreign office personnel. The atmosphere is friendly. A short walk from the hotel will take you to some of the best restaurants along King's Road. Tube: Sloane Square.

LONDON'S MOST ELEGANT B&B (FULHAM): Off Fulham Palace Road which runs from Hammersmith to Putney Bridge, at 10 Doneraile St., S.W.6 (tel. 731-2192), **Lady Hartley** has two comfortable doubles available at £18 ($31.50), single occupancy £28 ($49) double occupancy. In this elegant Edwardian house, renovated by Lady Hartley herself, you can come and go as you please.

The rooms are well furnished with comfortable beds. Guests share a bathroom but have their own tea- and coffee-making equipment. Knowing North American tastes, Lady Hartley willingly provides ice for your drinks.

Guests have the use of the front room to sit in, and this is where a substantial breakfast with hot croissants is served. Lady Hartley decided to take in guests purely because she and her two pug dogs enjoy meeting people. She does all she can to make you comfortable.

SOUTHEAST LONDON: This fairly remote section is still another possibility for finding rooms during the overcrowded months in the West End.

London Park Hotel, Brook Drive, S.E.11 (tel. 735-9191), is an enormous warehouse across the Thames that has been completely overhauled and turned into a streamlined modern hotel. It boasts 380 bedrooms, most with showers or tubs, plus a large restaurant, coffeeshop, and two bars. Rooms are very contemporary and contain built-in headboards with telephones, radios, and color TV. Bathless singles go for £14.50 ($25.38), increasing to £16.50 ($28.86) with private bath or shower. In a twin-bedded or double-bedded room, the cost is £24.50 ($42.88) nightly, rising to £27 ($47.25) with private bath or shower. Prices include a full English breakfast and VAT. There are fast elevators and one- or two-day laundry and dry-cleaning service. Meal prices are low for London: a set lunch is £6 ($10.50); a set dinner, £6.50 ($11.38). Numerous buses pass by the hotel, and there's a tube stop at Elephant and Castle.

Stonehall House Hotel, 35–37 Westcombe Park, Blackheath, S.E.3 (tel. 858-1595), is so pleasant that guests are willing to undergo an inconvenience in transportation to stay there. For bed (innerspring mattresses) and breakfast, the overnight charge is £10.50 ($18.38) per person. The hotel, which accommodates 50 guests, is near Greenwich Park, with its Royal Observatory. The hotel is only a short hike from Maze Hill Station (Southern Region), where you can catch trains for the City and the West End, a 20-minute ride. It is also convenient to bus stops, and for catching boats to Greenwich and the Tower of London. Guests are entitled to the use of the garden and television lounge. The house is owned by Tony and Kathleen Fagg, who also offer family rooms for up to four guests at a cost of £37 ($64.75) per night, including an English breakfast, VAT, and service. For stays of seven nights, you pay for only six nights. Tony was managing director of an agricultural tractor company, and he has traveled England and the U.S. extensively, along with the rest of the world. He has many useful tips for the visitor.

Bardon Lodge, 15 Stratheden Rd., Blackheath, S.E.3 (tel. 853-4051), was a Victorian gentleman's residence built in 1869 and still retains its original grandeur. It has now been converted into a small, friendly hotel where personal service is the norm. It's in a quiet residential area next to historic Greenwich, just six miles from London's center. Barbara and Donald Nott, the owners, readily advise guests on sightseeing expeditions and the most economical way of seeing London and its environs. London's center can be reached by train (20 minutes), bus, or boat which can be taken from Greenwich Pier for a leisurely journey up the Thames to the Tower of London and on to Westminster. Parking space is available in the hotel grounds. An English breakfast is served. Some rooms contain shower and TV. The inclusive price for a double room with breakfast is £26 ($45.50) daily.

WEST LONDON: A potential bonanza for finding a room. There are literally hundreds of private hotels scattered over a wide and attractive section of the West End. I'll first list the guest houses in the remotest sector, West Kensington, then follow with the Royal Borough of Kensington (west of Kensington Gardens and Hyde Park).

In the same vicinity is another good area, Bayswater, encompassing within its undefined borders Queensway and Notting Hill Gate. The already-mentioned Paddington district, surrounding Paddington Station, north of Hyde Park, is one of the major hunting grounds for budget hotels in London, with the prized Sussex Gardens in its lair. Finally, I'll conclude with St. Marylebone, a section that touches one corner of Hyde Park and is next to Regent's Park in the east, Edgware Road in the west. First I'll take up:

Kensington—B&B

Although the Royal Borough (W.8) draws its greatest number of visitors from shoppers (Kensington High Street), it also contains a number of fine middle-class bargain guest houses, lying, for the most part, west of Kensington Gardens. The district can be a convenient place at which to stay—so near the Kensington Palace where Queen Victoria was once a resident. Of course, in Victoria's day the rows of houses along Kensington Palace Gardens were inhabited by millionaires (although Thackeray also lived there). Today the houses are occupied largely by foreign ambassadors. But we'll have to skip off to less expensive streets for our lodgings.

Mr. and Mrs. A. Demetriou, 9 Strathmore Gardens, W.8 (tel. 229-6709), operate this small, privately owned guest house very close to Kensington Gardens and Hyde Park. Reader Joseph A. Wilson, a sergeant in the army, wrote, "They are without a doubt the most helpful, courteous, and gracious pair of hosts you could ever have the good fortune to meet. These kind people went out of their way to make me feel at home. The accommodations were immaculately clean. To coin the cliché, 'You could literally eat off the floor.'" Beautifully kept and decorated, the rooms are rented at a charge of £9.50 ($16.63) to £10 ($17.50) per person for B&B, the latter, a full English one, served in a sun-filled basement dining room.

Strathmore House, 12 Strathmore Gardens, W.8 (tel. 229-3063). You'd never guess this is a hotel. There's no sign, only a street number, and its location near Embassy Row and Kensington Palace make it appear like a private town house. It's a corner house, with a low wall and shrubbery. Mr. and Mrs. Haskell, the proprietors, charge from £7.50 ($13.13) to £9 ($15.75) per person per night inclusive, according to the length of your stay. Terms include a complete English breakfast, but don't expect private baths. The bed-sitting rooms, opening off the central hallway, are large and comfortable. There are some nice old pieces mixed in with the nondescript furniture, and the total effect is homey and immaculate. You get hot and cold running water in the rooms, as well as the free use of the corridor baths. Breakfast is brought to your room, and you have a gas ring and kettle so you can make your own tea or coffee. Tube: Notting Hill Gate.

Vicarage Private Hotel, 10 Vicarage Gate, W.8 (tel. 229-4030), is the domain of Ellen and Martin Diviney, who charge £9 ($15.75) per person, double occupancy, and £10 ($17.50) in a single. Some family rooms are also available. All rates include breakfast, and as of November 1 charges are reduced slightly. The rooms have pleasant furnishings. All have water basins, and there's a good supply of showers. Mrs. Diviney makes each breakfast individually. Vicarage Gate is handy for boutiques and restaurants on Kensington Church Street, and a laundromat is nearby. Parking is likely to be a major problem in case you bring a car into London. The nearest tube stops are Kensington High and Notting Hill Gate.

Clearlake Hotel, 19 Prince of Wales Terrace, W.8 (tel. 937-3274), is an ideal family hotel on a residential street facing Kensington Gardens. Remodeled from a row of early Victorian houses, the hotel offers several conveniences for the traveler weary of typical hotel life. You can, of course, rent the comfortable single and double rooms, but the real finds here are the two-room suites and the two- and three-room apartments with private baths and all-electric kitchenettes. Some apartments also have a full-size kitchen and two bathrooms. The larger apartments can accommodate as many as eight, with plenty of closet space to go around. Rates range from £8.50 ($14.88) for a bathless single up to £40 ($70) for a large apartment capable of housing four or more.

Avonmore Hotel, 66 Avonmore Rd., W.14 (tel. 603-4296), is easily accessible to West End theaters, yet is located in a quiet neighborhood, only two minutes from the West Kensington station of the underground's District line. It's also reached by bus, number 9, 27, or 73. The Avonmore, a bright, friendly place, boasts wall-to-wall carpeting, color TV sets, refrigerators, and central heating in each room. An English breakfast is included in the price of £20 ($35) for a double room in winter, £25 ($43.75) in summer. Clients requesting a single room will be placed alone in a double room at a cost of £12 ($21) in winter, £15 ($26.25) in summer.

Abbey House, 11 Vicarage Gate, W.8 (tel. 727-2594), is managed by Mr. Nayach and his helpful staff who see that it's kept very clean and comfortable.

There are color TV sets in the bedrooms, and the English breakfasts served in a pleasant dining room are satisfying. Every room is of good size, and the units have many extras such as shaver points and vanity lights. There is also hot and cold running water, and the corridor baths are adequate. The charge is £10.50 ($18.38) nightly for B&B, VAT and TV included. This family-run business stands on a typically Victorian square. Tube: High Street Kensington.

Bayswater—B&B

Lying north of Bayswater Road to the west of Hyde Park, Bayswater is another unofficial district with any number of well-recommended, budget lodgings. Many former town houses, converted into guest houses or private hotels, date back to the days when Bayswater spelled the good life to a prosperous upper middle class. Some of these town houses, often lined up in rows, open onto pleasant squares.

The West Two Hotel, 22–23 Kensington Gardens Sq., W.2 (tel. 229-7938), won the West London Challenge Shield for being the top B&B hotel in Paddington. Its standards are still high. It's a twin hotel, a true Gemini situation, a combination of two formerly private mansions. After a long renovation program, it has emerged fresh looking, enjoying a perch on an old square, only a block from Queensway. The owners are Alan G. Aldis, from Birmingham, and John K. Coles, from South Wales.

In the remodeling, they tried to slip in as much plumbing as possible—nine toilets, six baths—and enough space for 60 guests. The inclusive rate is £24 ($42) in a double, £16.50 ($28.86) in a single. In one of the bargain family rooms, suitable for four, the charge is £36 ($63). Each room has its own decorative theme, and everything is kept immaculate. The staff is selected not only for their competence, but because they "fit in."

The breakfast rooms, on a lower level, are in apple green, with sage green stoneware dishes, each of the twin dining salons overlooking a white shaftway garden with trailing ivy and potted flowers. Breakfast is freshly cooked, and it's a good English morning meal at that. In the evening, some guests congregate in the front lounge, with its Adam fireplace, color TV, and comfortably modern furnishings. Kensington Gardens is a block off Queensway, and the hotel lies within a three-minute walk from two tube stations, Bayswater and Queensway. It's a five-minute stroll from Hyde Park.

Garden Court Hotel, 30–31 Kensington Gardens Square, W.2 (tel. 229-2553), is operated by Mr. and Mrs. Stefan Lis, who fled Poland during World War II. The family found this old town house on a private garden square and began the long task of renewing and making it the homelike hotel that is it today. For the occupants of a double or twin room, the B&B charge is £17 ($29.75), plus VAT and service. Most of the rooms are singles, renting for £10 ($17.50) nightly, but families may be interested in one of the four triple rooms at £24 ($42). The eight double rooms with private bath go for £19 ($33.25). Each room has a water basin, along with telephone, radio, and intercom. You'll enjoy meeting and talking with guests from many lands who frequent the Garden Court; there's a bar-television lounge on the ground floor, where you can lower the stock of beer on hand and hear candid opinions about world affairs.

Kensington Gardens Hotel, 84 Kensington Gardens Square, W.2 (tel. 229-2913), is a family-run hotel, centrally located off Porchester Gardens only a short walk from Hyde Park. It overlooks its own gardens, so guests are virtually assured of a good night's sleep. A single rents for £10 ($17.50), a double going for £16 ($28), these tariffs including a full English breakfast,

VAT, and service. All of the comfortably furnished, centrally heated, immaculately clean rooms have water basins. A few of the doubles have private showers at an extra charge. From November to February a special winter tariff applies. Rates depend on length of stay.

Leinster Group of Hotels, 7–11 Leinster Square, W.2 (tel. 229-9641), consists of a group of three hotels, all on Leinster Square, the Leinster, the Linden, and the Camborne. These hotels offer clean, plain rooms, many with private showers or baths, renting from £6.10 ($10.68) to £11.50 ($20.13) in a single, and from £5.50 ($9.63) to £9.60 ($16.80) per person in a double, the rates depending on the plumbing. Tariffs include a continental breakfast plus VAT. There are also three- and four-bedded rooms, costing from £5.30 ($9.28) to £8.90 ($15.58) per person. Each hotel has a dining room where a set three-course meal, either lunch or dinner, is served for around £5 ($8.75) per person. There is a bar in the Leinster which also serves the Camborne, as well as a games room which is available to guests from all three hotels. TV is available in the evenings too. Write to the group office for reservations, and the staff there will confirm which hotel you will be staying at. Tube: Bayswater.

Shepherd's Bush

Gillet Hotel, 120 Shepherd's Bush Rd., W.6 (tel. 603-0784), is owned and operated by Mr. and Mrs. C. N. Gillet, whose place lies only 15 minutes by tube from Piccadilly Circus. The rooms have hot and cold water, television, and some have refrigerators. There are shower stalls on two floors and the price is £9.50 ($16.63) per person, including breakfast. The rooms are clean and adequately furnished. The breakfast, served in the dining room, is a typical, filling English one. The hotel is a short distance to the underground.

Paddington—B&B

Another popular hotel area, jammed with budget housing, is the Paddington section, around Paddington Station, just to the northwest of Kensington Gardens and Hyde Park. Here, you'll be within walking distance of Marble Arch, a central entrance into Hyde Park.

Again, you'd be well advised to telephone ahead before you make your search. If you have not obtained a reservation, then begin your trek by taking the underground to either Paddington or Edgware Road, and then by walking to **Sussex Gardens,** a long avenue flanked by bed-and-breakfast houses. As mentioned, postbreakfast hours, when guests have just checked out, are your best time for finding a vacancy.

If you're unable to find a room on Sussex Gardens, then try the satellite **Norfolk Square,** which lies near Sussex Gardens (even closer to Paddington Station) and contains additional guest houses. My recommendations on nearby Sussex Gardens, follow.

Camelot Hotel, 45 Norfolk Square, W.2 (tel. 723-9118), is a hideaway town house (now turned hotel), a remarkable bargain and a friendly oasis. It stands at the corner of an old, tree-filled square, only two minutes from Paddington Station. Peter Evans purchased the property in 1981 and completely refurbished it from top to bottom, installing some new showers and redesigning the dining room. A new lounge was also provided, and the hotel has been recarpeted throughout. All bedrooms have color TV, radio, and tea- and coffee-making facilities. Prices are fully inclusive of all facilities, and that means free luggage storage, ironing facilities, hair dryers, whatever. Mr. Evans's aim is to provide full hotel standards at a budget price. A single room rents for £13.50

($23.63), a double or twin-bedded room for £10 ($17.50) per person. Families may be interested in one of the three- or four-bedded rooms, renting at a cost of £8 ($14) per person. These tariffs include a three-course English breakfast and VAT. Wisely, Mr. Evans has hired Barbara Knox as his manager. She is very kind and helpful to guests.

St. George, 46 Norfolk Square, W.2 (tel. 723-3560), has clean, comfortable rooms, with a bath on each floor. Each pleasantly furnished unit is equipped with hot and cold running water, and the hotel enjoys central heating. Singles rent for £9 ($15.75), with doubles going from £17 ($29.75). Children sharing their parents' room are granted a reduced rate. The tariffs quoted include a well-prepared English breakfast.

Piccolino House, 14 Sussex Pl., W.2 (tel. 723-9360), is an elegant Victorian town house which was converted into a comfortable hotel. The guest rooms are pleasant and clean, and the English breakfast the next morning is good. The management is friendly and accommodating. The hotel has 18 bedrooms, all well furnished with TV, fitted carpets, innerspring mattresses, hot and cold running water, and razor points. Showers and toilets are found on all floors. A single goes for £10 ($17.50) a night, a double or twin for £17 ($29.75). A triple room costs from £25 ($43.75), and there are some family units at £30 ($52.50). Children 5 to 12 stay here for half price. A twin with shower costs £18 ($31.50). A front-door key is provided, and the management will also arrange theater tickets.

The **Lancashire Hotel,** 24–28 Norfolk Square, W.2 (tel. 723-2189), is an inviting choice at a very good price—from £8 ($14) per person in a double and from £5.50 ($9.63) in a triple. Only two minutes from Paddington Station, the hotel has a television lounge and a cocktail lounge. More than 200 beds are available in comfortably furnished rooms, all with hot and cold running water. Adjacent to the bedroom are baths and showers on the landings. In addition, all accommodations have radio and intercom. Overflow guests are put up at the Shannon Hotel, which is operated by the same management and also opens onto Norfolk Square.

ABC Hotel, 121 Sussex Gardens, W.2 (tel. 723-3945), is run by two Londoners, Mr. and Mrs. W. M. Landers, who try to make their guests as happy and comfortable as they can. All their accommodations contain hot and cold running water, tea- or coffee-making facilities, color TV, and radio, and are pleasantly furnished and immaculately kept. The rate in a double- or twin-bedded room is £9.50 ($16.63) per person, including a full English breakfast. Some family rooms are available as well. There is no limit on the baths and showers you use. The Landers couple welcome "our American cousins," and give good advice on how to see London in the easiest and cheapest way.

Dormers Hotel, 1 Talbot Square, W.2 (tel. 723-1726), between Sussex Gardens and Paddington Station, offers 24 well-groomed bedrooms spread out on four floors (bathrooms on all landings). Mr. and Mrs. John Davies, the resident proprietors, run this family hotel which is only a few minutes from Paddington Station and Hyde Park. Their charges are £12.50 ($21.88) for a single room and £11 ($19.25) per person in a double room. A full English breakfast is included. There are special rates for children under 12 who share a room with two adults. All rooms have hot and cold running water, comfortable beds, and radios. There is also a residents' lounge with color TV.

Nayland Hotel, 134 Sussex Gardens, W.2 (tel. 723-3380), has been a family-run hotel for more than 30 years. The friendly, helpful management offers clean and comfortable rooms equipped with TVs, radios, and tea- and coffee-making facilities. They provide a traditional English breakfast, as much as you can eat. There is a lounge with a log fire during cold weather and full central heating. Rates are from £9.50 ($16.63) per person nightly, fully inclusive. The hotel is one of the few in the whole area listed by both A.A. and R.A.C.

The **Century Hotel,** Craven Hill Gardens, W.2 (tel. 262-6644), is a neat and convenient place close to Paddington Station and the roads out of London to the north and west. All rooms have private bath, central heating, radio, color TV, and phone. There is a pleasant small bar. Comfortably furnished rooms rent for £22.50 ($39.38) in a single, but only £15 ($26.25) per person, in a twin or double. Triples are a bargain at £13.50 ($23.63) per person, including VAT and service. Breakfast is extra. (Under the same banner, the **Royal Eagle Hotel,** Craven Road, W.2 [tel. 723-3262], has similar facilities and the same overnight prices.) Tube: Paddington Station.

St. David's Hotel, 16 Norfolk Square, W.2 (tel. 402-9061), is run by George Neokleous, who offers not only clean and comfortably furnished bedrooms, but good English breakfasts and pleasant service. Rates are from £10.50 ($18.38) per person in units which contain hot and cold running water. There is central heating, and most rooms have TV as well. Guests have found the owner helpful, genial, and courteous. The hotel stands one minute from the Paddington and Lancaster Gate tube stations.

READER'S HOTEL SELECTION: "I could not have received a warmer welcome to London for the first time than I did at **Glais Guest House,** 119 Sussex Gardens, Hyde Park, W.2 (tel. 723-9785). This house is owned and operated by the N. K. Seymours, a Welsh couple who made me feel right at home. They charge from £11 ($19.25) per person per night, with an enormous breakfast and no limit on the baths. They were happy to give me a welcome when I arrived, and their rooms are nice, clean, and quiet, and all have hot and cold running water. They have radios and TV in all rooms" (Elsa Jo Carver, Huntington Beach, Calif.).

St. Marylebone—B&B

Below Regent's Park, lying northwest of Piccadilly Circus, is the principally Georgian district of St. Marylebone (pronounced Mar-li-bone), a residential section facing Mayfair to the south and extending north of Marble Arch at Hyde Park. A number of simple but gracious town houses in this section are being turned into private hotels, and little discreet bed-and-breakfast signs are popping up in the windows.

As you walk up and down some of these streets, you are certain to find them. For example, Upper Berkeley Street has some attractively priced accommodations. If you have arrived in London without a reservation in the peak months, then start at Edgware Road and walk past Seymour and Great Cumberland Place. Let the summer crowds fight it out in Bloomsbury.

Merryfield House, 42 York St., off Baker Street, W.1 (tel. 935-8326), is a refreshingly pleasant remake of a 19th-century pub, the Lord Keith. Former ale drinkers of old would look askance at the bright facade and the flower boxes filled with red geraniums. Owned by Mr. and Mrs. Tyler-Smith, the hotel is a haven for those who cling to the old English ways. Resisting TV sets and continental breakfasts, the manager, Bridget, serves a "jolly good breakfast" right in your room. According to the season and location, doubles (no twins or singles) range in price from £19 ($33.25) to £22 ($38.50). All rooms have private bathrooms. The house is small enough so that a tiny staff can keep everything shiny, polished, scrubbed, and laundered. The location is also convenient for shoppers, as it lies near Selfridges and Marks & Spencers. York Street is just two blocks south of Marylebone Road. Tube: Baker Street.

Rose Court Hotel, Great Cumberland Place, W.1 (tel. 262-7241), is well situated, lying just north of Marble Arch and Oxford Street. All rooms contain private bath, TV, central heating, radio, and phone. Surprising for the price, there is 24-hour porter service, along with friendly room service as well. A comfortable lounge and bar add to the other attractions of the old house, which once belonged to Lady Jennie Churchill. Her bedroom has been furnished in a period style, and there are two remarkable cantilevered staircases. Twins and doubles go for £15 ($26.25) per person, including VAT and service. Triples are rented for £13.50 ($23.63) per person, and four-bedded rooms cost from £12.50 ($21.88) per person. Breakfast is another £1.50 ($2.63) if continental, £2 ($3.50) if English. Tube: Marble Arch.

Hart House, 51 Gloucester Pl., W.1 (tel. 935-2288), is a well-preserved building, part of a group of Georgian mansions occupied by the French nobility during the French Revolution. The hotel is in the heart of the West End and is convenient for shopping and theaters. It is within easy walking distance of Oxford Street, Selfridges, Marble Arch, Hyde Park, Regent's Park, and the Zoo, along with Madame Tussaud's and the Planetarium. Hart House is centrally heated; all rooms have hot and cold running water, phones, radios, and razor points. This is a small family hotel, where the units are kept clean and comfortable. Mr. and Mrs. Bowden, the resident Welsh proprietors, charge from £17 ($29.75) in a single room, from £26 ($45.50) in a twin or double, provided it's without bath. With a private bathroom added, the rate jumps to £29 ($50.75). Some three-bedded rooms are rented as well, costing from £35 ($61.25) to £39 ($68.25), depending on the plumbing.

READERS' HOTEL SELECTIONS: "**Langford Court Hotel,** 50 Upper Berkeley St., W.1 (tel. 723-7888), charges £9 ($15.75) for bed and quite acceptable breakfast. It has a homey atmosphere. You can watch good-quality color TV in the dining room, and the staff is helpful. It is a private hotel, and while probably by no means outstanding, I think it's worth remembering for people who want to be near Central London as it is only about a ten-minute walk from the Marble Arch underground station and Oxford Street" (Mrs. Antoinette R. Mian, Scarborough, Ont., Canada.) . . . "I heartily recommend the guest house known as **Milford House,** 31 York St., W.1 (tel. 935-1935). Everything is spotless, breakfasts are ample and delicious, and the hostess, Ronnie, is a continuous help. As the house is in the Marble Arch area, it is near everything. The charge is £10.50 ($18.38) per person, VAT and service included" (Sally Julian, Tucson, Ariz.).

NORTHERN LONDON: London's most numerous cluster of budget hotels is to be found in the northern part of the city, a geographical designation that shouldn't discourage you. By northern I refer to an area which has as its southern border Oxford Street, New Oxford Street, and High Holborn. Its western border touches Regent's Park; its northern border, the terminals of Kings Cross, St. Pancras, and Euston Stations; its eastern border, Farringdon Road, the beginning of Finsbury. Most of the accommodations are centered in the southern part, known as Bloomsbury.

During the warmer months, June through mid-September, the hotels here are heavily booked. It is for that reason I suggest you seek out your summertime accommodations in the southwestern area of the city. If, nevertheless, you crave to live in the well-situated north, be sure to obtain advance reservations, or phone the hotels that sound attractive to you before appearing on their doorsteps. A timely call can spare you fruitless searching.

Bloomsbury—B&B

Northeast of Piccadilly Circus, beyond Soho, lies a world within itself. It is, among other things, the academic heart of London, where you'll find London University, several other colleges, the British Museum, and many bookstores. Despite its student overtones, the section is fairly staid and quiet. Its reputation has been fanned by such writers as Virginia Woolf, who lived within its bounds (it figured in her novel *Jacob's Room*). The novelist and her husband, Leonard, were once the unofficial leaders of a group of artists and writers known as "the Bloomsbury group"—nicknamed "Bloomsberries." At times, this intellectual camaraderie reached out to embrace Bertrand Russell.

The heart of Bloomsbury is **Russell Square,** and the streets jutting off from the square are lined with hotels and bed-and-breakfast houses. If you have not found a hotel room by phoning first, and prefer to make your search on foot, you might try the following itinerary:

From the Russell Square underground station (whose exit is on Bernard Street), walk first along Bernard Street, which contains many hotels. Then, one long block north of Bernard Street, try Coram Street, another hotel-lined block, and after that sample Tavistock Place, running one block north of Coram and parallel to it. North of Tavistock Place is Cartwright Gardens, which has a number of old converted town houses catering to overnight guests.

The Bernard Street–Coram Street–Tavistock Place hotels are, however, the most likely Russell Square establishments to be booked in summer. You'll have a better chance on the other side of Russell Square (opposite Bernard Street), where you'll find the relatively high-priced hotels of Bloomsbury Street (lined with publishing houses) and those on the less expensive Gower Street, where you'll be at the midpoint of the London University area. On Gower Street, for instance, you'll find the Royal Academy of Dramatic Art, across from which are a number of inexpensive B&B houses.

Garden House Hotel, 19 Bernard St., W.C.1 (tel. 837-5176), is a winsome choice on this residential street, where G. B. Shaw once trod. The hotel is friendly and comfortable, and the managers, Mr. and Mrs. Renato Ferdenzi, charge from £11 ($19.25) nightly in a single, the price rising to £17 ($29.75) in a double.

Avalon Private Hotel, 46–47 Cartwright Gardens, W.C.1 (tel. 387-2366), is the domain of Mr. and Mrs. A. J. Taylor, who have long been popular with overseas visitors. The centrally heated Avalon is part of a Georgian crescent of town houses built in 1810–1830 overlooking quiet gardens. For a good room and a full English breakfast, the Taylors charge £14 ($24.50) in a single, £20 ($35) in a double, including VAT. No additional service tax is added. They are pleased that their guests can use their private garden and the tennis courts. The Taylors will provide you with information on how to get around London by underground or bus; they will give you directions on ways to reach nearby cleaners, a druggist, the post office, railway stations, air terminals, tourist agencies, the shopping district, and car-rental places. If you want to wash your drip-dries, or iron your drip-wrinkles, facilities are provided.

Lonsdale Hotel, 9–10 Bedford Pl., W.C.1 (tel. 636-1812), is a Regency town house, within the shadow of the British Museum. It's positioned on an attractive tree-lined street midway between Russell and Bloomsbury Squares. It is a particular favorite of professors and scientists from the continent who find it a convenient place to stay while researching at the museum. The B&B rate in a double or twin is £26 ($45.50), although singles pay £16.50 ($28.86), including VAT. All rooms have razor outlets, and central heating assures cozy warmth. The hotel is privately owned and has a little garden in the rear. Tube: Russell Square.

Crescent Hotel, Cartwright Gardens, W.C.1 (tel. 387-1515), is a good economy choice in Bloomsbury. Its success is based in large part on the long-time management of its owner, Mrs. Bessolo, who hires an efficient, pleasant staff. Her rooms are well maintained, costing £12 ($21) per day in a single, rising to £20 ($35) for a twin- or double-bedded room. These rates include a full English breakfast and tax. In addition, she also rents out family rooms, consisting of two single beds and one double bed beginning at £26 ($45.50) daily. Children under 14 years of age pay half price in a family room. There's a TV lounge as well.

Gower House Hotel, 57 Gower St., W.C.1 (tel. 636-4685), is an attractive, clean, and friendly hotel run by P. and J. Borg, its owners who cater to families. In all, they offer 14 bedrooms, including some large family rooms, suitable for three to five persons. In these the rate is £8 ($14) per person nightly. Otherwise, singles pay £10 ($17.50) and doubles or twins go for £16 ($28). All tariffs include a full English breakfast and tax. Each well-furnished room contains hot and cold running water, and there is a breakfast room as well as a TV lounge.

Arran House Hotel, 77 Gower St., W.C.1 (tel. 636-2186), is run by Mr. W. J. Richards, an ex-army major, who commands a very good place. He lives at the hotel too, along with his family. The rooms are well maintained, containing hot and cold running water. All are centrally heated as well, and equipped with intercom. Near all bedrooms are baths, toilets, and showers. Rates in a single are £11 ($19.25) per person daily, rising to £17 ($29.75) in a twin or double. The special family rooms, with three and four beds, range in price from £21 ($36.75) to £25 ($43.75) daily, all tariffs including a full English breakfast. There is also a residents' lounge with a color TV.

Ruskin Hotel, 23–24 Montague St., W.C.1 (tel. 636-7388), stands next to the British Museum, within walking distance of London's shopping district and major West End theaters. A family-run business, the hotel is comfortably decorated, with many modern amenities added. All floors are serviced by an elevator. Listed as a building of historical interest, the hotel has retained many of its original architectural features. The television lounge has a mural ascribed to James Ward. The bedrooms have plenty of hot and cold running water and such amenities as shaver points, intercom, and electrical outlets. The rooms also enjoy central heating, and several have attached showers. The cost of a room, including a full English breakfast served in the dining room, is £14 ($24.50) in a single, from £22 ($38.50) in a double, including VAT.

READER'S HOTEL SELECTION: "I stayed at the **Ridgemount Hotel,** 65 Gower St., W.C.1 (tel. 636-1141). This guest house is run by Mr. and Mrs. Rees and is convenient to several underground stations. Singles rent at £10.50 ($18.38) and doubles at £9 ($15.75) per person nightly for B&B. Mrs. Rees made up a cold breakfast tray for me the night before my departure because my train to Edinburgh was to leave before the scheduled breakfast. I found the hospitality here to be first rate" (Ray LaFever, Arlington, Va.).

In and Around Hampstead

Sandringham Hotel, 3 Holford Rd., N.W.3 (tel. 435-1569). You'd never guess this is a hotel, because it stands on a residential street in one of the best parts of London. After getting off at the Hampstead tube station, you walk up Heath Street, past interesting shops, pubs, and charmingly converted houses. Shortly, at the Turpin Restaurant, you turn right into Hampstead Square which leads you into Holford Road. A high wall and trees screen the house from the street (if you have a car, you can park in the driveway). It is a well-built, centrally heated house, and the comfortable rooms often house professional people who want to be near the center of London yet retain the feel of rural life. The B&B charge is £10.50 ($18.38) per person (reduced for weekly stays), plus service and VAT. The breakfast room overlooks a walled garden. From the upper rooms you can see past the heath to a panoramic view of the center of London. You'll find a homelike lounge furnished with a color TV. Owners Mr. and Mrs. Dreyer and their two sons live on the premises.

In West Hampstead, a somewhat offbeat accommodation is provided by the **Charlotte Restaurant,** 221 West End Lane, N.W.6 (tel. 794-6476), an old established and inexpensive restaurant with a tasteful decor which offers B&B and a three-course dinner for an inclusive rate of £10 ($17.50) per person. The food is really good, and the chef will give you enough of it, both an English and a continental cuisine. Accommodations are simple but comfortable. The house lies only one minute to British rail, tube, and bus routes (17 minutes from the heart of London). The nearest underground station is West Hampstead.

Michael's Guest House, 1A Crossfield Rd. (tel. 722-9174), is small, quiet, and comfortable. All rooms have hot and cold running water and a TV, and guests are allowed to make use of two kitchens on the premises. A twin room rents for £14.50 ($25.38) nightly, and a single goes for £9.50 ($16.63), these tariffs including a continental breakfast and the service charge. The guest house is about a ten-minute ride from the center of London, and it's near local shops and restaurant. Tube: Swiss Cottage.

In a Northwest London Suburb

The Cottage, Handel Close, Canons Drive, Edgware (tel. 952-2104), provides a personal family style of London living, only 35 minutes by tube from the core of the theater and shopping areas. Handel, the composer, was a chapel master and musical director for two years in this area—hence Handel Close. The house itself is a detached corner structure in the Tudor style. For B&B on a daily basis, Mrs. Stein charges two persons from £16 ($28) to £19 ($33.25) in a double, from £11 ($19.25) to £13 ($22.75) in a single, plus service. There are tea-making facilities in each room. No private baths are available, but there are two bathrooms. The Cottage is attractively furnished in a personal style, some windows opening onto a landscaped garden with a sunken lawn and wishing well. Canons Drive has its own seven-acre lake, available to guests. Mr. Stein drives into London nearly every day, and is pleased to give free rides to his guests. Otherwise, the closest tube stations are Edgware and Canons Park.

READER'S HOTEL SELECTION: "An excellent B&B hotel is **St. Olaves Hotel,** 107 High Rd., in Loughton (on the tube system) just outside London (tel. 508-1699). The hotel is run by Joyce Heaton whom I found to be a warm and friendly hostess. Her charges are reasonable at £16 ($28) in a single and £21 ($36.75) in a double. In one of the family units, each person is charged £4 ($7) extra. She treats all her guests as if they are family and makes everyone feel at home. I have stayed at the St. Olaves on four different occasions, and each time I have been thoroughly satisfied with the friendly service and extremely clean rooms. The beautiful Epping Forest is within walking distance of the hotel. The town of Loughton is friendly, with many good stores for shopping at moderate prices. The tube makes it easy and inexpensive to go into London" (Gina Smith, Bedford, Texas).

3. London Airport Hotels

Most planes will land at Heathrow, although charter flights are likely to go to Gatwick. If you need to be near either airport, close to your point of departure, consider some of the following suggestions instead of the well-advertised and expensive operations at both airports.

HEATHROW: Close to the airport are several inexpensive but worthwhile suggestions.

The **Packhorse Hotel,** Thames Street, Staines, TW18 4SJ (tel. Staines 54221), is a solid riverside pub with terraces beside the stream where you can drink and ponder on a hot summer's evening. Solid bedrooms, some with bath, all with phone, radio, and TV, cost from £19 ($33.24) in a single and from £15.50 ($27.13) per person in a double or twin. Substantial meals are served in the evening, and there is good parking. The hotel is about a 30-minute drive from the airport.

The Swan, The Hythe, Staines, TW18 3JB (tel. Staines 52494), lies across the river on the Surrey side. It's an attractive old pub right over the river, with a good reputation for food. Rooms have central heating and radio, and the lone single rents for £14.50 ($25.38) nightly. Doubles cost £17.50 ($30.63) for two. A set dinner goes for £9 ($15.75), and you can choose from the selection of grills and roasts. Take your dinner in one of the small, sloping rooms which make up the restaurant of this ancient inn.

For bed and breakfast, try **Mrs. A. D. Sachs,** Upton Park Guest House, 41 Upton Park, Slough, Berkshire (tel. 0753/28797), about a 15-minute cab ride from Heathrow. If you preplan, Mrs. Sachs will send a local taxi to meet you, which is cheaper. The rooms have hot and cold running water, and there is a pleasant lounge with color TV. Tea- and coffee-making facilities are available for that refresher when you arrive between meals. The house is centrally heated, and there is ample car parking. Bed and a full breakfast costs about £7.50 ($13.13) per night.

Parkside Hotel, 1 Upton Court Rd., Slough, Berkshire (tel. 0753/22533), is a well-run place, offering B&B at a cost of £8.50 ($14.88) per person, plus VAT. All units have hot and cold running water and razor points. There is a TV lounge, plus another lounge which doubles as the breakfast room. Mr. and Mrs. Willmer, the owners, can provide local information about train services to London and buses to Windsor.

GATWICK: Since this airport is so far from London, you may want to find a convenient perch nearby while waiting for the departure of your flight. Some suggestions follow.

Goff's Park Hotel, 45 Goffs Park Rd., Southgate, Crawley RH11 8AX (tel. 0293/35447). This is a pleasant enough place where an overnight accommodation will cost from £20 ($35) in a single and from £30 ($52.50) in a double or twin equipped with phone, radio, and TV. Dinner is a simple meal at £3.50 ($6.13), and you can select mainly grills and fish dishes from an à la carte menu. The hotel lies about a 15-minute drive from Gatwick. If you have an early start, the management will arrange for a local taxi to take you across.

For B&B, try **Brookfield Farm House,** Winterpit Lane, Plummers Plain, Horsham, Sussex (tel. 040376/568), a much modernized farmhouse which is warm and cozy with an open log fire in the lounge. You are welcomed by Mr. and Mrs. Christian, who will even collect you from or take you to (or both) Gatwick Airport, if you give them sufficient warning. That is, you must give your flight number and arrival time. Rooms here rent for £9 ($15.75) per person for B&B, and an evening meal is provided upon request at £3.75 ($6.56). There is good parking as well.

Near Gatwick Airport

READER'S HOTEL SELECTION: **"Trumble's Hotel and Restaurant** on Stanhill (the road to Newdigate), Charlwood, Surrey (tel. Crawley 862212), is a wonderful place to stay overnight, or just to dine, if your plane comes in at Gatwick Airport. The hotel is only ten minutes by car from there, in lovely rolling country. Its rooms are large and beautiful, some furnished with fine antiques (one bedroom even has a 200-year-old canopied four-poster bed). All bedrooms have private bathrooms and color TV. There's nothing gloomy—everything's airy and cheerful and comfortable, and the 'full' heat is really that. The B&B rate for two persons, including a full English breakfast, VAT, and service, is £27.50 ($48.13) nightly. Proprietors Sue and Peter Trumble provide all kinds of services, including arranging for car rentals. Or they let you alone if that's your wish. Dinner here averages about £9 ($15.75) per person and is of gourmet quality. House specialties are traditional roast beef for Sunday lunch, roast duckling with orange sauce and fresh wheels of orange, very tender steaks, and plenty of fresh English fish. Menus are changed regularly as new dishes are created. Ask for the trifle, an English specialty. Also try the homemade meringue gâteau. Excellent wines and liqueurs are available. There's a small Victorian bar. Trumble's would be a splendid place to spend a week or two. As there are only five bedrooms, it is advisable to reserve ahead, and with mail delays, it is worth telephoning your reservation, but don't forget the time zone. International telephone number is + 44-293-862212. With a car, you could travel to Canterbury, Oxford, the South Coast, or Winchester, to name a few good spots, and get back in time for a memorable dinner. Also you can drive to Gatwick Airport, leave your car, and take the short train ride to London for the day. Trains run every 15 minutes during the day, every hour at night. Charlwood village is full of historic houses, some more than 500 years old. The church has a wall pre-William the Conqueror and 1066" (Mrs. Janet Kay, Rochester, N.Y.).

3. Flats, Services, and Hostels

YOUR OWN APARTMENT (for seven days or more): **London Tourist Holiday Flatlets,** 117 Sydney St., S.W.3 (tel. 351-0582), is run by the very helpful Bill Wiggins and Chris Kauntze, who will secure readers "flatlets" (small apartments) in the Kensington and Chelsea area. They charge from £ 30 ($52.50) per week for a nicely furnished single room with a full kitchen and shower. Doubles are available for £35 ($61.25) per week. All the flatlets contain TV sets, linen, and other equipment, and are near public transport.

Barbara and Roy Sheppard, 8 Woodsome Rd., N.W.5 (tel. 267-1782), offer some of the best value for apartments in London if you're interested in a self-catering holiday home. Their "flats" come with fully equipped kitchens, and bed linen is supplied. You can also expect a refrigerator and color TV, as well as metered electricity and a phone. The charge is £4 ($7) per day (half price for a child), plus the VAT, and there's a booking fee of £5 ($8.75), plus VAT. The Sheppards also offer a car rental at £10 ($17.50) a day, plus a £1 ($1.75) insurance waiver. VAT is extra, but the cars are rented on an unlimited mileage basis.

STAYING WITH A FAMILY: Many agencies in Britain can arrange stays with a private family, either in London or in the country. As much as is possible, interests are matched. This program is an intriguing way to involve yourself in the social life of a country, seeing it from the inside. Also it's a bargain when compared to hotels. Some agencies limit themselves to teenagers; others welcome older readers. Try one of the following:

Family Friendships Service, 22 Palmerston Crescent, Palmers Green, N.13 (tel. 882-5572), is run by April Strawson-Sykes and her partner, Kay

Steadman, and they give you personalized treatment. They provide family accommodations mainly in London and the southeast of England. However, given sufficient time, they will find accommodations in any area needed. They accept children from the age of 12, and can arrange B&B accommodations, half board, or full board in selected families on an "en famille" basis. Receiving families are interviewed so that guests can be sure of a good welcome by friendly hosts. Rooms are comfortable and clean, and all homes are well furnished and equipped with TV. Families are matched so that at least one shared interest will act as an "ice breaker."

Rates for B&B are from £42 ($73.50) weekly, going up to £49 ($85.75) weekly on the half-board plan. However, tariffs rise to £75 ($131.25) weekly for half-board in such areas as Kensington, which is a top-rate section.

London Home-To-Home, 26 Ascott Ave., W.5 (tel. 567-2998). When their children started to grow up, Anita Harrison and Australian Rosemary Richardson looked around for something to do. Since they both had always had a stream of overseas visitors staying with them, they hit on the idea of providing a "home-away-from-home" accommodation on a wider basis. Nowadays they have more than 100 houses on their books, mostly in the leafy London suburbs.

Each house must provide a comfortable accommodation with a full English breakfast, tea and coffee, access to the home and to the family living area at all times, use of TV and the lounge, and by arrangement, an evening meal at around £5 ($8.75) extra. All accommodations are by definition in private homes, with full use of bathrooms and washing and ironing facilities.

They try to match homes and guests, so you'll be asked to list your interests (briefly) when you book. For an additional £15 ($26.25), a transfer can be arranged from Heathrow Airport—more if you arrive at Gatwick. All arrivals are presented with a "holiday help pack" of maps, bus and tube timetables, sightseeing tour brochures, and so forth.

The amazing cost of this delightful service is £10.50 ($18.38) per night in a single, £17 ($29.75) per night in a twin or double. Family rooms for two adults and one child are £23 ($40.25) per night. All tariffs include a full breakfast.

You pay a small deposit on booking, then settle the balance with your hosts after you arrive. If you have to cancel, deposits are refunded, less a small administration charge if at least four-weeks' notice is given.

They also operate a very useful London Mail-Link, receiving and redirecting your letters and also acting as an accommodation address for airlines and tour companies who need to get in touch with you. All you have to do is to send your subscription of £3.50 ($6.13) per month and supply details of what you want done with your letters and messages. The Mail-Link registration form will be forwarded to you when you book your London accommodation.

In addition, **Family Holidays,** 2 Kirklands Ave., Baildon, Shipley, Yorkshire (tel. Bradford 584848), owned by Douglas Cummins, has a well-screened list of Britishers who ordinarily don't accept paying guests and who are not accessible from any other source. These include professional people and others who will welcome you into their homes, which are not only situated in London but in attractive areas by the sea or in the country in England, Scotland, and Wales. Upon application, you'll receive information about your host, his or her interests, age, and family. The cost of accommodations is the same: about $100 (U.S.) per person weekly for full board. Mr. Cummins adds a 15% service charge, and you'll pay no more. There's even an arrangement for what to do if you and your host don't get on too well!

Home from Home International Ltd. specializes in finding you genuine hospitality with a host family. Local knowledge and advice is readily given to make your stay enjoyable, whether it's in a country cottage, flat, farmhouse, or period house with antiques. Here is your chance to get to know the beautiful countryside of Surrey, Kent, Hampshire, Sussex, and the Cotswolds, or stay in London. B&B costs from £8 ($14) to £15 ($26.25) per person per night, and other meals are available on request. More information and brochures can be obtained from 30a High St., Haslemere, Surrey, GU27 2HJ (tel. 0428/53133).

Ball Tourist Services, 9 Norbury Ave., Thornton Heath, Surrey (tel. 01/653-8467), will arrange for accommodations with selected families living in the southwest suburbs of London, including Streatham, Norbury, Mitcham, and Thornton Heath. Only about 15 minutes by train to the center of London, the area is convenient for all sorts of recreational and sightseeing activities. Host-family accommodation is also available in Edinburgh, the Lake District, Cambridge, the southeast coast of England, and the Isle of Wight. Accommodation with English breakfast is from £7 ($12.25), and with English breakfast and an evening meal, £9.50 ($16.63). Prices include the booking fee and tax.

B&B IN PRIVATE HOMES: Thea Druce, who has operated a B&B establishment, now manages **London Homes,** 8 St. Dunstans Rd., Barons Court, W.6 (tel. 748-1504), which books visitors into private homes in the London area. These homes are in such districts as Finchley, Swiss Cottage, Hampstead, Richmond, Putney, Chiswick, and Hammersmith. All the homes, whether standard, superior, or deluxe, are well decorated, unlike the reputation of some London establishments as "Dickensian." Bedrooms offer subtle decoration, fitted carpets, wash basins, central heating, and a friendly atmosphere. All the homes are near the underground system, so traveling around is easy. In addition to the sections mentioned, London Homes also offers some B&B establishments right in the center of London—Kensington, Knightsbridge, and Sloane Square in Chelsea. A key is provided so that visitors can come and go as they wish. Accommodations are cleaned daily, and every morning a tasty English breakfast is provided. Best yet, there is a warm personal welcome waiting. Accommodations are in areas surrounded by good restaurants and typical English pubs. Daily rates begin at £8.50 ($14.88) per person, ranging upward. Brochures can be obtained by writing directly to London Homes.

HOUSE-SWAPPING: This custom is becoming more and more popular among those who spend three weeks or more in England. In exchange for a caretaker for your New York apartment or California bungalow, you can occupy a three-bedroom house close enough to London to make travel inexpensive and to give you a base for your holiday—and it's rent-free. Write to **Home Interchange Ltd.,** 8 Hillside, Farningham, Kent (tel. 0322/86-4527), to join the club for a fee of £16.50 ($28.86). You'll receive a copy of the Home Exchange Directory—and you're away. Members are required to give a reasonably accurate description of their home, including pets to be fed. This service, of course, does not apply only to houses near London. A range of properties throughout the country are available on the swap plan, including most countries in Europe.

STUDENTS: If you're a student, an International Student ID Card is your passport to all kinds of travel savings throughout the world. Substantial discounts on air and land transportation, cultural attractions, accommodations, and an automatic traveler's accident/sickness policy are some of the benefits of the ID card, which sells for $6 (U.S.). You can request a free copy of the *Student Travel Catalog,* packed with travel information as well as an application as well as an application and instructions for obtaining the card, from the **Council on International Educational Exchange,** 205 E. 42nd St., New York, NY 10017 (tel. 212/661-1414), the official U.S. sponsor of the card. High school, college, or graduate-level students are eligible for this document. Council travel offices throughout the U.S. are able to help all budget travelers with travel arrangements, including low-cost flights between the U.S. and Europe.

Making Friends

Want to meet an international assortment of fellow students? Many organizations in London will involve you in their social activities, and they extend a hearty welcome to foreign students. One in particular, **International House,** 106 Piccadilly, W.1 (tel. 437-9167), is a lively spot—and an ideal place for the lonely person to meet someone to talk to. The club, housed in an 18th-century mansion overlooking Green Park, was founded to provide education and a social life for overseas visitors. Nonmembers are welcomed without charge. Inexpensive excursions are offered, including, for example, four-day trips to Scotland and Wales. Four days in Scotland, including transportation from London, a tour bus, guide, accommodations, some meals, and some entertainment, is likely to run about £75 ($131.25).

Bargain Hotel for Students

Driscoll House, 172 New Kent Rd., Elephant and Castle, S.E.1 (tel. 703-4175), is an international hotel, offering accommodations for short or long terms. Some 200 rooms are offered, including many facilities and amenities. At a cost of £47 ($82.25) per week, a single room with full board is rented, among the least expensive accommodations in Central London. Rooms are centrally heated, and there are TV and table-tennis areas, as well as a library and a laundry. And there are a dozen pianos. About a quarter of the residents are students, and the rest are composed of civil servants, teachers, secretaries, whatever. In all, Mr. Driscoll has been host to people from some 158 countries. The hotel is about 20 minutes by bus from Victoria. In the main building are sitting rooms, including three for television, another for laundry, and a library. Social and cultural activities are organized. The hotel was founded in 1913 and opened by H.R.H. the Princess Louise.

YOUTH HOSTELS: In youth hostels, reservations are imperative—and must be made months or even a year in advance. In one season alone, the youth hostels of London turned away 33,000 written applications with deposits! You must, of course, comply with each hostel's restrictions, such as a membership card and in many cases a curfew. A great number also carry limitations on the number of nights you can stay.

In the United States, you can join the **American Youth Hostels Association** (contact them at: American Youth Hostels, Inc., 8th Floor, 1332 "I" St. NW, Washington, DC 20005, or call toll free 800/424-9426), by paying a membership fee of $14 if you're 18 or over. A junior membership for those under 18 years and 60 or over costs $7 for the year. Membership in AYH is honored at Youth Hostels in England as well as in 60 other countries.

Quest Hotel (formerly Coleman Court Student Hotel), 43 Queensborough Terrace (tel. 229-1619), is run by Joanna, a young, hip, blue-jeaned, eccentric American bird, with an international staff. They will share their fun and laughter along with their worldwide budget travel tips. Joanna is an expert on London, especially the theater world, and can point you to many inexpensive locations. If she is at the hotel, you may be asked to join in one of their fun evenings around London town. They cater to all age levels, even to touring 85-year-old hikers from New Zealand. The hotel is in the heart of London, next to Kensington Park, near two tube lines and a major bus line. The price per person is from £4 ($7) in a room shared with three to four other people and from £5 ($8.75) in a twin-bedded room. Breakfast is full English style, and a kitchen is available if you wish to cook your own meals.

The **Gayfere Hostel,** 8 Gayfere St., S.W.1 (tel. 222-6894), is dramatically positioned, just behind Westminster Abbey. Both young men and women (under the age of 25) are accepted at £4 ($7) per person nightly, not including breakfast but with cooking facilities. For one week, the charge per person is £22 ($38.50). Rooms must be shared. The hostel closes nightly at 11:45. The nearest underground station is Westminster (turn right, walk toward Millbank and turn right onto Great Peter Street).

Fieldcourt House, 32 Courtfield Gardens, S.W.5 (tel. 373-0152), keeps the student market firmly in mind, and is a hostel immaculately kept by its manager and his staff. It is a favorite among many of the economy tour operators. The residential hotel lies in a pleasant garden square near the West London Air Terminal on Cromwell Road, from which it's possible to obtain buses to all parts of London. The house is midway between Gloucester Road and Earl's Court underground stations (Piccadilly and District Lines). There is no curfew.

Fieldcourt was formed by combining two large Victorian mansions which were adapted to provide comfortable accommodations. There are central heating, wash basins, constant hot water, and ample showers, baths, and toilets in the public hallways. Other amenities include a quiet room for writing or study, plus a TV lounge with a color set. To keep hostel charges low, general cleaning is carried out by the staff, but residents are expected to make their own beds. Accommodation charges are payable weekly, in advance. A dormitory costs £5.50 ($9.63) per week. The most expensive unit, a single room, goes for £9.50 ($16.63) nightly. Otherwise, rates in a double room or a multibedded room, range in price from £9 ($15.75) to £6 ($10.50) per person nightly, these tariffs including VAT and a continental breakfast. A deposit of £10 ($17.50) is required on booking, and it's refundable on departure.

Baden-Powell House International Hostel, Queens Gate, S.W.7 (tel. 584-7030). You don't have to be a Boy Scout or Girl Guide to enjoy the facilities of this house across Queens Gate from the Natural History Museum. True, the place bustles with Scouts, and the bulletin board advertises club meetings and weekend trips for members. However, nonmembers and families are welcome to stay in the simple singles, twins, and dormitory accommodations. There are showers, baths, and other services available on each floor.

Rates go from £15 ($26.25) in a single, from £12.50 ($21.88) per person in a twin. Families are accommodated in three- or four-bedded units at £8 ($14) per person, including a full English breakfast, served in a self-service restaurant till 9 a.m., with views over the commuting London traffic on Cromwell Road.

Lunch in the restaurant is a three-course meal, Monday to Friday, costing £2.50 ($4.38). On Saturday and Sunday and every evening, a simpler two-course meal is featured at only £1.50 ($2.63). Packed meals can be provided for travelers if you order the night before. The Basement Snack Bar is equipped with vending machines providing sandwich rolls, cakes, fruit, and chocolates. There is a large lounge with color TV, plus a roof patio with views over London. Other services include a pay phone, a coin-operated laundry on the premises, and parking space in a garage. Tube: Gloucester Road.

Albert Hotel, 191 Queen's Gate, S.W. 7 (tel. 584-3019), is run by and primarily for young people. Its rooms have four six-bunk beds, plus shower and toilet. It advertises a friendly roof and a clean bed and lives up to its promise. You get your own key, and the place, unlike many hostels, stays open 24 hours a day. At a rate of £5.50 ($9.63) per person daily, you get a continental breakfast as well, served in the dining room/snackbar. There's also a 12-hour launderette service for guests. Meals are also inexpensive, a main course going for £2 ($3.50) and a packed lunch prepared for £1 ($1.75). The no. 52 bus from Victoria to the Albert Hall is convenient, or else the hostel is only two stops on the underground to South Kensington. The Albert is housed in a Victorian mansion, and it's centrally heated, its units cleaned daily.

"73," 73 Oakley St., S.W.3 (tel. 352-5599), is in Chelsea, near the Thames. It is run on friendly lines, offering bed and an English breakfast at £6 ($10.50) per person in a room shared with two others. For a twin, the charge is £7 ($12.25) per person, rising to £8 ($14) in a single. Deposits of £1 ($1.75) are required for room keys. There are no curfews, no age limits, and house telephones with extensions are provided in all rooms. A refrigerator and a cooker are in the kitchen for the use of guests, and everything but food is provided for preparing your own meals. In addition, a coin-operated washing machine and dryer are also available. If you ask for Roy or Eleanor, you'll receive a fine welcome.

38 Bolton Gardens, Earl's Court, S.W.5 (tel. 373-7083), is a youth hostel providing dormitory-style living for £3.95 ($6.91) per night for "seniors," £3.25 ($5.69) for "juniors." Breakfast costs £1.30 ($2.28). The premises are open from 8:30 to 10 a.m. and from 3 to 11:30 p.m. each day. The building is an old five-story mansion. Tube: Earl's Court.

Baron's Court Rooms, 5 Fairholme Rd., W.14 (tel. 385-6785), is a large Victorian-period terraced house in West Kensington that provides studio rooms ("bed-sitter" with a gas cooking stove and a food cabinet, etc.) for under-30s on tour. However, you must stay at least two weeks, at a cost that ranges (approximately) from $30 (U.S.) per week.

Don Ludwig House, 372 Gray's Inn Rd., W.C.1 (tel. 837-6543), at Kings Cross, is part of the International Students and Youth Centre. It provides accommodations for young travelers of both sexes up to the age of 30. Your bed will be in a small dormitory, holding up to four in a room. The bargain rate of £4 ($7) per night includes your bed linen, shared cooking facilities, showers, ironing facilities, and TV. There is central heating and hot and cold running water in the rooms. The hostel closes at midnight.

Catholic International Student Hostel, 16 Portland Rise, N.4 (tel. 802-1326), is open all year, accepting male guests 18 or over. There are 210 beds in one- to three-bedded rooms, costing from £3.80 ($6.65) to £5.29 ($9.26) daily. These rates include bed, breakfast, an evening meal, VAT, and service. However, on weekends, a midday meal is served instead of supper. It's a full-fledged hostel, approved by the British Council and I.L.E.A., with adequate recreational facilities, including sports equipment and a table-tennis room. Tube: Manor House (Piccadilly Line). Bus: 29, 253, or 279.

J.D. House, 285 Pentonville Rd., N.1 (tel. 278-5385), is a hostel northeast of Bloomsbury. It provides beds at £4 ($7) nightly, including your linen. The weekly rate is £17 ($29.75) to £20 ($35). Accommodation is in multiple rooms, with a maximum of four persons housed in each. Amenities include ironing and cooking facilities, as well as heating and television, with hot and cold running water in the rooms. The nearest underground station is Kings Cross, which is reached by at least seven buses that go near the student house.

READER'S HOSTEL SELECTION: "O'Callaghan's Nightly Tourist Accommodation, 205 Earl's Court Rd., S.W.3 (tel. 370-3000), is highly recommended. The charge is only

£4.80 ($8.40) per person in a room for four. Hot water and shower baths are available at all times of the day and night (even at 1 a.m.). I had my own key to my room and the front door. A perfectly charming, helpful, and concerned host was found in Mr. O'Callaghan, and his manager, George, reflected the same characteristics. Mr. O'Callaghan takes a fatherly interest in all the young people who stay there" (Arin Poller, Greenfield, Mass.).

LONDON ACCOMMODATION CENTER: Host & Guest Service, 592a King's Rd., S.W.6 (tel. 731-5340), will provide a place for you, at a cost that begins at £35 ($61.25) per person weekly for B&B. The service is run by Mrs. Carol Rutter, who has low-cost accommodations not only for students but also for older people and couples.

LONDON WALKABOUT CLUB: At 22 A Craven Terrace, Lancaster Gate, W.2 (tel. 402-9171), this club is run mostly by young people for young visitors to London. A life membership costs £8 ($14) and entitles you to reserve through this organization a very reasonable accommodation at one of its hotels, a free transfer from the airport, and the use of the clubhouse where you can meet people of your own age and find companionship for touring, sightseeing, or just pub-crawling. Information is also provided on cheap day excursions and bed-sitters or flats for those planning a longer stay. Other advantages of membership include swimming, luggage storage, mail service, welcome-to-London parties on Thursday, and a free London indoctrination (the club runs its own tours). Although the club's office is at 22 A Craven Terrace, the bar and meeting place is at 25–26 Craven Terrace. The bar incorporates a disco, restaurant, and coffeeshop. Ask about their "squash afternoons." There is also a Telex (22359) so that agents can arrange reservations at the last moment.

HELPING WITH CHILDREN: Visitors Welcome Ltd., 17 Radley Mews, W.8 (tel. 937-9755), is a competent organization whose business is escorting and caring for children. Founded in 1960, the service will arrange whole or half-day outings to keep your children entertained while you have the opportunity to spend some time on your own. The intelligent young staff is prepared to cope with any emergency, even putting up the children overnight if necessary. Such services as shopping escorts, tour guides, or theater and restaurant bookings are also available. Charges vary according to the time of day and the service rendered, but the daytime rate is usually about £4 ($7) per hour.

STUDENT JOBS: Students who want to live and work for a while in Britain can take advantage of a program operated by the British Universities North America Club in London. A $60 fee allows you to obtain a blue card, granting you permission to work in Britain for six months at any kind of job, even on a farm. Citizens enrolled in U.S. colleges are eligible, providing they are at least 18 years old and have at least $300 on landing in Britain. Information and application blanks can be obtained from the Council on International Educational Exchange, 205 E. 42nd St., New York, NY 10017 (tel. 212/661-1414).

FOR CHRISTIAN WORKERS: House of Rest for Christian Workers, 10 Finchley Rd., St. Johns Wood, N.W.8 (tel. 722-5765), is a slightly offbeat choice, although certain readers will find it ideal. It is a large Victorian house, well over 100 years old, which offers spacious rooms containing hot and cold running water and pleasant furnishings. The London Zoo and Regent's Park are within easy walking distance, as it is only a block from St. Johns Wood tube station (just a few yards from bus stops). Daily devotional services are scheduled, as the house caters to lay persons along with professional Christian workers. The cost is £14 ($24.50) per day for each person, this tab including both breakfast, room, and dinner. Meals are served family style, and usually there are representatives from about ten nations at the tables in the communal dining room. The warden is Eric J. Sutton.

In many ways, the task of the next chapter is even more intriguing, as we search out the restaurants and pubs of the West End and explore the ancient chophouses of "The City."

Chapter III

LONDON: RESTAURANTS, PUBS, AND WINE BARS

1. West End
2. Westminster and St. James's
3. The City
4. Holborn and Bloomsbury
5. Belgravia and Knightsbridge
6. Chelsea
7. Kensington
8. West London
9. East End
10. South of the Thames
11. Hampstead Heath
12. Thames Dining
13. Time Out for Tea
14. Almost-24-Hour Eateries

NOW THAT YOU'VE FOUND a hotel room, you'll want to know about the neighborhood bistros and pubs, the foreign and domestic restaurants, cafeterias and old chophouses in the heart of London. First, I'll survey the downtown district of London, by which I refer to a broad area embracing not only the theater district, but Piccadilly Circus, Soho, Covent Garden, the Strand, Trafalgar Square, and Leicester Square, as well as the elegant residential district of Mayfair and "Little America." South of here is the seat of government, Westminster and Whitehall, and the heart of royal and aristocratic London, St. James's (Buckingham Palace). To the east is the older part of London, which includes the financial square mile known as "The City," as well as the newspaper and publishing empire centered around Fleet Street.

Finally, I'll fan out to such residential districts as Bloomsbury (budget hotels and the British Museum), Chelsea, St. Marylebone, Brompton, and Kensington. And then, at the end of the chapter, I'll set forth my more remote recommendations—the pubs and bistros in Hampstead Heath, and a few scattered, but famous, inns, restaurants, and pubs either in the East End or along the Thames.

A word of warning: Pub hours are notoriously unpopular with foreign visitors, as well as with many of the British themselves. Generally speaking pubs are open from 11:30 a.m. to 3 p.m. and from 5:30 p.m. (7 p.m. on Sunday) to 11 p.m. (10:30 p.m. Sunday). Persons 17 years and under aren't allowed in licensed bars.

All restaurants and cafés in Britain are required to display the prices of the food and drink they offer, in a place where the customer can see them before entering the eating area. If an establishment has an extensive à la carte menu, the prices of a representative selection of food and drink currently available must be displayed as well as the table d'hôte menu, if one is offered. The cost for service and any minimum charge or cover charge must also be made clear, and, further, prices shown must include VAT.

However, the menu you receive in the restaurant does not necessarily show prices including VAT. You may find both VAT and service added at the end of your bill. You can also sometimes find that incidentals such as coffee or salad in place of vegetables are extras to a set-price meal.

1. West End

PICCADILLY CIRCUS: Garish, overneoned, crowded, but exciting, Piccadilly Circus keeps time with the heartbeat of a mighty city. If you're intrigued by Times Square at night, you'll find that Piccadilly Circus carries an equal fascination. Here from all sections of the city come the aristocrat, the housewife, the freak, the government official, the secretary, the pimp, the financier. They converge around the statue of Eros, named for love, about the only thing that occasionally unites these diverse elements of life which descend on Piccadilly.

Much of your London activity will be centered in and around here. Finding the right restaurant is most important, as many establishments in this area are unabashed tourist traps, or sleazy little joints aimed more at the "bangers-and-mash" palate. The following restaurants and pubs have been selected not only for the quality of their food but because they offer the best value for the money. Although definitely a splurge, my opening selection provides proper introduction to English cooking.

The Carvery, ground floor, Regent Palace Hotel, Glasshouse Street, W.1 (tel. 734-7000), just 20 feet from Piccadilly Circus, will fool you. Who'd think that for only £9.50 ($16.63) you could have all that your plate can hold of fabulous roasts and be able to go back for seconds—even thirds for those who suffer from one of the seven deadly sins? Yet that's the famous policy of this renowned, all-you-can-eat establishment; a winner with those seeking rib-sticking "joints," for which the English are known. The first course, perhaps a large slice of chilled melon, will be served at your table. After that, you can go to the horseshoe-shaped buffet carving table, where before you will be spread roast prime ribs of beef (choice of rare, medium, or well done), with Yorkshire pudding, roast leg of Southdown lamb with mint sauce, and a roast leg of English pork with apple sauce.

You carve the meat yourself, slicing off as much as you want, although carvers stand by to assist and give instructions on how to wield the knife. You may then heap your heated china plate with buttered peas, roast potatoes, new carrots, and gravy. In another area is a display of cold joints and assorted salads, whatever is in season. A plate of fresh fruit and a pitcher of thick cream are brought in for dessert, or you can select from the sweet trolley such desserts as meringue or chocolate and pineapple cake, perhaps a strawberry mousse. Well-brewed coffee for "afters" is included in the price. The Carvery is open on Monday through Saturday from noon to 2:30 p.m. and from 5:15 to 9 p.m., and on Sunday from 12:30 to 2:30 p.m. and 6 to 9 p.m.

Good news department: There are more Carvery establishments in London, with the same policy and the same menu. A favorite is within the Tower Hotel, ideal to combine with your Tower of London visit, although this is more expensive. Then there is the one in the Strand Palace Hotel, on the Strand. Here the decor is winning, eclectic, and dramatic: Chinese red chairs with rush seats, black tufted booths, a wood-paneled ceiling, decorative artifacts on the walls, a huge old wine press, modern paintings, rare Italian engravings, and converted baroque kerosene lanterns. At the Cumberland Hotel, at Marble Arch, the Carvery is more clublike, with tables on two levels, where you dine in a low-lit, seductive atmosphere. There's also a Carvery at the Kingsley Hotel, Bloomsbury Way, close to the British Museum.

The **Cockney Pride,** entrance on Jermyn Street, right off Piccadilly Circus, W.1 (tel. 930-5339), occupies the same spot as the former Criterion Restaurant. It is a clever reproduction, a latter-day tribute to the glory of Victoriana: button-tufted velvet banquettes, cut-glass mirrors, and converted brass oil lanterns. When ordering food in this pubby atmosphere, better take along a friend born within the sound of the Bow Bells. You'll need him or her for translations. For example, you can select such Cockney cuisine oddities as bangers and mash. The banger in this case is a super-sausage. Other dishes include beef curry and rice or shepherd's pie and baked beans. A simple meal here will cost from £4 ($7). Real ale goes for 85p ($1.49) a pint. On most nights you can hear a pub pianist and sometimes a singer.

The Crêperie, 56a South Molton St., W.1 (tel. 629-4794), is a pleasant and informal place, with bare wooden tables and chairs. The crêpes are cooked on the right as you enter, on pristine hotplates amid bubbling cauldrons of soup of the day. Main courses are buckwheat pancakes filled with a vast variety of goodies—onions, cheese, mixed salad, chicken, ratatouille, you name it. Prices range from £2 ($3.50) to £2.50 ($4.38) for a filling pancake, served with salad. For dessert, another pancake, made with plain flour this time, is filled with chestnuts, pineapple, bananas, or chocolate. Sweet ones cost from £1.75 ($3.06). In addition, a dish of the day—perhaps a Greek-style moussaka or a beef stew—bubbles alongside the soup. A two-floor restaurant, the Crêperie is in an alley off South Molton Street, amid many other eateries. A tortuous staircase leads up from the ground floor to the light airy dining room. The Crêperie is open seven days a week.

The Granary, 39 Albemarle St., W.1 (tel. 493-2978), serves a variety of dishes, all of which have a real home-cooked flavor. The whole place is under the watchful eye of John Shah, who opened it in 1974. In winter 25 hot dishes and five cold ones are served, and in summer 20 hot dishes and ten cold ones, plus desserts, are offered. An inexpensive meal of, say, meat pie, vegetables, chocolate cake, a glass of wine, and coffee, will cost around £5 ($8.75). The fare is likely to consist of spiced chicken, paella, and beef burgundy. Desserts are tempting, especially the tipsy cake and the upside-down cake. All portions are large, and everything can be taken away in containers to eat elsewhere (remember, no VAT is charged for food carried away). Hours are from 11 a.m. to 8 p.m. weekdays (on Saturday from noon to 2:30 p.m.); closed Sunday.

Wren at St. James's Coffee House, 35 Jermyn St., S.W.1 (tel. 437-9419). At this enterprising church, a two-minute walk from Piccadilly Circus, visitors can do brass-rubbings. It also boasts a cheerful coffeeshop right within its walls, offering good value. It's entered through a narrow door on Jermyn Street. You're greeted with bright paint, green and white tables, metal chairs, and windows overlooking the courtyard. A glass counter groaning with appetizing dishes is served to the lined-up patrons by pleasant, capable women. There is always a fresh soup of the day, along with cold appetizers such as carrot cocktail. Hot dishes include quiches, meat pies, and goulash, and desserts often feature the special, St. James pudding. A bill isn't likely to run more than £4.50 ($7.88). It's busy at lunchtime, particularly with local in-the-know office workers, when there is a minimum charge of £2 ($3.50). The full range of dishes is offered throughout the day. It's open from 11 a.m. to 6 p.m. from Monday to Friday. Tube: Piccadilly Circus.

McDonald's, 57 Haymarket, S.W.1 (tel. 930-9302). Yes, the real thing from America long ago arrived, and there are some 50 chain sisters in and around London. All produce, including meat, is purchased locally and is of high standard. A Big Mac costs £1 ($1.75); regular french fries go for 35p (61¢); shakes are 50p (88¢). If you eat in the restaurant, you pay VAT; but if you take the food out, the tax isn't assessed. The place is brash, brightly lit, and busy.

The **Mayfair Inn Sandwich Bar,** 61 Davies St., W.1 (tel. 629-4095), lies just off Oxford Street and opposite Grey's Antique Market, around the corner from the Bond Street underground station. The inn is actually a small, unobtrusive workingman's café at the end of a row of old London town houses. It's owned and run by Mary, with faithful assistance from Sadie, and it's open from around 7 a.m. They serve breakfast until 11 a.m., then start on the sandwich and lunch trade. An egg-and-bacon breakfast here costs only 85p ($1.49). Sandwiches such as a hot bacon one cost only 35p (61¢). Eat at one of the small tables with backless stools and listen to the banter between Sadie and the visiting taxi-drivers and office workers.

AROUND LEICESTER SQUARE: Named for the second Earl of Leicester, and once the site of the home of Sir Joshua Reynolds, Leicester Square has changed its colors today, bursting out as the cinema center of London. The 19th-century square is a congested area of stores, theaters, cinemas, even churches. And beyond those, it has some inexpensive restaurants and pubs in its little offshoot lanes and alleyways, where West End actors discreetly select their "local."

There's now a large paved pedestrian precinct rivaling Piccadilly Circus and Eros as a meeting place for travelers and locals. It's less dangerous than Piccadilly Circus for many reasons, among which is that there's no traffic.

The **Stockpot,** 40 Panton St., S.W.1, suggests good wholesome fare and lives up to its promise. Penny for penny, I'd hazard a guess that this cozy little member of a popular chain offers one of the best dining bargains in London. (Others are at 6 Basil St., S.W.3, and at 98 King's Rd., S.W.3.) All the Stockpots are favored by a young crowd, who know by heart the low prices charged for the well-cooked meals: a bowl of minestrone, 35p (61¢); spaghetti bolognese (the eternal favorite), 80p ($1.40); a plate of braised lamb, £1.40 ($2.45); the apple crumble (or other desserts), only 30p (53¢). Offering two levels of dining in a Scandinavian-style atmosphere, the Stockpot has a share-the-table policy during peak dining hours (open till around midnight). The little restaurant lies off Haymarket, opposite the Comedy Theatre.

If it's a charming ambience you're seeking, you'll find it in the heart of the theater district at the pubs and wine bars recommended below.

Slatters, 3 Panton St., S.W.1 (tel. 839-4649), lies off Haymarket, a split-level wine bar convenient for theater-goers. It makes a good rendezvous for pretheater and after-theater suppers. A stylish informality reigns. Classical and operatic tapes are played in the background and the paintings on the wall are for sale. The house wine is from France, and you can drink it at £1 ($1.75) a glass, along with food offered by owner Kenneth Slatter. The smoked trout goes for £2.50 ($4.38); the underdone pink roast beef, £4 ($7); a mackerel pâté served with french bread, £2 ($3.50); baked ham or chicken, £4 ($7); or the soup of the day, £1 ($1.75). Closed Sunday, it is open otherwise for lunch from 11 a.m. to 3 p.m. or dinner from 5 p.m. until midnight. Tube: Leicester Square or Piccadilly Circus.

Cork and Bottle Wine Bar, 44–46 Cranbourn St., W.C.2 (tel. 734-7807), is in the theater district, just off Leicester Square. Don and Jean Hewitson, the owners, devote a great deal of love and care to this establishment. Jean has revitalized the food, with a wide range of hot dishes, so that it is not a typical glass of wine and a slice of pâté type of bistro. Her most successful dish is her raised cheese-and-ham pie at £1.75 ($3.06). In just one week she sold 500 portions of this alone! She bagged, or else begged, the recipe for this from her favorite little bistro in the Rue Monge in Paris. It has a cream-cheesy filling, and the well-buttered pastry is crisp—not your typical quiche.

She also offers a machon Lyonnaise, a traditional worker's lunch in Lyon. The Hewitson's import their own saussiçon from a charcuterie in Lyon, serving it hot with warm potato salad, a mixed green salad, spicy Dijon mustard, and french bread for £2.75 ($4.81). They also offer an "American gourmet salad," at £1.75 ($3.06), consisting of lettuce, tomato, avocado, green beans, and croutons, in a spicy red stilton dressing. Don has expanded the wine list, and he doubts if anyone in the U.K. has a better selection of Beaujolais Cru and wines from Alsace. They also stock a good selection of California labels.

In fact, Don, a New Zealander, has been called "the kiwi guru of the modern wine bar movement." It is open Monday to Saturday from 11 a.m. to 3 p.m. and from 5:30 to 11 p.m. Tube: Leicester Square.

TRAFALGAR SQUARE AND THE STRAND: Between Leicester Square and Westminster, a former marshy meadow is known today as Trafalgar Square. The square is dominated by a monument honoring Lord Nelson, who died in the Battle of Trafalgar on October 21, 1805.

Beginning at the square, the Strand, south of Covent Garden, runs east into Fleet Street. Londoners used to be able to walk along the Strand and see the Thames, but the river, of course, has receded now. In the 17th century, the wealthy built their homes on the Strand, and their gardens stretched to the Thames itself. But today it is in transition to something less grand—flanked as it is with theaters (the Savoy, for example), shops, hotels, and such landmarks as Somerset House.

Peaceful lanes jut off from the Strand, leading to the Victoria Embankment Gardens along the river. Opposite the gardens is Cleopatra's Needle, an Egyptian obelisk, London's oldest (and perhaps dullest) monument. If the weather permits, you might want to stroll along the river.

Because this is such a major geographic and tourist center, you'll probably want to take some of your meals here. My recommendations follow.

The **Sherlock Holmes,** 10 Northumberland St., W.C.2 (tel. 930-2644), is for devotees of the legendary English detective and his creator, Arthur Conan Doyle. You can have your mug of beer and then look at the upstairs re-creation of the living room of 221B Baker Street, where get-togethers of "The Baker

Street Irregulars" are held. The homemade food, served upstairs, is simple and plain. The fare consists of grilled chops, steaks, fish such as sole or scampi, and a selection of desserts. All main dishes are served with three different potatoes and fresh vegetables (or in season a large bowl of salad). In the snackbar on the street level you can order a plate of cold meat including a salad or just a salad. Hot dishes include risotto, curry, liver and bacon, and a simple meal will cost around £5 ($8.75). Hours are noon to 3:15 p.m. and from 6:15 to 9 p.m.

The **Clarence Inn,** 53 Whitehall, S.W.1 (tel. 930-4808), just down from Trafalgar Square, is the haunt of civil servants from the nearby ministry offices. They enjoy such lunchtime delicacies as braised oxtail, Oriental pork chops, or the traditional shepherd's pie. There are always at least four hot dishes of the day, and a helping costs from £1.50 ($2.63) to £2 ($3.50). There is also a wide range of cold dishes and salads at around the same price, and the same food is available in the evening when the workers have gone home. Manager Don Stone offers a choice of six real ales in the bar, with its sawdust-strewn floor, church pews, and uncovered tables lit by flickering gaslights. Ancient farm tools and weapons decorate the smoke-blackened beams, and in the evening from Monday to Thursday a strolling minstrel makes light music in the bar.

The **National Gallery Restaurant,** Trafalgar Square, W.C.2 (tel. 930-5210). You can have lunch in this comfortable basement before you explore the gallery. Juicy quiches and flans are presented before you, along with a line-up of fresh crisp salads. Hot daily specials are likely to include chili with rice, coq au vin, and boeuf bourguignon. Count on spending from £4 ($7). The excellent house wine goes for about £4 ($7) a bottle.

Val Taro, 32 Orange St., W.C.2 (tel. 930-2939), is a white-painted, countrified place right in the heart of clubland, west of Trafalgar Square. It's a pleasant place in which to enjoy the fixed-price lunch or evening menu for £6.50 ($11.38). For that, you might begin with a prawn and celery cocktail, or perhaps a whitebait or chef's pâté. For a main course, you are likely to be served coq au vin with well-prepared vegetables. There's a wine bar in the basement if you want a lighter meal. Val Taro is open from noon to 3 p.m. and from 6 to 11 p.m. It is closed for lunch on Saturday and all day Sunday.

COVENT GARDEN: In 1970, London's flower, fruit, and "veg" market celebrated its 300th anniversary. But "Auld Lang Syne" might have been the theme song. Once a district of gambling dens and bawdy houses, east of Piccadilly Circus and north of the Strand, the historic, but congested, market was transferred in 1974 to a $7.2-million, 64-acre site at Nine Elms, in the suburb of Vauxhall, South London, 2½ miles away, across the Thames.

Covent Garden dates from the time when the monks of Westminster Abbey dumped their surplus home-grown vegetables here. Charles II in 1670 granted the Earl of Bedford the right to "sell roots and herbs, whatsoever" in the district. The king's mistress, Nell Gwynne, once peddled oranges on Drury Lane (later appearing on the stage of the Drury Lane Theatre).

Before that, in the 1630s Inigo Jones designed the square, hoping to have a plaza in the Florentine style, but the work bogged down. Even his self-tabbed "handsomest barn in England," St. Paul's Covent Garden, burned down in the late 18th century and was subsequently rebuilt: The English actress, Dame Ellen Terry (noted in particular for her letters to G. B. Shaw) is buried here.

St. Paul's eastern face looks down on the market where Professor Higgins in *Pygmalion* met his "squashed cabbage leaf," Eliza Doolittle, and later got reacquainted in *My Fair Lady.* Also in the area is the Royal Opera House on Bow Street housing the Royal Ballet and the Covent Garden Opera Company.

On Russell Street, nearby, Samuel Johnson met his admirer, Boswell, and coffeehouses in the district were once patronized by Addison and Steele. Just as chicly dressed people of fashion once flocked to Les Halles in Paris to have onion soup with butchers in blood-soaked smocks, so London revelers have dropped in at Covent Garden's pubs to drink with Cockney barrow boys in the early dawn hours. The tradition will be sadly missed.

The old central market is now reopened with expensive stores selling exclusive products jostled by the more temporary stalls in the center peddling unremarkable souvenirs, jewelry, baskets and wickerwork, clothing, and T-shirts. Occasional groups enliven the place with impromptu music.

There are exclusive clubs here, such as the Zanzibar and the Rock Garden. The Blitz offers snacks, and Brahms and Liszt offers drinks.

And the area has begun to attract art galleries, such as the Acme, the Hammond Lloyd, the Covent Garden, and the William Drummond.

It's appropriate that art galleries should be returning to Covent Garden. In the 18th century it was a beehive of artists, including Lely and Kneller (famous portrait painters, the latter of whom is buried at St. Paul's Church, around the corner). Others who lived there were Thornhill, Richard Wilson, Fuseli, Daniel Mytens, the sculptor Roubiliac, Zoffany, and Flaxman. The American painter Benjamin West also lived here after he got out of jail for trying to study in London during the Revolution.

In the popular Covent Garden complex is **Plummers Restaurant,** 33 King St., W.C.2 (tel. 240-2534). It is a friendly, informal sort of place where a woman can go on her own without attracting attention and where there is room enough between the tables so that you don't have to listen to someone else's conversation. The color scheme of cream and plum is enlivened by pretty print tablecloths and fresh flowers on the tables. Ferns and plants are reflected in mirrors around the walls.

Appetizers include avocado vinaigrette or clam chowder. Then there is a wide selection of main dishes including char-grilled pork chops, marinated in cider; lamb cutlets or liver and bacon; Californian chili with chef's salad and garlic bread; spare ribs; or veal escalope. There are Scottish beefburgers (100% meat) ranging from plain to Plummers Superburger topped with bacon, egg, and melted cheese. All burgers come with french fries or baked potato with sour cream and chives or butter, or with the chef's salad, but other vegetables are extra. Desserts include various flavors of ice cream and sorbets, and there is apple pie and cream. Coffee—as much as you can drink—finishes off the meal. A meal will cost around £9 ($15.75), but you can get away with £4.50 ($7.88) for a beefburger and coffee. VAT is included, but a 12½% service charge is added to all bills.

Johnny's Café, 33 Floral St., W.C.2, opposite the Dance Centre in the new Covent Garden complex, has an informal atmosphere with wooden benches and formica tables, but the food is the main attraction after Johnny and his wife. Lasagne is cooked fresh in enormous dishes from which they serve you an ample helping. Lamb casserole is good, as are Italian meatballs with sauce. The spaghetti, both bolognaise or milanaise, and a large mixed salad is offered. They serve super hunks of fresh brown and white bread to mop up the juices with. Fresh fruit salad plus the usual ices, fruit pies, and cakes round off the meal, which is likely to cost from £5 ($8.75). Everything is freshly prepared and very good. They are open most of the day and much of the night.

Tuttons, 11–12 Russell St., W.C.2 (tel. 836-1167). In the evening, what used to be a couple of tables on the pavement bursts into its own. A large glass-fronted modern building now houses Paul Tutton's busy, friendly, hurried restaurant where dishes of the day appear on the blackboard, and portions are extraordinarily large. Mainly salads and quiches, meat pies, and goulashes go for around £3.50 ($6.13). Of course, you'll pay far more for one of the exotic lobster salads or roast game. The daily special is a bowl of nourishing soup, followed by Cumberland sausage with potato salad and apple crumble for £4 ($7). A wide range of vegetarian dishes is priced from £2 ($3.50) and up. The ground-floor restaurant is rather free-wheeling; however, if you go downstairs, the atmosphere is more elegant, the service less rushed, and the tariffs higher.

Penny's Place, 6 King St., W.C.2 (tel. 836-4553), is a converted pub dating from 1660. However, it now has a real French ambience, serving customers from 11:30 a.m. to 3 p.m. and from 5:30 to 11:30 p.m. A large range of wines is offered—I counted more than 40 French labels—along with selections from the vineyards of Spain, Yugoslavia, Italy, and Germany. Prices range from 75p ($1.31) for a glass of house wine to £1.30 ($2.28) for a smooth French château-bottled claret. The blackboard lists the dishes available, and is likely to offer whitebait, coq au vin, liver in wine and orange sauce, or garlic mushrooms. Most dishes average £2 ($3.50) in price. The menu changes daily and depends largely on the whim of the Cordon Bleu chef and the state of the market. Downstairs in the cellar bistro, there's often live music, especially on Friday. Penny's is closed Sunday.

Diana's Diner, 39 Endell St., W.C.2 (tel. 240-0272), is a busy, noisy place, with no pretensions to elegance, but with a well-deserved reputation among local office workers for serving satisfying meals at very reasonable prices. The most expensive dish is the mixed grill at only £2.75 ($4.81), a grand selection of cutlet, steak, egg, sausages, mushrooms, and tomatoes. There are also massive three-egg omelets, steak pie, beef in cider, and a whole fried plaice served with the inevitable "chips." It is open Monday to Friday from 7:15 a.m. to 3:45 p.m. and on Saturday from 7:30 to 11:30 a.m. only.

Magno's Brasserie, 65a Long Acre, W.C.2 (tel. 836-6077), is very useful for pretheater meals if you're in the area. It offers a fixed-price menu of soup, a main meat course, a glass of wine, and coffee for only £5.25 ($9.19), including VAT and service. This meal is served only from 6 to 7:30 p.m. The brasserie is open from Monday to Friday for lunch and dinner, offering typical menus of grills and salads. It has a friendly atmosphere and service.

Porter's English Restaurant, 17 Henrietta St., W.C.2 (tel. 836-6466), is a rather sedate Victorian building, with a high ceiling and pillars. It offers no appetizers but a choice of ten homemade pies—cottage pie, lamb and apricot, steak, oyster, and clam pie, along with fish pie. Even the "puddings" are traditional, including jam rolypoly, suet pudding with treacle, and rhubarb crumble. There is also potted stilton, along with real ale and wine, a meal costing about £5.50 ($9.63), and you'll rise comfortably full to continue your wandering around Covent Garden. The restaurant is open daily from noon to 3 p.m. and from 5:30 to 11:30 p.m.

READER'S RESTAURANT SELECTION: "**Food for Thought,** 31 Neal St., W.C.2 (tel. 836-0239), is a very small place with inexpensive vegetarian food, meals costing from £3 ($5.25). Better go at odd hours, perhaps in the middle of the afternoon. Otherwise, it's likely to be crowded. Everybody ends up sitting with and often talking with everybody else. It's most congenial. The establishment is a tiny basement café in the heart of the theater and movie district. From the Covent Garden tube station, walk along Neal Street toward Shaftesbury Avenue. The restaurant will be in the second block on the left. It's open Monday through Friday from noon to 8 p.m." (Vicki Banks, London, England).

MAYFAIR: Mayfair (W.1), bounded by Piccadilly, Hyde Park, and Oxford and Regent Streets, is the elegant, fashionable section of London. Luxury hotels exist side by side with Georgian town houses and swank shops. Here are all the parks, names, and streets that have snob associations the world over. Grosvenor Square (pronounced Grov-nor) is nicknamed "Little America" because it contains the American Embassy and a statue of Franklin D. Roosevelt. Berkeley (pronounced Barkley) is the home of the English Speaking Union.

At least once you'll want to dip into the exclusive Mayfair section, or even make repeated trips to Carnaby, lying only one block from Regent Street.

Perhaps you'll prefer to have afternoon tea in Mayfair, or you might combine a luncheon with sightseeing. If so, you'll find that not all the establishments here charge rarefied prices. To prove my point, here are these budget recommendations:

Bubbles, 41 North Audley St., W.1 (tel. 499-0600), is another wine bar run by those ambitious and talented New Zealanders, Don and Jean Hewitson, who have made an outstanding reputation for themselves at the Cork and Bottle, 44–46 Cranbourn St., W.C. 2. Don doesn't believe in offering merely a dreary "red or white?" He offers a large variety of wines which are available by the glass. The food is limited but good, including a hot dish of the day. On my most recent rounds, it was poulet Dijonnaise at £3.25 ($5.69)—that is, a freshly roasted chicken in a creamy mustard sauce, served with potatoes and a green salad. Jean is also known for her raised ham-and-cheese pie at £2 ($3.50). Other dishes are likely to include Bubbles egg-and-shrimp salad at £2 ($3.50) and Maryland ham off the bone at £1.95 ($3.41). Desserts are always luscious, including marinated strawberries, raspberry mousse, and the inevitable chocolate cake. Hours are Monday to Friday from 11 a.m. to 3 p.m. and from 5:30 to 11 p.m.; on Saturday from 11 a.m. to 3 p.m. only. Tube: Bond Street.

The **Chicago Pizza Factory,** 17 Hanover Square, W.1 (tel. 629-2669), specializes in deep-dish pizza covered with cheese, tomato, and a choice of sausage, pepperoni, mushrooms, green peppers, onions, and anchovies. The regular-size pizza is enough for two or three diners, and the large one is suitable for four or five persons. This restaurant was introduced to London by a former advertising executive, Bob Payton, an ex-Chicagoan. The atmosphere is pleasant and friendly even though they are quite busy. It's one of the few places where a doggy bag is willingly provided. There are smoking and nonsmoking tables. The menu also includes stuffed mushrooms, garlic bread, salads, and homemade cheesecakes served with two forks. The cost begins at £6 ($10.50). The restaurant also has a large bar with a wide choice of cocktails, including a specialty known as the St. Valentine's Day Massacre. A video over the bar shows continuous American baseball, football, and basketball games. The 275-seat restaurant is full of authentic Chicago memorabilia, and the waitresses wear *Chicago Sun-Times* newspaper-sellers' aprons. The factory is just off Oxford Street behind Woolworth's, opposite John Lewis and within easy reach of Regent Street as well. The factory is open Monday to Saturday from 11:45 a.m. to 11:30 p.m. Tube: Bond Street.

Shampers, 4 Kingly St., W.1 (tel. 437-1692), is yet another adventure of Don and Jean Hewitson, who came to London to perk up the wine bar movement with their excellent and superb selection of wines and their imaginatively prepared food. You have a choice of seats: either upstairs or down. Or perhaps you'll prefer to perch on a stool alongside the bar. I prefer the cozy ambience of the downstairs. A meal for one person with wine comes to about £6 ($10.50) per person. Salads are a star, and look for the hot dish of the day including, perhaps, grilled marinated rabbit with mustard sauce. The selection of wines range from California to Germany to Australia. This might make an especially good choice if you're shopping in the area. Hours are Monday to Friday from

11 a.m. to 3 p.m. and from 5:30 to 11 p.m. The bar also serves lunch on Saturday. Tube: Oxford Circus.

Cranks Health Food Restaurant, Marshall Street, W.1 (around the corner from Carnaby Street), took its name from "cranks." But instead of the colloquial meaning of an eccentric, impractical person, the restaurant defines the word as those "who have the courage to pursue a line of thinking against the general stream of orthodox belief." Their "line," by the way, is excellent—the best of natural soups, salads, and breads made from wholemeal, compost-grown, stone-ground English flour. Cranks became famous when it operated on Carnaby Street, and first drew its young health-conscious clientele. The food-reform restaurant even tempts full-fledged carnivores by its fresh-tasting selections—such as the mix-it-yourself salad platter at lunch. If you've got a small waist, you can order a bowl of choice salads for £1.50 ($2.63), although if you've already lost the battle of the bulge, you may prefer a large plate at £2.50 ($4.38). Homemade cakes range from 50p (88¢) to £1.50 ($2.63). Cranks serves the best tiger's milk and dandelion coffee in town. It's open Monday from 10 a.m. to 7:30 p.m., Tuesday through Saturday from 10 a.m. to 11 p.m. (Dine and Wine by Candlelight service from 6:30 to 11 p.m.). Warning: At lunchtime, it gets crowded.

The **Widow Applebaum's Deli & Bagel Academy,** 46 South Molton St., W.1 (tel. 629-4649), is a useful place for those who don't wish to go to the East End of London to enjoy New York Jewish food in the strict environment of Bloom's. It's good for a pretheater meal, although you should avoid it during office lunch hours. The typists are mad about the salt (corned) beef sandwiches. Richard, the chef, drinking what I suspect is his 44th Coca-Cola of the day, assured me that the pastrami is flown in fresh daily from New York. Sandwiches, including roast beef and turkey, are topped with coleslaw and pickled cucumbers, and are accompanied by potato salad; they range in price from £1.75 ($3.06). You can enjoy the chopped liver or the chicken matzoh ball (dumpling) soup. An authentic 100% beef quarter-pound, charcoal-grilled hamburger on a toasted bun with lettuce, tomato, and french fries is also served. In addition to English beers, you can get a really decadent cocktail—a White Lady, a Rusty Nail, even a Bronx cocktail, at a cost ranging from £2.20 ($3.85). The front part of this narrow delicatessen is for take-out orders. Tables for sitdown meals are in the rear, going deep into the back. There you can order a plate of the corned beef with a salad for £3.50 ($6.13). Now that South Molton Street is a pedestrian precinct, tables are set outside in fair weather. Tube: Bond Street.

Justin de Blank, 54 Duke St., W.1 (tel. 629-3174), just off Oxford Street, offers breakfast, lunch, and dinner, and is a haven for tired shoppers. They serve a variety of hot dishes including lamb and eggplant casserole, barbecued spare ribs, cauliflower cheese, or you might like one of their many choices of salads. Desserts include fruit pie with cream, cheesecake, and fresh fruit salad. They bake their own breads and also have a "take-out" order department. One dish ranges in price from £1.85 ($3.24) to £3.50 ($6.13), and a three-course meal is likely to average £5.50 ($9.63). Wine is 80p ($1.40) a glass. Justin is open weekdays from 8:30 a.m. to 3:30 p.m. and from 4:30 to 9 p.m. On Saturday they are open only from 9 a.m. to 3:30 p.m., and are closed on Sunday.

Hard Rock Café, on Piccadilly at Hyde Park Corner, W.1 (tel. 629-0382), is a Downhome southern-cum-midwestern funky American roadside diner with good food at reasonable prices and service with a smile. A Downhome double burger in a sesame-seed bun with french fries and salad costs £3 ($5.25); hot chili and crackers, £2.50 ($4.38); and homemade ice cream, £1.30 ($2.28). The café is on two levels, with color TV at the end of the room and nonstop rock music. The bar is for solace while you wait for a table. Almost every night there is a line waiting to get in, as this is one of the most popular places in town for young people.

Shepherds Market

One of the curiosities of Mayfair is Shepherds Market, a tiny village of pubs, two-story inns, book and food stalls, and restaurants, all sandwiched between the slices of Mayfair grandness. At one corner you might be contemplating whether to buy that antique Rolls-Royce, then you suddenly turn down a street and are transplanted to a remnant of a village of old England, where the peddlers are hawking their wares. While here, you may want to drop in for a drink at one of London's best-known pubs.

Shepherds Tavern, 50 Hertford St., W.1 (tel. 499-3017), is a nugget, considered *the* pub of Mayfair. It attracts a congenial mixture of the kind of English who used to read *The Times* every morning and a rather pacey set of young things. There are many fine luxurious touches, including an exceptional collection of antique furniture; supreme among these is a sedan chair which once belonged to the son of George III, the Duke of Cumberland (it's now fitted with a telephone for those very private ring-ups). Many of the local habitués recall the tavern's association with the pilots in the Battle of Britain. On the second floor is a restaurant serving English food. Traditional English home-cooked food is served each weekday at lunchtime in the restaurant at reasonable prices. A homemade steak pie and two vegetables costs £2.50 ($4.38). Downstairs in the bar, hot individual shepherd's pies are served for £1.25 ($2.19) each and sizzling "bangers" are available.

The **Bunch of Grapes,** 16 Shepherds Market, W.1 (tel. 629-4989), is a place which is all bustle at lunchtime, when it's filled with local office workers. The action in summer spills out onto the pavement outside. Nevertheless, the foreign visitor is still welcome and expected to force your way with the others toward the bar to order real ale at 83p ($1.45) a half pint. For lunch you can select from a vast array of cold meats, pies, salads (such as coleslaw with orange), and hot dishes such as kidneys in sherry, braised brisket, and, in season, fresh poached salmon. Dishes run from around £2 ($3.50) to £4.50 ($7.88). No food is served on Sunday or in the evenings.

SOHO: This wedge-shaped section (W.1) of crisscrossed narrow lanes and crooked streets is the main foreign quarter of London, site of many of the city's best foreign restaurants. The unanglicized life of the continent holds forth in Soho: great numbers of French people are found here, and so are Italians and all other European nationalities, as well as Orientals. Traditionally, it has been known as the center of vice and prostitution in London.

Soho starts impudently at Piccadilly Circus, spreading out like a peacock and ending at Oxford Street. One side borders the theater center on Shaftesbury Avenue. From Piccadilly Circus, walk northeast and you'll come to Soho, to the left of Shaftesbury. This jumbled section can also be approached from the Tottenham Court Road tube station. Walk south along Charing Cross Road, and Soho will be to your right.

Of Gerrard Street, a correspondent wrote that "the smell of pickled ginger and roast duckling seeps from restaurant doors. The men scurry into stores from afternoon games of fan-tan and mah-Jongg. A lilting twang of Chinese rock 'n' roll envelops the downtown street." Although the East End's Limehouse made a small pretense, Gerrard Street has succeeded in becoming London's first Chinatown. Strip shows have given way to Chinese restaurants and bookstores keeping you informed of the latest developments in Hong Kong or China.

Soho in a sense is a Jekyll and Hyde quarter. In daytime it's a paradise for the searcher of spices, continental food, fruits, fish, and sausages, with at least two street markets offering fruit and vegetables, often at knock-down prices. At night it's a dazzle of strip joints, gay clubs, so-called blue movies, sex shops, and titillating bookshops, all intermingled with international restaurants which, because of the competition, are on their toes to offer value for money.

The French House, 49 Dean St., W.1 (tel. 437-2799), is popularly known as the French pub. Run by Monsieur G. R. Berlemont, it once was the unofficial headquarters of the French resistance in exile in London during the war. Nostalgic Frenchmen still come here, talking about the old days and purchasing outstanding "vins" by the glass. The pub has a plain exterior, and the decor is not remarkable. However, the hospitality of the patron is laudable, as are his bar-room snacks, especially the pâté and the excellent quiche Lorraine. Prices of wine by the glass begin at 70p ($1.23). A lot of authors, theater and film people are also attracted here.

The **Dumpling Inn,** 15a Gerrard St., W.1 (tel. 437-2567), in the small Chinese district of Soho, attracts a number of devoted regulars. Don't be fooled by the name or the Venetian murals—this is an elegant Chinese restaurant serving classical Mandarin dishes. The haute cuisine of China, Mandarin cooking dates back nearly 3000 years and employs a number of unique cooking rituals. The fact that this restaurant serves somewhat small portions can be turned into an advantage because it gives you an opportunity to sample a variety of this delectable cuisine. You can savor the special tastes of Mandarin cooking in the shark's fin soup, the beef in oyster sauce, or the grilled pork or beef dumplings. Pancakes stuffed with discreetly flavored minced meat are a house specialty. Main dishes such as prawns in chili sauce run about £3.50 ($6.13), and dumplings are priced from £2 ($3.50). Dinner reservations are recommended, and you should allow plenty of time for dining here since most dishes are prepared to your special order.

Pasticceria Amalfi, 31 Old Compton St., W.1 (tel. 437-7284), is a crowded, unusually good, bargain-priced Italian restaurant, one of the finest in Soho. It's popular with lunchers in an area where there are dozens of other luncheon possibilities. Its manager, Arnaldo Sassano, is a fanatic in his insistence that the cooking at his establishment be authentic. His is a friendly place, open every day from noon to 3 p.m. and from 6 p.m. to midnight, making it a good spot to head for, for an after-theater dinner. The pasta dishes are particularly recommended, ranging from spaghetti to tagliatelli to lasagne, at £1.50 ($2.63) to £1.80 ($3.15). Other starters include soup at 85p ($1.49). Pizzas average £1.85 ($3.24), and main dishes include sauté of veal in wine at £3.75 ($6.56) and other meat dishes costing from £3 ($5.25) to £5.50 ($9.63). Pastries, at 50p (88¢) to 80p ($1.40), are a specialty. There is a pâtisserie above the restaurant where these are freshly made daily by their own Italian pastry chefs.

The **Venus Kebab House,** 2 Charlotte St., W.1 (tel. 636-4324), is a zesty choice on a highly competitive street. It's a winner for Greek specialties and good food in the low-price range. Avgolemono, the Greek national soup, costs 70p ($1.23); it's made with chicken stock, rice, egg, lemon, and spices. You can have three lamb or pork kebabs for £2.50 ($4.38), or a large Greek salad, a main dish, at £2.30 ($4.03). The standard specialties, dolmades (vine leaves stuffed with lamb, beef, rice, tomatoes, and spices) and moussaka, go for £3.50 ($6.13) each. For dessert, try baklava (a light, flaky pastry made with blended honey and nuts). A corner restaurant, the Venus has outdoor tables in summer. It's open from noon to 11:30 p.m., Monday to Saturday.

Triano Restaurant, 53 St. Giles High St., is good public relations for the Cypriots. It serves excellent dishes, but keeps the prices low. You can have the popular moussaka with rice and peas for £3 ($5.25), although you may prefer the special shish kebab, £3.50 ($6.13). One of the specialties of Triano is kleftiko à la Greque garnished, costing £3.40 ($5.95). The restaurant is open daily from noon to 3 p.m. and from 5:30 to 11 p.m. For dessert, try the baklava.

Jimmy's, 24 Frith St., W.1 (tel. 437-9521), is across the street from Ronnie Scott's (see Chapter IV). I recommend a dinner at Jimmy's, then a visit to Ronnie Scott's later, where you need order only drinks and not its high-priced food. Jimmy's is a basement bistro, with the menu posted outside. Scruffy waiters, an unswept floor, and empty bottles on the bar create an atmosphere that ages ago used to be called bohemian. The cooking is basically Greek-Cypriot, with an international flavor. Appetizers include soups, taramasalata, and the like. Chops, kebabs, moussaka, and chicken dishes are the main courses, along with stuffed vine leaves. The helpings are huge, a complete meal costing around £4.50 ($7.88). There's music whenever the mood strikes. The restaurant is open daily except Sunday until 7 p.m.

Anemos, 34 Charlotte St., W.1 (tel. 636-2289), is the place for breaking plates, dancing, and joining the waiters in a rip-roaring Greek song. A typical meal of taramasalata, hummus, and kebabs, plus dessert, cheese, coffee, and a half bottle of wine, will run as much as £9.50 ($16.63). However, a smaller meal with, say, two courses only and no wine, will average around £5 ($8.75). You'll need a good digestion for you will be expected to dance on the tables, gyrate to bouzouki music, and drink retsina or Cyprus wines (others are expensive). The restaurant is closed on Sunday so the staff can clean up the mess.

Continental Bar, 30 Charing Cross Rd., W.C.2 (tel. 836-4233), is really just a snackbar but is open from 9 a.m. to midnight, and can satisfy your needs whatever the time of day, particularly after the theater. The service is quick and friendly. Salt beef (corned, to us) sandwiches are a featured selection, as are hearty soups such as bean and barley. Most soups cost 60p ($1.05), although you'll pay up to £2 ($3.50) for one of the house specialties, doner kebabs, which are spit-roasted lamb served in pita bread with relish and shredded salad. Moussaka is another house specialty, and the chef also prepares many different types of omelets.

Le Beaujolais, 25 Litchfield St., W.C.2 (tel. 836-2277), stands at Cambridge Circus. People go here to enjoy wine and cold snacks in a friendly atmosphere. Philippe M. Ruos has created this bar for those who like to chat and drink. House wines range from 75p ($1.31) to 90p ($1.58) per glass. By the bottle, prices start at £4 ($7) for the house wine, either white or red. He has cold food to accompany your wine, including French pâtés, cheeses, and chicken and ham, costing from £1.25 ($2.19).

2. Westminster and St. James's

This section (S.W.1) has been the seat of the British government since the days of Edward the Confessor. Dominated by the Houses of Parliament and Westminster Abbey, Parliament Square is the symbol of the soul of England. Westminster is a big name to describe a large borough of London, including Whitehall itself, the headquarters of many government offices. In addition, the sprawling area in and around Victoria Station (with many budget hotels) is also a part of Westminster, although sections of it fall into Pimlico.

After you've been photographed with Big Ben in the background, chances are you'll be ready for lunch.

The **Westminster College,** 76 Vincent Sq., S.W.1, is the luncheon find of the year. In a spacious dining room, with great windows opening onto a garden square, a complete midday meal, coffee included, is served for around £4 ($7), including VAT. The secret is that this is the finest school for hotel and restaurant catering in England, and the nonprofit meals are cooked and served by undergraduates. The young waitresses and waiters, with their efforts to do everything perfectly, give attentive service. It's really not amateur hour, as there is strict supervision. The food is of a high standard, but you must order whatever their "assignment" is for the day. You can reserve space by telephone (828-1222) between noon and 2 p.m. only, up to ten days in advance, or just arrive around noon to see whether there is space, have a drink in the lounge if you wish, and then be shown to your seat. If you are alone, you'll probably have to share. Naturally, the dining room is closed on weekends and college holidays from July through September.

Top Curry Centre, Tandoori House, 3 Lupus St., S.W.1 (tel. 821-7572), has the colossal advantage of listing the hotness and strength of the curries graded from one to nine, so you need not suffer the agonies if you prefer a mild dish. Nibble two bhajis with various fillings while you decide on your main curry dish. Curries include succulent chicken kurma, prawn and mushroom curry, egg or vegetable curry, beef or lamb curries. Side dishes include cauliflower or spinach bhajis and cucumber raita (in yogurt). Poppadums, chapatis, and, of course, rice accompany these, and the bill will come to around £5 ($8.75) per person for a highly satisfying meal. Drinks are available and you should certainly wash No. 9 curry down with lager unless you have an asbestos-lined palate. The center is open from 11:30 a.m. to 3 p.m. and 6 p.m. to midnight Monday to Friday, and 11:30 a.m. to midnight on Saturday. It is also open on Sunday from noon to midnight. All is under the care of Abdul Malik.

Grandma Lee's Bakery and Restaurant, 2 Bridge St., S.W.1 (tel. 839-1319), is a bright and cheerful place across the street from the Houses of Parliament and the tower of Big Ben. Bread, buns, and rolls are freshly baked on the premises, later to appear at the ground-floor service counter filled with your choice of an array of ingredients. You can either take these sandwiches out or else carry them upstairs to consume at the lightwood varnished tables and chairs. Everything comes in a bun, including breakfast, a bacon-and-egg bun served from 7 to 11 a.m. Along with juice, tea, and coffee, it comes to £1.35 ($2.36). Try a Grandwich Plate, a huge, thick slice of bread with your choice of filling. It's topped with another gigantic slice, served with coleslaw on the side and priced from £1 ($1.75) to £1.75 ($3.06), depending on your choice of filling. They also serve beef casserole with bread and chili with bread, each going for £1.30 ($2.28). It's open daily from 7 a.m. to 9 p.m. Tube: Westminster.

READERS' RESTAURANT SELECTIONS: "At the **Acropolis Kebab House,** 1 Denbigh St., S.W.1 (tel. 828-2471), for as little as £3 ($5.25), you can have a choice of several well-prepared pilafs. I especially recommend the dolmades, an exquisite stuffed grape leaves concoction. All entrees come with a mixed salad and pita bread. Prices include VAT, but there is a 25p (44¢) cover charge. It is open Monday to Saturday from noon to 2:30 p.m. and from 6 p.m. to midnight. 1 Denbigh St. is just one block off Belgrade Road" (Ms. Jean Pugh, Miami, Fla.). . . . "The **Seafresh Restaurant,** 80–81 Wilton Rd. (tel. 828-0745), lies about two blocks southeast of Victoria Station, within easy walking distance. It is a large, modern, and very clean restaurant patronized mostly by residents and tourists staying in this area. The prices are inexpensive, and the portions of cod, plaice, and skate are enormous, at least ten ounces. Most fish is lightly breaded and deep-fried. The plaice is cooked to perfection, the best fish meal I ever had, although I am not a fish fancier. This is undoubtedly the best value in the Victoria area. All fish is freshly caught, and service is prompt and efficient. Expect to spend from £6 ($10.50) plus your drink" (Robert C. Eckstein, Stockton, Calif.).

ST. JAMES'S: This section (S.W.1), the beginning of Royal London, starts at Piccadilly Circus, moving southwest. It's frightfully convenient, as the English say, enclosing a number of locations, such as American Express on Haymarket, many of the leading department stores, eventually encompassing Buckingham Palace.

But don't be scared off. There are luncheon bargains available in an atmosphere ranging from the world's most exclusive grocery store to a posh Victorian pub.

Fortnum and Mason PLC, 181 Piccadilly (tel. 734-8040), down the street from the Ritz, draws the carriage trade, the well-heeled dowager from Mayfair or Belgravia who comes seeking such tinned treasures as pâté de foie gras or a boar's head. She would never set foot in a regular grocery store, but Fortnum and Mason, with its swallow-tailed attendants, is no mere grocery story: it's a British tradition dating back to 1707. In fact, the establishment likes to think that Mr. Fortnum and Mr. Mason "created a union surpassed in its importance to the human race only by the meeting of Adam and Eve." In the Mezzanine Restaurant, you can mingle at lunch with the caviar and champagne shoppers. The Chocolate and Confectionery Department is on the first floor (ground floor, to the British). The Fountain Restaurant has both store and street entrances (Jermyn Street), and is open from 9:30 a.m. until 11:30 p.m., Monday to Saturday, for the benefit of theatergoers. The St. James's Restaurant on the fourth floor is open during normal store hours. One of the many departments of interest is luxury leather goods, and there's an enchanting children's carousel on the second floor. In the basement you can often pick up that odd gift to take home. At the fresh-food counter some very good take-away sandwiches are priced from £1.25 ($2.19), but where else can you buy a sandwich prepared by grocers who hold the Royal Warrant? Look for the Fortnum and Mason clock outside.

The **Red Lion,** 2 Duke of York St., St. James's Square, S.W.1 (tel. 930-2030), is only a short walk from Piccadilly Circus, near American Express on Haymarket. Ian Nairn compared its spirit to that of Edouard Manet's painting *A Bar at the Folies-Bergère* (see the collection at the Courtauld Institute Galleries). Try to avoid peak hours, so that you'll be able to introduce yourself to the friendly owners, Roy and Corinne Hamlin. They offer pub luncheons at noon: steak pie, £1.40 ($2.45); a wide variety of sandwiches, all on healthful brown bread, at 85p ($1.49) a "cutting," as they say. All roasts are £2 ($3.50). Everything is washed down with a pint of lager or cider in their jewel-like little Victorian pub, with its posh turn-of-the-century decorations such as patterned glass, deep-mahogany curlicues that recapture the gin-palace atmosphere. It's open six days a week from 11 a.m. to 3 p.m. and from 5:30 to 11 p.m., on Sunday from noon to 2 p.m. Single women can be at ease here, under the unofficial and kindly eye of the Hamlins.

The Captain's Cabin, 4 Norris St., S.W.1 (tel. 930-4767), just off Haymarket and close to Piccadilly Circus, is an old high London building on a narrow street with a maritime atmosphere. The restaurant has a carvery where a three-course meal can be had for £7 ($12.25). The snackbar offers traditional pies, salads, and ploughman's lunches. Try real English ale such as Directors Bitter or Best Bitter at 72p ($1.26) a pint.

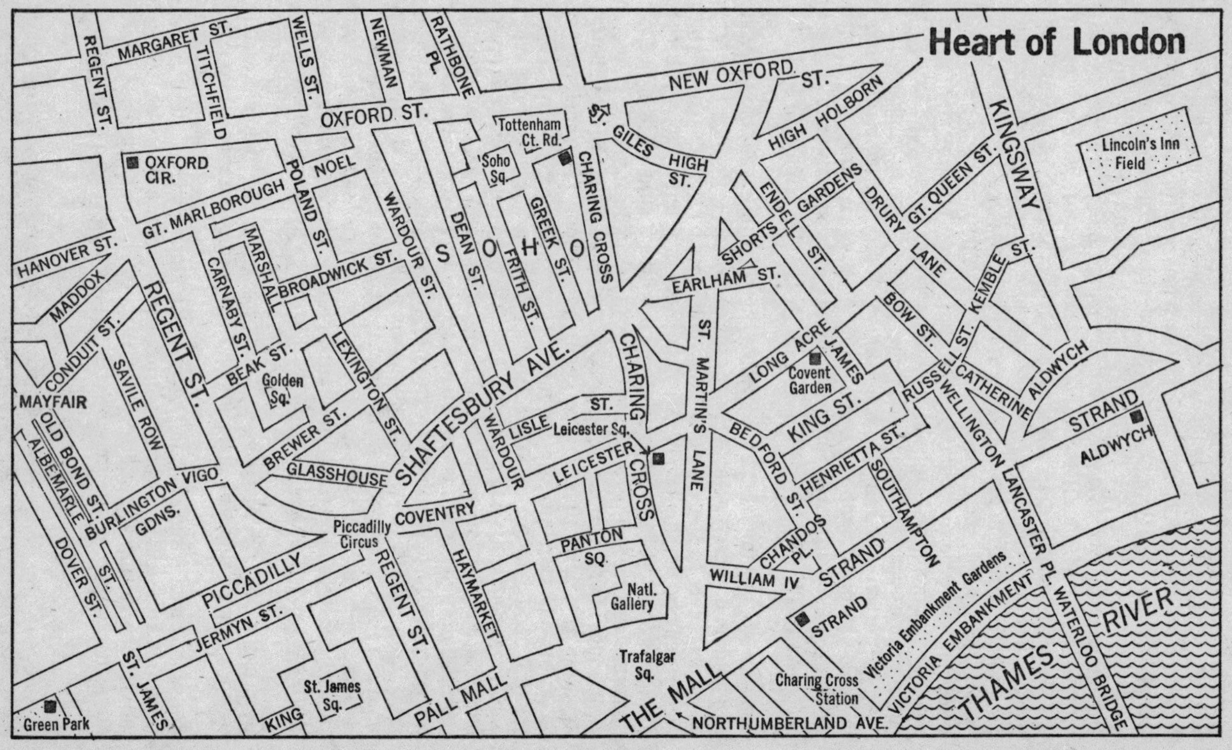
Heart of London
REGENT ST.
MARGARET ST.
TITCHFIELD
WELLS ST.
NEWMAN
RATHBONE PL.
NEW OXFORD ST.
OXFORD ST.
Tottenham Ct. Rd.
ST. GILES HIGH ST.
HIGH HOLBORN
KINGSWAY
Lincoln's Inn Field
OXFORD CIR.
NOEL
POLAND ST.
Soho Sq.
CHARING CROSS
ENDELL ST.
GARDENS
DRURY LANE
GT. QUEEN ST.
GT. MARLBOROUGH
WARDOUR ST.
DEAN ST.
FRITH ST.
GREEK ST.
SOHO
SHORTS
HANOVER ST.
MARSHALL
BROADWICK ST.
EARLHAM ST.
KEMBLE ST.
MADDOX
REGENT ST.
CARNABY ST.
BOW ST.
CONDUIT ST.
SAVILE ROW
LEXINGTON ST.
SHAFTESBURY AVE.
CHARING CROSS
ST. MARTIN'S LANE
LONG ACRE
JAMES
Covent Garden
RUSSELL ST.
CATHERINE
ALDWYCH
BEAK ST.
Golden Sq.
MAYFAIR
BREWER ST.
WARDOUR
LISLE
ST.
Leicester Sq.
KING ST.
WELLINGTON
STRAND
ALDWYCH
OLD BOND ST.
ALBEMARLE
BURLINGTON GDNS.
VIGO
GLASSHOUSE
LEICESTER
BEDFORD ST.
HENRIETTA ST.
SOUTHAMPTON
LANCASTER PL.
Piccadilly Circus
COVENTRY
PANTON SQ.
CHANDOS PL.
DOVER ST.
ST.
PICCADILLY
REGENT ST.
HAYMARKET
WILLIAM IV
STRAND
Natl. Gallery
Victoria Embankment Gardens
JERMYN ST.
STRAND
VICTORIA EMBANKMENT
RIVER
ST. JAMES
St. James Sq.
Trafalgar Sq.
THAMES
WATERLOO BRIDGE
Green Park
KING
PALL MALL
THE MALL
Charing Cross Station
NORTHUMBERLAND AVE.

The Dive Bar in the basement is a small, paneled, quiet bar with a regular clientele. Dimly lit, it was famous during the last world war as a rendezvous for airmen and servicemen on leave. Mementos from those days are still on the walls.

3. The City

When the English talk about "The City" (E.C.2, E.C.3), they don't mean London. The City is the British version of Wall Street. Not only is it an important financial and business square mile, but it contains much worth exploring.

Here are the buildings known all over the world: the Bank of England on Threadneedle Street (entrance hall open to the public); the Stock Exchange, where you can watch from a special gallery as fortunes are made and lost; and Lloyd's of London, on Leadenhall, one of the world's great insurance centers. Lloyd's will insure anything from a stamp collection to a giraffe's neck.

Typical English food—shepherd's pie, mixed grills, roast beef—is dished up in dozens of the old pubs of the City. Here you can eat along with the English, whether they be the man in the bowler worried about his country's balance of payments, or a Cockney clerk wanting to get back to the sound of the Bow Bells.

Many of the old pubs and wine bars date back to Elizabethan days, and lay claim to having entertained literary celebrities. For the most part, the following recommendations have been selected not only because of their well-prepared and inexpensive food, but because the buildings themselves have interest. The pub might have been designed by Sir Christopher Wren, or Shakespeare might have performed in one of them . . . whatever.

Have a good lunch.

Wren's Upstairs, 29 Watling St., E.C.4 (tel. 248-6252), is rich in associations with Sir Christopher Wren, having been rebuilt after the Great Fire of London in 1666. On the ground level is a mellow pub, with an intimate restaurant upstairs, serving lunch from noon to 2 p.m., Monday through Friday. Under oak beams and on trestle tables, you can have a good choice of English food, with such traditional dishes as steak-and-kidney pudding. Five hot dishes made on the premises daily are likely to include chicken-and-mushroom pie, beef-and-vegetable pie, chili con carne, costing from £2 ($3.50) to £2.75 ($4.81), including vegetables. For dessert? Sweets from the trolley go for around 70p ($1.23), including fresh cream.

The **George & Vulture,** 3 Castle Court, Cornhill, E.C.3 (tel. 626-9710), is for the enthusiast of Dickens, ye olde Pickwickian hostelrie and the like. This chophouse, founded in 1660, makes the claim that it is probably the world's oldest tavern, with reference to an inn on this spot going back to 1175. The George & Vulture no longer puts up overnight guests (although Dickens himself used to bed down here), but its three floors are still used for serving English meals. The Pickwick Club meets here now. Come here for lunch, Monday through Friday, noon to 3 p.m. In addition to the daily specials, the George & Vulture features a "loin chop, chump chop," fried filets of Dover sole with tartar sauce, or a more modest plaice. Every Thursday, the specialty is "Pickwick Pie," that is, steak, kidney, and oyster pudding. On other days the specialty is various roasts. Potatoes or buttered cabbage are served with most platters. The apple tart is always reliable. Meals begin at about £6.50 ($11.38) for two courses. After lunch, explore the intricate nearby passageways, discovering for yourself the maze of shops, wine houses, pubs, and old buildings surrounding the tavern.

Old King Lud, 78 Ludgate Circus, E.C.4 (tel. 236-6610), is a Victorian pub built in 1855 on the site of the Old Fleet Prison. The former dungeons are now the cellars of this old-world pub, which bills itself as the home of the original Welsh rabbit. However, it no longer serves that specialty for which it became famous. Rather, it offers a selection of pâtés at £1.20 ($2.10) which ranges from venison to duck with orange. Both hot and cold dishes are dispensed. One of the hot plates, such as beef curry with chutney and rice, costs £1.85 ($3.24). Wine is sold by the glass, selections including claret at 70p ($1.23) or Anjou at 65p ($1.14). You can also order good Marlow Bitter here. The decor is in varying shades of green, including the tufted banquettes. Tube: Blackfriars.

WINE BARS: **Mother Bunch's Wine House,** Arches F & G, Old Seacoal Lane, E.C.4 (tel. 236-5317), is a maze of vaults underneath the arches of Ludgate Circus. My favorite of all the wine houses, Mother Bunch's is one of the most atmospheric places for dining in the City, boasting a "well-stocked larder," with the best of hams and all manner of cheeses as well as game and other pies. Port wines of the most noted vintages are decanted daily "for gentlemen in the proper manner." In season, grouse, partridge, pheasant, and Scottish salmon are featured. Guests can dine in the mellow room downstairs or perhaps in the elegantly furnished upstairs room where many are seated around a large table and served family style. Sherry, port, and madeira "from the wood" begin at 95p ($1.66), and table wines by the glass start at 85p ($1.40). The favorite dish is a plate of smoked ham off the bone, costing £2 ($3.50), although game pie is £2.30 ($4.03). Strawberries and raspberries in season make the finest dessert, although you can always order cheese with french bread at £1.10 ($1.93). The wine house is open from 11:30 a.m. to 3 p.m. and from 5:30 to 8:30 p.m., Monday to Friday. Tube: Blackfriars.

Capataz Wine Store, 89 Old Broad St., E.C.2 (tel. 588-1140), is a City wine vault, under a shoe shop, that maintains a turn-of-the-century atmosphere, with sawdust covering the floors. You sit on simple wooden chairs grouped around wine cases and casks. At lunchtime a mainly male clientele patronizes this atmospheric cellar, selecting their favorite sherries or table wines. Wines, incidentally, are sold by the glass—a recently sampled red burgundy going for 75p ($1.31), Italian red and white wines for 65p ($1.14), and claret for 80p ($1.40). Food is not served. However, you can bring in and eat your own sandwiches and snacks, while enjoying a selection from some 70 different wines. The wine store has been under the management of the same family for more than a century. Hours are from 11:30 a.m. to 3 p.m., Monday to Friday. Tube: Bank, Liverpool Street, or Broad Street.

Bow Wine Vaults, 10 Bow Churchyard, E.C.4 (tel. 248-1121), has existed since long before the current wine bar fad. The atmosphere is staunchly masculine, and the vaults attract a loyal following of business and professional people who somehow manage to find their way back to their offices after a heavy eating and drinking session here. Sherries, port, and madeira are available by the glass, as are an assortment of table wines at prices ranging from 75p ($1.31) to £2.20 ($3.85). A cold buffet with a salad will run you £2.95 ($5.16) to £4.25 ($7.44). The vaults are open from 11:30 a.m. to 3 p.m. and from 5 to 7 p.m. but closed weekends and bank holidays. Tube: Mansion House.

Jamaica Wine House, St. Michael's Alley, off Cornhill, E.C.3 (tel. 626-9496), lies in a tangle of City alleyways, and if you do manage to find it, you'll be at one of the first coffeehouses to be opened in England. In fact, the Jamaica Wine House is reputed to be the first coffeehouse in the Western world. Pepys used to visit it and mentioned the event in his *Diary*. The coffeehouse was destroyed in the Great Fire of 1666, rebuilt in 1674, and has remained, more or less, in its present form ever since. For years London merchants and daring sea captains came here to lace deals with rum and coffee. Nowadays the two-level house dispenses beer, ale, lager, and fine wines to appreciative drinkers. The oak-paneled bar on the ground floor is more traditional, as the downstairs bar has been modernized. The Bank of England is only a stone's throw away. Tube: Bank.

Olde Wine Shades, 6 Martin Lane, off Cannon Street, E.C.4 (tel. 626-6876), is the oldest wine house in the City, dating from 1663. It was the only City tavern to survive the Great Fire of 1666, not to mention the blitz of 1940. Only 100 yards from the Monument, the Olde Wine Shades used to attract Charles Dickens who enjoyed its fine wines. In the smoking room the old oil paintings have appropriately darkened with age, and the 19th-century satirical political cartoons remain enigmatic to most of today's generation. Some of the fine wines of Europe are served here, and port and sherry are drawn directly from an array of casks behind the counter. The owners, El Vino, the famous City wine merchants, boast that they can satisfy anyone's taste in sherry. A candlewick bar and restaurant is found downstairs, but upstairs, along with your wine, you can order french bread with ham off the bone at £2 ($3.50), Breton pâté at £1.50 ($2.63), and sandwiches beginning at £1 ($1.75). Hours are from 11:30 a.m. to 3 p.m. and from 5 to 8 p.m. Men must wear a jacket and tie. The establishment is closed on Saturday, Sunday, and bank holidays. Tube: Monument.

FLEET STREET: This "street of ink" (E.C.4), as it is called, is a continuation of the Strand and is the gateway to the City, but it is famous as the center of London's newspaper and publishing world. The chances are that the person you are rubbing shoulders with in one of the old pubs is a writer or author, as people of letters gather in the historic pubs around here, just as they have been doing for centuries. Here you can eat steak-and-kidney pie.

Ye Olde Cock Tavern, 22 Fleet St., E.C.4 (tel. 353-9706), should inspire you to follow the long line of ghostly literary comrades, such as Dickens, who have favored this ancient pub with their presence. Downstairs you can order a pint as well as snackbar food. You can also order steak-and-kidney pie or a cold chicken-and-beef plate with salad at prices that range from £1.50 ($2.63) to £2 ($3.50). At the Carvery upstairs, you must reserve a table for lunch. The meal costs from £7.75 ($13.56) and includes a choice of five appetizers, such as soup or prawn cocktail, followed by all the roasts you can carve—beef, lamb, pork, or turkey. Naturally, you help yourself to as many vegetables as you desire, then follow with a choice of desserts, perhaps cheese and crackers.

Cheshire Cheese, Wine Office Court, 145 Fleet St., E.C.4 (tel. 353-6170), is one of the greatest of the old city chophouses, open and running since 1667. It is famous as the place where Dr. Johnson dined with his friends and entertained them with his acerbic wit. This is quite possible, and certainly Dickens was a customer. The two specialties of the house cost £4 ($7) each. The first is "ye famous pudding"—(steak, kidney, mushroom, and game)—and the other is roast beef, with Yorkshire pudding and horseradish sauce. The hot plate holds a giant joint of the roast beef, and the waiters will give you additional helpings, warning you "not to waste it." For dessert, "ye famous pancake" is £1.25 ($2.19), and there is "toasted cheese" at £1.25 also. Lunch is served from noon to 2:30 p.m. (last orders), and dinners from 6 to 9 p.m. Warning: It is advisable to reserve a table (the bars open at 11:30 and again at 5 p.m.). Closed Saturday and Sunday.

READER'S RESTAURANT SELECTION: "Slender's Health Food Restaurant, 41 Cathedral Pl., E.C.4, is exactly in front of St. Paul tube station. The menu at this fine eating place includes such items as tomato and watercress soup, 65p ($1.14); lasagne verdi, £1.50 ($2.63); and baked potato with butter, 60p ($1.05). Herb teas and decaffeinated coffee are also served. They serve luscious desserts, such as apple-date pie, apricot meringues, and cheesecake, all at reasonable prices. The young people serving you are most pleasant, the food very well prepared and attractive. One may either eat in the restaurant or take food out. Beans, whole grains, and dried fruits are also sold. Hours are 8:30 a.m. to 6:15 p.m., Monday through Friday" (Jean See, Spokane, Wash.).

4. Holborn and Bloomsbury

HOLBORN: In "legal London," you can join barristers, solicitors, and law clerks for food and drink at the following recommendations.

The Canteen, 4 Great Queen St., W.C.2 (tel. 405-6598), is owned and run by Messrs. Sulkin, Bryan, and Rudland, known to regulars as K.C., Joe, and David. On the second floor the 1940s are brought to life, and you can join in on the dance floor with a lively jitterbug or perhaps a dreamy foxtrot to the strains of the real live band which plays music from that era. It's a blue- and cream-colored place, with a raised stage for the musicians. The restaurant serves meat, fish, and chicken dishes, plus an appetizer and dessert, at a cost of £9 ($15.75) per head. In the jazz bar downstairs, snacks from the fast-service counter include southern fried chicken, hamburgers and a salad, and jacket potatoes with various stuffings. A meal here will cost from £4 ($7) to £6 ($10.50), a glass of wine going for 70p ($1.23). It's open every evening except Sunday from 8 p.m., and there is no admission charge.

My Old Dutch, 132 High Holborn, W.C.1 (tel. 404-5008), is a cheerful, friendly place, resembling a Dutch kitchen with scrubbed pine tables at which you can be served 101 different pancakes—all enormous—on huge Delft plates. Fillings and garnishes include cheese, meats, and vegetables, as well as sweet fillings, such as Adam's Downfall—that is, figs and avocado. There is also a selection of waffles and ice cream. The cost is from £2.75 ($4.81) and up, and one of these dishes makes a good meal. Coffee and tea are available to wash it all down. My Old Dutch opens at noon and remains open until late in the evening, depending on business.

Hennekey's Long Bar, 22–23 High Holborn, W.C.1 (tel. 242-7670), lays claim to being the oldest bar in England. Built in 1430, the pub is often visited by tourists after they've stopped over at the Silver Vaults on Chancery Lane. The food is good, the portions large. The food includes such hearty fare as steak-and-kidney pie, chicken casserole, and shepherd's pie, with dishes costing from £1.40 ($2.45). If you visit in winter, you can enjoy warmth from a three-sided fireplace, and while warming up, try to solve the mystery of how it works.

BLOOMSBURY: Spaghetti House, 15 Goodge St., W.1 (tel. 636-3582), is the big mamma of a chain of spaghetti and pizza houses. Chianti bottles enhance an inviting, Italian-oriented atmosphere on floor after floor. Most of the well-prepared pasta dishes hover in the £2 ($3.50) to £2.75 ($4.81) bracket, but you'll pay more, of course, for the meat courses. A worthy main dish is veal escalope in butter, served with vegetables. The minestrone is flavorsome. For dessert, cassata siciliana makes a soothing selection. Expect to pay at least £6 ($10.50) for a complete meal. The Spaghetti House is open Monday to Saturday from noon to 11 p.m., and from 5:30 to 10:30 p.m. on Sunday. It's across Tottenham Court Road in the vicinity of Russell Square. For Mayfair "trippers," its nearest chain sister is **Vecchia Milano,** at 74 Welbeck St. There are eight Spaghetti Houses in London, all part of the same chain. The one at 77 Knightsbridge was the location of the famous 1970s siege when gunmen held the staff hostage almost a week before surrendering.

But if you want pizza instead of spaghetti, walk down Goodge Street to the **Pizza House,** no. 56, W.1 (tel. 636-1346). Pizzas are in the £1.90 ($3.33) to £2.30 ($4.03) range.

The **Museum Tavern,** 49 Great Russell St., W.C.1 (tel. 242-8984), directly across the street from the British Museum, is a turn-of-the-century pub, with all the trappings: cut velvet, oak paneling, and cut glass. Right in the center of the London University area, it is popular with writers and publishers. At lunch you can order real, good-tasting, low-cost English food. Such standard English fare is featured as shepherd's pie or "sausage and mash." Hot pies are another featured selection. A cold buffet is offered, including herring, Scotch eggs, and veal and ham pies, as well as salads and cheese. Prices range from sandwiches at 65p ($1.14) to a large plate of cold meat with salad at £2.40 ($4.20). Hot dishes run around £2 ($3.50).

Green Parrot Restaurant, 146 Southampton Row, W.C.1 (tel. 837-3925), is one of the more traditional dining rooms convenient to the Russell Square tube station. A licensed restaurant, it features a three-course set menu from 11 a.m. to 3 p.m. The price of this table d'hôte begins at £1.70 ($2.98), going up to £3.75 ($6.56). It includes soup or juice, a main course, and dessert. Specials are steak pie served with french fries and vegetables, and apple pie for dessert. There is also a special Greek à la carte menu, which features a charcoaled shish kebab, served with salad and french fries. Other Greek dishes include stifado, meat cooked in red wine and served with vegetables and potatoes. Another is klefdigon, a very tender piece of lamb cooked in the oven with spices and served with vegetables and potatoes. Housed in an angular building, the Green Parrot seats quite a few guests every day of the year (except Christmas). Hours are from 10:30 a.m. to 3 p.m. and from 5 to 10 p.m. When you go in, ask for Mr. Alex, who will go out of his way to look after you.

Entrecôte, 124 Southampton Row, W.C.1 (tel. 405-1466), invites you to go downstairs to its Edwardian precincts. Attractive "resting" actresses are the waitresses, and they will serve you the house specialty, an entrecôte with french fries. Other daily specials are offered as well—perhaps coq au vin or beef bourguignon. A meal can cost as little as £4 ($7), and three courses average £6 ($10.50). In fact, the food is generally French inspired, and the wine list includes some Haut Médoc selections. The food is made fresh every day—no deep-freeze. In the evenings, a small disco atmosphere prevails, and sometimes there is dancing to live music. Hours are from noon to 3 p.m. and from 6 p.m. to 1 a.m. Tube: Russell Square.

Tagore, 8 Brunswick Centre, off Russell Square, W.C.1 (tel. 837-9397), is one of the finest Indian restaurants in London. It has an unobtrusive and rather unattractive entrance in this modern complex of apartments and shops. Hardly what you'd expect if you're seeking delicate Indian cookery, including the best of tandoori dishes. Colored lights inside illuminate a display of art objects and paintings. Sitar music is provided nightly, and there is dancing as well, so it becomes somewhat like a nightclub.

Specialties include pan-fried herring, heavily spiced, lamb pasanda, and tandoori king prawn masalla. Tagore is an ideal center for vegetarians who will find a special menu of tempting dishes. A dish costs from £2.45 ($4.29), although a typical three-course repast will average £5.50 ($9.63). Incidentally, if you're in the neighborhood, perhaps sightseeing at the British Museum, you might want to visit and sample the executive luncheon at £3.75 ($6.56). At the entrance is a large portrait of namesake Tagore, the Hindu poet and prose writer who died in 1941. The restaurant is open daily, including Sunday, from noon to 3 p.m. and from 6 till midnight. Tube: Russell Square.

READER'S RESTAURANT SELECTION: "Near the Holborn underground station, and convenient to Russell Square and Bloomsbury Square B&B hotels, is a small restaurant that specializes in light lunches and snacks, **Amandini's Salad and Sandwich Bar,** 3 Southampton Row, W.C.1 (tel. 405-6739). This little restaurant makes *fresh* sandwiches (123 different kinds!) and salads. We were delighted to find one of our favorite sandwiches on the menu, peanut butter and bananas. But the staff offers many more gourmet selections. Sandwiches cost from 65p ($1.14) to £1.50 ($2.63) a round, and salads are from 75p ($1.31) per portion. The place is inexpensive, quick, and delicious" (Mrs. Frank Welch, Seattle, Wash.).

READER'S PUB SELECTION (ISLINGTON): "While we were shopping for antiques at Camden Passage, Islington, N.I, northeast of Bloomsbury, we came upon **Camden Head** (tel. 359-0851), right in the middle of the antique center. It has a well-kept, typical Victorian interior, and the food is inexpensive yet good. Old mirrors and windows make this house one of the few authentic Victorian pubs in London. At exactly noon, trays of cold cuts and salad ingredients come out, and containers of hot food are set into their heat-keeping wells. Service is buffet style, and you pay for each individual item on a per-portion basis. The 'bubble and squeak' is authentic, as is cottage pie. Some continental dishes are featured as well. The cost for a one-dish meal averages £2 ($3.50), and you'll pay £2.75 ($4.81) for a two-course lunch. Get there on time, as the food goes quickly. Table service is offered on the terrace in front. On market days, Wednesday and Saturday, meat salads and a cheese board are provided in the upstairs Victorian dining room, and regular pub meals are served in the saloon bar" (Mrs. Robert H. Horen, Fairfield, Conn.).

5. Belgravia and Knightsbridge

BELGRAVIA: Belgravia (S.W.1), south of Hyde Park, is the so-called aristocratic quarter of London, challenging Mayfair for grandness. It reigned in glory along with Queen Victoria. But today's aristocrats are likely to be the top echelon in foreign embassies, along with a rising new money class—or at least young fashion models or actresses clever enough to secure a most desirable flat here. Belgravia is near Buckingham Palace Gardens (how elegant can your address be?) and Brompton Road. Its center is Belgrave Square (take the Piccadilly subway line to Hyde Park corner), one of the more attractive plazas in London.

Upper Crust in Belgravia, 9 William St., S.W.1 (tel. 235-8444). The menu hangs at the narrow frontage. Inside, the decor is welcoming, with natural-brick and pine walls and orange tiles on wooden tables. In all, it's a clean and friendly place with no pretension, recommended by visitors and local business people alike. The food is excellent and might begin with soup of the day or a country pâté—and here the staff knows the difference between a pâté and a terrine. Other appetizers include stuffed avocado, smoked mackerel with horseradish sauce, even Yorkshire pudding filled with chicken livers. Specialties include veal, tomato, and pimiento pie; turkey and cranberry pie; fisherman's pie; steak and pickled walnut pie; and, of course, shepherd's pie. Desserts are likely to feature Yorkshire pudding stuffed with sweet mincemeat and old English plum pudding and custard. Meals begin at £7 ($12.25) and range upward.

The **Antelope,** 22 Eaton Terrace, S.W.1 (tel. 730-7781), is on the fringe of Belgravia, at the gateway to Chelsea. This eatery caters to a hodgepodge of clients, aptly described as "people of all classes, colours and creeds who repair for interesting discussion on a whole gamut of subjects, ranging from sport to medieval, mid-European, wicker-work, bed-bug traps, and for both mental and physical refreshment." You can take lunch in a ground-floor chamber devoted to a cold buffet.

On the second floor (British first floor) food is served in a wine bar while the ground floor is devoted to drinks only. Prices for meals begin at £5 ($8.75), plus the cost of your drinks. The specialty is antelope soup. This is the base for English rugby football aficionados (not to be confused with those who follow the game of soccer). It's tougher than American football, because the players have no bodily protection. The trappings have long ago mellowed, as the history of the Antelope goes back to 1780.

The **Grenadier,** Wilton Row, Belgrave Square, S.W.1 (tel. 235-3400), is an oldtime pub on a cobblestone street, sheltered by higher buildings and protected from the noise of busy traffic. The Grenadier is one of the special pubs of London—associated with the "Iron Duke" himself, who used to play cards here with his officers. But today it's filled with a sophisticated crowd of Belgravia flatmates and chic stable-dwellers. English and continental dishes are served in front of fireplaces in two of the small rooms behind the front bar. Specialties include half an Aylesbury duckling; steak, kidney, and mushroom pie; and in honor of its former patron, filet of beef Wellington. A person can dine here in the range of £6 ($10.50) to £12 ($21) per person. However, snacks available include a plate of rare beef with salad and horseradish, rollmops, soup, sandwiches, Scotch eggs, or whatever, costing from £1 ($1.75) to £4 ($7) per portion. The bar is open from Monday to Saturday from 11 a.m. to 3 p.m. and from 5:30 until 11 p.m. On Sunday its hours are from noon to 2 p.m. and from 7 to 10:30 p.m. The grill room is open seven days a week for lunch until 2:30 p.m. and for dinner until the last orders are taken at 10 p.m. At the entrance to Wilton Row (in the vicinity of Belgrave Square), a special guard ("good evening, guv'nor") was once stationed to raise and lower a barrier for those arriving by carriage. The guard's booth is still there. Pub enthusiasts are fanatic about the Grenadier. If anyone tries to tear it down, he may meet his Waterloo. Tube: Knightsbridge.

Motcomb's, 26 Motcomb St., S.W.1 (tel. 235-6382), opposite Sotheby's Belgravia, is one of the handsomest and most charming wine bars and restaurants in London. On two levels, the bar is decorated with family paintings and wooden paneling. A complete range of food is served, and there is an excellent choice of wine as well, including several sold by the glass. Dishes are cooked to order, and recorded music is played at lunch along with live music some evenings, when a 75p ($1.31) cover charge is imposed for entertainment. Specialties include what may be the best calf liver and bacon in London, sea bass grilled with oil and lemon, and salmon trout grilled or poached to perfection. Meals begin at £10 ($17.50). To finish, coffee goes for 65p ($1.05). Motcomb's is open from noon to 3:30 p.m. and from 7 p.m. to midnight Monday through Friday. Tube: Knightsbridge.

KNIGHTSBRIDGE: Adjoining Belgravia is Knightsbridge (S.W.1), another top residential and shopping section of London, just south of Hyde Park. Knightsbridge is close in character to Belgravia, although much of this section; to the west of Sloane Street, is older, dating back (in architecture and layout) to the 18th century. This is where many Londoners go to shop, as several of the major department stores, such as Harrods, are here (take the Piccadilly Line to Knightsbridge).

Bill Bentley's, 31 Beauchamp Pl., S.W.3 (tel. 589-5080), stands on this restaurant- and boutique-lined street near Harrods. A small Georgian house, it offers tiny ground-floor rooms and a little sun-filled patio in back. Cozy and atmospheric, it presents a varied list of reasonably priced wines, including a fine selection of bordeaux. If you're in the neighborhood for lunch, you can enjoy a pub-style lunch, such as ham and salad. Hot main dishes are likely to include skate in black butter with capers and grilled lemon sole. However, they cost from £6 ($10.50). Extras such as vegetables, desserts, coffee, or appetizers, plus a 50p (88¢) cover charge and a 12% service charge, can mean a very high tab unless you stick just to sampling glasses of wine and some of the hot hors d'oeuvres such as fried whitebait. It's open daily from 11:30 a.m. to 3 p.m. and from 5:30 to 11 p.m.; Saturday, from 6:30 to 11 p.m. Closed Sunday and bank holidays. Tube: Knightsbridge.

Bistro d'Agran, la Beauchamp Pl., S.W.3 (tel. 589-3982), is a French-style bistro. Old coffeehouse benches have been used to make the booths. The walls are painted pink; otherwise, it's simple and clean. The lunch menu is likely to include such typical dishes as liver and onions fried in butter and served with a red wine sauce, or else steaks or spaghetti. Hot garlic bread, salmon steaks, thick soups, and creamy desserts provide further temptation. All main dishes include vegetables. You can usually have a good lunch for the minimum price of £4 ($7) per person. Dinner, however, is more expensive, costing about £7 ($12.25) per head, including a simple wine. Hours are Monday to Saturday from noon to 2:45 p.m. and from 7 to 11:30 p.m.

The **Chicago Rib Shack,** 1 Raphael St., Knightsbridge, S.W.7 (tel. 581-5595), serves real American barbecued foods—huge racks of baby back ribs, barbecued chicken, and barbecued beef sandwiches. The meat is cooked in imported smoking ovens and marinated in a barbecue sauce containing 15 secret ingredients. The shack is the creation of Bob Payton, an ex-Chicagoan who also owns the successful Chicago Pizza Factory in Hanover Square. The menu also includes their famous onion loaf which *Harper's & Queen* described as "either a Brobdingnagian French fried onion or the Illinois equivalent of an onion bhaji." Stuffed potato boats, salads, cheesecake, pecan pie, and ice cream round out the menu.

Visitors are encouraged to eat with their fingers, and bibs and hot towels are provided. The restaurant's vast bar has a special cocktail license for people preferring simply to drink without a meal. A video is suspended in the bar showing American sports games. There is an overwhelming number of Victorian architectural antiques which have been salvaged from demolished buildings all over the country. The 45-foot-long ornate mahogany and mirrored bar was once part of a Glasgow pub, and eight massive stained-glass windows came from a chapel in Lancashire. The restaurant's walls are covered with an ever-increasing collection of pictures, posters, and pottery farmyard animals—pigs and cows especially. The average tab comes to about £10 ($17.50) per head. The restaurant, which lies just 100 yards from Harrods, serves Monday to Saturday from 11:45 a.m. to 11:30 p.m. Tube: Knightsbridge.

Luba's Bistro, 6 Yeomans Row, S.W.3 (tel. 589-2950), is an oasis of moderately priced dining in tab-happy Knightsbridge. The atmosphere here is strictly business—just a big, narrow room with family-style tables covered with plastic cloths. The posters and paintings on the walls evoke a nostalgic feeling of early Bohemia. The food is good, and the chef believes in giving you enough of it. The management isn't licensed, so you have to bring your own bottle. For openers, I'd suggest Luba's Russian borscht or else kapoostniak (braised cabbage with prunes and sour cream). Main courses include beef Stroganoff, chicken Kiev, hussar's steak, stuffed green pepper, and shashlik (marinated pieces of lamb grilled on a skewer, with onion sauce, served with rice and vegetables). My latest tab came to £8.50 ($14.88), plus a 10% service charge. Bring your own wine, as there is no corkage charge. Hours are from noon to 3 p.m. and 6 p.m. to midnight, daily except Sunday. Tube: Knightsbridge.

READER'S PUB SELECTION: "In Knightsbridge walk about two blocks down Brompton Road to the **Crown and Sceptre,** at no. 132, S.W.3 (tel. 589-1615), for the best pub lunch you could desire. A pint of lager and lime followed by a plate of shepherd's pie, and I was all set to carry on for more of exciting London. They also have a good choice of other dishes, all steaming hot and under glass covers—most appetizing. Featured are steak-and-kidney pie, an excellent vegetable soup, and salads, including one made of beef, ham, and turkey. Prices begin at £2.50 ($4.38)" (Leslie Baker, Vernon, B.C., Canada).

6. Chelsea

In this area, comparable to the Left Bank of Paris or the more elegant parts of Greenwich Village, even the simplest stable has glamor. Here the diplomats and wealthy-chic, the stars of stage and screen, and successful sculptors and painters now live alongside a decreasing number of poor and struggling artists. To reach the area, take the Circle or District Lines to Sloane Square.

King's Road (named after Charles II) is the principal avenue, the main street of Chelsea, and activity is lively here both day and night. On Saturday mornings, Chelsea boutiques blossom with London's flamboyantly attired. What were once stables and garages, built for elaborate town houses nearby, have been converted and practically rebuilt, so that you see little alleyways with two-story houses, all brightly painted.

In the Mauve Era, Chelsea became popular with artists. Oscar Wilde found refuge here—so did Henry James, Whistler, and many more. The Chelsea Embankment, an esplanade along the Thames, is also found here. Homes of writers, such as the one once occupied by George Eliot, line the street. The best-known and most interesting part of the embankment, Cheyne Walk (pronounced Chain-y), contains some Georgian townhouses. It's a good place to go for a stroll around dusk. The most popular residents here are the Chelsea Pensioners, who live at the Royal Chelsea Hospital. These veterans and invalid soldiers, in uniform, can be seen perambulating up and down the riverfront.

This district boasts some of the city's finest restaurants, but not the cheap ones. Still, most readers will probably want to go to Chelsea. If so, they'll find the following restaurant, pub, and wine bar recommendations offering good and reasonable meals.

The **Chelsea Kitchen,** 98 King's Rd., S.W.3 (tel. 589-1330), is a favorite of those who know they can get large portions of good, plain cooking at inexpensive prices. The atmosphere is Nordic inspired, with compact booths and tables and bright, strong colors. The minestrone is good tasting, as is the steak-and-kidney pie. A strictly economy dish, most filling, is the stuffed marrow (in season), or you might prefer the coq au vin. To finish off, try either the apple crumble or ice cream. An average three-course meal will cost from £2.50 ($4.38). In the evening, you are likely to hear classical tapes played as background music.

King's Head & Eight Bells, 50 Cheyne Walk, S.W.3 (tel. 352-1820), is a historic Thames-side pub in a fashionable residential area of London, that has reopened after extensive redecoration and some reconstruction. It's popular with stage and TV personalities as well as writers. Many distinguished personalities once lived in this area. A short stroll in the neighborhood will take you to the former homes of such famous personages as Carlyle, Swinburne, and George Eliot. Press gangs used to roam these parts of Chelsea seeking lone travelers who were abducted for a life at sea. The snackbar has been upgraded to Cordon Bleu standards at pub prices. Tony and Veronica are in charge of catering, buying, preparing, and cooking everything. The best English beers are served here, as well as a goodly selection of wines and liquors. A large plate of rare roast beef is a favorite selection, followed by a choice of salad from the salad bar, celery and sultana, rice, beansprouts, for instance. Other tasty dishes include homemade game pie, if featured, or else steak-and-kidney pie. Chef Tony cooks and serves the dishes, and everything is displayed on a large old table in the corner. A slice of game-and-ham pie, with a choice of two salads, will cost around £3 ($5.25), plus another 95p ($1.66) for the plum pie and cream to follow.

Blushes, 52 King's Rd., S.W.3 (tel. 589-6640), stands across from the Duke of York's headquarters. Behind its red and white facade, it is usually busy in the evenings, attracting a lively King's Road crowd, drawn to its array of salads, cold meats, and hot dishes. The choice of wine is fair and reasonably priced. Hours are from noon to 3 p.m. and from 6 to 11 p.m. daily (on Sunday from noon to 2:30 p.m. and from 7 to 10:30 p.m.). Expect to pay around £5 ($8.75) for a light meal. Two chefs provide a wide choice of hot and cold dishes, including chicken à la king, coq au vin, and mackerel with horseradish sauce. Tube: Sloane Square.

Charco's/Searcy's, 1 Bray Pl., S.W.3 (tel. 584-0765), has an entrance on two streets in Chelsea, lying right off King's Road. A very bright crowd patronizes this establishment, enjoying the reasonably priced wines and the good and inexpensive food, such as salads, cold meats on the buffet, and such hot dishes as moussaka. Main dishes cost around £3.25 ($5.69). In summer you may dine at one of the sidewalk tables. The wine bar is open from 11 a.m. to 3 p.m. and from 5:30 to 11 p.m. daily except Sunday. Tube: Sloane Square.

For a super splurge, the **English House,** 3 Milner St., S.W.3 (tel. 581-2635), is a tiny restaurant in the heart of Chelsea. Guests have compared dining here to the experience of being a guest in an elegant private house. Michael Smith, who has a flair for color and fabrics, created and designed the place. Terracotta and blues predominate, and the walls are covered in printed cotton, using an old English design of blackcurrants and autumnal leaves. The fireplace makes everything cozy, and tables are well spaced. The garden room on the ground floor is whitewashed brick with panels of stylized flowers. The food includes many unusual dishes, and it isn't necessary to order a full two- or three-course meal. Appetizers and main dishes are interchangeable, and patrons can decide to take exactly what they wish, even only a bowl of soup.

The food is mainly English with such succulent offerings as homemade individual game pies, stilton soup, and syllabubs. The menu is extensive, including plenty of seafoods and salads. Interesting dishes are brie favors (pastry parcels of brie cheese marinated in lemon juice with a touch of garlic), elegant fish 'n' chips (sticks of sole crumbed with hazelnuts served in a basket with chips and a ramekin of Choron sauce), as well as grilled filet steaks, lamb and veal chops, and a homemade apple pie served with cream in the Yorkshire fashion. The chef's daily choices are included in a special luncheon menu at £7 ($12.25), including service and VAT. In the evening main courses, such as roast mallard with fennel and apricots, or mustard-baked chicken, begin at £8.50 ($14.88).

The restaurant is open daily, except Sunday, for lunch from 12:30 to 2:30 p.m. and dinner from 7:30 to 11:30 p.m.

The **Queens Elm,** 241 Fulham Rd., S.W.3 (tel. 352-9157), is an artists' pub, with a clublike atmosphere. Rampant, often provocative, conversation prevails (within an hour you're apt to hear Francis Bacon arguing about whether the late Anaïs Nin influenced the writing of Henry Miller, or vice versa, or William Redgrave expounding a theory of modern art). Just strike up a conversation with any of the friendly patrons, and you're likely to wind up in the middle of the group. Your pint of lager might be accompanied by a sandwich for 70p ($1.23). Prices start at £1.50 ($2.63) for the steak-and-kidney pie with a vegetable and potatoes. That's about the cheapest thing on the menu, and other dishes go up to £2.50 ($4.38). A collection of more than 200 smoking pipes, mostly antique, and from all over the world, is displayed on the walls. And they're most difficult to clean, the landlord confided.

FULHAM: Eel Pie and Mash Shop, 140 Wandsworth Bridge Rd., S.W.6 (tel. 731-1232), is a typical Cockney delight outside of the East End, and therefore more accessible to visitors. You can feast on jellied or stewed eels with mashed potatoes, on succulent homemade beef pie and mashed potatoes, or on "bangers and mash" (sausages and mashed potatoes). For the pie and mash, the cost is 90p ($1.58). Most main dishes cost £1.75 ($3.06), and the jellied eels go for £1 ($1.75). Served in simple pristine surroundings, it is something different, and you'll be sure to see some local color, for this sort of food is still much loved by Londoners. It's open Tuesday, Wednesday, Thursday, Friday, and Saturday from noon on. Your host is Mrs. Atkins.

7. Kensington

Most smart shoppers in London patronize two busy streets: Kensington High, with its long string of specialty shops and department stores, and the abutting Kensington Church, with its antique shops and boutiques. For a budget lunch or dinner right in the heart of this district, I recommend:

The **Twin Brothers Restaurant,** 51 Kensington Church St., W.8 (tel. 937-4152), is run by two identical twin brothers from Berlin. Tall and blond, they create an attraction in themselves, and they offer excellent and friendly service, good food, and a relaxed and happy atmosphere. The decor is enhanced by a collection of oil paintings. Detlef and Helge are master cooks and master carpenters. They made the chairs and benches. The restaurant is small, ideal for a tête-à-tête dinner. The menu is international—Bismarck herring ("our mother's recipe"), chicken à la Kiev served with paprika rice, wienerschnitzel. The salads have been called entertaining. The vegetables are fresh. A slice of apple strudel might rest happily on your plate. Every dish is freshly prepared for you. For a three-course meal, expect to pay from £4.75 ($8.31) to £7.50 ($13.13).

Edwardian Pullman Couch, Hypermarket, 26–40 Kensington High St. This is certainly a unique light-meal café, an Edwardian pullman railway dining car moved into the lower level of an antique emporium. You can have a sandwich or salad, lunch or tea, sitting in your high-backed compartment on a plush-covered seat. The proprietors, Yamin and Baqi, have kept the oldtime dining-car decorations intact. Your view is of the antiques in a few of the booths (isn't this true window shopping?). Open six days a week from late morning until 6 p.m., the café offers a variety of sandwiches—about ten, in fact. An average price is 85p ($1.49). A more filling three-decker with ham, lettuce, mayonnaise, and egg goes for £1.20 ($2.10). To finish, try a fresh cream pasty for 80p ($1.40).

SOUTH KENSINGTON: When you've grown weary of exploring this district's many museums, try a feast in one of the following recommendations, all in the big-splurge category.

Chanterelle, 119 Old Brompton Rd., S.W.7 (tel. 373-5522), used to be a part of the South Kensington Public Library. But times have changed. The smell is not of old books, but of highly original English and continental cookery in a restrained setting of wood paneling. The personable Stewart Grimshaw oversees the restaurant, and his partner, Fergus Provan, organizes the kitchen. They are open every day of the week for both lunch and dinner, including Sunday. Dinner is nightly from 7 p.m. to midnight. A three-course luncheon menu, costing £6 ($10.50), is changed every three days, and a fixed-price dinner menu, also consisting of three courses, is changed every two weeks, going for £9 ($15.75). Main courses at dinner are likely to include filets of sole stuffed with scallops and served with a champagne sauce, roast saddle of hare, and filet of veal sauteed in sage. Wines are limited but well selected. Reservations are advised.

Chompers, 2 Exhibition Rd., S.W.7 (tel. 589-8947), is probably the oldest established bistro in London. It boasts an art nouveau decor, but doesn't get lost in its stage setting. Chompers serves good food prepared on the premises at moderate prices. Helpings are generous, and the service is good. For an appetizer, I'd suggest hot ratatouille. Chompers has always been big for ratatouille. The main-course specialties include trout with capers, kidneys in sherry, sweetbreads in sherry and cream sauce, filet of plaice in prawn sauce, and steak with chilton cheese sauce. Meals cost from £5 ($8.75) to £10 ($17.50). The fully licensed Chompers is open from noon to 3 p.m. and from 6 p.m. to midnight Monday to Saturday. Reservations are recommended between 8 and 10:30 p.m. Tube: South Kensington.

READER'S RESTAURANT SELECTION: "We recommend **Daquise,** 20 Thurloe St., S.W.7 (tel. 589-6117), next to the South Kensington tube station. For people exhausted after a tour of the Natural Science Museum or the Victoria and Albert, this is the place. It serves Polish-Russian dishes and the continental pastries are fresh daily. A set lunch, costing £2.50 ($4.38), is served from noon to 3 p.m. Coffee is an extra 45p (79¢). The restaurant is fully licensed, open seven days a week. Hot meals are served from noon to midnight. The restaurant is owned by Serge Ganjou and Cz. Konarski. This was a real uplift to tired spirits and legs" (Dr. H. B. Collier, Edmonton, Canada).

8. West London

ST. MARYLEBONE: This area has quite a fine cross section of the best of what London has to offer in culinary treats.

The Baker & Oven, 10 Paddington St., W.1 (tel. 935-5072), may be in an out-of-the-way neighborhood, but it's a big success—a little corner bakery, with a sales shop converted into a tavern with a genuine pub atmosphere. The neighborhood people mingle with the fashionable West End visitors. Meals are served in the cellar kitchens, attractively done in a rustic style. The very English food often pleases the most critical; the portions are large, the tabs moderate. With a bit of luck, you'll be given a bare wooden table in one of the brick cove-ceilinged nooks, the former ovens.

The onion soup is a fine beginning at 95p ($1.66), as is the country pâté at £1.25 ($2.19). For the main course, there are several good choices, including roast Aylesbury duckling with stuffing and apple sauce for £4.25 ($7.44), and jugged hare with red currant jelly, £5.25 ($9.19). All entrees include vegetables. For dessert, you can order a hot fruit pie and cream at £1.25 ($2.19). The restaurant is open Monday to Friday from noon to 3 p.m. and from 6:30 to 11 p.m. On Saturday, it's open only in the evenings. The same prices are charged for both lunch and dinner.

Light of India, 59 Park Rd., near Regent's Park, N.W.1 (tel. 723-6753), doesn't require you to don a turban or sari to dine, although many homesick Indians will be wearing theirs. Happily, you can order varying strengths of curry, so have no fear about burning your throat if you're inexperienced. If there are several in your party, you can select a wide variety of plates—and share them, Chinese style. The traditional soup, of course, is mulligatawny. A number of curry dishes are priced at £2.50 ($4.38) to £3.25 ($5.69). Warning: Unless you'd like a sneak preview of Hades, avoid anything labeled *vindaloo*. The biryanis made in a variety of ways—chicken, mutton, prawn, even vegetable—are good for beginners. The restaurant also specializes in tandoori dishes which are cooked in a clay oven. Charcoal instead of the traditional gas fire is used. Some of these dishes include a tandoori chicken Masala, a mixed grill, king prawns, and naan, a levened bread, among others. Most Indian desserts average around £1 ($1.75). Service charge is not included in the prices. The Light of India is open from noon to 2:45 p.m. and from 6 till 11:30 p.m., including Sunday. The nearest tube station is Baker Street.

The **Victoria Tavern,** Strathearn Place, W.2 (tel. 262-4554), a three-in-one house, begins with a street-level old tavern, a most stylish Victorian pub, pleasantly coordinated, and on a par with the already-mentioned Salisbury in the theater district. Sit back over a lager and enjoy the polished mahogany, the cut and etched glass, a working fireplace, and the window seats with their soft moss-green cushions which match the swagged draperies. Coal fires burn in winter, making this place a snug rendezvous. Ask to see the check signed by Charles Dickens. The upper-level salon, called the **Gaiety Bar,** is a delightful place at which to entertain friends in the evenings. Here are the nostalgic memorabilia of the defunct Gaiety Theatre, including a playbill of the last performance, on July 4, 1903. The setting is one of top hats, opera glasses, and, of course, white and gilt boxes and chairs.

On the basement level, reached by an outer stairway, you enter the **Victorian Cellars Wine Bar.** To describe its atmosphere would make it sound artfully corny, but it isn't. The small dining room is placed in a simulated narrow street of 19th-century London, including an Old Curiosity Shop and a gas lamppost. The food is typical of wine-bar society—steak-and-kidney pie, smoked mackerel, or barbecued pork, for around £1 ($1.75) to £3.50 ($6.13). Quiches and salads go for the same price. Pâté or cheese with french bread is also sold. The restaurant is open from 11:30 a.m. to 3 p.m. and from 6:30 p.m. to midnight, Monday to Saturday. The restaurant is closed on Sunday, although the bar upstairs opens to serve drinks. For restaurant seating, telephone for reservations.

Garfunkels, Duke Street, W.1 (tel. 499-5000), is a coffeeshop operation with large glass walls which open onto the pavement onto which the tables spill in summer. The bright modern decor of plush benches and glass and chrome chairs and tables was designed to give a little privacy within the close quarters. There is a large, well-stocked salad bar from which you help yourself. Typical fare includes roast chicken, chili con carne, and hamburgers. With these, you might order jacket potatoes or fried potatoes, costing (with a main dish) from £3 ($5.25) to £4 ($7). Desserts feature a magnificent banana split, about six inches high and oozing with cream, ice cream, nuts, and sauce. There's also a children's menu for around £1.20 ($2.10). There are now several branches of this operation around central London.

BAYSWATER-QUEENSWAY: Queensway is a three-block-long street beginning at Kensington Gardens and Bayswater Road. At that corner are two tube stations, Bayswater and Queensway. The area is jam-packed with little all-purpose restaurants and about an equal number of take-away food places. With its ethnic cafés and restaurants, Queensway is not unlike Soho, but the tabs here are generally much cheaper. Along Queensway are two newsstands that sell periodicals from all over the world, testifying to the international flavor of the sector.

Il Barino, 39 Queensway, W.2 (tel. 229-0615), is a branch of a chain of Italian restaurants where the atmosphere is well styled, yet relaxed. Pasta specialties range in price from £1.45 ($2.54) to £1.85 ($3.24). Other specialties include minestrone alla Lombarda at 80p ($1.40) and such main dishes as Venetian-style liver, served with mashed potatoes £2.35 ($4.11). The sherry trifle with cream makes a good dessert at 90p ($1.58). Hours are from 8 a.m. to 11:30 p.m. seven days a week.

In the area is a dizzying variety of little restaurants that pack up their specialties for you. Many clients eat right on the street, others preferring to take their picnic to a nearby park, and still others sneaking back to their hotel rooms with their snacks.

Pizza Land, 76 Queensway, W.2 (tel. 229-1327), offers 18 varieties of pizza, plate size and succulent. Two pizza slices, a baked potato, and coleslaw costs £1.60 ($2.80). Pizzas range in price from £1.35 ($2.36) to £2.55 ($4.46), and spaghetti bolognaise goes for £1.25 ($2.19). It's open until midnight seven days a week.

Justin de Blank, 54 Duke St., W.1 (tel. 629-3174), also does excellent take-away meals to be selected from the range of dishes advertised on the blackboard. Served in earthenware crocks and pots, they can be easily warmed through when you get them home. What's nicer than a meaty casserole with fresh vegetables followed by crème brûlé on a cold spring or autumn day? Prices range from £1.85 ($3.24) to £3.35 ($5.86) per person for the main dish, plus a reasonable deposit on the crocks (which is refundable when you bring them back a day or so later).

READER'S RESTAURANT SELECTION: "**La Boîte,** 40a Notting Hill Gate, W.2 (tel. 229-2571), is in the Bayswater district. It is an Italian restaurant—small and intimate decor—dedicated to serving fine food at a reasonable price. The proprietor is Gennaro Di Landro, who comes from the southern part of Italy and has lived in England for more than 20 years. Two of us had a complete dinner, including wine, for just £11 ($19.25). La Boîte is open from noon to 3 p.m. for lunch and from 6 p.m. to midnight for dinner (on Monday, only dinners are served)" (Benjamin L. Crossley, Saginaw, Mich.).

NOTTING HILL GATE: **Hungry Viking,** 44 Ossington St., W.2 (tel. 727-3311), is a modern restaurant on a street of mews houses. You descend past flower-draped boxes into a Scandinavian parlor, where waitresses in national costume will help you select from a gigantic smörgåsbord for a set price of £8 ($14). It's called the traditional Viking table, and includes the usual array of food, such as prawns, herring, smoked fish, aspics, salads, cheeses, and meats, both hot and cold. The salads are especially good. The amount of food you can eat is your own capacity. The restaurant is closed on Monday but open otherwise Tuesday to Saturday from 6:30 to 11 p.m. (Sunday, 7 to 11 p.m.). Tube: Queensway or Notting Hill Gate.

To understand why the English became famous for fish 'n' chips, head for the following recommendation:

Geale's, 2 Farmer St., W.8 (tel. 727-7969), is worth the investment in a subway ride to the western part of London if you're seeking some of the best fish and chips in the English capital—all at prices for around £2 ($3.50). The fish is bought fresh daily, and it's not greasy as it is in most establishments in London. Cod, hake, and plaice are the featured mainstays of the menu. This corner restaurant, at the end of a mews street, is owned by Christopher A. Geale, who is proud, and rightly so, of his offerings. The place is run on very informal lines, and is open Tuesday to Friday from noon to 3 p.m. and 6 p.m. to midnight; on Saturday from noon to 3 p.m. and from 6 to 11 p.m. Tube: Notting Hill Gate.

PADDINGTON: Many guests find themselves near Paddington Station, having booked into a B&B house on, say, Sussex Gardens or Norfolk Square. If so, it's best to go Oriental if you're seriously economizing.

The best bargain is the **Keio Chinese Restaurant,** 168 Sussex Gardens, W.2 (tel. 402-9142). Fully licensed, it serves a complete meal for two persons for only £8 ($14). Your repast is likely to include soup, rice, and a combination of pork, chicken, and beef dishes. Only two blocks from Paddington Station, it stands on a corner and lies downstairs from the street level. Readers Bess and Steve Crider of New York write: "We ate there our first night in England and returned our last night because we could find nothing as cheap or as good!"

The Lotus House, 61–69 Edgware Rd., W.2 (tel. 262-4341), is a link in a Chinese dining chain created by energetic restaurateur John Koon. It provides interesting food in an attractive atmosphere, graced by music and dancing in the evening (open till 1 a.m. Sunday to Friday, 2 a.m. Saturday, and fully licensed). The choice bewilders—more than 200 suggestions, from roast breast of duck in the Cantonese style to Dublin bay prawns in oyster sauce. Interestingly, you can order both large and small portions (by choosing small dishes, you can sample a greater variety of the Lotus House wares). The management draws up a list of five different menus for four different parties, ranging from lone eaters to quartets. For example, one of the medium-priced meals—only £12 ($21) for two persons—includes soft pork noodles, fried crispy wonton with lobster balls in a sweet-and-sour sauce, chicken and mushrooms, chicken chop suey, sliced beef with green peppers, plus a special fried rice. The Lotus House is about a five-minute walk from Marble Arch.

Or if you're in the area and want something cheaper, try **Oodles,** 128 Edgware Rd., W.2 (tel. 723-7548). Just beyond the Marble Arch tube station, this aptly named place (one of several around London) fulfills the promise with well-filled plates of stews, curries, pies, and a wide range of vegetable dishes—leeks au gratin, stuffed eggplant, macaroni and cheese. Desserts are equally substantial, including country-style apple pie served from a deep dish with cream. Main dishes are priced from £1.50 ($2.63), with most meat dishes going for £2 ($3.50). A three-course meal with wine is about £5 ($8.75). The place is white, bright, and clean with wood tables and bench seats.

9. East End

At least once you may want to plunge into the colorful East End. In restaurants it has a few potent drawing cards. The most famous one is surveyed below.

Bloom's, 90 Whitechapel High St., E.1 (tel. 247-6001), is worth crossing over to the wrong side of the tracks (near the tube stop of Aldgate East). Overcrowded, with frantic service, Bloom's continues to tempt with kosher delights. Sunday lunch, however, is extremely busy, so try to schedule your visit at some other time. A chicken blintz might rest on your plate or borscht in your bowl. Main dishes include such specialties as boiled leg of fowl to salt beef (corned, to us). Try also the kreplach and kneidlach (dumplings) soup, very rich chopped liver and egg, sweet balls of chopped white fish (fried or boiled), and lockshen pudding. A good meal will cost around £6 ($10.50), but you can spend more. Don't forget that Bloom's is kosher, so don't expect milk in your coffee if you've ordered meat. Soup and sandwich customers are not allowed to sit down, that privilege being reserved for full-service dinner patrons.

CHINESE FOOD IN LIMEHOUSE: Remember *Limehouse Blues?* The lime kilns, after which the East End parish was named, were abolished before the war, but the legend lives on. On the north bank of the Thames, this particular district is unattractive, as it is filled with lots of ugly buildings. Ah, but herein lies its charm. Filled with down-and-out or retired seamen by day, Limehouse at night is often splashed with fashionable West Enders on a slumming spree. The big attractions are the Chinese restaurants known as "The Friends" (a few originals and a host of imitators). Some of them use ingredients that (to paraphrase the song) "came all the way from China."

Good Friends, 139 Salmon Lane, E.14 (tel. 987-5541), is so popular, it's adopted a reservations-only policy. The pocket-size restaurant, open noon to midnight, doesn't concern itself with decor—just food, and it happens to have a reputation for some of the best Cantonese dishes in England. To accompany your meal, bring your own wine (no corkage fee). Although the menu is filled with surprises (many diners call in advance to order special dishes), you'll fare handsomely just by sticking to the routine listings: items such as beef and peppers; crunchy, yet tender, spare ribs; sweet-and-sour pork; and chicken with almonds. For a complete meal, including dessert, tea, and coffee, expect to pay from £9 ($15.75) per person. Salmon Lane lies off Commercial Road before it forks at the West and East India Dock Roads.

Young Friends, 11 Penny Fields, E.14 (tel. 987-4276). This is the domain of Raymond Low, and many West Enders cross the city to sample his gray mullet (on 24 hours' notice). From the tiniest kitchen imaginable come excellent meals, served in a dining room that couldn't be more basic. Here are my suggestions for a memorable dinner: wonton soup, shark fin soup, stuffed chicken wings in oyster sauce, and roast duck. Other recommendable dishes include crispy pork, crab in a ginger sauce with black beans, sweet-and-sour fish, duck and ginger in an onion sauce, prawns with garlic, Singapore fried noodle, and prawns Chinese style. You can top off your dinner with lichee nuts. Expect to spend from £8 ($14) for a complete dinner. Penny Fields lies just off West India Dock Road. Lost? Call Raymond Low for directions.

10. South of the Thames

The **George Inn,** 77 Borough High St. (tel. 407-2056), across the bridge in Southwark, S.E.1, is a National Trust property, the last of the old galleried coaching inns of London. Known to Charles Dickens *(Little Dorrit),* the inn is a touch of olde England, tucked away in an alley. Some claim that Shakespeare and his troupe performed in an old inn that stood on the same ground, although the George today is essentially late 17th century. In fact, from the last week in June to August 10, a Shakespeare play is performed in the courtyard outside the pub from 3:30 p.m. You enter through a gateway into the Little Dorrit Chop House. On the ground floor there are two bars and a wine bar where hot chili, sausages and mash, along with shepherd's pie and beans are served at about £1.65 ($2.89) a portion. There is a serve-yourself salad table, with some dozen different mixtures. You can pile your plate for 60p ($1.05) and order a glass of wine at 76p ($1.33).

The restaurant upstairs serves meals Monday to Saturday from 6:30 to 9:30 p.m. It offers three set meals, with a fairly wide choice of dishes. The businessman's menu is £6.50 ($11.38), going up to £9.50 ($16.63) for the executive menu, and topped at £15 ($26.25) for the extraordinary menu.

The whole of the George yard is being revamped, the road taken up and cobbles laid, and small shops built to resemble a Dickensian street. Shops will be installed here, perhaps by the time of your visit. During the excavation, pieces of an old Viking ship were found.

No Name Place, 143 St. Johns Hill, S.W.11 (tel. 228-3043). You may think it's a bit out of the way, but you can quite easily reach the "No Name Place" by bus. It's well worth the effort. The restaurant is a converted shop, gleaming with highly polished wood and smartly set bistro-style tables and hanging plants. It's run by Rob and his French wife, Françoise, who cooks with enthusiasm. They provide superb appetizers, including mushrooms in garlic, avocado with stilton cheese, and cucumber mousse. Main dishes include a tasty continental selection, such as coq au vin, calf liver with avocado, and lamb cooked in lemon and garlic. Vegetables are always fresh (try, if featured, the ratatouille). For dessert, perhaps a French apple tart will rest on your plate. Everything is washed down with a presentable house wine. A good meal with wine is about £12 ($21) per person. They also do a set lunch on Sunday for £5.75 ($10.07). It is open otherwise for dinner from Tuesday to Saturday from 7:30 p.m. until last orders at 11 p.m.

555, 555 Battersea Park Rd., S.W.11 (tel. 228-7011), is a most unprepossessing café (in looks only) in a dreary commercial sector of London, south of the Thames. But surprise! The food is very good, the ingredients extremely fresh. A *gemütlich* feeling prevails at night, and soon you're joining in the fun. The posters on the walls are more permissive than ever. You can get a number of really good Baltic dishes here. Vera, the owner, oversees everything. By all means, try the homemade sausage. The pâté is also delicious, a bit crude but tasty. The suckling pig is highly recommended, and seems to be a house specialty. Vegetables come with everything; red cabbage is often featured. An entire meal will run you about £9 ($15.75). Meals are served to a very cosmopolitan crowd against a background of taped music. Vera says it's all in great fun, and I agree. Closed Sunday and Monday; it is open otherwise for dinner only from 7:30 p.m. till midnight. Take a taxi: you'll never find the place if you don't.

Royal Festival Hall Cafeteria, South Bank, S.E.1, is where you can get an inexpensive meal or snack in an unusual setting on the banks of the Thames. It's worth the five-minute trek over the bridge from the Embankment tube station to combine a meal with any of the activities at the Royal Festival Hall: a symphony orchestra, a string quartet concert, a showing of some old Griffith movies, a presentation of the National Film Festival Theatre, or perhaps the latest exhibition of a contemporary artist at the Hayward Gallery. You can have either a complete hot meal, a snack, or afternoon tea. Between noon and 2:30 p.m., and from 5 to 8 p.m., you can get hot food. Salads cost from £1.80 ($3.15) to £2.50 ($4.38), and desserts, such as apple pie, begin at 80p ($1.40). A glass of rosé is 85p ($1.49). Snacks are available until half an hour after any evening concert. The place is open seven days a week. There's always a view of London's skyline. When it's high tide, you can enjoy the tops of the river boats and the ships on the Thames. Between June and September, free concerts are given in the Charing Cross Gardens, adjacent to the tube station. For restaurant information, telephone 928-3246.

Goose and Ferkin, 47–48 Borough Rd., S.E.1 (tel. 403-3590), is a pub which brews its own beer. The owner of this enterprise is David Bruce, who worked as a brewer for one of the big companies for many years until his chance came to buy Goose and Ferkin. He obtained his own license to brew, and set about producing his own beers. He has now expanded his operation to include five other London pubs. A large mirror proclaims "Bruce's Brewery, established 1979." He brews three special strengths, Borough Bitter, 39p (68¢) for a half pint, Dog Bolter, 43p (75¢) for a half, and, for special occasions, Earth Stopper, 90p ($1.58) and only served in halves. Be warned: This one is a real man's beer, and your 90p worth is the equivalent of three measures of whisky in strength.

Food is also available in this lovely old London pub. Each day there is a different hot dish costing from around £1.75 ($3.06). Or else you can order extra-large baps (bread buns) filled with your choice of meat and salad, costing from 95p ($1.66).

The pub brewer is Nigel, who works away under the feet of the drinkers in the cellars below, and the pub is managed by Cornishman Bob Danby. From 8 p.m. onward, Crazy Jimmy plays the piano in the good old "knees up" style, and on Sunday at lunchtime there's more entertainment.

11. Hampstead Heath

The Georgian village of Hampstead (N.W.3), sitting high on a northern hill, is the most desirable residential suburb of London. The village borders a heathland containing acres of wooded dells and fields of heather. Yet the Northern Line of the underground reaches the edge of the heath, making it possible for the inhabitants to enjoy the countryside while living only 20 minutes from the heart of London. This combination of advantages has caused many young artists to discover what Keats could have told them years ago: Hampstead is the place to live. The little Georgian houses have never received so much attention.

The **Spaniards Inn,** Hampstead Lane, N.W.3 (tel. 455-3276), is a low, rambling, beamed building set right where the road narrows at the Old Toll House. Its history goes back to the times of the highwayman Dick Turpin, who, it is said, was at the inn before his mammoth ride to York to prove that he could not have committed a holdup in London Town. The inn was once the residence of the Spanish ambassador to the court of James I when it was run by two Spanish brothers who purchased it in 1620. The inn does a wide range of sandwiches from 65p ($1.14) and hot snacks from £1.20 ($2.10) for shepherd's pie and sausages and mashed potatoes to £3.10 ($5.43) for steak-and-kidney pie.

Pippin, 83–84 Hampstead High St., N.W.3 (tel. 435-6434), offers a fine array of strictly vegetarian dishes to tempt even the most skeptical nonvegetarian. The freshly baked breads and cakes are prepared from Pippin's own organically grown wheat flour. The restaurant's Copella pure apple juice is the favorite beverage to accompany any dish. Open daily from 10 a.m. to 11:30 p.m., Pippin offers morning coffee, lunch, afternoon tea, or dinner on its terrace restaurant. At night, meals cost around £4.50 ($7.88). During the summer diners can enjoy the village atmosphere of the High Street from the restaurant's balcony. The restaurant is owned and run by Dimitri Saterious.

READER'S RESTAURANT SELECTION: "**Manna,** 4 Erskin Rd., N.W.3 (tel. 722-8028), is open from 6:30 p.m. to midnight daily, except Monday. It's a little higher priced than Pippin, although not ridiculously so. The atmosphere is very nice. All foods served here are organically grown, skillfully cooked, with hot savories and casseroles featured. The rice is brown, the vegetables steamed and prepared in interesting ways, including with yogurt. The menu includes hizki-seaweed and vegetable casserole, celery and apple salad with curd cheese, stuffed pancakes, and organic cider, a complete dinner costing under £5 ($8.75) without wine. Stone floors and large old pine tables recreate a mellow farmhouse kitchen atmosphere. All the food is cooked on the premises, including the bread and yogurt. Manna is halfway between Regent's Park and Hampstead (north of Regent's Park and Primrose Hill), and within walking distance of the Chalk Hill tube station. From Adelaide Road, cross the bridge at Regent's Park Road and go along King Henry's Road. The restaurant is on your left at the corners of Ainger Road and Erskin Road" (Vicki Banks, London, England).

12. Thames Dining

When much of the West End is closed on Sunday, you'll find more life—if you take a taxi, tube, or bus to Aldgate East and spend a hectic hour or so at **Petticoat Lane.** That's the street market where, even if you don't want to buy the goods, you can see the full wit and expertise of the Cockney street vendors. Look for the one who sells tea services, or buy a toffee apple or a hot dog.

Then a short walk will bring you down to the Tower of London and, right beside it, just below Tower Bridge, **St. Katharine's Dock.** This is a new development, created out of the old London dock area where the "breakfast ships," carrying bacon and eggs from Holland, used to tie up. It has become a vast open-air pleasure area, but with a difference. At the dock lie many old and famous vessels, the Maritime Trust's Historic Ship Collection, Thames sailing barges, the elegant craft of visiting yachtsmen from all over the world.

By now, you should be ready for a splurge luncheon at the **Carvery** of the **Tower Hotel.** For about £9.50 ($16.63), you can retaliate by eating yourself silly on succulent hot roast beef, lamb, and pork.

Perhaps the main attraction is the **Dickens Inn** by the Tower, St. Katharine's Way, E.1 (tel. 488-1226), a very carefully reconstructed 19th-century warehouse. Incorporating the original redwood beams, stock bricks, and ironworks, it is a balconied pub/restaurant on three levels.

Sitting on a wooden chair and at an old table, you can enjoy such bar snacks as cockles at £1 ($1.75) or chicken liver pâté, £1.30 ($2.28) in the **Tavern Room,** the pub part of the building. It is open Monday to Saturday from 11 a.m. to 2:30 p.m. and from 5 to 11 p.m. (on Sunday from noon to 2 p.m. and from 7 to 10:30 p.m.). It is also open daily from 2:45 to 5 p.m. for snacks and nonalcoholic beverages.

In the **Pickwick Room** (tel. 488-2208), on the first floor, guests can order such dishes as roast loin of pork in pastry with a stilton and herb stuffing, sauté of veal cooked with mixed peppers, garlic, mushrooms, and onions, and half a duckling roasted with crème de Cassis and pears. A complete meal costs around £14 ($24.50), and hours are Monday to Friday from noon to 2:30 p.m. and from 6:30 to 10 p.m. On Saturday, service is only from 6:30 to 10 p.m. and on Sunday from noon to 3 p.m. The menu is à la carte except on Sunday at lunch when a family lunch table d'hôte style is featured for £9.50 ($16.63) for adults and £6 ($10.50) for children.

In the **Dickens Room** (tel. 488-9932), on the top floor, you'll find a fish restaurant serving such tasty main courses as Scottish salmon, whole lemon sole, and John Dory. The hors d'oeuvres are equally tempting, including whitebait and cockles and mussels in garlic butter. A complete meal costs from £12 ($21). Hours are noon to 3 p.m. and 5 to 10 p.m. daily.

If you're put off by the prices in the restaurant, remember that the bar snacks are quite adequate, and you'll enjoy more of the East End dock area flavor down there.

The **Warehouse Restaurant**, 52 St. Katharine's Way, St. Katharine's by the Tower (tel. 481-3356), is an old rum warehouse which has been renovated and decorated with brown carpets, brown and white tablecloths, and old prints and maps of the Thames hanging on the walls. The best tables overlook the river just below Tower Bridge. The restaurant is open Monday to Friday for lunch and dinner, dinner only on Saturday, and lunch only on Sunday. Most of your appetizers, which are likely to include avocado vinaigrette or Mediterranean prawns, are in the range of £1.50 ($2.63) to £3.50 ($6.13). For your main course, I'd recommend the grilled sole or else river trout with almonds, costing from £3.50 ($6.13) to £7.50 ($13.13). If you want a meat course, I'd suggest the veal Cordon Bleu or else the rump steak, these dishes in the neighborhood of £6 ($10.50) to £7 ($12.25). There is a cover charge of 75p ($1.31), and desserts begin at £1.50 ($2.63).

The **Prospect of Whitby**, 57 Wapping Wall, E.1 (tel. 481-1095), is one of London's oldest riverside pubs, having been founded originally in the days of the Tudors. In a traditionally pubby atmosphere, with a balcony overlooking the river, the Prospect has many associations—it was visited by Dickens, Turner, and Whistler, searching for local color. Come here for a tot, a noggin, or whatever it is that you drink. The Pepys room honors the diarist, who may—just may—have visited the Prospect back in rowdier days, when the seamy side of London dock life held sway here. Among the tempting appetizers are pâté country style or a hearty soup. Well-recommended main courses include poulet à la Kiev (breast of chicken stuffed and fried) and escalope of veal Cordon Bleu. Meals run about £10 ($17.50) per person. However, you can enjoy bar snacks such as hot sausages for 70p ($1.23). A small loaf of french bread, about eight inches, is filled with meat and served for £1.10 ($1.93). If you're having lunch upstairs, you'll have to call for a reservation if you want a table in the bow window overlooking the river. There's also live music almost every evening from 8:30 to 11 p.m. Take the Metropolitan Line to Wapping Station. When you emerge onto Wapping High Street, turn to your right and head down the road along the river. Wapping Wall will be on your right, running parallel to the Thames. It's about a five-minute walk. (It was around the area of Wapping Wall that lesser pirates were executed by tying them to rings in the wall at low tide and then letting the tide come up and finish the job.)

CRUISE AND DINE: The Regents Canal, which winds and twists through London, is the home of the **Fair Lady** cruising restaurant, departing from her moorings at 250 Camden High St. at 7:30 p.m. In comfortable surroundings, a three-course English dinner is offered for £14 ($24.50). Reservations are essential; telephone 485-4433. The *Fair Lady* also serves a Sunday lunch for £8.50 ($14.88), departing at 12:30 p.m.

Jason's Trip, opposite 60 Blomfield Rd., Little Venice, W.9, London's original canal cruise, offers 1½-hour trips along Regents Canal from Little Venice to Camden Lock, N.W.1. Lunch can be booked on the boat for £4.50 ($7.88), plus the cost of the fare. For details of departure times and other services, telephone 286-3428. Tube: Warwick Avenue.

13. Time Out for Tea

During the 18th century, the English from every class became enamoured of a caffeine-rich brew finding its way into London from faraway colonies. Tea-drinking became the rage of London. The great craftsmen of England designed furniture, porcelain, and silver services for the elaborate ritual, and the schedule of aristocrats became increasingly centered around teatime as a mandatory obligation. Even Alexander Pope found it expedient to be witty publicly as he satirized teatime as something uniquely English.

The taking of tea is having a renaissance in the lives of the English. Viewed as a civilized pause in the day's activities, it is particularly appealing to people who didn't have time for lunch or who plan an early theater engagement. Some hotels feature orchestras and tea-dancing in afternoon ceremonies, usually lasting from 3:30 to 6:30 p.m.

For an experience in a tradition that could have sparked the American Revolution (remember the 1773 Tea Party in Boston?), try the old-fashioned atmosphere of **Richoux,** where waitresses wear period dresses with frilly aprons and good-quality pastries are wheeled around on a cart. You might consider your tea there as a belated lunch (Richoux serves regular meals too). For £2.45 ($4.29) per person you can order four hot scones with strawberry jam and whipped cream, or six small sandwiches, perhaps sardine, anchovy, or egg salad. Of course, tea is obligatory.

There are three branches of Richoux in London. One stands opposite Harrods Department Store in Knightsbridge, at 86 Brompton Rd., S.W.3 (tel. 584-8300). Another is at the bottom of Bond Street, 172 Piccadilly, W.1 (tel. 493-2204), and the last is at 41A South Audley St., W.1 (tel. 629-5228).

Always specify lemon or cream, and one lump or two.

14. Almost-24-Hour Eateries

Sometimes you'll want to dine at odd hours, when most of the eating establishments in London are shut down. However, in a city as vast as London, some chef (not always a great one) is cooking. Here are some random selections.

Try **Canton Chinese Restaurant,** 11 New Port Pl., W.C.2 (tel. 437-6220), which is open 24 hours a day.

Or else patronize **Rockafella's Café,** 3 New Burlington St., W.1 (tel. 734-3075), which serves American and continental dishes, and has a full take-away service. It is open from midday until 6:30 a.m., and a cabaret is also presented at night.

You might also visit the appropriately named **Up-All-Night Restaurant,** 325 Fulham Rd., S.W.10 (tel. 352-1996).

Or else **Great British Success,** a restaurant at 85 Gloucester Rd., S.W.7 (tel. 370-4404), with another branch at 22 Terminus Pl., S.W.1, close to Victoria Station.

At London's **Heathrow Airport,** all three terminals serve hot food 24 hours a day.

Most branches of **Kentucky Fried Chicken** are open 24 hours a day. The most central one is at 247 Old Brompton Rd., S.W.5 (tel. 370-3951).

The **Wimpy Bar,** 27 London Rd., W.2 (tel. 723-4721), is also open 24 hours a day.

Hotels with 24-hour coffeeshops for nonresidents include the **Chelsea Lounge,** Carlton Tower Hotel, S.W.1 (tel. 235-5411), and the **Crescent Lounge,** Kensington Hilton Hotel, 179 Holland Park Ave., W.11 (tel. 603-3355).

The **24 Hour Supermarket,** 68 Westbourne Grove, W.2 (tel. 727-4927), never closes, serving the public seven days a week, 24 hours a day, 365 days a year.

Chapter IV

LONDON: WHAT TO SEE AND DO

1. Seeing the Sights
2. Shopping
3. London After Dark
4. Taking the Tours
5. Day Trips from London

DR. JOHNSON SAID: "When a man is tired of London, he is tired of life, for there is in London all that life can afford." "The Great Moralist" can say that again—even more so today.

Come along with me as I survey only a fraction of that life—ancient monuments, boutiques, debates in Parliament, art galleries, discos, Soho dives, museums, legitimate theaters, flea markets, and castles. Some of what we're about to see was known to Johnson and Boswell, even Shakespeare, but much of it is new.

1. Seeing the Sights

London is not a city to visit hurriedly. It is so vast, so stocked with treasures, that visitors planning to "do" London in two or three days do themselves a distinct disservice. Not only will a person miss many of the highlights, he or she will also fail to grasp the spirit of London and to absorb fully its special flavor, which is unique among cities. But faced with an infinite number of important places to visit and a timeclock running out, the tourist will have to concentrate on a manageable group. For those with a minimum of time, I'll survey first what I consider the indispensable sights of London, then follow with the best of the rest. But first, a digression—

BARGAIN TIP: The **Department of the Environment,** 25 Savile Row, W.1 (tel. 734-6010), offers **a Season Ticket to History** which allows the holder free and unlimited entry to all those places in England, Scotland, and Wales which are maintained by the British government. The cost of the ticket, payable only by international money order (sterling only), is £6 ($10.50) for adults, £3 ($5.25) for children under 16. Valid for one year, it can be purchased by mail only from the Department of the Environment, Room 32, Building 1, Vision Way, Victoria Road, South Ruislip, Middlesex HA4 ONZ, or in person at any

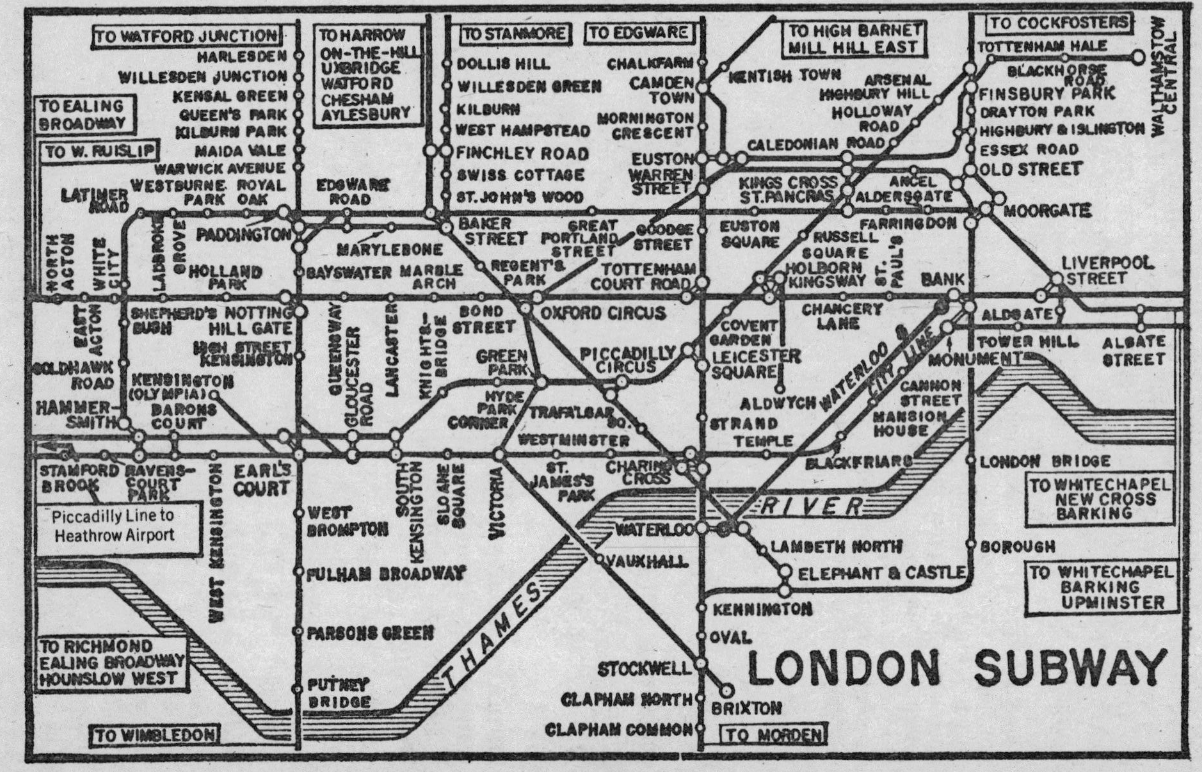
LONDON SUBWAY
TO WATFORD JUNCTION
TO EALING BROADWAY
TO W. RUISLIP
TO HARROW ON-THE-HILL UXBRIDGE WATFORD CHESHAM AYLESBURY
TO STANMORE
TO EDGWARE
TO HIGH BARNET MILL HILL EAST
TO COCKFOSTERS
TO RICHMOND EALING BROADWAY HOUNSLOW WEST
TO WIMBLEDON
TO MORDEN
TO WHITECHAPEL NEW CROSS BARKING
TO WHITECHAPEL BARKING UPMINSTER
Piccadilly Line to Heathrow Airport
HARLESDEN
WILLESDEN JUNCTION
KENSAL GREEN
QUEEN'S PARK
KILBURN PARK
MAIDA VALE
WARWICK AVENUE
WESTBOURNE PARK
ROYAL OAK
LATIMER ROAD
EDGWARE ROAD
DOLLIS HILL
WILLESDEN GREEN
KILBURN
WEST HAMPSTEAD
FINCHLEY ROAD
SWISS COTTAGE
ST. JOHN'S WOOD
CHALKFARM
CAMDEN TOWN
MORNINGTON CRESCENT
EUSTON
WARREN STREET
KENTISH TOWN
ARSENAL
HIGHBURY HILL
HOLLOWAY ROAD
CALEDONIAN ROAD
KINGS CROSS ST.PANCRAS
ANGEL
ALDERSGATE
TOTTENHAM HALE
BLACKHORSE ROAD
WALTHAMSTOW CENTRAL
FINSBURY PARK
DRAYTON PARK
HIGHBURY & ISLINGTON
ESSEX ROAD
OLD STREET
MOORGATE
NORTH ACTON
WHITE CITY
LADBROKE GROVE
PADDINGTON
HOLLAND PARK
MARYLEBONE
BAYSWATER
MARBLE ARCH
BAKER STREET
REGENT'S PARK
GREAT PORTLAND STREET
GOODGE STREET
TOTTENHAM COURT ROAD
EUSTON SQUARE
FARRINGDON
RUSSELL SQUARE
HOLBORN KINGSWAY
ST. PAUL'S
BANK
LIVERPOOL STREET
EAST ACTON
SHEPHERD'S BUSH
NOTTING HILL GATE
HIGH STREET KENSINGTON
QUEENSWAY
GLOUCESTER ROAD
LANCASTER
KNIGHTS-BRIDGE
BOND STREET
OXFORD CIRCUS
CHANCERY LANE
ALDGATE
GOLDHAWK ROAD
KENSINGTON (OLYMPIA)
HAMMER-SMITH
BARONS COURT
GREEN PARK
HYDE PARK CORNER
TRAFALGAR SQ.
PICCADILLY CIRCUS
COVENT GARDEN
LEICESTER SQUARE
ALDWYCH
WATERLOO & CITY LINE
TOWER HILL
ALDGATE STREET
MONUMENT
CANNON STREET
MANSION HOUSE
STRAND
TEMPLE
WESTMINSTER
BLACKFRIARS
STAMFORD BROOK
RAVENS-COURT PARK
WEST KENSINGTON
EARL'S COURT
WEST BROMPTON
SOUTH KENSINGTON
SLOANE SQUARE
VICTORIA
ST. JAMES'S PARK
CHARING CROSS
RIVER
LONDON BRIDGE
WATERLOO
LAMBETH NORTH
BOROUGH
VAUXHALL
ELEPHANT & CASTLE
FULHAM BROADWAY
KENNINGTON
PARSONS GREEN
THAMES
OVAL
STOCKWELL
PUTNEY BRIDGE
CLAPHAM NORTH
BRIXTON
CLAPHAM COMMON

of the Ancient Monuments which have custodians. A list of sights to be seen, including the Tower of London, Hampton Court Palace, Stonehenge, and Edinburgh Castle, giving opening times and available facilities, is given free with each ticket order.

An **Open to View** ticket sells for $21 (U.S.) for adults, $10.50 for children, and includes free admission to more than 500 properties in Britain, including Edinburgh Castle, Churchill's Chartwell, Woburn Abbey, Hampton Court Palace, and Windsor Castle. The ticket also entitles the holder to half-price admission to a further 200 historical sites. The Open to View ticket is good for one month after you first use it and covers all properties in the care of Britain's National Trust and those run by the Department of the Environment. It is estimated that anyone visiting as many as five of these sightseeing attractions will get back the initial outlay. In the U.S., inquire at BritRail Travel International Inc., 630 Third Ave., New York, NY 10017 (tel. 212/599-5400); 333 N. Michigan Ave., Chicago, IL 60601 (tel. 312/263-1910); or 510 W. Sixth St., Los Angeles, CA 90014 (tel. 213/626-5104).

1. THE TOWER OF LONDON: This ancient fortress and royal palace on the north bank of the Thames (tel. 480-6593) continues to pack 'em in because of its macabre associations with all the legendary figures who were either imprisoned or executed here, or both. James Street once wrote: ". . . there are more spooks to the square foot than in any other building in the whole of haunted Britain. Headless bodies, bodiless heads, phantom soldiers, icy blasts, clanking chains—you name them, the Tower's got them."

Back in the days of the axman, London was "swinging." Ranking in interest are the colorful attending Yeoman Warders, the so-called Beefeaters, in Tudor dress, who look as if they are on the payroll for gin advertisements (but don't like to be reminded of it).

Many visitors consider a visit to the Tower to be the highlight of their sightseeing in London, so schedule plenty of time for it. You don't have to stay as long as Sir Walter Raleigh (released after some 13 years), but give it an afternoon. Take either the Circle or District Line to Tower Hill Station (the site is only a short walk away). Or on a sunny day why not take a boat instead, leaving from Westminster Pier? You will be admitted March 1 to October 31 Monday through Saturday from 9:30 a.m. to 5 p.m. Admission costs £2 ($3.50) November to February; £2.50 ($4.38) March to June, September, and October; and £3 ($5.25) in July and August. Children pay half price. In winter the hours are from 9:30 a.m. to 4 p.m. The Tower is also open on Sunday from March to October, in the afternoon only (2 to 5 p.m.), but these times tend to be overcrowded. The Tower is closed on Good Friday, December 24, 25, and 26, and January 1.

Don't expect to find only one tower. The fortress is actually a compound, with the oldest and finest structure being the White Tower, begun by William the Conqueror. Here you can view the Armories, the present collection dating back to the reign of Henry VIII. A display of instruments of torture and execution is in the Bowyer Tower, recalling some of the most ghastly moments in the history of the Tower. At the Bloody Tower, the Little Princes (Edward V and the Duke of York) were allegedly murdered by their uncle, Richard III.

The hospitality today far excels that of years ago, when many of the visitors left their cells only to walk to the headsman's block on Tower Hill. Through Traitor's Gate passed such ill-fated, but romantic, figures as Robert Devereux, a favorite of Elizabeth I, known as the second Earl of Essex. Elizabeth herself, then a princess, was once imprisoned briefly in Bell Tower. At

Tower Green, Anne Boleyn and Katharine Howard, two wives of Henry VIII, lost their lives. The nine-day queen, Lady Jane Grey, also was executed here.

According to legend, the disappearance of the well-protected ravens at the Tower will presage the collapse of the British Empire (seen any around lately?).

By joining a Yeoman Warder's tour, which lasts an hour, you visit the Chapel Royal of St. Peter ad Vincula. The public is allowed free entry every Sunday morning to attend Holy Communion at 9:15 and Matins and sermon at 11, except during August.

For a well-spent 60p ($1.14) for adults, 30p (53¢) for children, you can see the Jewel House, where the Crown Jewels are kept, but go early in summer, as long lines usually form by late morning. Of the three English crowns, the Imperial State Crown is the most important—in fact, it's probably the most famous crown on earth. Made for Victoria for her coronation in 1838, it is today worn by Queen Elizabeth when she opens Parliament. Studded with some 3000 jewels (principally diamonds), it contains the Black Prince's Ruby, worn by Henry V at Agincourt, the battle in 1415 when the English defeated the French. In addition, feast your eyes on the 530-carat Star of Africa, a cut diamond on the Royal Sceptre with Cross. The Jewel House is closed in February each year for the annual cleaning and overhaul.

The Tower of London has an evening ceremony called the **Ceremony of the Keys.** It is, in fact, the ceremonial locking up of the Tower for yet another day in its 900 years. Nothing stops the ceremony. During World War II, a bomb fell within the castle walls during the ceremony, and nobody flinched—but the Tower was locked up two minutes late. Rumor has it that the guard that night was censured for tardiness, the pilot of the plane which dropped the bomb blamed as the culprit. The Yeoman Warder will explain to guests the significance of the ceremony. For free tickets, write to the Governor, Tower of London, London EC3N 4AB, England, requesting a specific date but also giving alternative dates you'd like to attend. At least one week's notice is required. With ticket in hand, you will be admitted by a Yeoman Warder around 9:35 p.m. All requests for permits must be accompanied by a stamped, self-addressed envelope or an equivalent amount of international postage coupons. For inquiries, telephone 709-0765.

Although its outward appearance is so familiar to Londoners and visitors alike, one of the most exciting new sights London offers is the **Tower Bridge** (tel. 407-0922), the one that certain American thought he'd bought when he purchased that other one farther up the river.

Tower Bridge was built during 1886 to 1894 with two towers 800 feet apart, joined by footbridges which provide glass-covered walkways for the public who can enter the north tower, take the elevator to the walkway, cross the river to the south tower, and return to street level. It's a photographer's dream, with interesting views of St. Paul's, the Tower of London, and in the distance, Big Ben and the Houses of Parliament. You can also visit the main engine room with its Victorian boiler and steam-pumping engines which raise and lower the roadway across the river.

There are models showing how the 1000-ton arms of the bridge can be raised in 1½ minutes to allow ships passage upstream. These days the bridge is only opened once or twice a week, and you'll be lucky to catch the real thing. You'll know if it is going to open, however, as a bell sounds throughout the bridge and road traffic is stopped. Admission is £2 ($3.50), with reductions for children. It is open daily in summer from 10 a.m. to 6:30 p.m. (to 4:45 p.m. in winter).

READER'S SIGHTSEEING TIP: "**All-Hallows-by-the-Tower** is a capsule of London's history. If one asks politely in the vicar's office and doesn't mind a peaceful wait, he or she can go down into the basement of the church where there are Roman floors and the Saxon walls of the original church (A.D. 690). Walk from the Tower" (Beth Daniell, Atlanta, Ga.).

2. WESTMINSTER ABBEY: No less than such an illustrious figure as St. Peter is supposed to have left his calling card at the abbey. If it's true, I wouldn't be surprised—for nearly everybody else, at least everybody in English history, has left his or her mark. But what is known for certain is that in 1065 the Saxon king, Edward the Confessor, rebuilt the old minster on this spot, overlooking Parliament Square (tube to Westminster) and founded the Benedictine abbey.

The first English king crowned in the abbey was Harold, in 1066, who was killed at the Battle of Hastings that same year. The man who defeated him, Edward's cousin, William the Conqueror, was also crowned at the abbey; the coronation tradition has continued to the present day, broken only twice (Edward V and Edward VIII). The essentially Early English Gothic structure existing today owes more to Henry III's plans than to any other sovereign, although many architects, including Wren, have contributed to the abbey.

Adults pay £1.20 ($2.10), students 60p ($1.05), and children 30p (53¢) to visit the Royal Chapels, the Royal Tombs, the Coronation Chair, the Henry VII Chapel, and the transepts. Hours are 9:20 a.m. to 4:45 p.m. (last ticket sold at 4 p.m.), Monday through Friday; 9:20 a.m. to 2:45 p.m. (last ticket at 2 p.m.) and 3:45 to 5:45 p.m. on Saturday (last ticket, 5 p.m.). On Wednesday the abbey, including the Royal Chapels, is open with free admission from 6 to 8 p.m. Only during this time may photographers snap away. On Sunday, the Royal Chapels are closed, but the rest of the church is open between services.

Built on the site of the ancient Lady Chapel, in the early 16th century, the Henry VII Chapel is the loveliest in Europe, with its fan vaulting, colorful Knights of the Order of the Bath banners, and Torrigiani-designed tomb of the king, in front of which is placed a 15th-century Vivarini painting *Madonna and Child.* The chapel represents the flowering of the Perpendicular Gothic style. Also buried here are those feuding sisters, Elizabeth I and Mary Tudor ("Bloody Mary"). Elizabeth I was always vain and adored jewelry. The effigy which lies on top of her tomb has been fitted out with a new set of jewelry, a gilded collar and pendant, a modern copy derived from a painting now at Hatfield House. The originals were stolen by souvenir hunters in the early 18th century. In one end of the chapel you can stand on Cromwell's memorial stone and view the R.A.F. chapel containing the Battle of Britain memorial stained-glass window, unveiled in 1947 to honor the R.A.F.

You can also visit the most hallowed spot in the abbey, the shrine of Edward the Confessor (canonized in the 12th century). In the saint's chapel is the Coronation Chair, made at the command of Edward I in 1300 to contain the Stone of Scone. Scottish kings were once crowned on this stone (in 1950 the Scots stole it back, but it was later returned to its position in the abbey). Nearby are the sword and shield of Edward III.

Another noted spot in the abbey is Poets' Corner, to the right of the entrance to the Royal Chapel, with its monuments to everybody from Chaucer on down—the Brontë sisters, Shakespeare, Tennyson, Dickens, Kipling, Thackeray, Samuel Johnson, "O Rare Ben Johnson" (his name misspelled), even the American Longfellow. The most stylized and controversial monument is Sir Jacob Epstein's sculptured bust of William Blake. The latest tablet commemorates the poet Dylan Thomas.

Statesmen and men of science, such as Disraeli, Newton, and Charles Darwin, are also either interred in the abbey or honored by monuments. Near the west door is the 1965 memorial to Sir Winston Churchill. In the vicinity of this memorial is the Tomb of the Unknown Soldier, symbol of British dead in World War I. Surprisingly, some of the most totally obscure personages are buried in the abbey precincts, including an abbey plumber.

Many visitors overlook such sights as the 13th-century **Chapter House** where Parliament used to meet (special shoes must be worn to walk across the 700-year-old floor). The Chapter House in the Great Cloister is open from 9:30 a.m. till 6 p.m. (closed on Sunday from March through September). It shuts down at 3:30 p.m. off-season.

Even more fascinating is the **Museum of Abbey Treasures** in the Norman undercroft (crypt), part of the monastic buildings erected between 1066 and 1100. The collection includes effigies—figures in wax, such as that of Nelson, and woodcarvings of early English royalty. Along with the wax figures, the abbey's answer to Madame Tussaud, are ancient documents, seals, replicas of coronation regalia, old religious vestments (such as the cope worn at the coronation of Charles II), the sword of Henry V, and the famous Essex Ring that Elizabeth I is supposed to have given to her favorite earl. The museum, which charges 25p (44¢) for adults, 10p (18¢) for children, is open from 10:30 a.m. to 4:30 p.m. seven days a week.

For tours of the abbey with an expert guide, the cost is £3 ($5.25) per person. These tours operate Monday through Friday at 10, 10:30, and 11 a.m. and at 2, 2:30, and 3 p.m.; on Saturday at 10 and 11 a.m. and at 12:30 p.m. These are called Super Tours and are conducted by vergers, members of the abbey staff. They last about 1½ hours, and visitors are shown parts of the abbey not open to regular visitors. Along the way, they are given a witty, fascinating commentary by guides.

For information on religious services, tours, and special functions, telephone 222-5152 or write to the Chapter Office, Westminster Abbey, Deans Yard, London, S.W.1.

Off the Cloisters, **College Garden** is the oldest garden in England, under cultivation for more than 900 years. Surrounded by high walls, flowering trees dot the lawns, and park benches provide comfort where you can hardly hear the roar of passing traffic. It is open on Thursday throughout the year, from 10 a.m. to 4 p.m. in winter, to 6 p.m. in summer. In August and September, band concerts are held at lunchtime from 12:30 to 2 p.m. Admission is free.

3. HOUSES OF PARLIAMENT: You may want to visit the Palace of Westminster at least twice. First, to see Western democracy at work (a debate in the House of Lords or the House of Commons), and again to explore the buildings themselves. The first is difficult, the second relatively easy.

Although I can't assure you of the oratory of a Charles James Fox or a William Pitt the Elder, the debates are often lively and controversial (seats are at a premium during crises). The chances of getting into the House of Lords when it's in session are generally better than they are in the more popular House of Commons (even the Queen herself isn't allowed there). The old guard of the palace informs me that the peerage speak their minds more freely and are less likely to adhere to party line than their counterparts in the Commons.

The general public is admitted to the Strangers' Gallery in the House of Commons on "sitting days"—normally about 4:15 p.m. Monday to Thursday (about 10 a.m. on Friday). Often there is considerable delay before the head of the public queue is admitted. You can speed up matters somewhat by applying at the American Embassy or the Canadian High Commission for a special pass, but this is too cumbersome for many. Besides, as reader Richard Grant put it, "The U.S. Embassy has only four tickets for daily distribution. Forget it and stand in line." It is easiest to get in during the early evenings Monday to Thursday. The House usually sits till after 10:30 p.m. Between 7 and 10 p.m. the waits are generally short.

The head of the queue is normally admitted to the Strangers' Gallery in the House of Lords after 2:30 p.m. from Tuesday to Thursday (often at 3 p.m. on Thursday). Line up at the St. Stephen's entrance.

No tours through other parts of the Houses of Parliament were permitted as this book went to press. It is not known when the guided tours through the handsomely decorated Robing Room and the Royal Gallery, with the sunburst theme on the ceiling, and the Princes' Chamber with portraits of Henry VIII and his many wives, will be available to the public. Incidentally, it was Henry VIII who packed his linen and moved from here to Whitehall. From the days of Edward the Confessor until Henry moved, the palace was a royal residence.

The House of Commons was destroyed by a German air attack on May 10, 1941, and was rebuilt by 1950. The famous Churchill Arch to the House of Commons remains in the damaged state in which it was found after the fire which destroyed the chamber. The stonework was cleaned but not restored in any way. The palace had been razed once before, in a fire in 1834.

Westminster Hall, scene of the trials of Guy Fawkes and of Charles I, is the oldest surviving structure in the complex. It is known for its hammer-beam roof built in the late 14th century by Richard II. Westminster Hall is open Monday to Thursday (unless either House is sitting) from 10 a.m. to 1:30 p.m., and on Saturday from 10 a.m. to 5 p.m. When both Houses are recessed, the time of opening is extended on Monday to Friday until 4 p.m. (5 p.m. on Saturday).

Further information about the work of the House of Commons is available by phoning 219-4272; House of Lords, 219-3107; or on the Post Office Prestel Viewdata system, frame 5000.

4. THE BRITISH MUSEUM: From its imposing citadel on Great Russell Street in Bloomsbury (tube to Holborn or Tottenham Court Road), the British Museum (tel. 636-1555) shelters one of the most catholic collections of art and artifacts in the world, containing seemingly countless treasures of ancient civilizations. To storm this bastion in a day is a formidable task, but there are riches to see, even on a cursory first visit. Basically, the overall storehouse splits into the National Museum of Antiquities and Ethnography and the Prints and Drawings division—each of which, in its separate way, has much to offer.

As you enter the front hall, you may want to head first to the Assyrian Transept on the ground floor, where you'll find the "winged and human-headed" bulls and lions that once guarded the gateways to the palaces of Assyrian kings, along with a rare Black Obelisk from about 860 B.C. From here you can continue into the angular hall of Egyptian sculpture to see the Rosetta Stone, whose discovery led to the cracking of the mysterious hieroglyphics (on the side opposite the stone is a booklet outlining the method of decipherment).

Also on the ground floor is the Duveen Gallery housing the famed Elgin Marbles, consisting chiefly of sculpture from a frieze on the Parthenon showing a ceremonial procession that took place in Athens every four years. Of the 92 metopes from the Parthenon, 15 are housed today in the British Museum. The metopes depict the to-the-death struggle between the handsome Lapiths and the grotesque, drunken Centaurs (see, in particular, the head of the horse from the chariot of Selene, goddess of the moon).

The classical sculpture galleries hold *The Caryatid* from the Erechtheum, a temple started in 421 B.C. and dedicated to Athena and Poseidon. Also displayed here is a statue of Mausolus, Prince of Caria in 353 B.C., whose tomb at Halicarnassus was listed among the seven wonders of the world. Look also for the blue-and-white Portland Vase, considered the "finest example of ancient cameo carving," having been made between 27 B.C. and A.D. 14.

The Department of Medieval and Later Antiquities has its galleries on the first floor, reached by the main staircase. Of its exhibitions, the Sutton Hoo funeral deposit, discovered at Ipswich, Suffolk, is, in the words of an expert, "the richest treasure ever dug from English soil"—containing gold jewelry, armor, weapons, bronze bowls and cauldrons, silverware, and the inevitable drinking horn. No body was found, although the tomb is believed to be that of a king of East Anglia who died in the seventh century A.D. In addition, you'll see the bulging-eyed Lewis Chessmen, Romanesque carvings by the Scandinavians in the 12th century, and the Ilbert collection of clocks and watches.

The featured attractions of the Upper Floor are the Egyptian Galleries, especially the mummies. The fourth Egyptian room is extraordinary, looking like the props for *Cleopatra,* with its cosmetics, domestic utensils, toys, tools, and other work. Some rare gems of Sumerian and Babylonian art—unearthed from the Royal Cemetery at Ur (southern Iraq)—lie in the room beyond: a bull-headed queen's harp (oldest ever discovered); a queen's sledge (oldest known example of a land vehicle); and a figure of a he-goat on its hind legs, crafted about 2500 B.C.! In the Persian Landing rests "The Treasure of Oxus," a hoard of riches, probably from the fifth century B.C.—containing a unique collection of goldsmith work, such as a nude youth, signet rings, a fish-shaped vase, and votive plaques.

One of the most popular attractions is a battered marble head which for years rested relatively forgotten in the gloomy basement of the museum. These days, dusted off, the one-foot-high head is displayed prominently, its identification by a U.S. scholar the subject of controversy. Dr. Iris Love of New York identified the head as that of the fourth century B.C. *Aphrodite* by Praxiteles. The head arrived at the British Museum in 1859 from an excavation site at Cnidus, in southwestern Turkey, on a peninsula overlooking the Aegean Sea. The Praxiteles *Aphrodite* has generally been regarded as lost. Some archeologists and scholars believe it still is—but not Iris Love and a host of believers.

The museum is open weekdays from 10 a.m. till 5 p.m. (Sunday, 2:30 to 6 p.m.). It's closed Good Friday, the first Monday in May, December 24, 25, and 26, and January 1.

The British Library

In the east wing the galleries form part of the British Library (tel. 636-1544). In the Greenville Library you'll see the Benedictional (in Latin) of St. Ethelwold, bishop of Winchester (A.D. 963-984), probably written by one of his monks, regarded as one of the most splendid medieval works of art in England. The next gallery is the Manuscript Saloon, with its collection of autographs by such men as Cromwell, Disraeli, Sir Walter Raleigh, Newton, Pepys, Wren, Milton, Dr. Johnson, Pope, Fielding, and Swift.

Among major exhibits of world interest on display are the Codex Sinaiticus (a Greek Bible, written in the fourth century A.D.); the Lindisfarne Gospels (a masterpiece, viewed by experts as one of the important treasures from early

Northumbria, written and illustrated about A.D. 698); Shakespeare's mortgage deed (with his signature, of course) to the Blackfriars Gate House; Captain Robert Scott's diary telling of his attempt to reach the South Pole in the expedition of 1910–1912; a memorandum by Admiral Nelson explaining his plans for engaging the allied French and Spanish fleet, taken from the *Victory* logbook, and a letter to Lady Hamilton written two days before he died in the Battle of Trafalgar; and finally, documents relating to Magna Carta, including the Articles of the Barons, demands accepted by King John at Runnymede in June 1215, along with John's seal of white wax and two of the four surviving exemplifications of Magna Carta issued over his seal.

In the King's Library rests a First Folio (1623) of the comedies, histories, and tragedies of Shakespeare. In addition, don't miss the Gutenberg Bible, the first substantial book ever printed from movable type (of the copies known, the British Library possesses one printed on paper, another on vellum—circa 1455). Also on display are Oriental manuscripts, bindings, stamps, and music.

Like the museum, the British Library often puts on special exhibitions, for example, to mark a centenary. The opening times of the British Library's exhibition galleries are the same as those of the museum. Admission is free.

The Museum of Mankind

The Museum of Mankind, the Ethnography Department of the British Museum, is housed at 6 Burlington Gardens, W.1 (tel. 437-2224), where the galleries are open to the public during the same hours as those of the Bloomsbury museum. It has the world's largest collections of art and material culture from tribal societies. A dazzling selection of treasures from five continents is displayed, and a number of large exhibitions show the life, art, and technology of selected cultures. New exhibitions are mounted every year. There is a large anthropology library which is open to the public on weekdays. Weekday hours are from 10 a.m. to 5 p.m., Sunday from 2:30 to 6 p.m., and there is no admission charged.

5. MADAME TUSSAUD'S: Strasbourg-born Marie Tussaud was to become world-famous as the madame of the macabre. She went to Paris at the age of six to join her uncle, Dr. Curtius. In 1770, he opened an exhibition of life-size wax figures. During the French Revolution, the head of almost every distinguished victim of the guillotine was molded by Madame Tussaud or her uncle.

After the death of Curtius, Madame Tussaud inherited the exhibition, and in 1802 she left France for England. For 33 years she toured the United Kingdom with her exhibition, and in 1835 she settled on Baker Street. The exhibition was such a success that it practically immortalized her in her day; she continued to make portraits until she was 81 (she died in 1850). The perennially popular waxworks are visited by some even before they check out Westminster Abbey or the Tower of London.

Some of the works displayed come from molds taken by the incomparable Madame Tussaud herself. But to keep from becoming stilted the waxworks continue to make new figures, whoever is *au courant.* Of course, good old reliables, such as Sir Winston, can always be counted on to be there. Some of the figures—that of Voltaire, for example—were taken from life. In the not-to-be-missed Chamber of Horrors, you can have the vicarious thrill of meeting such types as Dr. Crippen, in case you never had the dubious pleasure in real life. You can walk through a Victorian London street where special effects include the shadow presence of Jack the Ripper. The instruments and victims of death penalties contrast with present-day criminals portrayed within the confines of prison.

An enlarged Grand Hall, as well as high-speed elevators and air conditioning, are welcome improvements. In "Heroes," with a sequence of sound, light, and projection, each hero is presented in turn, including Elton John, Humphrey Bogart, John McEnroe, and Bjorn Borg. On the ground floor, you can relive the Battle of Trafalgar, complete with Nelson's recreated flagship. Madame Tussaud's costs £2.95 ($5.16) for adults, £1.65 ($2.89) for children under 16. You can visit the neighboring Planetarium for £1.65 ($2.89), £1.05 ($1.84) for children under 16. A combined ticket will save you money. Take the tube to Baker Street (entrance on Marylebone Road). Madame Tussaud's is open daily from 10 a.m. till 6 p.m. (5:30 p.m. October to March), including Saturday and Sunday. It's closed on Christmas Day only. For information, telephone 935-6861.

6. TATE GALLERY: This building, beside the Thames on Millbank, houses the best collection of British paintings from the 16th century on, as well as England's finest collection of modern art, from the French impressionists to contemporary. The Tate is open from 10 a.m. to 6 p.m. weekdays (on Sunday from 2 to 6 p.m.). To reach it, take the tube to Pimlico or bus 88 or 77. The number of paintings is staggering. If time permits, try to schedule at least two visits, the first to see the classic English works, the second to take in the modern collection (1860 to the present). Since only a portion of the collections can be shown simultaneously, the works on display vary from time to time. However, the most time-pressed individual may not want to miss the following, which are almost invariably on view:

The first giant among English painters, William Hogarth (1697–1764), is well represented, particularly by his satirical *O the Roast Beef of Old England, Calais Gate,* with its distorted figures, such as the gluttonous priest. The ruby-eyed *Satan, Sin, and Death* remains one of his most enigmatic works.

Two other famous British painters of the 18th century (exhibited in Galleries 4 and 17) are Sir Joshua Reynolds (1723–1792), and Thomas Gainsborough (1727–1788). Reynolds, the portrait painter, shines brightest when he's painting himself (two self-portraits hang side by side). Two other portraits, that of Francis and Suzanna Beckford, are typical of his work. His rival, Gainsborough, is noted for his portraits too, and also landscapes ("my real love"). His landscapes with gypsies are subdued, mysterious; *The View of Dedham* is more representative. One of Gainsborough's most celebrated portraits is of Edward Richard Gardiner, a handsome boy in blue (the more famous *Blue Boy* is in California). Two extremely fine Gainsborough portraits have recently been acquired: *Giovanna Baccelli* (1782), who was well known both as a dancer and as the mistress of the third Earl of Dorset, and *Sir Benjamin Truman,* the notable brewer.

In the art of J. M. W. Turner (1775–1851), the Tate possesses its greatest collection of the works of a single artist. Most of the paintings and watercolors exhibited here were willed to the nation by Turner (collection divided among the Tate, the National Gallery, and the British Museum). Of his paintings of stormy seas, none is more horrifying than *Shipwreck* (1805). In the Petworth series, he broke from realism (see his *Interior at Petworth*). His delicate impressionism is best conveyed in his sunset and sunrise pictures, with their vivid reds and yellows. Turner's vortex paintings, inspired by theories of Goethe, are *Light and Color—the Morning After the Deluge,* and *Shade and Darkness—the Evening of the Deluge.*

In a nation of landscape painters, John Constable (1776–1837) stands out. Some of his finest works include *Vale of Dedham* and *Flatford Mill, on the River Stour,* painted in 1817, both scenes from East Anglia.

American-born Sir Jacob Epstein became one of England's greatest sculptors, and some of his bronzes are owned and occasionally displayed by the Tate. Augustus John, who painted everybody from G. B. Shaw to Tallulah Bankhead, is also represented here with portraits and sketches.

The Tate owns some of the finest works of the Pre-Raphaelite period of the late 19th century. One of the best of the English artists of the 20th century, Sir Stanley Spencer (1891–1959) is represented by his two versions of *Resurrection* and a remarkable self-portrait (1913).

The Tate has many major paintings from both the 19th and 20th centuries, including Wyndham Lewis's portraits of Edith Sitwell and of Ezra Pound, and Paul Nash's *Voyages of the Moon.* But the sketches of William Blake (1757–1827) attract the most attention. Blake, of course, was the incomparable mystical poet and illustrator of such works as *The Book of Job, The Divine Comedy,* and *Paradise Lost.*

In the modern collections, the Tate contains Matisse's *L'Escargot* and *The Inattentive Reader,* along with the works by Dali, Chagall, Modigliani, Munch, Ben Nicholson (large collection of his works), and Dubuffet. The different periods of Picasso bloom in *Woman in a Chemise* (1905), *Three Dancers* (1925), *Nude Woman in a Red Armchair* (1932), and *Goat's Skull, Bottle and Candle* (1952).

Truly remarkable is the area devoted to the sculpture of Giacometti (1901–1966), and the paintings of two of England's most famous modern artists, Francis Bacon (especially gruesome, *Three Studies for Figures at the Base of a Crucifixion*), and Graham Sutherland (see his portrait of W. Somerset Maugham).

Rodin's *The Kiss* and Marino Marini's *Cavaliere,* both world-famous pieces of sculpture, are on show. In addition, sculptures by Henry Moore and Barbara Hepworth are displayed.

Downstairs is the internationally renowned, Rex Whistler–decorated, restaurant and a newly designed coffeeshop.

In the **Tate Gallery Restaurant,** Millbank, S.W.1 (tel. 834-6754), the menus, at least the main dishes, are selected from a vast array of dishes, some of which were concocted from old recipes handed down from Cromwellian or Elizabethan times. For example, you can order Elizabethan veal kidneys florentine, Hindle Wakes (a medieval dish of stuffed chicken from Lancashire), or Windsor veal pie made by an original recipe. "Accompanying salads" are large enough for a main course. The Joan Cromwell's Grand Sallet includes almonds, shrimp, raisins, pickled cucumbers, and french beans in a cream sauce. Desserts from the trolley include another traditional Pye and Fruyt Ryfshews. A meal will cost from £7 ($12.25) to £10 ($17.50). Pleasant young women conduct you to your table and take your order. Wine by the glass is available.

In the completely refurbished snackbar opposite the restaurant there is a serve-yourself salad bar, offering a selection of vegetable salads, tomato, potato, celery, lettuce, whatever is fresh. These salads go with pâté and terrine, along with slices of pie, to make a meal. There are also Danish open-face sandwiches, along with tea, coffee, and soft drinks. A meal here is much cheaper than in the Tate Gallery's restaurant, costing around £2 ($3.50) to £3 ($5.25).

7. NATIONAL GALLERY: On the north side of Trafalgar Square, in an impressive neoclassic building, the National Gallery (tel. 839-3321) houses one of the most comprehensive collections of European paintings, representing all the major schools from the 13th to the 19th centuries. The largest part of the collection is devoted to the Italians, including the Sienese, Venetian, and Florentine masters.

Of the early Gothic works, the *Wilton Diptych* in Room 1 (French school, late 14th century) is the rarest treasure. It stands in a niche by itself, and depicts Richard II being introduced to the Madonna and Child by such good contacts as John the Baptist and the Saxon king, Edward the Confessor.

A Florentine gem, a Virgin and grape-eating Bambino, by Masaccio (one of the founders of modern painting) is in Room 3. In Room 4 are notable works by Piero della Francesca, particularly his linear *The Baptism*.

In a specially lighted hall, Room 7, is the famous cartoon (in the fine arts sense) of *The Virgin and Child with Saint John and Saint Anne* by Leonardo da Vinci. Matter and spirit meet in the haunting nether world of the *Virgin of the Rocks,* a famous Leonardo painting, now hung in Room 8. Also in Room 8 are two other giants of the Renaissance—Michelangelo (represented by an unfinished painting, *The Entombment*), and Raphael (*The Ansidei Madonna,* among others).

The Venetian masters of the 16th century, to whom color was paramount, fill Room 9. The most notable works include a rare *Adoration of the Kings* by Giorgione; *Bacchus and Ariadne* by Titian; *The Beginning of the Milky Way* by Tintoretto (a lush galaxy, with light streaming from Juno's breasts), and *The Darius Family Kneeling Before Alexander the Great* by Veronese (one of the best paintings at the National). Surrounding are a number of satellite rooms, filled with works by major Italian masters of the 15th century—artists such as Andrea Mantegna of Padua *(Agony in the Garden);* his brother-in-law, Giovanni Bellini (his portrait of the Venetian doge, Leonardo Loredano, provided a change of pace from his many interpretations of Madonnas); finally, Botticelli, represented by *Mars and Venus, Adoration of the Magi,* and *Portrait of a Young Man* in Room 5.

The painters of northern Europe are well displayed. In Room 24, for example, is Jan van Eyck's portrait of G. Arnolfini and his bride, and Pieter Brueghel the Elder's Bosch-influenced *Adoration* (Room 25), with its unkingly kings and ghoul-like onlookers. In Room 28 the 17th-century pauper, Vermeer, is rich on canvas in a *Young Woman at a Virginal,* a favorite theme of his. Fellow Delft-ite Pieter de Hooch comes on sublimely in a *Courtyard of a House in Delft* (Room 28).

One of the big drawing cards of the National is its collection of Rembrandts in Rooms 15, 19, 26, and 27. Rembrandt, the son of a miller, became the greatest painter in the Netherlands in the 17th century. His *Self-Portrait at the Age of 34* shows him at the pinnacle of his life, his *Self-Portrait at the Age of 63* is more deeply moving and revealing. For another Rembrandt study in old age, see his *Portrait of Margaretha Trip* (Room 27). *The Woman Taken in Adultery* shows the artist's human sympathy. Rembrandt's portrait of his mistress, Hendrickje Stoffels, last displayed in public in the 1930s, has been bought and is now displayed by the National Gallery (Room 26). The picture is signed and dates from 1659. The purchase price has not been disclosed, but the market value is believed to be in the region of $2 million. Part of the prolific output of Peter Paul Rubens is to be seen in Room 20, notably his *Peace and War* and *The Rape of the Sabine Women.*

Five of the greatest of the home-grown artists—Constable, Turner, Reynolds, Gainsborough, and Hogarth—share their paintings with the Tate. But the National owns masterpieces by each of them. Constable's *Cornfield* is another scene of East Anglia, along with *Haywain,* perhaps his best-known work, a harmony of light and atmosphere. Completely different from Constable is the work of Turner, including his dreamy *Fighting Téméraire* and *Rain, Steam, and Speed.* Rooms 36 and 38 are essentially portrait galleries, hung with several works by Sir Joshua Reynolds, along with a Gainsborough masterpiece, *The Morning Walk,* an idealistic blending of portraiture with landscape. Finally, in a completely different brush stroke, Hogarth's *Marriage à la Mode* caricatures the marriages of convenience of the upper class of the 18th century.

The three giants of Spanish painting are represented in Rooms 41 and 43: Velázquez's portrait of the sunken-faced Philip IV; El Greco's *Christ Driving the Traders from the Temple;* Goya's portrait of the Duke of Wellington (once stolen) and his mantilla-wearing *Dona Isabel Cobos de Porcel.*

Room 33 is devoted to 18th-century French painters such as Watteau and Fragonard; Room 43, 19th-century French painters such as Delacroix and Ingres; Room 44, 19th-century French impressionists such as Manet, Monet, Renoir, and Degas; and Room 45, 19th-century French post-impressionists such as Cézanne, Seurat, and Van Gogh.

Samson and Delilah, a little-known painting by Peter Paul Rubens, is a more recent acquisition (Room 20). It cost $5.4 million and has been described as the most important Rubens to come on the market for many years.

The National Gallery (tube to Charing Cross) is open weekdays from 10 a.m. to 6 p.m. on Sunday from 2 to 6 p.m. Closed January 1, Good Friday, Christmas Eve, Christmas Day, Boxing Day, and bank holidays. Admission is free.

8. KENSINGTON PALACE: Home of the State Apartments, some of which were used by Queen Victoria, this is another of the major attractions of London, at the far western end of Kensington Gardens (tel. 937-9561, ext. 2). The palace was acquired by asthma-suffering William III (William of Orange) in 1689, and was remodeled by Sir Christopher Wren. George II, who died in 1760, was the last king to use it as a royal residence.

The most interesting chamber to visit is Queen Victoria's bedroom. In this room, on the morning of June 20, 1837, she was aroused from her sleep with the news that she had ascended to the throne, following the death of her uncle, William IV. Thus the woman who was to become the symbol of the British Empire and the Empress of India began the longest reign in the history of England. In the anteroom are memorabilia from Victoria's childhood such as a dollhouse and a collection of her toys.

In Queen Mary's bedroom, you can see her mid-17th-century writing cabinet with its tortoise-shell surface. Incidentally, Mary II reigned with William III, and is not to be confused with the late Queen Mary (1867–1953), who also has many relics at Kensington. The late Queen Mary was born in Victoria's bedroom.

As you wander through the apartments, you can admire many fine paintings, most of which are from the Royal Collection. The State Apartments are open Monday through Saturday from 9 a.m. to 5 p.m., on Sunday from 1 to 5 p.m., throughout the year. They are closed New Year's Day, Good Friday, Christmas Eve, Christmas Day, and Boxing Day. Admission fees are as follows: adults pay 80p ($1.40) and children, 40p (70¢). You enter from the Broad Walk, and you reach the building by taking the tube either to Queensway or Bayswater on the north side of the gardens, or High Street Kensington on the south side. You'll have to walk a bit from there, however.

The palace gardens, originally the private park of royalty, are also open to the public for daily strolls around Round Pond, near the heart of Kensington

Gardens. The gardens adjoin Hyde Park. Also in Kensington Gardens is the Albert Memorial to Queen Victoria's consort. Facing Albert Hall, it is a wart on the face of London, a statue that reflects all the opulent vulgarity of the Victorian era—it's fascinating, nonetheless.

9. ST. PAUL'S CATHEDRAL: During World War II, newsreel footage reaching America showed the dome of St. Paul's Cathedral lit by bombs exploding all around it. That it survived at all is miraculous, as it was hit twice in the early years of the Nazi bombardment of London. But St. Paul's is accustomed to calamity, having been burned down at least three times and destroyed once by invading Norsemen. It was in the Great Fire of 1666 that the old St. Paul's was razed, making way for a new Renaissance structure designed (after mishaps and rejections) by Sir Christopher Wren.

The masterpiece of this great architect was erected between 1675 and 1710. Its classical dome dominates the City's square mile. Inside, the cathedral is laid out like a Latin cross, containing few art treasures (Grinling Gibbons choir stalls an exception) and many monuments, including one to the "Iron Duke" and a memorial chapel to American servicemen who lost their lives in the United Kingdom in World War II. Encircling the dome is the Whispering Gallery, where discretion in speech is advised. In the crypt lie not only Wren but the Duke of Wellington and Lord Nelson, as well as Wren's Great Model and the Diocesen Treasury. It was in this cathedral on July 29, 1981, that Prince Charles married Lady Diana Spencer amid much pomp and ceremony.

The cathedral (tube to St. Paul's) is open daily from 8 a.m. to 5 p.m., but to 6 p.m. mid-April to September. The crypt and galleries, including the Whispering Gallery, are open only from 11 a.m. to 4:15 p.m. weekdays, to 3:15 p.m. in winter. Guided tours, lasting 1½ hours, and including the crypt and other parts of St. Paul's not normally open to the public, take place twice daily at 11 a.m. and 2 p.m. when the cathedral is open (except Sunday) and cost £2 ($3.50) for adults and £1 ($1.75) for children.

St. Paul's is an Anglican cathedral with daily services held at 8 a.m. and at 5 p.m. in summer, 4 p.m. in winter. On Sunday, services are at 10:30 and 11:30 a.m. and at 3:15 p.m. For more information, telephone 236-4128 or 248-2705. In addition, you can climb to the very top of the dome for a spectacular 360-degree view of all of London, costing 70p ($1.23) per person.

10. VICTORIA AND ALBERT MUSEUM: When Queen Victoria asked that this museum be named after herself and her consort, she could not have selected a more fitting memorial. The Victoria and Albert is one of the finest museums in the world, devoted to fine and applied art of many nations and periods, including the Orient. In many respects, it's one of the most difficult for viewing, as many of the most important exhibits are so small they can easily be overlooked. To reach the museum on Cromwell Road, take the tube to the South Kensington stop. The museum is open weekdays, except Friday, from 10 a.m. to 5:50 p.m., on Sunday from 2:30 till 5:50 p.m.

There is space only to suggest some of its finest art. The early medieval art in Room 43 includes many treasures, such as the Eltenberg Reliquary (Rhenish, second half of the 12th century). In the shape of a domed, copper-gilt church, it is enriched with champlevé enamel and set with walrus-ivory carvings of Christ and the Apostles. Other exhibits in this same salon include the Early English Gloucester Candlestick, and the Byzantine Veroli Casket, with its ivory panels based on Greek plays. Devoted to Islamic art, Room 42 contains the Ardabil carpet from 16th-century Persia (320 knots per square inch).

In the Gothic art exhibition (Rooms 22 through 25), there are some fine pieces, such as the Syon Cope, made in the early 14th century, an example of the highly valued embroidery produced in England at that time; a stained-glass window from Winchester College (circa 1400); a Limoges enameled triptych for Louis XII. The Gothic tapestries, including the Devonshire ones depicting hunting scenes, are in Room 38.

Renaissance art in Italy, Rooms 11 through 20, include such works as a Donatello marble relief, *The Ascension;* a small terracotta statue of the Madonna and Child by Antonio Rossellino; a marble group, *Samson and a Philistine,* by Giovanni Bologna; a wax model of a slave by Michelangelo. The highlight of the 16th-century art from the continent is the marble group, *Neptune with Triton,* by Bernini (Room 21).

In Room 48 are displayed the cartoons by Raphael, which are owned by the Queen. These cartoons, conceived as designs for tapestries for the Sistine Chapel, include scenes such as *The Sacrifice of Lystra* and *Paul Preaching at Athens.*

A most unusual, huge, and impressive exhibit is the Cast Room, with life-size plaster models of ancient and medieval statuary and architecture, made from molds formed over the originals.

Of the rooms devoted to English furniture and decorative art during the period from the 16th to the mid-18th century, the most outstanding exhibit is the Bed of Ware (Room 52), big enough for eight. In the galleries of portrait miniatures, two of the rarest ones are in Room 55, both by Hans Holbein the Younger (one of Anne of Cleves, another of a Mrs. Pemberton). In the painting galleries (8 and 9) are many works by Constable. His *Flatford Mill* represents a well-known scene from his native East Anglia.

The museum's phone number is 589-6371.

THE BEST OF THE REST: Now, for those with more time to get acquainted with London, we'll continue our exploration of a many-faceted city.

Royal London

From Trafalgar Square, you can stroll down the wide, tree-flanked avenue known as **The Mall.** It leads to **Buckingham Palace,** the heart of "Royal London" (English kings and queens have lived there since the days of Queen Victoria). Three parks—St. James's, Green, and the Buckingham Palace Gardens (private)—converge at the center of this area, where you'll find a memorial honoring Victoria.

London's most popular daily pageant, particularly with North American tourists, is the **Changing of the Queen's Guard** in the forecourt of Buckingham Palace (tube to St. James's Park or Green Park). The five regiments of the Guard's Division, in their bearskins and red tunics, actually are five regiments in one, including the Scots, Irish, and Welsh. The guards march to the palace from either the Wellington or Chelsea barracks, arriving around 11:30 a.m. for the half-hour ceremony. To get the full effect, go somewhat earlier. There is usually no ceremony when the weather is what the English call inclement. But remember that your idea of inclement may not be a weather-toughened Londoner's idea of inclement. At Buckingham Palace, the ceremony is daily from Easter to September and on alternate days for the rest of the year. The guard is changed daily, of course, but without the ceremony on nonpublic days. It is also changed daily at the Horse Guards throughout the year. For information, call 730-0791.

You can't visit the palace, of course, without an invitation, but you can inspect the **Queen's Gallery** (entrance on Buckingham Palace Road). The picture gallery may be visited from 11 a.m. to 5 p.m. Tuesday through Saturday (from 2 to 5 p.m. on Sunday), including bank holidays (closed Monday), for an admission of £1 ($1.75), 40p (70¢) for children. As is known, all the royal families of Europe have art collections, some including acquisitions from centuries ago. The English sovereign has one of the finest, and has consented to share it with the public. Of course, I can't predict what exhibition you're likely to see, as they are changed yearly at the gallery. You may find a selection of incomparable works by old masters, and sometimes furniture and objets d'art.

You can get a close look at Queen Elizabeth's coronation carriage at the **Royal Mews,** on Buckingham Palace Road (tel. 930-4832). Her Majesty's State Coach, built in 1761 to the designs of Sir William Chambers, contains emblematic and other paintings on the panels. Its doors were executed by Cipriani. It is used by sovereigns when opening Parliament in person and on other state occasions. Queen Elizabeth used it upon her coronation in 1953 and in 1977 for her Silver Jubilee Procession. It is traditionally drawn by eight gray horses. Many other official carriages are housed here as well, including the Scottish and Irish state coaches. The Queen's horses are also sheltered here. The mews is open to the public on Wednesday and Thursday from 2 to 4 p.m. and charges an admission of 30p (53¢) for adults, 15p (26¢) for children. It is closed during Ascot week in June.

Official London

Whitehall, S.W.1, the seat of the British government, grew up on the grounds of Whitehall Palace, which was turned into a royal residence by Henry VIII, who snatched it from its former occupant, Cardinal Wolsey. Beginning at Trafalgar Square, Whitehall extends southward to Parliament (Houses of Parliament and Westminster Abbey described earlier). On this street, you'll find the Home Office, the Old Admiralty Building, and the Ministry of Defence.

At Whitehall, **Winston Churchill's War Room** will be open to the public in the spring of 1984, after this guide is printed. It will be managed by the Imperial War Museum, Lambeth Road, S.E.1 (tel. 735-8922), whom you should contact for information as to opening hours and admission charges. The entrance to the war room is by Clive Steps, off Horseguards Road, and visits will be possible seven days a week.

It really should be known as the Cabinet War Room, as it was here that Winston Churchill, the prime minister of Great Britain, and members of his cabinet, senior members of his military staff, and nearly 500 civil servants, spent the dark days of World War II when London was blitz-bombed, from 1940 to 1945.

A number of Sir Winston's famous radio broadcasts—". . . We shall fight them on the beaches. . ."—among others, were made here. You can see the very table and the antiquated microphone he used for these broadcasts. The bed on which he spent many troubled nights is also shown, as well as the kitchen clock by which he timed events. Many other personal mementos can be seen as you walk through the bunker which Hitler failed to destroy.

You can also see the Map Room with the table set out for conferences, the transatlantic telephone box from which Churchill spoke to President Roosevelt for the long and highly secret calls which were necessary during the war.

Seventy feet below ground level, it was impossible to know the world's weather conditions. Therefore a system of boards, rather like old railway-station boards, was used with laconic phrases: wet, very wet, hot and sunny, dry and dull.

At the **Cenotaph** (honoring the dead in two World Wars), turn down unpretentious Downing Street to the modest little town house at **No. 10,** flanked by two bobbies. Walpole was the first prime minster to live here, Churchill the most famous.

Nearby is the **Horse Guards Building,** where the changing of the Queen's Life Guard takes place daily at 11 a.m. each morning (10 a.m. on Sunday). The ceremony lasts 20 minutes, a spectacle provided by the Life Guards and the Royal Horse Guards, combined to form the Household Cavalry. Mounted on their black horses, the guards in their white and red plumes, red and blue tunics, make for an exciting and dramatic show.

Across the street is Inigo Jones's **Banqueting House** (tel. 212-4785), site of the execution of Charles I. William and Mary accepted the crown of England here, but preferred to live at Kensington Palace. The Banqueting House was part of Whitehall Palace, which burned to the ground in 1698, although the ceremonial hall escaped razing. Its most notable feature today is an allegorical ceiling painted by Peter Paul Rubens. The Banqueting House may be visited weekdays from 10 a.m. to 5 p.m., except Monday (Sunday from 2 to 5 p.m.). The admission fee is 50p (88¢) for adults, 25p (44¢) for children.

Finally, you may want to stroll to Parliament Square for a view of **Big Ben,** the world's most famous timepiece, the very symbol of the heart and soul of England. Big Ben is actually the deepest and loudest bell, although the common name for the clock tower on the Houses of Parliament. Opposite, in the gardens of Parliament Square, stands the statue of Churchill by Oscar Nemon.

Legal London

The smallest borough in London, bustling Holborn (pronounced Hoburn) is often referred to as Legal London, the home of the city's barristers, solicitors, and law clerks. It also embraces the university district of Bloomsbury. Housing the ancient Inns of Court, Holborn was severely damaged in World War II bombing raids. The razed buildings were replaced with modern offices, housing insurance brokers, realtors, whatever. But the borough still retains quadrangle pockets of its former days.

Turn south from busy Fleet Street down Middle Temple Lane, leading to the Embankment. You'll come to an area known as **The Temple,** named after the medieval order of the Knights Templar (originally formed by the Crusaders in Jerusalem in the 12th century). Here you'll find the **Temple Church,** a Gothic building, one of four Norman "round churches" left in England. First completed in the 12th century, it has been recently restored. Look for the knightly effigies and the Norman door any time from 10 a.m. to 5 p.m. (4 p.m. in winter). Readers Manly and Mary Johnson, from Tulsa, Oklahoma, were impressed with "a circle of grotesque carved portrait heads which have to be seen to be believed—a goat in a mortar board, characters making faces, rolling their eyes, lolling tongues, and even a couple of them with little fierce creatures biting their ears. There's also a dungeon one flight up—ask the caretaker to show you."

The **Middle Temple** contains a Tudor Hall completed in 1570, with a double hammer-beam roof. It is believed Shakespeare's troupe played *Twelfth Night* here in 1602. A table on view is said to have come from timber from Sir

Francis Drake's *The Golden Hind.* The hall may be visited from 10 a.m. to noon and from 3 to 4:30 p.m. weekdays.

While in this district, you may also want to explore the area north of Fleet Street and the Temple. **Staple Inn,** near the Chancery Lane tube stop, is the last of the old Tudor fronts to be found in London. The inn, lined with shops, was constructed and reconstructed many times, originally having come into existence between 1545 and 1589. Dr. Johnson moved here in 1759, the year *Rasselas* was published.

On Chancery Lane you can visit the **Public Record Office** (see "The Best of the Museums"), or walk through a Tudor gateway into **Lincoln's Inn,** dating back to 1422. Another of the ancient Inns of Court, Lincoln's Inn (Cromwell lived here) forms another link in the architectural maze of London. In the 17th century Inigo Jones erected a chapel here. To the east of Lincoln's Inn is the large square known as **Lincoln's Inn Fields,** with the Soane Museum (see below). Near the south of the fields on Kingsway is the **Old Curiosity Shop,** immortalized by Charles Dickens.

North of Lincoln's Inn in High Holborn is the last of the four great Inns of Court—**Gray's,** restored after being heavily damaged by World War II bombings. Francis Bacon (not the modern artist) was the most eminent tenant to have resided here. Off Gray's Inn Road, it contains a rebuilt Tudor hall.

The Best of the Museums

The present **Guildhall,** on King Street in Cheapside (The City, E.C.2; tel. 606-3030; tube to Bank), was built in 1411. But the Civic Hall of the Corporation of London has had a rough time, notably in the Great Fire of 1666 and the 1940 blitz. The most famous tenants of the rebuilt Guildhall are *Gog and Magog,* two giants standing over nine feet high. The original effigies, burned in the London fire, were rebuilt only to be destroyed again in 1940. The present giants are third generation. Restoration has returned the Gothic grandeur to the hall—replete with a medieval porch entranceway; monuments to Wellington, Churchill, and Nelson; stained glass commemorating lord mayors and mayors; the standards of length; a 15th-century crypt; and colorful shields honoring fishmongers, haberdashers, merchant tailors, ironmongers, skinners, and some of the major Livery Companies. The Guildhall and Crypt may be visited Monday through Saturday, 10 a.m. to 5 p.m. (on Sunday, May to September only, from 10 a.m. to 5 p.m.).

The museum of the **Public Record Office,** on Chancery Lane (tel. 405-0741; tube to the Temple or Chancery Lane), is one of the finest of the small museums of London, deserving far more attention than it gets. A mere recitation of some of its exhibits is all the selling it needs. You'll find two volumes of the *Domesday Book,* a general survey of England ordered by William the Conqueror in 1086. Here also are the navy log of the H.M.S. *Victory,* showing Nelson's dispatches relating to the Battle of Trafalgar; Elizabeth II's signed oath "to govern Great Britain"; exemplars of Magna Carta (Case VIII); John Bunyan's preaching license; one of the six authentic signatures known of Shakespeare on his Last Will and Testament, dated March 25, 1616; a letter from George Washington (Case XII) to his "great and good friend," King George III; letters from Maria Theresa, Frederick the Great, Catherine the Great, Marie Antoinette, and Metternich; the first confession of Guy Fawkes about the gunpowder plot to blow up the king, signed November 9, 1605; scads of royal autographs—Richard II, Edward IV, Catherine Parr, Anne Boleyn. The museum is open Monday through Friday from 1 to 4 p.m. (free). It's closed on bank holidays.

Sir John Soane's Museum, 13 Lincoln's Inn Fields, W.C.2 (tel. 405-2107), is the former home of an architect who lived from 1753 to 1837. Sir John, who rebuilt the Bank of England (not the present structure, however), was a "spaceman" in a different era. With his multilevels, fool-the-eye mirrors, flying arches, and domes, Soane was a master of perspective, a genius of interior space (his art gallery, for example, is filled with three times the number of paintings a room of similar dimensions would be likely to hold). That he could do all this and still not prove a demon to claustrophobia victims was proof of his remarkable talent. Even if you don't like Soane (he was reportedly a cranky fellow), you may still want to visit this museum to see William Hogarth's satirical series, *The Rake's Progress,* containing his much-reproduced *Orgy,* and the less successful satire on politics in the mid-18th century, *The Election.* Soane also filled his house with paintings (Watteau's *Les Noces,* Canaletto's large *Venetian Scene*), and classical sculpture. Finally, be sure to see the Egyptian sarcophagus found in a burial chamber in the Valley of the Kings. Soane turned his house over to his country for use as a museum. It is open Tuesday through Saturday from 10 a.m. till 5 p.m. Take the tube to Chancery Lane or Holborn.

Just across the Thames in Lambeth Road, S.E.1, is the **Imperial War Museum** (tel. 735-8922; tube to Lambeth North or Elephant and Castle). This large domed building, built around 1815, the former Bethlehem Royal Hospital for the Insane, or Bedlam, houses the museum's collections relating to the two World Wars and other military operations involving the British and the Commonwealth since 1914.

A wide range of weapons and equipment is on display: aircraft, armored vehicles, field guns, small arms, and models, decorations, uniforms, posters, photographs, and paintings. You can see a Mark V tank, a Battle of Britain Spitfire, a German one-man submarine, and the rifle carried by Lawrence of Arabia, as well as the German surrender document, Hitler's political testament, and a German V2 rocket. As part of the reorganization of the galleries, there is an exhibition on trench warfare in the First World War and a show of uniforms, medals, and accoutrements which belonged to the Duke of Gloucester. Paintings on display include works by well-known war artists such as William Orpen, Paul Nash, Stanley Spencer, and Jacob Epstein. There is also a collection of propaganda posters from the First and Second World Wars, plus Field Marshal Montgomery's three campaign caravans. The museum is open Monday to Saturday from 10 a.m. to 5:50 p.m., on Sunday from 2 to 5:50 p.m.

The **Wellington Museum,** at Apsley House, 149 Piccadilly, Hyde Park Corner, W.1 (tel. 499-5676), takes us into the former town house of the Iron Duke, the British general (1769–1852) who defeated Napoleon at the Battle of Waterloo. Wellington's London residence was opened as a public museum in 1952. Once Wellington had to retreat behind the walls of Apsley House, even securing it in fear of a possible attack from Englishmen, outraged by his autocratic opposition as prime minister to reform. In the vestibule you'll find a colossal statue in marble of Napoleon by Canova—ironic, to say the least. Completely idealized, it was presented to the duke by King George IV. In addition to three good paintings by Velázquez, the Wellington collection includes Correggio's *Agony in the Garden,* Jan Steen's *The Egg Dance,* and Pieter de Hooch's *A Musical Party.* You can see the gallery where Wellington used to invite his officers for the annual Waterloo banquet (the banquets were originally held in the dining room). The house also contains a large porcelain and china collection—plus many Wellington medals, of course. Also displayed is a magnificent Sèvres porcelain Egyptian service, made originally for the Empress Josephine and given by Louis XVIII to Wellington. In addition, superb English silver and the extraordinary Portuguese centerpiece, a present from a grateful Portugal to its liberator, are exhibited. The residence was designed by Robert Adam and built in the late 18th century. The museum is open Tuesday, Wednesday, Thursday, and Saturday from 10 a.m. to 6 p.m.; Sunday, 2:30 to 6 p.m. Admission is 60p ($1.05). Tube: Hyde Park Corner.

The **Commonwealth Institute,** Kensington High Street, W.8 (tel. 603-4535; tube to Kensington High Street or no. 9 bus from Piccadilly Circus), is a center of information on the 47 countries of the modern Commonwealth. There are continuous exhibitions on each country, and you can capture some of the atmosphere and flavor of places as different as Sri Lanka and Papua, New Guinea, Malaysia, and Trinidad. Admission is free and there are also free film shows, an attractive and inexpensive restaurant, and a shop selling Commonwealth crafts, gifts, and books. The institute also has a free library and art gallery. The Commonwealth Arts Centre runs a continuous program of non-European visual and performing arts events: dance, drama, music, and poetry. It's open Monday through Saturday from 10 a.m. to 5 p.m., on Sunday from 2 to 5 p.m.

The **National Army Museum,** Royal Hospital Road, S.W.3 (tel. 730-0717), in Chelsea (tube: Sloane Square), traces the history of the British, Indian, and Colonial forces from 1485. (The Imperial War Museum above concerns itself with World Wars I and II.)

The National Army Museum stands next door to Wren's Royal Hospital. The museum backers agreed to begin the collection at the year 1485, because that was the date of the formation of the Yeomen of the Guard. The saga of the forces of the East India Company is traced, beginning in 1602 and going up to Indian independence in 1947. The gory and the glory—it's all here, everything from Florence Nightingale's lamp to the French Eagle captured in a cavalry charge at Waterloo, even the staff cloak wrapped round the dying Wolfe at Quebec. Naturally, there are the "cases of the heroes," mementos of such outstanding men as the Dukes of Marlborough and Wellington. But the field soldier isn't neglected either. A new gallery traces British military history from 1914 to 1980. The museum is open weekdays from 10 a.m. to 5:30 p.m., on Sunday from 2 to 5:30 p.m. It is closed on New Year's Day, Good Friday, from December 24 to 26, and on the May bank holiday.

In London's Barbican district, in the bombed-out World War II area around St. Paul's Cathedral, the **Museum of London,** 150 London Wall (tel. 600-3699), allows visitors to trace the history of London from prehistoric times to the present through relics, costumes, household effects, maps, and models. Exhibits are arranged so that visitors can begin and end their chronological stroll through 250,000 years at the main entrance to the museum. Of special interest to Anglophiles is a large number of relics, possessions, and costumes of the monarchs of England, including such gruesome items as a vest supposedly worn by Charles I at his execution and the death mask of Oliver Cromwell. But the pièce de résistance is the Lord Mayor's coach, built in 1757 and weighing in at three tons. This gilt-and-red, horse-drawn vehicle is like a fairytale coach. Visitors can also see the Great Fire of London in living color and sound; a Roman dinner, including the kitchen and utensils; cell doors in Newgate Prison made famous by Charles Dickens; and most amazing of all, a shop display with pre–World War II prices on the items.

The museum overlooks London's Roman and medieval walls and, in all, has something from every era before and after, including little Victorian shops and recreations of what life was like in London in the Iron Age. Anglo-Saxons, Vikings, Normans—they're all there, arranged on two floors around a central garden. With quick labels for museum sprinters, more extensive ones for those who want to study, and still deeper details for scholars, this new museum, built at a cost of some $18 million, is an enriching experience for *everybody.*

A small coffeeshop helps sustain the visitor with various soft drinks, tea and coffee, plus sandwiches and other cold snacks. Coffee and a piece of veal, ham, and egg pie costs 70p ($1.23). Sandwiches begin at 45p (79¢). At least an hour should be allowed for a full (but still quick) visit to the museum, which will surely rank as one of the most worthwhile hours you'd spend in any museum in London. Free lectures on London's past are given during lunch hours. These aren't given daily, but it's worth inquiring at the entrance hall. In addition, the museum holds special exhibitions throughout the year. You can reach the museum by going up to the elevated pedestrian precinct at the corner of the London Wall and Aldersgate, five minutes from St. Paul's. It is open Tuesday through Saturday from 10 a.m. to 6 p.m., Sunday from 2 p.m. to 6 p.m. Admission is free.

The **London Transport Museum,** Covent Garden, W.C.2 (tel. 379-6344), is in a splendidly restored Victorian building which formerly housed the flower market. Horse buses, motorbuses, trams, trolley buses, railway vehicles, models, maps, posters, photographs, and audio-visual displays illustrate the fascinating story of the evolution of London's transport systems and how this has affected the growth of London.

There are a number of unique working displays. You can "drive" a tube train, a tram, and a bus, and also operate full-size signaling equipment. The exhibits include a reconstruction of George Shillibeer's omnibus of 1829, a steam locomotive which ran on the world's first underground railway, and a coach from the first deep-level electric railway.

The museum is open every day of the year except Christmas and Boxing Day from 10 a.m. to 6 p.m. Admission charges are £1.60 ($2.80) for adults and 80p ($1.40) for children.

Linley Sambourne House, 18 Stafford Terrace, W.8, attracts lovers of Victorian art and furniture. It is open on Wednesday from 10 a.m. to 4 p.m. and on Sunday from 2 to 5 p.m., March 1 through October 31. Admission is £1.50 ($2.63). Unaccompanied children under 15 are not allowed to enter. Built in Kensington in 1874, the house was the property of the Sambourne family until it was sold to the Greater London Council in 1980, and it is now open to the public under the auspices of the Victorian Society (for information, telephone 994-1019). Mr. Sambourne was a political cartoonist at *Punch,* and some of his cartoons decorate the house. It is filled with all the overstuffed and opulent trappings of Victoriana, including bric-a-brac and objets d'art. Much use is made of stained glass which is typical of the period.

The **Royal Air Force Museum,** Grahame Park Way, Hendon (tel. 205-2266), covers all aspects of the history of the Royal Air Force and its predecessors and much of the history of aviation in general. The museum lies on ten acres of the former historic airfield at Hendon. Its aircraft hall, which occupies two hangars dating from World War I, displays some 40 aircraft from the museum's total collection of more than 100 machines. Admission is £1 ($1.75) for adults, 50p (88¢) for children, and hours are weekdays from 10 a.m. to 6 p.m. and on Sunday from 2 to 6 p.m. The nearest underground is Colindale on the Northern Line. The entrance is via the M1, the A41 (Aerodrome Road off Warford Way), or the A5 (Colindale Avenue off Edgware Road).

On a site adjacent to the main building the **Battle of Britain Museum** has been built. It contains a unique collection of British, German, and Italian aircraft which were engaged in the great air battle of 1940. The museum is a national memorial to the victorious forces and especially to "The Few." Machines include the Spitfire, Hurricane, Gladiator, Defiant, Blenheim, and Messerschmitt BF109. A central feature of the exhibition is a replica of the No. 11 Group Operations Room at RAF Uxbridge. Equipment, uniforms, medals, documents, relics, works of art, and other memorabilia of the period are included in the permanent memorial to the men, women, and machines involved in the air battle. Admission is £1 ($1.75) for adults, 50p (88¢) for children.

The **National Postal Museum,** King Edward Building, King Edward Street, E.C.1 (tel. 432-3851), contains the post office's collection of British postage stamps, a worldwide stamp collection from 1878, and philatelic correspondence archives covering postage stamps of 200 countries from 1855 onward. The museum is open Monday to Thursday from 10 a.m. to 4:30 p.m. and on Friday from 10 a.m. to 4 p.m.

A unique private museum in London, the home of **Dennis Severs,** 18 Folgate St., E.1 (tel. 247-4013), is a delight. Dennis is a young Californian who has lived in London since he was 16 years old and is utterly involved with England, the history and the culture of the place. He has restored a house on the edge of the City. Originally built in 1725, no. 18 was occupied by a Huguenot family who were silk weavers.

Now the home belongs to Dennis and his black cat Whitechapel (who claims to have been born on the grounds of Buckingham Palace). The ten rooms of the house recreate with sound and vision the world of the 18th and 19th centuries. You walk into the kitchen of Beatrix Potter, with its blackened range holding simmering pots, the gleaming coppers, and china glinting in the candlelight on the Welsh dresser. You explore the Dickens Room, the master bedroom (with Bob Cratchett's high desk in the corner). The withdrawing room with high-backed chairs and ornaments add up to a fascinating picture of bygone times.

To visit the house and its charming occupants, telephone in the morning only. There are three tours a week, in the evenings only, lasting 2¼ hours. It is not practical for more than eight people to try to tour together, and this is only really suitable for historians or sensitive people who want to step back into the past world of candlelight in a nonelectric, nongasoline age. The cost is £10 ($17.50) per person. The house is five minutes from Liverpool Street underground at the back of Spitalfields Market.

Another unique London museum is **Whitbread's Brewery,** Chiswell Street, E.C.1 (tel. 606-4455). Although beer is no longer brewed in Chiswell Street, the old brewery remains the headquarters of Whitbread's, which has opened the magnificent old building to the public. The most impressive of the rooms is the Porter Tun Room, completed in 1784 and renowned for its massive unsupported King Post timber roof, the second largest of its kind in Europe. The lower part of this room is now renamed the Overlord Room, and houses the remarkable Overlord embroidery, depicting the story of the invasion on June 6, 1944, of the Normandy beaches during World War II. The appliquéed embroidery, probably the largest of its kind—272 feet long and 3 feet high—was designed by Miss Sandra Lawrence and took 20 ladies of the Royal School of Needlework five years to complete. It is a remarkably complete record of the Allied Forces' progress into France. Admission to the embroidery is 75p ($1.31) for adults, 50p (88¢) for children, students, and senior citizens.

Also on display in the brewery is the Speaker's Coach. A magnificent affair of gold and finery, it was built in 1698 and is still used, drawn by dray horses, to convey the Speaker of the House of Commons on state occasions. The stables can be visited by appointment.

The coffeeshop is open Monday to Saturday from 8:30 a.m. to 5 p.m. and provides light snacks from £1.25 ($2.19) or a three-course meal from £5.50 ($9.63).

Across the road on the north side of Chiswell Street, in the vaults below the Georgian terraces, is a cellar wine bar. The vaults are a honeycomb of tunnel-like rooms with curved brick ceilings, sawdust on the floor, and tables and benches set between old wine barrels. From the vast selection of wines, a glass will cost about 85p ($1.49). Bottles start at £4 ($7). In one of the vaults, snacks are available. There is also a small restaurant area with tables and chairs and waitress service.

The Greatest of the Galleries

National Portrait Gallery, Orange Street, W.C.2 (tel. 930-1552; entrance around the corner from the National Gallery on Trafalgar Square), gives you a chance to outstare the stiff-necked greats and not-so-greats of English history. In a gallery of remarkable and unremarkable portraits, a few paintings tower over the rest, including Sir Joshua Reynolds's first portrait of Samuel Johnson ("a man of most dreadful appearance"). Among the best are Nicholas Hilliard's miniature of a most handsome Sir Walter Raleigh (Room 1); a full-length Elizabeth I (painted to commemorate her visit to Sir Henry Lee Ditchley in 1592), along with the Holbein cartoon of Henry VIII (sketched for a family portrait that hung, before it was burned, in the Privy Chamber in Whitehall Palace)—both in Room 1. Also in Room 1 is a portrait of William Shakespeare with a gold earring. The artist is unknown, but the portrait bears the claim of being the most "authentic contemporary likeness" of its subject of any work yet known. The John Hayls portrait of Samuel Pepys adorns Room 4. Whistler could not only paint a portrait, he could also be the subject of one (Room 24). One of the most unusual portraits (Room 17) in the gallery—a group of the three Brontë sisters (Charlotte, Emily, Anne)—was painted by their brother, Branwell. A turbaned, idealized portrait of Lord Byron (painted from life by Thomas Phillips) is pleased with itself in Room 14. For a finale, treat yourself to the likeness of the incomparable Aubrey Beardsley (Room 24). For sheer volume of portraiture, Queen Victoria reigns supreme. The gallery is open from 10 a.m. to 5 p.m. daily, on Sunday from 2 to 6 p.m. In addition, you might note the exhibitions that take place from time to time at the gallery.

The **Wallace Collection,** Manchester Square, off Wigmore Street (tel. 935-0687; tube to Bond Street), has an outstanding collection of works of art of all kinds bequeathed to the nation by Lady Wallace in 1897 and still displayed in the house of its founders. There are important pictures by artists of all European schools, including Titian, Rubens, Van Dyck, Rembrandt, Hals, Velázquez, Murillo, Reynolds, Gainsborough, and Delacroix. Representing the art of France in the 18th century are paintings by Watteau, Boucher, and Fragonard, and sculpture, furniture, goldsmiths' work, and Sèvres porcelain. Valuable collections also are found of majolica and European and Oriental arms and armor. Frans Hals's *Laughing Cavalier* is the most famous painting in the collection, but Pieter de Hooch's *A Boy Bringing Pomegranates* and Watteau's *The Music Party* are also well known. Other notable works include Canaletto's views of Venice (especially *Bacino di San Marco*); Rembrandt's *Titus;* and Gainsborough's *Mrs. Robinson (Perdita).* Worthy also is Boucher's portrait of the Marquise de Pompadour. The Wallace Collection may be viewed daily from 10 to 5 p.m., on Sunday from 2 to 5 p.m. Closed Christmas Eve, Christmas Day, Boxing Day, New Year's Day, Good Friday, and the first Monday in May.

The **Courtauld Institute Galleries,** Woburn Square (tel. 580-1015), is the home of the art collection of London University, noted chiefly for its superb impressionist and post-impressionist works. It has eight works by Cézanne alone, including his *A Man with a Pipe.* Other notable works include Seurat's *La Poudreuse,* Van Gogh's self-portrait (with ear bandaged), a nude by the great Modigliani, Gauguin's *Day-Dreaming,* Monet's *Fall at Argenteuil.* Toulouse-Lautrec's most delicious *Tête-à-Tête,* and Manet's *Bar at the Folies Bergère.* The galleries also feature classical works, including a *Virgin and Child* by Bernardino Luini, a Botticelli, a Giovanni Bellini, a Veronese, a triptych by the Master of Flémâlle, works by Pieter Brueghel, Matsys, Parmigianino, 32 oils by Rubens, oil sketches by Tiepolo, three landscapes by Kokoschka, and wonderful old master drawings (especially Michelangelo, Brueghel, and Rembrandt). The collection may be viewed Monday to Saturday from 10 a.m. to 5 p.m., on Sunday from 2 to 5 p.m. Tube: Euston Square, Goodge Street, or Russell Square.

The **Hayward Gallery,** South Bank, S.E.1 (tel. 629-9495), presents a changing program of major exhibitions organized by the Arts Council of Great Britain. The gallery forms part of the South Banks Arts Centre, which also includes the Royal Festival Hall, the Queen Elizabeth Hall, the Purcell Room, the National Film Theatre, and the National Theatre. Admission to the gallery ranges between about 80p ($1.40) and £2 ($3.50), with a one-day cheap entry, usually on Monday, and in the evening Tuesday through Thursday between 6 and 8 p.m. Hours are Monday to Thursday from 10 a.m. to 8 p.m.; Friday and Saturday, 10 a.m. to 6 p.m.; and Sunday, noon to 6 p.m. The gallery is closed between exhibitions, so check the listings before crossing the Thames.

The **Serpentine Gallery,** Kensington Gardens, W.2 (tel. 402-6075). The Old Teahouse, near the Albert Memorial, was an inspired choice for the Arts Council's London platform for professional artists whose work has not been seen in commercial galleries. Its four large rooms, spacious and adaptable, are well suited to the experimental, and large-scale works are often shown here. The fact that the gallery is in popular parkland not only means that there are excellent adjacent outdoor facilities for sculpture and events, but that it draws a crowd who generally would not think of going to a Bond Street exhibition. Usually a minimum of four artists is shown at a time and given freedom to use the space as they wish. The exhibitions are principally for those interested in the most outstanding contemporary trends and tendencies, and are carefully watched by the more far-sighted commercial gallery owners. The gallery has a winter program as well, and stages some international shows, exhibitions by more established artists, and occasional retrospectives devoted to just one artist. The gallery is open daily from 10 a.m. to 6 p.m., April through October, and 10 a.m. to 15 minutes before dusk during November through March. Admission is free. Closed Good Friday, Christmas Eve, Christmas Day, Boxing Day, and New Year's Day.

Homes of Famous Writers

Dr. Johnson's House: The Queen Anne house of the famed lexicographer is at 17 Gough Square (tel. 353-3745). It'll cost you 70p ($1.23), and it's well worth it. Students and children pay 50p (88¢). It was there that Dr. Johnson and his able copyists compiled his famous dictionary. The 17th-century building has been painstakingly restored (surely "Dear Tetty," if not Boswell, would approve). Although Johnson lived at Staple Inn in Holborn and at a number of other houses, the Gough Square house is the only one of his residences remaining in London. He occupied it from 1748 to 1759. It is open from 11 a.m. to 5:30 p.m., Monday through Saturday, May through September, closing half an hour earlier off-season. Take the tube to Blackfriars, then walk up New

Bridge Street, turning left onto Fleet. Gough Square is a tiny, hidden square, north of the "street of ink."

Carlyle's House: 24 Cheyne Row (tel. 352-7087), in Chelsea (bus 11, 19, 22, or 39). For nearly half a century, from 1834 to 1881, the handsome author of *The French Revolution* and other works, known as "the Sage of Chelsea," along with his letter-writing wife, took up abode in this modest 1708 terraced house, about three-quarters of a block from the Thames, near the Chelsea Embankment. Still standing and furnished essentially as it was in Carlyle's day, the house was described by his wife as being "of most antique physiognomy, quite to our humour; all wainscotted, carved and queer-looking, roomy, substantial, commodious, with closets to satisfy any Bluebeard." Now who could improve on that? The second floor contains the drawing room of Mrs. Carlyle. But the most interesting chamber is the not-so-soundproof "soundproof" study in the skylit attic. Filled with Carlyle memorabilia—his books, a letter from Disraeli, a writing chair, even his death mask—this is the cell where the author labored over his *Frederick the Great* manuscript. The Cheyne (pronounced chainey) Row house may be visited weekdays, except Monday and Tuesday, from 11 a.m. to 5 p.m., on Sunday from 2 to 5 p.m. (or till dusk if it falls earlier), for a £1 ($1.75) admission; children pay 50p (88¢).

Dickens's House: In Bloomsbury stands the house of the great English author Charles Dickens, accused in his time of "supping on the horrors" of Victoriana and read by Russians today to find out "what Britain is really like." Born in 1812 in what is now Portsmouth, Dickens is known to have lived at 48 Doughty St., W.C.1 (tel. 405-2127; tube to Russell Square) from 1837 to 1839. Unlike some of the London town houses of famous men (Wellington, Soane), the Bloomsbury house is simple, the embodiment of middle-class restraint.

The house contains an extensive library of Dickensiana, including manuscripts and letters second in importance only to the Forster Collection in the Victoria and Albert Museum. In his study are his desk and chair from the study at Gad's Hill Place, Rochester, on which he wrote his last two letters before he died (also the table from his Swiss Chalet on which he wrote the last unfinished fragment of *The Mystery of Edwin Drood*). Dickens's drawing room on the first floor has been reconstructed, as have the still room, wash house, and wine cellar in the basement. The house is open daily, except Sunday and bank holidays, from 10 a.m. to 5 p.m. Admission is 75p ($1.31) for adults, 50p (88¢) for students, and 25p (44¢) for children.

Keats's House: The darling of romantics, John Keats lived for only two years at Wentworth Place, Keats Grove, Hampstead, N.W.3 (tel. 435-2062); take the tube to Belsize Park or Hampstead or bus 24 from Trafalgar Square). But for the poet, that was something like two-fifths of his creative life, as he died in Rome of tuberculosis at the age of 25 (1821). In Hampstead Keats wrote two of his most celebrated *Odes,* in praise of a Grecian Urn and to the Nightingale. In the garden stands an ancient mulberry tree which the poet must have known. His Regency house is well preserved, and contains the manuscripts of his last sonnet *("Bright star, would I were steadfast as thou art"),* a final letter to the mother of Fanny Brawne (his correspondence to his Hampstead neighbor, who nursed him while he was ill, forms part of his legend), and a portrait of him on his death bed in a little house on the Spanish Steps in Rome. Wentworth Place is open weekdays from 10 a.m. to 1 p.m. and from 2 to 6 p.m.; Sunday, Easter, and spring and summer bank holidays hours are from 2 to 5 p.m. Admission is free.

Churches

St. Martin-in-the-Fields, overlooking Trafalgar Square, is the Royal Parish Church, dear to the heart of many a Britisher, especially the homeless. The present, classically inspired church, with its famous steeple, dates back to 1726; James Gibbs, a pupil of Wren's, was its architect. But the origins of the church go back to the 11th century. Among the congregation in years past was George I, who was actually a churchwarden, unique for an English sovereign. Because of St. Martin's position in the theater district, it has drawn many actors to its door—none more notable than Nell Gwynne, the mistress of Charles II. On her death in 1687, she was buried there. Throughout the war, many Londoners rode out an uneasy night in the crypt, while blitz bombs rained down overhead. One, in 1940, blasted out all the windows.

Floating History

The Maritime Trust's **Historic Ship Collection** is at St. Katharine's Dock, E.1 (tel. 481-0043), which has been for some years the home of the old Nore lightship. That vessel has now been joined by the Thames sailing barge *Cambria,* a schooner, an East Coast herring drifter, a stream coaster the *Robin,* and now the H.M.S. *Discovery,* the royal research ship which carried Captain Scott's first expedition to Antarctica in 1901.

The Trust provides walk-around guide leaflets to help visitors interpret what they see, and souvenirs are sold aboard the *Cambria.* While the *Discovery* is in dock, it will be possible to see restoration work carried out on her massive timbers by traditional shipwrights and riggers. There are plenty of spaces for a snack lunch or a pint in a pub, and, of course, the Tower of London is just across the road. The ships are open daily from 10 a.m. to 5 p.m. (until dusk in winter), charging an admission of £1.50 ($2.63) for adults, 50p (88¢) for children.

A floating museum, H.M.S. *Belfast,* Symons Wharf, Vine Lane, S.E.1 (tel. 407-6434), is an 11,500-ton cruiser, the last of the great British warships. She's moored on the opposite bank of the Thames, looking out onto the Tower of London. The first shots from her guns were fired during the sinking of the *Scharnhorst,* and she saw distinguished service during the D-Day bombardment of Normandy. She also was in action in Korea. Exhibitions show the history not only of the H.M.S. *Belfast* but of cruisers in general. The huge engine and boiler rooms can be seen, together with many other working and living spaces. The price of admission is £1.80 ($3.15) for adults, 90p ($1.58) for children. The hours are 11 a.m. to 5:50 p.m. daily. In winter the ship closes at 4:30 p.m. Nearest tube stations: Tower Hill, Monument, and London Bridge. Boats run from Tower Pier in summer and on weekends in winter.

The Dungeon

The **London Dungeon,** 34 Tooley St., S.E.1 (tel. 403-0606), simulates a ghoulish atmosphere designed deliberately to chill the blood while reproducing the conditions which existed in the Middle Ages. Set under the arches of London Bridge Station, the dungeon is a series of tableaux, more grizzly than Madame Tussaud's, depicting life in Old London. The rumble of trains overhead adds to the spine-chilling horror of the place. Bells toll and there is constant melancholy chanting in the background. Dripping water and live rats make for even more atmosphere.

The heads of executed criminals were stuck on spikes for onlookers to observe through glasses hired for the occasion. The murder of Thomas à Becket in Canterbury Cathedral is also depicted. Naturally, there's a burning at the stake, as well as a torture chamber with racking, branding, and fingernail extraction.

If you survive, there is a souvenir shop selling certificates which testify that you have been through the works.

The dungeon is open daily from 10 a.m. to 6 p.m. in summer (until 5:30 p.m. in winter), charging £3 ($5.25) for adults, £1.50 ($2.63) for children under 14.

Highgate Cemetery

At last, the ideal setting for a collection of Victorian sculpture. Described as everything from "walled romantic rubble" to "an anthology of horror," the 20-acre cemetery in North London's old Highgate section is a real treat for tombstone fanciers. The unkempt look of overgrown weeds, combined with the clutter of obelisks and crosses gives the graveyard a rare, Gothic kind of beauty. Several of the tombstones are masterpieces in themselves, including a full-size concrete grand piano, its top open as if ready for a concert, marked only with the name Thornton and a poetic phrase by Puccini. Another grave, that of a sporting-goods manufacturer, is decorated with crossed tennis rackets, cricket bats, and balls. The most tender marker is a lifelike statue of a small boy with a ball, placed over the grave of a five-year-old boy. Highgate's most famous grave is that of Karl Marx, the founder of modern Communism, who died in Hampstead in 1883. On his tomb is a huge bust of Marx, inscribed with his famous quotation, "Workers of all lands, unite." The grave is seldom without a wreath or bouquet of red flowers, usually placed there by an Eastern embassy or a local Communist group. The cemetery adjoins attractive Waterlow Park, a 29-acre landmark of Highgate. In the nearby community are also several historic houses, including the Cromwell House, dating from 1638, and the home of Samuel Taylor Coleridge.

Free Sights of London in Action

Those who have, by this time, grown museum-weary and gallery-bored might like to see the workaday London, engaged in its task of, say, trying to start a revolution at Speakers' Corner or sentencing a modern-day Jack the Ripper at Old Bailey.

Here are a few of the action items available to you:

First, at the northwest extremity of Mayfair, head for Marble Arch, an enormous *faux pas* that the English didn't try to hide, but turned into a monument. Originally it was built by John Nash as the entrance to Buckingham Palace, until it was discovered that it was too small for carriages to pass through. If you see a crowd of people nearby who look as if they are plotting revolution, you might be right. In this part of Hyde Park (Central Line subway to Marble Arch) is **Speakers' Corner,** where you will see English democracy at work. Everybody from Communists to Orgone theorists mounts the soapbox to speak his (or her) mind. The speeches reach their most violent pitch on Sunday, the best day to visit Marble Arch.

If, during your visit in the area of St. Paul's, you are intrigued with the operation of the courts, you may want to go to the **Central Criminal Court** on Old Bailey, E.C.4 (built on the site of the infamous Old Newgate Prison). Affectionately or otherwise known as Old Bailey, the criminal court has witnessed some great moments in the history of British justice . . . and some dubious distinctions. Guests queued up outside where the final public execution occurred in 1868. To visit the Public Gallery, go any time between 10:15 a.m. and 1:45 p.m., Monday through Friday. . . . For civil justice, you can visit the **Law Courts** on the Strand, W.C.2 (tube to Temple), which are open Monday through Friday, 10 a.m. to 4 p.m.

The **Stock Exchange** is one of the world's leading exchanges. On the trading floor of this famous money center, one of the most modern in the world, you can catch a glimpse of brokers and jobbers. Guides explain what the furious action means, and later you're shown a film in an adjoining cinema, giving you an insight into the world of high finance. The Visitors' Gallery entrance is in Old Broad Street, E.C.2 (tel. 588-2355), and the nearest underground station is Bank. Admission is free, and visiting hours are weekdays from 9:45 a.m. to 3:15 p.m.

London Zoo

One of the greatest zoos in the world, the London Zoo is more than a century and a half old. Among the thousands of animals, the most famous are the two giant pandas, Ching-Ching and Chia-Chia, a gift to Britain from the People's Republic of China. One of the most fascinating exhibits is the Snowdon Aviary. Many families budget almost an entire day to spend with the animals, watching the sea lions being fed, enjoying an animal ride in summer, and meeting the baby elephant on its walks around the zoo. Also of interest is the Moonlight World, where animals of the night, the "nocturnal beasties," wander in their special world, everything from Australian fruit bats to primitive echidnas.

The London Zoo occupies 36 acres of Regent's Park (tel. 722-3333), and is open every day except Christmas from 9 a.m. in summer and from 10 a.m. in winter, till 6 p.m. or dusk, whichever is earlier. You can go by underground to Baker Street or Camden Town and then take the no. 74 bus (Camden Town is nearer and an easy ten-minute walk). On the grounds are two fully licensed restaurants, one self-service, the other with waitresses. Admission is £3.50 ($6.13) for adults, £1.50 ($2.63) for children.

It costs about £1500 ($2625) to maintain a lion for one year in the zoo. You can become part of the action by adopting an animal. You need not go so far as to adopt a whole lion, but why not start with a gentle dormouse, a bushbaby, or a douroucoulis at £30 ($53.38), a flamingo or an owl at £90 ($157.50), or if you aim higher, a couple of crocodiles at £250 ($437.50) each? An elephant will cost a majestic £5000 ($8750) a year. Nevertheless, whatever animal you adopt, you'll have your name displayed on the notice board in the zoo and will receive a ticket of adoption, entitling you to one complimentary entry ticket or a discount off a group entry ticket. You'll receive a picture of your adopted animal and periodic reports as to its welfare and progress.

The Jewish Museum

The major communal building for English Jewry is **Woburn House,** Upper Woburn Place, W.C.1 (tel. 387-3081), near Euston Station. In these precincts you'll also come upon the hard-to-find Jewish Museum, tucked away on a lovely square. Walk along Euston Road, turning right onto Upper Woburn Place until you come to **Tavistock Square.** Turn right, and the entrance is on the right. After entering, you're invited to sign a guest book, then you're guided up to the museum itself, a large salon filled with antiques relating to the history of the Jews. You'll come across many artifacts used in Jewish rituals. All the exhibits, in fact, are of interest to those concerned with Anglo-Judaica. It is open Monday to Thursday from 12:30 to 3 p.m. and on Sunday from 10:30 a.m. to 12:45 p.m. It is closed on bank and Jewish holidays. The Jewish Historical Society runs the **Mocatta Library** at the neighboring University College on Gower Street.

Wembley Stadium

To the football buff, this stadium is the ultimate. A guided tour of the hallowed ground gives you a chance to visit the players' changing rooms, then walk up the players' tunnel to the roar of the crowd. You can even climb the steps to the box where the famous F.A. Cup is presented and later relax in the Royal Box and Retiring Rooms. There is also a multiscreen slide show, depicting the activities of Wembley. These include the first ever Wembley Cup Final and also Henry Cooper's fight with Muhammed Ali. Tours leave at 10 and 11 a.m., noon, and 2, 3, and 4 p.m., taking one hour and 10 minutes. Tours depart daily except Thursday and the day before, of, and after any event, as well as Christmas, Boxing Day, and New Year's Day. Admission is £1.80 ($3.15) for adults and £1 ($1.75) for children. For information, telephone 903-4864. Take the underground or British Rail to Wembley Central, Wembley Park, or Wembley Complex stations.

YOUNG LONDON: Most children from the age of 4 to 84 know that **Hamley's** on Regent Street is just about the best toyshop in the world and that **Pollock's Toy Museum** on Scala Street, W.1 (tel. 636-3452), has a wealth of old dolls, dollhouses, and teddy bears on view, as well as cut-out theaters, miniatures, and old-fashioned toys for sale. Admission is 40p (70¢) for adults, 20p (35¢) for students and children.

But London also has a vast selection of other attractions for the young at heart, including **Blenheim Gardens,** Brixton Hill, S.W.2, an early 19th-century tower mill.

At the **Royal Mews** (tel. 930-4832), children can see the Queen's horses, and royal and other state coaches. The entrance is from Buckingham Palace Road, S.W.1. Tickets are not required, and admission is by turnstile. The Royal Mews is open Wednesday and Thursday throughout the year between the hours of 2 and 4 p.m., with the exception of Royal Ascot Week, state visits to England, ceremonial processions, bank holidays which fall on open days, and other such times as published in the press.

After viewing the coaches, many parents take their children for a picnic lunch in **St. James's Park.** However, don't forget to take your papers and wrappers away with you.

Kew Bridge Engines and Water Supply Museum, Kew Bridge Pumping Station, Kew Bridge Road, Brentford (tube to Gunnersbury, then bus 237 or 267; tel. 568-4757), has two pumping stations and five steam-driven engines on display with traction engines, models, and water supply exhibits. It sounds wet, but it's interesting to the mechanically minded. It's open weekends and bank holidays. You can get there by river from Westminster or Richmond in summer.

The **Little Angel Marionette Theatre,** 14 Dagmar Passage, Cross Street, N.1 (tel. 226-1787), is unique in London. They stage shows every Saturday and Sunday at 3 p.m. throughout the year for children 6 years and over. Every Saturday morning at 11 throughout the year they also have shows for the 3 to 6 age bracket. For that 11 a.m. show, the charge is £1.25 ($2.19) for adults and

£1 ($1.75) for children, increasing to £2 ($3.50) for adults and £1.25 ($2.19) for children at the 3 p.m. show.

The **Unicorn Theatre,** 6 Great Newport St., W.C.2 (tel. 836-3334), has a variety of plays performed by marionettes and by real-life actors, totally suitable for children. It's best to telephone for details of performances and times.

Other sights, museums, monuments, and entertainment available for children are shown elsewhere in this guide.

2. Shopping

In London, a nation of shopkeepers displays an enormous variety of wares, and you can pick up values ranging from a still-functioning hurdy-gurdy to a replica of the crown jewels. For the best buys, search out the sensational clothing, as well as traditional and well-tailored men's and women's suits, small antiques and curios, woolens, tweeds, tartans, rare books, and Liberty silks, to name just a few. Here is a brief survey of the more attractive offerings, enough to get you started on your search.

ANTIQUE MARKETS (FOR CURIOS): Chelsea Antique Market, 245–253 King's Rd., S.W.3 (tel. 352-5689), is billed as the world's largest covered antique market. It's a gold mine where you can pan for some hidden little treasure. Sheltered inside a rambling old building, it offers endless browsing possibilities for the curio addict, stall after stall extending along a serpentine maze. In this ever-changing display you're likely to run across fur coats, Staffordshire dogs, shaving mugs, old books, prints, maps, paintings, Edwardian buckles and clasps, ivory-handled razors, old velours and lace gowns (most chic), wooden tea caddies, antique pocket watches, wormy Tudoresque chests, silver snuff boxes, and grandfather clocks. The market is open Monday through Saturday from 10 a.m. to 6 p.m. Closed Sunday. Tube: Sloane Square.

Antiquarius, 15 Flood St., S.W.3 (tel. 351-5353), is the most varied of the indoor markets of London, with more than 200 stalls leased to collectors as a showcase for their wares: souvenir spoons, silver decanter labels, old books, authentic Tudor and Elizabethan furniture, rare helmets, antique guns and swords, silver pill boxes, snuff boxes, fine bone china, Roman glass, pocket watches, teapots, ornate wooden boxes, lead toy soldiers, military buttons, wooden glasses, Oriental canisters, dolls of every size, age, and character, mechanical toys, unusual walking sticks, and an amusing collection of art nouveau statuary. Also there is a large selection of 1920s and 1930s fashion. Antiquarius is open from 10 a.m. till 6 p.m., Monday to Saturday; closed Sunday.

Alfies Antique Market, 13–25 Church St., N.W.8 (tel. 723-6066), is one of the cheapest covered markets in London. The dealers come to buy here, inspecting more than 185 stalls, showrooms, and workshops on 20,000 square feet of floor.

ARTS AND CRAFTS: On a Sunday morning along Bayswater Road, for more than a mile, pictures, collages, and craft items are hung on the railings along the edge of Hyde Park and Kensington Gardens. If the weather is right, start at Marble Arch and walk and walk, shopping or just sightseeing as you go along. Along Piccadilly, you'll see much of the same thing by walking along the railings of Green Park on a Saturday afternoon.

Slavonic Arts, 17 New Oxford St., W.C.1 (tel. 242-7344), is a gift shop, selling predominantly handcrafted works of art, mainly from the Slavic countries such as Bulgaria, Czechoslovakia, Poland, Russia, and Yugoslavia. The shop also stocks unusual handcrafted items from various other countries. The stock of amber jewelry is extensive, with prices beginning at £5 ($8.75). Slavic icons also begin at £5. Handmade laces and shawls start at £7 ($12.25), and inlaid and hand-painted enamel and lacquer works begin at £3 ($5.25). In addition, Slavonic displays a range of handcrafted dolls in national costumes, porcelain, wood and metallic works of art.

The **Crafts Council,** 12 Waterloo Pl., S.W.1 (tel. 930-4811), is a gallery that mounts temporary exhibitions of contemporary British crafts and houses a loan collection of objects which can be borrowed. If you're seriously interested in crafts, you may want to pay it a visit. Off Lower Regent Street, it charges no admission and offers for sale a wide selection of cards, posters, brochures, craft books, magazines, slides, and catalogues. It also provides an index of craftspeople. It's open Tuesday to Saturday from 10 a.m. to 5 p.m., on Thursday from 10 a.m. to 7 p.m., and on Sunday from 2 to 5 p.m. Tube: Charing Cross or Piccadilly Circus.

BEAUCHAMP PLACE: Of all the shopping streets of London, one has surfaced near the top. It's Beauchamp Place (pronounced Beecham), S.W.3, a block off Brompton Road, near Harrods department store. The *Herald Tribune* called it "a higgledy-piggledy of old-fashioned and trendy, quaint and with it, expensive and cheap. It is deliciously unspecialized." Whatever you're looking for—a place to revamp your old alligator bag, reject china, crystal, and pottery, second-hand silver, collages, custom-tailored men's shirts—you should find it here. It's pure fun even if you don't buy anything. Should you get hungry, you'll find some of the best-known restaurants in London here.

BOOKS: **W&G Foyle Ltd.,** 119–125 Charing Cross Rd., W.C.2 (tel. 437-5660), claims to be the world's largest bookstore, with an impressive array of hardcovers and paperbacks. The shop includes records as well, along with videotapes and sheet music.

The **Children's Book Centre Ltd.,** 229 Kensington High St., W.8 (tel. 937-6314), is thought to be the largest children's bookshop in the world and has thousands of titles, including volumes from both France and Germany. A feature of the bookshop is that fiction, both hardback and paperback, is arranged according to age. The large toy department, which has been described as the most imaginative in London, offers a wide selection of toys, games, and stationery for all ages. The store is open from 9:30 a.m. to 6 p.m. Monday through Saturday. Tube: High Street Kensington.

BRASS RUBBING: There is such a wealth of spectacular brasses in churches and cathedrals up and down the country that the pastime of brass rubbing is becoming more and more popular. The rubbing is made with a metallic wax on paper and can be done in about half an hour. The cost, depending on the size, ranges from around 45p (79¢) up to £5 ($8.75) for the largest and most important. Materials are provided at the centers which are in all parts of the country, including Stratford-upon-Avon, Oxford, York, Chester, Edinburgh, Coventry, and Chichester. It is wise to telephone ahead if you want to rub a particular brass. A complete list of centers is available from **Historycraft,** Cripps Road, Cirencester, Glos. (tel. 0285/3971).

READER'S SUGGESTION: "The **London Brass Rubbing Centre** is at St. James's Church, Piccadilly, W.1 (tel. 437-6023), a two-minute walk from Piccadilly Circus. I visited it to discover a dozen or more young Americans who had walked by, seen the sign, and entered. For those parents who want to rest a bit while teenagers are vigorously occupied, and for those grownups who are interested in making their own brass rubbings at little expense, this center is ideal. Twenty exact copies of celebrated bronze portraits are ready for use. The center furnishes the paper, rubbing materials, and instruction on how to begin your own rubbing. There are also some books and pamphlets for sale on the subject. I did a bronze rubbing (gold on black) of a medieval knight about three feet high. The only fee is for using their brass. For those who become bitten by the bug, they also sell materials to take with you. There is a similar center in an annex to Westminster Abbey, with different bronzes. However, tourists flow through the large hall, and the general environment is much more distracting. I would strongly recommend the center at St. James's Church (in the basement) as an inexpensive way to pass several hours and obtain a personal work of art which would cost considerably more if purchased. Hours are from 10 a.m. to 6 p.m. Monday to Saturday; noon to 6 p.m. Sunday" (William A. Knowlton, West Springfield, N.H.).

THE BURLINGTON ARCADE: Opposite Fortnum and Mason on Piccadilly, W.1, is the Royal Academy of Arts (tel. 734-9052), where there are remarkable art shows throughout the year. A door west of the Royal Academy is the Burlington Arcade, a glass-roofed passage from Piccadilly north for several hundred feet to the next street. It houses dozens of shops, all with tiny upper floors, devoted solely to the sale of luxuries almost beyond imagination. You can take a short stroll through it, or spend a day wandering up and down, protected from the weather, no small item in rainy London. You will see some of the best that London has to offer in the way of jewelry, both antique and modern, clothing for both men and women, fine arts, linen, bric-a-brac, all in profusion. It is possibly the greatest single concentrated bit of luxury shopping in London. Pomp and ceremony may be departing, but if you linger in the arcade until 5:30 in the afternoon, you can watch the beadles, those ever-present attendants, in their black-and-yellow livery and top hats, ceremoniously put in place the iron grills which block off the arcade until 9 the next morning, when they just as ceremoniously remove them, marking the start of the new business day.

If you're in the arcade at 5:30 p.m., you'll see a British tradition of 150 years' standing. A hand-bell called the Burlington Bell is sounded, signaling the end of trading. It's rung by one of the beadles, a member of the smallest police force in England (there are only two members). He's responsible for seeing that shoppers behave in the arcade—no music, no singing, no riotous behavior! Tube: Piccadilly Circus.

CHINA: The **Reject China Shop,** 33–34–35 Beauchamp Pl., and at Beauchamp Place Corner, S.W.3 (tel. 584-9409), is really four shops at Knightsbridge, near Harrods. They offer a wide choice of china firsts and seconds. From a single shop, they have expanded because of increased popularity. They offer excellent china at prices well below most other stores. The merchandise changes constantly and what you don't find today most likely will show up tomorrow. Good buys are offered in bone china dinner and coffee sets, earthenware, and crystal from leading British and European manufacturers. Tube: Knightsbridge.

In addition, **Wedgwood** has a showroom at 34 Wigmore St., W.1 (tel. 486-5181), at the corner of Regent Street (tube: Bond Street). The staff there will explain their export plan to save you money on your souvenir buying. The showroom is like a miniature museum and well worth a visit. In addition to porcelain, it also carries a collection of china, jewelry, pendants, earrings, and brooches. To look and buy, head for the Wedgwood shop at 266–270 Regent St., W.1, right on Oxford Circus (tel. 734-5656).

CLOCKS: **Strike One Ltd.,** 51 Camden Passage, N.1 (tel. 226-9709), offers clocks for collectors. The shop lies 25 yards to the south of Camden Walk in Islington (tube: Angel). Strike One clearly dates and prices each old clock, and every clock is guaranteed for a year against faulty workmanship. A wide selection of clocks is displayed, ranging from Victorian dial clocks to early English long-case. Strike One specializes in Act of Parliament clocks. The shop is owned by John and Ann Mighell. He was a former mining executive who loved clocks more than his job. He gave up his business more than a decade ago to found Strike One. Open daily, except Sunday, the clock strikes from 9 a.m. to 5 p.m. If you're looking for a special clock, John Mighell is the man to find it.

COVENT GARDEN ENTERPRISE: The old fruit market, that building bounded by the Piazza, has now completed its facelift, and elegant and expensive specialty stores line its ancient walls. These include names like Culpepper for herbal remedies and toiletries, Hammick's for books, Kickers for shoes. The center of the market is taken up with stalls normally rented on a daily or weekly basis, selling objets d'art, knickknacks, jewelry, and souvenirs. It is probably outside that area that the discerning bargain hunter will find satisfaction, in the side streets where the specialty shops cluster among the derelict warehouses and building projects.

The **British Crafts Centre,** 43 Earlham St., Covent Garden (tel. 836-6993), is a national crafts association with a gallery and display center promoting the best of British crafts through exhibitions, information, and events. Many of the leading craftspeople in Britain exhibit their work through the center, much of which is for sale. A program of changing exhibitions attempts to cover all the craft disciplines and their various applications, with the emphasis on contemporary original and professional work. The main exhibition program is complemented by a second display area with a fast-changing program of shows each month. The ceramics, glass, jewelry, leather, metal, silver, textiles, and wood shown in the center has a appeal for the serious collector of fine crafts through to the person wanting an individual gift for a friend. Information is available about craft organizations, galleries, and studios throughout Britain. The center is open Tuesday to Friday, 10 a.m. to 5:30 p.m.; Saturday, 10 a.m. to 4 p.m.

The **Covent Garden General Store,** 111 Long Acre, W.C.2 (tel. 242-2721), offers a conglomeration of household items, ranging from pots, pans, glass and china, cups, mugs, money boxes, walking sticks, handbags, and shopping bags. It's ideal for browsing to find that odd souvenir which will have some use. Prices range from a few pence to several pounds, and they also sell herb teas, sea salt, spices, and country jam, as well as natural soaps. There's also a soup and salad restaurant run by two Americans.

The Market, Covent Garden, W.C.2 (tel. 836-9136), is a specialty shopping and catering center with 40 stalls selling antiques on Monday and craft goods Tuesday through Saturday. Shopping hours are from 10 a.m. to 8 p.m.

At 21 Neal St., W.C.2 (tel. 836-5254), the **Natural Shoes Store** sells all manner of footware from thong sandals to climbing boots made of natural leather.

The **Neal Street Shops,** 23 and 29 Neal St., W.C.2 (tel. 240-0135 and 240-0136, respectively), have expanded to include an even larger selection of "godwotterie," chinoiserie, and Victoriana.

The Warehouse, 39 Neal St., W.C.2 (tel. 240-0931), specializes in beads and stones, providing the fittings, clasps, and strings to make necklaces and earrings.

Naturally British, 13 New Row, W.C.2 (tel. 240-0551), is owned and run by Jon Blake, who claims with total conviction that everything he sells is truly British—pottery, jewelry, knitwear, honey, toys, glass, woodwork, rocking horses, and wrought ironwork.

The **Glasshouse,** 65 Long Acre, W.C.2 (tel. 836-9785), sells beautiful glass, and also invites visitors into the workshops to see the craftspeople producing their wares.

Penhaligon's, 41 Wellington St., W.C.2 (tel. 836-2150), is an old established perfumery company, offering beautifully packaged, exquisite products.

Behind the Warehouse off Neal Street runs a narrow road leading to **Neal's Yard,** a mews of warehouses which seem to retain some of the old London atmosphere. The open warehouses display such goods as vegetables, health foods, fresh-baked breads, cakes, sandwiches, and in an immaculate dairy, the largest variety of flavored cream cheeses you are likely to encounter.

Coppershop, 48 Neal St., W.C.2 (tel. 836-2984), is another one of the enthusiastic enterprises to blossom in the market, this one selling a wide range of British-manufactured copper goods for the kitchen. Prices range from £1.60 ($2.80) for a copper ring—good for rheumatism—to £8.30 ($14.53) for a six-inch pure copper omelet pan (special pans are around £46 or $80.50). You can purchase an illustrated mail-order catalogue for £1.30 ($2.28). The shop is run by Sally and Michael Crosfield, and is an example of vendors of good English products at reasonable prices for those who don't want to go outside London and scour the countryside to find them.

There are a multitude of tiny shops, mostly of a specialized nature, where artists and craftspeople seem to have gathered to form a community. There are silversmiths, pewter, and copperware shops, and several small snackbars and restaurants. It's well worth making your own voyage of discovery and enjoy finding odd shops and souvenirs to take home.

The **London Transport Museum,** Covent Garden, W.C.2, sells merchandise of London Transport—that is, a map of the London underground system in its original size, books, souvenirs, photos, and hundreds of posters. In addition, there's a London Transport shop at the St. James's underground station (just beyond the ticket barrier, but still within the station complex. The station is on both the Circle and District Lines).

While in the area, you might drop in at the **Rock Garden,** corner of James Street and King Street, W.C.2 (tel. 240-3961), which offers live music in the evening. American groups are sometimes featured, and sets are at 9:45 and 11 p.m. Music is generally of a high standard and embraces everything from jazz to New Wave rock. Admission is £1.50 ($2.63) or more, depending on the group. In the restaurant you can order corn on the cob, £1.10 ($1.93); salad of cheese, fruit, and nuts, £3.50 ($6.13); or barbecued ribs, £3.75 ($6.56). Various hamburgers with relishes and fries go for around £2.15 ($3.76) and up. In summer, guests can also dine al fresco beneath the arcades designed by Inigo Jones. Videotapes are shown in both places at night. The restaurant is open from 8 a.m. and all night to 6 a.m. the following morning, every day.

DEPARTMENT STORES: Harrods, Brompton Road, at Knightsbridge, S.W.1 (tel. 730-1234), is the department store to end all department stores. As firmly entrenched in English life as Buckingham Palace and the Ascot Races, it is an elaborate emporium, at times as fascinating as a museum. In a magazine article about Harrods, a salesperson was quoted as saying: "It's more of a sort of way of life than a shop, really." Aside from the fashion department (including high-level tailoring and a "Way In" section for young people), you'll find such incongruous sections as a cathedral-ceilinged and arcaded meat market, even a funeral service. Harrods has everything: men's custom-tailored suits, tweed overcoats, cashmere or lambswool sweaters for both men and women, handstitched traveling bags, raincoats, mohair jackets, patterned ski sweaters, scarves of hand-woven Irish wool, pewter reproductions, a perfumery department, "lifetime" leather suitcases, pianos. Tube: Knightsbridge.

Much more economical, however, is **Selfridges,** on Oxford Street, W.1 (tel. 629-1234), one of the biggest department stores in Europe, with more than 550 divisions, selling everything from artificial flowers to groceries. The specialty shops are particularly enticing, with good buys in Irish linen, Wedgwood, leather goods, silver-plated goblets, cashmere and woolen scarves. There's also the Miss Selfridge Boutique, for the young or those who'd like to be. To help you travel light, the Export Bureau will air-freight your purchases to anywhere in the world, completely tax free. On the ground floor, the London Tourist Board will help you find your way around London's sights with plenty of maps, tips, and friendly advice. Tube: Bond Street.

Liberty, on Regent Street, W.1 (tel. 734-1234), celebrated its centenary in 1975. In 100 years the store became known worldwide for its exquisite fabrics. One whole floor of the store is devoted to fabrics of all kinds from all over the world, including Liberty printed cottons, silks, and pure wool. Liberty Print Tana lawn is sold by the meter, as is Liberty Print Silk. Liberty Print Silk squares in all sizes and colors, for both men and women, can be found in the country's largest scarf hall.

Other exciting departments include treasures from the Orient, antique jewelry, a wide range of modern furniture an extensive furnishing fabric department, including Liberty's own furnishing fabrics and wallpapers, and the best china and glass from all over the world.

From the clock on the Marlborough Street side of the building, figures emerge when the hour strikes—and photographers on the pavement wait in anticipation. Tube: Oxford Circus.

Marks & Spencer has several branches in London, attracting the British, who get fine buys, especially in woolen goods. The main department store is at 458 Oxford St., W.1 (tel. 486-6151), three short blocks from Marble Arch. However, there are a number of branches in London as well as in most towns of any size in Britain. This chain has built a reputation for quality and value, and now clothes about 70% of British workers—wholly or partially! It is said that 25% of the socks worn by men in Britain come from M&S. The prices are competitive even when you go as far as cashmere sweaters for women at £30 ($52.50). A man's suit goes for £45 ($78.75) to £60 ($105), and a pair of those ubiquitous socks at £1.45 ($2.54). All goods can be changed if you keep the tab and return it with the goods.

IRISH WARES: The **Irish Shop,** 11 Duke St., W.1 (tel. 935-1366), unites northern and southern Ireland by stocking so much stuff in such a small area. Directed by Charles Bruton and Anthony Tarrant, it is a useful place for those who missed buying souvenirs in Ireland. All products are genuine. Prices are reportedly as close to those you'd pay in Ireland as possible. Merchandise ranges from china to woolens, from "tea-cosies" to Celtic-design jewelry set with precious stones. Waterford crystal comes in all styles and types. Belleek china and Gaelic coffee glasses, single or in a set, are also featured. You can purchase hand-woven tweed at about £8.75 ($15.31) a yard. A 45" by 45" Irish linen tablecloth, hand-embroidered, will be yours for £35 ($61.25). As the jerseys are all hand-knitted, you have to rummage to find the exact one to suit your particular shape and size. Women's shirts and dresses in fine wool are offered as well. Duke Street is off Wigmore, a street running alongside Selfridges from Oxford Street. The shop also has a branch at 80 Buckingham Gate, S.W.1 (tel. 222-7132).

Ireland House Shop Limited, 150–151 New Bond St., W.1 (tel. 493-6219), can eliminate a trip to Ireland, if you were planning to go there just to pick up some of those wonderful Irish tweeds. Opened in conjunction with the Irish Tourism Bureau, this colorful shop provides fine hand-loomed tweeds, as well as hand-made apparel and accessories for both men and women. There is an interesting collection of long woven scarves in unusual colors.

MILITARY MINIATURES: **Tradition,** 5a and 5b Shepherd St., W.1 (tel. 493-7452), sells a bewildering array of military miniatures perfect in every detail. You name it, Tradition makes it—it has a vast stock of French cavalry figures, all sorts of British soldiers from the Napoleonic Wars, U.S. cavalrymen from the War of 1812 and the Civil War, to name but a few. What more fitting souvenir of London than a British Grenadier, a Beefeater, or a Chelsea Pensioner? The range is enormous, and the shop will sell you figures painted or unpainted, marching, running, firing, dying, even kneeling. The shop is open weekdays, 9 a.m. to 6 p.m.; Saturday, 9 a.m. to 3:30 p.m.

OLD MAPS: **The Map House,** 54 Beauchamp Pl., S.W.3 (tel. 589-4325), sells antique maps, engravings, and atlases. The shop also has a vast selection of old prints of London and England, both in the original and in reproduction. It's an ideal place to find an offbeat souvenir of your visit. The Map House is open from 9:45 a.m. to 5:45 p.m. Monday to Friday, and from 10:30 a.m. to 4 p.m. on Saturday.

County Hall, headquarters of the Greater London Council, is just across Westminster Bridge on the south side of the Thames, at 40 Northampton Rd., E.C.1. It houses the Greater London History Library (tel. 633-7132), which contains an extensive collection of books on London history, and topography and maps, prints, and photographs of the Greater London area from the 16th century to the present day. The library is open Tuesday to Friday from 10 a.m. to 4:45 p.m. It is open late on Tuesday till 7:30 p.m. It's closed on Monday and during the third and fourth weeks of October and between Christmas and New Year's Day. The nearest underground station is Farringdon on the Circle and Metropolitan Lines.

OLD PIECES: **Stanley Leslie,** 15 Beauchamp Pl., S.W.3 (tel. 589-2333), is a small shop stacked to the roof with a mass of old pieces, mostly small, of silver, plate, and pewter. It's just the place to spend hours ferreting around for a special present. It may look like junk, but the quality is very high, and it's amazing that Mr. Leslie knows what he's got there and how much is a fair price. He's a lovely London character, hovering ready to help in his glasses and jeweler's apron.

PHILATELY: The **National Postal Museum,** King Edward Building, King Edward Street, E.C.1 (tel. 432-3851), is open Monday to Thursday from 10 a.m. to 4:30 p.m., 10 a.m. to 4 p.m. on Friday, and houses a magnificent collection of postage stamps and allied material. It also sells postcards illustrating the collection and has a distinctive Maltese Cross postmark first used on the Penny Black. A letter mailed from Heathrow Airport is franked at Hounslow with an attractive Concorde cancellation. In country areas, the post office provides a postbus service between many remote and otherwise isolated villages. Often passenger tickets are cancelled with a special stamp of collector interest; and postcards, depicting places of interest along the routes, are issued and mailed from these buses. More specialized, many of the narrow-gauge and privately owned railways in the country issue and cancel their own stamps. Among these are the Ravenglass and Eskdale, the Keighley and Worth Valley Light Railway, and the Bluebell Railway, along with the Romney, Hythe, and Dymchurch Railway.

POSTERS: **London Transport Shop,** St. James's Park underground station, 55 Broadway, S.W.1 (tube: St. James's Park, Circle/District Lines), is open from 9:15 a.m. to 5 p.m.; closed Saturday, Sunday, and public holidays. This unique shop carries a fine selection of posters in a wide range, most costing £2 ($3.50). The London underground maps, in their original size as seen on every tube station, can be purchased here for £2.50 ($4.38). The shop also carries books, cards, T-shirts, and other souvenir items. London Transport also has a similar shop in its museum in Covent Garden.

SILVER: The **London Silver Vaults,** Chancery Lane, W.C.2 (tel. 242-3844), were established in Victoria's day (1882), and soon became the largest silver vaults in the world. You can shop in vault after vault for that special treasure. The vaults are open from Monday to Friday, 9 a.m. to 5:30 p.m., on Saturday to 12:30 p.m.; closed on bank holiday weekends. Tube: Chancery Lane.

SOUVENIRS: The **Old Curiosity Shop,** 13–14 Portsmouth St., off Lincoln's Inn Fields, W.C.2 (tel. 405-9891), was used by Charles Dickens as the abode of Little Nell. One of the original Tudor buildings still remaining in London and built in 1567, the shop crams every nook and cranny with general knick-knackery, what-nots, and souvenirs, including Charles Dickens first editions. A popular item is an unframed silhouette of Little Nell's grandfather for 50p (88¢), or horse brasses for £1.75 ($3.06) each. Old Curiosity Shop bookmarks cost only 50p (88¢), and ashtrays with Dickensian engravings go for £2 ($3.50) to £4 ($7). The shop is open every day of the week, including Sunday and holidays.

STEAM ENGINE MINIATURES: **Steam Age,** 19 Abingdon Rd., W.8 (tel. 938-1982), is for steam engine buffs, and offers a rare selection of miniature, but accurately scaled, models of locomotives and stationary, marine, and traction engines permanently on display. They also stock a large range of steam fittings for model engineers. It's open Tuesday through Friday from 9:30 a.m. till 5:30 p.m.; Saturday, 9:30 a.m. till 1 p.m. Tube: Sloane Square.

STREET MARKETS: Colorful street markets have played an important part in the life of London. They are recommended not only for bric-a-brac, but as a low-cost adventure. In fact, you don't have to buy a thing. But, be warned, some of the stallkeepers are mighty convincing. Here are the best ones:

Portobello Road Market

This Saturday market is one of the city's most popular flea markets. Take bus 52 from Hyde Park Corner to Portobello Road (W.11). Here you'll enter a hurly-burly world of stall after stall selling curios to tempt even the staunchest penny pincher. Items include everything from the military uniforms worn by the Third Bavarian Lancers to English soul food. Some of the stallholders are antiquarians, with shops in fashionable Kensington, Belgravia, and Chelsea, and they know the price of everything. Feel free to bargain, however. A popular pastime is dropping in for a pint of ale at one of the Portobello pubs. The best time to visit is on a Saturday between 9 a.m. and 6 p.m.

New Caledonian Market

Commonly known as the **Bermondsey Market** because of its location, this street market is on Long Lane, commencing on the west at the Borough underground station. At its extreme east end, it begins at Tower Bridge Road. It is also approachable by a longer walk from the tube stop at Elephant and Castle. The stalls are well known, and many dealers come in to London from the country. The market gets under way at 5 a.m.! But take a flashlight, as the light is bad at that time of the morning. This is even before the underground opens. Antiques and other items are generally lower in price than at Portobello Road and the other street markets.

Petticoat Lane

On Sunday morning (go before noon), throngs of shoppers join the crowds on Petticoat Lane (also known as Middlesex Street, E.1). The lanes begin at the Liverpool Street station on the Bishopgate side. Here you may buy clothing, food, antiques, and plenty of junk. There's also a good warehouse selling cut-rate sheepskin and leather coats. It's open on Sunday morning when the market is, but also from Monday to Friday. Nearest tube station is Aldgate East.

Camden Passage

Only 200 yards in length, this traffic-free antiques center contains 250 antique shops, three pubs, and half a dozen first-class restaurants. Open-air antiques-stall markets are in business on Tuesday, Wednesday, and Saturday, and an open-air book market offers its goods on Thursday and Friday. Offered are a wide range of antiques for everybody from the young collector to the international dealer. For information, telephone John Friend, 359-0190. Tube: Angel (Northern Line). Buses: 4, 19, 38, 38a, 43, 73, 171, 172, 179, 214, 239, 277, and 279.

Church Street

Along Church Street, N.W.8, you'll have to search through a wide assortment of junk, but you'll often come across a great buy. There's a lot of second-hand furniture that won't fit under your airplane seat, but you'll find smaller purchases as well. Business is conducted Monday to Saturday from early morning until evening (stalls may close earlier if trading is slow). Here's an opportunity to haggle and enter into a true market spirit, only don't forget that the vendor probably knows more about his or her merchandise than you and may give you an "earful" if you try some unfair or unnecessary bargaining. North of Marble Arch, Church Street crosses Edgware Road, one street beyond Harrow Road, and is reached by taking the tube to either Edgware Road or Marylebone.

Camden Lock

On Chalf Farm Road, Camden Lock is a five-minute walk from the Camden Town underground. It's a smaller and cozier version of Portobello. The stallkeepers sell old silver, jewelry, and other crafts, as well as unusual boots and shoes, even homemade cakes. This market is more out of the way than those previously recommended. Young women with spiky psychedelic hair stalk between the stalls, and you have the impression that sales are not vital to the stallkeepers, more a perk in life, the cream on the trifle. It's well worth a visit just for the atmosphere. They are open all day Saturday and Sunday.

Leather Lane

Leather Lane, E.C.1 (tube: Chancery Lane), is open from 11 a.m. to 2:30 p.m., Monday to Friday only. It provides a bewildering array of clothes, furniture, and food, plus plenty of atmosphere. The lane is patronized mainly by local office workers, but also is colorful to the foreign visitor as well.

Food at Open Markets

If you've decided to rent one of the previously recommended self-catering apartments, you may find that shopping for supplies in London can be an adventure.

Berwick Street, W.1, is quite the place with locals, extending from Rupert Street, past the porn shops and up Berwick. The emphasis here is heavy on fruit and vegetables. There is also good meat. At 11 Brewer St., **Richards (Soho) Ltd.** (tel. 437-1358) sells fish fresh from the sea—live lobsters and crawfish, hideous monkfish, sea bass, grey mullet, clams, prawns, and crabs. Oysters are offered in season, as are haddock, hake, and cod.

Visitors must realize that many of these markets are founded and maintained almost exclusively by local business and that, therefore, much of the merchandise is of a prosaic nature—food, clothes, household equipment. It's not often these days that you find the bargain of the century, gold disguised as brass, a Renoir posing as Homing Cattle. All the same, the atmosphere in the markets is something unique to the character of London and part of its way of life.

STYLISH CLOTHING: Carnaby Street, just off Regent, is a legend, and legends take time to build. Often, by the time they are entrenched, fickle fashion has moved on elsewhere. Alas, Carnaby no longer dominates the world of pace-setting fashion. But the street is still visited by the curious, and some of its shops display lots of claptrap and quick-quid merchandise. For value, style, and imagination in design, the **Chelsea** (King's Road) and **Kensington** boutiques have left Carnaby far behind.

TAILORS: Many men have a pipedream about owning a suit tailormade in London. If you have the time and money, several expert tailors will make you a 100% British suit. But this takes several weeks for fittings, and the foreign visitor rarely will have such chunks of time. A preferable and far less expensive way of getting a hand-cut made-to-measure suit is to visit one of the **Burton** stores. They are all over Great Britain, 66 branches in the Greater London area. Those nearest tourist attractions include Regent Street and Oxford Street in the West End, Cheapside in the City, and Kensington High Street, a short taxi ride from the West London Air Terminal. You can choose your made-to-measure suit from a vast selection of cloth patterns, and the comprehensive style books cover a wide range of modern designs. If you prefer to buy ready-made, then Burton's stores can show you a large collection of suits (medium to light-weight), topcoats, rainwear, leisure wear, including jackets in Harris tweed, suede, and leather, slacks, and an array of shirts, ties, and knitwear. Made-to-measure and ready-to-wear suits start at around £50 ($87.50), ranging up to £150 ($162.50) and more.

WELSH HANDICRAFTS: The **Welsh Craft Centre,** 91 Regent St., W.1 (tel. 439-0087), is a gallery of things Welsh, ranging from hand-woven rugs, tapestries, and tweeds to Welsh lovespoons, brass miners' lamps, horse brasses, pottery, and stoneware. You can learn about the people and the history of the goods before buying at very genuine prices. Tube: Westminster. There's also a branch store at 36 Parliament St., S.W.1 (tel. 839-5056).

WOOLENS: See **Selfridges** ("Department Stores," page 119), where the standard is high and the prices low. But for a specialty shop, **D. L. Estridge,** 61A Piccadilly, W.1 (tel. 493-7434), opposite the Ritz Hotel, and 62 Regent St., W.1 (tel. 734-0195), next door to the Café Royal, is a good choice (and it's not as expensive as one would judge from its location). Cashmere, camel hair, shetlands, tartan kilts and skirts—Estridge is a virtual showcase of Scottish crafts. Good values are to be found in sweaters and kilts. Authentic tartan kilts are from $45 (U.S.), with capes and scarfs to match. There is also a wide range of knitwear and tartans for men and children. Tube: Piccadilly Circus.

READERS' SHOPPING SELECTIONS: "In London, an outdoor (weather permitting) art show takes place on Saturday and Sunday on **Piccadilly at Green Park** (underground stop: Hyde Park or Green Park). The show extends for almost half a mile, and you can pick up good-quality drawings, watercolors, oils, and craft items for very little" (Ray R. Conley). . . . "In London, combine a Sunday afternoon outing at the Hyde Park Speakers' Corner with a stroll down Bayswater Road. Along the edge of the park, from Marble Arch for blocks toward Lancaster Gate, stretches an outdoor art fair. Every possible type of art and craft is exhibited, from paintings on velvet to handmade pottery—and most at very reasonable prices" (Phyllis and Steve Wilson, Chicago, Ill.). . . . "The best men's ready-made clothing I have seen during my five-month stay is sold at **Dunn & Co.,** with branches in London, the larger towns of England and Scotland, and main shops on Regent Street, Oxford Street, the Strand, and Piccadilly. Ready-to-wear suits and jackets are sold in sizes—regular, short, slim, long, and stout—to fit anyone. What I think are the best Harris tweed sports jackets available in England are sold here. A purchase mailed to the United States is exempt from VAT, a savings of approximately 15%. Dunn & Co. stores in London with large selections of woolen suits and Harris tweeds are on Regent Street and also on the Strand" (John W. Weber, Pullman, Wash.).

"There is a multifloor department store called the **Houndsditch Warehouse** at 123 Houndsditch, just one block from the famed Petticoat Lane market. This store is unusual in England in that it offers discounts (about 15%) on name-brand merchandise. The china department features such brands as Wedgwood, Royal Doulton, Lladro figurines, and Waterford crystal. The store will send your purchases if desired, through their export office, which will also fill out the papers for a refund of VAT charge if you decide to take your purchases with you. The store is open on Sunday" (Reuben S. Title, Chappaqua, N.Y.).

3. London After Dark

London is crammed with change-of-pace nighttime entertainment. You'll have a wide choice of action, from the dives of Soho to the elegance of opening night on Shaftesbury Avenue. So much depends on your taste, pocketbook, and even the time of year. Nowhere else will you find such a panorama of legitimate theaters, operas, concerts, gambling clubs, discos, vaudeville at Victorian music halls, strip joints, jazz clubs, folk-music cafés, nightclubs, and dance ballrooms. For information about any of these events, ask a newsstand dealer for a copy of *Time Out,* 60p ($1.05). *What's On* has now combined with *Where to Go* and sells for 50p (88¢), containing listings of restaurants, theaters, and nightclubs.

THEATERS: The fame of the English theater has spread far and wide. In London you'll have a chance to see it on its home ground. You may want to spend a classical evening at the "Old Vic" (now the National Theatre Company), or you may settle for a new play by some unknown writer. You might want to catch up on that Broadway musical you missed in New York, or be an advance talent scout for next year's big Stateside hit. Production costs are lower in London, and sometimes it's easier for people in the legitimate theater there to experiment.

For the average production, you pay around £2 ($3.50) for upper circle seats, around £15 ($26.25), sometimes more, for front stalls. You can either purchase your ticket from the theater's box office (the most recommended method), or from a ticket agency, such as the one operated from the reservations desk of American Express (agent's fee charged, however). In a few theaters you can reserve your spot in the gallery, the cheapest seats of all, but in some cases the less expensive seats are sold only on the day of performance. This means that you'll have to buy your gallery ticket early, then return about one hour before the performance and go around to the entrance to the balcony. Often you can rent a queueing stool from a man in charge. Occasionally, you can enjoy a preshow staged by strolling performers, called buskers, including next year's Chaplin—or last year's (the theater has its peaks and valleys).

It is also possible to telephone most of the theaters for reservations, quoting an American Express card number (if you possess such a thing). You then collect your tickets from the box office just before the performance.

If you want to see two shows in one day, you'll find that Wednesday, Thursday, and Saturday are always crammed with matinee performances. Many West End theaters begin their evening performances at 7:30.

Students and senior citizens get a break at most theaters (subject to availability) by being granted a discount at the local box offices. Currently, such discount tickets sell at a price beginning at £3.50 ($6.13) each.

The **Leicester Square Ticket Booth,** Leicester Square, W.C.2, sells theater tickets on the day of performance for half price, plus a 50p (88¢) service charge. Open from noon to 2 p.m. for matinee performances and from 2:30 to 6:30 p.m. for evening performances, they have a wide selection of seats available. Ask for the show you want to see, and they will offer alternatives if they cannot do it. Tickets for "hits" are obviously not available often. There is often a long line, but it moves quickly and is well worth the effort if you want to take in a lot of theater while you're in London—and want to save money. Many of the shows for which tickets are available are well displayed at the booth, so you can make up your mind on what to see as you wait in the queue.

Of London's many theaters, these are particularly outstanding:

The **National Theatre** is a concrete cubist fortress, a three-theater complex that stands as a $32-million landmark beside the Waterloo Bridge on the south bank of the Thames. It was first suggested in 1848, and it took Parliament 101 years to pass a bill vowing government support. Flaring out like a fan, the most thrilling theater in this complex is the **Olivier,** named after Lord Laurence Olivier, its first director when the company was born in 1962. (Olivier was succeeded in 1973 by Peter Hall, who created the Royal Shakespeare Company.) The Olivier Theatre bears a resemblance in miniature to an ancient Greek theater. It has an open stage and seats 1160. The **Cottesloe** is a simple box theater for 400 people. Finally, the 890-seat **Lyttelton** is a traditional proscenium arch house that doesn't have one bad seat for any theater-goer. In the foyers there are two bookshops, eight bars, a restaurant, and two self-service buffets (some open all day except Sunday), and many outside terraces with river views. For everyone, with or without tickets for a play, there is live foyer music, free, before evening performances and Saturday matinees, and free exhibitions. The foyers are open 10 a.m. to 11 p.m. except Sunday. Also guided theater tours are available daily, including backstage areas, for about £1.50 ($2.63).

For information and reservations for all three theaters, telephone 928-2252. However, for credit-card bookings, you should ring 928-5933. Prices of seats range from £3.20 ($5.60) to £11.50 ($20.13); however, there are many variations and reductions. The only way to find out is to know what you wish to see, the day and time, then call the theater, naming the particular auditorium. Otherwise, join the line before 10 a.m. on the day of the performance and obtain as much as a 75% reduction—generally a more reasonable 20%.

You may also be interested in the activities of the **National Film Theatre,** in the same South Bank complex (tel. 928-3232). It runs a fascinating cinema program, ranging around the world. For instance, you might see avant-garde French films, American imports, or something fascinating out of Germany. A visitor can obtain a week's membership for only 60p ($1.05). If booked in advance, tickets cost £2 ($3.50). Otherwise, you pay £1.55 ($2.71) if you line up right before a performance.

The **National Theatre Restaurant** (tel. 928-2033) will serve you a good meal for around £9 ($15.75), but at one of the coffee bars a snack will run around £2.25 ($3.94). If the weather is good, you can just sit and look out over the river and the London skyline spread before you. Tube: Waterloo Station.

The **Royal Shakespeare Company** has its famous theater in Stratford-upon-Avon and is also housed in the Barbican Theatre, Barbican Centre, E.C.2 (tel. 628-8795—tube to Barbican or St. Paul's—or Stratford 292-271). A program of new plays and Shakespearean and other classics is performed here. Plays run in repertoire and are presented two or three times a week each. The company also has two smaller theaters where new and experimental plays are performed as well as classics: **The Other Place** in Stratford-upon-Avon, and **The Pit,** also in London's Barbican Centre.

The **Barbican Centre,** Barbican, E.C.2 (tel. 638-4141), is the newly built arts and exhibition centre (tube: Barbican, Moorgate, Liverpool Street, or St. Paul's), considered to be the largest in Western Europe. It was created to make a perfect setting in which to enjoy good music and theater from comfortable, roomy seating.

The theater is now the home of the **Royal Shakespeare Company,** which of course performs a wide range of works other than the plays of the Bard. The Concert Hall is the permanent home of the London Symphony Orchestra and is host to visiting performers.

There are often lunchtime concerts where the admission is £2 ($3.50) for the 45 minutes or so. Otherwise, seats are priced from £2 ($3.50) to £7.50 ($13.13) for evening performances. Matinees in the theater start at £2 ($3.50), going up to £8 ($14), and evening seats range from £2 ($3.50) to £9.50 ($16.63).

There are a number of bars and the **Waterside Café,** Level 5, a self-service restaurant with a salad and wine bar, which is open from 10 a.m. to 8 p.m., Monday to Saturday (from noon on Sunday). It offers views over an artificial lake and seats outside on the terrace in good weather.

The Cut Above, Level 7, overlooks that same lake and St. Giles Church. It was decorated in brilliant mauves, pinks, and purples by the famous designer David Hicks. There is a bar and table service. It is open from noon to 3 p.m. and from 6 p.m. until the last orders are taken half an hour after the end of the last performance. For table reservations, call 588-3008.

Other useful numbers at the Barbican include: box office, reservations, and inquiries, 628-8795; credit-card bookings, 638-8891. For information on all events taking place at the center, a 24-hour recording information service is available by dialing 628-9760 or 628-2295.

Royal Court Theatre, Sloane Square, S.W.1 (tel. 730-1745: tube to Sloane Square). The English Stage Society has operated this theater since 1956. The emphasis is on new playwrights (John Osborne got his start here with the 1956 production of *Look Back in Anger*). Also on the premises is the Theatre Upstairs, a large room with an open stage suitable for unusual productions to supplement the main-house repertoire. Tickets range from £2 ($3.50) upward to £5.50 ($9.63). On Monday all seats sell for £2 ($3.50). A half hour before performance, students can get any available seats for £2 ($3.50) on any day of the week. The theater gets a grant from the Arts Council, so prices are somewhat artificial. Many shows presented here are experimental.

The **Young Vic,** The Cut, Waterloo, S.E.1 (tel. 928-6363), has a repertoire which includes such authors as Shakespeare, Ben Jonson, O'Casey, and Pinter, as well as specially written new plays, and although slanted toward young people, the productions have a general appeal. Performances begin normally at 7:30 p.m. All seats go for £2.50 ($4.38), including VAT. Reservations may be made by phone.

Sadler's Wells Theatre is on Rosebery Avenue, E.C.1 (tel. 837-1672). Apart from its resident company, Sadler's Wells Royal Ballet, it also plays host to other outstanding opera and dance companies. Prices fluctuate from £2 ($3.50) to £12 ($21). Take the underground to Angel Station (Northern Line). The theater is a three-minute walk. Or you can go by bus direct from Piccadilly (no. 19 or 38); from Holborn (no. 19, 38, or 172); to the Angel (no. 30, 43, 73, 104, 214, 277, or 279); and from Waterloo (no. 171 or 188), and change at Holborn.

Lyric Theatre, 23 King St., Hammersmith, W.6 (tel. 741-0824), stands on the edge of the site where the old Lyric stood for 80 years until 1965. The elegant auditorium from the old theater, designed in 1895, has been restored and incorporated in the new building and offers a variety of productions, musical and dramatic. The theater is open daily from 10 a.m. to 10:30 p.m. (noon to 10 p.m. on Sunday) for food in the buffet, and the bars are open during normal pub hours.

Many theaters will accept bookings by telephone if you give your name and American Express card number when you ring. Then all you have to do is go along before the performance to collect your tickets which will be sold at the theater price. All theater booking agencies charge a fee. Once confirmed, the booking will be charged to your account even if you don't use the tickets. Only card holders can collect the tickets charged to their accounts.

Theater Clubs

In addition to the productions in the regular theaters, several theater clubs also operate. These clubs are where the most experimental and avant-garde productions are staged. By stopping by at their box offices and paying a nominal fee, you can become a temporary member. The clubs include: **Mountview Arts Centre** and **Mountview Theatre School,** with two theaters, the Mountview Theatre and the Judi Dench Theatre, both at 104 Crouch Hill, N.8 (tel. 340-5885), have been established for about 40 years. Thirty plays and musicals are presented annually, plus 30 films. Membership is free. Many courses are offered, mainly full time, although some evening part-time courses are also offered. Affiliated theaters include the New Arts Theatre Club in London, the Hampstead Theatre Club, and the Traverse Theatre Club, Edinburgh. Performances on weekday evenings begin at 7:30 p.m. on Sunday at 7:30 p.m. Matinees are at 3:30 p.m. There is no charge for seats, although donations are invited for the students' scholarship fund. Take the subway on the Piccadilly Line to Finsbury Park and then a W2 or W7 bus (terminus). The theater is on the main road. For more detailed information, get in touch with John Rose at 889-4306.

St. Georges Theatre, Tufnell Park Road, N.7 (tel. 607-7978), is a skillfully converted church, made over as a London home for Shakespeare. It is acknowledged by scholars and historians as a valid recreation of the Elizabethan theater. The standard is highly professional, and the atmosphere is friendly and welcoming. Shakespeare plays are done in repertoire all year. Performances are every evening (except Sunday), and the seats are inexpensive. Telephone the theater for details of prices, times, and plays.

Fringe Theaters

There are now many club theaters, lunchtime shows, and out-of-London preview performances, offering everything from music hall and comedy to very serious modern theater and the classics performed by both professionals and amateurs. It is well to buy both *What's On* and *Time Out,* published weekly. With these two publications you'll be able to plan your entertainment along your own personal lines of preference. Most of the time the Cottesloe Theatre at the National presents repertory groups. Entrance charges range from free for many of the smaller productions up to £1.50 ($2.63) and £2.50 ($4.38) at the posher places. Clubs often charge a small membership fee, although this is waived sometimes for overseas visitors.

MUSIC HALLS: Players, Villiers Street (formerly the famous Gatti's "Under the Arches"), W.C.2 (tel. 839-1134). Nowadays, the Players is a Victorian music hall variety club. Top-notch performers in London often use these two-week engagements as fill-ins. The presentation is professionally staged, with the appropriate settings and costumes. The master of ceremonies (he's called the chairman) asks members to introduce their guests who stand for a bow (and comments). Insults are exchanged in jest, especially if a guest is from one of the "colonies."

You can enjoy the entire show having drinks only (even toasting the Queen—Victoria, that is). It's best to make an entire evening of it, staying for the dancing session after the show. To do that, you can have a generous dinner, à la carte. Temporary membership is available for £6 ($10.50) per week or £12 ($21) for three weeks. Forty-eight hours must elapse before a membership becomes valid. Application must be made in person. While members do not have to pay for seats, they are charged £3 ($5.25) for each guest. Guests are limited to four at any time. On Monday and Tuesday, if you bring more than two guests, one gets in free. The à la carte dinner offers fish, steaks, poultry, and the usual appetizers and desserts, and the average price for a three-course meal is £9 ($15.75). Performances are given every night except Sunday, but check in advance by calling the box office. Take the tube to Embankment station. Directly across the street from the Players is a house with a plaque, commemorating the fact that Rudyard Kipling lived there between 1889 and 1891.

The **Pindar of Wakefield,** 328 Gray's Inn Rd., W.C.1 (tel. 722-5395 for bookings), perpetuates the convivial world of the English music hall. Aided by tankards of foaming ale and authentic Cockney entertainment, the boisterous days of communal friendliness live on. As your chairman, the "garrulous glossarist" puts it, the Pindar is for "booze, ballads, and bonhomie," not to forget "bangers and mash, faggots, cockles and mussels." The admission charge is £3.50 ($6.13) at the door. However, the music hall is run by a separate organization, not the publican, and you can book in advance by writing to Aba Daba, 30 Upper Park Rd., N.W.3, paying only a £3 ($5.25) admission. In the pub you can order snacks from 7:30 p.m., including chicken and salad at £2 ($3.50) and scampi and fried potatoes at £2 ($3.50). The show is billed as "a gargantuan garish gala glorious gathering for your gracious gratifications." Usually six performers belt out tearjerkers, and you're given a song sheet to help in the sing-alongs. Performances start at 7:30 p.m. Take the tube to Kings Cross station.

The **Rheingold Club,** at 361 Oxford St., W.1 (tel. 629-5343), is a favorite rendezvous for singles in the West End. Its entrance is in Sedley Place, a small pedestrian alleyway leading into Mayfair. It is an appropriate location for London's oldest continental club, easy to find, being only 30 yards from the Bond Street tube station. Housed in a centuries-old wine cellar, this spacious nightspot conveys the old-world charm of an ancient Rhineland inn. It always features one of the best groups in town, usually a versatile dance band which can play everything from Johann Strauss to the latest pop music. A soft glow is cast across Rhenish coats-of-arms by wrought-iron lanterns, mellowing the dark wooden beams and historical copper etchings. The entertainment is provided for the most part by the patrons themselves, although from time to time a celebrity will be among the crowd and will perform for a midnight cabaret, usually on Monday night.

You purchase a temporary membership card at the club reception costing £5 ($8.75) for men and £4 ($7) for women. This entitles you to free admission on the night of the purchase. Typical German dishes such as bratwurst and eisbein (pickled pork knuckles) with sauerkraut cost from about £2 ($3.50) to £4 ($7). German draft beer by the half pint starts at 70p ($1.23) and German wines from 85p ($1.49) per glass or £4 ($7) by the bottle. The Rheingold is open every night except Sunday from 8 p.m. for dinner (optional) and drinks. Dancing begins at 9:30 p.m. to live music and goes on until about 2 a.m. from Monday to Thursday and until 2:30 a.m. on Friday and Saturday. Admission fees vary from nothing if you are a member and arrive early to £3 ($5.25), depending on the night of the week and if there is a cabaret. Until 10 p.m. women are admitted free.

READER'S MUSIC HALL SELECTION: "I found the **World's End,** 459 King's Rd., S.W. 10, in Chelsea (tel. 352-7992), to be a super-friendly place where old-style music is appreciated. It takes one back to the days of Queen Victoria, and the piano player has just the right style for the period. Many songs you'll know and want to join in; others are more traditionally English but North Americans learn quickly. Entertainment is on Friday and Saturday nights only" (Michael Marshall, London, England).

EAST END DRAG PUBS: In the East End is a series of pubs offering entertainment nightly. Drag acts (female impersonators) are the chief form of amusement. The English, especially the Cockneys of the East End, love to giggle and scream over the caricatures of men satirizing women. Many female impersonator acts find their way into the posh West End clubs which many of our readers will find too expensive. However, talent without all the fancy trappings appears almost nightly in some of these Victorian pubs. You pay no admission, no cover, no minimum—one of the bargain entertainment values in London.

Royal Vauxhall Tavern, 372 Kennington Lane, S.E. 11 (tel. 582-0833), is under new management, and although it is still a drag pub, it has been redecorated in the Victorian Music Hall style. Pat and Breda McConnon extend a warm welcome to tourists and maintain the original policy of no cover charge. So the price is for whatever drinks you buy. They also offer homemade hot and cold meals, day or night. The pub lies on the south of the Thames, over the Vauxhall Bridge and near the Vauxhall tube station. Live drag acts are presented nightly.

GAY NIGHTLIFE: The most reliable source of information on all gay clubs and activities is the **Gay Switchboard** (tel. 837-7324). The staff there runs a 24-hour service of information on places and activities catering openly to homosexual women and men.

Here are some suggestions; most are membership clubs which, nevertheless, welcome overseas visitors:

The **Salisbury,** 90 St. Martin's Lane, W.C.2 (tel. 836-5863), is one of the most famous of the Edwardian pubs of London, attracting today a large gay theater crowd. Its glittering cut-glass mirrors reflect the faces of English stage stars (and would-be stars), sitting around the curved buffet-style bar, having a cold snack. The Salisbury is now under the capable management of Jerry Wynne (no relation to that famous English spy of the '50s). Jerry has managed to walk away with several gold stars for the home-cooked meals served here, up to eight different dishes, including, of course, the traditional steak-and-kidney pie. Fresh vegetables are served, and the price is an unbelievable £1.75 ($3.06) a plate. The vegetarian is catered for at the same price, with a choice of three dishes daily, including leeks with cheese sauce. If you want a less prominent place to dine, choose the old-fashioned wall banquette with its copper-topped tables. The light fixtures separating the banquette wall complement the art nouveau decor, with its veiled bronze women in flowing togas holding up clusters of electric lights concealed in bronze roses. In the saloon, the grill, or the more sedate dining room, you'll see and hear the Olivier of yesterday and tomorrow.

Copacabana, 180 Earl's Court Rd., S.W.5 (tel. 373-3407), is a cellar disco with palms and cane furnishings. A smoke machine over the dance floor creates eerie effects.

Gateways, 239 Kings Rd., S.W.3 (tel. 352-0118), is for women only who gather to play darts, dominos, and card games. On three nights a week there's disco dancing.

Among pubs which cater to gays are **Boltons** and the **Coleherne** on Old Brompton Road, S.W.5. The already-previewed **Salisbury,** 90 St. Martin's

Lane, W.C.2 (tel. 836-5863), not only seats a theatrical rendezvous crowd, but is also a gay meeting place.

A new monthly magazine, called *Him*, is available at some newsagents in London or direct from **Zipper,** 283 Camden High St., W.1, costing £1 ($1.75). The magazine contains a lot of information on useful places to go in the homosexual world and people to know.

NIGHTCLUBS: The night scene of London changes so rapidly that it's difficult to keep abreast of it. There are several general situations to keep in mind:

First, the English are strongly addicted to jazz, and there are several clubs (dives) where you can fill up on a variety of jazz, whether it be the old-fashioned Louis Armstrong type or progressive. Many a rendezvous for jazz enthusiasts is found in Soho, right off Shaftesbury Avenue. Few are licensed for alcohol, so you'll have to adjust in some cases to soft drinks as you get lost in rhythmic forces.

There are several kinds of nightclubs where you can eat or drink, be entertained or allowed to dance—even gamble. Most often these clubs are private. To avoid the unpopular early closing hour (11 p.m.) for licensed public establishments, the private club has come into existence (many stay open till 3 and 4 a.m.). In most cases, the clubs welcome overseas visitors, granting them a temporary membership with proof of identity and perhaps a nominal charge. Many clubs offer dinner, a show, and dancing. Inquire before you commit yourself. No visitor to London should be afraid to ask about membership in a private club. After all, most of the clubs are in business to make money—and welcome foreign patronage. I'll survey a range—jazz, disco, and gaming clubs —that charge a low membership and a nominal entrance fee, beginning with:

The **Cockney Club,** 18 Charing Cross Rd., W.C.2 (tel. 408-1001), stands right in the heart of the West End, almost within the sound of Bow Bells. At the Cockney, the evening starts with a nip of Mother's Ruin (gin) or Gold Watches (scotch), while the honky-tonk piano turns out sing-along tunes. Then your Jim Skinner (dinner) will include loop (soup) and probably a Lillian Gish (fish), or else a feathered bird for the main dish followed by dessert. Unlimited beer and wines are provided during your meal, and it's finished off with a good old cuppa (tea). Then there's a cheerful, noisy cabaret, some time for dancing, followed by a second cabaret session before the end of the evening at midnight. Cost is £19.95 ($34.91) or you can pay just £15.95 ($27.91) and choose your own drinks at the bar. A £2 ($3.50) supplement is charged on Saturday.

Boulogne, 27 Gerrard St., W.1 (tel. 437-3186), is a supper club that has dancing to live music and serves a three-course dinner for about £15 ($26.25), from Monday through Saturday. If you don't dine, there's a £3 ($5.25) cover charge. The Victorian decor is original and authentic, and dates back to 1852. Soft background music is played from 9 p.m. until dawn at this popular Soho nightspot, and a cabaret is presented nightly at 11 p.m. and 1:30 a.m.

Eve, 189 Regent St., W.1 (tel. 734-0557), is London's longest established late-night club. Doyen of London's nightlife, owner Jimmy O'Brien launched it in 1953. Nude cabaret and erotic entertainment (at 1 a.m.) have replaced the floor shows previously presented. Dancing is to disco, alternating with live music of a high standard. Eve is open Monday to Friday from 10 p.m. to 3:30 a.m. Admittance is by membership only. Entrance is £5 ($8.75) per person, plus a £1 ($1.75) membership. But only one member of your party need join. Overseas visitors may be admitted on application without waiting the customary 48 hours. Charming girls, many of whom speak more than one language, are available as dining or dancing partners for unaccompanied men. A set-price menu is offered for £10.50 ($18.38).

The **London Room** is in the New London Centre at Drury Lane and Parker Street, W.C.2 (tel. 831-8863). This popular nighttime rendezvous is open daily, offering a four-course dinner with a choice of menu. Dancing is to the Johnny Howard band from 9:30 p.m. A spectacular revue, featuring international artists, follows. Monday to Friday the price is £20 ($35), going up to £22 ($38.50) on Saturday.

The Discos

A firmly entrenched London institution, the disco is, nevertheless, as vulnerable as the Stone of Scone. Many of them open, enjoy a quick but fast-fading popularity, then close. Some possible favorites that may still be going strong upon your arrival include the following:

The **Lyceum,** Wellington Street, W.C.2 (tel. 836-3715), was once the Covent Garden Opera House and the Henry Irving Theatre, its origins going back to 1772. One of the great old theaters of London, it reached its 200th birthday in 1972. But it keeps abreast of the times, paying attention to changing musical tastes. Its gilded, flamboyant gingerbread ceiling now shelters disco and punk rock music. Monday through Thursday there's disco, and admission is £2.50 ($4.38). On Friday evening Capital Radio runs the disco, and admission is £2.75 ($4.81). On Saturday nights there are two disc jockeys to enliven the music, and the price of admission, if you come early, is £2.50 ($4.38) rising to £3 ($5.25) after 11 p.m. Sunday is punk rock night—you must make a reservation—and admission is £3 ($5.25) with two live bands for your entertainment.

Samantha's, 3 New Burlington St., W.1 (tel. 734-6249), just off Regent Street, has been one of London's most popular discos and nightspots since it opened some 25 years ago. However, it is very much a club of the '80s, and it has recently acquired a completely new sound and light system and a new D.J. box. Now twice its original size, the club boasts a 30-foot cocktail bar with its own dance floor alongside, as well as Harry's Bar upstairs where you can relax to some quieter music. If electronic games are what you prefer, there's a room full of these to improve your skills. Admission is £4 ($7), and drinks average around £1.30 ($2.28).

La Valbonne Club, 62 Kingly St., off Regent Street, W.1 (tel. 439-7242), is surely one of London's most wildly versatile discos. The decor has changed to a garish mirror and flashing-light extravaganza, an ultramodern fun palace. There is a 100-inch video screen with constant pictures. The dance floor is an eye-catching feature with its multitude of flashing colored lights. Words and sentences are flashed on the walls, and in all this, bodies gyrate on the dance floor to live and disco music with a heavy beat. Admission Monday to Wednesday is £4 ($7) for men and £3 ($5.25) for women. Otherwise, for the rest of the week both men and women pay £5 ($8.75). There are three bars, one quieter than the rest for a bit of relaxation. À la carte meals range in price from £8 ($14) to £12 ($21) for three courses.

The **Marquee,** 90 Wardour St., W.1 (tel. 437-6603), is rightly considered one of the best-known centers for rock music in Europe. Its reputation goes back to the '50s, but it remains forever young, in touch with the sounds of the future. Famous groups, such as the Rolling Stones, played at the Marquee long before their names spread beyond the shores of England. Fortunately, you don't have to be a member—you just pay at the door. If you possess a student I.D. card from any country, it will cost you less to enter. The entrance fees vary, but usually fall in the $3 (U.S.) to $4 range, depending on who's appearing. There's a coffee and Coke bar for light snacks. Those 18 years of age or older can order hard drinks. Importantly, many well-known musicians are known to frequent the place regularly on their nights off. The quite-small and very crowded club is one of the few which features live music. Hours are from 7 to 11 p.m. seven nights a week. Tube: Piccadilly Circus.

Eroticism in Soho

When it comes to taking it off, London is one of the breeziest, barest capitals of Europe. The king of the nudity business, Paul Raymond of the Raymond Revuebar reportedly combs the continent, surveying bosoms in all dimensions, although concentrating mainly on the fair fräuleins of Germany. However, there is plenty of local talent as well, as any quick survey of one of the Soho dives will reveal.

Soho reigns supreme in the nude department, the dives lining whole sides of the streets (many of the strippers work several joints, hustling back and forth between engagements—sometimes doing a little street hustling on the side as well). Wardour, Frith, and Greek Streets are especially strong on disrobing. Some of the cheaper dens are really bleak—far removed from the humor and camp of such nudity emporiums as the Crazy Horse Saloon in Paris. Other, more lavish houses stage spectacular numbers.

Raymond Revuebar Theatre, Walkers Court, Brewer Street W.1 (tel. 734-1593), is a world center of erotic entertainment. The stage show, Festival of Erotica, is presented three times nightly, Monday to Saturday, at 7, 9, and 11 p.m. There are licensed bars, and patrons can take their drinks into the theater. The price of admission is £7.50 ($13.13), and there is no membership fee. Whisky is around £1.75 ($3.06) per large measure.

Jazz

The **100 Club,** 100 Oxford St., W.1 (tel. 636-0933), is a serious contender for the title of London's finest jazz center. The emphasis here is strictly on the music, which begins each evening at 7:30 p.m. and lasts until midnight or later. On Tuesday and Thursday nights, West Indian reggae is presented, but jazz—all kinds of jazz—is performed on the other five nights. The scheduled performers vary every night, so you'll have to phone ahead for that evening's program. However, you're sure to see the cream of jazz at the 100 Club, including such bands as Ken Colyer's All Star Jazzmen, Chris Barker's Jazz Band, and Mr. Acker Bilk and his Paramount Jazz Band. The club's menu features Creole food. There's also a fully licensed bar, serving liquor, wine, and beer. The club no longer requires membership, but imposes a door charge likely to range from £2 ($3.50) to £5 ($8.75), depending on which artist is appearing. Tube: Tottenham Court Road or Oxford Circus.

A much cheaper way to hear jazz is at one of the many pubs in the West End offering it on certain nights of the week. Some charge admission; others allow you to listen for the price of your drink.

Ronnie Scott's, 47 Frith St., W.1 (tel. 439-0747), has long held supremacy as the first citadel of modern jazz in Europe. Featured on almost every bill is an American instrumentalist, plus a top-notch singer (such as Carmen McRae or Blossom Dearie). The best of English and American groups are booked, including such names as Woody Herman and his orchestra. In the heart of Soho, a ten-minute walk from Piccadilly Circus via Shaftesbury Avenue, it's worth an entire evening of your time. You can not only saturate yourself in the best of jazz, but get reasonably priced drinks and dinners as well. There are three separate areas: the Main Room, the Upstairs Room, and the Downstairs Bar. You don't have to be a member, although you can join if you wish. The entrance fee to the main room depends on who's appearing. The average price of admission for nonmembers is £6 ($10.50) Monday to Thursday, rising to £7 ($12.25) on Friday and Saturday. Students with a valid I.D. card pay only half price all evening from Monday through Thursday.

Open Monday to Saturday, 8:30 p.m. to 3 a.m., the Main Room is built like an amphitheater, with tiered tables, providing clear vision and good sound. You can either sit at the bar to watch the show or at the tables. The Downstairs Bar is more intimate—a pine-paneled rustic atmosphere, where you can meet and talk with the faithful habitués, usually some of the world's most talented musicians. The Upstairs Room is separate. It's a disco called The Maze, and is open Monday to Thursday from 8:30 p.m. to 2 a.m., from 8:30 p.m. to 3 a.m. on Friday and Saturday. Tube: Tottenham Court Road.

The **Bull's Head,** Barnes Bridge, S.W. 13 (tel. 876-5241), offers live jazz all week, with musical happenings that sometimes get very lively indeed. The modern jazz is said by many to be the best in town. Weekdays it attracts shoppers and fashion designers to its old English snackbar, which is a fine place to meet for lunch.

Gambling

London was a gambling metropolis long before anyone ever heard of Monte Carlo and when Las Vegas was an anonymous sandpile in the desert. From the Regency period until halfway into the 19th century, Britain was more or less governed by gamblers. Lord Sandwich invented the snack named after him so he wouldn't have to leave the card table for a meal. Prime Minister Fox was so addicted that he frequently went to a cabinet meeting straight from the green baize table.

Queen Victoria's reign changed all that, as usual, by jumping to the other extreme. For more than a century games of chance were so rigorously outlawed that no barmaid dared to keep a dice cup on the counter.

The pendulum swung again in 1960 when the present queen gave her Royal Assent to the new Betting and Gaming Act. According to this legislation, gambling was again permitted in "bona fide clubs" by members and their guests.

Since London's definition of a "club" is as loose as a rusty screw in a cardboard wall, this immediately gave rise to the current situation, which continues to startle, amaze, and bewilder foreign visitors. For the fact is that you come across gambling devices in the most unlikely spots, such as discos, social clubs, and cabaret restaurants. All of which may, by the haziest definition, qualify as "clubs."

The most legitimate gambling clubs offer very pleasant trimmings in the shape of bars and restaurants, but their central theme is unequivocally the flirtation of Lady Luck. There are at least 25 of them in the West End alone, with many scattered through the suburbs. And the contrasts between them are much sharper than you find in the Nevada casinos.

Under the law, casinos are not allowed to advertise, and if they do, they are likely to lose their licenses. Their appearance in a travel guide that doesn't accept advertising is still considered "advertising"—hence I can't recommend specific clubs as in the past.

However, most hall porters can tell you where you can gamble in London. It is not illegal to gamble, just to advertise it. You'll be required to become a member of your chosen club, and must wait 24 hours before you can play the tables, then strictly for cash. The most common games are roulette, blackjack, punto banco, and baccarat. Most casinos, as mentioned, have restaurants where you can expect a good standard of cuisine at a reasonable price.

Spectacles

For good, family-oriented entertainment, the **Beefeater Club** by the Tower of London, Ivory House, St. Katharine's Dock, E.1 (tel. 408-1001), is open nightly from 8 to 11:30 p.m. It presents a medieval-style banquet in the historic vaults beneath the ivory warehouses. Long tables are set in the alcoves beneath the vaulted brick ceilings. Guests are greeted by "King Henry VIII" and his court with a glass of mead. Heralded by a choir of wenches and minstrels, the meal begins. It features Ye Potted Spiced Metes, then "thikke soup," fishes served with Nell Gwynn's sauce, joints of chicken brewed in cider, and finally, Anne Boleyn's baked apple flan, all washed down with unlimited wine and ale, followed by dancing. Tables must be reserved in advance. The cost for this meal is £20 ($35), and you can also enjoy the evening for £16 ($28) by making your own selection of drinks from more standard choices.

Folk Music

The 20th-century troubadour makes his way to a smoke-gets-in-your-eyes candlelit haven called the **Troubadour Coffee House,** 265 Old Brompton Rd., S.W.5 (tel. 370-1434), to sing of the woes of yesteryear. The Troubadour operates in the basement, open to nonmembers. At one time this club was young at heart, a pacesetter in a new kind of unpretentious, natural entertainment. It still offers many happy nights to an attractive young crowd (if you can squeeze in).

You can dine upstairs, again if you can find a seat. From the ceiling hang musical instruments of every shape and size; the walls are covered with unusual trade signs of Victorian era. Prices are quite reasonable: omelets for £1.60 ($2.80); spaghetti bolognese, £1.75 ($3.06); and salads, from £1.40 ($2.45).

A Cultural Complex

In the old **Riverside Studios,** Crisp Road, Hammersmith, W.6, an enterprising young group has developed a complex of theaters and exhibition rooms where, under the directorship of Jenny Stein, unknown and not-so-unknown artists can demonstrate their skills. In the film theater, seasons of movies demonstrate the producer's art or that of the camera person; visiting orchestras and dance teams perform nightly, and in the restaurant there is generally an exhibition of paintings or collages.

The restaurant is open from 11 a.m. to 11 p.m., serving mostly homemade meals. A filling repast will cost about £3 ($5.25). The bar serves real ale among other beverages during licensing hours. Current programs are available throughout London, and the studios are well worth a visit, lying just a five-minute walk from Hammersmith underground station. Telephone the box office at 748-3354. Prices for plays and concerts range from £2 ($3.50) to £6 ($10.50), depending on who's performing. For theater and musical workshops, the charge is only £1 ($1.75) per person.

FOR DANCING: Café de Paris, Coventry Street, off Piccadilly Circus (tel. 437-2036), W.1, is a legend. Once Robert Graves considered it a worthy subject for a book; the Duke of Windsor went there to see Noël Coward perform. Now part of the Mecca chain, it is elaborately decorated with chandeliers. Changing lights set the mood. Two bands alternate every night. Dancing is seven nights a week from 7:30 p.m. to 1 a.m. (later on weekends). Admission charges range from £2.35 ($4.11) to £3.60 ($6.30). There's a reasonable three-course meal offered for £6 ($10.50) to £8 ($14). Cabaret shows, however, are no longer featured. A tea dance is staged seven days a week from 3 to 5:45 p.m. when guests dance to both live and recorded music. At that time admission ranges from £1.70 ($2.98) to £1.90 ($3.33). Tube: Piccadilly Circus.

The biggest and one of the best places to dance in London is the **Empire,** Leicester Square, W.C.1 (tel. 437-1446), which caters to young people 18 to 25 who enjoy dancing to top sounds. The bandstand is a leaping, revolving, and ever-changing spectrum of light. Monday is disco night; otherwise, there is live music for most of the evening. Admission is from £2.50 ($4.38) to £4 ($7).

VAUDEVILLE: This lives on in London on a grand scale.

Palladium, Argyle Street, W.1 (tel. 437-7373). World famed for the best of vaudeville artistry, it is equivalent to the former Palace in New York, which Judy Garland was always singing about. Performers from America, the continent, and Britain can be seen here in acts that sometimes border on the spectacular. Seats range from £3 ($5.25) to £10 ($17.50) for orchestra stalls, but it depends on who's appearing. Prices can't go much higher. Tube: Oxford Circus.

Victoria Palace, Victoria Street, S.W.1 (tel. 834-1317), near Victoria Station, presents comedy, variety, and light entertainment. Seats range in price from £5 ($8.75), going up to £10 ($17.50). Tube: Victoria Station.

OPERA AND BALLET: London's **Royal Opera House** on Bow Street, Covent Garden (tel. 240-1200), provides performances of the highest caliber from September to August each year. It is the home of the Royal Opera and the Royal Ballet companies. The advance box office, 48 Floral St., W.C.2, is open from 10 a.m. to 7:30 p.m. Monday to Saturday, and tickets range in price from £4 ($7) to £19 ($33.25) for ballet and from £7.50 ($13.13) to £44 ($77) for opera. Sixty-five rear amphitheater seats are held for sale on the day of performance and are available, one per person, from 10 a.m., but you may have to queue up well before this for the most popular productions. Tube: Covent Garden.

English National Opera, London Coliseum, St. Martin's Lane, W.C.2, just off Trafalgar Square (box office, tel. 836-3161). The London Coliseum, built in 1904 as a variety theater and converted into an opera house in 1968, is London's largest and most splendid theater. The English National Opera is one of the two national opera companies, and performs a wide range of works, from great classics through operetta to world premières, and every performance is in English. The company has a large and enthusiastic following among young people. Balcony tickets are available for as little as £2.50 ($4.38), but many visitors prefer the Upper Circle or Dress Circle at about £6.50 ($11.38) to £12 ($21). During the opera season (usually from August to May), about 100 cheap seats in the balcony are held for sale on the day of performance, from 10 a.m. In early summer there are short guest seasons at the Coliseum by international ballet companies. Tube: Trafalgar Square.

The **D'Oyly Carte Company** has no permanent home in London or elsewhere. Information can be obtained from the company's office address: Tabard

House, 116 Southwark St., London SE1 OTA (tel. 928-7322). Enthusiasts can patronize the **Gilbert and Sullivan Pub,** John Adam Street, W.C.2, at **Grim's Dyke Country Hotel,** Old Redding, Harrow Weald, Middlesex (tel. 954-7666). Concerts are presented the first and third Sunday every month. For £14.50 ($25.38) you hear not only an operetta, but get a substantial three-course meal.

The **Barbican Centre,** The Barbican, E.C.2, is newly built and considered the largest art and exhibition center in Western Europe. It was created to make a perfect setting in which to enjoy good music and theater from comfortable, roomy seating.

The theater is now the home of the Royal Shakespeare Company who, of course, perform a wide range of works other than plays of the Bard. The Concert Hall is the permanent home of the London Symphony Orchestra and host to visiting performers.

There are often lunchtime concerts where the admission is £2.50 ($4.38) for the 45 minutes or so. Otherwise, seats are priced from £2.80 ($4.90) to £9 ($15.75) for evening performances. Matinees in the theater start at £1.75 ($3.06), going upward to £7 ($12.25). In the evening low-cost seats are still featured, although the best seats are likely to go for £9 ($15.75).

There are a number of bars and a self-service café and wine bar open from 9 a.m. to 10:30 p.m. Monday to Saturday and from noon to 10:30 p.m. on Sunday. Called the Waterside Café, it has views over the artificial lake. In good weather patrons can sit on the terrace in the open air.

The main restaurant, the Cut Above, also overlooks the lake, a more formal place with a Carvery open from noon to 3 p.m. and from 6 p.m. until the last orders are taken half an hour after the end of the performance. The cost of a meal where you can carve as much as you want from the succulent joints of meat is £10 ($17.50). Table reservations can be made by telephoning 588-3008.

The following numbers will be useful—628-8795 for the box office for seats for concerts and theatrical performances; 928-9760 for 24-hour information on performance of concerts; and 628-2295 for information about theatrical performances. Tube: Barbican.

CONCERTS: There are at least five major orchestras performing in London. They are: the London Philharmonic, the Royal Philharmonic, the BBC, the London Symphony, and the New Philharmonia.

These orchestras are to be heard mainly in the **Royal Festival Hall,** while in the adjoining **Queen Elizabeth Hall** and **Purcell Room** there are concerts of chamber music and lieder recitals, among other presentations. In all, roughly 100 events take place each month in these three concert halls. Tube to Waterloo Station. Tickets are available from the Royal Festival Hall box office (tel. 928-3191; credit card bookings, 928-6544), or the usual booking agents. They range in price from £1.50 ($2.63) to £8 ($14).

Royal Albert Hall, Kensington Gore, S.W.7 (tel. 589-8212). Acoustic improvements and other alterations have made this one of the world's finest auditoriums. The BBC Promenade Concerts are held here for eight weeks in summer. Throughout the year there are performances by top orchestras and artists, brass bands, and all manner of events ranging from covered court lawn tennis to the annual Royal British Legion Festival of Remembrance. Ticket prices vary according to the type of event.

Wigmore Hall, 36 Wigmore St., W.1 (tel. 935-2141). At this intimate auditorium, you'll hear excellent recitals and concerts. There are regular series, master concerts by chamber music groups and instrumentalists, song recital series, and concerts featuring special composers or themes throughout the year. In summer, Wigmore Summer Nights and Sunday morning concerts are featured. Many good seats are in the £2.20 ($3.85) range. A free list of the month's concerts is available from the hall. Tube: Bond Street and Oxford Circus.

City of Westminster Arts Council, Marylebone Library, Marylebone Road, N.W.1, sponsors concerts, recitals, and exhibitions throughout the year. These are held in small, often little-known halls around the city. For current information, refer to the address above. The average entrance charge is only £1.75 ($3.06), and some promotions, such as exhibitions, are free. In most cases, payment is at the door, and no advance reservations are necessary.

4. Taking the Tours

In addition to the sites you can see in London by foot, or by utilizing the underground, there are numerous attractions that can be reached via several coach tours. As an added bonus, there are dozens of fascinating trips that can be made on the Thames.

LONDON'S WEST END AND THE CITY: If you prefer a more detailed look at the city's sights, **London Transport** offers highly regarded guided tours.

For a look at the West End, a three-hour tour is featured, passing Westminster Abbey (guided tour), the Houses of Parliament, Trafalgar Square, and Piccadilly Circus. A visit to the Changing of the Guard at Buckingham Palace or the Horse Guards Parade is also included. The cost is £6 ($10.50) for adults and £4 ($7) for children under 14.

London Transport's other popular three-hour tour is of the City, including guided trips to the Tower of London and St. Paul's Cathedral. The fare for this one is £8 ($14) for adults and £5 ($8.75) for children under 14, including admission charges.

The tours leave from the Wilton Road Coach Station, close to Victoria Railway Station, at 10 a.m. and 2 p.m., respectively. Departures are daily except Sunday. There is a connecting bus service from Euston Bus Station one hour before departure for those who are staying in the Russell Square area.

To reserve seats, go to the London Transport Travel Information Centres at: St. James's Park, Piccadilly Circus, Kings Cross, Euston, Oxford Circus, Victoria, or the Heathrow Central tube stations. Reservations cannot be made over the phone.

Between their unguided round London tour and the more intensive guided tours, London Transport also has a two-hour, guided, nonstop tour, leaving from the Wilton Road Coach Station at 10 a.m., 1 p.m., and 3 p.m., costing £3.50 ($6.13) for adults and £2 ($3.50) for children under 14. The double-decker bus makes the rounds of the most celebrated landmarks, with a guide relating the history of the buildings as you pass.

BUS TOURS: Both **Back Street London** and the **Vintage Bus Service** are operated by Obsolete Fleet, 17 Air St., W.1 (tel. 437-8225), on behalf of London Transport. These tours use real vintage London buses dating from the 1920s and also an open-top bus which runs into the back streets of London—hence its name. One tour runs from Baker Street (corner of Allsop Place), heading for Hampstead. It costs £1 ($1.75) for adults and 50p (88¢) for children. This tour, lasting about 50 minutes and covering 11 miles, departs daily at 11:30 a.m., and 2, 3:30, and 5 p.m. You can also book a round trip for about twice the price. The Vintage Bus stops at most regular London Transport stops between Aldwich and Oxford Circus (look for the red 100 plate). A return fare is 70p ($1.23).

BOAT CRUISES ON THE THAMES: Some travelers might be interested in water tours of London. Touring boats operate in profusion on the Thames between April and September, with curtailed winter schedules, taking you various places within London, and also to nearby towns along the Thames.

Main embarkation points are Westminster Pier, Charing Cross Pier, and Tower Hill Pier, a system that enables you to take a "water taxi" to the Tower of London and Westminster Abbey. Not only are the boats energy-saving, bringing you painlessly to your destination, but they permit you to sit back in comfort as you see London from the river's point of view.

A number of companies operate these boats, which vary from large launches to smaller speedboats. Many have service every 20 minutes from 10:20 a.m. until dusk. Because of tides, however, no exact schedule is given; you must simply go to the pier and take your chance. But the wait is usually short.

The multitude of small companies operating boat services from Westminster Pier have organized themselves into the **Westminster Passenger Service Association,** Westminster Pier, Victoria Embankment, S.W.1 (tel. 930-4097). Boats leave the pier for cruises of varying length throughout the day and evening. A selection follows.

There is regular service from Westminster Pier to the Tower of London, the most popular ride, leaving every 20 minutes, April to October from 10:20 a.m. to 5 p.m. In winter the service is slightly curtailed. Boats continue from the Tower to Greenwich during the same period. From Westminster to the Tower costs £1 ($1.75) one way, £1.50 ($2.63) round trip. Children pay 80p ($1.40) for a single trip, £1.10 ($1.93) round trip.

London Launches Ltd. runs a twice-daily, 2½- to 3-hour tour downstream past the Tower to H.M.S. *Belfast,* Greenwich, and the Naval College, across the Meridian Line to the Thames Flood Barrier and back. The barrier is the largest movable flood barrier in the world, and the British are rather proud of it. The cruise is operated by *Zodiac,* a traditional London water bus. The skipper, Bill, keeps up an informal commentary during the journey, or you can wander below decks to sample pub food. Cost of the cruise is £2.65 ($4.64) for adults and £1.35 ($2.36) for children. Departures are usually at 10 a.m. and 1:30 p.m., but you should check as exceptional traffic on the river and other events may necessitate the cancellation of a departure or amendment to departure time.

Upstream service to Kew (Botanical Gardens), Richmond, and Hampton Court (the palace) are less frequent. You can generally get a boat every 30 minutes to Kew, and the trip takes 1½ hours. There are usually three sailings to Richmond (2½ hours) and Hampton Court (3 to 5 hours). You should telephone **Westminster Pier** (tel. 930-2062) for upstream service, as this is a novel and pleasant way to visit Hampton Court. You can always return by bus or train.

Evening departures also operate. You can take either a two-hour trip past the floodlit buildings of the West End and the City, or else a floodlit supper cruise, operated from May to October, lasting 1½ hours and including a cold supper. Adults pay £7.50 ($13.13); children, £5 ($8.75). They also operate a river-ride disco—noisy and popular on Friday and Saturday evenings at 7 or 8 p.m. The cost is £6.95 ($12.16), including a hot supper. If you can break away from the revelry and the beat down below, you can always use the observation decks to view the sights of the city.

There are traditional Sunday lunch tours and other-day-of-the week luncheon cruises. Among the latter, lunchtime cruises leave on Wednesday, Saturday, and Sunday from Westminster Pier, costing about £9 ($15.75). Ask for the Catamaran Cruisers if you telephone for information and reservations.

From Tower Pier (tel. 488-0344), the *Sir Thomas More* is a late-model luxury passenger motor cruiser, with panoramic viewing in good comfort. The trip features the history of the Thames in multiple-screen video with commentary by TV personalities. There are three sailings daily, costing £3.50 ($6.13) in the morning, including coffee; £8 ($14) at midday, including lunch; and £10 ($17.50) in the evening, including dinner. Children under 13 enjoy a discount price of £1 ($1.75).

Jenny Wren Canal Cruises, 250 Camden High St., N.W.1 (tel. 485-4433), will take you for a 1¼-hour trip along Regent's Park Canal past the zoo. The cost is £1.10 ($1.93) for adults, 65p ($1.14) for children. On Friday and Saturday there is a mystery cruise with a refreshment stop at a suitable hostelry which costs £3 ($5.25) per person. Reservations are essential.

London Transport also runs an afternoon tour to Richmond, where you embark on a river steamer for the journey up the Thames past Ham House to Hampton Court. After a guided tour of the state apartments, you return to London by coach. Departure is from Wilton Road Station on Thursday and Sunday at 1:30 p.m. The return is shortly before 6 p.m. The cost is £9 ($15.75) for adults and £6 ($10.50) for children under 14, including the boat and admissions.

London Transport's evening tour of the city and the river by night departs on Thursday at 7 p.m. from Wilton Road. First you're taken on a short drive around the sights, including St. Paul's, the Tower of London, Buckingham Palace, and Trafalgar Square. Then you go for a leisurely cruise on the river, with a buffet and wine served on board. The return to Westminster Pier is approximately at 10:30 p.m. The cost, including the boat ride and the meal, is £13.50 ($23.63). Reservations for these and other tours operated by London Transport can be made at any of their travel information centers.

A CANAL BOAT IN LITTLE VENICE: When you get tired of fighting the London traffic, you might want to come here and take a peaceful trip (1½ hours) aboard the traditionally painted Narrow Boat *Jason* and her butty boat *Serpens.* Come for lunch along the most colorful part of the Regent's Canal in the heart of London. The boat is moored in Blomfield Road, just off Edgware Road in Maida Vale. Little Venice is the junction of two canals and was given its name by Lord Byron.

To inquire about bookings, including the Boatman's Basket Luncheon Trip, get in touch with **Jason's Trip,** Opp. No. 60 Blomfield Road, Little Venice, W.9 (tel. 286-3428). Advance booking is essential during high season. If you come by tube, take the Bakerloo Line to Warwick Avenue. Face the church, turn left, and walk up Clifton Villas to the end and turn right (about two minutes). If you arrive early, you can browse around the shop which sells many brightly colored traditionally painted canal wares.

On the trip you'll pass through the long Maida Hill tunnel under Edgware Road, through Regent's Park, the Mosque, the Zoo, Lord Snowdon's Aviary, past the Pirate's Castle to Camden Lock and return to Little Venice. The season begins on Easter weekend and lasts through to the middle of October. During April and May, the boats run at 12:30 and 4:30 p.m. In June, July, and August, they run at 10:30 a.m. and at 12:30, 2:30, and 4:30 p.m. During September and October, trips leave at 12:30 and 2:30 p.m., but always telephone first. Refreshments are served on all trips, including a prebooked boatman's basket lunch on the 12:30 and 2:30 p.m. trips. The fare for a day trip is £1.95 ($3.41) for adults and 85p ($1.49) for children.

CITY WALKS: **J. W. Travel,** 66 St. Michael's St., W.2 (tel. 262-9572). John Wittich, who owns J. W. Travel, started walking tours of London in 1960. He is a Freeman of the City of London and a member of two livery companies as well as having written six books on London walks. He is also director of the London History Fellowship. There is no better way to search out the unusual, the beautiful, and the historic, than to take a walking tour. The walks are conducted by guides who really know their business, and you don't need an advance booking. Tours take place whatever the weather. The cost is £1 ($1.75) for adults, 50p (88¢) for students with identification cards, and free to children with adults. Some of the titles of the organized tours are "Wren's Churches," "Jack the Ripper," "Soho," and "Sherlock Holmes."

Hunt for ghosts or walk in the steps of Jack the Ripper, the infamous East End murderer of prostitutes in the 1880s. Discover the relics of Roman and Tudor London. Investigate the London of Dickens, Shakespeare, and Sherlock Holmes, or taste the delights of an evening's drinking in four historic pubs. These and many other walks (Roman London; 1660s: Great Plague and Great Fire; Legal and Illegal London—Inns of Court) are included in the program of unusual and historical walks organized by **London Walks,** 139 Conway Rd., Southgate, London N14 7BH (tel. 882-2763). Walks take place on weekends all through the year and during the week throughout the summer. The cost is £1.50 ($2.63) for adults; children under 16 go free. No booking is required. Get in touch with the above address for details. Send an International Reply Coupon.

Another small and enthusiastic company offering a vast variety of London walks is **Discovering London.** It's operated by a Scot, Alex Cobban, a historian of some note who insists that his guides are knowledgeable and sympathetic and who, perhaps, looks at the London which the Londoners take for granted. He is aided by Mrs. Cobban, also a highly qualified guide. Mainly on Sunday, but during the week as well, scheduled walks are planned, starting at easily found underground stations—to the London Dickens Knew, Finding Roman London, Inns of Court—Lawyers' London, Belgravia "Upstairs and Downstairs," Ghost, and Jack the Ripper tours, some 50 different titles. Mr. Cobban's knowledge of Sherlock Holmes is immense. No advance booking is necessary for most tours, and the walks cost £1.40 ($2.45); children under 16 go free, and students with I.D. cards are charged £1.20 ($2.10). Each walk takes about 1½ to 2 hours. A selection of tours of museums, galleries, Westminster Abbey, St. Paul's, and Kensington Palace is also offered. Write, enclosing an International Reply Coupon, for a detailed sheet of the walks available during your stay in London. The address is Discovering London, 11 Pennyfields, Warley, Brentwood, Essex CM14 5JP (tel. Brentwood 0277/213704).

Londoner Pub Walks set out every Friday evening from the Temple underground station at 7:30 p.m. to discover places full of interest and history. By exploring away from the more regular tourist areas, the walks offer a chance to meet the local people and to discover what it is that makes the English pub a unique institution. Reservations are not necessary, but further details may be secured from Peter Westbrook, 3 Springfield Ave., London, N.10 (tel. 883-2656). The charge is £1.75 ($3.06), and you buy your own drinks.

Guided London Outings and **Hidden London Tours** operate from 102 Newgate St., E.C.1 (tel. 405-6191). After working for many years of life in

London as a newspaper seller, John Dreamer now conducts three-hour tours, including visits to unusual and interesting houses and buildings, at a cost of £5 ($8.75) per person.

Citisights, 12 Alpha Pl., S.W. 3 (tel. 600-3699, ext. 281), is connected to the Museum of London. From those precincts, Paul Herbert works and conducts archeological walks daily, except Monday. Call during office hours only.

TOURS FOR CHILDREN: **Junior Jaunts,** 4A William St., S.W.1 (tel. 235-4750), is a responsible organization which will take children between the ages of 5 and 15 off your hands for the entire day. The service provides tours for parties of no more than six children at a time to various points of interest in London. The small number of each group assures you that your child will be carefully supervised and that his or her interests will be taken into consideration. Tours range from a visit to the Regent's Park Zoo to a trip to Buckingham Palace or the Tower of London to a museum tour which includes no less than six popular museums in London to choose from. Tours are flexible, and suggestions from the children are often incorporated into the activities. Tours are arranged from 10 a.m. to 4 p.m., and children are collected. Telephone for prices, as they vary, according to what your offspring wants to do. However, tariffs average around £15 ($26.25) for each child, including meals.

5. Day Trips from London

It would be sad to leave England without ever having ventured into her countryside, at least for a day. The English are the greatest excursion travelers in the world, forever dipping into their own rural areas to discover ancient abbeys, 17th-century village lanes, shady woods for picnic lunches, and stately mansions. From London, it's possible to avail yourself of countless tours—either by conducted coach, boat, or via a do-it-yourself method on bus or train. On many trips, you can combine two or more methods of transportation; for example, you can go to Windsor by boat and return by coach or train.

For some of the most interesting day trips from London, refer to the "home counties" chapter coming up.

DO-IT-YOURSELF: Many hidden sightseeing surprises are in store for the adventurous traveler who doesn't depend on guides and scheduled routes. And this is possible even if you don't rent a car. You can branch out in all directions, either extending a visit or cutting it short if fatigue sets in. Several means of transportation are available: coach, train, or boat.

Highly recommended are the previously described Green Line Coaches, operated by London Country Bus Service. You can go to the Green Line Enquiry Office at Victoria (Eccleston Bridge) and pick up Green Line timetables giving specific details on routes.

For longer tours—say, to Stratford-upon-Avon—you will probably find the trains much more convenient, or at least more comfortable. Often you can take advantage of the many bargain tickets outlined in Chapter 1. For further information about rail transportation to a specific location that you're interested in, go to the British Rail offices at Lower Regent Street, off Piccadilly, S.W.1.

LONDON TRANSPORT TOURS: The official bus company, London Transport (tel. 222-1234), takes the lead in guided tours to the places of interest in and around London. The tours are accompanied by an experienced guide,

TOURIST AREAS
N
Hadrian's Wall
NEWCASTLE
NORTH SEA
Lake District
Yorkshire Dales & Moors
YORK
ISLE OF MAN
HULL
IRISH SEA
Sherwood Forest
LIVERPOOL
Peak District
ANGLESEY
ENGLAND
COVENTRY
Cambridge
East Anglia
STRATFORD UPON AVON
WALES
HARWICH
Wye Valley
& Forest of Dean
Cotswolds
Oxford
Chilterns
Windsor Castle
LONDON
THAMES
RIVER
CARDIFF
BRISTOL
Thames Valley
Stonehenge
DOVER
RYE
FOLKESTONE
South Downs
SOUTHAMPTON
New Forest
BRIGHTON
NEWHAVEN
West Country
ISLE OF WIGHT
Dartmoor
PLYMOUTH
ENGLISH CHANNEL
SCILLY ISLES

and they start from Wilton Road Coach Station, Victoria. It is necessary to reserve seats; this is done at the London Transport Travel Information Centres at St. James's Park, Piccadilly Circus, Oxford Circus, Victoria, Heathrow Central, Kings Cross, and Euston tube stations.

An outstanding tour is offered to **Windsor Castle and Hampton Court Palace,** a day's adventure that also includes Runnymede and the Kennedy Memorial. Adults pay £15 ($26.25); children, £10 ($17.50). Rates include lunch and all admission charges.

THE BRITAINSHRINKERS: This is a bonanza for travelers who want to make several quickie trips into the heart of England, without having to check out of their hotel room in London. Scheduled full-day tours are operated by Road 'n' Rail Tours Ltd. in cooperation with British Rail. You're whisked out of London by train to your destination, where you hop on a waiting bus to visit the various sights during the day. You have a light lunch in a local pub, and there is also free time to shop or explore. A guide accompanies the tour from London and back to London. Your return is in time for dinner or the theater. Included in the rates are entrance fees and VAT.

For more information, telephone 589-0156. It's possible to call this number, even on weekends, providing you do so before 4:30 p.m.

On one-day trips you can visit such places as: Bath and Stonehenge; Warwick Castle, Stratford-upon-Avon, and Coventry Cathedral; Canterbury and Dover; Wales; York, Oxford, and the Cotswolds; Cambridge and Ely Cathedral; Brighton; or Devon for an average cost of £27 ($47.25) for adults and £16 ($28) for children under 16. There are also overnight trips to Scotland at a cost of £107.50 ($188.13) for adults and £71.60 ($125.30) for children. All the above tours have large discounts for holders of validated BritRail passes.

It's better to write Britainshrinkers, 22 Hans Place, London, S.W.1, than to get in touch with British Rail.

THE TOURIST CIRCUIT: If you have only a limited number of days to spend in England, I suggest the following trips: (1) Windsor Castle and Hampton Court, (2) Stratford-upon-Avon and Warwick Castle, (3) Oxford and the Cotswold villages, (4) Cambridge and East Anglia, and (5) the cathedral city of Canterbury and the old Cinque port of Rye on the Sussex coast.

HAMPTON COURT: On the Thames, 13 miles west of London, this 16th-century palace of Cardinal Wolsey can teach us a lesson. Don't try to outdo your boss, particularly if he happens to be Henry VIII. The rich cardinal did just that. But the king had a lean and hungry eye. Wolsey, who eventually lost his fortune, power, and prestige, ended up giving his lavish palace to the Tudor monarch. In a stroke of one upsmanship, Henry took over, outdoing the Wolsey embellishments. The Tudor additions included the Anne Boleyn gateway, with its 16th-century astronomical clock that even tells the high-water mark at London Bridge. From Clock Court, you can see one of Henry's major contributions, the aptly named Great Hall, with its hammer-beam ceiling.

Hampton Court had quite a retinue to feed. Cooking was done in the Great Kitchen, which may be visited. Henry cavorted through the various apartments with his wives of the moment, everybody from Anne Boleyn to Catherine Parr (the latter reversed things and lived to bury her erstwhile spouse). Charles I was imprisoned at one time, and temporarily managed to escape his jailers.

Although the palace enjoyed prestige and pomp in Elizabethan days, it owes much of its present look to William and Mary of Orange, or rather to Sir Christopher Wren. You can parade through the apartments, filled as they are with porcelain, furniture, paintings, and tapestries. The King's Dressing Room is graced with some of the best art, including Pieter Brueghel the Elder's macabre *Massacre of the Innocents.* Tintoretto and Titian deck the halls of the King's Drawing Room. Finally, be sure to inspect the Royal Chapel (Wolsey wouldn't recognize it). To confound yourself totally, you may want to get lost in the serpentine shrubbery Maze in the garden.

The State Apartments may be visited year round—April to September, weekdays from 9:30 a.m. to 6 p.m., on Sunday from 11 a.m. to 6 p.m.; October to March, weekdays from 9:30 a.m. to 5 p.m., on Sunday from 2 to 5 p.m. The admission is £1.80 ($3.15) for adults, 90p ($1.58) for children under 16. The off-season admission is 90p ($1.58) for adults, 50p (88¢) for children. There is an extra charge for admission to any special exhibition held at the palace.

Frequent trains run from Waterloo to Hampton Court Station. To come by boat, apply to Thames Passenger Services, Westminster Pier, S.W.1 (tel. 930-0921). Or take bus 201, 206, 216, or 264 weekdays; 267 on Saturday and Sunday only. Green Line coaches 716, 716A, and 718 will deliver you to Hampton Court in about half an hour from London.

KEW GARDENS: Nine miles southwest of central London at Kew, near Richmond, are the **Royal Botanic Gardens,** among the best known in Europe, containing thousands of varieties of plants. But Kew is no mere pleasure garden—rather, it is a vast scientific undertaking that happens to be beautiful. A pagoda, erected in 1761, represents the flowering of chinoiserie. One of the oddities of Kew is a Douglas fir flagstaff more than 220 feet high. The Palm House, built in the heyday of Victoria by Decimus Burton, is replete with torrid temperatures and cannibalistic-looking vegetation, a sort of south of Pago Pago setting.

Much interest focuses on the red-brick **Kew Palace** (dubbed the Dutch House), a former residence of King George III and Queen Charlotte. It is reached by walking to the northern tip of the Broad Walk. Now a museum, it was built in 1631 and contains memorabilia of the reign of George III, along with a royal collection of furniture and paintings. It is open only from April to October, 11 a.m. to 5:30 p.m. daily (Sunday from 2 to 6 p.m.). Admission is 60p ($1.05) for adults, 30p (53¢) for children. Kew Gardens is open daily from 10 a.m. until 4 or 8 p.m., according to the time of year. The museum opens at 10 a.m., the glass houses from 11 a.m., to closing time. Admission is only 10p (18¢). Closed Christmas Day, New Year's Day, and May bank holiday.

At the gardens, **Queen Charlotte's Cottage** has been restored to its original splendor. Built in 1772, it is half-timbered and thatched. George III is believed to have been the architect. The house has been restored in great detail, including the original Hogarth prints which hung on the downstairs walls. The cottage is open from mid-April to mid-October from 11 a.m. to 5:30 p.m. on Saturday, Sunday, and bank holiday Mondays. Admission is 30p (53¢) for adults and 15p (26¢) for children. The least expensive and most convenient way to visit the gardens is to take the District Line subway to Kew. The most romantic way to come in summer is via a steamer from Westminster Bridge to Kew Pier.

RICHMOND: Want to spend an afternoon in a river town on the Thames? Richmond is only a 30-minute ride from London, and can be easily reached by one of the underground trains (or else Green Line Coach 716 or 716a from Hyde Park Corner). But if you're feeling lighthearted, you can take a boat trip down the Thames. Turner himself came here for inspiration.

Richmond is only one mile from Kew with its botanical gardens. You may prefer a combined excursion to Kew Gardens and Richmond on the same day. One of the attractions of the Thames town is the 2500-acre **Richmond Park,** first staked out by Charles I in 1637. It is filled with photogenic deer and waterfowl. Richmond has long enjoyed associations with royalty: Henry VII's Richmond Palace stood there, and an even earlier manor was razed. Queen Elizabeth I died in the old palace in 1603. However, somebody's short-sighted thinking led to having the palace carted away (only a carriageway remains).

If you want to be like the English, you'll climb **Richmond Hill** for a view of the Thames, considered by some to be one of the ten best views in the world. The scene reminded William Byrd of a similar view near his home on the James River in Virginia, inspiring him to name the new city founded there in 1737—Richmond. As you scale the hill, you'll see a rising art colony, with several galleries exhibiting the work of local painters, potters, and sculptors.

A HALF-DAY IN GREENWICH: Greenwich Mean Time, of course, is the basis of standard time throughout most of the world, the zero point used in the reckoning of terrestrial longitudes since 1884. But Greenwich is also the home of the Royal Naval College, the National Maritime Museum, and the Old Royal Observatory. In drydock at Greenwich Pier is the clipper *Cutty Sark,* as well as Sir Francis Chichester's *Gipsy Moth IV.*

About four miles from "The City," Greenwich is reached by a number of methods, and part of the fun of making the jaunt is in the getting there. Ideally, you'll arrive by boat, as Henry VIII preferred to do on one of his hunting expeditions. In summer, launches leave at regular intervals from either the Charing Cross or Westminster Piers.

Actually, Westminster Pier is preferred because the boats from Charing Cross are usually filled with tour-group passengers. In addition, you can take the underground to New Cross, then bus 171a or 177. Buses 70 and 188 run from Surrey Docks underground station. The boats leave daily for Greenwich every 20 minutes from 10 a.m. to 7 p.m., costing only £3.20 ($5.60) for a round-trip ticket. The one-way fare is £1.80 ($3.15). Children pay half price.

Unquestionably, the *Cutty Sark*—last of the great clippers—holds the most interest, having been seen by millions. At the spot where the vessel is now berthed stood the Ship Inn of the 19th century (Victorians came here for whitebait dinners, as they did to the Trafalgar Tavern). Ordered built by Capt. Jock Willis ("Old White Hat"), the clipper was launched in 1869 to sail the China tea trade route. It was named after the Witch Nannie in Robert Burns's *Tam o'Shanter* (note the figurehead). Yielding to the more efficient steamers, the *Cutty Sark* later was converted to a wool-clipper, plying the route between Australia and England. Before her retirement, she knew many owners, even different names, eventually coming to drydock at Cutty Sark Gardens, Greenwich Pier, S.E.10, in 1954. For 80p ($1.40) for adults, 40p (70¢) for children, the vessel may be boarded weekdays from 11 a.m. to 6 p.m., on Sunday from 2:30 to 6 p.m. It closes at 5 p.m. in winter.

A neighbor to the *Cutty Sark*—and also in drydock—is Sir Francis Chichester's *Gipsy Moth IV,* in which he circumnavigated the world in 1967. He single-handedly fought the elements in his vessel for 119 days. For 20p (35¢)

for adults and 10p (18¢) for children, you can go aboard (same hours as *Cutty Sark*). It's usually closed Friday.

The **Royal Naval College** grew up on the site of the Tudor palace in which Henry VIII and Elizabeth I were born. William and Mary commissioned Wren to design the present buildings in 1695 to house naval pensioners, and these became the Royal Naval College in 1873. The buildings are a baroque masterpiece, in which the Painted Hall, by Thornhill (1708–1727) and the chapel are outstanding. Charging no admission, it is open to the public every day, except Thursday and Christmas, from 2:30 p.m. until 5 p.m.

The **National Maritime Museum,** built around Inigo Jones's 17th-century Palladian Queen's House, portrays Britain's maritime heritage. Actual craft, marine paintings, ship models, and scientific instruments are displayed, including the full-dress uniform coat that Lord Nelson wore at the Battle of Trafalgar. Other curiosities include the chronometer (or sea watch) used by Captain Cook when he made his Pacific explorations in the 1770s. The museum is open from 10 a.m. to 6 p.m. in summer and from 10 a.m. to 5 p.m. in winter (Saturday from 10 a.m. to 6 p.m.; Sunday from 2 to 5:30 p.m. in summer and from 2 to 5 p.m. in winter). Admission is free. Just off the Navigation Room, in the west wing, is a licensed restaurant.

Where to Eat and Drink

The **Cutty Sark Free House,** Ballast Quay, Lassell Street, S.E.10 (tel. 858-3146), has plenty of local color on its Thames-side perch. About half a mile from the railway station, this English riverside tavern will dispense drinks in an atmosphere in which you can eavesdrop on the conversation of oldtime salts (head to the second floor for the Captain's Bar). At lunch and dinner, traditional English fare, such as whitebait suppers and roast beef, is featured, costing around £5.50 ($9.63). Service is available until 11 p.m.

SYON PARK: Just nine miles from Piccadilly Circus, on 55 acres of the Duke of Northumberland's Thames-side estate, is one of the most beautiful spots in all of Great Britain. There's always something in bloom. Called "The Showplace of the Nation in a Great English Garden," Syon Park was opened to the public in 1968. A nation of green-thumbed gardens is dazzled here, and the park is also educational, showing amateurs how to get the most out of their small gardens. The vast flower- and plant-studded acreage betrays the influence of "Capability" Brown, who laid out the grounds in the 18th century.

Particular highlights include a six-acre rose garden and the Great Conservatory, one of the earliest and most famous buildings of its type, housing everything from cacti to fuchsias. In it is also housed a walk-through aviary full of exotic and brilliantly colored birds. In the old dairy you will find an interesting seawater aquarium. There is a quarter-mile-long ornamental lake studded with waterlilies and silhouetted by cypresses and willows, even a huge gardening supermarket, and the British Leyland Car Museum.

Operated by the Gardening Center Limited, Syon was the site of the first botanical garden in England, created by the father of English botany, Dr. William Turner. Trees include a 200-year-old Chinese juniper, an Afghan ash, an Indian bean tree, and a "Liquidambar." The gardens are open all the year (except for Christmas and Boxing Day). The gates open at 10 a.m. and close at dusk or 6 p.m. In winter, after October 31, gates close at 4 p.m. Admission is 75p ($1.31) for adults, 40p (70¢) for children.

On the grounds is **Syon House,** built in 1547, the original structure incorporated into the Duke of Northumberland's present home. The house was later remade to the specifications of the first Duke of Northumberland in 1766. The battlemented facade is that of the original Tudor mansion, but the interior is from the 18th century, the design of Robert Adam. Basil Taylor said of the interior feeling: "You're almost in the middle of a jewel box." In the Middle Ages, Syon was a monastery, later suppressed by Henry VIII. Katharine Howard, the king's fifth wife, was imprisoned in the house before her scheduled beheading in 1542. The house is open Easter until the end of September, daily except Friday and Saturday from noon to 5 p.m.

If you want to visit the house as well as the park, ask for the combined ticket, costing £1.30 ($2.28) for adults and 65p ($1.14) for children. For more information, telephone 560-0881.

THORPE PARK: This is a 400-acre site built around four lakes in old gravel pits. A "theme" park, it lies 20 miles west of London and can be reached by train from Waterloo Station to Staines and by London suburban bus from Victoria Station. Lying on highway A320 between Chertsey and Staines, it charges adults an admission of $4 (U.S.); children under 14 pay $2. One area of the park includes scenes from British history, with full-size replicas of Roman and Viking ships built at the same Devonshire shipyard which produced a replica of Sir Francis Drake's *Golden Hinde.* Other scenes include a Stone Age cave, a Norman Motte and Bailey Castle (the type used by William the Conqueror), and King John's Pavilion at the signing of Magna Carta. There's an entire section devoted to detailed reconstructions of World War I aircraft and the race-winning craft which took part in the Schneider Trophy Races for aircraft between 1913 and 1931.

SHIRE HORSE CENTRE: At Maidenhead in Berkshire, this center (tel. 5957/3917) is run by Courage, one of the breweries which used horses to deliver all their beer and ale in London. The Shire Horse Centre is a glimpse into a world which has almost ceased to exist. Just off the A4 at Maidenhead (take the M4 from London to Exit 8/9), the stables are constructed in the traditional style. There is a display of harnesses, with genuine horse brasses and prize rosettes won by the stables' inmates. Besides being an exhibition, the center breeds shire horses, and each spring there are foals to interest the visitor as well as the massive feathered-footed giants. It is open daily except Monday from 11 a.m. to 5 p.m. From November to February it is closed. The price of a ticket is £1.50 ($2.63) for adults, 75p ($1.31) for children. There are toilets but no restaurant, so go to the **Courage Shire Horse Inn** in Littlewick Green for a drink and a pub lunch.

A DAY AT THE RACES: Within easy reach of central London, there are horse-racing tracks at Kempton Park, Sandown Park, and the most famous of all, Epsom, where the Derby is the main feature of the summer meeting. Entrance to the courses for a day's racing can be as little as £1.50 ($2.63), but of course you pay more for a seat in a grandstand or on one of the most prestigious race days. Racing isn't conducted every weekend, so you should telephone United Racecourses at Epsom (tel. 03727/26311) for information of the next meeting. You can drive yourself, or if you want to travel by rail, call 01/928-5100 for details of train services.

Chapter V

WINDSOR, OXFORD, AND THE HOME COUNTIES

1. Windsor
2. Oxford
3. Hertfordshire
4. Buckinghamshire
5. Bedfordshire

WITHIN EASY REACH of London, the Thames Valley and the Chilterns are a history-rich part of London, and they lie so close to the capital they can be easily reached by automobile or Green Line coach. You can explore here during the day and return in time to see a show in the West End.

Here are some of the most-visited historic sites in England: the former homes of Disraeli and Elizabeth I, the estate of the Duke of Bedford, and, of course, Windsor Castle, 22 miles from London, one of the most famous castles in Europe and the most popular day trip for those visitors venturing out of London for the first time.

Of course, your principal reason for coming to Oxfordshire, our second goal, is to explore the university city of Oxford, about an hour's drive from London. But Oxford is not the only attraction in the county, as you'll soon discover as you make your way through Henley-on-Thames. The shire is a land of great mansions, old churches of widely varying architectural styles, and rolling farmland.

In a sense, Oxfordshire is a kind of buffer zone between the easy living in the southern towns and the industrialized cities of the heartland. In the southeast are the chalky Chilterns, and in the west you'll be moving toward the wool towns of the Cotswolds. In fact, Burford, an unspoiled medieval town, lying west of Oxford, is one of the traditional gateways of the Cotswolds (dealt with in a later chapter). The Upper Thames winds its way across the southern parts of the county.

The "Home Counties" are characterized by their river valleys and gentle hills. The beech-clad Chiltern Hills are at their most beautiful in spring and fall. This 40-mile chalk ridge extends in an arc from the Thames Valley to the old Roman city of St. Albans in Hertfordshire. The whole region is popular for boating holidays, as it contains a 200-mile network of canals.

1. Windsor

If you hop aboard a 701 or 704 Green Line Coach at Victoria Station, you'll be delivered in little more than an hour and a quarter to Windsor, site of England's greatest castle and its most famous boys' school.

You can also take an express nonstop bus (no. 700). The one-way fare is £1.70 ($2.98). However, a round-trip ticket can be purchased if you board the bus after 9 a.m. at a cost of £2.10 ($3.68). There is a Green Line bus which runs between London, Victoria, Hampton Court, and Windsor—useful if you want to visit Hampton Court as well. This fare will total £2.90 ($5.08); children pay half price.

THE SIGHTS: Your bus will drop you near the Town Guildhall, to which Wren applied the finishing touches. It's only a short walk up Castle Hill to the following sights:

Windsor Castle

It was William the Conqueror who founded a castle on this spot, beginning a legend and a link with English sovereignty that has known many vicissitudes. King John cooled his heels at Windsor while waiting to put his signature on Magna Carta at nearby Runnymede: Charles I was imprisoned here before losing his head; Queen Bess did some renovations; Victoria mourned her beloved Albert; who died at the castle in 1861; the royal family rode out much of World War II behind its sheltering walls. When Queen Elizabeth II and her entourage are at Windsor, the Royal Standard flies, which means the State Apartments are off-limits then. Otherwise, they may be visited weekdays from 10:30 a.m. to 5 p.m. from May to October, 10:30 a.m. to 3 p.m. from November to March. The price of admission is £1.20 ($2.10) for adults, 50p (88¢) for children. The apartments are closed for about six weeks at Easter and for around three weeks in June when the Queen and Prince Philip come here for the Ascot Races. The apartments contain many works of art, porcelain, armor, furniture, three Verro ceilings, and several Gibbons carvings from the 17th century. The world of Rubens adorns the King's Drawing Room and in his relatively small dressing room is a Dürer, along with Rembrandt's portrait of his mother, and Van Dyck's triple look at Charles I. Of the apartments, the grand reception room, with its Gobelin tapestries, is the most spectacular.

The castle precincts are open daily except June 13 between 10 a.m. and 4 p.m., charging no admission. The Changing of the Guard in many ways is more attractive than the London ceremony at Buckingham Palace. The castle backdrop lends itself to photographs, and you're able to get closer to the ceremony. The guard marches up through the town past Sir Christopher Wren's lovely Guildhall and into the castle for the ceremony daily at 11 a.m. The only time the routine is changed is when there is a state visit at Windsor or a special service in the chapel.

The Tourist Information Office in the Central Station opposite the castle can tell you of the few occasions when there will be no ceremony (tel. 07535/52010).

Old Master Drawings

The royal family possesses a rare collection at Windsor of drawings by old masters, notably Leonardo da Vinci. One Leonardo sketch, for example, shows a cat in 20 different positions; another is a study of a horse; still a third is that of Saint Matthew, a warmup for the head used in *The Last Supper.* In addition, you'll find sketches by William Blake, Thomas Rowlandson, and 12 Holbeins (don't miss his sketch of Sir John Godsalve). The drawing exhibition may be visited at the same time as the State Apartments for an admission of 50p (88¢) for adults and 20p (35¢) for children. It remains open, unlike the State Apartments, when the Court is in residence.

Queen Mary's Dollhouse

Just about the greatest dollhouse in all the world is at Windsor. Presented to the late Queen Mary as a gift, and later used to raise money for charity, the dollhouse is a remarkable achievement and re-creation of what a great royal mansion of the 1920s looked like, complete with a fleet of cars, including a Rolls-Royce. The house is perfect for Tom Thumb and family, and a retinue of servants. All is done with the most exacting detail—even the champagne bottles in the wine cellar contain vintage wine of that era. There's a toothbrush suitable for an ant. A minuscule electric iron really works. For late-night reading, you'll find volumes ranging from Hardy to Housman. In addition, you'll see a collection of dolls presented to the monarchy from nearly every nation of the Commonwealth. The Dollhouse may be viewed for an admission of 50p (88¢) for adults, 20p (35¢) for children, even when the State Apartments are closed.

St. George's Chapel

A gem of the Perpendicular style, this chapel shares the distinction with Westminster Abbey of being a pantheon of English monarchs (Victoria is a notable exception). The present St. George's was founded in the late 14th century by Edward IV near the site of the original Chapel of the Order of the Garter (Edward III, 1348). You enter the nave first with its fan vaulting (a remarkable achievement in English architecture). The nave contains the tomb of George V and Queen Mary, designed by Sir William Reid Dick. Off the nave in the Urswick Chapel, the Princess Charlotte memorial provides an ironic touch. If she had survived childbirth in 1817, she—and not her cousin, Victoria—would have ruled the British Empire. The Edward IV "Quire," with its imaginatively carved 15th-century choir stalls (crowned by lacy canopies and colorful Knights of the Garter banners), evokes the pomp and pageantry of medieval days. In the center is a flat tomb, containing the vault of the beheaded Charles I, along with Henry VIII and one of his wives (no. 3, Jane Seymour). Finally, you may want to inspect the Prince Albert Memorial Chapel, reflecting the opulent taste of the era of Victoria. The chapel is open Monday to Thursday, and Saturday, from 10:45 a.m. to 4 p.m. in summer, from 11 a.m. to 3:45 p.m. in winter. On Friday it is open from noon to 4 p.m. all year. Sunday hours are from 2 to 4 p.m. in summer, from 2:15 to 3:45 p.m. in winter. Closed in January, the chapel charges an admission of £1 ($1.75) for adults and 50p (88¢) for children 5 to 15 years of age. It's best to telephone Windsor 65538 in case of unexpected closings.

Footnote: Queen Victoria died on January 22, 1901, and was buried beside her beloved Prince Albert in a mausoleum at **Frogmore** (a private estate), near Windsor (open only three days a year, in May). The Prince Consort died in December 1861.

Royal Mews Exhibition

Entered from St. Albans Street, the red-brick buildings of the Royal Mews and Burford House were built for Nell Gwynne in the 1670s. They were named for King Charles II's natural son by her, the Earl of Burford. When the child was 14 years old, he was created Duke of St. Albans, from which the street outside takes its name. The exhibition contains large pictures of the queen, along with the Duke of Edinburgh driving his horses through a water splash in the Great Park, and other members of the royal family riding and driving.

There is a collection of state harness, much of it in regular use, along with other riding and driving bits, including the regimental ceremonial bridle of the Tenth Hussars. Three stalls are lined with straw as in former times and contain model horses to illustrate stable kit harness and riding tackle. Photographs show the various stages of training which the young horses go through before taking part in ceremonials. In the coach house is a magnificent display of coaches and carriages in mint condition and in constant use. In the souvenir shop, books, postcards, and small trinkets are on sale.

The exhibition is open from the end of October to the end of March from 10:30 a.m. to 3 p.m., Monday to Saturday. From April to October, it is open from 10:30 a.m. to 5 p.m., Monday to Saturday. However, from May 1 until the end of August, it is also open on Sunday from 10:30 a.m. to 4 p.m. Admission is 50p (88¢) for adults and 20p (35¢) for children.

Royalty and Railways

The famous company founded by Madame Tussaud in 1802 has taken over part of the Windsor Town railway station to present an exhibition of "Sixty Glorious Years of Victorian history." It's at the **Station Master's House** on Thames Street (tel. 07535/57837). At one of the station platforms is a replica of *The Queen,* the engine used to draw the royal coaches disembarking the life-size wax figures of guests arriving at Windsor for the Jubilee celebration. In one of the carriages, the Day Saloon, are Queen Victoria (in wax, of course) and her family. In the anteroom is her faithful Indian servant, Hafiz Abdul Karim, the Munshi. Among the famous guests portrayed are the Prince and Princess of Wales (Edward VII and Alexandra), the Empress Frederick of Prussia (Queen Victoria's eldest daughter), and the prime minister, Lord Salisbury.

The platform is busy with loyal servants, a flower seller and a newsboy, an Italian with a barrel organ, along with others who have come to see the arrival of the train. Drawn up in the courtyard are the troops of the Coldstream Guards and the horse-drawn carriage which will take the party to the castle.

With the sounds of military music in the background and the commands of the officers to their troops, you really feel you are present in the courtyard yourself at Her Majesty, Queen Victoria's arrival.

Afterward, at the end of the walkway through the Victorian Conservatory, you reach the 260-seat theater for a short audio-visual presentation, with life-size animated models giving further glimpses of life during Victoria's reign. The whole visit will only take 45 minutes and is certainly an opportunity for anyone with Victorian English ancestry to see. It is open daily except Christmas from 9:30 a.m. to 5:30 p.m., charging adults £1.85 ($3.24) for admission and children £1 ($1.75).

By the way, do say hello as you pass the train to Mr. Edwin Mutter, whose job it is constantly to clean and polish the royal train. He is the "alive" one, and like the men who paint the Golden Gate Bridge, he goes up one side and down the other.

Sunday Entertainment

There are often polo matches in **Windsor Great Park**—and at Ham Common—and you can often see Prince Charles playing and Prince Philip serving as umpire. The Queen herself often watches. For more information, telephone 07535/60633.

Also, at the gates into the park are maps showing attractive paths for walking. You can circumnavigate Royal Lodge and walk through the Deer Park before enjoying a pint at one of the pubs outside the park (there's a pub at almost every gate!).

The Town Itself

Windsor is largely a Victorian town, with lots of brick buildings and a few remnants of Georgian architecture. In and around the castle are two cobblestoned streets—**Church and Market Streets**—with their antique shops, silversmiths, and pubs. One shop on Church Street is supposed to have been occupied by Nell Gwynne (she needed to be within beck and call of the king's private chambers). Church is also a good street on which to find low-cost tearoom luncheons. After lunch or tea, you may want to stroll along the three-mile, aptly named Long Walk.

Round Windsor Sightseeing Tour

A 35-minute tour of Windsor and the surrounding countryside is offered in an open-top, double-decker bus with commentary. The ten-mile drive starts from Windsor Castle and passes the Royal Mews, the Long Walk, the Royal Farms, Albert Bridge, Eton College, and the Theatre Royal. The departure point is Castle Hill, near the King Henry VIII Gateway to Windsor Castle. Adults pay £1 ($1.75); senior citizens, 80p ($1.40); and children, 50p (88¢). The senior citizen ticket is not valid on weekends, holidays, and in August. Tickets, along with information about dates of operation and departure times, are available from **Windsorian Coaches,** 17 Alma Rd. (tel. 07535/56841).

Guided Tours

Every day except Sunday a guided tour of Windsor Castle and the town leaves from the **Tourist Information Centre** in the Central Station, the one opposite the castle. The walking tour includes a look at the Long Walk, then the Guildhall and Market Cross House, along with the changing of the guard when possible. In the castle precincts you'll visit St. George's Chapel, the Cloisters, and the Albert Memorial Chapel, finishing in the State Apartments. Subject to demand, the tour leaves at 10:15 a.m., costing adults £3 ($5.25) and children £1.50 ($2.63) for two hours. A one-hour tour is priced at £1.50 ($2.63) for adults and 75p ($1.31) for children. There are further departures during the day if demand merits it. All tours are accompanied by a licensed guide and include inside visits when possible.

Boat Trips on the Thames

From an embarkation point on the Promenade, at Barry Avenue, there are regular boat departures for 35-minute trips up to Boveney Lock. You pass the Windsor Horse Racecourse and cruise past Eton College's boathouses and the Brocas Meadows. On the return, you'll have one of the most perfect views of Windsor Castle to be captured by the camera's lens. The cost is 90p ($1.58) for adults, 45p (79¢) for children. However, you can also take a two-hour trip through Boveney Lock and up past stately private riverside homes, the Bray Film Studios, Queens Eyot, and Monkey Island at a cost of £2 ($3.50) for adults, £1 ($1.75) for children. The boats carry light refreshments and have a licensed bar. There are toilets on board, and the decks are covered in case of that unexpected shower, although your view of the river will be unimpaired.

WHERE TO EAT: The **William IV Hotel,** Thames Street, 100 yards from Eton Bridge (tel. 07535/51004), a lovely old place (circa 1500) with its armor, beams, and log fire, invites visitors in with its friendly and local atmosphere. Just outside is the Chapter garden where the Windsor martyrs were burned at the stake in 1544 for their religious beliefs. It was from this inn that they received their last cups of strong ale "in gratification of their last wish." The house built by Sir Christopher Wren for his own use is opposite the William IV, and the great architect of St. Paul's was reputedly a regular visitor to the old tap room, as were diarists Evelyn and Pepys. The present landlord is Ken Gardner, award-winning journalist and writer, and his son Guy. Rub shoulders here with newspapermen and actors (nearby is the Theatre Royal), artists and river folk, and drink traditional ale which is still pulled by old-fashioned beer engines. Food is home-cooked, and the portions are guaranteed to satisfy gargantuan appetites. Scottish beef is served by two motherly locals, Lottie and Gert, who are quick and accurate. Try a steak or one of the house regional specialties. At the bar, a lunch—perhaps liver, bacon, and a vegetable—goes for £2 ($3.50). At the restaurant in back, a three-course meal costs from £5.50 ($9.63). You can sit at a sidewalk table in a pedestrian area by the Eton Bridge, gazing up at the castle while enjoying your lunch. They have three rooms to rent, all twins with wash basins. A large breakfast is your reward after an early-morning jog along the Thames. Room, including breakfast, is £20 ($35) for two persons. The William IV lies at the bottom of Windsor Hill on the approach road to the bridge, which is now open to pedestrians only.

Country Kitchen, 3 King Edwards Court, Peascod Street (tel. 07535/68681). Walk from the castle gateway down Peascod Street to King Edwards Court for a good, home-cooked, whole-food meal in this light, airy, self-service restaurant above the shops. They make their own scones, tea bread, flans, cheesecake, and dessert. The soups, pâtés, and quiches are homemade, and only good vegetable oils, honey, lemon juice, herbs, and spices are used in the preparation of the main dishes. There's always a vegetarian dish, along with some low-fat, low-calorie ones. Choose your own salad from the ten different, freshly made concoctions at 95p ($1.66) or else pick one as a side dish at 25p (44¢). Hot dishes include chicken curry, lasagne, and chili con carne, and you can choose from the display of scrumptious desserts, including passion cake. They offer five different teas and herbs—decaffeinated if you wish—and fine house wines by the carafe or glass. You can eat here for around £4 ($7), plus the cost of your drink. They are open for morning coffee, lunch, tea, and an early evening meal in summer.

Crumbs, 43 St. Leonards Rd. (tel. 07535/58421), just around the corner from the Clarence Hotel, is a simple place, serving from 9 a.m. to 10 p.m. daily. Mr. Bhardwaj's sole purpose in life seems to be to feed and water as many people as he can. He willingly produces another pot of tea or another plate of chips. The menu starts the day with various breakfasts, including "The Big Fry" at £1.95 ($3.41). At lunch you might select one of the hamburgers with various toppings, including melted cheese at £1.85 ($3.24). Besides all this, there is a long menu of main dishes, including such standard English fare as roast chicken, mixed grills, and fried fish. Perhaps you'll try instead one of his special curries, such as chicken or keema at £2.15 ($3.76).

The **Drury House Restaurant,** 4 Church St. (tel. 07535/63734). The very British owner states with pride that all luncheons served in this wood-paneled 17th-century restaurant, dating from the days of Charles II, are home cooked "and very English." A visit here could be included in a tour of Windsor Castle, as the entrance to the restaurant is only a stone's throw apart. A typical meal could include soup followed by either roast beef and Yorkshire pudding or homemade steak-and-kidney pie, both served with vegetables and followed by a dessert such as apple pie. All this, and a dash of English history too, comes to about £4.30 ($7.53) per person. Owner Joan Hearne also serves a refreshing tea, including either homemade scones with jam and freshly whipped cream, or freshly made cream cakes, both offered with copious quantities of the obligatory tea, for £1.20 ($2.10). Drury House is open Tuesday through Sunday only from noon till 5:30 p.m.

London Steak House, 10 Thames St. (tel. 07535/66437), is a good choice following your visit to Windsor Castle. For its grills, it offers prime beef from Scotland, and there is also a selection of fish. The best value, however, is the fixed-price menu. For about £7 ($12.25) you can order an appetizer such as pâté maison, followed by a main course—perhaps beef Strogonoff—then seasonal vegetables or salads made to your choice, along with a choice of potatoes, climaxed by a dessert from the trolley and coffee. VAT is included but you must pay 12% extra for service. A reasonably priced wine list is also presented on back of the menu. The restaurant is open for lunch from Monday to Saturday from noon to 3 p.m. and from 6 to 11 p.m. On Sunday it serves lunch from 12:30 to 3 p.m. and dinner from 6:30 to 10:30 p.m.

WHERE TO STAY: The **Tourist Information Centre,** Central Station (tel. 07535/52010), is located in the railway station at the top of the hill opposite the castle. Here you can book a bed ahead if you're touring or else find an accommodation in and around Windsor. This is a very useful service, as many of the local guest houses have no signs. In summer only, there is also an Information Kiosk down by the river promenade.

The **Riverbank Holiday Cottages,** Clewer Court Road, in Windsor, are right down by the river on a Wind-in-the-Willowy backwater. This is a collection of modern, comfortable, and well-furnished holiday cottages. Cottages contain a large living room, phone, color TV, and a private terrace with a view across the grass to Millstream Island. Beyond the willows, you can see the Thames. Each unit has a well-equipped kitchen, bath, and two double bedrooms, the package renting for about £100 ($175) a week for four guests. The cottages are fully furnished, and all you need to do is provide your own food. They share the use of the island with a summer house and barbecue, and there are rowing dinghies available free to the more adventurous tenants. Car rentals can be arranged, and this is an ideal base from which to visit London each day.

For reservations, write to Windsor Boats, Clewer Boathouse, Mill Lane, Windsor S14 5JII (tel. 07535/62933). A deposit of 20% is required to secure a cottage. The staff will supply, upon request, groceries and other goods so you can just walk into your home away from home and take up from there. Cottages are not really suitable for families with children, and are designed more for adults who want a relaxing holiday on the river.

Clarence Hotel, Clarence Road (tel. 07535/64436). Two old town houses were joined to form this spotless, warm hotel with a snug lounge and color TV, along with a licensed bar. An English breakfast is provided in the room rate, and in the evening snack meals are served only to residents. You'll get chicken à la king, spaghetti bolognese, fish and chips, or pizza. Most dishes cost around £1.80 ($3.15). The place is managed by Joyce Lynch, who will willingly suggest other eating places in town or direct you to the castle, six minutes away. She tries to solve what other problems you may have. A double room is £8.25 ($14.14) per person, a single renting for £10.50 ($18.38). For a room with a private shower and toilet, you pay an extra 75p ($1.31) per person. VAT, an English breakfast, and service are included.

The **Christopher Hotel,** High Street in Eton (tel. 07535/52359), is across the river from Windsor town. It has 20 double and family rooms. At one time this was a noted coaching inn, and the stable around the courtyard has been converted into modern chalet bedrooms, superbly fitted with shower room, color TV, radio, pay phone, trouser press, refrigerator, hair dryer, and all the ingredients for a self-catered continental breakfast. A traditional English breakfast is also available in the hotel. There are bar snacks or restaurant facilities at lunchtime or a good dinner in the evening for around £9 ($15.75). The cost of a room is from £27 ($47.25) for two persons. The Christopher is only a five-minute walk from Windsor Riverside Railway Station with a service to Central London.

READERS' ACCOMMODATION SELECTIONS: "I stayed at the best B&B house in all my experience of this type of accommodation. It was at 86 Bulkeley Ave. (tel. 07535/63184), run by Mrs. Farrell. The rooms are delightfully bright and the food excellent. There are twin-bedded rooms at £8.50 ($14.88) per person and a double room with private bath at £10.50 ($18.38) per person. Mrs. Farrell is a lovely woman who lived in North America for 20 years, so she knows the likes and dislikes of people from there. The house is close to the Green Line bus service, and during the summer months a special express bus has been put on, no. 700, which takes you to London in 50 minutes" (Mrs. J. Roberts, Tiburon, Calif.). . . . "You can make reservations through the tourist agency office in the railroad station. We were fortunate to find accommodations in the home of **Mr. and Mrs. Allsopp,** 62 Clarence Rd. (tel. 07535/62640). It is a very well-kept, attractive house. At night when we came in cold and tired, we requested and were served a hot pot of tea in the comfortable, cozy parlor where a color TV was available. The next morning we were served a good, full breakfast. Mrs. Allsopp was kind enough to make porridge especially for us. The price is about £9 ($15.75) per person" (Mr. and Mrs. Sid Muskin, Sapulveda, Calif.).

"A short walk from the castle is the guest house of **Ms. P. B. E. Roberts,** 57 Alma Rd. (tel. 07535/66154). The accommodations are simple, homey, and comfortable, and a full English breakfast is served. The real find is Ms. Roberts herself, a gracious, caring individual with a good knowledge of Windsor and the surroundings. I found her to be one of Windsor's greatest attractions. From the town's main intersection, a block from the castle entrance, at Clarence Road, you follow that road a few blocks to its intersection with Alma road. Mrs. Roberts charges £7.50 ($13.13) per person for B&B" (Susan Magnuson, Minneapolis, Minn.). . . . "I stayed at the **Avarest Guest House,** run by Mrs. Sampson, at 74 Clarence Rd. (tel. 07535/60597), about a 15-minute walk from the castle. Singles rent for £9 ($15.75)" (Ray LaFever, Arlington, Va.). . . . "We found a very nice accommodation with **Mrs. Bowerbank,** a charming young woman, at 154 Arthur Rd. (tel. 07535/77742). The rooms are pleasant, the bath and toilet facilities good. A full English breakfast is served. The rate is £8.50 ($14.88) per person" (Mrs. K. L. Kiser, Trenton, N.J.).

ETON: For our final sight, from Windsor Castle we must cross over a bridge spanning the Thames:

Eton College

Largest and best known of the public (private) schools of England, Eton College was founded by a teenage boy himself, Henry VI in 1440. Some of England's greatest men, notably the Duke of Wellington, have played on the fields of Eton. Twenty prime ministers were educated at Eton, as well as such literary figures as George Orwell and Aldous Huxley. Even Ian Fleming, creator of James Bond, attended. The traditions of the school have had plenty of time to become firmly entrenched (ask a young gentleman in his Victorian black tails to explain the difference between a "wet bob" and a "dry bob"). For an admission fee of 50p (88¢) for adults, 20p (35¢) for children, or 30p (53¢) for students, the School Yard and Cloisters may be visited daily, 2 to 5 p.m., throughout the year, and also from 10:30 a.m. to 2 p.m. on school holidays, including most of July and all of August. There are also one-hour guided tours daily at 2:15 and 3:15 p.m., conducted by an upper former in the traditional black tails and pinstripe pants. You get to tour areas not permitted to the general admission payers. Tours cost 80p ($1.40) for adults, 70p ($1.23) for students, and include admission. If it's open, take a look at the Perpendicular chapel, with its 15th-century paintings and reconstructed fan vaulting.

Bernard Weinraub wrote, "Eton, the Gothic school on the Thames that has symbolized starched exclusiveness, is quietly lifting its cloak of privilege." In the future, along with the sons of diplomats and prime ministers, boys from poorer families will also be educated there, the tuition funded by scholarships. All of this represents the movement in England toward a classless society. One man put it this way, "The lifestyle of the young cuts across all classes—they're wearing the same clothes, listening to the same music, engaging in the same activities." However, the administration (at the moment) doesn't plan to go coed.

Life here is spartan. One travel agent made arrangements for a summer school, using the accommodations occupied at termtime by the boys of Eton. But he had to find an alternative, as the rooms required tougher occupants than the summer scholars.

For Meals

Eton Wine Bar, High Street (tel. 07535/54921), is owned and run by William and Michael Gilbey of the Gilbey's gin family, although no gin is served here. Just across the bridge from Windsor, it is a charming place set among the antique shops with pinewood tables and old church pews and chairs. There is a small garden out back. Hours are weekdays from 11:30 a.m. to 3 p.m. and from 6 to 11 p.m.; on Friday and Saturday, from 11:30 a.m. to 3 p.m. and from 6 to 11:30 p.m. Appetizers include borscht and a cheese-and-onion quiche. They also serve baked chicken with rosemary, Cornish smoked mackerel, cold roast beef, and salad. Each day a special dish is featured, and desserts include pineapple and almond flan and damson crunch. A meal of two courses will cost about £4 ($7), the price going up to £6 ($10.50) for roast beef with an appetizer and dessert. Wine can be had by the glass for 85p ($1.49).

Eton Buttery, 73 High St. (tel. 07535/54479), is just on the Eton side of the bridge from Windsor, a new building among the boathouses of the college with magnificent views over the river and up toward the town and castle. Open seven days a week from 9:30 a.m. to 10:30 p.m., it is decorated with plain red brick walls, brown carpets and tables, caneback chairs, and a mass of potted plants. This is an up-market self-service buffet owned by Doreen Stanton, owner of the House on the Bridge restaurant, opposite.

A traditional English Sunday lunch is served at the **House on the Bridge,** Eton (tel. 07535/60914). While the everyday operation of the House on the Bridge is beyond the price range of this guide, the Sunday luncheon deserves a mention. After a morning of sightseeing, relax at one of the tables overlooking the river and enjoy a choice of an appetizer, then roast Scottish sirloin of beef with Yorkshire pudding and horseradish sauce, or roast leg of lamb with mint sauce, along with buttered carrots and seasonal vegetables. Dessert is made from a sweet trolley or else you can order cheese and crackers before your coffee. The cost is £10.50 ($18.38) per person, plus service.

Food is well displayed along spotless counters. There are waitresses to clear away and to bring you wine and drinks; otherwise you help yourself to a variety of quiches, cold sliced meats, and specialty salads and pâtés. There is also a hot dish of the day. A meal will cost about £4 ($7), including a glass of wine.

NEARBY SIGHTS: Attractions of interest are in the surrounding area.

One of England's Great Gardens

The **Savill Garden,** Wick Lane, Englefield Green (tel. Windsor 60222), is in Windsor Great Park and clearly signposted from Windsor, Egham, and Ascot. Started in 1932, the garden is now considered one of the finest of its type in the northern hemisphere. The display starts in spring with rhododendrons, camellias, and daffodils beneath the trees; then throughout the summer there are spectacular displays of flowers and shrubs all skillfully presented in a natural and wild state. It is open March to October from 10 a.m. to 6 or 7 p.m., and the admission is £1.20 ($2.10) for adults, free for children. Salads, hot dishes, and sandwiches are available, a snack costing around £2.50 ($4.38), a meal going for about £5 ($8.75).

Adjoining the Savill Garden are the **Valley Gardens,** full of shrubs and trees in a series of wooded natural valleys running down to Virginia water. It is open daily, free, throughout the year.

Windsor Safari Park and Seaworld

In the safari craze sweeping the world, even the Royal Borough of Windsor hasn't been spared. The Safari Park and Seaworld, Winkfield Road (tel. 07535/69841), is open just two miles from Windsor Castle on a site 23 miles from London. There you can watch the performing dolphins and a killer whale, and drive through reserves of lions, tigers, baboons, giraffes, camels, and many other wild animals. It is open every day (except Christmas Day) from 10 a.m. There are catering facilities, but you can picnic on acres of green. If you have a soft-top car or come on public transport from Windsor, take the free safari bus through the reserve. Admission to Safari Park is £3.50 ($6.13) for adults, £3 ($5.25) for children 4 to 14. Seaworld and the parrot show and amusements are free. The charge is per occupant of a car.

Mapledurham House

The Elizabethan mansion home of the Blount family lies beside the river in the unspoiled village of Mapledurham, which can be reached by car from the A4074 Oxford to Reading road. A much more romantic way of reaching the old house is to take the boat, leaving the Promenade next to Caversham Bridge at 2:15 p.m. on Saturday, Sunday, and bank holidays from Easter to the end of September. The journey upstream takes about 40 minutes, and the boat leaves Mapledurham again at 5 p.m. for the journey back to Caversham.

This gives you plenty of time to walk through the house, viewing the Elizabethan ceilings and great oak staircase. You'll see portraits of the two beautiful sisters with whom the poet Alexander Pope, himself a frequent visitor, was in love. The family chapel, built in 1789, is a fine example of "modern Gothick."

Cream teas with homemade cakes are available at the house, and on the grounds is the last working watermill on the Thames. It still produces flour—100% whole-meal flour which can be purchased. The house is open from 2:30 to 5 p.m. on Saturday, Sunday, and public holidays from Easter Sunday until the end of September. The mill is open from noon on the same days in summer and in winter on Sunday from 2 to 4 p.m. Entrance to both the house and mill is £2.10 ($3.68) for adults and £1.10 ($1.93) for children. To visit only the mill costs adults 70p ($1.23) and children 40p (70¢). The boat ride from Caversham costs £1.50 ($2.63) for adults and 85p ($1.49) for children. Further details of the boat ride and others operated from Caversham Bridge can be obtained by getting in touch with **D & T Scenics Ltd.**, Mapledurham Village, Reading, RG4 7TR (tel. Reading 724123).

If you'd like to make an interesting day trip in Berkshire, I'd suggest the following:

THE WELLINGTON DUCAL ESTATE: **Stratfield Saye** (tel. Basingstoke 882882) lies between the A4 and the A30, just west of the city of Reading. It has been the home of the Dukes of Wellington since 1817 when the 17th-century house was bought for the "Iron Duke" to celebrate his victory over Napoleon at the Battle of Waterloo. Many memories of the first duke remain in the house, including his billiard table, battle spoils, and pictures. Recently, the funeral carriage which since 1860 had rested in St. Paul's Cathedral crypt was added to the ducal collection.

In the gardens is the grave of Copenhagen, the charger ridden to battle at Waterloo by the first duke. The lovely plain stone face of the house looks over a country park, with its lake, woods, and meadows.

There is a fascinating National Dairy Museum, with relics of 150 years of dairying. Other attractions include a riding school, nature trails, boating, and sailing on the lake. On summer weekends a miniature railway goes through the parklands.

The estate is open daily from March until the end of October from 10 a.m. to 5:30 p.m., charging an admission of £1.90 ($3.33) for adults and 95p ($1.66) for children. There are refreshments available, and plenty of parking space.

READERS' SIGHTSEEING TIP: "About midway between London and Oxford lies the model village of **Beaconscot.** With miniature towns, trees, mountains, a golf course, and operating model trains, it makes a welcome break for children who have seen enough full-size historic buildings. Take exit 2 off the M40 motorway and then head west along the A40 into the town of Beaconsfield. At the large rotary, turn right, and the village is about one mile further on, past the British Rail station" (Peter, Susan, and Eric Wildman, Lexington, Mass.). *Author's Note:* For information, telephone 04946/2919. Beaconscot is open April to October from Monday to Friday, 10 a.m. to 5 p.m. On Saturday, Sunday, and bank holidays, it is open from 10 a.m. to 5:30 p.m. Off-season it still opens at 10 a.m., but shuts down at dusk. Admission is 85p ($1.49) for adults and 40p (70¢) for children.

HENLEY-ON-THAMES: At the eastern edge of Oxfordshire, only 35 miles from London, Henley-on-Thames is a small town and resort on the river at the foothills of the Chilterns. It is the headquarters of the Royal Regatta held annually in July, the number one event among European oarsmen. The regatta dates back to the first years of the reign of Victoria.

The Elizabethan buildings, the tearooms, and the inns along its High Street live up to one's conception of what an English country town looks like—or should look like. Cardinal Wolsey is said to have ordered the building of the tower of the Perpendicular and Decorated parish church.

Life here is serene, and Henley-on-Thames makes for an excellent stopover en route to Oxford. However, readers on the most limited of budgets will find far less expensive lodgings in Oxford. The fashionable inns of Henley-on-Thames (Charles I slept here) are far from cheap. Warning: During the Royal Regatta rooms are difficult to secure, unless you've made reservations months in advance.

Thamesmead Private Hotel, Remenham Lane (tel. 04912/4745), is a Tudoresque and Victorian-style house, built of red brick with black and white timbers. Surrounding it is a pretty garden and hedge. This gem is owned by former London publican and his wife, Mr. and Mrs. R. G. Thompson, who bring a fresh approach to the hotel business. The rate is £12.50 ($21.88) per person nightly for B&B. A simple continental breakfast is served in your bedroom, as there is no dining room or guest lounge. They have furnished the rooms with many modern pieces, interspersed with antiques and interesting objects. Call or write early for space. A wing has been built in style sympathetic to the spirit of the house, and there's a parking area.

Sydney House Hotel, Northfield End (tel. 04912/3412), is a 16th-century inn at the edge of town, yet within walking distance of the center and the river. Simon Hamlin, the owner, has put his energies into making the hotel and restaurant attractive, without spoiling their original beauty. The bedrooms have been successfully updated with modern comforts. He asks £15 ($26.25) in a single and £25 ($43.75) in a double, including a full English breakfast and VAT. He has done a fine job with his brick-walled dining room and drinking lounge. You'll find Windsor chairs and some other English period pieces. A set dinner with several choices is offered for £10 ($17.50). On one recent occasion, I had a creamy onion soup with coriander, beef wrapped in olive leaves (served with fresh vegetables), and a dessert of raspberry mousse, followed by coffee. Don't expect bellboys and lots of uniformed maids. Mr. Hamlin runs a personal, friendly hotel.

From Henley on Thames it is only a 24-mile drive to Oxford.

2. Oxford

A walk down the long sweep of The High, one of the most striking streets in England; a mug of cider in one of the old student pubs; the sound of a May Day dawn when choristers sing in Latin from Magdalen Tower; the Great Tom bell from Tom Tower, whose 101 peals traditionally signal the closing of the college gates; towers and spires rising majestically; the barges on the upper reaches of the Thames; nude swimming at Parson's Pleasure; the roar of a cannon launching the bumping races; a tiny, dusty bookstall where you can pick up a valuable first edition. All that is Oxford—57 miles from London and home of one of the greatest universities in the world. An industrial city, the center of a large automobile business, as well as a university town, Oxford is better for sightseeing in summer. The students are wherever Oxford scholars

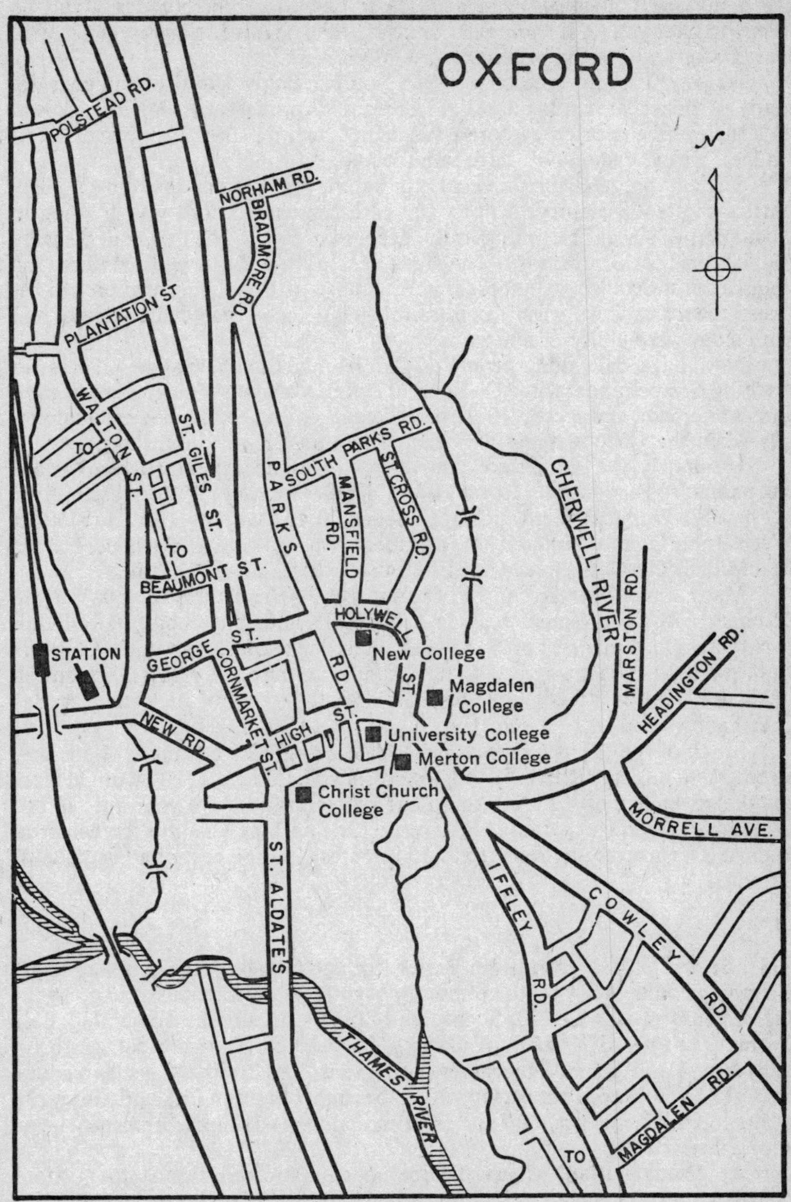
OXFORD
N
POLSTEAD RD.
NORHAM RD.
BRADMORE RD.
PLANTATION ST
WALTON ST.
TO
ST. GILES ST.
SOUTH PARKS RD.
PARKS
MANSFIELD RD.
ST. CROSS RD.
CHERWELL RIVER
TO
BEAUMONT ST.
HOLYWELL
STATION
GEORGE ST.
CORNMARKET ST.
RD.
ST.
New College
Magdalen College
MARSTON RD.
HEADINGTON RD.
NEW RD.
HIGH ST.
University College
Merton College
Christ Church College
MORRELL AVE.
ST. ALDATE'S
IFFLEY RD.
COWLEY RD.
THAMES RIVER
MAGDALEN RD.
TO

go in the summer (allegedly they study more than they do at term time), and the many B&B houses—vacated by their gown-wearing boarders—will be happy to offer you an accommodation. But you'll be missing a great deal if you view Oxford without glimpsing its life blood.

However, at any time of the year, you can enjoy a tour of the colleges, many of them representing a peak in England's architectural kingdom, as well as a valley of Victorian eyesores. Just don't mention the other place (Cambridge), and you shouldn't have any trouble.

The city predates the university; in fact, it was a Saxon town in the early part of the tenth century. And by the 12th century, Oxford was growing in reputation as a seat of learning at the expense of Paris. The first colleges were founded in the 13th century. The story of Oxford is filled with conflicts too complex and detailed to elaborate here. Suffice it to say, the relationship between town and gown wasn't as peaceful as it is today. Riots often flared, and both sides were guilty of abuses.

Nowadays, the young people of Oxford take out their aggressiveness in sporting competitions, with the different colleges zealously competing in such games as cricket and soccer. However, all colleges unite into a powerful university when they face matches with their traditional rival, Cambridge.

Ultimately, the test of a great university lies in the men it turns out. Oxford can name-drop a mouthful: Roger Bacon, Samuel Johnson, William Penn, John Wesley, Sir Walter Raleigh, Edward Gibbon, T. E. Lawrence, Sir Christopher Wren, John Donne, William Pitt, Matthew Arnold, Arnold Toynbee, Harold MacMillan, Graham Greene, A. E. Housman, and Lewis Carroll.

Many Americans arriving in Oxford ask, "Where's the campus?" If an Oxonian shows amusement when answering, it's understandable. Oxford University is, in fact, made up of 28 colleges, including five just for women (scholars in skirts in years past staged, and won, the battle for equal rights). To tour all of these would be a formidable task. Besides, a few are of such interest they overshadow the rest.

Much of the city is either closed to motor traffic or is a maze of one-way streets. You might end up in Woodstock by mistake. Therefore, you might want to take advantage of the **Park and Ride** scheme. You leave your auto in one of the designated car parks, then take the free parking bus into the center of Oxford. Departures are every 10 to 15 minutes, and the cost of a bus ticket is 40p (70¢).

THE SIGHTS: In season (from Easter through October), the best way to get a running commentary on the important sightseeing attractions is to go to the **Oxford Information Centre,** St. Aldate's Street, opposite the Town Hall, near Carfax (tel. Oxford 726871). Walking tours through the major colleges leave daily from Easter to mid-November at 10:45 a.m. and 2:15 p.m., last two hours, and cost £1.50 ($2.63) per person. Of all the tours I know in England, this ranks at the top, both for economy and information. No booking is necessary—you simply arrive.

At **Punt Station,** Cherwell Boathouse, Bardwell Road (tel. Oxford 55978), you can rent a punt at a cost of £2 ($3.50) per hour on weekdays, £2.40 ($4.20) per hour on weekends, plus a £10 ($17.50) deposit. Similar charges are made on rentals at Magdalen Bridge Boathouse and at the Folly Bridge Boathouse.

A Word of Warning

The main business of a university, is, of course, to educate—and unfortunately this function at Oxford has been severely interfered with by the number of visitors who have been disturbing the academic work of the university. So, with deep regret, visiting is now restricted to certain hours and small groups of six or fewer. In addition, there are areas where visitors are not allowed at all, but your tourist office will be happy to advise you when and where you may "take in" the sights of this great institution.

Christ Church

Begun by Cardinal Wolsey as Cardinal College in 1525, Christ Church, known as The House, was founded by Henry VIII in 1546. Facing St. Aldate's Street, Christ Church has the largest quadrangle of any college in Oxford.

Tom Tower houses Great Tom, the 18,000-pound bell referred to earlier. It rings at 9:05 nightly, signaling the closing of the college gates. The 101 times it peals originally signified the number of students at the time of the founding of the college. The student body number changed, but Oxford traditions live on forever.

In the 16th-century Great Hall, with its hammer-beam ceiling, are some interesting portraits, including works by those old reliables, Gainsborough and Reynolds. Prime ministers are pictured, as Christ Church was a virtual factory turning out actual and aspiring prime ministers: men such as Gladstone and George Canning. There is a separate picture gallery.

The cathedral, dating from the 12th century, was built over a period of centuries. (Incidentally, it is not only the college chapel, but the cathedral of the diocese of Oxford.) The cathedral's most distinguishing features are its Norman pillars and the vaulting of the choir, dating from the 15th century. In the center of the Great Quadrangle is a statue of Mercury mounted in the center of a fish pond. The college and cathedral can be visited between 9:30 a.m. and 4:30 p.m. Entrance fee is 50p (88¢).

Magdalen College

Pronounced "maud-len," this college was founded in 1458 by William of Waynflete, bishop of Winchester and later chancellor of England. Its alumni range all the way from Wolsey to Wilde. Opposite the botanic garden, the oldest in England, is the bell tower, where the choristers sing in Latin at dawn on May Day. The reflection of the 15th-century tower is cast in the waters of the Cherwell below. On a not-so-happy day, Charles I, his days numbered, watched the oncoming Roundheads. But the most celebrated incident in Magdalen's history was when some brave Fellows defied James II. Visit the 15th-century chapel, in spite of many of its latter-day trappings. The hall and other places of special interest are open when possible.

A favorite pastime is to take Addison's Walk through the water meadows. The stroll is so named after a former alumnus, Joseph Addison, the 18th-century writer and poet noted for his contributions to *The Spectator* and *The Tatler.* The grounds of Magdalen are the most extensive of any Oxford college, containing a deer park. You can visit Magdalen each day from 2 to 6:15 p.m.

Merton College

Founded in 1264, this college is among the trio of the most ancient at the university. It stands near Corpus Christi College on Merton Street, the sole survivor of Oxford's medieval cobbled streets. Merton College is noted for its library, one of the oldest in England, having been built between 1371 and 1379. In keeping with tradition, some of its most valuable books were chained. Now only one book is so secured, to show what the custom was like. One of the treasures of the library is an astrolabe (astronomical instrument used for measuring the altitude of the sun and stars), thought to have belonged to Chaucer. You pay only 30p (53¢) to visit the ancient library, as well as the Max Beerbohm Room (the satirical English caricaturist who died in 1956). Both are open from 2 to 4 p.m. from Monday to Friday, and, in addition, 10 a.m. to 4 p.m. on Saturday and Sunday. You can also visit the chapel, dating from the 13th century, at these times.

University College

On the High, University College is the oldest one found at Oxford, tracing its history back to 1249 when money was donated by an ecclesiastic called William of Durham. More fanciful is the old claim that the real founder was Alfred the Great! Don't jump to any conclusions about the age of the buildings when you see the present Gothic-esque look. The original structures have all disappeared, and what remains today represents essentially the architecture of the 17th century, with subsequent additions in Victoria's day, as well as in more recent times. For example, the Goodhart Quadrangle was added as late as 1962. Its most famous alumnus, Shelley, was "sent down" for his part in collaborating on a pamphlet on atheism. However, all is forgiven today, as the romantic poet is honored by a memorial erected in 1894. The hall and chapel of University College can be visited during university vacations from 10 a.m. to noon and from 2 to 4 p.m. (otherwise, 2 to 4 p.m.).

New College

New College was founded in 1379 by William of Wykeham, bishop of Winchester and later lord chancellor of England. The college at Winchester supplied a constant stream of candidates. The first quadrangle, dating from before the end of the 14th century, was the initial quadrangle to be built in Oxford, forming the architectural design for the other colleges. In the antechapel is Sir Jacob Epstein's remarkable modern sculpture of *Lazarus* and a fine El Greco painting of St. James. One of the treasures of the college is a crosier (pastoral staff of a bishop) belonging to the founding father. In the garden you can see the remains of the old city wall and the mound. The college (entered at New College Lane) can be visited from 2 to 5 p.m. weekdays at term time (otherwise, 11 a.m. to 6 p.m.). On weekends, it is open from noon to 6 p.m.

Salters River Thames Passenger Services

It's possible to do a day trip down river to historic Abingdon and back, passing through Iffley and Sandford Locks. Boats leave Folly Bridge (tel. Oxford 243421) in Oxford at 9 a.m. and 2:30 p.m., arriving at Abingdon less than two hours later. The return boats depart at 11 a.m. and 4:45 p.m., so you can spend the middle of the day in Abingdon if you wish. Cost is £3.20 ($5.60) for adults (round trip) and £2.20 ($3.85) for children.

From Reading, Caversham Bridge, there's also a daily service to Henley-on-Thames at 1:30 p.m., but you'll have to remain on the boat at Henley if you want to come back by river. The boat turns straight around and arrives back at Reading at 6:30 p.m. The cost of a round-trip ticket is £3.05 ($5.34) for adults, £1.95 ($3.41) for children. Services run from mid-May to mid-September.

ACCOMMODATIONS: When the tourist rush is on, why tire yourself further? **The Oxford Association of Hotels and Guest Houses** has provided an efficient accommodation secretary, Mr. J. O'Kane, who also operates the Earlmont Guest House at 322/4 Cowley Road (tel. Oxford 240236). If Mr. O'Kane cannot accommodate you himself, he will spare no effort in helping you to find the kind of lodgings you require. For B&B the tariffs begin at £6.50 ($11.38) per person. Advance bookings can also be made, long or short term, single person or party booking. No fees are charged.

The **Oxford Information Centre,** St. Aldates Chambers (tel. Oxford 726871), operates a room-booking service for personal callers for a fee of 50p (88¢) per person, from Easter to September. Families should take note that the maximum charged for a booking is £1 ($1.75). If you'd like to seek out lodgings on your own, the staff at the center will provide a list of accommodations, or you may try one of the following recommendations:

Bed and Breakfast

The Old Parsonage Hotel, 3 Banbury Rd. (tel. Oxford 54843), is so old it looks like an extension of one of the ancient colleges. Originally a 13th-century hospital named Bethleen, it was restored in the early 17th century. Today it's slated for designation as an ancient monument. Near St. Giles Church, it is set back from the street behind a low stone wall and sheltered by surrounding trees and shrubbery. However, most of the rooms are in a modern wing which is more institutional in character. The owners charge from £15 ($26.25) per person nightly for B&B in a single, from £25 ($43.75) in a double or twin. Should you want a private shower, the price is increased to £30 ($52.50) for two persons. A family room for four rents for £38 ($66.50) nightly, including a full English breakfast, VAT, and service. Some of the large front rooms, with leaded-glass windows, are set aside for tourists. You have breakfast in a pleasant modern dining room, overlooking the garden. A licensed restaurant and bar are on the premises. In the restaurant you order à la carte. If you want only one dish, you can pay as little as £2.80 ($4.90). The cost of an average three-course meal is £5 ($8.75).

Mr. and Mrs. Conrad Adams, 302 Banbury Rd. (tel. Oxford 56118), operate a clean, comfortable guest house. They offer gracious hospitality, good beds, central heating, and an individually prepared English breakfast. Shower and bath facilities are available at no extra charge. Shopping amenities are nearby, and the city and university areas are a short bus ride away. Rates are from £9 ($15.75) per person per night, inclusive.

Lonsdale Guest House, 312 Banbury Rd. (tel. Oxford 54872), is another pleasant accommodation. This one is run by Roland and Christine Adams, who have established a gem of a little guest house. A comfortable bedroom, with hot and cold running water, and free use of the corridor bath, plus an individually prepared breakfast, costs from £9 ($15.75) per person nightly (less for longer stays). Lonsdale offers twin beds, lounge chairs, occasionally an antique chest of drawers, innerspring mattresses, comforters of soft down, wall-to-wall carpeting, and central heating. If you arrive at term time, you may think you're in a fraternity house. Students of all races stay here (it's odd to hear a young Chinaman speaking with a broad Oxonian accent). A heated indoor pool is about a two-minute walk from the house. It's called the **Ferry Pool,** and charges are 65p ($1.14) for adults, 35p (61¢) for children.

Mrs. K. Andrews, 26 St. Michael's St., off Cornmarket (tel. Oxford 242101), has a few rooms which she lets to students from nearby St. Peter's College. But she always sets aside some rooms for tourists, charging them £9 ($15.75) per person nightly for B&B. Her little rooms are tidy, clean, and pleasingly comfortable. She takes care of the guests in a friendly, hospitable manner.

Westgate Private Hotel, 1 Botley Rd. (tel. Oxford 726721), lies close to the railway station, right near the city center and university, which are no more than half a mile away. Dave and June Lester run this small family business, giving you a warm, friendly welcome. All units have hot and cold running water, and some have showers. There is also double glazing on the windows to help keep out the noise, and each room has a color TV. Singles rent for £13 ($22.75), doubles going for £23 ($40.25). Home-cooked evening meals are also available, and the hotel has a residential license. Mr. and Mrs. Lester also own the **Walton Guest House,** 169 Walton St. (tel. Oxford 52137), lying at the city end of Walton Street, 100 yards from the bus station and half a mile from the rail station. All the pleasantly furnished rooms have hot and cold running water, shaver points, central heating, and TV. Terms are from £9 ($15.75) per person here, including a first-class English breakfast. In both hotels, they can accommodate a total of 50 persons.

Earlmont Guest House, 322 Crowley Rd. (tel. Oxford 240236), is run in a friendly way by Jim and Anne O'Kane, who offer a high standard of accommodation, some rooms containing private showers. All of the units have hot and cold running water and central heating, and breakfast is with "traditional Irish helpings." Tariffs are £7.50 ($13.13) per person inclusive, although units with showers cost an additional 50p (88¢) per person. Reductions are granted families with children. Jim and Anne now welcome guests who require vegetarian, vegan, or whole-food breakfast. Ann mixes her own muesli and makes granola from an old American recipe. It's really good, with fresh fruit and homemade yogurt. Of course, traditional breakfasts that have made Earlmont such a popular choice over the years are still served. Earlmont is just a mile from the city center, and buses pass nearby every five to ten minutes. The O'Kanes are helpful in offering advice about seeing Oxford and the sights in its environs.

Belmont, 182 Woodstock Rd. (tel. Oxford 53698), is the domain of Mr. and Mrs. Bellamy, who operate this house in a tree-shaded residential section of Oxford, at the junction of Woodstock Road and Moreton Road, about a mile from the heart of the city. Woodstock is the main road from the city leading north to Woodstock, Bladon (burial place of Sir Winston Churchill—about five miles away), Stratford-upon-Avon, Birmingham, and the Midlands. Belmont is an attractive house, once a private home. All rooms are centrally heated, and all have hot and cold running water basins. Baths and showers are available. The rate for B&B, inclusive of taxes, is from £7.50 ($13.13) to £9 ($15.75) in a single, from £15 ($26.25) to £17 ($29.75) in a double. Accommodations are pleasantly decorated, each overlooking the surrounding gardens.

Ascot Guest House, 283 Iffley Rd. (tel. Oxford 240259), is ideally located in the quiet outskirts of Oxford, yet only minutes away by bus or car from the city center. The owner, Mrs. Neville, combines friendliness, high standards, and reasonable prices in her recently refurbished home. All rooms have wall-to-wall carpeting, telephones, and hot and cold running water. The per-person charge of £9 ($15.75) per night includes breakfast and VAT. Parking facilities are plentiful here, and it's usually less expensive and more convenient to leave your car at the guest house and take the frequent buses into the city proper. When Mrs. Neville is unable to accommodate any more guests, she will cheerfully recommend other guest houses in the area.

Kerry and Suzanne Bunt, 228 Abingdon Rd. (tel. Oxford 44725), have a Victorian terraced house overlooking the University Cricket Ground and a country field, yet it's only ten minutes from Christ Church College. This friendly couple offers two twin rooms and one family unit (with four single beds), charging from £7.50 ($13.13) per person for B&B. They also cater to children from the age of six months, and have hot and cold running water in all their accommodations. The house also has central heating and a color TV set for the use of guests.

The **Galaxie Private Hotel,** 180 Banbury Rd. (tel. Oxford 55688), is owned by H. and M. Harries-Jones, whose rooms are spotlessly clean. A bus service on Banbury Road will take you the one mile to the center of town. All of the 21 bedrooms are equipped with reading lights, electric shaving points, hot and cold running water, central heating, and TV (mostly color). Many of the units have showers en suite, for which you'll pay more, of course. For a bed and typical filling English breakfast, the cost per person daily for a single is £14 ($24.50), a double is £10 ($17.50) per person. There is central heating, and parking space is available.

In Iffley Village

The **Elms and Hawkwell Hotel,** Church Way in Iffley (tel. Oxford 778529), just a few minutes ride from the center of Oxford, on a main road toward London, is suitable for motorists. The two buildings, several hundred feet apart, stand in three acres of lawns and gardens and were the private residences of English gentry until 1946. The Elms has nine bedrooms, each with TV and facilities for making tea or coffee. There are two communal bathrooms. The Tartan Bar, with more than 100 brands of whisky, is popular with both residents and the public. The price is £17 ($29.75) in a single, £22 ($38.50) a double, including VAT, service charge, and English breakfast. The Hawkwell has a TV lounge, and one bath to each five bedrooms. Take bus 4 or 10A, or a taxi.

READERS' GUEST HOUSE SELECTIONS: "We found the **Conifer Guest House,** 116 The Slade (tel. Oxford 63055), run by Mr. and Mrs. Grant, to be the best we stayed at in Europe. The accommodations were extraordinary for £8 ($14) per person per night. The B&B was superb, even the electric sockets took American plugs, and, what is even more rare, the bathroom was great. The Grants have added an extension to the property, offering more rooms, three of which have private bath/showers, at a cost of £10 ($17.50) per person" (Mr. and Mrs. Jerome Bump, Austin, Tex.). . . . "**Mr. and Mrs. J. King** operate a well-run guest house at 363 Iffley Rd. (tel. Oxford 41363). Our rooms had basins and a shower, and there was a toilet nearby. There is a car park, and a little picnic area in the garden for families who like to have their evening meal on their own. Rates are £8.50 ($14.88) to £9.50 ($16.63) per person. The Kings are very helpful hosts" (Mrs. K. L. Kiser, Trenton, N.J.).

WHERE TO EAT: All Oxford undergraduates aren't the sons or daughters of wealthy dukes, as you'll soon discover when you see its numerous restaurants and cafés where you can get good food at reasonable prices. Here are my recommendations, which will be followed by my pub selections.

The **Cherwell Boathouse Restaurant,** Bardwell Road (tel. Oxford 52746), is owned and run by Tony Verdin, with the help of two or three nice young women. Everyone does anything that needs to be done, and preparation of menus and the cooking is taken in turns. Their menu contains items which have come from friends (the pork with mushrooms, for example). Two fixed menus which are never repeated are offered at each meal, and the cooks admit they change the menu every two weeks to allow for the availability of fresh vegetables, fish, and meat. Appetizers include soups or fish or meat pâtés, followed by casseroles, pies, and hot pots, then some exotic dessert—cikolatak pasta, rum soufflé, or fruit fool.

There is a very reasonable wine list, including brandy after dinner. The restaurant is open every evening from 8 to 10 p.m. and for Sunday lunch. For a regular dinner, the charge is £7.70 ($13.48), and Sunday lunch is £7.40 ($12.95), plus VAT. It's recommended that you make a reservation. Children, if they don't order a full meal, are granted half price. In summer the restaurant also does an all-day cold buffet in the Marquee for thirsty punters for around £2.50 ($4.38). This place surely must be one of the most English, most attractive, and least known of the eating establishments of Oxford. It also provides an opportunity to observe a most important aspect of Oxford undergraduate life.

The **Turf Tavern,** 4-5 Bath Place (tel. Oxford 43235), is on a very narrow passage in the area of the Bodleian Library, off New College Lane. A 13th-century tavern, it is surely the find of the year. The proprietor, a Yorkshireman, Wally Ellse, although he is no longer actually always present on the premises, maintains an excellent establishment through his resident manager. Thomas Hardy used the place for the setting of *Jude the Obscure.* It was "the local" of Burton and Taylor when they were in Oxford some years ago making a film, and today's stars include such names as Kris Kristofferson and John Hurt. At night, the old tower of New College and part of the old city wall are floodlit, enabling you, in warm weather, to enjoy an al fresco evening in a romantically historical setting. In winter braziers are lighted in the courtyard and gardens which adds a beautiful atmosphere.

Inside the low-beamed hospice, you can order traditional English food such as steak-and-kidney pie, jacket potatoes, and old English casseroles and stews. Prices range from £1.50 ($2.63) to £3 ($5.25). More impressive, however, is a table about eight feet long and four feet wide, covered with meats, fish, fowl, eggs, cheeses, bread puddings, sausages, cakes, and salads (all cold), and a selection of hors d'oeuvres, freshly prepared daily. You can fill your plate for about £4 ($7). Old English brews from the wood, plus a range of country wines, are served all year, and a special punch is offered in winter to warm you through.

The **Nosebag,** 6-8 St. Michael's St. (tel. Oxford 721033), is perhaps one of the most popular places to eat among students at Oxford. It's a self-service upstairs cafeteria on a side street off Cornmarket, opposite St. Michael's Church. Two floors of light wood-paneled furniture and cushioned benches greet you. But if you arrive at the busy main mealtimes, you'll probably have to queue (line up) on the stairs. The manager, Ray Hartman, keeps order out of the muddle. At lunch you can get a homemade soup for 65p ($1.14), followed by the dish of the day, perhaps hot peppers and rice at £2.50 ($4.38). Baked potato with a variety of fillings is a good accompaniment at £1 ($1.75), as is the hot garlic bread at 55p (96¢). Wine—white, red, or rosé—is available by the glass at 95p ($1.66). The Nosebag is open Monday to Friday from 10 a.m. to 5:30 p.m., Saturday from noon to 5:30 p.m., and Friday and Saturday nights from 6:30 to 9:30 p.m.

Bookshop and Coffee House, 94 St. Aldate's (tel. Oxford 722970), is almost opposite the entrance to Christ Church College, adjacent to St. Aldate's Church. An offbeat suggestion for eating, it is a bookshop/coffeehouse. The bookshop offers a wide range of first-class paperbacks suitable for holiday reading. Head for the back where you'll find a large restaurant with counter service run by the church. You receive value for money here, together with quantity. All the food is homemade, including soups and salads from fresh produce daily. The range of fresh baked scones and cakes brings the English fireside and cozy atmosphere right into the center of Oxford. Meals are priced around £3 ($5.25), but you can order à la carte.

Burlington Bertie's, 1 Market Ave., 9A High St. (tel. Oxford 723342), is a restaurant and coffeehouse over a covered market. A continental cuisine is served in a world of cut-glass mirrors and Edwardian-style chairs. Continental specialties, including moussaka or cannelloni, begin at £2.75 ($4.81) and are served with a mixed salad and herb or garlic bread. "The main event," is the main course, and it's likely to be chicken chasseur or boeuf bourguignon, the cost of a meal beginning at £6 ($10.50). Daily specials are also written on the blackboard, and breakfast is served from 9:30 to 11:45 a.m. The desserts and ice cream sundaes are delectable. You can also visit Bogie's Pizza Parlour upstairs, serving some of the best pizzas in town. A children's menu is also available. The place stays open daily until midnight.

Go Dutch, 18 Park End St. (tel. Oxford 40686), is a bright and cheerful place where even the furnishings evoke the Netherlands, with clean wooden chairs and tables. Pancakes are served with savory fillings, such as bacon with apple or perhaps ham, corn, and green pepper. If you don't like the advertised stuffings, make up your own at 40p (70¢) to 60p ($1.05) extra for each selection. To go with your pancake, order one of the crisp, fresh salads as a side dish. Those intrepid diners who like their pancakes sweet will face a choice of such selections as black currant and mandarin. There is an extra-special concoction with banana ice cream, chocolate sauce, and Tia Maria. If you can't face a pancake, the kitchen also does grilled sandwiches. Count on spending from £4 ($7). Plenty of green plants have been placed about. The establishment is open from 11:45 a.m. to 2:30 p.m. and from 6 to 10 p.m. Monday to Friday, from noon to 11 p.m. on Saturday and Sunday.

Yeadon's Restaurant, 61–63 George St. (tel. Oxford 43084), stands opposite the old fire station in an upstairs complex in the Omni shopping center in the middle of the city. A mass of tables, chairs, and old church bench seats are separated by bamboo screens. You'll hear musical background noise as you proceed to the self-service counter to make your selection from the hot dishes of the day—vegetable samosas, cheese, onion, and pepper quiche, steak-and-kidney pie, and the increasingly popular stuffed potatoes (try the garlic or curry filling). These dishes are served after, perhaps, french onion or vegetable soup, accompanied by roll and butter and a side-dish selection from the salad bar. If you still have room for dessert, try homemade flapjacks or sponge cake, perhaps a chocolate biscuit cake. A filling and wholesome meal will cost about £2.50 ($4.38) for three courses. They do some excellent teas, including Earl Grey and Ceylon in addition to the regular Indian. The place is very much student oriented, and is the sort of establishment that's handy after you're browsed through the discount shopping center.

The **Coffee Mill and Wine Bar,** Magdalen Street, is a busy, ordinary place, but as a coffee bar it offers cheap, good meals, served Monday to Saturday from 10 a.m. to 7:30 p.m. You get the regular fare here, including homemade soup to begin with, followed by a choice of chicken and "chips," or perhaps the slightly more exotic curry and rice. If you're dining simply, rolls are filled with delitype meats, and to go with that, you can order a mixed salad, followed by a fruit pie. Wine is sold by the glass at 60p ($1.05). Depending on your selection, your lunch might cost only £3 ($5.25).

Brown's, 7 Woodstock Rd. (tel. Oxford 511995), is large and noisy, with pop music played in the background. It's popular with students who know of its quick snack meals. There is always a hamburger on the grill, and the staff will make you a hot pastrami on rye or perhaps a club sandwich. They also serve spaghetti with various sauces, including a Brighton seafood concoction. Salads include the usual chicken and tuna, and you can also order such main dishes as fish pie topped with potatoes. Check the blackboard for the day's specials. You'll spend from £4 ($7) to £5 ($8.75), much less if you're snacking. The decor is simple, with dark wood tables and potted plants. Brown's is open from 11 a.m. (from noon on Sunday) until 11 p.m. daily.

Maxwell's, 36 Queen St. (tel. Oxford 42192), is a big, airy room with steel supports set into the ceiling. It attracts homesick Americans with its cuisine. There is nothing corny, however, about Maxwell's, except for the grilled corn on the cob served as an appetizer. The Yankee theme is carried throughout the menu, which includes quarter-pound burgers served with practically anything, including a No Bunburger with lots of salad at £2.40 ($4.20). A large chef's salad costs £2.85 ($4.99). Soda-fountain specials include malts, sundaes, and banana splits, costing about £1 ($1.75) apiece. Maxwell's is open daily from 11:30 a.m. to midnight.

Opium Den, 79 George St. (tel. Oxford 4868), attracts only those "addicts" who desire good Cantonese food at reasonable prices. Sizable dinners can be ordered in special fixed-price menus for one, two, three, or four diners. There is an enormous selection from which to choose. A typical dinner might include grilled Chinese dumplings in soy sauce, followed by king prawns with baby corn in a sweet-and-sour sauce. This, plus an aromatic pot of Chinese tea, would bring the bill to £5.80 ($10.15). Budgeteers could select two courses from a wholesome variety of less expensive items for around £4.50 ($7.88). From Monday to Saturday, hours are from noon to 2:30 p.m. and from 6 p.m. to midnight. On Sunday, hours are from 1 to 2:30 p.m. and from 6 p.m. to midnight.

Raffles Tea Room, 90 High St. (tel. Oxford 241855), is a new branch of this tea-room chain system, part of the House of Tweed. In Oxford, the tea room, which opened in the summer of 1983, offers convenient refreshment for tired shoppers or visitors. The variety of beverages served, all in the 40p (70¢) range, remind me of a Parisian café, but the ambience is definitely English. Teatime can be an event, particularly if you order two scones with jam and cream, along with a pot of Ceylon or Earl Grey tea, costing £1.35 ($2.36). There's a wide choice of cakes and eclairs, averaging about 65p ($1.14), and hot dishes and cold salads which could be a satisfying lunch or supper for around £2.50 ($4.38). For lighter appetites, Raffles offers Cona Toasties, a Scottish-derived formula for "closed toasted sandwiches," including ham and cheese with chutney for £1.30 ($2.28). It is open from 9:30 a.m. to 7 p.m. (from 10:30 a.m. to 4:30 p.m. on Sunday) in summer, and from 9:30 a.m. to 5 p.m. Monday through Saturday in winter.

Crest of the Wave is a traditional fish 'n' chip shop at the bus station off George Street. You can eat it there or take it away. It is open daily from Monday through Saturday from 11 a.m. to 11 p.m., from 6 to 11 p.m. on Sunday. Lovely fresh fish and chips can be eaten on the premises at only 90p ($1.58). A jumbo plate goes for £1.25 ($2.19). Sadly, the fish these days is not wrapped in newspaper, as in days of yore, but in hygenic, greaseproof containers. They also do steak-and-kidney pie, hamburgers, and sausage, chicken, and mushroom pie.

THE SPECIAL PUBS OF OXFORD: The **Bear Inn,** Alfred Street, is an Oxford tradition, a short block from the High overlooking the north side of Christ Church College. It's the village pub. Its swinging inn sign depicts the bear and ragged staff, old insignia of the Earls of Warwick, who were among the early patrons. Built in the 13th century, the inn has been known to many famous people who have lived and studied at Oxford. Over the years, it's been mentioned time and time again in English literature.

The Bear has served a useful purpose in breaking down social barriers, bringing a wide variety of people together in a relaxed and friendly way. You might talk with a rajah from India, a university don, a titled gentleman—and Clive and Debbie Wright, who are the latest in a line of owners that goes back more than 700 years.

They may explain to you their astonishing hobby: collecting ties! Around the lounge bar you'll see thousands of snipped portions of neckties, which have been labeled with their owners' names, the most famous of which is Lord Ismay, former head of NATO. For those of you who want to leave a bit of yourself, a thin strip of the bottom of your tie will be cut off (with your permission, of course) with a huge pair of ceremonial scissors. Then you, as the donor, will be given a free drink on the house. After this initiation, you may want to join in some of the informal songfests of the undergraduates.

The shelves behind the bar are stacked and piled with items to nibble on: cheese, crisp rolls, cold meats, flans. Homemade pie with french fries and beans costs £1.50 ($2.63); a ploughman's lunch, £1.25 ($2.19); and many salads are offered, from £1.50 ($2.63).

The **Trout Inn,** 195 Godstow Rd., near Wolvercote, lies on the outskirts of Oxford. Ask any former or present student of Oxford to name his or her most-treasured pub, and the answer is likely to be the Trout. Hidden away from visitors and townspeople, the Trout is a private world where you can get ale and beer—and top-notch meals. Have your drink in one of the historic rooms, with their settles, brass, and old prints, or go out in sunny weather to sit on a stone wall, where you can feed crumbs to the swans that swim in the adjoining weir pool. Take an arched stone bridge, stone terraces, architecture that has wildly pitched roofs and gables, throw in the Thames River, and you have the Trout. If you don't have a car, take bus 520 or 521 to Wolvercote, then walk.

Daily specials are featured for lunch. The seafood platter's popular, as is a tempting eight-ounce entrecôte. Soup of the day is hearty fare. For dessert, try the fruit tart with cream. Meal prices range from £7 ($12.25) to £9 ($15.75), but a single plate of meat and salad will be around £3.75 ($6.56). The inn is open from noon to 2 p.m. and from 7 to 10 p.m. Salads are served during the summer, and grills in the winter.

On your way there and back, look for the view of Oxford from the bridge. And go ahead and talk with the undergraduates, who usually like telling about their university. They may even ask you to have tea at one of their colleges, where the average visitor rarely penetrates.

READERS' RESTAURANT SELECTION: "Want to say you've gone through Oxford? If you're lucky, you'll meet a scholar-cum-guide who'll walk you by the Thames, where, during the last week in May, there takes place a crewing competition between some 30 schools which make up Oxford. Next, to witness the discretion and objectivity of this educational tradition, visit a classroom. And for dinner, mug it with Oxford's prodigal sons at the **Welsh Pony Hotel,** Gloucester Green (tel. Oxford 242998), outside and to the right of the bus station, where you can have lasagne and beer for £2 ($3.50). Various other snacks are priced from 70p ($1.23). All food for thought" (Anne Fuchs, Southfield, Mich.; Linda Klein, Pittsburgh, Pa.).

From Oxford, you can visit one of England's greatest attractions.

BLENHEIM PALACE: This extravagant baroque palace regards itself as England's answer to Versailles. Blenheim is the home of the 11th Duke of Marlborough, a descendant of the first Duke of Marlborough (John Churchill), an on-again, off-again favorite of Queen Anne. In his day (1650-1722), the first duke became the supreme military figure in Europe. Fighting on the Danube near a village named Blenheim, Churchill defeated the forces of Louis XIV. The lavish palace of Blenheim was built for the duke as a gift from the queen. It was designed by Sir John Vanbrugh, who was also the architect of Castle Howard. Landscaping was carried out by Capability Brown.

The palace is loaded with riches: antiques, porcelain, oil paintings, tapestries, and chinoiserie. But more North Americans know Blenheim as the birthplace of Sir Winston Churchill. His birthroom forms part of the palace tour, as does the Churchill exhibition, four rooms of letters, books, photographs, and other Churchilliana. Today, the former prime minister lies buried in Bladon Churchyard, near the palace.

Blenheim Palace is open every day from April to October, inclusive, from 11:30 a.m. to 5 p.m. The last tour is at 5 p.m., and the last admittance to the palace is at 4:45 p.m. On spring bank holidays, Sunday, and Monday charity events take place in the park when different prices and times apply. The admission fee is £2.50 ($4.38) for adults, £1.25 ($2.19) for children. For information, telephone Woodstock 811325.

In the park is the Blenheim Model Railway, second longest in Britain, which you can usually ride on weekends in season. The palace is at Woodstock, eight miles north of Oxford on the A34 Road to Stratford-upon-Avon. From Oxford, do-it-your-selfers take bus 420 or 421 from Kohl Market Street, which stops at the gate of Blenheim Palace.

READER'S FOOD AND LODGING SELECTIONS (OUTSIDE OXFORD): "The **Sunset House,** Milton-under-Wychwood (tel. Shipton-under-Wychwood 830581), is a B&B find on the edge of the Cotswolds close to Burford. Bedrooms are attractive in this refinished 250-year-old home, away from the noise of the city. It's run by two gracious hosts, Tony and Elizabeth Durston. The typical English breakfast was the best we had during our stay in England. All of this, plus directions to the best pubs in the area, costs only £7 ($12.25) to £8.50 ($14.88) per person. . . . **The King's Head** is a 16th-century inn on the green, with beer gardens serving real ale in a small Cotswold village. A hot menu and cold buffet are served daily at lunchtime and in the evenings. The King's Head is in Bledington (tel. Kingham 365). Owners are Frank and Joan Powell. The varied menu starts with French onion soup and features a well-prepared steak pie served in a casserole and baked in wine, spare ribs (with finger bowl), steaks, chops, and other typical English treats. Unquestionably, this was the best dinner we had during our two-week stay, and the price, including some cold ale, was under £7 ($12.25) apiece. The innkeepers offer B&B for around £9 ($15.75) per person, and this would have to be the best bargain for you if you're going through the Cotswolds" (Charles W. Lassen, Philadelphia, Pa.).

WOODSTOCK: This small country town, the birthplace of the Black Prince, is a good choice for lodgings if you want to be on the outskirts of Oxford and conveniently near Blenheim Palace.

The **Marlborough Arms Hotel** (tel. Woodstock 811227), is a pleasant 15th-century coaching inn, with an arched alleyway leading to the courtyard. Alistair McEwen and his staff of cheerful local help are used to passing travelers. Their bar snacks are ample and succulent. They also do a set lunch for £4.60 ($8.05) and a dinner for £8 ($14). Bedrooms are simple and comfortable, containing color TV. The charge in a single is £16 ($28), rising to £30 ($52.50) in a double or twin with bath. With a private bath, a double or twin rents for £36 ($63) nightly. Corridor baths are ample.

The **Star Inn,** Market Place (tel. Woodstock 811373), is a small pub opposite the super-splurge Bear Hotel, offering home-cooked pies and quiches in the bar daily. All ingredients are fresh. Rooms cost £22 ($38.50) for two persons, including a large breakfast. Owner Rees Hicks has only two rooms to rent, but they're worth grabbing if you have the chance.

READER'S PUB SUGGESTION: "Do have lunch at the **Potato Pub.** They serve more than 51 different toppings on their baked potatoes. I had the curried shrimp, and it was very tasty. For £2 ($3.50), it's the best buy in England. Just ask anyone on the street for the Potato Pub, and they will direct you. But you may have to wait. It's the busiest place in Woodstock" (Bob Knox, Pittsburgh, Penna.).

3. Hertfordshire

Like a giant jellyfish, the frontier of Greater London spills over into this county, once described by Charles Lamb as "hearty, homely, loving Hertfordshire. " This fertile land lies northwest of London and supplies much of that city's food, although industry has crept in. Hertfordshire is sometimes called "the market basket of England."

Its most important attraction, which is usually visited on a day trip from London, follows.

HATFIELD HOUSE: One of the chief attractions of Hertfordshire, and one of the greatest of all English country houses, Hatfield House (tel. Hatfield 62823) is just 21 miles north of London. To build what is now the E-shaped Hatfield House, the old Tudor palace at Hatfield was mostly demolished. The Banqueting Hall, however, remains.

Hatfield was much a part of the lives of both Henry VIII and his daughter Elizabeth I. In the old palace, built in the 15th century, Elizabeth romped and played as a child. Although Henry was married to her mother, Anne Boleyn, at the time of Elizabeth's birth, the marriage was later nullified (Anne lost her head and Elizabeth her legitimacy). Henry also used to stash away his oldest daughter, Mary Tudor, at Hatfield. But when Mary became Queen of England, and set about earning the dubious distinction of "Bloody Mary," she found Elizabeth a problem. For a while she kept her in the Tower of London, but she eventually let her return to Hatfield (Elizabeth's loyalty to Catholicism was seriously doubted). In 1558, while at Hatfield, Elizabeth learned of her ascension to the throne of England.

The Jacobean house that exists today contains much antique furniture, tapestries, and paintings as well as three much-reproduced portraits, including the famed ermine and rainbow portraits of Elizabeth I. The Great Hall is suitably medieval, complete with a minstrel's gallery. One of the rarest exhibits is a pair of silk stockings, said to have been worn by Elizabeth herself, the first lady in England to don such apparel. The park and the gardens are also worth exploring. The Riding School and Palace Stables contain a number of interesting historical and costume exhibitions.

Hatfield is usually open from March 25 through the second Sunday in October, daily, except Monday, from noon to 5 p.m. (Sunday from 2 to 5:30 p.m.). Admission is £2.25 ($3.94) for adults, £1.60 ($2.80) for children. The house is across from the station in Hatfield. From London, take Green Line coach 716, 716a, or 724, or the fast trains from Kings Cross. Luncheons and teas are available in the converted coach house in the Old Palace yard.

Elizabethan banquets are on stage Tuesday, Thursday, Friday, and Saturday, with much gaiety and music. Guests are invited to drink in an anteroom, then join the long tables for a feast consisting of typical English food, ending with the classic syllabub. Wine is included in the cost of the meal, but you're expected to pay for your predinner drinks yourself. The best way to get there from London is to book a coach tour for an inclusive fee. If you book with Evan Evans or Frames and use their coach from London, it will cost £20 ($35) on Tuesday, Thursday, and Friday, the price going up to £21.50 ($37.63) on Saturday. The Evan Evans agency has tours leaving from Russell Square or from 41 Tottenham Court Rd. The coach returns to London after midnight. If you get there under your own steam, the cost is £14.50 ($25.38) on Tuesday, Wednesday, and Thursday, £16 ($28) on Friday and Saturday. For reservations, telephone Hatfield 62055.

In Old Hatfield, a fine place for light lunches and good lager is **Eight Bells,** a pub on Park Street. For Dickens fans, it was the inn where Bill Sikes and his dog found temporary refuge after the brutal murder of Nancy. It's a rickety old corner inn with a central bar for drinks and dining nooks—in all, a forest of time-blackened beams, settles, and pewter tankards. A bowl of homemade soup is reasonably priced, and the cook's specialty is smoked mackerel filet. A light luncheon here will cost about £1.75 ($3.06).

HERTFORD: This old Saxon city is the county town, containing many fine examples of domestic architecture, some of which date back to the 16th century. Hertford is reached via the A1 or A10 from London. Samuel Stone, founder of Hartford, Connecticut, was born here. The town's Norman castle has long been in ruins, and part of the still-standing keep dates from the 16th century.

For food and lodgings, try the **Salisbury Arms Hotel,** Fore Street (tel. Hertford 53091), which has been called "always Hertford's principal inn." For 400 years, it's been feeding and providing lodgings to wayfarers, or giving a hot grog to the coachman, a stable for his horses. Although the stables have long given way to a car park, a sense of history still prevails. In the cellar is medieval masonry predating the 16th-century structure around it. Cromwell is said to have lodged here, and both Royalists and Roundheads have mounted the Jacobean staircase. Bedrooms now spill over into a modern extension, a total of 22 functionally furnished rooms added to the 10 more antiquated original ones. Rates depend on the room occupied—singles, doubles, or twins. Singles start at £15.50 ($27.13), going up to £18 ($31.50) for those requiring a private bath. Two persons pay from £24.50 ($42.88) to £29 ($50.75). Family rooms rent for £31 ($54.25). Good, wholesome English "fayre" is provided. At lunch, when most visitors stop by, a cut from the roast of the day goes for £4 ($7) with vegetables. A paneled and intimately partitioned dining room provides traditional meals as well as a full Chinese menu. There is, as well, a well-stocked cellar. Dinners are from £7 ($12.25).

ST. ALBANS: This cathedral city, just 21 miles northeast of London, dates back 2000 years. It was named after a Roman soldier, the first Christian martyr in England. Don't ask a resident to show you to the **Cathedral of St. Albans.** Here it's still known as "The Abbey," even though Henry VIII dissolved it as such in 1539. Construction on the cathedral was launched in 1077, making it one of the early Norman churches of England. The bricks, especially visible in the tower, came from the old Roman city of Verulamium at the foot of the hill. The nave and west front date from 1235.

The new Chapter House, the first modern building beside a great medieval cathedral in the country, which also serves as a pilgrim/visitor center, was opened by the Queen in 1982.

The **Verulamium Museum** (tel. St. Albans 54659) at St. Michael's stands on the site of the Roman city. Here you'll view some of the finest Roman mosaics in Britain. Part of the Roman town wall, a hypocaust, and a theater and its adjoining houses and shops are still visible. Visit in summer from 10 a.m. to 5:30 p.m. weekdays (on Sunday from 2 to 5:30 p.m.), and in winter from 10 a.m. to 4 p.m. weekdays, 2 to 4 p.m. on Sunday, paying 50p (88¢) for adults, 30p (53¢) for children.

The **Clock Tower** at Market Place was built in 1402, standing 77 feet high, a total of five floors.

From St. Albans you can see **Gorhambury House,** a classic-style mansion built in 1777, containing 16th-century enameled glass and historic portraits. It's open, May to September, only on Thursday (2 to 5 p.m.), charging adults £1 ($1.75) for admission; children pay 60p ($1.05). The location is 2½ miles north of St. Albans off the A414.

On the outskirts, the **Mosquito Aircraft Museum,** the oldest aircraft exhibit in Britain, lies on the grounds of Salisbury Hall, just off the main A6 London to St. Albans road near London Colney, about five miles south of St. Albans. The hall is no longer open to the public, but the museum can be visited from Easter Sunday to October 1 on Sunday from 2 to 6 p.m. (also on bank holiday Mondays from 11 a.m. to 6 p.m.). Displayed is the prototype of the de Havilland "Mosquito" aircraft which was designed and built at Salisbury Hall in World War II. There are also three Mosquitos. Admission is 50p (88¢) for adults, 25p (44¢) for children. For more information, telephone Bowmansgreen 22051, or write Box 107, St. Albans.

Back in St. Albans, I offer the following recommendations for food and lodgings:

Melford House, 24 Woodstock Rd. North (tel. St. Albans 53642), is a 12-bedroom hotel-cum-guest house in the best residential area away from the busy town center, charging moderate prices for B&B: £14.38 ($25.17) nightly in a single room, £23 ($40.25) nightly in a twin-bedded room, and £31.05 ($54.34) for three persons in a family room. A full English breakfast is included in the tariffs. Each unit has its niceties, and each is immaculately kept, with full central heating. There is a spacious residents' lounge with color TV. The house is licensed for beer and liquor, and there is a car park and a garden. The resident owners are Yvonne and Cecil Green who are experienced hoteliers of long standing who have managed large luxury hotels abroad.

For dining, **Zorbas Greek Restaurant,** 3 French Row (tel. St. Albans 60609), seems an incongruous choice in such an historic English town, but it is a good and moderately priced eating place. Right in the old part of town, it is reached by going along a pedestrian mall. The Josephedes family welcomes you if you've come to dine, although I've seen them politely turn away English women who drop in just for afternoon tea, which they don't serve, incidentally. The house specialty, served with rice, is a kebab. You might prefer, to begin with, a Greek salad or hummus (ground chickpeas with garlic). Pita bread is also served, as is the classic Greek moussaka. Another house specialty is stuffed vine leaves. A dinner begins at £10 ($17.50). However, a set lunch is offered for just £3 ($5.25). Although closed on Sunday and holidays, the restaurant is open otherwise until 3 p.m., and for dinner from 6 to 11 p.m.

SHAW'S CORNER: Just southwest of Ayot St. Lawrence, three miles northwest of Welwyn, stands the home where George Bernard Shaw lived from 1906 to 1950. The house is practically as he left it at his death. In the hall, for example, his hats are still hanging, as if ready for him to don one. His personal mementos fill the four rooms which can be seen in March and November on Saturday and Sunday and then from April to October on Wednesday to Sunday from 11 a.m. to 1 p.m. and from 2 to 6 p.m. Admission is £1.20 ($2.10) for adults, half price for children. For information, telephone High Wycombe 28051.

4. Buckinghamshire

This is a leafy county, lying north of the Thames and somewhat to the west of London. Its identifying marks are the wide Vale of Aylesbury, with its sprawling fields and tiny villages, and the long chalk range of the Chilterns. Going south from the range, you'll find what is left of a once-great beech forest.

A good center for touring the Chilterns is—

AYLESBURY: Gourmets still speak of its succulent ducks, a prize-winning dish on any table, although ducks bearing that name are usually raised elsewhere these days. The county town, Aylesbury has a number of timbered inns, old houses, and a wide Market Square. Less than 40 miles from London, it remains cozily old world.

Six miles northwest of Aylesbury on the Bicester Road (A41), **Waddeson Manor** (tel. Aylesbury 651211) contains an outstanding collection of French decorative art of the 17th and 18th centuries and an exhibition of dresses of a lady in the 1860s. Among the paintings are portraits by Reynolds, Gainsborough, and Romney. The manor was built in the late 19th century for Baron Ferdinand de Rothschild in the style of the French Renaissance and stands in 150 acres of ground with rare trees, an aviary, and a herd of Sika deer. Visiting times are from March 23 to October 30, Wednesday to Sunday, from 2 to 6 p.m. The admission to the house, grounds, and aviary is £1.70 ($2.98).

Back in Aylesbury itself, you can find big-splurge food and lodgings at the **Kings Head,** Market Square (tel. Aylesbury 5158), a half-timbered hotel that was once a 15th-century coaching inn. It is one of the finest examples of Tudor architecture in Buckinghamshire. Its 15 bedrooms overlook a cobbled courtyard. Because of its heavy patronage by business people on weekdays, I've never been able to get a room unless reserved well in advance. Rooms, incidentally, cost from £27 ($47.25) in a double, plus VAT, and from £19 ($33.25) in a single, plus VAT. No unit has a private bath. Lunch is served from noon to 2 p.m. and dinner from 7 to 9 p.m. (from 7:30 to 10 p.m. on Saturday). Try to have a predinner drink in the cozy pub in back, with its collection of weapons. A three-course luncheon or dinner goes for £8 ($14), although there is an à la carte menu as well. The inn was much frequented by Cromwell, and his chair is still on view in the lounge bar. He slept in the Cromwell Room upstairs with its extra-large bed.

BUCKINGHAM: This old market town on the River Ouse was once the county town of Buckingham. It has a fine 13th-century Chantry Chapel and some 18th-century houses.

If you're motoring through, try to plan a luncheon or dinner stopover at **Old Market House,** Market Hill (tel. Buckingham 2385), housed in the oldest and perhaps the most interesting building in town, a black-and-white timbered structure with leaded-glass windows dating from 1430. A special Sunday luncheon is served for £5.50 ($9.63). On weekdays, you can choose from the à la carte menu or else order the table d'hôte at £4 ($7) for three courses. The cuisine is traditional home style. Fish, poultry, game, and meat dishes are always available. All vegetables used are fresh, not frozen. Main courses cost around £5.50 ($9.63) from the à la carte menu. Specialty dishes include chicken chasseur, old English pork, and steak-and-kidney pudding. Luncheon is served from noon to 2 p.m. and dinner every evening except Sunday from 7 to 10 p.m. The resident proprietors are Sheila and John Rawlings, who offer an extensive wine cellar.

JORDANS VILLAGE: **Old Jordans,** Jordans Lane, in Jordans Village (tel. Chalfont St. Giles 4586), is a farm dating back to the Middle Ages. But its recorded history starts in the early 17th century when one Thomas Russell, sitting tenant, bought the freehold, signing the deed with his thumbprint. The house was added to over the years, and in the mid-17th century William Penn, founder of Pennsylvania, and other well-known Dissenters stayed here and worshipped.

Now the property of Quakers, the house is run as a conference center, but they have several simply furnished rooms available for overnight guests at £12 ($21) in a single, £18 ($31.50) in a double, including breakfast.

On the grounds is the Mayflower Barn, built almost undisputably from timbers from the ship *Mayflower* in which the first Pilgrims sailed to the New World. These days the beams ring to the strains of concert music and recitals performed by top-notch artists.

Morning tea or coffee with crackers goes for 50p (88¢), and an afternoon tea of scones and jam for 85p ($1.49). These are served in the great kitchen-dining room of the hall. Supper at £3 ($5.25) is served at 7 p.m., and reservations are necessary.

It's a very peaceful place, full of history, and perhaps a little isolated from today's bustle.

MILTON'S COTTAGE: The modern residential town of Gerrards Cross is often called the Beverly Hills of England, as it attracts the wealthy-chic who settle here in many beautiful homes. Surrounding this plush section are several tucked-away hamlets, including **Chalfont St. Giles,** where the poet Milton lived during the Great Plague in 1665. He completed *Paradise Lost* here, and the cottage he lived in contains a small museum of Miltoniana.

John Milton's Cottage (tel. Chalfont St. Giles 2313) is open daily except Monday from February 1 to October 31, 10 a.m. to 1 p.m. and 2 to 6 p.m. (on Sunday from 2 to 6 p.m.), charging adults an admission of 60p ($1.05) and 20p (35¢) for children under 15. It is closed in November, December, and January. Allow time to visit the beautifully maintained garden.

West of Gerrards Cross, the town of Beaconsfield, with its broad, treelined High Street, enjoys many associations with Disraeli. Visitors pass through here en route to—

HUGHENDEN MANOR: Outside High Wycombe, in Buckinghamshire, sits a country manor that gives us not only an insight into the age of Victoria, but acquaints us with a remarkable man. In Benjamin Disraeli we meet one of the most enigmatic figures of 19th-century England. At age 21, Dizzy published anonymously his five-volume novel *Vivian Grey.* But it wasn't his shining hour. He went on to other things, marrying an older widow for her money, although they developed, apparently, a most successful relationship. He entered politics and continued writing novels, his later ones meeting with more acclaim.

In 1848 Disraeli acquired Hughenden Manor, a country house that befitted his fast-rising political and social position. He served briefly as prime minister in 1868, but his political fame rests on his stewardship as prime minister during 1874-1880. He became Queen Victoria's friend, and in 1877 she paid him a rare honor by visiting him at Hughenden.

In 1876 Disraeli became the Earl of Beaconsfield: he had arrived. Only his wife was dead, and he was to die in 1881. Instead of being buried at Westminister Abbey, he preferred the simple little graveyard of Hughenden Church.

His library is preserved much as he left it. In fact, Hughenden contains an odd assortment of memorabilia, including a lock of Disraeli's hair. The letters from Victoria, the autographed books, and especially a portrait of Lord Byron, known to Disraeli's father.

If you're driving to Hughenden Manor on the way to Oxford, continue north of High Wycombe on the A4128 for about 1½ miles. If you're relying on public transportation from London, take coach 711 to High Wycombe, then board an Alder Valley bus (323, 324, 333, or 334). The manor house and garden are open daily except Monday and Tuesday, April to October, from 2 to 6 p.m. (from 12:30 to 6 p.m. on Sunday and bank holidays). In March and November, they're open on Saturday and Sunday only from 2 to 5 p.m. (or sunset if earlier). Admission for adults is £1.30 ($2.28), half price for children. It is closed all December, January, and February, and on Good Friday. For more information, telephone High Wycombe 28051.

WEST WYCOMBE: Snuggled in the Chiltern Hills 30 miles west of London, the village of West Wycombe still has an atmosphere of the early 18th century. The thatched roofs have been replaced with tiles, and some of the buildings have been removed or replaced, but the village is still two centuries removed from the present day.

In the mid-18th century, Sir Francis Dashwood began an ambitious building program at West Wycombe. His strong interest in architecture and design led Sir Francis to undertake a series of monuments and parks which are still among the finest in the country today. He also sponsored the building of a road using the chalk quarries on the hill to aid in the support of the poverty-stricken villagers. The resulting caves became the meeting place of "The Knights of St. Francis of Wycombe," later known as "The Hellfire Club." The knights consisted of a number of illustrious men drawn from the social circle surrounding the Prince of Wales. Its members "gourmandized," swilling claret and enjoying the company of women "of a cheerful, lively disposition . . . who considered themselves lawful wives of the brethren during their stay."

You can tour the caves today, wandering through a quarter mile of winding passages, past colorful waxwork scenes brought to life by sound and light effects.

A visit to **West Wycombe House,** home of the Dashwoods, is of both historical and architectural interest. Both George III and Ben Franklin stayed here, but not at the same time. The house is one of the best examples of Palladian-style architecture in England. The interior is lavishly decorated with paintings and antiques from the 18th century.

Admission to the caves, café, and gift shop is £1.50 ($2.63) for adults and 75p ($1.31) for children. The caves are open daily from the end of February until the end of October from 1 to 6 p.m. On Saturday, Sunday, and bank holidays they open at 11 a.m. The house and grounds may be viewed from 2:15 to 6 p.m. on Monday to Friday in June, July, and August (also on Sunday and bank holidays in July and August). Admission is £1.60 ($2.80) for adults and 80p ($1.40) for children. For more information, write to West Wycombe Park Office, West Wycombe, Buckinghamshire HP14 3AJ (tel. 0494/24411).

Other sights at West Wycombe include the **Church of St. Lawrence,** perched atop West Wycombe Hill and topped by a huge golden ball. Parts of the church date from the 13th century; its richly decorated interior was copied from a third-century Syrian sun temple. The view from the church tower is worth the trek up the hill. Near the church stands the Dashwood Mausoleum, built in a style derived from Constantine's Arch in Rome.

During your tour, you may also wander freely through the village, stopping for lunch at one of the public houses. Four miles of nature trails also meander about the village, through woods and farmlands.

5. Bedfordshire

This county contains the fertile, rich Vale of Bedford, crossed by the River Ouse. Most visitors from London head here on a day trip to visit historic Woburn Abbey (previewed below). Others know of its county town—

BEDFORD: On the Ouse, Bedford contains many riverside parks and gardens, but is better known for its associations with Bunyan. In Mill Street stands the 1850 **Bunyan Museum** (tel. Bedford 52539), erected on the site of a barn where Bunyan used to preach. Panels on the doors illustrate scenes from *Pilgrim's Progress.* The Bunyan Museum contains the surviving relics of Bunyan and a famous collection of the *Pilgrim's Progress* in 165 languages. It is open Tuesday to Saturday, April to October, from 2 to 4 p.m., charging an admission of 20p (35¢) for adults and 10p (18¢) for children.

About 1½ miles south of Bedford lies Elstow, close to Bunyan's reputed birthplace. Here you can visit **Elstow Moot Hall,** a medieval market hall. In it is housed a collection of 17th-century relics associated with Bunyan. It is open Tuesday to Saturday from 10 a.m. to 1 p.m. and from 2 to 5 p.m. (dusk in winter) (Sunday from 2 to 5:30), charging 20p (35¢) for adults, 10p (18¢) for children. For more information, telephone Bedford 66889.

The **Swiss Garden,** Old Warden, near Biggleswade, is an unusual romantic site dating from the early 19th century. It contains original buildings and features, together with many interesting plants and trees, some of great rarity. A lakeside picnic area in adjoining woodlands is open at all times. Hours for the garden are from 2 to 6 p.m. (last admission is at 5:15 p.m.) on Wednesday, Saturday, Sunday, bank holiday Monday, and Good Friday from March 27 to October 24. The garden lies approximately 2½ miles west of Biggleswade adjoining the Biggleswade–Old Warden road about two miles west of the Al. For more information, telephone Bedford 63222, ext. 30.

Stevington Windmill, dating from about 1770, is a particularly fine example of a post mill, fully restored in 1921. The Bedfordshire County Council acquired the mill in 1951, when further extensive restoration work was carried out. Stevington Mill was probably the last windmill in the country working with four common (i.e., cloth-covered) sails. Visitors to the mill may borrow the keys between the hours of 10 a.m. and 7 p.m. (dusk in winter) from the landlord, Royal George, Silver Stevington. The location is half a mile southeast of Stevington. For more information, telephone Bedford 63222, ext. 30.

WOBURN ABBEY: Few persons visiting Bedfordshire miss the Georgian mansion of **Woburn Abbey** (tel. Woburn 666), the seat of the Dukes of Bedford for more than three centuries. The much-publicized 18th-century estate is about 42 miles from London outside of Woburn. Its State Apartments are rich in furniture, porcelain, tapestries, silver, and a valuable art collection, including paintings by Van Dyck, Holbein, Rembrandt, Gainsborough, and Reynolds. A series of paintings by Canaletto, showing his continuing views of Venice, grace the walls of the dining room in the Private Apartments (Prince Philip said the duke's collection was superior to the Canalettos at Windsor—but Her Majesty quickly corrected him!). Of all the paintings, one of the most notable from a historical point of view is the *Armada Portrait,* of Elizabeth I. Her hand rests on the globe, as Philip's invincible armada perishes in the background.

Queen Victoria and Prince Albert visited Woburn Abbey in 1841. Victoria slept in an opulently decorated bedroom (her night dress is still there). In 1954, another queen—this one of the cinema, Marilyn Monroe—slept in the same bed as a publicity stunt. Victoria's Dressing Room contains a fine collection of 17th-century paintings from the Netherlands. Among the oddities and treasures at Woburn Abbey are a Grotto of Shells, a Sèvres dinner service (gift of Louis XV), and a chamber devoted to memorabilia of "The Flying Duchess." Wife of the 11th Duke of Bedford, she was a remarkable woman, who disappeared on a solo flight in 1937 (the same year as Amelia Earhart). The duchess, however, was 72 years old at the time.

In the 1950s, the present Duke of Bedford opened Woburn Abbey to the public to pay off some $15 million in inheritance taxes. In 1974 he turned the estate over to his son and daughter-in-law, the Marquess and Marchioness of Tavistock, who reluctantly took on the business of running the 75-room mansion. And what a business it is, drawing more than a million visitors a year and employing more than 300 persons to staff the shops and grounds.

Today, Woburn Abbey is surrounded by a 3000-acre park containing many rare and exotic animals (ten varieties of deer). Some visit just to see the animals. While seated in one of 57 gondolas on the two-mile cable lift, you pass over lions, elephants, and giraffes. What would Humphry Repton, the designer of the estate's park in the 18th century, say?

Woburn Abbey is outside Woburn, near Dunstable. It is hard to reach by public transportation from London, so you may prefer to take one of the organized tours.

From April 1 to October 31 the abbey is open weekdays from 11 a.m. to 5:45 p.m. (on Sunday, from 11 a.m. to 6:15 p.m.). Off-season the abbey is open from 1 to 4:45 p.m., except when it's closed in December and January. The last entry is always three-quarters of an hour before closing time. Admission is £2.20 ($3.85) for adults and £1 ($1.75) for children. If you wish to explore only the park by car, the charge is £1.70 ($2.98), including passengers. Many shows and special events take place at Woburn Abbey. Make a phone call if you want to, say, catch a Scottish clan gathering or witness a hot-air balloon race.

To visit the Deer Park by car, the fee is £2 ($3.50), inclusive of passengers. The Deer Park entrance charge doesn't apply to visitors who purchase their abbey tickets as they enter the park. To visit the Woburn Wild Animal Kingdom as a coach passenger costs £1.50 ($2.63) for adults and 75p ($1.31) for children. However, if you're driving, a car with up to six occupants is admitted for £5 ($9.75), plus 50p (88¢) for the guidebook.

After visiting the abbey, a good spot for lunch is the **Woburn Wine Lodge,** 13 Bedford St. Authentic, flavorsome food is served here on scrubbed wooden tables seven days a week. A hot and cold buffet is offered daily, and wine is sold by the glass or bottle. Expect to spend from £5 ($8.75).

If you've decided to stay in Bedford for the night, the best place to head is the **Greek Villager Restaurant,** a taverna and kebab house at 36 St. Peters St. (tel. Bedford 41798). It features dining and dancing to live Greek music on Friday and Saturday. Bouzouki and guitars, along with Serina, a belly dancer, are featured, as well as Yioryos and his superb Cypriot and Greek dancing. Costas amuses with his glass dance. The restaurant is open seven nights a week: until midnight Monday to Thursday, until 2 a.m. Friday and Saturday, and until 11:30 on Sunday. A special feature of the chef is small portions of about 14 different Greek dishes served on separate plates at a cost of £9 ($15.75) per person. Otherwise, you get the usual appetizers such as hummus and taramosalata, followed by such typical Greek dishes as moussaka and dolmades (stuffed vine leaves). Meals begin at £8 ($14), plus the cost of your wine.

READER'S GUEST HOUSE SELECTION: "**Homeleigh Guest House,** 26 De Pary's Ave. (tel. Bedford 59219), was a timely and delightful discovery for us. Only a short walk from downtown Bedford and on a broad street with good parking, this house was recently opened under the direction of Gianna and Ken White. It is a large Victorian building, but the Whites are renovating it as a B&B establishment. Although I don't know the exact number of rooms, I know that it is one of the largest B&B places at which we stayed. Our room was spacious and had hot and cold water. The breakfast was tasty. I think this will become a popular stopover in Bedford. The cost for two is £17 ($29.75) for B&B" (Hugh Wamble, Kansas City, Mo.).

READER'S SIGHTSEEING TIP: "You should not miss seeing the **Shuttleworth Collection** of vintage airplanes and automobiles. It is at the Old Warden Aerodrome, two miles west of the A1 roundabout at Biggleswade, about eight miles southeast of Bedford. The Shuttleworth Collection contains dozens of pre–World War II aircraft, and all are maintained in flying condition. Several of the aircraft are the only air-worthy specimens of their type in existence. The collection also houses unique vintage automobiles, also maintained in running order. A flying day is held the last Sunday of each month between May and October, at which time most of the aircraft are actually flown. Admission is £1 ($1.75) for adults, 50p (88¢) for children, with special rates for flying days. The collection is open throughout the year" (Capt. H. Michael Bartley, APO New York).

Chapter VI

KENT, SURREY, AND SUSSEX

1. Canterbury
2. Dover
3. Tunbridge Wells
4. Haslemere
5. Rye
6. Winchelsea
7. Hastings and St. Leonards
8. Battle
9. Alfriston and Lewes
10. Brighton
11. Hove
12. Arundel
13. Chichester

LYING TO THE SOUTH and southeast of London are the shires (counties) of Kent, Surrey, and the Sussexes. Combined, they form a most fascinating part of England to explore—and are easy to reach, within commuting distance of the capital.

Of all the tourist centers, **Canterbury** in Kent is of foremost interest, but the old Cinque ports of **Rye** and **Winchelsea** in East Sussex are almost equally exciting, as is the resort of **Brighton** in a completely different way. In and around these major meccas are dozens of castles and vast estates, monuments, homes of famous men (Churchill, for example), cathedrals, yachting harbors, and little villages of thatched cottages.

The range of accommodations varies from an old-world smugglers' inn in the ancient seaport of Rye to a clean, comfortable Georgian guest house in the heart of medieval Canterbury. Regardless of the price range in which you travel, you'll discover some superb bargains throughout the counties of the South Coast. The reason is simple. The English come to these coastal counties for the sun, and most of the tariffs are in keeping with their pocketbook, as they will be with yours.

In the fog-choked cities of north England, the great dream for retirement is to find a little rose-covered cottage in the south, where the living's easier. The

South Coast is also a potent magnet for London's East Enders. Come with me as we examine the lure, beginning with:

KENT

Fresh from his cherry orchard, the Kentish farmer heads for his snug spot by an inglenook, with its bright-burning fire, for his mellow glass of cherry brandy. The day's work is done. All's right with the world.

We're in what was once the ancient Anglo-Saxon kingdom of Kent, on the shirttails of London itself, yet far removed in spirit and scenery. Since the days of the Tudors, cherry blossoms have pinkened the fertile landscape. Not only orchards, but hop fields abound. The conically shaped oasthouses with kilns for drying the hops dot the rolling countryside. Both the hops and orchards have earned for Kent the title of the "garden of England." And in England the competition's rough for that distinction.

The country is rich in Dickensian associations, and for that reason Kent is sometimes known as Dickens Country. His family once lived near the naval dockyard at Chatham.

ROCHESTER: In the cathedral city of Rochester, 30 miles from London, you can visit the **Charles Dickens Centre** and **Dickens Chalet** in Eastgate House, built in 1590. This center, on High Street in Rochester, is open seven days a week from 10 a.m. to 12:30 p.m. and 2 to 5:30 p.m. Admission is £1 ($1.75) for adults and 50p (88¢) for children. The museum has tableaux depicting various scenes from Dickens's novels, including a Pickwickian Christmas scene, then the fever-ridden graveyard of *Bleak House,* scenes from *The Old Curiosity Shop* and *Great Expectations,* along with *Oliver Twist* and *David Copperfield.* There is clever use of sound and light. Information is also available at the center on various other sights in Rochester associated with Dickens, including Eastgate House and, in the garden, the chalet transported from Gad's Hill Place, where Dickens died, as well as the Guildhall Museum, Rochester Cathedral, and the mysterious "6 Poor Travellers' House." Pick up a brochure which includes a map featuring the various places and the novels with which each is associated. For further information, telephone Rochester 44176.

Three miles from Rochester stands **Gads Hill Place,** which was the home of Dickens from 1858 to 1870. Standing on the A226, it can only be visited by prior arrangement.

At Broadstairs, the favorite seaside resort of the novelist, the **Dickens House Museum** has been installed on the main seafront. This museum (tel. 0843/62853), was once the home of Mary Pearson Strong, on whom he based much of the character of Betsey Trotwood, David Copperfield's aunt. It is open April to October daily from 2:30 to 5:30 p.m. from June to September. It is also open on Tuesday, Wednesday, and Thursday evening from 7 to 9 p.m. Admission is 35p (61¢) for adults and 15p (26¢) for children.

You can also visit **Bleak House** (tel. 0843/62224), which is open from Easter to June and during October and November from 10 a.m. to 6 p.m. From July to September its hours are from 10 a.m. to 9 p.m. It charges the same admission.

An attraction for Canadian readers is the square, red-brick, gabled home where James Wolfe, the English general who defeated the French in the battle for Québec, lived until he was 11 years old. Called **Québec House,** a National Trust property, it contains memorabilia associated with the military hero, who was born in Westerham (Kent) on January 2, 1727. The house which Wolfe's parents rented may be visited March to October on Monday, Wednesday, Friday, and Sunday from 2 to 6 p.m., charges an admission of £1 ($1.75) for adults and 50p (88¢) for children.

Kent suffered severe destruction in World War II, as it was the virtual alley over which the Luftwaffe flew in its blitz of London. After the fall of France, a German invasion was feared imminent. Shortly after becoming prime minister in 1940, Churchill sped to Dover, with his bowler, stogie, walking cane, and pin-striped suit. Once there, he inspected the coastal defense and gave encouragement to the men digging in to fight off the attack. But Hitler's "Sea Lion" (code name for the invasion) turned out to be a paper tiger.

In spite of much devastation, Kent is filled with interesting old towns, mansions, and castles. The most famous pilgrimage is to:

CHURCHILL'S HOME: For many years, Sir Winston lived at **Chartwell,** (tel. Edenbridge 866368), which lies 1½ miles south of Westerham in Kent. Churchill, a descendant of the first Duke of Marlborough, was born in grand style at Blenheim Palace on November 30, 1874. Chartwell doesn't pretend to be as grand a place as Blenheim, but it's been preserved as a memorial, administered by the National Trust. The rooms remain as Churchill left them, including maps, documents, photographs, pictures, and other personal mementos. In two rooms are displayed a selection of gifts that the prime minister received from people all over the world. There is also a selection of many of his well-known uniforms. Terraced gardens descend toward the lake with its celebrated black swans. In a garden studio are many of Churchill's paintings. Go if you want to see where a giant of a man lived and worked. The house is open from March 1 to November 30 on Tuesday, Wednesday, and Thursday from 2 to 6 p.m.; Saturday and Sunday from 11 a.m. to 6 p.m. Admission to the house and gardens is £1.75 ($3.06) for adults, £1 ($1.75) for children. To visit the gardens only is 75p ($1.31) for adults, 40p (70¢) for children. A restaurant serves morning coffee, light lunches, and afternoon tea.

KNOLE: Begun in the mid-15th century by Thomas Bourchier, archbishop of Canterbury, Knole (tel. Seven Oaks 53006) is one of the largest private houses in England. It was an archbishop's palace from 1456 until the day Henry VIII's eye fell covetously upon it. He spent considerable sums of money on Knole, but there is little record of his spending much time there after extracting the gift from the reluctant Archbishop Cranmer. History records one visit only, in 1541. It was then a royal palace until Queen Elizabeth I granted it to Thomas Sackville, first Earl of Dorset, whose descendants have lived at Knole ever since. The building was given to the National Trust in 1946. The Great Hall and the Brown Gallery are Bourchier rooms, early 15th century, both much altered by the Earl of Dorset, who made other additions in about 1603. The earl was also responsible for the Great Painted Staircase. The house covers seven acres and has 365 rooms, 52 staircases, and seven courts. The elaborate paneling and plasterwork provide a background for the 17th- and 18th-century tapestries and rugs, the Elizabethan and Jacobean furniture, and the family portraits. Knole, in Seven Oaks, is five miles north of Tonbridge and 25 miles south of London. It is open April to September, Wednesday to Saturday, bank holiday Mondays, and Good Friday, from 11 a.m. to 5 p.m. (Sunday from 2 to 5 p.m.). In October and November, you can see the house on guided tours only, except on weekends. In those months, the hours are 11 a.m. to 4 p.m. on weekdays, 2 to 4 p.m. on Sunday. Last admission is one hour before closing.

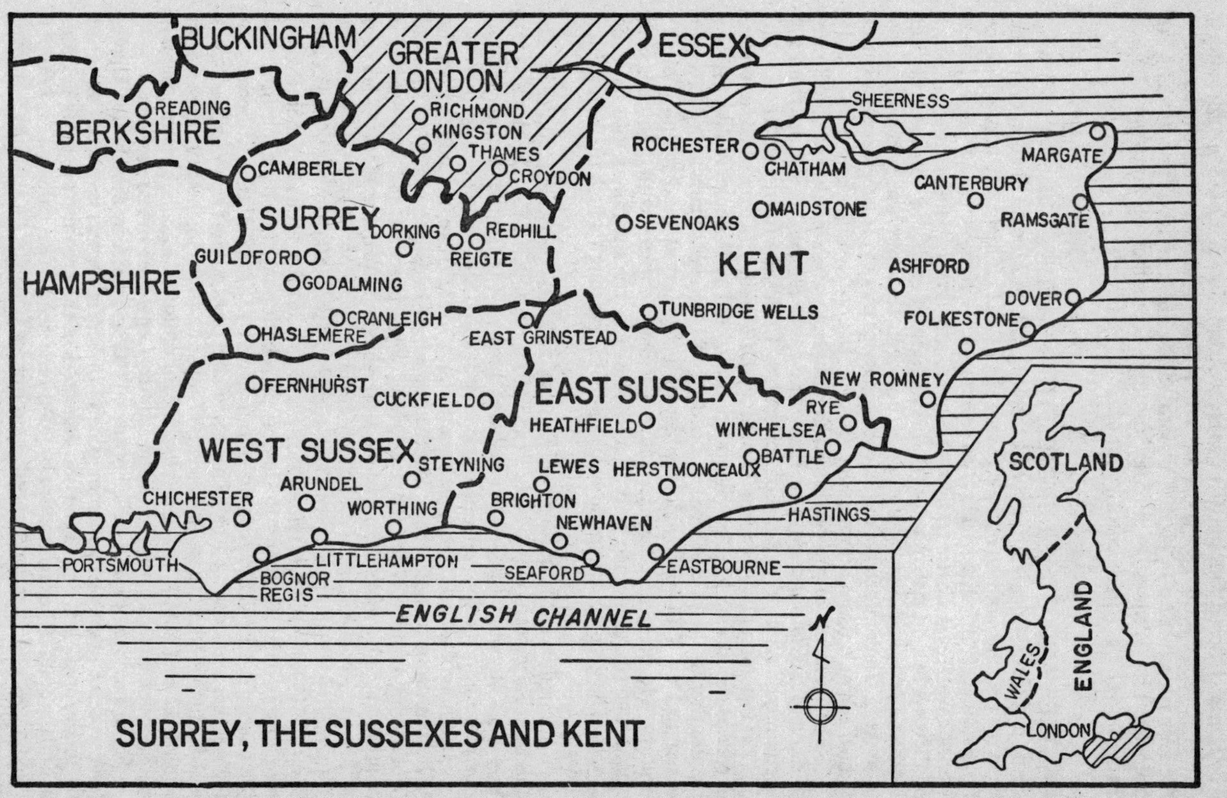

SURREY, THE SUSSEXES AND KENT

The house is closed December to March. Admission is £2 ($3.50) for adults, £1 ($1.75) for children. If you want a tour that includes several extra rooms, the cost rises to £2.50 ($4.38) for both adults and children. The gardens are open the first Wednesday in May through September by courtesy of Lord Sackville. The car park costs yet another £1 ($1.75).

CASTLES AND OTHER SIGHTS: **Hever Castle** is a 13th-century moated castle just three miles southeast of Edenbridge. It has the distinction of having been the residence of two of the wives of Henry VIII. The family home of Anne Boleyn, it was forfeited by Henry's second wife—along with her head. Later, Henry gave Hever Castle to his proxy wife, the "great Flanders mare," Anne of Cleves when he discovered that this mail-order bride did not live up to her Holbein portrait. Anne did not mind, however, since she was perfectly happy to settle into a comfortable castle with plenty of money. It was certainly better than the king's usual alternative.

The forecourt of the castle and the gardens were used during the filming of *Anne of a Thousand Days* in 1969. The castle is open to visitors from the beginning of April to the end of September. Hours are from 11:30 a.m. until 5 p.m. (last entry) daily except Thursday and Monday. Also available to view is part of the unique "Tudor village" built in 1903 by William Waldorf Astor, grandfather of the present owner, Lord Astor of Hever. The whole estate was redesigned by William Waldorf when he bought it at the beginning of the century. He created a formal Italian garden complete with fountains and classical statuary, a maze, and an avenue of yew trees trimmed into fantastic shapes. The grounds also include a 35-acre lake through which the River Eden flows.

Admission to the gardens only costs £1 ($1.75) for adults, 50p (88¢) for children. To visit the castle costs £2 ($3.50) for adults, £1 ($1.75) for children. You can't buy admission to the castle without paying for the gardens as well. For more information, telephone Edenbridge 865224.

Chilham Castle Gardens (tel. Canterbury 730319) can be reached from the M2 Faversham turnoff, the A252 (Canterbury-Maidstone road), or the A20 (Folkestone-London road). It is a former royal property and was used as a hunting lodge by more than one royal personage until King Henry VIII sold it. The gardens are closed on Monday and Friday. From March 27 to October 2, the hours are noon to 6 p.m., and admission is £1.50 ($2.63) for adults and 75p ($1.31) for children, reduced to £1.35 ($2.36) for adults and 65p ($1.14) for children from October 4 to October 30. On Sunday they have jousting, and the charge is £2 ($3.50) for adults and £1 ($1.75) for children. If because of the weather the jousting is cancelled, weekday rates apply. On holiday Sundays and Mondays when there are medieval jousting tournaments, the cost for an adult is £2.80 ($4.90), and £1.30 ($2.28) for children. Each afternoon, there is a display of birds of prey from the Raptor Centre set in the gardens.

The Jacobean castle, built between 1603 and 1616 by Sir Dudley Digges (whose descendant was governor-general of Virginia), was reputedly designed by Inigo Jones. It is one of the best examples of the architecture of its day and is built around a hexagonal open-ended courtyard. The gardens, laid out by Readescant and later landscaped, possibly by Lancelot "Capability" Brown, are visually magnificent and look out over the Stour Valley.

The village has a lovely little square with a church at one end, the castle at the other, and a mass of half-timbered buildings in between interspersed with old red brick houses.

The **White Horse Inn** dates from the 15th century and has good bar snacks, with prices starting at 90p ($1.58).

At Haddon Cottage, the **Copper Kettle Tearooms,** The Square (tel. Chilham 303), offers a daily lunchtime special, dishes such as pepper steak, chicken suprême, or plaice meunière, costing from £3 ($5.25). Salads are from £3 also, and omelets with various fillings cost from £2.25 ($3.94) to £3.50 ($6.13). They also do morning coffee and afternoon teas and sell homemade cakes, postcards, pottery, and gifts. However, they are closed in the evening.

Penhurst Place, a magnificent English Gothic-style mansion, one of the outstanding country houses in Britain, lies 33 miles from London and 3½ miles west of Tonbridge on the Tunbridge Wells Road. Sir John de Pulteney, four times mayor of London, built the stone house whose Great Hall forms the heart of Penshurst, even after more than 600 years. The boy king, Edward VI, presented the house to Sir William Sidney, and it has remained in this family ever since, becoming, in 1554, the birthplace of the soldier-poet, Sir Philip Sidney. In the first half of the 17th century, Penshurst was known as a center of literature, attracting such personages as Ben Jonson.

Visitors are shown through the premises, including the splendid State Dining Room and Queen Elizabeth's Room. In the Stable Wing is an interesting Toy Museum. The place is open daily, except Monday, from April 1 until the first Sunday in October. It is also open on Good Friday and all bank holiday Mondays. The gardens, home park, Venture Playground, nature trail, and countryside exhibition are open from noon to 6 p.m. The house is open from 12:30 to 5:30 p.m. Admission is £2.25 ($3.94) for adults, £1 ($1.75) for children.

Leeds Castle, Maidstone, once described by Lord Conway as the loveliest castle in the world, dates from A.D. 857. Originally built in wood, it was rebuilt in 1119 in its present stone structure. It is surrounded by a moat and is an almost impregnable fortress.

The castle has strong links with America through the sixth Lord Fairfax who, as well as owning the castle, owned five million acres in Virginia and was a close friend and mentor of the young George Washington.

Within the surrounding parkland, there is a wild wood garden and duckery where rare swans, geese, and ducks can be seen, and the aviaries contain a superb collection of birds, including parakeets and cockatoos. Dogs are not allowed here, but dog lovers will enjoy the Great Danes of the castle and the unique collection of dog collars dating from the Middle Ages. A 9-hole and an 18-tee golf course are open to the public daily.

Leeds is open in April and May daily except Monday from noon to 5 p.m. From June until the end of September it is open from noon to 5 p.m. daily, and from October until the end of March its hours are from noon to 4 p.m. on Saturday and Sunday only. Admission is £2.95 ($5.16) for adults and £1.95 ($3.41) for children. Should you wish to visit only the grounds, the fee is £1.95 ($3.41) for adults and 95p ($1.66) for children. Disabled people are admitted free. Those who can't face the half-mile or so walk from the car park to the castle can take a free ride on a tractor-drawn farm wagon bus.

Kentish evenings at the castle are presented every Saturday throughout the year from 7 p.m. to 1 a.m., starting with a sherry cocktail reception, then a guided tour of the castle and Fairfax Hall, exploring also a 17th-century tithe barn converted into an attractive banqueting hall for a feast of mousse, followed by broth and a slice of beef carved at your table and served with seasonal vegetables. The meal is rounded off by dessert, cheese, fruit, and coffee. A half bottle of wine is included in the overall price of £17 ($29.75) per person. During the meal musicians play and sing songs fitting to the surroundings and the occasion.

It is worth checking with British Rail and with London tour operators for the price of a package unless you want to drive there yourself.

A Sunday lunch at the castle costs £8.75 ($15.31) for adults and £5.75 ($10.07) for children. A four-course meal with a sherry when you arrive and a glass of wine with your meat is offered from November to March at noon. Advance reservations can be made by telephoning 0622/65400. After lunch, diners are taken on a free tour of the castle.

Haxted Mill, near Edenbridge (tel. Edenbridge 862914). There seems to have been a watermill on this site since 1361, but the present mill was built on the original foundations in 1680, the eastern half added in 1794. The three pairs of grinding stones which you can see today have been grinding corn for more than 250 years, and the waterwheel which drives them is more than 140 years old. The old building is a museum in itself, but it contains a fascinating collection of mill machinery, early mill gas engines, and an old wooden drive shaft from Horsten Keynes mill. Woody Woodrow is the curator. After you've seen the mill pool and the waterwheels, you can go across the courtyard to a small tea room where light refreshment is served. The mill is open most afternoons from Easter to September. Drive west out of Edenbridge on an unnumbered road toward Haxted and Lingfield. Admission is 40p (70¢) for adults and 20p (35¢) for children.

Squerryes Court at Westerham (tel. 0959/62345), is a William and Mary–period manor house built in 1681 and owned by the Warde family for 250 years. Besides a fine collection of paintings, tapestries, and furniture, in the Wolfe Room is a collection of pictures and relics of the family of General Wolfe. The general received his military commission in the grounds of the house at a spot marked by a cenotaph. See also the Museum of the Kent Sharpshooter Yeomanry Regiment. The house and grounds are open from March to October on Saturday, Sunday, and bank holidays (also Wednesday from May to September). Hours are 2 to 6 p.m., and admission charges are £1.20 ($2.10) for adults and 60p ($1.05) for children.

Postscript: **Violet Bourne,** 70 High St., Milton Regis, near Sittingbourne (tel. Sittingbourne 23762 in the evenings), owns the Elizabethan house in which she lives and has filled it with Victoriana. Each room has been furnished absolutely to period down to the last ornament and trinket—a tiny purse made of shells, polished and lacquered musical boxes, and chiming clocks. She is delighted to take visitors around, charging 50p (88¢) to see her lovely collection. She prefers afternoon visitors.

Ightham Mote, Ivy Hatch, at Seven Oaks (tel. 0732/62235). The house is open only on Friday afternoon throughout the year and on Sunday afternoon as well from April to September. But it is worth knowing about, as it is one of the most complete remaining examples of a medieval moated manor house in England. The house was extensively remodeled in the early 16th century, and the Tudor chapel with its painted ceiling, the timbered outer walls, and the ornate chimneys reflect that period. A stone bridge crosses the moat, leading into the great central courtyard which is overlooked by the magnificent windows of the Great Hall. The rest of the house is grouped around the courtyard, and from the Great Hall a Jacobean staircase leads to the old chapel on the first floor. You go through the Solar with its oriel window to the Tudor chapel.

Unlike many other ancient houses in England, Ightham has passed from family to family, and each has left its mark on the place. The present owner is Charles Henry Robinson of Portland, Maine, a visitor who found the house for sale in 1953 and promptly purchased it. He has been responsible for a great deal of the restoration and hopes to be able to leave the place to the National Trust. It is open from 2 to 5 p.m. in summer, until 4 p.m. in winter. Admission is £1.10 ($1.93) for adults and 70p ($1.23) for children.

1. Canterbury

Under the arch of the ancient West Gate journeyed Chaucer's knight, solicitor, nun, squire, parson, merchant, miller, and cook—filled with racy tales. Straight from the pages of *The Canterbury Tales,* they were bound for the shrine of Thomas à Becket, archbishop of Canterbury, who was slain by four knights of Henry II on December 29, 1170. (It is said that the king later walked barefoot from Harbledown to the tomb of his former friend, where he allowed himself to be flogged in penance.) The shrine was finally torn down in 1538 by Henry VIII, as a part of his campaign to destroy the monasteries and graven images. Canterbury, then, has been an attraction of long standing.

The medieval Kentish city, on the Stour River, is the mother city of England, its ecclesiastical capital. Mother city is an apt title, as Canterbury was known to have been inhabited centuries before the birth of Christ. Julius Caesar once went on a rampage near it. Although its most famous incident was the murder of Becket, the medieval city has witnessed other major moments in English history, including Bloody Mary's ordering that nearly 40 victims be burned at the stake. Richard the Lion-hearted came back this way from crusading, and Charles II passed through on the way to reclaim his crown.

Canterbury was once completely walled, and many traces of its old fortifications remain. In the 16th century, weavers—mostly Huguenots from northern France and the Low Countries—fled to Canterbury to escape religious persecution. They started a weaving industry that flourished until the expanding silk trade with India sent it into oblivion.

The old city is much easier to reach today than it was in Chaucer's time. Lying 56 miles from London, it is within a 1½-hour train ride from Victoria Station.

In the Middle Ages, as now, the goal of the pilgrim remains:

CANTERBURY CATHEDRAL: The foundation of this splendid cathedral (tel. Canterbury 61954) dates back to the coming of Augustine, the first archbishop, from Rome in A.D. 597, but the earliest part of the present building is the great Romanesque crypt built circa 1100. The monastic choir erected on top of this at the same time was destroyed by fire in 1174, only four years after the murder of Thomas à Becket on a dark December evening in the northwest transept, still one of the most famous places of pilgrimage in Europe. The destroyed choir was replaced by a magnificent early Gothic one immediately, and first used for worship in 1180. The cathedral was the first great church in the Gothic style to be erected in England and set a fashion for the whole country. Its architects were the Frenchman, William of Sens, and "English" William who took Sens's place after the Frenchman was crippled in an accident in 1178 which later proved fatal.

This part of the church is noteworthy for its medieval tombs of royal personages such as King Henry IV and Edward the Black Prince, as well as numerous archbishops. To the later Middle Ages belongs the great 14th-century nave and the famous central "Bell Harry Tower." The cathedral stands in spacious precincts amid the remains of the buildings of the monastery—cloisters, chapter house, and Norman water tower, which have survived intact from the Dissolution in the time of King Henry VIII to the present day.

Becket's shrine was destroyed by the Tudor king, but the site of that tomb may be seen in Trinity Chapel, in the vicinity of the High Altar. Becket is said to have worked miracles. The cathedral contains some rare stained glass depicting those feats. Perhaps the only thing miraculous is that the windows escaped Henry VIII's agents of destruction and Hitler's bombs as well (part of the cathedral was hit in World War II). East of the Trinity Chapel is "Becket's Crown," in which is a chapel dedicated to "Martyrs and Saints of Our Own Time." St. Augustine's Chair, one of the symbols of the authority of the archbishop of Canterbury, stands behind the high altar.

ROMAN PAVEMENT: This site is off High Street down Butchery Lane. It contains some fine mosaic pavement remains and treasures from excavations in the city. The Pavement is open daily from 10 a.m. to 1 p.m. and from 2 to 5 p.m. (afternoons only, in winter). The entrance charge is 25p (44¢), or you can obtain a combined ticket to the Roman Pavement and the West Gate Towers Museum for 35p (61¢).

GUIDED TOURS: Guided tours of Canterbury are organized by the **Guild of Guides,** Virginia House, 12 St. Thomas Hill (tel. Canterbury 59779), costing 85p ($1.49) per person. Tours of the cathedral are arranged by the Guides office at 11B, The Precincts (tel. Canterbury 64212). They take place generally from April to October at 11:20 a.m. and 2:30 p.m. Monday to Friday and at 11:20 a.m. on Saturday. No tours are conducted on Sunday. There is no charge to enter the cathedral, although tours cost 60p ($1.05) per person.

ACCOMMODATIONS: Before you can begin any serious exploring, you'll need to find a room. You have several possibilities within the city itself and on the outskirts, both budget guest houses and splurge hotels.

Bed and Breakfast

Cathedral Gate Hotel & Restaurant, 37 Burgate (tel. Canterbury 64381), is for modern-day pilgrims who want to rest their bones at an inn shouldering up to the cathedral's gateway. In 1620 the former hospice became one of the earliest of the fashionable coffee and tea houses of England. Its facade was added in the 19th century, however. The interior reveals many architectural features of the 17th century. Mr. P. Shingler, the proprietor, has improved the amenities while retaining the hotel's old-world charm. Two curved bay windows in the living room overlook the little square in front of the gateway. The bedrooms and public rooms are warmed by gas central heating. Each of the 33 bedrooms has hot and cold running water, and some contain private baths. The single rate goes from £10.50 ($18.38) to £13.50 ($23.63); the double tariff, from £15 ($26.25) to £22 ($38.50). A full English breakfast is an additional £3.50 ($6.13). The ground-floor restaurant serves both luncheon and evening snacks and is licensed.

The **Georgian Guest House,** 69 Castle St. (tel. Canterbury 61111), is a venture of Mrs. Kennett, who has restored and preserved the old architectural features of a 1502 building near the center of Canterbury. She has updated it with water basins, baths, and heating. The home is gracious and pleasant, furnished with antiques. Your timbered bedroom may have either a half-tester Victorian bed, or a slim four-poster, making sleeping here a retreat to Pickwickian days. The cost of a sleep in a treasured bed plus an abundant breakfast is

£7.50 ($13.13) per person. She rents out three singles, three doubles, and, most interesting for families traveling with children, two family rooms suitable for three to four persons. The back drawing room is made from the old cellar kitchen, overlooking the rear garden. Guests enjoy the restored Tudor exterior —wooden corbels, tile-hanging—at the back of the house and the garden. Mrs. Kennett is just the type for a stack of books beside a high-backed chair in front of the fireplace, ready for an evening's conversation on any subject. She's also considered one of England's authorities on Dr. Johnson.

Pilgrims Guest House, 18 The Friars (tel. Canterbury 64531), dates back in part more than 300 years, and is just a three-minute walk from the cathedral. Owners Patricia and Peter Malin believe in making guests feel thoroughly at home. Comfort is assured by such items as innerspring mattresses, hot and cold running water in all the rooms, some with their own toilet and shower, enough corridor baths and toilets, and an efficient central heating system. The charge is from £8.50 ($14.88) nightly for B&B. The breakfast fortifies you for the day. In the evening, guests congregate in the lounge for conversation and to watch television. There's an adjoining concrete car park.

Ersham Lodge, 12 New Dover Rd. (tel. Canterbury 63174), is a Tudor-style, 19th-century building at the edge of town. The owners, Mr. and Mrs. Pellay, have acquired this pleasant lodge, and the whole place has been redecorated and is as fresh as a country morning in Kent. All rooms contain TV, radio, telephone, and shower. Paying guests are accepted at a charge of £11.50 ($20.13) per person for B&B in a single room, £22 ($38.50) for two in a double. There are some rooms with TV, private bath, and toilet renting for £27 ($47.25) for two. A full English breakfast is included. The house is gracious in style—set back from the road and in the midst of many shade trees, with a back garden for children to play in. From the two-story living room, a winding staircase leads to the spacious and comfortably furnished corner bedrooms.

St. Stephen's Guest House, 100 St. Stephen's Rd. (tel. Canterbury 62167), is in a quiet part of the city, yet close to the main attractions. One of the most attractive buildings in Canterbury, St. Stephen's is owned and managed by Richard and Jean Ganther, who give visitors a friendly welcome. The house, set in well-kept gardens and lawns, with its discreet extensions, has retained its character and yet also offers modern accommodations for the guests. There are nine bedrooms, all with central heating and hot and cold water. The house can also boast of its own water softener and sleeps up to 18 people. Tariffs include B&B and use of bath or shower. A single room rents from £8 ($14) per person nightly, a double room from £15 ($26.25). The guest house also has a residential liquor license.

The **House of Agnes Hotel,** 71 Saint Dunstan's St. (tel. Canterbury 65077), remains much as Dickens described it in *David Copperfield,* as the home of Agnes Wickfield, heroine of the novel. Built in the 16th century, the House of Agnes is an authentic, Tudor black-and-white timbered building—historic surroundings at budget prices. The Frost family, who run it, quote B&B terms (depending on the room and the time of year) ranging from £9 ($15.75) to £15 ($26.25), inclusive. Some of the bedrooms are handsome and cozy; all ye olde chambers have hot and cold running water and color TV. The hotel has its own car park and full central heating.

Abbey Gate Guest House, 7 North Lane (tel. Canterbury 68770), offers friendly and personal service. The spotlessly clean rooms, although small, have central heating and lots of hot water. There are laundry facilities, and a bath or shower on the premises. If you need it, babysitting services are available. The Abbey is centrally located in Canterbury, and all fire regulations have been completed. Price (including a very good breakfast) per person daily is from

£6.50 ($11.38). Children are most welcome.

Carlton Guest House, 40 Nunnery Fields (tel. Canterbury 65900), is operated by the very helpful Ian and Alison Williams, who enjoy meeting guests. All their rooms have radio, TV, and a refrigerator, and are clean and comfortable. The cost is £7.50 ($13.13) per person nightly for B&B. The road on which the guest house lies is very quiet, and there is private parking. The town center is about a six-minute walk from Carlton, the cathedral about a ten-minute walk. The main station and the bus station also lie nearby. In the summer Mr. and Mrs. Williams will offer you an evening meal with traditional English cooking.

Yorke Lodge Guest House, 50 London Rd. (tel. Canterbury 51243), is spacious and comfortable, a Victorian guest house close to the center of town and the cathedral. The resident owner, Mrs. Sharron Rockhill, is charming and helpful to guests. The charge is from £8.50 ($14.88) per person for B&B. All units contain hot and cold running water, and there are two large shower rooms which are popular with American visitors. The house also has a comfortably furnished television lounge and a pleasant sun lounge looking onto the garden. An evening meal, offering traditional English fare with local produce when available, can be arranged.

The **Seven Stars Inn,** Orange Street, (tel. Canterbury 63774), is a lovely old Victorian pub where they have traced the innkeepers back to 1680 and a charmer called Catherine Gill. They could have gone further back if they weren't so busy catering to the needs of the present-day clientele. Today John Lytton is mine host, presiding over the hand pumps which served traditional Kentish ale to the crowds who frequent the pub. It's very popular with the young, particularly members of Kent University. It sometimes seems that the whole campus is there on any given evening.

Beyond the bars, inn-style bedrooms cost £8 ($14) per person, including a continental breakfast. If you want a big English breakfast, expect to pay another £2.25 ($3.94). There are only three doubles and two singles.

Lunch or dinner, mostly grills, consists of such dishes as sirloin with mushrooms, onion, tomato, and fried potatoes and peas at a cost of £4 ($7). Cheaper is the chicken or ham with fried potatoes, £1.85 ($3.24).

Kingsbridge Villa, 15 Best Lane (tel. Canterbury 66415), is a bright, friendly, and spotless guest house run by Barbara Williams close to the cathedral in the oldest part of the city. She rents out a dozen rooms at a rate of £9 ($15.75) per person nightly. There's a small restaurant and bar in the basement which is reached through the house or else by area steps past a medieval well where they once found a coin dating from A.D. 163. Clay pipes adorn the red brick walls, and there are comfortable settle seats around the bar. All ingredients used in the kitchen are fresh, and they bake their bread and make their own cakes. A set lunch of typically English fare goes for £3.50 ($6.13). Dinner, which is likely to include some continental dishes, costs about £6 ($10.50), including VAT.

READERS' GUEST HOUSE SELECTIONS: "I would like to recommend a lovely woman in Canterbury whose home is a 15-minute walk (or less) from the cathedral. She's Mrs. Eve Osborn who has **Allwyn House,** 51 Whitstable Rd. (tel. Canterbury 64769). To reach it you go right past the old city gate, and it's one block from the road to London. The rooms are bright, fresh flowers abound, and Mrs. Osborn will bring breakfast to your room. The cost for B&B ranges from £7 ($12.25) to £8.50 ($14.88), depending on the season" (Eleanor Pantar, Watertown, Mass.). . . . "Just off the main road, right downtown, is a delightful place called **St. John's Court Guest House,** St. John's Lane (tel. Canterbury 56425). The proprietors, Ross and Joyce Skinner, are friendly and accommodating, the rooms are nice with good on-the-hall bath facilities, and a good-tasting breakfast is served. The guest house is not large, taking 22 persons, and has private parking spaces for ten cars. I had an excellent stay at this establishment, and I was especially pleased at its location, a two- or three-minute walk from the cathedral. The rate is £9 ($15.75) per person" (Fred H. Cate, Oxford, England). . . . "**Mrs. K. Sylvester,** 11 Nunnery Rd. (tel. Canterbury 68665), runs a real guest house where Stan and Kay, who formerly lived in South Africa and have many artifacts from there, welcome you with open arms. You are really more like a house guest than just another B&B-er. They give you a home-cooked breakfast, comfortable beds, and bath down the hall. The place is within easy walking distance of both the train and bus station. The Sylvesters charge £8.50 ($14.88) per person for B&B" (Judith Reusswig, Washington, D.C.).

DINING IN CANTERBURY: **Queen Elizabeth's Restaurant,** 44–45 High St. (tel. Canterbury 64080), has the original room where Queen Elizabeth I entertained the Duke of Alençon, while she was trying to decide whether to marry him. The 16th-century interior, with its outstanding relief and wall paneling, recaptures the past admirably. The food is fresh and home-cooked—and very English as well, from the rich-tasting soups, such as cream of pea for 35p (61¢), to the roast pork with apple sauce and vegetables, £2 ($3.50), to the deep-dish apple pie with heavy cream for dessert, 85p ($1.49). If you go early enough, select the seat next to the window so you can look down the High Street. You can spot the restaurant easily by its gabled facade, which has plaster carving. Meals are served every day except Sunday and Monday, and the restaurant is open from 10 a.m. to 6 p.m.

The **Castle Restaurant,** 71 Castle St. (tel. Canterbury 65658), is frequented by in-the-know "Canterburians" as one of the choicest dining spots in the medieval city—the building dates back to 1485—choice not only because of its refined cuisine, but because of economy too. It is directed by Mr. and Mrs. Benjamin, who keep it unpretentious and unspoiled. For suggestions: The soups have rarely been found disappointing—a choice of two is offered daily for 70p ($1.23). The specialties run to grills and fish dishes (prices include chips and garden peas), with such favorites as rainbow trout for £4 ($7). Two grilled lamb chops go for £3.10 ($5.43). The desserts are good and varied, often featuring a gooseberry tart with fresh cream, costing £1.20 ($2.10). On Saturday it's imperative to book before 4 p.m. The restaurant is open daily from 10 a.m. to 10 p.m. The Benjamins also run the more expensive and plush **Adelaide Restaurant,** Adelaide Place, which is part of the Castle Restaurant.

The **Ben Jonson Steak House,** Guildhall Street (tel. Canterbury 69189), has leaded-glass windows with plants on the sills, as well as a small bar and a warm, quiet restaurant where obviously the specialties are steaks. Rump, porterhouse, and entrecôte, along with a T-bone, can come plain and simple from the grill or else you may prefer them more adorned, as in steak Diane. Vegetables are in addition to the price of the meat, as are desserts, and you can order wine by the glass at 75p ($1.31). Because of the expensive cuts of meat, you'll pay more, of course, than in some of the establishments we've been considering—that is, from £7 ($12.25) for a meal.

The **Mayflower Restaurant,** 59 Palace St. (tel. Canterbury 65038), stands on the corner of Palace and Sun Streets. The restaurant is well known in the area which is largely made up of junk-food eating houses. There are very few good English home-cooking establishments in the whole city, and the Mayflower is one of them. This is also an area of the city where many of the Pilgrim Fathers who sailed for America on the *Speedwell* and *Mayflower* came from. C. F. Byrom and his family run the establishment, offering good value on all their dishes. On the first floor is the Pilgrims Bar, where a large variety of snacks are served. The downstairs restaurant has been completely refurbished and decorated in keeping with the old-world surroundings of the building which dates back to 1601. Breakfast and coffee are offered from 10 a.m., lunch and grills from 11:15 a.m. to 2:15 p.m., and dinner or light meals from 6 to 10 p.m. daily except Sunday.

Specialty dishes include Mrs. Byrom's homemade individual beefsteak pudding or pie, roast topside of beef served with Yorkshire pudding, or roast chicken with a sage and onion stuffing. The family also serves two varieties of trout and a lemon sole cooked in wine and mushroom sauce. The portions on all dishes are large. Several continental dishes including coq au vin are also featured. The most expensive three-course dinner with wine and coffee would be under £12 ($21), and the cheapest full meal with wine and coffee would be under £5 ($8.75).

The **House of Agnes,** 71 Saint Dunstan's St. (tel. Canterbury 65077), is a 16th-century hotel, the fictional home of the heroine of *David Copperfield,* Agnes Wickfield (see the hotel discussion). In a cozy, old-world atmosphere, it offers some of the finest "ye fare" in Canterbury. Meals are served in a timbered room, which has several oak settles drawn up to softly lit tables. A table d'hôte luncheon, from £4.50 ($7.88), is served daily, the price including VAT and service charge. On the à la carte menu, the carefully prepared food is likely to include a soup of the day from 85p ($1.49); succulent fowl, such as stuffed duckling with seasonal vegetables, about £5.50 ($9.63); fish platters such as sole from the nearby waters off the White Cliffs of Dover, from £7.50 ($13.13); and large helping of dessert, served with Kentish cream.

Longport Eating House, Longport (tel. Canterbury 53063), is a family-run business that stands at the end of Longport Street. There Peter and Anne Payne welcome you to their cheerful, licensed eatery. They serve meals seven days a week—lunches from noon to 2:30 p.m. and dinners from 6:30 to 11 p.m. You are likely to pay about £6 ($10.50) per head, and wine by the glass is priced at 75p ($1.31). Anne is a Cordon Bleu-trained chef. There is a daily choice of freshly made salads and specialties, and special vegetarian dishes are also available. Good nut roasts, lamb chops, and roasted chicken are regularly featured.

Alberrys Wine and Food Bar, 38 St. Margaret's St. (tel. Canterbury 52378), is fun—even the Victorian cartoons on its wine list claim that "Tomorrow morning you'll be able to perform great feats of strength if you drink plenty of wine tonight." Today, in the same area where slaves of the Romans once toiled (part of the exposed foundation was a section of a Roman amphitheater), there is Latin jazz, disco, and rock/pop music performed live on Monday, Wednesday, and Thursday nights, completely free to customers.

Alberrys offers an inexpensive and frequently changing repertoire of well-prepared food. Cream of mushroom soup, then Alberrys "jumbo" (a big roasting potato filled with pork sausage, cheese, garlic butter, and relish), followed by passion cake, costs only £2.65 ($4.64). Pizzas and quiches are available, and are less expensive. Beer and mixed drinks are served, and wine is available by the glass. It is open daily from noon to 2:30 p.m. and on Tuesday evening from 6:30 to 11 p.m. On other evenings it is open from 6:30 p.m. to midnight. Closed Sunday.

LIVING ON THE OUTSKIRTS: If you should arrive in Canterbury during the peak season, you might be better off to live in a country home or a farmhouse in and around the city, as the center is likely to be overcrowded. And if you have a car, you might prefer to do this regardless of the time of year. You get better and more spacious rooms—and even friendlier service, yet you can be back in the city after a short drive. I'll set forth, first, my inexpensive suburban accommodation recommendations where you'll receive B&B.

At Elham: A 15th-century Hotel and Restaurant

The Abbot's Fireside, Elham (tel. Elham 265), has been a famous restaurant for many years. The inn has been owned by the Prebble family for the past decade or so, although the family has roots in the village dating back to the 14th century. The building is circa 1480, an example of pre-Renaissance architecture. Its wooden mullions and transoms have been well preserved. The whole structure leans forward, as if it's been standing too long. Latticed windows and grotesquely carved wooden brackets give an old-world aura. In one room is a great old fireplace, carved by a monk, from which the establishment takes its name. The Duke of Wellington made this his garrison headquarters when he was mustering his army for battle against Napoleon. Charles II and the Duke of Richmond are reported to have hidden in the chimney while pursued by Roundheads. The inn also has a rare Parliament Clock, thought to be 16th century, and in the restaurant a "coat of chain mail" from the 14th century, reputedly worn by the Black Prince.

Try to schedule at least a luncheon visit, enjoying a set meal featuring standard English fare for about £5 ($8.75). If you fall in love with the place, you can stay over in one of nine bedrooms, all of which have washbasins. They are sparsely, but adequately, furnished. For your B&B and evening meal, you're charged £17 ($29.75) nightly. B&B is £12 ($21) nightly, including VAT. Service is extra.

In the area is the **Romney, Hythe & Dymchurch Light Railway Co.,** the world's smallest public railway. The engines are all steam driven, the carriages covered so there is no fear of getting wet. The line is 13½ miles long from Hythe (Kent) to New Romney and Dungeness, and the trains are one-third-size miniature versions of the kind of trains that ran on English or North American line railways in the 1920s. The line has a complicated rail fare, depending on the distance traveled. Otherwise, you can purchase a runabout ticket valid for unlimited travel, costing about £7 ($12.25) per day. Children travel for one-third the adult fare. It operates daily from Easter to the end of September and on weekends from March through October. The railway is reached by road along the A259. The ride takes about half an hour. Naturally, the ticket includes the freedom to travel for a whole day as services permit on the R.H.&D. Railway. Telephone New Romney 2353 for train times. The terminal of the railway, Hythe, is near Folkestone, which can be reached by frequent trains from London.

To get to Hythe, leave Canterbury on the Dover road, five miles out, then turn right a further five miles to Hythe.

At Northbourne: A Former Rectory

Parsonage House, Northbourne, near Deal (tel. Deal 5826), was once the village rectory. It stands in two acres of garden close to the Norman church of St. Augustine, just 12 miles from Canterbury. The house, run by Mr. and Mrs. R. W. Stiles, is within easy reach of the Channel ports, beaches, golf courses, and the Kentish countryside. B&B is offered to no more than six guests at a time, each of whom is charged from £10 ($17.50). Three spacious double rooms are offered, each with hot and cold running water. There's also a lounge with TV and a billiards room. Evening meals can be served if arranged in advance. The Stiles are a very accommodating and helpful couple, and their English breakfast has been called "super."

Near Maidstone: An 18th-Century House

Dial House, East Street, Harrietsham, near Maidstone (tel. 0622/859-622), was built in the 18th century by the ancestors of the present owners. The Bottle family (isn't that a wonderful English name?) has been living there ever since the house was built, and in the village two centuries before that. Dial House is a typical Kent tile hung house with an inglenook fireplace in the lounge and a large garden. The Bottles accommodate up to ten people in two double rooms, one single, and a two-room annex, sleeping four to five persons with a private bathroom en suite. Terms are from £8.50 ($14.88) per person with no extras. Mrs. Bottle serves a full English breakfast with homemade jams and a fruit compote.

Although Dial House and its cottage annex are old properties, they have been fully modernized, with full central heating, hot and cold running water in the double rooms, fitted carpets, and excellent bathroom facilities. The house lies 7 miles from Maidstone and 11 miles from Ashford. The A20 divides the village of Harrietsham; at the A20 traffic lights, follow the sign to Sandway. Just 200 yards on the left is Dial House, standing opposite the Bell Inn. Anchored here, you're four miles from Leeds Castle and a ten-minute walk from Pilgrims Way.

Fifteen miles from Canterbury is our next stopover:

2. Dover

One of the ancient Cinque ports, Dover is famed for its white cliffs. In Victoria's day, it basked in popularity as a seaside resort, but today it is of importance mainly because it is a port for major cross-Channel car and passenger traffic between England and France (notably Calais). Sitting in the open jaws of the white cliffs, Dover was one of England's most vulnerable and easy-to-hit targets in World War II. It suffered repeated bombings that destroyed much of its harbor.

Hovering nearly 400 feet above the port is **Dover Castle,** one of the oldest and best known in England. Its keep was built at the command of Becket's fair-weather friend, Henry II, in the 12th century. You can visit the keep all year, generally from 9:30 a.m. to 5:30 p.m. in summer (it closes earlier off-season), for an admission of £1 ($1.75); children pay 50p (88¢). Admission to the underground works is 50p (88¢) for adults, 25p (44¢) for children. Admission to the castle grounds is free. The ancient castle was called back to active duty as late as World War II. The "Pharos" on the grounds is a lighthouse built by the Romans in the first half of the first century. The Romans landed at nearby Deal in 55 B.C. and 54 B.C. The first landing was not successful. The second in 54 B.C. was more so, but after six months they departed, and did not return until nearly 100 years later, A.D. 43, when they occupied the country and stayed 400 years.

An excursion from Dover can be made to **Lympne Castle,** near Hythe. This small castle was built in the 14th century on land given in the 18th century to the church at Lympne. There is mention of a Saxon abbey on the site in the *Doomsday Book* of 1085. Right on the edge of a cliff, the castle has magnificent views over the channel and across Romney Marshes to Fairlight. An ideal lookout against invasion, it has a Norman tower in the east and a medieval one to the west with turret stairways leading to the main rooms. It's open daily from 10:30 a.m. to 6 p.m., June to September.

ACCOMMODATIONS: Because Dover operates in a sellers' market, owing to the cross-Channel traffic, prices for lodgings tend to run high. But below you'll find some top bargains.

St. Martins Guest House, 17 Castle Hill Rd. (tel. Dover 205938), stands a few blocks away from the cross-Channel ferries and the Hoverport, on the hillside leading up to Dover Castle. The house is more than 130 years old, and is maintained and furnished to high standards, with full central heating. Bedrooms with double-glazed windows also contain color TV sets and private showers. B&B only is provided, from £8 ($14) per person. Ample parking is available.

The house is run by Mr. and Mrs. Morriss, who have proved to be very popular with their North American visitors. Mrs. Morriss had been connected with catering before taking over the guest house, and was in charge of some restaurants in London's West End. However, her dream was always to own her own guest house, and now that has come true.

Mildmay Hotel, 78 Folkestone Rd. (tel. Dover 204278), is a brick Edwardian-style hotel run by Mr. and Mrs. Hedgecock. By their refurbishing touches, they have transformed it from a guest house into a hotel, where they charge £13 ($22.75) per person, including VAT and service. All rooms have private bathrooms. Mildmay has a license for drinks, and Mrs. Hedgecock will serve an evening dinner to her guests on their way to and from the continent. The management is polite and friendly, the service is efficient, and there's a free car park out back. Maj. George F. Hanson, New York City, writes: "This was without a doubt the best for the money that we found anywhere in England!"

Number One Guest House, 1 Castle St. (tel. Dover 202007), is one of Dover's oldest remaining homes. It is centrally situated for visits to the town, port, banks, and restaurants. Mrs. Adeline Reidy and her family run this "grade one" guest house, offering doubles, twins, and family rooms, all with private shower, TV, and heating. Three rooms contain complete private showers and toilets. A full English breakfast, included in the rate, is served in your room. Terms are from £8.50 ($14.88) per person daily. Both Adeline and her husband, John, extend a warm welcome to their guests.

Westbank Guest House, 239 Folkestone Rd. (tel. Dover 201061), is one of the best B&B houses in the area. Gwen and Bill Tennant welcome you, housing guests in one of their well-appointed, clean, and comfortable units, each with hot and cold running water. In season, the cost of a twin-bedded room is £7.50 ($13.13) per person. That tariff includes a well-prepared breakfast. They also cater for stays of three days at reduced rates. For example, in the height of season (August), a family of four sharing a room can have bed, breakfast, and evening meal for £87 ($152.25) for three days. In all, they can accommodate 21 guests. Gwen is a cook of high standard, and if given a few hours notice, she offers an evening meal at £3 ($5.25) per person. All guests receive a welcome tray of tea or coffee along with biscuits on arrival.

READERS' HOTEL SELECTIONS: "We stayed at the **Cleveland Guest House,** which is just off the bottom of Castle Hill in Dover. It is a delightful B&B house run by Mr. and Mrs. Kaczor. The address is 2 Laureston Pl. (tel. Dover 204622). Mr. and Mrs. Kaczor were two of the most helpful people with whom we stayed on our entire trip. Their home is extremely clean. Their charge is £9 ($15.75) per night, and there is adequate parking space on the street in front of their home" (Michael L. Lowry, Atlanta, Ga.). . . . "At the recommendation of friends and family, we stayed at the **Gladstone**

House, 3 Laureston Pl. (tel. Dover 208457). It is within minutes of Dover Castle, good restaurants, shopping, and the Hoverport. Owners Karen and Keith Davies are easily the nicest and most helpful acquaintances we made during our entire trip in England. They gave us a real flavor and insight into the British way of life. Their house is tastefully and traditionally decorated, with a large Tudor dining room and spacious bedrooms. An exceptional breakfast completed our stay with them. The total cost for B&B for two is £15 ($26.25)" (Fran and Mike Young, Alexandria, Va.).

"Mr. and Mrs. D. Bowles own **Linden Guest House,** 231 Folkestone Rd. (tel. Dover 205449). We stayed there and were treated very kindly. The rooms are beautifully appointed, clean, and warm. A lovely cup of tea and cookies were provided for supper. B&B is from £8.50 ($14.88) per person" (Mr. and Mrs. E. J. Mullen, Gisborne, New Zealand). . . . "We spent the night in Dover at the **Beulah House,** 94 Crabble Hill (tel. Kearsney 824615). It's right in town along the A256 (A2) to London. It was a delightfully attractive, clean, and well-decorated home. There was a huge garden in the back surrounded by rose bushes and sculptured yews. The breakfast was huge, hot, and delicious. The proprietors, Donald and Beulah Abate, were very gracious. The price is £10 ($17.50) per person" (Anne Hixson, APO New York). . . . "We found a place which we would label 'England at its best.' East of Dover, we discovered, just five minutes from the docks by car, **Wallett's Court,** West Cliffe, St. Margarets-at-Cliffe (tel. Dover 852424), a historic building that dates back 900 years. The owners, Chris and Lea Oakley, renovated it with much love for every detail, and we happened to be the first guests. We highly recommend it to everyone who is interested in history and who not only wants a place to sleep and eat but who appreciates the little things that make such a stay enjoyable (magnificent sight from the bedroom window across the sea, fresh flowers in the bedroom, an extra tea at night, a large English breakfast, and pleasant conversation with the hosts). Charges are £8 ($14) per person for B&B. Children are charged half price" (Wolfgang Gatzka, Essen, Germany).

WHERE TO EAT: **Wrens,** 40 Castle St., is ideal for morning coffee or lunch, as it is open from 9 a.m. to 2 p.m. daily except Sunday. Despite its flighty name, it offers down-to-earth prices. Lying only two blocks from the harbor, it was one of the few little buildings to survive the bombing. It has a small Georgian curved bay window facing the street and two tiny rooms for dining on the street floor. The delightful ladies who prepare and serve the home-cooked meals are English to the bone. They seat you at tiny tables, then tempt you with the likes of, say, a rich, stock-based soup for 35p (61¢), followed by a large home-cooked main dish for £1.75 ($3.06). The homemade fruit pies or steamed puddings are the best for dessert, 45p (79¢).

For our next and final stopover in Kent, we go inland—37 miles from London—to a once-fashionable resort:

3. Tunbridge Wells

Dudley, Lord North, courtier to James I, is credited with the discovery in 1606 of the chalybeate spring that started it all. His accidental find led to the creation of a fashionable resort that reached its peak in the mid-18th century under the foppish leadership of "Beau" Nash. "Beau" or Richard Nash (1674-1761) was a dandy of a style-setter in his day, the final arbiter of what to wear and what to say—even how to act (for example, he got men to take off their boots and put on stockings). But, of course, most of his time was devoted to Bath.

Even so, Tunbridge Wells enjoyed a prime spa reputation from the days of Charles II through Victoria's time. Because so many monarchs had visited, Edward VII named it "Royal Tunbridge Wells" in 1909. Over the years "the cure" was considered the answer for everything from too many days of wine and roses to failing sexual prowess.

The most remarkable feature of Tunbridge Wells is its Pantiles, a colonnaded walkway for shoppers, tea-drinkers, and diners, built near the wells. At the Assembly Hall, entertainment (opera, vaudeville) is presented.

Alas, there's nothing sadder in tourism than a resort that's seen its day: Tunbridge Wells is more for Jane Austen than Jane Fonda. Still, it's worth a visit just for a fleeting glimpse at the good old days of the 18th century.

Canadians touring in the area may want to seek out the grave of the founder of their country's capital. Lt.-Col. John By of the Royal Engineers (1779-1836) died at Shernfold Park in Frant, East Sussex, near Tunbridge Wells, and is buried in the churchyard there. His principal claim to fame is that he built the Rideau Canal in Upper Canada and established what was later to be the capital of the Dominion of Canada, the city of Ottawa.

The Rideau Canal, some 124 miles long, links the city of Kingston on the St. Lawrence River with the city of Ottawa on the Ottawa River. Between 1826 and 1832 John By successfully constructed the canal through an unexplored wilderness for the British government. At the northern end of the canal he laid out "Bytown." Twenty years later this was renamed Ottawa, and it became the capital of the united Canada. His grave near Tunbridge Wells is marked with a plaque erected by the Historical Society of Ottawa in 1979.

WHERE TO STAY: **The Swan Hotel,** Pantiles (tel. Tunbridge Wells 27590), backs up against the historic arcade. A Scottish and Newcastle Breweries Hotel, it offers better-than-average amenities. The rate for B&B is £10 ($17.50) in a single, £17 ($29.75) for two in a double, including service and VAT. The rooms have the basic requirements, such as water basins, but they lack élan. The corridor baths are adequate. In addition, you'll find a bar and a pleasant lounge, where food is served. The famous Scottish soup—cock-a-leekie—(if it's on the menu) is well worth a try. For your main course, you get such typical fare as roast rib of beef with Yorkshire pudding and vegetables, or half a Surrey chicken. A hot fruit pie with fresh cream generously rounds out a most filling repast. Lunch, costing around £5 ($8.75), is served between 12:30 and 2 p.m.; dinner, at £6.50 ($11.38), from 7 to 8 p.m.

Cosack House, Victoria Road, Southborough (tel. 32633), belongs to Mrs. Pamela Paradise, who has three double bedrooms and two singles. She has set the daily per-person rate of £10 ($17.50), which includes one of her popular breakfasts, where she prepares eggs and bacon the way you prefer. Her tidy and homelike bedrooms have hot and cold running water, and there's a parking lot for your car.

Thornedene Guest House, 108 St. Johns Rd. (tel. Tunbridge Wells 21712), is a moderately priced place to stay in a high-priced area. Mr. and Mrs. R. J. Jose, the owners, charge £9 ($15.75) per person daily for B&B. It's a simple place, unpretentious, but well-kept.

Grosvenor Guest House, 215 Upper Grosvenor Rd. (tel. Tunbridge Wells 32601), is one of the better B&B houses at the spa. That's because it's owned by Virginia and Colin Clark, who are fine hosts, seeing that each guest is made comfortable. They charge from £9 ($15.75) for a good bed and a "very fattening" English breakfast. They rent out three double bedrooms and two family rooms, and the house has full central heating and hot and cold running water in all units. In addition, there is parking space for five cars.

READERS' GUEST HOUSE SELECTIONS: "We arrived at **Brian and Ann Moore's** home, 34 Pennington Rd., Southborough (tel. Tunbridge Wells 37986), totally worn out, and it was everything exhausted travelers dream of—spotlessly clean, freshfully and tastefully decorated, and quiet. The dining room looks out on a small, flower-filled garden. Ann fixed a big, good breakfast which included orange juice, cereal, bacon, eggs, toast, and wheat rolls. In the evening, they let us use a spare black-and-white TV which they were not using. It was a wonderful, homey place which we enjoyed as an exploring base. The charge is £7.50 ($13.13) per person per night, and we considered it one of the best bargains in all our travels" (Mrs. Robert Merrill, Kansas City, Mo.). . . . "A charming, well-kept B&B home is run by **Mrs. Joan Still,** 80 Ravenswood Ave. (tel. Tunbridge Wells 23069). The cost is £6.50 ($11.38) per person. Our breakfast was enormous: cereal, two kinds of sausages, tomatoes, beans, eggs, potatoes, toast, and of course tea, quite the best we had in England. To add to the homey feeling, the dining room is decorated with fresh flowers from their own attached greenhouse. Mrs. Still's daughter two doors down takes in any overflow of guests" (Gregg and Wendy Wheeler, Helena, Mont.).

WHERE TO EAT: Most travelers are content with a luncheon stopover in Tunbridge Wells.

If so, **Hole in the Wall,** 9 The High St. (tel. Tunbridge Wells 26550), is a suitable choice. George Lawson is "mine host" of this popular 1880s-style pub. The fare is simple, consisting mainly of stews, salads, and soups, accompanied by crisp fresh bread. A Kentish ploughman's lunch with a half pint of cider will cost around £1.30 ($2.28) and should set you up nicely for the rest of the day. A plate of meat with salad goes for £1.75 ($3.06).

Bruin's Bar and Ristorante Orso, 5 London Rd. (tel. Tunbridge Wells 35757). In Italian, "orso" means bear, but that isn't one of the specialties here. The Brown brothers run Bruin's, with the help of dozens of teddy bears decorating this friendly pub which is a combination of ale house and Italian restaurant. The food is excellent here. Beer and ale go well with the snacks served in the bar. These include steak-and-kidney pie with potatoes or lasagne and salad, each for £1.85 ($3.24). In the restaurant upstairs, you might order mussels in garlic butter, followed by beef casserole in red wine, at a cost of £5.55 ($9.72). A variety of cheaper pasta dishes is available. The brothers are open Monday through Saturday from noon to 3 p.m. and from 7 until 11 p.m.

Instead of leaving London for Kent, you might head directly south of the capital to inviting Surrey.

SURREY

This tiny county has for some time been in danger of being gobbled up by the growing boundaries of London and turned into a sprawling suburb, catching the overflow of a giant metropolis. But although it is densely populated in the area bordering the capital, Surrey still retains much unspoiled countryside, largely because its many heaths and commons form undesirable land for postwar suburbanite houses. Essentially, Surrey is a county of commuters (Alfred Lord Tennyson was among the first), since a worker in the city can practically travel to the remotest corner of Surrey from London in anywhere from 45 minutes to an hour.

Long before William the Conqueror marched his pillaging Normans across its chalky North Downs, Surrey was important to the Saxons. In fact, early Saxon kings were once crowned at what is now Kingston-on-Thames (their Coronation Stone is still preserved near the Guildhall).

RUNNYMEDE: Two miles outside Windsor is the meadow on the south side of the Thames, in Surrey, where King John put his seal on the Great Charter. John may have signed the document up the river on a little island, but that's being technical. Today, Runnymede is also the site of the **John F. Kennedy**

Memorial, one acre of English ground given to the United States by the people of Britain.

4. Haslemere

A quiet, sleepy town, Haslemere attracts because Early English musical instruments are made by hand there. Ever hear a harpsichord concert? An annual music festival (see below) is the town's main drawing card. Over the years the Dolmetsch family has been responsible for the acclaim that has come to this otherwise unheralded little Surrey town, lying in the midst of some of the shire's finest scenery. Haslemere is only an hour's train ride from Waterloo Station in London, about 42 miles away.

THE FESTIVAL: It isn't often that one can hear such exquisite music played so skillfully on the harpsichord, the recorder, the lute, or any of the instruments designed so painstakingly to interpret the music of earlier centuries. Throughout the year, the Dolmetsch family makes and repairs these instruments, welcoming visitors to their place on the edge of Haslemere. They rehearse constantly, preparing for the concerts that are held in July, and last nine days.

You can get specific information by writing to the **Haslemere Festival Office,** Jesses, Grayswood Road, Haslemere (or telephone Haslemere 2161 between 9 a.m. and 12:30 p.m. daily). During the festival, matinees begin at 3:15 p.m., evening performances at 7:15 p.m. For seats in the balcony, prices range from £2 ($3.50) to £3 ($5.25), with stall seats going from £1 ($1.75) to £2.50 ($4.38).

For Pub Snacks

The **Swan Hotel,** High Street (tel. Haslemere 4608), is a pub in the center of the village. Just because it has hotel in its name doesn't mean that it contains rooms to rent. Built in the late 19th century, it was the descendant of an inn of the same name erected in 1601. Much of the old quaintery still exists, including low black beams. The Swan is a good restaurant, with all English meals, such as homemade steak-and-kidney pie with chips and peas and cottage pie with vegetables. Pub snacks are always available, including sandwiches at 70p ($1.23) and cold meat pie with salad at £1.90 ($3.33). Otherwise, expect to spend from £4 ($7) for a simple meal.

GUILDFORD: The old and new meet in the county town on the Wey River, 40 minutes by train from Waterloo Station in London. Charles Dickens believed that its High Street, which slopes to the river, was one of the most beautiful in England. The Guildhall has an ornamental projecting clock which dates back to 1683.

Lying 2½ miles southwest of the city, **Loseley House** (tel. Guildford 571881), a beautiful and historic Elizabethan mansion visited by Queen Elizabeth I, James I, and Queen Mary, has been featured on TV and in five films. Its works of art include paneling from Henry VIII's Nonsuch Palace, period furniture, a unique carved chalk chimneypiece, magnificent ceilings, and cushions made by the first Queen Elizabeth. The mansion is open from the end of May to the end of September on Wednesday, Thursday, Friday, and Saturday from 2 to 5 p.m., charging £1.10 ($1.93) for adults, 65p ($1.14) for children.

Back in Guildford, I'd suggest the following accommodations:

Brian & Jenny Newman's Guest House, 24 Waterden Rd. (tel. Guildford 60558), is a simple but immaculate guest house with a swimming pool. Mr. and Mrs. Newman charge from £9.50 ($16.63) per person for B&B, including VAT and a big English breakfast. For guests traveling by train, the guest house is just a two-minute walk from the London Road Station in Guildford. There is direct rail link to Gatwick Airport, plus a rail and coach link to Heathrow. The breakfast room at the guest house is unique, with its vast collection of copper and curios.

The **Carlton Hotel,** London Road (tel. Guildford 575158), is used by some guests so as to be out of the big crush of London. It's just a three-minute walk to the London Road Station on the London (Waterloo) to Guildford line via Cobham. The tab here is £12 ($21) in a single, £10 ($17.50) per person in a double, although if you require a private shower, a single is £17 ($29.75) and a double is £11 ($19.25) per person. You can spend the day visiting the London museums or theater and come home here and have a £3.50 ($6.13) evening meal. All these prices include VAT and service. Bedrooms are centrally heated with hot and cold running water, and have a radio and intercom. For an evening's relaxation, there is color TV in the lounge, plus a saloon bar.

Mrs. Linda Atkinson, 129 Stoke Rd. (tel. Guildford 38260), is most reasonable for B&B, considering the warmth of the welcome and the quality of the rooms. Mrs. Atkinson includes VAT, service, and the use of washing facilities in her charge of £9 ($15.75) per person daily. Her breakfasts are plentiful and well prepared.

READER'S RESTAURANT SELECTION: "Absolutely the best food of our entire trip was found at the **Tudor Rose,** 144 Milkhouse Gate (tel. 0483/63887), which opens onto High Street in downtown Guildford. The food is delicious. We had dinner there three nights, and for a full meal, with soup, entree, and several vegetables, plus wine, the bill came to an average of £8 ($14) per person" (Norman S. Wells, Arcadia, Calif.).

DORKING: This country town lies on the Mole River, at the foot of the North Downs. Within easy reach are some of the most scenic spots in the shire, including Silent Pool, Box Hill, and Leith Hill. Three miles to the northwest and a mile south of Bookham Great stands **Polesden Lacey** (tel. Bookham 53401), a former Regency villa containing the Greville collection of antiques, paintings, and tapestries. In the early part of this century, it was enlarged to become a comfortable Edwardian country house when it was the home of a celebrated hostess, who frequently entertained royalty here. The 18th-century garden is filled with herbaceous borders, a rose garden, and beech walks, and in all, the estate consists of 1000 acres. It's open in March and November on Saturday and Sunday from 2 to 5 p.m.; April to the end of October, on Tuesday, Thursday, and Saturday from 2 to 6 p.m. The gardens are open daily from 11 a.m. to sunset. Admission to the gardens is 70p ($1.23), with the house costing an extra 90p ($1.58). Children 16 years of age or under are admitted for half price (under 5 get in free). A licensed restaurant on the grounds is open from 11 a.m. on the days the house can be visited.

Back in Dorking, you can find accommodations at the following:

Just Home, 74 Chalkpit Lane (tel. Dorking 889199), is a tiny guest house owned by Mrs. E. Dawson, who points out that her house is only 25 miles from London, that a fast train from "the bottom of the road" goes into the center of London in just 35 minutes. And "Just Home" is only eight miles from Gatwick Airport where so many charter flights arrive. Mrs. Dawson charges £8.50 ($14.88) per person in a double or single, and provides a well-prepared breakfast. Her rooms are clean and comfortable.

READER'S GUEST HOUSE SELECTION: "We were especially impressed with the B&B operated by Mrs. Vivienne Bundy, **Woodlands,** Betchets Green Road, South Holmwood (tel. Dorking 889522). She is an outstanding hostess and her breakfast was good-tasting and plentiful. The price is £8 ($14) per person, which made our visit economical and extremely pleasant" (Mrs. Roger Hemmer, St. Louis, Mo.).

THE SUSSEXES

If King Harold hadn't loved Sussex so much, the course of English history might have been quite different. Had the brave Saxon waited longer in the north, he could have marshaled more adequate reinforcements before striking out south to meet the Normans. But Duke William's soldiers were ravaging the countryside he knew so well, and Harold rushed down to counter them.

Harold's enthusiasm for Sussex is understandable. The landscape rises and falls like waves. The country is known for its Downlands and tree-thickened Weald, from which came the timber to build England's mighty fleet in days gone by. The shire lies south of London and Surrey, bordering Kent in the east, Hampshire in the west, and opening directly onto the sometimes sunny, resort-dotted English Channel.

Like the other sections in the vulnerable south of England, the Sussexes witnessed some of the most dramatic moments in the country's history, notably invasions. Apart from the Norman landing at Hastings, the most life-changing transfusion of plasma occurred in the 19th century, as middle-class Victorians flocked to the seashore, pumping new spirit into Eastbourne, Worthing, Brighton, including old Hastings itself. The cult of the saltwater worshippers flourished, and has to this day. Although Eastbourne and Worthing are much frequented by the English, I'd place them several fathoms below Brighton and Hastings, which are much more suitable if you're seeking a holiday by the sea.

Far more than the resorts, the old towns and villages of the Sussexes are intriguing, particularly Rye and Winchelsea, the ancient towns of the Cinque Ports Confederation. No Sussex village is lovelier than Alfriston (and the innkeepers know it, too). Arundel is noted for its castle, and the cathedral city of Chichester is a mecca for theater buffs. Traditionally, and for purposes of government, Sussex is divided into East Sussex and West Sussex. I've adhered to that convenient designation.

I'll begin in East Sussex, where you'll find many of the inns and hotels within commuting distance of London.

5. Rye

"Nothing more recent than a Cavalier's Cloak, Hat and Ruffles should be seen in the streets of Rye," exuded Louis Jennings. He's so right. This ancient town, formerly an island, was chartered back in 1229. Rye, 65 miles below London, near the English Channel, and neighboring Winchelsea were once part of the ancient Cinque Ports Confederation. Rye flourished as a smuggling center, its denizens sneaking in contraband from the marshes to stash away in little nooks (even John Wesley's firm chastisements couldn't stop an entrenched tradition).

But the sea receded from Rye, leaving it perched like a giant whale out of water, still carrying its mermaid-like veil of antiquity. Its narrow, cobblestone streets twist and turn like a labyrinth. It has long been considered a special place by the English themselves, having attracted any number of famous men, including Henry James, who once lived in the Georgian Lamb House on Mermaid Street.

Attacked several times by French fleets, Rye was practically razed in 1377. But it rebuilt sufficiently, decking itself out in the Elizabethan style. Queen Elizabeth I, during her visit in 1573, bestowed upon the town the distinction of Royal Rye.

Today the city has any number of specific buildings and sites of architectural interest, notably the 15th-century St. Mary's Parish Church, with its unusual clock.

Attractions include **Lamb House,** on West Street at the top of Mermaid Street. Henry James lived here from 1898 to 1916, and there are many mementos of his day. The walled gardens are warm and peaceful. The house is open on Wednesday and Saturday from 2 to 6 p.m., April to October, charging an admission of 70p ($1.23).

Rye Museum (tel. Rye 3254) is housed in the Ypres Tower, a fortification built circa 1250 by order of Henry III as a defense against French raiders. It's open from Easter to mid-October from 10:30 a.m. to 12:30 p.m. and 2:15 to 5 p.m. The charge is 50p (88¢).

FOOD AND LODGING: The former seaport offers a wide variety of accommodations at several price levels.

Bed and Breakfast

Monastery Hotel, 6 High St. (tel. Rye 3272), is an early 17th-century building that grew up over the ruins of a 13th-century friary of the Augustinian order. Its own monastic garden backs up against the walls of the old friary. Nowadays, the house offers eight modernized double- and twin-bedded rooms (with hot and cold running water, central heating, and razor points), renting at £12 ($21) per person in a room with shower, rising to £15 ($26.25) per person with private bath. Six of the units contain private showers and one room has a bathroom en suite. There is a comfortable lounge, with color television, and a restaurant installed in an attractive room overlooks the Old Friary Chapel. For nearly 50 years, the Monastery has been receiving guests, the welcome today provided by the resident proprietor, Colin G. Coombes.

Little Saltcote, 22 Military Rd. (tel. Rye 223210), owned by Barbara McKenzie, is an attractive guest house five minutes from the town center, yet with a peaceful rural setting. The well-appointed rooms, complete with TV, central heating, razor points, and coffee- and tea-making facilities, are from £7.50 ($13.13) per person nightly including an English breakfast with a good choice of menu. Guests are provided with forecourt parking and may wander freely in the large garden.

Meals in Rye

Fletcher's House, Lion Street (near St. Mary's Church), is housed in an ancient vicarage converted into a tea room, serving morning coffee, hot or cold luncheons, and afternoon tea. A typical and very English lunch might begin with homemade vegetable soup, 75p ($1.31), followed by a two-course lunch at £5 ($8.75). The tea room is particularly noted for its Devonshire cream, served on request with any dessert for 50p (88¢). John Fletcher, the Elizabethan dramatist and contemporary of Shakespeare, was born in the house in 1579, when his father was vicar of Rye. It still retains many of its original architectural features, such as the old hidden-away front door with its design of York and Tudor roses, and an impressive oaken room. Do look at the clock on that church. It contains animated figures.

The **Mermaid Inn,** Mermaid Street (tel. Rye 3065), is the most famous of the old smugglers' inns of England—known to the band of cutthroats, the real-life Hawkhurst Gang, as well as to Russell Thorndike's fictional character, Dr. Syn. One of the present bedrooms, in fact, is called Dr. Syn's Bedchamber, and is connected by a staircase, set in the thickness of a wall, to the bar. The Mermaid had been open for 150 years when Elizabeth I visited Rye in 1573. The inn has 20 comfortable bedrooms, three four-posters, and central heating. It is owned by the Gregory family.

The inn, the most charming tavern in Rye, serves good food—English with frills. For £6 ($10.50) you can have a table d'hôte luncheon such as this typical one: a rich and heavy kidney soup, followed by poached sea trout with hollandaise sauce (superb), accompanied by three vegetables, including string beans. English cheese or traditionally made fruit pies, such as black currant and apple, round out the repast. Luncheon is served from 12:30 to 2 p.m. At the dinner, from 7:30 to 9 p.m., your tab for four courses may average around £8 ($14). The dining room, with its linenfold paneling, Caen-stone fireplaces, and oak-beamed ceiling, makes for an ideal setting. Even if you're not dining at the Mermaid, drop in to the old Tudor pub, with its 16-foot-wide fireplace (look for a priest's hiding hole).

For a splurge, the **Flushing Inn,** Market Street (tel. Rye 3292), is in a 16th-century inn on a cobblestone street. It has preserved the best of the past, including a wall-size fresco in the restaurant dating from 1544 and depicting a menagerie of birds and heraldic beasts. A rear dining room overlooks a carefully tended flower garden. A special feature is the Sea Food Lounge Bar, where sandwiches and plates of seafood are available from £1.50 ($2.63) to £4 ($7). In the main restaurant, luncheons are offered for from £6 ($10.50), dinners from £9 ($15.75). Besides these lunches and dinners, gastronomic evenings are held at regular intervals between October and April. For one of these specially prepared meals, including your aperitif, wine, and after-dinner brandy, you pay £19 ($33.25) per person. Fine Wine evenings cost £20 ($35) per person. The inn is closed Monday night and all day Tuesday, three weeks in October, two weeks after Christmas, and one week after Easter.

The **Monastery Restaurant,** 6 High St. (tel. Rye 3272), recommended previously, is also excellent for dinner, costing about £10 ($17.50) per person. A meal is likely to feature such items as an excellent fish soup with croutons, chopped herbs, and cream, or six oysters in Guinness batter with a pepper sauce. Main-course specialties include monkfish and prawn on a skewer, served with a green pepper sauce, and half a duck roasted with honey and served with apricots. Another favorite, which is served only to two diners, is a Romney saddle of lamb roasted with an orange stuffing, garlic, and rosemary. A selection from the dessert trolley might include a raspberry and almond flan.

The **Swiss Patisserie and Tea Room,** 6 Cinque Port St. (tel. Rye 222830), is where expatriate Swiss-born Claude Auberson concocts creamy Swiss cakes, cream meringues, buns, and pastries. Everything is very good and fattening, and it's to be washed down in a tiny tea room with coffee or Swiss-style hot chocolate. A cream tea goes for £1.25 ($2.19), and there is a selection of hot savory snacks baked daily on the premises. These are likely to include Cornish pastries, sausage and eggroll, or ravioli with cheese sauce, ranging from 40p (70¢) to 75p ($1.31).

The Quayhole, Strand Quay (tel. Rye 3638), is a restaurant and beefburger bar in three of the original warehouses, built as early as 1720, down by the Rother River. Joanne and Ron Harding have created a delightful establishment, keeping the rough brick walls and stone floors, along with dark-wood settles (comfortably cushioned) with tables to match. Pictures of Old Rye and articles used during the working life of the warehouses are an added spice of interest.

Appetizers include dolmades—that is, lamb, peppers, currants, and rice, enclosed in vine leaves and cooked in fresh cream and spices—or a Rye bay cocktail of raw fish steeped in lemon juice with mixed herbs, olives, and chopped avocado pears, each costing about £1.75 ($3.06). The fish dishes include Indonesian ikan panggang—trout cooked with spices and banana and served with a coconut sauce. Meat dishes include barbecued pork at £3.75 ($6.56), together with a selection of steaks at £5 ($8.75). The menu is long and varied to cater to all tastes. A set lunch with a choice of appetizer, plaice, and crêpes will cost about £4 ($7). A 10% service charge is added to bills.

On a final shopping footnote, adjoining the Beefburger Bar you will be able to make a purchase from a large selection of English desserts together with ice-cold drinks and a range of ice cream and other goodies.

About 2½ miles away is our next target for exploration:

6. Winchelsea

The sister Cinque port to Rye, Winchelsea too has witnessed its waters ebbing away. It traces its history back to Edward I, and has experienced many dramatic moments, such as those from the sacking French. But today it is a staidly dignified residential town (Ellen Terry's former cottage can be seen huddling up to Strandgate, on the road to Rye). In the words of a now-almost-forgotten 19th-century writer, Winchelsea is "a sunny dream of centuries ago." Its finest sight is a badly damaged 14th-century church, containing a number of remarkable tombs.

The **Strand House** (tel. Winchelsea 276) is an eye-catcher—a weathered historic house and cottage set in a garden at the foot of a hill, and separated from the sea by meadows in which sheep graze. The house is a cliché: a mixture of thick brick and stone walls with tiled roof, rambling roses, and a lawned garden with flowering shrubs and rockeries. The owners, Peter and Irene Wareham, are conscious of comforts, and their high standard includes hot and cold basins in all rooms, wall-to-wall carpeting, and central heating in all bedrooms. One of the rooms includes a four-poster bed. Reserved for the guests is a private dining room with a huge inglenook fireplace. There is ample parking for guests' cars within the hotel grounds. The house is open most of the year and charges from £18 ($31.50) for two, including a choice of a full English breakfast. The cottage can be hired on a self-catering basis for those wishing independence. The house is well over 500 years old and has irregular oak floors. The heavy oak ceiling beams have been taken from ships and are quite low, as are some of the doors (duck or bump your head). The stairs are open and, in fact, much safer than they look. It is believed that a tunnel near the house leads up to Winchelsea Town and is a relic of the days when smuggling was one of the main industries of the area. In World War II the wooded bank at the rear of the house was used to store rifles and ammunition in the event of a Nazi invasion (the meadow below was flooded to deter foot soldiers bent on invasion).

Becket (tel. Winchelsea 226) is a beautiful old home on the edge of town, owned by a delightful and charming hostess, Mrs. Mary Barling. In terms of a personalized accommodation, it is the finest place to stay in Winchelsea. She has decorated her home in excellent taste, and everything is kept in immaculate condition. Breakfast is served in a 16th-century room with a beamed inglenook fireplace. Old china and antiques abound in this large, airy, and most comfortable home. Rates are £9 ($15.75) per person, including breakfast.

Snailham House, Broad Street, Icklesham, near Winchelsea (tel. Icklesham 556), has been honored by the Automobile Association as "guest house of the year." Irene and Denis Coxell run this country guest house which lies about three miles from the coast and Winchelsea, and half a mile off the A259, attracting those who like its bucolic location. Surrounded by landscaped gardens, it has views from all its attractively furnished bedrooms which rent for £14 ($24.50) per person daily for half board. B&B is £9 ($15.75) per person nightly. This former farmhouse stands in the midst of a fruit and sheep farm. In colder weather, log fires burn in the lounges. The cookery is good and pleasantly served, and there is a residential license for drinks.

READER'S HOTEL SELECTION AT CROWHURST: "We found **The Inn at Crowhurst,** East Sussex (tel. Crowhurst 488), to be worthy of special mention. It is an imposing structure, built in 1902. Its features include comfortable rooms with hot and cold running water, oil paintings (believed to be the work of the Victorian artist Augustus John) on each of the bedroom doors, down-the-hall baths equipped with showers, washcloths, and huge bath towels, an oak-beamed restaurant featuring good food, an on-the-premises pub, an adjacent coach house (one of the last to be built in England), and extremely friendly and helpful Christine and Mike Pierce, who offer B&B for £9.50 ($16.63) per person per night. They also have a Monday through Thursday special of bed, breakfast, and dinner for £45 ($48.74) per person for the four days." (Mrs. E. G. Philipson, St. Paul, Minn.).

7. Hastings and St. Leonards

The world has seen bigger battles, but few are as well remembered as the Battle of Hastings—1066. When William, Duke of Normandy, landed on the Sussex coast and lured King Harold (already fighting Vikings in Yorkshire) southward to defeat, the destiny of the English-speaking people was changed forever. It was D-Day in reverse. The actual battle occurred at what is now Battle Abbey (seven miles away), but the Norman duke used Hastings as his base of operation.

Hastings suffered other invasions, being razed by the French in the 14th century. But after that blow an old Tudor town grew up in the eastern sector, and it makes for a good stroll today. The more recent invasion threat—that of Hitler's armies—never came to pass, although the dragons' dentures put up across the countryside stood waiting to bite into Nazi tanks.

Linked by a three-mile promenade along the sea, Hastings and St. Leonards were given a considerable boost in the 19th century by Queen Victoria, who visited several times. Neither town enjoys such royal patronage or prestigious name guests today; rather, they do a thriving business with middle-class Midlands traffic who shun the wicked ways of the continent to bask in the highly unreliable English sun. Hastings and St. Leonards have the usual shops and English sea-resort amusements. Lying only 63 miles from London, the coastal resorts are serviced by fast trains from Victoria Station.

THE SIGHTS: This area has two major attractions of interest.

Hastings Castle

In ruins now, the first of the Norman castles to be built in England sprouted up on a western hill overlooking Hastings, circa 1067. Precious little is left to remind us of the days when proud knights, imbued with a spirit of pomp and spectacle, wore bonnets and girdles. The fortress was ordered torn down by King John in 1216, and later served as a church and monastery until it felt Henry VIII's ire. Owned by the Pelham dynasty from the latter 16th century to modern times, the ruins have been turned over to Hastings. From the mount, you'll have a good view of the coast and promenade. It is open from 10 a.m. to 12:30 p.m. and 1:30 to 5 p.m. daily from Easter to the end of September, charging an admission of 50p (88¢) for adults, 25p (44¢) for children.

The Hastings Embroidery

A commemorative work, the Hastings Embroidery (tel. Hastings 424242) was first exhibited in 1966. It is a remarkable achievement that traces 900 years of English history through needlework. Depicted are some of the nation's greatest moments (the Battle of Hastings, the coronation of William the Conqueror) and its legends (Robin Hood). In all, 27 panels, each nine feet wide (243 feet total), depicting 81 historic scenes, are exhibited at the Town Hall. The history of Britain comes alive—the murder of Thomas à Becket, King John signing Magna Carta, the Black Plague, Chaucer's pilgrims going to Canterbury, the Battle of Agincourt with the victorious Henry V, the War of the Roses, the Little Princes in the Tower, Bloody Mary's reign, Drake's *Golden Hind,* the arrival of Philip's ill-fated Armada, Guy Fawke's gunpowder plot, the sailing of the *Mayflower,* the disastrous plague of 1665 and the great London fire of the following year, Nelson at Trafalgar, the Battle of Waterloo, the Empress of India, Victoria, the Battle of Britain, and the D-Day landings at Normandy. In the center is a scale model of the battlefield at Battle, depicting William's one-inch men doing in Harold's small soldiers. The embroidery may be viewed from October to May, Monday to Friday from 11:30 a.m. to 3:30 p.m. From June to September, it is open Monday to Friday from 10 a.m. to 5 p.m. and Saturday from 10 a.m. to 1 p.m. and 2 to 5 p.m. An admission of 60p ($1.05) is charged for adults and 35p (61¢) for children.

BED AND BREAKFAST: **Seafoam Guest House,** 3 Pelham Crescent (tel. Hastings 431903), is a small (two singles, six doubles) establishment with a winning location, directly overlooking the sea. It is one of a row of well-preserved Regency houses, complete with a half-moon balcony and the traditional wrought-iron decoration. Even in high season, the B&B rate is from £8.50 ($14.88) per person nightly. The owners, Mr. and Mrs. D. H. Evans, believe in giving you your money's worth: soft beds, a fine breakfast, good-size rooms, a friendly and pleasant ambience, and a roomy lounge opening onto the water.

Fairlight Lodge Hotel, Fairlight Road (tel. Pett 862104), lies away from the center of Hastings, 600 feet above the sea on the road to Rye. Surrounded by several acres of its own parkland and trees, it offers two pleasantly furnished and well-equipped single rooms, six doubles, and four family rooms, for which the B&B rate is £9 ($15.75) per person daily. Open all year, the licensed lodge also quotes an inclusive weekly term of £85 ($148.75), including all the extras, such as afternoon tea, baths, whatever. The quiet and dignified retreat, a former country estate, is owned by Mr. and Mrs. Papaspyrou.

Wise-Campbell Guest House, 143 Marina, St. Leonards (tel. Hastings 427282), is a well-appointed seafront house, offering B&B prices ranging from £9.50 ($16.63) per person. It is just past a block of apartments built like the old *Queen Elizabeth,* and separated from the sea by the promenade and bowling green. All rooms contain hot and cold running water, shaver points, and

TV. Mrs. Wise, the owner, does not accept children or pets, but invites prior inspection. There is plenty of parking space nearby.

Gresford Guest House, 12 Devonshire Rd. (tel. Hastings 424745), stands 250 yards from the main-line station and seafront. Your hosts are Penny and Patrick O'Brien, whose son lives in California. Most of their tastefully decorated bedrooms overlook a large green cricket field. As a backdrop there is the Norman castle. In addition to being a good cook, using fresh ingredients, Penny is a competent artist and guitar player. The O'Briens have a genuine hospitality, and will often convey guests by private car to such places as Bodiam Castle. They charge from £8.50 ($14.88) per person for a bed and full English breakfast. Hot showers are always available, and they have both color TV and a liquor license.

READER'S GUEST HOUSE SELECTION: "The **Keats Guest House,** 11 Cornwallis Terrace (tel. Hastings 433249), is run by Mr. and Mrs. R. D. Houghton. There isn't a speck of dirt in the whole five-story Victorian house. Everything is clean, newly painted, and nicely furnished, and there is lots of hot water. Electric heaters are in the bedrooms and bathrooms. There is a comfortable parlor on the second floor for the use of guests. Here one can sit and watch color TV. B&B costs £8 ($14) per night per person. With the evening meal included it's £10.50 ($18.38) per night. The best part is that the house is just around the corner from the railroad station" (Jean Hartley, Sacramento, Calif.).

WHERE TO DINE: Hastings is a fishing center, with a multitude of very competitive small seafood restaurants along the street fronting the beach at the east side of the city (on the way to the old part of town).

Martlets, 11 Grand Parade, St. Leonards-on-Sea (tel. Hastings 437589), is owned and run by Peter Sharrard, who named it after the Sussex coat-of-arms. He doesn't like any frozen food, so his vegetables are fresh and well cooked. The cuisine is award-winning. Lunch is served from noon to 2 p.m. Tuesday to Sunday, and dinner from 7 to 10 p.m. Tuesday through Saturday. A three-course luncheon or dinner costs from £4.50 ($7.88) to £7.50 ($13.13), including roll and butter as well as coffee. There is also a full à la carte menu available, including Dover sole, filet steak stuffed with prawns and laced with mushroom sauce, and homemade pâtés and a seafood soup.

Judge's Restaurant, High Street (tel. Hastings 427097), is run by Mrs. Inwood, who does the cooking, using only fresh ingredients. There is a choice of a roast joint or chicken or shepherd's pie and a variety of cold meats and salads. High Street is in the old town fishing quarter of Hastings, and local fish also appears on the menu daily. Main-dish prices range from £2 ($3.50) to £2.50 ($4.38). There are homemade desserts such as apple and blackberry pie, apple crumble, or a trifle. Judges is open for lunch from 12:15 to 2 p.m. and for morning coffee and afternoon teas, 10 to 11:30 a.m., and 3:30 to 5:30 p.m. It is closed Sunday and Monday. The son of the owner runs a bakery adjoining the restaurant, where a variety of freshly baked bread, buns, and cakes are available.

Brant's, on the High Street, serves a wide variety of unusual salads with savoury pies or quiches, cheese and vegetable pie, and homemade puddings, cheesecake, and other rich confections. All the food is prepared and/or cooked on the premises. A meal will cost around £3.50 ($6.13), and the establishment is open 10 a.m. to 5 p.m. daily, except Sunday.

The Lifeboat, 14 East Parade, is a good fish 'n' chips shop right near the harbor, where the boats are pulled up on the shingle. Plaice and chips costs £1.75 ($3.06); skate and chips, £2.25 ($3.94); and there are other fish dishes too, all served in traditional style with bread and butter and a cup of tea.

If you have a car, you might leave Hastings and head for **Crossways,** corner of Waites Lane, at Fairlight, near Hastings (tel. Pett 2356), a country village restaurant and B&B establishment about five miles away. It is known for its food, and many English residents in Sussex journey for miles around to enjoy the hospitality of Len and Babs Nevill. They offer a reasonable luncheon for a fixed price of £3 ($5.25) between 12:30 and 2 p.m., and a three-course à la carte evening meal for £6 ($10.50) and up. A typical lunch might consist of soup, followed by roast leg of lamb or a homemade steak-and-kidney pie. Dessert might be a fruit sponge cake with fresh cream. Dinner, served between 7:30 and 9:30 p.m., might include pâté, followed by chicken Kiev, then a choice of desserts. Crossways also rents one single room, one double room, and a family room big enough to sleep five. Breakfast is included in the fee of £6 ($10.50) per person nightly. While no private sitting room is available to guests, they can use the bar or the restaurant as a social area. All rooms have central heating with hot and cold running water, along with shared bath and shower facilities.

8. Battle

Nine miles from Hastings, in the heart of the Sussex countryside, is the old market town of Battle, famed in history as the setting for the Battle of Hastings in 1066. King Harold, last of the English kings, encircled by his housecarls, fought bravely, not only for his kingdom but for his life. In the battle Harold was killed by William, Duke of Normandy, and his body was dismembered. To commemorate the victory, William the Conqueror founded **Battle Abbey,** some of the stone for which was shipped from his own lands at Caen, in northern France.

During the dissolution of the monasteries in 1537 by King Henry VIII, the church of the abbey was largely destroyed. Some buildings and ruins, however, remain in what Tennyson called "O Garden, blossoming out of English blood." The principal building still standing is the Abbot's House, which is leased to a private school for girls and not open to the general public. Of architectural interest is the Gatehouse, with its octagonal towers, standing at the top of the Market Square. All of the north Precinct Mall is still standing and one of the most interesting sights of the ruins is the ancient Dorter Range, where the monks once slept.

The town of Battle grew up around the abbey, but even though it has remained a colorful medieval market town, many of the town's old half-timbered buildings regrettably have lost much of their original character because of stucco plastering carried out by past generations. The abbey is generally open from 9:30 a.m. to 6:30 p.m. (winter hours are from 9:30 a.m. to 4 p.m.). On Sunday, hours are generally more restricted. From April through September the admission for adults is £1 ($1.75), 50p (88¢) for children. Winter tariffs are 50p (88¢) for adults, 25p (44¢) for children. Children under 5 are always admitted free.

FOOD AND LODGING: The **Nonsuch Hotel,** 27 High St. (tel. Battle 2255), formerly known as the Bull Inn, was rebuilt in 1688 using stones from the Battle Abbey kitchen, which was demolished in 1685. In the cozy restaurant is a large inglenook fireplace where logs are burned. A selective à la carte menu, with specialty dishes using local farm products (fresh fish, venison, and wild duck), is cooked by chef-proprietor R. Retzlaff. All rooms have central heating with individual controls, radio, house phone, and some have private bath/

showers. There are a TV lounge and a bar lounge. A bed and English breakfast costs £12 ($21) per person, and dinner is from £5 ($8.75) per person. All prices include service and tax.

Ittington, London Road (tel. Battle 3782), run by Mr. and Mrs. A. Wright, is a large country Tudor house with gardens, sun roof, conservatory, and inglenook fireplaces. A peaceful spot with horses, the guest house lies only a mile from Battle Abbey and about eight miles from the sea. Rooms are pleasantly maintained and comfortably maintained, costing £9.50 ($16.63) per person for a bed and a full English breakfast, this tariff including mid-morning and afternoon tea or coffee. The house is centrally heated, and the Wrights have a TV lounge as well.

Pilgrim's Restaurant, Battle Village Green, High Street (adjacent to Battle Abbey; tel. Battle 2314), is an early 14th-century, black-and-white timbered house, the preferred place for morning coffee, lunch, or afternoon tea while in town. You'll not only receive good portions of homemade food, but you'll encounter an authentic atmosphere. Recommended is the set lunch for £5 ($8.75), which includes a choice of appetizers, a main-course choice, and a special English dessert. There is also a light-meal menu where the choice is wide and varied. A 10% service charge is added. The restaurant is licensed. You may have your meal in the Long Room, the Great Hall, or in the garden with its view of the ancient stones of Battle Abbey Gate. For afternoon tea you can have a pot of tea, a Sussex cream tea, cakes, or something more substantial. The Pilgrims Rest, with its inglenook fireplace and king-post supported roof, is an interesting example of its age. Hosts are Peter and Heather Randall-Mason. Hours are daily from 10:30 a.m. to 6 p.m.

The **Gateway Restaurant,** 78 High St. (tel. Battle 2856), is owned and run by John and Moira Gregson. He did his training as a chef on the Orient Line ships, was torpedoed in the war, and then became head chef at the BBC—for radio and then TV. Moira was in service to members of the Mountbatten family, and their son and wife are also in the catering business. And that is only a small part of the family's accomplishments.

The meals offered show their skills; everything that can be is homemade. The steak-and-kidney pie is superb, and there is always a joint roasted to perfection and served with fresh vegetables. Follow this with, perhaps, black currant pie or melt-in-the-mouth suet pudding (the old-fashioned kind) with syrup. Your meal is likely to cost from £3.50 ($6.13). The accent is on English dishes, and the menu changes according to season. They are open at 10 a.m. for coffee, closing after the last tea is served around 5 p.m. In mild weather you can sit out on the smooth lawn, smell the roses, and enjoy the view of the abbey across the road. The restaurant is closed on Sunday and also on Monday in winter.

Life at a 15th-century Farmhouse

Kitchenham Farm, Bodiam, Robertsbridge (tel. Sandhurst 357), is a 15th-century farmhouse, owned and operated as a farm by Mrs. Daws and her family. They grow hops and have flocks of sheep and cattle. Their house is typical of East Sussex: weather boarded, with an interior boasting a wealth of old beams, a fireplace with an inglenook, and a well-kept garden that grows raspberries, red and black currants, and strawberries. The farm was originally called St. Christopher, because it was a resting place for pilgrims en route to Canterbury from Chichester.

The homey farmhouse is comfortable, modestly furnished, with all the necessary amenities. You'll be charged £8.50 ($14.88) per person for B&B.

Breakfast is prepared farm style, including bacon, grilled tomatoes, freshly laid eggs, and homemade jam. The farm is on the Sussex border, half a mile from Bodiam Castle, built in 1386, the last military castle in Britain. That's only eight miles from Battle Abbey, the same distance from Rudyard Kipling's former home, and just 54 miles from London.

9. Alfriston and Lewes

ALFRISTON: Nestled on the Cuckmere River, Alfriston is one of the most beautiful villages of England. Its High Street, with its old market cross, looks like one's fantasy of what an English village should be. Some of the old houses still have hidden chambers where smugglers stored their loot. Alfriston has several old inns, the best known of which is the Star, now a Trust House hotel with its heraldic carvings outside.

During the day, Alfriston is likely to be overrun by coach tours (it's that lovely, but that popular). The village lies about 60 miles from London, northeast of Seaford on the English Channel, in the general vicinity of the resort of Eastbourne and the modern port of Newhaven.

Guest Houses Built of Stone

Deans Barn Guest House (tel. Alfriston 870274) is at the edge of the village. An 18th-century farmhouse with a white picket fence, it is surrounded by gardens and a lawn shaded by tall trees. The B&B rate is £10.50 ($18.38) per person, inclusive of service charge and VAT. The hosts, Mr. and Mrs. Powell, longtimers in Alfriston, have adapted their spacious and interesting home to the needs of paying guests. They really enjoy sharing their English ways with responsive overseas visitors ("They are usually so charming, so appreciative of our home. They seem to love our antiques and the old beams and timbers," to quote Mr. Powell). The Powells receive guests from February when the snowdrops and crocuses carpet the lawn until the end of November when the log fire crackles in the hall.

Riverdale Guest House, Seaford Road (tel. Alfriston 870397), is a small guest house with chimneys, bays, and gables, just outside the village, commanding a view across the valley to the Downs. The owners, Rosalind and John Keble, supervise everything personally, making for a comfortable stay. Their well-furnished and carpeted bedrooms come with hot and cold running water and a shaver socket. There are also tea- and coffee-making facilities in each bedroom. Visitors have been fascinated by the stained-glass front doors and have spent many hours photographing them. Daily bed, breakfast, and evening dinner terms are from £18 ($31.50), inclusive of VAT. B&B only goes for £11.50 ($20.13), and weekly rates including dinner are from £85 ($148.75). A good, filling four-course evening meal is assured. Home-grown fruit and vegetables and fresh eggs are a feature of the cuisine.

Pleasant Rise (tel. Alfriston 870545) is a brick farmhouse standing on 100 acres of Downland with indoor and outdoor tennis courts, along with badminton. The hosts are Mr. and Mrs. Savage, who are very helpful to their guests. From the porch there are views of the Downs. Accommodations are pleasant and attractive, renting for £8.50 ($14.88) per person.

LEWES: An ancient Sussex town, Lewes is worth exploring. Centered in the South Downs, Lewes lies 51 miles from London. Since the home of the

Glyndebourne Opera is only five miles to the east, the accommodations of Lewes are often frequented by cultured guests.

The county town has many historical associations, listing such residents as Thomas Paine, who lived at Bull House, High Street, now a restaurant. The half-timbered **Anne of Cleves House,** so named because it formed part of that queen's divorce settlement from Henry VIII, is now a Museum of Local History and is cared for by the Sussex Archaeological Society (tel. Lewes 4379). Anne of Cleves never lived in the Anne of Cleves House, and there is no proof that she ever visited Lewes. The museum has a furnished bedroom and kitchen and displays of furniture, local history, the Wealden Iron Industry, and other local crafts. It is found on Southover High Street and is open weekdays from mid-February to November from 10 a.m. to 5 p.m.; on Sunday, April to October, from 2 to 5 p.m. Admission is 60p ($1.05) for adults and 35p (61¢) for children.

Lewes, of course, grew up around its Norman castle. From the tower you can obtain a fine view of the surrounding countryside. To visit **Lewes Castle and Museum,** a joint ticket costs adults 80p ($1.40); children, 40p (70¢). The castle is open Monday through Saturday from 10 a.m. to 5 p.m. or dusk throughout the year. It is also open on Sunday, April to October, from 2 to 5 p.m.

Accommodations are difficult during the Glyndebourne Opera Festival, but adequate at other times.

Food and Lodging

Lamb House, 3 Chapel Hill (tel. Lewes 3773), is owned by Joan Welton, who is proud that artists, producers, conductors, and others connected with the Glyndebourne Opera House gravitate to her place. They stay here when there's room, enjoying the quiet walled garden in the rear. Lamb House was a hospice for pilgrims. The 16th-century building was given a new facade in 1716 (note the date by the front porch). For B&B you pay from £8.50 ($14.88) per person. There are many nearby inns and taverns within walking distance, where you can dine well during the day. The furnishings are simple, but in keeping with the old. Try to get one of the small bedrooms overlooking the garden.

The **Tatler Guest House,** 83 High St. (tel. Lewes 2510), is a fine, traditional town house dating back some 200 years. It boasts an original oak-paneled coffeeshop and restaurant. The ten quiet and well-appointed bedrooms have good views of the Sussex countryside and Lewes Castle. Bed and English breakfast cost £11 ($19.25) in a single, £17 ($29.75) in a double or twin, including VAT. Luncheons go for £3.50 ($6.13), dinners for £5 ($8.75), on the table d'hôte menu. A reasonably priced à la carte menu is available in the evening. The wine list offers moderately priced wines to compliment the menu selections. The coffeeshop is open from 9:30 a.m. to 5 p.m. Monday to Saturday for teas, coffees, and light refreshments.

The **Bull House,** 92 High St. (tel. Lewes 3936), lies at the West Gate in the oldest part of the town. There is a car park opposite. A coaching inn in 1450, a knight's home in the 16th century, the scene of a fight between Cavaliers and Roundheads in the 17th-century English Civil War, the Bull House has had a checkered career. Thomas Paine, who coined the name United States of America, lived here from 1768 to 1774. The restaurant in this historic house specializes in traditional home-cooked English dishes. It is closed on Sunday evening and all day on Tuesday and Wednesday. A set lunch goes for £4.50 ($7.88), the traditional Sunday lunch for £6.50 ($11.38). The dining price is based on the main-dish choice, but count on spending from £6.95 ($12.16) to

£8.50 ($14.88) for a three-course meal. A meal is likely to begin with a homemade soup or an orange with a chicken and prawn filling, then follow with roast lamb or pork, perhaps sliced beef in a horseradish and stilton sauce, topped off by a dessert from the trolley.

THE BLUEBELL RAILWAY: This railway is at Sheffield Park Station, near Uckfield in East Sussex (tel. Newick 2370) on the A275 from Lewes to Danehill. It takes its name from the spring flowers which grow alongside the track, running from Sheffield Park to Horsted Keynes. A railway buff's delight, the steam locomotives date from 1872 with Fenchurch to the 1950s and the end of steam in England. You can visit the locomotive sheds and works, plus a museum and a souvenir and bookshop. There's a carriage shed at Horsted Keynes. The Victorian room on the platform at Horstel Keynes offers refreshments while you wait for your train. The journey from Sheffield Park, climbing out of the Ouse Valley through lovely countryside, takes 15 minutes, costing adults £1.60 ($2.80), and children 80p ($1.40). There are several daily services from May to September. In spring and autumn service is restricted mainly to Wednesdays and weekends, and in December, January, and February trains operate on Sunday only.

Only eight miles from Lewes is the royal resort of:

10. Brighton

Back in 1753, when Dr. Russell propounded the seawater cure—even to the point of advocating the drinking of an oceanic cocktail—he launched a movement that was to change the life of the average Britisher, at least his vacation plans. Brighton was one of the first of the great seaside resorts of Europe.

The original style-setter who was to shape so much of its destiny arrived in 1783, just turned 21; he was the then Prince of Wales, whose presence and patronage gave status to the seaside town.

Fashionable dandies from London, including Beau Brummell, turned up. The construction business boomed, as Brighton blossomed out with charming and attractive town houses, well-planned squares and crescents. From the Prince Regent's title came the voguish word "Regency," which was to characterize an era, but more specifically refers to the period between 1811 and 1820. Under Victoria—and in spite of her cutting off the patronage of her presence—Brighton continued to flourish.

Alas, in this century, as the English began to discover more glamorous spots on the continent, Brighton lost much of its *joie de vivre.* It became more aptly tabbed as tatty, featuring the usual run of fun-fair-type English seaside amusements ("let's go down to Brighton, ducky"). Happily, the state of affairs has changed, owing largely to the huge numbers of Londoners moving in (some of whom have taken to commuting, as Brighton lies only one hour's—frequent service—train ride from Victoria Station). It's London by the Sea.

The Lanes, a closely knit section of alleyways off North Street in Brighton (many of the present shops were formerly fishermen's cottages) were frequented in Victoria's day by style-setting curio and antique collectors. Many are still there, although sharing space with boutiques.

Still, the eternal attraction remains—

THE ROYAL PAVILION: Among the royal residences of Europe, the Pavilion at Brighton (tel. Brighton 603005), a John Nash version of an Indian mogul's palace, is unique. Ornate and exotic, it has been subjected over the years to the most devastating wit of English satirists and pundits. But today we can examine it more objectively as one of the outstanding examples of the Orientalizing tendencies of the romantic movement in England.

Originally, the Pavilion was built in 1787 by Henry Holland. But it no more resembled its present look than a caterpillar does a butterfly. By the time Nash had transformed it from a simple classical villa into a Oriental fantasy, the Prince Regent had become King George IV. He and one of his mistresses, Lady Conyngham, lived in the place until 1827.

A decade passed before Victoria, then queen, arrived in Brighton. Although she was to bring Albert and the children on a number of occasions, the monarch and Brighton just didn't mix. The very air of the resort seemed too flippant for her, and the latter-day sea-bathing disciples of Dr. Russell trailed Victoria as if she were a stage actress. Further, the chinoiseries of the interior and the mogul domes and cupolas on the exterior didn't set too well with her firm tastes—even though the pavilion would have been a fitting abode for a woman who was to bear the title Empress of India.

By 1845 Victoria and Brighton had had it. She began packing, and the royal furniture was carted off. Its tenants gone, the Pavilion was in serious peril of being torn down. By a narrow vote, Brightonians agreed to purchase it. Gradually, it has been restored to its former splendor, enhanced in no small part by the return of much of its original furniture on loan by the present tenant at Buckingham Palace.

The caretakers put out the silverware, gold plates, and porcelain during the annual Regency Exhibition in July, August, and September. But at any time you can walk through the world of crustacean ceilings, winged dragons, silk draperies, lacquered furniture, water-lily chandeliers, gilt dolphins, Chinese mythological figures, and serpents who hold everything up.

Of exceptional interest is the domed Banqueting Hall, with a chandelier of bronze dragons supporting lily-like glass globes. In the Great Kitchen, with its old revolving spits, is a collection of Wellington pots and pans, his *batterie de cuisine,* from his town house at Hyde Park Corner. In the State Apartments, particularly the domed Salon, dragons wink at you, serpents entwine, lacquered doors shine. The Music Room, with its scalloped ceiling, is a salon of water lilies, flying dragons, sunflowers, reptilian paintings, bamboo, silk, and satin. In the second-floor gallery, look for Nash's views of the Pavilion in its elegant heyday. Finally, don't miss the sitting room of the king's "wife," Mrs. Fitzherbert, with some of her former furniture.

Currently the Royal Pavilion is undergoing an extensive program of structural and decorative restoration. This inevitably results in occasional inconvenience to visitors, although the work is, in its own right, absolutely fascinating. The pavilion is open daily from 10 a.m. to 5 p.m., October to June, and from 10 a.m. to 6 p.m., July to September. It is closed Christmas and Boxing Day. According to the time of the year, adults pay an admission ranging from £1.30 ($2.28) to £1.75 ($3.06); children, 60p ($1.05) to 80p ($1.40).

READER'S TOUR SUGGESTION: "**Mr. Cliff Edwards** (tel. Brighton 26450) conducts a walk-around tour of the old landmarks and points of interest in Brighton. He leads this most informative and entertaining tour, quoting poetry, historical facts, and even a bit of song, each Tuesday at 2:30 p.m., Wednesday at 10:30 a.m., and Thursday at 7:30 p.m. All tours start from the Marlborough House, which is also the Tourist Information Centre. The walk takes about 1½ hours, costing 65p ($1.14). The tour is sponsored by Watneys Red Lion and is quite a bargain. Mr. Edwards finishes up at the local cemetery, describing some of the people buried there, and their exploits. This takes an extra half hour and is optional" (Paul Engel, Palo Alto, Calif.).

WHERE TO STAY: Hundreds of accommodations are to be found in all price ranges. I'll give you only a representative sampling in Brighton itself.

Malvern Hotel, 33 Regency Square (tel. Brighton 28517), only a stone's throw from the seafront, is an 1820 Regency building on an attractive square. It's run by Mr. and Mrs. Douglas Foster. He was a former engineer for Westinghouse, living in Kansas City and Pittsburgh. Their rooms are clean and brightly furnished, containing hot and cold running water, color TV, and tea- and coffee-making facilities. In a room without shower, a single rents for £11 ($19.25), rising to £19 ($33.25) in a double. With shower, the cost is £15 ($26.25) in a single, from £26 ($45.50) in a double. You can order dinner as well from £6 ($10.50). There's a small lounge bar with a residential license.

Ryford Private Hotel, 6 and 7 New Steine (tel. Brighton 681576), on a Regency square adjacent to the Marine Parade, is within minutes of the seafront, the Palace Pier, and the Aquarium. The comfortable lounge and some of the guest rooms offer views of the sea. All the rooms are carpeted and immaculate, complete with hot and cold running water. B&B rates per person per night are about £10 ($17.50). Dinner is also available in the spacious dining room where excellent cuisine is prepared and served under the personal supervision of the resident proprietors.

The **Cambridge Hotel,** 23 Portland Pl. (tel. Brighton 605203), is another recommendable and economical hotel about half a block from the seafront. It offers six doubles and six singles, with B&B rates ranging from £8.05 ($14.09) to £8.90 ($15.58) in a single, from £16.10 ($28.18) to £17.80 ($31.15) in a double or twin, including a full English breakfast. At the licensed restaurant on the premises, an evening meal is available at £4 ($7) for two courses.

Churchill Palace Hotel, 2–3 and 5 Middle St. (tel. Brighton 21817), lies just off the Brighton seafront and is most convenient for the main shopping centers, entertainment facilities, and cinemas. This completely modernized hotel offers comfortable accommodations together with a cheerful and friendly atmosphere as well as personal service. Most of the rooms have private baths and toilets. Full central heating and an elevator add to the comfort. Music and dancing are occasionally offered. Prices are quite a bargain at £12.50 ($21.88) per person in a room with private bath. A three-course evening meal is served for £4.50 ($7.88).

Rowland House, 21 St. George's Terrace, Kemp Town (tel. Brighton 603639), is open all year, has full central heating and units with shower, TV, room call, and courtesy coffee. Run by R. E. Davis and R. W. Smith, it is a well-furnished house of ten bedrooms, located just behind the Royal Crescent in Marine Parade, 250 yards from the beach. No rooms are higher than the second floor. Rates are from £11 ($19.25) for a bed and full English breakfast. The house has a table license and serves an optional evening dinner. The food is good, and so is the attention from the hosts.

Downlands Hotel, 19 Charlotte St. (tel. Brighton 601203), is a well-run, small hotel, only a short walk from the Palace Pier and Royal Pavilion. The rooms are comfortably furnished and contain hot and cold running water, plus razor points and electric fires. The B&B rate ranges from £52 ($91) per person weekly. Should you prefer also to take your evening meal in the hotel's large dining room, you'll pay a partial-board rate of £80 ($140) per person weekly. Owners Maxine and John Salter attract many Americans to their pleasant hotel. When writing for a reservation, enclose a deposit of £5 ($8.75).

Trouville Private Hotel, 11 New Steine, Marine Parade (tel. Brighton 697384), offers rooms that are nicely furnished, bright, cheerful, and exceptionally clean. Showers and toilets are also large and well kept. The proprietors are most gracious and helpful, and their food is good. For a double room and breakfast, their charge is from £16 ($28) nightly.

READERS' HOTEL SELECTIONS: "**Fyfield House,** 26 New Steine (tel. Brighton 602770), is across the wide park-like divided street from Ellesmere Private Hotel. The proprietor, Mr. P. Culpeck, is friendly and offers a good, hearty breakfast in a spotless guest house. The charge is £8.50 ($14.88) per person for one night rising to £9.50 ($16.63) per person if the room has a private shower. There is no extra charge for baths" (Mrs. Edward Chait, Los Angeles, Calif.). . . . "The **Acropolis Hotel,** 14 Burlington St. (tel. Brighton 698195), owned by N. and M. Olympios, is delightful, a clean place with a full English breakfast served in an attractive room in the basement. The owners are friendly and helpful. They even helped carry in our luggage. There is parking on the street. Showers, with soap provided, are on the first floor, and an excellent French restaurant is just around the corner (reservations are necessary). The charge for a room and breakfast is £9.50 ($16.63) per person" (George and Lillian Schmidt, San Gabriel, Calif.).

DINING OUT: Outside of London, in the south of England you'll find the best food, the widest choice of restaurants, in the resort of Brighton. New restaurants of widely varying cuisine and standards are popping up all the time, and the foreign invasion isn't confined solely to Chinese and Indian. My sampling represents the best of the budget eating establishments.

Tureen, 31 Upper North St. (tel. Brighton 28939), is one of my favorite Brighton bistros, a rare one that makes available (see the blackboard for daily specials) some of the best of the English and continental dishes at low prices—including an always-delicious soup "from the tureen" or a homemade pâté. Among the delectable fare you'll find half a roast local duckling and sweetbreads in white wine and cream. All main-course prices include a selection of four fresh vegetables. To finish, I suggest the lemon syllabub. A three-course set daily lunch goes for £3.75 ($6.56), increasing to £5.95 ($10.41) on Sunday. A three-course dinner costs around £8.50 ($14.88), these tariffs including VAT and service. The restaurant is open Tuesday through Saturday from noon to 2 p.m. and from 7 to 9 p.m. On Sunday, lunch is served from noon to 2 p.m.

Ceres Health Food Restaurant, 23 Market St., may give you a "raw deal," but you'll love it. For those who like naturalism, it's unbeatable. Everywhere, the good basic value of the unadorned dominates, such as the natural pine settles, tables, and stools, or the simple hanging basket lamps. Food is served in handmade pottery. On the walls are Japanese paintings and prints. You help yourself, selecting from such offerings as freshly made soup for 60p ($1.05), or a fruit salad, 75p ($1.31). The most imaginative entrees are the freshly made flans and salads, priced from 80p ($1.40) to £2 ($3.50), according to choice. It is also licensed to sell wine, which costs about 75p ($1.31) a glass. The Ceres is open all day, serving coffee from 9:30 to 11:45 a.m.; luncheon, 11:45 a.m. to 3 p.m.; high tea from 3 to 5:30 p.m.

The **Market Wine House,** 20 Market St. (tel. Brighton 23829), is a wine bar and restaurant, featuring soups, salads, steaks, cheeses, and continental dishes. Housed in a black-and-white Regency building in the center of a boutique district, the wine house will serve you a whole plaice on the bone. The seafood platter is popular as well. Various chicken dishes, such as Kiev, are featured also. Pietro Addis owns and runs the establishment. He offers a three-course meal of, say, chilled melon or avocado with prawns, plus a choice of plaice, steak, and chicken with vegetables and potatoes, dessert, and coffee, for about £6 ($10.50). The decor of the cellar bar consists of natural wood booths, stacks of french bread, barrels of sherry, and candlelight—not to mention the talented instrumentalists and singers who entertain by flickering candlelight in the evening. The Market Wine House is open from noon to 2:15 p.m. and again from 6 to 10:30 p.m., seven days a week.

Nanking, 21 Market St., is one of the best of the budget Chinese restaurants in Brighton. Right in the shopping district, it offers a three-course luncheon, served from noon to 2:30 p.m., for £1.50 ($2.63). A choice of six dishes, different each day, is featured. In the evening, two people can order a dinner for £6 ($10.50), comprising chicken and mushrooms, port with mixed vegetables, sweet-and-sour king prawn balls, cashew nuts with pork, and boiled rice. The Nanking, established for more than a quarter of a century, also lists a number of tempting dishes on its à la carte menus, beginning as low as £1.90 ($3.33). The fully licensed restaurant has a fine selection of European, Chinese, and Japanese wines.

Allanjohn's, 8 Church St. (tel. Brighton 683087), is not a fish 'n' chips shop but a fascinating display of winkles, cockles, shrimp, crab, and lobster fresh from the sea to be eaten with brown bread and butter, salt and vinegar. A well-filled bowl of fresh crabmeat costs £1.75 ($3.06), and you can also order a seafood plate with a salad at £3 ($5.25). If you're lunching light, a salmon sandwich costs £1.60 ($2.80); a crab sandwich, 95p ($1.66). Lobster and crab are only available when the fish are running. Nigel Rodway is your host.

11. Hove

Hove is Brighton's sister city, Siamese linked—they are often referred to as Brighton and Hove. Its waterfront flanked by Regency architecture, Hove abounds with B&B houses as well, such as—

BED AND BREAKFAST: Chatsworth Private Hotel, 9 Salisbury Rd. (tel. Brighton 737360), is a small hotel that meets the tests of cleanliness, good food, sleep-producing beds, and a comfortable lounge with television—not to mention the Swiss-style personal services of Francis Gerber. The B&B rate is from £9 ($15.75) per person nightly. The bedrooms are large and suitably furnished, and there's a bathroom and toilet on every floor.

The **Tatler,** 26 Holland Rd. (tel. Brighton 736698), a few hundred yards from the sea, is a quiet and efficiently run hotel of Regency charm and modern comfort that charges £11 ($19.25) per person for B&B. The clean, comfortable rooms have tuckaway water basins (rods for drip-dries), and are well furnished (good beds). Some rooms are family size. The resident proprietors, Kay and John Collier, are fond of their North American and continental guests. The top floor even has a shower room, and there is a licensed bar for residents opening out to a patio garden.

The **Albany Hotel,** corner of St. Catherine's Terrace and Albany Villas (tel. Brighton 773807), is a small hotel on the Hove seafront on level ground, one mile from Brighton's West Pier, with a sea view from the lounge/diner and the front bedrooms. The King Alfred sports and entertainment complex is nearby. Bedrooms are on the ground, first, and second floors, and there is no elevator. The hotel contains central heating throughout, as well as a lounge with color television. All bedrooms have color TV, coffee-making facilities, and private showers or baths. The price per person, daily, including breakfast is £9 ($15.75), based on double occupancy. The resident proprietors are Mr. and Mrs. C. C. Wardle.

ST. MARY'S AND THE NATIONAL BUTTERFLY MUSEUM: At Bramber, in West Sussex, St. Mary's (tel. Steyning 813158), is a perfectly preserved timbered house dating from the 15th century. It has splendid paneled rooms and a unique painted room decorated for Elizabeth I. The house was the last stop on the escape route of Charles II, and you can still see the entrance to the underground tunnel to Bramber Castle.

The Burgess Hall, added later, houses the National Butterfly Collection, which attracts more than just the lepidopterist. It is one of the largest private collections in the world, the exhibition including dioramas, an artificial jungle, and a gift shop. It's open daily from May to October from 10 a.m. to 5 p.m., charging an admission of £1.15 ($2.01) for adults and 65p ($1.14) for children.

12. Arundel

This small and beautiful town in West Sussex, only 58 miles from London, four miles from the English Channel, nestles at the foot of one of England's most spectacular castles. The town was once an Arun River port, its denizens enjoying the prosperity of considerable trade and commerce. The harbor traffic is gone, replaced by coaches filled with visitors who come in summer to hike through the vastness of—

ARUNDEL CASTLE: The seat of the present Duke of Norfolk, this baronial estate is a much-restored mansion of considerable importance. Its legend is associated with some of the greatest families of England, the Fitzalans and the powerful Howards of Norfolk. But Arundel Castle traces its history back to King Alfred, while its keep goes back to the days before the Norman landing at Hastings.

Over the years, Arundel Castle suffered destruction, particularly during the Civil War when Cromwell's troops stormed its walls, perhaps in retaliation for the 14th Earl of Arundel's (Thomas Howard) sizable contribution to the aid of the faltering king. In the early 18th century, the castle virtually had to be rebuilt. In late Victorian times, it was remodeled and extensively restored again. Today it is filled, as you'd expect, with a good collection of antiques, along with an assortment of paintings by old masters such as Van Dyck and Reynolds.

The castle is open April to October, Sunday to Friday, from 1 to 5 p.m. From June to August and bank holidays, it is open daily from noon to 5 p.m. For full details, get in touch with the Administrator, Arundel Castle Trustees Limited, Arundel Castle, West Sussex, BN18 9AB (tel. Arundel 883136). Admission is £2 ($3.50) for adults, £1 ($1.75) for children.

Arundel Toy and Military Museum at "Doll's House," 23 High St. (tel. Arundel 882908), displays a delightful and intriguing family collection spanning many generations of old toys and games, small militaria, dolls, dollhouses, tin toys, musical toys, Britain's animals and soldiers, arks, boats, rocking horses, and crested military models. Housed in a Georgian cottage in the heart of historic Arundel, it is open most days from Easter to October (winter, weekends only), or it may be seen at any time by arrangement. Admission is 50p (88¢) for adults, 25p (44¢) for children.

READER'S SIGHTSEEING TIP: "The little **Museum of Curiosity,** 6 High St. (tel. Arundel 882420), will delight children (and their parents) with its displays of small animals in storybook tableaux, including the life work of the Victorian naturalist and taxidermist, Walter Potter. It is open April to September on Monday to Friday from 10:30 a.m. to 5:30 p.m.; on Saturday and Sunday from 11 a.m. to 5:30 p.m. It closes for lunch from 1 to 2:15 p.m. It is also open daily in October from 2:15 to 5 p.m. or dusk (lunch as before). Admission is 50p (88¢) for adults and 25p (44¢) for children" (Ralph Williams, Falls Church, Va.).

FOOD AND LODGING: **St. Mary's Gate Inn,** London Road (tel. Arundel 883145), is an old inn on the crest of a hill near the Catholic Church of St. Philip Neri. There is a large car park. At a lounge bar and pub you can enjoy after-dinner drinks. The food is well recommended. You can have homemade soup for 65p ($1.14) or a huge order of fried plaice for £5 ($8.75). The kitchen offers excellent Dover sole at £7 ($12.25). Lobster and crab are also offered when available.

Partners Sandwich Bar and Restaurant, 25 High St., does a range of sandwiches (some of them hot), costing from 55p (96¢) to £.1.25 ($2.19). Salads, many of them made from meat, go for anywhere from £1.25 ($2.19) to £2 ($3.50).

Arundel House Restaurant, 11 High St., opposite the post office, is a pleasant licensed restaurant run by Mr. and Mrs. Rogers. It is open for morning coffee, as well as good-tasting lunches, including main dishes consisting of such fare as homemade chicken pie or steak-and-kidney pie, served with three vegetables at a cost of £2.25 ($3.94). Also served, and inevitably popular, is fish and chips along with peas, £2 ($3.50). The staff also offers pork sausages or Cornish pasties with chips at £1.05 ($1.84). In the afternoon a Sussex cream tea goes for £1.05 ($1.84) per person, which is very good value.

READER'S GUEST HOUSE SELECTION: "In Arundel at the A27 roundabout near the railroad station is **Portreeves Acre** (tel. Arundel 883277), a modern B&B with five twin-bedded or double-bedded rooms, each with bath. Charging only £9.50 ($16.63) per person, it is spotlessly clean with comfortable beds. It's a three-minute walk to town. There's a beautiful garden, plus a TV room" (Robert and Bea Thacher, Minneapolis, Minn.).

13. Chichester

According to one newspaper, Chichester might have been just a market town if the Chichester Festival Theatre had not been established in its midst. One of the oldest Roman cities in England, Chichester is in vogue, drawing a chic crowd from all over the world who come to see its presentations.

Only a five-minute walk from Chichester Cathedral and the old Market Cross, the 1400-seat theater with its apron stage stands on the edge of Oaklands Park. It opened in 1962 (first director: Lord Laurence Olivier), and its reputation has grown steadily, pumping new vigor and life into the former walled city. The Chichester theater has given fresh stimulus to the living theater in England.

THE FESTIVAL THEATER: Booking generally opens in the middle of March, although the season might not start till the middle of May (it continues until late September). The price range is from £2 ($3.50) for an unreserved seat bought at the time of the performance up to £4 ($7) for the cheapest reserved seat or for any seat for a Thursday matinee performance. The best seats cost about £8.50 ($14.88). Reservations made over the telephone will be held for a maximum of four days (call Chichester 781312). It's better to mail inquiries and checks to the box office, **Chichester Festival Theatre,** Oaklands Park, Chichester. Matinee performances on Thursday and Saturday begin at 2:30 p.m., evening shows at 7 p.m., except Friday and Saturday when they start at 7:30 p.m.

How to get there: If you would like to come down from London, 62 miles away, for a matinee, then catch the 11:28 train from Victoria Station which will deliver you to Chichester by 1:05 p.m., in plenty of time. For an evening performance, board the 4:28 p.m. train from Victoria Station, arriving at 6:05 p.m. Regrettably, there is no direct late train back to London after the show. Visitors who must return can make a connection via Brighton, arriving at Victoria Station shortly after midnight.

ACCOMMODATIONS: **The Bedford,** Southgate (tel. Chichester 785766), is one of the best all-around budget accommodations in the city. It is charming and comfortable, and also quiet, in spite of its location near the railroad and bus stations. The host is Peter Musgrave, who has given up his dangerous hobby of racing cars in favor of riding horses. He and his wife charge £12 ($21) per person, this rate including breakfast. An old-fashioned English tea is offered in the lounge. The Bedford has 26 bedrooms, each with hot and cold running water and central heating.

READER'S HOTEL SELECTION: "In **Chidham,** four miles west of Chichester, between Bosham and Southbourne, is **St. Marlo House,** owned by friendly Mr. and Mrs. Voller. The big front and back yards of this country house make one feel especially at home, and the generous English breakfast is an excellent way to welcome the new day. The price for B&B is from £8.50 ($14.88) per person. The house is 400 yards south of Barley Corn Public House, off the A27. The address is St. Marlo, Cot Lane, Chidham, Chichester (tel. Bosham 573230)" (Ron Dodge, San Francisco, Calif.).

WHERE TO EAT: The **Roussillon Coffee Shop,** Dolphin & Anchor, West Street (tel. Chichester 785121), serves snacks and light meals from 10 a.m. to 10 p.m. daily. Those on the sightseeing run might settle happily for a cheese and bacon burger at £3.15 ($5.51), although fish dishes and sirloin steak (ten ounces uncooked weight, served with french fries) are also featured. A complete hot meal is likely to cost from £7.50 ($13.13). Children under 14 may choose from the main menu at half price.

The Coffee House, 4 West St. (tel. Chichester 784799), is straightforward and simple in its presentation. You don't get a lot of fanciness here with a lot of labels. But what you do get is low-cost, well-prepared food, made with fresh ingredients. Look for a plat du jour which is likely to include everything from shrimp salad to cold ham with french fries. Omelets come in a variety of flavors, or you can make your selection from the cold buffet. A fried fish is usually featured, and you can also count on a bowl of nourishing soup being offered. Expect to spend around £5 ($8.75) for a lunch here, maybe less. Hours are Monday to Saturday from 10 a.m. until 5 p.m.

The Local Pub

Royal Arms, East Street, near the Market Cross, is a pub built in 1575 and known locally as the Punch House, as it became famous in the early 19th century for the making and sale of Chichester milk punch. Hosts Tim and Val Biggs offer a full range of hot and cold bar snacks, lunchtime and evening. Prices range from £1 ($1.75) to £2.50 ($4.38).

On the Outskirts

The **Ship Inn,** Itchenor (tel. Birdham 512284), stands in a colorful yachting village, only seven miles from the center of Chichester. A restful and attractive place to stay, the inn is gabled with brick and timbering. Its front area has lushly planted flowering shrubbery. The owner, Derek Woods, rents four double and two single rooms, some having harbor views, all with tea- and coffee-making facilities. There are two guest bathrooms. A traditional breakfast is served, and from May 1 to September 30 an extensive cold food buffet is offered at lunch and dinner. Featured are Selsey crabs and lobsters when available. The B&B rate is £11 ($19.25) per person in a single or double, plus service. A full English breakfast is included, and a buffet, presented April to October, carries with it a minimum cost of £3.75 ($6.56). You'll pay a lot more for lobster, of course.

Hunters Lodge, Lavant (tel. Chichester 527329), dates back to the early 16th century, and its present facade was added in the 18th century by the Duke of Richmond. In the 1940s it was the center for the Goodwood motor racing fraternity, and now with extensive modernization is an inn where you can find pleasant rooms and excellent meals, featuring fresh fish dishes. It's just two miles north of Chichester and, although on the roadway, its side and rear gardens have many old trees and flowering shrubbery. Another acre provides fruit and vegetables for the kitchen. The bedrooms overlook the garden, and are nicely appointed with hot and cold running water (a few have showers), and the charge per person, including VAT, service, and a complete bacon-and-egg breakfast is £11 ($19.25). There's a lounge bar where drinks are served, and in winter an open fireplace provides cheer and warmth.

WEALD AND DOWNLAND OPEN AIR MUSEUM: This museum stands on a 40-acre downland site, at Singleton, six miles north of the cathedral city of Chichester on the A286 (London road). In a natural woodland country park rescued historic buildings, in which people lived and worked from the Middle Ages to the 19th century, are being reassembled. The museum is open every day except Monday, from 11 a.m. to 5 p.m., April 1 to October 31 (open bank holidays and on Monday in June, July, and August). Admission for adults is £1.30 ($2.28). Children and students pay 80p ($1.40). Although still developing, the museum shows the history of traditional buildings in southeast England. Exhibits include a Tudor market hall; timber-framed medieval houses dating from the 14th to the 16th centuries with wattle-and-daub walls; a working watermill; a blacksmith's forge; plumbers' and carpenters' workshops; a toll cottage; a 17th-century treadwheel; agricultural buildings, including thatched barns and an 18th-century granary; and a charcoal burner's camp. For further information, telephone Singleton 348.

FISHBOURNE: A trip well worth the taking and just a few miles away from Chichester is to the largest Roman palace as yet discovered. It's called the **Fishbourne Roman Palace and Museum,** Salthill Road (tel. Chichester 785859). Built in A.D. 43, it is architecturally pure Italian, and you will be amazed to discover it has an underground heating system. There is good parking and a cafeteria on the premises that serves coffee and sandwiches. Admission is £.1.10 ($1.93) for adults, 40p (70¢) for children, and 70p ($1.23) for students.

Chapter VII

HAMPSHIRE AND DORSET

1. Portsmouth
2. Southampton
3. New Forest
4. Isle of Wight
5. Winchester
6. Bournemouth
7. Wool
8. Wareham
9. Dorchester
10. Bridport
11. Chideock
12. Charmouth
13. Lyme Regis

STONE FARMHOUSES—conjuring up images of Burke's *Landed Gentry*—all this belongs to the countryside of the 17th century: fireplaces where stacks of logs burn gaily; wicker baskets of apples freshly brought in from the orchard (ever had homemade apple butter?); chickens stuffed with dressing and roasted with strips of bacon on top to keep them tender and juicy; milk that doesn't come from bottles; and mellowed village houses, now run as hotels. Beyond the pear trees, on the crest of a hill, are the ruins of a Roman camp. And a village pub, with two rows of kegs filled with varieties of cider, is where the hunt gathers.

You're in Hampshire and Dorset, two shires guarded zealously by the English, who protect their special rural treasures. Everybody knows of Southampton and Bournemouth (Dorset), but less known is the undulating countryside lying inland. Your car will take you through endless lanes, revealing tiny villages and thatched cottages—untouched by the industrial invasion.

HAMPSHIRE

This is Jane Austen country—firmly middle class, largely agricultural, its inhabitants doggedly convinced that Hampshire is the greatest spot on earth. The English spinster left six novels of manners, including *Pride and Prejudice* and *Sense and Sensibility,* that earned her a room at the top among 19th-century English novelists. Her books provided a keen insight into the solid middle-class English who were to build such a powerful empire. Although the details of the life she described have now largely faded ("at five o'clock the two ladies retired to dress, and at half-past six Elizabeth was summoned to dinner"), much of the mood and spirit of Hampshire depicted in her books remains.

Born in 1775, Miss Austen was the daughter of the rector at Steventon. Although she lived outside Hampshire for a while in Bath, and for a troubled time in Southampton, she spent most of her life at **Chawton,** near Alton (tel. Alton 83263), where her home may be visited today. You can see the writing desk on which she penned such memorable novels as *Emma* (her "handsome, clever, and rich" heroine, Emma Woodhouse). There is an attractive garden in which visitors are invited to have picnics, and an old bakehouse with Miss Austen's donkey cart. About a mile from the station, Miss Austen's home is open daily, including Sunday, from 11 a.m. to 4:30 p.m., for a 75p ($1.31) admission; children under 14, 25p (44¢). It is closed Monday and Tuesday from November 1 to March 31.

Like a loving mother, Hampshire reaches out to embrace the New Forest (don't expect anything in England labeled "new" to be new), the South Downs, the Isle of Wight (Victoria's favorite retreat), the passenger port and gateway city of Southampton, and the naval city of Portsmouth.

Going west from Southampton, you'll come to the **New Forest,** more than 90,000 acres selfishly preserved by William the Conqueror as a private hunting ground (poachers met with the death penalty). William lost two of his sons in the New Forest, one killed by an animal, the other by an arrow. Today, it is a vast and unspoiled woodland and heath ideal for walking and exploring.

LUNCHEON STOPOVERS ON THE WAY: For those driving down to Winchester and the New Forest, there is a good lunch stop at **Selborne.** After traveling the A31 from London to Chawton to see Jane Austen's home, take the signposted B3006 to Selborne, five miles away. In the 18th century, Gilbert White, the famous author of the *Natural History of Selborne* and a pioneering botanist, lived here.

Today the **Gilbert White Museum** is housed in the "Wakes" in Selborne. His natural history was written in this house. Two rooms on the ground floor are furnished in the style of the 18th century; one of these is White's study. The upper floor of the museum includes exhibits related to the travels of Frank Oates in Central America (1872) and in Africa (1873-1875), and of Capt. Lawrence Oates who was on Scott's last, ill-fated expedition in the South Pole. The museum is open from March until October every day of the week except Monday from noon to 5:30 p.m., charging adults 75p ($1.31) admission; children pay 35p (61¢).

At the **Queens Hotel** (tel. Selborne 272), you can order either a pub luncheon of homemade soup, Queensburger, and Welsh rarebit for £1.40 ($2.45), or eat in the fantastically decorated dining room under a canopy of brass jugs, bits of farm equipment, corn cobs, and God-whattery, hanging from old oak beams. The owner, Blake Paton, ladles out the special Peggy Paton's homemade soup (his wife's recipe) and large portions of freshly roasted beef with all the trimmings. That means Yorkshire pudding, roast potatoes, and properly cooked cabbage—just *al dente* with a little butter and some pepper. On other days there is lamb with mint sauce and red currant jelly. Desserts are homemade—fruit pies and cream, trifles, or a good cheeseboard with bread or crackers. Wines can be ordered by the glass, and peppermints and book matches are handed out with the coffee and the bill—which, including VAT, comes to around £4.50 ($7.88) per person.

The hotel is open for lunch from 12:30 to 1:45 p.m. and for dinner from 7:30 to 8:45 p.m. Mr. Paton also makes and sells candy, fudge, chocolates, and honey, plus other local goodies. If you're not too stuffed to drive after dining here. Winchester is not too far away. Retrace your steps to the A31.

If you'd like to stay over, B&B terms in a double range from £20 ($35) to £22 ($38.50) a night, the latter for units with private bath or shower.

Alternatively, at Hurstbourne, between Andover and Whitchurch, on the B3400, stands the **Portsmouth Arms** (tel. Whitchurch 2000), another country pub serving mainly pub food. Wine can be ordered by the glass. Various sandwiches, steak-and-kidney pie, cottage pie, and other dishes are offered, at prices ranging from 60p ($1.05) to £1.75 ($3.06). Salads with cold meats are made up to order, ranging in price from £2.20 ($3.85) to £3.50 ($6.13).

You can also find lodgings here, a bed and a very satisfying English breakfast, a large one, going for £10 ($17.50) in a single, from £17.50 ($30.63) in a double or twin. Everything is run by Jill Papps.

The country pub is open for lunch between noon and 2:30 p.m. and for dinner between 7 and 10:30 p.m.

1. Portsmouth

Virginia, New Hampshire, and Ohio may have their Portsmouths, but the daddy of them all is the old port and naval base on the Hampshire coast, about 70 miles south of London. German bombers in World War II virtually leveled the city, destroying or hitting about nine-tenths of its buildings. But the seaport has recovered admirably.

Its maritime associations are famous. From Sally Port, the most interesting district of the Old Town, "naval heroes innumerable have embarked to fight their country's battles." That was certainly true on June 6, 1944, when Allied troops set forth to invade occupied France.

THE SIGHTS: Of chief interest is Lord Nelson's flagship, H.M.S. *Victory,* a 104-gun, first-rate ship of the line, now at No. 2 Dry Dock in Portsmouth (tel. Portsmouth 22351). Although she first saw action in 1778, her fame was earned on October 21, 1805, in the Battle of Trafalgar when the British destroyed the combined Spanish and French fleets. It was in this battle that Lord Nelson lost his life. The flagship, after being taken to Gibraltar for repairs, returned to Portsmouth with Nelson's body on board (he was later buried at St. Paul's in London). It is open March 1 to November 1 weekdays from 10:30 a.m. to 5:30 p.m., on Sunday from 1 to 5 p.m. From November 1 to March 1, weekdays, hours are from 10:30 a.m. to 4:30 p.m.; on Sunday from 1 to 4:30 p.m. There is no admission charge.

One of the top tourist attractions in the south of England in 1984–1985 will surely be the *Mary Rose.* The summer of 1982 saw the culmination of years of investigation and effort when the *Mary Rose,* the Tudor warship, pride of Henry VIII's navy, finally broke the surface of the Solent, 437 years after she sank in full view of the horrified monarch and his party. After elaborate preservation, the hull will lie in a dry dock alongside H.M.S. *Victory* and will be open to view. It will probably be reconstructed to show what life aboard a Tudor man-of-war was like. At present, artifacts, cooking pots, eating irons, a complete surgeon's kit, shoes, and clothing are on view in Southsea Castle.

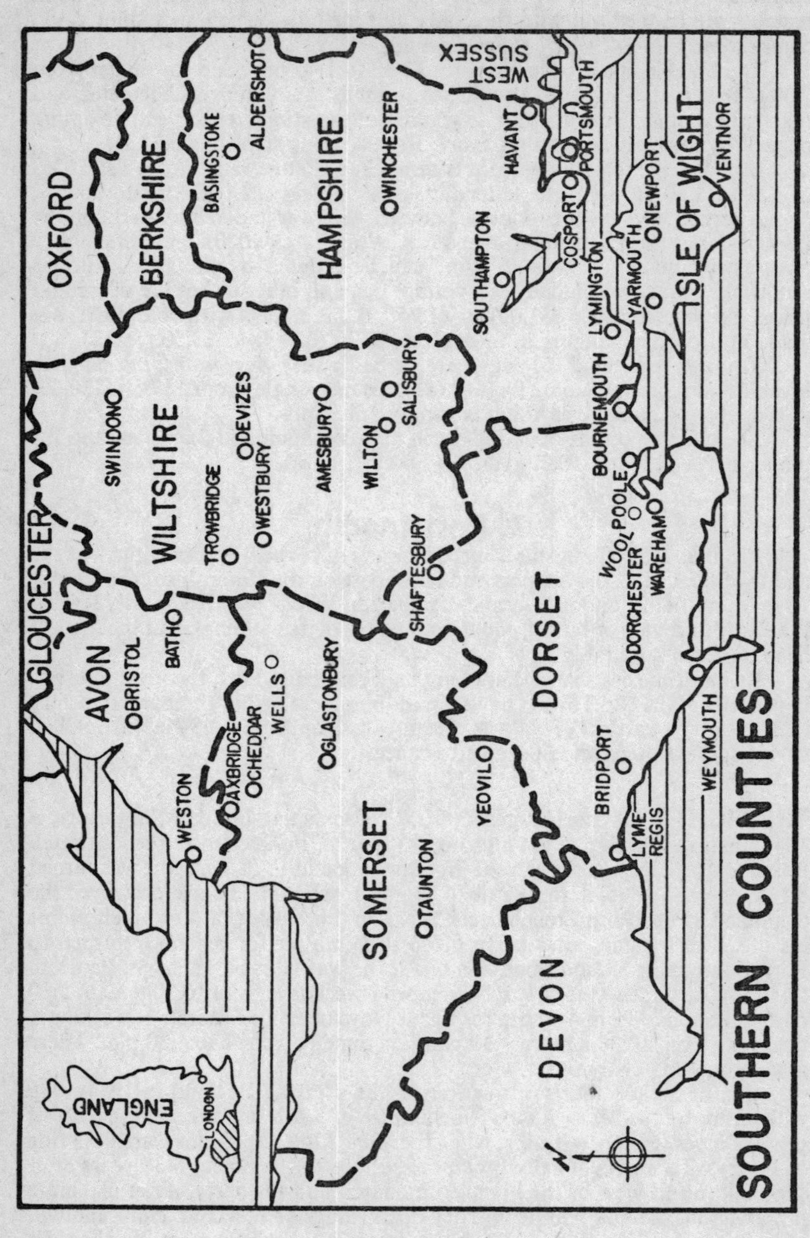
SOUTHERN COUNTIES
OXFORD
BERKSHIRE
HAMPSHIRE
WEST SUSSEX
SLE OF WIGHT
WILTSHIRE
GLOUCESTER
AVON
SOMERSET
DORSET
DEVON
ALDERSHOT
BASINGSTOKE
WINCHESTER
HAVANT
PORTSMOUTH
SOUTHAMPTON
COSPORT
LYMINGTON
YARMOUTH
NEWPORT
VENTNOR
SWINDON
DEVIZES
TROWBRIDGE
WESTBURY
AMESBURY
WILTON
SALISBURY
SHAFTESBURY
BOURNEMOUTH
POOLE
WOOL
WAREHAM
DORCHESTER
WEYMOUTH
BRIDPORT
LYME REGIS
YEOVIL
BATH
BRISTOL
WELLS
GLASTONBURY
CHEDDAR
AXBRIDGE
WESTON
TAUNTON
ENGLAND
LONDON

The remains of the ship—not the complete hull—and the artifacts are in fantastically good condition. At press time, admission charges haven't yet been decided.

The **Royal Naval Museum** stands next to Nelson's flagship, H.M.S. *Victory,* in the heart of Portsmouth's historic naval dockyard. The only museum in Britain devoted exclusively to the general history of the Royal Navy, it contains relics of Nelson and his associates, together with unique collections of ship models, naval ceramics, figureheads, medals, uniforms, weapons, and other naval memorabilia. Special displays include the Victorian navy, the Second World War at sea, and the modern navy.

The museum is open daily from 10:30 a.m. to 5 p.m. (on Sunday from 1 p.m.), closing at 4:30 p.m. in the winter. An admission charge of 50p (88¢) is levied as part of a joint ticket which also gives access to the nearby *Mary Rose* displays. There is a buffet and a souvenir shop in the museum complex.

For more information about either the H.M.S. *Victory,* the Royal Museum, or the *Mary Rose,* telephone Portsmouth 822351.

Portsmouth was the birthplace of Charles Dickens. Fortunately, the home of the Victorian novelist was spared the bombardments of World War II. It serves to commemorate the birth of the writer on February 7, 1812. Called the **Dickens' Birthplace Museum,** it is at 393 Old Commercial Rd., Mile End (tel. Portsmouth 827261). It has been restored and furnished to illustrate the middle-class taste of the early 19th century (only one or two items are directly connected with Dickens, e.g., his inkwell, paperknife, and snuff box, and the couch on which he died). It is open daily from 10:30 a.m. to 5:30 p.m. Admission charges are 30p (53¢) for adults and 12p (21¢) for children. Family tickets, admitting four persons, sell for 60p ($1.05).

Jutting out into the harbor, **Portchester Castle** is the finest example of a complete Roman fortress in Europe. Within its walls, enclosing seven acres, stand Norman castle and Norman church. You can explore the Roman stone walls and bastions. It was here that Henry V assembled his men for the assault on Agincourt in 1415.

Overnighting in Portsmouth? If so, I have the following recommendations.

LIVING IN OLD PORTSMOUTH: Fortitude Cottage, 51 Broad St. (tel. Portsmouth 23748), is a charming small house in Old Portsmouth, on Camber inner harbor. It is a narrow, four-story structure, with a steep staircase, almost in Dutch fashion, that leads to the compact home of Carol Harbeck. There are several rooms available, and the charge is £7.50 ($13.13) nightly for B&B. Mrs. Harbeck has demonstrated her excellent taste in the designing and furnishing of the home. It is airy, colorful, modern, yet not too extreme, and the views from the rooms are good. Her breakfasts are on a "what you want" basis.

Mrs. Fisher, 9 Bath Square, Old Portsmouth (tel. Portsmouth 823683), is the mother of Mrs. Harbeck and also has a delightful terraced house offering accommodation to overnight guests. It faces the harbor entrance directly opposite H.M.S. *Dolphin* at the submarine base. She has two double bedrooms costing £7.50 ($13.13) per person nightly. Breakfast is on a "what you want" basis.

DRINKING AND DINING: The **Lone Yachtsman** (tel. Portsmouth 24293), at the Point (head up Broad Street), is a revamped pub that is the center of much of the local life of Old Portsmouth. Decorated in a nautical theme, it commands a view of the harbor from its perch on the end of a promontory.

You can drink in both the Sir Alec Rose bar (popular with yacht people) or dine at the Lively Lady (hot luncheons Monday to Saturday from noon to 2:30 p.m.). Among the usual entrees are such tempting items as soup of the day and steak, kidney, and mushroom pie. A set lunch costs £4 ($7). The Dover sole, depending on size, is excellent, although it costs from £6.50 ($11.38). A tradition is the hot fruit pie, served with thick cream, for 85p ($1.49).

The Hungry One, 15 Arundel Way, Arundel Street (tel. Portsmouth 817114). Owner Michael See runs this clean, relaxing snackbar. His wife Shirley tells me she really runs it, because Michael is always playing golf—but actually they both do a very good job, offering sandwiches, ranging in price from 65p ($1.14) to £1 ($1.75). You can eat a three-course meal for less than £5 ($8.75). Mr. and Mrs. See remain open Monday to Saturday from 9:30 a.m. to 5 p.m. The Hungry One is on a street off Commercial Road, close to the Guildhall and the town railway station, a short bus journey from the Dockyard, H.M.S. *Victory,* and the *Mary Rose.*

Between Portsmouth and Southampton lies an increasingly popular attraction in this part of the country—

BROADLANDS: At Romsey (tel. Romsey 516878), Earl Mountbatten of Burma lived until his assassination in 1979 while traveling in Ireland. On their honeymoon, he lent his mid-16th-century house to H.M. the Queen when as Princess Elizabeth she married Prince Philip. More recently, Prince Charles and Princess Diana spent the first nights of their honeymoon there. Now a shrine to Britain's last war hero, the 40-room Georgian mansion lies 87 miles southwest of London.

Originally constructed as an adjunct to Romsey Abbey, the house was purchased by Lord Palmerston in 1736 and later decorated in a fine Palladian style. Capability Brown landscaped the gardens, and Broadlands today still retains some 6000 acres of park and farmland. There is a fine exhibition and show depicting the highlights of Lord Mountbatten's brilliant career as a sailor and diplomat until his partial retirement from public life.

In the dining room you'll find four Van Dyck oil paintings, plus grilles by Whistler. The house is open daily, except Monday (daily including Monday in August and September), April to September, from 10 a.m. to 6 p.m. Admission is £2.25 ($3.94) for adults and £1 ($1.75) for children.

If you'd like to stay over, the **Wessex Guest House,** 5 Palmerston St. in Romsey (tel. Romsey 512038), is run by Mrs. Patricia Edwards. Her comfortable house stands close to Broadlands. It's a good base from which to tour the New Forest area or to make trips to Winchester and Salisbury. Bed and a good breakfast is £6.50 ($11.38) per person. Evening meals aren't provided, but there are one or two very pleasant inns in the village.

2. Southampton

To many North Americans, England's premier passenger port, home base for the Cunard's *Queen Elizabeth 2,* is the gateway to Britain. Southampton is changed today, a city of wide boulevards, parks, and shopping centers. It was rebuilt after German bomb damage, which destroyed hundreds of its old buildings.

In World War II, some 3½ million men embarked from here (in the First World War, more than twice that number passed through Southampton). Its supremacy as a port has long been recognized and dates from Saxon times when the Danish conqueror, Canute, was proclaimed king here in 1017.

Southampton was of special importance to the Normans, keeping them in touch with their homeland. And it shares the dubious distinction of having "imported" the bubonic plague in the mid-14th century that wiped out a quarter of the English population. In the vicinity of the docks is a memorial tower to the Pilgrims, who set out on their voyage to the New World from Southampton on August 15, 1620.

If you're waiting in Southampton between boats, you may want to use the time to explore some of the major sights of Hampshire that lie on the periphery of the port—the New Forest, Winchester, the Isle of Wight, and Bournemouth in neighboring Dorset.

THE BEST PUB IN TOWN: The **Red Lion,** High Street (tel. Southampton 333595), is one of the few architectural jewels to have survived World War II. This pub has its roots in the 13th century (a Norman cellar), but its high-ceilinged and raftered "Henry V Court Room" is in the Tudor style. The room was the scene of the trial of the Earl of Cambridge and his accomplices, Thomas Grey and Lord Scrope, who were condemned to death for treason in plotting against the life of the king in 1415. The Court Room is adorned with coats-of-arms of the noblemen who served as peers of the condemned trio. All this bloody history needn't deter you. The Red Lion is a friendly, fascinating place at which to stop in for a drink and a chat. Bar snacks begin at 75p ($1.31) for a sandwich, going up to £2.20 ($3.85) for a plate of cold meat and a salad.

LIVING ON THE OUTSKIRTS: Finding an accommodation directly in Southampton isn't as important as it used to be. Very few ships now arrive, and the places to stay just outside the city are in the main far superior to what one finds directly in the heartland. Also, the recommendations to follow are in far more attractive surroundings.

Grove House, Newtown Minstead, near Lyndhurst (tel. Southampton 813211), is owned and run by Marion Dixon, who offers accommodations in her own family's home. She has a comfortable family room to accommodate from two to four persons, facing south and west and going for £8.50 ($14.88) per person per night, including a large breakfast. An evening meal can be arranged from £5.50 ($9.63) per person. This pleasant farmhouse lies at the rural end of the village with the New Forest a quarter mile away up a country lane.

Lyndhurst House, 35 Romsey Rd., Lyndhurst (tel. Lyndhurst 2230), is a solid, turn-of-the-century house opposite Pat's Garage in the town. It's the home of Sydney and Yvonne Renouf, who rent several rooms in their main house, plus three more in a chalet behind, at a cost of £8 ($14) per person nightly. Yvonne turns out an enormous breakfast of eggs, sausages, bacon, tomatoes, toast, jam, tea or coffee. The house is close to the New Forest and to shops.

Bentley, Sway Road, Brockenhurst (tel. Lymington 22407), is a lovely New Forest house run by a friendly couple, Michael and Inez Lancaster. They offer rooms at £9.50 ($16.63) per person nightly, including a good hot breakfast. They rent out two family rooms, two doubles, and one single, and can provide bunk beds for kids. There is a warm lounge with TV, plus a car park, and the whole place is surrounded by a large garden. Wild forest ponies wander around, and the open forest itself is just around the corner. If given a warning in time, they'll prepare a dinner for you, the fare consisting mainly of chops, chicken, or roast. The cost is about £5 ($8.75) per person. They'll also make a picnic lunch for you if you want to go exploring the next day.

Rose and Crown Inn, Lyndhurst Road, Brockenhurst (tel. Brockenhurst 22225), is a pleasant 300-year-old inn run by Ennio Cantini, who charges from £11 ($19.25) to £12 ($21) per person in a room with private bath. A large breakfast is served in the pub dining room. There is a self-service buffet at lunchtime, with both hot and cold dishes, as well as quiches and salads, costing from £1.80 ($3.15) to £3 ($5.25) per plate, depending on your choice of meats. Dinner, a more sober affair, costs £5 ($8.75) for two courses and £6.50 ($11.38) for four courses.

The **Old Well Restaurant and Guesthouse,** Copythorne, Cadnam (tel. Cadnam 2321). Pat and Laurie Martin's family used to own the village grocery store, and they are true forest folk. In 1960 they bought the Old Well, which now opens at 9 a.m. and closes according to the departure of the last guest. Breakfast is a good meal of homemade bread and local free-range eggs, bacon, and sausages; then morning coffee leads to lunch, a set meal going for £4 ($7). On Sunday they always have a traditional roast joint or something from the à la carte menu such as New Forest lamb chops. Cream teas at £1.35 ($2.36) take over after lunch. If you decide to stay over, they have five rooms to rent in the main house, three more in the annex, and the charge is £8 ($14) per person, including that large and wholesome breakfast. This is a friendly place, offering excellent value.

An Excursion Back to the Past

If postwar Southampton is too modern for your tastes and you want to capture the flavor of merrie olde England, then strike out for the **Fox and Hounds Inn,** Hungerford Bottom, Old Bursledon (tel. Bursledon 2784), between Southampton and Portsmouth—not far from the ferry to the Isle of Wight, and in the vicinity of the Bursledon Railroad Station. It would take the writing ability of Charles Dickens and the visual techniques of William Hogarth to capture the spirited image of this inn, which dates back to 1338. You can have your wine-tasting experience in either the Hunter's Bar or the Farmer's Kitchen. Against a backdrop of horse brasses, a heavily beamed ceiling, and an open fireplace, the legendary mead, known to both the English and the Vikings, is dispensed. The Saxons considered it an elixir, and it is believed that the honey-based drink was the customary toast following a wedding—hence the term honeymoon. Between lifting your maple and silver "mazer," you can sample Hampshire farm cheese served with good-tasting cottage bread. The Fox and Hounds, run by Bill and Joy Rout, is also noted for its English wines, which can be ordered on draft. If you've tasted cowslip before, you surely haven't sampled damson dandelion. From your beer-barrel seat, you can also take your chance on some sloe gin. English wines cost 60p ($1.05) per glass; a half pint of draft cider or beer, 45p (79¢). At the rear of the inn is a timbered barn serving as both a museum of farming artifacts (old farm wagons, carts, and smithy tools) and a self-service dining room. Here you dine on benches at one of the longest, oldest tables in England. During winter, the table nearest the ten-foot-wide fireplace is favored. Summertime, tables are also available in the courtyard beside an ancient wine press, under a rose arbor. A ploughman's lunch costs from £1.25 ($2.19).

Directions: Take the A27 from Southampton, toward Portsmouth. Go past Lowford, turn right onto Long Lane, pass the school on School Road and you'll reach a road called Hungerford Bottom. The Fox and Hounds is on your right.

BEAULIEU ABBEY: This stately home in the New Forest (tel. Beaulieu 612345) draws more visitors than Woburn Abbey, already previewed. The abbey and palace house, as well as the National Motor Museum, are on the property of Lord Montagu of Beaulieu, at Beaulieu, five miles southeast of Lyndhurst and 14 miles south of Southampton. Originally, a Cistercian abbey was founded on this spot in 1204, and the ruins can be explored today. The palace house was the great gate house of the abbey before it was converted into a private residence in 1538. The house is surrounded by gardens. On the grounds, one of the best and most comprehensive motor museums in the world, with more than 200 vehicles, was opened to the public, tracing the story of motoring from 1895 to the present day. Famous autos include four land-speed record-holders, among them Donald Campbell's "Blue Bird." The collection was built on the foundation of Lord Montagu's family collection of vintage cars. All the facilities are open every day from 10 a.m. to 6 p.m. (to 5 p.m. November to March). Inclusive admission to museum, house, abbey ruins, and gardens is £2.80 ($4.90) for adults, £1.40 ($2.45) for children.

3. New Forest

The New Forest came into the limelight in the times of Henry VIII, who loved to hunt here, as venison abounded. Also, with his enthusiasm for building up the British naval fleet, he saw his opportunity to supply oak and other hard timbers to the boatyards at Buckler's Hard on the Beaulieu River for the building of stout-hearted men-o'war. Today you can visit the old shipyards, and the museum with its fine models of men-o'war, pictures of the old yard, and dioramas showing the building of these ships, their construction, and their launching. It took 2000 trees to build one man-o'-war.

Stretching for about 92,000 acres, New Forest is a large tract 14 miles wide and 20 miles long. William the Conqueror laid out the limits of this then-private hunting preserve. Those who hunted without a license faced the executioner if they were caught, and those who hunted but missed had their hands severed.

Nowadays New Forest is one of those places traversed by a motorway by those motorists bound for the southwest. However, I'd suggest you stop a moment and relax.

This used to be a forest, but now the groves of oak trees are separated by wide tracts of common land which is grazed by ponies and cows, hummocked with heather and gorse, and frequented by rabbits. Away from the main arterial roads, where signs warn of wild ponies and deer, there is a private world of peace and quiet.

While you're in the New Forest area, try to visit the village of **Bucklers Hard** on the Beaulieu River. It was there that wooden-walled ships were built in the 18th century, among them Nelson's *Agamemnon.* Oak trees from the forest were felled and fashioned to make the hulls which were then towed round to Portsmouth Harbour for fitting-out. Entrance to the village and the car park is £1 ($1.75) per adult; children pay 50p (88¢). The car gets in free. You can visit free a delightful museum, with its collection of models, among them the *Agamemnon.* You'll see the tools used to build them along with the way of life of an 18th century man-o'-war. There is also much information on present-day sailors, Sir Francis Chichester included.

The **New Forest Butterfly Farm,** Longdown, Ashurst, near Southampton (tel. 042129/2166), is probably not everyone's cup of tea, but if you're interested in Orange-tips, Jezebels, or Delias, this is the place for you. This farm keeps not only endangered species of British butterflies, but exotic numbers from Malaysia, Brazil, and Africa. They are bred in a paradise of lemon trees, bougainvillea, and passion flowers. Outside on the ponds, dragonflies and damselflies hover over the water and breed naturally among the reeds. More exotically, there are also locusts, mantids, and tarantula spiders carefully protected behind observation glass.

There are five acres of woodland, a tea shop, and a gift shop where you can buy mounted butterflies, jewelry, butterfly books, and caterpillars for home breeding. At the Old Spud Shed, a relic of some former garden, you can purchase tropical plants and good old-fashioned dandelions, thistles, and nettles to encourage butterflies in your own garden. The farm is open from April 1 to October 31, daily from 10 a.m. to 5 p.m., charging adults an admission of £1.50 ($2.63) and children, 80p ($1.40).

FOOD AND LODGING: My recommendations for food and lodging in the New Forest include a few inexpensive places for overnighting.

The **Compton Arms,** Stoney Cross (tel. 042127/2134), stands in a village on the A31, close to the Rufus Stone. It is a Georgian-style inn, with large gardens and lovely views over New Forest. All rooms have radio and TV, and there are facilities for dry cleaning. Rates go from £6.50 ($11.38) per night in a single to £13 ($22.75) in a double or twin. A good set dinner is £6.50 ($11.38), or else you can order à la carte.

Copythorne Lodge, Romsey Road, Cadnam, near Southampton (tel. 042127/2127), is a large country house with a small dairy farm which provides fresh produce for the substantial farm breakfasts which Mrs. Garrett serves. There is a cozy lounge with TV, and one of the bedrooms has its own bath. The others must share showers and a toilet. The overnight charge is £6 ($10.50) per person, a little bit more for the room with private plumbing.

4. Isle of Wight

Four miles across the Solent from the South Coast towns of Southampton, Lymington, and Portsmouth, the Isle of Wight is known for its sandy beaches and its ports, favored by the yachting set. The island, which long attracted such literary figures as Alfred Tennyson and Charles Dickens, is compact in size, measuring 23 miles from east to west, 13 miles from north to south. You can take regular ferryboats over, although hydrofoils cross the Solent in just 20 minutes from Southampton.

Visitors who'd like to explore the Isle of Wight for the day can take an **"Around the Island"** six-hour bus tour which leaves from the Cowes Coach Park at 11:40 a.m. daily from May to October. The price is £3 ($5.25) for adults, £2 ($3.50) for children. For further information, telephone Cowes 524221.

The ferry from Southampton to the Isle of Wight costs £2.55 ($4.46) for a round-trip ticket, or else you can take a ferry/hydrofoil combination, a round-trip ticket costing £3.75 ($6.56).

The Lymington–Yarmouth (Isle of Wight) ferry charges £14 ($24.50) for each passenger on a day round-trip ticket. The more usual way of reaching the island is by ferry from Portsmouth Harbour or by hovercraft from Southsea, both of which take you to Ryde, a busy seaside town in summer, the railhead for the island's communications system. Arriving in Yarmouth, however, is something else. It's a yacht harbor, with pubs cluttering the wall.

Long a favorite of British royalty, the island has as its major attraction **Osborne House,** Queen Victoria's most cherished residence, lying a mile southeast of East Cowes. Prince Albert designed the Italian-inspired mansion which stands in lush gardens, right outside the village of Whippingham with its much-visited church. The rooms have remained as Victoria knew them, right down to the French piano she used to play and with all the cozy clutter of her sitting room. Grief-stricken at the death of Albert in 1861, she asked that Osborne House remain as it was, and so it has been. Even the turquoise scent bottles he gave her, decorated with cupids and cherubs, are still in place. It was at her bedroom in Osborne House that Victoria died on January 22, 1901. The house is open to the public from Easter Monday to June, Monday to Saturday from 11 a.m. to 5 p.m. In July and August, from Monday to Saturday it is open from 10 a.m. to 5 p.m. In September and early October, it is open Monday to Friday from 11 a.m. to 5 p.m. Admission is £2 ($3.50) for adults, £1 ($1.75) for children.

A completely different attraction, **Carisbrooke Castle** is where Charles I was imprisoned by the Roundheads in 1647. This fine medieval castle is in the center of the island, 1½ miles southwest of Newport. Everybody heads for the Well House, concealed inside a 16th-century stone building. Donkeys take turns treading a large wooden wheel connected to a rope which hauls up buckets of water. The castle is open weekdays from mid-March until mid-October from 9:30 a.m. to 6:30 p.m. (from mid-October to mid-March, to 4 p.m.). However, Sunday hours are different. From mid-March until March 31 and from October 1 to mid-October, it is open on Sunday from 2 to 6:30 p.m. From April 1 to September 30, it is open on Sunday from 9:30 a.m. to 6:30 p.m., and from mid-October to mid-March, Sunday hours are from 2 to 4 p.m. From April to September, adults pay an admission of £1.20 ($2.10); children, 60p ($1.05). Off-season prices are 60p ($1.05) for adults, 30p (53¢) for children.

You have a choice of several bases on the Isle of Wight unless you're what the English call a "day-tripper."

Cowes is the premier port for yachting in Britain. Henry VIII ordered the castle built there, but it is now the headquarters of the Royal Yacht Squadron. The seafront, the Prince's Green, and the high cliff road are worth exploring. Hovercraft are built in the town, and it is also the home and birthplace of the well-known maritime photographer, Beken of Cowes.

Along the southeast coast are the twin resorts of **Sandown,** with its new pier complex and theater, and **Shanklin,** at the southern end of Sandown Bay which has held the British annual sunshine record more times than any other resort. Keats once lived in Shanklin's Old Village.

Farther along the coast, **Ventnor** is called the "Madeira of England," because it arises from the sea in a series of steep hills.

On the west coast, the sand cliffs of **Alum Bay** are a blend of many different colors, a total of 21 claimed. The Needles, three giant chalk rocks, and the Needles Lighthouse, are further features of interest at this end of the island. If you want to stay at the western end of Wight, refer to my recommendations under **Totland Bay,** and **Freshwater Bay.**

Newport is the capital, a bustling market town lying in the heart of the island.

Ventnor

Madeira Hall, Trinity Road (tel. Ventnor 852624), is perhaps one of the nicest places to stay on the Isle of Wight. In an estate garden of lawns, tall trees, and flowering shrubs stands this stone manor house, with mullioned windows, gables, and bay windows. It has housed interesting people, such as Lord Macaulay, who wrote some of his well-known essays here. And there are associations with Charles Dickens and some of his characters. On the grounds is a heated swimming pool and an 18-hole putting course. Some units have private bathrooms, and all contain hot and cold running water. There are ample baths and toilets in the corridors. Mr. and Mrs. Waring quote a B&B rate ranging from £10.50 ($18.38) to £13.50 ($23.63) per person nightly. The half-board rate is £14.50 ($25.38) to £18 ($31.50) per person daily.

Delamere, Belle Vue Road (tel. Ventnor 852322) is a modest family-operated and -owned hotel a few blocks up the hill from Ventnor Bay and the pier. John and Jackie Morris have accommodations for only 22 guests, which means everyone gets personal attention. This is one of the best bargains on the island. The Morrises provide an ample, home-cooked evening dinner. The bedrooms face either the sea or the Downs, and are comfortably furnished. The beds have innerspring mattresses, and each room has hot and cold running water and bedside lamps. For B&B and evening dinner, the charge is only £12 ($21) per person daily. Children are granted reduced rates if they share a room with their parents. Mr. and Mrs. Morris like meeting Americans and Canadians, but wish they'd stay around longer so they could get to know them.

Sandown

Cliff House Hotel, Cliff Road (tel. Sandown 403656), is a substantial, well-cared-for, mustard-brick building with a white trim, on a quiet road overlooking Sandown Bay, as near to the sea as the cliff will allow. Although small—only 17 bedrooms, some with private bath—it has many amenities. In high season the daily half-board rate ranges from £18 ($31.50). Inside, an oak-pillared archway leads to the open dining room and drinking lounge, all in beiges, oranges, and browns. Open all year, Cliff House is supervised by Mrs. E. M. Gibbs and Alan and Diana Holbrook.

Shanklin

Westhill Manor, Westhill Road (tel. Shanklin 2783), is one of the most unusual places to stay on the island. It is a fine old stone manor house with a square tower, a half-timbered wing, and a lawn with a garden including a flagstone-edged open-air swimming pool. Adapted to the needs of guests, the architectural features have not been spoiled, only enhanced, with subtle and excellent choice of colors. The oak-paneled library has antiques and a platter collection. The Picasso blue-and-moss-colored dining room retains its original marble fireplace, and tables are set in its bay window. All bedrooms have two-channel radio, an intercom, and a water basin. The unusual feature of Westhill Manor is the Great Baronial Hall. The room rate is £8 ($14) per person in low season, rising to £13 ($22.75) in peak season. A private bath will cost an extra £1 ($1.75) per person. A table d'hôte dinner is available to guests for only £3 ($5.25), or else you can order à la carte, paying from £4.75 ($8.31) to £9 ($15.75) for three courses.

Afton Hotel, Clarence Gardens (tel. Shanklin 3075), is a substantial red brick hotel with ornate white Victorian trim under its gables. Owned by the enterprising John and Anita Williams, who have as their motto "Home Sweet

Afton," they bring to their guests charm and consideration. They have brought flair and style to the decorations and furnishings, and sound comforts as well, including full double glazing. The dining room, opening onto a sun terrace, is furnished with mahogany armchairs set around polished tables, and an interesting wicker bird stand. The living room has an ornate kelly-green and mahogany Victorian sofa and armchairs, with rose medallion wallpaper and a white trim. The intimate drinking lounge, the Shakespeare Bar, also has the Victorian touch. The bedrooms have central heating, lots of hot water, plenty of clean towels, soap, reading lights, and radio. Several units have private shower and toilet, and one has a four-poster bed and color TV. Anita does all the cooking, and if you have a special diet she'll happily comply with your needs. Generally, she's best at traditional cooking. Daily terms include B&B and evening dinner, costing a peak £15 ($26.25) per person daily. A five-course dinner goes for another £6 ($10.50).

Totland Bay

Randolph Private Hotel, Granville Road (tel. Freshwater 752411), has the look of a two-story traditional suburban home built at the beginning of this century. Owned and managed by Mrs. Bridget Mary Lodowski and daughter Bonita, it's not too large so you get plenty of personal attention. Each of the nicely furnished rooms has hot and cold running water, bed lights for night reading, innerspring mattresses, radio, and intercom, and is centrally heated. Mrs. Lodowski takes true pride in her home-cooking—"plain but tasty and nourishing." On short-term stays, the cost is £11 ($19.25) per person daily, including bed, breakfast, and evening dinner. Half price is charged for children.

Freshwater Bay

Saunders Hotel, Coastguard Lane (tel. Isle of Wight 752322), is an area not spoiled commercially. Set in a secluded bay with uninterrupted views of the sea and the downs, it is only 150 yards from the water. It is a fine converted Victorian private hotel with gables, tall chimneys, and several bay-view windows, surrounded by its own gardens. Guests are received all year. The dinner, bed, and breakfast rate, including VAT, is £15 ($26.25) per person daily. Mr. and Mrs. Keith Brettell are the resident owners.

Twelve miles from Southampton is the ancient city of:

5. Winchester

The most historical city in all of Hampshire, Winchester is big on legends. It's even associated with King Arthur and the Knights of the Round Table. In the Great Hall, the remains of Winchester Castle, a round oak table, with space for King Arthur and his 24 knights, hangs on the wall. But all that spells undocumented romance. What is actually known is that when the Saxons ruled the ancient kingdom of Wessex, Winchester was the capital.

The city is also linked with King Alfred, who is honored today by a statue and is believed to have been crowned there. The Danish conqueror, Canute, came this way too, as did the king he ousted, Ethelred (Canute got his wife Emma in the bargain). The city is the seat of the well-known Winchester College, whose founding father was the bishop of Winchester, William of Wykeham. Established in 1382, it lays claim to being the oldest public (private) school in England.

Traditions are strong in Winchester. It is said (although I've never confirmed the assertion) that if you go to St. Cross Hospital, now an almshouse, dating from the 12th century, you'll get ye olde pilgrim's dole of ale and bread (and if there's no bread, you can eat cake). Winchester, 65 miles from London, is essentially a market town, on the downs on the Itchen River.

WINCHESTER CATHEDRAL: For centuries Winchester Cathedral (tel. Winchester 53137) has been one of the great mother churches of England. The present building, the longest cathedral in Britain, dates from 1079, and its Norman heritage is still in evidence. When a Saxon church stood on this spot, St. Swithun, bishop of Winchester and tutor to young King Alfred, suggested modestly that he be buried outside. When he was later buried inside, it rained for 40 days. The legend lives on; just ask a resident of Winchester what will happen if it rains on St. Swithun's Day, July 15.

Of the present building, the nave with its two aisles is most impressive, as are the chantries, the reredos (late 15th century), and the elaborately carved choir stalls. Of the chantries, that of William of Wykeham, founder of Winchester College, is perhaps the most visited (it's found in the south aisle of the nave). The cathedral also contains a number of other tombs, notably those of novelist Jane Austen and Izaak Walton (exponent of the merits of the pastoral life—*The Compleat Angler*). The latter's tomb is to be found in the Prior Silkestede's Chapel in the South Transept. Miss Austen's grave is marked with a commemorative plaque. Winchester Cathedral contains in chests the bones of many of the Saxon kings and the remains of the Viking conqueror, Canute, and his wife Emma, in the presbytery. The son of William the Conqueror, William Rufus (who reigned as William II in 1087), is also believed to have been buried at the cathedral.

The Crypt is flooded for a large part of the year, and at such times is closed to the public. When it's not flooded, there are regular tours at 10:30 a.m. and 2:30 p.m. The Library, in which is displayed the *Winchester Bible* and other ancient manuscripts, is open for limited hours throughout the summer (except Monday mornings and Sunday) and on Wednesday and Saturday for the rest of the year (except January, when it's open only on Saturday). The Treasury is open during the summer season from 11 a.m. to 5 p.m. It is small and does not require a guide.

OTHER SIGHTS: The **Royal Hussars Museum,** Southgate Street (tel. Winchester 61781, ext. 239), traces the history of the famous regiment in tableaux and pictures. You go from the days when the original regiments, the 10th and 11th Royal Hussars, were engaged in the Peninsular War and fought at Waterloo, to their mechanization in 1928 and their amalgamation in 1969. All sorts of questions are answered, including why the 11th is known as "Cherrypickers." The answer to that one is that they had an engagement with the French in a cherry orchard during the Peninsular War. The word "Hussar," you'll learn, is a derivation from old Hungarian relating to the method of conscripting "one in twenty" from the men of each village. The museum is open from Easter until the end of October, Tuesday to Friday, from 11 a.m. to 4 p.m. On Saturday and Sunday, its hours are from 2 to 4 p.m. Admission is 20p (35¢) for adults and 10p (18¢) for children.

The **Royal Green Jackets Museum,** Peninsular Barracks, Romsey Road (tel. Winchester 61781, ext. 288). In the same military complex as the Royal Hussars Museum, this other exhibition hall has a collection of weaponry and uniforms illustrating the history of the Oxfordshire and Buckinghamshire Light Infantry. Along with that, you'll see other mementos of the King's Royal Rifle Corps and the Rifle Brigade, which together form the Royal Green Jackets. The museum is open in March from 10:30 a.m. to 12:30 p.m. and 2 to 4 p.m., Monday to Saturday. From April to September, it's open Monday to Friday from 10:30 a.m. to 12:30 p.m. and 2 to 4:30 p.m. On Saturday hours are 2:30 to 4:30 p.m.

LODGING: **Winton Court Hotel,** 49 Southgate St. (tel. Winchester 53664), is a remake of a group of gracious 18th-century town houses painted in aqua and trimmed in white. All accommodations have radio and telephone, central heating, and hot and cold running water. All floors are served by elevator. The single rate is £13.80 ($24.15); the twin or double rate, £22.50 ($39.38). Family rooms go for £11 ($19.25) per person. Twins or doubles with private bath or shower and toilet cost £25.50 ($44.63). VAT is added to all rates. The pine-paneled and rugged stone drinking lounge has a rock garden and fountain, and there is a comfortable lounge with color TV. Meals are served in the paneled dining room, decorated in strong primary colors. Parking is available at the rear of the hotel, which lies a few minutes' walk from the city center.

The **Winchester Hotel,** St. Cross Road (tel. Winchester 3507), is just outside the heart of the city, set back from the busy Southampton road. It is comprised of two Edwardian brick houses blended together. Hot and cold water and central heating are in all rooms. At present there are 22 singles, 11 doubles, five family rooms, and one twin. Singles range from £8.50 ($14.88) to £10.50 ($18.38); twins or doubles, from £17 ($29.75) to £25 ($43.75), the latter with private bath. Tariffs include breakfast, VAT, and service. Many public bathrooms are available, as is a comfortable television lounge. There is an excellent restaurant open seven days a week, but in the evening only. You must tell the staff if you want a meal before 4:30 p.m. The cost is £6 ($10.50) to residents.

Southgate Hotel, Southgate Street (tel. Winchester 51243), is a brick house in the center of Winchester. It opens onto a rear garden with flowerbeds and an old walnut tree. Christopher Wren designed and built Southgate in 1715, and many of the original architectural details remain (note the front entry with the glass lights over the doorway). All the bedrooms are equipped with hot and cold running water. The B&B rate is £13 ($22.75) per person, to which 10% is added for service. There is an excellent cuisine, from gourmet à la carte meals to economy bar grub.

Stratton House, Stratton Road, St. Giles Hill (tel. Winchester 63919), is an old Victorian house (circa 1890) set in an acre of ground in an elevated position on St. Giles Hill, overlooking the city. It is about a five- to ten-minute walk from the center. Single, double, twin-bedded, and family units are available throughout the year. The charge for B&B is about £9 ($15.75) per person. An evening meal can be arranged for another £4 ($7). All bedrooms have TV, and there is ample parking in a private courtyard.

READER'S GUEST HOUSE SELECTION: "**The Doves,** 28 Egbert Rd. (tel. Winchester 61059), provided the friendliest and most homey accommodation on my tour. The impeccably clean home is about a five-minute walk from the train station and less than ten minutes from downtown. Joyce Dove runs the house which takes up to seven persons. Her full English breakfast is the best I experienced. The price per person is £7.50—$13.13" (Ed Hunter, Denver Colo.).

FOOD AND DRINK: The **Wessex Hotel,** Paternoster Row (tel. Winchester 61611), just by the cathedral, has a bright coffeeshop with a separate entrance from the street where hot and cold snacks are available all day. A typical meal of soup, breaded plaice with fried potatoes, apple pie and cream, plus coffee, will cost about £5 ($8.75).

They also do a traditional afternoon tea when you help yourself from the sideboard, which has a selection of sandwiches, along with scones with butter, jam and cream, pastries and cakes. The whole spread, as much as you want, costs £2.40 ($4.20) for adults and £1.20 ($2.10) for children.

From noon to 2 p.m. the cocktail bar in the hotel has a beef-and-seafood table, with various dishes, including open-face sandwiches, beef on rye, salade Niçoise. There is a good selection of cheese and cake served with cream. The average price for a helping is £1.75 ($3.06). A large meal will set you back about £4 ($7).

Splinters, 9 Great Minster St. (tel. Winchester 64004). The Sherret family runs two restaurants at this address. The upstairs restaurant serves an imaginative continental cuisine, but may be beyond our budget guidelines. However, the ground-floor brasserie offers good-value light lunches of, for example, quiche Lorraine with salad for around £1.65 ($2.89). Tempting desserts cost around 75p ($1.31) apiece. Splinters is open for lunch Monday through Saturday from 11 a.m. till 2:30 p.m.

Minstrels, 18 Little Minster St. (tel. Winchester 67212), serves a variety of functions: it's ideal for morning coffee and a pâtisserie, quick and reasonably priced lunches, and afternoon teas extending to light suppers suitable for family and friends. Run by R. M. Powell and J. A. Ayre, it was once known as Banners, during which it developed a devoted following. The menu is limited, simple fare such as homemade soup, leek and potato pie, fisherman's pie, and chili con carne. Continental dishes, however, also appear. Thus on any given day you are likely to find ratatouille, quiche, moussaka, and lasagne. Expect to spend no more than £4 ($7), unless you're ravenously hungry. A half liter of the house wine goes for £2.75 ($4.81). A hot menu is available all day, and there is take-away service. Hours are Monday to Saturday from 10 a.m. to 6 p.m.

Mr. Pitkin's Wine Bar & Eating House, 4 Jewry St. (tel. Winchester 69630), has been installed in a fine Victorian town house in the heart of the city. Anthony Pitkin used to be in advertising in London, but he gave that up, and along with his wife Magda, opened what has become one of the most popular rendezvous points in Winchester. And with good reason.

The place is active and bustling, and live music is a regular feature in the bar where snacks begin at £1 ($1.75). At lunch hot dishes are featured for around £2 ($3.50). The restaurant on the first floor offers English fare. A daily luncheon menu, with three courses, costs from £6.50 ($11.38), although if you skip a course you can dine for less. This table d'hôte is served daily from noon to 2 p.m. At night from 7 p.m. you can order a three-course meal, including coffee, at £9.50 ($16.63).

The **Royal Oak Pub** (tel. Winchester 61136) is to be found in a passageway next to the God Begot House in the High Street. This pub contains the oldest bar in England. Luncheons are served at the bar from noon to 2 p.m., Monday through Saturday. Various snacks and hot meals are available for prices that begin at £1.50 ($2.63). Live New Orleans jazz is featured on Monday and Thursday evenings. Admission is free. This is a busy, friendly pub with plenty of atmosphere where the hosts and staff enjoy serving good food and drink.

To continue your pub crawl, try:

The **Old Market Inn,** The Square, ideal for those who enjoy a local pub. It offers a relaxed, friendly, unself-conscious atmosphere, a proper background in which to drink a pint. The corner pub sits opposite the cathedral in the oldest, most historic district of Winchester. It's mellowed enough to have timbers galore, cozy nooks, and comfortable chairs. A good selection of hot and cold bar snacks is available at lunchtime, including home-cooked steak-and-kidney pie, cottage pie, and chicken-and-mushroom pie. Prices begin at £1.75 ($3.06). The owners don't think their establishment merits international publicity, but they welcome individual travelers who stray in.

If time remains, you might now continue your trip westward into the too-often-neglected county of:

DORSET

This is Thomas Hardy country. You may have seen the film *Far from the Madding Crowd,* or perhaps read *Tess of the D'Urbervilles* or have seen the recent film *Tess,* about one of the most memorable of all Victorian heroines. Dorset is the Wessex of Hardy novels. Some of the towns and villages, although altered considerably, are still recognizable from his descriptions—however, he changed the names to protect the innocent. Poole, for example became Havenpool; Weymouth converted to Budmouth. The last of the great Victorians, as he was called, died in 1928 at the age of 88. Although his tomb rests in a position of honor in Westminster Abbey, his heart was cut out and buried in his beloved Dorsetshire.

One of England's smallest shires, Dorset stretches all the way from the Victorian seaside resort of Bournemouth in the east to Lyme Regis in the west (known to Jane Austen, who couldn't find where all the action was). Dorset is a southwestern county, bordering the English Channel. It's big on cows, and Dorset butter is served at many an afternoon tea. Mainly, it is a land of farms and pastures, with plenty of sandy heaths and chalky downs.

The most prominent tourist center of Dorset is the Victorian seaside resort of Bournemouth. If you don't anchor there, you might also try a number of Dorset's other seaports, villages, and country towns. For the most part, I've hugged closely to the impressive coastline.

Incidentally, Dorset, as the vacation-wise Britisher might tell you if he or she wanted to divulge a secret, is a friend of the budget traveler.

6. Bournemouth

The South Coast resort at the doorsteps of the New Forest didn't just happen: it was carefully planned and manicured, a true city in a garden. Flower-filled, park-dotted Bournemouth contains great globs of architecture inherited from those arbiters of taste, Victoria and her mischievous boy, Edward. Its most distinguishing feature is its Chines (shrub-filled, narrow, steep-sided ravines) along the zigzag coastline. The walking English strike out at, say, Hengistbury Head, making their way past sandy beaches, both the Boscombe and Bournemouth Piers—finally reaching Alum Chine, a distance of six miles away, but a traffic-free walk to remember.

It is estimated that of the nearly 12,000 acres which Bournemouth claims for its own, about one-sixth is turned over to green parks, stage-setting-type waters, even flowerbeds, such as the Pavilion Rock Garden, through which amblers pass both day and night. The total effect, especially in spring, tends to be dramatic and helps explain Bournemouth's long-established popularity with the garden-loving English. Bournemouth was discovered back in Victoria's day, when sea-bathing became a firmly entrenched institution, often practiced with great ritual. Many of the comparatively elegant villas that exist today (now largely B&B houses and hotels) once privately housed eminent Victorians.

Bournemouth, which along with Poole and Christchurch forms the largest urban area in the south of England, is not as sophisticated as Brighton. Increasingly, it is retirement acres for widowed or spinster English ladies who have found their place in the sun by playing the wicked game of Bingo. Increasingly, too, Bournemouth and its neighbors have a floating population of some 20,000 students attending one of its schools or colleges and in their off-hours exploring places written about or painted by such poets and artists as Shelley, Beardsley, and Turner.

The resort's amusements are wide and varied. At the Pavilion Theatre, for example, you can see West End-type productions from London; the Bournemouth Symphony Orchestra is justly famous in Europe; and there's the usual run of golf courses, band concerts, variety shows, and dancing.

Bournemouth is about 104 miles from London, easily reached in about an hour and 40 minutes on an express train from Waterloo Station in London. It makes a good base for exploring a history-rich part of England. On its outskirts are the New Forest, Salisbury and Winchester, and the Isle of Wight (an island that lies 15 miles away, the former seaside retreat of Victoria).

ACCOMMODATIONS: **Park View Hotel,** 27 Spencer Rd. (tel. Bournemouth 28955), stands on a hillside, away from the bustle of Bournemouth center, although there is an impressive view of the resort. Bill Rowan welcomes guests at a cost of £7.50 ($13.13). Rooms come with hot and cold running water, and are comfortably furnished. Parking is available in the forecourt. Dinner is an extra £2.50 ($4.38) per person.

Dale Guest House, 34 St. Michael's Rd. (tel. Bournemouth 20265), is under the ownership of Mrs. Y. Jones. Dale House is on the West Cliff in the heart of Bournemouth. The street is quietly residential, leading directly to the seafront (some 600 yards). One of Bournemouth's best shopping areas is only 400 yards away, with regular bus services to the station. The Winter Gardens, Pavilion, pier shows, and cinemas are all within easy walking distance. The centrally heated rooms are well furnished with comfortable beds, hot and cold running water, and electric razor points in all accommodations. You can stay here for £8.50 ($14.88) per person nightly, including a good solid English breakfast. Evening meals can be arranged for those who wish to dine in, and luncheon/picnic baskets are also available. Depending on the menu, dinner is a full three-course meal which costs £4.50 ($7.88) to £5.50 ($9.63). All meals are homemade.

Belgravia Hotel, 56 Christchurch Rd., East Cliff (tel. Bournemouth 20857), is a gracious brick mansion in a posh section of the resort, set in its own garden, the pride of the owners. For from £8 ($14) per person daily, plus VAT, you can stay here and have B&B. Dinner is available on request at £4 ($7) per person. The Belgravia is a five-minute walk along a zigzag path to the water. It's a pleasant house, with a mansard roof and a multitude of bay windows. The bedrooms are sun-filled and roomy. The beds have innersprings, and the rooms contain built-in wardrobes, bedside lamps, and armchairs. Reservations of only a night or two are almost impossible to get during the summer season (when the one-weekers are given priority, of course).

Fenn Lodge, 11 Rosemount Rd., Alum Chine, Bournemouth West (tel. Bournemouth 761273), is the domain of Mr. and Mrs. D. Spring, who devote considerable energy to making their licensed guest house a friendly, clean, and comfortable place to stay. They charge £8 ($14), plus VAT, for bed and an English breakfast. Mrs. Spring takes pride in a high standard of service. During the peak holiday season, they take guests for at least a week only, but they do accept fill-ins, during the off-peak months. Single visitors are welcome. The weekly rate for B&B and an evening meal ranges from £80 ($140), plus VAT. In this way you can use Bournemouth as your base for exploring this part of England. There is no service charge. All bedrooms have hot and cold running water, and many of them overlook a small garden and Alum Chine. Public rooms are centrally heated. It is only a few minutes' walk through the chine to the sea and Bournemouth Bay. Parking in the front courtyard is free.

Sunnydene, 11 Spencer Rd. (tel. Bournemouth 22281), is a substantial, gabled house on a tree-lined road between the Central Station and Bournemouth Bay. The carpeted rooms contain hot and cold running water and are well kept and comfortable. The cost for B&B is £9 ($15.75) per person daily. An evening meal of four courses with coffee will cost an extra £4 ($7). Daily accommodation is usually available during April, May, June, September, and October. Bill and Marion Jackson, the proprietors, are efficient and most solicitous in their attentions. They serve excellent meals, and seem to pride themselves on running a bright private hotel.

South Beach Hotel, 112 Overcliff Dr., Southbourne (tel. Bournemouth 428928), is a small family hotel operated by resident owners W. J. Grimshaw and H. A. Grafton. Lying along the "Shell House," it has good views of Bournemouth Bay and the English Channel. There are some large family rooms with balconies, and children sharing a room with their parents are granted reductions. The rate for half board is a reasonable £10.50 ($18.38) per person. The owners have a comfortable lounge with color TV plus a private car park.

Mrs. H. M. Cameron (tel. Christchurch 483128) has accommodations at 46 Stour Rd. at nearby Christchurch, five minutes from the railway station. She offers B&B from £9.50 ($16.63) nightly. For many years Mrs. Cameron ran a guest house at another location and her friendship with many overseas guests still continues. Christchurch has a delightful ancient priory which attracts thousands of visitors. Christchurch is close to Bournemouth, Winchester, Southampton, Salisbury, and New Forest, and an hour's journey from the Isle of Wight.

EATING OUT IN BOURNEMOUTH: The **Old England,** 74 Poole Rd., Westbourne (tel. Bournemouth 766475), lives up to its name in food and decor. H. L. and J. L. Pyper run a friendly, comfortable restaurant, offering good value, and their efforts have gained increasing attention in town. A set daily lunch or supper menu goes for £4.75 ($8.31) or a child's portion for £3 ($5.25). This menu is served daily including Sunday. I recently enjoyed the roast Hampshire pork with a savory stuffing. You can also order from a large à la carte menu, including such well-prepared English fare as roast fresh Dorset chicken, roast Scottish beef, and the mixed grill "Old England." However, expect to spend from £10 ($17.50). For dessert, I'd suggest the homemade apple pie, served either with custard or cream. Hours, Tuesday through Sunday, are from 9:30 a.m. to 3 p.m. and 6 to 10:30 p.m.

Ann's Pantry, 129 Belle Vue Rd., Southbourne Crossroads, Southbourne (tel. Bournemouth 426178), stands on the corner, looking very much like an Edwardian drinking tavern. Near the seafront, it is actually a licensed restaurant which also provides a holiday accommodation. The owners, Geoffrey and Mary Thayne, offer one of the best bargain three-course lunches at the resort. For £2 ($3.50) and up, you get a three-course meal, beginning with soup, including one main dish such as Madras beef curry and rice, and ending with a typically English dessert. All the food is home-cooked and fresh. A three-course evening meal at £4 ($7) is also offered, including such main courses as seafood platter and pork chop, along with coffee following your dessert. There is also a more comprehensive and expensive à la carte menu. Hours are Tuesday to Saturday from 10:30 a.m. to 2 p.m. and 6:30 to 10 p.m. (on Sunday, 10:30 a.m. to 2 p.m. only).

Planters, 514 Christchurch Rd., Boscombe (tel. Bournemouth 302228), is an American-style restaurant and cocktail bar with a cinema backdrop. Ian Lancashire keeps his place open seven nights a week from 6:30 to 11 p.m. (also from noon to 2:30 p.m., Monday to Saturday). In the Bayou-style bar, a rather extraordinary array of cocktails is offered (for restaurant patrons only), ranging from a Dizzy Blond to a Margarita. Some are quite exotic, including the Freddy Fudpucker (that's Fudpucker), made with Tequila, Galliano, and orange juice. The price from is from £1 ($1.75) up to £4.50 ($7.88). Specials are featured, including a char-grilled Oregon lamb (marinated in wine and herbs) and chili con carne with pita bread and a side salad. A dozen different burgers are offered as well; each burger weighs about a quarter of a pound. Meals begin at £5 ($8.75), ranging upward. Desserts include such traditional American offerings as apple pie and a banana split.

Trattoria Tosca, 12 Richmond Hill (tel. Bournemouth 23034), is run by Eddie Cobelli, who serves some of the finest Italian dishes at this seaside resort. Hours are Monday to Sunday from 11:30 a.m. to 2:30 p.m. and 6 to 11:30 p.m. It's best to reserve a table on weekends, when the little restaurant on the square can get very busy. The Italian soups, such as pastina in brodo and minestrone, are good, as is the pasta selection. My favorite is his tasty and rich spaghetti alla carbonara. To please the English palate, he offers the usual boring selections. However, I recommend you visit strictly for his Italian specialties, which are well prepared and tasty, including the charmingly named filleto Casanova (filet seasoned with black pepper, cooked in brandy and marsala, and served with pâté). Fresh vegetables are served every day. About the cheapest you can dine here for is £7 ($12.25), plus the cost of your wine.

The **Salad Centre,** Post Office Road (tel. Bournemouth 21720), is for devotees of vegetarian and "whole-food." Against a sparkling, pristine backdrop, it places its emphasis on fresh ingredients. There is always a large selection of salads, and you can also count on a fresh soup every day. Various quiches are presented, as are vegetable flans. Instead of roast beef, you get a nut roast. There is no fixed menu, however, and the center is more or less cafeteria style. Meals begin at £2.50 ($4.38), and hours are Monday to Friday from 10 a.m. to 5 p.m., and on Saturday from 10 a.m. to 2:30 p.m. The center is run by the Sloan family who provide a warm welcome.

READER'S HOTEL SELECTION: "We were fortunate to find **The Hawthorns,** 183 Holdenhurst Rd. (tel. Bournemouth 24250). Owned by Brenda and Edwin Richards, the guest house is run as a 'tight ship,' in keeping with Mr. Richard's former occupation of naval officer. Convenient to shopping, the shore, restaurants, and churches, the house charges £6 ($10.50) per person, including breakfast. Mrs. Richards has some American ties and goes out of her way to be helpful to her guests. As with most English guest houses, The Hawthorns is very comfortable and clean. Off-street parking is provided" (Charles E. McCabe, McLean, Va.).

ON THE OUTSKIRTS: The **Fisherman's Haunt Hotel,** Winkton, Christchurch (tel. Christchurch 484071), dates back to 1673. An old wisteria-covered country house, it is run by James Bochan, of Ukrainian origin, who came to England with the Polish forces in 1943. He and his wife Isobel welcome guests all year, charging £13 ($22.75) for bathless singles, going up to £25 ($43.75) in a bathless double. Doubles with private baths and toilets cost £27 ($47.25), those with four-poster beds going for £31 ($54.25). Authentic regional British dishes are the fare of the dining room which overlooks the River Avon. Open from 12:30 p.m., the restaurant at Fisherman's Haunt Hotel offers a set luncheon for £4 ($7). Dinners on weeknights are served from 7 to 10 p.m. A special feature of the restaurant is the traditional Sunday midday meal. If you do stay over, you will be served a full English breakfast in the morning. All bedrooms have full central heating and tea- or coffee-making facilities. Bedroom windows afford views of the garden, the river, and the meadows. The hotel lies only seven miles from Bournemouth and a mile and a half from Christchurch.

READERS' GUEST HOUSE SELECTIONS (CHRISTCHURCH): "By far the best accommodation we had in terms of comfort, price, and luxury was **Brantwood,** 55 Stour Rd., Christchurch (tel. Christchurch 473446), run by Mr. and Mrs. Brackstone. They have twins and doubles, two large family rooms, very modern, and a most nutritious and filling breakfast, with offers of seconds. From October to June 1, their rates are £7 ($12.25) per person for B&B. In the summer months, the rate rises to £9 ($15.75) per person. In winter, an evening meal is available if desired. The Brantwood is within easy walking distance of one of the best amusement parks and model villages found in all of England, **Tucktonia"** (Mr. and Mrs. D. Weller, Pembroke, Bermuda). . . . "The comfortable guest house of **Mrs. A. J. White,** 39 Wick Lane (tel. Christchurch 473095), is less than a five-minute walk from downtown Christchurch. There is a regular bus service to Bournemouth, which joins Christchurch. The guest house has a small number of rooms, each with TV, and there is ample car space if needed. We had a large, lovely room facing the quiet street with the Isle of Wight in the background. Mr. and Mrs. White live next door. Mrs. White has a kitchen in the guest house and will cook breakfast for a person at any time requested. Mr. White is a photographer and perhaps could also be called the town historian for the many ancient records he possesses. Now for the clincher—Mrs. White charges £6.50 ($11.38) per person per night" (Lindsay S. Reeks, Pleasant Hill, Calif.).

SAIL ON A TALL SHIP (AT POOLE): The *Biche,* built in 1934, is the last existing Breton sailing ship built for tunny-fishing. More than 100 feet long and 22 feet wide, she was once the pride of Ange "Biche" Stephan, who still sails her when she visits Britanny. Now the pride of Charles Booth, she lies at Poole Harbour, Dorset. Used for participative sail crewing and training, she spends her days cruising, taking day trips in safe local waters, but also goes on weekend cruises offshore and on longer charters when the Atlantic is child's play to this ocean-going ship. She can sleep 12 in comfort, has a well-stocked galley and bar, and comes with a crew of two, Charles and one of his two mates, all vastly experienced in sailing. They're also good cooks. A day trip, including lunch, costs £10 ($17.50) per person for four or more. Departure is at 10:30 a.m., returning about 6 p.m. *Biche* can also be rented for fishing. Further details and reservations can be obtained from **Seaways Leisure Venture Club,** 9 Blackstone Rd., Wallingford, Oxon, OX10 8JR (tel. Wallingford 35531 or Abingdon 25998).

7. Wool

Set in the midst of pastoral scenery and known to readers of Hardy, the sleepy hamlet of Wool, about 19 miles west of Bournemouth, is one of the most charming in East Dorset. On the Frome River, it has thatched cottages with plastered walls on either side of the road. The stream that winds its way through the maze of streets and lanes lures potential waders.

The district was also known to T. E. Lawrence, Lawrence of Arabia, who died in a motorcycle crash in 1935. His former home, **Clouds Hill,** lies four miles to the northwest (one mile north of Bovington Camp). It is open Wednesday, Thursday, Friday, and Sunday from 2 to 5 p.m. from April to the end of September. From October to the end of March, it is open only on Sunday, from 1 to 4 p.m. Admission is £1 ($1.75) for either an adult or child, and no photography is allowed.

8. Wareham

On the Frome River, this historic little town is about a mile west of Poole Harbour. Many find it a good center for touring the South Dorset coast and the Purbeck Hills. It contains remains of early British and Roman town walls, plus the Saxon church of St. Martin has an effigy of Lawrence of Arabia. If you're stopping over, you'll find food at—

The Old Granary, The Quay (tel. Wareham 2010), a riverside country pub near a double-arched bridge. You dine either inside or on a terrace overlooking the boats and swans. The interior dining room has a charm of its own, with bentwood chairs, saffron cloths, a wine rack, a natural wood sideboard, and white walls displaying a collection of locally painted watercolors. A gracious and informal atmosphere prevails. The secret behind the success of the Old Granary is its fine cuisine; the owners, Mr. and Mrs. Michael Hipwell, try hard to stick to natural country foods. Homemade soups go for 75p ($1.31); pâté for £1.50 ($2.63); a filet of pork in a barbecue sauce, £6 ($10.50); Dorset lamb chops with cheese and onion, £6 also. A hefty portion of homemade fruit pie with cream is 80p ($1.40). The restaurant is open every day. If you wish to overnight here, the charge is £17 ($29.75), plus tax, per person for B&B.

9. Dorchester

Thomas Hardy, in his 1886 Victorian novel *The Mayor of Casterbridge,* gave it literary fame. But Dorchester was known to the Romans. In fact its Maumbury Rings, south of the town, are considered the best Roman amphitheater in Britain, having once resounded with the shouts of 12,000 spectators screaming for gladiator blood. Dorchester, the county town, was the setting of another blood-letting, the Bloody Assize of 1685, when Judge Jeffreys, suffering from "the stone," dispensed the ultimate in justice to the poor wretches condemned for supporting the Duke of Monmouth's ill-fated attempt to become the English monarch.

But it is mostly through Hardy that the world knows Dorchester. Many of his major scenes of love and intrigue took place on the periphery of Dorchester. The land was best known to Hardy, since he was born in 1840 at **Higher Bockhampton,** three miles northeast of Dorchester. His home, now a National Trust property, may be visited by the public from March to October, from 11 a.m. to 6 p.m. or dusk, whichever is earlier. But to go inside, you must make an appointment with the tenant. You may write in advance to **Hardy's Cottage,** Higher Bockhampton, Dorchester, Dorset, England, or telephone Dorchester 62366. You approach the cottage on foot, a seven-minute walk after parking your vehicle in the space provided in the wood. The admission is £1 ($1.75), and the cost of a guided tour is 50p (88¢). Within easy reach of the cottage is **Rainbarrow,** mentioned by Hardy in *Return of the Native.*

You may also want to browse around the **Dorset County Museum** on High West Street (next to St. Peter's Church; tel. Dorchester 62735), with memorabilia of Thomas Hardy. In addition, you'll find prehistoric and Roman relics, plus natural history exhibits and others pertaining to the geology of the region. There is also a rural craft section of bygones. The museum is normally open on weekdays from 10 a.m. to 5 p.m., but may close between 1 and 2 p.m. on Monday and Saturday. Admission is 50p (88¢) for adults, 25p (44¢) for children.

Five miles east of Dorchester, on the Dorchester-Bournemouth road (A35), stands **Athelhampton,** one of England's great medieval houses, considered the most beautiful and historic in the south. It was begun in the reign of Edward IV on the legendary site of King Athelstan's palace. It was Thomas Hardy's Athelhall. A family home for more than 500 years, it is noted for its 15th-century Great Hall, its Tudor Great Chamber, its state bedroom, and King's Room. The house stands on ten acres of formal and landscaped gardens, with a 15th-century dovecote, river gardens, fish ponds, fountains, and rare trees. It is open to the public on Wednesday, Thursday, Sunday, and bank holidays, from the Wednesday before Easter to the first Sunday in October, 2 to 6 p.m. In August it is also open on Tuesday and Friday. Admission is 75p ($1.31) to the garden and another 75p to the house.

FOOD AND LODGING: The **Wessex Hotel,** High West Street (tel. Dorchester 62660), is an architecturally interesting Georgian structure built on medieval foundations. In the town center, the hotel offers 20 bedrooms with full residential services. Room rates range from £12 ($21) for a single room to £21.75 ($38.06) for a double or twin. Prices include a full English breakfast and VAT. The Wessex has a full residential and restaurant license and a popular public restaurant with an extensive menu and a good wine list.

Judge Jeffrey's Restaurant, 6 High West St. (tel. Dorchester 64369), opposite the County Museum, is an attractive stop on your cross-country jaunt. Dating back to the 14th century, it had the dubious distinction of lodging that cantankerous alcoholic, Judge Jeffreys, during the Bloody Assize. The restaurant today offers different services in each room. The owners, Tony and Ann Coletta, call their pub grub "lunch snacks," and these range from a toasted cheese sandwich at 95p ($1.66) to fish and chips at £2.50 ($4.38). A three-course lunch at £3.95 ($6.91) includes coffee, and à la carte main courses start at £4.50 ($7.88) for the scampi Provençale. In winter from the end of October to early March, they are closed during the week but open on Saturday evening and for the traditional Sunday lunch at £4.50 ($7.88). Saturday night is jazz night throughout the year. An admission of £1.50 ($2.63) includes a sandwich. Food service is from 9:30 a.m. to 5:30 p.m. and then from 7 to 10 p.m. The proprietors take pride in the old English atmosphere of massive oak beams, an oak spiral staircase, stone-mullioned windows, paneled rooms, Tudor fireplaces. Most important, the restaurant's haunted. During its restoration in 1928, parts of a human skeleton were discovered in a bricked-up part of the east wall.

Staying at a Manor House

A highly recommended place to stay is **Moonfleet Manor,** only nine miles outside the town. It has 40 bedrooms, 21 with their own color TV. Rooms are updated and comfortably furnished, renting for from £10.50 ($18.38) per person nightly for B&B. There is a heated swimming pool on the premises. Reservations can be made by telephoning 0305/786948. The manor was the site of Thomas Hardy's novel *Moon Fleet.*

A Working Farm

Coombe Farm, Litton Cheney (tel. 03083/248), is a working sheep farm, an old and comfortable thatched farmhouse in a secluded valley south of the main A35 Dorchester–Bridport road. You are invited to join the Percival family in their attractive home, to appreciate the period furniture, and to doze by a log fire over a book or watching TV. They are only too willing to advise on places and houses to see, excursions to make in their delightful Dorsetshire countryside. Dinner, bed, and breakfast will cost from £12.50 ($21.88) per person, even for the room with a four-poster bed. The chambers have tea- and coffee-making facilities, and electric blankets in cold weather. One unit has a private bath, for which you'll pay extra.

On the Outskirts

Brace of Pheasants, Plush (tel. Piddletrenthide 357). Joan Chandler runs this charming country restaurant which has beautiful views through its little dormer windows, opening onto a rural setting. To reach it, take the B3143 out of Dorchester to Piddletrenthide, turning off at the sign to Plush. The inn, open Monday through Saturday with one sitting at 8 p.m., is on your left. Mrs. Chandler does the cooking, a French/Cordon Bleu cuisine. The restaurant upstairs is painted red with open beams, and the downstairs bar is cream colored with chintz covers, old paintings, and antique tables. Charcoal grills are the specialties of the Steak Bar, and not only steaks but cutlets and game dishes are available seven days a week. In summer Mrs. Chandler offers grilled lobster and prawns. She also has a covered patio in the garden which is great fun in summer. The variety of food offered in this complex is enormous, including at least eight appetizers and six main courses, along with a large selection of desserts. The cost is about £10 ($17.50) per person, including VAT. This place seems to get better every year. Reservations are necessary.

READER'S HOTEL SELECTION AT FRAMPTON: "Our very favorite place on our entire trip was **The Court** at Frampton, a tiny village in Dorset, near Dorchester in the Thomas Hardy country (tel. Maiden Newton 20242). The Court is a beautiful manor house, elegantly furnished, run by two lovely women. It's on a secluded land and contains 16 acres of gardens, a pond, and a charming menagerie of ducks, chickens, a golden retriever, a Siamese cat, and a pair of peacocks. There are ample bathrooms and a shower room. Our breakfast, served in their first-floor dining room overlooking the garden and pond, included hot homemade rolls, fresh milk and homemade butter from their Jersey cows, and generous servings of sausage, bacon, and eggs, with, of course, marmalade and tea. We had electric kettles in our rooms, and Mrs. Goddard brought us a doily-lined tray with a bone china cup and saucer and teapot for our early morning tea. There was also a small covered pitcher of cream, sugar, and tea bags. You can be served dinner also, but they like to have notice. B&B and evening dinner in the best English manor tradition is £18 ($31.50) per person. No children are accepted" (Alice L. Jones, Au Sable Forks, N.Y.).

FLEET AIR ARM MUSEUM: This museum at the Royal Naval Air Station, Yeovilton in Somerset (tel. Ilchester 840551), contains the largest collection of historic military aircraft in Europe, including the Concorde 002. It also displays scale models and other memorabilia associated with the RN Air Service and the Fleet Air Arm. Flying displays from the airfield can be viewed from the car park area. The museum, charging an nominal entrance fee, is open daily from 10 a.m. until 5:30 p.m. or dusk. There are a tea room and a picnic area.

From Dorchester, we continue west 15 miles to:

10. Bridport

In Thomas Hardy's fictional Wessex terrain, Bridport was Port Bredy. The town lies inland, although there is a harbor one mile away at the holiday resort of West Bay, near the end of Chesil Beach. Ropes and fishing nets are Bridport specialties. Many a man dangled from the end of a Bridport dagger—that is, a rope—especially when some home-grown rebels were carted off to Dorchester to face Hanging Judge Jeffreys.

FOOD AND LODGING: **The Old Bakery,** 126 North Allington (tel. Bridport 23400), is a friendly guest house owned by Michael Farmer and his American-born wife, Eleanor. Their holiday suggestions include exploring the local unspoiled countryside, the dramatic coastline, seaside resorts, and stately homes. They rent out two doubles and one single at a rate of £7 ($12.25) per person nightly, which includes a full English breakfast. There is a private bathroom and toilet for guests. A nearby pub serves good meals.

The **Bull Hotel,** East Street (tel. Bridport 22878), a 16th-century coaching inn, now houses modern wayfarers in its 27 bedrooms, all with hot and cold running water. A single ranges from £9.50 ($16.63) to £10.50 ($18.38), and a double goes for £18 ($31.50) to £19 ($33.25). The atmosphere is old-worldish, complete with a minstrels' gallery and enough bars to satisfy anybody. The bedrooms are simply, but comfortably, furnished. In 1939, George VI stopped off at the Bull. The hotel remains open all year, and nonresidents may patronize its restaurants, such as the Dorset Room, where table d'hôte luncheons cost £4 ($7), and a set dinner goes for £4.25 ($7.44).

Only one mile west of Bridport lies the little village of:

11. Chideock

A model village of West Dorset, Chideock is bathed in charm. For in this main-road hamlet of thatched houses, a mellowed stone is used for most of the buildings. A dairy farm is found in the village itself. About a mile from the coast, it's a gem of a place for overnight stopovers or even longer stays. The beautiful countryside, with its rolling hills, makes excursions a temptation.

FOOD AND LODGING: The **George Inn** (tel. Chideock 789419) is the oldest establishment in the village, right on the A35 and dating from 1685. The owners, Mike and Marilyn Tuck, extend a warm welcome to all and offer excellent food either in the bar or dining room. Three-course meals can be obtained for prices from £2.10 ($3.68) to £8.05 ($14.09), depending on your choice of entree. B&B in the well-equipped bedrooms will cost £7.50 ($13.13) per person, the price including tea- and coffee-making facilities and TV. All bedrooms have hot and cold running water. The George Inn is fully licensed, with facilities for children, a game room, and a well-kept Beer Garden. Prices include VAT.

Betchworth House (tel. Chideock 478) is a 17th-century guest house on the main road at the edge of the village. Owned by Mr. and Mrs. David Scott, it purveys accommodations that are immaculate, homey, and a good bargain—£8.50 ($14.88) per person for B&B. It is preferred that guests stay a week. When evening dinner is included, add another £4.50 ($7.88) to the bill. The Bartons will point out the way to the beach, a mile walk along a quiet road. The house opens in February, closing at the end of November. There's a large free car park just opposite the house, and a pretty walled garden in back of the building where you can sit and enjoy the peace among the flowers.

Chideock House Hotel (tel. Chideock 242) is perhaps the prettiest thatched house in Chideock, a village of winners. Set near the road, with a protective stone wall, the house opens onto a rear garden of flowers, shrubs, and fruit trees. A driveway through the gardens leads to a large car park in the rear. You go directly into the beamed lounge, with its wide fireplace (wood-burning fires on cool days). You can stay here on a B&B basis at a cost beginning at £15 ($26.25) per person nightly. The hotel has been extended, and most of its bedrooms have baths en suite. The cuisine reflects the skill of a Swiss chef. In addition to the à la carte restaurant, Chatters grill room offers a range of large steaks, fish, homemade dishes, and a salad table. Especially interesting is the Tudor part of the house, and the Adam fireplace in the lounge. The house quartered the Roundheads in 1645, and the ghosts of the village martyrs are still said to haunt, as their trial was held at the hotel. Resident owners are Barbara and Alf Way and Kevin and Alison Davies.

The **Thatch Cottage** (tel. Chideock 473). You'd never suspect that under the thatch of this 17th-century cottage are the comforts of home. The owner, Mrs. Pat Shayler, accepts paying guests all year. While this is essentially a summer resort, there are those who welcome the idea of staying winter weekends, snugly sitting in front of the fireplace after enjoying good home cooking. A table d'hôte dinner at £7 ($12.25) is featured, although you may order à la carte as well. Fresh local produce is a specialty. Most of the year, the charge is £8 ($14) per person for B&B. With dinner, the rate becomes £13.50 ($23.63) per person. If you want to walk to the beach, you can ask your hostess to pack a picnic lunch. It's best to make Chideock your center for a week, exploring the many sights in the area on day trips. Reservations are necessary from June to September.

A short ride and we're at:

12. Charmouth

On Lyme Bay, Charmouth is still another winner. A village of Georgian houses and thatched cottages, Charmouth contains some of the most dramatic coastal scenery in West Dorset. The village lies to the west of Golden Cap, which is—according to the adventurers who measure such things—the highest cliff along the coast of southern England.

The Court (tel. Charmouth 60255) offers old-style living at reasonable cost. This village Regency house, surrounded by its own gardens, is alongside the busy highway (once the Roman road) and entered through a formal driveway. The building is partially covered by a bignonia vine. In the rear is a high stone wall, a croquet lawn, old apple trees, and a short, formal, tree-lined walk for your morning constitutional. The owners, Mr. and Mrs. Stapleton, provide half board on a daily or weekly basis. The rates vary according to the season, ranging from £15 ($26.25) to £17 ($29.75) per person daily, including your evening meal. B&B only can be taken at £9 ($15.75) to £10 ($17.50) per person. Reductions are allowed for children sharing their parents' room. The bedrooms are spacious and well kept, satisfying one's need for physical comfort, with soft beds, hot and cold running water, and bedside lamps. Each room also has shaver points, radio, electric heater, and an electric kettle. The Stapletons believe in good home cooking, using the best ingredients, including, whenever possible, fresh fruit and vegetables from their own garden. One may take wine, beer, or local cider with the meal. The food and coffee draw many favorable comments. During the season, nonresidents may take morning coffee and cream teas in the garden or dining room.

The **Queens Armes Hotel** (tel. Charmouth 60339). Catherine of Aragon, the first of Henry VIII's six wives and the daughter of Ferdinand and Isabella of Spain, stayed in this hotel near the sea. A small medieval house, it also figured in the flight of the defeated King Charles, the Roundheads in hot pursuit. Since the Queens Armes is right on the road, you may not suspect its inner charm: a rear flower garden, oak beams, old doors with creaky hardware, a dining room with dark oak tables and Windsor chairs, and the living room with its Regency armchairs and antiques. Records don't reveal what the hotel charged for housing royalty. But you can stay here in one of the simply furnished rooms for £12.95 ($22.66) per person for bed and breakfast or £19.95 ($34.91) for dinner, bed, and breakfast. If you wish, you can also take all your meals. Lunch is à la carte from 70p ($1.23) to £3.75 ($6.56); dinner, £7.50 ($13.13). The hotel specializes in well-prepared English fare, with some continental dishes. The owners, Mr. and Mrs. P. G. Miles, have pleasantly added their own touches to the house.

Two miles west is—

13. Lyme Regis

On Lyme Bay near the Devonshire border, the resort of Lyme Regis is one of the most attractive centers along the South Coast. For those who shun such big commercial holiday centers as Torquay or Bournemouth, Lyme Regis may be ideal—the true English coastal town, with a highly praised mild climate. Sea gulls fly overhead; the streets are steep and winding; walks along Cobb Beach brisk and stimulating; the views, particularly of the craft in the harbor, photogenic. Following Lyme Regis's career as a major seaport (the Duke of Monmouth landed here to begin his unsuccessful attempt to become king), one finds it was a small spa for a while, catering to such visitors as Jane Austen, who was also fond of nearby Charmouth.

The stone breakwater, the Cobb, was immortalized in *The French Lieutenant's Woman.* As you walk on the Cobb—and everybody does—the waves crash around you, and as a backdrop you have the Dorset cliffs which seem to tumble into the sea. The actors stayed in the town's two main hotels. John Fowles, its author, is a resident of Lyme Regis.

The town also boasts the 1979–1980 world champion and best dressed town crier. Richard Fox is just maintaining a tradition which has been handed down for 1000 years in Lyme Regis when he announces the local news. He'll also take visitors on a two-hour tour of the resort on Tuesday and Thursday at 2:30 p.m. to see the Cobb, the harbor from which ships sailed to fight the Spanish Armada. The walks head up old Broad Street. Mr. Fox can be reached at the Witchcraft Gallery, Broad Street (tel. Lyme Regis 3803).

The surrounding area is a fascinating place for fossilism. Mary Anning discovered in 1810 at the age of 11 one of the first articulated ichthyosaur skeletons. She went on to become one of the first professional fossilists in the country. Books telling of walks in the area and the regions where the fossils can be seen are available at the local information bureau in the Guildhall on Bridge Street.

ACCOMMODATIONS: **Kersbrook,** Pound Road (tel. Lyme Regis 2596), lives up to its boast of being the "dream house of the Dorset Riviera." Built of stone, Kersbrook is crowned by a thatched roof and placed on a ledge above the village, which provides a panoramic view of the coast. There's even a century-old terraced garden in the rear. Many of the bedrooms have their own private shower/baths and toilets. The tariff is from £11 ($19.25) per person per day for B&B. Dinner is also available, and the hotel is licensed.

The White House, 47 Silver St. (tel. Lyme Regis 3420), is a friendly, small, centrally heated guest house run by Mr. and Mrs. D. T. Morris. It is only a few minutes' walk from the harbor and the center of town. The house is attractively furnished and well maintained, offering B&B from £7.50 ($13.13) daily. Dinner is £4 ($7) extra. A large lounge with color television is set aside for residents. The meals, incidentally, are good home-cooking.

READERS' GUEST HOUSE SELECTIONS: "In Lyme Regis, where most hotels are simply too expensive for the budget traveler, the **Guildhall House,** 6 Bridge St., run by Mrs. E. W. Nute, is a traveler's find. Its comfortable, clean rooms, baths with showers, and choice location make it a steal at £7 ($12.25) per person. Without doubt, Mrs. Nute serves one of the best breakfasts a traveler will find. The house has six rooms, a comfortable TV lounge, and friendly clientele" (David Leon Higdon). . . . "**Shamien House,** 8 Pound St. (tel. Lyme Regis 742339), is owned by John and Diane Drummond. We had a lovely, comfortable, quiet room with a glimpse of the ocean, hot and cold water, a bathroom across the hall, a huge English breakfast, and parking in the rear, all for £9 ($15.75) a night. The best part was the cleanliness. The Drummonds are charming, friendly, and helpful. A nearby path through the gardens takes you quickly to the ocean" (Lillian and George Schmidt, San Gabriel, Calif.).

Chapter VIII

DEVON AND CORNWALL

1. Beer and Seaton
2. Exeter
3. Dartmoor
4. Chagford
5. Torbay (Torquay)
6. Totnes
7. Dartmouth
8. Plymouth
9. Clovelly
10. Combe Martin and Lynton-Lynmouth
11. Looe
12. Polperro
13. Fowey, Truro, and Portloe
14. St. Mawes
15. Falmouth
16. Penzance
17. The Scilly Isles
18. Newlyn, Mousehole, and Land's End
19. St. Ives
20. Port Isaac
21. Tintagel

THE GREAT PATCHWORK-QUILT area of the southwest of England, part of the West Countree, abounds with cliffside farms, rolling hills, foreboding moors, semitropical plants, and fishing villages—all of which combine to provide some of the finest scenery in England. The British themselves approach the sunny counties of Devon and Cornwall with the same kind of excitement one would normally reserve for hopping over to the continent. Especially along the coastline, the British Riviera, many of the names of the little seaports, villages, and resorts have become synonymous with holidays in the sun: Penzance, Looe, Polperro.

It's easy to involve yourself in the West Country life, as lived by the British vacationers. Perhaps you'll go pony-trekking across moor and woodland, past streams and sheep-grazing fields, stopping off at local pubs to soak up atmosphere and mugs of ale. Chances are your oddly shaped bedroom will be in a barton (farm) mentioned in the *Domesday Book* or in a thatched cottage neither straight, level, nor true.

Fishermen may catch their lunch (salmon and trout in such rivers as the Dart), then take it back to the kitchen of their guest house to be grilled. Life is often most informal. Your hosts, many being of farming stock themselves, don't like to muck about putting on airs for tourists. In the morning your landlady might be out picking string beans for your dinner. Later she'll bring up pails from the milk house, and you can watch her create her own version of clotted Devonshire cream cooked on the back of the stove. For dessert that night, you'll get a country portion heaped on your freshly picked gooseberries.

A SPECIAL BUS TICKET: The two main bus companies of Devon and Cornwall have combined to offer a Rambler ticket, granting unlimited travel anywhere on the two networks for any seven consecutive days at a cost of £8.50 ($14.88) for adults and £4.25 ($7.44) for children under 14. You can plan your journeys from the maps and timetables from any Western National/Devon General offices when you purchase your ticket. But you should bear in mind that there are no connecting services between Devon and Cornwall. If you wish to combine the two counties, you must purchase another ticket to cross the border. The fee is £2.75 ($4.81) per person for the shortest journey, Bodmin to Plymouth. Further information may be obtained from **National House,** Queen Street, Exeter EX4 3TE (tel. 0392/74191).

Our adventure begins in:

DEVON

When a Devonian invites you to walk down the primrose path, he or she means just that. The primrose is practically the shire flower of this most beautiful of counties. Devon is a land of jagged coasts—the red cliffs in the south facing the English Channel, the gray cliffs in the north opening onto the Bristol Channel. Sandwiched between them is some of the most widely varied scenery in England, ranging from heartlands and wooded valleys to buzzard-haunted combes. Aside from the shores, a great many of the scenic splashes appear in the two national parks, **Dartmoor** in the south, **Exmoor** in the north. First, we'll explore:

SOUTH DEVON

It can be the lazy life in South Devon, as you recline in an orchard, enjoying the view of the coast from which native sons Raleigh and Drake set sail. Almost every little hamlet, on some level, is geared to accommodate visitors, who flock here in great numbers from early spring to late fall. There is much to see and explore (although a minimum of historical sights). But mainly the tranquil life prevails.

1. Beer and Seaton

Only seven miles from the last stopover in Dorset (Lyme Regis), Beer no longer is a center for smugglers, but remains still colorful, with its small fleet of fishing craft, its sandy beach, white cliffs, and a pebbly cove. Tucked away into the only chalk cliffs on Devon's south coast, Beer offers safe boating and bathing, plus deep-sea fishing. The village has an interesting history, stretching back beyond the time when the Romans quarried stone here. Honiton lace-

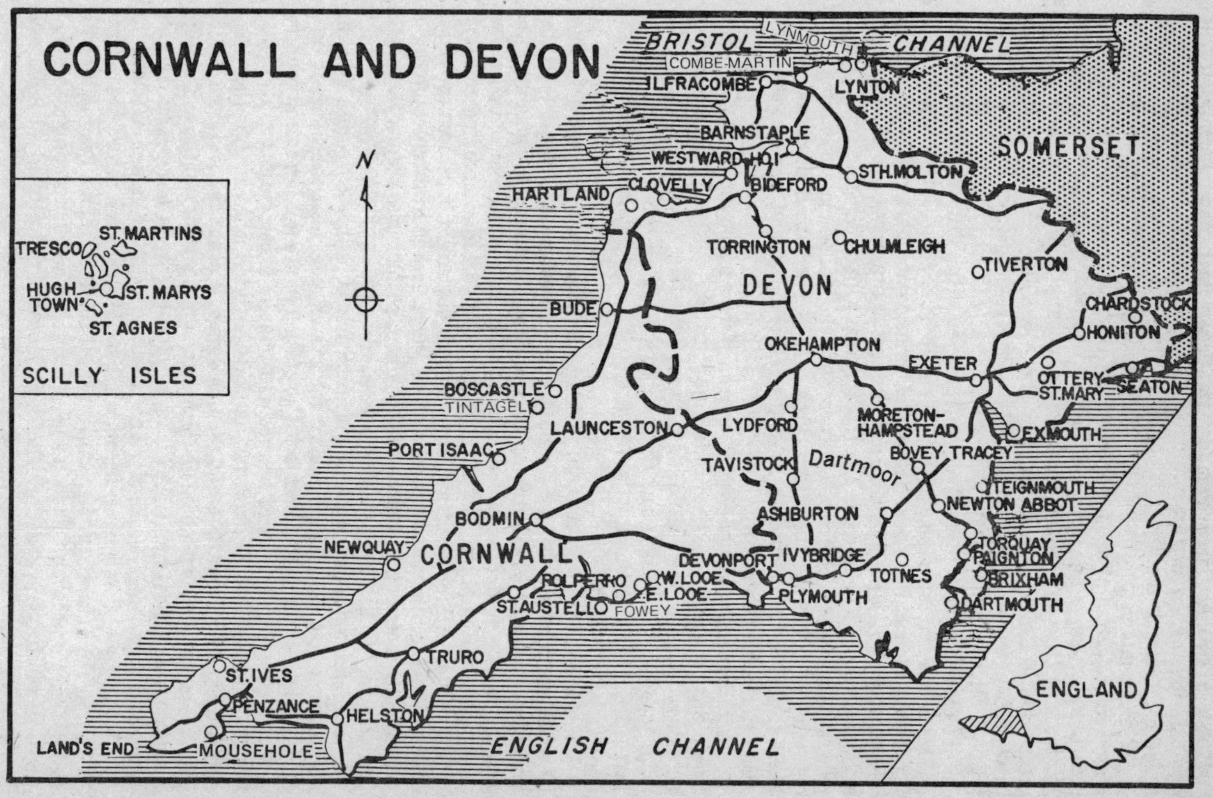
CORNWALL AND DEVON
BRISTOL CHANNEL
LYNMOUTH
COMBE-MARTIN
ILFRACOMBE
LYNTON
BARNSTAPLE
SOMERSET
WESTWARD HO!
STH.MOLTON
HARTLAND
CLOVELLY
BIDEFORD
TORRINGTON
CHULMLEIGH
TIVERTON
DEVON
BUDE
CHARDSTOCK
HONITON
OKEHAMPTON
EXETER
OTTERY ST.MARY
SEATON
BOSCASTLE
TINTAGEL
LAUNCESTON
LYDFORD
MORETON-HAMPSTEAD
EXMOUTH
PORT ISAAC
TAVISTOCK
Dartmoor
BOVEY TRACEY
TEIGNMOUTH
NEWTON ABBOT
ASHBURTON
BODMIN
NEWQUAY
CORNWALL
DEVONPORT
IVYBRIDGE
TORQUAY
PAIGNTON
BRIXHAM
POLPERRO
W.LOOE
E.LOOE
TOTNES
PLYMOUTH
DARTMOUTH
ST.AUSTELL
FOWEY
TRURO
ST.IVES
PENZANCE
HELSTON
ENGLAND
LAND'S END
MOUSEHOLE
ENGLISH CHANNEL
N
TRESCO
ST.MARTINS
HUGH TOWN
ST.MARYS
ST. AGNES
SCILLY ISLES

making was introduced from Flanders, and Beer women made Queen Victoria's wedding dress. There are four golf courses within nine miles, and tennis and riding are available locally.

Almost incongruously in the small seaside town of Seaton is a lovingly preserved collection of open-topped double-decker tramcars painted with authentic advertising. The collection lies on Harbour Road and is called the **Seaton and District Electric Tramway Company** (tel. Seaton 21702). The gentle ride to Colyton, three miles up the Axe Valley, passes through fields between hedgerows. There are several departures daily from May to October (also on Sunday from Easter to May).

I can think of no better way to acquaint you with the fine accommodations of Devon than to introduce:

Bovey House, Beer, near Seaton (tel. Branscombe 241), on the edge of the village, about 1½ miles away. Picture the sort of dreams you're likely to have at Bovey House, sleeping in the Charles II room, with its designed ceiling which tells the story of how the king finally escaped the Roundheads by hiding in an oak tree. After poking about, knocking, and old-fashioned snooping, you're likely to find a concealed door leading to an underground passageway to the sea, a mile and a half away.

A 12th-century manor with an avenue of trees leading to the village road, Bovey was presented to Queen Catherine Parr by King Henry VIII as part of her dowry following the dissolution of the monasteries. It is the favorite property of its present owner, Lord Clinton. In one of his off-moments, he was persuaded to let his tenant, Mrs. Joy Roberts, accept paying guests under the guise of house parties.

When you see the antique furnishings in the drawing room, you'll want to whisk them away into the night. Adam, Chippendale, Georgian—all the important furniture periods are represented here. The linenfold paneling in the dining room is museum caliber. There are collections of old china, silver, paintings, and sculpture. The spacious bedrooms contain antiques and beds that blend in with the atmosphere. A famous playwright once used the house as the model for the setting in one of his plays. In the drawing room you'll occasionally meet political leaders of England, perhaps stage stars, those who love this way of life.

Tea- and coffee-making facilities are provided in the bedrooms. You can also arrange to have a lunch packed for a later meal near the shore or on a picnic walk. Be sure to find a secluded, protected spot—this is hunting country, and one often sees a pack of hounds and hunters chasing a fox.

I've deliberately held off telling you the price till last. It's the nicest surprise of all! For your B&B and evening dinner, you are charged from £13.50 ($23.63) per person, depending on the location of the room and the season, plus a small service charge and VAT. Bovey House is open mid-March to mid-November and winter weekends. This is one of the best values in England.

In Beer you can stay at **Durham House Hotel,** Fore Street (tel. Seaton 20449), in the main street 500 yards from the sea. This small family hotel is run by Jenny and Brian Clinch, a friendly couple who offer accommodation all year in their 100-year-old Cornish granite house. You will find a comfortable lounge with color TV, a bar, and a dining room with an excellent reputation for good food and personal service. For B&B and an evening meal you pay £11.50 ($20.13) per person nightly, plus VAT. Durham House is probably the best of the small, inexpensive hotels in the village, and makes an ideal base for touring.

2. Exeter

The county town of Devonshire, on the banks of the Exe River, Exeter was a Roman city founded in the first century A.D. Two centuries later it was encircled by a mighty stone wall, traces of which remain today. Conquerors and would-be conquerors, especially the Vikings, stormed the fortress in the centuries ensuing. None was more notable than William the Conqueror. Irked at Exeter's refusal to capitulate (perhaps at the sheltering of Gytha, mother of the slain Harold), the Norman duke brought Exeter to its knees in short order.

Under the Tudors the city grew and prospered. The cocky Sir Walter Raleigh and Sir Francis Drake cut striking figures strolling through Exeter's medieval and Elizabethan streets. Regrettably, in May of 1942 the skies over Exeter were suddenly filled with German bombers. When their merciless task was over, Exeter was in flames. One of the most beautiful and historic cities of England was a mere shell of its former self. Exeter grew back, of course, but the new, impersonal-looking shops and offices couldn't replace the Georgian crescents, the black-and-white timbered buildings with their plastered walls. Fortunately, much was spared, including the major architectural treasure—

EXETER CATHEDRAL: Owing its present look to the Decorated style of the 13th and 14th centuries, the Exeter Cathedral of St. Peter actually goes back to Saxon times. Even Canute, the Viking conqueror, got in on the act of rebuilding around 1017. The Norman cathedral of Bishop Warelwast came into being in the early 12th century, and the north and south towers serve as reminders of that period. The remarkable feature of the present Gothic building is the nave, with its tierceron vaulting, stretching out for some 300 feet, broken only by an organ. The cathedral did suffer damage in the 1942 German bombings, which destroyed its St. James's Chapel (subsequently restored). But most of the treasures remain intact, including the rows of sculpture along the west front, the 14th-century Minstrels' Gallery, and the bishop's throne. The cathedral asks that visitors contribute at least 50p (88¢) toward its upkeep for the future.

EXETER MARITIME MUSEUM: This museum stands on The Quay (tel. Exeter 58075), displaying a delightful collection of boats from all over the world, lovingly preserved. You'll find none of your fiberglass here; rather, the boats are wooden, steel hulled, rowing types, sailing varieties, curraghs, cobles, guffas, and shashas. Some have been rowed across the Atlantic; others are too fragile to do more than lie in the sunshine. Brunel's drag boat *Bertha* was built in 1844 and still works. You can even hire a rowing boat, an exotic Portuguese chata, and navigate the three miles of the River Exe and the canal for about £1 ($1.75) an hour. Admission to the museum collection is £1.90 ($3.33) for adults and 95p ($1.66) for children; it's open daily from 10 a.m. to 6 p.m. in summer (till 5 p.m. in winter). There's also a tea room, plus a maritime gift and book shop.

OTHER MONUMENTS: Much of the old remains. The **Exeter Guildhall,** a colonnaded building on the High, is regarded as the oldest municipal building in the kingdom. The earliest reference to the Guildhall is contained in a deed of 1160. The Tudor front which straddles the pavement was added in 1593. Inside is a fine display of silver in the gallery. It contains a number of paintings as well, including one of Henrietta Anne, daughter of Charles I (she was born in Exeter in 1644). The ancient hall is paneled in oak. The Guildhall is open throughout the year, Monday to Saturday, from 10 a.m. to 5:30 p.m., and admission is free.

The present headquarters of the Devon County Council, **Rougemont Castle,** with its Norman gateway, is now largely a memory. Although a Saxon fortification was built on the same site, Rougemont was created for William the Conqueror. Over the centuries the castle fell into ruins. Now there has been some small-scale restoration, and it is pleasant to stroll through Rougemont Gardens.

If time remains, see also **St. Nicholas Priory,** the Mint, lying off Fore Street (founded in 1080—now partially restored); **Tucker's Hall,** Fore Street, a 15th-century craft building; and the underground passageways of **Princesshay** (the subterranean water supply channels of medieval times).

On the Outskirts

Powderham Castle, Powderham (tel. Starcross 890243), lies eight miles south of Exeter off the A379 Dawlish road. A castle here was built in the late 14th century by Sir Philip Courtenay, sixth son of the second Earl of Devon, and his wife Margaret, granddaughter of Edward I. Their magnificent tomb is in the south transept of Exeter Cathedral. The castle suffered damage during the Civil War and was restored and altered in the 18th and 19th centuries, but its towers and battlements are still pure 14th century. The castle contains much fine furniture, including a remarkable clock which plays full tunes at 4, 8, and 12 o'clock, some 17th-century tapestries, and a chair used by William III for his first Council of State at Newton Abbot. The staircase hall contains some remarkable plasterwork set in bold relief against a brilliant turquoise background, more than two centuries old. The chapel dates from the 15th century, with hand-hewn roof timbers and carved pew ends. It contains a detailed pedigree of the Courtenay family, a document more than 12 feet high. The castle is open Easter Sunday and Monday and then Sunday only until the end of May. From May to September, it is then open daily from 2 to 6 p.m., charging an admission of £1.75 ($3.06) for adults and 80p ($1.40) for children.

A HILL OF BUDGET GUEST HOUSES: In the vicinity of Exeter's two main-line railway stations, near the center of the city, is a row of brick Edwardian-style guest houses, similar architecturally—but with variations in price and in the way they're run. For our low-budget selections, I've chosen the following:

Oakcliffe Private Hotel, 73 St. David's Hill (tel. Exeter 58288), is the first choice of my budget grouping. Mrs. Kenshole charges £8 ($14) per person nightly for bed and an English breakfast. She keeps her white-gabled, brick house immaculate, ever ready to receive guests. The furnishings are plain—nothing fancy, just solid comfort, including hot and cold running water and showers. Her front door is opposite Hele Road, near the top of the hill. There is a car park.

The **Radnor Private Hotel,** St. David's Hill (tel. Exeter 72004), is run by Mrs. J. E. Parish, who charges £8.50 ($14.88) for B&B, plus VAT. The rooms contain water basins and comfortable beds, and some have private showers. The house also has full central heating. In addition, there are two shower rooms. Mrs. Parish will prepare an evening dinner for £5 ($8.75). Close to the city center and the railway stations, this warm and homey hotel is for economy living. In the rear is a car park.

The **Lea-Dene,** 34 Alphington Rd. (A377), St. Thomas (tel. Exeter 57257), is a semi-detached Edwardian house with gardens, lying within walking distance of the cathedral, city center, and Maritime Museum, among other attractions. Mr. and Mrs. Rogers offer a lot of extras, including a large free car park behind the house, a double garage, a choice of evening meals, family rooms (with cots and highchairs), full central heating, a public phone, a color TV lounge (although the units also have private color TV sets), and free baths and showers. They'll also provide a babysitting service, packed lunches, and will even arrange for special diets if given advance notice. Each bedroom is carpeted and well furnished, and rates are from £8 ($14) per person for B&B, and an evening meal can be ordered for another £4.50 ($7.88).

READERS' HOTEL SELECTIONS: "A small hotel that is clean, courteous, and inexpensive is the **Regents Park Hotel,** owned and operated by Mr. and Mrs. Doug Jeffries on Polsloe Road (tel. Exeter 59749). The rates are £9 ($15.75) for a room and an old-style English breakfast served in a cheerful dining room. I guarantee any traveler will get his or her money's worth here. It offers a convenient location a half mile from the central bus station and three-quarters of a mile from the city center" (Lin E. Nixon, Pine Bluff, Ark.). . . . "The **Willowdene Hotel,** 161 Magdalen Rd. (tel. Exeter 71925), has immaculate rooms, as well as a bath on each floor and a shower in the second-floor bathroom and on the first floor. A lounge with color TV is on the ground floor. Mr. and Mrs. Walker were gracious enough to take my two girls and myself at the last minute. Oh, yes! Lovely gardens are in front of the house. The charge is £8 ($14) per person nightly. The house was built in 1810 and is a Georgian period property and can't be altered in any way without specific government permission. Willowdene is a ten-minute walk from the coach station, or else the F or S bus leaves from a stop adjacent to the station, stopping at the corner of Barrack Road, immediately behind the hotel" (Mrs. David F. Lee, Fort Worth, Texas).

WHERE TO EAT: The **Ship Inn,** Martin's Lane (tel. Exeter 72040), a short walk from the cathedral, was often visited by Sir Francis Drake, Sir Walter Raleigh, and Sir John Hawkins. Of it Drake wrote: "Next to mine own shippe, I do most love that old 'Shippe' in Exon, a tavern in Fyssh Street, as the people call it, or as the clergie will have it, St. Martin's Lane." The pub still provides tankards of stout and lager and is still loved by both young and old. The reconstructed dining room on the second floor also retains the early English atmosphere: settles, red leather and oak chairs. The fare is hearty English, the service friendly. At either lunch or dinner, you can order such temptations as onion soup, grilled rainbow trout, or grilled rump steak. Expect to spend from £5 ($8.75) up for a meal. The price of the main courses includes vegetables, roll, and butter. The portions, as in Elizabethan days, are large. The restaurant is open from noon to 2 p.m. and from 6:30 to 10:30 p.m. Monday through Saturday; closed Sunday and all bank holidays. The bars are open from 11 a.m. to 2:30 p.m. and 5 to 10:30 p.m. weekdays, until 11 p.m. on Friday and Saturday.

The **Port Royal Inn,** The Quay (tel. Exeter 72360), stands close to the Maritime Museum. With such a name, the pub reminds one of smugglers in the Caribbean, intrepid explorers, and the famous navigators. The bar food offered will revive the inner person in a more modern way. Salads are tempting, and you can also order a ploughman's lunch or pâté and toast at around £1.30 ($2.28). Sandwiches made from granary bread and filled with meat or cheese cost from 60p ($1.05) to 80p ($1.40) a serving. There are also mini-loaves for the starving, white or granary bread filled with salad, cheese, or meat for 95p ($1.66). Each day they do two or three hot specials such as seafood, roast chicken, and roast lamb at around £2 ($3.50) a serving. There are also desserts and coffee with cream, and the pub serves real ales from various breweries, including Flowers, Eldridge Pope, and Hall and Woodhouse. Barry Weeks is in charge.

The **Milkmaid,** 15 St. Catherine St. (tel. Exeter 77438), offers self-service on the first floor, and, upstairs, a restaurant serving such dishes as salads, omelets, and quiches for around £2 ($3.50). Homemade scones, shortbreads, and fruit cakes undo the slimming qualities of other dishes. There's also traditional fare to take away.

The **Cafeteria** at the **Exeter Bus Depot,** just off the main street, is a clean, friendly, and efficient place, serving good sandwiches, salads with cold meats, steak-and-kidney pie with vegetables, shepherd's pie, pastries, and cakes. A three-course meal of soup, main dish, pudding, and coffee is around £3 ($5.25). A snack meal for two with tea or coffee will cost around £2 ($3.50).

Coolings Wine Bar, 11 Gandy St. (tel. Exeter 34183). The family who runs this place welcomes guests as friends, even if they don't know you. It's a little hideaway that is both unpretentious and enjoyable. The beams overhead are familiar enough, and the bright tables create an English version of a bistro. You're also allowed to dine below in the cellar, which is most atmospheric. A blackboard informs you of the specials of the day, and I generally prefer these, although everything tastes fresh here. Try the steak-and-kidney pie, if featured, or one of the Italian pasta dishes, most tasty and filling. At the serve-yourself counter, you can make up your own smörgåsbord-inspired plate. Expect to spend from £4 ($7) and up, depending on what you order. Hours are from noon to 2 p.m. Monday to Saturday and from 5:30 to 11 p.m. for dinner.

Poppys, 12 South St. (tel. Exeter 73779) is quite suitable if you want a light meal. Hamburgers (generous ones at that) come in a variety of sizes, accompanied by a crisp fresh salad and potato. Quiches are also on the bill of fare, and you can fill up nicely for around £3 ($5.25) and more. If you're a vegetarian, ask for the nutburger. This very busy place has a tendency to fill up quickly. It's open from 5:30 to 11 p.m. Monday to Saturday, from 6:30 to 11 p.m. on Sunday.

LIVING ON THE OUTSKIRTS: Perhaps the finest way to enjoy the cathedral city of Exeter, especially if you have a car, is to live on the outskirts, from 10 to 19 miles from the heart of the city.

At Whimple

Nine miles from the seaside resort at Sidmouth, ten miles from Exeter, is **Down House** (tel. Whimple 822475), the friendly domain of Mrs. Pinn, who accepts paying guests all year at her brick Victorian-type house. Down House has numerous gables, tall chimneys, and bay windows overlooking a well-tended garden with flowers and shrubbery. If possible, get one of the bedrooms with those sunny bays. The cost of half board is from £9.50 ($16.63) per person. B&B costs from £7.50 ($13.13) per person. This is a bargain, as the dinners (and breakfasts, too) are substantial. Whimple makes a good center for touring Devon.

At Bickleigh

In the Exe Valley, four miles south of Tiverton and ten miles north of Exeter, lies a hamlet with a river, an arched stone bridge, a mill pond, and thatched-roof cottages—a cliché of English charm, one of the finest spots in all of Devon. In this village, you have a choice of two arrangements for living:

Bickleigh Cottage Guest House, Bickleigh Bridge (tel. Bickleigh 230), is a thatched, 17th-century guest house, with a riverside garden leading down to the much-photographed Bickleigh Bridge. Add to this image swans and ducks gliding by to get your leftover crumbs from tea on the lawn. Mr. and Mrs. Stuart Cochrane, the friendly owners, charge from £8.50 ($14.88) per person nightly for B&B. In a room with a private bath, the rate is from £10 ($17.50) nightly. Meals are unforgettable. The raspberries and gooseberries come fresh from the garden, topped with generous portions of Devonshire cream. Dinner is priced from £6 ($10.50). Inside, the rooms are cozy, with oak beams and old fireplaces. The no. 354 bus runs between Exeter and Tiverton, if you don't have a car.

The **Fishermen's Cot Hotel** (tel. Bickleigh 237) sits like a picture postcard across the way from Bickleigh Bridge. Even though it's thatched and blends beautifully into the local setting, it is newer than most of the houses here, and has all the heating and plumbing necessary. The B&B rate is £10.50 ($18.38) per person nightly in a bathless room, £12 ($21) with bath. You'll be served some of the best food in Devon. They offer excellent fish dishes on the dinner menu as well as a good range of bar snacks at lunchtime, including homemade soup and crusty bread, cottage pie or steak-and-kidney pie, along with steak-and-onion sandwiches, costing from 60p ($1.05) to £2.65 ($4.64) a portion. There are also cold salads and sandwiches, as well as a ploughman's lunch with cheddar or stilton cheese, and a homemade pâté. The price range is from 50p (88¢) for a humble cheese-and-tomato sandwich to £2.50 ($4.38) for crab or prawns with salad. Cream teas, Devonshire style, are served from 3 to 5:30 p.m. Fishermen particularly like the place, because they can catch salmon and trout right in front of the hotel on the banks of the Exe. The hotel is fully licensed.

Trout, on the main Tiverton–Exeter road, the A396, four miles south of Tiverton (tel. Bickleigh 339), is a former 17th-century coaching inn, transformed into three pubs and a restaurant. The thatched roof is long and low with tiny leaded windows. Former stables have been converted into rooms for dining. One of the favored pubs contains an old fireplace, made from the original bridge stone. A sign indicates that the inn was built in 1630 as a trout hatchery. Pub lunches are available from noon to 1:30 p.m. Homemade soups are hearty, and "freshly cut" and garnished sandwiches might tempt, or else you can order a cold plate of meat and salad. In the restaurant, you can select such dishes as beef Stroganoff or lamb cutlets (local produce). The buffet lunch goes for £5 ($8.75), and evening snacks are served in the bar seven days a week during pub hours.

READER'S HOTEL SELECTION: "**Front House,** East Street, Bovey Tracey (tel. 832202), is a charming old house once reputed to have seen Oliver Cromwell. It proved a superb choice from which to make sorties into Devon and Cornwall. The property is owned by Mr. and Mrs. J. C. Bornet, who have brought to Front House a wealth of experience gathered all over the world. You'll enjoy the attractive English garden with its own swimming pool. Bathless rooms have hot and cold running water. B&B is £8 ($14) per person bathless, £9 ($15.75) with bath and four-poster. Self-catering cottages and apartments are also available. An evening meal by prior arrangement is served for only £4.75 ($8.31)" (Mary E. Learich, Green Brook, N.J.).

READER'S PUB SELECTION: "We were pub crawling in the area and found **Coombe Cellars Inn** (tel. Shaldon 2423), halfway between Shaldon and Newton Abbot, right on the west bank of the Teign River. The pub's history dates back to the 17th century when it was a notorious smuggler's haunt. The view from the bar of the Devon sunset is beautiful. John and Val Moore, the proprietors, were most hospitable. The rate for half board is £11 ($19.25) per person daily" (Bruce and Jane Woods, Toronto, Ontario, Canada).

3. Dartmoor

Antiquity-rich Dartmoor lies in the southern part of the shire. The Tors, huge rock formations of this granite mass, sometimes soar to a height of 2000 feet. The national park is a patchwork quilt of mood changes: gorse and purple heather, gorges with rushing water, a foreboding landscape for the experienced walker only. Look for the beautiful Dartmoor pony.

Some 13 miles west from Exeter, the peaceful little town of **Moreton Hampstead,** perched on the edge of Dartmoor, makes a good center. The heavily visited Dartmoor village of **Widecombe-in-the-Moor** is only seven miles from the town. Moreton Hampstead contains much that is old, including a market cross and several 17th-century colonnaded almshouses.

Accommodation information and a booking service are now available from the **Dartmoor Tourist Association,** Pencroft, Widecombe Road, Postbridge (tel. Yelverton 3501). Local information centers will also provide a list of accommodations.

The **National Park Authority** operates a summer bus service throughout the moor. Services have such inviting names as the Pony Express and the Transmoor Link, and are an ideal way to get onto the moor to hike the 500 miles of foot- and bridgepaths. The country is rough, and on the high moor you should always make sure you have good maps, a compass, and suitable clothing and shoes. Don't be put off, however. Unless you are a professional hiker, it is unlikely that you will go very far from the well-trodden paths.

For bus service information, apply at **Plymouth City Transport,** Bretonside Bus Station in Plymouth (tel. Plymouth 664014), or at the **Exeter Bus Station,** Western National, in Exeter (tel. Exeter 56231). Apart from the regular service of buses linking the various villages and towns on the moor, the National Park Authority runs guided walks from selected starting points.

There are also guided walking tours of varying difficulty, ranging from one hour up to six hours for a trek of some 9 to 12 miles. All you have to do is turn up suitably clad at your selected starting point, and there you are. Details are available from the Dartmoor National Park Information Centres or from the **Dartmoor National Park Board,** Parke, Haytor Road, Bovey Tracey, Newton Abbot (tel. Bovey Tracey 832093). The charge for walks is 50p (88¢) for 1½ hours, 85p ($1.49) for up to three hours, or £1.20 ($2.10) for six hours.

Throughout the area are stables where you can arrange for a day's trek on horseback across the moors. For horse-riding on Dartmoor, there are too many establishments to list. All are licensed, and you are accompanied by an experienced rider/guide. The moor can be dangerous, with sudden fogs descending without warning on treacherous marshlands. All horse-rental stables are listed in a useful free publication, the *Dartmoor Visitor,* obtainable from tourist and visitor centers or by mail. Send an International Reply Coupon to the Dartmoor National Park Board (address above). Prices are around £3 ($5.25) per hour, £6 ($10.50) for a half day, and £12 ($21) for a full day.

The **Wild Life Gallery and Bird Sanctuary,** Mearson Manor, Cross Street in Moretonhampstead (tel. Moretonhampstead 483). Terry and Betty Tilson-Chowne, who own the manor, decided that the house should be put to good use. They have opened the halls and rooms to house a great collection of contemporary paintings and sculpture. You can browse through these rooms until you find just the one you want. There are beautiful, delicate pastels and crayon drawings of wildlife on Dartmoor by Brian Carter, otters, a fox chasing a pheasant, whatever. Unframed they go for £20 ($35), or you can buy reproductions for as little as £8 ($10.50). Other rooms contain Eastern brassware and bronze work, among other items. The oldest part of the house is, in fact, a restaurant, with two magnificently preserved fireplaces. The food is entirely homemade—scones with fresh butter, Devonshire cream teas at £1.15 ($2.01), and cakes at 50p (88¢) a portion. They do light lunchtime snacks as well. Before you leave, say hello to the talking crow and the other birds in the aviary.

The **Museum of Dartmoor Life** is at the rear of 3 West St., Okehampton (tel. Okehampton 3020). The market town of Okehampton owes its existence to the Norman castle built by Baldwin de Bryonis, sheriff of Devon, under orders from his uncle, William the Conqueror, in 1068, just two years after the Conquest. The Courtenay family lived there for many generations until Henry VIII beheaded one of them and dismantled the castle in 1538. The museum is a number of authentic buildings grouped around a courtyard. These include two 19th-century cottages, an agricultural mill, and a printer's workshop. They display farm machinery and some old vehicles, a Devon box wagon of 1875, a 1922 Bullnose Morris motorcar, a 1937 motorcycle. There is a reconstructed wheelwright's shop, a farm kitchen, a dairy, and much more. It is open from April to October, daily except Sunday from 10:30 a.m. to 4:30 p.m. Admission is 40p (70¢) for adults and 20p (35¢) for children. The castle is open from mid-March to mid-October, Monday to Saturday, from 9:30 a.m. to 6:30 p.m. (on Sunday from 2 to 6:30 p.m.). In winter it closes at 4 p.m. Admission is 40p (70¢) for adults and 20p (35¢) for children.

FOOD AND LODGING: **Leusdon Lodge Guest House,** Poundsgate (tel. Poundsgate 304), is a 150-year-old stone country house, with gables, chimneys, and, beyond the garden, views of Dartmoor National Park. Its owners are Neelia and Denis Hutchins, who know a lot about this area. Denis was once the chairman of the Dartmoor Tourist Association and likes to help visitors with their problems. He can guide you to horseback riding, to the best local sights, to a picnic beside a crystal-clear brook, or tell the history of the moor and its folklore. On cool nights, he lights a log fire in the living room and joins the guests in conversation. Seven rooms are available, with soft beds and hot and cold water basins, at a charge of £16.50 ($28.86) per person nightly for half board. Your breakfast will be abundant and varied. Dinners are English at their best, traditional food served in the dining room with hand-carved paneled walls and an ornate fireplace. Specialties are shepherd's pie, steak-and-kidney pudding, and boiled beef and carrots. In the family atmosphere at the lodge, you'll be looked upon more as a new friend than a room number. In winter there is full central heating, along with a festive Christmas house party.

Lydgate House Hotel, Postbridge (tel. Tavistock 88209), is an attractive residence set on 35 acres by a rushing stream, right in the middle of Dartmoor National Park. The hotel is run by Brian and Penny Ward and Mrs. Ward's mother, Mrs. René Howell. Their guests are assured of a warm welcome, comfortable accommodation, and plenty of good English food. Friendliness is the keynote of this hotel.

The breakfasts are as super-generous as the dinners. The house is quite old, but it's been fully restored, the dining room extended out to the garden. Big windows allow views of the river. There are several comfortable lounges set aside for get-acquainted conversations or quiet retreats. In a snug bar, predinner drinks are served. Mr. Ward will arrange horseback riding, and Mrs. Ward will pack a lunch for £1.25 ($2.19) if you want to hike across the moors.

The daily rate for B&B, including VAT, is £11 ($19.25) per person in season, lowered to £8 ($14) per person off-season. By the week, it's cheaper. From Exeter take the A38 Plymouth road to Peartree Tree Cross (signposted

Ashburton and Dartmoor), follow the B3357 to Two Bridges, and turn right onto the B3212. Postbridge is approximately three miles away.

Old Walls Farm, Ponsworthy, near Widecombe-in-the-Moor and Newton Abbot (tel. Poundsgate 222), is a substantial, stone-colored plastered country home set remotely on a working farm and reached by very narrow lanes. Here you are comfortably in the heart of the moors, and in the safe, knowing hands of owner Bill Fursdon, an expert on the area. He is a genial, handsome, white-haired gentleman with a gracious smile who is by avocation a naturalist. He'll take you on a short walk around his farm, showing you his collection of cows, Jack Russell terriers, ducks, a pet goat (its milk is served at breakfast, but it's strictly optional), and a beautiful little river, which gives electric power to the house. He'll make handmade maps, pinpointing the places of interest within driving distance.

His house is a living tribute to a fast-disappearing era. He is assisted by his wife Elizabeth, who plays the organ on Sunday at the village church, and their son who lives in a separate home close by. Guests relax around a stone fireplace in the drawing room, or else on a sunny day enjoy a crescent-shaped, all-glass sun room. From the latter, the view of the moorland is exceptional. The living room has an old grand piano, a Victorian card table, a soft arm sofa, and armchairs placed in a curving bay recess.

The B&B rate is about £9 ($15.75) per person. Breakfast is a special event in the dining room, and you can have as much food as you want, including muesli, a concoction of oats, bran, wheat germ, and raisins or dates, served with brown sugar, goat's milk, and a glob of clotted Devonshire cream.

Old Walls Farm is reached from the A38 dual carriageway between Exeter and Plymouth. Turn right past Ashburton onto the B3357, then right at Poundsgate onto the Ponsworthy–Widecombe road. Go through the hamlet of Ponsworthy, passing the all-purpose post office and store, and look for the B&B sign on the left about 600 yards on.

Scobitor Farm, Widecombe-in-the-Moor, near Newton Abbot (tel. Widecombe 254), is run by Capt. and Mrs. Roger Curnock. Theirs is a large farmhouse of much character, lying 1000 feet up on Dartmoor, with good views overlooking the moor. It's approached down a long tree-lined entrance drive, some 1½ miles outside the village of Widecombe. The present house is mainly from 1725 with later alterations, although the property dates back to before the *Domesday Book.* Fully modernized, it still retains its charm and atmosphere. The emphasis is on comfort and good food, and the house has full central heating along with log fires.

A working farm, Scobitor accepts guests all year. The Curnocks cater very much to families, with suites of two bedrooms and a private bath, along with a large playroom and early suppers for younger children. For adults there is a drawing room. Dinners are excellent, mainly based on Cordon Bleu recipes. A very large amount of the food coming from their kitchen is home-produced. Captain Curnock will arrange riding and hunting for guests. Charges range from £26 ($45.50) daily per person for half board based on double occupancy. Children in a unit with their parents are charged £19 ($33.25). No service charge or VAT is added.

Dowerland Farm, Mary Tavy, near Tavistock (tel. Mary Tavy 345), is an immaculate, simple farmhouse, ideal for tranquility seekers. Near a little village, it lies only a few minutes via a country lane from the main highway, the A386. A 50-acre farm, Dowerland produces vegetables, including five different kinds of potatoes, sold in the local shops. The owner, Mrs. I. M. Hogg, is motherly and thoughtful, kindness itself—and a good cook! She charges £7 ($12.25) per person for B&B, and if notified in advance will prepare a homemade supper. She opens her farm to paying guests all year, except in December, which she sets aside as "our family month." The living room is snug, with chairs for relaxing gathered around an open fire. On cold nights a hot-water bottle is placed in your bed.

Lydford House Hotel, Lydford, near Okehampton (tel. Lydford 347), is a family-run country-house hotel, standing in some three acres of grounds on the outskirts of Lydford, just on the edge of Dartmoor. It was built in 1880 for the Dartmoor artist William Widgery, and several of his paintings hang in the residents' lounge. Owners Ron and Ann Boulter offer varied and interesting menus, all of which feature home-cooking using local produce. The rates are £12.50 ($21.88) per person per night for a room with private bath/shower and toilet and a full English breakfast, while a table d'hôte dinner costs £6 ($10.50). Reductions are allowed for seven or more nights, especially off-season. All prices include service charge and taxes. The hotel is seven miles south of Okehampton, just off the A386, and it's on your right as you approach the hamlet of Lydford.

The **Castle Inn,** Lydford, near Okehampton (tel. Lydford 242), is a 16th-century inn next to Lydford Castle. The low inn, with its pink facade and row of rose trellises and clematis, is the hub of the village, along with the all-purpose grocery store and post office. The inn's owners, Mr. and Mrs. Reed, have maintained the character of the commodious rustic lounge, with its collection of old furniture and accessories, including wing chairs, a grandfather clock, a large collection of Victorian ribbon plates, and antique prints. One room is called the "Snug," containing a group of high-backed oak settles arranged in a circle. Meals are served buffet style, from noon to 2 p.m., a great spread set out on a long table. The cost depends on your selection of a main course. The salads are on a help-yourself basis, costing from £3 ($5.25) to £3.50 ($6.13). Snacks are available as well, and you can take your plate, along with a lager, and sneak off to an inviting nook. À la carte dinners are available in the evening, going for £4 ($7) to £7 ($12.25). For a bed and a large country-style breakfast, the charge is £11 ($19.25) per person nightly. The bedrooms, although not large, are well planned and attractively furnished, often with mahogany and marble Victorian pieces, each room with its own color scheme.

Stoanen, The Green, Widecombe-in-the-Moor (tel. 03642/325). Doug Somerton, tired of life in the city as production manager from ICI, brought his wife Diane to this historic moorland village to run their home as a guest house. They charge £7 ($12.25) per person nightly for a warm bed and a scrumptious breakfast that might include kippers. The bedrooms have wash basins and are equipped with tea- and coffee-making facilities. But there is no TV—savor the peace of the countryside instead. Doug and Diane are keen on walking and will provide maps and details of routes across the moors. Horse-riding can be arranged in the village.

A pub nearby does excellent meals. It's the **Ring O' Bells,** where a set dinner costs £6.95 ($12.16). In September Widecombe holds its annual fair when the famous ride of Old Uncle Tom Cobbley is commemorated.

The Old Inn, Widecombe-in-the-Moor (tel. Widecombe 207), is a real traditional old country inn run by James Lapraik. There are the usual bars, such as the public and the saloon, each well patronized by local farmers. At lunch and in the evening, bar snacks include cornish pasties, ploughman's plates, pâté, steak-and-kidney pie with chips, and a cold roast meat platter and salad. The curry is made from a special Kenya recipe and served with rice, mango, chutney, and poppadums. There is usually an apple or cherry pie, perhaps a plum tart with custard. Two courses will cost about £2.80 ($4.90).

Otherwise, sandwiches, pasties, or sausages are in the 70p ($1.23) to 90p ($1.58) range.

The **White Hart Hotel,** Moretonhampstead (tel. 06474/406), is a 300-year-old inn, a Georgian post house right on the main street, with a white hart on the portico over the main door. Most of the rooms have bath and hot and cold running water, and all have tea- or coffee-making facilities. A few contain TV sets. The units vary in size and decor, and many of the chambers come with beamed ceilings, attractive bed linen, country quilts, and flowery curtains. One of the two lounges has TV, and meals are taken in the polished dining room with a splendid carved sideboard and a grandfather clock lit by silver chandeliers. Afterward, a drink is in order, served in a cheerful, oak-beamed bar, sharing the warmth of the log fire with the locals.

Dinner might include the chef's chicken liver pâté, followed by grilled rainbow trout and duck in orange sauce. Or you can enjoy home-cooked ham or stuffed leg of pork. Desserts include a treacle tart with Devon clotted cream. A three-course meal will cost about £7.60 ($13.30). "Mine host" is Peter Morgan, who has lived most of his life in Devon and has run a hotel for more than 20 years. Overnight rates are from £11.50 ($20.13) per person, including an English breakfast and VAT.

The **White Horse Inn,** Moretonhampstead (tel. 06474/242), is a simple country inn with plain bedrooms, all with good heating and hot and cold running water. Three contain private baths. There is a friendly local bar, plus a dining room where you can enjoy a three-course meal for under £5 ($8.75). The fare is typically English, including lamb cutlets with mint sauce and liver and bacon with onions, followed by a homemade fruit pie with cream. The overnight charge is £9.50 ($16.63) per person, including an English breakfast. Henry White and Les Billington, both ex-oilmen, run the White Horse, along with their wives, and they willingly recommend long walks and will organize horseback riding trips and fishing expeditions.

Alexanders, 8 Cross St., Moretonhampstead, is a café offering home-baked cakes and cream teas. You can order a real budget meal here, including soup, roll, and butter, along with fish and chips or perhaps a mixed grill, then fruit pie and cream, all for about £2.50 ($4.38). They also have a daily roast joint, served with potatoes and vegetables at £3.25 ($5.69). Upstairs they have some simple rooms to rent at a cost of £5.50 ($9.63) per person nightly, including a large breakfast.

The **Bell Inn,** The Square, Moretonhampstead. Mr. Emerson does a very good line in hot, fresh bar snacks, hamburgers, french-fried potatoes, and peas, costing from 90p ($1.58). There are also fat sandwiches and a ploughman's lunch for around 95p ($1.66).

Great Sloncombe Farm, Moretonhampstead (tel. 06474/595), is a farmhouse dating from the 13th century. It has open beams and log fires, a cobbled courtyard, and the heads of contented horses nodding in looseboxes in the stables. Trudie Merchant cooks wholesome meals for her family and guests, using produce from the farm, including eggs, milk, and meat. Bedrooms have welcoming open fires and warm, comfortable beds. An overnight's stay, including a good supper, will cost around £10 ($17.50) per person.

READER'S FARMHOUSE AND COUNTRY HOME SELECTION: "Going to **Widecombe-in-the-Moor,** I was directed about a half mile or so down a lane, to **Higher Venton Farm,** Newton Abbot (tel. Widecombe 235), a lovely, thatch-roofed cottage. It has two stories and is about 500 years old. A warm, very hospitable family lives there, who, aside from making their living operating the small farm, also rent rooms. There are one family and two double bedrooms. The charge for B&B is £6 ($10.50) or else £8.50 ($14.88) per person for half board. The rooms are cheerful and clean, the meals plentiful, and the family very nice. The person you rent from is the mother, Mrs. B. Hicks" (Arnold Chapman, Los Angeles, Calif.).

4. Chagford

Six hundred feet above sea level, Chagford is an ancient Stannary Town. With the moors all around it, it is a good base for your exploration of the region of North Dartmoor. It is approximately 20 miles from Exeter, Torquay, and Plymouth. Chagford overlooks the Teign River in its deep valley, and is itself overlooked by the high granite tors. There's good fishing in the Teign (ask at your hotel). From Chagford, the most popular excursion is to Postbridge, six miles to the southwest, a village with a prehistoric clapper bridge.

Near Chagford stands **Castle Drogo,** in the hamlet of Drewsteignton (tel. Chagford 3306). This massive granite castle was designed and built by Sir Edward Lutyens and the castle's owner, Julius Drewe, in the early 20th century. It stands high above the River Teign, with gorgeous views over the moors. The family can trace its origins back to the Norman Conquest. Julius Drewe wanted to create a home worthy of his noble ancestors. He found the bleak site high above the moors. Between them, he and Lutyens created a splendid modern castle. The tour includes the elegant library, the drawing room, the dining room with fine paintings and mirrors, and a simple chapel, along with a vault-roofed gun room. There is a restaurant open daily from 11 a.m. for such snacks as soups at 65p ($1.14) and salads, costing from £1.75 ($3.06) to £1.95 ($3.41). It closes at 6 p.m. The castle is open from April until the end of October from 11 a.m. to 6 p.m., charging an admission of £1.60 ($2.80) for adults. If you wish to visit only the grounds, the fee is £1 ($1.75). Children are admitted for half price.

FOOD AND LODGING: There are several good possibilities in the area.

The **Great Tree Country House Hotel,** Sandypark (tel. Chagford 2491). Although you may have to consider this place as your luxury for a night or two, it is well worth the expense just to be able to walk in the eight acres of grounds at eight o'clock in the morning and hear nothing but the birds and the sound of running water from the nearby stream, mingling with the occasional moo of a cow.

Mr. Whyte, who owns the hotel, brings a very considerable experience to this attractive establishment. He offers a well-prepared, four-course dinner for £9.50 ($16.63). Bar snacks are varied at lunch. Try the home-cooked ham and a salad, preceded by a country soup. You pay only £2 ($3.50) for the lot.

When the weather is fine, Devonshire cream teas are served on the terrace overlooking Dartmoor and the forest. If it rains, you can sit in the lounge and gorge yourself on scones, jam, cream, cakes, and tea.

Bedrooms are simple and countrified. The beds are good, and all units have baths, phone, and radio, and a few have their own television sets. The rate of £23 ($40.25) per person includes a bountiful breakfast the next morning.

The **Three Crowns Hotel** at Chagford (tel. Chagford 3444), is a 16th-century granite inn built to withstand the rigors of the climate, with open fireplaces, roaring log fires, and firelight dancing on old oak beams. Much of the furniture is of the period, although the old manor house has modern conveniences, central heating, hot water, and bathrooms. A single rents for £10 ($17.50) to £12 ($21) with breakfast, a double going for £18.50 ($32.38) to £24.50 ($42.88). All rates include breakfast, but service and VAT are extra.

The bar snacks are very good. Served at lunch and in the evening too, they include basket meals of chicken, fried fish, or sausages, as well as steak-and-kidney pie with vegetables, home-cooked ham and pastries, at prices ranging from £1 ($1.75) to £3 ($5.25) a portion. They also do a set lunch for £5 ($8.75), and a dinner from £7 ($12.25). Some specialty dishes include coq au vin, half a roast duckling with apple sauce, beef Stroganoff, and escalope of Devon veal. There are desserts and a good selection of cheese assortments to finish off with.

Moor Park Hotel at Chagford (tel. Chagford 2202), is a cheerful, chintzy inn with comfortable bedrooms going for around £13 ($22.75) per person, including breakfast but not VAT. The Tavern Bar is a pleasant pubby place with bar billiards and small tables grouped around the open fire. Set meals of four courses and coffee are about £8 ($14), plus VAT. However, the bar snacks are adequate, including homemade soup for 70p ($1.23) and quickies such as rump steak and chips, plaice and chips, or an omelet in the £1.20 ($2.10) to £3 ($5.25) range.

Glendarah Guest House at Chagford (tel. Chagford 3270) is a very neat and clean guest house run by John Philip and his wife. Mrs. Philip does most of the cooking, providing ample cooked breakfasts and an excellent four-course dinner every night. Rooms are comfortable, and all have hot and cold running water (there are ample bathrooms shared by guests). The lounge has a TV, and the B&B rate is £8.50 ($14.88), plus VAT. The half-board charge, £13 ($22.75) per person nightly, is preferable. The Glendarah has a quiet, respectable atmosphere.

Claremont Guest House at Chagford (tel. Chagford 3304), is a charming small house just down the hill from the town square. All rooms have hot and cold running water, central heating, and good comfortable beds which rent for £8 ($14) a night, including breakfast. An evening meal of good fresh local food is £4 ($7), and they will do a packed lunch of sandwiches and goodies for £1.25 ($2.19) for walkers and sightseers. The lounge has plenty of information to keep holiday-makers busy, and the owners, Brian and Judith Cosford and their family, know Dartmoor and can suggest walks and drives to places of interest nearby.

Ely House, Nattadon Hill (tel. Chagford 2404), is a country-house hotel converted from a former rectory. A short walk from the village of Chagford, it is set in five acres of grounds with sweeping lawns. The house is elegantly furnished with antiques, and some bedrooms have four-poster beds and private baths. Mr. and Mrs. G. B. Thompson welcome you, offering a total of five double bedrooms with bath, two doubles without, plus a single without. In all, they take a maximum of only 15 guests, which makes for a house-party atmosphere. For half board, the tariff ranges from £14 ($24.50) to £15.50 ($27.13) per person daily. When the weather's cool, a log fire burns in the comfortable lounge. The house, however, is centrally heated, and all bedrooms have hot and cold running water, along with coffee- or tea-making equipment. Small children are not accepted. The cuisine is good home-cooked food, using produce from Ely House's garden whenever possible. Although the hotel isn't licensed, guests can bring their own wine or liquor.

A VISIT TO AN ABBEY: **Sir Francis Drake's House,** Buckland Abbey, Yelverton, was originally a Cisterian monastery in 1278. It was dissolved in 1539 and became the country seat of Sir Richard Grenville and later Sir Francis Drake (two great sailors). It remained in the Drake family until 1946 when the abbey and grounds were handed over to the National Trust. The abbey is now a museum, housing portraits, mementos, including Drake's drum, banners, and a superb collection of model ships. The abbey lies three miles west of Yelverton off the A386. It is open Monday to Saturday from 11 a.m. to 6 p.m. (on Sunday, from 2 to 6 p.m.). In winter it is open only on Wednesday, Saturday, and Sunday from 2 to 5 p.m. Admission is £1.30 ($2.28) for adults and 70p ($1.23) for children.

The largest collection of hotels on the Devon Coastline is found in:

5. Torbay (Torquay)

In April 1968, the towns of Torquay, Paignton, and Brixham combined to form the County Borough of Torbay, as part of an overall plan to turn the area into one of the super three-in-one resorts of Europe. Escapees from the factories of the Midlands find it easier to bask in the homegrown Devonshire sunshine than to make the pilgrimage to Rimini or the Costa del Sol.

Torquay, set against a backdrop of the red cliffs of Devon, contains 11 miles of coastline, with many sheltered pebbly coves and sandy beaches. With its parks and gardens (including numerous subtropical plants and palm trees), it isn't hard to envision it as a Mediterranean-type resort (and its retired residents are fond of making this comparison, especially in postcards sent back to their cousins in Manchester). At night, concerts, productions from the West End (the D'Oyly Carte Opera appears occasionally at the new Princess Theatre), vaudeville shows, and ballroom dancing keep the holiday-makers (and many honeymooners) regally entertained.

If you suddenly long for an old Devonshire village, you can always ride the short distance to **Cockington,** still in the same borough, which contains thatched cottages, an old mill, a forge, and a 12th-century church.

Furthermore, if you want to visit one of the great homes of England, you can call on **Oldway,** in the heart of Paignton (tel. Torquay 550711). Started by the founder of the Singer sewing-machine dynasty, Isaac Merritt Singer, and completed the year after he died (1875), the neoclassic-mansion is surrounded by about 20 acres of grounds and Italian-style gardens. Inside, if you get the feeling you're at Versailles, you're almost right, as many of the rooms were copied. It's open May to September, Monday to Saturday, from 10 a.m. to 1 p.m. and 2:15 to 5 p.m. (on Sunday from 2:30 to 5:30 p.m. or dusk). In winter it's open Monday to Friday from 10 a.m. to 1 p.m. and 2:15 to 5:15 p.m. or dusk. The gardens are always open. Admission is free.

BED AND BREAKFAST: For B&B accommodations, I've focused on one of the choicest hotel and residential districts of Torquay. The prices, especially the weekly partial-board terms, are moderate.

Lanscombe House, Cockington Village (tel. Torquay 607556), is a Georgian house set in a large garden in this beautiful village. Built nearly 250 years ago, it resembles a church rectory, with large lounges and dining rooms opening onto views. The owners, Mr. and Mrs. Malcolm Goldby, have ten rooms going for around £15 ($26.25) in high season—May 1 to October 31—for B&B, plus an evening meal. Without dinner, the charge is £10.50 ($18.38). The furnishings are comfy English, overstuffed chairs et al. The bar-lounge has bare white walls and a beamed ceiling, the coziest place in the house (it was once the woodshed). The dinner is home-cooked, typically English fare. Readers Mr. and Mrs. Charles Aarons write, "Those who like to carry the calm and grace of a bygone age beyond the hotel grounds can take a horse-drawn carriage from the village to the beach!" Mr. Charles A. Haigh adds: ". . . a real pearl with excellent hosts, the food was just great, and it's ideal for a family."

Anstey's Lodge Guest House, 307 Babbacombe Rd. (tel. Torquay 27261), is a small guest house run by Mr. and Mrs. Manders and Mr. and Mrs. Griffiths, who quote B&B terms beginning at £8 ($14) per person nightly, a low price for a resort as popular as Torquay. Their house is somewhat on the outer fringe of town, overlooking Walls Hills Downs. The rooms themselves are simply, but pleasingly, furnished, containing water basins and comfortable beds with innerspring mattresses. For the lone traveler, two single rooms are available at £8.50 ($14.88) each, although the house caters mostly to couples. There is free car parking on the grounds, and a bus stops 75 feet from the door, taking one into Torquay for shopping or amusements. An evening meal can also be prepared, costing from £4.50 ($7.88).

Kelvin House, 46 Bampfylde Rd. (tel. Torquay 27313), is a former private home, and is within walking distance of the sea as well as the center of town. Green with white trim, the guest house provides sunny rooms that are extra clean, sufficiently comfortable, and moderately priced—from £7 ($12.25) per person for B&B. The cost of half board is from £9.50 ($16.63) per person. There's no skimping, since the bedrooms have innerspring mattresses and basins with hot and cold running water. In addition, the resident owners, Mr. and Mrs. J. Haynes, have provided a lounge for television.

Colindale, Rathmore Road (tel. Torquay 23947), is a good choice. And it's about as central as you'd want, opening onto King's Garden, as well as lying within a five-minute walk of Corbyn Beach, and three minutes from the railway station. The B&B rate, set by Mr. Spencer and Mr. Gold, is £10 ($17.50) per person in high season. But the best arrangement in one of their nine well-kept double rooms is to take the weekly half-board rate of £80 ($140) per person. The hotel has a cocktail bar and a resident's lounge and dining room. Colindale is one of a row of attached brick Victorian houses, with gables and chimneys. It's set back from the road, with a tiny parking court in front.

Blue Haze Hotel, Seaway Lane (tel. Torquay 607186), is an old home built for a wealthy family who wanted gracious holiday living near the sea. In a pleasant residential area overlooking Torbay, it is painted a sea blue, in keeping with the view. The house is well built and large, with comfortably high-ceilinged rooms. For one of the dozen well-furnished rooms, along with a substantial English breakfast, you pay from £8 ($14) to £10.50 ($18.38) per person, depending on the season. Half board costs £11.50 ($20.13) to £13.50 ($23.63) per person per day. The hosts, Doug and Hazel Newton, will give you a warm welcome, good home cooking, and a holiday to remember. There's a large private car park, and the hotel is licensed and has a game room.

Chelston House Hotel, Chelston Road (tel. Torquay 605200), is a gracious old mansion on its own grounds. The hotel is 250 yards from the beach and the railway station and three-quarters of a mile from the old-world village of Cockington, with its gardens and church. Open all year, Chelston House charges from £9.50 ($16.63) to £12.50 ($21.88) per person for B&B. The rooms, 14 doubles and four singles, are cheerful and spotless, with hot and cold running water and razor points. Three units with private bathrooms cost £1.50 ($2.63) per person per day extra. Some of the accommodations have sea views through curving bay windows. Lounges are devoted to sun-seeking, television, and drinks. The owners, Freda and Bill Smith, do everything possible to make their guests comfortable. For half board on a weekly basis, the rate ranges from £79 ($138.25) to £99 ($173.25) per person.

Castle Mount Hotel, Castle Road (tel. Torquay 22130), is a little out of the way, but well worth the effort to reach it because of the reasonable prices and immaculate rooms. Mr. and Mrs. John C. Bruch, Santa Barbara, California, write: "An evening with the proprietors was a Torquay highlight!"

Castle Mount is a converted private home, lodged high on a terrace and surrounded by lawns and gardens, just a few minutes' walk below to bus routes and the town center. Bay windows overlook the garden. The main rooms are centrally heated, and in chilly weather, bedrooms have heaters and electric blankets. All accommodations have hot and cold running water and inner-spring mattresses. Evening meals are a bargain, so I suggest the half-board tariff, £12 ($21), inclusive, per person. Room and breakfast is £7.50 ($13.13), inclusive. Mrs. Bradbury or Mrs. Tapping, the resident owners, will pack lunches for £1.50 ($2.63). The hotel is approached from the harbor via the one-way system to Castle Circus. Castle Road is opposite the Town Hall.

Avenue House, Avenue Road (tel. Torquay 25329), is recommended for comfort, food, and friendliness. Anna and Barry Carswell, as well as their family, are most hospitable. Their pleasantly furnished house rents units with hot and cold running water at a rate of £9 ($15.75) per person for B&B, or £12 ($21) with half board. Their house looks across Torre Valley Park and is central to the station, shops, sports, and bus routes. The location is only a few minutes' level walk to Torre Abbey Sands through Torre Abbey and Gardens.

WHERE TO EAT: **South Devon Technical College,** Newton Road (tel. Torquay 35711), serves inexpensive but gourmet lunches during the school terms (closed July, August, and the first two weeks in September, as well as on weekends). You pay a set £4 ($7), including coffee. Wines are inexpensive as well. The menu changes daily, and lunch is served at 12:15 p.m. (table reservations are made no more than seven days in advance; telephone between 10:30 a.m. and 4:30 p.m.). Special regional meals are offered on certain days, giving you a chance to try the Italian, German, and Provençale styles of cuisine. The usual bill of fare offers an hors d'oeuvre, soup, possibly an egg or farinaceous dish, followed by fish (perhaps filet of sole in white wine). The main course may be duck or an entrecôte steak chasseur, with vegetables, and finally you are served a dessert. The modern restaurant setting is enhanced by beautifully crisp table linen, sparkling silver and glassware, and the smartest of young students waiting at table. The college is well worth a visit.

The **Strand Restaurant** (tel. Torquay 22498) is a family dining room opposite the harbor. Right in the hub of Torquay, it serves typical English fare. For an appetizer, try the soup of the day. A good-size plate of fried scampi is served, or try roast Devonshire chicken with french fries and peas. All these main dishes are garnished generously with well-cooked vegetables, included in the price. Three-course lunches cost from £4 ($7). Most popular is the window table, virtually on the pavement. A set three-course dinner is offered for £6 ($10.50). The Strand opens at 10 a.m. for coffee, staying so until the last person leaves at night.

6. Totnes

One of the oldest towns in the West Countree, the ancient Borough of Totnes rests quietly in the past, seemingly content to let the Torbay area remain in the vanguard of the building boom. On the Dart River, 12 miles upstream from Dartmouth, Totnes is so totally removed in character from Torquay that the two towns could be in different countries. Totnes shelters a number of historic buildings (none worth making a special pilgrimage to, however), notably the ruins of a Norman castle, the ancient Guildhall, and the 15th-century church of St. Mary, made of red sandstone. In the Middle Ages, the old cloth town was encircled by walls, and the North Gate serves as a reminder of that period.

Broombrough House Farm (tel. Totnes 863134) is a gracious 100-year-old, many-gabled stone manor house, set on a hill about a 15-minute walk from Totnes. Owner Joan Veale loves to show guests around the farm, relating that the place was designed by Sir George Gilbert Scott, who also designed the Albert Memorial and Kings Cross Station. Four spacious and well-furnished bedrooms are on the first floor (two baths are shared). They are centrally heated, each containing twin beds, innerspring mattresses, and hot and cold running water. A week's stay costs £58 ($101.50), and includes morning tea, a farm-style breakfast, plus your evening meal. The daily charge is £9 ($15.75) per person for B&B, plus another £5.50 ($9.63) for the evening meal. Guest lounges are spacious and comfortable. The place is highly recommended, especially to those who have never experienced life on a farm. From the farm, a view opens onto Dartmoor National Park.

LIVING ON THE OUTSKIRTS OF TOTNES: In and around this area is some of South Devon's most beautiful scenery. The hamlets, such as Harberton and Dartington, are especially pleasing, and each motorist approaches them with the freshness of a personal discovery. To the southeast is the pleasant little village of Stoke Gabriel. You'll find intriguing living accommodations on both the economy and splurge price levels.

At Stoke Gabriel

About four miles southeast of Totnes sits the little village of Stoke Gabriel, one of the loveliest in Devon. Famous as a fishing hamlet, it lies on a creek of the Dart River. Dartmouth is only six miles to the south of the village (equidistant to Torquay).

For a splurge, the **Gabriel Court Hotel** (tel. Stoke Gabriel 206) is a manor which until recently had been owned by one family since 1485. What must the ghosts have thought when Michael and Eryl Beacom acquired it and guests started to fill up the rooms, chasing away the cobwebs of the past? The gleaming white house is surrounded by gardens, hedges, and magnolia trees. A heated swimming pool is on the grounds. B&B rates are from £17.50 ($30.63) per person, and what a breakfast! It's the old-fashioned English kind. You might get a room in the new wing, containing eight bedrooms, all with private baths, or one of the rooms in the old building which are tastefully decorated and furnished and most of which now have their own private shower or bathroom and toilet facilities, although a few feature hot and cold running water only. Gabriel Court holds a high reputation for its well-cooked English food. Game is often available, including Exmoor venison. Or you may be offered Brixham scallops, trout and salmon from the River Dart, and poultry from the nearby farms, enhanced with vegetables from the garden. The hotel has a bar/cocktail lounge. Wines are moderately priced. The hotel remains open all year.

At Paignton

Formosa, 34 Totnes Rd. (tel. Paignton 559850), is in the center of Paignton, although the location is quiet. You're near the shops, beaches, and only a ten-minute walk from the railway station. Mrs. Anne Keene welcomes you in comfort at £7.50 ($13.13) nightly for B&B. In cold months, electric blankets are provided, and tea and cookies are offered in the evening.

At Dartington

For such a small hamlet, Dartington attracts a surprising number of international visitors, mainly because of **Dartington Hall,** an experimental Anglo-American alliance dating back to 1925. A Yorkshire man and his American-born wife (one of the Whitneys) poured energy, courage, imagination, and money into the theory that such a village could be self-sufficient. They used historic Dartington Hall, built in the late 14th century and restored by them after 1925, as their center. In the surrounding acres of undulating hills and streams, several village industries were created: housing construction, advanced farming, milling of cloth, and an experimental school. One famous activity here is the College of Arts, in which students live and work in a series of modern buildings erected since the formation of the college in 1961. The Summer School of Music spends the month of August here, occupying the school and college buildings and giving numerous concerts. During the day, visitors are welcome to tour the extensive grounds and can make purchases of handmade crafts in the community store. The Cider Press Centre is a complex designed to introduce visitors to the history of the Dartington enterprise and provide a showcase for the work of leading British crafts people. You'll find a craft gallery and shop, a print gallery, souvenir shop, toy shop, and a Cranks health-food restaurant. One of the shops sells Dartington glass "seconds," along with many interesting souvenirs. A glass swan or a set of cocktail glasses begins at 70p ($1.23), going up to £12 ($21).

Cranks Health Food Restaurant, Dartington Cider Press Centre, Shinners Bridge (tel. Totnes 862388), owes its concept to its parent restaurant in London, where it instantly became the leading health-food restaurant. Now, here among the creative craft center of Dartington, in an old Devonshire farmstead, it has found new dimensions. The center, with its handmade chairs, tables, and pottery, displays the work of various craftspeople. It's strictly self-service, and there's a buffet featuring creatively conceived salads. They use compost-grown vegetables when available, and serve freshly made vegetable soup, also live yogurts and freshly extracted fruit and vegetable juices. The Devonshire cream teas with Cranks' newly baked whole-meal scones are very popular. The restaurant is open Monday to Saturday from 10 a.m. to 5 p.m. Meals begin at £4 ($7), with most hot savories costing around £2.50 ($4.38). A small salad plate costs £1.25 ($2.19); a large plate, £2.50 ($4.38). Cakes range from 42p (74¢) to £1 ($1.75).

The **Cott Inn** (tel. Totnes 863777), on the old Ashburton–Totnes turnpike, is the second-oldest inn in England, built in 1320. It is a low, rambling, two-story building of stone, cob, and plaster, with a thatched roof and walls three feet thick. The owners, Nigel Shortman and Neville Yeadon, charge £16 ($28) per person, including service and VAT, for a full English or a continental breakfast and occupancy of one of their low-ceilinged old beamed rooms upstairs, where modern conveniences, including hot and cold running water, have been installed.

The inn is a gathering place for the people of Dartington, and here you'll feel the pulse of English country life. Even though it is a lowly pub, it is sophisticated—and you'll hear good talk here. In winter, log fires keep the lounge and bar snug. You'll surely be intrigued with the tavern, perhaps wanting to take a meal there. A crock of hot soup and a ploughman's lunch (hunks of cheese, bread, and pickles) go for £2 ($3.50). Dinner is not a light meal! A buffet is laid out (lunchtime as well), priced according to your choice of dish. You can eat for as little as £2.50 ($4.38), or as much as £7 ($12.25), for a choice likely to include pork escallope, rabbit pie, steak-and-kidney pie,

Scottish rib of beef, home-cured ham, or local trout. Salads are crisp and fresh, the array of desserts appetizing. Even if you're not staying over, at least drop in at the pub (seven beers on draft).

READER'S FARMHOUSE SELECTION: "I want to heartily recommend a farm B&B establishment. **Wyses Englebourn,** Harberton (tel. Harbertonford 548), is a 16th-century farm about three miles from Totnes. The proprietors, Marjorie and Richard German, are lovely people who made our stay most pleasant. Such touches as hot-water bottles in our beds and teddy bears for the children made us feel quite at home. The cost for our family of four was £14 ($24.50) a night for two rooms, morning and afternoon tea, and breakfast. Portions are enormous, and dinner can be purchased for £4 ($7) per person, £2.50 ($4.38) for children" (Lawrence Coe Lanpher, Washington, D.C.).

From Totnes, we head south to the old town of:

7. Dartmouth

At the mouth of the Dart River, this ancient seaport is the home of the Royal Naval College. Traditionally linked to England's maritime greatness, Dartmouth sent out the young midshipmen who saw to it that "Britannia ruled the waves." You can take a river steamer up the Dart to Totnes (book at the kiosk at the harbor). The scenery along the way is breathtaking, as the Dart is Devon's most beautiful river.

Dartmouth's 15th-century castle was built during the reign of Edward IV. The town's most noted architectural feature is the Butterwalk, lying below Tudor houses. The Flemish influence in some of the houses is pronounced.

FOOD AND LODGING: **Ridgeway Cottage,** 27 Ridge Hill (tel. Dartmouth 2799), owned by Mrs. Elizabeth Crotty, is a small guest house with one twin-bedded room facing the river and one single room fronting the Naval College. Both rooms have the exclusive use of Mrs. Crotty's own bathroom and shower, with a separate toilet. For B&B, per person, according to season and length of stay, the cost goes from £7.50 ($13.13) to £8 ($14).

The **Victoria Hotel,** Duke Street (tel. Dartmouth 2572), is an unheralded little hotel just 150 yards from the harbor, and a favorite retreat of the officers of the Naval College (at times, you feel that Gilbert and Sullivan wrote their operettas there). A bathless double or twin costs from £19 ($33.25) to £21 ($36.75), a twin with bath going for £21 ($36.75) to £24 ($42) nightly. These tariffs include a full English breakfast, VAT, and service. A favorite place for before-dinner drinks is one of the Victorian slipper chairs in front of the lounge fireplace. The bedrooms are immaculate, tidy, and personal; the beds fresh and restful. Recommended on the à la carte menu are the chef's own pâté, beef Stroganoff, or roast Devonshire duckling with orange sauce. All main dishes include vegetables.

The **Bay Tree Restaurant,** Fairfax Place (tel. Dartmouth 3167), is perhaps the most tea-roomy of Dartmouth's restaurants. Here you can order an authentic Devonshire lunch for £3.50 ($6.13), a typical offering including roast chicken and stuffing, plus the dessert of the day. The rich-tasting soups are good, and the Devonshire cream also. True to its type, the Bay Tree is graced with ladderback Jacobean chairs, tiptop tables, and prints on the walls. It is open for morning coffee, lunches, and afternoon cream teas at £1.50 ($2.63). The restaurant is licensed to serve drinks at tables.

An alternate possibility is the **Scarlet Geranium,** Fairfax Place (tel. Dartmouth 2491), a charming old restaurant off the Quay. Built originally in 1333, it was once known as the Albion Inn. Try it for morning coffee or a three-course table d'hôte luncheon (noon to 2:30 p.m.) for £2.75 ($4.81), which features such temptations as roast leg of lamb or baked Wiltshire ham. When available, you can order the locally caught and dressed crab for £3.60 ($6.30), or fresh-caught salmon, £3.80 ($6.65). From April to October, the Scarlet Geranium blooms at night, too. Two licensed bars are on the premises. It is open from March until November.

READER'S RESTAURANT SELECTION: At the **Cherub**, Higher Street (tel. Dartmouth 2571), we had excellent bar snacks for less than £2.50 ($4.38) apiece. The Cherub has been in existence since about 1380 and maintains its original decor. This attractive and friendly pub is run by Roy and Lois Thwaites. There's also an evening dining room for fresh seafood and lobster from the tank" (Benjamin L. Crossley, Saginaw, Mich.).

Thirty miles west from Dartmouth is our final stopover on the South Devon coast:

8. Plymouth

The historic seaport is more romantic in legend than in reality. But this was not always so. In World War II, the blitzed area of Greater Plymouth lost at least 75,000 buildings. The heart of present-day Plymouth, including the municipal civic center on the Royal Parade, has been entirely rebuilt, the way it was done the subject of controversy.

For the old you must go to the Elizabethan section, known as the Barbican, and walk along the quay in the footsteps of Sir Francis Drake (once the mayor of Plymouth), and other Elizabethan seafarers, such as Sir John Hawkins, English naval commander and slave trader. It was from here in 1577 that Drake set sail on his round-the-world voyage. An even more famous sailing took place in 1620 when the Pilgrim Fathers left their final port in England for the New World. That fact is commemorated by a plaque at the harbor.

While playing bowls on Plymouth Hoe, Drake was told that the Spanish Armada had entered the Sound. In what must surely rank as one of the greatest displays of confidence of all time, he finished the game.

Still a major base for the British navy, Plymouth makes for an interesting stopover.

Apart from the Hoe, the most interesting part of the city is the area around the departure point of the Pilgrim Fathers in 1620, the already-mentioned **Barbican.** Here you'll find the Memorial Gateway to the Waterside whence, as tradition has it, they embarked on the *Mayflower.* Here too is the Black Friars Refectory Room, dating from 1536, in Southside Street. The building is a national monument and one of Plymouth's oldest surviving buildings. It's now owned by Plymouth Gin Distillery, which welcomes visitors Monday to Friday to see the small exhibition of the history of the building. It was here that the Pilgrims met prior to setting sail for the New World.

The Barbican is a mass of narrow streets, old houses, and quayside shops selling antiques, brasswork, old prints, and books. Fishing boats still unload their catch at the wharves, and passenger-carrying ferry boats run short harbor cruises. A one-hour trip includes a visit to Drake's Island in the Sound, the dockyards, and naval vessels, plus a view of the Hoe from seaside. A cost is £2.80 ($4.90) per person. For other cruises, get in touch with **Millbrook Steamboat and Trading Co.,** Cremyll Quay (tel. Plymouth 822202).

The **Barbican Craft Centre,** White Lane, in the Barbican, has workshops and showrooms where you can watch and talk to people engaged in crafts. You'll see such sights as a potter throwing a special design or a glassblower fashioning a particular glass. Woodcarvers, leather workers, and weavers are also busy, and you can buy their products at reasonable prices, even commissioning your own design if you're lucky.

WHERE TO EAT: If you're pressed for time and are only passing through, try at least to visit the Barbican—perhaps for a meal. A good dining choice is **Green Lanterns,** 31 New St., The Barbican (tel. Plymouth 660852). A 16th-century eating house, on a Tudor street, the Green Lanterns lies 200 yards from the Mayflower Steps, about as close to the Pilgrim Fathers as you can get. Even to this day, it's a good restaurant. At lunch a three-course meal is available for £5 ($8.75).

In the evening (you can dine until 10:30 p.m.), the price of the main dish includes fresh vegetables of the day. Specialty dishes include harriett steak, hare royal, and "pepperpot" (diced lamb cooked with spices, prawns, hot chili peppers, and topped with baby dumplings). À la carte dinner prices are from £7 ($12.25) for a main course with fresh vegetables. All the desserts are served with Devonshire cream. Family owned, the Green Lanterns is run by Sally M. Russell and Kenneth Pappin, who are fully aware that voyaging strangers like the Elizabethan atmosphere, traditional English fare, and personal service. The restaurant is near the municipally owned Elizabethan House. It's licensed until 11:30 p.m. and closed Sunday. Reservations for dinner are available.

The Ship, Barbican (tel. Plymouth 67604), is a lovely two-story frame house whose ground floor is the pub. The restaurant, where all dishes are prepared individually, is on the second floor. An à la carte three-course meal costs from £5.50 ($9.63) to about £8 ($14), according to your choice.

Martins Restaurant, 2 Windsor Villas, Lockyer Street (tel. Plymouth 28133), is run by Bill Proudman and his wife Anne. Their à la carte menu offers a wide range of dishes—try their homemade soup, chicken chasseur with three fresh vegetables, then a dessert, all for £4.40 ($7.60). In such a fishing port, you can, of course, order lobster or less exotic fresh fish. Bill and Anne try to vary the evening's fare, so perhaps you'll have moussaka and dolmades, or else an Italian repast with pasta, perhaps a barbecue. They also have a popular Poor Man's Night with filling desserts and pies. Their place is open Monday to Saturday from noon to 2 p.m. and 6 to 9:30 p.m.

The **Barbican Wine Lodge,** Quay Road in the Barbican (tel. Plymouth 660875), lies right on the quayside, across the water from the Customs House. Owned and run by Alastair Orr Ewing, the lodge is an old building with wooden floors softened by sawdust. Vintage wines are stacked in racks behind the bar under an oak-beamed ceiling. Parking is possible directly outside if you can find a space among the local cars, as this is a popular place. It is open from 11 a.m. to 2:30 p.m. and 6 to 10:30 p.m. Monday to Saturday (closed on Sunday).

This is an ideal place to stop while exploring Plymouth. There is a good ambience, plus a wide range of snacks to sate the appetite, including avocado vinaigrette, pâtés, hot soups, quiches, salads, and cold plates of meat. They also feature fresh crab, Dunster chicken, and Barbican vol-au-vents, as well as steaks. No main dish costs more than £3.50 ($6.13), and you can usually dine for far less. A glass of wine is 75p ($1.31).

The **Queen Anne Tea and Coffee House,** White Lane, in the Barbican (tel. Plymouth 262101), stands next to the previously recommended Barbican Craft Centre. It's a bow-fronted, white-painted tea shop where from 11 a.m. to 1 p.m. you can order fresh coffee, tea, savories, cakes, delicacies, and sandwiches which, as the menu says, titillate the tastebuds. White wood tables and chairs, along with white-paneled walls, make for a bright and cheerful place. It's ideal for a quick snack or a Devonshire cream tea, costing £1 ($1.75). You can also drop in, ordering just a large mug of coffee for 60p ($1.05). This is one of the very few places I've found in the heart of Plymouth, within a moment's walk of the spot where the Pilgrim Fathers set sail.

BED AND BREAKFAST: Present-day pilgrims from the New World who didn't strike it rich are advised to head for Smeaton Terrace, in one of the most colorful parts of Plymouth, West Hoe. Here they'll find a number of inexpensive B&B houses on a quiet, peaceful street near the water. My recommendations for overnighting follow:

The **Imperial Hotel,** 3 Windsor Villas, Lockyer Street (tel. Plymouth 27311), is for anyone who prefers a small, friendly place, rather than a commercial hotel. The proprietors are great characters who enjoy making guests feel at home. Mr. Brooks was a rubber planter in Malaya, but retired here and he and Mrs. Brooks bought this attractive Victorian house. The hotel is tastefully furnished, indicating the experienced travel background of its owners. The B&B rate is £10 ($17.50) per person, including service. VAT is extra. Some ground-floor rooms are offered for those who have difficulty with stairs. Twelve rooms have private showers and toilets. There is ample car parking on the premises for guests.

The **Wiltun,** 39 Grand Parade, West Hoe (tel. Plymouth 667072), is set on Plymouth's historic foreshore overlooking Drake's Island and Plymouth Sound. This Victorian house has many modern facilities, but retains several of the architectural features of the 1850s. Pat and Alan Rendle, owner-proprietors, offer friendly service throughout the year. Family rooms are available. There's a private lawn to relax on and watch the ships go by. Major credit cards are welcome. The charge is £10 ($17.50) per person per day, including a large English breakfast. The well-prepared evening meal goes for £5 ($8.75), plus VAT.

The **Anchorage,** Grand Parade, West Hoe (tel. Plymouth 668645), boasts a choice location, on the Grand Parade by the sea, overlooking Plymouth Sound. Owned by Mr. and Mrs. Willmott, the hotel is simply furnished in a modified modern style. Without flair or frills, it provides its own drama. The rooms have innerspring mattresses, hot and cold running water, and electric heaters. The rate for B&B is from £8 ($14) to £9 ($15.75) per person.

St. Rita's, 76 Alma Rd. (tel. Plymouth 667024), is close to the Plymouth railway station in a row of blue-painted Victorian houses on the main bus route to the city center, approximately one mile away. The hotel furnishings aren't style setters, but the place is well kept and clean. Mr. and Mrs. Sheehan are only too willing to help. They offer 28 comfortable rooms, each with a wardrobe and chest. The tariff varies with the room, but averages £8 ($14) per person nightly, including breakfast. The accommodations at the back are quieter. Evening meals are offered only from October to May. However, you have to have something to eat if you want to drink because of license requirements. There is good parking at the rear of the hotel.

Camelot Hotel, Elliott Street, The Hoe (tel. Plymouth 669931), stands on a small road just off the grassy expanse of the Hoe. It is a neat tall house with a pleasant small bar and restaurant, with set menu meals and a short à la carte menu in the evening. There is a lounge with color TV and video, or else you can watch from your own set in your bedroom. Accommodations go for £10.70 ($18.73) in a single without bath, rising to £14.75 ($25.81) with bath. Two persons can stay here in a bathless chamber for £20.75 ($36.31), the price going up to £26.35 ($46.11) with private bath. These tariffs include a full English breakfast, service, and VAT. There are facilities for laundry and dry cleaning, a boon when you're traveling.

READER'S GUEST HOUSE SELECTION: "The absolutely most lovely, airy, charming B&B we stayed at in England was the **Parkview Guest House**, 9 Tothill Ave., St. Jude's (tel. Plymouth 23016). Rooms are in a totally restored Victorian mansion, furnishings are in exquisite good taste, and it is beautifully situated just across a lovely little park within easy walking distance of the Barbican and Plymouth Harbor. Mrs. F. Michael, the host, is a gracious woman. A well-prepared breakfast is everything from cereal through eggs, bacon, and sausage. The price is from £12 ($21) in a double" (Gary W. Fentress, Beverly Hills, Calif.).

Most tourists at this point will want to continue their trip into Cornwall. However, if you're entering Devon from Somerset, you may first want to explore:

NORTH DEVON

"Lorna, Lorna . . . Lorna Doone, my lifelong darling," is the wailing cry you're likely to imagine from your farmhouse bed in North Devon. A wildness seems to enter the air at night on the edge of the moody Doone Valley. Much of the district is already known to those who have read Victorian novelist R. D. Blackmore's romance of the West Country, *Lorna Doone.*

The coastline is mysterious. Pirates and smugglers used to find havens here, in crooked creeks and rocky coves. The ocean crashes against the rocks, and the meadows approach so close to the cliff's edge that you wonder why they don't go spilling into the sea, sheep and all. The heatherclad uplands of Exmoor, with its red deer, spill over into North Devon from Somerset, a perfect setting for an English mystery thriller. Favorite bases are Clovelly, the twin resorts of Lynton and Lynmouth, and Combe Martin.

Our first stopover is the best:

9. Clovelly

This most charming of all Devon villages becomes overpopular in summer. Still, it remains one of the main attractions of the West Country. Starting at a great height, the village cascades down the mountainside, with its narrow, cobblestone. High which makes travel by car impossible (you park your car at the top and make the trip by foot). Supplies are carried down by donkeys. Every yard of the way provides views of tiny cottages, with their terraces of flowers lining the main street. The village fleet is sheltered at the stone quay at the bottom.

If you don't want to climb back up the slippery incline, go to the rear of the Red Lion Inn and "queue up" for a Land Rover. In summer the line is often long, but considering the alternative it's worth the wait. Two Land Rovers make continuous round trips, costing 50p (88¢) per person each way.

Tip: To avoid the flock of tourists, stay out of Clovelly from around 11 in the morning till teatime. After tea, settle in your room, and have dinner, perhaps spend the night in peace and contentment. The next morning after breakfast, you walk around the village or go for a swim in the harbor, then visit the nearby villages during the middle of the day when the congestion sets in. Bideford, incidentally, is 11 miles away.

Be forewarned: It's not easy to get a room in Clovelly. Advance reservations, with a deposit, are imperative during the peak summer months, although you can telephone in advance and *possibly* get a bed.

WHERE TO STAY: The New Inn (tel. Clovelly 303), about halfway down the High Street, possesses the principal village pub, a good meeting place at sundown. It offers some of the best lodgings in the village. The B&B price ranges from £10 ($17.50) per person, inclusive. If you're not stopping over, then this little country inn is recommended for meals. A wide choice of moderately priced à la carte meals is offered in the oak-beamed dining room. The local fare, including genuine Devonshire cream, is featured whenever possible. Locally caught lobsters are prepared by a skilled chef exactly as you want them. The hotel is open most of the year. Motorists can park in the car park at the top of the street. It is advisable to pack an overnight case, as the luggage has to be carried down (but is returned to the top by donkey).

Red Lion, The Pier (tel. Clovelly 237), may well occupy the jewel position of the village, at the bottom of the steep cobbled street, right on the stone seawall of the little harbor. Rising three stories, with gables and a courtyard, it is actually an unspoiled country inn, where life centers around an antique pub, and village inhabitants, including sea captains, gather to satisfy their thirsts over pints of ale. Most of the bedrooms look directly onto the sea, and all of them contain hot and cold running water and adequate furnishings. The cost is £9.50 ($16.63) per person nightly, including breakfast. Other meals are available in the sea-view dining room. Lunches always include a roast joint, a homemade steak-and-kidney pie, or a cold meat and salad. Prices range from £1 ($1.75) for a sandwich and tea, going up to £6 ($10.50) for a crab salad. Dinner goes for £7 ($12.25) with a choice of four main dishes, two of which are always fresh local fish, then a choice from the dessert trolley. The manager can arrange for boating in the bay, and suggests that the Red Lion is not suitable for children under 7 years of age.

Bed and Breakfast in Higher Clovelly

Overflow lodgings in summer are available in the tiny hamlet of Higher Clovelly, lying above the main village. Although Higher Clovelly has none of the charm of Clovelly, you don't have to face the problem of carting luggage down that steep cobblestone street. To get you started on your search for a room here, I'd recommend—

Mrs. Kelly, Jonquil House, Burscott Road, Higher Clovelly (tel. Clovelly 346), has been taking in guests since 1945. Her mother did the same before her, so there's plenty of experience in running this spotless home. Guests are welcomed with or without children at a rate of £6 ($10.50) per person. This includes a warm room, a comfortable bed, and a large breakfast. If lethargy sets in, you can relax in the small sunny garden.

READERS' GUEST HOUSE SELECTIONS: "In a total of two weeks of traveling seven countries of Europe with two kids, the most perfect lodging that we remember was B&B at **Mid-Way House,** 84 High St. (tel. Clovelly 382), operated by Vic and Dot Smith. We felt like we were special guests in a private home of rare charm, antiques, and artifacts. Clovelly boasts that it is the safest city in the world for traffic, as only donkeys and people on foot can ascend and descend its only street, which goes 47 stories up from a sea-level quay. Its location on the street gives the Smiths' house its name, and longtime residents are in top physical shape as getting around is hard, either uphill or down. Rooms are handsomely decorated. How romantic to awaken to seagulls, an ocean view, and rooftops, and Dot Smith bearing a tray of tea for each room! Vic Smith directs guests to sensational hikes and beaches, will pack a great lunch, and one evening he served 'cut rounds with Devon clotted cream,' a local specialty. The rate is a bargain at £8 ($14), as breakfast included the usuals plus half a broiled tomato and mushroom caps, as well as poached (not fried) eggs" (David Gibson Butterworth, D.D.S., Evanston, Ill.). . . . "Our best breakfast, tasty and varied, with fried eggs, bacon, sausage, tomato, and mushrooms, plus juice and toast as well as a 'fried in bacon and beef drippings' piece of toast, was at the lowest-priced guest house we found. The **Old Smithy**, Slerra, Higher Clovelly (tel. Clovelly 202), is run by Mrs. Vanstone, who charges £6.25 ($10.94) per person. An evening meal can be provided if requested. It's well worth stopping there when you're driving into Clovelly on the B3237" (Michael and Arlien Wesa, Thunder Bay, Ont., Canada).

10. Combe Martin and Lynton-Lynmouth

COMBE MARTIN: One of the best bases for excursions into Exmoor, Combe Martin is a lovely village, lying in a valley or combe. Cliffs, ideal for rambles, soar on both sides. After you've traversed its High Street, you've about seen the village. Its old church is built in the Early English and Perpendicular styles. The English like to sunbathe and swim nearby in the sheltered little coves, with their pebblestone beaches. Combe Martin lies six miles from Ilfracombe.

Staying over? I suggest the following accommodations:

Where to Stay

Saffron House, King Street (tel. Combe Martin 3521), is an old farmhouse successfully adapted into a popular small, licensed, family hotel offering all-year accommodation with the benefit of full central heating for those early and late holidays. The hotel, which is set back from the road, is just a short walk away from the beach and harbor, and commands extensive views of the village and surrounding countryside, as well as the famous "Hangman Hill." The owners, Mr. and Mrs. Chantler, are sincerely interested in your comfort, being well traveled themselves, and from the moment of your friendly reception you know that you are going to have an enjoyable stay. The guest rooms vary in size and are clean and comfortable. You will find two lounges, a private heated swimming pool, a garden, and a sun terrace, as well as laundry and drying facilities. B&B rates are about £8 ($14) per adult, including VAT, with reductions for children. The Chantlers will point out the areas of interest and, if not too busy, will accompany you on a walk through the cliff paths.

The **London Inn** (tel. Combe Martin 3409) is a roadside inn at the upper part of the village road, standing fresh and prim. The owner, Mrs. Denham, charges £9.50 ($16.63), plus VAT, per person for B&B, based on double occupancy. The lounge tavern, heavy beams and all, is the meeting place for the nearby villagers, as well as residents. All are warmed by old features—four settles, a stone fireplace with logs on a raised hearth, a copper hood, and shelves of pewter and copper steins and mugs. The living room is comfortably furnished, as are the pleasantly decorated bedrooms. The emphasis is on comfort, good food, and cleanliness. On the rear lawn, you can sit quietly, listening to the movement of the nearby trout stream at the bottom of the garden, later enjoying music and dancing in the bar.

Twelve miles to the east is still another good base for exploring Exmoor—

LYNTON-LYNMOUTH: The north coast of Devon is set off most dramatically in Lynton, a village some 500 feet high. It is a good center for exploring the Doone Valley and that part of Exmoor that spills into the shire from neighboring Somerset. The Valley of Rocks, west of Lynton, offers the most spectacular scenery.

The town is joined by a cliff railway to its sister, Lynmouth, about 500 feet lower. The East Lyn and West Lyn Rivers meet in Lynmouth, a popular resort with the British. For a panoramic view of the rugged coastline, you can walk on a path halfway between the towns that runs along the cliff. From Lynton, or rather from Hollerday Hill, you can look out onto Lynmouth Bay, Countisbury Foreland, and Woody Bays in the west. This area offers the same kind of scenic excitement that Big Sur does in California.

Where to Stay

Countisbury Lodge, at Lynmouth (tel. Lynton 2388), is a former vicarage overlooking Lynmouth and the West Lyn River. The hosts, Peter and Kathy Hope, are enthusiastic innkeepers, providing for one's comfort. Their basic tariff is £10 ($17.50) per person for bed and a full English breakfast. Dinner is £5 ($8.75), these prices including VAT. The lodge offers eight double rooms, some with twin beds, some with matrimonial beds. A few rooms contain private baths. The lodge has a unique bar which was built into the rock face of Countisbury Hill.

Sandrock, Longmead (tel. Lynton 3307), is a substantial, three-story house on the edge of Lynton, one of the best economy oases in North Devon. The house is on the lower part of a hill beside the road, with most of its bedrooms opening onto views. You can see the beginning peaks of the Valley of Rocks. Fortunately, it's a hotel with many windows, and the rooms are sunny and bright. The bedrooms, generally quite large, are interestingly shaped; the third floor has dormer windows, which make the rooms even cozier. Each accommodation has its own water basin; the beds have innerspring mattresses, and there are plenty of spanking-clean bathrooms in which you can soak after those long walks. The high-season rate for your B&B and evening dinner ranges from £15 ($26.25) to £16 ($28) per person, depending on the plumbing. The owners, Mr. and Mrs. Harrison, manage everything at the Sandrock, and they do it well, taking a personal interest in the welfare of their guests. Their baked goods are a delight, especially the deep-dish apple and rhubarb pie, which are tasty, tart, and sweet at the same time. In the Anglers' Bar, foreign visitors meet the Lynton locals after dinner.

The **Rising Sun Hotel** (tel. Lynton 3223) is perhaps one of the most colorful thatched inns in England, especially as it's right at the end of the quay at the mouth of the Lyn River. Not only is the harbor life spread before you, but you can bask in the wonder and warmth of an inn in business for more than 600 years. In bedroom after bedroom, with crazy levels and sloping ceilings, you'll have views of the water, the changing tides, and bobbing boats. Mr. Wade and Mr. Jeune, the owners, have skillfully worked matters out between Lynmouth regulars and voyagers from faraway lands. They charge £11 ($19.25) to £15 ($26.25), plus service and VAT, per person nightly for B&B, with rooms facing the sea going at the higher rate. Guests willing to stop in Lynmouth for a week pay £92 ($161) for half board. The inn is open all year. Even if you're not staying over, you may want to sample the English cuisine: dinners are from £6.50 ($11.38). It's a delight dining at the Rising Sun, as everything is 101% British in the dining room, with its deeply set window and fireplace. See the original 14th-century fireplace in the bar.

Bonnicott Hotel, Watersmeet Road in Lynmouth (tel. Lynton 3346), was built 150 years ago as a rectory. Pam Holford and George Rainbow run it as a private hotel, and they are most helpful. Each of their nine bedrooms is distinctive and attractively decorated, with views over Lynmouth Bay or the Lyn Valley. On cooler days a log fire burns in the lounge and bar. Pam is an excellent cook, which means you'll want to ask for the half-board terms which range from £15 ($26.25) to £16 ($28) per person nightly. If given notice, Pam will gladly prepare special diets and vegetarian dishes. At Christmas, Pam and George invite you to a house party.

Where to Dine (Lynmouth)

Ye Olde Cottage (Spinning Wheel Restaurant) (tel. Lynton 3297) is a miniature quayside inn, centered in this tiny resort with an unspoiled view of the harbor. Here, under pleasant and homey circumstances, you can get teas and meals. For five generations, the Wakeham family has been operating the inn. It's a favored spot for a Devonshire cream tea, costing £1.25 ($2.19), with all the trimmings. At lunch you can order a three-course meal for £3.50 ($6.13), based on such traditional English "fayre" as roast beef or West Country chicken and homemade pies and tarts. From the à la carte menu you can select from such choice delights as rainbow trout, £4 ($7); Lyn salmon, £5 ($8.75); and a full range of prime steaks, from £5 also. Chef Peter Wakeham has introduced a line of dishes cooked in wine and cider, his own recipes, at prices that begin at £3.75 ($6.56).

READERS' HOTEL SELECTIONS: "**Longmead House,** 9 Longmead, Lynton (tel. Lynton 2523), is owned by Pat and Reg Silcock. The house is at the end of Lynton at the mouth of the Valley of Rocks. It is a small private hotel of some ten double bedrooms, with car parking. It has a pleasant and happy atmosphere; beautiful furnishings; clean, spacious bedrooms with sinks; plenty of hot and cold water all the time; towels, soap, and heat if needed; a snug bar and a lounge with color TV. You can enjoy a very good English breakfast with coffee in the dining room. B&B costs £8 ($14), with a four-course evening meal going for £5 ($8.75). Mr. and Mrs. Silcock make you feel wanted" (Irene and Ed Duguay, Amesbury, Mass.). . . . "The **Croft Guest House,** Lydiate Lane, Lynton (tel. Lynton 2391), is far and away the 'best buy' in all of England. For £11 ($19.25) per night per person, you can have a spacious bedroom, mammoth breakfasts, and four-course dinners. Mrs. J. Moisey and Mrs. B. Mander are the most hospitable hostesses we've encountered in five visits to Europe" (Marlene and Bill Klett, St. Joseph, Minn.).

After Devon, sunny Cornwall beckons.

CORNWALL

The ancient Duchy of Cornwall is the extreme southwestern part of England—often called the toe. But Cornwall is one toe that's always wanted to dance away from the foot. Although a peninsula, it is a virtual island, if not geographically, then spiritually. Encircled by coastline, it abounds with rugged cliffs, hidden bays with fishing villages, sandy beaches, sheltered coves, and secluded creeks where the age-old art of smuggling was once practiced with consummate skill. Many of the hillside-clinging cottages in some of the little seaports are reminiscent of towns along the Mediterranean, although Cornwall retains its own distinctive flavor.

The true Cornish people are generally darker and shorter than the denizens with whom they share the country. These characteristics reflect their Celtic origin, which still lives on in superstition, folklore, and fairy tales. King Arthur, of course, is the most vital legend of all. When Cornish men speak of King Arthur and his Knights of the Round Table, they're not just handing out a line for the tourist. To them, Arthur and his knights really existed, romping around Tintagel Castle, now in ruins—Norman ruins, that is—lying 300 feet above the sea, 19 miles from Bude.

This ancient land had its own language up until about 250 years ago. And some of the old words ("pol" for pool, "tre" for house) still survive. As you move into the backwoods, you'll encounter a dialect more easily understood by the Welsh than by those who speak the queen's English.

The Cornish men, like the Welsh, are great miners (tin and copper), and they're fond of the tall tale. Sometimes it's difficult to tell when they're serious. One resident, for example, told me that he and his wife had been out walking in the woods near twilight but had lost their way. He claimed that the former owner of the estate (in Victoria's day) appeared suddenly in a dog-carriage and guided them back to where they'd taken the wrong turn. If this really happened I wouldn't be surprised, at least not in Cornwall.

Traditionally, the typical oldtimer in Cornwall is a man involved in a vendetta. I heard of one rich and wicked moneylender in Victorian times who wanted to live in total seclusion, but was frustrated in this ambition by two spinster sisters who kept a neighboring farm. So he bought a public chiming clock from Looe, placed it in the tower over the house, and set the quarter-only chimes going only at night—until he finally drove the good ladies out. The Cornish, they are a colorful lot.

The English come here for their holidays in the sun. I suggest anchoring in at one of the smaller fishing villages, such as East and West Looe, Polperro, Mousehole, or Portloe, where you'll experience firsthand the charm of the duchy. Many of the villages, such as St. Ives, are artists' colonies. In some of the pubs and restaurants frequented by painters, a wonderful camaraderie prevails, especially in the nontourist months. Recently, for instance, at one of the artists' hangouts, three young men who had finished dining brought out their guitars and spontaneously launched into folk songs for the rest of the evening. Detecting the accent of some visiting Americans, they sang (with appallingly perfect accents) several country music favorites, although it was their repertoire from Ireland and Wales that cast the greater spell. Living here with these artists is like going back 30 years, experiencing dependence upon yourself and your associates for entertainment. By all means, cross over the Tamar from Devon and see what Cornwall is up to.

Except for St. Ives and Port Isaac, most of my recommendations lie on the southern coast, the so-called Cornish Riviera, which strikes many foreign visitors as being the most intriguing. However, the North Coast is not without its own peculiar charm.

POLDARK MINE: **Wendron** (tel. Helston 3173) stands three miles north of Helston on the B3297. As you have driven around Cornwall, the old workings of the tin mines will have been evident everywhere. Here you have the chance to visit a mine and walk through the old works which extend for several miles beneath the surface. They have discovered yet another cavern, and the tour of the mine will soon take longer than the present three-quarters of an hour. Above ground is a museum of mining artifacts, mining equipment, steam engines, drills, and a history of mining. There is a souvenir shop and another selling good-quality local products, a snackbar, and a children's play area if they don't want to see the exhibits. Admission is £1.80 ($3.15) for adults, 90p ($1.58) for children. The mines are open seven days a week from 10 a.m. to 6 p.m.

TALL TREES RIDING CENTRE: At Davidstow, near Camelford (tel. Otterham Station 249), Mrs. Margaret Harrison, with her two daughters and various other assistants and working pupils, runs stables of 23 horses and ponies. They offer weekly courses when days are spent on long rides over majestic Bodmin Moor, through forests, and along bridle paths and country lanes. Accommodation, including breakfast and supper, is £55 ($96.25) per week for adults, plus VAT. If you can't spare the time for a week, a day's riding, including lunch, is £12 ($21) or £4 ($7) per hour.

WALKING TREKS: **Backpack Man,** 11 Church St., Moulton, Northampton (tel. 0604/48559), is a small organization of dedicated enthusiasts who plan walking treks in the West Country for those who like their adventure accompanied by comfort and good food. During the trek, all baggage is carried by a support vehicle, and overnights are spent where the food and comfort are the best available. Their most strenuous walk is the South West Way, which runs for 572 miles from Minehead in Somerset to Bournemouth in Dorset, but the walks are usually of a shorter distance. The Poldark Trek covers 100 miles from St. Ives to St. Mawes. Walkers are met and returned to London's Heathrow Airport. Lunchtime stops are usually in village pubs, and overnight stopovers can be in another comfortable pub hotel or in a first-class clifftop hotel. Visits are paid at Geevor tin mine, St. Michael's Mount, and local industries. You'll also hear concerts by male choirs. Ken Ward is the trek leader, the president of the British Backpackers Club, an ex-parachutist and expedition leader in the Everest foothills and Swedish Lapland.

11. Looe

After your visit to Plymouth about 15 miles away, you can either take the Tamar Suspension Bridge to Cornwall, or cross by ferry from Plymouth. You'll soon arrive in the ancient twin towns of East and West Looe, connected by a seven-arched, stone bridge which spans the river. In the jaws of shrub-dotted cliffs, the fishing villages present a stark contrast to Plymouth. Houses scale the hills, stacked one on top of the other in terrace fashion.

In both fishing villages you can find good accommodations and meet interesting people. Fishing and sailing are two of the major sports, and the sandy coves, as well as East Looe Beach, make choice spots for sea bathing, as uniquely practiced by the British. Beyond the towns are cliff paths and downs worth a ramble.

In these villages are several levels of life, the most traditional of which is that followed by the Cornish villagers, many of whom are fishermen (go down to the harbor and watch the pilchard boats come in). Then there is a sophisticated group whose members enjoy the unspoiled atmosphere. A large transient group, representative of no special class, trips down for a week or so, mostly in the summer months. But all year you can watch the artists and craftspeople who live and work here.

Looe is noted for its shark-angling, but you may prefer simply walking the narrow, crooked medieval streets of East Looe, with its colorful harbor and 17th-century Guildhall.

FOOD AND LODGING: Space and prices are at a premium in July and August.

New Barbican Farm, Barbican Road (tel. 05036/2773), overlooks the sea and the river. It is only open to guests from April to the end of September. There is a large garden where you can sit and enjoy the view. In the dining room, Mrs. Lawson Toms provides excellent breakfasts and evening meals, using as much local and home-grown produce as she can find. The charge for dinner, bed, and breakfast is £9.50 ($16.63) per person.

Lodging on the Outskirts

Shutta, Stoke Climsland, near Callington (tel. Stoke Climsland 70389), is a B&B place par excellence. Peter and Joan Davis welcome guests to their lovely 16th-century home where breakfast is served in the ancient beamed cider house of the old structure. They have only two rooms, one with two beds, the other with a large double bed. Both have private bath and TV. They charge £9.50 ($16.63) per person for bed and a massive breakfast. To get there, drive on the A388 from Callington toward Bodmin Moor and bear right at the Swingle Tree toward Stoke Climsland. Shutta is on the right.

Lyndhurst, 17 Beech Terrace, West Looe (tel. Looe 4305), is a private family house lying on the main Polperro road out of Looe, about a ten-minute walk from beaches and a five-minute walk from the principal shopping center of East Looe. Accommodations include a double room, a large family room, and one extra single room. All the comfortably furnished units contain hot and cold running water. The tariff is £7 ($12.25) per adult or £5 ($8.75) per child. There is a guest lounge with a dining room where you can order an optional evening meal at £3.75 ($6.56). It's served early: at 5:45 p.m. Families are welcome, and a babysitting service is available on request. Free parking is available at the rear of the premises.

Northeast of Looe, in the village of Widegates, **Rosellen Guest House** (tel. Widegates 403) is run by a dental surgeon and his wife, Bob and Sue Treggiden. Their rooms are nice and fresh and pleasantly decorated, renting from £6 ($10.50) in a single and £7 ($12.25) per person for a family room with toilet, shower, and wash basin. Their food is well prepared, and you'll surely want to return from the bustle of the Looes and Polperro to enjoy a candlelight dinner for £5.50 ($9.63). You might, for example, order a homemade soup, followed by boeuf bourguignon, plus a variety of desserts.

READERS' HOTEL SELECTIONS: "On a recent trip our best find was the **Turtle's Rest Hotel,** Market Square, East Looe (tel. Looe 2821). For £9 ($15.75) per person in a double, including VAT and service charge, Alan and Audrey Robson provide you with an immaculate, comfortable room, a lounge with bar and TV, a tasty breakfast, and a warm welcome. For £5 ($8.75) and with a couple of hours' notice, Alan will cook you dinner, the nicest we had in England. The small hotel has seven well-appointed bedrooms with hot and cold running water. There is a cozy bar/lounge for guests. The Robsons are helpful, friendly people who made us feel more like houseguests than paying customers" (Mrs. A. R. Dick, Thornhill, Ont., Canada).

"The highlight of our trip to England was discovering the friendliness of **Coombe Farm,** just southwest of the village of Widegates off the south side of the B3253 to Looe (tel. Widegates 223). The house is English country style overlooking ten acres of beautiful, unspoiled meadows and wooded land. The dining room, lounge, and all eight guest rooms have a spectacular view of the garden, rolling hills, and the sea sculpted in the distance. The charge is £9.50 ($16.63) per person, plus VAT, and all rooms are beautifully color coordinated, sparkling clean, and furnished with antiques and paintings belonging to the family of Alexander and Sally Low, the gracious hosts, who retired from London to open this guest house. Alex is a world-renowned freelance photographer as well as an author and producer who traveled around the world on assignments in more than 75 countries. Sally, also an artist, prepares the best breakfast and home-cooked meals we had in England. The dinner menu is excellent, priced at around £7 ($12.25). A whole plaice fried in butter with peas and creamed potatoes was sensational. Our dinners were served in front of a cheery fire. After dinner, we retired for coffee to another crackling fire in the lounge. There is a fine selection of liquors and wines to complement dinner. On a scale of 1 to 10, the Lows' Coombe Farm rates a 10" (Ray L. Benedicktus, Los Angeles, Calif.). . . . "The **Allhays Guest House,** Talland Bay near Looe (tel. Polperro 72434), has all the best features of an English country manor: spaciousness, beautiful English furniture, lawns, views, cozy living and dining rooms with real fireplaces and real fires, plus central heating and electric blankets for winter visitors. The estate is hidden away in rolling green hills dotted with grazing sheep and cows and has the sea at its feet. We woke up every morning to some of the loveliest scenery in England and had breakfast, tea, and dinner by roaring fireplaces. Edna and Bill Payne, the hosts, made us feel very special and at home. Edna is a talented cook, and Bill looked after our every need. Room, a full English breakfast, and dinner cost £13.50 ($23.63) per person. Allhays is a real find in English hospitality and accommodations" (Luigi and Bianca Miller, New York, N.Y.).

If you wish, you can strike out from Looe on the cliff walk—a distance of 4½ miles—to Polperro. The less adventurous will drive.

12. Polperro

This ancient fishing village is reached by a steep descent from the top of a hill. Motorists in summer are forbidden to take their cars down unless they are booked in a hotel. Why? Because otherwise they'd create too much of a traffic bottleneck in July and August. The British have long known of the particular charm of this unspoiled Cornish village.

At one time it was estimated that nearly every man, woman, and child in the village spent time salting down pilchards for the winter, or else was engaged in the art of smuggling. Today, tourists have replaced the contraband.

You'd have to search every cove and bay in Cornwall to come up with a village as handsomely mellowed as Polperro, which looks almost as if it had been removed intact from the 17th-century. The village is tucked in between some cliffs. Its houses—really no more than fishermen's cottages—are bathed in pastel-wash. A small river, actually a stream called the Pol, splits its way through Polperro. The heart of the village is its much-photographed, much-painted fishing harbor, where the pilchard boats, loaded to the gunnels, used to dock.

ACCOMMODATIONS: In and around Polperro, you'll find a number of quite good and colorful cottages and houses that receive paying guests.

Noughts and Crosses Hotel (tel. Polperro 72239). One side of this 16th-century pub-hotel faces a narrow street, and the other the five-foot-wide River Pol which goes through the center of the village. The Noughts and Crosses charges £8.50 ($14.88) nightly for B&B. Only doubles are available. Children are not accepted, and bookings in season must be for at least three nights. Its name came from the bookkeeping habits of a baker, its one-time owner. The education of bakers being what it was in those days, she was forced to make a small "o" whenever she sold a small loaf of bread and a large "O" when she sold a large loaf. When the loaves were paid for, she would check them off with an "X." The hotel has windows opening on the Pol. The bedrooms are pleasingly furnished, with hot and cold running water and beds with innerspring mattresses. Basket meals, snacks, real ale, and chilled beer are served in the two well-equipped bars. Steak and chips costs £5 ($8.75), although scampi and chips goes for £3.75 ($6.56). There is a dining room upstairs where residents have breakfast and can take their basket meals to eat in peace.

Landaviddy Manor (tel. Polperro 72210) is a 200-year-old manor house, built of gray Cornish stone, on a secluded ledge on a hill above the village on the west side of Polperro. The manor stands in a peaceful and attractive setting, commanding a view of Polperro Bay and the coast. It adjoins National Trust land, giving access to cliff paths and coves along the coast. The Cornish moors and Dartmoor are easily accessible, as are numerous beaches nearby. Landaviddy retains its old character, yet all its bedrooms have hot and cold running water and innerspring mattresses. Some have private facilities. There is central heating as well, plus a comfortable lounge with TV, a cozy bar, and a licensed dining room.

The owners, Bert and Irmgard Lester, give personal service, and run the place in a friendly and informal way. They charge from £10.50 ($18.38) in a single, from £19 ($33.25) in a double, including an English breakfast. For one-nighters a surcharge of 10% is made. Dinner of four courses and coffee is £7 ($12.25) per person. All prices include VAT.

WHERE TO EAT: The **Captain's Cabin,** Lansallos Street (tel. Polperro 72292), a big-splurge restaurant, is owned by the Moore family, who are pleased when Americans come by. While they don't have bedrooms for overnight guests, they have been known to give travelers tips about where to find a room. You'll surely want to dine with the Moores, among the antique furniture in their low-beamed dining room. The cuisine is very comprehensive, and they enjoy a fine reputation for their fish dishes, from among which you may order crab mornay, trout à la Bretonne, grilled sole, plus many other choices. An à la carte dinner, excluding wine, will cost about £13 ($22.75) per person, or else you can select the table d'hôte at £10 ($17.50). The Moores also have individually cooked dishes and salads for lunch along with snacks.

Nelsons (tel. Polperro 72366) is owned and run by the Nelson family, not only Peter and Betty but Tony as well. Peter and Tony do the cooking, and Betty takes care of everything up front. They always have at least three soups—fish, crab, lobster, vegetable, meat. Each pot is homemade and priced from 90p ($1.58) to £1.20 ($2.10) with bread. Before your main course rests on your plate, it was probably swimming. However, you can also order home-cooked ham or beef, served with vegetable and a salad. Prices of main courses range from £1.75 ($3.06) to £3.95 ($6.91). For dessert, you can settle for a simple ice cream at 60p ($1.05), or else something more elaborate, crêpes suzette at £2.40 ($4.20). The place is likely to be very crowded on Saturday and Sunday.

Crump's (tel. Polperro 72312). It used to be hard to find an inexpensive place to eat in Polperro until this family-owned and -run bistro and wine bar opened. Mr. and Mrs. Costello selected a farmhouse with heavy beams which is well on its way to three centuries of life. This pleasant little place always gives you a warm welcome. Most visitors seem to pass through here for lunch, enjoying fairly light fare such as quiches and good-tasting, crisp salads. You can also get a pizza. Expect to escape for around £3 ($5.25). If you're lucky enough to get to spend at least one night of your life in Polperro, you can partake of more substantial fare, ordering from a set menu. Count on spending at least £5 ($8.75) for a filling repast. It's well worth a visit anytime from Monday through Sunday—11 a.m. to 6 p.m. and 7:30 to last orders at 9:30 p.m.

THE VILLAGE PUB: The **Three Pilchards,** near the harbor, is where the locals and sophisticates alike go for their evening pints of beer and social activity. It's a large L-shaped room with a fireplace that burns brightly at night. Black oak is used almost everywhere. Why don't you sit in the windowseat and listen to the talk of the villagers? That isn't really as rude as it sounds, as you may not be able to understand a word of their thick Cornish dialect. You may like the absence of quaint bits of decor in this honest, unvarnished pub, the center of life in Polperro.

13. Fowey, Truro, and Portloe

FOWEY: Called the Dartmouth of Cornwall, Fowey is an old town of historical interest, one of the most ancient seaports in the West Country. Once the Fowey Gallants sailed the seas and were considered invincible when raiding French coastal towns. At the time of the Armada, Fowey sent more ships than London. With its narrow streets and whitewashed houses, the town has remained unspoiled over the years, enjoying a sheltered position on a deep-water channel. Its creeks and estuary attract sailors and fishermen. If you climb to St. Catherine's Point, you'll be rewarded with a view of the harbor. There are sandy beaches and coves to explore here, as well as an 18-hole golf course within easy reach of Carlyon Bay.

Food and Lodging

The **King of Prussia,** Town Quay (tel. Fowey 2450), is a modest hotel with royal pretensions, right in the heart of the village, opening onto a boat landing. It's named after a former local character who made himself a king. Aside from having a rather formal appearance and a central exterior staircase, it is quite informal. It is the best low-priced hotel in Fowey. The charge is £9.50 ($16.63) per person for B&B. Each room has hot and cold running water and TV. Everything is well kept. In a bar overlooking the river a variety of snacks are available at lunchtime, and you can also order Cornish ale "from the wood" (that is, from traditional wooden barrels).

Riverside, Passage Street (tel. Fowey 2275), is the all-purpose ferry-landing hotel of Fowey, all under the watchful eye of Mr. Featherstone the owner. Directly on the water as well as the main street at Fowey, the hotel is at the little car-ferry station where regular crossings leave for Bodinnick. The establishment has an individualistic decor. Most have views of the river, and from your window you can observe the passing river craft and ferries. All 14 of the hotel's bedrooms have hot and cold running water, but only six are equipped with private baths or showers. Rates are based on the time of the year, the plumbing, and the view. Bed and a full English breakfast costs from £15 ($26.25) to £20 ($35) per person daily. For stays of more than two nights, a half-board rate of £23 ($40.25) to £28 ($49) per person nightly will be quoted. The chef specializes in hot and cold salmon and lobster dishes; the produce caught locally is fresh and tasty.

TRURO: This ancient town on the Truro River is the only cathedral city in Cornwall. As such, it is the ecclesiastical center of Cornwall. The Cathedral Church of St. Mary was begun in 1880 in the Early English style (the spires are in the Norman Gothic design). The town is within 8 to 20 miles of the Cornish beaches. It can be used as a base to explore the countryside, ranging from bleak Bodmin Moor to fertile farmland and the Winter Roseland of the Falmouth Estuary.

My accommodations choice here is:

Pencowl, 12 Ferris Town (tel. Truro 74946), rents rooms on a self-catering basis. Single, double, and twin-bedded rooms are available, each supplied with color TV, electric kettle and toaster, refrigerator, table, and chairs. Also available are three kitchens for guests who want to cook their own food. The owners also rent out a twin-bedded apartment with its own kitchen. The rate is £8 ($14) per person nightly. For this, guests get their rooms cleaned and their beds made every day except Sunday.

READER'S RESTAURANT SUGGESTION: "We found a marvelous restaurant, **The Bear Essential,** 19 Bridge St., just behind the cathedral. The menu was innovative and exciting, including a nice array of fish, lamb, veal, and beef. It was handwritten and changed regularly. Everything was individually prepared and served piping hot. We had a superb seafood au gratin appetizer, lamb chops beautifully cooked with a pâté and onion sauce, potatoes, carrots, a local zucchini-type vegetable which was perfectly done and crisp but tender, a bottle of wine, and the pièce de résistance, the dessert. My husband had something called a cherry brandy chocolate slice. I had warm apple pie with cream—a quarter of a pie. The cost, with coffee and service, was about £18 ($31.50) for the two of us. This is a splurge, but entrees, including vegetables and potatoes, began at £3.50 ($6.13), so the tab could be less" (Judith Bell, Ann Arbor, Mich.).

PORTLOE: If you really want to get away from it all and go to that hidden-away Cornish fishing village, then Portloe may be for you. On the slope of a hill opening onto Veryan Bay, it is reached by a road suitable for cars.

Portloe might be an ideal stopover on the South Cornish coast if you're traveling to the West Country in July and August, which are the months when the popular tourist centers, such as Looe and St. Ives, are overrun with sightseers. Here, in Portloe, the living's more relaxed.

The **Lugger Hotel,** Portloe, near Truro (tel. 0872/501322), was built originally in the 17th century, but has been carefully modernized since to provide some of the comforts expected in modern life. On the water's edge in this delightful cove, the Lugger is owned and run by Steve Powell and his family, who believe in making you feel welcome in their old smugglers' inn. There are 21 rooms, all with bath or shower, radio, room call, and tea- or coffee-making facilities. Some of the accommodations in the main building are traditionally furnished, while others in the annex are decorated in a more modern idiom. There is a cozy sitting room as an escape from the bar where life ebbs and flows through the french doors onto the terrace in summer. Meals include ingredients such as fish, shellfish, vegetables, and meat from the local stock. The daily rate includes dinner chosen from a four-course menu, a full breakfast, early-morning tea, and afternoon tea with crackers. The low-season tariff is £23 ($40.25) per person, rising to £27 ($47.25) from May to September, but there are reductions for stays of five days or more. At lunch sandwiches and salads, hot potatoes with cheese or butter, or baked ham are served in the bar, along with soups and terrines. Fruit pies and ice cream complete your meal.

14. St. Mawes

Overlooking the mouth of the Fal River, St. Mawes is often compared to a port on the Riviera. Because it's sheltered from the northern winds, subtropical plants are found here. From the town quay, you can take a boat to Frenchman's Creek, Helford River, and other places. Mostly, St. Mawes is noted for its sailing, boating, fishing, and yachting. Half a dozen sandy coves lie within 15 minutes by car from the port. The town, built on the Roseland Peninsula, makes for interesting walks, with its color-washed cottages and sheltered harbor. On Castle Point, Henry VIII ordered the construction of St. Mawes Castle. Falmouth, across the water, is only two miles away.

FOOD AND LODGING SPLURGES: **The Rising Sun** (tel. St. Mawes 270233) is a colorful inn on the seafront—made of a row of white fishermen's cottages, with a slate roof, and a flagstone terrace out front. Inside, every square inch oozes with tasteful charm. The locals gather in the pub, with its Windsor chairs grouped around the fireplace. The dining room has lush gold walls with paintings by Michael Oelman in the form of two poems, Kubla Khan and Jacob's Ladder. English gentility reigns here. The proprietor, Mrs. Campbell Marshall, sets the gracious pace, and is known for her cuisine. If you're just dropping in for lunch, you can order hot or cold bar food. A three-course à la carte dinner costs £10 ($17.50) to £12 ($21), plus service. Without a private bath, the B&B rate begins at £21 ($36.75), increasing to £24 ($42) with a bath.

Braganza, Grove Hill (opposite the Catholic church); (tel. St. Mawes 270281), is a Regency house, furnished with antiques and furniture of the period. It offers three twin-bedded rooms, two with private baths. All are centrally heated. Visitors gather in the lounge to watch television. The staircase is a perfect Regency one. The charge ranges from £10 ($17.50) to £11 ($19.25) per person per night. These tariffs include VAT and an English breakfast. The house has an extensive garden overlooking the harbor of St. Mawes where yacht racing takes place twice a week in the summer. Lord Byron, who stayed in Falmouth in 1809, may have visited this house, for he mentions its name in one of his poems. It's said that his limping step can be heard at the Braganza on windy nights.

The **Idle Rocks,** St. Mawes (tel. St. Mawes 270771), is a solid old building right on the sea wall, with gaily colored umbrellas and tables lining the terrace. Water laps at the wall, and the site opens onto views over the river and the constant traffic of sailing boats and dinghies. The bar serves tasty lunchtime snacks, including fresh seafood caught locally. The bedrooms mostly have sea or river views, and they're equipped with central heating, tea- or coffee-making facilities, radio, and intercom. All of them contain private baths or showers, renting for £22 ($38.50) per person in winter, that tariff rising to £24 ($42) from June to September, including dinner, a full breakfast, and morning and afternoon tea. Considerable reductions are granted for stays of five days or more.

15. Falmouth

A lot of cutthroat smugglers used to live in the area. In fact, when John Killigrew, a leading citizen, started to build a lighthouse on Lizard Head, they protested that the beacon in the night would deprive them of their livelihood and "take awaye God's Grace from us." Falmouth, 26 miles from Penzance, is today a favorite base for the yachting set, which considers it one of the most beautiful harbors in Europe. On a small peninsula, Falmouth's old section overlooks the land-locked inner harbor. The newer part, center for most of the hotels, faces the bay and commands a panoramic sweep from St. Anthony's Lighthouse to Pendennis Castle. Warmed in winter by the Gulf Stream, Falmouth has become an all-year resort. Built on a promontory overlooking the fjord-like estuary of the Fal, it was once occupied in part by the captains of old mail-carrying packet ships. Many find it a good center for touring the rugged Cornish coastline. It's possible, for example, to take a ferry from Falmouth to St. Mawes, a 20-minute ride.

Pendennis Castle, now the Youth Hostels Association (tel. Falmouth 311435), was once part of Henry VIII's coastal defense system. It dates from 1544 when the central circular keep with semicircular bastions enclosed by a curtain wall was completed on the site of a prehistoric fortress. Since Tudor days it has protected the entrance to Falmouth Harbour. During the Civil War it suffered seige. Henrietta Maria, wife of Charles I, found shelter here as she fled to France. The castle was beseiged in 1646 by Parliamentary forces into surrender, but because of the bravery of the governor, his soldiers and citizens were allowed to march out with drums beating, colors flying, and trumpets sounding.

Nowadays it is a more peaceful place, besieged only by tourists and sightseers. It is host to the Youth Hostels Association, who run a successful hostel in the old barrack block. The standard charge is only £2.60 ($4.55) a night in a dormitory accommodation (sexes separated). Children pay only £2.05 ($3.59), or if under 5, £1.70 ($2.98). That's the tariff for YHA members. If you're not part of the association, you must pay £4.70 ($8.23) for adults and £3.95 ($6.91) for children. You can rent sheets and sleeping bags for 65p ($1.14). A shop on the premises sells bread, eggs, milk, and a variety of canned goods. If you just decide to visit the castle briefly, admission is 50p (88¢) for adults and 25p (44¢) for children.

During most of the year, sightseeing craft ply up and down the River Fal from the Prince of Wales Pier in Falmouth to the Town Quay in Truro. There are also morning and afternoon **cruises** to view the docks and the castle, St. Just, as well as romantic creeks, stately riverside mansions, and smugglers' cottages. The cost is £1.60 ($2.80) for adults and 80p ($1.40) for children. The trip, taking two hours, leaves at 10:30 a.m. and again at 2:30 p.m. There is usually a luncheon cruise at 11:45 a.m., including a stopover at the Heron Inn at your own expense. The cost of this cruise is £1.60 ($2.80) for adults and 80p ($1.40) for children. For further details, contact **Enterprise Boats,** 66 Trefusis Rd., Flushing (tel. Penryn 74241), or else telephone the Prince of Wales Pier, Falmouth (tel. Falmouth 313234) from 9 a.m. to 3 p.m.

During the summer, sailing trips leave **Mylor Yacht Harbour,** just downstream from Falmouth. The 32-foot yacht departs at 10 a.m. for a cruise in the Fal estuary, with views of Pendennis Castle and Falmouth Castle. Coffee and then a light lunch are served, and you return to Mylor about 4 p.m. The price is £12.50 ($21.88) per person, including lunch. Times depend sometimes on tides and weather conditions. For further inquiries, telephone Mevagissy 843480.

WHERE TO STAY: A pair of large, gracious Tudor-style houses (turned hotels) stand side by side in the most attractive residential area of Falmouth. Although attached, they have individual owners and private gardens. Both are eye-catching, with tall black-and-white gables, towering chimneys, and graveled entry drives leading to tailored gardens.

The **Tudor Court,** Melvill Road (tel. Falmouth 312807), has a country-house quality. Mr. and Mrs. Jeff Jefferys run the Court, and Mrs. Jefferys is a Cordon Bleu chef and does all the cooking. Their bedrooms are carpeted and double glazed, with radios, hot and cold running water (some with private baths), and views of the side or rear garden. Most are of conventional size, and large family rooms are also available. The management prefers weekly bookings, but will accept shorter stays. Tudor Court is open all year, and the Jefferyses offer special package rates for golfing holidays and the Christmas period. Higher rates are charged from July to September. The cost of a bed, an English breakfast, and a home-cooked evening meal is £13 ($22.75) per person nightly. Dinner includes a choice of appetizers, a main dish, dessert cheese and biscuits, and coffee. An à la carte menu is also available.

Grove Hotel, 1 Grove Pl. (tel. Falmouth 311417), has a star position, overlooking the harbor. It is, in fact, a modest little hotel, offering sound value for your pound. Yet it's large enough to have a combination bar and guest lounge and a dining room with separate tables (most with a view of the water). The modestly furnished accommodations rent for £10 ($17.50) for B&B, plus £5 ($8.75) for your evening dinner. These are daily terms. The majority of bedrooms now have bath/shower and toilet en suite. There is a games room.

Maenheere Hotel, Grove Place (tel. Falmouth 312009), is a converted, stately 18th-century harborfront house, with Georgian windows and an attractive and popular bar. The furnishings are well chosen, and you get plenty of local atmosphere. It's a good buy, owing to its position. Highest rates are charged from June to August, when B&B costs £9.50 ($16.63) daily, although you can get half board for £12.50 ($21.88) per person daily, plus VAT and service. Launderette service is available.

Harbour Hotel, 1 Harbour Terrace (tel. Falmouth 311344), is a small, family-run establishment, operated by Ron and Carole Corfield. It gives personal service and has a homey atmosphere. The cost of one of the six bedrooms is £10.50 ($18.38) for B&B, including a toilet and shower en suite. The hotel has central heating throughout, and each unit has tea- or coffee-making facilities. The hotel has views overlooking Falmouth Inner Harbour and 4½ miles beyond. There is also a licensed bar.

READERS' GUEST HOUSE SELECTION: "**Lisnaveane House,** 43 Melvill Rd. (tel. Falmouth 311465), is perched on the shoulder of Melvill Road. The proprietor knew we were expected and drove down the hill to meet us at the train stop. This was the first of many kind touches that Mary Wakefield gave to our two-day stay in Falmouth. Mrs. Wakefield offers accommodations in small but clean and modernized rooms for from £9 ($15.75) per person. Her clients are primarily English, but we think others should know of her hospitality. We had an intriguing discussion on private and public education with her and got a primer on the BBC programs as well, not to mention the bountiful breakfasts and wonderful roast beef and Yorkshire pudding dinner she provided. The dinner is optional and costs an extra £4.50 ($7.88), and ours was probably the best British cookery we had" (Diana and Paul Colvin, Lake Oswego, Ore.).

WHERE TO EAT: **Pickwick's Oven,** 47 Arwenack St. (tel. Falmouth 312947), is a cheerful, whitewashed brick building opposite the Customs House and the main quay area of the town. It's owned and run by Geoff Gower, who was once in the photographic business. Perhaps that's the reason for the dark tables and chairs which turn the place into a kind of "negative." Hot, freshly cooked jacket potatoes are the main ingredient of the snack meals. You can order them plain with butter at 50p (88¢) or with a variety of stuffings. Other dishes include crab salad, prawn and coleslaw, or hot chili. Slices of cake and soft drinks are sold, and you rarely need to spend more than £3 ($5.25). The food is to take away or else to eat in the rear downstairs or in the upstairs restaurant.

The **Cornish Kitchen** and **Bistro Chives,** 28 Arwenack St. The kitchen opens at 10 a.m., finally closing at 10:30 p.m. It is a small tea shop backing up to the water. In its confined area, you can order a hot soup and crusty bread or perhaps a big cheesey pizza, certainly fried chicken and "chips." My crab sandwich "bulged," and I could also have ordered the local crab salad. A simple meal will cost £3.50 ($6.13). The cream tea is good at £1 ($1.75), and if you still have room, try the homemade apple pie to fill the cracks. Michael McDonald and his wife Connie also own the Bistro Chives, which is open only in the evening from 6 to 10:30 p.m. Connie cooks excellent dishes, especially lobster bisque and french onion soup. Main dishes include local lemon sole grilled with prawns and chives, to honor the bistro's namesake. Grecian lamb kebabs with curried rice and beef strips are cooked in real ale and served with a fresh salad and crusty brown bread. There are simple desserts as well. A three-course meal with a glass of wine will cost about £5 ($8.75).

A SIDE TRIP TO LIZARD: The most southerly point of England is the Lizard, an unremarkable spot with jagged rocks reaching out into the sea where cormorants and gulls fish.

Right on the point, beneath the lighthouse, is the workshop of a man who must surely be one of the most perfect one-man cottage industries in the country. Mr. Casley runs **Lizard Point Serpentine Works** in one of the small shacks by the car park. There he turns, polishes, and fashions into pots, vases, ashtrays, and dishes the serpentine stone found only in this part of the country. The veins in the stone can be green, gray, or sometimes red. A small vase will cost about £4 ($7), or a larger one £6 ($10.50).

Ornamental barometers and clocks are a lot more, but these are absolutely genuine souvenirs made by a man who is entirely at peace with himself and the country he lives in. The family, his son, and his brother assist with the quarrying of the stone which comes from under Coonhilly Down close by, the site of the country's largest radio receiving and space-tracking station. Mr. Casley's son, another blue-eyed Cornishman, is fast learning the trade so there is every hope that in 50 years there will still be someone whistling happily in the tiny workshop at the tip of Lizard.

Mrs. Snowden, Villa Clare, Lizard Point (tel. 0326/290300), must be the owner of the most southerly bedroom in England. Her home is definitely the most southerly house in the country, built on solid granite with a terraced garden. It opens onto fantastic views over the sea and the cliff edge from the garden fence some 170 feet above sea level. Despite this, the house is frequently showered by spray from the breakers below during storms, much to the annoyance of the Siamese cat who much prefers to sun himself in the large garden and to fuss around guests. Mrs. Snowden, who settled here from Germany some 30 years ago, charges £6 ($10.50) per person for B&B. If she can't take you in, she'll recommend one of her friends in the village.

16. Penzance

This little Gilbert and Sullivan harbor town is the end of the line for the Cornish Riviera Express. A full 280 miles southwest from London, it is noted for its equable climate (it's one of the first towns in England to blossom out with spring flowers), and summer throngs descend for fishing, sailing, and swimming. Overlooking Mount's Bay, Penzance is graced in places with subtropical plants, as well as palm trees.

The harbor is used to activity of one sort or another. *The Pirates of Penzance* were not entirely fictional. The town was raided by Barbary pirates, destroyed in part by Cromwell's troops, sacked and burnt by the Spaniards, and bombed by the Germans. In spite of its turbulent past, it offers tranquil resort living today.

The most westerly town in England, Penzance makes a good base for exploring Land's End, the Lizard Peninsula, St. Michael's Mount, the old fishing ports and artists' colonies of St. Ives, Newlyn, Mousehole, and the Scilly Isles.

THE SIGHTS: **St. Michael's Mount** is reached at low tide by a causeway three miles east of Penzance. Rising about 250 feet from the sea, St. Michael's Mount is topped by a partially medieval, partially 17th-century castle. At high tide the mount becomes an island, reached only by motor launch from Marazion. A Benedictine monastery, the gift of Edward the Confessor, stood on this spot in the 11th century. The castle, with its collections of armor and antique furniture, is open on Monday, Wednesday, and Friday from 10:30 a.m. to 4:45 p.m. from April 1 to October 31. At other times of the year it can be visited on conducted tours leaving at 11 a.m., noon, and 2 and 3 p.m. on Monday, Wednesday, and Friday, weather and the tide permitting. It charges £1.50 ($2.63) for adults, 70p ($1.23) for children. From Penzance take bus 20, 21, or 22, then get off at Marazion, the town opposite St. Michael's Mount. To avoid disappointment, it's a good idea to telephone the office of St. Michael's Mount (tel. Penzance 710507) to learn the state of the tides, especially during the winter months when a regular ferry service does not operate. After a longish walk over the causeway, be warned that there is quite a hard climb up cobble streets to reach the castle. You must wear sensible shoes.

The **Minack Theater** in Porthcurno, nine miles from Penzance, is unique. It's carved out of the Cornish cliff-face with the Atlantic as its impressive backdrop. In tiered seating, similar to that of the theaters of Ancient Greece, 550 persons can watch the show and the rocky coast beyond the stage. The theater is generally open to visitors who come sometimes just for sightseeing, although you may want to attend an evening performance. To reach Minack, leave Penzance on the A30 heading toward Land's End. After three miles, bear left onto the B3283 and follow the signposts to Porthcurno. Or you can take bus 4 or 4A from Penzance. For details, telephone St. Buryan 471 during the season, lasting from the end of June to mid-September. Seats cost around £2 ($3.50) at the box office.

WHERE TO STAY: The **Abbey Hotel,** Abbey Street (tel. Penzance 66906), is a well-preserved oldish place that is frequented by discerning guests. The bonus is its situation—on a narrow side street on several terraces directly overlooking Penzance Harbor. You can take only your room and breakfast at the Abbey, or have all of your meals in the restaurant downstairs which is open only to hotel guests. The B&B rate per person averages around 14 ($24.50). Behind the hotel, which is built close to the street, is a tiny formal garden on two tiers, each with a view of the water. Here the herbs are grown that are used to spice the delicately flavored meats in the restaurant downstairs. The owners, Michael and Jean Cox, have brought their vitality, style, and charm into the hotel business.

The Pirates of Penzance, The Cliff (tel. Penzance 3686), offers a sunbasking situation, on a raised terrace, with only the coast road between it and the harbor. It's a substantial, well-appointed hotel, close to the railway station and the heliport, and most of its bedrooms have an unobstructed view of Mount's Bay. The sunsets are spectacular from any point of view. Rooms in the main building all have bath and toilet, renting for £13.50 ($23.63) in low season, rising to £14 ($24.50) per person in high season. In the annex there is one rate throughout the year: £10 ($17.50) per person for B&B. The rooms are pleasantly furnished, containing water basins, innerspring mattresses, and bedside lamps. A restaurant on the premises serves from 7 to 8:15 p.m. The evening meal is a mixed table d'hôte and à la carte menu, with main dishes priced from £3.75 ($6.56) to £6 ($10.50).

Mincarlo, Chapel Street (tel. Penzance 2848), is a guest house built directly on the sidewalk. Owned by Mrs. Welsh, it is across the street from the Admiral Benbow restaurant. Mrs. Welsh tends to the large house herself, serving hearty Cornish breakfasts in her dining room, which is packed with antiques. Bright of spirit and most hospitable, she charges £6 ($10.50) per person daily for B&B. In one room a four-poster was installed by popular demand. Mincarlo is neat and adequate.

Richmond Lodge, 61 Morrab Rd. (tel. Penzance 5560), is a comfortable early Victorian house with a nautical flavor, lying a few steps from Market Jew Street (the main street) and within an easy walk of the Promenade along the sea wall. The Morrab Gardens is across the street. The host-owners, Jean and Pat Eady, have warm courtesy, down-to-earth friendliness, and an unrehearsed charm. A Cornish woman, Mrs. Eady is an excellent cook, specializing in traditional English dishes. Her husband serves with Her Majesty's Royal Navy as a chief petty officer. They give faultless service and operate a clean, bright, homey place. Charges are £42 ($73.50) per person weekly for B&B. Evening meals are an additional £4 ($7) per person per day.

Kimberley House, 10 Morrab Rd. (tel. Penzance 2727), lies between the Promenade and the center of town, opposite Penlee Park and near the Morrab Gardens. Avril and Rex Mudway have run this house since his retirement after a long sea-going career. They are friendly and gracious to their guests, not only providing good food and accommodations but offering tips about what to see in the area. B&B costs around £9.50 ($16.63) per person, and a rather large dinner goes for £5.50 ($9.63).

Carnson Guest House, East Terrace (tel. Penzance 5589), is personally run by Pat and Richard Hilder, two friendly owners. Close to the harbor, town center, station, and beach, their house is convenient for train, coach, and bus travelers. They charge from £9 ($15.75) daily for B&B, plus another £4.50 ($7.88) for dinner. At certain times of the year, they also serve a light cooked supper from an à la carte menu as an alternative to a full three-course dinner. All bedrooms have automatic tea- or coffee-making machines for your early-morning drink. Guests can also make use of a comfortable lounge with TV. The Hilders are also licensed to serve alcohol, and they provide a tourist information service on local "things to do." They are also ticket agents for local bus and coach tours as well as steamer trips to the Scilly Isles.

Con Amore, 38 Morrab Rd. (tel. Penzance 3423), is a small, homey, completely modernized Victorian guest house run by Prissie and Denis Holwill. It's recommended for its comfort, friendliness, situation, and cleanliness, along with good service and varied food. There is a TV set in each bedroom, plus a TV lounge. Mr. and Mrs. Holwill aim to make friends of their guests, treating them as if they were sharing their home instead of checking into an impersonal guest house. Their policy of a different breakfast each day is very popular and not the usual practice in England. Even the traditional bacon-and-egg English breakfast gets a little boring after a few weeks. Each unit is color schemed and so named: the Purple Room, the Gold Room, the Rose Room. Even the soaps have individual color. Rates for B&B are from £7.50 ($13.13) per person. There are reductions for children sharing a room with adults. As an added bonus, there are no service charges or VAT. Con Amore lies opposite the subtropical Morrab Gardens.

Penalva Guest House, Alexandra Road (tel. Penzance 2068), is a clean, comfortable guest house on a tree-lined road leading directly to the seafront. Mrs. Wendy Lorens is Cornish, and she's traveled all over the world, working in telecommunications. She's also taught dancing and yoga, and extends a special welcome to students. Her rooms are pleasantly furnished, with hot and cold running water and shaver points. Her B&B rate is from £8.50 ($14.88) per person. She offers both an English breakfast and a "whole-food" breakfast, the latter with her homemade granola. She doesn't offer a full evening meal, but light meals and snacks are available. Children are granted reductions. As a "local," she is able to help her guests with touring information.

READER'S GUEST HOUSE SELECTION: "The **Yacht Inn,** right across the street from the sea, offers a superb view of the island and Mousehole. The place is immaculate, warm, and cozy. Tea and coffee makings are provided in the rooms, and fresh roses are on the dining tables and in the hallways. The vegetables served us at dinner were home-grown in a garden plot just behind the inn, along with the flowers. B&B costs £8 ($14), and a well-prepared dinner is £4 ($7)" (Marcella R. Bonsall, South Pasadena, Calif.).

Overnight for Train Travelers

Those arriving by train will find some good B&B cottages on nearby Leskinnick Street (so close you don't need a taxi to transport your luggage). The houses lie off the main road which makes them comparatively quiet. All are similar architecturally, the differences manifesting in their color and their front gardens. There must be fierce competition among the landladies for distinction. Each of the guest houses offers fairly comfortable lodgings, with hot and cold running water in the rooms, corridor baths, and English breakfasts.

WHERE TO EAT: The **Admiral Benbow,** Chapel Street (tel. Penzance 3448), is a restaurant-cum-museum dedicated to the sea. What started out as a simple, two-story timbered inn has grown into a showcase of nautical objects. Open every day of the week (10:30 a.m. to 2:30 p.m. and 6 to 11 p.m.), it serves meals on the lower floor with its nooks and crannies, benches and booths. On the upper level there's a lounge bar (you wait here for a table if Admiral Benbow can't take any more on board downstairs). The nearby museum rooms are filled with portions of vessels, masts, lanterns, bow sculpture, model ships, smuggling tools. The inn used to be owned by Roland Morris, a professional diver who had been discovering treasure for years on old wrecks around Cornwall and the Scilly Isles.

When you get a table, consult the "Vittals Chart and Grog Log," the latter studded with everything from Hungarian Bull's Blood to Yugoslavian Tiger's Milk. You'll find Cornish crab soup a fine appetizer. Among the principal à la carte selections are Aylesbury duck with orange sauce and vegetables, fried scampi, and fried chicken with bread sauce and vegetables. For dessert, try one of the old English standbys, such as a home-cooked fruit tart, although an order of Cornish cream would make it sparkle. The price of a meal averages around £8 ($14) from the à la carte menu. Otherwise, you can order a bar meal from the cold buffet, consisting of meat pies and salads, in addition to two hot dishes, the cost ranging from £1.75 ($3.06) to £3 ($5.25).

Attached to the inn is a nightclub, open from 9 p.m. till 1 a.m. It charges half price to the patrons of the restaurant and also offers chilled draft lager. Otherwise, admission charges range from £1 ($1.75) to £1.75 ($3.06) per person.

Rosie's Restaurant, 12 Chapel St. (tel. Penzance 3540). Yes, Virginia, there really is a Rosie. She's red-haired and friendly, and seems to run everything around this place. In the heartbeat of everything, Rosie's is open from 12:30 a.m. to 2:30 p.m. and from 6:30 to 9:30 p.m. Monday to Saturday; closed Sunday. An informal, bustling little place, it is decorated in a style increasingly known as "English bistro." A dish of the day greets you and might satisfy, although the menu has a repertoire of both English and continental-inspired dishes, some from faraway Greece. Even a Texas-style chili appears on the menu. Food is prepared with obvious care from good materials, and your tab is likely to be no more than £5 ($8.75).

READER'S GUEST HOUSE SELECTION AT MEVAGISSEY: "**Mrs. Anne Gilbert** has a clean, warm, and friendly B&B on the main road to Land's End (tel. Mevagissey 2505).

It's reached by going through the town of Mevagissey, then up a hill. A beautiful view of the English Channel unfolds from all the rooms. She also has a parking area in front. Upon our arrival, Mrs. Gilbert offered us tea and cookies. She has a lovely dining area overlooking the Channel, and large comfortable rooms, tastefully furnished, with TV provided. We were able to get tasty sandwiches for our lunch, and with prior notice, Mrs. Gilbert will provide a good supper. She also serves a full English breakfast. The charge is £8.50 ($14.88) per person for B&B" (D. C. Iler, Toronto, Ont., Canada).

17. The Scilly Isles

Perhaps the most important and scenic excursion from Penzance is a day trip to the Scilly Isles, lying off the Cornish coast, about 27 miles southwest of Land's End. The granite isles are noted for their sandy beaches, palm trees, and warm climate (Gulf Stream–protected flowers bloom in December). One looks at flowers and gardens a lot in the Scillies, but the islands also have bird sanctuaries and seal colonies. **St. Mary's** is the largest inhabited island, and the site of most tourist facilities. From there, you can take a motor launch to the major sightseeing attraction, the **Tresco Abbey Gardens,** on the **Isle of Tresco.** Not only can you explore terraced gardens, but you can also duck inside the **Valhalla Ship Museum,** a collection of figureheads gleaned from wrecks in the islands. The gardens are open all year, weekdays only, including Saturday, from 10 a.m. to 4 p.m.

From Penzance, the Scilly Isles may be visited by helicopter or by sea. A ship, *Scillonian III,* maintains year-round connections to St. Mary's. For details of sailings and fares, apply to **Isles of Scilly Steamship Co. Ltd.,** Quay Street (tel. Penzance 2009). **British Airways Helicopters** at the Heliport in Penzance (tel. Penzance 3871) flies regularly to the Isles of Scilly, the one-way flight taking only 20 minutes. A special one-day return excursion fare is available any day except Saturday from May to early September. The round-trip day fare is £31 ($54.25) per person. The peak return fare is £44 ($77).

Hanjague, St. Mary's (tel. Scillonia 22531), is a modern bungalow near the center of the island, offering good views stretching from the heliport in the southwest. Owners Dorothy and David Oxford will meet arriving guests at the heliport or quay if notified in advance. For B&B, the Oxfords charge £14 ($24.50) per person. The half-board rate is £19 ($33.25) per person nightly. Rooms are comfortably furnished and heated, containing hot and cold running water. In the studio lounge is a fine display of wildlife prints by the artist William Timym.

Now we turn to the outlying district of Penzance, beginning first on the eastern side of the bay at St. Hilary, then heading south to Newlyn and Mousehole.

18. Newlyn, Mousehole, and Land's End

NEWLYN: From Penzance, a promenade leads to Newlyn, a mile away, another fishing village of infinite charm on Mount's Bay. In fact, its much-painted harbor seems clogged with more fishing craft than that of Penzance. Stanhope Forbes, now dead, founded an art school in Newlyn, and in the past few years the village has gained an increasing reputation for its artists' colony, attracting both the serious painter and the Sunday sketcher. From Penzance, the old fishermen's cottages and crooked lanes of Newlyn are reached by bus. For a dining or overnighting recommendation, try the following:

The Smugglers Hotel and Restaurant, Fore Street (tel. Penzance 4207), is the central mecca for those who create in clay and paint. An artist's dream, this little two-story inn lies right on the roadside, across from the Newlyn Harbor. You pay £13 ($22.75) in a single, £22 ($38.50) in a double for a good bed and a big Cornish breakfast. The rooms are bright and sparklingly clean, with innerspring mattresses and water basins. Several bedrooms have full private baths and a double rents for £26 ($45.50), a single for £17 ($29.75). Good shore dinners are served till around 10 p.m. from £6 ($10.50). Conversation in the lounge or in the dining room is often most rewarding, particularly if you talk to the owners, Ann and Dave Reeve. The bar is found in the granite-walled cellars, with tables and benches made from local driftwood. The original tunnel used by smugglers, although now blocked, can still be seen.

MOUSEHOLE: Still another Cornish fishing village, Mousehole lies three miles south of Penzance (take bus 9), two from our last stopover in Newlyn. The hordes of tourists who flock here haven't changed it drastically—the gulls still squawk, the cottages still huddle close to the harbor wall (although they look as if they were built more to be photographed than lived in), the fishermen still bring in the day's catch, the salts sit around with their smoking tobacco talking about the good old days, and the lanes are as narrow as ever. About the most exciting thing that's occurred was the arrival in the late 16th century of the Spanish galleons, whose ungallant sailors sacked and burnt the village. In a sheltered cove, off Mount's Bay, Mousehole (pronounced mou-sel) today has developed the nucleus of an artists' colony. For rooms and meals, try the following recommendations, all within the village:

Food and Lodging

Tavis Vor (tel. Mousehole 306) is the only place in Mousehole with direct access to the sea through its own grounds. It has a marvelous view overlooking the harbor and St. Michael's Mount. Almost directly opposite is a small island on which there are the remains of a monastery. The first building on the sea side when you enter Mousehole, it accommodates 18 guests, costing £9 ($15.75) per person for B&B. The owners, John and Kathleen Hanley, keep the house open all year, offering rooms with sea views (one accommodation, the studio at the top of the house, has a four-poster bed and a bath en suite). Mrs. Hanley does the cooking.

Renovelle, The Parade (tel. Penzance 258), is a pretty little villa, all fresh blue and white, at the edge of the village. It's aptly perched right beside the sea, on a cliff, which makes the view memorable. Mrs. Stella Bartlett, the owner, has made it charming and comfortable. Her guests keep returning year after year, and pay a B&B rate of £8 ($14) per person nightly. Each bedroom is comfy, equipped with water basins—and they have good views of the sea. It's a pleasure to have breakfast set before you in the sunny little dining room.

Pam's Pantry, Brook Street (tel. Mousehole 532), is a small and cheerful café and kitchen which is open from 11 a.m. daily. Most of the dishes served here feature fish which comes straight from the harbor. You can order a crab salad, a summer favorite, or else grilled or fried plaice or sole. The cost of a meal is about £4 ($7).

LAND'S END: Craggy Land's End, where England comes to an end, is where you'll find the last of everything. It lies nine miles west of Penzance and is reached by bus 1 or 1B. America's coast is 3291 miles away to the west of the rugged rocks which tumble into the sea beneath Land's End.

Big business has taken over Britain's most southwesterly peninsula where you are often blown almost horizontal by transatlantic winds. There is now a crafts center where young artists and artisans practice and demonstrate their crafts. You can purchase pots, jewelry, and souvenirs. The snackbar has simple fare if you're hungry. If you fall in love with this rugged country, as many others have, you can stay overnight at the following.

Old Success Inn, Sennen Cove, Land's End (tel. Sennen 232). Just before you reach Land's End, turn right and follow the road down to Sennen Cove. The Old Success lies at the bottom, facing the sea and wide sandy beaches. Surfing rollers come in from the Atlantic almost to the foot of the sea wall beneath the 17th-century fishermen's inn. Over the years it has been extended and modernized, now offering bright, clean rooms, many with private bath, all with radio, tea and coffee maker, electric heater, and wash basin.

Downstairs there is a lounge with color TV and fantastic panoramic views over the Atlantic, a cozy lounge bar, and Charlie's Bar where the locals and fishermen join the residents of the evening. The chef, Don Woodward, provides bar snacks at lunch and a set three-course meal for £7.50 ($13.13). Fresh local fish with fresh vegetables are featured. Try the grilled river trout or the fresh Cornish crab with salad.

For those who seek more energetic exercise than an evening walk along the sand, there is the Surf Bar by the beach which is separated from the inn by a large car park. Disco music is played on summer evenings. Gillian and Tony Webster have run the inn for the past few years. B&B is £9 ($15.75) in low season, rising to £12 ($21) per person in high season. Packed lunches can be provided, and all rates include VAT.

19. St. Ives

This north coast fishing village, with its sandy beaches, is England's most famous art colony. Only 20 miles from Land's End, ten from Penzance, it is a village of narrow streets and well-kept cottages. The artists settled in many years ago and have integrated with the fishermen and their families.

The art colony was established long enough ago to have developed several schools or splits, and they almost never overlap, except in pubs where the artists hang out, at an occasional café, and where classes are held. The old battle continues between the followers of the representational and the devotees of the abstract in art, with each group recruiting young artists all the time. In addition, there are the potters, weavers, and other artisans, all doing things creatively and exhibiting and selling in this area. There are several galleries to visit, with such names as the Sail Loft.

A word of warning: St. Ives becomes virtually impossible to visit in August, when you're likely to be trampled underfoot by busloads of tourists, mostly the British themselves. However, in spring and early fall, the pace is much more relaxed, and a visitor can have the true experience of the art colony.

Park and Ride

During the summer months, many of the streets in the center of town are closed to vehicles. You may want to leave your car in the **Lelant Saltings Car Park,** three miles from St. Ives on the A3074, and take the regular train service into town, an 11-minute journey. Departures are every half hour. It's free to all car passengers and drivers, and the car park charge is about £1.50 ($2.63) a day. Or else you can use the large **Trenwith Car Park,** close to the town center, for 25p (44¢) a day and then walk down to the shops and harbor or else take a bus, costing 16p (28¢) for adults and 8p (14¢) for children.

WHERE TO STAY: Avoid the snug, suburban houses built on the edge of St. Ives and go instead to the end of the peninsula, or island as it's called (it's not actually). In these winding streets, you'll find the studios of the working artists, the fishermen, and the unusual places set aside to show and sell works of art. And you'll also find here a number of B&B guest houses and cottages. For the most part, they are easy to find; simply look for B&B signs as you walk along the narrow streets.

Garrack Hotel, Higher Ayr (tel. St. Ives 796199), from its two-acre knoll, commands a panoramic view of St. Ives and Portmeor Beach. The vine-covered little hotel, once a private home, is reached by heading up a narrow lane. It's one of the friendliest and most efficiently run small medium-priced hotels on the entire coast, with every room furnished in a warm, homey manner. The atmosphere in the living room is inviting, with a log-burning fireplace, antiques, and comfortable chairs. The Garrack belongs to Mr. and Mrs. Kilby, who are proud of their meals. Each bedroom has an innerspring mattress and hot and cold running water (most with private baths). Prices vary because of the view, the size of the room, and the season. B&B is from £9.13 ($15.98) to £13.80 ($24.15) per person in a room without bath, rising to £14.95 ($26.16) to £16.10 ($28.18) per person in rooms with bath or shower. Half-board terms are quoted on stays of more than three days. A set dinner costs £7.25 ($12.69). But if you care to order before 10 a.m., they will provide a special meal from the shellfish menu—everything will have been brought in that morning by the fishermen, prepared, cooked, and served in the evening.

Lamorna, 11 Barndoon Terrace (tel. St. Ives 795376). I tried very hard to find a real Cornish landlady, and my search ended on the cliffs above the town, but only four minutes or so from the harbor and shops. Margaret Bunn is a lovely lady married to a fisherman. Her son is duty coxwain of the lifeboat, and the family goes back seven or eight generations in St. Ives. They have always been connected to the sea. She rents out four rooms, all with wash basins. Guests are welcome to stay in whenever they like, making use of the comfortable lounge where a TV is provided. B&B, a large nourishing meal, is £5.50 ($9.63) per person, or else you can stay here on the half-board terms of £8 ($14) per person. Evening meals are three courses, or you can walk down to the harbor to sample the delights of the town. Advance booking isn't necessary, although you may find it full. If you can plan ahead and reserve for a week, the charge is £38.50 ($67.38) per person for B&B or £56 ($98) per person for half board. There is a good car park behind the typical 1930s Cornish solid house.

Hobblers Guest House and Restaurant, The Wharf (tel. Penzance 796439), is right on the harbor side, a black-and-white building next to a shellfish shop. Paul Folkes has rooms available at £6 ($10.50) per person, including breakfast. But his main interest is the restaurant on the ground and first floors. In paneled rooms decorated with pictures of ships and seascapes, you are served the local catch—fresh sole, skate, mackerel, and plaice. Of course these dishes come with "chips" and peas, priced from £1.95 ($3.41) to £2.50 ($4.38) for an ample portion.

Trecarrell, Carthew Terrace (tel. St. Ives 795707), is a pleasant old house where you can enjoy the personal attention of the proprietors, who offer B&B for £8.25 ($14.44) per person, including a large English breakfast. They also do a set evening meal for £4.50 ($7.88), or you can choose from the small range of à la carte dishes. There is a lounge with TV, plus radios in the bedrooms. Good parking and ironing facilities add to the suitability of Trecarrell.

READERS' GUEST HOUSE SELECTIONS: "The best guest house we found in southern England was **Island View,** 2 Park Ave. (tel. St. Ives 795363). Trevor and Sheila Portman have a completely refurbished house—clean and bright, with comfortable beds equipped with hot-water bottles on a chilly night. There is hot and cold running water in each room and a bath on the same floor. We discovered Mrs. Portman to be such an excellent cook that we took dinners in addition to breakfast during our stay. The charge was £7 ($12.25) per person for B&B. For evening dinner, you pay £3.50 ($6.13) extra. Island View is perfect as the name of the house—it sits so high it commands a view over all of the town, the harbor, and out to the Atlantic beyond. The Portmans invite their guests to enjoy their living room, the view, and their books and magazines as well" (Mrs. Eleanor W. Loucks, Chapel Hill, N.C.). . . . "Four miles out of St. Ives on the road to Penzance, there's a small sign advertising B&B at **Tremadda Farm** (tel. Penzance 796935). The farm is half a mile from Zennor on the St. Ives side. Following the rocky road toward the ocean, you come upon an old farmhouse (200 to 250 years old), whose front door is difficult to find. It's a big sliding wooden door inside of which lies a real treat—a U-shaped farmhouse built around a garden plot. The rooms are spacious and open onto porches, the water is always hot, the hostess, Mrs. Berryman, is very congenial, the breakfasts are excellent, and the price is right—£6.50 ($11.38). The house will only hold about six guests, so telephone ahead" (Suzanne Shay, San Francisco, Calif.).

WHERE TO EAT: The **Chef's Kitchen,** Halsetown (tel. St. Ives 6218), stands on a point above St. Ives on a back road to Penzance. It's in an old granite post office, fitted in pine with large tables and soft lighting. When you reserve a table (and reservations are imperative), you have it for the night. Lunch is served from noon to 2 p.m., dinner from 7 p.m. and "onwards." Jenni and Ken Wright, the owners, run what they call an "up market" restaurant, specializing in homemade foods cooked to a high international standard. Fish dishes depend on the catch and availability. On my most recent rounds, I enjoyed a paupiette de sole à la Dieppoise—that is, wine-poached filets of Dover sole coated in a shellfish sauce of scallops, prawns, mussels, and mushrooms, and glazed with an egg saboyonne. The meat dishes are especially well prepared. Order, if featured, a suprême de volaille Jules Janin—a boneless breast of chicken, filled with a stuffing of pâté, artichoke hearts, and mushrooms, and garnished with asparagus and coated in a cream and mushroom sauce. All main courses are served with three fresh vegetables and salad. The desserts are homemade, the coffee freshly ground. Prices begin at £9 ($15.75).

Garrack Hotel, Higher Ayr (tel. Penzance 796199), the domain of Mr. and Mrs. Kilby, is outstanding, producing an excellent cuisine and, when possible, using fresh ingredients from their own garden. The hotel dining room, open to nonresidents, offers regular à la carte listings, plus a cold buffet or snacks at the bar, and a £7.25 ($12.69) dinner from 7 to 8:30 p.m. The menu features some of the finest of English dishes, such as roast shoulder of lamb with mint sauce, fried fillet of plaice, and a wide choice of continental fare, such as filet of bass meunière and escalopes de veau Cordon Bleu. A 10% service charge and VAT are added. Coffee is served in the lounge. The Kilbys' son Michael has joined his parents in the operation of the hotel and restaurant after completing a training period with Claridges in London.

The Sloop Wine Bar, The Wharf (tel. Penzance 796584), is to be found behind the Sloop on the harbor side. It is an atmosphere of stone walls and low beams, but on warm days you can take your food and drink outside and enjoy the view as you munch. Ian Barnes, the landlord, offers salad platters, chicken, ham, and turkey. The specialty, if there is one, is the seafood salad with prawn or crab. Count on spending around £4 ($7). A glass of wine, depending on your selection, ranges from 50p (88¢) to 90p ($1.58).

The Balancing Eel, Back Lane (tel. Penzance 796792), is almost a traditional fish and chips shop where you line up at the take-out counter and receive your supper wrapped—not in newspaper these days, pity!—or take it upstairs to eat in the restaurant. A bag of sole and chips is only 75p ($1.31). There are the usual bottles on the counter—vinegar, catsup, chutney, and pickled onions. It's open from noon to 2:30 p.m. and from 5:30 p.m. onward seven days a week. It's close to the Wharf Post Office and Chy-an-Chy Street.

The **Pudding Bag Restaurant,** in the Sloop Craft Market in St. Ives (tel. Penzance 797214), is open daily from 10 a.m. to 10 p.m. A long, narrow cafeteria opens into a seating area, where Phyllis cooks gargantuan pasties for Tuesday's Cornish pasty night at 90p ($1.58) each. In one of her steak pies, the meat alone weighs half a pound. You're served vegetables too. There's always a soup and the inevitable mixed grill. A good and filling meal can be ordered here at a cost of only £2.50 ($4.38), including a beer and coffee. If you don't enter through the Craftmarket, you can go to the entrance on Back Road West. Phyllis also bakes her own bread and cakes on the premises.

Tilley's Continental Café, beneath the Eastern National Bus car park, does a good breakfast—egg, two sausages, beans, tomatoes, toast, marmalade, and a pot of tea for only £1.80 ($3.15). It's about the best bistro-style café in St. Ives, with its small balcony overlooking the harbor. During the day they serve hamburgers, pizzas, and more substantial dishes, but their cream teas at 95p ($1.66) are notable.

BARBARA HEPWORTH MUSEUM: At Trewyn Studio and Garden, on Barnoon Hill (tel. St. Ives 796226), the former home of Dame Barbara Hepworth contains a museum of sculpture by the artist from 1929 until her death in 1975, together with photographs, letters, and other papers documenting her life and background. The garden, too, contains sculpture and is well worth a visit. The museum is open year round from 10 a.m. to 5:30 p.m., Monday to Saturday. It is closed on Sunday and bank holidays and charges an admission of 50p (88¢) for adults and 25p (44¢) for children. There is limited parking some 200 yards away, but visitors may like to leave their cars at Lelant Station some three miles away and use the park-and-ride service into St. Ives.

A ST. IVES GRAB BAG: Trophy Motorcycles, 36 Hayle Terrace, Hayle, St. Ives (tel. Penzance 794601), offers Mopeds for rent at £5 ($8.75) per day or £25 ($43.75) a week. Helmets are supplied, and the Moped is ideal in this hilly country. You must present a car license or a full motorcycle driving license to be able to rent a vehicle.

Oates Travel, The Harbour Office, The Wharf (tel. Penzance 795343), has regular bus tours to Land's End, the Lizard, and the villages of Looe and Polperro, and also day trips to the Scilly Islands. Prices vary, and full details are available at the office. They also do evening trips to St. Austell when there are concerts, returning to St. Ives afterward.

The **Sloop Craft Market** in St. Ives is the original craft market of the town where you can watch craftspeople making pottery, polishing stones and shells, and working in silver and gold. Objects are for sale from 70p ($1.23). You'll find rings set with semiprecious stones, candle holders, inlaid boxes, vases, and small pots, as well as leather goods.

20. Port Isaac

The most unspoiled fishing village on the north Cornish coastline is Port Isaac, nine miles from Wadebridge. This Atlantic coastal resort retains its original character, in spite of the intrusions of large numbers of summer visitors. You can wander through its winding, narrow lanes, gazing at the white-washed fishermen's cottages with their rainbow trims.

For meals, try the **Harbour Café,** Fore Street (tel. Port Isaac 237), in the center of the village. It has a special fame, featured several times on British television and once in scenes from the Sherlock Holmes thriller, "The Devil's Foot." The unique café is designated as a building of architectural and historic interest, and is one of several buildings on this treacherous stretch of coast that used the timber of wrecked ships in construction. The owners offer complete meals as well as snacks. In addition they have a table-wine license. On the menu are such local dishes as crab and mackerel salads, plus a number of other homemade specialties. Meals begin at around £2.50 ($4.38). Perhaps you will arrive in the afternoon, when you can have a Cornish cream tea, and if your appetite is still unsatisfied, you may care to try a piece of homemade gâteau topped with a portion of clotted cream.

Another good bet is the **Cornish Café** (tel. Port Isaac 256), a licensed family restaurant owned by David Phelps, who also is the proprietor of Trewetha Farm (see below). Port Isaac is known for its crabs and lobsters, and Mr. Phelps does superb crab salads. He also prepares spicy curries along with grilled steaks. Cornish cream teas are a specialty, and snacks are available all day. Prices begin at £4.50 ($7.88). Introduce yourself to Mr. Phelps, who is interesting to talk to.

For accommodations, try **Tre-Pol-Pen Hotel** (tel. Port Isaac 232), a simple but well-run establishment in the modern part of the village. Rooms are attractively furnished and well maintained, costing £12 ($21) per person in the high season for B&B. This tariff includes a large English breakfast where you have a choice of ingredients. Hot and cold water has been installed in all bedrooms, and the beds have innerspring mattresses. In winter electric blankets keep you toasty warm. Your hosts are Mr. and Mrs. P. A. Mason, who give personal service, and will provide picnic lunches if desired. Guests gather in the lounge to watch color TV or else enjoy a drink in Sally's bar overlooking Port Isaac Bay, with a good view of the sea and the coastline up to Tintagel. Open throughout the year, the hotel serves good food and Cornish cream teas in the afternoon. Reservations are imperative in the summer months.

Rouges Retreat, Roscarrock Hill (tel. Port Isaac 566), is a licensed guest house run by Frank and Jill Gadman, who are marvelous hosts even though this is their first venture at innkeeping (perhaps that's why they're so good). They rent seven comfortable bedrooms, with hot and cold running water and coffee- or tea-making facilities. Their charge of £8 ($14) per person nightly is most reasonable. The guest house has good views over the fishing village and harbor. It lies adjacent to a National Trust footpath where walkers can enjoy the scenery of the coast and deserted coves. An evening meal with a selection of fine wines is served from 7 p.m. in a cozy dining room. Table settings are color coordinated in royal blue and white down. The half-board rate is from £12 ($21) per person, with children sharing a parent's room granted reductions.

READERS' HOTEL SELECTIONS: "The **Hathaway Guest House** (tel. Port Isaac 416) is beautifully situated on the cliff on the eastern side of Port Isaac harbor. The licensed house overlooks not only the village and harbor, but also the western coastline and beyond. Resident proprietor Enid Andrews offers colorfully decorated rooms with breakfast at £7 ($12.25) per person in April, May, and June, and £8 ($14) in July, August, and September. Dinner is available for £4 ($7). It is less than a five-minute walk to the pub and shops. A two-mile cliff walk begins at the door. There's a car park and children are welcome. It's open all year" (A. Emerson Smith, Columbia, S.C.). . . . "Just outside Port Isaac, on a bend in the main road into town, is **Trewetha Farm** (tel. Port Isaac 256), run by Mr. and Mrs. David Phelps. It is a B&B place during the off-season, and during the summer they open the farm to tenters and caravans as well. The cost of B&B is £7 ($12.25) per person, rising to £9 ($15.75) per person for half board. Things like cleanliness and a great breakfast are provided. In addition, we felt David to be a new friend, and his son took us to see the newborn chicks. We were awakened by the roosters in the morning and looked out of our window to see David scattering grain to the fowl and shooing them out of the barn" (Susan Thomas, London, England).

"**Harbour Heights,** Rosehill (tel. Port Isaac 502), lies on its own two-acre meadow, complete with a patio, fenced-in goats and ducks, and the best view of the town, the harbor, and that magnificent coastline. Vickie and Ken Overall are superb hosts. There are five double rooms, and children are welcome, either in the same room as the parents or in separate rooms. Babysitting is available in the evenings. Each room has a hot and cold water basin, and one of the bathrooms has a shower. Breakfast, either continental or English, is served in the dining room overlooking the harbor and cliffs. Rooms go for £7 ($12.25) per person" (Sue and John Magod, East Brunswick, N.J.).

21. Tintagel

On a wild stretch of the Atlantic coast, Tintagel is forever linked with the legends of King Arthur, Lancelot, and Merlin. The Norman ruins, popularly known as "King Arthur's Castle," stand 300 feet above the sea on a rocky promontory. The colorful writing of Lord Tennyson in *Idylls of the King* greatly increased the interest in Tintagel, as did the writings of Geoffrey of Monmouth. The ruins, which date from Geoffrey's time, are what remains of a castle built on the foundations of a Celtic monastery from the sixth century.

The **Old Post Office** at Tintagel is a National Trust property. It was once a 14th-century manor, but since the 19th century it has had connections with the post office. In the village center, it has a genuine Victorian post room which is open, April to October, daily from 11 a.m. to 6 p.m. or sunset if that is earlier. Admission is 70p ($1.28), including a guidebook.

In summer, many visitors make the ascent to Arthur's lair, 100 rock-cut steps. You can also visit Merlin's Cave.

If you become excited by legends of Knights of the Round Table, you can even go to **Camelford,** just five miles inland from Tintagel. The market hall there dates from 1790, but, more interestingly, the town claims to be Camelot.

Trenowan Hotel, Treknow, near Tintagel (tel. Camelford 770255), is a small, family-run hotel, not sophisticated, but offering personal service and homestyle cooking. Peter Saville is your host, and he and his wife Christine make you comfortable inside their quiet home, on its own grounds overlooking the coast near Trebarwith Sands. Some 20 guests are accommodated in well-furnished rooms, costing from £13 ($22.75) per person for half board. The dinner uses home-grown and farm produce. Their house is open from Easter until the end of September. Meals have to be planned ahead, so it's best to notify them of your intended arrival at least 24 hours in advance, rather than appearing at 5 p.m. without warning, as many visitors tend to do.

Pennallick Hotel, Treknow, near Tintagel (tel. Camelford 770296), is another small, family-run hotel, where the living is relaxed and homey. Mr. and Mrs. Wilson welcome you to their house on the coastline, about a mile from Tintagel. Their 11 bedrooms contain hot and cold running water, and most of the units have showers as well. In the peak summer months they charge £12 ($21) per person for half board. If you're touring the next day, a packed lunch will be provided. There is also a comfortable licensed lounge bar and a TV room.

Pendragon Guest House, Tintagel (tel. Camelford 770426), is a modern guest house only a ten-minute walk from Tintagel, close to King Arthur's Castle and the Trebarwith Sands. All rooms face the sea and miles of coastline, and all are pleasantly kept with hot and cold running water. Miss M. C. Hayne prefers weekly bookings in season, although she will accept B&B guests at a cost of £7 ($12.25) per person nightly. For those wanting to use her place as a base for exploring this part of Cornwall, she will quote half-board weekly terms of £58 ($101.50) per person.

Trebrea Lodge, Trenale, near Tintagel (tel. Camelford 770410), may appear as a dignified stately home, but in truth it looks and feels inside like an old Cornish farmhouse. It dates back to 1315, and was lived in by the same family for more than 600 years. The house, owned by Ann and Guy Murray, looks straight out across fields to the sea, and each bedroom has a good view. Rooms are available in many sizes, and each has hot and cold water, color TV, radio, intercom, and even a baby-listening service. Evenings are cozy in the drawing room around an open fire. The original first-floor drawing room has been restored, and there is a traditional Victorian smoking room in addition to the bar. You can have drinks in another lounge with a fireplace. Dining is most informal, and all food is homemade by Mrs. Murray, who has mastered true English recipes. The cost is £16 ($28) per person for half board.

Bossiney House Hotel (tel. Camelford 770240) stands in an inviting spot on the right as you approach Tintagel from Boscastle. Two brothers, John and Reg Wrightam, and their families operate the hotel, and everybody combines to make guests feel welcome. The hotel is comfortable, with a TV lounge and a well-stocked bar/lounge which has a fine view of surrounding meadows marching right up to the tops of the cliff, as well as of the wide expanse of lawn with a putting green. Rooms are comfortably furnished and have private baths and central heating. The large dining room, where a big English breakfast is served and you can enjoy other well-prepared meals brought to you by smiling Cornish women, is so situated as to give a view of the front, side, and back lawns. The price is £18 ($31.50) per person for a room with dinner, breakfast, and morning tea served in your room before breakfast. The Wrightams will direct you to interesting places you might otherwise miss seeing in the area. The hotel is closed from early October until spring. Look for the old phaeton and farm implements in the front garden.

A FARMHOUSE NEAR BUDE: **Forda Farm,** Morwenstow, near Bude (tel. Morwenstow 275), is a 250-year-old farmhouse nestled in a wooded coombe about 1½ miles from the sea. Miss Manfield likes to keep guests to a minimum so "they will feel more like a friend of the family than a paying guest." Guests, rarely more than six, gather around the table at night, as the farm is noted for its excellent cuisine, using wholesome foods, including their own dairy products and home-grown vegetables. Breakfast is in the traditional Cornish style, and a picnic lunch will be provided if you want to go touring during the day.

Daily rates, including bed, breakfast, early-morning tea, and a table d'hôte dinner, are from £20 ($35) per person, plus another £2.50 ($4.38) for a packed lunch. You can also go on guided tours at £6 ($10.50) per person. Readers Dr. and Mrs. William Douglas write, "We arrived in time for haying and milking. We pitched in with the family and later shared a warm evening and a wonderful meal together. One can walk through lovely meadows overlooking the sea to Ireland and share from the local inhabitants the charm of one of the loveliest parts of England."

READERS' GUEST HOUSE SELECTIONS: "We found the best hospitality and the lowest prices of our trip at **Castle View,** 2 King Arthurs Terrace (tel. Camelford 770421), a B&B where the price is £5.50 ($9.63) for a friendly welcome, a good room, and an excellent breakfast. Proprietors Brian and Sandy Spiller searched for the most rugged coastline setting before settling on Tintagel. They say the area is particularly rugged in winter, a season when Americans predominate in their guest house" (Thomas M. Wagner, Bloomington, Minn.). . . . "We found a real jewel of a place, **Channel Villa,** Bossiney Road (tel. Camelford 770287). Mrs. R. M. Deacon is a congenial hostess, serving one of the best breakfasts we had on our trip. B&B costs £6.50 ($11.38) per person" (Sally Julian, Tucson, Ariz.). . . . "One of the best guest houses is **Belvoir House** in Tregatta, Tintagel (tel. Camelford 770265). Joyce Martin and her husband were kind enough to chase us halfway across southern England after we forgot our copy of Frommer. When they couldn't catch up with us, they mailed it to one of our next stops. The food was tasty. The charge is £12 ($21) per person per night for lodging, breakfast, and a gourmet dinner" (Marlene and Bill Klett, St. Joseph, Minn.).

In our next chapter, we'll conclude our trek through the West Country by exploring Wiltshire, Somerset, and Avon.

Chapter IX

WILTSHIRE, SOMERSET, AND AVON

1. Salisbury
2. Castle Combe
3. Wells
4. Bleadney
5. Glastonbury
6. Exmoor
7. The Caves of Mendip
8. Bath
9. Bristol

FOR OUR FINAL LOOK at the West Countree, we move now into Wiltshire, Somerset, and Avon, the most antiquity-rich shires of England. When we reach this area of woodland and pastoral scenes, London seems far removed from the bucolic life here.

On cold, windswept nights in unrecorded times, the Druids used to steal across these plains armed with twigs. Sheltered by boulders, they'd burn their sloe with rosemary to ward off the danger of witchcraft.

Most people seem to agree that the West Country, a loose geographical term, begins at Salisbury, with its Early English cathedral. Nearby is Stonehenge, England's oldest prehistoric monument. Both Stonehenge and Salisbury are in Wiltshire.

Somerset is even more varied, the diet richer not only in historical cities, but in wild scenic grandeur, especially in Exmoor, the home of the red deer. The legendary burial place of King Arthur at Glastonbury and the cathedral city of Wells also await you on your visit to Somerset. The old Roman city of Bath is the main target in the county of Avon.

WILTSHIRE

When you cross into Wiltshire, you'll be entering a county of chalky, grassy uplands and rolling plains. Most of the shire is agricultural, and a large part is devoted to pastureland. Wiltshire produces an abundance of England's dairy products, and is noted for its sheep raising. In this western shire, you'll traverse the Salisbury Plain, the Vale of Pewsey, and the Marlborough Downs (the last gobbling up the greater part of the land mass). Unquestionably, the crowning achievement of Wiltshire is:

1. Salisbury

Long before you've made the 83-mile trek from London, the spire of Salisbury Cathedral comes into view, just as John Constable painted it so many times. The 404-foot pinnacle of the Early English and Gothic cathedral is the tallest in England. But Salisbury is also a fine base for touring such prehistoric sights as Stonehenge.

Market days are generally on Tuesday and Saturday. There is a general market in the Market Place, where stalls sell anything from meat by auction to clothes and household goods, plants, and sweets.

THE SIGHTS: Salisbury, or New Sarum, lies in the valley of the Avon River. Filled with Tudor-style inns and tea rooms, it is known to readers of Thomas Hardy as Melchester and to the Victorian fans of Anthony Trollope as Barchester.

Salisbury Cathedral

You can search all of England, but you'll find no purer example of the Early English, or pointed, style than Salisbury Cathedral. Its graceful spire has already been mentioned, but the ecclesiastical building doesn't depend totally on the tower for its appeal. Construction began on the structure as early as 1220, then took 38 years to complete, which was jet-age speed in those days (it was customary to drag out cathedral building for three centuries at least). The spire was to soar at the end of the 13th century. Despite an ill-conceived attempt at revamping in the 18th century, the architectural harmony of the cathedral was retained.

The cathedral's octagonal Treasury (note the fine sculptures) is especially attractive, dating from the 13th century. The Library contains one of the four copies of Magna Carta. The Cloisters enhance the beauty of the cathedral. The Close, with at least 75 buildings in its compound (some from the early 18th century, although others predate that), is exceptionally large, setting off the cathedral most fittingly. An interesting clock in the north transept is considered the oldest working mechanism in Europe. The cathedral now charges an admission of 50p (88¢), although strong objectors are still admitted free.

The cathedral has a good **Brass Rubbing Centre** where you can choose from a selection of exact replicas molded perfectly from the original brasses. The small charge made for each rubbing includes the cost of materials and a donation to the church from which it comes. The center is open at the cathedral from early June to early September, Monday to Saturday, from 10 a.m. to 5 p.m., from 2 to 5 p.m. on Sunday.

One of the houses in the Close is **Mompesson House,** built by Charles Mompesson in 1701. It was the home of the Townsend family for more than a century, and is well known for its fine plasterwork ceilings and paneling. There is also a magnificent collection of 18th-century drinking glasses. It is open April to October, daily except Thursday and Friday, from 12:30 to 6 p.m. or dusk, charging an admission of £1 ($1.75).

Also in the Close is the **Regimental Museum** of the Duke of Edinburgh's Royal Regiment, the Berkshire and the Wiltshire. Admission is 60p ($1.05) for adults and 30p (53¢) for children.

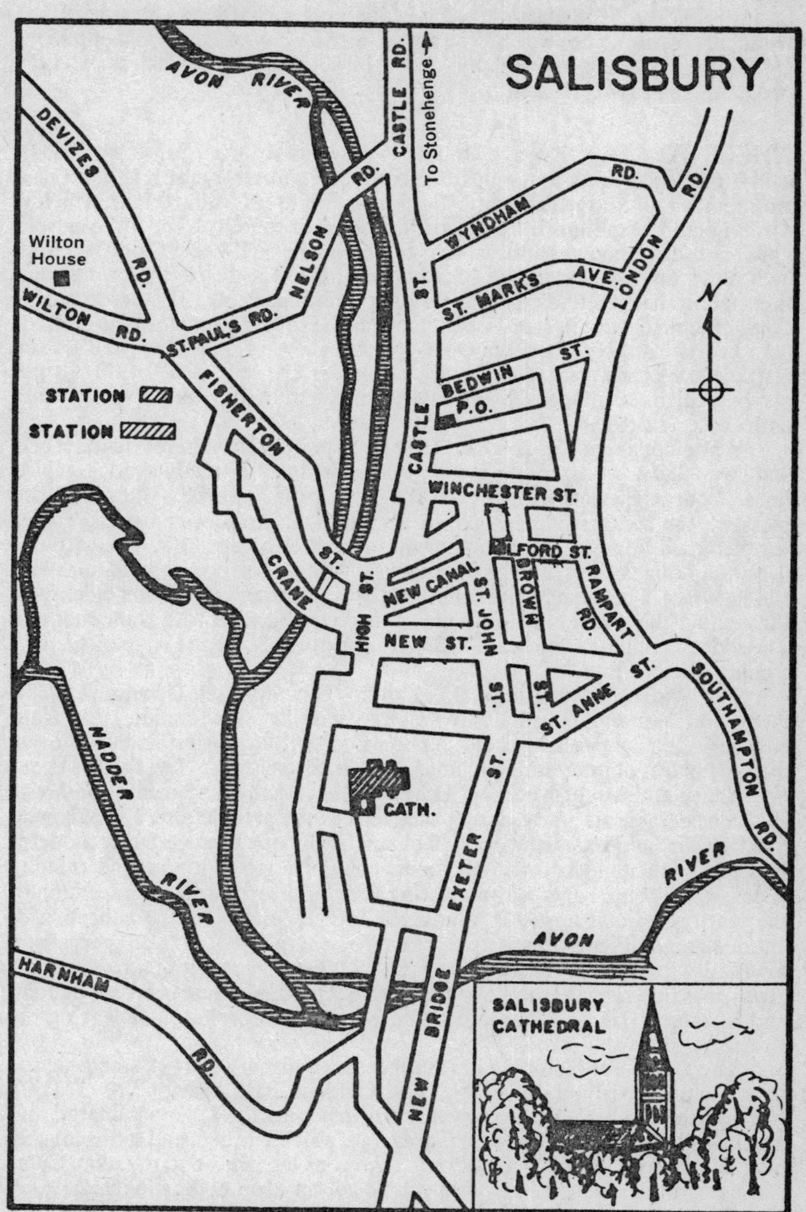
SALISBURY
AVON RIVER
CASTLE RD.
To Stonehenge
DEVIZES RD.
NELSON RD.
Wilton House
WILTON RD.
ST. PAUL'S RD.
WYNDHAM RD.
LONDON RD.
ST. MARK'S AVE.
N
CASTLE ST.
BEDWIN ST.
P.O.
STATION
STATION
FISHERTON ST.
WINCHESTER ST.
LFORD ST.
CRANE ST.
HIGH ST.
NEW CANAL
ST. JOHN ST.
BROWN ST.
RAMPART RD.
NEW ST.
ST. ANNE ST.
SOUTHAMPTON RD.
NADDER RIVER
CATH.
EXETER ST.
RIVER AVON
HARNHAM RD.
NEW BRIDGE
SALISBURY CATHEDRAL

GUIDED TOURS: Daily throughout the summer at 6:30 p.m., and also at 2:30 p.m. on Wednesday, registered guides conduct walking tours around Salisbury, through the City Chequers, visiting St. Thomas's Church and the Cathedral Close. The starting point is the notice board on the side of the Guildhall, facing Queen Street. The cost is 70p ($1.23) for adults and 30p (53¢) for children. There is also a family ticket for £1.70 ($2.98) which is good for two adults and two children.

WHERE TO STAY: **Byways House,** 31 Fowlers Rd. (tel. Salisbury 28364), is in a residential area that consists mostly of Victorian houses. It is about a ten-minute walk to the cathedral. Turn to the right off Milford Hill, which is a continuation of Milford Street in the center of the city. The 100-year-old house is in very good condition, and the garden is well kept. Front windows look down onto the cathedral. Mr. and Mrs. Neil Castle are the owners and their family backgrounds include farming and innkeeping. The accommodations, of course, vary in size. A bungalow in the garden provides four ground-floor bedrooms. Five of the units have private showers and toilets, and for the rest adequate showers and baths are available. The cost is £10 ($17.50) per person, which includes tax, breakfast, heating, and baths. Rooms with private baths cost £12 ($21).

White Lodge, 68 London Rd. (tel. Salisbury 27991), is the residence of Mr. and Mrs. Law, who receive paying guests in their attractive, brick-gabled house, charging about £10.50 ($18.38) per person for B&B. The rooms are pleasant, the breakfasts personalized. In addition, the Laws have taken over another good house, a few doors down, to handle the overflow. The entrance to White Lodge is, in reality, a greenhouse, with lots of potted geraniums and trailing vines. The main hall is dominated by an antique grandfather clock, and throughout the house you'll find nice old pieces, blended with some modern. The lodge is opposite St. Mark's Church, on the A30 at the edge of the city coming in from London.

The **Warren Guest House,** 15 High St., Downton (tel. Downton 20263), is in an attractive and unspoiled Wiltshire village just a ten-minute drive from Salisbury. It's an excellent center for touring, as it lies within an hour's drive of many places of interest, including Longleat, Stonehenge, New Forest, Beaulieu Abbey and Motor Museum, H.M.S. *Victory,* and Old Sarum. The house is of considerable antiquity, dating back to the time of Sir Walter Raleigh, who lived nearby, and retains its original character, having been carefully modernized to a high standard, with all rooms equipped with hot and cold running water, razor points, and central heating. The furniture (with the exception of the mattresses, of course), is almost all antique, and a superb collection of antique grandfather clocks is on display. The charge is £9 ($15.75) per person for B&B without bath, rising to £10 ($17.50) per person with bath. Breakfast always has free-range eggs and filtered coffee. The guest house is owned by John and Elizabeth Baxter. Now retired, he was a metal broker after leaving the British army.

The **Cathedral Hotel,** Milford Street (tel. Salisbury 20144), stands across from the old Red Lion. Its double rooms without bath rent for £18 ($31.50), going up to £21 ($36.75) with private bath, including VAT, service charge, and a full English breakfast. The rooms are large, well furnished, and immaculately maintained. Add to that an elevator to take your luggage up to the rooms, plus extremely pleasant personnel, and you've got an ideal night's lodging.

Stratford Lodge, 4 Park Lane, Castle Road (tel. Salisbury 25177), is run by Jill and Bill Bayly, who give you a friendly welcome at their B&B, charging from £10 ($17.50) per person nightly. Their lodge stands in a residential area, across from Victoria Park. Whenever possible, home produce is offered, and the cookery is just fine—so good in fact that you should ask for the half-board rate of £16 ($28) per person nightly. From the cathedral city of Salisbury, take the A345 road to Amesbury. You'll see a sign.

On the Outskirts

The **Cross Keys Hotel,** Shaftesbury Road at Fovant (tel. Fovant 284), is ideal if you're motoring. Stone built, it dates from the late 15th century and is said to have been frequented by the notorious highwayman Jack Rattenbury. Mrs. Story not only does B&B at £8 ($14) per head, but she prepares excellent English fare, including pheasant on occasion (this is likely to cost from £6.50 or $11.38), along with venison, local trout, and duck in orange sauce. Cottage pie is regularly featured, and you can always get a steak. Usually there is a choice of a dozen main courses, along with about seven appetizers and the equivalent number of desserts. For a typical meal, expect to spend from £6 ($10.50). Hours are from 7:30 a.m. to midnight every day; however, alcoholic beverages can only be served during regular licensing hours.

Netton Old Farmhouse, Bishopstone, (tel. 072/278565), is a stone farmhouse under a thatch roof dating from 1637. It is believed that King Charles I stayed in the house during the early years of the Civil War. The house has recently been renovated to a very high standard, and the accommodations available include two double bedrooms (one with its own bath) and two twin-bedded rooms. The house stands in 1½ acres of traditional English garden in the middle of the small village of Bishopstone, next to a trout stream. The village is only four miles southwest of Salisbury, and is convenient for exploring Stonehenge and Wilton House. The New Forest is only a half-hour drive from the house, and there are two golf courses nearby. B&B costs from £8.50 ($14.88) in a single, from £14.50 ($25.38) to £16.50 ($28.86) in a double. Dinner isn't offered, but there are a number of excellent thatched old pubs nearby, serving good meals at reasonable prices. The owner, Peter Burke, will direct you. Children are welcome, and the Burkes have children of their own who will let others ride their pet donkey.

READERS' GUEST HOUSE SELECTIONS: "Try the **Lazy Corner,** 145 Rampart Rd. (tel. Salisbury 27585), the house of Mrs. I. F. Van Dyke. The price of a twin-bedded room and two very good breakfasts is £7 ($12.25) per person per night. Mrs. Van Dyke's accommodations are somewhat difficult to find, as they are separated from the center of the city (the bus station, the train station, and the cathedral) by a highway, yet they are only a five-minute walk from the center of the city" (Christian J. Mixter and Glenn E. Morrical, Columbus, Ohio). . . . "A lovely B&B place I stayed in is the home of Mr. and Mrs. Spiller, at Nuholme, Ashfield Road (tel. Salisbury 336592). It is a spacious row house, and the Spillers are exceptionally friendly. They generally have three rooms to rent, which are warm and well furnished. The railroad station is an eight-minute walk from their home, and they are only too happy to let guests use the bath (very modern) or go for a walk in their pleasant garden. The low price of £6 ($10.50) per night, per person, includes a home-cooked breakfast" (Jeffrey Spiegler, Cleveland, Ohio).

"Of all the B&Bs we stayed in during our trip to England, we most enjoyed and highly recommend the home of Mr. and Mrs. Marks, **Hayburn Wyke Guest House,** 72 Castle Rd. (tel. Salisbury 24141). The price per person in a double-bedded room with a fantastic breakfast is £8 ($14) per night, including VAT and service. This 2½-story B&B consists of six spacious bedrooms, a dining room, a comfortable lounge with color TV, and a shower. Bill and Doreen Marks are charming hosts and most anxious to please. Their home is immaculate and beautifully decorated with plush carpeting throughout. Bill is also licensed for taxi service and can pick you up at the station, although they are only a ten-minute walk from the city center. Also, there is ample parking for three to four cars" (Larry and Vilma Anderson, Laguna Niguel, Calif., and Kenneth and Shirley

Raemsch, Tajunga, Calif.). . . . "At the **Motorish Motel** on the A38 outside Salisbury, we stayed in a modern motel facility. We were pleased by the rural setting and the chance to walk along the quiet country roads nearby. The duck dinner we had in the pleasant, cozy, wood-paneled dining room was good and the service attentive. The large breakfast we had the following morning was one of the best of our trip. B&B costs £18 ($31.50) for a double room. The duck dinner goes for about £9 ($15.75) per person, including cocktails, dessert, and a tip" (Susan M. Kocik, New York, N.Y.).

READER'S HOTEL SELECTION AT AMESBURY: "The **Fairlawn Hotel,** High Street (tel. Amesbury 22103), is ideally located for an in-depth visit to the archeological sites on Salisbury Plain. It is only two miles from Stonehenge and one mile from Woodhenge and Durrington Walls. The hotel is a Georgian building well into its third century. A single goes for £9 ($15.75), a double or twin for from £17.50 ($30.63), and three- to four-bedded family rooms range in price from £24.75 ($43.31) to £32 ($56). A double with private shower rents for £18.50 ($32.28), VAT included. The rooms are immaculate and sunny. The hotel has a cocktail lounge and restaurant. Gerald Hawkins, author of *Stonehenge Decoded,* stayed at the Fairlawn when he visited the area. The Tourist Information Centre in Salisbury will gladly make your reservations to assure the availability of a room before you start to Amesbury" (Edward Pasahow, San Diego, Calif.).

READERS' GUEST HOUSE SELECTION NEAR HINDON: "A fine accommodation in Chicklade on the A303 east of its junction with the A350 in Wiltshire is **The Old Rectory** (tel. Hindon 226). This 17th-century rectory, next to the Chicklade Church which is even older, is operated as a guest house by Mr. and Mrs. David Head. B&B is £9 ($15.75) per person, and B&B with dinner costs £13 ($22.75) per person. The evening meal is worth an early reservation. We had steak-and-kidney pie for the first dinner and roast lamb for the second. Both were excellent. Chicklade is central to Stonehenge, Salisbury, Winchester, and the Roman baths in Bath, as well as to the seacoast towns of Bristol and Exeter. All these attractions can be reached by day trips. There are eight spacious bedrooms, one single, two double, and three twin-bedded. All have hot and cold running water. Baths and showers are available at all times. We were so impressed that we drove 100 miles out of our way to stay there a second time just before leaving England" (Mr. and Mrs. J. Lombard, Phoenix, Ariz.).

DINING: Michael J. R. Snell, 8 St. Thomas's Square (tel. Salisbury 6037), is the best all-around tea room and pâtisserie in Salisbury. His specialty is tea and coffee along with handmade chocolates. Trained in Switzerland, Mr. Snell is a friendly, considerate owner-manager. He keeps his place open Monday to Saturday from 9 a.m. to 5:30 p.m. In fair weather the atmosphere becomes quite continental, with umbrella-shaded tables placed out on the square. In the afternoon you can enjoy a Wiltshire clotted cream tea with scones at £1.50 ($2.63) per person. Among the dessert specialties, I'd make a detour for a slice of his forêt noire gâteau at £1 ($1.75), a Black Forest cake. Try also his black cherry cheese cake for the same price. A reasonable luncheon menu, which is likely to include everything from New Forest venison pâté to pizza flan, is offered until 2:30 p.m., costing from £2.50 ($4.38) per person. Each main dish is served with a choice of salads. Coffee is roasted right on the premises, and you can see the coffee-roasting room by the river. Children's portions are also available.

The **Old House,** 471 New St. (tel. Salisbury 4651), is a 15th-century, oak-beamed tea room owned and managed by Jack and Breeda Falconer. The central hall is filled with antique furniture and old copper, and on the walls are original oil paintings of scenes of village life. The well-prepared luncheon is a bargain, usually including a bowl of vegetable soup, a meat entree with vegetables, followed by an English dessert, such as apple charlotte. On weekdays, lunches go for £2.70 ($4.73), going up to £3 ($5.25) on Saturday, £4.50 ($7.88) on Sunday. Morning coffee is also available at 45p (79¢), and a three-course dinner for around £5.95 ($6.91).

The **Haunch of Vension,** Minster Street (tel. Salisbury 22024), deserves its popularity. Right in the heart of Salisbury, this creaky timbered, 14th-century chophouse serves some excellent dishes, especially English roasts and grills. Stick to its specialties and you'll rarely go wrong. Diners with more adventurous palates will sample a bowl of game soup. The pièce de résistance of the inn is its local New Forest haunch of venison, with chestnut puree and red currant jelly. A set lunch goes for around £4.75 ($8.31). If you avoid the à la carte menu in the evening, you can order a set dinner at only £8 ($14). All this good food and hospitality are offered in a treasured building, dating back to 1320. The centuries have given a gleam to the oak furnishings, and years of polishing have worn down the brass. Twisting steps lead to tiny, cozy rooms (there is one small room with space for about four to sit where you can saturate yourself in the best of England's yesterdays and todays). Two windows of the barroom overlook St. Thomas's cloisters (naturally, it's called the Cloisters Chamber). Dancing fires are kept burning in the old fireplace; heavy beams are overhead; antique chairs encircle the tables. The restaurant is run by Mr. Leroy, and the chef is Tim Philbrick. It is closed Sunday and open Monday in the evening only. Otherwise, hours are from noon to 2 p.m. and from 7 to 10 p.m.

The **Red Lion Hotel,** Milford Street (tel. Salisbury 23334), is too stately to roar. But since the 1300s, it's been putting up wayfarers who rumbled in stagecoaches from London across the Salisbury Plain to the West Countree. Cross under its arch into a courtyard with a hanging and much-photographed creeper, a red lion, and a half-timbered facade, and you'll be transplanted back to the good old days. An à la carte luncheon is from £5 ($8.75). The recommendable dinner ranges from £9 ($15.75) for a three-course meal. House specialties include jugged hare with red currant jelly, roast venison, steak-and-kidney pie, and roast beef with horseradish sauce. Meals are served from 12:30 to 1:45 p.m. and from 7 to 9 p.m.

The **White Hart Hotel,** St. John Street (tel. Salisbury 27476), has a particularly good set lunch menu, beginning with such tempting appetizers as prawns in aspic or turkey and ham mousse. You might follow with a roast joint or vegetable, or a choice from the cold salad and meats buffet, all for a cost of about £6 ($10.50), including service and VAT. The cold buffet, incidentally, is laden with roast beef, hams, homemade chicken and ham pie, pâtés of chicken liver, duck, and brandy, as well as smoked fish. There are also relishes and salads to accompany such selections. The snackbar in the hotel also offers a variety of light dishes, including corned beef for around £1.50 ($2.63).

The **New Inn,** 43 New St. (tel. Salisbury 27679), isn't new at all. Backing up to the Cathedral Close wall, it's a bit of old England. The center of the inn is the serving bar, which is a common counter for three outer rooms—one, a tiny sitting area; another, a tavern with high-backed settles and a fireplace; the third, a lounge with a dart game. You'll find stacks of little pork pies for 28p (49¢), to be eaten cold and washed down with pints of ale. A half pint of draft cider costs 52p (91¢). Snacks include a ploughman's lunch at 90p ($1.58) or sandwiches, which begin at 65p ($1.14). You'll know instantly that this is the pub of the people, relatively undiscovered.

Harper's Restaurant, 7–9 Market Place (tel. Salisbury 3118), is run by Adrian Harper, who has a cosmopolitan, continental menu. Previously named Claire's, it recently reopened upstairs under its new name, with its reputation and clientele intact. This pleasantly decorated restaurant offers a large quiche of the day, including a customer's foray to the salad bar, costing £3 ($5.25). A variety of inexpensive daily specials are offered. You might find hot ratatouille on the menu, along with grilled English lamb chops with orange and mint sauce, followed by a homemade lemon and treacle tart with cream, costing £4.65 ($8.14). Children's portions of fish fries and hamburgers cost around £1.40 ($2.45). Harper's is open Monday through Saturday from noon to 2:30 p.m. and 6:30 to 10 p.m.

Raffles Tea Room, Mitre House, 37 High St. (tel. Salisbury 3705), lies in the House of Tweed, offering convenient refreshment for visitors or shoppers. Light meals are served, including cona toasties, a Scottish-derived formula for closed toasted sandwiches, which include ham and pineapple at £1.30 ($2.28). A fixed-price, refreshing English tea at Raffles includes two scones with jam and cream, and naturally a large pot of Earl Grey or Ceylon tea, for £1.35 ($2.36). There is a wide choice of cakes and eclairs, averaging about 65p ($1.14), as well as hot dishes and cold salads—a satisfying meal in themselves—for around £2.50 ($4.38). Raffles is open from 9:30 a.m. to 7 p.m. (from 10:30 a.m. to 4:30 p.m. on Sunday) in summer, and from 9:30 a.m. to 5 p.m., Monday through Saturday only, in winter.

Bay Tree Restaurant and Cake Shop, High Street, is really a "quick meal" place opposite Woolworth's. Although modern, this bow-fronted café blends with the ancient buildings around it. Waitresses move fast between the tables, serving very typically English fare, including mixed grills and fish and chips. A line of cold salads is also presented. A simple meal can be ordered here for around £4 ($7). It is open daily from 11 a.m. to 9:30 p.m., taking a short break from 5 to 6 p.m. when they mop up.

Sarah's, Blue Boar Row, is a useful, quick, and spotless self-service cafeteria where you can take out the food or stay to eat it in the restaurant behind the shop. The restaurant is hung with continental sausages and garlic cloves. Sandwiches are made from bread rolls with a variety of fillings, and there is a good selection of salads and a choice of pies. You can order chicken flan and an apple in Sarah's lunchbox for only 92p ($1.62). Sandwiches run from 42p (74¢) to 80p ($1.40).

When you've finished shopping, relax in the **Blue Boar Restaurant,** above Debenham's store, just off the Market Place. The restaurant is a historian's paradise of oak hammer beams, open fireplaces, and wheelback chairs. Tables are set off by the warm red carpet. It's a good example of an old building put to modern use. It's open from 9 a.m. to 5:30 p.m., Monday to Saturday, offering a wide range of dishes, including steak-and-kidney pie, fried filet of plaice, and prawn salad with mayonnaise. They also offer three-decker club sandwiches. You won't spend more than £3.50 ($6.13) at the most.

Reeve the Baker, Butcher Row, does sandwiches made from rolls, along with small french battens, baps, and french bread to take away stuffed with all sorts of goodies—cheese and pickle, liver sausage, ham, watercress, cold beef. You can make up your own picnic. Salads are priced from 25p (44¢) to 36p (63¢). There are also cakes and scones to round off your picnic.

READER'S RESTAURANT SUGGESTION: "The **Asia (Indian) Restaurant,** 90 Fisherton St. (tel. Salisbury 27628), is an excellent eating place we found between trains after visiting Stonehenge. For very little money, we had a shrimp-and-rice dish, a chicken-and-rice dish, Oriental vegetables, and tea. The cost is about £4.85 ($8.49) each, a beautiful and bountiful bargain. The service is excellent, too" (Mrs. Seymour H. Kaplan, Mercer Island, Wash.).

SIDE TRIPS FROM SALISBURY: Less than two miles north of Salisbury is **Old Sarum,** the remains of what is believed to have been an Iron Age fortification. The earthworks were known to the Romans as Sorbiodunum, and later to the Saxons. The Normans, in fact, built a cathedral and a castle in what was then a walled town of the Middle Ages. Parts of the old cathedral were disassembled to erect the cathedral at New Sarum. It is open March to October from 9:30 a.m. to 6:30 p.m. weekdays and from 2 to 6:30 p.m. on Sunday. From October to March it has a shorter schedule: from 9:30 a.m. to 4 p.m. weekdays and 2 to 4 p.m. on Sunday. Admission is 40p (70¢).

Wilton House

In the small borough of Wilton, less than three miles to the west of Salisbury, is one of England's great country estates, Wilton House (tel. Wilton 3641), the home of the Earl of Pembroke. The stately house in the midst of 20 acres of grounds dates from the 16th century, but has seen modifications over the years, as late as Victoria's day. It is noted for its 17th-century state rooms by Inigo Jones. Many famous personages have either lived at or visited Wilton. It is believed that Shakespeare's troupe entertained here. Plans for the D-Day landings at Normandy were laid out here by Eisenhower and his advisers, in the utmost secrecy, with only the silent Van Dycks in the Double Cube room as witnesses. The house is filled with beautifully maintained furnishings, especially a collection of Chippendale. Wilton House displays some of the finest paintings in England, including works by Rembrandt, Rubens, Reynolds, and the already-mentioned Van Dycks.

The estate lies in the midst of gardens and grounds, with Cedars of Lebanon, the oldest of which were planted in 1630. The Palladian Bridge was built in 1737. Wilton House may be visited Tuesday through Saturday and bank holidays from 11 a.m. to 6 p.m., and on Sunday from 1 to 6 p.m. Guided tours are conducted daily except Sunday from March 29 to October 9. Admission is £1.80 ($3.15) for adults, £1 ($1.75) for children under 16.

The excellent, fully licensed, self-service restaurant is open during house hours and offers homemade cooking. Cold buffet with a selection of cold meats and quiches costs from 70p ($1.23) a portion, with a selection of fresh salads priced from 35p (61¢). Hot dishes can be had by ordering ahead. Don't miss a Wilton House cream tea.

There is an Adventure Playground for children, plus an exhibition of 7000 model soldiers and "The Pembroke Palace" dollhouse. You can also visit "England's Heritage in Miniature," the new model railway which is in the 14th-century almonry.

Stonehenge

Two miles west of Amesbury and about nine miles north of Salisbury is the renowned Stonehenge, believed to be anywhere from 3500 to 5000 years old. This huge oval of lintels and megalithic pillars is the most important prehistoric monument in Britain.

Some North Americans have expressed their disappointment after seeing the concentric circles of stones, which have been fenced off to protect the stones from the ravages of visitors. However, you can get within about 20 feet of the stones. Admittedly, they are not the pyramids, and some imagination has to be brought to bear on them. Pyramids or not, they represent an amazing engineering feat. Many of the boulders, the bluestones in particular, were moved hundreds of miles, perhaps from southern Wales, to this site by the ancients. If you're fanciful, you can always credit Merlin with delivering them on clouds from Ireland.

The widely held view of the 18th- and 19th-century romantics that Stonehenge was the work of the Druids is without foundation. The boulders, many weighing into the tons, are believed to have predated the arrival in Britain of that Celtic cult. Recent excavations continue to bring new evidence to bear on the origin and purpose of Stonehenge. The prehistoric site was a subject of controversy following the publication of *Stonehenge Decoded* by Gerald S. Hawkins and John B. White, which maintained that Stonehenge was in fact an astronomical observatory. That is, a Neolithic computing machine capable of predicting eclipses.

Others who discount Hawkin's decoding would prefer to adopt Henry James's approach to Stonehenge, which regards it as "lonely in history," its origin and purposes (burial ground, sun-worshipping site, human sacrificial temple?) the secret of the silent, mysterious Salisbury Plain.

Admission is 60p ($1.05) for adults and 30p (53¢) for children. In March, April, and October, hours are from 9:30 a.m. to 5:30 p.m.; May to September, to 7 p.m., and November to February, to 4:30 p.m. There is a small snackbar, offering very nice fresh sandwiches, hot pies and cakes, soft drinks, tea and coffee. There's also a free car park.

If you don't have a car, getting to Stonehenge can be difficult unless you're athletic. First, take the bus to Amesbury, then walk about 2½ miles to Stonehenge. The British do this all the time, and they don't complain. But if that is too strenuous, you'd better take one of the organized coach tours out of Salisbury.

To protect these ancient stones, Stonehenge has been fenced off.

READERS' GUEST HOUSE SELECTION: "Mrs. Podger at **Seend Bridge Farm**, Seend, Melksham (tel. Seend 534), charges £7 ($12.25) per night per person for B&B and £5 ($8.75) for a good, bountiful evening meal. English guests were also staying (this in itself is an excellent recommendation), and between them and Mrs. Podger we learned of local prehistory and several fascinating nearby places to visit, including Silbury Hill constructed by the ancestors of Stonehenge and the Elizabethan village of Lacock" (Gail and Keith Randall, Glendale, Calif.).

Longleat House

Between Bath and Salisbury, Longleat House (tel. Maiden Bradley 551) lies four miles southwest of Warminster, 4½ miles southeast of Frome on the A362. The first view of this magnificent Elizabethan house, built in the early Renaissance style, is romantic enough, but the wealth of paintings and furnishings within its lofty rooms is enough to dazzle. The Venetian ceilings were added in Queen Victoria's time by the fourth Marquess of Bath.

A tour of the house, from the Elizabethan Great Hall, through libraries, the State Rooms, and the Grand Staircase, is awe inspiring in its variety and splendor. The State Dining Room is full of silver and plate, and fine tapestries and paintings adorn the walls in rich profusion. The Victorian kitchens are open during the summer months, offering a glimpse of life below the stairs in a well-ordered country home. Various exhibitions are mounted in the Stable Yard, and the Safari Park contains a vast array of animals in open parklands. During the summer months, a program of outside events is arranged on weekends.

The house is open all year except Christmas Day. The Safari Park closes in winter. Admission to the house is £1.75 ($3.06) for adults, 75p ($1.31) for children. The Safari Park costs £1.95 ($3.41) per adult and £1.32 ($2.31) per child. The road toll is 60p ($1.05) per adult—maximum £1 ($1.75) per car—at the entrance to the grounds, giving access to the gardens, picnic areas, and parking facilities. There are many attractions within the grounds, including a 15-inch gauge railway ride, safari boats, pets' corner, and a doll's house.

A maze, believed to be the largest in the world, has been added to the attractions by Lord Weymouth, son of the marquess. It has more than 1½ miles of paths among yew trees. The first part is comparatively easy, but the second part is very complicated, with bridges adding to the confusion. It knocks the Hampton Court maze into a cocked hat, as the British say. The house also contains more than 39,000 magnificent books and rare manuscripts, some of which are on display to the public.

Stourhead

After Longleat, you can drive six miles south down route A3092 to Stourton, a village just off the A3092, three miles northwest of Mere (A303). Stourhead (tel. Bourton 840587), a Palladian house, was built in the 18th century by the banking family of Hoare. The pleasure grounds became known as *le jardin anglais,* in that they blended art and nature. Set around an artificial lake, the grounds are decorated with temples, bridges, islands, and grottos, as well as statuary. It is open April to October from 2 to 6 p.m. on Monday, Wednesday, Saturday, and Sunday. From May to the end of September it's open daily except Friday from 2 to 6 p.m. Admission is £1.60 ($2.80) to the house and £1.20 ($2.10) to the garden. The gardens are open daily from 8 a.m. to 7 p.m. or dusk.

Avebury

One of the largest prehistoric sites in Europe, Avebury lies about six miles west of Marlborough on the Kennet River. It is gaining in popularity with visitors now that the British have had to rope off the sarsen circle at Stonehenge. Explorers are able to walk the 28-acre site at Avebury, winding in and out of the circle of more than 100 stones, some weighing up to 50 tons. They are made of sarsen, a sandstone found in Wiltshire. Inside this large circle are two smaller ones, each with about 30 stones standing upright. Native Neolithic tribes are believed to have built these circles. The village of Avebury, taken over by the National Trust, bisects the prehistoric monument, and is worth exploring.

Dating from before the Conquest, **Avebury Manor** (tel. Avebury 203) was built on the site of a Benedictine cell. An early Elizabethan manor house, it stands beside the great stone circle of Avebury. The manor is carefully restored and is now a family home which can be visited in May and September on Saturday and Sunday, 2 to 5 p.m.; in June, July, and August, daily from 2 to 5 p.m. Admission charges are £1 ($1.75) for adults and 50p (88¢) for children. Inside you'll find oak-paneled rooms and coved plasterwork ceilings. The state rooms were visited by Queen Anne and Charles II. Throughout is much early oak and fine furniture in a period setting. Portraits date from 1532. The Queen Anne bedroom, with its imposing state bed, is of particular note, and is the Cavalier bedroom, linked with tales of the supernatural and recounted by more than one visitor staying at the manor. The surrounding garden and parkland are equally intriguing. The topairy—old yew and box—pleasantly emphasize the historic atmosphere. Outside attractions include the walled garden, herb border, wishing well, and a 16th-century dovecote. Car parking is within the manor grounds.

The **Alexander Keiller Museum** (tel. Avebury 250) houses an important collection of archeological finds from the Avebury area, and a display illustrating prehistoric monuments. From mid-March to mid-October, it is open from 9:30 a.m. to 6:30 p.m. weekdays (on Sunday from 2 to 6:30 p.m.). Off-season hours are from 9:30 a.m. to 4 p.m. weekdays (from 2 to 4 p.m. on Sunday). Admission is 50p (88¢) for adults, 25p (44¢) for children under 16.

The **Wiltshire Folk Society Great Barn** (tel. Avebury 333) is a center for the display and interpretation of Wiltshire during the past three centuries. It houses a museum dealing with local geology, farming, craftsmen, and domestic life. From April to October it is open from 10 a.m. to 5:30 p.m., Monday to Saturday (from 10:30 a.m. to 5:30 p.m. on Sunday). Admission is 60p ($1.05) for adults, 30p (53¢) for children. Or else you can purchase a ticket for your whole family at £1.20 ($2.10).

After sightseeing—and still in the same vicinity—you may be ready for a "cuppa."

On the A350 Blandford road, 20 miles from Warminster, stands **Milestones,** Compton Abbas, near Shaftesbury in Dorset (tel. Fontmell Magna 811360), a 17th-century tea room right next to the church, with gorgeous views over the Dorset hills. This spotless little place is presided over by two delightful women who serve real farmhouse teas at £1.50 ($2.63), or a ploughman's lunch at £1.30 ($2.28). Fresh sandwiches are also offered for 50p (88¢) to 65p ($1.14). This is really the ideal English tea room, and the women who run it are charming and friendly. Morning coffee is served from 10 a.m. to 1 p.m. and afternoon tea from 2:30 to 5:30 p.m. except Thursday.

Lacock

Lacock is a National Trust village, with an abbey dating from 1232 and a famous photographic museum. It's a good base for exploring Bath, Castle Combe, and Longleat.

Your best accommodations bet is **The Old Rectory,** Cantax Hill, Lacock, near Chippenham. Mrs. Margaret Addison welcomes visitors to her old house which was built in 1866. The house stands in its own grounds of eight acres, with ample car parking space just off the A350 Chippenham–Melksham road. In comfortably furnished rooms, B&B is offered at a rate of £8.50 ($14.88) per person. A lounge with TV is provided for guests, and each unit has a kettle for making your own coffee.

2. Castle Combe

Once voted Britain's prettiest village, Castle Combe was used for location shots for *Dr. Doolittle.* About ten miles from Bath, this little Cotswold village is filled with shops selling souvenirs and antiques. The village cottages are often set beside a trout stream, and are made of stone with moss-laden roofs. The church is unremarkable except for its 15th-century tower. An old market cross and a triple-arched bridge are much photographed.

No accommodation but plenty of local color is offered at the **White Hart,** on the main road through the village (tel. Castle Combe 782295). It's a painted-white pub built of Cotswold stone and covered with a stone tile roof. Dating from either the 13th or 14th century, it has low ceilings (in the cellars are Norman arches). The main bar is divided into two parts, with a cold buffet counter for meals. The garden is also open to visitors, and the parlor bar admits children. This is the first venture of Dennis and Cath Wheeler (she calls it "my husband's indulgence"). Den, as he is known, works in London, commuting daily, and Cath is helped by her attractive daughters. Den's specialty is a landlord's pâté, and he claims the ingredients aren't "poached." Home-cooked ham or beef, with cole slaw and bread and butter, is offered at from £3 ($5.25). In winter, hot soups, chili, hot pasties, and toasted sandwiches are available.

Bitter beer from traditional wooden barrels is popular with the locals. They have a black cat, Pussy Galore, who drinks milk with her paws from a wine glass. This is one of the few traditional English pubs in the Cotswolds recommended for evening life.

READER'S GUEST HOUSE SELECTION: "Our favorite place is called the **Old Rectory** (tel. Castle Combe 782366), run by Fred and Barbara Rigby who are absolutely delightful. They welcomed us into their living room and shared their television and several hours of conversation. They offered all sorts of refreshment, served a wonderful breakfast, and gave us scones from their tea shop to take on the road the next morning. Our room had a fireplace and a private bath. The price of £22 ($38.50) is the least expensive in the village, and it's a bargain" (Ellen Fader, New York, N.Y.).

SOMERSET

When writing about Somerset, it's difficult to avoid sounding like the editor of *The Countryside Companion,* waxing poetic over hills and valleys, dale and field. In scenery, the western shire embraces some of nature's most masterly touches in England. Mendip's limestone hills undulate across the countryside (ever had a pot-holing holiday?). The irresistible Quantocks are the pride of the west, especially lovely in spring and fall. Here, too, is the heather-clad **Exmoor National Park,** a wooded area abounding in red deer and wild ponies, much of its moorland 1200 feet above sea level. Somerset opens onto the Bristol Channel, with Minehead being the chief resort.

Somerset is rich in legend and history, and is particularly fanciful about its associations with King Arthur and Queen Guinevere, along with Camelot and Alfred the Great. Its villages are noted for the tall towers of their parish churches.

Of the many Norman castles erected in the country, the most important one remaining is **Dunster Castle** (tel. Dunster 314), three miles southeast of Minehead in the village of Dunster, just off the A39. The National Trust owns the property and 30 acres of surrounding parkland. Terraced walks and gardens command good views of Exmoor, the Quantock Hills, and the Bristol Channel. Outstanding among the contents within are the 17th-century panels of embossed painted and gilded leather depicting the story of Antony and Cleopatra, and a remarkable 16th-century portrait of Sir John Luttrell shown wading naked through the sea with a female figure of peace and a wrecked ship in the background. The 17th-century plasterwork ceilings of the dining room and staircase and the finely carved staircase balustrade of cavorting huntsmen, hounds, and stags are also particularly noteworthy. The castle may be visited from April 3 until the end of September every day except Friday and Saturday from 11 a.m. to 5 p.m. (last admission 4:30). In October it is open on Tuesday, Wednesday, and Sunday from 2 to 4 p.m. Admission is £1.80 ($3.15) for adults, 90p ($1.58) for children.

A quiet, unspoiled life holds forth in Somerset. You're likely to end up in a vine-covered old inn, talking with the regulars about staghounds. Or you may anchor at a large estate that stands in a woodland setting—surrounded by bridle paths and sheep walks (Somerset was once a great wool center). Maybe you'll settle down in a 16th-century, thatched, stone farmhouse, set in the midst of orchards in a vale. Somerset is reputed (and I heartily concur) to have the best cider anywhere. When you lounge under a shady Somerset apple tree, downing a tankard of refreshingly chilled, golden cider, everything you've drunk in the past tastes like apple juice.

My notes on Somerset, accumulated over many a year, would easily fill a book. But space and limited schedule being what they are, I confined the following comments in the main to the shire's two most interesting towns, Wells and Glastonbury. Still, I'll throw in a few farmhouse recommendations off the beaten path, for those who want rural atmosphere.

3. Wells

In Wells, we meet the Middle Ages. At the south of the Mendip Hills, the cathedral town is a medieval gem. It lies only 21 miles from Bath, but 123 from London. Wells was a vital link in the Saxon kingdom of Wessex—that is, important in England long before the arrival of William the Conqueror. Once the seat of a bishopric, it was eventually toppled from its ecclesiastical hierarchy by the rival city of Bath. But the subsequent loss of prestige has paid off handsomely in Wells today. After experiencing the pinnacle of prestige, it fell into a slumber, and for that reason much of its old look remains. Wells was named after wells in the town, which were often visited by pilgrims to Glastonbury in the hope that their gout could be eased by the supposedly curative waters. The crowning achievement of the town is:

WELLS CATHEDRAL: Dating from the 12th century, Wells Cathedral is a well-preserved, mellow example of the Early English style of architecture. The medieval sculpture (six tiers of hundreds of statues now undergoing preservation work) of its West Front is without peer in England. The western facade was completed in and around the mid-13th century. The landmark central tower was erected in the 14th century, with its attractive fan vaulting attached later. The inverted arches were added to strengthen the top-heavy structure.

Much of the stained glass dates from the 14th century. The fan-vaulted Lady Chapel, also from the 14th-century, is in the Decorated style. To the north is the vaulted Chapter House, built in the late 13th century. Look also for a medieval astronomical clock in the north transept.

After a visit to the cathedral, walk along its cloisters to the moated Bishop's Palace of the Middle Ages. In the moat, the swans ring a bell when they're hungry. Its former Great Hall, built in the 13th century, is now in ruins. Finally, the small lane known as the Vicar's Close is one of the most beautifully preserved streets in England. The facade of the cathedral is currently being restored, a project under the sponsorship of Prince Charles.

WHERE TO STAY: You may want to base at Wells, as its budget establishments are better than equivalent-priced lodgings at Bath.

Ancient Gatehouse Hotel, Sadler Street (tel. Wells 72029). Its front is on Sadler Street, and the back overlooks the cathedral and the lovely open lawn in front of the cathedral's west door. Run by Francesco Rossi—known as Franco to everyone—the Gatehouse has nine rooms to rent. Two rooms at the front of the hotel, with adjoining shower and toilet facilities, rent for £27 ($47.25) in a double. Doubles with shared baths cost £22 ($38.50) nightly, the price lowered to £12 ($21) in a single. They also offer a "mini-break" tariff at £37 ($64.75) to £40 ($70) per person for rooms with showers, including two breakfasts, one lunch, and two dinners, as well as VAT. Mr. Rossi also rents out a double room with a four-poster bed and a private bath.

Franco also runs the Rugantino Restaurant attached to the hotel, where pastas and Italian dishes are a specialty. A large spaghetti bolognaise goes for £2.25 ($3.94), or you can order lasagne or ravioli for the same price. A specialty is chicken in red wine with mushrooms and onions at £3.50 ($6.13), and there's an intriguing list of appetizers, beginning at 80p ($1.40) for a fresh homemade soup. Vegetables are supplied fresh whenever possible, and include some imported out-of-season delicacies.

The **Sherston Hotel,** Prior Road (tel. Wells 73743), is a pleasant, friendly pub on the edge of town, with car parking, offering B&B for £10 ($17.50) per person, which includes a full English breakfast and VAT. The rooms are comfortable and clean, and have tea and coffee facilities. There is a small lounge with color TV. The pub has low ceilings, an open log fire in winter, and brasses and copperware abounding. Here bar meals and snacks are served daily from about £1 ($1.75) to £5 ($8.75). There is also a Steak Restaurant offering prime English beef and various other dishes from about £3 ($5.25) to £6 ($10.50). Beers and wines are reasonably priced. Roy and Sheila Hampshire are the proprietors. Roy does all the cooking, having been a chef for many years.

Flagstones, 26 Chamberlain St. (tel. Wells 72178), dates from the 17th century and is the friendly domain of Mr. and Mrs. Leggett. Their living room, where guests chat informally, contains a wide bay window fronting the street. A huge old fireplace in the lounge is kept burning on winter nights. Throughout is a conglomeration of antiques. The rear dining room and some bedrooms open onto the gardens. The breakfast is good and plentiful, the toaster is kept right in the dining room, and the charge is £8 ($14) per person nightly for B&B, which hardly compensates for the human consideration witnessed around here. At night you can park on the street and during the day in a nearby metered lot.

King Charles Hotel and Inn, 6-8 High St. (tel. Wells 73920), is another charming 16th-century building in this ancient city, housing a warm and cozy inn with old stone fireplaces, beams, and crooked floors. Bedrooms are equipped with tea- and coffee-making facilities, and the room rate is £11 ($19.25) in a single, from £18.50 ($32.38) in a double. These tariffs include a substantial cooked breakfast as well as VAT.

Philip Hansom and his wife also run the popular bars here, catering to both the local trade as well as passing visitors. Bar snacks include smoked mackerel with lemon salad, chili con carne, or turkey kebab with french fries, costing around £1.50 ($2.63) a portion. Sandwiches, ploughman's lunches, and bread and cheese are also available.

At dinner there's a minimum charge of £3 ($5.25), but for this you can order chicken or scampi in a basket, and for very little more try rump steak or a quarter roast chicken served with vegetables, followed by ice cream or a fruit cup. Lunchtime sees such staunch favorites as steak-and-kidney pie, savory meat pies, and quiches, all available for around £2.25 ($3.94).

The **Star Hotel,** High Street (tel. Wells 73055), is run by Mr. and Mrs. P. Nandi. This is a 16th-century coaching inn, with a cobbled yard and low beamed ceilings. Some of the bedrooms have four-poster beds and all are equipped with color TV, coffee- or tea-making facilities, and are centrally heated (some have private baths). An overnight stay, including a full English breakfast, is £10.50 ($18.38) to £15 ($26.25) in a single, from £18 ($31.50) to £25 ($43.75) in a double. Bar meals are available seven days a week, and prices start at £2 ($3.50) per person. In the restaurant, a three-course meal begins at £5 ($8.75) per person. These prices include VAT. All meals are served with fresh vegetables.

READERS' GUEST HOUSE SELECTIONS: "In Wells, we were directed to the **Mermaid,** Tucker Street (tel. Wells 72343), our first pub. The management had a twin room available, and we couldn't have been more pleased. It was clean and neat and cost £7.50 ($13.13) each. The breakfast was good, and a sitting room with TV was provided for guests" (Mrs. John T. Atkinson). . . . "We passed a B&B sign right on entering town on the A371 from Shepton Mallett. It turned out to be the **Tor Guest House** (tel. Wells 72322), with attractive gardens, and as a bonus a view out the windows of the front room of the Bishop's Palace and the east wing of the cathedral that is postcard-perfect. It is a lovely, three-story, 350-year-old home with a beautiful Queen Anne shell front porch. Its front yard contains the oldest magnolia tree in Europe. Jean and Ted Towers are the charming owners. Tor Guest House would be a good place to go first when looking for accommodations in Wells, because if the Towerses do not have room in their house, they will try to find someone for you who does. They have nine rooms: one double, one single, and seven family, and there are showers as well as baths. They charge £8.50 ($14.88) per person for B&B" (Jill L. Adams, Arlington, Va.). . . . "We stayed at a charming B&B, **Burleigh House,** Priory Road, an extension of the Glastonbury road (A39; tel. Wells 74344). It is within walking distance of the cathedral. Mrs. Burridge is a gracious hostess who serves a good breakfast in her sunny, glass-enclosed porch. Her home is immaculate, full of polished oak and brass and brightly colored carpets and furnishings. The price for B&B is £7.50 ($13.13) per person" (Marsha and David Scherbel, Washington, D.C.).

WHERE TO EAT: The **City Arms,** 69 High St. (tel. Wells 73916), is the former city jail, but it's been converted into a local pub and steak bar. It has a high beamed ceiling, and around the dining tables are dark-oak Windsor chairs. On the ground floor is a pub, with an open-air courtyard and umbrella-crowned tables, a popular gathering place for the youth of Wells. The restaurant is upstairs. On my most recent rounds, I ordered an old-style leek-and-potato soup, followed by filet of plaice, with peas and chips. Try the jailhouse chop, a double lamb chop with peas, mushrooms, lettuce, tomato, cucumber, and a baked potato. Meals begin at £5 ($8.75), plus the cost of your drink. Even if you're not hungry, drop in for a pint and soak up the atmosphere.

The **Crown Hotel,** Market Place (tel. Wells 73457), has a sign outside which says that William Penn, founder of Pennsylvania, preached to a vast congregation from a window of the inn in 1685. Appetizers in the cozy dining room include pâté, soups, and other good dishes, along with such main courses as roast topside of beef, trout, T-bones, and cold meats, and salads. At the £1.75 ($3.06) buffet lunch, you can order cold meat and a salad. The chef always has a special dish of the day, such as curry, and there's the invariable steak-and-kidney pie, so beloved by the English. A set three-course dinner is presented for £7.75 ($13.56).

On the Outskirts

Motorists may want to consider the **Manor Farm,** Old Bristol Road, Upper Milton, near Wells (tel. Wells 73394), on the slopes of the Mendips. An Elizabethan manor house of stone, it is supported by the proceeds of 130 acres of farmland. Its owner, Mrs. Janet Gould, has renovated three corner rooms with the best views ("clear to the Bristol Channel on a day that's not misty"), and has made them comfortably suitable for B&B guests. And in an uninhibited moment, she transformed the attic room into a vivid bathroom. Mrs. Gould charges around £7.50 ($13.13) per person for bed and a breakfast that includes about five choices as a main course. The sister-in-law of the owner, Mrs. Sheila Stott, prepares traditional English home-cooked meals, a three-course dinner costing £4.50 ($7.88). Children under 12 eat for half price. Meal time is 7 p.m. (except Sunday), and Mrs. Stott must be given 24 hours' notice. Summer days and evenings are often spent on a flagstoned terrace, overlooking the meadow and enjoying the pale roses climbing over the stone walls. The manor lies about a mile from Wells. Take the A39 from Wells in the Bristol direction. Bear left at the mini-roundabout at the north of the city, then take the second turning left 250 yards past the roundabout. Turn right into Old Bristol Road, and Manor Farm is up the hill.

Long House, at Pilton, near Shepton Mallet (tel. Pilton 283), is a 17th-century building run by Paul Foss and Eric Swainsbury. Guests coming here for the first time, particularly Americans, comment on the comfortable beds, "the best coffee in England," the plentiful towels, and the excellent food. Paul, an experienced chef, shuns instant or so-called convenience foods. They treat their guests as they would wish to be treated—that is, with an easy graciousness.

Bedrooms are attractively furnished, and most of the units have private bathrooms with showers. For half board the rate ranges from £16 ($28) to £21 ($36.75) per person nightly. Guests are encouraged to stay at least three nights, using Long House as a base for touring sights nearby, including Wells (5 miles away); Shepton Mallet, with its 14th-century marketplace and cross (3½ miles); and Glastonbury, with its ancient abbey ruins (6 miles).

Facilities at Long House include a comfortably furnished lounge and dining room that's like that of a private home, plus a well-stocked bar. There your hosts are likely to talk to you about everything from architecture to zoology. As a word of warning, I caution that there are two Piltons in Somerset, and this has led to some confusion. Long House has a postal code of BA4 4BP.

The Old Vicarage, Pilton, near Shepton Mallet (tel. Pilton 573), is an old stone vicarage, dated 1866, standing in 1½ acres of grounds. It's convenient to Wells, Bath, Stonehenge, Avebury, and Exmoor, along with the Cheddar Gorge and Glastonbury. The emphasis is on an informal and friendly family atmosphere. The charge for a bed and a full cooked English breakfast is from £10 ($17.50), with a special rate of £5.50 ($9.63) for children. A three-course evening meal can be arranged for £4.50 ($7.88) per person. There is no service charge or VAT. Mr. and Mrs. Colin J. Stevenson are your hosts. Mrs. Stevenson is a potter and is always pleased to give a demonstration to those interested. On the premises is a busy pottery and showroom.

Worth House Hotel, at Worth, near Wells (tel. Wells 72041), is an imposing house, parts of which date back four centuries. Margaret and John Mason, the resident owners, offer six double bedrooms, one of which has a private bath. They charge from £7.50 ($13.13) daily for B&B or else from £12 ($21) per person for half board. They offer a liquor license, and dinner is served in the intimate Stable Door restaurant. In addition, guests have a choice of two lounges, one with color TV. The house is set in a valley with views of the Mendip hills. It is also tastefully furnished, offering a comfortable accommodation with full central heating.

READER'S GUEST HOUSE SELECTIONS ON THE OUTSKIRTS: "**Walnut Farm** (tel. Wells 73587), just east of the A39 in Coxley, south of Wells, costs £6.50 ($11.38) per person per night. The ancient house contains three guest bedrooms and a hostess, Mrs. Palmer, who treats everyone like a member of the family. She makes a point of introducing guests to one another and providing a pot of tea on arrival. At 7:45 a.m. we were served tea in bed, followed by a full English breakfast in the lounge 45 minutes later. The residents' lounge offers TV, radio, table games, and a variety of literature" (Julianna M. Niemann, APO New York).

4. Bleadney

The unspoiled character of the West Country has been preserved in the quiet rural village of Bleadney, just four miles west of Wells on the B3139. Overlooking the moors toward the Cheddar Valley and the Mendip Hills, the village is a convenient center for the exploration of the beauty and history of Somerset with its medieval castles and cathedrals as well as its serene countryside and miles of coastline.

Threeways Hotel and Restaurant (tel. Wells 78870) stands on its own five acres of land right in the center of Bleadney, where guests can waken to a refreshing view of the moors and valleys surrounding the village. The inn provides clean, comfortable double or twin-bedded rooms. Some of the rooms contain private baths and color TV sets. A standard double rents for £7 ($12.25) per person, the cost going up to £9 ($15.75) per person in a deluxe unit. These tariffs include a continental breakfast, but for a full English breakfast you must pay an additional £1.50 ($2.63) per person, including service but not VAT. In the restaurant you can enjoy a snack at the bar for £1 ($1.75) or a filet steak in the restaurant at a cost of about £7 ($12.25). The restaurant serves mainly grills, and salads are available in the summer. Most North American guests seem to prefer the grilled rainbow trout. Horseback riding of about three-hour treks around the country lanes and bridle paths are available on Wednesday evening during the summer. Your hosts are Maureen and Ray Brandon.

Six miles southwest of Wells and we're at:

5. Glastonbury

GLASTONBURY ABBEY: The goal of the medieval pilgrim, Glastonbury Abbey, once one of the wealthiest and most prestigious monasteries in England, is no more than a ruined sanctuary today. But it provides Glastonbury's claim to historical greatness, an assertion augmented by legendary links to such figures as Joseph of Arimathea, King Arthur, Queen Guinivere, and St. Patrick.

It is said that Joseph of Arimathea journeyed to what was then the Isle of Avalon, with the Holy Grail in his possession. According to tradition, he buried the chalice at the foot of the conically shaped Glastonbury Tor, and a stream of blood burst forth. (You can scale this more than 500-foot-high hill today. A 15th-century tower rests atop it.)

At one point, the early saint is said to have leaned against his staff, which immediately was transformed into a fully blossoming tree. A cutting alleged to have survived from the Holy Thorn can be seen on the abbey grounds today. It blooms at Christmastime and in the early summer. Some historians have traced this particular story back to Tudor times.

Joseph, so it goes, erected a church of wattle (reeds and branches) in Glastonbury. In fact, excavations have shown that the town may have had the oldest church in England.

The most famous link, fanned for Arthurian fans in the Victorian era by Alfred Lord Tennyson, concerns the burial of King Arthur and Queen Guinivere on the abbey grounds. In 1191, the monks dug up the skeletons of two bodies on the south side of the Lady Chapel, said to be that of the king and his queen. In 1278, in the presence of Edward I, the bodies were removed and transferred to a black marble tomb in the choir. Both their alleged burial spot and their shrine are marked today.

A large Benedictine Abbey of St. Mary grew out of the early wattle church. St. Dunstan, who was born nearby, was the abbot in the tenth century, later becoming archbishop of Canterbury. At its most powerful stage in English history, Edmund, Edgar, and Edmund (Ironside)—three early English kings—were buried at the abbey.

In 1184, a fire of unknown origin swept over the abbey, destroying most of it, along with what must have been vast treasures. It was eventually rebuilt after much difficulty, only to be dissolved by Henry VIII. Its last abbot, Richard Whiting, was hanged by the neck at Glastonbury Tor. For years after, the abbey, like the Roman Forum, was used as a stone quarry.

The modern-day pilgrim to Glastonbury can visit the ruins of the Lady Chapel, which is linked by an early English "Galilee" to the nave of the abbey. The best preserved building on the grounds is a 14th-century octagonal Abbot's Kitchen, where oxen were once roasted whole to feed the wealthier of the pilgrims (that is, the biggest donors). You can visit the ruins from 9:30 a.m. till dusk, for 50p (88¢) for adults, 25p (44¢) for children under 16.

Glastonbury may be one of the oldest inhabited sites in Britain. Excavations have revealed Iron Age lakeside villages on its periphery. Some of the discoveries dug up may be viewed in a little museum in the High Street.

After the destruction of its once-great abbey, the town lost prestige. It is a market town today. The ancient gatehouse entry to the abbey, by the way, is a museum, its principal exhibit a scale model of the abbey and its community buildings as they stood in 1539, at the time of the dissolution. The above fees include entry to the abbey museum.

SOMERSET RURAL LIFE MUSEUM: **Abbey Farm,** Chilkwell Street (tel. Glastonbury 32903), is a museum explaining the history of the Somerset countryside over the last 100 or so years. The main part of the exhibition is Abbey Barn, the home barn of the abbey, built in 1370. The magnificent timbered roof, the stone tiles, and the sculpture outside, including a head of Edward III, make it special. There are also a Victorian farmhouse and various other exhibits illustrating farming in Somerset during the "horse age" and domestic and social life in Victorian times. In summer they have demonstrations of buttermaking, weaving, basketwork, anything which has reference to the rural life of the country, now rapidly disappearing with the invention of the engine, the freezer, and the instant meal. The museum is open daily from 10 a.m. to 5 p.m. (2 to 6:30 p.m. on Saturday and Sunday; 2:30 to 5 p.m. in winter). Admission is 50p (88¢) for adults, 20p (44¢) for children. There is a snackbar for light meals and soft drinks.

ACCOMMODATIONS: Although I'll document some exceptional places to stay in the area, you might need emergency assistance if you arrive when all the rooms listed are taken. In that case, there is a nonprofit **Accommodation Center** run by volunteers. The center (tel. Glastonbury 32954) is about 15 yards from Northload Street. Look for a narrow passage at the end of which is a pleasant terrace of flower-bedecked old brick cottages (the tourist office is in the first cottage). It is open from May to September from 9:30 a.m. to 5 p.m. daily except Sunday.

St. John's Vicarage, Lambrook Street (tel. Glastonbury 32362), is just up the High Street (turn to the right on the Shepton Mallet Road). On your left, about 150 yards along, is a Georgian house (facing down Silver Street) which can accommodate up to eight persons at a B&B charge of from £6 ($10.50) per person nightly. The house is actually a peaceful vicarage, run by the vicar's wife, Mrs. Alan Clarkson. It belongs to St. John's Church, one of Glastonbury's historic sights. The front door is approached through beautiful lawns in a garden surrounded by a stone wall. Mrs. Clarkson is attractive and charming, and she will accommodate you if she can, although her regular following tends to fill up the rooms. Those units are pleasant, and a nice homelike atmosphere prevails.

Guests have one of the living rooms for their own use, an area for home-cooked breakfasts, and another with comfortable chairs around a TV set. Other furnishings are oak antiques. The central hall has a glass window on the stair landing, where you can see the rear vegetable and flower garden. The front rooms overlook the garden and the rear of the abbey grounds.

Market House Inn (tel. Glastonbury 32220) is a village inn and pub, right on the main street, across from the abbey ruins. It's owned and managed by Mr. and Mrs. W. McVay who have made their bedrooms quite up-to-date, even installing TV sets (although there are no private bathrooms). They charge £12 ($21) nightly in a single, £24 ($42) in a double, and this includes a homemade breakfast as well. Evening meals are served for £5 ($8.75).

Tor Down, Ashwell Lane (tel. Glastonbury 32287), is a well-cared-for house on the edge of the town (on the road to West Pennard). The landlady, Miss Parfitt, charges from £8 ($14) to £9.50 ($16.63) per person for a comfortable bed in a centrally heated room and a large breakfast. There's an expansive view from the Tor of the Isle of Avalon. Miss Parfitt will pack lunches, if asked, and dinner can be served if a prior arrangement is made. Guests gather in the parlor in the evening for tea and crackers.

Yet another establishment offering B&B is **Beckets Inn**—see "Where to Dine," below, for details.

WHERE TO DINE: **Beckets Inn,** 43 High St. (tel. Glastonbury 32928), is what the English call a fully licensed house, which means this fairly old tavern, a Queen Anne building with a Regency facade, has three informal bars. In front of a tiny old fireplace with a copper kettle, you can order substantial snacks, along with real ale from the wood. Across the central hall is the Georgian Room for a proper sitdown meal. It is considered by the villagers the best middle-priced restaurant in town. Starting at 7 p.m., dinners feature a soup of the day with crusty bread at 60p ($1.05), deep-fried scampi and potatoes, £2.20 ($3.85), followed by an apple turnover with ice cream, 75p ($1.31). In fair weather, meals are served in the rear garden, and there is room on the grounds to park your car.

Upstairs, two double rooms are pleasantly furnished and comfortable, although you must make use of the hallway bath and toilets. The B&B rate is £10 ($17.50) per person. In addition, a self-contained apartment is rented in the garden above the old stable block, complete with shower, kitchen, and TV. It can sleep up to four in two bedrooms with double beds.

LIVING IN THE ENVIRONS: **Cradlebridge Farm,** Cradlebridge (tel. Glastonbury 31827), is a secluded farmhouse, about two miles from Glastonbury, where you can get not only bed and breakfast, but an evening meal as well. In this unsophisticated atmosphere, Mr. and Mrs. Henry Tinney will go out of their way to make you comfortable and will prepare old-fashioned meals. They have three doubles and one single for which they charge £8.50 ($14.88) per person nightly for B&B. There is a "family bath and toilet," although one bedroom has its own private bath. You reach the farm by taking the A39 road from Glastonbury. Turn at the second right after passing the Morlands Shoe Factory, then take the first left, and Cradlebridge Farm will be at the end of the road.

For a deeply rural setting, head five miles south of Glastonbury to **The Vicarage,** Compton Dundon (tel. Somerton 72324). Nowadays run by Joy Adams, it was built of local stone in 1867 on the site of a medieval manor and next to a medieval church. A well in the vicarage cellar is part of the ancient house. There are two double bedrooms, one with private bath. Both units have views over the unspoiled hills where deer can sometimes be seen. In the house are some interesting antiques, including a grandfather clock and a Welsh dresser. In addition to central heating, log fires burn on cooler days. For a bed and a full English breakfast, the charge is from £7.50 ($13.13) per person. A three-course dinner is served for £5 ($8.75). The two-acre garden surrounding the property includes a real Somerset orchard. All the food served here, including the bread, is homemade, and in summer vegetables from the Adams garden are used.

6. Exmoor

Heather-clad Exmoor National Park is a vast wooded area where red deer and wild ponies roam. Those interested in bucolic charm may want to anchor into a B&B in the vicinity, instead of in one of the larger cities. Minehead, the popular resort on the broad sands of the North Somerset coast, has the most tourist facilities, but in some ways such villages as Exford have more charm.

The small village of Exford, on the River Exe, is the headquarters of the Devon and Somerset Staghounds. It's possible from this base and others to explore the Quantocks and Brendon Hills. You can also make excursions to Dunster Castle, Horner Woods, Dunkery Beacon, and Selworthy village.

Winsford is another pretty Exmoor village on the wooded River Exe. It's a good center for Exmoor and the Brendon Hills.

In Exford, Dormobiles and tent-campers are welcome at **Westermill Farm,** Exford, near Minehead (tel. 064383/238). There are showers and flush toilets, a pay phone, and a small shop for essentials. The farm is right in the middle of the moor, and there are some beautiful walks. Fishing and bathing are possible in the area. Prices start at £1 ($1.75) for a small tent for two persons. Write to Mrs. E. Edwards to make reservations.

Or, alternately, you can stay at **Edgcoot House,** in Exford, near Minehead (tel. 064383/495). This is a large old country house with a sheltered garden close to the village. It offers comfortable bedrooms, some with private baths, and a warm lounge with an open fire. A typical country atmosphere prevails. Enormous breakfasts are served, and if prearranged, evening dinners. Your hostess, Mrs. Lamble, is a very friendly person and a good cook. She charges from £8.50 ($14.88) per person for B&B and from £12.75 ($22.31) for half board.

Another possibility is **Westerclose Country House Hotel,** in Withypool (tel. 064383/302). This is a small licensed hotel run by the Burnett-Wells family. The house stands above the village of Withypool, opening onto views of the surrounding moor. Some of the warm, well-furnished bedrooms contain private baths. Dinner, bed, and breakfast costs from £15 ($26.25) per person nightly, increasing to £17 ($29.75) per person should you desire a private bath. The breakfast is large, and the evening meal includes fresh local produce.

At **The Tufters,** in the village of Winsford (tel. 064383/318), Mrs. Babbage provides dinner, bed, and breakfast at £11 ($19.25) per person nightly, or else £7 ($12.25) per person for only B&B. In her modern cottage, the beds are comfortable, and all units contain wash basins. There are adequate bathroom facilities as well. Riding and fishing are available in the area, and she can babysit for children overnight if you want to sample the rustic "fleshpots" of Dulverton or Minehead. Mrs. Babbage also has a self-catering cottage available, but only for a minimum of seven days, a general requirement throughout the country.

Emmetts Grange Farm, Simonsbath, near Minehead (tel. 064383/282), is a hill stock farm on the B3223 in the middle of Exmoor. Mrs. Brown provides well-furnished rooms with wash basins. She has adequate bathroom facilities as well. There is a residents' lounge with color TV to watch before the log fire. Breakfast and the four-course dinner include much local produce, cream, butter, and meat. A bed and a full breakfast is £7.50 ($13.13), increasing to £13.50 ($23.63) with half board.

7. The Caves of Mendip

The Caves of Mendip are two exciting natural sightseeing attractions in Somerset—the great caves of Cheddar and Wookey Hole, both easily reached by heading west out of Wells. After leaving Wells, you'll first come to **Wookey Hole** (tel. Wells 72243), less than two miles away, the source of the Axe River. In the first chamber of the caves, you can see, as legend has it, the Witch of Wookey turned to stone. These caves were believed to have been inhabited by prehistoric man at least 60,000 years ago. Even in those days there was a housing problem, with hyenas moving in and upsetting real-estate values! A tunnel opened in 1975 leads to chambers unknown to early man and previously accessible only to divers.

Leaving the caves, you follow a canal path to the mill, where paper has been made by hand since the 17th century. Here you can watch the best-quality paper being made by skilled men according to the traditions of their ancient craft. Also in the mill is housed Lady Bangor's Fairground Collection, an extraordinary and colorful assembly of relics from the world's fairgrounds, and Madame Tussaud's storeroom, where molds of the famous and infamous have been brought from the London exhibition for safekeeping. Adults pay £2.50 ($4.38), children under 16 pay £1.50 ($2.63), for a guided tour which lasts about 1½ hours. Free car parking is provided, and there are a cafeteria and picnic area. Wookey Hole is open every day from 10 a.m. The last visitors are admitted at 6 p.m. from April to September, and at 4:30 p.m. from October to March.

At **Cheddar,** eight miles from Wells, you'll find an attractive village, famous for its cheese and an underground river (the Yeo), powerful enough to hollow out the spectacular Cheddar Gorge, a two-mile-long pass through 450-foot-high limestone cliffs. It's unlawful to try to mount the cliffs, except by way of Jacob's Ladder, an exhausting 322 steps to the top. Your "heavenly" reward will be panoramic views of the Mendip Hills and the Somerset moors. The cost of the climb is 30p (53¢) for adults, 15p (26¢) for children. The main attractions of the gorge, however, are below the limestone cliffs, in **Gough's Cave** and **Cox's Cave,** with their stalactites and unique rock formations. The museum contains exhibits of prehistoric man taken from the caves and dating as far back as 10,000 B.C. Gough's Cave, with an admission price of 85p ($1.49), is open all year, every day except Christmas, from 10 a.m. to 6 p.m. Cox's Cave, with an admission price of 60p ($1.05) is open from Easter to mid-October, also from 10 a.m. to 6 p.m. There is a concession ticket available which gives admission to all facilities at a cost of £1.80 ($3.15) for adults, £1.10 ($1.93) for children. For more information, telephone Cheddar 742343.

THE CHEESE TOUR: Chewton Cheese Dairy, Priory Farm, Chewton Mendip (tel. Chewton Mendip 560), is one of the six remaining dairies in England still making cheddar in the traditional way. Visitors are welcome to watch the cheesemaking process, which takes place every morning. Midmorning is the best time to arrive. After you look around, you may wish to purchase a "truckle" (or wheel) of mature cheddar to send home. The knowledge that Prince Charles is also a customer adds even more flavor to one of England's unique products.

This dairy is owned by Lord Chewton. The best time to make the tour is either at 9:15 a.m. or 1 p.m. when the curds and whey come down to the cheese table and the actual cheese making is done by Pepe D'Ovido. The admission of 50p (88¢) includes a guidebook. You should allow about an hour for the interesting tour. A 4½-pound truckle of cheddar cheese will cost about £6.75 ($11.81), and if you pay double that price, they'll ship your truckle back home for you.

WHERE TO STAY: In and around this area you'll find some interesting accommodations, as typified by the **George Hotel** (tel. 0934/712124) which lies three miles south of the Cheddar Gorge in the modest village of Wedmore. Here, King Alfred made peace with the Danes and their ruler, Guthrum in A.D. 878, forcing him to be baptized. Faced with such antiquity, nothing but an old-world coaching inn will do. The George, part of which dates back to the 1350s, has for centuries been giving strangers a refreshing pint of ale and a restful night's sleep in one of the 12 upstairs bedrooms. The B&B rate is £12 ($21) per person nightly. There is no set lunch, but you can compose a two-courser of bar snacks for £3 ($5.25) to £4.50 ($7.88). In the evening you're presented with an à la carte menu and are likely to spend from £5.50 ($9.63) to £7 ($12.25).

Behind the cellar bar are barrels of ales and beer, and rows of mugs hang from an overhead, time-blackened beam. Everywhere there is a sense of living in the past. It was in 1926 that the custom of holding "court leet of Wedmore" (a special type of manorial court) was abandoned, but the inn still functions as the center of village life. Kenneth and Valerie Harper, who own and manage the inn, are aware of this heritage—and its responsibilities.

In Cheddar, the best base is the **Gordons Hotel,** Cliff Street (tel. Cheddar 742497), which lies at the foot of Cheddar Gorge. Mr. and Mrs. E. C. Barker welcome visitors to their licensed hotel, offering 14 bedrooms, each with hot and cold running water, shaver points, and views of the Mendip Hills. For B&B, they charge from £10 ($17.50) daily. There is a comfortable lounge with color TV, plus a well-stocked bar where not only drinks but bar snacks are sold. The beamed restaurant, definitely "olde worlde," offers game when available. Dinner ranges from £3.50 ($6.13) to £7 ($12.25) for three courses. Outside is a garden with lawns and fruit trees, and there's plenty of room for children to play.

A 16th-Century Farm

Churchill Green Farm, Churchill Green, Churchill (tel. Churchill 852438), is a good base for exploring the Mendips. Janet Sacof has modernized this 16th-century farmhouse without endangering its old-world charm and character. But down-on-the-farm life has never been better since she added a swimming pool. In peak season, she charges from £68 ($119) per person weekly for partial board, or £15 ($26.25) daily, plus VAT. Children sharing a room with two adults are granted reductions.

She offers a number of reasons for you to stay with her: a pleasant lounge with plenty of books (she is university educated herself); a large and ancient dining room; plenty of hot water; good beds (particularly the canopied Edwardian tester-bed hung with red brocade); cots for children; central heating throughout the house; log fires to sit by on those dull days; and Somerset cider or wine and spirits served in her "ye olde world bar."

If these aren't reasons enough, she suggests some more: she will babysit; horseback-riding is available (and it's beautiful riding over the ancient British encampment on Dolebury Hill and among the young pine forests of Mendip); and the gardens face due south, looking out onto the foothills. If you still aren't satisfied, she grows most of the food, including beef, and she bakes bread fresh every day. Although she doesn't provide midday meals, she will pack you a lunch. The house is furnished with well-selected antiques.

A Farm Near Bridgwater

Pear Tree Guest House, 16 Manor Rd., Catcott, near Bridgwater (tel. Chilton Polden 722390), is a 300-year-old converted farmhouse standing in a history-rich part of England. The village of Catcott, on the slopes of the Polden Hills halfway between Glastonbury and Bridgwater on the A39, was once the camping ground of the Danes in 610. Facing Pear Tree Farm is a 13th-century church and tarry house, once used by the pilgrims on their way to Glastonbury, seven miles away. On the crest of the hill, you can look down on the battleground of Sedgemoor, the last major battle on English soil, between supporters of James II and forces loyal to the Duke of Monmouth.

Bridgwater itself was the home of Admiral Robert Blake (now turned into a museum). On the outskirts of Bridgwater at Nether Stowey (on the A39), you can visit the cottage where S. T. Coleridge *(The Rime of the Ancient Mariner* and *Kubla Khan)* lived in the closing years of the 18th century. It is open (parlor only) daily, except Saturday, from March to October from 11 a.m. to 1 p.m. and from 2 to 5 p.m. charging 35p (61¢) for admission.

David and Sheila Horsell, the owners of Pear Tree, offer good, wholesome, farm-style living. Their B&B rate is £7.50 ($13.13). If you take evening dinner (highly recommended), the charge is £11 ($19.25).

Memory item: Give-and-take after-dinner conversations in the living room while sitting in front of the log fire; the abundant, hearty meals prepared in the large kitchen-family room; the deep-dish apple pie—not too tart, not too sweet —and with a flaky crust riding the crest of its rich sauce.

READER'S FARMHOUSE SELECTION: "I was most impressed with **Critchill Farm,** Nunney Road, in Frome (tel. Frome 62766), between Frome and the village of Nunney where there is a quaint ruined castle. There, a young couple, Susan and Peter Austin, are reconstructing an ancient farmhouse with tender loving care. It is a working farm, illustrated by the fresh milk that accompanies the bountiful breakfast. In the nearby stream, you'll find collectible fossils, and the farm is convenient to places of interest such as Salisbury, Longleat House and Safari Park, Bath, Wells, and Cheddar. Susan and Peter are much involved in the local scene and willing to talk. They also like cars and horses, competing in local autocrosses and horse shows. The price is £7.50 ($13.13) per person. It's an ideal stop for someone driving" (Joseph A. Withey, Hanover, Ind.).

READER'S GUEST HOUSE SELECTION AT WINSFORD: "Of the multitude of pretty villages in England, and specifically Somerset, Winsford (12 miles southwest of Dunster on the River Exe within Exmoor National Park) is most notable. Winsford is an old-world village, amid glorious scenery, noted for its bridges and quietude. I recommend **Karslake Guest House** (tel. Winsford 242), an ancient malt house, at the foot of Winsford Hill just behind the impressive 12th-century thatched Royal Oak Inn. B&B (single) at Karslake is £11 ($19.25) and Richard Jenkins will happily make out an itinerary of Somerset villages to visit. Garage parking is available" (Robert F. Fera, Orchard Lake, Mich.).

AVON

Avon is the name that has been given to the area around the old port of Bristol, an area that used to be in Somerset.

8. Bath

Victoria didn't start everything. In 1702, Queen Anne made the 115-mile trek from London to the mineral springs at Bath, thereby launching a fad that was to make the city the most celebrated spa in England. Of course, Victoria hiked up too, in due time, to sample a medicinal cocktail (which you can still do today), but Bath by then had passed its zenith.

The most famous personage connected with Bath's scaling the pinnacle of fashion was the 18th-century dandy, Beau Nash. Dressed in embroidered white, he was the final arbiter of taste and manners (as one example, he made dueling déclassé). The master of ceremonies of Bath, he cut a striking figure as he made his way across the city, with all the plumage of a bird of paradise. Dispensing (at a price) trinkets to the courtiers and aspirant gentlemen of his day, Beau was carted around in a liveried carriage.

The gambler was given the proper setting for his considerable social talents by 18th-century architects John Wood the Elder and his son. These architects designed a city of stone from the nearby hills, a feat so substantial and lasting that Bath today is the most harmoniously laid out city in England.

This Georgian city on a bend of the Avon River has, throughout history, attracted a following among leading political and literary figures, among them Dickens, Thackeray, Lord Nelson, and William Pitt. Canadians may know that General Wolfe lived on Trim Street, and Australians may want to visit the house at 19 Bennett St. where their founding father, Admiral Philip, lived. Henry Fielding came this way, observing in *Tom Jones* that the ladies of Bath "endeavor to appear as ugly as possible in the morning, in order to set off that beauty which they intend to show you in the evening."

Bath has had two lives. Long before its Queen Anne, Georgian, and Victorian popularity, it was known to the Romans as Aquae Sulis. The foreign legions founded their baths (which may be visited today) here, so they might ease their plight of rheumatism in the curative mineral springs.

That Bath retains its handsome look today is the result of remarkable restoration and careful planning. The city suffered devastating destruction from the infamous Baedeker air raids of 1942, when Luftwaffe pilots seemed more bent on bombing historical buildings, such as the Assembly Rooms, than in hitting any military target.

The major sights today are the rebuilt Assembly Rooms, the abbey, and the Pump Room and Roman baths. But if you're intrigued by architecture and city planning, you may want to visit some of the buildings, crescents, and squares. The North Parade, where Goldsmith lived, and the South Parade, where Fanny Burney (English novelist and diarist) once resided, represent harmony, the work of John Wood the Elder. The younger Wood, on the other hand, designed the Royal Crescent, an elegant half-moon row of town houses copied by Astor architects for their colonnade in New York City in the 1830s. Queen Square is one of the most beautiful (Jane Austen and Wordsworth used to live here, but hardly together), showing off quite well the work of Wood the Elder. And don't miss his Circus, built in 1754, as well as the shop-flanked Pulteney Bridge, designed by Robert Adam and compared aptly to the Ponte Vecchio of Florence.

Since Bath suffers from a proliferation of one-way streets and traffic congestion, it is best to park in the heart of the city and explore its wonders on foot.

BATH ABBEY: Built on the site of a much larger Norman cathedral, the present-day abbey is a fine example of the late Perpendicular style. When Queen Elizabeth I came to Bath in 1574, she ordered that a national fund be set up to restore the abbey. The west front is the sculptural embodiment of a Jacob's Ladder dream of a 15th-century bishop. When you go inside and see its many windows, you'll understand why the abbey is called the "Lantern of the West." Note the superb fan vaulting, achieving at times a scalloped effect. Beau Nash was buried in the nave and is honored by a simple monument totally out of keeping with his flamboyant character.

PUMP ROOM AND ROMAN BATHS: In A.D. 75, the Romans founded their baths, dedicated to the native goddess Sul (similar to Minerva). Like many of their other baths, the one in Bath was in its day an engineering feat, and even today it is considered the finest Roman remains in the country. It is still fed by the original hot spring, which rises under the King's Bath. When the Romans departed, the baths decayed, and were buried until mid-18th century, although it was late in Victoria's day before major excavations were undertaken. A museum connected to the baths contains the most interesting objects from the digs (look for the head of Minerva). You can have coffee in the Pump Room or a drink at the licensed restaurant on the terrace. The Pump Room and the Roman Baths and Museum (tel. Bath 61111) are open daily in summer from 9 a.m. to 6 p.m. In winter weekday hours are from 9 a.m. to 5 p.m.; on Sunday from 11 a.m. to 5 p.m. Admission is £1.30 ($2.28).

THE ASSEMBLY ROOMS: Lying right off the Circus on Alfred Street, the Assembly Rooms (tel. Bath 61111) were originally designed by John Wood the Younger in 1769. Damaged by 1942 air raids, the rooms have been restored to the height of their 18th-century elegance, when the fashionable beaux and their ladies paraded about. Today they house a Costume Museum, founded on the collection of Mrs. Doris Langley Moore, and greatly enlarged and enriched by donations from many sources. The display of clothes covers more than 400 years of fashion history—Madame Recamier's lounging ladies, Jane Austen's upper-middle-class look, styles right out of Watteau paintings, the Alice B. Toklas post–World War I garb, up to Dior haute couture and a mini by Mary Quant.

Men's apparel isn't neglected in the exhibition and ranges from a splendid silver-embroidered brown cloth coat, with matching silk stockings, of the early 18th century, another in green velvet decorated with sequins (which Liberace would love), right up to today's jeans. The museum is open weekdays in summer from 9:30 a.m. to 6 p.m.; Sunday, 10 a.m. to 6 p.m. Winter hours are 10 a.m. to 5 p.m. weekdays, 11 a.m. to 5 p.m. on Sunday. Admission is £1.10 ($1.93) for adults, 60p ($1.05) for children.

BATH FESTIVAL: This annual festival of the performing arts lasts 17 days and takes place at the end of May and beginning of June. Essentially it's a festival of music under the artistic direction of Sir William Glock. Concerts are held in the Assembly Rooms, the Guildhall, the Abbey, Wells Cathedral, and many other historic houses and churches in the area. The varied program includes concerts by the major British and foreign choirs and chamber orchestras, opera, dance, an international lineup of soloists and chamber groups, exhibitions, lectures, garden and church tours. The festival runs its own art gallery which provides exhibitions of paintings, sculpture, and crafts throughout the year, with a special exhibition by an artist or group of artist of international standing during the period of the festival. All information can be obtained from the Bath Festival Office, 1 Pierrepont Pl., Bath, BA1 1JY (tel. Bath 62231; box office, Bath 63362). Finally, on the outskirts of Bath stands this leading attraction:

A GEORGIAN HOUSE: **No. 1 Royal Crescent** (tel. Bath 28126) was given to the Bath Preservation Trust by Bernard Cayzer in 1968. By 1970 it had been carefully restored and the main rooms decorated and furnished to create an authentic 18th-century interior. Thus visitors may see for themselves what the inside of a house in Bath looked like in its heyday. It is open from March through October, Tuesday to Saturday from 11 a.m. to 5 p.m.; on Sunday, from 2 to 5 p.m. (closed Monday). Admission is 60p ($1.05) for adults, 35p (61¢) for children.

CLAVERTON MANOR: Some 2½ miles outside Bath, you get a glimpse of life as lived by a diversified segment of American settlers until Lincoln's day. It was the first American museum established outside the United States. A Greek Revival house, designed by a Georgian architect, Claverton Manor sits proudly in its own extensive grounds above the Avon Valley. Among the authentic exhibits shipped over from the States are a New Mexico room, a Conestoga wagon, an early American beehive oven (ever had gingerbread baked from the recipe of George Washington's mother?), the dining room of a New York town house of the early 19th century, and (on the grounds) a copy of Washington's flower garden at Mount Vernon. You can visit the museum from March to October, daily except Monday, from 2 to 5 p.m. Adults pay £1.60 ($2.80); children, £1.40 ($2.45). For more information, telephone Bath 60503.

READER'S SIGHTSEEING TIP: "The Mayor's **Corps of Honorary Guides** conducts free walking tours of the City of Bath on Sunday during the winter, every day during the summer (end of May until the end of September), and on bank holidays. Tours leave from the abbey churchyard, outside the Pump Room. These guides are all unpaid volunteers and act in an honorary capacity. They do not accept tips. A tour of the city lasts about 1¾ hours, and visitors see the historical and architectural features of the city but are not shown into any buildings. For further information, write to Mr. J. Clifton, Assistant Director, Department of Leisure and Tourist Services, Pump Room, Bath, BA1 1LZ (tel. Bath 61111)" (R. Alter, Lexington, Ky.).

Back in Bath, we take up the problem of finding accommodations.

WHERE TO STAY: The home of **Mrs. Wellesley-Colley,** 22 Royal Crescent (tel. Bath 24477), stands out with its yellow front door and window blinds on this beautiful terrace of Georgian houses. Four floors overlook grass and gardens. Most of the furnishings are antique. The first-floor drawing room has many family portraits, comfortable chairs, and a peaceful atmosphere. A continental breakfast is served in the dining room around a big family table. There are three double rooms and two single, the occupants of which share three bathrooms. All accommodations are equipped with do-it-yourself morning tea-

and coffee-making equipment. Singles rent for £10 ($17.50) a night, doubles from £14 ($24.50). Again, the furnishings are elegant, with parquet flooring and rich carpeting—truly an English private house, befitting a descendant of the Duke of Wellington, as Mrs. Wellesley-Colley is. Apropos of nothing, there is a private chapel in the house. It's worth staying here for the venue and the view, although it's quite a walk up the hill to get here.

Dorset Villa, 14 Newbridge Rd. (tel. Bath 25975), is a Georgian-style private home, with a front garden and car park. It has been converted by Mr. and Mrs. Ivor Ham into a well-operated hotel. A double-decker bus will whisk you into the heart of Bath in about ten minutes. The Hams will tuck you in at £7.50 ($13.13) per person nightly, in a spacious, tidy, and pleasant room with hot and cold running water. No singles are offered except in off-season, when doubles are sometimes rented out to lone travelers. The atmosphere is personal, the owners genial and charming. There's a pleasant lounge with TV, a bright and cheerful breakfast room, and a place to park your car.

Arden Hotel, 73 Great Pulteney St. (tel. Bath 66601), is run by John H. Spillane, whose aim is to operate the pleasantest and cheapest small hotel in Bath. A Georgian building, the hotel is licensed and has a dozen bedrooms. It stands on one of the city's most famous streets, a few minutes' walk from the abbey, the Roman Baths, and the Royal Crescent. Recently redecorated and refurnished, the hotel has attractive rooms, often with private facilities. The rate in a single is £12 ($21), lowered to £10.50 ($18.38) per person in a double or twin without bath, rising to £13 ($22.75) per person with private bath. Guests can enjoy a cocktail bar or else relax in the lounge, watching color TV.

Jane's Hotel, Manvers Street (tel. Bath 65966), is just down the road from the railway station and within a two-minute walk of the abbey and the Roman remains. There is ample car parking opposite behind the police station. The hotel is a Victorian building welded from a row of terrace houses. It provides clean rooms with comfortable beds, color TV, and plenty of hot water, at a cost ranging between £15 ($26.25) and £16 ($28) per person, including breakfast. Rooms with shower cost more. Jane's is run by Adrian Leonards, a Cornishman who, along with his partners, has spent the last few years repainting and improving the hotel. He reckons that Jane's must be the cheapest hotel in the country providing color TV in all rooms. Mr. Leonards is "assisted" by his Great Dane, Gefjon, who has a tendency to walk about, joining tour groups. He has to be collected when he tires from his wandering—the local police know him well!

The restaurant, **La Crêperie,** which is run by the proprietor's son, Christopher Bradshaw, has a homey, pleasant atmosphere, is fully licensed, and carries a varied cocktail list (something rare in Bath). It also has the largest selection of foreign beers and lagers in the area. The French crêpes are excellent value, with a choice of many different fillings. For those who want something a little different, hamburgers and steaks are available, as well as side orders such as salads, baked potatoes, french bread, and garlic bread. The menu varies between £1.50 ($2.63) and £3 ($5.25). Under the hotel is the **Beau Nash Club,** Bath's top nightclub and disco. Entry for nonmembers is from £1.25 ($2.19) to £2.50 ($4.38), but it is free to residents of Jane's Hotel. The club is ideal for the over-20s looking for late-evening entertainment.

Apsley Garden House Hotel, Newbridge Hill (tel. Bath 21368), is a charming country house dating back to the reign of William IV, just a mile from the center of Bath. It's set in its own gardens, stately, with a square tower, arched windows, a walled garden with south views. The owners, Mr. and Mrs. K. Baird, have made improvements and are providing high standards. They ask £25 ($43.75) for two in a double, £15 ($26.25) in a single, including breakfast and VAT. They have such a comprehensive breakfast menu that you'll not need a meal until teatime. If you would like dinner as well, add another £6.50 ($11.38) to the bill. The food is served in an elegant dining room of classic Georgian proportions. There is a sympathetic response to North American requests such as for strawberry jam for breakfast, ice, ice water, and toasted waffles. There are ten well-appointed bedrooms with radio and a call system. Drinks are served in an intimate cocktail bar, and there is a comfortable lounge for TV. Directions: From Bath, on the A4, go to Upper Bristol 1 Road and fork right at traffic signals into Newbridge Hill.

Grove Lodge Guest House, 11 Lambridge (tel. Bath 310860), is a typical Georgian home dating from 1787, with well-furnished and spacious rooms, most with large windows overlooking a stone terrace, attractive garden, and the surrounding wooded hills. Just a few minutes from the city center, the lodge is serviced by frequent buses at the front gate. A warm welcome and personal attention are guaranteed by the owners, Alec and Diana Thompson, who have made many improvements in the house to increase service and comfort. There is a selection of single, twin, and double rooms, as well as large family rooms sleeping three or four persons. All rooms are equipped with TV, hot and cold running water, and wall-to-wall carpeting. There are ample shared bathroom and shower facilities. Drinks of all kinds are served until 11 p.m. The basic cost of a room, including a full breakfast and VAT, is £10 ($17.50) per person, but reductions are available for the larger rooms shared by three or more persons.

Richmond Hotel, 11 Great Pulteney St. (tel. Bath 60953), stands on a street laid out by Thomas Baldwin in 1798. It leads to the Pulteney Bridge with its delightful shops on either side, built over the River Avon. The hotel is within a few minutes' walk of the center of Bath. It is a listed Georgian building, centrally heated, and has 31 bedrooms, with lovely views from both front and back. All rooms are comfortably furnished, some with four-poster beds and antiques. Many units have private bathrooms, and color TVs are installed in the lounge and all principal bedrooms. There is a variety of car-parking facilities nearby. The cost per person daily without private bath is from £11 ($19.25); with private bath, from £12 ($21). Pay the top price and you'll find yourself in a traditional four-poster bed for a cost from £16 ($28) per person. Breakfast is typically English, ample and well prepared. If you want dinner, let the resident manager David Edwards know by 10 a.m., and you will be served a four-course meal for £7 ($12.25).

Highways House, 143 Wells Rd. (tel. Bath 21238), is an elegant Victorian family home within minutes of the historic center. There is parking for eight cars, plus a garage for another three vehicles, a rare facility within a city built when the sedan chair and coach and horses reigned supreme. Highways is the home of Guy and Jenny Simmins and their family. For seven years he was assistant director of tourism at the Pump Room and Roman Baths. They offer single, double, and family rooms, and some units have a shower and toilet en suite, as well as color TV. Singles cost from £10 ($17.50), and doubles or twins go for £16 ($28) to £20 ($25), with family rooms costing from £23 ($40.25). These tariffs include service, VAT, and a full English breakfast. Both Guy and Jenny know a lot about Bath and its environs and always show a willingness to help guests in their planning. Their ironing facilities may come in handy in an emergency, and drinks and snacks can be arranged.

Millers, 69 Great Pulteney St. (tel. Bath 65798), stands on a residential street of Georgian buildings, close to the heart of the city. Run by M. J. Miller, it offers a dozen colorful, relaxing rooms, two of which have their own private baths. The hotel is centrally heated, and each unit can be controlled to the desired temperature. A single rents for £13 ($22.75), a twin or double going for £21 ($36.75). With bath, a twin or double increases to £26 ($45.50) a night. Some units house three to four persons at rates ranging from £34 ($59.50) to £41 ($71.75). All these tariffs include a full English breakfast, service, and VAT. There is a comfortable dining room with an adjoining licensed lounge bar. This small hotel is unusually well managed and offers excellent value.

Mr. Smith's Steak & Chophouse, Queen Street (tel. Bath 61728), is known primarily as a restaurant (see below), but it also offers good accommodations. The Smiths run a centrally heated, pleasantly furnished guest house, accommodating overnight visitors and serving a full English breakfast. They rent two singles, three doubles, two twin rooms, plus some family-size units with private baths. One twin has a shower and toilet, and all rooms are equipped with hot and cold running water, TV, radio, and intercom. The cost of B&B ranges from £8.50 ($14.88) to £9.50 ($16.63) per person nightly. Considering its facilities and heartbeat location, it's a good choice for value.

"The Orchard," 41a Warminster Rd., Bathampton, outside Bath (tel. Bath 66115), is an excelent B&B run by Mrs. Judith Pye. Motorists can reach it on the A36, a five- to ten-minute drive from the heart of the city. If you don't have a car, it is also conveniently situated on a local bus route. In semi-rural surroundings, it's a peaceful and tranquil choice, and there is off-street parking. The double rooms, costing from £9.50 ($16.63) per night, are bright and cozy, and there are private baths en suite, along with tea- or coffee-making facilities, color TV, and central heating. A large traditional English breakfast is served. The house is kept very neat and clean, and Mrs. Pye makes all her guests feel comfortable.

READERS' GUEST HOUSE SELECTIONS: "We stayed at the home of **Mrs. H. F. Millburn,** 41 Crescent Gardens, Upper Bristol Road (tel. Bath 24725). She has a large comfortable house with good beds and a large breakfast. The charge is £8 ($14) per person for adults, £5.50 ($9.63) for children under 10. Also, Mrs. Millburn's is within ten minutes' walk of most of the major sights in Bath. She is very helpful about giving directions and recommending eating establishments" (Mrs. Edward Lacy, Ottenhofen, Germany). . . . "At **Kingsleigh House,** Box Road, Bathford (tel. Bath 858440), Mr. and Mrs. P. Gillen are delightfully cordial. Our bedroom was the most comfortably heated one (central heating) we occupied in England. It is on the eastern outskirts of Bath. For B&B, the charge is £8 ($14) per person in a single room, from £7 ($12.25) per person in a double" (Dr. and Mrs. Thomas F. Paine, Nashville, Tenn.).

"At the beautiful **Emdene Guest House,** Lansdown (tel. Bath 310961), Mr. and Mrs. Flook provide you with a fantastic breakfast and room for £7.50 ($13.13) each. The house furnishings are antiques of fine wood. The hallway is lined with shelves of character mugs and steins collected by the Flooks. The house is in Lansdown, a suburb of Bath. This place is perfect for travelers who want to be out in the country, yet not far from a city. One disadvantage that we found not really one is that after the final bus stop on Lansdown Road, you must walk a half a mile to the Emdene. The path is paved and surrounded by farm fields, so it is an enjoyable trek. The house has a giant guest lounge, and the whole place is centrally heated" (Patti Bradley, Tustin, Calif.). . . . "The **North Parade Hotel,** North Parade (tel. Bath 60007), rents hard-to-find singles at £11.50 ($20.13) and doubles at £20 ($35). The price includes an English breakfast and VAT. Tipping is at the discretion of the guests. The hotel is very clean and centrally located, only two or three blocks away from the bus and train stations (saving taxi fare), the abbey, the information bureau, the Roman baths, and the shopping area, and only a little farther from the Market which is opposite the post office" (A. R. Sockman, Forest Hills, N.Y.). . . . "**Wentworth House,** 106 Bloomfield Rd. (tel. Bath 310460), operated by Sylvia and Geoff Alger, is an attractive Victorian house in a quiet, pleasant neighborhood on the south side of Bath, just across the river from the city center. The house is immaculate, attractively furnished, licensed for adult beverages, and offers a swimming pool, black-and-white TV in all rooms, and a lounge with color TV. We had a room with private bath and an excellent dinner of young spring lamb, all for £30 ($52.50) for two. It seemed a bargain" (Dr. Colin Fell, Hastings-on-Hudson, N.Y.).

WHERE TO EAT: Mr. Smith's Steak & Chophouse, Queen Street (tel. Bath 61728), is the kind of dining establishment usually known to the locals who have resided in the city for some time. It's hidden from the usual visitors on a narrow street in the heart of Bath. The protruding bay window lets in the sun, and you can sit in the front and watch the passing parade.

Meals in the little dining room are prepared with care. The food is typically English, as reflected by the roast beef, Yorkshire pudding, boiled potatoes, peas, and carrots. A rump or sirloin steak, including vegetables, begins at £5.50 ($9.63). The house specialty is chicken à la Mr. Smith at £4.50 ($7.88), and at lunch there is homemade steak-and-kidney pie, plus other specials. The restaurant is open for lunch from noon to 2 p.m. and for dinner from 6:30 to 11 p.m.

Beaujolais, 5 Chapel Row (tel. Bath 23417), is run by Jean-Pierre Philippe on true bistro lines. You enter through the undistinguished front door and find a seat in one of the three rooms of brightly clad tables. Then you're greeted by a member of the friendly and knowledgeable staff. You'll definitely need to give notice if you want one of the more private tables for four with settles.

This little restaurant is a bastion of France in the center of the city. It is close to the theater and popular with the actors. French provincial cooking produces uncomplicated dishes based on the freshest ingredients. The menu is à la carte and changes daily. It includes a variety of fresh fish. A typical choice might be a classic onion soup, followed by an entrecôte steak with green peppercorn sauce and creamed celeriac, with a tangy sorbet to finish. The service has that delightfully French nonchalance. Reservations are necessary. Expect to spend about £12 ($21) per person, including wine. Between noon and 12:30 p.m. you can feast on Thai food for less than £2 ($3.50), inclusive. The Beaujolais is open daily, except Sunday and bank holidays, from 7:30 to 11:30 p.m. On Friday and Saturday, it also opens for lunch from 12:30 to 2:30 p.m. Faint music plays in the background, and the atmosphere is informal, the value excellent.

Evans Fish Restaurant, 7–8 Abbeygate St., only a three-minute walk from the abbey itself, features superb fish dinners at moderate cost. Created by Mrs. Harriet Evans in 1908, it is a family-style restaurant where you can have a three-course luncheon for as little as £4 ($7). The set meal might include the soup of the day, fried filet of fish with chips, and a choice of desserts. Mrs. Hunt carries on today in the fine traditions established by the Evans family.

Only the freshest of fish is served in this restaurant, but—just so it won't smell fishy—the staff comes in extra early on Monday morning, when every square inch is scrubbed clean. The lower floor has a self-service section for quickies. On the second floor is an Abbey Room which caters to families. The preferred dining spot is the Georgian Room—so named after its unspoiled arched windows and fireplace. You can order a number of crisply fried fish specialties, such as deep-fried scampi with chips for £2.55 ($4.46), and many other main-dish fish courses cost as little as 80p ($1.40) from the take-out section. The restaurant is open Monday from 11:45 a.m. to 2:30 p.m., Tuesday through Saturday, from 11:30 a.m. to 6 p.m. serving lunches and high teas.

Evelyn & Owen's, 1 St. Andrew's Terrace, Bartlett Street (tel. Bath 333233), is named in memory of Evan and Owen, the Bath department store whose former premises the restaurant now occupies. Bob Payton, a former advertising executive and ex-Chicagoan, opened the restaurant in 1982. It serves a wide-ranging menu, including deep-dish pizza, barbecued ribs, chicken and hamburgers, as well as stuffed mushrooms, cheese and carrot cake, and ice cream. A lunchtime special pizza and salad costs around £2 ($3.50), and you are likely to spend from £6 ($10.50) in the evening at dinner. The building the restaurant occupies was designed by the Bath architect, John Wood the Younger. The room is light and airy and filled with original advertising and publicity material from around the turn of the century. The restaurant is almost opposite the Assembly Rooms, and it has both smoking and no-smoking tables as well as a take-out service. Hours are Tuesday to Sunday from 11:45 a.m. to 11 p.m.

Tranter's Restaurant, 2 Saracen St. (tel. Bath 60868). One of our readers called this seafood restaurant "a magical place," and a quick visit here might confirm that impression. Owners Tina Tranter and Geoff Glover once worked as photographers and movie camera operators (he worked on *Star Wars* and *The Empire Strikes Back*). Today the city of Bath benefits from their successful transition from the visual to the culinary arts, although both partners continue their former career as well. A special seafood soup with all the trimmings—big enough for a meal in itself—costs £4.90 ($8.58). This, followed by a scallop, bacon, and prawn kebab, would come to about £9 ($15.75). Game dishes such as venison chops are also a specialty. Tranter's is open Monday to Saturday for lunch from 12:30 to 2:30 p.m. Dinner begins every night except Sunday at 6:30 p.m. Morning coffee is served Wednesday and Saturday from 10 to 11:30 a.m.

If you'd like a simple luncheon, I'd suggest the **Danish Food & Wine Bar,** Pierrepont Place (tel. Bath 61603). The space here might be a little cramped, but that's quickly forgotten as an array of smörebrød (those open-faced Danish sandwiches) is brought out. You can make selections from fish, cheese, and beef for about £1 ($1.75) per serving. The salads, costing more, are good, crisp, and fresh. Perhaps you'll sample the Scandinavian-style "cold board," where for about £2.75 ($4.81) you can self yourself an array of tempting food. Visit any time from 11:30 a.m. to 2:30 p.m. Monday to Saturday.

The Laden Table, 7 Edgar Buildings (tel. Bath 64356), attracts the vegetarian. Even when there's only a dozen diners, it seems a little crowded around here. The music is kept at a safe decibel level, as you make your selection from chef/owner Peter Slotter's repertoire. The menu on the blackboard changes, depending on their shopping for the day. The food is fresh and well prepared, and the cuisine is international. Hopefully, you'll be there on the day curry is offered. Tabs rarely run more than £4 ($7). Hours are from noon to 3 p.m. Monday to Saturday and from 6 to 11 p.m. for dinner Monday to Sunday.

A Landmark Coffeehouse

Sally Lunn's House, North Parade Passage, is a tiny gabled stone coffeeshop, with a Georgian bay window, original early Tudor fireplaces, and "bow and arrow" cupboards. The house is a landmark in Bath, built in 1482 and considered to be the oldest structure in the city. Sally Lunn was known by legend to all Bathonians for her buns baked in the cellars here in 1680. It's like going back 500 years to have a bite with a glass of wine in the cellars alongside the original ovens and cooking paraphernalia, or take coffee, tea, or hot chocolate at a natural-wood tavern table or in a settle. Coffee with a toasted Sally Lunn bun with "lashings" of fresh butter costs 75p ($1.31). You can have toasted sandwiches at 85p ($1.49) or salads with meat and smoked oyster pies, eel pies, or succulent quiches for around £2.80 ($4.90). Sally Lunn's is especially noted for continental pastries and cake, all baked on the premises by Susan Greenaway, pastry chef par excellence. The house is licensed and sells wines, including English country products such as blackberry and dandelion wines by the glass or bottle. The house is easy to spot—near the abbey, off Church Street.

READERS' PUB SELECTION: "**Crystal Palace** pub and lounge in Abbey Street is a charming place, just around the corner from Bath Abbey. It opens from a tiny square shaded by a large plane tree. The lounge, with a low, dark-beamed ceiling and paneled fireplace, has soft floral patterned carpet and tapestried chairs and banquettes. Whitewashed walls, deep red curtains at the windows, and hurricane lamps all add to a feeling of gracious warmth and welcome. The owner, Roy, was posting the menu in front as we walked by looking for a place to have lunch, and he chatted amiably with us. Our chicken pot pie and shepherd's pie were tasty and steaming hot. With a pint of lager, the total check for two was £6 ($10.50). Roy came by, sat down, and had a bit of a natter with us as we ate, and later as we walked through the enclosed, flowered courtyard in the rear, he called his wife Jeannette to come out and meet us and pose for a picture. Roy is a gracious, witty, and cordial host who serves an excellent hot lunch in delightful surroundings" (Carol and Don Green, San Diego, Calif.). [*Author's Note:* This is one of the few places in England where you can order Thomas Hardy ale, an expensive drink with the highest alcohol content of any beer in the world!]

ON THE OUTSKIRTS: The **Wheelwrights Arms,** Monkton Combe, near Bath (tel. Limpley Stoke 2287), is a high-grade accommodation in a converted stable block, a unique place of character run by Ric and Monica Gillespie as a "free house." To reach it, take the A36 out of Bath in the direction of Warminster. All visitors have one word to describe it: "quaint." The Wheelwrights Arms was a very old British pub which was refurbished to receive paying guests. Such rooms are equipped with twin beds, complete with private bath and *showers that work.* The charge is from £10 ($17.50) per person for B&B. The olde worlde dining room is especially inviting.

Mrs. Jenny Swinley, Bellsburn, Lower Street, Rode, near Bath (tel. Frome 830375), is a charming hostess, acting as a guide to visitors to Bath. Her husband is an officer in the Royal Navy. One of her ancestors saved Bath Abbey by buying it from Oliver Cromwell. She offers one twin-bedded room with an adjoining bath and sitting room en suite (a sofa bed in the sitting room is for a third person if required). Guests have their own private entrance from the enchanting garden in the rear. Rates are £9 ($15.75) per person for B&B. The traditional English breakfast is excellent. Evening meals can be arranged in advance. The warm, intimate country cottage contains its original beams. Guests can be met free at Bath or Westbury Station, only 75 minutes from London.

9. Bristol

Bristol, the largest city in the West Country, is a good center for touring western Britain. Its location is 10 miles west of Bath, just across the Bristol Channel from Wales, 20 miles from the Cotswolds, and 30 miles from Stonehenge. This historic inland port is linked to the sea by seven miles of the navigable Avon River. Bristol has long been rich in seafaring traditions and has many links with the early colonization of America. In fact, some claim that the new continent was named after a Bristol town clerk, Richard Ameryke! In 1497 John Cabot sailed from Bristol which led to the discovery of the northern half of the New World.

In Bristol, the world's first iron steamship and luxury liner is being restored to her 1843 glory. She's the 3000-ton S.S. *Great Britain,* and was created by Isambard Brunel, a Victorian engineer. Visitors can go aboard this "floating palace" between 10 a.m. and 5 p.m. for an admission of $2 (half price for children).

At the age of 25 in 1831, Brunel began a Bristol landmark, a suspension bridge over the 250-foot-deep Avon Gorge at Clifton.

The city's floating harbor was formed by damming up the Avon River in 1809. A tour boat leaves from the harbor daily at noon and again at 2, 3, and 4 p.m., costing £1.25 ($2.19) for adults and 60p ($1.05) for children. For more information about these tours, telephone Bristol 28157.

Bristol Cathedral, College Green (tel. Bristol 24879), was begun in the 12th century and was once an Augustinian abbey. The central tower was added in 1466. The Chapter House and Gatehouse are good examples of late Norman architecture, and the choir is magnificent.

Another church, **St. Mary Redcliffe,** was called "the fairest, the goodliest, and most famous parish church in England" by such an authority as Elizabeth I. Built in the 14th century, it has been carefully restored.

Cobbled King Street is known for its **Theatre Royal,** the smallest English playhouse and the oldest in continuous operation. For information about shows being offered, call the theater box office at Bristol 27466.

Many old taverns line this quayside area, principally the 17th-century **Llandoger Trow,** once the haunt of pirates. A few blocks up King Street from the Lightship, Llandoger Trow is reputed to have figured in *Treasure Island* by Robert Louis Stevenson. Guests drop in for a drink at the Smuggler's Bar or else the Old Vic Bar, later perhaps enjoying a plaice or steak dinner in an atmosphere of time-worn beams and old fireplaces.

This is also the home of the **Bristol Old Vic,** the city's repertory company. For information about tickets or its current presentation, telephone the box office at Bristol 27466.

Guided walking tours are conducted in summer, and these last about 1½ hours, leaving from the Exchange on Corn Street. On Monday and Tuesday the tour departs at 11 a.m., at 2:30 p.m. on the other days of the week. On Sunday, guided tours are conducted through Clifton, a suburb of Bristol which has more Georgian houses than the just-previewed Bath. These walking tours cost about 60p ($1.05) per person.

Additional information on special walks is provided by **Bristol Tourist Information,** Colston House, Colston Street (tel. Bristol 293891).

If you prefer to see the city from the water, you can take a boat tour on the *Bristol Packet,* costing £1 ($1.75) for adults and 60p ($1.05) for children. You embark in Wapping Way, going through the car park for the S.S. *Great Britain.* For information, telephone Bristol 28157.

LODGINGS: Instead of finding lodgings in Bristol itself, many visitors prefer to seek out accommodations in the leafy Georgian suburb of Clifton, near the famous suspension bridge, already mentioned.

There you'll find **Oakfield Hotel,** Oakfield Road, Clifton, off Whiteladies Road (tel. Bristol 735556), an impressive guest house that would be called a town house in New York, with an Italian facade. It's on a quiet street, and everything is kept spic and span under the watchful eye of Mrs. D. L. Hurley. Every pleasantly furnished bedroom has hot and cold running water and central heating. The charge is £9.50 ($16.63) daily in a single and £7.50 ($13.13) per person, based on double occupancy, these tariffs including breakfast but not VAT. For another £3.50 ($6.13) you can enjoy a good dinner.

Westbury Park Hotel, 37 Westbury Rd., in Bristol (tel. Bristol 620465), is a small, privately owned and run hotel on the A4018, one of Bristol's main arteries, linking the city center with the M4 and M5 motorways. The hotel stands about three miles from exit 17 on the M5 and about two miles from the city center. After a two-minute walk, you'll be at the Durdham Downs, which are acres of open park stretching from the Avon Gorge to Brunel's suspension bridge. Heather Jenkins has brought new vitality and a high standard of innkeeping to the place. The house is a stone structure, with bay windows opening onto a walled garden. There's a well-kept library, and drinks are served in the lounge. A good English breakfast starts the day. In a single, the B&B rate is £11.50 ($20.13), rising to £18.50 ($32.38) in a double, although VAT is extra. Some bedrooms are available with private bath and toilet, costing £16 ($28) in a single, £23.50 ($41.13) in a double. In the dining room you have an interesting table d'hôte menu for £6.50 ($11.38). Dishes are personally prepared with only fresh food, including vegetables.

Alandale Hotel, Tyndall's Park Road, Clifton (tel. Bristol 735407), is an elegant early Victorian house that retains a wealth of its original features, including a marble fireplace and ornate plasterwork. Note the fine staircase in the imposing entrance hall. The hotel is under the supervision of Mr. Johnson, who still observes the old traditions of personal service. For example, afternoon tea is served, as are sandwiches, drinks, and snacks in the lounge (up until midnight). A continental breakfast is available in your bedroom until 10 a.m., unless you'd prefer the full English breakfast in the dining room. Terms are from £9 ($15.75) per person nightly in a twin-bedded unit, including VAT.

Washington Hotel, St. Paul's Road, in Clifton (tel. Bristol 733980), makes up in quality for its smallness. Joan Steele, who manages it, is considerate in her hospitality. The hotel is on a quiet street, just north of the city center, with space for car parking. Each of the bedrooms has a radio, electric blankets, central heating, and, best of all, a decent price for B&B—£10.50 ($18.38) per person. Even better, this includes VAT and the service charge. Guests congregate in the pleasant lounge for conversation or else to view TV.

The Willow, 209 Gloucester Rd., Patchway (tel. Almondsbury 612276), is simple, clean, and comfortable, a nice little guest house run by J. S. Abrahams who always seems pleased to receive visitors "from so far away!" For B&B, the tariff is £8 ($14) nightly, going up to £11 ($19.25) with an evening meal included. Depending on their ages, children are granted reductions.

The **Dunraven Hotel,** Upper Belgrave Road, Clifton (tel. Bristol 737475), is a white brick three-story hotel with five rounded bay windows, on the main A38 road from the Midlands and South Wales (via the Severn Bridge) to the southwest. A mile from the city center, the hotel stands on major bus routes, facing the Clifton Downs. At the rear are good views of Bristol. The rates, not including VAT, are £11 ($19.25) in a single, rising to £18 ($31.50) in a double. An evening meal—good home-cooking—is served for £6 ($10.50). The rooms are nicely furnished and centrally heated, containing hot and cold running water. There are two lounges, each with TV, and the hotel is licensed.

Rockdale Guest House, 512 Bath Rd., Brislington (tel. Bristol 712831), is owned by Mrs. Whitfield, who also has the house next door. In all, she rents out ten rooms, including three family rooms and seven twin-bedded units. The charge is £8 ($14) per person nightly, although you are assessed another £1 ($1.75) if you stay only one night. Children sharing their parents' room pay only half price. Mrs. Whitfield makes all her guests feel right at home, and she keeps her rooms spotlessly clean. When she has the time, she often sits and chats with her guests after serving them a tasty breakfast. All her units have hot and cold running water, along with shaver points. There's a TV lounge for the use of guests, and there is also limited car parking space.

Orchard House, Bristol Road, Chew Stoke, about ten miles from Bristol (tel. Bristol 733143), is run by a charming and hospitable couple, Bill and Dorothy Young. Their rooms are very comfortable and immaculately clean, with coffee-making facilities. Their baths are well kept, and they serve an excellent breakfast. The house is 200 years old, and there is a nearby lake for trout fishing. B&B costs from £9.50 ($16.63) per person nightly. There is a generous four-course meal offered for £6 ($10.50), and it's followed by tea or coffee. Garden produce is used when available, and the homemade soups and desserts are indeed worthy. House wines are served. Chew Stoke is a good center for touring Bristol, Bath, Wells, Glastonbury, Longleat, and Stonehenge.

Hotel Clifton, St. Paul's Road (tel. Bristol 736882), has been improved greatly. On a peaceful street near the University of Bristol, it offers attractively furnished rooms that contain color TV, tea- or coffee-making facilities, and often a private bath or shower. Doubles range in price from £17 ($29.75) to £20 ($35), and singles cost from £10 ($17.50) to £12 ($21). The hotel has an intriguing vaulted bar converted from the old cellars and a licensed supper room serving traditional home cooking.

WHERE TO EAT: The **Guild Restaurant,** 68–70 Park St. (tel. Bristol 291874), forms a section of the Bristol Guild Shop, right in the heart of town. While traffic in the distance roars down Park Street, you dine here in a secluded atmosphere of style and comfort. In the cold months its terrace is covered, but come spring, patrons dine al fresco. It's open from 9:30 a.m. (drop in for coffee) to 5 p.m., Monday to Friday; however, it shuts down at 1 p.m. on Saturday and is closed all day on Sunday.

Soups at lunch are hearty and homemade, although you might prefer one of the pâtés or quiches to launch your repast. Salads are outstanding here, and casseroles are hot, good tasty and filling. Many of the dishes are inspired by the continental kitchen. Expect to spend from £5 ($8.75) for a complete meal.

La Romanina, 25 The Mall, in Clifton (tel. Bristol 34499), is ideal if you, like most readers, are staying in Clifton and don't want to venture into the city center to dine. In recent times, a trattoria and pizzeria craze seems to have swept over Bristol, and La Romanina has surfaced near the top. It serves Monday to Saturday from noon to 2:30 p.m. and reopens for dinner at 7 p.m. (last orders around 11 p.m.).

Homemade pastas and pizzas draw a crowd of all ages, and you can order a simple meal or a savory Italian feast, depending on your appetite and pocketbook. The waiters, at least on my latest rounds, have sunny dispositions, in keeping with the bright, florid atmosphere. For pasta or pizza, the charge begins at around £2.50 ($4.38), going up. Of course, if you order one of the main courses, such as a tender veal, the cost will rise. Still, you are likely to escape for around £6 ($10.50). With main dishes fresh vegetables are included.

Flipper, at 6. St. James Barton (no phone), at the edge of Breadmead, is said to serve the best fish 'n' chips in town. If you want to take out your dinner, it'll cost only £1.20 ($2.10), a little more if you prefer to sit down and eat it on the premises. Good-tasting cod or halibut, served with crisp chips, is freshly prepared daily.

Behind a Georgian facade, **Parks Restaurant and Brasserie,** 51 Park St. (tel. Bristol 28016), is a favorite hangout of university students. It serves meals all day from noon to 11 p.m., Monday through Sunday. Its decor is attractive and inviting. For £3.25 ($5.69) you can order a Breton crêpe with a salad on the side, such as chicken and mushroom or cheese and spinach. For £4.50 ($7.88) the chef prepares a steak, kidney, and mushroom pie, served with jacket potatoes and vegetables. Homemade ice creams, such as prune and cognac, apricot and almond, whatever, cost from £1.35 ($2.36).

READER'S RESTAURANT SUGGESTION: "May I suggest **Munchers Café,** 31 Victoria St. (tel. Bristol 214585), near the Courage Brewery by the Bristol Bridge? It's convenient to the city center, St. Mary Redcliffe, and S.S. *Great Britain.* The hours are from 8:30 a.m. to 3 p.m. Sandwiches are made to order on six kinds of freshly baked bread delivered daily. Also featured are fresh quiches, salads, jacket potatoes with cheese, cheesecake, brownies, and carrot cake. The North American influence is strong because the owner/cook, Kate Sommerfield, lived in Cambridge, Mass., for four years. The building dates from 1435, and the café has been recently refurbished and even has occasional small shows of works by local artists" (Jessica Ferguson, Cambridge, Mass.).

Chapter X

THE COTSWOLDS

1. Burford, Minster Lovell, and Bibury
2. Cirencester and Painswick
3. Cheltenham
4. Royal Sudeley Castle
5. Malmesbury
6. Tetbury
7. Wotton-under-Edge
8. Shipton-under-Wychwood and Chipping Norton
9. Bourton-on-the-Water
10. Lower Swell and Stow-on-the-Wold
11. Moreton-in-Marsh
12. Broadway
13. Chipping Campden

THE COTSWOLDS, a once-great wool center of the 13th century, lie mainly in the county of Gloucestershire, although parts dip into Oxfordshire, Warwickshire, and Worcestershire. If possible, try to explore the area by car. That way you can spend hours surveying the land of winding goat paths, rolling hills, and sleepy hamlets, with names such as Stow-on-the-Wold, Wotton-under-Edge, Moreton-in-Marsh, Old Sodbury, Chipping Campden, Shipton-under-Wychwood, Upper and Lower Swell, and Upper and Lower Slaughter (often called the Slaughters). These most beautiful of English villages keep popping up on book jackets and calendars.

Cotswold lambs used to produce so much wool that they made their owners rich, wealth they invested in some of the finest domestic architecture in Europe, made out of the honeybrown Cotswold stone. The wool-rich gentry didn't neglect their church contributions either. Often the simplest of villages will have a church that in style and architectural detail seems to rank far beyond the means of the hamlet.

"Come on in through the kitchen" is all you need hear to know that you've found a homelike place where naturalness and friendliness prevail. Many readers will want to seek out comfortable (although decidedly unchic) accommodations in little stone inns that exist in the midst of the well-known and sophisticated hotels that advertise heavily. Perhaps you'll be served tea in front of a two-way fireplace, its walls made of natural Cotswold stone. Taking your long pieces of thick toasted bread, saturated with fresh butter, you'll find the flavor so good you won't resist putting on more chunky cherry jam.

Or maybe you'll go down a narrow lane to a stately Elizabethan stone manor, with thick walls and a moss-covered slate roof. Perhaps you'll arrive at haying time and watch the men at work in the fields beyond, as well as the cows and goats milked to produce the rich double cheese you'll be served later. Your dinner that night? Naturally, a roast leg of Cotswold lamb. If you arrive at a different season, you can enjoy the warmth and crackle of the logs on the fire in the drawing room.

Or you may want to settle down in and around Cheltenham, where the view from your bedroom window of the Severn Valley to the Malvern Hills to the Welsh mountains is so spectacular that old King George III came for a look. The open stretches of common, woodlands, fields, and country lanes provide the right setting for picnics. Life inside your guest house may be devoted to comfort and good eating—baskets of fresh eggs, Guernsey milk, cream, poultry, and a variety of vegetables from the garden.

If your tastes are slightly more expensive, you may seek out a classical Cotswold manor (and there are dozens of them) featuring creamy fieldstone, high-pitched roofs, large and small gables, towering chimneys, stone-mullioned windows, a drawing room with antique furnishings, a great lounge hall, an ancient staircase, and flagstone floors. Such Cotswold estates represent England at its best, with clipped hedges, rose gardens, terraces, stone steps, sweeping lawns, age-old trees, and spring flowers. You can revel in a fast-disappearing English country life, perhaps rent or borrow a pink coat (actually, it's red), and go on a genuine hunt, chasing a sly fox.

The adventure begins in:

1. Burford, Minster Lovell, and Bibury

BURFORD: In Oxfordshire, Burford is the gateway to the Cotswolds. This unspoiled medieval town, built of Cotswold stone, lies 19 miles to the west of Oxford, 31 miles from Stratford-upon-Avon, 14 miles from Blenheim Palace, and 75 miles from London. Its fame rests largely on its early Norman church (c. 1116) and its High Street, lined with coaching inns. Oliver Cromwell passed this way, as (in a happier day) did Charles II and his mistress, Nell Gwynne. Burford was one of the last of the great wool centers, the industry bleating out its last breath as late as Victoria's day. You may want to photograph the bridge across the Windrush River where Queen Elizabeth I once stood. Burford is definitely equipped for tourists, as the antique shops along the High will testify.

Food and Lodging

The **Corner House Hotel,** High Street (tel. Burford 3151), is informally run by Mr. and Mrs. Bateman, who like company. Actually, their hotel is an extension of their home. They've taken over this 15th-century stone-and-timbered overgrown cottage, adding a living room facing the rear garden. The inn is built of Cotswold stone. The B&B cost ranges from £12 ($21) to £13 ($22.75) per person nightly. The rooms are pleasant, neat, and comfortable, and you can take your meals at the Corner House. At noon, a three-course luncheon is served from £4 ($7), and dinner costs from £6 ($10.50). The steak-and-kidney pie is a treat. The Corner House is closed in December and January.

THE SOURCE OF THE THAMES: In your exploration of the Cotswolds, you may want to stop by the **Trout Inn,** St. John's Bridge, Lechlade, in

Gloucestershire (tel. Lechlade 52313). Lawns run down to the river, and you can sit out enjoying a peaceful drink in summer. Bar snacks are also served, including soup with crisp, crusty bread at £1.20 ($2.10), or sausages with pickle or mustard at 75p ($1.31).

This old inn beside the Thames is at St. John's Lock, the first on the river. Actually the spot is just about the source of the great river. You can walk across the fields to find the spring source, and here you'll see a statue of Father Thames erected by the Thames Conservancy Authorities. This place is as far as you can navigate the river in any case.

MINSTER LOVELL: From Oxford along the A40, you pass through Witney. Soon after, you turn right at the Minster Lovell signpost, about half a mile off the highway between Witney and Burford. Long since passed by the main road, the village is visited because of **Minster Lovell Hall,** the remains of a moated house in which an early Lovell is said to have hidden and subsequently starved to death after a battle in the area.

It was in the village that the legend of the mistletoe bough originated by the Windrush River. Minster Lovell is mainly built of Cotswold stone, with thatch or stone-slate roofs. It's rather a pity that there is a forest of TV aerials, but the place is still attractive to photographers.

BIBURY: Bibury, on the road from Burford to Cirencester, is one of the loveliest spots in the Cotswolds. In fact, the utopian romancer of Victoria's day, poet William Morris, called it England's "most beautiful village." On the banks of the Coln River, Bibury is noted for **Arlington Row,** a gabled group of 15th-century cottages, its biggest and most-photographed drawing card. The row is protected by the National Trust.

Arlington Mill (tel. Bibury 368) dates from the *Domesday* survey and was in use until the outbreak of World War I. There are four floors in the mill and three in the cottage, with 16 exhibition rooms. It contains a collection of 19th-century mill machinery, along with Peter Waals furniture, Victorian costumes and furniture, and Staffordshire china. The mill is open March to October and winter weekends from 10:30 a.m. to 7 p.m., and charges 80p ($1.40) admission for adults, 30p (53¢) for children.

From Bibury, we head down the road for seven miles to:

2. Cirencester and Painswick

CIRENCESTER: Don't worry about how to pronounce the name of the town. Even the English are in disagreement. Just say "siren-cess-ter" and you won't be too far wrong. Cirencester is often considered the unofficial capital of the Cotswolds, probably a throwback to its reputation in the Middle Ages when it flourished as the center of the great Cotswold wool industry.

In Roman Britain, five roads converged on Cirencester, which was called Corinium in those days. In size, it ranked second only to London. Today it is chiefly a market town, a good base for touring, as it lies 34 miles from Bath, 16 from the former Regency spa at Cheltenham, 17 from Gloucester, 36 from Oxford, and 38 from Stratford-upon-Avon. The trip from London is 89 miles.

Corinium Museum

On Park Street, the museum houses the archeological remains left from the Roman occupation of Cirencester. The mosaic pavements found on Dyer Street in Cirencester in 1849 are the most important exhibit. And the provincial Roman sculpture (Minerva, Mercury), the pottery, the bits and pieces salvaged from long-decayed buildings, provide a remote link with the high level of civilization that once flourished here. The museum has been completely redeveloped and modernized. It's open from 10 a.m. to 6 p.m. weekdays, 2 to 6 p.m. on Sunday. Admission is 30p (53¢) for adults; children, 10p (18¢). For information, telephone Cirencester 5611.

Cirencester Parish Church

Dating back to Norman times and Henry I, the Church of John the Baptist overlooks the Market Square. (Actually, a church may have stood on this spot in Saxon times.) In size, the Cirencester church appears to be a cathedral, not a mere parish church. It is, in fact, one of the largest parish churches in the country. The present building represents a variety of styles, largely Perpendicular, such as its early 15th-century tower. Among the treasures inside are a 15th-century pulpit and a silver-gilt cup given to Queen Anne Boleyn two years before her execution.

Food and Lodging

The **Marlborough Arms,** Sheep Street (tel. Cirencester 3926), is a traditional stone Cotswold village house with dormers and chimneys. It has had a reputation as a good hostelry for several centuries. Most of the age-old traditions of this post house remain, although many modern facilities have been added. The owners, Doug and Nora Colbourne, maintain old English hospitality. They have three double rooms with adjacent bathroom, each unit nicely furnished and equipped with wash basin and electric heating. In a single, they ask £12 ($21) nightly per person, but lower it to £11 ($19.25) if you stay more than one night. In a double, the rate is £10 ($17.50) per person for one night, and £9 ($15.75) per person for the following night. The rates include a traditional morning fare. They'll even provide early-morning tea and your favorite newspaper if requested. According to inn traditions, you can get bar snacks and lunches at either of the bars.

If you don't want to stay at a hotel, you might try **La Ronde Guest House,** 52–54 Ashcroft Rd. (tel. Cirencester 4611), run by Mr. and Mrs. N. E. Shales, who charge £10 ($17.50) per person for B&B. They have both family rooms, as well as doubles, twins, and singles. In the town center, within walking distance of Cirencester Park, the abbey grounds, and the museum and parish church, the small hotel is licensed. The dining room offers a varied menu and an extensive wine list. Dinner is from £7.50 ($13.13). The hotel offers central heating, hot and cold running water in all the rooms, and has a color TV lounge as well. A cocktail bar has been added which visitors find cozy and attractive. La Ronde can serve as your center for touring the Cotswolds. The owners will give you a printed leaflet, describing in detail 14 different tours that can easily be done in one day while based at their premises.

Wimbourne Guest House, 91 Victoria Rd. (tel. Cirencester 3890), is a Cotswold stone house, built in the Victorian era (1894). It is near the town center and marketplace which is dominated by the parish church. Nearby lie Cirencester Park, with 3000 acres of beautifully wooded parkland, the abbey grounds, and the Corinium Museum. Rates are £9 ($15.75) to £10.50 ($18.38) per person for B&B, with half board costing £14 ($24.50) to £15.50 ($27.13) per person. A friendly and welcoming atmosphere is provided by the owners, Miss Hagar Butler and Miss Joyce Degg. Television is available in the sitting room, and all bedrooms have wash basins with hot and cold running water and shaving points.

Raydon Guest House, 3 The Avenue (tel. Cirencester 3485), is only five minutes from the town center, yet is in a peaceful residential area adjoining an attractive garden complex. This Victorian mansion is owned by Mr. and Mrs. Ron Cupitt, who rent ten of their large bedrooms. They charge £10 ($17.50) per person nightly, whether in a single or a double, including VAT. Mrs. Cupitt will prepare one of her special English breakfasts. They'll reduce their rates for children under 14, and if you come in late you can have a light snack in the well-furnished lounge. If you are driving, there is space for your car in the parking area. From Market Place, drive along Cricklade Street and Watermoor Road, turning left on The Avenue.

The **Crown Hotel,** West Market Place (tel. Cirencester 3288), was a coaching inn from the 14th century. Today, it's just a good pub opposite the old parish church. Many of the Crown's original architectural features have been preserved, and the beams still tell a story of long ago. A hot and cold buffet is served in the bar and in the old Swan Inn across the cobbled courtyard. Prices range from £1.25 ($2.19) to £3 ($5.25).

Cottage of Content, 117 Cricklade St., is a delightful little restaurant owned and run by Mr. and Mrs. Pugh, who cook, serve, and even do the washing up. A lunch of soup, main course, and pudding costs about £2 ($3.50). In the evening they have a variety of succulent meals, or T-bone steaks, the latter costing £7 ($12.25), all served with fresh vegetable, salads in season, and a dessert. They are open daily except Sunday, Monday, and bank holidays from noon till 2 p.m. and from 7:30 to 9:30 p.m.

PAINSWICK: The sleepy little town of Painswick, four miles northeast of Stroud, is considered a model village. All its houses, although erected at different periods, blend harmoniously, because the former villagers used only Cotswold stone as their building material. The one distinctive feature on the Painswick skyline is the spire of its 15th-century parish church. The church is linked with the legend of 99 yew trees, as well as its annual Clipping Feast (when the congregation joins hands and circles around the church as if it were a Maypole, singing hymns as they do). Ancient tombstones dot the churchyard.

Where to Stay

For accommodation, try the **Painswick Hotel and Restaurant** in Kemps Lane (tel. Painswick 812160). This was formerly the Cranham Wood Hotel. Completely refurbished, this beautiful Georgian house was once a royal vicarage and has terraces of formal gardens of beauty and tranquility. The hotel reception area was once the private chapel. There are rooms both with and without private bath, and the rates for B&B start at £17 ($29.75). This tariff includes VAT, and there is no service charge. For guests staying two nights or more, the hotel offers a half-board rate of £20.50 ($35.88) per person daily, including VAT, except on bank holiday weekends. The hotel has been awarded rosettes for its high standard of cuisine and service, both by the Automobile Association and the Royal Automobile Club.

Where to Dine

The **Country Elephant** (tel. Painswick 813564), is an excellent restaurant serving fine, English country-style cuisine. Owned and operated by Michael and Jane Medforth, the restaurant has a distinct personal touch. Mrs. Medforth does the cooking, keeping the menu limited so that only the freshest ingredients are used. In the simple dining room done in modern style, you may dine on steak-and-mushroom pie with bacon and red wine, pork chops stuffed with apricots, almonds, and raisins and baked in cider and herbs, or a fresh grilled trout with cream and chives. Most entrees cost about £7 ($12.25). Appetizers may include a homemade cream of watercress soup or an individual prawn-and-cheese quiche, ranging from £1 ($1.75) to £2.50 ($4.38). On Sunday a three-course set lunch is offered for £6.50 ($11.38). The menu changes twice a week, sometimes even more often depending on what is available at the local markets. The restaurant is open Tuesday through Saturday from 7 to 11 p.m., and also for Sunday lunch from 12:30 to 2:30 p.m.

3. Cheltenham

In a sheltered area between the Cotswolds and the Severn Vale, a mineral spring was discovered by chance. An interesting legend is that the people of this Cotswold stone village noticed pigeons drinking from a spring, and observed how healthy they were. As a result of this story, the pigeon has been incorporated into the town's crest.

Always seeking a new spa, George III arrived in 1788 and launched the town. In trouble because of a liver disorder, the Duke of Wellington also is responsible for fanning its praise. Lord Byron came this way too, proposing marriage to Miss Millbanke.

Some 100 miles from London, Cheltenham is one of England's most fashionable spas. Its architecture is mainly Regency, with lots of ironwork, balconies, and verandas. Attractive parks and open spaces of greenery make the town inviting.

The main street, the Promenade, has been called "the most beautiful thoroughfare in Britain." Rather similar to the Promenade are such thoroughfares as Lansdowne Place and Montpellier Parade. The design for the dome of the Rotunda was based on the Pantheon in Rome. Montpellier Walk, with its shops separated by caryatids, is one of the most interesting shopping centers in England.

Guided walking tours of Cheltenham leave from the **Tourist Information Centre,** Promenade.

WHERE TO STAY: **Carr's Hotel,** 42 Clarence St. (tel. Cheltenham 24003), is a Georgian hotel, taken over and redecorated by Mr. and Mrs. Douglas and their son John. Carr's is close to the National Coach Station and the local bus station. It is right in the heart of Cheltenham, opposite the art gallery, museum, and library. The Douglas family are warm and friendly, creating an inviting atmosphere. The hotel has 18 bedrooms, renting for £11 ($19.25) in a single, and from £18 ($31.50) or £19 ($33.25) in a double or twin. Special rates will be quoted for the family rooms. There is an extensive menu for a traditional English breakfast and a choice from the table d'hôte or a grill menu if you'd like to take dinner at your hotel.

Eveleigh, 56 Prestbury Rd. (tel. Cheltenham 512692), is a large Victorian guest house run by Mrs. Luker, who charges £9 ($15.75) per person nightly for B&B. The house is well kept, tastefully decorated, and furnished with firm and comfortable beds. There are facilities for making tea and coffee. This is a suitable choice for those seeking budget accommodations. Rooms contain hot and cold running water, and there is access to the showers and toilets on the landing. A bus leads to the center of Cheltenham, a ten-minute walk away (six, if you're speedy).

North Hall Hotel, Pittville Circus Road (tel. Cheltenham 20589), is a substantial and attractive house, which lies close to the center of town as well as the race course and Pittville Park. There's free parking in the private forecourt. The house is nicely appointed, with full central heating. Rooms, well furnished and comfortable, contain hot and cold running water, electric heaters, and razor plugs. In a double, the rate is £16 ($28), dropping to £10 ($17.50) in a single. Children are granted reductions. There's a lounge and dining room which serves good but simple English-style food, such as roast chicken with savory stuffing or roast beef with horseradish sauce, a complete meal costing from £4 ($7). VAT is extra.

READERS' HOTEL SELECTIONS: "The **Lawn Hotel,** 5 Pittville Lawn (tel. Cheltenham 26638), is a meticulous and comfortable Regency town house within the impressive wrought-iron gates to Pittville Park and Gardens. In a quiet, lovely residential area, the Lawn is conveniently near the Promenade and town center, as well as the two coach stations where buses depart on regular runs to countless, charming, old-world Cotswold villages and to Oxford, Stratford-upon-Avon, and Wales. The experienced, efficient, and friendly resident-proprietors of the Lawn, Mr. and Mrs. J. C. Richards, are warm and cordial hosts. B&B is £8.50 ($14.88) per person, and tasty snacks and evening meals are cheerfully served upon request. The half-board rate is £12 ($21) per person. Besides comfortable rooms (accommodating in total 14), the facilities include a TV lounge, bulletin board with notices of local events, guests' phone, shower and bath, hot and cold washing facilities in each room, adequate electric heaters, and free parking" (Mrs. Mary Hamilton Moe, Potomac, Md.). . . . "We found Mrs. Williams's **Clairmont,** 94 St. Georges Rd. (tel. Cheltenham 35393), to be a home on a central tree-lined street with spacious rooms and a well-prepared breakfast. Mrs. Williams is a warm, friendly person. Each evening she would arrive with tea and cookies. Some rooms with private bathroom and/or kitchen facilities rent for £10 ($17.50)" (Jean Wootton, Victoria, B.C., Canada).

DINING IN CHELTENHAM: **Montpelier Wine Bar and Bistro,** Bayshill Lodge, Montpelier Street (tel. Cheltenham 27774), is an imposing Regency building converted from an old established shop to a cellar bistro and a first-floor wine bar. Very busy at lunchtime, but worth the effort to get in, it offers a choice of some 12 wines by the glass at around 80p ($1.40). Then you can select a hot meal from the blackboard menu. A hot soup is always featured among the various appetizers, then cold meats and salad, hot meat pies, smoked fish, lasagne, interesting salads, and a good selection of desserts. You'll pay around £4.50 ($7.88) for a very satisfying meal either in the cellar or, in good weather, on the terrace. It is open from Monday to Saturday from noon to 2:30 p.m. and from 6 to 10:30 p.m., and on Sunday from noon to 2 p.m. only.

Forrest's Wine House, Imperial Lane (tel. Cheltenham 38001). Wines are sold here by the glass, which you can sip while admiring the lofty ceilings of this room which was once used to sell bread. The menu changes daily, but could include an orange and tomato soup, followed by a plat du jour of pork casserole with cider, apples, and cream, served with red cabbage and bavarian potatoes. All this, plus gooseberry and ginger fool, would come to only £4.80 ($8.40). A variety of less expensive dishes, such as Mexican pancakes filled with chili con carne and served with salad, are available for around £1.50 ($2.63). The wine house is open daily from 10:30 a.m. to 2:30 p.m. and from 6 to 10:30 p.m. (on Friday and Saturday till 11 p.m.).

Mister Tsang, 63 Winchcombe St. (tel. Cheltenham 38727), and his family take Chinese cooking seriously. Their well-chosen menu lists a thoughtful selection of Cantonese specialties subtly prepared in large quantities. A chicken-and-mushroom soup, followed by sweet-and-sour boneless fish, or a Cantonese lamb casserole served with fried or steamed rice, would come to only £4.55 ($7.96). When two or more order from a selection of fixed-price Chinese combination plates, with enough food to make a warlord happy, the price per person goes down somewhat. His restaurant offers one of the best quality for value meals in Cheltenham, and is a good change of pace from typically English cookery. Hours of opening, known in England as "trading hours," are Monday from 5 to 11:30 p.m.; Tuesday and Friday from noon to 2 p.m. and 5 to 11:30 p.m., and Saturday all the way from noon to midnight.

Around the town are the **Mini-Restaurant/Coffeehouses,** useful for quick, inexpensive meals. Very clean and white, they evoke the film *2001,* filled with extreme modernistic trappings and black and white plastic. The friendly staff serves soups and fruit juices, a quarter-pound beefburger, omelets, and pastries. Expect to pay from £1.75 ($3.06) for a light meal or else £3 ($5.25) for a more substantial meal, including, for example, vegetable soup, a Spanish omelet, followed by pastry and coffee. The chain runs two restaurants, one (the more central) at 112 Promenade (tel. Cheltenham 23985). The other is called the Jules Mini-Restaurant, and it's at 5 Winchombe St. They serve from 9 a.m. to 11 p.m. daily.

That Sandwich Place, 69 Regent St. (tel. Cheltenham 29575), just back of Cavendish House department store, offers 200 different sandwiches to choose from. You can eat there, cafeteria style (get your order at the counter and find a table), or take out your choice to your car. There is also a large tea garden where you can eat one of the inexpensive sandwiches. For a cheese and tomato you pay 50p (88¢); a tuna fish sandwich costs 50p also; tea is 28p (49¢) and coffee is 25p (44¢), while soft drinks are 30p (53¢). They also serve a choice of some 12 salads and fresh white or whole-meal bread is used. Desserts include cakes, rum babas, and eclairs from 38p (67¢) up.

4. Royal Sudeley Castle

In 1962 Elizabeth Chipps of Lexington, Kentucky, met and married Mark Dent-Brocklehurst, the wedding taking place in the 16th-century chapel of Royal Sudeley Castle. In 1970 her husband died, and Elizabeth inherited the 15th-century castle in the Cotswold village of Winchcombe, six miles northeast of Cheltenham. The history of the castle dates back to Saxon times, when the village was the capital of the Mercian kings.

Elizabeth remarried in 1979 and now lives at Sudeley as Lady Ashcombe. The castle remains in trust for her two children, Henry and Mollie Dent-Brocklehurst. Lady Ashcombe first reopened the castle to visitors shortly after her first husband's death. As one of England's finer stately homes, Sudeley Castle attracts visitors from all over the world. There are works of art by Constable, Turner, Rubens, Van Dyck, and many others. The ancient dungeon tower houses a unique collection of toys and dolls spanning four centuries. Exhibits include the rocking horse that once belonged to the beheaded King Charles I.

Peacocks strut in the formal gardens which are set in a landscape of rolling farmland and parks. Water fowl abound on the lake beside the castle. The exquisite herb garden dates from the time when Queen Catherine Parr, sixth and surviving wife of King Henry VIII, lived and died at Sudeley.

The castle also has a coffeeshop good enough to participate in the "Taste of England" scheme, offering a variety of cold salads and home-cooked meats for £3.50 ($6.13). Soup at 85p ($1.49) and a hot meal of the day, £3 ($5.25), are also part of the daily menu. A more simple ploughman's lunch can be obtained for approximately £1.50 ($2.63). A selection of desserts is also available. The cream teas are mouthwatering.

The castle is open daily from noon to 5:30 p.m., March 1 to October 31. The grounds are open from 11 a.m. Admission prices are £2.50 ($4.38) for adults, £1.75 ($2.19) for children.

A telephone call to the secretary at Sudeley Castle (tel. Winchcombe 602308) will provide you with any up-to-the-minute information you may wish before visiting.

Unknown to most visitors, it's possible to have your own home on the estate grounds, as there are four cottages to rent, the Woodman's, the Old Smith's, and the Carpenter's Cottages which are close to the village, and Wadfield Cottage which is farther away on the grounds. The buildings are old timber-beamed farm cottages with tiled roofs, dormer windows, and creepers around the door. Inside, there is a spacious living room with comfortable chairs, color TV, a dining area, and a fully equipped kitchen. Upstairs the beds are ready-made—duvets for easy repair in the morning. Your room looks out onto a small patio where you can sit in privacy among the trees and flowers, admiring the peace of the countryside. Bathrooms are modern, and central heating provides raging hot water for that welcome bath after a long country walk.

Cottages hold from two to seven people, and rentals range from £30 ($52.50) per person in low season to £60 ($105) per person weekly in high season. The minimum rent is for three nights, and a cottage here is a good base for two days of touring in the Cotswolds.

The rent on the cottage includes entrance to the castle whenever you wish to wander through the woods or formal gardens. The cottages are serviced before and after your stay, but you're encouraged to do for yourself. Linen is changed once a week, on Saturday.

If you feel like a meal outside, wander down to the village to **Isbourne House,** Castle Street, Winchombe, Gloucestershire (tel. 0242/602281), a period Cotswold stone house surrounded by a well-kept garden, stone walls, and wrought-iron gates. Here Ted Saunders and his friend and colleague Dick provide elegant dinners for £12 ($21) per person for three or four courses, including half a bottle of excellent wine.

In the house, part Elizabethan, part Georgian, they also do B&B, charging from £22 ($38.50) to £25 ($43.75) for two guests per night, depending on whether you have the room with bath and toilet or just a shower. Dinner is likely to include an appetizer such as chicken liver pâté, then veal escalope in ginger sauce or pigeon breasts with juniperberry sauce, followed by salad and a dessert, perhaps a strawberry and pernod mousse. Meals for nonresidents are provided only by arrangement.

5. Malmesbury

At the southern tip of the Cotswolds, the old hill town of Malmesbury in the county of Wiltshire is moated by the Avon River. In the center of England's Middle West, it makes a good base for touring the Cotswolds. Cirencester is just 12 miles away; Bibury, 19 miles, and Cheltenham, 28 miles. Malmesbury is a market town, with a fine market cross. Its historical fame is reflected by the Norman abbey built there on the site of King Athelstan's grave.

Malmesbury is considered the oldest "borough" in England, as it was granted its charter by Alfred the Great in 880. In 1980 it celebrated its 1300th anniversary. Some 400 years ago the Washington family lived there, leaving their star-and-stripe coat-of-arms on the church wall. In addition, Nancy Hanks, Abraham Lincoln's mother, came from Malmesbury. The town still has members of the family, noted for their lean features and tallness. The Penns of Pennsylvania also originally came from Malmesbury.

WHERE TO EAT: The **Apostle Spoon,** Malmesbury Cross (tel. Malmesbury 3129), run and owned by Mr. and Mrs. Smalley, is open for lunch and dinner with a comprehensive snack selection. An à la carte menu is offered. Snacks are from 85p ($1.49) to £2.20 ($3.85). The à la carte menu has seven appetizers in the 80p ($1.60) to £2.20 ($3.85) range and 11 main courses, costing from £5 ($8.75) to £9 ($15.75). The Spoon is open every day. The building housing the restaurant adjoins the abbey, facing the octagonal market cross, and it is reputed to be the oldest house in the oldest borough in England.

6. Tetbury

In the rolling Cotswolds, Tetbury was never in the mainstream of tourism (like Oxford or Stratford-upon-Avon). However, ever since an attractive man and his lovely bride moved there and took the Macmillan place, a Georgian building on nearly 350 acres, it is now drawing crowds from all over the world.

Charles and Diana will, of course, one day be King and Queen of England. Their nine-bedroom mansion, Highgrove, can be spotted at a bend of the A433 road just outside the town on the way to Westonbirt Arboretum. Usually that spot is filled with rubber-neckers, and has become one of the most visited places in England.

The town itself has a 17th-century Market Hall and lots of antique stores along with trendy boutiques (one called Diana's). Visitors can often catch a glimpse of the Princess shopping in the village.

Its inns, even before the couple moved in, have never been budget minded. Apparently, it costs to live so close to royalty. However, if you're game, here are my selections.

The White Hart, Market Place (tel. Tetbury 52436), is a 16th-century inn in the village center. Sympathetically modernized, the hotel has lovely bedrooms with private baths, while downstairs it retains its old-world charm. Log fires, stone walls, and lots of copper antiques adorn this privately owned hotel. Everybody drops in for Sunday lunch, costing £6.50 ($11.38). If you're passing through for the day, enjoy their bar snacks which cost from 75p ($1.31) to £1.75 ($3.06). Should you wish to stay over you'll find bedrooms renting for £18 ($31.50) per person, including a full breakfast and VAT. Units are fully equipped with color TV, phone, central heating, and double glazing.

The Close, Long Street (tel. Tetbury 52272), is the preferred place to stay, and almost the most expensive. Once the home of a wealthy wool merchant, it dates from 1695 and takes its name from a Cistercian monastery to which it was linked. Architecturally, it was built of warm honey-brown Cotswold stone, with gables and stone-mullioned windows. The ecclesiastical-type windows in the rear overlook a garden with a reflection pool, a haven for doves.

Inside, you'll find a Georgian room with a domed ceiling, where predinner drinks are served and you can peruse the menu. Dining is in one of two rooms. Owners Jean-Marie and Sue Lauzier have spared none of their attractive antiques and silver, proudly sharing their treasures with guests. Candlelight on winter evenings, floral arrangements, sparkling silver, and glassware are just the proper background for the first-rate cookery.

The cooking is superb, and an à la carte menu offers specialty dishes such as guinea fowl. Main dishes feature chicken cooked in champagne and encased in light pastry, as well as steaks, beef, and fish. A dinner costs from £14 ($24.50) per person. Fixed menus are also offered for lunch for £6.50 ($11.38) and up.

There are only a dozen rooms, each with a private bath. A single ranges from £19 ($33.25) to £27 ($47.25), a double from £17.50 ($30.63) to £28 ($49) per person. A continental breakfast, service, and VAT are included.

7. Wotton-under-Edge

At the western edge of the Cotswolds, in Gloucestershire, Wotton-under-Edge is in the rural triangle of Bath (23 miles), Bristol (20 miles), and Gloucester (20 miles). Many of its old buildings indicate its former prosperity as a thriving wool town. One of its obscure claims to fame is that it was the home of Sir Isaac Pitman, who invented shorthand. Its grammar school is one of the oldest in England, founded in 1384 and once attended by Dr. Edward Jenner, the discoverer of the vaccine against smallpox.

WHERE TO STAY: The **Falcon,** Church Street (tel. Wotton-under-Edge 2138), is a typical plastered Cotswold stone inn in the heart of the village, with attractively priced accommodation rates. B&B costs £9 ($15.75) per person, inclusive of VAT and service. The owners are Irene and Bill Suffell and Cath and Tony Stephenson, who watch after the needs of their guests very well. They run their 17th-century coaching house as a family concern and will provide bar meals and snacks as well as evening meals upon request.

8. Shipton-under-Wychwood and Chipping Norton

SHIPTON-UNDER-WYCHWOOD: Taking the A361 road, enroute from Burford to Chipping Norton, you arrive after a turnoff at the little village of Shipton-under-Wychwood, in Oxfordshire. It's about four miles north of Burford, but don't blink—you'll pass it right by. The monks of Bruern Abbey used to run a hospice in the village.

CHIPPING NORTON: Just inside the Oxfordshire border, Chipping Norton is another gateway to the Cotswolds. Since the days of Henry IV it has been an important market town. Its main street is a curiosity in that it follows along a slope, making one side terraced over the lower part. The highest town in Oxfordshire, at 650 feet, Chipping Norton has long been noted for its tweed mills. Seek out its Guildhall, its church, and its handsome almshouses. If you're touring, you can search for the nearby Rollright Stones, more than 75 stones forming a prehistoric circle 100 feet in diameter, the Stonehenge of the Cotswolds. Chipping Norton lies 11 miles from Stratford-upon-Avon.

Where to Stay (Big Splurge)

The **Crown and Cushion Hotel,** High Street (tel. Chipping Norton 2533), dates back to 1497 and was originally a coaching inn. All bedrooms are centrally heated and equipped with hot and cold running water. Six bedrooms come with private baths with showers, telephones, and color TV if requested. Rates are £13 ($22.75) per person without bath, £17.50 ($30.63) per person with bath. All tariffs include an English breakfast and VAT. The refurbished bar provides hot and cold meals morning and evening. The restaurant is à la carte. There's a color TV lounge, plus a residents' reading room. The hotel has a sauna and solarium, and golf, squash, horseback riding, and fishing are available nearby. This is an ideal center for touring the Cotswolds, and it's close to Oxford, Stratford-upon-Avon, Cheltenham, and Silverstone. Resident proprietors are Jim and Margaret Frasor.

Food at an Old Inn

On the B4450 across country from Chipping Norton to Stow-on-the-Wold, right on the village green at Bledington, lies the **King's Head,** Bledington, Oxfordshire (tel. Kingham 365). This 16th-century inn has been catering to travelers for more years than it's possible to remember. Nowadays, Joan Powell provides real ale to be quaffed in the beer garden or in the low-ceilinged bars. Lunchtime and in the evenings a buffet provides an ample meal of smoked mackerel, Scotch eggs, steak-and-wine pie, and pâtés which complement the usual bar snacks. There is always a steaming pot of soup going, and chocolate cream cakes are there if you don't want cheese. You can eat for as little as £1.40 ($2.45), or the most extravagant dish will cost around £6.95 ($12.16).

READER'S GUEST HOUSE SELECTION AT GREAT WOLFORD: "We enjoyed staying with **Robin Duggan** (tel. Barton-on-the-Heath 225), who is postmistress in Great Wolford, about eight miles northwest of Chipping Norton. She charges £7.50 ($13.13) per person in her lovely old Cotswold house. It is quiet, clean, pleasant, and friendly" (Daniel Driver, Albion, Calif.).

9. Bourton-on-the-Water

In this most scenic Cotswold village, you can be like Gulliver, voyaging first to Brobdingnag, then to Lilliput. Brobdingnag is Bourton-on-the-Water, lying 85 miles from London, on the banks of the tiny Windrush River. Its mellow stone houses, its village greens on the banks of the water, and its bridges have earned it the title of the Venice of the Cotswolds. But such a far-fetched label as that tends to obscure its true charm.

To see Lilliput, you have to visit the **Old New Inn.** In the garden is a near-perfect and most realistic model village. It is open daily from 8:30 a.m. till dusk, and costs 60p ($1.05) for adults, 30p (53¢) for children. (The Old New Inn is also recommended as a lodging place, below.)

Among the attractions in the area, **Birdland** (tel. Bourton-on-the-Water 20689) is a handsomely designed garden set on about five acres, containing from 600 birds of 160 different species. Exotic birds and flowers include the most varied and largest collection of penguins in any zoo, with underwater viewing and a tropical house. In the latter are hummingbirds. Many of the birds are at liberty for the first time in England. An art gallery has been installed in the Box Bush gift shop. Hours are March to November from 10 a.m. to 6 p.m.; otherwise, from 10:30 a.m. to 4 p.m. Admission is £1 ($1.75) for adults and 50p (88¢) for children to 14 years.

Also in the area, the **Windrush Trout Farm** stands on Rissington Road (tel. Bourton-on-the-Water 20541). On the River Windrush, it offers you can chance to wander among the ponds and enjoy your own picnic while watching the trout which can be fed with food obtained at a shop. It is open daily from 10:30 a.m. to dusk from March to November. Admission is 50p (88¢) for adults and 25p (44¢) for children.

If you're coming to the Cotswolds by train from London, you'll find the nearest rail station is Moreton-in-Marsh, eight miles away. However, buses make connections with the trains.

WHERE TO STAY: **Brookside Hotel** (tel. Bourton-on-the-Water 20371) was originally a private house, built of sturdy Cotswold stone in the center of the village, standing on the banks of the River Windrush. All of its original character has been retained, and it has the atmosphere of a gracious country home. It is owned and managed by Mr. and Mrs. Hardie. The entrance hallway with its antique sideboard is filled with display china, and the antique chairs and grandfather clock are most attractive. There is a tiny drinking lounge at the front with a large bow window, commanding a view of the river and village green, and here you can drink and let life slow down.

Even the dining room, with its dark polished wood, time-blackened Windsor chairs, and bright and cheery fabrics, is an ideal setting for an English cuisine. Homemade soups, pies, and pastries, with liberal amounts of fresh produce, even trout and local game when in season, are offered. Every bedroom is centrally heated, with emphasis on comfort and simplicity rather than sophistication. All rooms have hot and cold running water, radio, and intercom, and some of the larger rooms have a private bathroom. The B&B rate is £13 ($22.75) to £15 ($26.25) per person in a double. VAT is included, but not service. You can have a typical English dinner in the dining room for only £5.50 ($9.63), or, if you wish, bar snacks are available at £1.20 ($2.10) and up.

The **Old Fosseway Hotel** (tel. Bourton-on-the-Water 20387) was built at the turn of the century in the timbered Tudor style, standing in its own gardens, with grassy lawns and tall trees. It lies just one mile south of the Bourton-on-the-Water turnoff on the A429 Fosseway and is owned and managed by Mr. and Mrs. R. Browning, who rent rooms on a daily basis between January and November. The rate for half board per person is £12 ($21) daily. Occasional lunches can be had for just £3.50 ($6.13). A greater bargain is the full-board rate on a weekly basis of £93 ($162.75). These rates do not include VAT. The bedrooms have pleasant views of the garden, hot and cold running water, and central heating, and are attractively furnished in a simple manner. There's a color TV in the spacious living room. On the grounds are stables with riding facilities and a school.

Duke of Wellington Inn (tel. Bourton-on-the-Water 20539) provides simple yet comfortable accommodations in a most fashionable area. Tony Wisdom, the owner, charges £9.50 ($16.63) nightly per person for a bed and a full breakfast, including VAT. He doesn't serve meals other than breakfast, as there are so many excellent restaurants in the area.

Chester House Hotel & Motel (tel. Bourton-on-the-Water 20286) is a weathered, 300-year-old Cotswold stone house, built on the banks of the Windrush River. Owned and managed by Mr. J. Davies, the hotel is a convenient place at which to stay. A double room without bath rents for £24.40 ($42.70), increasing to £29.60 ($51.80) with bath and TV.

The **Old New Inn** (tel. Bourton-on-the-Water 20467) can lay claim to being the leading hostelry in the village. Right in the center, overlooking the river, it's a good example of Queen Anne design. But it is mostly visited because of the miniature model village in its garden (referred to earlier). Hungry or tired travelers are drawn to the old-fashioned comforts and cuisine of this most English inn. The B&B rate is £16.50 ($28.86) per person nightly, including service charge and VAT. The rooms are comfortable, with homey furnishings, soft beds, and hot and cold running water. Packed lunches at £3 ($5.25) will be provided for your excursion jaunts. You may want to spend evenings in the pub lounge, playing darts or chatting with the villagers. Nonresidents may also want to stop in for a meal, with lunches at £6 ($10.50), dinners from £9 ($15.75). The bar snacks at lunchtime enjoy great popularity among some of the local residents.

READERS' INN SELECTION ON THE OUTSKIRTS: "We recommend the **Lamb Inn** at Great Rissington between Burford and Bourton-on-the-Water (tel. Great Rissington 20388). The owners, Richard and Kate Cleverly, welcome you with warm hospitality, excellent food, fine ales, and lovely accommodation in rooms with antique furniture and English chintz. The inn is more than 300 years old and commands a superb view across the Gloucestershire countryside. Bed and a full English breakfast cost £7.50 ($13.13) per person. This is truly a rare find in the expensive Cotswolds" (Rosemary and Bob Knox, Bethel Park. Penna.).

10. Lower Swell and Stow-on-the-Wold

LOWER SWELL: In the vicinity of Stow-on-the-Wold, Lower Swell and its twin sister, Upper Swell, are small villages in the Cotswolds. You may want to anchor in for the night or stop over for a meal at the following recommendation.

Old Farmhouse Hotel (tel. Stow-on-the-Wold 30232) is a small, intimate, 16th-century hotel in the heart of the Cotswolds. It is owned by Susan van de Pol, who has built up a reputation for excellent food and a warm, friendly atmosphere. The hotel is pleasantly furnished, and the cocktail bar (which only has a restaurant-and-residential license) and restaurant are popular with locals and visitors alike.

The bedrooms are comfortable and have central heating and color TV. A bathless double, inclusive of a full English breakfast and early morning tea, costs from £13 ($22.75) per person nightly. For a room with private bath, expect to pay from £4 ($7) to £6 ($10.50) per person extra. Light lunches (soup, smoked salmon, chicken-in-the-basket, sandwiches, ice cream, etc.) are served à la carte Monday to Saturday, from 12:15 to 2 p.m., while on Sunday a traditional English lunch is featured. Dinner is served from 7:30 p.m. Monday through Saturday, and is likely to be a mouthwatering, filling repast from around £9 ($15.75) per person.

STOW-ON-THE-WOLD: This is an unspoiled Cotswold market town, in spite of the busloads of tourists who stop off en route to Broadway and Chipping Campden, nine to ten miles away. The town is the loftiest in the Cotswolds, built on a wold (rolling hills) about 800 feet above sea level. In its open market square, you can still see the stocks where offenders in days gone by were jeered at and punished by the townspeople throwing rotten eggs. The final battle between the Roundheads and the Royalists took place in Stow-on-the-Wold. The town, which is really like a village, is used by many for exploring not only the Cotswold wool towns, but Stratford-upon-Avon, 21 miles away. The nearest rail station is at Moreton-in-Marsh, four miles away.

White Hart (tel. Stow-on-the-Wold 30674) is a guest inn, owned by Maurice and Margaret Bird, who flew in from Stratford-upon-Avon. They've redecorated this old pub-inn, making it a pleasant place to stay. In high season, they ask an inclusive £18.50 ($32.38) per person for B&B and evening dinner. Their pleasing little bedrooms are color coordinated and most tidy, each containing its own water basin, plus facilities for making tea or coffee, even a TV set. You may be drawn to the front lounge, with its collection of horse brasses, a horse collar, and crude tables made of elm by a local woodmaker (all pegged —no nails).

The **Kings Arms Hotel** (tel. Stow-on-the-Wold 30602) is a 500-year-old post house, opening onto the market square. The much-traveled Charles I slept here, on May 8, 1645. You can too, surrounded by some fine antiques, for £14 ($24.50) per person nightly for B&B, plus service and VAT. The lucky ones get the King Charles room with its carved bed and open fireplace. The other bedrooms are all furnished with television and tea-making facilities, and have all the modern comforts, such as innerspring mattresses, bedside lamps, and water basins. You can also have your meals here, as the food is quite good and traditional English. A dinner averages around £7 ($12.25). Hot snacks are available in the bar at a cost of £2.50 ($4.38).

READER'S GUEST HOUSE SELECTION: "At **West View,** Fosseway (tel. Stow-on-the-Wold 30492), Nancy White supplies a tantalizing English breakfast (you choose the time) and beds that are comfortable and clean, for £6.50 ($11.38) per person. Guests have the run of the upstairs of her cottage. Her bathroom contains a shower unit. It's a cheerfully cheap place in an area of the country generally so extravagant" (David Rubin, New Orleans, La.).

Lunches and Teas

St. Edwards, The Square, is a little tea room that's easy to spot, as it opens onto the market square. It has a formal facade with fluted stone pilasters. Inside, you can have morning coffee, lunches, or afternoon tea, while sitting on Windsor chairs in front of an open fireplace. Lunch is served from noon to 2:30, for £4 ($7). A typical one, prepared with great care, might include homemade soup, a steak "pastie," apple pie with fresh cream, and coffee. The set afternoon tea is £1.50 ($2.63), and includes freshly baked muffins and cake.

11. Moreton-in-Marsh

Connected by rail to Paddington Station in London (83 miles away), Moreton-in-Marsh is an important center for British Rail passengers headed for the Cotswolds because it is so near many villages of interest—Bourton-on-the-Water (8 miles), Stow-on-the-Wold (4 miles), Broadway (8 miles), Chipping Campden (7 miles), Stratford-upon-Avon (17 miles away).

Each of the stone Cotswold towns has its distinctive characteristics. In Moreton-in-Marsh, look for a 17th-century Market Hall, an old Curfew Tower, and then walk down the High, where Roman legions trudged centuries ago. The town once lay on the ancient Fosse Way. Incidentally, if you base here, don't take the name "Moreton-in-Marsh" too literally. Marsh derives from an old word meaning border.

Black Bear Inn, High Street (tel. Moreton-in-Marsh 50705), is a fair choice for B&B lodgings. The polite owners, Fred and Doll Weaver, don't put on airs; they know they run a pub-inn rather than a fancy hotel. With a modicum of amenities, the Weavers receive overnight guests, charging them an inclusive £8 ($12.25) per person for B&B. They provide a large number of snacks and salads, and arrange musical evenings with an electric organ. Near the clock tower, the Black Bear is built of stone from a nearby quarry, and fits pleasantly into the village.

The Rectory (tel. Moreton-in-Marsh 50387) offers B&B in the attractive manor home of Bridget and Tom Cekin, a charming young couple with a vast fund of information about the Cotswolds. Their rooms are well cared for and comfortably furnished, as is their bath. One room has a private living room overlooking their garden and a private entrance. Each morning a full English breakfast is served. Their smaller bedroom rents for £10 ($17.50) nightly, their larger one for £12 ($21). It's worth paying the extra pounds for the larger unit if you can secure it.

12. Broadway

This is the best-known Cotswold village. Its wide and beautiful High Street is flanked with honey-colored stone buildings, remarkable for the harmony of their style and design. Overlooking the Vale of Evesham, Broadway, a major stopover for bus tours, is mobbed in summer. That it retains its charm in spite of the invasion is a credit to its character.

Broadway lies near Evesham at the southern tip of Worcestershire, more than just a sauce familiar to steak lovers. Many of the prime attractions of the Cotswolds as well as the Shakespeare Country lie within easy reach of Broadway: Stratford-upon-Avon is only 15 miles away. The nearest rail stations are at Evesham and Moreton-in-Marsh.

For lodgings, Broadway has the dubious distinction of sheltering some of the most expensive inns in the Cotswolds. The guest houses can also command a good price—and get it.

BED AND BREAKFAST: Olive Branch Guest House, 78 High St. (tel. Broadway 853440), is a budget oasis in the heart of an expensive village. You can get an English breakfast and a comfortable bed, as the guest of Mr. and Mrs. Riley, for £9.50 ($16.63) per person nightly. They have eight bedrooms (two singles, one double, and five large family rooms), all with running water. A shower is available. Behind the house is a large garden and car park. The house retains its old Cotswold architectural features. Guests are allowed a discount in the attached antique shop.

Half Way Guest House, 89 High St. (tel. Broadway 852237), is a little treasure in this picture-postcard village. True to its name, it lies halfway between the village green and the edge of town. Formerly a coaching inn, built in 1600, it has a carriage passageway to a rear courtyard. It is now a first-rate guest house, owned by the salty and dynamic Mrs. Brodie, who used to operate one of Broadway's fine antique shops. She is assisted by her daughter, Gillian, and they rent out six bedrooms. They charge from £10 ($17.50) per person for B&B. In the olden days you'd have come out for less, as an old inn sign they display will testify—"4 pence a night for bed, 6 pence with pot luck. No more than five to sleep in one bed."

For the antique-lover, the house is sheer heaven, as Mrs. Brodie brought with her an excellent collection of furniture and bric-a-brac, enough to make each bedroom as well as the living room special and tasteful. Even the bathroom, opening onto the rose garden has a gilt cherub and a Cromwellian chair.

Milestone House, 122 High St. (tel. Broadway 853432), is the kind of place to be found only in England. Mary and Neville Sargent have created a homelike atmosphere in this little private hotel. Once an inn, known as the Fox & Dog, it now receives B&B guests for £15 ($26.25) per person nightly. The rooms have soft, downy beds and are immaculately kept. Nor have modern comforts been neglected; there is central heating and plenty of hot and cold running water. Excellent English breakfasts are prepared. In addition, you can order dinner at £8 ($14), and they are licensed to sell drinks.

Bankside House, 140 High St. (tel. Broadway 852450), is in the exclusive residential area of Broadway—and isn't allowed to put out a sign—but it accepts B&B guests who want to live in the atmosphere of a private home. Its owner, Elizabeth B. Oldham, tells the story quite aptly: "My bacon is crisp and my toast is hot! And I'm an American doing B&B in Broadway." Double rooms go for £11.50 ($20.13) per person nightly, with extra-wide twin beds and a large breakfast. Singles cost £16 ($28). The house dates from the 15th and 16th centuries, and is said to have belonged to Catherine Parr, one of the wives of Henry VIII. It is a honey, with its low beams, huge fireplaces, and garden. But it is the geniality and helpfulness of Mrs. Oldham that makes a stopover here a highlight of your Cotswold jaunt.

WHERE TO DINE: **Hunter's Lodge Restaurant** (tel. Broadway 853247) is set back quietly from the long High Street, surrounded by its own lawns, flowerbeds, shady trees, and flowering shrubs. The stone gables are partially covered with ivy, and the windows are deep-set with mullions and leaded panes. There is a formal entrance, with a circular drive and a small foyer furnished with antiques. The restaurant serves outstanding food, prepared by its chef-patron of international reputation. The menu, which is changed every month, features high-quality seasonal food and fresh vegetables. Also, homemade chocolates are available. Lunches are served from 12:30 to 2 p.m., and dinners from 7:30 to 10 p.m. Lunch with a wide menu is reasonably priced, costing from £7 ($12.25) per person, and dinners begin at £11 ($19.25) per person. The Lodge is closed on Sunday night and all day Monday.

Goblets Wine Bar, High Street (tel. Broadway 852258), is a 17th-century inn built of Cotswold stone, with black-and-white timbered walls. It is filled with antiques which are much enjoyed by the people of Broadway themselves, who frequent the place along with tourists. Additions to the menu are marked on the blackboard, and orders should be placed at the bar. The menu is limited but tasty. It begins with such appetizers as taramasalata and goes on to such daily specials are chicken marengo or duckling in orange sauce. About four desserts appear daily, including, for example, a hot gingerbread pudding. The coffee is well made, and the welcome is warm and friendly. The house wine goes for £3.75 ($6.56) a bottle, and dinner costs from £6 ($10.50). Hours are from 11:30 a.m. to 2:30 p.m. except Sunday when Goblets is open from noon to 2 p.m. In the evening the doors open at 6, closing at 10:30 p.m. (until 11 p.m. on Friday and Saturday).

Cotswold Café & Restaurant, The Green (tel. Broadway 853395), is an old favorite. Mrs. Susan Webb keeps the same high standards, serving meals all day. She specializes in good, English food, offering a two-course lunch for £2.50 ($4.38) that is likely to include roast beef, or pork or chicken. Fresh vegetables are served with it, along with a homemade dessert. The homemade ice cream has been a feature of the establishment for decades. Each customer gets personal service as well. Hours are Monday to Friday from 10 a.m. to 6 p.m. In summer Mrs. Webb keeps her place open for suppers, the last booking at 8 p.m. From soup to coffee, including a glass of French wine, the charge is from £7 ($12.25). At the high tea you are likely to find the Broadway locals. In season ask from a "fruit tea," which is likely to include fresh strawberries or raspberries along with homemade ice cream or fresh cream.

READERS' GUEST HOUSE SELECTION: "We stayed in a beautiful home in the Cotswold village of Willersey, one mile from Broadway, three from Chipping Campden, 13 from Stratford, and well situated for exploring all of the Cotswolds. **Chestnut House** (tel. Broadway 853259) is a Queen Anne-period stone house. It was recently restored by

Hamish and Thelma Pender who are retired from business and farming. Family antiques furnish every room. The Penders provided fresh flowers from their formal garden each day, and hot-water bottles warmed our beds each evening. We were invited to share their sitting room and TV nightly. Rates are £22 ($38.50) double, £12 ($21) single, including VAT, bath, and a full English breakfast. Inquiries may be addressed to the Penders, Chestnut House, Willersey, Broadway, Worcs. WR127PJ" (Warren and Nedra Seibert, West Lafayette, Ind.).

13. Chipping Campden

The English, regardless of how often they visit the Cotswolds, are attracted in great numbers to this town, once a great wool center. It's neither too large nor too small. Off the main road, it's easily accessible to major points of interest, and double-decker buses frequently run through here on their way to Oxford (36 miles away) or Stratford-upon-Avon (12 miles away).

Chipping Campden was the winner of the best-kept-village award in the Bledisloe Cup competition. Rich merchants built homes of Cotswold stone along its model High Street. They have been so well preserved that Chipping Campden to this day remains a gem of the Middle Ages. Its church dates from the 15th century, and its old Market Hall is the loveliest in the Cotswolds. Look also for its almshouses.

FOOD AND LODGING: **Seymour House Hotel,** High Street (tel. Evesham 840429), has remained unspoiled and relatively undiscovered, even though it's right in the center of this much-trodden town. It's a little inn, with an inner courtyard dominated by a large grape arbor. The owners, Mr. and Mrs. Hitchman, are proud of their establishment, and rightly so, as it's been designated by the government as a site of historical and architectural interest. The owners have preserved its old-world atmosphere while at the same time turning it into a functional and comfortable hotel. Half of their rooms have private bath, and each bed has an innerspring mattress. A single costs £10.50 ($18.38); a double with bath, £23 ($40.25) nightly.

Sandalwood House, Back Ends (tel. Evesham 840091), is a newly built Cotswold stone house, belonging to Mrs. D. Bendall. It's just a three-minute walk from the High Street, the village center. It's one of three similar houses up a very short lane. Each of the bedrooms is quite comfortable, immaculate, and contains hot and cold running water. The price is right for such a popular area, £9 ($15.75) per person nightly. This includes an English breakfast served in the separate dining room. Mrs. Bendall does not encourage smoking and definitely does not permit it in the bedrooms, as the smoke will permeate the fabrics for the next guest. If you must smoke, you can go out into the garden. You'll have the use of the living room, with its color TV, the books for reading, and games for guests.

Island House Restaurant, High Street (tel. Evesham 840598), is a tiny restaurant which has a few bedrooms for rent—and is not even a true guest house. But in this posh, expensive Cotswold village, it's an excellent place for stopovers. The owner is Elizabeth Barker who works alongside her management team of Andrew Porter and Rosemarie Strange. She has two bedrooms to rent, each fitted with carpeting and a private color TV. The charge is £20 ($35). This includes a well-cooked, generous breakfast. The dining room of the restaurant is separate and provides lunches, afternoon teas, and evening dinners. The house is right in the heart of the village.

The Dragon House, High Street (tel. Evesham 840734), stands close to the Market Place. It is run by pleasant and friendly Australian proprietor Mrs. Valerie James, who serves you tea in the evening as well as an excellent and plentiful breakfast the next morning. Rooms are attractively decorated and quite comfortable, costing from £7 ($12.25) per person for a bed and filling breakfast, quite a bargain for high-priced Chipping Campden. There is a separate house out in the backyard with two double bedrooms and one modern bath. There's also a living/dining room area with TV.

Trinder House, High Street (tel. Evesham 840869), is where Mrs. Hart rents out three rooms at a rate of £7 ($12.25) per person nightly for B&B. Dorothy Hart is young and attractive, and runs her house like a real home. The front door is an often-open stable door with hanging flowers framing the woodwork.

The **Badger Wine Bar,** High Street, is a very attractive little Cotswold shop with a bar and tables all made of pinewood. A comfortable, cheerful place, it offers such items as soup at 55p (96¢) and pâté and toast at £1 ($1.75). Tongue, chicken, quiche, game, or chicken and ham pie range in price from £1.55 ($2.71) to £2.70 ($4.73), and this includes a salad. Desserts such as cheesecake go from 85p ($1.49). Every day the cook prepares a dish of the day, such as steak, kidney, and potato pie with vegetables (mostly meat, not overdone with potatoes), at a cost of £2.50 ($4.38).

Of the more expensive hotels in town, the **Noel Arms** (tel. Evesham 840317) is good if you want a splurge meal in more elegant surroundings. A three-course meal will cost about £8.50 ($14.88), and is likely to include such good-tasting English fare as grilled plaice, roast leg of lamb, ham steaks, or a carbonnade of beef. A selection of vegetables is served with the main dishes. Appetizers include the usual soups and prawn cocktails. Desserts are served from a selection of fruit pies and cakes.

The **Kings Arms,** The Square, is still fantastic for bar snacks. You're likely to be tempted with artichokes with stilton dressing, baked eggs, crab with gruyère cheese and cream, fresh filet of mackerel with a mustard cream sauce, taramasalata with hot toast, these items vying with the more prosaic soups and pâtés, all in the 65p ($1.14) to £2.95 ($5.16) price range. They also do a Sunday lunch, but it is the variety and originality of their snacks which marks this pretty old pub.

READERS' GUEST HOUSE SELECTIONS: "We found an excellent B&B, **M'Dina,** run by Mr. and Mrs. Hughes on Park Road (extension of High Street at the west end of the town center) (tel. Evesham 840052). The charge is £8 ($14) per person, all inclusive. The mattresses were the best we had in England, the breakfasts were tasty, and Mrs. Hughes was very helpful. They have two rooms in their modern home at present and plan to expand in family-owned buildings around a courtyard" (Irving E. Lempert, Glenview, Ill.). . . . "Three miles north of Chipping Campden, in the town of Mickleton on the A46, is the **Chatsworth Cottage Tea Rooms** run by E. R. and M. L. Bostock. Their large, spotlessly clean rooms, excellent meals, and most of all their wonderful hospitality made this stop one of our most pleasant in all of England. The cost is £9.50 ($16.63) per person in a large double with hot and cold running water" (Mr. and Mrs. Thaine W. Reynolds, Fairview Park, Ohio).

Now it's time to pay our respects to the Bard.

Chapter XI

STRATFORD AND THE HEART OF ENGLAND

1. Stratford-upon-Avon
2. Warwick
3. Kenilworth Castle
4. Coventry
5. Hereford and Worcester
6. Salop (Shropshire)
7. Staffordshire

SO CLOSE TO LONDON, so rich in fascination, the Shakespeare Country in the heart of England is that district most visited by North Americans (other than London, of course). Many who don't recognize the county name, Warwickshire, know its foremost tourist town, Stratford-upon-Avon, the birthplace of England's greatest writer.

The county and its neighboring shires form a land of industrial cities, green fields, and sleepy market towns dotted with buildings, some of which have changed little since Shakespeare's time. Here are many of the places that have magic for overseas visitors, not only Stratford-upon-Avon, but also Warwick and Kenilworth Castles, as well as Coventry Cathedral.

Those who have time to penetrate deeper into the chapter will find elegant spa towns, such as Great Malvern, historic cathedral cities such as Hereford and Worcester, and industrial archeology at Stoke-on-Trent (the famous potteries). Scenery in Salop ranges from untamed borderlands to gentle plains which give way in the north to wooded areas and meres.

1. Stratford-upon-Avon

The magnitude of traffic to this market town on the Avon River, the oldest and most attractive in Warwickshire, is one of the phenomena of tourism. Actor David Garrick really got the shrine launched in 1769 when he organized the first of the Bard's birthday celebrations. It is no secret by now, of course, that William Shakespeare was born in Stratford-upon-Avon.

Surprisingly little is known about his early life, as the frankest of his biographers concede. Perhaps because documentation is so lacking about the writer, much useless conjecture has arisen (did Elizabeth I really write the plays?). But the view that Francis Bacon authored Shakespeare's body of work would certainly stir up *The Tempest,* if suggested seriously to the innkeepers of Stratford-upon-Avon. Admittedly, however, some of the stories and legends connected with Shakespeare's days in Stratford are largely fanciful, invested belatedly to amuse and entertain the vast number of literary fans making the pilgrimage.

Today's magnet, in addition to Shakespeare's Birthplace, is the Royal Shakespeare Theatre, where Britain's foremost actors perform during a long season that lasts from Easter until late October. Stratford-upon-Avon is also a good center for trips to Warwick Castle, Kenilworth Castle, Sulgrave Manor (ancestral home of George Washington), Compton Wynyates, and Coventry Cathedral. The market town lies 92 miles from London, 40 from Oxford, and 8 from Warwick.

THE SIGHTS: In addition to all the attractions on the periphery of Stratford, there are many Elizabethan and Jacobean buildings in this colorful town, many of them administered by the Shakespeare Birthplace Trust Properties. One ticket, costing £2.70 ($4.73) for adults, £1.10 ($1.93) for children, will permit you to visit the five most important sights. You should pick up the ticket if you're planning to do much sightseeing (obtainable at your first stopover at any one of the Trust properties). Shakespeare's Birthplace and Anne Hathaway's Cottage are open all year except Good Friday and from December 24 to 26. From April to October hours are weekdays from 9 a.m. to 6 p.m. (often till 7 p.m. in summer but only until 5 p.m. in October). On Sunday the in-season hours are from 10 a.m. to 6 p.m. From November to March the weekday hours are from 9 a.m. to 4:30 p.m.; on Sunday, 1:30 to 4:30 p.m. Mary Arden's House, New Place, and Hall's Croft are open all year except Good Friday and December 24 to 26. From April to October, weekday hours are from 9 a.m. to 6 p.m. (only until 5 p.m. in October); on Sunday, 2 to 6 p.m. From November to March, these three properties are open on weekdays only from 9 a.m. to 4 p.m.

Shakespeare's Birthplace

On Henley Street, the son of a glover and whittawer was born on St. George's day (April 23) in 1564, and died 52 years later on the same day. Filled with Shakespeare memorabilia, including a portrait, and furnishings of the writer's time, the Trust property is a half-timbered structure, dating from the early years of the 16th century. The house was finally bought by public donors in 1847 and preserved as a national shrine. You can visit the oak-beamed living room, the bedroom where Shakespeare was born, a fully equipped kitchen of the period (look for the "baby-minder"), and a Shakespeare Museum, illustrating his life and times. Later, you can walk through the garden out back. It is estimated that some 660,000 visitors pass through the house annually. If visited separately, admission is £1 ($1.75) for adults, 30p (53¢) for children. Next door to the birthplace is the modern Shakespeare Centre, built to commemorate the 400th anniversary of the Bard's birth. It serves both as the administrative headquarters of the Birthplace Trust and as a library and study center. An extension to the original center, opened in 1981, includes a Visitors' Centre providing reception facilities for all those coming to the birthplace.

Anne Hathaway's Cottage

One mile from Stratford in the hamlet of Shottery is the thatched, wattle, and daub cottage where Anne Hathaway lived before her marriage to the poet. In sheer charm it is the most interesting and most photographed, it would seem,

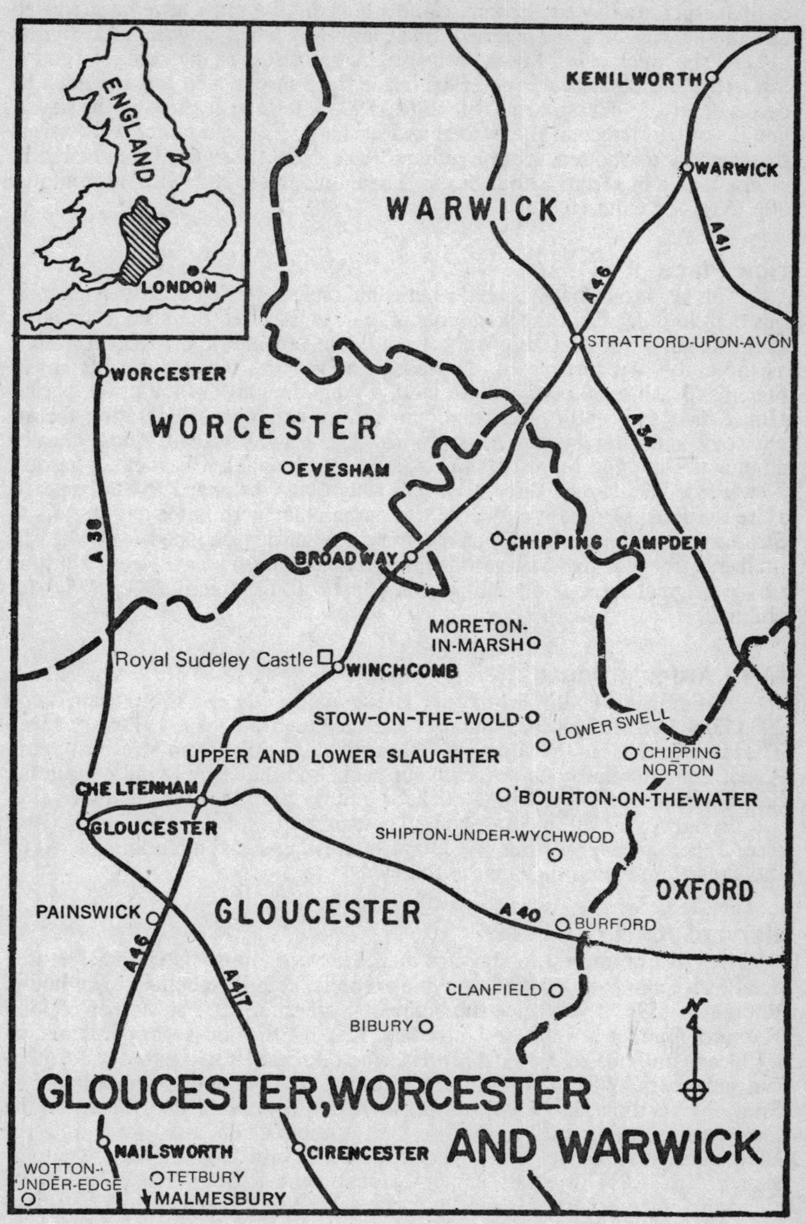
ENGLAND
LONDON
KENILWORTH
WARWICK
WARWICK
A41
A46
STRATFORD-UPON-AVON
A34
WORCESTER
WORCESTER
EVESHAM
A 38
CHIPPING CAMPDEN
BROADWAY
MORETON-
IN-MARSH
Royal Sudeley Castle
WINCHCOMB
STOW-ON-THE-WOLD
LOWER SWELL
UPPER AND LOWER SLAUGHTER
CHIPPING
NORTON
CHELTENHAM
BOURTON-ON-THE-WATER
GLOUCESTER
SHIPTON-UNDER-WYCHWOOD
OXFORD
PAINSWICK
GLOUCESTER
A 40
BURFORD
A46
A417
CLANFIELD
BIBURY
N
GLOUCESTER, WORCESTER
AND WARWICK
NAILSWORTH
CIRENCESTER
WOTTON-
UNDER-EDGE
TETBURY
MALMESBURY

of the Trust properties. The Hathaways were yeoman farmers, and aside from its historical interest, the cottage provides an insight into the life of a family of Shakespeare's day. If the poet came a-courtin', he must have been treated as a mere teenager, as he married Miss Hathaway when he was only 18 years old and she much older. Much of the original furnishings, including the courting settle, and utensils are preserved inside the house, which was occupied by descendants of Shakespeare's wife until 1892. After a visit through the house, you'll want to linger in the garden and orchard. You can either walk across the meadow to Shottery from Evesham Place in Stratford (pathway marked), or else take a bus from Bridge Street. The admission is 90p ($1.58) for adults, 30p (53¢) for children.

New Place

This site is on Chapel Street, where Shakespeare retired in 1610, a prosperous man to judge from the standards of his day. He died there six years later, at the age of 52. Regrettably, only the site of his former home remains today, as the house was torn down. You enter the gardens through Nash's House (Thomas Nash married Elizabeth Hall, a granddaughter of the poet). Nash's House has 16th-century period rooms and an exhibition illustrating the archeology and later history of Stratford. The heavily visited Knott Garden adjoins the site and represents the style of a fashionable Elizabethan garden. New Place has its own Great Garden, which once belonged to Shakespeare. Here the Bard planted a mulberry tree, so popular with latter-day visitors to Stratford that the cantankerous owner of the garden chopped it down. The mulberry tree that grows there today is said to have been planted from a cutting of the original tree. The admission is 60p ($1.05) for adults, 20p (35¢) for children.

Mary Arden's House

A timbered Tudor farm, this is the house (tel. Stratford-upon-Avon 293455) where Shakespeare's mother, the daughter of a yeoman farmer, lived. The farmstead lies in the village of Wilmcote, three miles from Stratford-upon-Avon. Look for the stone dovecote out back, and the farming museum in the barns. The admission is 60p ($1.05) for adults, 20p (35¢) for children.

By now, you will have seen the Trust properties, except for Hall's Croft (see "Where to Eat" further on). Other interesting sights not administered by the Trust foundation include the following:

Harvard House

Not just of interest to Harvard men, Harvard House on High Street (tel. Stratford-upon-Avon 204507) is a fine example of an Elizabethan town house. Rebuilt in 1596, it was once the home of Katherine Rogers, mother of John Harvard, founder of Harvard University. In 1909, the house was purchased by a Chicago millionaire, Edward Morris, who presented it as a gift to the American university. With a profusion of carving, it is the most ornate house in Stratford. Its rooms are filled with period furniture, and the floors, made of the local flagstone, are authentic. Look for the Bible Chair, used for hiding the Bible during the days of Tudor persecution. Harvard House, charging admission of 75p ($1.31) for adults, 25p (44¢) for students and children, is open April through September from 9 a.m. to 1 p.m. and 2 to 6 p.m. on weekdays, 2 to 6 p.m. on Sunday; October through March, 10 a.m. to 1 p.m. and 2 to 4 p.m. weekdays, closed Sunday.

Holy Trinity Church

In an attractive setting near the Avon, the parish church of Stratford-upon-Avon is distinguished mainly because Shakespeare was buried in the chancel ("and curst be he who moves my bones"). The Parish Register records his birth and death (copies of the original, of course). No charge is made for entry into the church, described as "one of the most beautiful parish churches in the world," but visitors wishing to view Shakespeare's tomb are asked to donate a small sum, at present 25p (44¢) toward the restoration fund.

A Motor Museum

Stratford-upon-Avon Motor Museum, 1 Shakespeare St. (tel. Stratford-upon-Avon 69413). Just around the corner from Shakespeare's birthplace is a small but interesting museum, started in 1974 by Bill Meredith-Owens, internationally known motor rally driver; it is now run by his son. The Roaring '20s era is portrayed and consists of many Rolls-Royces (specially built for the maharajas of India, among others), Bugattis, Hispano Suizas, early Jaguars, and many others. They also have a reconstructed garage of the '20s and a specialty bookshop where maintenance books on the old models and vintage cars are for sale, as well as a collection of car badges (not for sale). Admission is £1 ($1.75). The museum is open daily, except Christmas Day, from 10 a.m. to 5:30 p.m.

A Theater of History

The *World of Shakespeare* at the **Heritage Theatre,** Waterside (tel. Stratford-upon-Avon 69190), stands opposite the Royal Shakespeare Theatre. This multimedia presentation is a new concept in presenting history. It is designed to portray the progress of Queen Elizabeth I in the summer of 1575 from London to Kenilworth Castle (ten miles from Stratford-upon-Avon), as she escaped the plague-ridden city. The 25-minute presentation consists of a series of 76 costumed figures, making up 25 tableaux in costumes and settings of the time. The action takes place in sound and light through the tableaux positioned around the perimeter of the circular theater with the audience standing in the center of the darkened auditorium. It is an educational experience, for the materials used have been meticulously researched to provide authenticity. It's a good bet for a wet day or if you have an hour to kill. The theater is open from 9:30 a.m. until 5:30 p.m. from September to July and 9:30 a.m. until 8:30 p.m. from July to September, with performances every half hour. Admission is £1.60 ($2.80) for adults, £1.20 ($2.10) for children and students. Facilities include a gift shop and Bureau de Change.

A Wax Museum

Louis Tussaud's Waxworks, 60 Henley St. (tel. Stratford-upon-Avon 5880), illustrates the comedies, tragedies, and histories of Shakespeare, including scenes from *Romeo and Juliet* and *A Midsummer Night's Dream.* The location is near Shakespeare's Birthplace, and opening hours are daily from 9:30 a.m. to 5:30 p.m., including Sunday. Adults pay 85p ($1.49) admission, and children are charged 45p (79¢). The best buy is the family ticket, admitting two adults and two children at a cost of £2 ($3.50).

GETTING THERE: The Shakespeare Connection "Road and Rail" leaves from London's Euston Station at 8:35 a.m., allowing you to spend a whole day in Shakespeare Country. It's the only way you can attend the Royal Shakespeare Theatre and return to London the same day. If you wish to attend an evening performance at the Royal Shakespeare Theatre, the Shakespeare Connection is again your best bet. Trains depart London's Euston Station at 5:10 p.m. It returns to London at 11:40 p.m. The service is operated by British Rail and **Guide Friday Ltd.,** whose offices are at 13 Waterside in Stratford-upon-Avon (tel. Stratford-upon-Avon 294466). The price is £10.75 ($18.81) for a one-day round trip, £16 ($28) for a round trip valid for one month, and £9.55 ($16.72) for a single fare. Ask for a Shakespeare Connection ticket at London's Euston Station or any British Rail London Travel Centre. British Rail passholders using the service simply pay the coach fare from Coventry Station to Stratford-upon-Avon.

TOURS: Once in Stratford-upon-Avon, you may want to take one of the tours offered by **Guide Friday,** 13 Waterside, in *The World of Shakespeare* audio-visual theater, across the road from the Royal Shakespeare Theatre. Guide Friday's phone number is Stratford-upon-Avon 294466. The office is a tourist reception center for the Shakespeare Country, dispensing free maps and offering tours. For £2 ($3.50) there is a short tour of Stratford, lasting 1½ hours, with a guide that goes out at 9:30 a.m., 11:15 a.m., 2 p.m., and 3:45 p.m. Riding in an open-top double-decker bus, the tour makes stops at Anne Hathaway's Cottage, Mary Arden's House in Wilmcote (four miles away), and gives visitors a general look at the town. For £4 ($7), a tour departs at 9:30 a.m. and 2 p.m., visiting Warwick and Kenilworth Castles. At 11 a.m. a tour of the Cotswolds leaves, stopping for lunch in a typical country pub, at a price of £4.50 ($7.88). At 11:15 a.m. a tour of Blenheim and Bladon, the birth and burial places of Sir Winston Churchill, departs, costing £5 ($8.75).

CAUGHT WITHOUT A ROOM? During the long theater season, the hotels in Stratford-upon-Avon are jampacked, and you may run into difficulty if you arrive without a reservation. However, if you should visit from April to October during regular office hours (9 a.m. to 5:30 p.m. weekdays, 2 to 5 p.m. Sunday) you can go to the **Information Centre** at the Judith Shakespeare House, 1 High St. (tel. Stratford-upon-Avon 293127).

Here a staff person, who has had much experience with travelers on all budgets, will get on the telephone and try to book a room for you in the price range you are seeking.

It is also possible to reserve accommodations if you write well enough in advance. By writing to the Information Centre, you'll be spared having to get in touch with several hotels on your own and running the risk of getting turned down. If you do write, specify the price range and the number of beds required. The centre often gets vague letters, and the staff doesn't know whether to book you into a private suite at the Shakespeare Hotel, or else lend you a cot to put in front of the Royal Shakespeare Theatre. Don't be surprised. Stratford-upon-Avon visitors are a varied group. Recently a young man not only slept in front of the theatre, but was seen frying an egg there over an open fire the next morning.

BED AND BREAKFAST: **Midway Guest House,** 182 Evesham Rd. (tel. Stratford-upon-Avon 204154), has four good double rooms, with hot and cold running water, electric heaters, and razor sockets—for which charges range from £7 ($12.25) per person for B&B (less for longer stays). The rooms have been modernized, making them homelike and comfortable.

The **Marlyn Hotel,** 3 Chestnut Walk (tel. Stratford-upon-Avon 293752), is a Victorian family house which has been welcoming B&B guests since 1890. It is pleasantly and conveniently situated near Hall's Croft, the former home of Shakespeare's daughter, and is within a five-minute walk of the town center and the Royal Shakespeare Theatre. The hotel is centrally heated throughout, each bedroom contains tea- and coffee-making facilities, and there is a small lounge with TV. If you don't want to pack your Shakespeare, don't worry. A copy of the complete works of the Bard is available for reference in every bedroom. Free and unrestricted parking is available under the chestnut trees opposite the hotel. The owners, Mr. and Mrs. C. Allen, who have owned the hotel since 1973, endeavor to provide guests with comfortable accommodation throughout their stay. Daily rates are not more than £10 ($17.50) for bed and an English breakfast, inclusive of tax.

Glenavon Private Hotel, Chestnut Walk (tel. Stratford-upon-Avon 292588), is a fresh-looking pink-and-white corner house, three minutes' walk from the theater and the town center, with bay windows in front and a small walled garden in the rear. There is a large, free area for overnight parking opposite the hotel. Owned by Mr. and Mrs. David Wilson, it is in the best tradition of *Separate Tables.* The daily B&B rate is £8 ($14) per person in low season, going up to £9 ($15.75) in high season. The Wilsons have done much to make guests comfortable—central heating, hot and cold water in all the bedrooms, and facilities for children.

Stratheden Hotel, Chapel Street (tel. Stratford-upon-Avon 297119), is a small, tuck-away hotel, in a weathered building dating back to 1673, with a tiny rear garden and top-floor rooms with slanted, beamed ceilings. Owned by Mr. and Mrs. Wells (she's from Northern Ireland, he's a native of Warwickshire), the house has improved in both decor and comfort, with fresh paint, new curtains, and good beds. The charge for B&B ranges from £8 ($14) to £12 ($21), plus VAT. Some rooms have private showers and toilets along with TV.

The entry hallway has a glass cupboard, holding family heirlooms and collector tidbits. The house is sprinkled with old pieces. The dining room, with a bay window, has an overscale sideboard that once belonged to the "insanely vain" Marie Corelli, the eccentric novelist, poet, and mystic who wrote a series of seven books, beginning with *A Romance of Two Worlds* and ending with *Spirit and Power and Universal Love.* Queen Victoria was one of her avid readers. The Victorian novelist (1855-1924) was noted for her passion for pastoral paintings and objets d'art. In one room you can see an example of her taste in bedchamber furniture: a massive mahogany tester bed.

Avon View Hotel, 121 Shipston Rd. (tel. Stratford-upon-Avon 297567), is a small Georgian house which has been extensively remodeled into a hotel. It's owned by Mr. and Mrs. Rooney, who charge from £9.25 ($16.19) in a single, from £18 ($31.50) in a twin (bathless) and from £23.20 ($40.60) in a twin with bath. Rooms are comfortable and pleasantly furnished. They also run an adjoining fully licensed restaurant. It's called **Duneiden,** which is Gaelic for Edinburgh, from whence Mr. Rooney originates.

Wayside Hotel, 11 Warwick Rd. (tel. Stratford-upon-Avon 292550), is a small six-bedroom hotel, at the edge of town in the direction of Warwick (a convenient five-minute walk to the theater). The owners, the Heynes family, charge from £9 ($15.75) nightly for B&B, including VAT and service. The rooms are comfortable, although not lavishly furnished, and contain hot and cold running water. However, showers and toilets are shared. Run separately from the hotel is the **Buccaneer Restaurant,** offering French and Italian cuisine. Open nightly, except Monday, from 7 to 11:30 p.m., this fully licensed restaurant features an à la carte menu or a choice of meals of three courses, including coffee and VAT, for £10 ($17.50). The cost of your wine is extra. The hotel and restaurant have free car parking close by.

Hunters Moon, 150 Alcester Rd. (tel. Stratford-upon-Avon 292888), is a family-owned and -operated guest house on the fringe of Stratford. The owners, Mr. and Mrs. J. H. Monk, who have run it for 25 years, also operate another guest house just a few doors away, so you may be housed there. Hunters Moon has been completely modernized and extended. Shower rooms have been built, and in some cases there are showers and toilets in some of the bedrooms, along with tea- or coffee-making facilities. Between the two guest houses Hunters Moon can accommodate 40 persons. There is a very good selection of rooms (singles, doubles, twins, or family rooms), and the price is from £8 ($14) per person nightly, including breakfast. I have received many letters of praise concerning Hunters Moon's cleanliness, neatness of the rooms, and general helpfulness. Guests arriving in Stratford without transportation can telephone and a car will be sent free.

Craig Guest House, 69 Shipston Rd. (tel. Stratford-upon-Avon 297473), is a family-run place, under the management of its owners, Mr. and Mrs. Giles. There is a comfortable guest lounge with TV and just five bedrooms to rent, costing £7.50 ($13.13) nightly per person for B&B. Two coin-operated showers are available, and no VAT is added. Their house lies across the old Clopton Bridge from Stratford. Incidentally, this bridge was standing in Shakespeare's time. It's also possible to reach the house by taking a footbridge across the Avon. If you do take the footbridge, you can see punts and even boats which use the lock from the Stratford Canal.

The Croft, 49 Shipston Rd. (tel. Stratford-upon-Avon 293419), is a B&B guest house that has been in business many years and is kept up-to-date. A visitor's book testifies to all those who have been pleased. The Croft stands on the A34 close to the center of town and the Memorial Theatre. Fully modernized, the house has central heating and hot and cold running water in all units. Some family rooms are available. Tony and Rhoda Lapish are your friendly hosts, offering a freshly cooked breakfast and a twin-bedded room with private bath at the rate of £11.50 ($20.13) per person nightly. A bathless double rents for £9.50 ($16.63) per night, a single going for £10 ($17.50). Family rooms suitable for three to five persons cost from £22 ($38.50) to £32 ($56) nightly.

Ashburton House, 27 Evesham Pl. (tel. Stratford-upon-Avon 292444), is a guest house with a restaurant license and is one of the better selections in Stratford. Evening dinners, particularly pretheater ones, are a specialty. Rooms are handsomely furnished and well equipped with color TV available in all units. The establishment is centrally heated, and hot water is available for baths and showers at all times. Hosts are Mr. and Mrs. Fraser, formerly of Zambia when it was Northern Rhodesia, where she taught physical education and he was an agricultural land use and conservation specialist. He is still involved in his specialty as a consultant. The Frasers have settled into Stratford, where they are delighted to receive foreign visitors, charging them £10.50 ($18.38) for bed and full menu breakfast. Dinners are optional and cost £9.50 ($16.63) for the four-course pretheater repast served at 6 p.m., in good time before the eight-minute walk to the Royal Shakespeare Theatre. A six-course dinner at a more leisurely hour for nontheater-goers costs £14 ($24.50) per person. After-theater service is available to guests by arrangement. Salmon and trout fishing can be arranged, and Ashburton House will provide transportation for guests at reduced rates. Advance reservations by letter with a £5 ($8.75) deposit are strongly recommended. All charges are inclusive of service charge and tax.

Ravenhurst Hotel and Gingers Restaurant, Broad Walk (tel. Stratford-upon-Avon 292515), is run by Tina Roderick. This eight-room guest house, set in a quiet street of Old Town, is within easy reach of the historic town center. B&B costs £9 ($15.75) per person. Should you want an easy lunch or casual evening meal, you can eat in the Bistro for about £5 ($8.75) per person, including wine. For a more elegant meal, choose Gingers, which has excellent food and a delightful atmosphere. The restaurants are open seven days a week, and snacks are always available. Tina is helpful with information and tries to make one's stay as pleasant as possible.

Grosvenor Villa, 9 Evesham Pl. (tel. Stratford-upon-Avon 66192), is owned and run by Mr. and Mrs. John Wells (he used to run a pub). Eight spotless rooms are available, and the nightly rate is £8 ($14) per person, including an English breakfast. They will serve an evening meal by arrangement, for £3.50 ($6.13). There is a comfortable lounge with color television and a small licensed bar. On the second floor, hot tea, coffee, and soups are available. Each room has a wash basin and hot running water, and there are several bathrooms. There's parking for two cars. The house is on the main road toward Evesham, and is only a few minutes from Market Place and about eight minutes from the theater.

Aidan Guest House, 11 Evesham Pl. (tel. Stratford-upon-Avon 292824), is a large Victorian family house, belonging to Diane and Raymond Smith. It has retained some of the best features and character of its architectural period. Close to the town center, the house lies within a five-minute walk of the theater and railway station. All rooms have central heating as well as hot and cold running water. The place is particularly recommended for parents traveling with small children, as babysitting can be arranged. Children's cots are also available. Charges are £7.50 ($13.13) per person nightly, including breakfast, service, and taxes. The Smiths keep their place impeccably clean and have tastefully furnished it. Fresh flowers abound. Di will occasionally babysit for infants, and she and her husband are attentive in every way.

READERS' HOTEL SELECTIONS: "The **Salamander Guest House,** 40 Grove Rd. (tel. Stratford-upon-Avon 205728), is a very large, well-kept home run by Mr. and Mrs. J. Copestick facing a small wooded park. There are seven rooms available, which I found quite cheerful. There is also a comfortable sitting room available to the guests which I found useful in which to read the copy of Shakespeare's plays that the Copesticks make available. Breakfast is well prepared and ample. The Salamander is about 5 minutes from the center of Stratford, 10 minutes from the theater, and about 15 minutes' walk from the bus depot. The overnight charge is £8.50 ($14.88) per person nightly. There are separate toilet, shower, and bathrooms. Perhaps the nicest feature of the Salamander Guest House is the congeniality of the owners. They are personable and seem to enjoy conversing with their guests. Also, they are willing to answer questions and suggest possible points of interest" (Anthony H. Feldhus, Dearborn Heights, Mich.). . . . "I can recommend highly **Argos Hotel,** 5 Arden St. (tel. Stratford-upon-Avon 204321), just a two-minute walk from the station—close enough that we were able to carry our own bags. The bedrooms (five singles and five doubles), halls, two shower rooms, a bathroom, lounge, and dining rooms—all were spotlessly clean. You get lots of hot water, hot enough to use in a hot-water bottle. The hotel is quiet at night. Breakfast is included in the rate per room. The owners, Mr. and Mrs. Stan Shaylor, are friendly and helpful. They made our stay most enjoyable. A single room is £8.50 ($14.88); a double, £15 ($26.25). All tariffs include VAT and service. I do not hesitate to recommend Argos to anyone desiring friendliness, cleanliness, and comfort away from home" (Mrs. Alison Good, Calgary, Alberta, Canada).

"Mr. and Mrs. B. Smith, owners of the **Linhill Guest House,** 35 Evesham Pl. (tel. Stratford-upon-Avon 292879), personally see to the needs of their guests. The house is centrally heated, and there is hot and cold running water in all rooms. Also, all units have color TV. Bed and an ample breakfast cost £7 ($12.25) per person per night. The house is conveniently situated close to Anne Hathaway's cottage, only a few minutes' walk from both the town center and the theater. There are seven bedrooms—a single, four twins, and two family rooms" (Gauden Galea, Malta). . . . "**Chadwyns,** 6 Broad Walk (tel. Stratford-upon-Avon 69077), is brightly decorated and spotlessly clean. Each room has hot and cold water, and the house is equipped with numerous toilets, a bathroom, and a separate shower room, plus central heating and car-parking space. The tariff is £7.50 ($13.13) per person, all inclusive, for a room and a good breakfast. Mrs. Diana O'Halleran, the owner, made us feel at home, supplied us with a map of the town, and shared with us a lot of stories about the Royal Shakespeare Theatre where she worked as a costumer for several years. She is even glad to suggest B&Bs in other parts of the country of which she is absolutely sure of the quality. In short, she cares, and she is a real find in a town that is perhaps just a little too tourist oriented" (Michele M. Krebs, New York, N.Y.).

"I can recommend highly the **Payton Hotel,** 6 John St. (tel. Stratford-upon-Avon 66442). It is a small hotel, five double rooms, but one of the most pleasant in which we stayed. Mrs. J. G. Haighton is a charming woman, most accommodating. We also had a small black-and-white TV in our room. The hotel is only a couple of blocks from all the tourist attractions but on a small, quiet street, with parking available. The tariff was only £8.50 ($14.88)" (Mrs. W. Bracken, Aptos, Calif.). . . . "Even though I've used Frommer's guidebooks since *England on $5 a Day,* I've never felt compelled to recommend any place I've been to. Selfishly, whenever I do find a great place, either a restaurant or lodgings, I want to keep it to myself. Nevertheless, I feel I owe something to the Barnacles in Stratford-upon-Avon for the wonderful kindness and service they've extended to me. It's **Mrs. P. J. Barnacle,** 41 Grove Rd. (tel. Stratford-upon-Avon 297239), where I've been stopping for more than 12 years now, and the hospitality has never wavered. If anything, the Barnacles become more patient as the years go on. I must confess that at £8.50 ($14.88) per person per night, it's a bargain in the England of today. That price includes one of the best breakfasts you can have to begin a long and busy day of sightseeing—pots of coffee or tea, cereal, juice, eggs, bacon, fried bread, racks of toast, butter, and marmalade. No need for lunch with that under your belt" (W. N. Warnken, New York, N.Y.).

WHERE TO EAT: Cobweb Restaurant & Confectionery, 12 Sheep St. (tel. Stratford-upon-Avon 292554), is a black-and-white timbered building, with a high gabled wing, dating from the early 16th century. It's steeped in associations with the days of Shakespeare. On the ground floor are cases of goodies for sale, but you may want to go to the second floor, where there's a maze of three rooms filled with antique oak tables, Windsor chairs, and settles. The shop is noted as one of the finest in England for its cakes, pastries, cream gâteaux (especially chocolate and sherry gâteau), meringues, apple strudel, and cheesecake.

The luncheons and dinners are excellent, and the kitchen provides the traditional English "Fayre." The soups are tasty—each costing from 60p ($1.05). A full lunch of three courses costs from £4 ($7), and dinners are around £6 ($10.50) and up. After morning coffee and luncheon, the next major event is teatime. A good-size pot of tea is 60p ($1.05), and the Cobweb offers at least 60 varieties of English and continental cakes from 45p (79¢) upward. The Cobweb is also open for teas on Sunday from 3 to 6 p.m.

Thatch Restaurant, Cottage Lane, Shottery (tel. Stratford-upon-Avon 293122), is two doors from Anne Hathaway's Cottage and two miles from Stratford-upon-Avon. Almost hidden by the entrance to the big coach park, this tea room provides a relaxed meal away from the hurly-burly of the town of Stratford. Apart from morning coffee which costs 35p (61¢) a cup, and afternoon cream teas at £1.40 ($2.45), the Thatch offers a four-course roast beef lunch for £5.50 ($9.63). The staff also offers soup, a sandwich, and a dessert for £2 ($3.50), or a three-course chicken supper for £5 ($8.75). Wine, liquor, or beer is available to have with your meal. It is run by Guy and Denise Belchambers, an enthusiastic couple, who suggest you might like to sit outside on the covered patio and watch the visitors lining up to see Anne Hathaway's house, or just listen to the chirping of the birds. The food is good, the prices reasonable, and the atmosphere pleasant.

Hathaway Tea Rooms, 19 High St. (tel. Stratford-upon-Avon 292404), is housed in a mellowed 374-year-old building, timbered and rickety as is its across-the-street neighbor, Harvard House. You pass through a bakery shop up to the second floor, into a forest of olden beams. Sitting at the English tables and chairs you can order wholesome food made from time-tested recipes. Lunch is offered from noon to 2 p.m., including Sunday, but the tea room is closed in the evening. The soup of the day is homemade, costing 50p (88¢). Usually, you have a choice of six entrees every day, such as roast beef with Yorkshire pudding or steak-and-kidney pie, at prices ranging from £2.30 ($4.03). The classic steaming hot fruit pies go for around 50p (88¢). Teatime swarms with the tweedy English.

The **Dirty Duck,** Waterside Street (tel. Stratford-upon-Avon 297312), was formerly known as the Black Swan. By whatever bird it's called, it's been popular since the 18th century as a favorite hangout of Stratford players. Autographed photographs of its patrons, such as Lord Laurence Olivier, line the wall. The front lounge and bar crackles with intense conversation. The choices change daily, and in the bar you'll find good value and quick service, everything washed down with mellow beer.

In the Dirty Duck Grill Room meals are served from noon to 2:30 p.m. and from 6 to midnight. Typical English grills, among other dishes, are featured. You're faced with a dozen appetizers, most of which would make a meal in themselves. They're priced at around £1 ($1.75) each. Main dishes, including braised kidneys with rice, are priced from £3 ($5.25) to £7 ($12.25), and desserts or cheese go for 50p (88¢).

The **Horseshoe Buttery and Restaurant,** 33–34 Greenhill St. (tel. Stratford-upon-Avon 292246), is a family-run business offering good old-fashioned, straightforward English cookery at reasonable prices. Centrally situated opposite the cinema, the café is open daily from 9 a.m. to 9 p.m., serving grills, snacks, salads, sandwiches, along with burgers and pizzas, with prices beginning at £1.50 ($2.63). In the restaurant, open from noon to 3 p.m. and 5 to 9 p.m. daily, the fare runs to steaks, chops, cutlets, scampi, fish, chicken, and salads, at prices between £2.50 ($4.38) and £4 ($7). A two- or three-course luncheon is served daily for only £2.50 ($4.38).

The best dish to order is a homemade steak-and-kidney pie, or a roast joint, each served with fresh vegetables, creamed or boiled potatoes. Because of their 50% patronage by Americans or Canadians, ice water is always available. But you can also order iced lagers, beer, ales, and wines by the glass. The owner, Mr. G. J. Roughlem, also rents out two bedrooms, offering B&B at a cost of £8.50 ($14.88) per person nightly. Rooms are attractively furnished and comfortable, with sliding doors to a roof garden.

YOUR PRIVATE CLUB: The **Hall's Croft Festival Club,** in Old Town (tel. Stratford-upon-Avon 297848), makes for an ideal headquarters during your stay. This preserved timbered Elizabethan building can become your private club, where you can congregate with fellow Shakespeare enthusiasts and order meals. Hall's Croft was the original town house of Susanna, daughter of William Shakespeare, and her husband, Dr. John Hall. Parts of the authentically furnished house may be visited on your £2.70 ($4.73) ticket admitting you to the Shakespeare Trust Properties. The house lies about five blocks from the Royal Shakespeare Theatre and a block from the Avon. The cost of membership (see the attendant in the entry lounge) is £2 ($3.50) weekly. As a member, you'll be entitled to use the facilities of the club, including the comfortable rooms for lounging, lunching, or reading, and the beautiful garden. Lectures and poetry readings are held, books and pamphlets sold—and you can also get your mail here.

Eating at the club is inexpensive, and the food is quite good. A typical luncheon selection might include oxtail soup, roast lamb with mint sauce, roast potatoes, carrots, and cabbage, followed by apple crumble and custard—all for approximately £5 ($8.75), including coffee. Luncheon is served from noon to 2 p.m. After these hours, snacks are available. The club is open from April till the end of October, six days a week, from 10:30 a.m. till 5 p.m. It is closed Sunday.

ATTENDING THE THEATER: The **Royal Shakespeare Theatre** (tel. Stratford-upon-Avon 292271) on the banks of the Avon is the number one theater for Shakespearean productions. The season runs for nine months from March to January, with a winter festival of music and ballet in February. The present theater was opened in 1932, after the old Shakespeare Memorial Theatre, erected in Victoria's day, burned down in 1926. The theater employs the finest actors and actresses on the British stage. In an average season, five Shakespearean plays rotate in repertory.

Usually, you'll need reservations: there are three successive booking periods, each one opening about two months in advance. You can best pick these up from a North American or an English travel agent. If you wait until your arrival in Stratford, it may be too late to get a good seat. The price of seats generally ranges from £3 ($5.25) to £11.50 ($20.13). The theater box office holds back about 14 stall seats, and these go on sale the day of each performance at 10:30 a.m. Predictably, they are almost always grabbed up at once.

In the Victorian wing of the old Memorial Theatre, spared by the fire of 1926, is the Picture Gallery, opened more than a century ago. The permanent collection has portraits of Shakespeare, 18th- and 19th-century romantic interpretations of his plays, and portraits of famous actors and actresses. Various special exhibitions are planned throughout the season. Backstage/gallery tours are available. The gallery is open April to October weekdays from 10 a.m. to 1 p.m. and 2 to 6 p.m.; matinee days, 10 a.m. to 6 p.m.; Sunday, 2 to 6 p.m. December to March, open Sunday only. Admission is 40p (70¢) for adults, 20p (35¢) for children.

For the first time, the Royal Shakespeare Theatre is introducing packages of its own, the **Shakespeare Stop-over.** These packages are available in three prices, beginning at £24 ($42), going up to £28 ($49), and peaking at £33 ($57.75). The package includes dinner at the Box Tree restaurant in the theater, a seat (either stalls or circle) for any Monday-to-Friday performance, and an overnight in a choice of six hotels and two guest houses. The selection of hotel determines the cost of the package. There is also a budget package which includes a balcony seat and a pizza or lasagne in the Terrace Restaurant after the performance, all for a cost of £5.50 ($9.63), including service and VAT. Reservations are made by calling Val Mellini at the Royal Shakespeare Theatre, Waterside (tel. Stratford-upon-Avon 67262) from 9 a.m. to 10:30 p.m.

The RST's small studio theater, **The Other Place,** also opens from March to January, and presents a varied program, from Shakespeare to contemporary authors. All seats cost £4 ($7). Throughout the summer there are also Saturday morning workshop and discussion sessions at The Other Place, led by RST directors, designers, and actors. Seats cost £1 ($1.75).

The new **Box Tree Restaurant,** the Royal Shakespeare Theatre, Waterside (tel. Stratford-upon-Avon 293226), has dibs on the best position in town, in the theater, with walls of glass providing an unobstructed view of the Avon and its swans. You can also dine on the outer terrace where tables are placed in fair weather. The meals and service are worthy of its unique position. Luncheon is served from 12:30 to 2 p.m., with a table d'hôte going for £7 ($12.25). A pretheater dinner is featured from 6 to 7:30 p.m.; then during intermission there is a snack feast of smoked salmon and champagne. After each evening's performance, you can dine by flickering candlelight. Dinner and supper are à la carte, and cost from £8 ($14) to £15 ($26.25) per person. Classical cuisine is served and supervised by chef patron Toni Carbonari. Be sure you book your table in advance, especially on the days of performances (there's a special phone for reservations in the theater lobby).

Overlooking the Avon, the **River Terrace Restaurant** is open to the general public as well as theater-goers. A colorful coffeeshop and restaurant serves typical English and pasta dishes. Afternoon teas are offered on a self-service basis. Meals cost from £2 ($3.50) to £4 ($7). It is open from 10:30 a.m. until after the show.

A TUDOR PUB: The **Garrick Inn,** High Street, is a black-and-white timbered Elizabethan pub named after one of England's greatest actors, David Garrick. It has its own kind of unpretentious charm. The front bar is decked out with tapestry-covered settles, an old oak refectory table, and an open fireplace where the locals gravitate. The back bar has a circular fireplace with a copper hood—plus a buffet bar serving "ploughman's lunches" and steak-and-kidney pie, among other dishes. Prices begin at £2 ($3.50).

NEARBY FARMHOUSE ACCOMMODATIONS: Motorists may find it better to live in one of the farmhouse accommodations on the outskirts of Stratford-upon-Avon. Especially good choices include the following:

Grafton House Farm, Temple Grafton (tel. Bidford-on-Avon 772289), is near Alcester, five miles from Stratford-upon-Avon between the A439 and the A422 roads. The Fisher family charges from £9 ($15.75) to £10 ($17.50) per person per night in high season for B&B. The farm is quite old, but they have modernized the bedrooms—one single, two double, and two family rooms. All are good-size. A small restaurant and licensed bar, adapted from the old stable and blacksmith forge, offer facilities for evening meals costing from £6 ($10.50).

The Goodwins, Long Marston, near Stratford-upon-Avon (tel. Stratford-upon-Avon 730326), is where you can submerge yourself in the best of Old England, at low cost. It's a 17th-century stone farmhouse, with four front gables and mullioned windows. In an unspoiled country atmosphere, you can relax on this 700-acre farm, complete with a pond, a gaggle of geese, sheep grazing in the meadows, and cows in their pastures. Yet you're only seven miles from the heart of Stratford, five miles from Chipping Campden, eight from Broadway. En route to Stratford, you can pass through the little village of Welford-on-Avon and see its much-photographed Boat Lane.

Mr. and Mrs. Hodges, the owners, have doubles and twin-bedded rooms, each with hot and cold running water. The cost ranges upward from £10 ($17.50). There is a guest lounge with color TV. Light meals are available, and an afternoon English "cuppa" is served daily. The farm Aviation Club offers microlight flying, gliding, and parachute jumping at moderate rates.

In the nearby village of Loxley, just 3½ miles from Stratford-upon-Avon, is an ancient community, boasting a Norman church and historic **Loxley Farm** (tel. Stratford-upon-Avon 840265). Roderick and Anne Horton live in a real dream of a thatched cottage with windows peeping from the thatch and creeper climbing up the old walls. The garden is full of apple blossom, roses, and sweet-scented flowers. A stone path leads across the grass and into the flagstone hall, with nice old rugs and a roaring fire. Blackie the cat welcomes you, and Flossy, the gray pony with a touch of Arab, whinnies from the paddock. They have two double rooms and one family room, which go for £7 ($12.25) per person nightly, including a farmhouse breakfast. Roderick leaves for work each day in the farm chemical industry, but Anne is on hand to prepare a packed lunch if required, and to have an evening meal ready for you. However, you must give her advance warning if you plan to eat in. The cost of a meal is £5 ($8.75), including an appetizer, then a roast with three vegetables, a dessert, and coffee. Incidentally, the dining room table is made from a panel from the wall of the Royal Mint in London.

ON THE OUTSKIRTS: **Kings Lodge,** Long Marston (tel. Stratford-upon-Avon 720705), lies six miles from Stratford-upon-Avon. From Stratford, take the A34 Oxford road; on the outskirts of town, fork right on to the A46 Cheltenham road and continue for 4½ miles. Turn right at the signpost to Long Marston and proceed to a "T" junction, turning right. Once a manor house, which has now largely disappeared, it was a place where Charles II hid out as a manservant after the Battle of Worcester.

George and Angela Jenkins accept only six guests at a time, sheltering them in comfortably furnished and centrally heated bedrooms, with hot and cold running water. One bedroom features a traditional four-poster bed hewn from timber grown on the estate. For B&B the charge is from £10 ($17.50) per night, increasing to from £16.50 ($28.86) in a double (slightly more for the room with the four-poster). For £6 ($10.50) you can enjoy a three-course dinner with coffee at an oak table in what was once part of the manor's Great Hall. The restored room is dominated by a large stone inglenook fireplace. Mullioned windows frame vistas of green lawns and stately trees.

If you're planning to do a lot of touring in the area, you might ask to rent one of three self-contained apartments on the grounds which are fully equipped for self-catering.

Broom Hall Hotel, Broom, near Bidford-on-Avon (tel. Bidford-on-Avon 773757), is a privately owned, 16th-century licensed pub-hotel, lying about six miles outside Stratford-upon-Avon. A black-and-white timbered structure, it is set back from the main highway. The tree out front is more than six centuries old, one of the rarest of its kind in Britain. Tina and Robin Barrett own the hotel, and they're assisted by their daughter and her husband, Nina and George Downie. George is the resident chef, offering a number of bar meals, plus an impressive menu with a limited but select number of à la carte specialties, including duckling à l'orange and steak au poivre. Meals cost from £7.50 ($13.13). A special Sunday family luncheon is also offered. There are four double or twin-bedded rooms and two singles, of which three of the former have private baths. Rates are from £12.50 ($21.88) in a single, from £22 ($38.50) in a double, including a full English breakfast and VAT.

READERS' FARMHOUSE SELECTIONS: "**Whitfield Farm,** Ettington, near Stratford-upon-Avon (tel. Stratford-upon-Avon 740260). Bernard and Janet Wakeham are a young couple, with two children, who own the farm on which Mr. Wakeham was born and reared. His father gave it to him when he married, and himself retired. The house has been remodeled. We had a large room with twin beds. I should call these people extremely well-to-do; the furnishings are solid and well chosen. This is a working farm, specializing in sheep. The charge is £5.50 ($9.63) per person, per night, for a bed and an enormous breakfast. I should call this place exceptional. There is a parlor downstairs, with a television set where we were invited to sit in the evening—and where we were brought tea when we got home from our travels. There is only one bathroom, with very modern fittings; but we had no problems about the traffic. All bedrooms contain sinks" (Mary L. Nunn, Pacific Palisades, Calif.). . . . "The friendly and helpful Irene and Robert Bolton run an old farmhouse, **Lower Andrews,** Crimscote, Stratford-upon-Avon (tel. Alderminster 356). The B&B charge is £7.50 ($13.13) each. We had large, comfortable bedrooms and a delicious breakfast that featured Mrs. Bolton's homemade jams and marmalade, with home-baked brown bread. The farmhouse is right on the River Stour, with plenty of sheep and ducks, making it an ideal place for children. Mrs. Bolton, a retired English teacher, knows her Shakespeare very well and will gladly obtain tickets to the Shakespeare Festival if you give her advance notice. The farmhouse is five miles south of Stratford, so a car is necessary" (Glynn Mapes, Brooklyn, N.Y.).

READER'S HOTEL SELECTION IN THE ENVIRONS: "The award-winning **Broad Marston Manor,** Pebworth (tel. Stratford-upon-Avon 720252), is the ideal place for the traveler who loves antiques, old stately homes, and peace and tranquility. Eight miles south of Stratford-upon-Avon, the manor is 12th century, made of Cotswold stone, furnished with family heirlooms, including two antique four-posters, and has an interior of open-hearth fireplaces, beamed ceilings, and creaky floors. In a word, it's charming. Mrs. Rochfort, the owner, has seven rooms for B&B. The grounds are immaculate, and it was a delight to sit on a bench under a centuries-old chestnut tree reading a history of England with not a sound except for an occasional car and a few chirping birds. It's not cheap. A double room costs £11.50 ($20.31) per person, but it is well worth going over the budget to have the privilege of enjoying a night's lodging here. The four-poster rooms rent for £15 ($26.25) per person" (Judith Reusswig, Washington, D.C.).

Most travelers approach our next stopover, Warwick, via the A46 from Stratford-upon-Avon, eight miles away. The town is 92 miles from London and is on the Avon.

2. Warwick

Visitors seem to rush through here to see Warwick Castle; then they're off on their next adventure, traditionally to the ruins of Kenilworth Castle. But the historic center of medieval Warwick deserves to be treated with greater respect. It has far more to offer than a castle.

In 1694, a fire swept over the heart of Warwick, destroying large segments of the town, but it still retains a number of Elizabethan and medieval buildings, along with some fine Georgian structures from a later date. (Very few traces remain of the town walls except the East and West Gates.) Warwick looks to Ethelfleda, daughter of Alfred the Great, as its founder. But most of its history is associated with the Earls of Warwick, a title created by the son of William the Conqueror in 1088. The story of those earls—the Beaumonts, the Beauchamps (such figures as "Kingmaker" Richard Neville)—makes for an exciting episode in English history, but is too detailed to document here.

WARWICK CASTLE: Perched on a rocky cliff above the Avon, this magnificent 14th-century fortress encloses a stately mansion in the grandest late 17th-century style.

The importance of the site has been recognized from earliest times. The first important work at Warwick was the Mound, built by Ethelfleda, daughter of Alfred the Great, in A.D. 915. The same Mound was enlarged at the time of the Norman Conquest, and a Norman castle of the motte and bailey type was built. There are now no remains of the Norman castle, as this was sacked by Simon de Montfort in the Barons War of 1264.

The Beauchamp family, the most illustrious medieval Earls of Warwick, are responsible for most of the castle as it is seen today, and much of the external structure remains unchanged from the mid-14th century. When the castle was granted to the ancestors of the Greville family in 1604, Sir Fulke Greville spent £20,000 constructing a mansion within the castle fortifications, although this has been much altered over the years. The Grevilles have held the Earl of Warwick title since 1759, when it passed from the Rich family.

The State Rooms and Great Hall house fine collections of paintings, furniture, arms, and armor. The armory, dungeon, torture chamber, ghost tower, clock tower, and Guy's tower give vivid insights into the castle's turbulent past and its important part in the history of England. Surrounded by gardens, lawns, and woodland, where peacocks roam freely, and skirted by the Avon, Warwick Castle was described by Sir Walter Scott in 1828 as "that fairest monument of ancient and chivalrous splendor which yet remains uninjured by time."

Many new features include the Rampart Walk, the River Island with magnificent views of the south face of the castle, the Conservatory Exhibition which is a fantasy exhibition reflecting the spirit of the 18th century, and a Victorian Occasion consisting of a reconstruction of a Victorian weekend party of the 1890s by Madame Tussaud's in the former private residential wing of the castle.

The castle is open daily except Christmas Day. From March 1 through October 21, hours are 10 a.m. to 5:30 p.m.; November 1 through February 28, 10 a.m. to 4:30 p.m. All-inclusive admission is £2.75 ($4.81) for adults, £1.75 ($3.06) for children.

The private apartments of Lord Brooke and his family, who recently sold the castle to Madame Tussaud's company, of waxworks fame, have been opened to visitors to display a carefully constructed Royal Weekend House Party of 1898. The major rooms contain wax models of celebrities of the time: Winston Churchill, the Duchess of Devonshire, Winston's widowed mother Jennie, and Clara Butt, the celebrated singer, along with the Earl and Countess of Warwick and their family. In the Kenilworth bedroom, the Prince of Wales, later to become King Edward VII, reads a letter, and in the red bedroom, the Duchess of Marlborough prepares for her bath. Among the most lifelike of the figures is a little uniformed maid, bending over a bathtub into which the water is running, to test the temperature.

OTHER SIGHTS: Other nearby sights worth exploring include the following:

St. Mary's Church

This church was destroyed, in part, by the fire of 1694, and is characterized by its rebuilt battlemented tower and nave, considered among the finest examples of the work of the late 17th and early 18th centuries. The striking aspect of St. Mary's is that it's unusually lofty, dominating the surrounding countryside. The Beauchamp Chapel, spared from the flames, encases the Purbeck marble tomb of Richard Beauchamp, a well-known Earl of Warwick who died in 1439 and is commemorated by a gilded latten effigy. The most powerful man in the kingdom, not excepting Henry V, Beauchamp has a tomb considered one of the finest remaining examples of Perpendicular-Gothic as practiced in England in the mid-15th century. The tomb of Robert Dudley, Earl of Leicester, a favorite of Elizabeth I, is against the north wall. The choir, another survivor of the fire, dates from the 14th century. It too is built in the Perpendicular-Gothic style. The Norman Crypt is another fine example of this period, as is the 14th-century Chapter House. For more information, get in touch with the Rectory, Warwick (tel. Warwick 491132).

Lord Leycester Hospital

At the West Gate, this group of half-timbered almshouses was also spared from the great Fire. The buildings were erected in about 1400, and the hospital was founded in 1571 by Robert Dudley, the Earl of Leicester, as a home for old soldiers. It is still in use by ex-servicemen today. On top of the West Gate is the attractive little chapel of St. James, dating from the 12th century, although much restored. The hospital may be visited weekdays from 10 a.m. to 5:30 p.m. (closed Sunday) for 75p ($1.31) for adults, 25p (44¢) for children. Off-season it closes at 4 p.m.

Warwick Doll Museum

Housed in one of the most charming Elizabethan buildings in Warwick, this doll museum is on Castle Street, near St. Mary's Church. Its seven rooms house an extensive private collection of dolls in wood, wax, and porcelain. The house once belonged to Thomas Oken, a great benefactor of Warwick. In summer (May to October) the house is open from 10 a.m. to 5 p.m.; otherwise, from 11 a.m. to 4 p.m. Admission is 60p ($1.05) for adults, 30p (53¢) for children.

Warwickshire Museum

At the Market Place, this museum was established in 1836 to house a collection of geological remains, fossils, and a fine grouping of British amphibians from the Triassic period. There is also much for the natural historian. The history collections include church plate, coins, firearms, and the famous Sheldon tapestry map of Warwick. It is open weekdays from 10 a.m. to 5:30 p.m.; Sunday in summer from 2:30 to 5 p.m.

St. John's House

A 17th-century mansion at Coten End, St. John's House (tel. Warwick 493431) is a five-minute walk from the castle and houses the Warwickshire Museum social history collection. Displays include a Victorian classroom used by local schoolchildren in costume; an Edwardian nursery where visitors are invited to sit and play replica games; the old kitchen with cooking and laundry exhibits in an appropriate setting, plus changing displays of costume, furniture, musical instruments, and craft tools. A study room for costume enthusiasts is available by appointment where those with a serious interest are welcome to study drawings and photographs of the reserve collection of more than 300 dresses dating from the mid-18th century to the present day. On the first floor is a military exhibition tracing the history of the Royal Warwickshire Regiment from 1674 on. Admission is free. The house is closed Monday; open Sunday afternoon in summer.

BED AND BREAKFAST: The **Warwickshire Licenced Hotel,** 82 Emscote Rd. (tel. Warwick 492927). Despite its formal and somewhat forbidding name, this is a friendly place where Maria and Pepe Sanchez offer bed and a "succulent" English breakfast for £8 ($14) per person nightly. During the day he is a catering manager in the nearby Birmingham Exhibition Centre. All rooms have comfortable beds, central heating, and hot and cold running water, along with TV and tea- and coffee-making facilities. After 22 years in England, Maria and Pepe know what goes into a full English breakfast, served in the basement dining room. If you ask in advance, they will also provide a three-course dinner for £3.50 ($6.13), including a choice of three or four appetizers, a roast or a casserole, followed by a simple dessert. They are so anglicized as to have an English spaniel dog, Pepe II, which spoils the illusion, and an obvious cat called Ginger. It's a comfortable place, close enough to Stratford-upon-Avon to be your base for touring the Shakespeare Country.

The Woolpack Hotel, Market Place (tel. Warwick 496191), started life as a coaching inn and managed to survive the Great Warwick Fire of 1694. So today it is an authentic part of the old town. Comfortable modern bedrooms go for £10 ($17.50) per person in a twin, including a full English breakfast and VAT. Some rooms have private facilities, and for these the tariff goes up to £12 ($21) per person. In the bar and restaurant you can order set dinners or make selections from an à la carte menu. Sunday lunch is an event here. You sit down to an appetizer of fruit or pâté, then follow with a roast rib of beef with a selection of vegetables. The cost, including a glass of wine, is £4.70 ($8.23) per person.

Avon, 7 Emscote Rd. (tel. Warwick 491367), is a B&B down the hill from the Town Gate in the Leamington direction, about ten minutes from Warwick Castle. The house is on the left just before an iron bridge. Mrs. Stringfellow has been running this house for many years, charging £7.50 ($13.13) per person nightly in rooms with hot and cold running water. She does not offer an evening meal. You get good value in pleasant surroundings. The rooms are comfortable, and the welcome is friendly. The house is opposite a park and the Avon River. In the rear is a lock-up car park.

READER'S GUEST HOUSE SELECTION: "Undoubtedly the cleanest, cheeriest place we stayed at was the **Cambridge Villa Guest-House,** 20A Emscote Rd., in Warwick (tel. Warwick 491169). Here you pay £6.50 ($11.38) per person, based on double occupancy. The managers offered to babysit for our son, and Mr. Parker even drove us to Coventry to catch a train one morning on his way to work. The 518 bus, which goes through some marvelous countryside on its way to Stratford-upon-Avon, runs right down Emscote Road" (T. Cleve Callison, Madison, Wisc.).

WHERE TO DINE: The **Porridge Pot,** Jury Street (tel. Warwick 491641), near the East Gate, serves good English food in an old-world setting. This historic building was originally a trader's dwelling, erected circa 1420 and refaced in 1694 after the Great Fire of Warwick destroyed many neighboring dwellings. The owners, Ken and Jackie Smith, provide excellent meals, many of the recipes taken from a 1717 cookbook. Especially recommended is the English beefsteak pie for £4.50 ($7.88). The Pot is open seven days a week for lunch, and from Tuesday to Saturday a full à la carte menu is offered in the evening, beginning at £10 ($17.50) per head. Dinner hours are from 7 to 10 p.m. Medieval banquets are available for parties of 50 or more. The unique setting with its crooked beams, brass pots and pans, and a collection of oil paintings and prints gives you a glimpse of life in old England.

Tudor-House Inn & Restaurant, West Street (tel. Warwick 495447), was built in 1472. It's at the edge of town, on the main road from Stratford-upon-Avon leading to Warwick Castle. It is a stunning black-and-white timbered inn, one of the few buildings to escape the fire that destroyed the High Street in

1694. Off the central hall are two large rooms, each of which could be the setting for an Elizabethan play. In the corner of the lounge is an open turning staircase, waiting for the entrance of a minstrel player. A regular meal in the restaurant and steak bar costs from £7 ($12.25). The inn has nine bedrooms, all with wash basins, although some have baths en suite. The cost ranges from £14 ($24.50) to £27 ($47.25) per room nightly. Two of the rooms have doors only four feet high. There's the usual resident ghost—an old man who gets up early in the morning, leaving the front door open and heading toward Stratford-upon-Avon, without paying his bill. In addition, the old priest's hiding hole has become the **Priest Hole Bar.**

The **Saxon Mill,** Guy's Cliffe (tel. Warwick 492255), is a mill that predates the Norman Conquest, and it still has a turning waterwheel. The old mill has gone through a lot of changes in fortune, but has emerged as a cheerful and economical roadhouse, offering a very good bar-snack menu during the day. Fresh salads are accompanied by home-cooked meats, and prices range from 60p ($1.05) to £2.25 ($3.94). Hot dishes are also available. Bar specials include chili con carne, lasagne, and chicken curry, all priced at around £2 ($3.50). For a more relaxed lunch in the restaurant, or for dinner, the cost will be about £6.75 ($11.81) for lunch and £7.95 ($13.91) for dinner. Appetizers are likely to include prawn cocktail, and a choice from the carvery of meats and poultry. An à la carte menu includes some good fish, such as trout and Dover sole, and you can also order a T-bone. A carafe of the house wine sells for £3 ($5.25). The Saxon Mill is about one mile outside Warwick on the old road to Coventry.

Bar Roussel, Market Place, is the lair of Katherine O'Hara, a bistro and wine bar which is open daily except Sunday from noon to 2:30 p.m. for lunches and nightly from 7 to 10:30 for supper. There is a choice of some 50 wines, beers, and "spirits." A glass of wine with your meal costs 70p ($1.23). Every day there is a freshly made soup going for 50p (88¢), followed by a homemade dish of the day, a hot casserole or a meat pie, each costing £1.85 ($3.24). The cheese board features nine different selections with crackers and bread at 70p ($1.23).

Nicolinis Bistro, 18 Jury St. (tel. Warwick 458817), brings a touch of Italy and its savory cuisine to staid Warwick. Lynne and Nicky, as they are known, welcome you to their attractive restaurant, which is made most inviting with much greenery. Pause at the enclosed counter to check out the crisp salads and luscious Italian desserts. The lighting is also kind. You're faced with an array of appetizers, pizzas, pastas, salads, and desserts, and I haven't even gotten to the main courses. Pizzas come in sizes of 6½ to 9 inches, and Nicolinis choice includes "everything," costing from £1.70 ($2.98) to £2.40 ($4.20), depending on its size. For a main course you can order chicken Kiev with potatoes at £3.55 ($6.21), although the lasagne would be more typical at £2.30 ($4.03). The restaurant serves Tuesday through Sunday from 9:30 a.m. to 10:30 p.m.

3. Kenilworth Castle

In magnificent ruins, this castle, the subject of Sir Walter Scott's romance *Kenilworth,* once had walls that enclosed an area of seven acres. It lies 5 miles north of Warwick, 13 from Stratford-upon-Avon. In 1937, Sir John Davenport Siddely purchased the castle and placed it in the care of the Office of Works (now the Department of the Environment).

The castle dates back to the days of Henry I, having been built by his chamberlain, Geoffrey de Clinton. Of the original castle, only Tower Keep, with its 16-foot-thick walls, remains. Edward II was forced to abdicate at Kenilworth in 1326, before his murder at Berkeley Castle in Gloucestershire in 1327. Elizabeth I in 1563 gave the castle to her favorite, Robert Dudley, Earl of Leicester, who built the Gatehouse. Elizabeth I, surrounded by courtiers, visited on several occasions after Leicester moved in. Parts of the castle were destroyed on orders from Parliament after the Civil War. The castle is open from March 15 to October 15 on weekdays from 9:30 a.m. to 6:30 p.m. and on Sunday from 2 to 6:30 p.m. From October 16 to March 14 hours are 9:30 a.m. to 4 p.m. on weekdays, 2 to 4 p.m. on Sunday. Admission is 50p (88¢) for adults, 25p (44¢) for children.

FOOD AND LODGING: Hollyhurst Guest House, 47 Priory Rd. (tel. Kenilworth 53882), is a modest little nine-bedroom guest house run by Mr. and Mrs. J. Smart, who charge from £6.75 ($11.81) to £7.25 ($12.69), depending on the room. Their space is too limited to provide meals other than breakfast, but they will recommend various restaurants nearby. Their rooms are modestly furnished, with hot and cold running water, and there is a lounge for guests who enjoy TV.

The Magnolias, 58 Priory Rd. (tel. Kenilworth 56173), is a pleasant although small guest house where one has to reserve a room in July or August. The owner, Mrs. Iris Eyles, is an interesting personality, and makes her guests very much at ease. She charges £8 ($14) per person nightly, whether in a single or double room. In the height of the season she can't offer dinners in the evening, although she can provide coffee, tea, and sandwiches if needed.

Tudor Cottage (tel. Kenilworth 56702) is a 450-year-old half-timbered structure right across the street from the castle. Its little restaurant is a delightful spot for a refreshing afternoon tea following a tour of Kenilworth. The friendly owner, Frank Hart, is happy to share his wealth of knowledge about the interesting history and the sights of the area. If you decide to spend the night, B&B will cost you an all-inclusive £8 ($14). Also served is afternoon tea, as well as a three-course luncheon, costing £3.50 ($6.13) weekdays, rising to £4.50 ($7.88) on Sunday. Mr. Hart always has a roast with vegetables and trimmings.

READER'S GUEST HOUSE SELECTION: "Enderley Guest House, 20 Queens Rd., Kenilworth (tel. Kenilworth 55388), is on a quiet side street. It offers a room with tea/coffee-making facilities and serves a large breakfast, and the total cost is £9 ($15.75) per person. A bar is open to guests, light snacks being always available, as is a lounge with color TV. It is, of course, close to Kenilworth Castle and Warwick Castle, and a few miles between Stratford-upon-Avon and Coventry. Joy and Dennis Street, the owners, are friendly and full of helpful advice" (Robert P. Kennedy, Yorba Linda, Calif.).

4. Coventry

The Midlands city of Coventry, home of motorcar and cycle manufacturing, is principally industrial, but you'll want to pay it a visit to see Sir Basil Spence's controversial **Coventry Cathedral,** consecrated in 1962. The city was partially destroyed during the blitz bombing in the early '40s, but the rebuilding was miraculous. No city symbolizes more dramatically England's power to bounce back from adversity.

Before the war, Coventry was noted in legend as the ancient market town through which Lady Godiva made her famous ride, giving birth to a new name in English: Peeping Tom. The Lady Godiva story is clouded in such obscurity that the truth has probably been lost forever. It has been suggested that the good lady never appeared in the nude, but was the victim of scandalmongers, who, in their attempt to tarnish her image, unknowingly immortalized her.

The cathedral grew up on the same site as the 14th-century Perpendicular building. Many Coventry residents maintain that the foreign visitor is more disposed to admiring the structure than the Britisher, who perhaps is more tradition-laden in his concept of cathedral design.

Outside is Sir Jacob Epstein's bronze masterpiece, *St. Michael Slaying the Devil.* Inside, the outstanding feature is the 70-foot-high altar tapestry by Graham Sutherland, said to be the largest in the world. The floor-to-ceiling abstract stained-glass windows are the work of the Royal College of Art. The West Window is most interesting, with its engraved glass and rows of stylized saints and monarchs with jazzy angels flying around among them.

After visiting the cathedral, you may want to have tea in a nearby patio, listening to the chimes.

St. Mary's Guildhall, Bayley Lane (tel. Coventry 25555). Up a flight of steps leading from a small yard off Bayley Lane is one of the most attractive medieval guildhalls in England, dating from 1342. It was originally built as a meeting place for the guilds of St. Mary, St. John the Baptist, and St. Catherine. It is now used for the solemn election of the Lord Mayors of the city and for banquets and civic ceremonies. Above the north window is an arras (tapestry), added in the 15th century, and a beautiful oak ceiling with its original 14th-century carved angels which was rebuilt in the 1950s. There is a Minstrel's Gallery and a Treasury, and off the Armoury, Caesar's Tower where Mary Queen of Scots was imprisoned in 1569. By appointment only, you can also see a magnificent collection of 42 original watercolors by H. E. Cox, depicting Coventry before the bombings of 1939. City pensioners conduct guided tours.

Ford's Hospital, Greyfriars Lane, is a house built in the very early 16th century to house the poor of the city. Today it is a wealth of old beams and mullioned windows restored during 1953. It is now the home once more of elderly Coventry residents. There is a beautiful inner courtyard surrounded by timbered walls hung with geraniums, ferns, and ivy. It is open from 10 a.m. to 5 p.m. daily throughout the year and is well worth a visit.

At the **Coventry Information Centre,** 36 Broadgate (tel. Coventry 20084 or 51717), you can obtain free a useful brochure on the city, listing the main sights and where to eat cheaply or magnificently. It also guides you to shopping bargains, including those of the indoor retail market off Market Way and the craft shops on Spon Street.

The **Museum of British Road Transport,** on Cook Street, is some five minutes' walk from Coventry Cathedral in the city center. It houses the largest municipally owned collection in the United Kingdom, possibly in the world. The oldest car is an original Daimler, dating from 1897 (the first English Daimler was built in Coventry only one year before). The museum also displays some of the most antique vehicles still running, with six of them being regular participants in the annual London–Brighton run (only vehicles manufactured before 1905 are eligible). Curiosities include a 1910 Humber taxi whose mileage is listed at more than one million. Exhibits are diversified, as the museum has the ambitious task of covering the total history of transport in the Midlands, internationally recognized as the home of the British transport industry. Indeed, Coventry has been the home of some 116 individual motor vehicle manufacturers, many of whom are represented in the collections. Among the military vehicles is the staff car in which Montgomery rode into Berlin after the defeat of the Nazis. The museum is open daily throughout the summer (Easter through September) and on Friday, Saturday, and Sunday from October through March, although prebooked parties can gain entry outside the public hours in winter. Admission charges are £1.30 ($2.28) for adults, half price for children. For further information, telephone the Director of Leisure Services, Jordan Well, Coventry (tel. Coventry 25555, ext. 2315).

Coventry is 19 miles from Stratford-upon-Avon, 11 from Warwick, and 6 from Kenilworth.

WHERE TO STAY: **Falcon,** 16 Manor Rd. (tel. Coventry 58615), is a pleasant splurge hotel just off the Coventry ring road and 100 yards from the station. This old house has been completely modernized to accommodate today's traveler, while retaining its charm and character. Single rooms range from £17 ($29.75) per day without bath to £21 ($36.75) with full private bath, double rooms from £22 ($38.50) to £28 ($49), these prices including a full English breakfast. All rooms are centrally heated, and they come with radio, TV, and telephone. No lunch is served on Saturday; otherwise, lunch and dinner are presented daily in the Carvery, a midday meal going for £6 ($10.50), rising to £7.50 ($13.13) in the evening.

Croft Hotel, 23 Stoke Green (tel. Coventry 457846), is a 14-bedroom licensed Victorian hotel, just ten minutes from the city center and the cathedral. Owned by Peter and Loraine Llewellyn, it's an all-purpose hotel, where single travelers are as welcome as families. The daily rate for B&B is £14 ($24.50); double or twin-bedded rooms cost £22 ($38.50) per night. An extra £1 ($1.75) is assessed if guests stay only one night. A room with a private shower is available at an extra cost of £1.50 ($2.63). Bedrooms are centrally heated and have radios and alarm clocks. Mr. Llewellyn prepares a hefty breakfast, and Mrs. Llewellyn caters for evening meals and a Sunday lunch which goes for £5.25 ($9.19). The hotel also offers a selection of bar snacks.

Rochelle Guest House, 33 Westminster Rd. (tel. Coventry 22925), owned by Denise Warren, is modest but homelike. She has central heating, hot and cold running water in all of the pleasantly furnished bedrooms, and there are corridor toilets and bath. Guests gather in the lounge to watch color TV. The cost per person, whether single or double, is £8 ($14) nightly. An evening meal, typical English fare is served for £4 ($7). It's just a four-minute walk from the station—ideal for those who are traveling by train.

Sapphire House, 11 Park Rd. (tel. Coventry 20992), offers low terms for a bed and full English breakfast, just £9 ($15.75) per night in a single, and £16 ($28) per night in a double, including everything. It's owned by Mr. and Mrs. C. W. Webster, who will willingly prepare evening snacks, which they serve in their TV lounge. Each bedroom has hot and cold running water, radio, morning call system, and central heating. If you're driving, there's plenty of parking space, and if you arrive by train, Sapphire House is just a few minutes from the railway station.

READERS' GUEST HOUSE SELECTION: "We stayed at the **Spencer Guest House,** 2 Spencer Ave. off Warwick Road, Earlsdon (tel. Coventry 713274), where the hostess, Mrs. S. Pithers, was gracious in every way, and her accommodations above average. Our bedroom bay window overlooked a large playing field and park, all of which was on a high hill overlooking downtown Coventry. The rate of £8 ($14) per person includes a delicious breakfast, and tea and cookies when desired" (Wilson and Maxine Spencer, Celina, Ohio).

WHERE TO EAT: **Ostlers Eating House,** 166 Spon St. (tel. Coventry 26603), lies some five to eight minutes from the cathedral. Spon Street itself is being restored to its original state as it was in medieval England, with some adjustments to the 20th century of course. Ostlers is a traditional eating house where a very satisfying meal will cost around £5 ($8.75). You're presented with a choice of appetizer, then perhaps roast chicken with baked potato or a grilled steak with salad and potato. Chili con carne or a meat-and-potato pie costs only £2 ($3.50). Desserts go for 85p ($1.49); a glass of wine, 70p ($1.23). The place is good for atmosphere in a city that has had to be almost totally rebuilt.

Coventry Town Wall Tavern, Bond Street, is the domain of "mine host" Ray. It's a haven for draft brass drinkers (58p, or $1.02, a pint) where the bars are called "The House of Lords" and "Make Room." The public bar, of course, is "The House of Commons." Bar snacks include Chester pie at 75p ($1.31), a creation of minced meat, onions, peppers, and green beans, topped with Lyonnaise potatoes. A more prosaic sandwich will cost less, and you might also order one of the meat pies, the prices ranging from 90p ($1.58) to £1.10 ($1.93). Both Ostlers and the Town Wall Tavern are convenient to the Bond Street car park, which is close to the cathedral.

Corks Wine Bar & Bistro, 4–5 Whitefriars St. (tel. Coventry 23628), evokes a stylized belle époque atmosphere, with its dark colors and antique lighting fixtures. Daily fixed-price menus are displayed on chalkboards, costing anywhere from £1.30 ($2.28) to £2 ($3.50). From the handwritten à la carte menu, you can select a filling meal of soup, pâté salad, or lasagne, along with a dessert, for around £2.75 ($4.81). If you're really hungry for something to sink your teeth into, try the entrecôte bordelaise with a salad or french fries at a cost of £3.95 ($6.91). Monday to Saturday lunches are served from 11 a.m. to 2:30 p.m. Dinner is offered Monday to Thursday from 6 to 10:30 p.m., until 11 p.m. on Friday and Saturday, and on Sunday from 7 to 10:30 p.m.

Nello Pizzeria, 8 City Arcade (tel. Coventry 23551), is an informal and heavily frequented bistro, specializing in lasagne and pizza dishes, ranging in price from £1.20 ($2.10) to £2.50 ($4.38). It is open daily except Sunday from 10 a.m. to 11 p.m.

For a picnic before your tour of the countryside, go and visit **Tommy Tucker,** on Hertford Street. He will supply "anything you can imagine" served in a bread roll. I don't know if anyone has ordered a kipper-and-marmalade concoction yet, but try one of his corned beef and salad sandwiches or whatever is your favorite.

TOURING A GLASSWORKS: **Royal Brierley Crystal,** North Street, Brierley Hill, West Midlands DY5 3SJ (tel. 0384/70161). If you telephone ahead to arrange a visit, a tour of this glassworks, taking 1½ hours, is quite fascinating. You are shown the process of mixing the ingredients, including white sand, red lead, and arsenic (yes, the poison). You also see the melting of ingredients in a giant furnace in the center of the great hall, and the progress to smaller furnaces around the walls. There, the glass is collected, blown, cut, and decorated. Every item is handmade and unique.

The craftspeople are so skilled that items of a set are almost identical, and very few, comparatively, end up in the Seconds Shop. But some do, and to the layperson's eye they look almost perfect anyway. Tours take place at 11 a.m. Monday to Friday and at 1 p.m. Monday to Thursday for a charge of 20p (35¢). But you can visit the Seconds Shop any day except Sunday from 9 a.m. to 4 p.m. to buy goods at very advantageous prices.

Items include export rejects and discontinued lines, as well as slightly imperfect glasses and vases. Anything can be packed for you for shipment overseas. The Tea Shop is open for lunch or tea, serving soups, quiches, chili con carne, and plain whole-meal bread sandwiches, along with cakes. For three courses and tea or coffee, expect to pay around £2.70 ($4.73).

To get there, turn off the M5 at exit 4 on to the A491 Bromsgrove–Wolverhampton road, turning right to Brierley Hill.

5. Hereford and Worcester

The Wye Valley contains some of the most beautiful river scenery in Europe. The river cuts through agricultural country, and there is no population explosion in the sleepy villages. Wool used to be its staple business, and fruit growing and dairy farming are important today.

The old county of Herefordshire has now combined with Worcestershire to form "Hereford and Worcester"-shire. Worcestershire's name, of course, has become famous around the world because of its sauce familiar to gourmets. It is one of the most charming of Midland counties, covering a portion of the rich valleys of the Severn and Avon.

Herefordshire's Black Mountains border the Welsh Brecon Beacons National Park, and between the two cathedral cities of Hereford and Worcester the ridge of the Malverns rises from the Severn Plain.

The heart of England is the best point to travel to by train from Paddington Station in London if you wish to use your BritRail Pass. The train takes you through many of the previously mentioned towns and villages, and you can stop and visit Windsor, Henley-on-Thames, and Oxford, not to mention the numerous Cotswold villages such as Chipping Campden. It must be one of the best train rides in the country, and you can also take a side trip by bus from Evesham to Stratford-upon-Avon, too. Or else take the bus back from Stratford to Oxford via Woodstock, then the train back into London.

HEREFORD: One of the most colorful old towns of England, the ancient Saxon city of Hereford, on the Wye River, was the birthplace of both David Garrick and Nell Gwynne. Dating from 1079, the red sandstone **Hereford Cathedral** (tel. Hereford 59880) contains all styles of architecture, from Norman to Perpendicular. One of its most interesting features is a library of chained books—more than 1600 copies—as well as one of the oldest maps in existence, the Mappa Mundi of 1290. There is also a newly established Treasury in the crypt.

Hereford is surrounded by both orchards and rich pasturelands. Hence it has some of the finest cider in the world, best sampled in one of the city's mellow pubs. Hereford cattle sold here are some of the finest in the world, too.

The Old House, High Street (tel. Hereford 68121, ext. 207), is preserved as a Jacobean period museum, with the appropriate furnishings. The completely restored half-timbered structure, built in 1621, also contains superb 17th-century wall paintings and local history items. On Monday, hours are from 10 a.m. to 1 p.m.; on Tuesday and Friday, from 10 a.m. to 1 p.m. and 2 to 5 p.m. On Saturday in summer, hours are from 10 a.m. to 1 p.m. and 2 to 5:30 p.m. (on Saturday in winter, 10 a.m. to 1 p.m.). Admission is 20p (44¢) for adults, 10p (18¢) for children.

Where to Stay

Burton Lodge, 168 Whitecross Rd. (tel. Hereford 269073), was someone's great private home when Queen Victoria was fading from the English scene. It's built of solid brick with every kind of fancy ornate woodwork trim, gables, and sunny bay windows. Operated by David and Kaye Robertson as a high-level guest house, it's a bargain. For a bed and an excellent English breakfast, they charge, per person, whether in a single or double, £8.50 ($14.88), and they add no VAT or service charge. Each unit has bedside lamps, is centrally heated, and contains hot and cold running water. In the corridor a bath or shower is always available. Even more of a bargain is to have dinner as well. If English TV interests you, there's a set in the living room. Since Burton Lodge is three-quarters of a mile from the center of the city, you'll get a peaceful sleep.

Alexander House Hotel, 61 Whitecross Rd. (tel. Hereford 274882), offers moderately priced accommodations for 15 guests in a lovely house, half a mile from the city center. It's on the A438 Hereford–Brecon road, and easy to spot. Owners Sylvia White and Eileen Jennings charge £9.50 ($16.63) per person nightly whether in a single or double, and for an additional £4 ($7) to £7 ($12.25) you can have one of their home-produced dinners. The cooking is family style, with fresh vegetables used whenever available. They are licensed for alcoholic beverages as well. They'll even prepare packed lunches for you. Each bedroom is commodious, with hot and cold running water, bedside lights, and central heating. On each floor there is a bathroom with toilet and shower. Early-morning tea or coffee is served in the bedrooms, and substantial snacks are available for those guests who don't require a three-course dinner.

Ferncroft Hotel, Ledbury Road (tel. Hereford 265538), is a simple, comfortable hotel with no pretensions, offering an economy accommodation. Rates are £10 ($17.50) per person nightly for B&B. For just £15 ($26.25) per person daily you can stay here on half-board terms. In the chillier months there is central heating, and each of the nicely furnished bedrooms contains hot and cold running water. The location is off St. Owens Street, a short walk from the railway station and the Wye River.

Bowes Guest House, 23 St. Martins St. (tel. Hereford 267202), is just across the River Wye, about a five-minute walk from the cathedral. John and Eileen Bowes own a nice old town house with leaded windows, leading straight from the street into the hallway. The 19th-century listed building was built by the Duke of Norfolk to accommodate his fishing guests, and there is a large garden at the back. Parking is close by. There are 13 bedrooms, with hot and cold running water and central heating. Baths are down the hall. Singles rent for £8.50 ($14.88), with doubles and twins ranging from £14 ($24.50) to £15 ($26.25). Some triple rooms are available at £20 ($35) a night. These rates include a large breakfast that just might offer haddock or kippers in addition to the regular bacon and eggs. They'll pack a picnic lunch for you if you give them warning, costing £1.25 ($2.19) for an ample meal. Eileen Bowes is a local person and will recommend tourist sights and give directions to places further afield.

Westdene, 200 Whitecross Rd. (tel. Hereford 50438). Harvey and Myfanwy Payne are real Herefordshire locals. They love the city and surrounding countryside and welcome guests into their comfortable home to share their enjoyment of the region. Their Victorian house is about five minutes from the center of the city by car, and there is a lounge with TV. In the evening, when Harvey comes home from his work in the construction business, Myfanwy provides an evening meal, mainly stews and roasts, served with fresh vegetables. Four courses cost £3.50 ($6.13). Bed and a large English country breakfast, along with morning and evening coffee, cost £7 ($12.25) per person and up. Mrs. Payne will pack a picnic lunch for another £2 ($3.50). The house is centrally heated.

On the outskirts, if you're a motorist you can seek out a farmhouse accommodation. Gladys and Frank Lee own and run **Cym Craig** at Little Dewchurch in Hereford (tel. 0432/70250). This is a mixed farm, 180 acres around a solid Victorian farmhouse where bed and a farm breakfast costs £6 ($10.50) per person. There is a comfortable sitting room with TV and a grander drawing room, with a baby grand which the family—and guests—are encouraged to play. During the day, guests are invited to walk around the farm, but not through the "milking parlours," when milking is in progress. Son Anthony provides an interesting guide when he's not away driving heavy trucks around the country. Glenys completes the family, the daughter who works as a secretary to the local antiques company. Then there are three dogs. The large spotless bedrooms have snug beds to sink into, and there is a bathroom and separate shower down the passage, along with two toilets. How to get there from Hereford: take the Ross road, the A49, over the river and turn left at the traffic lights by the church. Follow this road to a pedestrian crossing, turning left and driving for four miles to the village. Once there, turn left. Cym Craig is the first farm on the left.

READER'S GUEST HOUSE SELECTION AT WORMELOW: "From Hereford, take the A49 to the A466 to Wormelow, and **Lyston Smithy** (tel. 0981/540368) is about half a mile on the road to Monmouth. Mrs. Elizabeth Jones, the hostess, is most gracious, greeting guests with a pot of tea and cookies. We had a lovely room with bath attached, very comfortable accommodations. Both Graham and Elizabeth Jones are helpful and friendly. Mrs. Jones serves a delightful full English breakfast in her dining room, using a lace cloth and fine crystal and silver. We were also encouraged to enjoy the lounge, where color TV is provided. The Joneses went out of their way to phone a local pub and arrange for us to get dinner only a five-minute drive away, where we had a long-to-be-remembered meal. The charge is £8.50 ($14.88) per person for B&B" (D. C. Iler, Toronto, Ont., Canada).

Food and Drink

Saxty's Restaurant and Wine Bar, 33 Widemarsh St. (tel. Hereford 57872), is a Victorian restaurant and wine bar with good food, atmosphere, and fine specialties. It features many dishes Herefordshire chefs have done well for years—roast beef, steak-and-kidney pie, and saddle of lamb, at prices beginning at £4 ($7). The small restaurant is open from noon to 2:30 and from 7:30 to 10:30 p.m. Closed Sunday.

The **Tudor Restaurant,** Broad Street (tel. Hereford 277374), is a good luncheon choice, following your visit to the red sandstone Hereford Cathedral. The roof of this restaurant is still supported by the interior rough beams of the 17th-century building which houses it. Windsor chairs and white tablecloths serve as the appropriate setting for the wholesome and inexpensive luncheons prepared by a staff directed by the owners, Messrs. Cook and Whaley. The menu is simple and very English. A steamy soup is followed by, say, a mixed grill or you may prefer the rump steak or roast chicken. Especially tempting might be one of the oversize salads, loaded with ham and greenery. Count on spending from £4 ($7). A children's menu offers a hamburger served with french fries at £1 ($1.75). Hours from Easter Sunday to October are daily from 10:30 a.m. to 4:30 p.m. After that, it's open only from Monday to Saturday, 9:30 a.m. to 5 p.m.

Cathedral Restaurant, Church Street (tel. Hereford 265233), is known locally as John Browne's place. Huddling close to Hereford Cathedral, it's a good choice, either for lunch or dinner. Old beams and eggshell-colored walls evoke the heart of England, as does the menu which, to break the monotony, always includes some continental fare as well. Hours are Tuesday to Saturday from 10:30 a.m. until 2:30 p.m. and from 7 to 10:30 p.m. Mr. Browne also opens for a traditional Sunday lunch, a popular choice in Hereford from 11:30 a.m. to 2:30 p.m. Your dinner is likely to cost from £7 ($12.25), plus the cost of your drink. For a main course I selected pork cathedral style—that is, seasoned and cooked in cream with Hereford cider and herbs and served with apples. Entrees are served with vegetables and potatoes. The wine list is limited but adequate. At lunch you can order roast beef or fried plaice, a meal costing around £5 ($8.75).

Shopping in Hereford

The **Museum of Cider,** The Cider Mills, 21 Ryelands St. (tel. Hereford 54207), displays everything connected with the making of cider, often called the wine of England. There is a reconstruction of a 16th-century farm cider house, cider mills, presses, barrels, and barrel-making tools, along with jugs and bottles. The shop sells cider from 90p ($1.58) a bottle to £1.40 ($2.45) for a rare old cider brandy guaranteed to be at least ten years old. They also sell recipe books, miniature bottles and barrels of cider, mugs, teacloths, and post-cards. The tea shop sells light refreshment during the day. Entrance is 80p ($1.40) for adults and 40p (70¢) for children. It is open daily, June through September, but closed on Tuesday in April, May, and October, and closed completely from November to March. To reach the museum, take the A438 Hereford–Breacon road, turning off onto Grimmer Road.

Gaffers, Brewers Passage, Commercial Street, in Hereford, is an interesting place, useful for many purposes. After a visit to the cathedral, a short walk brings you to this cheerful café, noisy with enthusiastic young people. Tea here costs a mere 15p (26¢), and a baked potato with butter, to be eaten with a bowl of vegetable soup, costs 65p ($1.14). A slice of pizza goes for 35p (61¢).

Upstairs is the **Gallery** where young craftspeople demonstrate their various arts—glassblowing, blacksmithery, furniture making, fine art painting, and pottery. They run the place as a cooperative, attracting passers-by to the café. By so doing, they try to sell their work, although there is no pressure to buy. If she has time, Karlin Rushbrooke will blow glass to your design. Sim Lawrence, the blacksmith and secretary of the group, will discuss the finer points of wrought ironwork and will recommend some small souvenir for you to fly home with. A small Grecian-style vase will cost £2.25 ($3.94); a glass goblet or an intricate paperweight, £10 ($17.50). Gaffers is open from 10 a.m. to 5 p.m. Monday to Saturday. For a phone contact, it's Sim Lawrence again (tel. 098-16-236).

At Hay-on-Wye, an attractive market town in the Wye Valley, which is a good center for touring on both sides of the border, you'll come upon the **Hay Cinema Bookshop,** on Castle Street, Hay-on-Wye (tel. 0497/820071). Once upon a time, an enthusiastic young man started a tiny secondhand bookshop which expanded rapidly into the largest secondhand bookshop in the world. Still in the old cinema where it started, the bookshop flourishes. This is the place to find that specialist book you've sought for so long. Just to browse through the vast stocks is a delightful way to spend an afternoon. You'll probably find some title you can't imagine having done without for so long: e.g., *Nurse and Spy in the Union Army,* published in Hartford, Connecticut, in 1865.

Browsing is hungry work, and **The Granary,** by the clock tower in Hay-on-Wye (tel. 0497/820790), will provide food and drink. It is open daily for lunch and on Friday and Saturday evening for dinner. They serve soups and appetizers, followed by typical English main dishes, such as chicken pie and vegetables. A meal will cost a mere £3 ($5.25), and it's washed down with beer at 50p (88¢) or wine at 70p ($1.23) a glass. Once the town's grain store, the Granary has a long counter where you can order your choice from the blackboard to be served at the casual wooden tables.

A Country Hotel near Ledbury

Ledbury is a charming old-world market town and center for the Malvern Hills. From here you can explore Eastnor Castle, two miles to the east, which has a collection of paintings, tapestries, and armor. If you'd like accommodations in the area, you'll find them at—

The Verzons, Trumpet, near Ledbury (tel. Trumpet 381). Philip and Mary Stanley welcome you to their establishment, which is a free house, bistro bar, and B&B hotel. It is a beautiful Georgian house, standing on four acres overlooking the Malvern Hills. It lies on the A438 road, some two miles from Ledbury. Most of the bedrooms have private baths or showers en suite and are pleasantly furnished. The Stanleys charge from £10.50 ($18.38) in a single and from £26 ($45.50) in a double, including a full English breakfast, VAT, and service. Much of the food served is made with home produce in their kitchen—salads from the garden, individual chicken-and-ham or duck-and-bacon pies. Garlic-fried potatoes are served, as well as chunky jacket potatoes deep-fried and offered with homemade garlic mayonnaise. A three-course meal will cost from £4 ($7). The Verzons lies on the A438 road, some two miles from Ledbury.

An Inn on the Border

The **Rhydspence Inn,** Whitney on Wye, Hereford (tel. 04973/262), is a timbered inn right on the border of England and Wales, dating from the 16th century. It has a fascinating gabled porch through which you enter the gleaming bar where a log fire crackles in the chimney. The locals are used to welcoming travelers to share the excellent meals and snacks prepared by David Wallington. These include thick homemade soups at 80p ($1.40) a bowl. A specialty is the landlord's favorite "Homey," a soup made with chopped ham and eggs, or "Fishy," made with smoked haddock, anchovies, mushrooms, and cream. You should also try their local cider as an alternative to beer in the area. David worked for a U.S. chemical company, but he and Flo (Florence) wanted to settle down in Hereford. The inn was the answer.

They have only two rooms to rent, one with shower and the other with private bath. Both have central heating, color TV, and tea- or coffee-making facilities. They charge from £12.50 ($21.88) per person for B&B or else £17.50 ($30.63) per person for half board, providing you stay for more than three nights. In addition to the bar food there is a restaurant, where David applies himself to grills, roasts, and tasty country dishes. Dinner costs about £7.50 ($13.13), and wine can be ordered by the glass at 70p ($1.23).

This is an excellent place from which to tour Herefordshire and the Wye Valley. The locals, too, are friendly, and you can join them in the bar in the evening for a game of darts, or more novel, quoits. It is closed on Monday, and on Tuesday they don't do lunch.

WORCESTER: This historic cathedral city, famous for its gloves and porcelain, stands 27 miles from Birmingham and 26 miles from Stratford-upon-Avon.

Offering views of the Malvern Hills, **Worcester Cathedral** stands on the banks of the Severn River. Dating from 1084, it contains the Quire (rebuilt in 1224) which shelters King John's Tomb from 1216. The Chapter House, with its massive central supporting column, is considered one of the finest in England. A refreshment room and gift shop are in the cloisters. The cathedral is open from 7:30 a.m. to 6 p.m. daily (in summer until 7:30 p.m.).

A visit to the **Royal Worcester Porcelain Factory** is worthwhile. At the factory, a two-hour tour, including an introductory talk by a member of the staff, a souvenir guidebook, and tea or coffee, costs £4.50 ($7.88). For the more hurried visitor, there is a shorter tour for £1.40 ($2.45) for adults, 60p ($1.05) for children, allowing you to see the craftspeople at work. Unfortunately it's necessary to book ahead if you wish to take a tour, but everyone can enjoy browsing in the shop at the factory. There you can buy examples of their craft. Many pieces are "seconds," all marked as such and sold at low prices. Most of the time you won't be able to tell why. There is a magnificent museum as well.

The city is rich in other sights as well, including the **Commandery,** a fine 15th-century timber-framed structure which was originally founded about 1085 as a hospital. It was also a Civil War site visited by Charles II. Purchased by the City of Worcester in 1973, it contains a great hall with a hammer-beam ceiling and oriel window. It features displays on the city's history from Roman times. It's open Tuesday to Saturday from 10:30 a.m. to 5 p.m. (Sunday from April 1 to October 1 only, 2:30 to 5 p.m.) Admission is free. For information, telephone Worcester 25371.

If time remains, see **King Charles' House,** where Charles II stayed before the Battle of Worcestershire in 1651; **Queen Elizabeth's House,** and the **Queen Anne Guildhall,** built in 1723 (outside, the Royalists honored Charles I and II with statues); and **St. Helen's,** the nation's oldest church, which may date back to 680.

For information on guided walking tours and boats on the River Severn, call the **Heart of England Tourist Board** at 0905/29511.

Food and Lodging

The **Talbot Hotel,** 8 Barbourne Rd. (tel. Worcester 21206), most certainly is a bit of old England—a long, half-timbered coaching inn, with tiny dormers, a tower bay window, and leaded-glass windows. It's owned by Mr. and Mrs. Ray and Daphne Cross, who welcome overnight B&B guests at reasonable rates—£10 ($17.50) in a single, £18 ($31.50) for a double, VAT included. Ask about a family room, renting for £24 ($42) nightly. Each bedroom has hot and cold running water, heating, intercom, and a radio. All other meals are extra and available in the timbered, old-style dining room. À la carte meals are served in the evening, including, for example, a prawn cocktail followed by a ham steak, at £3.60 ($6.30). Dessert is an extra 50p (88¢). Snacks are offered in the pub lounge.

Chatsworth, 80 Barbourne Rd. (tel. Worcester 26410), is a good clean guest house with car parking, where an overnight stay will cost £6.50 ($11.38) per person, including a full breakfast. It's run by Patricia Grinnel, whose husband, Dennis, is a radio ham. His call sign is G4MKO, so if you care to make your advance reservations by radio, give him a call. Incidentally, a licensed ham will be allowed to use Dennis's equipment.

The **Fiveways Inn,** Angel Place (tel. Worcester 27065), is a pub right in the middle of the town, with good clean bedrooms that contain central heating and wash basins. There are toilets and baths down the landing. Singles with TV rent for £8 ($14), doubles or twins with TV for £15 ($26.25), and triples for £20 ($35.88). Prices include VAT and a large breakfast. Steve Wilding is the host, and the busy bar serves good snacks every evening and at lunch from Monday to Saturday. There is usually a special such as shepherd's pie or chili and rice. You should put together a meal for about £3.50 ($6.13).

Park House Hotel, 12 Droitwich Rd. (tel. Worcester 21816), is a neat guest house with pleasantly decorated, centrally heated rooms, with radio and hot and cold running water. There is a TV lounge as well. The charge is £9.50 ($16.63) in a single and from £8.50 ($14.88) per person, based on double occupancy, including VAT and an English breakfast. There is a residents' license for serving alcoholic drinks, and they provide a good range of snacks and light meals. Dinner can be provided by arrangement for £4.45 ($7.79). Wynn and June Davies are the owners.

For meals, I suggest **Bottle's Wine Bar & Bistro,** 5 Friar St. (tel. Worcester 21958), perhaps the favored rendezvous right in the historic center, particularly among young people. It's managed by John Anderson. The decor is handsomely subdued, with black-painted wickerwork tables, and the selection of cold foods is very good. I prefer the clove-studded freshly baked ham, along with a nice crisp salad. In addition, the good-tasting soups are also homemade. The roast joints, seafood dishes, and at least one hot specialty every day are also recommended. You might end your meal with a brie or a stilton cheese. A plate of food costs from £2.20 ($3.85) to £2.60 ($4.55), with cheese going for another 85p ($1.49). The wine bar is open from noon to 2 p.m. and from 6:15 to 10 p.m. (on Friday and Saturday, it's open until 11 p.m.). Closed Sunday.

Inglenooks Restaurant, 34 Sidbury (tel. Worcester 21444), must be the most traditional tea shop in the country, with its brick walls, crooked beams, and wheelback chairs arranged around lots of small, flowery-tableclothed tables. The decor is enhanced by knickerleg shades on the yellow lights and a large wood stove burning quietly in the corner. The place is staffed by friendly people under the watchful eye of Mrs. Clark-Hyslop, the owner. They will go so far as to serve you roast beef for breakfast at 9:30 a.m. if you really want it. But I'd suggest you start with morning coffee and a slice of homemade cake at 55p (96¢). If you're still ensconced at lunchtime, continue with the £3.25 ($5.69) set meal of, say, roast beef, Yorkshire pudding, potatoes, and vegetables. They also serve stuffed baked potatoes, quiches, stews, cold meats, and salad. At teatime, a cream tea with jam and scones is priced at only £1.25 ($2.19), and they also do good hot fruit buns with butter. It is open daily, Monday to Saturday, from 9:30 a.m. to 5:30 p.m., on Sunday from 12:30 to 5:30 p.m.

Museums on the Outskirts

Avoncroft Museum of Buildings, Stoke Heath, Bromsgrove, Worcester (tel. Bromsgrove 31886), is 11 miles from Worcester and 21 miles from Stratford-upon-Avon. It is open daily from March 1 to November 30 from 10:30 a.m. to 5:30 p.m. or dusk if it falls earlier; closed Monday in March and November. Admission is £1.20 ($2.10) for adults, 65p ($1.14) for children. The museum's cafeteria is open from 11 a.m. for coffee, lunch, and afternoon tea. Lunch includes quiches, pâtés, and a selection of salads with cold meats, and snacks are also available. The museum is an open-air site where a number of historic buildings have been saved from destruction and reconstructed. There are a windmill in working order, a timber-framed merchant's house from the 15th century, an Elizabethan house, chain- and nail-making workshops, and a blacksmith's forge. Recent additions include a cockfight theater, a stable, and a wagon shed, all of the 18th century. This gives one a fascinating insight into the construction of those buildings as done by our forefathers. The 14th-century Guesten Hall roof from Worcester has been reconstructed at ground level so that you can see how the joints were made by the skill of craftsmen of the past. These are just a few of the things on display on this ten-acre site. Car parking is available.

Sir Edward Elgar's Birthplace at Upper Broadheath is a brick cottage surrounded by stables and a coach house built by his father and uncle in the early 19th century. Nowadays the house contains a museum of photographs and drawings, original scores of his music, and mementos of his youth. Musicians and conductors come from afar to check his music and their interpretations of it. To reach the house, drive out of Worcester on the A44 toward Leominster. After two miles, turn off to the right at the sign. The house is in the village, 2½ miles along a side road. There is a small admission charge, and it is open daily from 1:30 to 4:30 p.m.

The **Jinney Ring Craft Centre,** Hanbury, Worcestershire (tel. 052784/272), is in the same area as the Avoncroft Museum, five miles away in the village of Hanbury on the B4091 from Stoke Prior to Vernon Arms. Two old farm buildings have been carefully restored and converted by ex-farmers Richard and Jenny Greatwood into artists' studios and craft workshops on 20 acres of land. The eight small studios house a jeweler, blacksmith, wood turner, stained glass designer, weaver, and toy-maker, all of whom will demonstrate their craft. Many of the items they show can be purchased in the center's shop. It is open Easter to Christmas on Wednesday to Saturday from 10:30 a.m. to 5 p.m. and on Sunday from 2:30 to 5:30 p.m. They also do tasty lunchtime snacks served from noon to 2:30 p.m., a light meal costing about £2.50 ($4.38). By the way, the Jinney Ring was one of the first implements in the mechanization of farming. A series of complicated cogs and drives linked the cider press or the chaff-cutter with the patient horse who plodded ever onward around the ring to drive the grinding wheels.

Also in the area, **Hanbury Hall** is a Wren-style red-brick building erected in the early 18th century. It is remarkable for its outstanding painted ceilings and magnificent staircase by Thornhill. It is open April to October, Saturday and Sunday (and also Easter Monday and Tuesday), from to 2 to 5 p.m. From May until the end of September, it is open Wednesday to Sunday and bank holidays from 2 to 6 p.m. The admission charge is £1.50 ($2.63) for adults and 55p (96¢) for children. Teas are served in the hall.

Lodging on the Outskirts

Oaklands Farm, Main Evesham Road, near Pershore in Worcestershire (tel. 2420/860323), is a horticultural farm of five acres where the actor James Mason, among others, come to buy plants and shrubs sold by the owner, the extroverted John Ownsworth. In the house, his wife Marlene dispenses good food and comfort to overnight guests. Their home is superbly furnished and decorated, and they allow guests to share in the pleasure of using solid silver cutlery, fine crystal glass, and porcelain. The three double rooms have twin beds, and there are ample facilities down the landing. Rooms cost £8 ($14) per person, including a big breakfast. They prefer guests to stay more than one night if possible. Dinner at £5.50 ($9.63) is four courses, usually including a roast joint with the usual trimmings. They have a collection of china and another of horse brasses. Tea is served from a silver teapot before the fire under a glistening chandelier.

6. Salop (Shropshire)

Immortalized by A. E. Housman's *A Shropshire Lad,* this hilly country borders Wales, which accounts for its turbulent history. The bloody battles are over today, and the towns of Salop, with their black-and-white timbered houses, are peaceful and quiet. Salop makes a good base for touring in the Welsh mountains.

SHREWSBURY: Lying within a horseshoe bend of the Severn River, Shrewsbury is the capital of Salop. The river almost encloses the town. Known for its cakes and ale, Shrewsbury contains one of the best-known schools in England. It was also the birthplace of Charles Darwin.

Considered the finest Tudor town in England, Shrewsbury is noted for its black-and-white buildings of timber and plaster, including Abbot's House from 1450 and the tall gabled Ireland's Mansion from 1575 standing on High Street. It also has a number of Georgian and Regency mansions, some old bridges, and handsome churches, including the Abbey Church of Saint Peter and St. Mary's Church.

Shrewsbury Castle is 900 years old and was saved from destruction in 1790 when an engineer, Thomas Telford, had it restored as a private house. Built of red sandstone on a hill dominating the town, it is now a visitor center with permanent displays of the history of Shrewsbury. Called the Information Centre, it stands on the Square (tel. Shrewsbury 52019).

Rowley's House on Barker Street has a fine collection of Roman artifacts from Viroconium (Wroxeter), and is open weekdays from 10 a.m. to 1 p.m. and 2 to 5 p.m. This building is adjacent to Rowley's Mansion which opened as a museum in 1982, covering art, local history, numismatics, Roman archeology, geology, minerals, prehistory, costumes, and natural history. The great treasures of these museums are the Hadrianic inscription (second century) and silver mirror (third century), both from Wroxeter.

Clive House Museum, on College Hill (tel. Shrewsbury 54811), has displays of local ceramics, industrial archeology, art, costumes, and a Georgian room, besides being the regimental museum of the Queen's Dragoon Guards. Hours are from 10 a.m. to 1 p.m. and 2 to 5 p.m., except Monday when hours are from noon to 1 p.m. and from 2 to 5 p.m.

At **Coleham Pumping Station,** Longden Coleham, you can see displayed compound rotative pumping engines from 1900, on Wednesday and Friday from 2 to 5 p.m.

Where to Stay

Abbey Court House, 134 Abbey Foregate (tel. Shrewsbury 64416), is a small, but well-kept hotel, owned by Mr. and Mrs. Turnock, who charge a modest £7.50 ($13.13) nightly for a single room, £7 ($12.25) per person in one of their comfortable doubles. Mrs. Turnock provides a complete breakfast, and if you ask, she'll make your bacon "crispy."

The White House, Hanwood, near Shrewsbury (tel. Shrewsbury 860414), is the only half-timbered black-and-white building in the village and it supposedly dates back to the 16th century. It has always been a private house except for a brief period between 1920 and 1940 when it was used by the village butcher. The slaughterhouse and winding gear have been preserved. Rates are £8.50 ($14.88) per person nightly, including a large English breakfast. There is an extensive à la carte menu and wine list or a three-course set dinner for £4.50 ($7.88) and up. There are five bedrooms for guests, a family room, twins and doubles, plus a single with a wide bed. All are furnished in the spirit of the period, with hot and cold running water and full central heating. If you enjoy color TV, there is a comfortable lounge for guests only. The location is 2½ miles from Shrewsbury.

Glynndene, Abbey Foregate (tel. Shrewsbury 52488), is a small, well-run guest house presided over by Mr. and Mrs. Knight. Their rooms are comfortable and clean, renting for £6 ($10.50) per person nightly for B&B. If you request it, Carol Knight will serve tea or coffee in your room before breakfast. She is pleasant and hospitable, and her breakfast is one of the most generous in Shrewsbury. The guest house lies left of Abbey Church.

READERS' HOTEL SELECTIONS: "We found an excellent place to stay, one of the best of our trip, the attractive and immaculately clean **Berwyn House** on Holywell Street (tel. Shrewsbury 54858). It is run by Mrs. J. Ellis. For £7 ($12.25) a night per person, we had a large double room with hot and cold water, delicious breakfast, and a hostess who was friendly and cheerful. The house is centrally heated, and there is a shower in the bathroom. Snacks are available upon request, and there is a TV room" (Robert and Virginia Chute, Mt. Vernon, Me.). . . . "Who could resist the charm of a 400-year-old farmhouse complete with mud and wattle wall? Mr. and Mrs. Christmas welcome you as their guest as you step back into Elizabethan times with sloping floors and old timbered walls at **Pulley Hall Farmhouse,** Bayston Hill, Shrewsbury (tel. Bayston Hill 2900). It's a real find for £7 ($12.25) per person for B&B. Mr. Christmas will give you clear instructions on how to find his farmhouse" (Mr. and Mrs. Robert Gifford, Lutherville, Md.). . . . "**Mrs. Mills's B&B,** 36 Cotton Crescent (tel. Shrewsbury 4513), is about six blocks from the railway station, a pleasant ten-minute walk along the Severn complete with ducks in the river and cows on the banks. Friendly, helpful Mrs. Mills charges £6.50 ($11.38) per person and will rent to singles" (Doris Pinnock, Jersey City, N.J.).

Where to Dine

The **Cavalier Restaurant,** Prince Rupert Hotel, Butcher Row (tel. Shrewsbury 52461). The hotel has three restaurants, of which the Cavalier is the most outstanding choice. White tablecloths, oil paintings, and a beamed ceiling live up to the tourist's conception of the heart of England. A fixed-price lunch menu, costing £5.50 ($9.63), includes a tempting choice of a well-prepared cuisine, such as a mortadella salad, followed by poached filet of plaice mornay, with potatoes and two vegetables, plus cheese. A fixed-price dinner might include smoked mackerel with horseradish sauce, poached sweetbreads mexicaine, along with vegetables and a freshly prepared dessert. This restaurant is popular with local residents, as well as clients of the hotel. Lunch is daily from noon to 2:30 p.m. Dinner is served from 7 to 10:30 p.m. Guests can also patronize the Steak Bar and the Royalist Restaurant.

Delany's, St. Julian's Craft Centre (tel. Shrewsbury 60602), is a wholefood vegetarian self-service restaurant, run entirely by women in the vestry of a disused church, now turned into a craft center. It is open Monday to Saturday from 10 a.m. to 5 p.m., serving both morning coffee and afternoon tea, along with a selection of home-baked cakes. At lunch, from noon to 2:30 p.m., hot food is offered. You get very imaginative soups, including carrot and lemon, curried peanut, and fennel and potato. At this place the "burger of the day" is made with a base of cheesy nuts and curried lentils and served on a sesame bun. There is also a flan of the day, often a spicy leek and potato. Hot dishes of the day are likely to include cheese bakes with fresh vegetables. There is also an array of fresh salads, six bowls daily. They even bake their own bread, and you're invited to have a glass of wine at lunch. A meal will cost around £3.50 ($6.13).

The **Steak and Pizza Bar,** 50 Mardol (tel. Shrewsbury 4834). John Collins, the managing director of this steak, pizza, and burger emporium, says he tries to emulate the enthusiasm he found among employees in restaurants in the United States. His staff seems to respond admirably, and the pizza is reported to be the best for miles around. All burgers are made on the spot, and all of the steaks come from the local Shropshire beef (which is tender and tasty, although slightly different from the Texas steers to which you might be accustomed). Pizzas start at £1.30 ($2.28), half-pound burgers with french fries at £2.25 ($3.94), and the most expensive item on the menu, the finest filet steak with garnish and french fries at £5.75 ($10.07). Desserts average £1 ($1.75) each. This happy place is open daily from 11:30 a.m. to 2:30 p.m. and 6 to 11 p.m.

WHITTINGTON: Many motorists in Salop drive across the county to eat at the **Whittington Inn,** at Whittington, near Stourbridge on the main Kidderminster–Wolverhampton road (tel. Kinver 2496). The inn is the original manor house of Sir William de Whittington, Dick Whittington's grandfather, who built it in 1310. Dick Whittington, of course, was the enterprising lad from a merchant family who became one of the principal bankers to English kings and later Lord Mayor of London, elected three times between 1398 and 1420.

Today the ancestral home boasts an attic bistro and wine bar. The interior is white-painted brick, and the menu offers a selection from a cold buffet with items priced from £1.75 ($3.06) to £3 ($5.25). You can also order sandwiches and a wide selection of English cheeses. Hours of the wine bar are from noon to 2:30 p.m. (on Sunday, noon to 2 p.m.) and from 7 to 10:30 p.m. In addition to the bistro, the inn operates three oak-paneled and beamed bars with fires burning in wintertime, and a Tudor walled garden, where traditional real ale is served. The restaurant part of the operation is open from Monday to Saturday in the evening and for Sunday lunch, offering both a table d'hôte menu and a more expensive à la carte menu than that served in the wine bar.

LUDLOW: Looking down on the Teme River, this is a mellow old town with a historic Norman castle. Many Georgian and Jacobean timbered buildings stand on its quiet lanes and courts. The most colorful street is known as "Broad," rising from the old Ludford Bridge to Broadgate, the one remaining gateway from walls erected in the Middle Ages. See, in particular, the Church of St. Laurence, Butter Cross, and Reader's House.

Bed and Breakfast

Wadboro Thatch, Thriftwicket Lane, Hayton's Bent, near Ludlow (tel. Stoke St. Milborough 75249), is a genuine 16th-century thatched cottage. It is in a completely secluded position in beautiful countryside, yet only a five-minute drive from Ludlow, the historic market town with a castle. From the Wadboro Thatch base, you can branch out to visit Worcester, Hereford, Shrewsbury, Stratford-upon-Avon, the Cotswolds, and Wales. Golf is also available nearby, the course rather unusual, as it is encircled by the Ludlow racecourse.

The cottage has been fully restored, yet its original features have been maintained—in fact, it's a perfect example of an old English country cottage. Although not large, it's very traditional, with its upper rooms tucked under the thatch, latticed windows, oak beams, and an inglenook fireplace with a bread oven. Accommodation comprises two doubles with private baths. Constructed of stone, the walls are nearly two feet thick. This, together with the thatched roof, combines to keep it cool in summer, warm in winter.

Formerly belonging to the Earls of Plymouth, the cottage has comparatively recently come into private hands—those of Mrs. Pamela Allcock-Brown. She loves people and is very used to meeting them and making them feel at home. A room with bath and an English breakfast rents for £8.50 ($14.88) per night per person, plus another £5.50 ($9.63) per person charged for an evening meal. The owner specializes in good traditional English food, including local Hereford beef and Welsh lamb, as well as fresh vegetables and fruits from her own half-acre garden.

Bromfield Manor, Bromfield, near Ludlow (tel. Bromfield 279), is a stone manor house with six gables, three groups of tall chimneys, and a surrounding park-like garden well back from the A49, three miles from Ludlow. Bromfield Manor is owned by Norman and Joy Cooke, who have been happily welcoming Canadian and American guests into their home at a moderate rate. Mrs. Cooke charges £9 ($15.75) per person daily, including VAT, for B&B in a single or double. Her bedrooms have hot and cold running water and tea- or coffee-making facilities. The living room is pleasantly furnished, and you can arrange for an evening meal. Mrs. Cooke also can direct you to several very good eating houses in Ludlow.

READERS' GUEST HOUSE SELECTION: "The **Croft Guest House,** Dinham (tel. Ludlow 2076), is a beautiful old house, complete with flower boxes in the windows. It is on the south side of Ludlow Castle, facing the castle gardens. The center of Ludlow is just a minute's walk away. The best pub in England, the Church Inn, is near the Church of St. Laurence, five minutes from the guest house. The rooms at Croft House are large, the breakfast real English. As a bonus in the spring, we had fresh mushrooms. Rate is £15 ($26.25) for a double, and there are no extra charges. The proprietor, Mrs. M. G. Davis, furnishes electric hot-water kettles and the makings, so early risers can have their pre-breakfast coffee or tea" (Alice and Bill Bristor, Baltimore, Md.).

IRONBRIDGE: Ironbridge Gorge is the location of an intriguing complex of museums, said to be the birthplace of the Industrial Revolution.

The **Ironbridge Gorge Museum,** open daily, includes the Blists Hill Open Air Museum with its restored blast furnaces and shops; the 18th-century Bedlam Furnaces, the restored riverside Severn Warehouse, the 1779 Iron Bridge (first major iron bridge in the world), the restored Coalport Pottery Museum, the Coach House Gallery (industrial art housed in stables), and the Coalbrookdale Blast Furnace dating back to 1638. The museum (tel. Ironbridge 3522) charges adults £2.50 ($4.38), and children and students, £1.60 ($2.80). A family ticket, good for two adults and up to five children, costs £6.50 ($11.38).

For an accommodation in the area, I suggest **The Hall,** Hope Bowdler, near Church Stretton (tel. Church Stretton 722041), which charges £8.50 ($14.88) per person for B&B. Hope Bowdler, on the B4371, is only 1½ miles from Church Stretton, an attractive small resort in the Shropshire Hills. The house has recently been modernized, providing two twin-bedded and one single room for guests. There are two baths with showers, plus hot and cold running water and central heating in each unit. The house is really the home of the Inglis family, direct descendants of Bishop Charles Inglis, rector of New York's Trinity Church at the time of the War of Independence, and later the first bishop of Nova Scotia. The house contains many interesting historical family pictures and possessions. Here's a chance to stay in a peaceful English country house at a reasonable price.

WORFIELD: This is a good base for exploring Ironbridge and Coalport, the birthplace of the Industrial Revolution, as well as Shrewsbury (see above), Ludlow, Worcester, the Malvern Hills, Clee Hills, and Wenlock Edge. Excursions can also be made to many famous glassworks, including Royal Worcester.

The **Old Vicarage Hotel,** Worfield, near Bridgnorth (tel. Worfield 498), is set in two acres of grounds on the edge of a conservation village. All the bedrooms have either private baths or showers and are well furnished. Each bedroom is named after a local Shropshire village. Victorian reception rooms are furnished with antiques, and log fires blaze in cooler evenings. Carefully restored, the house retains its turn-of-the-century character. Christine and Peter Iles welcome you to a relaxed, informal atmosphere, offering an excellent cuisine and a good wine cellar. For a superb dinner, a full English breakfast, and your room, you'll be charged from £23 ($40.25) per person nightly, although reductions are granted for longer stays. Reservations are necessary.

7. Staffordshire

Stoke-on-Trent is the name of the five towns called as the Potteries, the "Five Towns" of Arnold Bennett's novels. The Potteries are known throughout the world for the excellence of their fine porcelain and china.

The so-called "Black Country" of steelworks and coal mines has almost disappeared, although you can visit a coal mine and descend in the "cage" to the worked-out seams.

Within easy reach of the industrial town of Dovedale is a valley with some of England's most beautiful scenery, forming part of the Peak District National Park.

STOKE-ON-TRENT: Because of the worldwide interest in the making of pottery, this town has found itself something of a tourist attraction. It's the home of the pottery made famous by Josiah Wedgwood, along with other well-known names such as Coalport, Minton, and Spode.

The **Wedgwood Visitor Centre,** at Barlaston (tel. Barlaston 4141), charges 50p (88¢) for adults and 25p (44¢) for children, and is open from 9 a.m. to 5 p.m. Monday to Friday except over Christmas. In the demonstration hall you can watch the slip, the clay, built up on the potter's wheel, see how the raised motifs so well known on Wedgwood blue pottery are made and added to the pieces, as well as witness how delicate flowers are made and painted and plates turned and fired, then painted.

The young people working at the benches are often apprentices, but the work they produce is of the highest quality. They are happy to answer your questions about their special occupation.

There's a continuous film show in the large cinema, and the beginning of the movie is announced on the public address system. In the shop you can see samples of all the sorts of items made at the factory, and purchase souvenirs. Prices are the same as elsewhere, but they do sometimes have items of discontinued lines and some "seconds" available at reduced prices.

The fascinating museum has exhibits of more than 200 years of craftsmanship, showcases of old bills, working details, experimental pots and goblets, and drawings of machines invented by Josiah Wedgwood two centuries ago and still used daily in the factory.

When you need a rest, there's a lounge with a snack cafeteria where for £1.50 ($2.63) you can get a bowl of soup, a sandwich, or some steak-and-kidney pie with a glass of wine. Here you can write your postcards to home and have them franked with a special stamp to say they were mailed at the Wedgwood Centre.

Afterward, a visit to the past is in order. The **Gladstone Pottery Museum,** Uttoxeter Road at Longton (tel. Stoke-on-Trent 319232), is an old building with a paneled hallway leading to rooms piled with ancient machines and equipment used in the pottery trade. Tiles and saggers (something to do with the piling of plates in kilns) are stacked everywhere. There's a marvelous exhibit of washstand bowls and jugs, plus toilets of all shapes and sizes, including the original flush toilet made for Queen Elizabeth I in 1596. Called the Harrington Water Closet, it is still in working order. It was here that the tiles used in the Capitol in Washington were made, and they have examples displayed on the floor. Outside is a replica of a typical potter's home, plus a working pottery with its old Victorian bottle ovens, the last few in the area where there used to be several thousand. The area around the museum is known as Potters Acre because of the number of shops specializing in rejects and discontinued lines. Here you may be able to replace that broken cup. Admission to the museum is £1 ($1.75) for adults, 50p (88¢) for children. It is open Monday to Saturday from 10:30 a.m. to 5:30 p.m. (closed on Monday in winter). It is also open on Sunday in summer from 2 to 6 p.m.

The **Stoke-on-Trent City Museum,** on Broad Street in Hanley (tel. Stoke-on-Trent 29611), surely must contain the most comprehensive collection of ceramics in the world. The enthusiastic curator tells me that they have twice as much stored away as they can possibly show at any time. Even those who aren't museum buffs must find this a beautiful collection. There are also exhibitions of modern art as well as prehistoric local remains, all housed in a delightful contemporary building. The museum is open Monday to Saturday from 10:30 a.m. to 5 p.m.

Afterward all that, sustenance is required, and where better than at **Heath's Wine Bar,** Albion Street, at Hanley (tel. Stoke-on-Trent 272472), almost opposite the museum? The long bar groans beneath great dishes of pâté, cold meats, pies (veal, ham and egg, steak and kidney, grosvenor), chili, salads (several varieties), dressed crab, and hot soup. Mounds of french bread are stacked up, and jacket potatoes are a favorite item. For dessert, try the cheesecake or a fruit salad. Everything is fresh, and there is much that is homemade. Order and collect your meal and repair to one of the low coffee tables surrounded by sofas or the wheelbacked chair-surrounded tables. The music is soft, the atmosphere warm and red. A two-course meal will cost around £2 ($3.50) to 3 ($5.25). Wine begins at 60p ($1.05) a glass.

The **New Minton Museum** at London Road, Stoke-on-Trent (tel. Stoke-on-Trent 47771), is the starting place for a 1½-hour tour through the major departments of the factory, where they specialize in heavily decorated work. A phone call or a letter in advance is needed to join the 50p (88¢) tour, but your understanding of the processes will be complete when you have seen how to raise patterns and scour and burnish gold relief. It takes 45 minutes to finish the decoration on one plate, so you can see how much a dinner service would cost.

Free-hand-painting from some 1800 patterns is also shown during the tour. It is here that you can get that unique souvenir, a personalized free-hand-painted plate or other piece of china. Simply arrange to discuss with one of the artists the photo or picture you wish to have, and they'll do the rest. The cost of the plate can be as much as £130 ($227.50), and it'll take from 2 to 12 months to complete, depending on the demand for orders. But you'll have an elegant and totally different souvenir. For more information, see Mrs. Joan Jones, the museum's curator.

The **Chatterley Whitfield Mining Museum,** at Tunstall, Stoke-on-Trent (tel. Stoke-on-Trent 813337), is the only place in England where you can visit a coal mine, going down to the coal face. You are "kitted out" with lamp and helmet, and you can get overalls to cover your clothes. Stout shoes are also recommended. This mine was the first to produce one million tons of coal in a year. Coal was mined for 140 years, but the mine has been closed now for five years. The 700-foot shaft is 80 years old, and it takes 1½ minutes to descend to the face. Each party is accompanied by a retired miner. Mine was Joe, who was born in Poland but settled in England in the 1940s. He explains the techniques of mining, feeding you much information, including how the steam-winding engines work. The tour takes about an hour, costing £2.25 ($3.94).

STAFFORD: The county town was the birthplace of Izaak Walton, the British writer and celebrated fisherman. Its main industry is boot making, and it contains many historic buildings, notably St. Chad's, the town's oldest church; St. Mary's, with its unusual octagonal tower; and the **William Salt Library,** with its interesting collection of folklore.

Food and Lodging

Swan Hotel, 46 Greengate St. (tel. Stafford 58142), is a Berni hotel, with rooms that have been pleasantly modernized. For B&B you'll pay £20 ($35) in a single, £35 ($61.25) in a double, with private baths and showers. Meals offered in the grill are tasty. Most of the main dishes include vegetables, potato, bread, butter, and dessert. A lunch averages around £6 ($10.50), a dinner going for from £8 ($14).

LICHFIELD: Fans of Samuel Johnson pay a pilgrimage here to this historic city where he was born in 1709, son of an unsuccessful bookseller and parchment maker. The city is noted for its **cathedral,** whose three spires are known as "Ladies of the Vale." The tallest spire rises more than 250 feet, and the west front of the cathedral was built from about 1280. You can walk around the beautiful close and see a bit of the Vicars Close, with its half-timbered houses, along with the 17th-century Bishop's Palace.

Dr. Johnson's Birthplace on Breadmarket Street contains mementos and pictures of the author and his contemporaries. It is open from 10 a.m. to 5 p.m., closing at 4 p.m. off-season. The admission charged is 40p (70¢) for adults, 20p (35¢) for children.

Across the street from Dr. Johnson's Birthplace stands the **Heritage Centre & Treasury** in Lichfield's Market Square. Adults pay an admission of 50p (88¢), and children are charged 25p (44¢). Hours are daily from 10 a.m. to 5 p.m. (except Monday). Exhibits depict everything from burnings at the stake to plagues. Wax models are displayed of many of the city's galaxy of visitors, including David Garrick, the actor. The treasury displays goldsmiths and silversmiths over the centuries.

You can also visit the **Guildhall** (across the road from Heritage Centre), over the city dungeons dating from the Middle Ages. The Guildhall was rebuilt in 1846. Prisoners were jailed here before they were burned at the stake in Market Square.

Incidentally, market days are Friday and Saturday in Lichfield.

Where to Stay

Mrs. Pauline Duval's Guest House, 23 Dam St. (tel. Lichfield 24303), is a modest town house of historic and architectural interest owned and kept tidy by its helpful, friendly landlady. She has one single, a double, and one family room, all with hot and cold running water, one public and one private bath. She charges £8.50 ($14.88) per person, including a home-cooked breakfast, and willingly prepares evening meals or snacks as you wish. There is TV, a radio, and tea- and coffee-making facilities in each room. There's central heating, and if you are driving, off-street parking is available. Dam Street on which her guest house stands was mentioned in the *Domesday Book* of 1086. Opposite the guest house stands Brooke House where a general in Cromwell's army was shot in 1647. A plaque on the street commemorates where Johnson was taught English in 1714 at Dame Oliver's school.

"Gaialands," 9 Gaiafields Rd. (tel. Lichfield 23764), is a well-kept, small hotel within walking distance of the cathedral and Minster Pool. Mr. and Mrs. Robert White give their guests a true Staffordshire welcome in a quiet secluded environment. If you ask her, Mrs. White will prepare a home-cooked four-course dinner for £5 ($8.75). She charges £10 ($17.50) per person for B&B in either a double- or twin-bedded room. Units have central heating, pedestal hand basins, and the bathrooms are closely adjacent.

Oakleigh Guest House, 25 St. Chad's Rd. (tel. Lichfield 22688), is a country house standing on its own grounds adjoining a sailing lake, Stowe Pool. The owners, Nick and Hilary Hine, have greatly improved the house both in decor and comfort. Visitors are assured a high standard of cleanliness and service. Only a dozen guests are accommodated at one time in one of the spacious rooms with full central heating. Rates are £10 ($17.50) in a single, from £7.50 ($13.13) per person in a double. You might also enjoy an evening meal with Mr. and Mrs. Hine at a cost of £4 ($7) per person. Around four o'clock you can order tea and cookies at 50p (88¢).

READER'S GUEST HOUSE SELECTION AT ENDON: "The **Old Vicarage** (tel. Stoke-on-Trent 503686) is on Leek Road in the town of Endon, northeast of Stoke-on-Trent. This area is very short of overnight accommodations, so a recommended B&B should be welcomed by all who wish to visit the numerous potteries and discount potteries without having to travel a long distance for the night. Mr. and Mrs. Gray have a lovely, newly decorated home which they run with charm and grace. There was a vase of fresh blossoms on the dresser in our room, and on a bedside table we had the fixings for tea, bone china teacups and saucers, and even a container of cookies. There is a small, pleasant TV lounge. The charge is £8 ($14) per person per night" (Julianna M. Niemann, APO New York).

Chapter XII

CAMBRIDGE AND EAST ANGLIA

1. Cambridge
2. Ely
3. Thaxted
4. Saffron Walden
5. Finchingfield
6. Dedham
7. Long Melford
8. Lavenham
9. Woodbridge and Aldeburgh
10. East Bergholt
11. Norwich
12. North Norfolk

"WE ARE FARMERS, great animal lovers," say two spinster sisters who run a small farm in Essex. They delight in receiving paying guests at their old farm, feeding them fresh vegetables and home-grown fruit. They are not atypical of the East Anglians. The four counties of East Anglia—Essex, Suffolk, Norfolk, and Cambridgeshire—are essentially low-lying areas, where the bucolic life still reigns supreme.

East Anglia was an ancient Anglo-Saxon kingdom, under heavy domination of the Danes for many a year. Beginning in the 12th century, it was the center of a great cloth industry that brought it prosperity, as the spires of some of its churches testify to this day. In part it is a land of heathland, fens, marshes, and "Broads" in Norfolk.

Cambridge is the most visited city in East Anglia, but don't neglect to pass through Suffolk and Essex, the Constable country, containing some of the finest landscapes in England. Norwich, the seat of the Duke of Norfolk, is less visited, but the fortunate few who go that far toward the North Sea will be rewarded.

1. Cambridge

A young man and woman lying in an open green space between colleges, reading the romantic poets . . . rowing under the Bridge of Sighs . . . spires and turrets . . . droopy willows that witness much punting . . . dusty secondhand

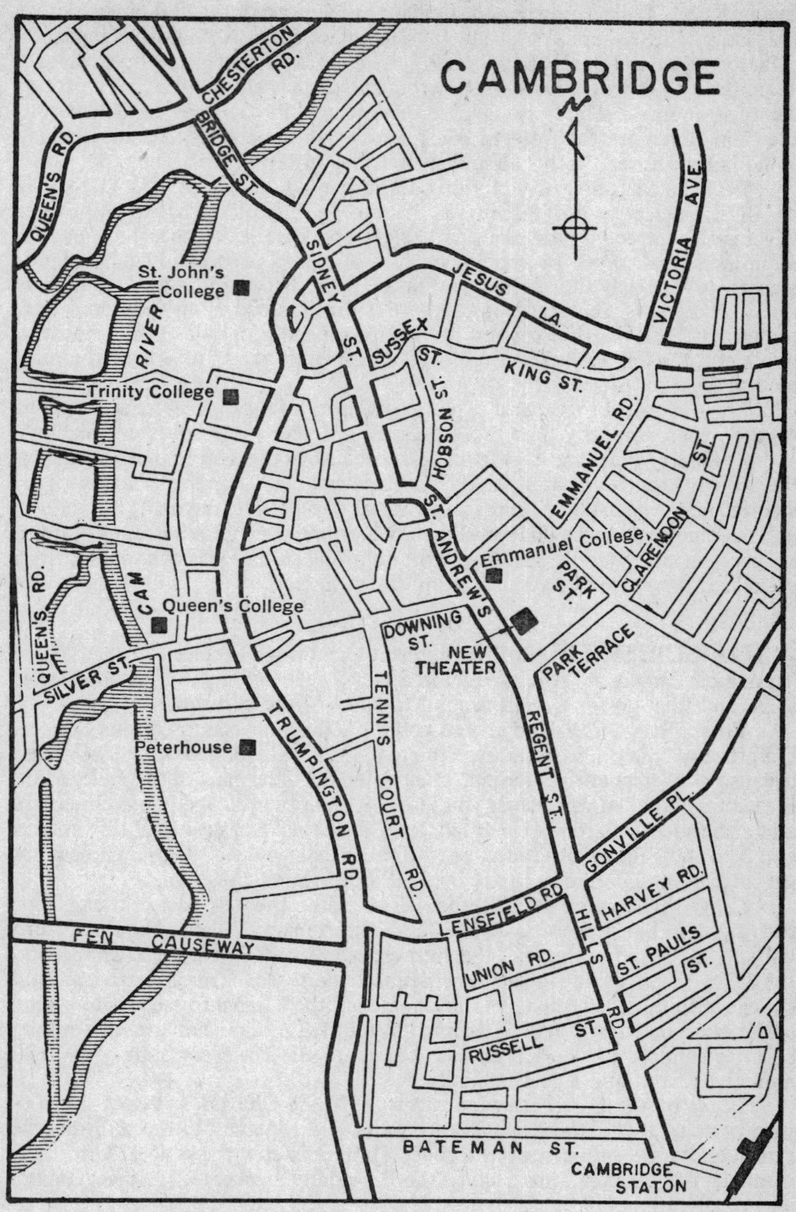
CAMBRIDGE
CHESTERTON RD.
QUEEN'S RD.
BRIDGE ST.
SIDNEY ST.
JESUS LA.
VICTORIA AVE.
St. John's College
RIVER
SUSSEX
ST.
KING ST.
Trinity College
HOBSON ST.
EMMANUEL RD.
ST. ANDREW'S
Emmanuel College
CLARENDON ST.
PARK ST.
QUEEN'S RD.
CAM
Queen's College
DOWNING ST.
NEW THEATER
PARK TERRACE
SILVER ST.
TENNIS COURT RD.
REGENT ST.
Peterhouse
TRUMPINGTON RD.
GONVILLE PL.
HARVEY RD.
LENSFIELD RD
HILLS RD.
FEN CAUSEWAY
ST. PAUL'S ST.
UNION RD.
RUSSELL ST.
BATEMAN ST.
CAMBRIDGE STATON

bookshops . . . daffodils blowing in the meadows . . . carol singing on Christmas Eve in King's College Chapel . . . dancing till sunrise at the end of the school year balls . . . the sounds of Elizabethan melodies from the throats of madrigal balladeers . . . the purchase of horse brasses at a corner in the open market . . . narrow lanes where Darwin, Newton, and Cromwell also trod . . . a protest demonstration . . . The Backs, where the lawns of the colleges sweep down to the Cam River . . . the tattered black robe of an upperclassman, rebelliously hanging by a thread to his shoulder as it flies in the wind.

We're in the university city of Cambridge, which, along with Oxford, is one of the ancient seats of learning in Britain. The city on the banks of the Cam River is also the county town of Cambridgeshire, 55 miles northeast of London, 80 miles from Oxford. In many ways, the story of Oxford and Cambridge is similar, particularly the age-old conflict between "town and gown" (impoverished scholars vs. rent-gouging landlords). But Oxford is an industrial city, sheltering a thriving life beyond the campus. Cambridge has some industry, too. Yet if the university were removed, I suspect it would revert to an unpretentious market town.

There is much to see and explore in Cambridge, so give yourself time to wander, even aimlessly. For those pressed, I'll offer more specific directions.

A Word of Warning: Unfortunately, because of the disturbances caused by the influx of tourists to the university, Cambridge has regretfully had to limit visitors, and even exclude them from various parts of the university altogether, and in some cases, even charge a small fee for entrance. Small groups of up to six persons are generally admitted with no problem, and you can inquire from your local tourist office about visiting hours here.

A SELF-GUIDED TOUR: The center of Cambridge is closed to cars. There is good parking at the Anchor Pub in Silver Street, so why not leave your car there and then go for a walk around to some of the colleges?

Cross Silver Street Bridge, and you'll see the entrance to Queens College. Go into the college, crossing over the mathematical wooden bridge, so called because of its geometrical design. Then enter the older part of the college into the center of a quadrangle, and you'll see much of the Elizabethan architecture and also the doors around the quad, leading to the "staircases" of tiny studies and bedrooms for undergraduates within the college itself. Those who cannot get an accommodation here are boarded out around the city.

Leave through the fine Elizabethan arch into the new part of the college; turn right and, just past the Chapel, take the doorway open to the road. Turn left and at the end of the road the archway leads to King's College Chapel and the college. Just inside is a very well-defined "staircase." This is also a beautiful college with lawns sweeping to the Cam. Visit the Chapel to see the *Adoration of the Magi* by Rubens hanging over the High Altar. You can attend evensong at King's almost every night at 5:30. There are services every Sunday at 10:30 a.m., 3:30 p.m., and again at 6 p.m.

Leave by the Porter's Lodge and walk to the Church Tower of the 800-year-old parish church of St. Edward Saint and Martyr. Within its walls the reformers of the 16th century preached and ministered the gospel. Turn right into the main Market Square where there is a daily market for fruit, vegetables, and other produce.

Leave on Wheeler Street, leading on to Benet Street. Opposite St. Benet's Church in St. Benet's Lane you will see two doors leading to a passage which will bring you to the **Eagle Pub** on the grounds of Corpus Christi, arguably the only galleried inn in Cambridge. It is little known by visitors but much frequented by locals. The usual bar snacks are provided to mop up the beer.

Totter back to Benet Street and you'll be back where you started at the Anchor where you left your car. Without stopovers, this walk will take you about one hour of leisurely observation.

This tour is best done when the colleges aren't in session. Otherwise, many colleges at term time are, of course, closed in the morning.

GUIDED TOURS OF THE CAMBRIDGE COLLEGES: Leisurely walking tours of about two hours' duration take place daily from April to early November (Saturday only in winter). They start from the **Tourist Information Centre,** Wheeler Street (tel. Cambridge 358977). With a qualified and knowledgeable guide you will explore the small streets and courts of the major colleges. These are places of work, and at term time some of the buildings may be in use or closed. Kings College Chapel, for example, may be in use for a choir practice. Only Fellows and their guests may walk on the grass, and staircases lead to the accommodations of students and are private. The cost of these tours is £1.10 ($1.93) per person. Tours vary in direction, but always contain as much of interest as is available at the time. Departure times also vary according to demand, but there are usually four departures a day during July to September when the colleges are "down" in any case.

CAMBRIDGE UNIVERSITY: Oxford University predates the one at Cambridge. But in the early 13th century scholars began coming up to Cambridge. The choice of the market town as a seat of learning just happened, perhaps coming about because a core of important masters, dissatisfied with Oxford, elected to live near the fens. Eventually, Cambridge won partial recognition from Henry III, rising and slumping with the approval or disdain of subsequent English monarchs. In all, the University of Cambridge consists of 29 colleges for men, most of which are for both men and women. But if you have time for only one sight, then make it:

King's College Chapel

The teenage Henry VI founded the college on King's Parade in 1441. But most of its buildings today are from the 19th century. The Perpendicular chapel is not only its crowning glory, but one of the architectural gems in England inherited from the Middle Ages. The chapel, owing to the altogether chaotic vicissitudes of English kings, wasn't completed until the early years of the 16th century.

Its most characteristic features are its magnificent fan vaulting, all of stone, and its Great Windows, most of which were fashioned by Flemish artisans between 1515 and 1531 (the west window, however, dates from the late Victorian period). The stained glass, in hues of blues, reds, and ambers, reflects biblical stories. The long range of the windows, reading from the first on the north side at the west end, right around the chapel back to the first on the south side, tell the story of the birth of the Virgin, the Annunciation, the Birth of Christ, the Life, Ministry, and Death of Christ, the Resurrection, the Ascension, the Acts of the Apostles, and the Assumption. The upper range contains Old Testament parallels to the New Testament stories—that is, the logic of the windows derives from the story of Christ. The rood screen is from the early 16th century. Henry James called King's College Chapel "the most beautiful in England."

It is open during vacation time on weekdays from 9 a.m. to 5 p.m., and on Sunday from 10:30 a.m. to 5 p.m. During term time, the public is welcomed to choral services which are at 5:30 p.m. on weekdays (service said on Monday) and at 10:30 a.m. and 3:30 p.m. on Sunday. In term the chapel is open to visitors from 9 a.m. to 3:45 p.m. on weekdays, from 2 to 3 p.m. and from the end of evensong (approximately 4:30) to 5:45 p.m. on Sunday. The chapel may be closed at other times of the year for recording sessions. Closed December 26 to January 1.

Peterhouse

This college on Trumpington Street is visited largely because it is the oldest seat of learning at Cambridge, having been founded as early as 1284. The founding father was Hugo de Balsham, bishop of Ely. Of the original buildings, only the Hall remains, but this was restored in the 19th century and now contains stained-glass windows by William Morris. Old Court was constructed in the 15th century, but refaced in 1754, and the chapel dates from 1632. Parties of not more than 12 at a time may visit the college between 1 and 5 p.m. Ask at the porter's lodge.

Trinity College

On Trinity Street, Trinity College, the largest at Cambridge (not to be confused with Trinity Hall), was founded in 1546 by Henry VIII from a number of smaller colleges that had existed on the site. The Great Court is the most spacious court in Cambridge, built when Thomas Nevile was master. Sir Christopher Wren designed the library. This college has Sir Isaac Newton, Lord Byron, and Prince Charles among its former members. For admission to the college, apply at the porter's lodge or telephone Cambridge 358201 for information.

Emmanuel College

On St. Andrew's Street, Emmanuel was founded in 1584 by Sir Walter Mildmay, chancellor of the exchequer to Elizabeth I. John Harvard, founder of that university, studied here. With its attractive gardens, it makes for a good stroll. You might visit the chapel designed by Sir Christopher Wren in 1677. The chapel is open daily, except when in use, from 9:30 a.m. to 12:15 p.m. and from 2 to 6 p.m. The gardens and paddock are open daily until dusk.

Queens' College

On Queens' Lane, Queens' College (tel. Cambridge 65511) is considered by some old Cambridgeites as the loveliest in the architectural galaxy. Dating back to 1448, it was founded, then refounded, by two English queens—one the wife of Henry VI, the other the wife of Edward IV. Its second cloisters are the most interesting, flanked with the half-timbered President's Lodge, dating from the first half of the 16th century. The college may be visited during the day. An admission fee of about 25p (44¢) is charged and a short printed guide issued. Normally, individual visitors are admitted between 2 and 4:30 p.m. only, but during July, August, and September the college is also open to visitors from 10:15 a.m. to 12:45 p.m. Entry and exit is by the Old Porters' Lodge in Queens' Lane only. The college is closed between mid-May and mid-June. The Old Hall and chapel are normally open to the public when not in use.

St. John's College

On St. John's Street, the college was founded in 1511 by Lady Margaret, mother of Henry VII. A few years earlier she had founded Christ's College. Before her intervention, an old monk-run hospital had stood on the site of St. John's. The impressive gateway bears the Tudor coat-of-arms, and Second Court is a fine example of late Tudor brickwork. But its best-known feature is the Bridge of Sighs, crossing the Cam, built as late as the 19th century, patterned after the bridge in Venice. It connects the older part of the college with New Court, a Gothic revival, on the opposite bank, from which there is an outstanding view of the famous Backs. Wordsworth was an alumnus of this college. The Bridge of Sighs is open from October till Easter but is best viewed from the neighboring Wren Bridge. The chapel is open from 10 a.m. to noon and 2 to 4 p.m. daily except Monday. The college is closed to visitors from late April until early June.

Other College Sights

The preceding form only a representative selection of some of the more interesting-to-visit colleges. **Magdalene College** on Magdalene Street was founded in 1542; **Pembroke College** on Trumpington Street was founded in 1347; **Christ's College** on St. Andrew's Street was founded in 1505; and **Corpus Christi College** on Trumpington Street dates from 1352. Only someone planning to anchor into Cambridge for a long time will get around to them. Magdelene is open daily from 9 a.m. to 6:30 p.m.; Pembroke daily till dusk; Christ's College weekdays. For Corpus Christi times, inquire at the porter's lodge.

Colleges aren't the only thing to see in Cambridge, as you'll assuredly agree if you explore the following attractions:

THE FITZWILLIAM MUSEUM: On Trumpington Street, near Peterhouse, this museum was the gift of the Viscount Fitzwilliam, who in 1816 gave Cambridge University his paintings and rare books, along with £100,000 to build the house in which to display them. He thereby knowingly or unknowingly immortalized himself. Other gifts have since been bequeathed to the museum, and now it is one of the finest in England. It is noted for its porcelain, old prints, archeological relics, and oils (works by such masters as Titian and Veronese). The museum is open weekdays from 10 a.m. to 5 p.m., Sunday from 2:15 p.m. till 5 p.m. However, only half of the exhibits are open in the morning, the other half in the afternoon, owing to the lack of staff. Closed Monday, Good Friday, and December 24 to January 1 inclusive. Admission is free.

GREAT ST. MARY'S: Great St. Mary's (tel. Cambridge 350914), opposite King's College Chapel on King's Parade, is the university church. It is built on the site of an 11th-century church, but the present building dates largely from 1478. It was closely associated with events of the Reformation. The cloth which covered the hearse of King Henry VII is on display in the church. A fine view of Cambridge may be obtained from the top of the tower.

BOAT RENTALS: Scudamore's, on Granta Place, by the Anchor Pub, has been in business since 1910. Costs are by the hour—£3 ($5.25) for a punt, £2.80 ($4.90) for a rowboat, and £2.60 ($4.55) for a canoe. A deposit is required, £15 ($26.25), refundable if you don't wreck the boat.

Upriver you can go all the way to Grantchester, a distance of about two miles, made so famous by Rupert Brooke. Downstream you pass along the Backs behind the colleges of the university.

READER'S BOATING SUGGESTION: "In summer, some enterprising undergraduates offer a delightful combination luncheon and boat tour of the campus called the **Picnic Punt,** with embarkation point at the foot of the bridge over the Cam on Silver Street. My wife and I enjoyed a lunch served on the punt as we were slowly poled up and down the Cam along grassy banks lined with lots of holiday trippers and students enjoying the sun. Our waiter and punt propeller gave a running commentary on the history of the college buildings and bridges we passed. We ate a lamb curry on rice, a side plate of celery and carrots, and strawberries in Devonshire cream. Lunch is served at your departure on plywood planks attached to the gunwales, after you are comfortably seated on pillows in the punt. The price is £4.50 ($7.88) per person for all—punt ride, lunch, and tour comments. Wine is not provided, but the helpful woman doing the reservations steered us to a good wineseller who supplied us with a splendid Vouvray. The trip lasts 50 minutes and is a wonderful experience" (Gordon Beck, Olympia, Wash.).

BICYCLE RENTALS: **Geoff's Bicycle Hire,** 164 Mill Rd. (tel. Cambridge 249374), and **University Cycle and Electrical Shop,** 9 Victoria Ave. (tel. Cambridge 355517), have bicycles for rent in the university city for £2 ($3.50) per day or else £5 ($8.75) per week. A deposit of £20 ($35) is required.

PERSONALIZED TOURS: The person to know if you're in the Cambridge area is **Mrs. Isobel Bryant,** who runs Heritage Tours from her 200-year-old cottage, Manor Cottage, Swaffham Prior, Cambridge (tel. Newmarket 741440). A highly qualified expert on the area, she will arrange tours, starting from, say, your Cambridge hotel to Saffron Walden, Thaxted, and Audley End, for example, or to the U.S. military cemetery at Madingley, then Ely, Anglesey Abbey, and the lovely timbered villages of Suffolk.

Lunch is often organized in beautifully furnished private manor houses, so that you have the chance of meeting local people. The day's trip costs around £35 ($61.25) for three people. Lunch and admission charges are extra—probably about £6 ($10.50) per person more.

Mrs. Bryant can also arrange accommodations with local families in their lovely country houses. The charges range from £16 ($28) to £30 ($52.50) for two persons per night in double rooms with private baths, these tariffs including a full English breakfast. Often dinner with the family can be arranged at around £6 ($10.50) per person, including wine.

There are also walking tours around the colleges of Cambridge and, if you can make up a party of 15 or more persons, a fascinating tour of Newmarket, center of the horse-racing industry. On that tour, you visit a racing stable, sales paddock, and the elegant rooms of the Jockey Club, headquarters of racing since 1771, as well as a stud farm and other places of interest connected with racing. A whole day costs £10 ($17.50) per person; a half day, £6 ($10.50). If you want lunch arranged at a private house with Cordon Bleu cookery, the cost is around £5 ($8.75) per person.

ACCOMMODATIONS: In the center of the city are numerous buildings and homes where the students live and eat, most of them conveniently within walking distance of the major attractions. The most concentrated group of little B&B guest houses is on Jesus Lane. The tree-lined street runs about three blocks, along one side of the gardens and buildings of Jesus College, founded in 1496. It should be pointed out, however, that Jesus Lane isn't a "lane," but a busy street all night with cars accelerating from a stop. Try for the back rooms.

The **Tourist Office** (tel. Cambridge 358977) is at Wheeler Street, opposite the Arts Theatre and behind the Guildhall on Market Place. The staff there will give you information on available accommodations, as they run a booking service, charging 60p ($1.05) per person for finding a room in or around Cambridge.

During the vacation periods, there are rooms available for tourists, but most of them are used by students in term time. If you have no reservation, check your luggage and go directly to the beginning of Jesus Lane on Chesterton Road, knocking on front doors as you proceed. I'll survey the pick of the accommodations there, then include scattered B&B choices in other parts of Cambridge.

Miss M. A. Sampson, 4 Malcolm St. (tel. 0223/353069), can accommodate tourists only when her university students go on vacation: that is, from mid-June till the end of September. Her home is a convenient place at which to stay, in the center of Cambridge, just off Jesus Lane. Her B&B rate ranges from £7.50 ($13.13) per person, and you'll be nestling down at one of the finest lodging choices on this guest-house-filled lane. Miss Sampson's home lies just past All Saints' Church.

Portugal Street is only a stone's throw from the most interesting colleges and the center of Cambridge—yet the street is a good choice for finding an inexpensive B&B. **Mrs. Clough,** 22 Portugal St. (tel. Cambridge 357769), opens her private home to paying guests. She charges £7.50 ($13.13) per person for B&B. Normally modest, she does pride herself on the abundance of her English breakfast. The extensively modernized rooms she offers are small and tidy, containing comfortable beds. All units contain basins with hot and cold running water. Mrs. Clough has a large and varied collection of antique dolls, and she is also quite an authority on monumental brass rubbing and where to find the best ones around Cambridge. Just ask.

If she doesn't have room for you, you might try the nearby house of **Mrs. Holland,** 9 Portugal St. (tel. Cambridge 357350). This is the sister of the previously recommended Mrs. Clough. So as not to compete, Mrs. Holland charges the same rate for B&B as her sister—£7.50 ($13.13) per person nightly. Her rooms are pleasantly furnished, and her breakfast is a full English one. If you lodge here, you'll be near the Cam where students go punting.

Ayeone Cleave Guest House, 95 Gilbert Rd. (tel. Cambridge 63387), is a well-run guest house in a quiet part of the city with its own private car park. All the well-furnished rooms are centrally heated and contain hot and cold running water, television, radio, and razor sockets. Showers are available. Rates, which include a full English breakfast, are £10 ($17.50) in a single, £17.50 ($30.63) in a double or twin. A twin with private shower is £19.50 ($34.13), and with private shower and toilet, £21 ($36.75). Tea, coffee, cold drinks, and sandwiches are served on request. Your hostess is Mrs. E. Humphries, who is helpful in providing information.

Mr. and Mrs. D. Griffiths, 51 Jesus Lane (tel. Cambridge 66801), welcome you into their home, charging £7.50 ($13.13) per person for B&B. They offer clean, comfortable rooms, with convenient facilities. Although accommodation is limited during university terms, a room is always kept for transient guests.

Suffolk Guest House, 69 Milton Rd. (tel. Cambridge 352016), was built as the home of a well-known Cambridge doctor, but it has been converted into a contemporary guest house owned by Mr. and Mrs. Ball. Although they have retained some of the qualities of the old house, they have installed such modern conveniences as central heating, razor points, and TV sets in the rooms. Some units have private bath/shower. You can bathe or shower at no extra cost, other than the £9.50 ($16.63) per person charged for B&B. The helpful hosts will also offer you their garden in summer for tea or coffee, and if given notice will serve you a dinner Monday through Thursday. Children up to 10 years of age sharing a double room with their parents are granted reductions.

The Bridge Guest House, 151–153 Hills Rd. (tel. Cambridge 247942), is owned and run by Mr. and Mrs. Dalla-Libera, who also manage a popular restaurant in Cambridge, La Taverna. Their guest house stands a mile from their restaurant, and they offer rooms that are comfortable and agreeable. Fully licensed, their establishment charges from £7.50 ($13.13) to £8.50 ($14.88) in a single, the cheaper price for guests ordering the continental breakfast, the higher tab for the English breakfast. A double costs from £16 ($28), and three persons are housed in one room for £20 ($35). A family room, suitable for four, is also rented for £20 too. You can also order a three-course evening meal for £4.50 ($7.88).

If you have a car, you might want to try **Mrs. Carol Noble,** 22 St. Margaret's Rd., Girton (tel. Cambridge 276103), who does B&B. Her delightful home is only a mile from the center of Cambridge, offering a good night's lodging along with tranquility on a tree-lined avenue only a stone's throw from Girton College. For the charge of £7.50 ($13.13), Mrs. Noble includes a large breakfast. She is also pleased to help plan day trips to neighboring towns and villages, as she knows the area well. To reach the home from the center of Cambridge, take the A1307 north, turning off in the direction of Girton.

READERS GUEST HOUSE SELECTIONS: "The **Belle Vue Guest House,** 33 Chesterton Rd. (tel. Cambridge 351859), is a typical B&B house that charges from £7.50 ($13.13) to £8.50 ($14.88) per person. The plumbing is in hall bathrooms off each landing. Particular advantages include: (1) when approached from the North Chesterton Road, the house can be reached without having to battle Cambridge traffic; (2) the Belle Vue is close to the colleges, city center, and gardens which can be visited on foot; (3) it provides off-street parking; and (4) there are other overnight hotels on Chesterton Road should Belle Vue not be able to accommodate you" (Margaret E. Moody, Carmel, Calif.). . . . "At the residence of **Mrs. T. V. Smith,** 38 Montague Rd. (tel. Cambridge 353757), we had a beautiful room with constant hot and cold water and use of the bath with a shower from 9:30 a.m. to 10:30 p.m. The food was marvelous, the host great. I would recommend her residence to anyone, and the price is £6 ($10.50) per person a night for B&B" (Mr. and Mrs. B. J. Bentley, Toronto, Ont., Canada). . . . "We recommend the B&B home of **Mr. and Mrs. Fordham,** 2 Tenison Rd. (tel. Cambridge 64081). We had a beautiful room filled with antiques and one of the best English breakfasts on our trip in the dining room in front of a window overlooking a flower garden. The Fordhams are gracious hosts, and the price of £8 ($14) per person is a bargain. They recommended that we eat in the restaurant across the street, and we found it to serve the best Cantonese food we had eaten outside of Hong Kong, an unexpected treat for us both. The house is a nice walk from the railway station and the city center" (Rosemary and Bob Knox, Bethel Park, Penna.).

"At **Warkworth House,** Warkworth Terrace (tel. Cambridge 363682), a young couple, Timothy and Kathleen Collins, have joined two houses together to make accommodations for more than 30 persons in their bed-sitters (two singles, five twins, two doubles, three family rooms). The rooms are large, airy, heated, and well furnished, all with hot and cold water. The charge is £8 ($14) per person, including an English breakfast, baths, heat, service, and VAT. It's best to telephone two or three days ahead. The house is just off Parker's Piece and convenient to points of interest" (Joseph Horrell, Lexington, Va.). . . . "We spent five weeks at Mrs. Marie Byerley's **Homestead,** 23 Tenison Ave. (tel. Cambridge 362854), and we would have been hard put to find a B&B spot of greater cleanliness, quiet, comfort, or convenience (a ten-minute walk to the center of town, three minutes to the rail station). Mrs. Byerley and her daughter Sylvia did everything they could to make our stay a happy one. A full English breakfast is served and will send you humming through the day. The rate of £7.50 ($13.13) covers everything, including facilities for having tea in your room" (L. Davidson, Charlottesville, Va.). . . . **"Mrs. Leverett's B&B,** 55 Jesus Lane (tel. Cambridge 59439), was one of our most pleasant experiences. Mr. and Mrs. Leverett are helpful hosts. Mrs. Leverett keeps students from Jesus College during the school term and other guests in July and August. The rooms are lovely, and the number of guests is small enough so there is no 'traffic problem' for the shower and toilet facilities. The house is conveniently situated, and there is nearby parking. Mrs. Leverett serves a full breakfast in a cheerful breakfast room. The rate is £7.50 ($13.13) per person per night" (Mrs. K. L. Kiler, Trenton, N.J.).

WHERE TO EAT: Trinity Street Restaurant, 14 Trinity St. (tel. Cambridge 356845), is housed in a building reputedly the oldest in the university city. This black-and-white timbered facade conceals three restaurants. On the first floor the Carvery is Tudor style in decor, and a white-hatted chef will carve what you want from a large succulent joint of roast beef, pork, or turkey. You'll first be served an appetizer, such as soup or smoked mackerel, then help yourself to the vegetables (quite a selection). Including a dessert from the trolley, the total cost is about £4.50 ($7.88). You can wash it down with beer or wine.

In the bargain range, the **Granary** in the cellars advertises some eight or more hot dishes, such as beef casserole, goulash, curried lamb, and sweet-and-sour pork, all going for around £2 ($3.50). There are also snack dishes, quiches, and omelets for about £1.50 ($2.63), and the puddings and desserts go for around 75p ($1.31). The à la carte restaurant in the same building is more expensive. The Carvery is open Monday to Thursday from noon to 3 p.m. and 6 to 11 p.m.; Friday and Saturday from noon to 3 p.m. and 6 p.m. to midnight. The Granary is open from 10:30 a.m. to 10:30 p.m. daily, except Sunday when its hours are from 10:30 a.m. to 6 p.m.

Varsity Restaurant, 35 St. Andrew's St. (tel. Cambridge 56060). The Greek dishes offered here are eaten in a bare whitewashed room with black beams and pictures of boats and islands on the walls. Kebabs are served with rice and salad, and there are other Greek dishes along with some continental ones for less adventurous palates. A meal, including a glass of wine and coffee, will cost about £6 ($10.50). Service is fast and cheerful, and hours are Monday to Saturday from noon to 3 p.m. and from 5:30 to 11 p.m.

Martin's Coffee House, 4 Trumpington St. (tel. Cambridge 361757), is just past the Fitzwilliam Museum. It's a small coffeehouse, but has high standards, offering some of the best filled sandwiches in Cambridge. Whole-meal rolls are filled with turkey, ham, beef, salad, cheese, and eggs, from 75p ($1.31) for a mouth-filling snack. Homemade cakes and doughnuts are 25p (44¢) each. You can also have steak-and-kidney pie and two vegetables, £1.75 ($3.06); casseroles, curries, pâtés, and omelets for around the same price. Desserts are 65p ($1.14), and fresh, good coffee, 35p (61¢). All marketing is done daily so everything is fresh and wholesome.

Pentagon and Roof Garden, 6 St. Edward's Passage (tel. Cambridge 59302), is a self-service restaurant above the Arts Theatre, which is open Monday through Saturday from 9:30 a.m. to 8 p.m. That is, the Roof Garden is. The Pentagon is open from noon to 2 p.m. and from 6 to 11 p.m. The Pentagon has become a meeting place for the leading lights in the English theater, and boasts a picture gallery of stars who have visited. You can sit in the sunshine on the Roof Garden for breakfast or lunch. The Pentagon has a cold buffet along with hot dishes. A meal here is possible for around £1.50 ($2.63), but more likely you will spend £3.50 ($6.13).

Strudel's Restaurant, University Pitt Club Building, Jesus Lane (tel. Cambridge 311678), occupies part of a building which was originally constructed as an elegant Turkish bath. Since 1866 it has been used by the exclusive University Pitt Club, a young gentlemen's dining club founded in memory of William Pitt. Part of the building, including the original club dining room, with its high ceiling, huge central glass dome, and oak paneling, is now Strudel's Restaurant. Tables are draped in white, with fresh flowers and candles. In colder weather, a large glowing fire makes for a warm, inviting atmosphere.

The restaurant is run by Christopher Ryan and his partner, Alan Boorman. Mr. Ryan, who likes everything fresh as much as possible, does most of the cooking, shopping in the market every day for vegetables. Although the à la carte menu is fairly expensive, these men serve a three-course lunch for £6.50 ($11.38) and a three-course dinner for £8.50 ($14.88). The restaurant specializes in continental dishes, often using old family recipes, many of which date back more than 100 years.

When available, fish and game, such as Sussex pheasant, are featured. The restaurant is closed Sunday but otherwise serves lunch daily from noon to 2:30 p.m. and dinner from 6 to 11 p.m. Reservations are necessary.

READER'S RESTAURANT SUGGESTION: "The **Corner House Restaurant** on King Street, between Jesus Lane and the marketplace and a five-minute walk from most of the colleges (tel. Cambridge 59962), is where the students go for a good, filling meal at the right price. The efficient waiter served my husband and me heaping portions of delicious food, and most dishes are priced right. Almost everything listed costs £2.25 ($3.94) or less. For example, fish and chips go for £1.65 ($2.89); roast chicken or lamb, vegetable, and chips costs £1.75 ($3.06); moussaka, mixed salad or vegetable, and chips are £1.60 ($2.80); and apple pie and ice cream costs 60p ($1.05). It's recommended for hearty meals for reasonable prices" (Roi-Ann Bettez, Lexington, Ky.).

ENTERTAINMENT: An outstanding attraction in Cambridge is the **Arts Theatre,** 6 St. Edward's Passage, with its entrance on Peas Hill, fitted into a maze of lodging houses and shops. It provides Cambridge and the surrounding area with its most important theatrical events. Almost all of the leading stars of the British stage have performed here at one time or another. Call Cambridge 352000 to find out what's playing. Seats for most productions are £4 ($7) and £5 ($8.75).

Nearby, on Market Passage, you'll find the principal film house, the **Arts Cinema,** which usually has three separate showings daily. Seats for the evening performances are bookable by telephone Cambridge 352001.

2. Ely

The top attraction in the fen country, outside of Cambridge, is **Ely Cathedral.** The small city of Ely lies 70 miles from London, but only 16 miles north of Cambridge. Ely used to be known as the Isle of Ely, until the surrounding marshes and meres were drained, forcing the sea to recede. The last stronghold of Saxon England, Ely was defended by Hereward the Wake, until his capitulation to the Normans in 1071.

ELY CATHEDRAL: The near-legendary founder of the cathedral (tel. Ely 2078) was Ethelfreda, the wife of a Northumbrian king, who established a monastery on the spot in 673. But the present structure dates from 1083. Seen for miles around, the landmark octagonal lantern tower is the crowning glory of the cathedral. A remarkable engineering achievement, it was erected in 1322, following the collapse of the old tower.

EAST ANGLIA
N
SKEGNESS
LINCOLN
BOSTON
GRANTHAM
WELLS
BLAKENEY
CROMER
NORTH WALSHAM
CAISTER
GREAT YARMOUTH
KING'S LYNN
NORWICH
NORFOLK
WISBECH
PETERBOROUGH
LOWESTOFT
NORTHAMPTON
THETFORD
BUNGAY
ELY
CAMBRIDGE
BEDENHAM
HUNTINGDON
ALDEBURGH
BURY ST. EDMUNDS
STOWMARKET
NEWMARKET
SUFFOLK
WOODBRIDGE
CAMBRIDGE
NEEDHAM MARKET
IPSWICH
CLARE
BEDFORD
SUDBURY
HARWICH
COLCHESTER
ESSEX
WITHAM
CLACTON ON SEA
HERTFORD
CHELMSFORD
HERTFORD
TILBURY
THAMES
GREATER
GRAYS
LONDON
MARGATE
CHATHAM
MAIDSTONE
KENT
EAST
SUSSEX
ENGLAND
WALES
LONDON
ENGLISH CHANNEL

You enter the cathedral through the beautiful Galilee West Door, a good representation of the Early English style of architecture. The already-mentioned lantern tower and the Octagon are the most notable features inside, but don't fail to visit the Lady Chapel. Although it's lost much of its decoration over the centuries, it still is a handsome example of the Decorated style, having been completed in the mid-14th century.

The city, really a market town, is interesting—at least momentarily so—as it seems to be living in the past. Nevertheless, the attractions of Cambridge are close by, too alluring for most visitors to want to spend much time in Ely, once they've experienced the lacelike cathedral. Still, here are my recommendations, which take in overnight guests should you succumb to the charm of Ely.

FOOD AND LODGING: **Nyton Guest House,** Barton Road (tel. Ely 2459), is an attractive twin-gabled guest house in a quiet residential sector of Ely, surrounded by a two-acre flower garden with lawn and trees. Additional beauty is gained by the adjoining 18-hole golf course with uninterrupted views over a wide area of the Fenland. Arthur and Rosalyn Setchell, the joint owners, are rightly proud of their guest book list of pages and pages of pleased former clients who attest to the hospitality offered at Nyton. Only B&B is provided. A double room with shower/toilet costs £20 ($35) per night, although showerless doubles go for £18 ($31.50). A single room rents for £11 ($19.25), all these tariffs including a full English breakfast. Each bedroom has an electric kettle with the materials for an early-morning tea. Barton Road is easily accessible from the cathedral and railway station. It's on the A142 Ely–Newmarket road, off the Ely road (A10).

The **Old Fire Engine House,** St. Mary's Street (tel. Ely 2582), opposite St. Mary's Church, is one of the finer restaurants in East Anglia, worth a detour. It enjoys an interesting setting, in a complex of buildings with an art gallery. The restaurant was converted from a fire station, and it has a walled garden. It is open for lunch from 12:30 to 2 p.m. and for dinner from 7:30 till 9 p.m. (except Sunday). Reservations are required.

All the good English cooking is the result of the staff, a harmonious combination of unusual people who really care about food preparation. Food materials are all fresh. The menu is surprisingly large and varied, including various soups such as "lovage" (in season only). Main courses are likely to include such seasonal and other dishes as hot game pie, eel pie, pigeon casserole in red wine, casserole pheasant, jugged hare, and beef braised in beer. Expect to pay from £9 ($15.75) for a complete meal. Lunches are about £1 ($1.75) less. In summer, you can dine outside in the garden and also order a cream tea.

A TOUR TO GRIME'S GRAVES: On the B1108, off the main A1065 from Swaffham to Mildenhall road east of Ely, you can visit **Grime's Graves.** This is well worth the short detour, as it is the largest group of Neolithic flint mines in the country. This is fir-wooded country with little population, and it's easy to imagine yourself transported back to ancient times.

The mines are well signposted, and you soon find yourself at a small parking lot presided over by a bearded enthusiast and his aging Labrador. Because the mines have no head machinery and are spread around a common area, they are all securely enclosed. But on your arrival the custodian will open up one or several of the shafts, allowing you to enter ancient Britain.

Climb down the ladder of the pit and imagine what must have been going on even before the time of the Anglo-Saxons. Restoration has been carried out during the intervening years, and it is now possible to see where work took place and, if you're lucky, you may find a worked flint of your own to present to the custodian. He has a vast knowledge of the working methods and the implements used in those far-off days.

The mines are close to the air force bases so well known to countless American air crews during World War II. The place is open for most of the year from 9:30 a.m. to 4 p.m. (longer in summer), charging adults an admission of 40p (70¢); children pay 25p (44¢).

AN AIRCRAFT MUSEUM: The **Imperial War Museum** (tel. Cambridge 833963), on the A505 Newmarket–Royston road, is housed approximately at Duxford Airfield, the former Battle of Britain station. In airport hangars which date from World War I, you'll find a huge collection of historic civil and military aircraft, including the B-17 Flying Fortress, the Super Sabre, and Concorde 01, Britain's preproduction specimen of the controversial jet. Other exhibits include midget submarines, British and German tanks, and a variety of field artillery pieces, plus such additions as a P-51 Mustang and a prototype TSR-2. The museum is open daily from mid-March to the first week in November, from 11 a.m. to 5:30 p.m. Admission is £1.20 ($2.10) for adults, 60p ($1.05) for children, and parking is free.

Duxford was also a U.S. Eighth Air Force fighter station in World War II. There are now more than 70 aircraft on display, including the only B-29 Superfortress in Europe, plus a BE2c and an RE8 from World War I. Other exhibits include a giant 140-ton coastal artillery gun from Gibraltar and a special historical display on the U.S. Eighth Air Force in World War II.

ESSEX

Even though it borders London, and is heavily industrialized in places, Essex still contains unspoiled rural areas and villages. Most motorists pass through it on the way to Cambridge. What they find, after leaving Greater London, is a land of rolling fields. In the east are many seaside towns and villages, as Essex opens onto the North Sea.

The major city is Colchester, in the east, known today for its oysters and roses. Fifty miles from London, it was the first Roman city in Britain, the oldest recorded town in the kingdom. It's a rather dull-appearing city today, although parts of its Roman fortifications remain. A Norman castle has been turned into a museum, containing a fine collection of Roman Britain. Among the former residents of Colchester were King Cole, immortalized in the nursery rhyme, and Cunobelinus, the warrior king, known to Shakespearean scholars as "Cymbeline."

However, Colchester is not in the pathway of most visitors, so I have concentrated instead on three tiny villages in the western part of Essex—Saffron Walden, Thaxted, and Finchingfield, all three representative of the best of the shire. You can explore all of them quite easily on your way to Cambridge or on your return trip to London. Roughly, they lie anywhere from 25 to 30 miles south of the university city.

3. Thaxted

Some 43 miles north of London, the Saxon town of Thaxted sits on the crest of a hill. It contains the most beautiful small church in England, whose graceful spire can be seen for miles around. Its bells are heard throughout the day, ringing out special chimes to parishioners who attend their church seriously. Dating back to 1340, the church is a nearly perfect example of religious architecture.

Thaxted was well known to newspaper and magazine readers because of the late iconoclastic Conrad Noel, the so-called Red Vicar.

During the summer, folk dancing is performed by the townspeople, both in and out of the church. The London Philharmonic Orchestra comes up to play. The vicar has encouraged the church to use music, and you can hear both the old and the experimental. The denizens of Thaxted are divided about the activities of the church, but one thing they like: their town is alive and flourishing because of it.

Thaxted also has a number of well-preserved Elizabethan houses and a wooden-pillared Jacobean Guildhall.

FOOD AND LODGING: The **Swan Hotel,** Watling Street (tel. Thaxted 830321), is a 14th-century coaching inn, right in the middle of everything. From several of the bedroom windows, you can see the church and have a box seat if a procession should pass by. For many centuries, the townspeople have patronized the Swan for drinks and gossip. It is owned by Alma and Sam Carter, who respect the heritage of the inn. Singles begin at £10 ($17.50), rising to £18.50 ($32.38), according to location and facilities. Doubles range from £15 ($26.25) for the simple bedrooms, all the way to £37($64.75) for the chambers with private baths. If you're just passing through for the day, you may want to consider the three-course lunch for £5 ($8.75), plus VAT, consisting, say, of cream of mushroom soup, roast leg of pork with apple sauce, and a lemon mousse with cream for dessert. You can also have a three-course dinner from £8.50 ($14.88), plus VAT.

The **Recorder's House,** Town Street (tel. Thaxted 830438), near the Guildhall, was built in 1450 and is believed to have incorporated part of the medieval Thaxted Manor House. It derived its name from the recorder who used to live there, collecting taxes for the crown. Apparently, there were objections to these taxes, as the winding staircase was built with steps that pitch outward, so that an attacking swordsman would be thrown off balance.

As you dine in front of an inglenook fireplace (where Edward IV did when he brought his queen here for their honeymoon), you'll surely be pleased with the linenfold paneling, the carefully preserved wide oak floors, and the candlelight at night. The food, reflecting a continental influence, is the best in the area.

At luncheon, a three-course table d'hôte is offered from 12:30 to 2:30 p.m., for an inclusive price of £6 ($10.50). Dinner, from 7 to 9:30 p.m., includes fine steaks and seafood cooked on the charcoal broiler, in addition to the small but well-planned à la carte menu. Prices begin at £10 ($17.50) for a three-course meal. Specials could include roast haunch of venison. The owners, Michael and Maria Smith, try to serve as much homemade cookery as possible, including the bread rolls.

4. Saffron Walden

In the northwestern corner of Essex, a short drive from Thaxted, is the ancient market town of Walden, renamed Saffron Walden because of the fields of autumn crocus that used to grow around it. Although it lies only 44 miles from London, it still hasn't succumbed to heavy tourist traffic. Some residents of Cambridge, 15 miles to the north, escape to this old borough for their weekends.

One mile west of Saffron Walden (B1383 road) is **Audley End House** (tel. Saffron Walden 23207), considered one of the finest mansions in all of East Anglia. This Jacobean estate was begun in 1603, built on the foundation of a monastery. James I is reported to have said, "Audley End is too large for a king, though it might do for a Lord Treasurer." At the north end of the hall, a screen dates from the early 17th century and is considered one of the most ornamental in England. It is open from April to the end of September daily, except Monday, from 1 to 6 p.m., for an admission of £1.80 ($3.15) for adults, 90p ($1.58) for children.

Many of the houses in Saffron Walden are distinctive in England, in that the 16th- and 17th-century builders faced their houses with parget, a kind of plasterwork (sometimes made with cow dung) used for ornamental facades.

In accommodations, Saffron Walden innkeepers charge fairly high prices, but at least the buildings are romantic.

FOOD AND LODGING: **Cross Keys Hotel,** The High (tel. Saffron Walden 22207), opposite the post office, is a museum piece of black-and-white architecture built in 1449. Mr. and Mrs. Knott not only tend to locals at their neighborhood pub, but provide overnighters with pleasant and adequate lodgings in their upper-floor bedrooms. They have partially restored the interior, discovering an inglenook fireplace with a priest hole. In a single the charge is £12.50 ($21.88) without bath, rising to £14.50 ($25.38) with shower and toilet. Bathless doubles start at £20 ($35), going up to £25 ($43.75) with facilities, all these tariffs including a hearty English breakfast, service, and VAT.

One of the least expensive ways to eat in town is to patronize **The Take Away,** 10 George St., which is open lunchtime and evenings until midnight. It features such fare as beefburgers, curry chicken pie, pizza, barbecued chicken, and plaice or cod in bread crumbs. Prices of main dishes begin at 75p ($1.31). There is no sales tax on take-away food.

5. Finchingfield

This little village, only a short drive east of Thaxted, puts in a serious claim for being the model village of England. Even though you may have another personal favorite, you still must admit it's a dream village, surrounded by the quiet life of the countryside. If you're staying in either Saffron Walden or Thaxted, you might want to motor over here. It makes for an interesting jaunt.

FOOD AND LODGING: The **Manse** (tel. Great Dunmow 810306) is a small six-bedroom guest house, two hours from London Airport, overlooking the village pond in the center of one of the prettiest villages in Essex. All rooms have central heating, wall-to-wall carpeting, hot and cold running water, shaving points, and TV. Joe and Joan King bend every effort toward making their visitors comfortable and welcome. The cost, including VAT and a full English breakfast consisting of farm produce, is £10 ($17.50) per person per night.

The **Fox Inn** (tel. Great Dunmow 810151) is an attractive old pub with authentic pargeting (raised plaster) design on the facade. John and Joan Plester welcome all visitors and serve lunch from noon to 2 p.m., evening meals from 6 to 9 p.m. They provide a real fill-up for £3.50 ($6.13), including coffee. Their homemade soup costs 60p ($1.05), and steak-and-kidney pie goes for £2.50 ($4.38).

READERS' RESTAURANT SELECTION: "**Ye Olde Nosebag Restaurant,** on the Green in Finchingfield (tel. Great Dunmow 810258), is adjacent to the Fox Hotel and pub. Barry and Eileen Webb are an exceptional pair. The outstanding feature of the place is the food, which is gourmet quality. Prices are very moderate and middle range. Luncheon prices are from £2 ($3.50), and evening meals are available from £4.50 ($7.88). Since Barry was a pilot in World War II, he has the place dramatically decorated with one of the finest collections of color photographs of World War II aircraft I have encountered, and both the Webbs give their personal attention to customers in a most enjoyable atmosphere" (Ralph and Marjorie Berry, Santa Rosa, Calif.).

6. Dedham

Remember Constable's *Vale of Dedham?* In this little Essex village on the Stour River, you're in the heart of Constable country. Flatford Mill is only a mile farther down the river. The village, with its Tudor, Georgian, and Regency houses, is set in the midst of the water meadows of the Stour. Constable immortalized its church and tower. Dedham is right on the Essex-Suffolk border, and makes a good center for exploring both North Essex and the Suffolk border country.

In the village is **Castle House** (tel. Colchester 322127), home of Sir Alfred Munnings, the president of the Royal Academy (1944–1949), and painter extraordinaire of racehorses and animals. The house and studio contain sketches and other works, and are open from mid-May to mid-October, Wednesday and Sunday from 2 to 5 p.m., charging adults an admission of 50p (88¢); children pay 15p (26¢).

LODGING: Half a mile from the village, **Mrs. E. M. Watson,** Upper Park (tel. Colchester 323197) does B&B in her attractive private home, with fine views over Constable country. To reach her place, you pass Dedham church on your left, driving through the village and up the hill. Some 200 yards from the top of the hill by a letter box on the corner, turn right. Travel another 100 yards and Upper Park will be the first house on the right. Her charge for B&B is £9 ($15.75) per person nightly, or else £12 ($21) per person if you desire a private bath.

SUFFOLK

The easternmost county of England, a link in the four-county chain of East Anglia, is a refuge for artists, just as it was in the day of its famous native sons, Constable and Gainsborough. Many of the Suffolk landscapes have ended up on canvas.

A fast train can make it to East Suffolk from London in approximately an hour and a half. Still, its fishing villages, dozens of flint churches, historic homes, and national monuments remain relatively unvisited by overseas visitors.

The major towns of Suffolk are Bury St. Edmunds, the capital of West Suffolk, and Ipswich in the east, a port city on the Orwell River. But to capture the true charm of Suffolk, you must explore its little market towns and villages. Beginning at the Essex border, we'll strike out toward the North Sea, highlighting the most scenic villages as we move easterly across the shire:

7. Long Melford

Long Melford has been famous since the days of the early clothmakers. Like its sister, Lavenham (coming up), it grew in prestige and importance in the Middle Ages. Of the old buildings remaining, the village church is often called one of the glories of the shire. Along its High Street are many private homes erected by wealthy wool merchants of yore. While London seems far removed here, it is only 61 miles to the south.

EATING AND SLEEPING: If you're passing through, try to have a drink at the **Bull Hotel** (tel. Sudbury Suffolk 78494), one of the old (1540) inns of East Anglia. It was built by a wool merchant, and is considered Long Melford's finest and best-preserved building. Incorporated into the general inn is a medieval weavers' gallery and an open hearth with Elizabethan brickwork. The dining room is the outstanding portion of the Bull, with its high-beamed ceilings, trestle tables, settles, and handmade chairs, as well as a ten-foot fireplace. You can order a set three-course lunch for £7.75 ($13.56), a table d'hôte dinner for £9.95 ($17.41). Bar snacks, however, cost only £1.60 ($2.80) to £3.25 ($5.69), and they are served at both lunch and dinner. You're likely to get minced beef with beans or lasagne.

If you're staying over, consider one of the following recommendations:

The **Crown Inn,** Long Melford (tel. Sudbury 77666), is an attractive Suffolk inn on the main village road. Its restaurant and bedrooms, some with private baths, open onto a small but lovely garden kept private from the road by a high stone wall. It's owned and run by Jytte and Brian Sell, who will assure you of a warm personal welcome and will help you with your tour. While not ancient, the Crown has a country cottage flavor, with a sitting room for guests filled with comfortable armchairs and a fireplace. The charge for B&B in one of the pleasantly furnished, well-kept bedrooms is from £14 ($24.50) per person. Lunches cost from £4.25 ($7.44) and evening meals are from £10 ($17.50) à la carte or £6 ($10.50) table d'hôte. Real ale brewed locally is served from original hand pumps. Many fine wines are stored in the pre-Tudor cellars. One of the bars contains some of the finest theatrical stained glass in England, and many of the rooms are furnished with family antiques.

The **Black Lion,** Long Melford (tel. Long Melford 310302), is a typical corner village pub at the edge of the green, overlooking Melford Hall (which is National Trust property). Publicans Joe and Vera Westley offer homey, overnight accommodations as well as a saloon with lots of local color. It's easy to find, painted sage green, on the A1092 at the approaches to the Holy Trinity Church. Single rooms cost £8 ($14) and doubles run £15 ($26.25), plus VAT. Home-style cooking is featured in the bar and restaurant, and there is sometimes entertainment on Sunday evening. Old English teas are also served in the afternoon.

8. Lavenham

Once a great wool center, Lavenham is filled with a number of beautiful, half-timbered Tudor houses, washed in the characteristic Suffolk pink. Be sure to visit the church, with its landmark tower, built in the Perpendicular style. Lavenham lies only 7 miles from Sudbury, 11 from Bury St. Edmonds.

WHERE TO STAY: The **Angel Hotel,** Market Place (tel. Lavenham 247388), is the best little B&B in town. Mr. and Mrs. Graves welcome you, giving you a good bed and a bountiful breakfast the next morning, all at a cost of £12 ($21) per person nightly. It's also possible to order a three-course dinner from the inn's à la carte menu, paying from £4 ($7).

WHERE TO EAT: **Timbers Restaurant,** High Street (tel. Lavenham 247218), is popular with villagers and tourists alike. Sue and Paul Prentice provide well-cooked, traditional English-style meals for moderate prices. On Sunday a set dinner of roast beef and Yorkshire pudding goes for £5.50 ($9.63). Or in the evening you can try, for example, hare and venison pie, baked in whisky, for £5.60 ($9.80), or another specialty, beef casserole in ale at £4.20 ($7.35). If featured, I'd also suggest the stuffed quail (two) in a white grape sauce at £5.20 ($9.10). There is also an evening three-course table d'hôte with a choice of dishes, going for £5.50 ($9.63). On the regular luncheon menu during the week you can order such favorites as a homemade steak-and-kidney pie at £2.25 ($3.94) or a shepherd's pie at £2 ($3.50). The establishment is open from noon to 2:30 p.m. and 7 to 9:30 p.m. except Monday. In the quiet season they are often closed during the week, so it's best to phone and ask, as it merits a visit.

The **Old Tea Shop** in Lavenham (tel. Lavenham 247248) is a pink-washed, thatched cottage opposite the church with old leaded windows and coach lamps outside, along with low beams and wheelback chairs inside. Home-cooked lunches run from about £3 ($5.25), with fresh vegetables and well-seasoned pies and goulashes. Afternoon teas include scones with jam and cream, crumpets, and home-baked cakes.

Food and Lodging in the Environs

The **Bell Inn** at Kersey, off the A11 from Lavenham to Hadleigh, is in an attractive village with a watersplash right in the middle of the main street. Presided over by Geoffrey Slater, the Bell offers good bar snacks in the timbered bar with glinting horse brasses. In the grill room, lunches and dinners start with appetizers ranging from 75p ($1.31) to £3.95 ($6.91). Then there is a selection of main courses, good-tasting English fare such as steak-and-kidney pie (individually prepared), game pie, honey-roasted ham, or a filet steak. These dishes range from £2.50 ($4.38) to £5.75 ($10.06). The grill room operates during pub hours from 11:45 a.m. to 1:45 p.m. at lunchtime and from 7 to 9:30 p.m. in the evening.

Also off the A1141, on the B1115, is Chelsworth, which is typical of the villages of the area. There the **Peacock Inn,** The Street (tel. Bildeston 740758), spreads its feathers. The inn is run by Tony and Lorna Marsh. It dates back to the 14th century, a genuine oak timbered inn, with inglenook fireplaces and its own unique character. It stands just across the road from the banks of the Brett River. At lunchtime they have a hot and cold table with a fresh soup, cold ham, chicken curry, homemade game pie, and salads, a meal costing from £3 ($5.25). A three-course evening dinner, beginning at £6 ($10.50), is also featured. Seasonal specialties are afternoon teas (from May onward) and spit beef roasted over an open log fire in winter. Most of the food is homemade on the premises, and is available seven days a week.

The Peacock also offers five bedrooms, consisting of four doubles and one single, each with hot and cold running water. All are furnished traditionally. The cost is £12.50 ($21.88) per person.

9. Woodbridge and Aldeburgh

WOODBRIDGE: A yachting center, 12 miles from the North Sea, Woodbridge is a market town on a branch of the Deben River. Its best-known, most famous resident was Edward Fitzgerald, the Victorian poet and translator of the *Rubáiyàt* of Omar Khayyám (some critics consider the Englishman's version better than the original). The poet died in 1883 and was buried nearly four miles away at Boulge.

Woodbridge is a good base for exploring the East Suffolk coastline, particularly the small resort of Aldeburgh, noted for its Moot Hall. The town is also a good headquarters for excursions to Constable's Flatford Mill, coming up.

Where to Dine

The **Captain's Table,** 7 Quay St. (tel. Woodbridge 3145), is a good choice for intimate dining run by Tony Prentice. The food, mainly seafood, is well prepared, the atmosphere near the wharf colorful. The facade of this cozy nook is painted a Suffolk pink. The licensed restaurant serves a number of specialties, including rainbow trout. Many of the main dishes are traditionally English, especially beef cooked in beer and home-cooked ham and salad. Vegetables are extra, and desserts are rich and good-tasting. A three-course lunch is likely to cost around £4.25 ($7.44), a dinner going for £7.50 ($13.13). The day's specials are written on a blackboard—oysters, sea salmon, turbot in lobster sauce, plaice, sole, whatever.

The **Wine Bar,** 17 The Thoroughfare (tel. Woodbridge 2557), is an upstairs bar, whose managers, known to everyone as Richard and Sally, offer an alternative to the pub and restaurant. In a very laid-back atmosphere, you can select a dish to suit your pocket and appetite. Tasty and freshly made appetizers include locally smoked fish pâtés, Suffolk game terrines, and soups. Savory crêpes, game pies, and stuffed vegetables of the season, rounded off with homemade dessert, go for around £5 ($8.75). They insist, however, that you don't have to eat to visit the bar. Why not sit with a glass or bottle of one of the excellent house wines for £3.50 ($6.13) to £4 ($7) a bottle, a glass of beer, or a cup of coffee? The Wine Bar is open from noon to 2:30 p.m. and from 7 to 11 p.m. daily except Sunday and Monday (open in the evening on bank holiday Mondays).

ALDEBURGH: Pressed against the North Sea, Aldeburgh is a favorite retreat of the in-the-know traveler, even attracting some Dutch people who make the sea crossing via Harwich, the British entry point for those coming from the Hook of Holland. The late Benjamin Britten, the renowned composer *(Peter Grimes, The Rape of Lucretia),* lived in the area. But the festival he started at Aldeburgh in 1948 is held at Snape in June, a short drive to the west. A second festival, sponsored by Benson & Hedges, is now held in early autumn, featuring major international singers. Less than 100 miles from London, the resort was founded in Roman times, but legionnaires have been replaced by fishermen, boatmen, and fanciers of wildfowl. A bird sanctuary, Havergate Island, lies about six miles south of the town in the River Alde. Some take time out from their sporting activities (a golf course stretches 3½ miles) to visit the 16th-century **Moot Hall.** In August, the time of the regatta and a carnival, accommodations tend to be fully booked.

For our final look at Suffolk, we move south toward the Essex frontier to:

10. East Bergholt

The English landscape painter, John Constable (1776-1837), was born at East Bergholt. Near the village is **Flatford Mill,** subject of one of his most renowned canvases. The mill, in a scenic setting, was given to the National

Trust in 1943, and since has been leased to the Fields Studies Council for use as a residential college. Weekly courses are arranged on all aspects of the countryside and the environment, including landscape painting and photography. None of the buildings contains relics of Constable nor are they open to the general public, but students of all ages and capabilities are welcome to courses. Details may be obtained from the Warden, Flatford Mill Field Centre, East Bergholt, Colchester CO7 6UL (tel. Colchester 298283). Beside a bridge nearby sits a 16th-century cottage, where you can have drinks and sandwiches.

The final stop in our journey in East Anglia will be in the shire of Norfolk, with its famed Broads and the cathedral city of Norwich.

NORFOLK

Bounded by the North Sea, Norfolk is the biggest of the East Anglian counties. It's a low-lying area, with fens, heath, and salt marshes. An occasional dike or windmill makes you think you've been delivered to the Netherlands. One of the features of Norfolk is its network of Broads, miles and miles of lagoons, shallow in parts, connected by streams.

Summer sports people flock to Norfolk to hire boats for sailing or fishing. From Norwich, **Wroxham,** the capital of the Broads, is easily reached, only eight miles to the northeast. Motorboats regularly leave from the resort, taking parties on short trips. Some of the best scenery of the Broads is to be found on the periphery of Wroxham.

11. Norwich

Some 20 miles from the North Sea, Norwich still holds to its claim as the capital city of East Anglia. The county town of Norfolk, Norwich is a charming and historic city, despite encroachments by industry.

Norwich is the most important shopping center in East Anglia and is well provided with hotels and entertainment. In addition to its cathedral, there are more than 30 medieval parish churches built of flint.

There are many interesting old houses in the narrow streets and alleyways, and a big open-air market, busy every weekday, where fruit, flowers, vegetables, and other goods are sold from stalls with colored canvas ıoofs.

The **Assembly House** (see below) is a Georgian building (1752) restored to provide a splendid arts and social center. The **Maddermarket Theatre,** the home of the Norwich Players, is an 18th-century chapel converted by Nugent Monck in 1921 to an Elizabethan-style theater. On the outskirts of the city, the buildings of the University of East Anglia are strikingly modern in design and include the Sainsbury Centre (1978).

There is a **Tourist Information Centre** at Augustine Steward House at 14 Tombland, near the cathedral.

THE SIGHTS: In the center of Norwich, on a partly artificial mound, sits **Norwich Castle,** formerly the county gaol (jail). Its huge 12th-century Norman keep and the later prison buildings are used as a civic museum and headquarters of the county-wide Norfolk Museums Service (tel. Norwich 611277, ext. 279). The museum houses an impressive collection of pictures by artists of the Norwich School, of whom the most distinguished were John Crome, born 1768, and John Sell Cotman, born 1782. The castle museum also contains a fine collection of Lowestoft porcelain and Norwich silver. These are shown in the new rotunda. Two most recently completed displays are the Ecology Gallery, showing Norfolk's flora and fauna, and the Ceramics and Glass Gallery, including a fine collection of teapots. There are two sets of dioramas, one showing Norfolk wildlife in its natural setting, the other illustrating scenes of Norfolk life from the Old Stone Age to the early days of Norwich Castle.

The castle museum is open weekdays from 10 a.m. to 5 p.m. and on Sunday from 2 to 5 p.m. Adults pay 50p (88¢) from spring to September; otherwise, it's 25p (44¢). Children pay 5p (9¢) all year. There's a coffee bar, and the licensed buttery is open from 10:30 a.m. to 2:30 p.m. You can also visit a geology gallery and a permanent exhibition in the keep, "Norfolk in Europe."

The **Norwich Cathedral,** principally of Norman design, dates back to 1096. It is noted primarily for its long nave, with lofty columns. Its spire, built in the late Perpendicular style, rises 315 feet, and shares distinction with the keep of the castle as the significant landmarks on the Norwich skyline. On the vaulted ceiling are more than 300 bosses (knoblike ornamental projections) depicting biblical scenes. The impressive choir stalls with the handsome misereres date from the 15th century. Edith Cavell—"Patriotism is not enough"—the English nurse executed by the Germans in World War I, was buried on the cathedral's Life's Green. The quadrangular cloisters go back to the 13th century, and are among the most spacious in England.

A short walk from the cathedral will take you to **Tombland,** one of the most interesting old squares in Norwich.

The **Sainsbury Centre for Visual Arts** was the gift in 1973 of Sir Robert and Lady Sainsbury, who contributed their private collection to the University of East Anglia. Along with their son David, they gave an endowment to provide a building to house the collection. The center, designed by Foster Associates, was opened in 1978, and since then the design has won many national and international awards. A feature of the structure is its flexibility, allowing solid and glass areas to be interchanged, and the superb quality of light which allows optimum viewing of the works of art. The Sainsbury Collection is one of the foremost in the country, including modern, ancient, classical, and ethnographic art. Other displays at the center include the Anderson collection of art nouveau and the university aggregation of 20th-century nonfigurative art. There is also a regular program of special exhibitions.

The center (tel. Norwich 56161) is open from noon to 5 p.m. from Tuesday to Sunday. Admission to the permanent collections is 50p (88¢) for adults and 25p (44¢) for children.

The restaurant on the premises offers a self-service buffet from 10:30 a.m. to 2:30 p.m. Monday to Friday. Meal service is available from 12:30 to 2 p.m., also Monday to Friday. In the coffee bar, snacks are served from 2:30 to 4:30 p.m. Tuesday to Friday and from noon to 4:30 p.m. on Saturday and Sunday.

The **Mustard Shop,** 3 Bridewell Alley (tel. Norwich 27889), first opened in 1973, on the 150th anniversary of Jeremiah and James Colman's partnership. This delightful Victorian shop is a wealth of mahogany and shining brass. There is an old cash register to record your purchase, and the standard of service and pace of life also reflect the personality and courtesy of a bygone age. In the Mustard Museum is a series of displays illustrating the history of the Colman company and the making of mustard, its properties and origins. There are old advertisements, as well as packages and "tins." You can browse in the shop, selecting whichever of the mustards you prefer. Really hot, English-type mustards are sold, as well as the continental blends. Besides mustard, the shop sells aprons, tea towels, chopping boards, pottery mustard pots, and mugs, all of which are also available by mail order from the attractive free brochure provided. The shop and museum are open from 9 a.m. to 5:30 p.m. from Monday to Saturday (closed all day Thursday).

Before I begin my recommendations for finding lodgings, I'll lead off with a tip about how to find a room in a hurry.

ACCOMMODATIONS: Norwich is better equipped than most East Anglian cities to handle guests who arrive without reservations. The **Norwich City Tourist Information Centre** maintains an office at Augustine Steward House, 14 Tombland, opposite the cathedral (tel. Norwich 20679), and the friendly personnel there will help. Each year a new listing of accommodations is drawn up, including both licensed and unlicensed hotels, as well as B&B houses, and even living arrangements on the outskirts.

A street called **Earlham Road** abounds in budget hotels and guest houses. You can almost pick and choose. To drive there, go west along St. Giles Street from the north side of City Hall. The guest houses were mostly built at the turn of the century, and they offer widely varying prices.

Bed and Breakfast

Heathcote Hotel, 1723 Unthank Rd. (tel. Norwich 25639), is managed by Mrs. Grace Pendle, a Norwich woman whose pleasant personality will soon make you feel at home. Established in 1904, the hotel, which is only a few minutes' walk from the city center, has recently undergone some major alterations which have increased its bedroom capacity to 45 rooms and provided a comfortable TV lounge and cocktail bar. The heated rooms, which are well furnished, have hot and cold running water, radios, and tea-making facilities. The charge is £14 ($24.50) per person nightly for bed and a full English breakfast. A three-course evening meal is available at £5.50 ($9.63). Prices are subject to VAT, but there is no service charge.

Santa Lucia Hotel, 38–40 Yarmouth Rd. (tel. Norwich 33207), is one of the best for value of the hotels outside Norwich, only 1½ miles from the center. The hotel offers not only an inexpensive accommodation, but an attractive setting and a friendly atmosphere. You pay from £8.50 ($14.88) nightly for B&B. The food is quite good too, costing from £4.50 ($7.88) for a dinner. Each room has running water and a clock radio. There are sun terraces for relaxing, modern bathrooms and showers, and plenty of parking space. Two buses pass by the door heading for the center of the city.

Ferry Hotel, 22 Riverside Rd. (tel. Norwich 23674), is a small hotel of only seven bedrooms, lying opposite the yacht station. Three of the units are rented to singles, one is a twin, and the other three are doubles. Derek J. White, the owner, charges £9 ($15.75) per person, including a full English breakfast. Guests have use of the lounge where they can watch TV. Mr. White prides himself on giving good value for money, and in particular he is pleased to present his large breakfast, consisting of fried bread, sausages, bacon, tomato, and egg. Rooms are clean and comfortably furnished.

DINING IN NORWICH: **Briton Arms Coffee House,** Elm Hill (tel. Norwich 23367), in the heart of the old city, overlooks the most beautiful cobbled street in Norwich. Over the years it's had several names, and traces its history back to the days of Edward III. Now it's one of the least expensive eating places in Norwich, certainly one of the most intimate and informal. The coffeehouse has several rooms, including a back one with an inglenook. You'll find old beamed ceilings and Tudor benches. It is open daily, except Sunday, from 10 a.m. to 5 p.m.

The procedure here is to go to the little counter, where you purchase your lunch and bring it to the table of your choice. Everything I've tried was well prepared, and the items are homemade. Every day a different kind of soup is offered. You can eat here for as little as £1 ($1.75), although you're likely to pay about £3 ($5.25) for a substantial, two-course meal. It's a good place to stop after your inspection of the cathedral, only a block away.

The **Assembly House,** Theatre Street (tel. Norwich 26402), is a good example of Georgian architecture. You enter the building through a large front courtyard, which leads to the central hall, with its columns, fine paneling, and crystal chandelier. The restaurant is administered by H. J. Sexton Norwich Arts Trust.

On your left is a high-ceilinged room with paneling, fine paintings, and a long buffet table ready for self-service. After making your selection, take your plate to any one of the many tables. Often you'll share—perhaps with an artist. You'll find an unusually varied selection of hors d'oeuvres. A big bowl of homemade soup costs only 50p (88¢); hot entrees range from £1.80 ($3.15), salad from £1.30 ($2.28). The restaurant is open first for coffee, 10:30 a.m. to noon; then lunch, between noon and 2 p.m. Teatime is from 3 to 5 p.m., and the supper hour is from 5 to 7:30 p.m.

After dining, you may want to stroll through the rest of the building. Art exhibits are usually held regularly in the Ivory and Hobart Rooms, open from 10 a.m. to 5:30 p.m. Concerts are sponsored in the Music Room, with its chandeliers and sconces. There's even a little cinema.

The **Wine Press,** Woburn Court, 8 Guildhall Hill, serves lots of homemade fare. The hot dish of the day, costing £2.50 ($4.38), is often chicken curry or beef-and-mushroom pie. Various salads and homemade puddings are also offered. Wine is 70p ($1.23) a glass. It is open Monday to Saturday from 9 a.m. to 3 p.m.

Le Bistro, 2a Exchange St. (tel. Norwich 24452), in terms of value, is among the best accommodations in Norwich. Mr. Squires offers a three-course English lunch for just £2.75 ($4.81) and a three-course English and French lunch for £4 ($7). In the evening you can enjoy a three-course English and French dinner for only £5.50 ($9.63). On a typical menu you are likely to find frog legs, snails in their shells, roast leg of pork (with a sage-and-onion stuffing), and roast duck, perhaps chicken Maryland. French fries and seasonal vegetables are served with the main dishes. At least ten desserts are offered, perhaps raspberry sorbet with blackcurrants and cream. All prices include VAT. Lunch is served Monday to Saturday from 11:30 a.m. to 2 p.m. and grills are offered Tuesday to Friday from 2 to 5 p.m. Evening meals are served from 5 to 9:30 p.m.

12. North Norfolk

This part is already well known by members of the American Eighth Air Force, as many Liberators and Flying Fortresses took off and landed from this corner of the country. Their captains and crews sampled most of the local hostelries at one time or another. Now it is just feathered birds that fly overhead, and the countryside is quiet and peaceful.

THE SIGHTS: The area is of considerable scenic interest, as the Queen of England herself will surely agree. It's extremely convenient for a weekend out of London, as it lies only a three-hour drive away.

SANDRINGHAM ESTATE: In the Norfolk countryside, some 107 miles northeast of London, Sandringham Estate is the famous country home in East Anglia where the British royal family spends many of its holidays. The gardens plus a section of the interior are open to the public. The house and grounds are open from Easter Sunday until the last Thursday in September, inclusive, from Sunday through Thursday of each week. The house is closed for a certain period during the summer (normally the last two weeks in July and the first week in August). The house is open from 11 a.m. (noon on Sunday) to 4:45 p.m., and the grounds can be visited from 10:30 a.m. (11:30 a.m. on Sunday) to 5 p.m. For a combined ticket to the house and grounds, adults pay £1.30 ($2.28) and children are charged 70p ($1.23). The grounds are not open when the Queen or any member of the royal family is in residence.

The house dates from the mid-19th century and stands on the site of one bought for Edward VII when he was Prince of Wales. There are picnic areas, a souvenir shop, and a cafeteria. The museum, first opened in 1973, includes cars and a fire engine, big-game trophies, and a gallery of local archeological finds. The cars include a 1900 Daimler Tonneau of Edward VII, which was the first car bought by a member of the royal family. It still works!

Traditionally, the royal family welcomes in the new year at Sandringham. Sandringham lies eight miles northeast of the ancient port and market town of King's Lynn.

Near the estate, there's another **Royal Museum** in the village of **Wolferton,** where generations of royal visitors arrived for Sandringham until the line from King's Lynn to Hunstanton was closed in 1969. Now, the downside platform and its buildings are the home of Mr. and Mrs. Eric Walker, who have opened the paneled retiring rooms as a museum of royal railway travel. In one corner nestles Queen Victoria's traveling bed, made for her when a young girl in 1828. The museum is open daily except Saturday from 11 a.m. to 6 p.m. and on Sunday from 2 to 6 p.m. Admission is 50p (88¢) for adults and 25p (44¢) for children.

Blickling Hall

A long drive, bordered by massive yew hedges towering above and framing your first view of this lovely old house, leads you to Blickling Hall, near Aylsham (tel. Aylsham 733471). A great Jacobean house built in the early 17th century, it is perhaps one of the finest examples of such architecture in the country. The Long Gallery has an elaborate 17th-century ceiling, and the Peter the Great Room, decorated later, has a fine tapestry on the wall. The house is set in ornamental parkland with a formal garden and an orangery. Meals and snacks are available. It is open from April 2 until the end of October, except Monday and Thursday, from 2 to 5:30 p.m. The house is also open from 11 a.m. to 1 p.m. daily, except Monday and Thursday, from June to September. Admission is £1.60 ($2.80) for adults, 80p ($1.40) for children. For information, telephone Aylsham 3084.

Norfolk Lavender Ltd.

At **Caley Mill** at Heacham (tel. Heacham 70384), you can see how lavender is grown, the flowers harvested, and the essence distilled before appearing prettily packaged as perfume, aftershave, potpourri, and old-fashioned lavender bags to slip between your hankies. Much of the lavender is grown on the nearby Sandringham royal estate, so you may end up with a regal product. The grounds and shop are open from 10 a.m. to 6 p.m. from May to September, from 9 a.m. to dusk in winter. Admission is 30p (53¢) for adults and 15p (26¢) for children. The **Miller's Cottage Tea Room** serves cream teas with homemade cakes, scones, and buns, from late May to September. The best time to see the lavender in bloom is mid-July to early August. You will be able to discuss the merits of the various varieties and their suitability for your particular garden.

Alby Crafts Ltd.

This brainchild of Valerie Alston, on Cromer Road, Erpringham (tel. Hanworth 761590), is open from Easter to Christmas, daily except Monday, from 10 a.m. to 5 p.m. The craft center is housed in an old Norfolk stone farmhouse and its outbuildings. Mrs. Alston scours the country to find genuine articles of country craft, including leatherwork, woodcarving, and ceramics. A rocking chair model, perfect in every detail, yet only four inches high, costs about £18 ($31.50). Bronze and wrought ironwork can be made to order, a piece costing as little as £2.50 ($4.38), although prices can run much, much higher. There are sometimes demonstrations and specialist exhibitions, and several of the workshops are made available to local craftspeople. The delight of this place is that the articles come from all over the country and are entirely genuine craftware. Homemade dishes and cakes are served throughout the day in the tea room.

Sutton Windmill

At Sutton (1½ miles southeast of Stalham off the A149) is the tallest mill in the country. But its main claim to fame, in a county where many of the windmills still work, is the exceptional quality and interest of the working machinery. Chris Nunn, the young man who owns the mill, decided it was time he put something back into the country instead of taking it out. So he left the construction business and now devotes his days to restoring the mill. When money runs short, he works on North Sea oil rigs for a time. He hopes shortly to be grinding corn again, but the lower floors—there are nine in all—house a collection of tools and bygones reflecting the mill's 100 years of history. From April 1 to mid-May hours are 1:30 to 6 p.m. From May 15 to September 30, hours are daily from 9:30 a.m. to 6 p.m. Admission is 60p ($1.05) for adults and 35p (61¢) for children. There is a telescope on the top floor, and the view over the countryside is magnificent. Crafts, pottery, books, and gifts are on sale. Telephone Stalham 81195 for more information.

The Thursford Collection

Just off the A148 which runs from King's Lynn to Cromer, at **Laurel Farm,** Thursford Green, Thursford, near Fakenham (tel. Thursford 3839), George Cushing has been collecting and restoring steam engines and organs for more years than you'd care to remember. His collection is now a trust, and the old painted giants are on display, a paradise of traction engines with impeccable pedigrees such as Burrells, Garretts, and the Ruston Proctors. There are some static steam engines, the sort that run merry-go-rounds at fun fairs, but the most flamboyant exhibits are the showman's organs, the Wurlitzers and concert organs with their brilliant decoration, moving figures, and mass of windpipes. The organs play at 4 p.m. There is a children's play area, and a Savages Venetian Gondola switchback ride with Gavoili organ, which operates daily. It was built at nearby King's Lynn, and Disneyland has been after it for years. On many days during the summer, the two-foot-gauge steam railway, the

Cackler, will take you around the wooded grounds of the museum. There is a refreshment café and a souvenir shop to buy photographs, books, and records of the steam-organ music. The collection is open daily from 2 to 5:30 p.m. from the beginning of April until the end of October. On Sunday it is open throughout the year. Admission is £1.20 ($2.10) for adults and 90p ($1.58) for children. There are live Wurlitzer concerts every Tuesday evening at 8 p.m. from June to September.

The North Norfolk Railway

This steam railway plies from Sheringham to Weybourne. The station at Sheringham (tel. Sheringham 822045) opens daily at 10 a.m. from Easter to October. Admission is 50p (88¢) for adults and 30p (53¢) for children. There are two museums of railway paraphernalia, steam locomotives, and historic rolling stock. The round trip to Weybourne by steam train takes about 45 minutes through most attractive countryside. Days and times of departures vary, so you should telephone between 10 a.m. and 5 p.m. before you go there. The round-trip journey will cost £1.25 ($2.19) for adults and 65p ($1.14) for children.

KING'S LYNN: The **Pilgrims Restaurant,** The Priory, Litcham, King's Lynn (tel. Litcham 262), is equidistant from Swaffham, Dereham, and Fakenham. This restaurant, aside from giving you a good meal, could come in handy, as there are few eating places in the area, and it's not far from several American military bases. The building looks as if it were built 500 or 600 years ago, since old materials were used. Indicative of the care and concern which has gone into this place, the owners have even provided a bathroom for invalids.

The restaurant is open only on Wednesday, Thursday, Friday, and Saturday evenings, and for lunch on Sunday. Real ale and modestly priced wines complement the menu. Sunday lunch, when everybody seemingly shows up, costs around £6.50 ($11.38), including VAT. Main courses are likely to include trout stuffed with herbs or braised oxtail. The regular table d'hôte evening menu at around £10 ($17.50) is much larger with a selection of continental dishes such as pot-au-feu (boiled topside of beef) or braised lamb kidneys in madeira sauce, all served with fresh vegetables or mixed salad. The service is friendly, efficient, and polite, and, in all, the Pilgrims Restaurant is a rewarding choice.

In the Middle Ages the Priory was an overnight house of rest for pilgrims on the long journey to Walsingham, its visitors including such notables as Catherine of Aragon and Henry VIII.

Chapter XIII

EAST MIDLANDS

1. Northamptonshire
2. Leicestershire
3. Derbyshire
4. Nottinghamshire
5. Lincolnshire

THE EAST MIDLANDS contains several widely varied counties, both in character and scenery. This part of central England, for instance, offers miles of dreary industrial sections and their offspring row-type Victorian houses, yet the district is intermixed with some of Britain's noblest scenery, such as the Peak District National Park, centered in Derbyshire. Byron said that scenes there rivaled those of Switzerland and Greece. There are, in short, many pleasant surprises in store for you, from the tulip land of Lincoln to the 18th-century spa of Buxton in Derbyshire, from George Washington's ancestral home at Sulgrave Manor in Northamptonshire to what remains of Sherwood Forest.

1. Northamptonshire

This sprawling county in the middle of England is rather undistinguished in scenery, although its meadows are pleasant in summer. The county town is—

NORTHAMPTON: This has long been an important shoe-making center, and the **Central Museum** on Guildhall Road (tel. Northampton 34881) commemorates that fact. In its collection it traces footwear through the ages, some of which dates back to Roman times. It can be visited free from Monday to Saturday, 10 a.m. to 6 p.m. Most visitors pass through here en route to Sulgrave Manor, previewed below.

A Luncheon Stopover

Squirrels Inn, Main Road, Duston, outside Northampton (tel. Northampton 51930), is a converted thatched cottage with stone walls, a beamed ceiling, and an open fireplace. At the central bar you can enjoy a buffet, with such dishes as hot steak-and-kidney pie, quiche, macaroni and cheese, and ham steak in a cider sauce with three vegetables. There are cold dishes as well, including roast meats, a cold meat pie, and pâtés served with vegetable or salad. Everything is self-service, and you'll rarely spend more than £2 ($3.50), plus another 80p ($1.40) if you want dessert. The inn is open from noon to 2 p.m., until 10:15

p.m. on Friday and Saturday. It is closed for Saturday lunch and all day Sunday.

SULGRAVE MANOR: On your way from Oxford to Stratford-upon-Avon, you can visit Sulgrave Manor, the ancestral home of George Washington. First, you'll come to **Banbury**, a market town famed in the nursery rhyme, immortalizing the lady upon the white horse. The old Banbury Cross was destroyed by the Roundheads, but was replaced in Victoria's day. Eight miles northeast of Banbury will take you to Sulgrave Manor, a small Tudor manorial house, built in about the mid-16th century. Follow the A422 east from Banbury toward Brackley. Go left on the B4525 toward Northampton until you pick up the signs to Sulgrave.

As part of Henry VIII's plan to dissolve monasteries, he sold the priory-owned manor in 1539 to Lawrence Washington, who had been mayor of Northampton. George Washington was a direct descendant of Lawrence (seven generations removed). The Washington family occupied the Sulgrave for more than a century. In 1656, Col. John Washington left for the New World.

In 1914 the manor was purchased by a group of English people in honor of the friendship between Britain and America. Over the years, major restoration has taken place (a whole new wing had to be added), with an eye toward returning it as much as possible to its original state. The Colonial Dames have been largely responsible for raising the money. From both sides of the Atlantic the appropriate furnishings were donated, including a number of portraits—even a Gilbert Stuart original of the first president. On the main doorway is the Washington family coat-of-arms, two bars and a trio of mullets, which is believed to have been the inspiration for the "Stars and Stripes."

The manor is open from February to December, daily except Monday and Wednesday, from 10:30 a.m. to 1 p.m. and 2 to 5:30 p.m. (till 4 p.m. in winter). Admission is 70p ($1.23). For more information, telephone 029576/205.

Food and Lodging

Across from Sulgrave Manor is the **Thatched House Hotel** (tel. 029576/232), a long, low group of 17th-century cottages, with a front garden full of flowers. Even if you're just passing through, it's a good place to stop for tea following your visit to Sulgrave Manor. Afternoon teas cost from 75p ($1.31) to £2.65 ($4.64) for a great spread with sandwiches, homemade cakes, scones with thick cream and jam, and strawberries in season. Tea is served at a table in either the beamed living or dining room, furnished with antiques.

If you're lucky enough to stay over, Ron Walpole, the owner and manager, has modernized the bedrooms, installing private baths or showers to accommodate overnight guests. They are charged from £16 ($28) in a single and from £25 ($43.75) in a double, including a full breakfast and VAT. Set lunches start at only £3.75 ($6.56), and a table d'hôte dinner is served for £5.50 ($9.63).

THE SPENCER HOME: Althorp, Northampton (tel. East Haddon 209), is the home of Earl and Countess Spencer, parents of the former Lady Diana Spencer, now Princess of Wales. The house lies six miles northwest of Northampton and one mile from the village of Harlestone. Built in 1508 by Sir John Spencer, the house has undergone many alterations over the years.

It now contains a fabulous collection of pictures by Van Dyck, Reynolds, Gainsborough, and Rubens, as well as fine and rare French and English furniture, along with Sèvres, Bow, and Chelsea porcelain. The collection is quite as magnificent as that in better known stately homes. The present countess helps in the gift shop, and Lord Spencer's own favorite sideline is the excellent cellar and wine store. There is a tea room for light refreshment.

The house is open daily all year (except Monday in August) from 2:30 to 5:30 p.m. The house is also closed on Friday (except in August). Admission is £2 ($3.50) for adults and £1 ($1.75) for children.

WATERWAYS MUSEUM: The Waterways Museum, at Stoke Bruerne, near Towcester in Northamptonshire (tel. 0604/862229), is on the Grand Union Canal at Stoke Bruerne, just south of the Blisworth Tunnel (take the A508 from the M1 junction 15 and the A5). The three-story grain warehouse has been lovingly restored and adapted to give an insight into the working lives of canal boatmen and their families. On display is a full-size replica of a "butty" boat cabin, complete with cooking range, brassware, and lace curtains, along with the traditional painted ware, tools, and teapots. There is also an early semi-diesel Bolinger boat engine, a boat-weighing machine once used to determine canal toll charges, and a shop where you can buy posters, books, illustrations of canal life, hand-painted miniatures of traditional canalware, models, and badges. The museum is open from 10 a.m. to 6 p.m. It is closed on Monday from October to Easter and but open otherwise until 4 p.m. Admission is 60p ($1.05) for adults and 30p (53¢) for children.

If you find yourself in the area, you'll be able to partake of one of the most delightful dining adventures in Northamptonshire.

The **Boat Inn,** Stoke Bruerne, near Towcester (tel. 0604/862428), started as a row of humble cottages in the 17th century and has gradually progressed without losing its original character. It is still a limestone building with a thatched roof overlooking the Grand Union Canal and the Stoke Bruerne Waterways Museum. The Public House is the oldest part, with stone floors and open fires, along with pictures depicting canal boats and life. Bar food includes the usual soup of the day, steak-and-kidney pie, cornish pasty, and ploughman's lunch. You can also order sandwiches, salads, and basket meals. Count on spending around £4 ($7). Next to the pub is a traditional Northamptonshire skittles room where you can try your skill at throwing the "cheese," the flattened puck used to knock the skittles down.

The restaurant offers a full range of dishes, including smoked salmon, snails in garlic butter, and an interesting apple and stilton soup. There are several fish dishes, including a whole lobster thermidor, and guinea fowl and grouse are served in season, along with such elegant continental dishes as tournedos Rossini or steak Diane. A three-course meal, finished off with a choice from the dessert trolley or the cheese board, then coffee and mints, will cost around £8.50 ($14.88), including VAT but excluding the service charge. That is, unless you started with poached oysters, followed by lobster thermidor, and rounded off with roast grouse! On Sunday they do a Great British Sunday lunch, costing £4.50 ($7.88) for adults and £2.95 ($5.16) for children. There is also a traditional cream tea in the afternoon, costing £1.30 ($2.28).

The Woodward family has owned and run the Boat Inn since 1877, and recently "twinned" their inn with Ratcliffe's Restaurant in Dallas, and promotions and exchanges are now being arranged between the two establishments.

BRACKLEY: This is an ancient market town mentioned in the *Domesday Book.* If you're in the area, I suggest a stopover at **The Sun** at Whitfield, near Brackley (tel. Syresham 232), a colorful country inn. Its exterior has a high peaked roof, large chimneys, bay windows, and flower boxes. The inn stands close to the town's church with its square steeple. The interior has been restored, and many of the old features have been retained. The dining room has its original oak beams, as well as Windsor chairs and trestle tables. A single without bath rents for £13 ($22.75), the price going up to £15.50 ($27.13) with bath. In a twin or double, the bathless chambers go for £20 ($35), rising to £24 ($42) with bath. The owners provide both table d'hôte lunches and à la carte dinners, as well as morning coffee. A meal, including soup, steak, and dessert, would cost around £7 ($12.25) in the restaurant. The Sun Inn lies on the A43, between Brackley (2 miles) and Towcester (9 miles). It's a handy base for such sights as Sulgrave Manor (6 miles) and Oxford (24 miles).

The **Old Crown Hotel,** Market Place (tel. Brackley 702210), is an old-world posting house, parts of which date back to the 12th century. The Duke of Wellington stopped here in 1814, a year before the Battle of Waterloo. A single rents for £12.75 ($22.31); a double or twin costs £21 ($36.75). Some chambers are rented to three at a rate of £30 ($52.50), and there are some four-bed family rooms at £34 ($59.50). All these tariffs include a full English breakfast and VAT. The bedrooms are comfortably furnished, and all have hot and cold running water, a radio, and an intercom. There's a babysitting service for a nominal fee. The original character of the Old Crown has been preserved. There are heavy, time-aged beams, open brick fireplaces, and oak paneling in the lounge. There's a traditional bar, a lounge where you can have afternoon tea in front of the Tudor-style fireplace, and in the evenings you can dine by candlelight. A traditional Sunday roast beef lunch goes for £4 ($7). For lunch you can have snacks of soup, steak, and dessert at £5 ($8.75). The same meal in the restaurant would cost £6.50 ($11.38).

2. Leicestershire

Virtually ignored by most North American tourists, this eastern Midland county was the home of King Lear and is rich in historical associations.

LEICESTER: The county town is a busy industrial center, but it was once a Roman settlement and has a Roman wall and bath site that remind one of those days.

It also has a Norman castle-hall, a period museum, a costume museum in a late medieval building, a 15th-century Guildhall (Shakespeare is said to have played here), and many interesting gardens. On its abbey park and grounds are the remains of Leicester Abbey, Cardinal Wolsey's grave, a boating lake, paddling pool, riverside walks, a miniature railway, ornamental gardens, and an aviary.

You can ask at the **Leicester Information Bureau** (tel. 0533/20644), at 12 Bishop St., for details of guided walks around the city.

Also inquire at **City Transport** (tel. 0533/556691) on Rutland Street about double-decker bus tours.

Daval Hotel, 292 London Rd., Stoneygate (tel. Leicester 708234), is a historical building of architectural interest, built in 1889 during the reign of Queen Victoria. There are rooms of all sizes: singles, doubles, twins, and family size. All are modern with hot and cold running water, shaver points, bedside lights, radio, intercom, and wall-to-wall carpeting. Charges, which include a full English breakfast and all taxes, are £13.50 ($23.63) in a single, £21.50 ($37.63) for two persons in a room with a double bed, and £21.50 ($37.63) for two persons in a twin-bedded room. Some units contain private showers, and cost an extra £2 ($3.50) per night. Family rooms with three or four beds are offered on a pro rata basis. There is a cozy restaurant where home-cooked evening meals are available, including steaks, chicken, duckling, scampi, and other specialties. Emphasis is on personal and friendly service, and the owners, Mr. and Mrs. Tolley and their son Martin, will make you feel welcome. The hotel has its own licensed bar with a TV lounge. The Daval is ideally situated for touring and visiting the Midlands. It is on the main A6 trunk road. For those traveling by train or bus, it is just a few minutes' ride away from the stations.

Alexandra Hotel, 342 London Rd. (tel. Leicester 70356), is a modest hotel owned by Mr. and Mrs. Andrew and Terri Warzynski, who not only provide B&B but will offer a four-course dinner for £6.50 ($11.38) per person. Mrs. Warzynski will also prepare a light snack for you when required. Singles begin at £12 ($21), and doubles go for £16.25 ($28.44).

The Old Tudor Rectory, Main Street, Glenfield (tel. Leicester 312214), near Leicester and the M1, is a much-added-to building where you can find spacious and comfortable accommodations. It stands in its own three-quarter-acre garden—a Tudor rectory with extensive additions made during the reign of Queen Anne—although 20th-century comforts have been added. There's central heating, for one thing, and in the dignified living room, color TV. Single rooms are £12 ($21), and doubles or twins run £8 ($14) per person. Children are given reduced rates.

The owners, Beryl and Maurice Weston, also run a licensed restaurant serving bar snacks at 50p (88¢) and à la carte meals at £7.50 ($13.13).

TOURING THE COUNTRY: As long as people continue to read Sir Walter Scott's *Ivanhoe,* they will remember **Ashby-de-la-Zouch,** a town that retains a pleasant country atmosphere. Mary Queen of Scots was imprisoned in an ancient castle here.

On the northern border of Leicestershire, **Belvoir** (pronounced beaver) **Castle** has been the seat of the Dukes of Rutland since Henry VIII's time, overlooking the Vale of Belvoir. Rebuilt by Wyatt in 1816, the castle contains paintings by Holbein, Reynolds, and Gainsborough, as well as tapestries in its magnificent state rooms. The location is seven miles west-southwest of Grantham, between the A607 to Melton Mowbray and the A52 to Nottingham. The castle was the location of the movie *Little Lord Fauntleroy,* and in summer it is the site of medieval jousting tournaments. From March 22 to October 1 it is open on Tuesday, Wednesday, Thursday, and Saturday from noon to 6 p.m. On Sunday its hours are noon to 7 p.m. After October 1, it is open until the end of that month only from 2 to 6 p.m. Admission is £1.60 ($2.80) for adults and 90p ($1.58) for children. Further details are available from Jimmy Durrands, Estate Office, Belvoir Castle, Grantham, Lincolnshire (tel. Grantham 870262).

Other interesting towns to visit in Leicestershire include **Melton Mowbray,** a fox-hunting center and market town which claims to be the original home of stilton cheese and is renowned for its pork pies.

For a sample of this town's gastronomy, I'd recommend **Dickinson & Morris Ltd.,** 10 Nottingham St., in Melton Mowbray (tel. Melton Mowbray 62341), in a 17th-century structure. By tradition, the first Melton pork pie was baked in this bakery and confectionary, and you can sample it today, based on an old recipe, costing from £1.50 ($2.63). The Melton Hunt cake (rich fruit) is made in the bakery shop to the rear, going for 85p ($1.49) a serving.

The **Olde Mill House,** Redmile (tel. Bottesford 42460), is a charming old farmhouse with cozy open fires which brighten the chill of a cold summer evening, although the place is centrally heated. All bedrooms have hot and cold running water, and there are ample bathroom and toilet facilities down the hall. B&B will set you back £8 ($14) per person nightly, including service and VAT. There are reduced terms for longer stays. A four-course dinner is willingly provided for £5 ($8.75), including a glass of wine. Then you can repair to the games room to work off your sloth at the billiard table, with a quick game of table tennis or a less energetic game of darts. They'll tell you the rules if you haven't played before. This is a good center for horseback riding in the shires. Mr. and Mrs. Murray Barton are gracious hosts in this 250-year-old house built on the site of an old mill near the borders of Leicestershire and Nottinghamshire. The farm is near Belvoir Castle and overlooks the Vale of Belvoir.

3. Derbyshire

The most magnificent scenery in the Midlands is found within the borders of this county, lying between Nottinghamshire and Staffordshire. Derbyshire has been less defaced by industry than its neighbors. The north of the county, containing the **Peak District National Park,** is by far the most exciting for touring. In the south the land is more level, and the look becomes, in places, one of pastoral meadows.

Some visitors avoid this part of the country, because it is ringed by the industrial sprawl of Manchester, Leeds, Sheffield, and Derby. To do so, however, would be a pity, as this part of England contains the rugged peaks and leafy dales which merit a substantial detour, especially Dovedale, Chee Dale, and Millers Dale.

Chatsworth House, home of the Dukes of Devonshire, and **Haddon Hall,** home of the Duke of Rutland, are worth a visit. Melbourne Hall, Kedlestone, and Hardwick Hall are also open to view.

OTHER PLACES TO SEE: In addition to majestic scenery, you may want to seek out the following specific sights:

National Tramway Museum, Crich, near Matlock (tel. Ambergate 2565). One young 65-year-old whom I know spends as much of his free time as his wife will allow in the paradise of trams—electric, steam, and horse-drawn. Your admission ticket is £1.50 ($2.63) for adults and 80p ($1.40) for children. This ticket allows you to ride on the tram which makes a round trip to Glory Mine with scenic views over the Derwent Valley, then back through Wakebridge where a stop is made to visit the Peak District Mines Historical Society display of lead mining. It also includes admission to the tramway exhibition. It is open daily except Friday from April to October, then weekends only until the end of October. Hours are from 11 a.m. until some time in the late afternoon.

Peak District Mining Museum, the Pavilion, Matlock Bath (tel. Matlock 3834), is open year round, daily (except for Christmas), from 11 a.m. to 4 p.m. Admission is 75p ($1.31) for adults and 45p (79¢) for children. The main exhibit of this display of 2000 years of Derbyshire lead mining is a giant water-pressure engine, used to pump water from the mines and itself rescued from 360 feet underground by members of the society before being brought to the museum. The most popular feature is the children's climbing shaft, a twisting tunnel through which they crawl.

The **Royal Cave** at Matlock Bath (tel. Matlock 3654) is just off the A6 main road beside the Pavilion. Before going underground, you are given a brief audio-visual explanation of man's activities under the earth. Then you descend into the cavern, with its series of sound and light shows depicting the life of the earliest cavemen through hardships and disasters, as well as the life of the first Romans in Britain and on to the present day. There's a mineral museum, and after the tour, the Gallery Cafeteria will revitalize or sustain you. The cave is open daily from Easter until the end of September from 11 a.m. to 4:30 p.m. (sometimes closed on Friday).

Magpie Mine, at Sheldon, near Bakewell, has been the site of much desperate toil, murders, vendettas, and enormous financial losses. In summer the surface remains of the lead mine (the underground workings are dangerous) are open to view from 2:30 to 4 p.m. The cost is 40p (70¢) for adults and 30p (53¢) for children. This is definitely a specialist tour, but it's representative of conditions which existed in the 18th- and 19th-century English countryside.

The **Clock Warehouse,** London Road, Shardlow (tel. Derby 792844), was built in 1780 on the Trent and Mersey Canal at the junction with the navigable River Trent. It became part of the inland port where merchandise was stored on arrival by narrow boat and river barge. Nowadays, the old building houses the Canal Story exhibition which fills its three floors. There are life-size models of boats and barges, historic photographs, artifacts, and a dioramas showing the history of the canal system and the flourishing trade carried on along the waterways. The Canal Shop will sell books, souvenirs, and mementos. Look out for the authentic canal boat painted buckets, jugs, and boxes. The Lace Plate Restaurant is a simple beamed room decorated with dozens of authentic "lace-plates" peculiar to the canals. It serves snacks and refreshments throughout the day. You may be lucky enough to be able to take a short trip on the canal in an authentic narrow boat. Admission is 50p (88¢) for adults and 30p (53¢) for children. The warehouse is open during most of the year, but telephone to make sure.

As a final note, you may be interested in renting a **bicycle.** There are three centers where cycles can be rented by the day or the week for touring holidays in the Peaks and Dales of Derbyshire. Tandems and tricycles are also available, but only with prior notice. The centers which rent are at Ashbourne and Middleton south and southeast of the Dales, at Parsley Hay on the High Peak Trail, and at Derwent in Derwent Dale, north of the Hope Valley. Charges are £2.60 ($4.55) per day or £15.40 ($26.95) per week. Children under 16 pay less. A £2 ($3.50) deposit is required on each cycle. Write to the **Peak Park Joint Planning Board,** Aldern House, Baslow Road, Bakewell, Derbyshire DE4 1AE (tel. 062981/4321). That is, all except for Middleton Top. There you should get in touch with the **County Planning Officer,** County Offices, Matlock, Derbyshire DE4 3AG (tel. 0629/3411, ext. 7121). You can either just follow your nose along the country lanes or follow one of the marked routes from each of the centers. These are marked by red arrows displayed by the roadside and shown on the free map provided when you hire your bike.

BUXTON: One of the loveliest towns in Britain, Buxton was built in the 18th century to rival the spa at Bath. Although it eventually fell into a decline, it is now being considerably revived. The 18th-century opera house, for years the local movie palace, has been restored, and is the centerpiece for a festival featuring Britain's National Theatre. Buxton is 20 miles southeast of Manchester and 163 miles northwest of London.

Of its old buildings, the finest is the Crescent, built by the fifth Duke of Devonshire between 1780 and 1784. Pump Room, opened in 1894, now houses the Tourist Information Centre, in which you may drink the water from Buxton's natural springs.

Poole's Cavern, Buxton Country Park, Green Lane, in Buxton (tel. Buxton 6978), is a cave that was once inhabited by Stone Age man, but now the only inhabitants are its visitors who marvel at the natural vaulted roof bedecked with stalactites. Explorers walk through the spacious galleries, viewing the incredible horizontal cave, electrically illuminated. It is open from Easter until the first week in November, from 10 a.m. to 5 p.m., charging a small admission fee.

Some 20 minutes away in Grin Low Woods is **Solomon's Temple,** a folly built in 1895, on a tumulus which dates from the Neolithic Age. Climb the small spiral staircase inside the temple for impressive views over Buxton and the surrounding countryside.

Accommodations

Ashwood Park Hotel, Bakewell Road (tel. Ashwood 3416), is an impressive stone building in the heart of the spa, owned by M. Jean Howarth. It's set back from the busy roads, facing the well-tended public gardens with a small stream and lawns. It's more of a country inn, with the entire ground floor being a bar-lounge, decorated in oranges and browns with a collection of glittering brass and copper. The charge for B&B in a double is £8 ($14) per person daily, and there are no evening meals. The hotel is open only from May 1 until the end of October.

The Old Manse Guest House, 6 Clifton Rd., Silverlands (tel. Buxton 5638), is one of the lovely old buildings in a quiet area, yet close to everything. Owner Joan Power accepts guests on either a B&B or half-board arrangement. For B&B she charges £7 ($12.25) and offers another bargain, £11 ($19.25) daily for bed, breakfast, and evening meal (served at 6 p.m.). The menu is varied, with use of local products when possible, and the dining room is licensed. In the lounge, guests congregate for either friendly chats or viewing TV. Rooms have hot and cold running water, with central heating. There's space for parking cars.

Hartington Hotel, Broad Walk (tel. Buxton 2638), is a substantial stone Georgian-style building with gardens facing the boating lake. The Whibberley family has owned and run this hotel for a quarter of a century. Your view is of the River Wye, the gardens, and surrounding hills—a true pastoral setting, yet close to the town center. The hotel has been fully adapted to provide service and comfort, and as a thoughtful extra, some ground-floor bedrooms with private baths and showers have been added and made suitable for disabled guests. The well-proportioned living room is furnished in an English homelike style, with some antiques. The dining room is dignified and has a garden view as well. All bedrooms have a radio, and hot and cold running water, although a few have private baths/showers. Bathless singles are £12 ($21). Bathless doubles cost from £18 ($31.50) to £20 ($35); with your own bath and TV, £22 ($38.50) to £24 ($42). Evening meals can be obtained starting at £5 ($8.75) for four courses. These rates include VAT, and there is no service charge.

The **Egerton Hotel,** St. John's Road (tel. Buxton 6770), is a dignified stone building surrounded by its own gardens. It is a simple square Victorian, with a pair of bay windows. Its location is fine, opposite the Pavilion Gardens. The Egerton has been well adjusted for guests, with an elevator, central heating, and a TV lounge. The living room is decorated in a homey fashion with floral green fabrics and carpets. All singles have private bath, costing from £10 ($17.50) nightly. Doubles or twins rent from £15 ($26.25) to £18 ($31.50), according to the season. You pay an extra £3 ($5.25) for a private bath. The half-board rate is £27 ($47.25) daily for two persons. Horseback riding is arranged for guests.

On the Outskirts

The **Pack Horse Inn,** Crowecote, near Buxton (tel. Longnor 210), is a 300-year-old inn which makes a good center for touring the Peak District. Just seven miles from Buxton, one mile from Longnor, it enjoys a position on one side of the Dove Valley. At this fully licensed free house, guests are warmly received by John and Doris Shirley, who charge £10.50 ($18.38) daily in a single and £19 ($33.25) in a double, including a full English breakfast. Since the food is good, it's best to order dinner at £6 ($10.50).

Upperdale Farm, Monsal Dale, near Buxton (tel. Great Longstone 420), lies in the heart of one of the prettiest Derbyshire dales. Upperdale is an old, rather plain stone farmhouse, owned and run in a hospitable manner by Barbara and Alan Gilbert. The home-style cooking accounts for many return guests who enjoy such regional dishes as cottage pie and peas with red cabbage and roast shoulder bacon with broad beans. Rooms are tidy, comfortable, and clean, costing from £9.50 ($16.63) for B&B daily, and from £13 ($22.75) per person for bed, breakfast, and an evening meal. The Gilberts will guide you to nearby sights, including Chatsworth House, a 15-minute drive away.

Crewe & Harpur Arms Hotel, Longnor, near Buxton (tel. Longnor 883205), is a long, low, red-brick inn with Georgian portions, set in a village in the hills of the Peak District, six miles from Buxton. The twin rivers, Dove and Manifold, are a couple of miles away. In the village square, with its cobbled street and market hall, you are linked quickly with the past when it stood at the crossing of the old wagon trails from Leicester to Liverpool. Owners Graham and Lorraine Deighan have furnished their hotel with discretion and taste. All bedrooms have hot and cold running water and electric heaters. Their Georgian dining room is a fine background for both table d'hôte and à la carte meals, although guests can have hot or cold snacks in the pub bar. You'll be charged £11.50 ($20.13) per person for B&B and £6 ($10.50) for an evening meal; bar snacks start at £1 ($1.75). If you want to fish, the charge is £1 ($1.75) per day. And if you want to try horseback riding, it can be arranged at a nearby riding school.

ASHBOURNE: This old market town has a 13th-century church, a 16th-century grammar school, and ancient almshouses.

For accommodations, I recommend—

Green Man Hotel, (tel. Ashbourne 42017), in the town center, has many historical connections going back to 1710. In 1777, Dr. Samuel Johnson and his biographer, James Boswell, stayed at the inn, and Boswell writes, "I took my postchaise from the Green Man, a very good inn." In the Tap Room you can still see the chairs of Boswell and Johnson. Princess Victoria and her widowed mother, the Duchess of Kent, halted here and gave the inn the right to add "Royal" to its name. This red-brick posting inn has retained its traditional character, although modern amenities have been added. There are 17 bedrooms, each well decorated, and prices include a full English breakfast, early-morning tea or coffee, as well as VAT and service charge. The charge is £12 ($21) per person nightly, plus another £2 ($3.50) per person for a private bath or shower. Luncheons and evening dinners are offered in the Shrovetide Restaurant, selections made from an à la carte menu.

DOVEDALE: Overhung by limestone crags, this beautiful wooded valley forms part of the Peak District National Park, with its views of Thorpe Cloud, a conical hill 900 feet high. It's best explored on foot. Fishermen know of its River Dove trout stream, because of its associations with such famous anglers as Izaak Walton and Charles Cotton.

READER'S B&B SELECTION IN DARLEY DALE: "Mrs. L. Haywood and her husband Ralph receive guests at **The Homestead,** 24 Main St., Darley Bridge, Darley Dale, near Matlock (tel. 062983/3254), in a stone cottage behind an English cottage garden. The rooms are clean, cheerfully decorated, have hot and cold running water, and the beds are comfortable. The toilet and shower are new and modern, the very hot water is plentiful, and the location is only a short walk from all the bedrooms. But what makes this a gem of a B&B are the gourmet meals Mrs. Haywood prepares, with vegetables and fruit from her own garden and trout from the garden stream. A guest could hardly ask for anything more, but they do get more, because Mrs. Haywood and her husband are perfect hosts, always available to be of assistance but never intruding in their guests' privacy. All of this—a good room, a full English breakfast, and a gourmet evening meal—costs £10 ($17.50) per person, all inclusive" (Michael J. Davies, Sea Isle City, N.J.).

4. Nottinghamshire

"Notts," as it is called, was the county of Robin Hood and Lord Byron. It is also Lawrence country, as the English novelist, author of *Sons and Lovers* and *Lady Chatterley's Lover,* was also from here, born at Eastwood.

Sherwood Forest is probably the most famous woodland in the world, yet very little of it was forest, even in the days of Robin Hood and his men. The area consists of woodland glades, fields, and agricultural land, along with villages and hamlets.

The **Sherwood Forest Visitor Centre,** Sherwood Forest National Park at Edwinstowe, near Mansfield (tel. Mansfield 823202), has been opened in the area just by the Major Oak, popularly known as Robin Hood's tree. It's the center of many marked walks and footpaths through the woodland. There's an exhibition of life-size models of Robin Hood and the other well-known outlaws, as well as a shop with books, gifts, and souvenirs. The center, some 18 miles north of Nottingham city off the A616, will provide as much information as remains of Friar Tuck and Little John, along with Maid Marian and Alan-a-Dale, as well as the other Merry Men. Little John's grave can be seen at Hathersage, Will Scarlet's at Blidworth. Robin Hood is believed to have married Maid Marian at Edwinstowe Church, close to the Visitors Centre. Nearby is the Major Oak, 30 feet in circumference, where the outlaws could easily have hidden in the hollow trunk.

Robin Hood's Larder offers light snacks and meals, with an emphasis on traditional English country recipes. It's open daily except Monday from 11 a.m. However, it's closed on Friday in winter. There is no admission charge to the center which is on the B6034 north of Edwinstowe village, seven miles north of Mansfield.

Nottinghamshire is so rarely visited by foreign tourists that its beautiful landscapes could almost be called "undiscovered," although British trippers know of its hidden villages and numerous parks.

NOTTINGHAM: The county town is a busy industrial city, 121 miles north of London. On the north bank of the Trent, Nottingham is one of the most pleasant cities in the Midlands.

Overlooking the city, **Nottingham Castle** (tel. Nottingham 411881) was built by the Duke of Newcastle on the site of a Norman fortress in 1679. After restoration in 1878, it was opened as a provincial museum, surrounded by a charmingly laid-out garden. See, in particular, the collection of medieval Nottingham alabaster carvings. The works of Nottingham-born artists are displayed in the first-floor gallery. The castle is open from April to September, daily from 10 a.m. to 5:45 p.m. Otherwise, its hours are daily from 10 a.m. to 4:45 p.m. Admission is free except on Sunday and bank holidays, when a small fee is charged. Closed Christmas Day.

For 40p (70¢), you'll be taken on a conducted tour at the castle of Mortimer's Hole and underground passages. King Edward III is said to have led a band of noblemen through these secret passages, surprising Roger Mortimer and the Queen, killing Mortimer, and putting his lady in prison. A statue of Robin Hood stands at the base of the castle.

More recently opened, the **Brewhouse Yard Museum** consists of five 17th-century cottages at the foot of Castle Rock, presenting a panorama of Nottingham life in a series of furnished rooms. Some of them, open from cellar to garret, have much local historical material on display, and visitors are encouraged to handle these exhibits. The most interesting features are in a series of cellars cut into the rock of the castle instead of below the houses. This is not a typical folk museum, but attempts to be as lively as possible, involving both visitors and the Nottingham community in expanding displays and altering exhibitions on a bimonthly basis. Open all year, the admission-free museum (tel. Nottingham 411881, ext. 48) may be visited from 10 a.m. to 5 p.m. except during the lunch hour from noon to 1 p.m. It is closed Christmas.

An elegant row of Georgian terraced houses, the **Museum of Costume and Textiles** at 51 Castle Gate (tel. Nottingham 411881), presents lace, textile, and costume collections of one of the city's great industries. You'll see everything from the 1632 Eyre map tapestries of Nottingham to "fallals and frippery." The admission-free museum is open daily from 10 a.m. to 5 p.m.; closed Christmas Day.

On the outskirts of Nottingham, at Linby, **Newstead Abbey** (tel. 06234/2822) was once Lord Byron's home. It lies 11 miles north of Nottingham on the A60 (the Mansfield road). Some of the original Augustinian priory, bought by Sir John Byron in 1540, still survives. In the 19th century the mansion was given a neo-Gothic restoration. The poet's bedroom is as he left it. Mementos, including first editions and manuscripts, are displayed inside, and later you can explore a parkland of some 300 acres, with waterfalls, rose gardens, a Monk's Stew Pond, and a Japanese water garden.

Admission to the grounds and gardens is 60p ($1.05) for adults, 20p (35¢) for children. To visit the abbey costs adults 50p (88¢); children, 10p (18¢). There is an additional charge if you take the special tour around the abbey, which is open from Good Friday to September 30 from 2 to 6 p.m. (last admissions at 5:15). The gardens are open all year from 10 a.m. to dusk.

Also on the outskirts of Nottingham, **Wollaton Hall** is a well-preserved Elizabethan mansion, housing a natural history museum, with lots of insects, invertebrates, and British mammals, along with reptiles and crustaceans, some a long way from their former home in the South Seas. The mansion is open, April to September, daily from 10 a.m. to 7 p.m. and on Sunday from 2 to 5 p.m. From October to March its hours are 10 a.m. to 5:30 p.m. (Sunday, 1:30 to 4:30 p.m.). From November to February it is open from 10 a.m. to 4:30 p.m.

Admission is free except on Sunday and bank holidays when a modest charge is made. The hall is surrounded by a deer park and gardens.

Where to Stay

The **Rufford Hotel,** 53 Melton Rd., West Bridgford (tel. Nottingham 811233), is approximately 1½ miles from the city center, in a relatively quiet suburb, and within easy access of the M1. It's an adaptation of a clean-cut, rather attractive private house, but fully converted to receive overnight guests. Owners Mr. and Mrs. Michael Fellows charge £24 ($42) for a double and £16 ($28) for a single, including B&B but not VAT. Most rooms have private shower and toilet, and coffee-making facilities, and all have color TV. From Monday through Thursday an evening meal is also available, although over the weekend inexpensive bar snacks are on hand.

Cotswold Hotel, 332 Mansfield Rd. (tel. Nottingham 623547), is a comfortable private home turned guest house, owned by Peter and Brenda Smart. They've given the lounge, dining room, and bedrooms a fresh look with decorations and pleasant furniture. There is full central heating, hot and cold running water in each bedroom. In the invitingly homelike living room, color TV is offered. They charge a set fee of £11 ($19.25) per person nightly, which includes an English breakfast, although VAT is extra. Many of the rooms have their own shower and color TV, plus tea- and coffee-making facilities. Monday through Thursday you can order moderately priced evening meals. The hotel is easy to find, on the A60, one mile north of Nottingham center. It is on the road and has a Tudor-style facade.

Windsor Hotel, 4 Watcombe Circus (tel. Nottingham 621317), is a small, well-run hotel, just two miles north of Nottingham city center via the Mansfield road (A60). The entire hotel is centrally heated and pleasantly furnished, offering bedrooms with hot and cold running water. There are ample baths and toilets as well. For B&B, a single costs £10 ($17.50) daily, that fee rising to £17 ($29.75) in a twin. The owner, P. J. Smith, makes reductions for children. The Windsor is a remake of an Edwardian gabled private home, with bay windows and terraced gardens.

The **Flying Horse Hotel,** Poultry (tel. Nottingham 52831), is one of the hotels owned by Barni Inns, and in this case provides adequate accommodation near St. Peters Church. The public rooms have been modernized, and many have a private bath. Depending on the plumbing, singles range from £15.50 ($27.13) to £19.50 ($34.13), with doubles going for £27 ($47.25) to £31 ($54.25). In one of two restaurants, main courses begin at £4 ($7) for plaice, rising to £8.50 ($14.88) for a T-bone steak. There are nine bars (count them), including a wine bar. The inn celebrated its 500th birthday in 1983.

Food and Drink

Eviva Taverna, 25 Victoria St. (tel. Nottingham 580243). The political squabbles between Greece and Britain are over, at least during a meal in this joyful tavern. Do you like to watch Greek dancing and smash plates? If so, this is the place, although you'll be charged extra for the plates demolished. Chef's specialties include stiffado, a Greek stew of beef, onion, and herbs, cooked in wine vinegar, and kleftico, a thick piece of lamb cooked very slowly in the oven with herbs. Of course there are the inevitable dolmades, stuffed vine leaves. The owner, J. Kozakis, runs a kebab house above the tavern, offering kebabs of lamb, pork, and steak. A meal here will cost from £7.50 ($13.13), plus your wine. And plate smashing! Hours are Monday through Saturday evenings from 7 p.m. till 2 a.m.

Ben Bowers, 128 Derby Rd. (tel. 413388), is a three-in-one complex, all part of the same chain. The same phone number is valid for each member of the trio: Ben Bowers, the Palms Bar and Diner, as well as Betty's Buffet Bar. At Ben Bowers, a fixed-price luncheon menu of culinary items from around the world goes for £4.35 ($7.61). This would include, for example, salmon in tarragon cream sauce, then beef Stroganoff, topped by an almond Malakoff (whipped cream, ground almonds, vodka, and chopped fruit). An à la carte dinner would be more expensive. A three-course selection of barquettes des champignons (a pastry boat filled with mushrooms, bacon, and cheese in a brandy and cream sauce), followed by breast of chicken Balmoral (sauteed chicken breast stuffed with pâté, mushrooms, and raisins, in a Drambuie cream sauce), then perhaps a banana split Tia Maria, would come to £8.45 ($14.79). Hours are from 11 a.m. to 2:30 p.m. and 6 to 10:30 p.m. Monday to Saturday, and noon to 2 p.m. and 7 to 10:30 p.m. on Sunday.

For a more informal atmosphere, and an equally satisfying but less expensive meal, try the à la carte menu at the Palms, next door. Drinks sell for 25% off every evening until 8. A special lunch menu is offered on Sunday from noon to 2 p.m. An à la carte three-course meal, including palm hearts with prawns, then chicken à la king, followed with a rum raisin sundae, would come to £5.60 ($9.80). In the basement of Ben Bowers, Betty's Buffet Bar is the most economical choice, offering a goodly selection of bar snacks, cold meats, and salads for around £2 ($3.50).

Mr. Haddock, 103–111 Derby Rd. (tel. Nottingham 412138), offers good value. It's a fast-service place for travelers rushing through Nottingham. After a simple appetizer of soup or fruit cocktail, you can enjoy the excellent fresh fish dishes. Naturally, the chef offers haddock, but you can also be served halibut or plaice along with "chips." With bread and butter, and a cup of coffee as well, expect to pay only £2.80 ($4.90) to £3.58 ($6.27). If you're more extravagant, try the fisherman's platter, a selection of three different types of fish, served with chips and a drink at a cost of £3.95 ($6.91). For dessert, they specialize in ice creams with transatlantic names—New York butter almond, Brazilian rippled chocolate—each costing 80p ($1.40). On the side-dish extra list is "mushy peas," quite an experience to the visitor at 27p (47¢), but much beloved by the local populace.

Ye Olde Trip to Jerusalem, Brewhouse Yard, Castle Road (tel. Nottingham 43171), claims to be the oldest inn in England. It was a traditional stopover for the Crusaders on their way to the Holy Land. Founded in the 12th century, it was built right into the castle rock, and served, because of its coolness, as the castle brewery. Scientists can't fathom how the speaking tube, cut through the rocks, works—but it does. The two bars are literally cut out of the rocks, and the fireplace chimney is nearly 45 feet high, also cut out of the rock. Ginger wine is 42p (74¢), and draft cider is 68p ($1.19) a pint. Various sandwich rolls, depending on the filling, range in price from 25p (44¢) to 38p (67¢).

Grange Farm, Toton (tel. Long Eaton 69426), is a small old-world farmhouse turned restaurant which has grown and grown in size, and now does a record lunch and dinner business. It is surrounded by a suburban complex, a mile from Long Eaton, near enough to Nottingham to have many diners from there. Although somewhat touristy and gimmicky, it does provide a true English cuisine. There's a £6.50 ($11.38) set lunch, including VAT, service, and coffee in the lounge. The first course offers a choice of 18 interesting appetizers such as battered mushrooms with sweet-and-sour sauce or filet of smoked mackerel with creamy horseradish sauce. The second course presents 14 substantial dishes such as curried chicken with rice or roast loin of pork with gooseberry sauce. You'll get generous helpings of vegetables. There are 16 kinds of desserts such as apple and raspberry pie with custard, or steamed treacle sponge pudding with custard. Evening meals cost £8.50 ($14.88) and include an extra course. Lunch is served between noon and 1:45 p.m. Reservations are necessary for Friday and Saturday dinner. There are two evening settings, one at 7 p.m., another at 8:30 p.m. All is run by the Ackroyd family.

About a half-hour drive from Lord Byron's Newstead Abbey leads to—

SOUTHWELL: This ancient market town is a good center for exploring the Robin Hood country. Byron once belonged to a local amateur dramatic society here. An unexpected gem is the old twin-spired cathedral, **Southwell Minster,** which many consider the most beautiful church in England. James I found that it held up with "any other kirk in Christendom." Look for the well-proportioned Georgian houses across from the cathedral.

East of Southwell, near the Lincolnshire border, is—

NEWARK-ON-TRENT: Here is an ancient riverside market town, on the Roman Fosse Way, lying about 15 miles across flatlands from Nottingham. King John died at **Newark Castle** in 1216. Constructed between the 12th and 15th centuries, the castle, now in ruins, survived three sieges by Cromwell's troops before falling into ruin in 1646. From its parapet, you can look down on the Trent River and across to Nottingham. The delicately detailed parish church here is said to be the finest in the country. The town contains many ancient inns, reflecting its long history.

Linked to the castle by a riverside walk, the **Millgate Museum of Folk Art** (tel. Newark-on-Trent 79403) was a 19th-century oil-seed mill, then a warehouse. Today it houses a fascinating collection of local products, domestic items set in room settings, dress, toy, and art shops. You'll see demonstrations of local crafts, such as matting, blacksmithing, and wood-turning. Alongside are craft workshops where a host of young and enthusiastic craftspeople demonstrate and sell their wares. You can be sure of getting a unique and genuine article to take home.

On the outskirts, I'd suggest the following for food and lodgings:

Newcastle Arms Hotel, Tuxford (tel. Tuxford 870208), has been a village inn since 1701, welcoming such guests as Margaret Tudor, Charles II, and Mr. Gladstone. It's a Georgian-style, two-story corner building, with a plain facade, except for a pair of bay windows flanking the small pillared entrance. Furnishings are in the style of an English country inn. A single without bath rents for £16 ($28), rising to £19 ($33.25) with bath. A double or twin, depending on the plumbing, goes from £20 ($35) to £24 ($42). All units contain phones and television sets. Fully licensed, the hotel offers good food and wine. The chef does not only good-tasting English dishes, but classically continental ones along with many Asian specialties. Luncheons run from £6 ($10.50), and dinner is from £7 ($12.25). The location is on the A1, 12 miles north of Newark, 20 miles south of Doncaster.

THE DUKERIES: In the Dukeries, portions of Sherwood Forest, legendarily associated with Robin Hood, are still preserved. These are vast country estates on the edge of industrial towns. Most of the estates have disappeared, but the park at **Clumber,** covering some 4000 acres, is administered by the National

Trust, which has preserved its 18th-century beauty, as exemplified by Lime Tree Avenue. Rolling heaths and a peaceful lake add to the charm. You can visit Clumber Chapel, built in 1886-1889 as a chapel for the seventh Duke of Newcastle. It is open April 1 to September 30 on Monday to Friday, 2 to 7 p.m. On weekends its hours are noon to 7 p.m. Off-season hours are daily, 1 to 4 p.m. There is no admission fee for visiting the chapel, but vehicles entering the park are charged. The location is at Clumber Park, five miles southeast of Worksop.

A few miles south of Clumber stands the greatest Victorian house in the Midlands, **Thoresby Hall.** Built by Salvin in 1864, it is the only mansion in the Dukeries still occupied as the home of the original owners. Barton & Skills run tours from Nottingham, as it is open only by appointment. The hall lies four miles north of Otterton, just west of the Bawtry road (A614).

EASTWOOD: Because of the increased interest in D. H. Lawrence these days, many literary fans like to make a pilgrimage to Eastwood, his hometown. The English novelist was born there on September 11, 1885. Mrs. Brown, a member of the D. H. Lawrence Society, conducts parties of visitors around the "Lawrence country." Hopefully, at the end, you'll make a donation to the society. If you're interested in taking a tour, write her in advance—Mrs. M. Brown, D. H. Lawrence Society, c/o 8a Victoria St., Eastwood, Nottingham (tel. Langley Mill 68139).

The Lawrence birthplace at 8a Victoria St. has been turned into the **D. H. Lawrence Information Centre and Museum** (curator's home telephone is Langley Mill 66611), now authentically depicting a miner's home as it was in 1885. The Eastwood Library houses a unique collection of Lawrence's works and the headstone from his grave on the French Riviera. Hours are 1:30 to 4 p.m. on Sunday, Monday, Tuesday, Thursday, and Friday, from 9:30 a.m. to noon on Wednesday, and from 9:30 a.m. to 4 p.m. on Saturday. Admission is 25p (44¢).

SCROOBY: This is a tiny village of some 260 inhabitants where in 1566 William Brewster, a leader of the Pilgrim Fathers, was born. His father was bailiff of the manor and master of the postes, so it may have been in the Manor House that the infant Brewster first saw the light of day. The original house dated from the 12th century, and the present manor farm, built on the site in the 18th century, has little except historical association to attract.

Brewster Cottage, with its pinfold where stray animals were impounded, lies beside the village church of St. Wilfred. But it's uncertain whether the Pilgrim Father ever lived there.

The village also contains Monks Hill on the River Ryton, now almost a backwater but once a navigable stream down which Brewster and his companions may have escaped to travel to Leyden in Holland and on to their eventual freedom.

In the 18th century the turnpike ran through the village, and there are many stories of highwaymen, robberies, and murders. The body of John Spencer hung for more than 60 years as a reminder of the penalties of wrongdoing. He'd attempted to dispose of the bodies of the keeper of Scrooby toll-bar and his mother in the river.

READER'S SEARCH FOR PILGRIM ROOTS: "Since so many North Americans are descended from the Pilgrims, I feel certain that there are many who, like me, might be eager to see the area from which their ancestors came. The Separatist movement started in an area north of Nottingham and south of York. The towns from which its members came are all in a small area and include **Blyth, Scrooby, Austerfield, Bawtry,** and **Babworth.** Both the Scrooby and Babworth churches welcome North American visitors. William Brewster, the Pilgrim Father, lived in Scrooby, and his farmhouse is still standing, identified by a plaque. William Bradford's birthplace was a manor house in Austerfield, still standing and well maintained. It can be visited by arrangement with the occupant. We did not see Babworth, but of the other towns, Blyth was the most delightful, a village of 900 with a beautiful green surrounded by beautiful old houses. The parish church was developed from the 11th-century Norman nave of a Benedictine priory church, and on the green is a 12th-century stone building, once the Hospital of St. John.

"Blyth can also boast of a fine, small hotel with an excellent dining room, the **Fourways Hotel** (tel. Blyth 235). Rates for a large room and breakfast are about £24 ($42) for two persons.

"This Blyth, by the way, is not to be confused with the Blyth on the northeastern coast of England" (Miriam C. Timbrell, Hackettstown, N.J.).

5. Lincolnshire

This large East Midlands county is bordered on one side by the North Sea. Its most interesting section is Holland, in the southeast, a land known for its fields of tulips, its marshes and fens, and windmills reminiscent of the Netherlands. Although much of the shire is interesting to explore, time is too important for most visitors to linger long. Foreigners, particularly North Americans, generally cross the tulip fields, scheduling stopovers in the busy port of Boston before making the swing north to the cathedral city of Lincoln, lying inland.

BOSTON: This old seaport in the riding of Holland has a namesake that has gone on to greater glory, and perhaps for this reason it is visited by New Englanders. At Scotia Creek, on a riverbank near Boston, is a memorial to the early Pilgrims who made an unsuccessful attempt in 1607 to reach the promised land. They were imprisoned in the Guildhall in cells that can be visited today. A company left again in 1620 and fared better, as anybody who has ever been to Massachusetts will testify. Part of the ritual here is climbing the Boston Stump, a church lantern tower with a view for miles around of the all-encircling fens. In the 1930s, the people of Boston, U.S.A., paid for the restoration of the tower, known officially as St. Botolph's Tower. Actually, it's not recommended that you climb the tower, as the stairs aren't in good shape. The tower, as it stands, was finished in 1460. The city fathers were going to add a spire, making it the tallest in England. But because of the wind and the weight, they feared the tower would collapse. Therefore, the tower became known as "the Boston Stump." An elderly gentleman at the tower assured me it was the tallest in England—that is, 272½ feet tall. Boston is 116 miles north from London, and 34 miles southeast of Lincoln.

Accommodations

The attractive **White Hart** (tel. Boston 64877) is a Berni Inn right by the bridge with some rooms overlooking the river. There is good car parking. Singles range from £16 ($28) to £21 ($36.75), including a full English breakfast, service, and VAT. Doubles go from £28 ($49) to £34 ($59.50). The difference in price depends on the room's location and whether or not it has a private bath. The location is right in the center, near the Boston Stump and the courthouse and prison. The inn has two restaurants. The Steak and Duck is a self-service salad bar, with prices about 10% higher than in the Steak and Chicken, where you can order soup, fish, vegetables, and a dessert for £3.95 ($6.91) or £5.90 ($10.33) if you go for the steak.

Fairfield Guest House, 101 London Rd. (tel. Boston 62869), is an economy oasis where you can spend the night in a gracious stone Victorian house set in its own garden. Built originally for a large family, it has been adapted successfully to receive overnight guests. Yet the personal quality hasn't been sacrificed. At the edge of Boston, it is reached by a driveway leading to a formal entry. The bedrooms have hot and cold running water and are centrally heated and pleasantly furnished. For B&B, you'll be charged £9 ($15.75) per person nightly, and you can order an evening meal for £5 ($8.75). The owners are L. P. and F. Shanley.

Causeway Guest House, Causeway, Wyberton (tel. Boston 66260), is a Georgian-style farmhouse built in 1850 and is on the Causeway, just off Saundergate Lane and the A16. It is only two miles from Boston, and is owned by Mr. and Mrs. Philip Harris who have adapted their home to accommodate guests. They charge £8 ($14) per person for B&B, and if you want one of Mrs. Harris's home-cooked dinners, the cost is only £4 ($7). Each room has hot and cold running water, there's plenty of car parking space, and for evenings there's a TV lounge.

READER'S GUEST HOUSE SELECTION: "We stayed at **Holgate Guest House,** on the 105 London Rd. in Boston (tel. Boston 64648). Because of the beautiful decor, comfortable facilities, friendly reception of the owners, and reasonable price, we feel this one deserves special mention. Mr. and Mrs. J. R. Wells have converted this old squire's house into something special, with a foyer containing tiles, hunting prints, and various brass and furniture antiques. The dining room has impressive dark stained tables, a high ceiling, and large windows overlooking the garden. Our spacious room had a sink. The bathroom was next door, and toilet facilities were nearby. The price in a single is £9.50 ($16.63), going up to £18 ($31.50) in a double. An evening meal begins at £3.50 ($6.13)" (Mrs. Kenneth Kelley, Boyds, Md.).

Where to Dine

The Carving Table, New England Hotel, Wide Bargate (tel. Boston 65255), offers the best food value in town. In its carving room guests are invited to choose their main dish from a selection of freshly roasted joints of prime meat, carved by the hotel chef. You help yourself to vegetables or else decide on a good-tasting cold meal served direct from a buffet. The special luncheon price is £5.50 ($9.63). In the evening the price goes up to £6 ($10.50), and children are served for £3.50 ($6.13). A choice of desserts from the trolley include fruit salad and fruit pie, all served with fresh cream. A cheese board is also presented. Appetizers are priced extra, but I found that one is unnecessary considering the amount of food offered at the fixed price. Carving room hours are noon to 2 p.m. and 7 to 10 p.m. seven days a week. In addition the hotel also serves bar snacks Monday to Saturday from noon to 2 p.m. Prices range from 50p (88¢) to £1.75 ($3.06).

LINCOLN: One of the most ancient cities in England, and only 135 miles north of London, Lincoln was known to the Romans as Lindum. Some of the architectural glory of the Roman Empire still stands to charm the present-day visitor. The renowned Newport Arch (the North Gate) is the last remaining arch left in Britain that still spans a principal highway. For a look at the Roman relics excavated in and around Lincoln, head for the **City and County Museum,** Broadgate (tel. Lincoln 30401), open daily from 10 a.m. to 5:30 p.m. (2:30 to 5 p.m. on Sunday). Admission is 25p (44¢) for adults, 10p (18¢) for children.

Two years after the Battle of Hastings, William the Conqueror built **Lincoln Castle** on the site of a Roman fortress. Used for administrative purposes, parts of the castle still remain, including the walls, the 12th-century keep, and fragments of the gateway tower. In addition, you can visit the High Bridge over the Witham River, with its half-timbered houses (you can have a meal in one of them). This is one of the few medieval bridges left in England that has buildings nestling on it.

Lincoln Cathedral

Towering over the ancient city, the Minster forms a grand sight, with its three towers. The central one is 271 feet tall, making it the second tallest in England, ranking under the Boston Stump, mentioned earlier. However, the central tower at Lincoln was once the tallest spire in the world (525 feet) until it blew down in 1549. The Norman cathedral was consecrated in 1092, but only the west front remains. The cathedral represents the Gothic style, particularly the Early English and Decorated periods. The nave, in its present form, was built in the early 13th century. In the Early English Great Transept, you can see a rose medallion window, known as the Dean's Eye. The rose window at the opposite end of the transept, in the Decorated style, is known as the Bishop's Eye. The Angel Choir, in the eastern end, completed in the 13th century, was named after the sculptured angels displayed in it. The exquisite carving in the choir dates from the 14th century. The black font of Tournai marble is from the 11th century.

In the Seamen's Chapel is a window commemorating Lincolnshire-born Capt. John Smith, one of the pioneers of early settlement in America and the first governor of Virginia.

The Library, in the Cloister, was built in 1674 by Sir Christopher Wren. It contains many fine books and manuscripts, some of which are on view in the adjoining Medieval Library, together with one of the four remaining original copies of Magna Carta of 1215, the Cathedral Charter of 1072, and the Foresters' Charter of 1225. The Library is open Monday through Saturday, 10:30 a.m. to 4:30 p.m. May through September, and in winter by appointment (tel. Lincoln 21089). Cost is 20p (35¢).

In the Treasury (open weekdays from 2:30 to 4:30 p.m., May through September), there is fine gold and silver plate from churches in the diocese.

In line with many other great churches, the cathedral has adopted the medieval custom of asking for admission fees. If you refuse, you will still not be excluded, however. Adults are asked to contribute 50p (88¢); children, 20p (35¢). All monies gathered are devoted to maintenance and repair of the ancient structure. There is a Minster Shop where you can contribute more funds by purchasing the attractive souvenirs, and the Coffee Shop run at the entrance to the library stairs also helps out.

Where to Stay

Hillcrest Hotel, 15 Lindum Terrace (tel. Lincoln 26341), is a fine red-brick house built in 1871 as the private home of a local vicar. And although it has been converted into a comfortable small licensed hotel, it retains many of the features of its original use. It is suitable for those who appreciate a homey atmosphere where personal tastes can be accommodated. It is in a quiet tree-lined road overlooking 26 acres of parkland, in the old high town and within easy walking distance of Lincoln Cathedral and the Roman remains. It is the home of the proprietors, Mr. and Mrs. Baker, who have made substantial improvements in recent years. There are color TV and wash basins in all rooms. The charge is from £14.75 ($25.81) in a single and from £23 ($40.25) in a double, with a £2 ($3.50) supplement assessed for a room with private bath. The à la carte restaurant serves a three-course meal for around £7.50 ($13.13).

St. Catherine's South Park Hotel, 21 St. Catherine's (tel. Lincoln 20498), is centrally located, opposite the South Commons. Its Edwardian architecture with its ornate triple front dormers and bay windows make it a delightful place to stay. The price of a single room here is £12.50 ($21.88), the same rate per person for either single or double occupancy. By the time of your arrival, some rooms may contain private baths and will cost more. Monday through Friday you can have an à la carte lunch or dinner for £8 ($14). A set meal goes for £4.50 ($7.88). It's worth considering as the cook knows and uses Lincolnshire recipes. Amenities available: a coin-operated launderette, showers, a car park, a patio with a rock garden, and a fish pond in the rear garden. There's also a bar with medieval decor.

The **Hollies Hotel,** Carholme Road (tel. Lincoln 22419), owned by the Williams family, provides clean, comfortable accommodations at fair prices. Including VAT and a tasty breakfast, the per-person rate in a single or double is £10 ($17.50) nightly. Each room is centrally heated, with hot and cold running water and a radio. During the day it's possible to obtain a light meal, but no evening meal is served. There's a free car park as well.

Fircroft Private Hotel, 398 Newark Rd. (tel. Lincoln 26522). Chris and Pete Vasey run a very friendly, clean, and comfortable B&B house, for which they charge £11 ($19.25) in a single, from £19 ($33.25) in a double, and from £23 ($40.25) in a triple. All these charges include a full English breakfast and VAT. All their pleasantly furnished rooms have tea- and coffee-making facilities and are heated. There are three showers, and the individual units contain hot and cold running water. In the lounge is a color TV. They have a Tudor-style dining room and a small cocktail bar, serving an evening meal for £5 ($8.75) per head. Sandwiches are usually available at most times when the dining room is closed.

Delph Guest House, 177 Carholme Rd. (tel. Lincoln 29578), is run by Mrs. Dorr, who offers clean, pleasantly furnished rooms, charging £7 ($12.25) per person for B&B, including the service charge and VAT. An evening meal can be ordered in advance for only £3 ($5.25).

On the outskirts, you'll find **The Graffoe,** Hall Lane, at Branston (tel. 0522/791452), less than five miles from the center of Lincoln at Branston on the B1188. Mrs. Jean Stevenson offers B&B in her charming country house. A bed and a large, cooked-to-order breakfast costs only £5.50 ($9.63) per person. An evening meal, a three-course family type, costs £3.50 ($6.13). Drive to Branston, then turn right at the Waggon and Horses for Mrs. Stevenson's red-brick house.

READER'S FARMHOUSE SELECTION (NEAR LINCOLN): "Mr. and Mrs. Bradshaw, Sturton-by-Stow (tel. Gainsborough 788309), have a farmhouse B&B in the center of the village. Mr. Bradshaw operates a 350-acre mixed farm, with cattle, sheep, and horses, as well as grain fields. Mrs. Bradshaw, extremely hospitable, met us with tea and cookies. Their home has been modernized, with full central heating, new carpets, and antiques for decoration. Rooms are spotlessly clean and well furnished, renting for £9.50 ($16.63) per night per person. Light evening meals are available at a nearby pub. There is color TV in the lounge, and the breakfast is quite good. The Bradshaws' home is near a championship golf course and about 12 minutes from Lincoln. This is one of the best farm B&Bs we found on our trip" (Robert B. Miller, Poway, Calif.).

Where to Dine

High Bridge, 207 High St. (tel. Lincoln 23548), is a 16th-century tea room built over the medieval bridge that is one of the sightseeing attractions of Lincoln. If you're seeking only tea and coffee, R. W. Stokes & Sons are specialists. The building is timbered with black-and-white beams. From the room on the top floor there is a view of the river and bridge. You reach the tea room by going through a little shop on the bridge level. Food here is a bargain. A complete luncheon, including a main course such as roast beef with Yorkshire pudding, vegetables, and a dessert (perhaps steamed blackberry and apple pudding), costs around £2.40 ($4.20). Lunch is served from 11:50 a.m. to 2:15 p.m. (no dinners).

The **Grand Hotel,** St. Mary's Street (tel. Lincoln 24211), opens its restaurant to nonresidents—in fact, it seats 150 diners who know that they're getting economical if unimaginative food. The waitresses serve with a personal touch. From 7 to 8:30 p.m. a table d'hôte dinner is offered for £5.60 ($9.80). Meals are inclusive, priced according to the entree. The food is not only good and typically English, but the portions are ample.

The first course usually consists of a bowl of soup. Then comes the meat course, such as a roast leg of pork with apple sauce and a big bowl of vegetables, served family style. For dessert you can select desserts from the trolley. But that's not all: even cheese and biscuits (crackers) are included in the price. You can also lunch at the Grand from noon to 2 p.m. A buttery is open from 10:30 a.m. to 10 p.m.

The **Duke William Hotel,** 44 Bailgate (tel. Lincoln 30257), has an 18th-century pub which offers good food and drink at its location near the cathedral. An unpretentious but savory lunch is served here from noon to 2:30, Monday to Saturday. Only cold snacks are offered on Sunday from noon to 1:45 p.m. A ploughman's or fisherman's lunch will cost £1 ($1.75), while sandwiches go for only 80p ($1.40). You might order soup and french bread, followed by steak-and-kidney pie, at only £2.30 ($4.03). Dinners, served Monday to Saturday from 7:30 to 9:30 p.m., are more elaborate. For about £7 ($12.25), you can compose a three-course meal beginning with pâté and toast, following with pork marsala and fresh vegetables, then dessert.

Crust, 46 Broadgate (tel. Lincoln 40322), is a century-old building, an olde-worlde-style restaurant that occupies a site on the Old Roman Road. The chef-patron, Malta-born Victor Vella, has won a number of gold and silver medals for his cookery. He is assisted by his wife, Sylvia. They offer one of the best restaurant bargains in Lincoln, a fixed-price lunch for only £1.95 ($3.41). For that, you get three courses of well-prepared food. Other fixed-priced luncheon menus cost £3.50 ($6.13) and £4.95 ($8.66). The à la carte dinner menu is more elaborate, including such specialties as escalope of veal maréchale and steak Diane. You'll spend a lot more too, from £10 ($17.50) and up. A special luncheon menu, served from noon to 1:45 p.m. on Sunday, costs only £3.75 ($6.56) and includes the traditional roast beef and Yorkshire pudding. Morning coffee and cake are served from 10:30 to 11:30 a.m., lunch from 11:30 a.m. to 2:30 p.m., and dinner from 7 to 10:15 p.m., Tuesday to Thursday. On Friday and Saturday last orders are taken at 11:15 p.m.

Harvey's Cathedral Restaurant, 1 Exchequer Gate, Castle Square (tel. Lincoln 21886), is just around the corner from the cathedral and castle. A small split-level eatery, it is bright and clean and owned by Bob and Adrienne Harvey. You get a very filling two-course meal here for around £2.50 ($4.38). You'll always find steak-and-mushroom pie, or its equivalent, on the menu, along with a dessert such as apple crumble. On Sunday a magnificent rib of beef is the centerpiece of a three-course meal costing £6 ($10.50). Harvey's is open Monday to Saturday from noon to 2 p.m. and from 7 to 11:30 p.m. (on Sunday from noon to 2 p.m. only).

STAMFORD: This is a charming stone market town. One mile to the southeast stands **Burghley House,** a magnificent Elizabethan house, the home of the Marquess of Exeter.

The **Crown Hotel** in Stamford (tel. Stamford 3136) stands on All Saints Place, a cobbled street near the church. It's a reasonable alternative to the much higher priced George Hotel, and the establishment is also useful to those visiting Burghley House. Modest bedrooms rent for anywhere from £15 ($26.25) to £17 ($29.75) in a single and from £20 ($35) to £25 ($43.75) in a double, including breakfast. Meals served in the bar include fish dishes from £4 ($7) to £6 ($10.50), and roast beef from the trolley, at £4 ($7).

Mrs. Mary Taylor, 44 Rutland Rd. (tel. Stamford 3459), provides a good B&B, offering only three bedrooms whose guests must share the bath. Breakfast is served in a conservatory dining room looking out onto a large private garden. The house lies on a quiet suburban road. The rate for B&B is from £6.50 ($11.38) per person daily, with vegetarians getting a slight reduction.

READER'S GUEST HOUSE SELECTION (FOLKINGHAM): "While driving north on the A15 toward Sleaford, we chanced upon the charming village of Folkingham, a tiny place where the 18th-century houses have maintained their original appearance. **Mrs. Mary Bradley,** 31 Market Pl. (tel. Folkingham 281), and her husband run a wonderful guest house within one of these houses. Not only is the village charming, the Bradleys are as well. They are avid nature lovers and told us of some choice birdwatching spots in the area. They also informed us about the history of the town and its medieval church. The rooms are comfortable, and the breakfast was perhaps the best we had in a month of traveling in Britain. The elegant exterior of the house made us fear that it would be quite expensive, but we were charged only £7 ($12.25) per person for B&B. Folkingham is a serene village on the edge of the Fens, worth a stop, and it is strategically located between the cities of Peterborough, Boston, Lincoln, Nottingham, and Leicester" (Marshall Cohen, Newton, Mass.).

Chapter XIV

CHESHIRE, LIVERPOOL, AND THE LAKES

1. Chester
2. Nantwich
3. Liverpool
4. Kendal
5. Windermere
6. Ambleside
7. Rydal
8. Grasmere
9. Hawkshead
10. Keswick
11. Bassenthwaite
12. Penrith

ONE OF ENGLAND'S most popular summer retreats in Queen Victoria's day was the Lake District in the northwest. It enjoyed vogue during the flowering of the Lake Poets, including Wordsworth, who was ecstatically moved by the rugged beauty of this area. In its time, the district has lured such writers as S. T. Coleridge, Charles Lamb, Shelley, Keats, Alfred Lord Tennyson, Matthew Arnold, and Charlotte Brontë.

The Lake District is a miniature Switzerland condensed into about 32 miles, principally in Cumbria, although it begins in the northern part of Lancashire.

As an added bonus, I've included Liverpool, plus Cheshire, a county that lies south of Lancashire. I suggest that you make a pilgrimage to the ancient city of Chester, with its medieval walls, near the border of Wales.

The northwest of England is one of the special parts of the country, yet is rarely visited by the agenda-loaded foreigner who considers it too far removed. In many ways, however, its remoteness is part of its charm. Have you ever seen one of those English-made films depicting the life of the Lake District? A soft mist hovers over the hills and dells, sheep graze silently on the slope of the pasture—and a foggy enchantment fills the air.

But first—

CHESHIRE

This county is low lying and largely agricultural. The name it gave to a cheese (Cheshire) has spread across the world. This northwestern county borders Wales, which accounts for its turbulent history. The towns and villages of Cheshire are peaceful and quiet, forming a good base for touring North Wales, the most beautiful part of that little country. For our headquarters in Cheshire, we'll locate at:

1. Chester

Chester is ancient, having been founded by a Roman legion on the Dee River in the first century A.D. It reached its pinnacle as a bustling port in the 13th and 14th centuries, declining thereafter following the gradual silting up of the river. The upstart Liverpudlians captured the sea-trafficking business. The other walled medieval cities of England were either torn down or badly fragmented, but Chester still retains two miles of fortified city walls intact.

The main entrance into Chester is Eastgate, itself dating back to only the 18th century. Within the walls are half-timbered houses and shops. Of course, not all of them came from the days of the Tudors. Chester is freakish architecturally in that some of its builders kept to the black-and-white timbered facades even when erecting buildings during the Georgian and Victorian periods, with their radically different tastes.

The Rows are double-decker layers of shops, one tier on the street level, the other stacked on top and connected by a footway. The upper tier is like a continuous galleried balcony. Shopping upstairs is much more adventurous than down on the street. Rain is never a problem. Thriving establishments operate in this traffic-free paradise: tobacco shops, restaurants, department stores, china shops, jewelers, and antique dealers. For the most representative look, take an arcaded walk on Watergate Street.

At noon and at 3 p.m. daily at the City Cross, the world's champion town crier issues his news (local stuff on sales, exhibitions, and attractions in the city) at the top of his not-inconsiderable voice, to the accompaniment of a hand bell, at the junction of Watergate, Northgate, and Bridge Streets.

After exploring The Rows, focus your attention on:

CHESTER CATHEDRAL: The present building, founded in 1092 as a Benedictine abbey, was created as a cathedral church in 1541. Considerable architectural restorations were carried out in the 19th century, but older parts have been preserved. Notable features include the fine range of monastic buildings, particularly the cloisters and refectory, the chapter house, and the superb medieval wood carving in the quire (especially the misericords). Also worth attention are the long south transept with its various chapels, the consistory court, and the medieval roof bosses in the Lady Chapel. A free-standing bell tower, the first to be built in England since the Reformation, was completed in 1975 and may be seen southeast of the main building. For more information, telephone Chester 25920.

HERITAGE CENTER: The **Chester Heritage Centre,** St. Michael's Church, Bridge Street Row (tel. Chester 317948), is open from April to September, Monday to Saturday, except Wednesday, from 10 a.m. to 5 p.m. (on Sunday from 2 to 5 p.m.). From October to March, it is open every day except Wednesday from 1:30 to 4:30 p.m. Admission for adults is 50p (88¢), and children pay 25p (44¢). The center contains an audio-visual display on the character of

Chester and its historic buildings. This provides an excellent introduction to the city for visitors. There is also a permanent exhibition on the conservation of the city's heritage and the continuous program of restoration work which is arranged by Chester City Council.

The City Record Office in Chester has responsibility for the administration of the Heritage Centre, and the City Archivist arranges for special temporary exhibitions to be shown. These generally have a local and historic theme but can include the work of local craftspeople.

READER'S SIGHTSEEING TIP: "In the center of the town, we noticed an interesting old clock mounted on a wall. It is possible to climb a flight of steps to the top of the wall, and from a point on the wall near the old clock, you can follow the wall back to your original point. We spent an absorbing 1½ hours on this walk. The wall seems to pass through thousands of years of English history. We passed by men playing cricket, had views of the River Dee which was formerly a major trade artery, and went by many old buildings of 18th-century vintage, some of which were being renovated. The wall also goes past some Roman ruins, and it was possible here to leave the walkway on the wall to explore the ruins further. The entire walk is charming, not strenuous, and free" (Susan M. Kocik, New York, N.Y.).

ACCOMMODATIONS: The **Cavendish Hotel,** 44 Hough Green (tel. Chester 675100), is attractive, well furnished, and reasonable. It is a well restored and elegantly furnished Edwardian residence set in its own landscaped garden. There is a large car park, and the city center is within walking distance. Each bedroom is fully equipped with hot and cold running water, central heating, and color TV. The charge is £12.50 ($21.88) in a single, £20.50 ($35.88) in a double. The lounge recreates the mood of the Edwardian era, both in its decor and the antiques that furnish it. The dining room serves a limited but select menu, with dinner around £6 ($10.50), and packed lunches are available upon request. There's also a small residents bar. In all, it has a lot of cozy charm.

Ye Olde King's Head, 48 Lower Bridge St. (tel. Chester 24855), is a 17th-century museum piece of black-and-white architecture. From 1598 to 1707, it was occupied by the well-known Randle Holme family of Chester, noted heraldic painters and genealogists (some of their manuscripts have made it to the British Museum). Since 1717, the King's Head has been a licensed inn. The host rents out a dozen handsomely groomed bedrooms, charging from £12 ($21) to £17 ($29.75) in a single and from £18 ($31.50) to £24 ($42) in a double, including a full English breakfast, VAT, and service. There are reductions for two nights or more. The rooms are linked with the past, with soft mattresses and eiderdown covers. Many of the walls and ceilings are sloped and highly pitched, and the decor is enhanced by exposed beams.

The residents' lounge, with its massive beams overhead, boasts a Tudor fireplace, along with authentic furnishings, such as an elaborate grandfather clock, an octagonal card table, high-backed Jacobean oak chairs, and soft upholstered pieces. The main lounge has a number of wall settles, barrel tables, wood paneling, and a Tudor fireplace. The 17th-century dining room is also a showcase of timberwork, with old furnishings, such as a Welsh cupboard and pewter and copper pieces. A set lunch costs £4 ($8.75). Dinner, served from 6:30 to 9 p.m., might include the following: a steaming bowl of nutritious soup, roast Cheshire chicken with stuffing and three vegetables, and deep-dish fruit pie with cream. The set price is £5.50 ($9.63).

Eaton House, 36 Eaton Rd. (tel. Chester 671346), lies in a quiet residential area within walking distance of the town center and the main tourist attractions, including the medieval rows and the city walls. There is car parking on the grounds. Each unit contains hot and cold running water, and three of the accommodations are large family rooms. The charge for B&B is £7 ($12.25) per person daily, the tariff increasing to £9 ($15.75) per person with an evening meal included. There is a comfortable TV lounge, and a full English breakfast is served in the attractive dining room. For parents traveling with children, cots, high chairs, and bunk beds are available on request. Thoughtful extras include packed lunches and morning tea in the rooms. Evening snacks are also available. Car tours to Snowdonia and the Lake District can be arranged.

The **Eversley Private Hotel,** 9 Eversley Park (tel. Chester 373744), lies off Liverpool Road, about a mile from the heart of old Chester. Richard and Vera Roberts have fully modernized this select little nine-bedroom hotel, for which they charge from £8.50 ($14.88) per person nightly. They also quote a half-board rate of £13 ($22.75) per person daily. Rooms are comfortably furnished, and the house stands in a peaceful residential section.

Upstairs Downstairs Guest House, 49 Lower Bridge St. (tel. Chester 21139), is run by Pat and Lilian, who provide good beds and a pleasant, inviting atmosphere at a most reasonable price—from £6.50 ($11.38) in a single, from £12 ($21) in a double, including breakfast. Everything is maintained spotlessly clean. The house dates from some four centuries ago but has been well kept. It stands within walking distance of the center of Chester.

READERS' GUEST HOUSE SELECTIONS: "The house was immaculate, and our room was furnished in a much finer manner than most B&B houses provide. We had hardly gotten our coats off when Mr. Cowie was at the door, with tea and digestive biscuits (cookies to me). The house is in walking distance of Chester city center, and Mr. Cowie told us a lot about the attractions. The food was very good and served so happily that I wish we could have stayed longer. The charge for B&B is £6 ($10.50) per person per night, including VAT. The name of the place is **Elgin,** 2 Princes Ave., City Road (tel. Chester 23372)" (Mrs. James K. Drew, Jr.). . . . "I stayed at **Mrs. Edmund's B&B,** 14 Queens Rd., off City Road (tel. Chester 316192). It is three minutes from the train station, and from there you can get a bus to the city center for 10p (18¢). Singles rent for £7.50 ($13.13) per night for B&B" (Ray LaFever, Arlington, Va.).

WHERE TO EAT: The **Courtyard,** 13 St. Werburgh St. (tel. Chester 21447), was originally a stable courtyard, opposite the south transept of the cathedral. Today, it's been turned into one of the finest dining spots in Chester. The narrow entrance, with its black-and-white decorative motif, sets the stage for a two-in-one restaurant. Opening into the inner courtyard and up a steep flight of steps is the ingeniously designed split-level bistro, which offers an à la carte and a buffet luncheon from noon to 2:30 p.m.

A smörgåsbord lunch is individually priced with hot dishes, cold meats, and salads. Prices range from 75p ($1.31) per helping. From 6 to 10 p.m., the restaurant offers a bistro dinner where you serve yourself for an inclusive price of £7.50 ($13.13). It's good value. A more elaborate à la carte menu is available from 7 to 10 p.m., including items such as roast rib of beef with savory butters (for two people), carved at the table, at around £9 ($15.75) per person. A specialty appetizer is Raymond's homemade pâté or oeufs sur le plat florentine. The chef's specialty desserts are Mercedes gâteau and walnut fudge gâteau. The Courtyard is open from 10:30 a.m. Monday through Saturday. There is dancing Monday to Friday.

Bear & Billet Inn, Lower Bridge Street (tel. Chester 21272), with its intricately timbered and highly decorative facade from the mid-17th century, is one of the most famous buildings in Chester. The restored pub and restaurant was once a city house belonging to the Earls of Shrewsbury. It still preserves its traditional atmosphere. Mr. and Mrs. Stanley Rix have recently taken over this landmark inn and have brought about major changes, opening the first- and second-floor restaurants. A traditional time-tested English menu is served, and that means such classic dishes as cockles and mussels, the original "Sir Loin" (that's sirloin steak), and old dessert favorites such as bread pudding and syllabub. Much research went into the menu which a reader, Roscoe E. Hill, dean at the University of Denver, called "the most authentic in the kingdom." I concur. Expect to spend from £7 ($12.12) or a lot more for your dinner.

The **Witch's Kitchen,** Frodsham Street (tel. Chester 311836), is in the center of town, just a short walk from the station. It seats 100 and has old-world charm and good service. The ground-floor restaurant is 15 yards from the city walls and Chester Cathedral. It is open every day for morning coffee (10 a.m.); luncheon (11:30 a.m. till 5:30 p.m.), high tea (5 to 6:30 p.m.), afternoon tea (3 to 5 p.m.) and dinner (7 to 10:30 p.m.). À la carte meals are served all day, and the Kitchen is open seven days a week. Luncheon is a three-course meal, costing from £2.25 ($3.94) to £3.50 ($6.13), beginning with juice or soup, a choice of three different roasts (beef, pork, or chicken), fried filet of plaice or a salad, vegetables, and a choice of potatoes, ending with a dessert or coffee. And for £4 ($7) a traditional three-course Sunday luncheon is served which includes soup or fruit juice, roast beef and Yorkshire pudding with horseradish sauce, vegetables, and a choice of dessert. The Cheshire chicken is a favorite dish. Traditional roasts are served all day every day, costing about £3 ($5.25).

Jean's Kitchen, St. Anne Street (tel. Chester 381313), is open midday for lunch and from 5:30 to 7 p.m. for the set dinner. The restaurant serves both à la carte and complete meals. Ask for the "Rougier" menu for a three-course meal that includes tax and service charge for around £3.50 ($6.13). The food is excellent and prepared with a different touch. The kitchen is open until 10 p.m., and it is advised that you make a reservation if you plan to dine after 7 p.m.

Pierre Griffe Wine Bars, 4–6 Mercia Square, off Frodsham Street (tel. Chester 312635), is a warmly decorated bar a stone's throw from the cathedral. It specializes in selling vintage wine by the glass, along with a changing menu of wholesome food written on a blackboard. You can choose, for example, chicken-and-leek soup, then veal in a sherry and cream sauce, served with rice, and finally, a black cherry cheesecake—all for a cost of only £3.10 ($5.43). If you'd prefer a lighter lunch from the cold buffet of salads, English cheeses, and homemade pâtés, it will run about £1.85 ($3.24). The wine bars are open daily from 11:30 a.m. to 3 p.m. and from 5:30 to 10:30 p.m. (until 11 p.m. on Friday and Saturday).

The **Gallery Restaurant,** 24 Paddock Row, Grosvenor Precinct (tel. Chester 47202), is festooned with masses of green plants which make walking in here a little like going into an indoor garden. Mr. Jones, the host and owner, has created a conservatory atmosphere by the use of green and white walls and curtains, along with the plants and hanging baskets. A varied menu is displayed on a chalkboard. Three courses with wine can be enjoyed for under £5 ($8.75) at lunch from noon to 2:15 p.m. daily except Sunday, and for under £7 ($12.25) at dinner from 6:30 to 9:30 p.m. except Sunday. Afternoon tea is served here every day except Sunday from 3 to 5 p.m., which makes for a relaxing diversion after shopping and sightseeing.

The **Carriage Restaurant,** Mercia Square, off Frodsham Street (tel. Chester 23469), is part of the Deering restaurant chain. Its modern glass facade conceals the pseudo-Gothic ceiling with iron and wood arches. An à la carte menu offers attractive choices of salads, grilled meats, and fish, all for around £2.70 ($4.73) to £5.75 ($10.05). But an attractive fixed-price menu offers better value at £3.40 ($5.95) for two courses and £3.95 ($6.91) for three courses. Selections include, for example, a homemade soup, followed by roast chicken with bacon and stuffing, served with giblet gravy. Desserts feature a large eclair packed with ice cream and topped with hazelnuts. Hours are from noon to 2:30 p.m. and 5:30 to 10 p.m., Monday through Saturday.

The **Farmhouse Serve-Yourself Kitchen,** 9–13 Northgate St. (tel. Chester 311332), offers some of the most inexpensive—and best—meals in the city in a friendly setting above a sporting goods outlet. There is no menu, but lots of plants frame a blackboard where daily specials are written. Chicken in wine sauce or a Greek-inspired moussaka, accompanied by a fennel or beansprout salad, would cost only £2.20 ($3.85). At least 16 different, freshly made salads are displayed daily, ranging from Waldorf to pineapple and celery. A selection of homemade hot dishes is also offered daily, including a wide range of what they call "old favourites." A host of desserts, all for under 70p ($1.23), completes a satisfying meal. Hours are from 9 a.m. to 5 p.m. (till 5:30 p.m. in summer).

Claverton's Wine Bar, Lower Bridge Street (tel. Chester 319760), is very popular with the locals in the evening, a good way to see—if not to meet—the people of Chester. The place is attractively decorated, the food good and reasonable. No wonder it's such a popular choice. Begin, perhaps, with the leek-and-potato soup, followed by fisherman's pie (cod, mushrooms, and potatoes in a white sauce), or a selection from the cold buffet. A large salad is included with the meal, and this, along with homemade apple pie with cream, would come to only £3.25 ($5.69). The buffet, incidentally, is exceptional, in that it often includes game pie and fish mousse. An unusual dish, at least to Americans, is the fresh trout served with a gooseberry sauce. In addition to the regular mixed drinks, wines are available by the glass, as are "mocktails" for drivers or those nursing a hangover from the day before. Claverton's is open Monday to Saturday from 11 a.m. to 3 p.m. and 5:30 to 10:30 p.m. Sunday hours are 11 a.m. to 3 p.m. and 7 to 10:30 p.m.

AN EXCURSION TO CONWY CASTLE (WALES): The most popular excursion from Chester is to the castle and walled town of Conwy in Wales, a distance of some 48 miles. The town contains many interesting old buildings, including the National Trust property of Aberconwy, Plas Mawr, and what is said to be the smallest house in Britain.

However, the major interest, of course, centers on **Conwy Castle,** built between 1283 and 1289 and considered a perfect specimen of medieval fortifications in Britain. Following the contours of a narrow strip of rock, the eight towers of the castle dominate the estuary of the River Conwy. The castle stands at the harbor where the river finds its way to the sea. From these old walls you can see the small fishing fleet at anchor in the sheltered harbor. Fishermen bring in their catch of mussels and Conwy dabs here.

The castle (tel. Conwy 2358) is open from 9:30 a.m. to 6:30 p.m. from mid-March to mid-October. Otherwise, it is open weekdays from 9:30 a.m. to 4 p.m. and on Sunday from 2 to 4 p.m. The summer admission charge is 85p ($1.49) for adults and 60p ($1.05) for children and senior citizens. In winter, charges are reduced to 40p (70¢) for adults and 20p (35¢) for children.

The town wall, which protected the borough laid out by Edward I below the castle, is still nearly intact. It is flanked by 21 towers and pierced by three twin-towered gateways.

2. Nantwich

The old market town on the Weaver River lies only 15 miles southeast of the county town of Chester, and can easily be tied in with a visit to that city. The town is particularly outstanding because of its black-and-white timbered houses. The most spectacular one, Churche's Mansion, is a dining recommendation.

FOOD AND LODGING: Churche's Mansion Restaurant, Hospital Street (tel. Nantwich 625933), is the most enchanting old restaurant in Cheshire, lying in Nantwich at the junction of Newcastle Road and the Chester bypass. Many years ago, the late Dr. and Mrs. E. C. Myott learned that this historic home of a wealthy Elizabethan merchant had been advertised for sale in America, and asked the town council to step in and save it. Alas, no English housewife wanted such a gloomy and dark home, so the Myotts attended the sale and outbid the American syndicate who wanted to transport it to the United States. They sought out the mysteries of the house: a window in the side wall, inlaid initials, a Tudor well in the garden, a long-ago love knot with a central heart (a token of Richard Churche's affection for his young wife). Today the house, now run by the Myotts' son, is widely known and recommended for its quality meals. Lunch is offered daily, Monday to Friday for £4 ($7), increasing to £5 ($8.75) on Saturday and Sunday. Dinner, Monday to Friday, costs £10 ($17.50), going up to £11 ($19.25) on Saturday. All meals consist of four courses, and tariffs include VAT and coffee. The mansion restaurant is closed on Sunday night. You need to reserve a table, especially for dinner. Guests dine at candlelit tables. The mansion is "open to view" throughout the day for 50p (88¢), and refreshments are available.

Crown Hotel and Restaurant, High Street (tel. Nantwich 65283), is a black-and-white timbered structure, with leaded windows and an archway for carriages. The hotel was built in 1583 after a fire. Most attractive, the Crown offers guest rooms where you can immerse yourself in the charm of old England for £11 ($19.25) in a bathless single, £14 ($24.50) in a single with bath, £18 ($31.50) in a bathless double, £28 ($49) in a double with bath, these tariffs including breakfast, VAT, and service. The plank floors are so slanted you have to be careful not to lose your balance. The tavern and lounge blend antiquity with charm. The unique Georgian Assembly Room attached to the Crown has been restored, redecorated, and refurnished in the style of the period, and is now used as a dining and ballroom. Light snacks such as sandwiches are served in the lounge bar, starting from as little as 75p ($1.31). The hotel specializes in typically English dishes, and there is a good à la carte menu available at both lunch and at dinner. Meals range from £6.50 ($11.38) to £10 ($17.50).

READER'S FARMHOUSE SELECTION: "There is a delightful farmhouse which takes in guests, run by Mrs. Margaret Clayton right off the main road. The address is **Alvaston Farm,** Barony Road (A51), Nantwich (tel. Nantwich 625647). She charges £8.50 ($14.88) per person for B&B, and she's an excellent cook. Each room has a washbasin and a private toilet, plus tea-making facilities. There is a lack of accommodations in this area" (Mrs. James Walther, Dublin, Ireland).

3. Liverpool

Liverpool, with its famous waterfront on the Mersey River, is a great shipping port and industrial center that gave the world everybody from Fannie Hill to the Beatles. King John launched it on its road to glory when he granted it a charter in 1207, and it quickly became a port for shipping men and materials to Ireland. At the time Victoria came to the throne, Liverpool had become Britain's biggest port.

Liverpudlians, as they are called, are rightly proud of their city, with its new hotels, two cathedrals, shopping and entertainment complexes (as exemplified by St. John's Centre, a modern pedestrian precinct), and the parks and open spaces (2400 acres in and around the city, including Sefton Park with its Palm House). Liverpool's main shopping street, Church, is traffic free for most of the day.

The **Metropolitan Cathedral of Christ the King** was built in a record-breaking short time—only five years—yet it has taken 120 years to reach fruition. It is called the Metropolitan Cathedral because Liverpool, in Catholic terms, is the mother city, the "metropolis" of the north of England. Yet it has had its own Catholic cathedral only since 1967. The cathedral's most striking feature is its Lantern Tower, containing more than 25,000 separate pieces of stained glass in a continuous progression of every color in the spectrum. Beneath the central tower lies the white marble high altar. It's been called a "space age" cathedral.

Want to visit the early Liverpool beginnings of the Beatles? Go to the **Tourist Information Centre,** 29 Lime St. (tel. Liverpool 227-5234), in front of the main railway station. You will be able to buy Beatles souvenirs, a self-guide Beatle trail book for £1.75 ($3.06), arrange a private guided tour for from £8.50 ($14.88), join one of the scheduled weekly walking tours for 60p ($1.05) or coach trips for £2.30 ($4.03), or even book an inclusive Beatles weekend holiday, which will run you about £58 ($101.50).

The unofficial gathering spot for pilgrims who come to worship the Beatles is the **Cavern Mecca,** 18 Mathew St., a Beatles museum run by Mr. and Mrs. Jim Hughes. The Mecca displays a large collection of memorabilia on the Beatles and has a full-size replica of the Cavern, where many Liverpudlians first heard the Beatles. The museum is open Tuesday through Saturday from 10 a.m. to 5:30 p.m., charging an admission of 35p (61¢).

Among Liverpool's historic buildings, **St. George's Hall,** designed by a 24-year-old architect who never saw it realized, was completed in 1854. It has been called "England's finest public building." It contains law courts, and in the rear are pleasantly laid-out gardens.

Many visitors head for Liverpool these days just to see one attraction, the great new Anglican edifice, the **Cathedral Church of Christ,** largely completed 74 years after it was begun in 1903. On a rocky eminence overlooking the Mersey River, the cathedral might possibly be the last Gothic-style one to be built on earth. Dedicated in the presence of Queen Elizabeth II in 1978, it is the largest church in the country (the fifth largest in the world). England's poet laureate, Sir John Betjeman, hailed it as "one of the great buildings of the world." Its vaulting under the tower is 175 feet high, the highest in the world, and its length of 619 feet is second only to that of St. Peter's in Rome. The architect, who won a competition in 1903 for the building's design, was Giles Scott. He later went on to rebuild the House of Commons, gutted by bombs after World War II. He personally laid the last stone on the highest tower pinnacle. The organ of the world's largest Anglican Cathedral contains nearly 10,000 pipes, the biggest found in any church. The tower houses the highest (219 feet) and the heaviest (31 tons) ringing peals of bells in the world, and the Gothic arches are the highest ever built.

WHERE TO STAY: Hanover Hotel, Hanover Street (tel. Liverpool 709-6223), is an all-purpose modernized hotel right in the center of the city, just a few minutes from the central railway station. Hanover Street adjoins Church Street and Ranelagh Street in the center of the Liverpool shopping complex, and is at the heart of the entertainment district. This has been a family hotel for more than 50 years and has undergone constant upgrading, providing attractive bedrooms with built-in units for hot and cold running water, drawers, and wardrobes. There is a fingertip heating control, intercom, and radio. Bathless singles are £14.50 ($25.38); with bath, £16 ($28). Bathless doubles or twins rent for £23 ($40.25); with bath, £25 ($43.75). Rates include an English breakfast and all taxes. There are four bars—the Cavalry in the cellar provides quick, economical meals; the Shire offers drinks and sandwiches; and Portcullis features a popular buffet; and the Tartan Bar offers music in the evening. There's a homey lounge with black leather chairs, a fireplace, and a TV set.

Solna Hotel, Ullet Road, Sefton Park (tel. Liverpool 733-1943), is a rambling turn-of-the-century house converted to a hotel on the outskirts of Liverpool. It's 2½ miles from the heart of the city and three miles from the airport, standing in its own gardens overlooking Sefton Park. The B&B rate is £14 ($24.50) per person nightly in a single, dropping to just £12 ($21) per person in a double or twin. You'll find all required amenities: push-button radios, central heating, hot and cold running water, color TV, and good breakfasts, as well as dinners at £5.50 ($9.63). There's plenty of parking space, plus a bar.

Aplin House Private Hotel, 35 Clarendon Rd., Garston (tel. Liverpool 427-5047), is a well-kept B&B hotel run by Mr. and Mrs. Atherton, who have a good many repeat guests. Mrs. Atherton makes breakfast "as you want it." Her charges include VAT and service. Singles are £11.50 ($20.13) nightly. In July and August add £1 ($1.75) nightly. The rate in a twin-bedded room per person is £10 ($17.50) in May and June, rising to £11 ($19.25) per person in July and August.

Orrell Park Hotel, 109 Orrell Lane (tel. Liverpool 525-4018), while five miles from the true city center, is only a five-minute walk from the railway station. The M57 motorway is two miles from the hotel. The terms for B&B, excluding VAT, are £11 ($19.25) in a single, £19 ($33.25) in a double, all bathless. There are a few rooms with private bath, renting for £13 ($22.75) in a single and from £22 ($38.50) in a double. Some family rooms can also be negotiated. Offered are 21 bedrooms in all, eight with bath, five with toilets. Monday through Thursday you can get a full evening meal for £6 ($10.50). Guests, often business representatives, gather in the licensed bar or TV lounge.

Aachen Hotel, 89 Mount Pleasant (tel. Liverpool 709-3477), has one flat rate per person, £9.50 ($16.63), including VAT. You tip as you see fit. Mr. F. P. Wilson, the owner, provides complete English breakfasts. Each of his modernized bedrooms has hot and cold running water, hairdryer, shower, color TV, and an electric heater. Mr. Wilson will help you with your Liverpool visit, as he knows the city well. The location is about five minutes from the center of the city.

READERS' HOTEL SELECTION: "There is a row of B&Bs on Lord Nelson Street, which is between the Lime Street train station (British Rail) and the Empire Theatre. We stayed at the **Atlantic Hotel** on this street. It was adequate, and the charge is £10 ($17.50) per night per person. The best thing about it is the huge breakfast, which consists of all the juice you can drink, two eggs, two kinds of meat, and cereal. We were full for most of the day after breakfast there" (Jan and Lisa Hubbard, Fort Worth, Texas).

EATING AND DRINKING: For some really good old English cooking, go to the **Feathers Hotel,** 119–125 Mount Pleasant (tel. Liverpool 709-9655), a long-standing favorite decorated in peacock colors. Here you can sample the famous Lancashire hot-pot, a casserole where the lamb chops are layered with onions and potatoes. It's traditionally eaten with pickled red cabbage. To finish your meal, I suggest a "Wet Nelly," a pastry sandwich of cake bits which have been doused in syrup. Meals begin at £6 ($10.50). It's open from noon to 2 p.m. and from 6:30 to 8:30 p.m. The hotel also rents out rooms, which are expensive. Depending on the plumbing, the single rate ranges from £13.50 ($23.63) to £16 ($28); the double charge is from £23.50 ($41.13) to £27 ($47.25).

La Grande Bouffe, 48a Castle St. (tel. Liverpool 236-3375), sports a menu which illustrates what might be an Englishwoman and a Frenchman discreetly embracing, which is perhaps a symbol of the way the British residents of Liverpool have embraced the Gallic cuisine of the patronne, Juliet Shield. An inexpensive luncheon menu is written on a blackboard, and might consist of a chilled yogurt-and-cucumber soup, followed by a bacon-and-mushroom quiche. This could be finished off with a slice of nectarine and lemon curd tart, all for a deliciously low total of £2.40 ($4.20). Dinner is more elaborate and much more expensive, although a pretheater supper is served early in the evening for just £4.95 ($8.66). A fixed-price menu of £7.50 ($13.13) is available every night until closing. An à la carte dinner might include La Bouffe's coarsely chopped chicken liver pâté (the menu warns that it's "very alcoholic"), followed by sauteed breast of chicken stuffed with cream cheese and an herb pâté, then homemade ice cream for dessert. As in France, a 10% service charge is automatically added. Hours are Monday from 10 a.m. to 4:30 p.m.; Tuesday through Friday, to 11:30 p.m., and Saturday only from 6 p.m. till midnight. Teas, coffee, and cakes are served on weekdays before noon and after 3 p.m.

Villa Italia, 9–13 Temple Court (tel. Liverpool 227-5774), is one of the best of the reasonably priced trattorie of Liverpool. It's operated in conjunction with the **Ristorante del Secolo** at 36–40 Stanley St. (tel. Liverpool 236-4004). At the Villa Italia, which is the more reasonably priced of the two, you're faced with a large selection of dishes, not only a dazzling array of antipasti, but a lot of good pasta dishes as well. Try tortellini del Secolo. Among the main courses, I'd recommend the sirloin steak in a tomato and garlic sauce. For dessert, why not a cassata, the typical Sicilian ice cream? Expect to spend from £7.50 ($13.13) for a meal. It's open Tuesday to Saturday from noon to 2:30 p.m. and 5:30 to 10 p.m. The Ristorante del Secolo serves a £7.25 ($12.69) set lunch and an £8.50 ($14.88) table d'hôte dinner.

Bistro Everyman, 9 Hope St. (tel. Liverpool 708-9545), is informal, crowded on weekends, and fun. Pauline Gaskill, the manager, keeps the prices low and the food tempting. The menu is limited but select, and everything is homemade. A three-course meal, using lots of fresh produce, might consist of a spicy lentil-and-vegetable soup, followed by a flambé of pork with apricots and white rice, and topped by a rhubarb fool for dessert. This, with coffee, would come to a modest total of £3.75 ($6.56). The bistro is open from noon to 11:30 p.m., Monday to Saturday.

Everybody's favorite pub is at the **Philharmonic Hotel,** 36 Hope St. (tel. Liverpool 709-1163), which has all those splendid turn-of-the-century architectural decorative features that are now so much in vogue—stained glass, carving, plasterwork, you name it. You pass through wrought-iron gates into a selection of several bars, some with rosewood paneling. The heart of the pub is the Horseshoe Bar, with a mosaic floor and stained glass, fine Edwardian flamboyance. You can have a few pints and play dominoes. The feeling is like a private club, and almost any regular will advise a stranger what kind of local ale is good. The habitués refer to it as "The Phil," and it attracts art, drama, and music students as well as actors. If you're a man, I suggest you pay a visit to the gent's urinal, even if you don't need to go. It's a work of art! Landlord is Michael Cross, who offers stuffed rolls priced from 65p ($1.14) and up. There's always a hot dish of the day, along with a well-displayed buffet from which a plate is priced at £2.50 ($4.38).

CUMBRIA

Driving in the wilds of this northwestern shire, the Lake District, is fine for a start. But the best activity is walking, which is an art best practiced here by both young and old with a crooked stick. Don't go out without a warning, however. There is a great deal of rain and heavy mist, and sunny days are few. When the mist starts to fall, try to be near an old inn or pub, where you can drop in for a visit and warm yourself beside an open fireplace. You'll be carried back to the good old days, as many places in Cumbria have valiantly resisted change. If you strike up a conversation with a local, you must make sure you know something about hounds.

The far northwestern part of the shire, bordering Scotland, used to be called Cumberland. Now part of Cumbria, it is generally divided geographically into a trio of segments: the Pennines dominating the eastern sector (loftiest point at Cross Fell, nearly 3000 feet high), the Valley of Eden, and the lakes and secluded valleys of the west, by far the most interesting. The area, so beautifully described by the romantic Lake Poets, enjoys many literary associations. Wordsworth ("when all at once I saw a crowd, a host of golden daffodils") was a native son, born at Cockermouth.

The largest town is **Carlisle** in the north—not a very interesting tourist center, but a possible base for explorations to Hadrian's Wall. The wall stretches from Wallsend in the east to Bowness on the Solway, a distance of about 75 miles. It was built in the second century A.D. by the Romans.

Brockhole National Park Centre, between Ambleside and Windermere, is well worth a visit.

A traditional gateway to the district is from the south, approached via:

4. Kendal

A simple market town, Kendal contains the ruins of a castle where Catherine Parr, the last wife of Henry VIII, was born. With its 13th-century parish church, Kendal makes for a good stopover en route to the lakeside resort of Windermere, beginning about nine miles away. Kendal is 270 miles from London.

The town was also associated with George Romney, the 18th-century portrait painter (Lady Hamilton his favorite subject), who used to travel all over the Lake District trying to get someone to sit for him. He held his first exhibition, married, and raised a family in Kendal. He deserted them in 1762, not returning until the end of his life. He died in Kendal in 1802.

FOOD AND LODGING: Hillside, 4 Beast Banks (tel. Kendal 22836), is a comfortable guest house just two blocks from the main street of Kendal. Carl and Brenda Denison are the gracious and helpful owners of this neat, clean accommodation. There is a lounge with color TV, and all rooms have new and modern sinks with plenty of hot water. The toilets are separate from the shower and bathrooms. The charge is £8.50 ($14.88) per person per night.

The **Brewery Arts Centre,** Highgate (tel. Kendal 25133). At lunchtime, this popular restaurant is frequented by local businesspeople who savor its unpretentious selection of quiches, fish dishes, meat pies, and salads. For a

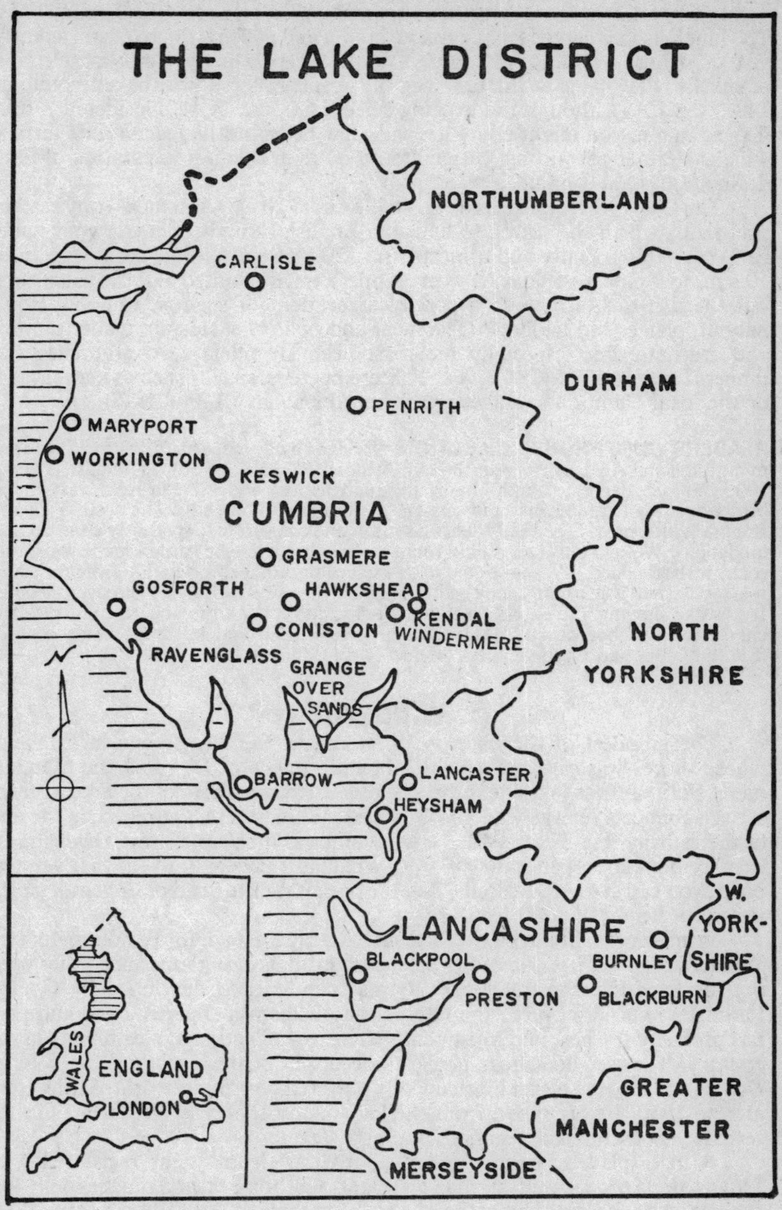
THE LAKE DISTRICT
NORTHUMBERLAND
CARLISLE
DURHAM
PENRITH
MARYPORT
WORKINGTON
KESWICK
CUMBRIA
GRASMERE
GOSFORTH
HAWKSHEAD
KENDAL
CONISTON
WINDERMERE
NORTH
YORKSHIRE
RAVENGLASS
GRANGE
OVER
SANDS
LANCASTER
BARROW
HEYSHAM
W.
YORK-
SHIRE
LANCASHIRE
BLACKPOOL
BURNLEY
PRESTON
BLACKBURN
WALES
ENGLAND
LONDON
GREATER
MANCHESTER
MERSEYSIDE

regional English dish, try the ham steak (they call it gammon), served with two vegetables, followed by a simple dessert and coffee, all for about £2.60 ($4.55). The lunch itself is served from noon to 2 p.m., and coffee is offered from as early as 10 a.m. until 3 p.m. From 7 to 10:30 p.m. (except Sunday) a modest selection of snacks is available at the bar. Try the shepherd's pie with baked potato at £1.20 ($2.10). Although the evening selection is not to be considered a full-fledged menu, you might enjoy having a few beers on the restaurant's terrace which, weather permitting, turns into an outdoor media presentation of film, drama, dance, and mime.

The Cherry Tree, 24 Finkle St. (tel. Kendal 20547), is a tuck-away restaurant that's worth the search to find. Ian English (how British can your name get?) runs this friendly and atmospheric 120-seat establishment, serving from 10 a.m. to 9 p.m. seven days a week. Appetizers are limited and the usual sort, but the fish dishes include a goodly assortment of scampi, rainbow trout, halibut, plaice, and haddock. The meat and poultry salads are made to order and are quite fine, especially the roast beef. He offers savory lunches and dinners for around £5 ($8.75). For lighter appetites, snacks such as hamburgers or the local Cumbria sausages are served for about £1.35 ($2.36).

READERS' GUEST HOUSE SELECTION: "Bridge House at Garnett Bridge is just a few minutes off the A6 as it runs north from Kendal (tel. Selside 288). The house is about 300 years old, decorated with charm and imagination, and situated right next to the bridge over the River Sprint amid small farm plots and rolling hills. The hosts, Tom and Brenda White, provide perfectly delicious meals and comfortable, spotlessly clean accommodations. We had our own dining room looking out over the garden, our own sitting room with fireplace, TV, and a marvelous selection of books where after-dinner coffee was served, and a charming, snug bedroom under the eaves with a view out over the hills. It was like slipping into an old-fashioned English novel but with modern comforts. The charge for half board is £11 ($19.25) per person. Bed and breakfast alone cost £7 ($12.25)" (Bill and Phyllis Levers, Menlo Park, Calif.).

5. Windermere

The grandest of the lakes is Windermere, the largest one in England, whose shores wash up against the adjoining towns of Bowness and Windermere. Both of these lakeside resorts lie on the eastern shore of the lake. A ferry service connects Hawkshead and Bowness. Windermere, the resort, is the end of the railway line. From either town, you can climb up **Orrest Head** in less than an hour for a panoramic view of England's lakeland. From that vantage point, you can even see **Scafell Pike,** the peak pinnacle in all of England, which rises to a height of 3210 feet.

Windermere Steamboat Museum, Rayrigg Road in Windermere (tel. Windermere 5565), is one of the most delightful working museums it has been my lot to visit for many years. It was founded and developed by George Pattinson, who discovered the fascination of steam many years ago and now has probably the best and most comprehensive collection of steamboats in the country. The wet boatsheds house some dozen boats, including the veteran *Dolly,* probably the oldest mechanically powered boat in the world, dating from around 1850. It was raised from the lake bed in the early 1960s and run for several years with the original boiler and steambox.

Also displayed is the *Espérance,* an iron steam yacht registered with Lloyds in 1869, as well as many elegant Victorian steamlaunches and ferryboats. Attached to the boathouses is the speedboat *Jane,* dating from 1938, the first glider-plane to take off from the water in 1943, and the hydroplane racer, *Cookie*—all jostling Beatrix Potter's rowing boat and other Lakeland craft for position.

There's a small shop selling books, postcards, and souvenirs of historic craft. The museum is open from Easter to October, charging an admission of 95p ($1.66) for adults and 50p (88¢) for children. The *Osprey* is regularly in steam, and visitors can make a 40-minute trip on the lake at £1.75 ($3.06) for adults and £1.40 ($2.45) for children.

It's also possible to make trips on Ullswater and on Coniston, and there is regular steamer service around Windermere, the largest of the lakes, which serves the outlying villages as well as operating for visitors in summer. Ken Crowther is curator. He retired there in recent times, and is totally absorbed in the craft and concept of the museum.

WHERE TO STAY: **Willowsmere Hotel,** Ambleside Road (tel. Windermere 3575), is a handsome Edwardian stone hotel, along the A591, about a ten-minute walk from the railway station and Windermere shops. Willowsmere is owned by David F. Scott, who is assisted by his daughter, Heather, the fifth generation of the Scott family to be catering in the Lake District. Heather's husband, Alan Cook, also helps run the business. Regular guests say that it is most appropriate that Heather's married name is now Cook, as her father receives many glowing compliments on her culinary abilities. The best way to stay here is to request the dinner and B&B rate of £17 ($29.75) per person nightly. The evening meal is a well-prepared four-courser. Bedrooms contain hot and cold running water, shaver points, and unmetered heat. For just B&B, expect a rate ranging from £12 ($21) to £14 ($24.50). Guests gather at night to socialize and watch the "telly." If you want to go on a lakeside ramble the next day, Heather will pack you a lunch for about £2.50 ($4.38).

Waverley Hotel, College Road (tel. Windermere 5026), stands only a short walk from town, about three minutes from the rail station. It is owned by Bryan and Beryl Lewis, who charge from £10 ($17.50) in a single, from £18 ($31.50) in a double, including B&B and VAT. Dinner is a four-course table d'hôte meal with an appetizer, main course, and a selection from the dessert trolley, along with tea or coffee. It costs £5 ($8.75). Or else you can order à la carte with a choice of main courses, costing from £7 ($12.25) to £8 ($14) for four courses.

The Guest House, 1 St. Michaels Villas, Crescent Road (tel. Windermere 4691), can be highly recommended for its friendly atmosphere and general standard of comfort. The charge is from £8 ($14) per person per night for bed and an English breakfast. An evening meal costs from £4.50 ($7.88). A newly equipped launderette and same-day dry-cleaning service are opposite, and the guest house is only a short walk from the railway station and is in the center of town.

Prospect House Guest House, High Street (tel. Windermere 4205), is an old Lakeland stone house right in the center of town. It's a family home where Marjorie Clarke manages to offer a warm welcome to guests while lovingly dealing with her husband Albert, her daughters, and the most important members of the family, Trudi and Fred, the cairn terriers. All her rooms are centrally heated and contain hot and cold running water, TV, and tea- or coffee-making facilities. There is a small dining room, plus a comfortable lounge with color TV and video. Marjorie and Albert have always spent holidays in the Lake District, and now that they live here are only too anxious to pass on local information on walking, riding, and sailing. Open throughout the year, their guest house charges £7.50 ($13.13) per night for a bed and a large Lakeland breakfast. Packed lunches can be arranged, and you can return to a well-cooked meal, beginning with soup and followed by perhaps a braised steak or coq au vin, along with a dessert, at a cost of £5 ($8.75) per person, including VAT.

Rockside Guest House, Ambleside Road (tel. Windermere 5343). Nev (Neville) Fowles always wanted to live in the Lake District, and when he bought Rockside his wish was achieved. He and Mavis, formerly a schoolteacher, offer B&B for £7.50 ($13.13) per person, with a variety of singles, doubles, twins, and family rooms, all with central heating and hot and cold running water. There are two lounges, one with a small well-stocked bar for residents. Good evening meals are served each day. There is adequate parking, and packed lunches can be provided by Nev for your day's touring.

Waverley Hotel, College Road (tel. Windermere 5026). The call of the lakes and a peaceful country life persuaded Bryan and Beryl Lewis to leave the city and their flourishing printing company to set up their guest house. From all reports, life hasn't been nearly as quiet as they expected. They are now enjoying the challenge of catering to a stream of guests from all parts of the world, helping them to enjoy the countryside and to relax a little. B&B is from £7.50 ($13.13) per person, including VAT. Evening meals are provided, three simple courses prepared from fresh local produce whenever possible, costing from £5 ($8.75) per person. Beryl is a great walker, and she also likes needlework and flower arrangements, while Bryan loves sailing. So you'll probably find much to talk about during the evening.

On the Outskirts

Belsfield Guest House, 4 Belsfield Terrace, Kendal Road, Bowness-on-Windermere (tel. Windermere 5823), is a small, family-style guest house near the lake. It's owned by Joan and Jack Jackson, who have modernized the house. Their welcome is personalized, and they offer cleanliness and a friendly atmosphere. Their B&B rate is £8.50 ($14.88) per person nightly. They offer family rooms, doubles, and twins, and receive guests from Easter week until November.

Town End House (tel. Ambleside 2172) lies in the little village of Troutbeck, about three miles outside Windermere. A private house built of Lakeland stone in 1889, it is run by Mrs. A. E. Wilson. From the guest rooms, views open onto the hills and valley. The house is approached from the A591 at Troutbeck Bridge, about a mile past Windermere where the village road turns to the right. Open all year, Town End House charges £7.50 ($13.13) per person for a room and a full English breakfast. It's a peaceful spot away from the main road. Town End House is not to be confused with Townend Farm, which is nearby.

READERS' ACCOMMODATION SELECTIONS (IN AND NEAR WINDERMERE): "A particular find was the **Elim Lodge Guest House,** in Bowness-on-Windermere (Biskey Howe Road; tel. Windermere 4271), just a mile or two south of Windermere itself. It has six rooms, all with hot and cold running water, and our room was huge, with a double and two singles, for families during the school holidays, we were informed. The owners serve an evening meal for £5 ($8.75), if you arrive early enough. The cost is £8 ($14) per person for B&B. The house is three stories, and was redecorated. It is spotlessly clean, bright, and cheery" (William E. Hager, American Embassy, N.Y.). . . . "**Mr. and Mrs. S. J. Kendall** operate a B&B at 7 Park Ave. (tel. Windermere 2175). The cost is £7 ($12.25) per person. Mrs. Kendall is one of those special women who takes great pride in her housekeeping and food preparation, and the result is near perfection. She offers an optional evening meal which is truly a gourmet feast, exquisitely prepared. The half-board rate is £10 ($17.50) daily. She serves a 10 p.m. tea which includes her homemade scones" (Barbara Larson, Rockford, Ill.).

"Only the demands of time caused us to depart from the care, cleanliness, and very rewarding tea and cake conversations with Mr. and Mrs. William Evans and their other guests at the guest house, **Oakfield,** 46 Oak St. (tel. Windermere 5692), near the Windermere railroad station. The charge for B&B is £7 ($12.25) per person nightly" (Walter S. Dewey, De Kalb, Ill.). . . . "In Windermere, we found a lovely home of an interior designer, **High Garth,** Park Road (tel. Windermere 2880), for £7 ($12.25) per person. Sid and Mary Dobbs are delightful people, with Mary a real sketch. After a good steak-and-kidney pie dinner downtown, we and other guests gathered in the dining room where we supplied the beer and all laughed the night away. The rooms are beautiful, and those in front look down on Lake Windermere in the distance" (John B. Fassett, Fort Myers, Fla.). . . . "The finest B&B was offered us in the Lake District by Mrs. Hellier of **Mylne Close,** Holly Road (tel. Windermere 2229). She and her sister are exceptionally gracious in sharing their beautifully decorated home. Breakfasts were ample and tasty, and tea and scones were offered in the evening as we watched TV in the private guest sitting room. The huge bedroom was appointed with several comfortable chairs, reading lamps, and paperback books. A large, immaculate bathroom was used by the occupants of only two other rooms. All this costs £8 ($14) each" (Marilyn and Ed Foodim, Northport, N.Y.).

WHERE TO EAT: **Millers Restaurant,** 31–33 Crescent Rd. (tel. Windermere 3877), in the center of town, has a simple tea-room decor, and offers good, inexpensive food. Special lunches and dinners are offered for £2.50 ($4.38), including such dishes as homemade steak-and-kidney pie, two vegetables, new potatoes, and a choice of dessert. A three-course fish dinner is featured from £3.50 ($6.13). When available, char, a fish from Lake Windermere, is offered for £4.25 ($7.44). The restaurant is owned and run by Mr. Lord, who is responsible for the carefully prepared, traditional dishes.

LAKE DISTRICT TOURS: **Mountain Goat Holidays,** Victoria Street, Windermere (tel. Windermere 5161), offer two types of holidays in the Lake District, based in Windermere and Keswick, Touring Holidays or, for the more energetic, the Valley or Mountain Walking Holidays.

Touring Holidays start at approximately £120 ($210) per week in guest houses going up to about £150 ($262.50) per week in hotels. The price includes dinner, bed, a full English breakfast, five Mountain Goat tours, plus such other extras as a welcome drink, a Lakeland gift and photo, a welcome pack, and comprehensive insurance.

Walking Holidays start at about £125 ($218.75), rising to about £170 ($297.50), and include seven nights of half board in a hotel or guest house and four full-day walks with a guide.

Mountain Goat Tours, available on a day-to-day basis, can be bought on the spot at the Mountain Goat offices in Windermere and Keswick. Most of the full-day and half-day tours are in 12-seater minibuses with fully qualified driver/guides. Prices start at £4.50 ($7.88) for a half-day tour, going up to £8.50 ($14.88) for a full-day tour. Half-day picnic tours cost £6.75 ($11.81), including the picnic.

Mountain Goat / British Rail Short Break to the Lakes is a package which can be purchased from any British Rail Travel Centre in London, in the south of England, and in Manchester. The price, from £49.50 ($86.63), includes two nights' B&B in a guest house or hotel, a Sealink Cruise on Lake Windermere, a full-day Mountain Goat Tour, and a taxi transfer from the station to your hotel.

6. Ambleside

A good and idyllic retreat, Ambleside is one of the major centers of the Lake District, attracting pony-trekkers, fell-hikers, and rock-scalers. The charms are here all year, even in late autumn when it's fashionable to sport a mackintosh. Ambleside is superbly perched, at the top of Lake Windermere. Traditions are entrenched, especially at the Rushbearing Festival, an annual event.

WHERE TO STAY: The **Romney Hotel,** Waterside (tel. Ambleside 2219), is a substantial but plain hotel up on a ledge above the road and waterfront. The view is superb. You drive up a steep, winding drive to the entry and car park. It's a busy place with groups of visitors from many countries enjoying the situation and reasonable prices. B&B in a single is £12.50 ($21.88) daily; in a double it's £12 ($21) per person. Most guests stay here on a half-board rate of £18 ($31.50) in a single, £17.50 ($30.63) per person in a double. These rates include VAT and a service charge. A packed lunch can be provided for only £1.75 ($3.06), if you are going for a walk through the hills. The restaurant, incidentally, is licensed for drinks. The hotel, named after the painter George Romney, is personally supervised by Mrs. Boow and Mrs. Nevinson.

The Gables Private Hotel, Church Walk, Compston Road (tel. Ambleside 3272), is a half-timbered manor house with eight gables, in the heart of the village, yet set aside on a quiet street overlooking the park, the tennis courts, and Loughrigg Fell. The owners, Mr. and Mrs. K. Robinson, have furnished the bedrooms comfortably, with color-coordinated bedcovers and draperies. For half board, the cost is £12.40 ($21.70) per person nightly. Around 10 in the evening tea and cookies are served in the lounge. There are two very comfortable and well-furnished living rooms for guests, and the dining room overlooks the gardens. Importantly, there's a free car park.

Ghyll Head Hotel, Waterhead (tel. Ambleside 2360), stands on the main road along the lake, one minute from the pier and its passenger steamer, yet it is high on a ledge surrounded by two acres of garden. It's a large Edwardian estate home adapted for guests. The charge is £14 ($24.50) in a single, rising to £28 ($49) in a double. An evening meal can also be arranged for about £6 ($10.50). The roomy, informal atmosphere attracts many groups of young guests, who arrive in hiking attire and walking boots. It's all very friendly.

Rothay Garth Hotel, Rothay Road (tel. Ambleside 2217), is a stone country house set in an idyllic spot surrounded by lakes, mountains, and streams. The well-kept private gardens overlook tennis courts and a par-3 golf course. It is only a three-minute walk from the center of Ambleside. All rooms are tastefully decorated, warm, and comfortable. Most bedrooms have private bathrooms. There is a luxury sun lounge, a TV lounge, and a cozy bar. A traditional English breakfast is served, along with excellent table d'hôte and à la carte dinner menus. High standards and good value are assured by the personal attention of the resident owners, Doreen and David Clark. B&B is £17.50 ($30.63) per person daily, and dinner, bed, and breakfast costs £22.50 ($39.38) per person per day.

READERS' GUEST HOUSE SELECTION: "We were treated to the finest hospitality we've found throughout our entire six-month visit to Europe, when we discovered a truly fantastic place to stay with John and Sue Horne at **Horseshoe Guest House,** Rothay Road (tel. Ambleside 2000). An architect from London by profession, John has left the big-city life behind and is creating an enviable lifestyle for Sue and himself in the Lake Country. For £17 ($29.75) per night for a double, you can stay in a large and immaculate room, bath down the hall, in a former church-owned residence. John, an avid outdoorsman and member of the local Mountain Rescue Squad, has a complete knowledge of the surrounding area and he will gladly direct you to places of interest. Sue is up bright and early in the morning to fix breakfasts of eggs, bacon, and sausage, all included in the room cost. In a newly built south wing of the house, all the bedrooms have their own showers, toilets, and balconies. A supplement is charged for these rooms" (Phil Pritulsky and Pauline Dainty, Norfolk, Va.).

WHERE TO DINE: **Jacaranda Restaurant,** Compston Road (tel. Ambleside 2430), in the center of town, with seating for 70 persons, provides traditional English home cooking and confectionery. Most main dishes range in price from £2.40 ($4.20) to £6 ($10.50). A typical three-course meal could include corn on the cob at 90p ($1.58), roast chicken in red wine sauce at £3.10 ($5.43), and a fruit cheesecake dessert at 65p ($1.14). The restaurant opens for evening meals at 5 p.m.

Gemini Restaurant, Lake Road (tel. Ambleside 2528), is an informal roadside restaurant run by Jill and David Smith. It offers good value in a pleasant setting. A lunch of egg mayonnaise followed by local Cumberland sausage with croquette potatoes and a homemade dessert will cost £3.63 ($6.39). Dinner is more elaborate, consisting of, say, tomato antibise, a ripe tomato stuffed with tuna and apples, followed by filet of pork normande in a mushroom and cream sauce, with apples and fresh vegetable, then a homemade dessert of cheese, at a cost of £5.65 ($9.90). A children's menu goes for £1.50 ($2.63), and the restaurant is licensed to serve alcohol. Lunch is daily from noon to 2:30 p.m., and dinner begins every evening at 6:30 p.m. Closed Sunday. An art gallery attached to the restaurant features paintings by Cumbrian artists. Michael, the establishment's talented chef, prepares his own specialty every day.

Apple Pie Eating House, Rydal Road (tel. Ambleside 3679), makes its own apple pie, and does so exceedingly well, a thick slice with fresh cream going for 51p (89¢). The cooks make very good quiches, including the Lorraine classic at £1.30 ($2.28). Everything tastes better with their freshly ground coffee with cream, 35p (61¢). The homemade meat pies at £1.25 ($2.19) are also recommended. The eating house is also a bakery, and the quality of the baking is so good you may want to take away with you some cakes, pastries, or scones. Hours are from 9 a.m. to 6 p.m. It is closed November to Easter.

Harvest Wholefood Vegetarian Restaurant, Compston Road (tel. Ambleside 3151), offers homemade fare, far better than some of the bland vegetarian restaurants opening in England. The home-cooking is pure and simple, and fresh produce is used. A rich-tasting soup goes for 65p ($1.14), and most vegetable-based main dishes with a crisp, fresh salad cost £2.50 ($4.38).

7. Rydal

Between Ambleside (the top of Lake Windermere) and Wordsworth's former retreat at Grasmere is Rydal, a small village on one of the smallest lakes, Rydal Water. Wordsworth lived at Rydal Mount, overlooking the lake, from 1813 until his death in 1850. The house is now a museum. The village is noted for its sheep-dog trials at the end of summer.

WHERE TO STAY: **Rydal Lodge** (tel. Ambleside 3208), beside the roadway between Ambleside and Grasmere, is a good center for walking and touring the whole of the Lake District. The Rothay River runs beside the pleasant and secluded gardens; and Rydal Water, a beautiful lake, is at the end of the garden. Mr. and Mrs. Warren provide meals of high quality, and the menus are well planned. Strawberries and other fruit from the garden are provided in season, and the lodge has a license to serve wine with main meals. The bedrooms are equipped with hot and cold running water, shaving points, electric blankets, heaters, and innerspring mattresses. There are two bathrooms as well as a private car park. Terms are from £11.50 ($20.13) for B&B, with dinner costing from £8.50 ($14.88), including VAT. Rydal Lodge is of historical interest. Matthew Arnold stayed here, and it is connected with Harriet Martineau. The older part of the house was an inn in 1655.

READERS' GUEST HOUSE SELECTION: "We wish to commend **Nab Cottage,** Rydal (tel. Grasmere 311). This establishment and its proprietors stood out. First, for its unique historical background; it dates from 1702, and this date is inscribed above the porch. Hartley Coleridge, son of the famous poet, Samuel Taylor Coleridge, lived here, as did writer Thomas De Quincey. The house is beautifully sited on the shore of Rydal Water, about two miles from Grasmere, with lovely views of the lake from its bedroom windows. Mr. and Mrs. A. Hunt are continually endeavoring to make their guests' stay as pleasant as possible. Mr. Hunt personally serves at table. The table settings are gracious and elegant, the food served as you would expect in a first-class restaurant. And the food! Mrs. Hunt must have studied 'Cordon Bleu'—the food is so delicious! And the charge is £11 ($19.25) per person for B&B. With a three-course dinner included, the half-board rate is £17 ($29.75) per person" (W. B. and A. J. Renfredy, Melbourne, Australia).

8. Grasmere

Grasmere, on the lake which bears its name, was the home of Wordsworth from 1799 to 1808. Along with his sister, Dorothy (the English writer and diarist), the nature poet lived at **Dove Cottage** (tel. Grasmere 544), which is now a museum administered by Dove Cottage Trust. Wordsworth died in the spring of 1850, and was buried in the graveyard of the village church at Grasmere. The other famous tenant of Dove Cottage was Thomas De Quincey *(Confessions of an English Opium Eater),* who lived there from 1808 to 1835. Nearby is the **Grasmere & Wordsworth Museum,** which displays many of Wordsworth's manuscripts together with the history and geology of Grasmere Vale. For a combined ticket costing £1.50 ($2.63) for adults, 75p ($1.31) for children, you can visit both Dove Cottage and the Wordsworth Museum, with its collection of his manuscripts and memorabilia. The Trust property is open weekdays from 9:30 a.m. to 5:30 p.m., Easter to October, and from 11 a.m. to 5:30 p.m. on Sunday. Off-season, the properties open at 10 a.m. and close at 4:30 p.m. on weekdays, from 11 a.m. to 4:30 p.m. on Sunday.

WHERE TO STAY: The **Moss Grove Hotel** in Grasmere (tel. Grasmere 251) is one of those places you are glad to have found. This old Lakeland house in the center of town is owned and run by Ken and Shirley Wood. Ken deals with the reception and reservations, and he's a man who always remembers your name, greeting you with a genuine and cheery "good morning." Shirley does the cooking. Ken used to work for a brewery, and she is a physicist. Both loved the area and came here more than a decade ago. They spend at least one day a week walking in their beloved hills and will take guests with them and will advise on walks and special scenery to be viewed. Ken is white-bearded and lean from leading an outdoor life, and his gentle eyes reflect a relaxed attitude to life.

The hotel is well furnished and warm. Rooms go for £12 ($21) per person, including VAT and a large, wholesome Lakeland breakfast. There are two lounges, one with TV, the other with a small bar. Dinner during the week is a well-cooked meal with a roast joint or poultry, fresh vegetable, and on Sunday, a cold buffet including various cold meats, some 14 choices of salad, and a quiche, followed by dessert or cheese. Such a meal costs about £7.50 ($13.13).

Titteringdales, Rye Lane (tel. Grasmere 439), is a small private guest house run by Mrs. Vera Watson. Away from traffic noise, it opens onto views of Silverhow, Fairfield, and Helm Crag. Surrounded by its own gardens, the house is well run and comfortable, with full central heating. Mrs. Watson has a family room, and children sharing accommodations with their parents are given one-third reductions in prices. The owner takes pride in her English home-cookery and her personal service, trying and succeeding in achieving that home-away-from-home appeal. B&B costs from £9.50 ($16.63) per night, and an evening meal is provided for another £5 ($8.75). Packed lunches and afternoon tea are available on request.

WHERE TO EAT: The **Cumbria Carvery** (tel. Grasmere 515) offers lunches and dinners until 9 p.m. It's a cheerful, friendly place, and the food is simple, the prices reasonable. A three-course meal of prawn cocktail followed by halibut with tartar sauce and a dessert of sherry trifle would cost around £4.80 ($8.40). Of course, omelets—a satisfying meal in themselves—would cost less at £1.50 ($2.63), while a salad of cold ham, egg, cheese, or fish would come to about £2 ($3.50). The restaurant is under the warm supervision of Elaine and Louis Diomedous.

The **Shepherd's Crook,** Stock Lane (tel. Grasmere 342), is a small bar with red carpets, wheelback chairs and benches, and a warm and friendly atmosphere. Appetizers range from 30p (53¢) for fruit juice to 70p ($1.23) for pâté. Steaks start at £2.60 ($4.55), and for about the same price there are grills, chops, scampi, or plaice, all served with vegetables and the inevitable "chips." The house specialty is a farmhouse grill of chop, sausage, bacon, egg, tomato, and mushrooms at £3.70 ($6.48) or the smaller Cumberland grill at £3 ($5.25). The place is open daily from 5 to 8 p.m., and also does lunch Monday to Friday from noon to 2 p.m. It's close to the main car park on Stock Lane and to Chris Reekie's shop.

The **Coffee Bean** is right in the center of Grasmere, offering soups, sandwiches (toasted or not), coffee, tea, chocolate, pastries, pies, and cookies. Nothing costs more than 75p ($1.31), including VAT, and can be eaten there or taken away. They will fill flasks of hot tea or coffee for you. Everything is freshly made and much is home-baked.

9. Hawkshead

Discover for yourself the village of Hawkshead, with its 15th-century grammar school where Wordsworth went to school for eight years (he carved his name on a desk that still remains). Near Hawkshead, in the vicinity of Esthwaite Water, is the 17th-century **Hill Top Farm,** former home of Beatrix Potter, the author of the Peter Rabbit books, who died during World War II.

At Coniston, four miles away from Hawkshead, you can visit the village famously associated with John Ruskin. Coniston is a good base for rock climbing. The Coniston "Old Man" towers in the background at 2633 feet, giving mountain climbers one of the finest views of the Lake District.

Ruskin moved to his home, **Brantwood** (tel. Coniston 396), on the east side of Coniston Water in 1872 and lived there until his death in 1900. The house today is open for visitors to view much Ruskiniana, including some 175 pictures by him. Also displayed are his coach and boat, the *Jumping Jenny.*

An exhibition illustrating the work of W. J. Linton is laid out in his old printing room. Linton was born in England in 1812 and died at New Haven, Connecticut, in 1897. Well known as a wood engraver and for his private press, he lived at Brantwood, where he established his printing business in 1853. He published *The English Republic,* a newspaper and review, before emigrating to America in 1866, where he set up his printing press in 1870. The house is owned and managed by the Education Trust, a self-supporting registered charity. It is open daily from Easter to the end of October from 11 a.m. to 5:30 p.m.; closed on Saturday. The admission is £1 ($1.75) for adults, 50p (88¢) for children. Part of the 250-acre estate is also open as a nature trail, costing 35p (61¢) for adults, 20p (44¢) for children. A special £2.50 ($4.38) family day ticket (mother and/or father and children up to the age of 16) covers the house and nature trail. There is a gift and Ruskin Book shop, and tea and coffee are available.

Literary fans may want to pay a pilgrimage to the graveyard of the village church, where Ruskin was buried; his family turned down a chance to have him interred at Westminster Abbey.

ACCOMMODATIONS: **Ivy House Hotel** (tel. Hawkshead 204) is a friendly Georgian house that warms the austere Lake District. It's an ideal headquarters from which to branch out for visits on Lake Windermere. On a daily basis, the half-board rate begins at £16.50 ($28.86) per person. Two units have private shower/toilet and cost an extra £1 ($1.75) per day per person. The hospitable proprietors, Mr. and Mrs. Williams, are used to welcoming overseas visitors, and Mrs. Williams tries to take a personal interest in all her lodgers. But because of her charming house and lovely situation, she is heavily booked—so it's imperative that you reserve well in advance. Some other points worth noting: All the rooms are centrally heated and have hot and cold running water. A modern, motel-type annex, with unrestricted electric heating, handles overflow guests. The house is open March to October only.

A good headquarters for touring the northern Lake District is:

10. Keswick

Lying 22 miles north of Windermere, Keswick opens onto Derwentwater, one of the loveliest lakes in the district. Robert Southey, poet laureate, lived for four decades at Greta Hall, and was buried at Crosthwaite Church. Coleridge lived there too, depending on Southey for financial aid. Sir Hugh Walpole, the novelist, in a different era also resided near Keswick.

Keswick is the natural geographical starting point for car tours and walks of exploration in the northern Lake District, including the John Peel country to the north of Skiddaw (quiet and little known), Borrowdale, Buttermere, and Crummock Water, as well as Bassenthwaite, Thirlmere, and Ullswater.

And you too, following in the footpaths of Charles Lamb and Shelley, will seek out an accommodation.

WHERE TO STAY: The **George Hotel,** St. John Street (tel. Keswick 72076), is a 400-year-old coaching inn, known to Southey and Coleridge. Still offering unvarnished charm, it lies in the middle of town, near the market square, which comes alive on Saturday morning. For B&B, guests are charged £16 ($28) in a single, £26 ($45.50) in a double, plus another £7 ($12.25) for dinner. The rooms are well appointed and maintained. The inn, particularly the two old-world bars, offers a relaxed atmosphere.

Linnett Hill Hotel, Penrith Road (tel. Keswick 73109), has been thoroughly modernized, yet it retains oak beams and other typical characteristics. This private town house dates from 1812, and its decorations in the main are Victorian. Mr. and Mrs. Baxter offer three double rooms and one single (two of these units are spacious enough to serve as family rooms). They charge from £10 ($17.50) per person for B&B, or else from £15 ($26.25) with a good dinner included. Meals are not only large, but beautifully served and prepared. The hosts offer every assistance. Each bedroom is provided with hot and cold running water, electric shaver points, and an electric heater. There is a comfortable lounge with color TV, plus a small private bar. The house also has a private car park. The little hotel is pleasantly situated, opposite Gretna River and Fitz Park with open views of Skiddaw Range and Latrigg.

The Bay Tree, 1 Wordsworth St. (tel. Keswick 73313), offers B&B to travelers for £7.50 ($13.13) per night. You can also choose half-board terms for what represents good value at £11.50 ($20.13) per person. Rooms are comfortable and attractively furnished, and the service is friendly and efficient. The restaurant serves meals both to residents and nonresidents. Appreciating the Victorian antiques of its dining room is part of the fun of going there. Lunch is not served, but a fixed-price meal is offered every evening except Sunday from 7 to 9:30 p.m. It consists of a choice of four or five appetizers, a main course such as veal filet with cream sauce or fresh poached salmon with hollandaise sauce, both served with a platter of fresh vegetables, followed by a dessert, for £7.50 ($13.13). Advance bookings are essential.

WHERE TO EAT: Yan, Tyan, Tethera, 70 Main St. (tel. Keswick 70233), is named for the way local farmers count sheep. Judith Szucs, the owner, specializes in seafood dishes with a distinctive flair all her own. There is even a note on the menu saying "No service charges or gratuities, please. . . . just come back!" A three-course meal of delicately seasoned pâté followed by jumbo shrimp in a white wine sauce, with cherry pie, might cost £4.75 ($8.31). The restaurant is popular locally, so be sure to book in advance.

11. Bassenthwaite

With its fine stretch of water in the shadow of the 3053-foot Skiddaw, Bassenthwaite makes a good center for exploring the western Lakeland. In the village, you can stay at a splurge recommendation.

For a big splurge, the **Pheasant Inn,** Bassenthwaite Lake, Cockermouth (tel. Bassenthwaite Lake 234), is a 16th-century inn with a neat exterior set against a wooded mountain backdrop. Inside, the bar is wood-paneled and smoke-mellowed. Old hunting prints dot the walls, and real ale is on tap. The beamed dining room is bright and cheerful, with spotless white tablecloths and a menu of good-quality roasts, fish, and poultry with fresh vegetables. A set lunch is £6 ($10.50), a set dinner is £9 ($15.75), and the staff will pack you a lunch for £3 ($5.25). There are three pleasant lounges with an open log fire, and fresh flowers abound. The bedrooms are spotless and bright with chintz. Twelve have a bath or shower room attached, and there are electric blankets on the beds. There are also three bedrooms in the annex, which is a bungalow on the grounds. B&B starts at £18.50 ($32.38) per person, including VAT and a service charge. With a private bathroom the charge is £20 ($35). A double room costs £36 ($63); with bath, £39 ($68.25).

12. Penrith

This is an old Lakeland border town with a turbulent history. See the red ruins of Penrith Castle and the ancient church with its Giant's Grave. It is a good area for exploring not only Hadrian's Wall, but the rolling hills of the

Lake District, the small and ancient stone hamlets that still carry Norse and Danish names, having been settled by the Vikings, and an occasional Norman tower.

In and around this area—but not in Penrith itself—I have selected a random sampling of widely varied accommodations in case you'd like to anchor in and do some exploring.

Armathwaite Castle, in the tiny hamlet of Armathwaite, just off the M6, between Penrith and Carlisle (tel. Armathwaite 287), was built in the heyday of the border wars of the 14th century as a defensive "Tower House." During a lull in the hostilities in the 17th century it was converted into a private home. Today, Charles Francis, the genteel owner, lives there, accepting B&B clients in his historic home, charging them £12 ($21) per person nightly. His brother is a chef, so you can count on a good breakfast. The place still has no central heating, and it can be cold, so be duly warned. Otherwise, if you throw yourself into the spirit of the place, you'll have a good stopover. Don't expect showers either. Reader Elizabeth S. Paltz, of Wayland, Mass., who discovered the place for me, writes: "This is not a hotel but a large English country house with lots of dogs."

Nunnery House, Staffield, near Penrith (tel. 076883/537). If you're driving past the Lake District without time to visit the better known places, come off the M6 at Carlisle or Penrith and go east into the Valley of the Eden River. There you can stay with the Armstrongs in their 18th-century house, built on the site of an ancient nunnery. Bed and a substantial breakfast costs £8.50 ($14.88). There is a lounge and bar, so after a day's trek in the Nunnery Walks along the Eden and Croglin Rivers, you can sink into a chair with a well-earned drink at your elbow before enjoying a pleasant evening meal. For £4 ($7) you are served an appealing appetizer, then a meat or fish course with vegetables, followed by dessert.

Nearer to Kendal, on the A685 in Gaisgill, is **Barbara's Cottage,** Gaisgill, Tebay, near Penrith (tel. 05874/340). Anne and Tony Raw own this 17th-century cottage, with open beams and roaring log fires. They provide comfortable overnight accommodations where guests have their own bath and dining room and lounge with color TV. The cottage is part of a small-holding which provides many fresh vegetables for the wholesome meals. The farmyard and fields are home to a number of almost exotic animals such as Jacob sheep and Muscovy ducks and bantams. The overnight charge is £6 ($10.50) per person, including a full breakfast. An evening meal goes for £4.50 ($7.88). It is a good center for fishing in the River Lune, birdwatching, walking, and sightseeing. Nearby is Appleby Castle with its perfect Norman keep, or you can visit Langrigg Pottery at Winton, or Wetherriggs Country Pottery at Clifton Dykes, an ancient industrial monument where pottery is still produced by means of a steam engine, blunger, settling pans, and pug mill.

Longthwaite Farm, Watermillock, near Penrith (tel. Pooley Bridge 584), was built in 1695, and it's been modernized with hot and cold running water in the bedrooms along with central heating. Although old, the house is in fine shape with black oak floorboards and some of the original doors. Edward and Mary Graham, the owners, take a limited number of paying guests at any time of the year, charging them £14 ($24.50) for two persons, including a full English breakfast. In fact the farm is an ideal center for touring the English lakes. Mr. and Mrs. Graham will direct you to a number of old castles open to the public, as well as to festivals, exhibitions, and sheep-dog trials. If you're writing for reservations, and an answer is required, send an International Reply Coupon.

Chapter XV

YORKSHIRE AND NORTHUMBRIA

1. York
2. North Yorkshire
3. West Yorkshire
4. Durham
5. Tyne and Wear
6. Northumberland

FOR THE CONNOISSEUR, the northeast of England is rich in attractions.

Yorkshire, known to readers of *Wuthering Heights* and *All Creatures Great and Small,* is the Texas of Britain, embracing both the moors of North Yorkshire and the Dales. With the radical changing of the old county boundaries, the shires are now divided into North Yorkshire (the most interesting from the tourist's point of view), West Yorkshire, South Yorkshire, and Humberside.

Away from the cities and towns that still carry the taint of the Industrial Revolution, the beauty is wild and remote. It's characterized by limestone crags, caverns along the Pennines, many peaks, mountainous uplands, rolling hills, the chalkland Wolds, heather-covered Moorlands, broad vales, lazy rivers, and tumbling streams.

Yorkshire lures not only in inland scenery, but with some 100 miles of shoreline, with its rocky headlands, cliffs, sandy bays, rock pools, sheltered coves, fishing villages, bird sanctuaries, former smugglers' dens, and yachting havens.

Across this vast region came the Romans, the Anglo-Saxons, the Vikings, the monks of the Middle Ages, kings of England, lords of the manor, craftsmen, hill farmers, wool growers, each leaving their mark. You can still see Roman roads and pavements, great abbeys and castles, stately homes, open-air museums, and craft centers, along with parish churches, old villages, and cathedrals. In fact, Yorkshire's battle-scarred castles, Gothic abbeys, great country manor houses (from all periods) are unrivaled anywhere in Britain.

Northumbria is made up of the counties of Northumberland, Cleveland, and Durham. Tyne and Wear is one of the more newly created counties, with Newcastle upon Tyne as its center.

The Saxons who came to northern England centuries ago carved out this kingdom, which at the time stretched from the Firth of Forth in Scotland to the banks of the Humber in Yorkshire. Vast tracts of that ancient kingdom remain natural and unspoiled. Again, this slice of England has more than its share of industrial towns, but you don't go here to see those. Set out to explore the wild hills and open spaces, crossing the dales of the eastern Pennines.

The whole area evokes ancient battles and bloody border raids. Castles, Saxon churches, and monastic ruins abound in Northumbria, none more notable than the Roman wall, one of the wonders of the Western world. The finest stretch of the wall lies within the Northumberland National Park between the stony North Tyne River and the county boundary at Gilsland.

1. York

Few cities in England are as rich in history as York. It is still encircled by its 13th- and 14th-century city walls—about 2½ miles long—with four gates. One of these, Micklegate, once grimly greeted visitors coming up from the south with the heads of traitors. To this day you can walk on the footpath of the walls of the Middle Ages.

The crowning achievement of York is its minster or cathedral, which makes the city an ecclesiastical center equaled only by Canterbury. In spite of this, York is one of the most overlooked cities on the cathedral circuit. Perhaps foreign visitors are intimidated by the feeling that the great city of northeastern England is too far north. Actually, it lies about 195 miles north of London on the Ouse River, and can easily be tied in with a motor trip to Edinburgh. Or after visiting Cambridge, a motorist can make a swing through a too-often-neglected cathedral circuit: Ely, Lincoln, York, and Ripon.

There was a Roman York (Hadrian came this way), then a Saxon York, a Danish York, a Norman York (William the Conqueror slept here), a medieval York, a Georgian York, a Victorian York (the center of a flourishing rail business), and of course, a 20th-century York. A surprising amount of 18th-century York remains, including Richard Boyle's restored Assembly Rooms.

SEEING THE SIGHTS: The best way to see York is to go to the **Tourist Information Centre,** DeGrey Rooms, Exhibition Square (tel. York 21756) at 10:15 a.m. and 2:15 p.m. daily from Good Friday to the end of October, where you'll be met by a voluntary guide who will take you on a 1½-hour walking tour of the city, revealing its history and lore through numerous intriguing stories. There is no charge. Additional tours are made at 7:15 p.m. daily during June, July, and August.

At some point in your exploration, you may want to visit **The Shambles,** once the meat-butchering center of York, dating back before the Norman Conquest. But this messy business has given way, and the ancient street survives. It is filled with jewelry stores, cafés, and buildings that huddle so closely together you can practically stand in the middle of the pavement, arms outstretched, and touch the houses on both sides of the street.

Recently, special interest has been focused on discoveries of the Viking era, from 867 to 1066, when the city was known as Jorvik, the Viking capital and major Scandinavian trade center. During excavations under York's Coppergate prior to development, a wealth of artifacts was unearthed in the late 1970s and early 1980s, including entire houses and workshops of the Viking age. For information on the period of history and treasures found in the excavations, inquire at the **Vikings in England Information Office,** 3 Kings Court, Kings Square (tel. York 32342).

Incidentally, the suffix *gate* for streets and sites in York is from the Scandinavian word for street, a holdover from the era when the Vikings held sway here.

York Minster

One of the great cathedrals of the world. York Minster traces its origin back to the early seventh century. The present building, however, dates mainly from the 13th century. Like the minster at Lincoln, York Cathedral is characterized by three towers, all built in the 15th century. The central tower is lantern shaped, in the Perpendicular style.

Perhaps the distinguishing characteristic of the cathedral is its medley of stained glass from the Middle Ages in glorious Angelico blues, ruby reds, forest greens, and ambers. See in particular the large east window, the work of a 15th-century Coventry glass painter. In the north transept is an architectural gem of the mid-13th century, the "Five Sisters," with its lancets. The choir screen, from the late 15th century, has an impressive line-up, everybody from William the Conqueror to the overthrown Henry VI.

The undercroft is open Monday to Saturday, from 10 a.m. to dusk (Sunday from 1 to dusk), charging adults 50p (88¢) for admission; children pay 25p (44¢). The central tower is open Monday to Saturday, April to September, from 10 a.m. to 7 p.m. (October to March, 10:30 a.m. to 3:30 p.m.), costing adults 80p ($1.40) and children 50p (44¢). The chapter house is open Monday to Saturday from 10 a.m., costing adults 20p (35¢); children, 10p (18¢). The bookshop is open Monday to Saturday from 9 a.m. to 5 p.m. (Sunday from 2 to 5 p.m.). The crypt is shown during conducted tours only. At an Information Desk near the south aisle of the minster parties can be put in touch with a guide, if one is available, for a conducted tour. No charge is made, and the guides do not accept gratuities. Gifts toward the maintenance of the minster are, however, always welcome. For more information, telephone York 24426.

The Treasurer's House

In the Minster Yard, the Treasurer's House stands on a site which dates from Roman times. But the main part of the house was erected in the early 17th century when it became the official residence of the treasurer of York Minster. The house contains much fine furniture and an exhibition with tape and slide shows, illustrating the traditions and some of the interesting people associated with the city and the house. It is open from April until the end of October from 10:30 a.m. to 6 p.m., except on Good Friday. Admission is 90p ($1.58) for adults and 40p (70¢) for children. On some evenings in summer the house is open from 8 to 10 p.m., when you can enjoy coffee by candlelight in the main hall, then music in the drawing room.

York Castle Museum

On Tower Street, the York Castle Museum (tel. York 53611) is one of the finest folk museums in the country. Its unique feature is the shop-flanked Kirkgate, the re-creation of a cobble street, with authentic facades moved to the site (including a silversmith). The present exhibition was inspired mainly by a Dr. Kirk who on his travels through Yorkshire acquired a large collection of antiques and old relics.

Upstairs rooms range from a formal, neoclassic Georgian interior to an overstuffed and heavily adorned Victorian living room. In the debtors' prison, former prison cells have been converted into workshops, such as one cubicle where a blacksmith plies his trade.

On the main floor, a collection of costumes ranges from a gown a Georgian debutante would have worn to a fancy-dress ball all the way to the grandmother of the mini of the post–World War I era. Firearms and armor are also displayed.

Part of the debtors' prison is the Half-Moon Court, a re-creation of an Edwardian street, with a gypsy caravan, a sheriff's coach, and a pub that would have attracted the eye of Dickens. Finally, you can visit a mill powered by the water of the Foss River. The museum is open April to September, Monday to Saturday, 9:30 a.m. to 6 p.m.; Sunday, 10 a.m. to 6 p.m. From October to March, hours are from 9:30 to 4:30 p.m. weekdays; 10 a.m. to 4:30 p.m. on Sunday. Admission is £1.25 ($2.19) for adults, 65p ($1.14) for children.

National Railway Museum

The first national museum to be built away from London, the National Railway Museum, Leeman Road (tel. York 21261), was adapted from an original steam locomotive depot. The museum gives visitors a chance to look under and inside steam locomotives or see how Queen Victoria traveled in luxury. In addition, there's a full-size collection of railway memorabilia, with an early 19th-century clock and penny machines for purchasing tickets to the railway platform. On display are more than 20 full-size locomotives including diesel and electric. One, the *Agenoria,* dates from 1829, and is a contemporary of Stephenson's well-known *Rocket.* It's almost identical to the first American locomotive, the *Stourbridge Lion,* brought over from England in 1828. Of several royal coaches, the most interesting is the century-old Royal Saloon, in which Queen Victoria rode until her death. It's like a small hotel, with polished wood, silk, brocade, and silver accessories. Items on exhibition change from time to time, but a popular display is *Mallard,* the fastest steam locomotive in the world. The museum can be visited weekdays from 10 a.m. to 6 p.m. and Sunday from 2:30 to 6 p.m. Admission is free. It is closed on some public holidays.

Theatre Royal

Theatre Royal, on St. Leonard's Place (tel. York 23568), is an old traditional theater building with modern additions to house the box office bars and restaurant. It is worth inquiring about the current production, as the Royal Shakespeare Company includes York in its tours. The Arts Council presents dance, drama, and opera, and visiting celebrities appear in classics. There is also an excellent resident repertory company.

Seats go from £1.50 ($2.63) to £4 ($7) when there are visiting celebrities. The glass-walled, ground-floor restaurant does pre- and post-performance meals. The ground-floor snackbar serves coffee, along with such fare as soup, baked potatoes with cheese, ham and baked beans, priced from £1 ($1.75). Upstairs the Salad Bowl does a variety of cold dishes, costing from £1.75 ($3.06) to £2.30 ($4.04). A three-course business lunch is featured from £2.20 ($3.85), and evening specialties begin at £2.45 ($4.29). You don't have to buy a ticket to eat here, and it's quite a relaxing experience to sit outside with your drink and a snack, looking out on the world passing by.

Brass Rubbings

At St. Williams's College, the **York Brass Rubbing Centre** is open from 10 a.m. to 5 p.m. daily (except Sunday when it is open only from 12:30 to 5 p.m.). The lovely old building was once the home of William Fitzherbert, great-grandson of William the Conqueror. Now a hive of activity, it offers rubbings ranging from 20p (35¢) for a small dog to £2 ($3.50) for an elaborate medieval lady. Or else you can purchase readymade rubbings.

Afterward you can go to **The Restaurant,** across the courtyard, for coffee and homemade cakes and scones, served from 10 a.m. to noon. Lunch is from noon to 2 p.m., and tea follows from 2 to 4 p.m. At lunch, costing from £2.75 ($4.81), you can order such dishes as homemade soups, herb-flavored quiches, steak, kidney, and mushroom pie, chicken paprika, and wine by the glass. Among the more delectable desserts are lemon or chocolate mousse, honey pie, or a butterscotch tart.

An Unguided Walk-About

Starting from York Minster, walk down past Young's Hotel, the birthplace of Guy Fawkes. Turn right into Stonegate, a pedestrian area with old shops, a 12th-century house on the right, and some old coffeehouses. Continue across Davygate into St. Helen's Square to see the Guildhall and Mansion House, then go left into Coney Street, taking a right into Lower Ousegate.

At the beginning of Ouse Bridge, take the steps down to Kings Staithe, with a pub on the left for refreshment, before continuing on into South Esplanade and St. George's Gardens beside the river.

At the bridge, join the road again, turning left and in front of you stand the Castle Museum, the Assize Courts, and Clifford's Tower. Walk up Tower Street and Clifford Street to Nessgate. Turn right into High Ousegate and continue across Parliament Street to the beginning of the Shambles on the left.

Walk up the Shambles past the attractive shops and ancient buildings to Kings Square, then bear right into Goodramgate. Walk down Goodramgate and, at the end, cross Deangate into College Street with St. William's College on the right. At the end a narrow road leads to the Treasurer's House.

You're now behind the east end of the Minster. Walk around to the west end and then up Bootham Bar, through the city gate and turn left into Exhibition Square. The Art Gallery is on the right, the Tourist Information Centre to the left, and beside it, York's Theatre Royal. Continue down St. Leonard's Street to the crossroads, turning right into Museum Street. Cross the river and go right to join part of the old Roman wall which you follow all the way to Skeldergate Bridge. Then follow the river's course upstream again to the center of York.

A Horse-Drawn Carriage Tour

While in York, what about a 15-minute trip in a horse-drawn Danish carriage around the city? One or two horses pull up to five persons, and an umbrella protects you in case it rains. The cost is only £1 ($1.75) for adults and 55p (96¢) for children. Call Mr. B. W. Calam (tel. York 769490) for more information, or else just turn up at the cathedral's west doors where he is likely to be found. He also takes visitors on evening trips, with lantern lights, the price depending on the time.

WHERE TO STAY: Galtres Lodge, Low Petergate (tel York 22478), is a Georgian brick building, presided over by James and Elizabeth Adams. Rates range from £12.50 ($21.88) per person for third-floor rooms to £15.50 ($27.13) per person for second-floor accommodations. If possible the Adamses will give you a room with a view of the rose window of the cathedral. Two rooms contain private showers. Lunch is offered à la carte from noon to 2 p.m., costing about £4 ($7). Tariffs quoted include VAT. Dinner is à la carte, averaging around £6 ($10.50). The location of Galtres is faultless, lying only a hop from the minster and in the vicinity of the railway station. Incidentally, the name of the street (Petergate) is a holdover from the Danish occupation in pre-Norman days. Gate is not used in the English sense, but in the Scandinavian way, meaning street. Historical note: There is a plaque attached to the wall outside the hotel, showing that the street was once the "Via Principalis" of the old Roman fortress of Eboracum.

Bootham Bar Hotel, 4 High Petergate (tel. York 58516), is a charming place, a well-run, clean, 18th-century house with bedroom views over various city sights. Right by the minster, it is well situated for walking in the evening. Mr. and Mrs. M. Warren offer ten bedrooms at a rate of £9 ($15.75) per person nightly, including an English breakfast, although VAT is extra. A £5 ($8.75) deposit will secure a room. All the accommodations, incidentally, are heated and contain wash basins and radios. There is a small lounge with TV. Mrs. Warren's tiny staff is pleasant and helpful.

The **Sycamore Hotel,** 19 Sycamore Pl. (tel. York 24712), was built as a private dwelling in 1902, but has been carefully converted to maintain much of its original splendor. Now it's a family-owned and -run hotel, offering a high level of accommodation for £8.50 ($14.88) per person, including a full breakfast. The location is close to the city center (a 10-minute walk to the minster, a 15-minute walk to the rail station), yet it occupies a position in a quiet cul-de-sac. All rooms have hot and cold running water, central heating, tea- and coffee-making facilities, and TV. There are two toilets, a bathroom, and a shower. Guests frequent the lounge with its color TV. Keys are provided each guest, and car parking is available.

Parkside Hotel, 100 Bishopthorpe Rd. (tel. York 33365), is a family-run hotel giving personal attention. Close to the museums of the city center as well as the minster, it is run by the Johnson family, who offer 15 neatly furnished bedrooms, some of which contain private showers and toilets. All units, however, have hot and cold running water, shaver points, and central heating. Charges begin at £8.50 ($14.88) per person, this tariff including breakfast. There is a large comfortable lounge with color TV, plus a separate dining room.

Dairy Guest House, 3 Scarcroft Rd. (tel. York 39367), is a Victorian house decorated throughout with ideas and furnishings in the "Habitat Sanderson's–Laura Ashley" style, with emphasis on pine and plants. It lies only 200 yards south of the ancient city walls, within easy access of car parking. Units have hot and cold running water and shaver points. Two of the accommodations are family rooms, one with private shower and toilet. There is also a lounge with TV. Rates for B&B are from £8 ($14) per person nightly.

Gleneagles Lodge Guest House, 27 Nunthorpe Ave. (tel. York 37000), is a handsomely decorated, spotlessly maintained, and comfortable guest house which is nicely furnished. On a quiet street, it is within walking distance of the center of York, including the train station, Micklegate Bar, and a number of restaurants serving good but reasonably priced food. The success of Gleneagles has everything to do with the hospitality of Mr. and Mrs. Jones, who go far out of their way to make your stay a memorable one. With them, good conversation comes easy, and they are kind and gracious, as well as sensitive to your needs. Mrs. Jones will prepare a superb home-cooked evening meal if you make arrangements in advance. For B&B, the charge is from £9 ($15.75) per person nightly. Children are granted reductions. Don't be surprised if coffee and fresh scones are brought in to greet you one evening. The next morning you are likely to hear music while your hearty breakfast is being served in a delightful room.

Youngs Hotel, High Petergate (tel. York 24229), was the birthplace of Guy Fawkes. It is one of the best situated budget hotels of York, standing just across the road from the minster and at the beginning of a road leading to the medieval Shambles. Mr. and Mrs. Thomas did a much-needed facelifting when they took over the hotel, improving it greatly after a slump of many years. They installed new wash basins, carpets, beds, and other items for your comfort. The charge is from £12.50 ($21.88) per person for B&B. Their food is excellent. In the evening you can order from a choice à la carte menu, although there is a cheaper menu for lunch as well as a very popular Sunday lunch. Bar meals are also served.

Cranleigh House Hotel, 28–29 East Mount Rd. (tel. York 20837), is an attractive and comfortable Victorian town house, lying in a quiet cul-de-sac near the city walls and Micklegate. It is also within walking distance of the National Railway Museum, the Castle Museum, and the railway station itself. B&B is £9.50 ($16.63) per person nightly, or with dinner included the tariff jumps to £14 ($24.50) per person. The hotel is known locally for its cleanliness and comfort, and there are those who claim it's the most outstanding guest house in all of York.

Grasmead House Hotel, 1 Scarcroft Hill (tel. York 29996). One American guest departing was overheard to remark, "This hotel is just like an Alice in Wonderland place—so super inside." It doesn't have any white rabbits or mad hatters, but it does boast genuine four-poster beds in all the rooms. It's been refurbished with excellent fabrics and made very comfortable with made-to-measure mattresses. Diana and Bill Sissons, the resident owners, give you a real welcome and personal service. Their small family-run hotel lies within easy walking distance of the center, close to the Castle Museum. Some rooms look out toward the city walls and minster. All units have their own private bath, with easy chairs, color TV, and tea- or coffee-making equipment. Prices are from £14.50 ($25.38) per person nightly, including an English breakfast and VAT.

Astoria Hotel, 6 Grosvenor Terrace, Bootham (tel. York 59558), is a guest house lying a four-minute walk from the city center and York Minster. Mrs. Jill Hameed receives guests in single-, double-, twin-bedded, and large family-type rooms, charging them £8 ($14) per person, including a full English breakfast. Each room contains hot and cold running water, and most have private showers. A room with private shower and toilet costs £10 ($17.50) per person. Guests gather in the TV lounge in the evening, and the hotel is licensed for drinks.

READER'S HOTEL SELECTIONS: "The **Carlton House Hotel,** 134 The Mount, an extension of Blossom Street, just a short walk beyond Micklegate Bar (tel. York 22265), is owned by Mr. and Mrs. Greaves. It was the best B&B hotel in which I stayed in all of England. There are both central heating (which runs 24 hours when needed) and metered heaters. Unlike other places where I have stayed, I was given three bath towels. There were several lights and mirrors in my room. The full English breakfast was fantastic. There was a choice of fried, poached, or scrambled eggs. One great joy is a hot shower. All this costs just £9 ($15.75) per person per night or £10 ($17.50) with a private shower" (Harriett Burns, San Diego, Calif.). . . . "**Minster View Guest House,** 2 Grosvenor Terrace (tel. York 55034), was the best B&B find of our entire 70-day Europe tour. Proprietors Pat and Laurie Watson offer clean, quiet rooms at £6 ($10.50) per person, plus helpful sightseeing and shopping tips. A pleasant TV lounge is provided. Their best act, however, was the absolutely superb breakfast served: orange juice, grapefruit sections, cereal, bacon, sausages, egg, mushrooms, tomato, and potatoes or beans, plus toast, honey, and lots of hot coffee. It's a 15-minute walk from the railway station and convenient to the city center" (Hayden Rand, Huntington Beach, Calif.).

"I hope you have the pleasure of staying with Mr. and Mrs. Wood at **The Mount,** 11 Park St. (tel. York 54971), only a few blocks from the railroad station. For £7 ($12.25) I got a large, comfortable, very clean room and a huge breakfast. Mrs. Wood also serves tea and all kinds of goodies in the evening while you're relaxing and watching TV" (David Zarri). . . . "We enthusiastically recommend the comfortable, immaculate accommodations of the **Priory Hotel,** 126 Fulford Rd. It is conveniently on the main route into the city from the south. B&B is £8 ($14) per person, plus VAT—and it was the biggest breakfast offered us on the entire trip" (Mr. and Mrs. Rex Vail, Rochester, N.Y.). . . . "The B&B establishment of **Mrs. J. R. Rankin,** 32 Claremont Terrace, Gillygate (tel. York 27054), is so satisfactory I had to write. I have traveled through various parts of Great Britain, but nowhere was the breakfast as fresh, tasty, and plentiful as that served by Mrs. Rankin. The room was wonderfully clean and light, the living room with TV accessible, and I received complimentary pots of tea with cookies in the evenings. Mrs. Rankin is friendly and helpful. She even washed and ironed my clothes for a fair fee. I felt more at home in her household than in any other English lodgings. The rate is £8 ($14) per person, double occupancy. There is also a private car park. It's a ten-minute walk from the train station, five from York Minster" (Jeffrey A. Stonehill, New York, N.Y.).

"We strongly recommend the **Acomb Road Guest House,** 128 Acomb Rd. (tel. York 792321), owned and operated by Mrs. Eastwood and family. It is a B&B house but, given sufficient time, Mrs. Eastwood will prepare an enjoyable three-course dinner and all is reasonably priced. B&B costs £8 ($14) per person. When we were there, the house had been recently redecorated and had new carpets and bedding. There is a large private car park" (Mrs. D. E. McKillop, Hamilton, New Zealand). . . . "My find is **Margaret's,** 77 Nunthorpe Rd. (tel. York 26396). Nunthorpe Road is an extension of Moss Street, which crosses Blossom Street not far from Micklegate Bar. Mrs. Margaret Stephenson has three rooms. Her rate is £7 ($12.25) per person for B&B. She serves a full English breakfast in each of the comfortable, large bedrooms, which have black-and-white TV sets. The quality of the accommodation is higher than that of many places which cost more. Perhaps the best feature is Margaret herself. Originally from County Durham, she has lived in York for a number of years and takes a great interest in both the welfare of the city and the comfort of its visitors. She treats her guests like personal friends" (Miss Susan E. Leas, Atlanta, Ga.).

"Alan and Serena Coulter at the **Hazlemere Guest House,** 65 Monkgate (tel. York 55947), are wonderful people with a marvelous, clean house and large, good-tasting breakfasts. Color TV may be watched in the living room with tea served at a small charge in the evening if you wish. The charge is £8 ($14) to £10 ($17.50) per person, breakfast included. They will pick up visitors who telephone from the rail or coach station, and they are also within easy walking distance of the center of the city" (Mrs. Philip Reisman, New York, N.Y.). . . . "**The Gables,** 50 Bootham Crescent, Bootham (tel. York 24381), owned by Mrs. Sandy Hare, is one of the cleanest and friendliest places we found in all of England. We rated it 8+ on our personal 1 to 10 rating system. The bed in our room was very firm and comfortable. We particularly appreciated the fact that Mr. Hare drove to the railway station to pick us up. The house is only a few minutes' walk from the minster and the city center. Breakfasts are good, and the cost is reasonable at £8.50 ($14.88) per person per night, including VAT" (Mr. and Mrs. H. Ray Burkhart, Corvallis, Ore.). . . . "We stayed at **Ascot House,** 80 East Parade (tel. York 25782), which is owned by Mr. and Mrs. Greensmith, a delightful, friendly, accommodating couple. Their rooms are clean, and all contain a shower or bath. The cost is £12 ($21) per night per person for B&B, and the breakfasts are good" (Carol A. Helmholz and Phyllis J. Chatham, Tucson, Ariz.).

"**Hazelwood,** 24 Portland St., Gillygate (tel. York 26548), is a very nice guest house. Several items place it in a class above the ordinary. There is an electric tea kettle in each room with a supply of coffee, tea, sugar, and powdered cream. Also, breakfasts are varied by serving hot fresh homemade biscuits each morning. One morning, an omelet was served and the next morning a fried egg was garnished with mushroom slices. The price is £9 ($15.75) per night per person. Owners June and Harry Simpson enlisted their son to carry our luggage up to the room, and Mr. Simpson parked our car for us around at the back which was a little confusing to find. We didn't need the car during our stay, as the guest house is within easy walking distance of York Minster" (Jane E. Phillips, Santa Rosa, Calif.). . . . "**Birchfield House,** 2 Nunthorpe Ave., Scarcroft Road (tel. York 36395), is in a prime position. Everything is so near, and in my opinion it cannot be beaten for genuine, friendly hospitality at absolutely giveaway prices. The price is £7 ($12.25) per night per person for the choice of a double or twin-bedded room. The rooms are large and beautifully decorated, and the place was so clean, it puts some of our North American places to shame. The price includes an English tea and biscuits on arrival and a large English breakfast. You can eat just as much as you want. We tucked in every morning and didn't want to eat again until evening. Each bedroom had hot and cold running water, and you can shower whenever you wish. There is a lounge where guests can write letters, watch color TV, or just relax. The place has central heating and was always warm, but this was nothing to the warmth and friendliness we got from Stella and Joe, the owners" (Mrs. Monroe, Pitcairn Cypress, Calif.). . . . "**Wold View House,** 173–175 Haxby Rd. (tel. York 32061), is a short mile walk from the walled city. The charge is £9 ($15.75) per person, plus a tremendous, well-cooked English breakfast that will last till dinnertime. We also enjoyed an excellent evening meal for £5 ($8.75) more. The service is good and the proprietors, Doreen and Arthur Rawlings, are pleasant and friendly. Mr. Rawlings picked us up at the railway station at no extra charge" (Mr. and Mrs. David Dilley, Indianapolis, Ind.).

WHERE TO EAT: Betty's Restaurant, St. Helen's Square (tel. York 22323), is one of the best all-around eating houses in York, regardless of the price range in which you travel. The restaurant opened in the 1930s and has retained the decor and style of that period. First, at its second-floor self-service restaurant, luncheons are served from 11:30 a.m. to 2 p.m., averaging £3.80 ($6.65) for a meal consisting of a main course, including vegetables. The food is traditionally English, including roast beef and Yorkshire pudding, roast pork and seasoning, and steak-and-vegetable pie. All dishes are well prepared and attractively served.

In the Oakroom in the basement, with bar and waitress service, a set meal is featured for £6 ($10.50). A good choice also at lunchtime is an open buffet. The Oakroom Bar is well known for its links with the Second World War, when it was known as Betty's Dive. A mirror bearing the names of military air crews from all over the world attracts attention. On the ground floor is a confectionery, gift shop, and tea room offering quality products and service. The restaurant is closed on Sunday.

Petergate Fish Restaurant, 97 Low Petergate (on the old Roman *Via Principalis;* tel. York 28167), between the minster and the Shambles, is a typical fish 'n' chips café, with a front counter for take-out orders. For those who can't manage the fine art of consuming fish and chips as they stroll along sightseeing, there is a back room for sitdowns—a modest, basic "caff" in the old English style. Quick fish plates, always accompanied by "chips," are served at the tables. A plate of fish and chips goes for £1.90 ($3.33). Or you may want savaloys at 65p ($1.14) or meat pies and chips from £1.60 ($2.80). The place is open from 11:30 a.m. to 2 p.m., except Thursday and Friday when it closes at 10:30 p.m.

Dean Court Hotel, Duncombe Place (tel. York 25082), has a coffeeshop with an entrance from a basement door just by the minster. A sandwich and coffee will cost about £1.20 ($2.10). They also do hot dishes for £1.35 ($2.36), including sardines on toast, welsh rabbit, or chicken liver pâté. Desserts include peach and banana sundaes at 75p ($1.31), and they also have a good selection of afternoon tea specialties, such as scones with cream and strawberry jam. Service and VAT are included in the prices on the menu, so you know exactly what you're paying.

The **Century Coffee Lounge and Grill,** Petergate, is fresh and green, with a mass of ferns and potted plants in the window, along with wheelback chairs and wooden tables inside. The day's special of chicken, lamb, or pork, with potatoes and fresh vegetables, costs £2 ($3.50), or you can order an à la carte meal of soup, steak and chips, and ice cream for £5 ($8.75). Burgers, sausages, meat pies, and fried plaice go for £1.60 ($2.80) to £3 ($5.25) a portion.

Kooks Bistro, 108 Fishergate (tel. York 37553), is an informal, relaxed eating place run by the owners, Stephanie Cooke and Richard P. Thiel, whose idea is "If you don't enjoy it, we don't." Pleasantly decorated in fresh greens and browns with plants and flowers, it features a varied and unusual menu of English, American, Mexican, French, and vegetarian dishes. All main courses are served with a choice of baked potato, french fries, or a side salad included in the price. Kooks Cheapies range from £1.75 ($3.06), while the most expensive, Posh Kooks, is £6 ($10.50). Special features include help-yourself french bread and unlimited coffee. The service is friendly and the atmosphere is relaxed, with interesting background music and handmade jigsaws, games, and puzzles on every table. Kooks is fully licensed and open daily except Monday from noon to 3 p.m. and 7 p.m. to midnight. It is within walking distance of the center of the city, and there is also plenty of easy parking.

Charlie's Bistro, Tanner Row, in the County Hotel (tel. York 25120), goes back to the Hollywood of the 1920s for its inspiration. The Charlie in the title is a reference to slapstick comedian Charlie Chaplin, whose pictures decorate not only the walls but the menu. Look to the blackboard for the chef's daily specials, which include both continental and traditional English dishes. For an appetizer, try the homemade soup (made fresh every day) or a herb pâté. There is the usual assortment of items to order as a main course, including hamburger, pizza, and lasagne, or you can get more elaborate, going for a T-bone steak or a chicken roasted with garlic. Depending on your selection of a main course, you can dine here for only £3 ($5.25), although at dinner you could spend more than £5 ($8.75), plus the cost of your wine, which, incidentally, is sold by the glass at 55p (96¢). Service is from noon to 2:30 p.m. and 6 to 9:30 p.m. daily (except on Friday and Saturday when it stays open another two hours).

Restaurant Bari, 15 The Shambles (tel. York 33807), stands in one of York's oldest and most colorful streets, originally the street of the butchers and mentioned in the *Domesday Book.* In a continental atmosphere, you can enjoy a quick single course or a full leisurely meal. Ten different pizzas are offered from £1.80 ($3.15). Lasagne and cannelloni at £2.20 ($3.85) are superb. Lunch can cost as little as £3 ($5.25) and dinner from about £4 ($7). A main-dish specialty is escalope Sophia Loren (veal cooked with brandy and cheese with a rich tomato sauce).

Bess's Coffee House, Royal Station Hotel, Station Road (tel. York 53681), is named after the unfortunate heroine of Alfred Noyes's *The Highwayman.* It is a coffeeshop in this landmark British Transport hotel, presenting a simple but reasonably priced menu of "fast food" English dishes. You can order a belly-warming three-course lunch or dinner for around £4.50 ($7.88). You might begin with the chef's pâté, then follow with shepherd's pie with baked beans and a strawberry cream cake. The coffeeshop serves lunch Monday to Saturday from 12:30 to 2:30 p.m. (till 2 p.m. on Sunday) and dinner from 6 to 9 p.m. daily (except on Sunday when it's closed). All prices include service and VAT.

Dreamville, Kings Square (tel. 36592), opposite the Shambles, glorifies the "great American hamburger," naming them after such fun people as Al Capone, Lucky Luciano, and Machine Gun Jack. Burgers are made from 100% selected beef, which is then double-chopped for extra tenderness. They come in three sizes: the quarter-pounder, half-pounder, and, for trenchermen, the "three-quarter-pounder." They're served on a hot toasted sesame seed bun, with a crisp salad, french fries, and American-style relishes. Depending on their size, these burgers range from £2.10 ($3.68) to £4 ($7), the latter for the Bugsy

Siegal bacon and cheeseburger, weighing in at three-quarters of a pound. For dessert, there are 36 varieties of ice cream, and Dreamville serves daily from 10:30 a.m. to 10:30 p.m.

The Bread Basket, 30 Goodramgate (tel. York 32643), is a bright and cheerful "egg-and-chips"–type place, owned by Ron Murphy. It offers quick service for snacks, sandwiches, and fast food. If you're watching the carbohydrates, steer clear. Otherwise, a good meal will cost around £2 ($3.50). As for its "royal patronage," Prince Andrew, the Queen's second son, bought a sandwich when he was stationed with the air force closeby. The Bread Basket is open daily except Sunday and Wednesday afternoon from 9 a.m. to 5 p.m.

Rooney's Bar and Fish & Chip Restaurant, Blake Street, is just around the corner from the minster and Stonegate. In the garden fish and chip restaurant, foliage, hanging baskets of flowers, plants, and fish tanks provide an almost open-air setting for dining the traditional British way. The fish and chips are cooked on a frying range in the usual way, and the fish is delivered daily from local ports to guarantee freshness. A small wine bar is also on the premises. Expect to spend from £4 ($7) and up. The restaurant is open daily from 11 a.m. to 11 p.m.

Taylors in Stonegate, 46 Stonegate (tel. York 22865). Downstairs the bow-windowed shop is filled with bags and jars of coffee. The old-fashioned till bears the prices of the various teas for sale. They boast 36 varieties of teas and coffee. When you see the shop, you'll know that is no idle boast. Teas come all the way from China and India, including exotic Moroccan mint and passion fruit. Upstairs the coffeeshop dispenses these same beverages at 55p (96¢) for a pot of tea for one, 85p ($1.49) for a pot of coffee for one. They advertise a late breakfast for £2 ($3.50). You can also order Welsh rabbit, Yorkshire ham, and omelets with various fillings, costing around £2.50 ($4.38). Spiced Yorkshire teacakes and cinnamon toast are also on the menu. Service is from 9 a.m. to 5:15 p.m.

LODGING ON THE OUTSKIRTS: The **Manor Country Guest House,** Acaster Malbis (tel. York 706723), is a large country mansion surrounded by six acres of lawns, gardens, a small lake and island, a sundial, an 11th-century chapel, and woodlands adjoining the River Ouse. It lies about 12 minutes or so from York by car or bus. The manor is 2¼ miles from the A64 at unspoiled Acaster Malbis, via Copmanthorpe or Bishopthorpe (home of the archbishop of York). Originally the manor was a small farmhouse, but it was enlarged at the turn of the century.

All bedrooms are comfortably furnished and have central heating and hot and cold running water. Some have showers. Most of the guest bedrooms are in the front of the house, overlooking the grounds, lake, and woods. The tariff is £10.70 ($18.73) per person for the first night and £9 ($15.75) per person for succeeding nights. Between October 1 and Easter, these rates are reduced to £9 ($15.75) per person for the first night and £8.35 ($14.61) per person afterward. A week costs only £46 ($80.50) per person. These charges cover room, a full, hot English breakfast, and VAT. The breakfast is buffet style and all you can eat. When children share their parents' room, a reduction can be made according to age up to 12 years. Packed lunches can be provided at £1 ($1.75) and at 6 p.m. a cold buffet meal is offered at £5 ($8.75) for all courses, including VAT. Please send four International Reply Coupons with inquiries.

READER'S FARMHOUSE SELECTION ON THE OUTSKIRTS: "**Moor House Farm,** Moor Lane, Bishopthorpe (tel. York 703143), is on the outskirts of a small village,

Bishopthorpe, only four miles from the center of York. Regular bus service connects it with the city center. Susan Whittaker is your hostess. The farm has been in her family for several generations. The original part of the farmhouse dates back to the 1700s. Susan is a gracious hostess, and her children are able and willing helpers when needed. The farmhouse rooms are large and well furnished, and an attractive guest lounge is provided. The farm is in a quiet area which provides the opportunity to stroll along country lanes. This is a working farm with a large herd of cattle. B&B costs £8 ($14) per person. There are several good restaurants serving food at reasonable prices within a mile of the farm, but Mrs. Whittaker can provide an excellent dinner with sufficient notice" (Ulric Morley, Sacramento, Calif.).

2. North Yorkshire

For those seeking legendary untamed scenery, I recommend a tour of North Yorkshire, which also takes in the already-previewed historic cathedral city of York.

North Yorkshire contains England's most varied landscape. Its history has been turbulent, often bloody, and many relics of its rich past are still standing, including ruined abbeys. North Yorkshire is little known to the average North American visitor, but many an English traveler knows of its haunting moors, serene valleys, and windswept dales.

The hospitality of the people of North Yorkshire is world renowned, and if a pudding which originated there doesn't accompany a slab of roast beef, the plate looks naked to the British. The people of North Yorkshire, who speak an original twang often imitated in English cinema, are, in general, hardworking and industrious, perhaps a little contemptuous of the easy living of the south. But they are decidedly open and friendly to strangers, providing you speak to them first.

CASTLE HOWARD: In its dramatic setting of lakes, fountains, and extensive gardens, the 18th-century palace designed by Sir John Vanbrugh is undoubtedly the finest private residence in North Yorkshire. The first major achievement of the architect who later created the lavish Blenheim Palace near Oxford, Castle Howard was begun in 1699 for the third Earl of Carlisle, Charles Howard, whose descendants still call the place "home." The striking facade is topped by a painted and gilded dome, reaching more than 80 feet into the air. The interior boasts a 192-foot "Long Gallery," as well as a chapel with a magnificent stained-glass window by the 19th-century artist, Sir Edward Burne-Jones. Besides the collections of antique furniture, tapestries, porcelains, and sculpture, the castle contains a number of important paintings, including a portrait of Henry VIII by Holbein, and works by Rubens, Reynolds, and Gainsborough.

The seemingly endless grounds around the palace also offer the visitor some memorable sights, including the domed Temple of the Four Winds, by Vanbrugh, and the richly designed family mausoleum by Hawksmoor. There are two rose gardens, one with old-fashioned roses, the other featuring modern creations. The stable court houses the Costume Galleries, the largest private collection of 18th- to 20th-century costumes in Britain. The authentically dressed mannequins are exhibited in period settings. Castle Howard, just 15 miles northeast of York, is open to the public daily from March 25 through the end of October; the grounds from 10:30 a.m., the house and Costume Galleries from 11:30 a.m. to 5 p.m. Admission is £2.50 ($4.38) for adults, £1.10 ($1.93) for children. There is a self-service cafeteria where you can order sandwiches and hot dishes, the latter for around £2 ($3.50). Good wines are served. The cafeteria opens at 11 a.m. For information, telephone Coneysthorpe 333.

Castle Howard had the "title role" in *Brideshead Revisited,* the popular television mini-series.

HARROGATE: If you head northeast from York for 20 miles, you reach Harrogate, North Yorkshire's second-largest town after York. In the 19th century, Harrogate was a fashionable spa. Most of the town center is surrounded by a 200-acre lawn called "The Stray." Boutiques and antique shops, which Queen Mary used to frequent, make Harrogate a shopping center of excellence, particularly along Montpellier Parade. Harrogate is called England's floral resort, deserving such a reputation because of its gardens, including Harlow Car Gardens and Valley Gardens. The former spa has an abundance of guest houses and hotels, including the expensive Swan where Agatha Christie hid out during her mysterious disappearance—still unexplained—in the 1920s.

Where to Stay

Gilmore, 98 King's Rd. (tel. Harrogate 503699), is a small, privately owned guest house run by Mr. and Mrs. Gill that has been added to over the past 20 years, and now provides quite good accommodations at painless rates. It's half Edwardian, half no style at all, but under a coat of sparkling paint it appears fresh. B&B costs £10 ($17.50) daily in a single and £9.50 ($16.63) per person in a double. Two bedrooms with private showers rent for £11 ($19.25) per person. Dinner is optional, costing another £5 ($8.75). Bedrooms have colorful bedcovers, hot and cold running water, and there are three public rooms, including a bar lounge.

Wessex Hotel, Harlow Moor Drive (tel. Harrogate 65890), is in an attractive part of Harrogate overlooking and with immediate access to the Valley Gardens. It is only a ten-minute walk from the center of town. The family-run Wessex Hotel provides hospitality in the Yorkshire style, combined with comfort and personal service, with special emphasis on good food served in their spacious dining room. There is central heating throughout the hotel, and all 15 bedrooms are equipped with radios and shaver points. Most bedrooms have shower/toilet en suite, and have been refurbished. A pleasantly decorated and well-furnished television lounge is available for relaxation after a busy day of sightseeing or shopping. Or you can have a drink in the comfortable bar lounge and unwind by getting to know your fellow guests. For £15 ($26.25) per person you get a very clean and airy room and a standard English breakfast. The proprietors, Mr. and Mrs. H. Kirkby, will be happy to direct you to the Valley Gardens with its beautiful floral displays; or the facilities for tennis, 18-hole mini-golf course, horseback riding, and if you are a racing fan, there are four racecourses within easy distance of the hotel.

Ashley House Hotel, 36/40 Franklin Rd. (tel. Harrogate 57474), is a comfortable family-run licensed hotel with excellent food and friendly atmosphere. There are 18 guest rooms, all equipped with coffee- and tea-making facilities, TV, and alarm-clock radios. Some rooms are available with shower and toilet en suite. A good selection of wines is available with meals in the spacious dining room, and in the evening guests may relax and meet fellow visitors in the cozy "olde worlde" bar. There are two lounges for guests, both with color TV, and there is full central heating throughout. The hotel is in a quiet, residential part of town, although it is only a five-minute walk to the center. It's a convenient site for visiting York and the Yorkshire Dales. Wendy and Richard Wood assure you of every comfort and attention. They charge £9 ($15.75) per person daily in a double or twin room, including a full English breakfast. Single rooms are £9.50 ($16.63) daily. A four-course dinner is served each evening at £4.25 ($7.44) a head, including coffee. Weekly half-board terms are available at a 10% reduction. All prices are fully inclusive.

The **Manor Hotel,** 3 Clarence Drive (tel. Harrogate 503916), is an impressive Victorian stone concoction with complex architectural details—a square tower and off-balance gables. A former private home, with its own gardens, it is close to the Valley Gardens and is now under the personal supervision of Elizabeth Cooper, who has set the following rates: For B&B, guests pay £13.23 ($23.15) per person daily, VAT included. She also caters to special diets.

READER'S HOTEL SELECTION: "**Alexandra Court Hotel,** 8 Alexandra Rd. (tel. Harrogate 502764), is run by Mr. and Mrs. G. Keeler, who are most hospitable. The hotel is very well run, with large and tastefully furnished rooms. Everything is of the best. The breakfast is excellent, and you can relax in a comfortable TV lounge. The price for B&B is £18 ($31.50) in a double, and dinner costs £5 ($8.75). Some rooms have private baths for which you pay slightly more. We found this hotel an excellent center for us to tour the Yorkshire Dales" (Betty Presto, Waikanae, Wellington, N.Z.).

MOORS AND DALES: The rural landscape is pierced with ruins of once-great abbeys and castles. North Yorkshire is a land of green hills, valleys, and purple moors. Both the Yorkshire Dales and the Moors are wide open spaces, two of Britain's finest national parks, with a combined area of some 1200 square miles. However, the term "national" can be misleading, as the land is managed by foresters, farmers, and private landowners. In fact, more than 90% of the land is in private ownership. The Dales rise toward Cumbria and Lancashire to the east, and the Moors stretch to the eastern coastline.

Of course, York, the major center, has already been previewed. But those with the time may want to explore deeper into the rural roots of England. From Harrogate, our last stopover, you can enjoy the wildest scenery of the region by heading out on day trips, anchoring at one of the inns coming up if you don't want to return to the old spa.

After leaving Harrogate, you can discover white limestone crags, drystone walls, fast-rushing rivers, and isolated sheep farms or else clusters of sandstone cottages.

Malhamdale receives more visitors annually than any dale in Yorkshire. Of the priories and castles to visit, two of the most interesting are the 12th-century ruins of **Bolton Priory,** and a 14th-century pile, **Castle Bolton,** to the north in Wensleydale.

In contrast, the Moors, on the other side of the Vale of York, have a wild beauty all their own, quite different from that of the Dales. They are bounded by the Cleveland and Hambleton Hills. The white horse of Kilburn can be seen hewn out of the landscape.

Both **Pickering** and **Northallerton,** two market towns, serve as gateways to the Moors. Across the Moors are seen primordial burial grounds and stone crosses. The best-known trek in moorland is the 40-mile hike over bog, heather, and stream from Mount Grace Priory inland to Ravenscar on the seacoast. It's known as **Lyke Wake Walk.**

Along North Yorkshire's 45 miles of coastline are such traditional seaside resorts as **Filey, Whitby,** and **Scarborough,** the latter claiming to be the oldest seaside spa in Britain, standing on the site of a Roman signaling station. It was founded in 1622, following the discovery of mineral springs with medicinal properties. In the 19th century, its Grand Hotel, a Victorian structure, was acclaimed "as the best in Europe." The Norman castle on big cliffs overlooks the twin bays.

In and Around Helmsley

This attractive market town, with a market every Friday, is a good center for exploring the surrounding area. It is called the key to Ryedale and is the mother town of the district, standing at the junction of the roads from York, Pickering, Malton, Stokesley, and Thirsk.

Helmsley is on the southern edge of the North Yorkshire Moors National Park and is well known as a center for walking and "potholing." It is in an area among many places and things of interest: remains of Bronze and Iron Age existence on the moors; prehistoric highways, Roman roads, and of course the ruins of medieval castles and abbeys. Beyond the main square of the town are the ruins of its castle with an impressive keep. This castle was built between 1186 and 1227.

A good reason for selecting Helmsley as a stopover is because it is near York and well located, but the hotel rates are far below those of York.

Three miles to the north of Helmsley, are the ruins of **Rievaulx** (pronounced "Reevo") **Abbey.** The abbey was named for Rye Vallis, valley of the River Rye. It was the first Cistercian house in northern England and was founded in 1131 by monks who came over from Clairveaux in France. At its peak it had 140 monks and 500 lay brothers. In its size, its architecture, and its setting, even its ruins are among the most impressive in the country. The land was given by Walter l'Espec, a Norman knight, who later entered the community as a novice and died and was buried here.

Rievaulx Terrace, now a property of the National Trust, is a landscaped grassy terrace about half a mile long, which was laid out in the mid-18th century by Thomas Duncombe of Duncombe Park. The visitor, after a picturesque woodland walk, emerges onto a wide lawn near a circular "temple," known as the Tuscan Temple. The walk along the terrace gives frequent views of the abbey ruins in the valley below. On a windy North Yorkshire spring day, this walk is truly a constitutional.

At the opposite end from the Tuscan Temple is the Ionic Temple, whose interior is beautifully decorated and furnished, with a classically painted ceiling and gilded wood and rose-velvet upholstered furniture. In the basement are two rooms which were originally used by servants to prepare food for guests above. This temple was planned by Thomas Duncombe III as a banqueting house and a place of rest and refreshment after the long carriage ride from Duncombe Park.

Admission is 80p ($1.49) for adults, 40p (70¢) for children.

Crown Hotel, Market Square at Helmsley (tel. Helmsley 70297), is of undetermined age, but quite old and colorful. It's built of stone, standing at the edge of the village green, and the walls are covered by creepers, giving it charm. The owner, Mr. Manders, has spared no effort to make every room not only attractive, but comfortable. Five of the bedrooms now have showers, all contain hot and cold running water, and, wherever possible, in the restoration old beams have been left exposed. The dining room is well furnished; there are two bars, one public and one better furnished for residents. In addition, there are two living rooms. A single ranges from £15 ($26.25) to £17 ($29.75), a double or twin renting for anywhere from £30 ($52.50) to £33 ($57.75). Set lunches are from £4 ($7), dinners from £8 ($14), and the food is typically English. There's always a roast plus two different fresh East Coast fish on the menu.

At Coxwold

Coxwold is on the southern border of the park, one of the most attractive villages in the Moors.

Fauconberg Arms, The High (tel. Coxwold 214), is a fine old Yorkshire inn, on the main street of this village of stone houses. The social center of the village, it attracts residents with a lounge bar, where a fire burns brightly in a stone fireplace topped by a 15-foot oak beam. There are black oak settles, Windsor armchairs, a stone floor, horse brasses, and in spring a bowl of flowers in the wide bay window overlooking the street. Here you can literally settle in for a premeal drink in front of the fire. If it's Thursday, the maid starts her weekly round of polishing the impressive collection of brass and copper. The dining room is cozily decorated, and you can get a set lunch for £5.50 ($9.63). The cuisine is traditional English, including roast pork with apple sauce or roast chicken with bread sauce. Hopefully, the cook will make a rhubarb pie served with a dollop of thick cream. Dinners are à la carte and include poultry choices and meat dishes for around £12 ($21) per person. There are three attractively decorated rooms which share a corridor bath, costing £21 ($36.75), rising to £24 ($42) with shower, in a double. Bathless singles go for £15 ($26.25), the tariff going up to £16 ($28) with shower. If you can get it, the best room, the fourth one, is a double complete with shower and television.

In and Around Settle

Golden Lion Hotel, Duke Street (tel. Settle 2203), has been accepting overnight guests since 1671 when travelers would arrive via the covered entryway and descend from the carriage in the inner courtyard. Each of the 13 attractive guest rooms has hot and cold running water and is centrally heated. The rate for B&B is £10 ($17.50) per person, including VAT and service. The rooms have old-style furnishings and are of a good size. There are two lounge bars, each colorful, with open fires in cold weather. They have real ale. Bar snacks include chicken and chips at £2.10 ($3.68). The menu in the dining room has simple but well-prepared Yorkshire fare, including a roast and a fish dish. A three-course set meal costs about £6.10 ($10.68).

Close House, Giggleswick, near Settle (tel. Settle 3540), is a 17th-century farmhouse of great charm with all the required modern amenities, a delightfully relaxing place. The owner, Mrs. B. T. Hargreaves, has tastefully furnished the rooms with antiques and a collection of horse brasses, and other objects, all making it an unusual stopover retreat. Close House and its 230 acres of farmland lie at the end of a tree-lined private drive in the Yorkshire Dales. It's 1½ miles from Settle (off the A65 Lancaster, Skipton road). The rate for B&B in a single is from £14.50 ($25.38), or else it's from £13.50 ($23.63) per person in a double, including VAT. A home-prepared evening meal is graciously presented for £8.50 ($14.88). The service charge is left to your discretion. Close House does not cater to children.

Near Skipton

The **Buck Inn,** Malham, near Skipton (tel. Airton 317), is a Victorian stone inn where Dale explorers can find excellent ale, a comfortable and cozy room, and a good breakfast and dinner. There are two bars, one especially for hikers, the other for residents. The inn offers ten centrally heated bedrooms, each with a wash basin, only one with a private bath. A single ranges from £14 ($24.50) to £16 ($28), and a double goes for £23 ($40.25) to £27 ($47.25), the latter for units with private bath or showers. The half-board tariff is in the range of £19 ($33.25) to £21 ($36.75) per person nightly. You can order bar lunches noon and evenings if you don't want a full meal.

Sparth House, Malham, near Skipton (tel. Airton 315), is a stone property, part of which dates from 1664 with an extension from 1879. It's a family affair, run by Alan and Gillian Cooper, who offer inexpensive accommodations for those who want to use their place as a base for exploring the Dales, the Lake District, and Brontë country. Singles, twins, and family rooms are rented. A single costs £12 ($21) in high season, and a double ranges from £19.60 ($34.30) to £24 ($42). The evening meal served here costs £6 ($10.50) for three courses, £8 ($14) for four courses. There is one room with a private bath and toilet. The Cooper family members do the cooking, and the cuisine is well prepared, using home-grown vegetables and fruit in season, as well as homemade marmalade and cakes.

In and Around Richmond

Richmond, the most frequently used town name in the world, stands at the head of the Dales as the mother of them all. It's an old market town built beside the River Swale and dominated by the striking ruins of its Norman castle. In the center of the cobbled marketplace stands an ancient church and a tall stone pillar known as the Market Cross. It's a good touring center for the surrounding countryside.

The Georgian Theatre here, which was constructed in 1788, has a resident amateur company of the highest quality.

For an accommodation in the area, try the following recommendation:

West View, Ravensworth, near Richmond (tel. 0325/718504), is a country cottage in the small village of Ravensworth, above the market town of Richmond. Here Mrs. Bainbridge offers a warm welcome and genuine Yorkshire hospitality. B&B is from £6.50 ($11.38) per person nightly. There is a TV lounge, with an open log fire, and a walled garden where you can sit in the evening. There's also a good village pub nearby which will provide an evening meal or you can drive down into Richmond.

READERS' GUEST HOUSE SELECTION: "We stayed at **Windsor House,** 9 Castle Hill (tel. 0748/3285), just off the main market square and only a short walk from Richmond Castle. Accommodations are pleasant, the breakfast is good, and Mrs. Mary Turner provides friendly and helpful management. The charge is £8 ($14) per person per night" (Carol A. Helmholz and Phyllis J. Chatham, Tucson, Ariz.).

READER'S B&B SELECTION AT BELLERBY (NEAR RICHMOND): "We stayed at **Myrtle House,** Bellerby, near Leyburn (tel. Wensleydale 23309). It was our most surprising B&B. We entered an old stone house behind a wall to find an extremely modern interior with chrome furniture, a grand piano, and many pieces of art. Rates are from £8 ($14) per person. Also in this village we found a real tea room, **Olde Post Office Tea Room** (tel. Wensleydale 23123). The proprietor, Anne-Margaret Lonsdale, finds that the custom of tea rooms is being revived. In winter she serves beautiful dinners by her description. Certainly our high tea was something out of a novel" (Barbara Benda Jenkins, Amherst, Mass.).

In and Around Bedale

Ainderby Myers, Bedale (tel. 0609/748668). At this 16th-century manor house, Mrs. Anderson offers B&B, charging from £6.50 ($11.38) per person nightly. There are mentions of the manor in the *Domesday Book.* She offers four rooms with hot and cold running water and good heating, plus a lounge with TV. In the pleasant garden, you can sit and enjoy a view of the rolling

Yorkshire countryside. An evening meal can be provided for £5 ($8.75), but there are some very good places to eat out in the area, of which Mrs. Anderson will provide details if required. To reach the village, turn off the A1 at the Hackforth turning.

Burtree Farm, Crakehall, near Bedale (tel. 0677/22833), is another farm just off the A1, with large airy rooms which contain heating and hot and cold running water. There are adaptations for disabled visitors. There is a ground-level shower and toilet. This is a working farm, and there is always lots of activity from which to escape to the comfort of the TV lounge. B&B is from £6.50 ($11.38) per person nightly, and an evening meal at £4 ($7) can be provided by arrangement. Mrs. Shields will take great pains to see that guests are well looked after.

Mill Close Farm, Patrick Brompton, near Bedale (tel. 0677/50257), is another farm close to Bedale, where Mrs. Knox provides B&B at a cost of £7 ($12.25) per night. Visitors join in the life of the house, which is surrounded by an attractive garden with a variety of rare animals, deer, sheep, and water-fowl. No evening meals are provided, so a drive into Bedale is indicated.

In and Around Ripon

Ripon has an ancient tradition of the watchman blowing a horn in the center of town every night at 9 p.m., a custom dating back to 886. This cathedral city, 27 miles north of Leeds by road, was once a Saxon village where a Celtic monastery was founded in 651.

Beneath the central tower of **Ripon Cathedral,** the site of a Norman cathedral dating from 1154, is the original crypt built by St. Wilfrid more than 1300 years ago. This is one of the oldest buildings in England, and the original plaster is still on the walls. The crypt contains silver chalices and patens dating from 1500 to the present.

Archbishop Roger built the nave of the Norman cathedral, the north transept, and part of the choir stalls. The twin towers of the west front are Early English, from about 1216, and the library (once the "Lady Loft") is from some time in the 14th century. The canons stalls were hand-carved and were completed in 1495. Two sides of the tower date from the original construction in 1220, but in 1450 an earthquake caused the other two to collapse. They were reconstructed and the central tower and south transept were added at the beginning of the 16th century. The completion of all the work was never carried out, as King Henry VIII took away all the cathedral endowments. Until 1664 the towers had tall spires, which were removed to prevent fires caused by lightning.

Today the cathedral is a lively Christian Centre, with a study center and a choir school. It is the mother church of the Diocese of Ripon, which spreads over most of the Yorkshire Dales to the fifth-largest city in England, Leeds. For further information, telephone Ripon 4108.

Three miles west of Ripon lie the ruins of **Fountains Abbey,** which I consider the most magnificent abbey ruins in England. Founded in 1132, this former abbey was Cistercian in origin. It is set in 100 acres of meadow and woodland, with ornamental gardens, Fountains Hall, and a deer herd.

Newby Hall, lying on the northeast bank of the Ure River between Ripon (four miles) and Boroughbridge (3½ miles), is a famous Adam house set in 25 acres of garden, filled with sunken gardens, magnolias, azaleas, and countless flowering shrubs, along with many rare and unusual species. The house, built for Sir Edward Blackett circa 1695, is in the style of Sir Christopher Wren. In the mid-18th century Robert Adam redesigned the house, extending it to display the antique sculpture, tapestries, and furniture of its then owner, William Weddell, a connoisseur and art collector. Robert Compton is the present owner. Displayed are the Gobelins Tapestries, one of only five sets completed, with medallions by Boucher, appointed first painter to Louis XV.

On the grounds is a miniature railway, the Newby 10¼" gauge, providing rides for both children and adults.

In April, May, and September, the house is open from 1 to 5:30 p.m. on Wednesday, Thursday, Saturday, and Sunday, and from June to August daily except Monday. The gardens are open April 1 to September 30 daily except Monday from 11 a.m. to 5:30 p.m.

To visit the hall, park, and gardens costs about £2 ($3.50) for adults; children, half price. For more information, telephone Boroughbridge 2583.

The **Nordale,** 1 North Parade, Ripon (tel. Ripon 3557), is a bargain at the daily per-person rate of £9 ($15.75), which includes not only a complete full-course breakfast but VAT. All rooms have hot and cold running water, and there is a shower room in the corridor. Some units have showers en suite. Consider having a Yorkshire dinner as well, and this costs £14 ($24.50) per person including your room and breakfast. Mrs. Richmond, the owner, will pack a picnic lunch for you if you are making a day trip. All her bedrooms are attractively furnished, with twins and doubles, according to your wish. Children can stay at reduced rates. The Nordale is a good center for exploring the Yorkshire Dales. Mr. Richmond, who assists in the running of the Nordale, has a keen interest in the city of Ripon and a knowledge of its history and traditions, and he can arrange for the viewing of the "City Regalia" for those who wish. He also has forged new links with the Ripons of America, one in Wisconsin and more recently the Ripon in California.

Black-a-Moor Inn, Risplith, near Ripon (tel. Sawley 214), is a stone country inn well known for its hospitality and convivial atmosphere. It's on the Ripon to Pateley Bridge road, the B6265, five miles from Ripon, just perfect for visits to Fountains Abbey, the Brimham Rocks, and the Dales. Owners Patricia and Bryan Brader have decorated the three bedrooms with taste, installing central heating as well as hot and cold running water. They charge £16 ($28) per person for B&B in a single, £21 ($36.75) in a double, including VAT and the service charge. They offer country grill breakfasts, and some of their specialties include homemade steak-and-kidney pie, venison in black cherries, and guinea fowl in a red wine sauce. Two dessert concoctions they are known for include lemon meringue pie and "Old Perculier Cake" with Wensleydale cheese.

READER'S RESTAURANT SUGGESTION: "For lunch, I recommend the **Cathedral View Coffee Shop** on the second floor of a furniture store close to the cathedral. The atmosphere is charming, and you have a choice of generous salad plates from £1.50 ($2.63) up, including french bread, lots of butter, and tea or coffee. This is a good bargain, mealwise" (Mrs. Audrey Fawcett, Victoria, B.C., Canada).

At Thirsk

This pleasant old market town, north of York, has a fine parish church, lying in the Vale of Mowbray. But what makes it such a stopover for visitors is the fame brought to the village by James Herriot, author of *All Creatures Great and Small.* Mr. Herriot still practices in Thirsk, and visitors can photograph his office, perhaps get a picture of his partner standing in the door.

If you'd like to stay over, **Brook House,** Ingramgate (tel. Thirsk 22240), is a large Victorian house set in 1½ acres of land, some of which is filled with flower beds. It overlooks the open countryside, but a three-minute walk brings you to the Market Square. Mrs. Margaret McLauchlan charges from £9 ($15.75) per person for B&B, although she makes reductions for children. She is charming and kind, and has even been known to do a batch of washing for guests at no extra cost (however, I can't promise that!). She serves a good Yorkshire breakfast, hearty and filling, plus an English tea in the afternoon. She has a spacious and comfortable living room with color TV, and her bedrooms are large and airy. The experience of knowing John and Margaret McLauchlan and enjoying their hospitality will remain long in your memory. They are personal friends of Mr. Herriot.

Church Farm, at Sowerby, near Thirsk (tel. Thirsk 23655), offers rural peace. It's reached by a footpath from the town center, about a five-minute walk from Thirsk Market Square. It is both a Cordon Bleu restaurant and a farm offering accommodations. The owners, Roy and Olga Sheppard, were born in Yorkshire, and they are most helpful to guests touring in the area. Their home is some three centuries old, but it has been brought up to date and handsomely furnished, often with family heirloom pieces. Outside stand large lime trees which were planted to honor Queen Victoria's Jubilee. Bedrooms are nicely furnished and have a personalized touch. My favorites are the two double rooms and a family room, all with en suite bath, installed in a former hayloft. The en suite accommodation is rented for £13 ($22.75) per person, or if you take one of the other double rooms the charge is lowered to £9 ($15.75) per person.

The six-stall horse barn has been converted into the Sheppard's Table. It is possible to enjoy a quiet drink and a candlelit dinner on the very spot where James Herriot ministered to the horses. The walls are of rough brick, and dark wood and farm equipment make for a rustic atmosphere. The cuisine is excellent because all the ingredients that go into making it are bought fresh daily. The cookery is both imaginative and served with flair. A traditional Sunday lunch is featured for £5.50 ($9.63) and a dinner from £8.50 ($14.88) to £12 ($21). An extensive lunch menu is available Tuesday to Saturday including, for example, chicken breast in mushroom sauce at £3 ($5.25). There's also a full à la carte menu if you prefer. Lunch is served from noon to 2 p.m. and dinner from 7 p.m. The stable is closed Sunday evening and Monday. Reservations are advised.

READER'S HOTEL SELECTION (WHITBY): "The **Saxonville Hotel,** Ladysmith Avenue, Whitby (tel. 0947/602631), is run by Mr. and Mrs. R. Newton and their two married sons, Roger and Peter. From the time we checked in until we left, some member of the family was always on hand to make sure we were comfortable or just to visit if we felt like it. Our room was pleasantly furnished and immaculate. All the 22 rooms have radio, intercom, and facilities for making tea or coffee. Some have private showers and toilets. The food, which is primarily Roger's responsibility, is superb. The hotel is in a quiet area yet is within easy walking distance of the beach and the town center. It has private parking spaces for 20 vehicles. If one wanted a base for exploring that area of North Yorkshire, the hotel, open from around mid-May to mid-October, would be an ideal place to stay. Rates for a bed and full English breakfast are £15 ($26.25) per night per person, including service and VAT. A bigger bargain is to take the excellent five-course dinner as well. For dinner and B&B, the per-person rate is £20 ($35) per day, again including VAT and service" (Theodore Peterson, Urbana, Ill.).

READER'S GUEST HOUSE SELECTION (CRACOE): "The Dale country in Yorkshire is primarily walking country, but just driving-through is worthwhile. In particular we want to recommend the **Idrick House** in the village of Cracoe, owned by Mr. and Mrs. G. F. Drake. This is a converted church and has rooms on the second floor. We had B&B for £8 ($14). The beds were fine, the entire house immaculate, breakfast was very good, and tea was served at night. Mr. and Mrs. Drake make you feel more like old friends than like paying guests. There's a TV set in the lounge" (Kirk Cargill).

3. West Yorkshire

HAWORTH: In West Yorkshire, this ancient stone village lying on the high moors of the Pennines—45 miles west of York via Leeds and 21 miles west of Leeds—is world famous as the home of the Brontë family. The three sisters—Charlotte, Emily, and Anne—distinguished themselves as English novelists. They lived a life of imagination at a lonely parsonage at Haworth.

Anne wrote two novels, *The Tenant of Wildfell Hall* and *Agnes Grey,* and Charlotte's masterpiece was *Jane Eyre,* which depicted her experiences as a governess and enjoyed popular success in its day.

But, of course, it was Emily's fierce and tragic *Wuthering Heights* which made her surpass her sisters, as she created a novel of such passion, intensity, and primitive power, with its scenes of unforgettable, haunting melancholy, that the book has survived to this day, appreciated by later generations far more than those she'd written it for.

From Haworth (pronounced "How-worth"), you can walk to Withens, the "Wuthering Heights" of the immortal novel. In Haworth, Charlotte and Emily are buried in the family vault under the church of St. Michael's.

The parsonage where they lived has been preserved as the **Brontë Parsonage Museum** (tel. Haworth 42323). Emily and Charlotte died there. It may be visited daily from April 1 to September 30 from 11 a.m. to 5:30 p.m. In winter it is open from 11 a.m. to 4:30 p.m. The admission is 50p (88¢) for adults, 25p (44¢) for children.

Haworth is the second most visited literary shrine in England, after Stratford-upon-Avon. Frequent bus and train service is available from Haworth to Keighly and Bradford and Leeds in West Yorkshire. The popular Worth Valley Steam Railway is one of the best preserved steam lines in England. At Keighley it connects with British Rail, running up the Worth Valley to Oxenhope via Haworth. From Haworth you can visit the tiny market towns of Settle as well as Skipton with its canal and castle.

Food and Lodging

The **Tourist Information Centre,** 2–4 West Lane (tel. Haworth 42329), offers an accommodation booking service for the local area, but cannot recommend individual establishments. The office is open daily throughout most of the year (usually closed for one week around Christmas). If you don't avail yourself of this service, then you might stay at one of the recommendations below.

The **Old White Lion Hotel** (tel. Haworth 42313) stands at the top of a cobbled street. It was built around 1700 with a solid stone roof almost next door to the church where the Reverend Brontë preached and to the parsonage where the family lived. June and Ken Cousins welcome Brontë buffs in their warm, cheerful, and comfortable inn. They charge them from £23 ($40.25) to £26 ($45.50) in a double, from £14 ($24.50) to £16 ($28) in a single. For an additional £2 ($3.50) per person, you'll be given a room with a bath or shower. Dinners, except Sunday, are à la carte, and good local meats and fresh vegetables are used at a cost of £4 ($7), usually featuring a roast. Bar snacks include the usual favorites—ploughman's lunch, hot pies, and sandwiches at 90p ($1.58) a portion.

The **Black Bull,** Main Street (tel. Haworth 42249), owned by Ron and Kath Bennett, stands close to the parish church where Patrick Brontë was incumbent for 41 years and is closely associated with the son, Branwell Brontë. Although renovated and improved since Branwell's day, it is still interesting to spend time within the walls that drew him so strongly and even to sit in the chair which he occupied on his many visits to the place, still on the premises. Today the Black Bull is as comfortable an inn as you will find.

Conversion of the restaurant, which seats 40, has made use of a thick stone wall in forming a central arch. This is the room where Branwell's chair sits and here is the original bell pull and bell which he used to ring for his many drinks. Luncheon and bar snacks are served from noon until 2:30 p.m. A three-course lunch with roast beef and Yorkshire pudding costs around £5 ($8.75). Snacks and assorted sandwiches are served in the lounge area. Chicken, scampi, and haddock with chips and peas or homemade steak pie are offered for around £2 ($3.50). Dinner is served from 7 until 10:30 p.m. The cuisine is excellent, and the à la carte menu, with a good supporting wine list, gives an ample choice. Morning coffee and high tea are served on Sunday. The Bennetts charge £20 ($35) for a double room, £12 ($21) in a single, including a good breakfast.

The **Brontë Bookshop,** 1 Church St. (tel. Haworth 42243), was the post office in the Brontës' time. Today, Mrs. Tricia Richmond runs a spotlessly clean B&B accommodation at the address, charging £8.50 ($14.88) per person, including a large Yorkshire breakfast. She and her husband spent many years in Africa before returning to Haworth. Mrs. Richmond admits to being from Lancashire, but "as my father was from Yorkshire, they let me in." She has accommodations for families, couples, or singles, with the best location in town for sightseeing. Next door stands the Chocolate Box, which some have called "the sweetest candy store in England."

Mrs. D. Alderman, 30 West Lane (tel. Haworth 44540), accepts B&B guests are her homey Heathcliffe Cottage, right in the center of Haworth, lying only a minute from the Parsonage and Black Bull. In this 400-year-old cottage, overnight guests are welcomed at a cost of £5.50 ($9.63) per person nightly, including a full English breakfast. Appointments are comfortable, and the hospitality of Mrs. Alderman is winning.

On the Outskirts

On the Haworth Moor stands a Brontë landmark, **Ponden Hall,** Stanbury, near Keighley (tel. Haworth 44154), a distance of some three miles from Haworth. It lies half a mile from the main road on a wide rough track which is the Pennine Way. An Elizabethan farmhouse built in 1560 and extended in 1801, this reputedly is the model for Thrushcross Grange, Catherine's home after her marriage to Edgar Linton.

Today the hall provides a farmhouse accommodation, a hand-loom weaving studio, a residential weaving course, a bunkhouse accommodation, as well as camping.

The hall is restricted to accommodating only six guests, and supplies evening meals for residents only. For B&B the charge is only £9 ($15.75) per person nightly, with subsequent reductions for longer stays. The food is good, and log fires burn brightly. Guests often gather around the piano for spontaneous entertainment.

To fulfill the needs of Pennine Way walkers, Roderick Taylor has converted a traditional, two-story farm cottage in the yard above the hall to provide simple self-catering accommodations for nine persons. You need your own sleeping bag. Booking isn't really necessary, and the charge is only £3 ($5.25) per person nightly. However, between Easter and October there's a maximum stay of two nights. An evening meal goes for £4 ($7).

HARWOOD HOUSE AND BIRD GARDEN: In West Yorkshire, at Junction A61/659, midway between Leeds and Harrogate, and five miles from the A1 at Wetherby, stands the home of the Earl and Countess of Harewood. One of the "Magnificent Seven" homes of England, this 18th-century house was designed by John Carr and has always been owned by the Lascelles family. The fine Adam interior has superb ceilings and plasterwork, and furniture made especially for Harewood by Chippendale. There are also important collections of English and Italian paintings and Sèvres and Chinese porcelain.

The Capability Brown landscape includes a 4½-acre bird garden which borders the lake. It contains exotic species from all over the world, including penguins, macaws, flamingoes, and snowy owls, and there is an undercover extension. The spacious grounds offer terraces, lakeside and woodland walks, exhibitions, shops, and a restaurant and cafeteria. Car parking is free, and there is a picnic area, plus an adventure playground for the children.

Harewood is open daily from April 1 to October 31 at 10 a.m. The house, bird garden, and adventure playground are also open on Sunday, Tuesday, Wednesday, and Thursday in November, February, and March. The bird garden and adventure playground are open daily from December 26 for nine days. Admission, reduced for children under 16, and closing times vary at different times of year but may be ascertained by calling Visitor Information (tel. Harewood 886225).

Incidentally, Harewood is on a regular bus route (Leeds/Harrogate/Ripon), but the stop is about a mile from the house. Summer excursions run on varying days from those cities served by the regular buses from York and Bradford among other places. Ask at local tourist information centers and at your hotel for details.

LEEDS: In the 18th and 19th centuries, Leeds grew into a great industrial center. Today it is a business and cultural center—once described "as a fascinating amalgam of the totally unexpected and the completely predictable."

Leeds is the center of England, lying about 200 miles from London and Edinburgh, respectively. It is directly on the M1 leading north-south and the M62 going east-west.

The public libraries are extensive, the atmosphere Victorian, and the museums crammed with history from Roman times to the Industrial Revolution which gave Leeds fame and prestige.

The city lies at the crossroads of the Yorkshire Dales—Ilkley Moor is "just along the road"—and there are main roads and rail links to vast stretches of the Yorkshire coastline. Its university is widely known throughout Britain.

In summer such places as York and Harrogate become full of visitors and accommodation can be difficult. However, Leeds is but a short distance away and has many hotels giving a wide range of services.

Among them, I'd recommend **Ann-Marie House,** 47 Cliff Rd., near Hyde Park Corner, Headingley (tel. Leeds 758856). Mr. and Mrs. K. W. T. Smith operate this family-run place, which lies in a cul-de-sac with a parkland at the rear. The hotel is within ten minutes of the University of Leeds and barely one mile from the city center. York, Harrogate, The Dales, and the motorways are easily reached without having to go through the center of Leeds.

The building was constructed of York stone in the early 19th century at the height of the Industrial Revolution. A single room with a continental breakfast rents for £8 ($14), a twin, double, or triple room costing from £7.50 ($13.13) per person, also with continental breakfast. For another £1 ($1.75) you can enjoy a full English breakfast. You can also order an evening grill for

£4 ($7). Children are welcome and given a reduced price.

The hotel has a residential license as well. Each unit has hot and cold running water, and there are ample shower facilities. Every guest is given a front-door key. In a secluded back garden, guests can sit and order refreshments, depending on the weather. Sometimes on weekend evenings, barbecue parties are planned here, along with a background of music and lanterns.

4. Durham

This densely populated county of northeast England is too often pictured as a dismal, foreboding place, with coalfields, ironworks, mining towns, and shipyards. Yet it contains valleys of quiet charm and a region of wild moors in the west. Therefore, if you have the time, it would be interesting to explore the Durham Dales, especially Teesdale with its waterfalls and rare wild flowers and Weardale with its brown sandstone villages.

DURHAM: The county town is built around a sandstone peninsula. It possesses a Norman **cathedral** which ranks as one of the most important in England. Adjoining the cathedral is **Durham Castle** (tel. Durham 65481), a Norman structure of the prince bishops which has been used by Durham University since 1832. Except on the occasion of university or other functions, the castle is open to visitors all year. From July to September, hours are from 10 a.m. to noon and from 2 to 4:30 p.m. weekdays only. During the rest of the year it is open from 2 to 4 p.m. on Monday, Wednesday, and Saturday. Admission is 75p ($1.31) for adults, 35p (61¢) for children.

Food and Lodging

Drumforke, 25 Crossgate Path (tel. Durham 42966), is a modest guest house owned and run by Mrs. D. B. Greenwell, who for years has catered to small families. She asks £7.50 ($13.13) per person for a room, the rate including a hefty breakfast. She reduces the tariff for children sharing one of the good-size rooms with their parents.

Market Tavern, Market Place (tel. Durham 62069), right in the center of town, remembers associations of more than a century ago with one of England's first trade unions, reputedly organized on the premises. Lunchtime finds this pub busy and bustling with people who work in the area. They enjoy hot dishes, including roast beef and lamb chops, beginning at £1.75 ($3.06).

READERS' RESTAURANT SELECTION: "An unexpected find in Durham Cathedral was the **Undercroft Restaurant,** The College (tel. Durham 63721). Under the ancient roof and arches, you eat snacks, pastries, and sip a glass of wine" (Peter, Susan and Eric Wildman, Lexington, Mass.).

BARNARD CASTLE: Near the River Tees, in the town of Barnard Castle, stands the **Bowes Museum** (tel. Teesdale 37139), at the eastern end of town. It was built in 1869 by John Bowes and his wife, the Countess of Montalbo, to house and display their art collection. Here you'll find masterpieces by Goya and El Greco, plus many fine tapestries and porcelains. There are also collections of French and English furniture, superb costumes, musical instruments, a children's gallery, and many other things of interest. A tea room and ample parking are found on the premises. It is open all year except some days around Christmas, weekdays from 10 a.m. to 5:30 p.m., on Sunday from 2 to 5 p.m., charging 80p ($1.40) for adults, 20p (35¢) for children. It closes at 4 p.m. from November to February.

Food and Lodging

The **Montalbo Hotel,** Montalbo Road (tel. Teesdale 37342), is a stone roadside inn, away from the noise of the town. Mr. and Mrs. Dominick rent out ten nicely furnished bedrooms at a rate of £10 ($17.50) per person nightly for B&B, including VAT. Two bathrooms are available. In addition, they run the Four Lanterns Bar. Bar meals are provided, but there is also a dining room open to nonresidents. From the à la carte menu, a typical dinner would cost about £8 ($14) per person.

The **Market Place Tea Shop,** 29 Market Pl. (tel. Teesdale 37049), is a charming place for good-tasting meals, with a rustic interior and rugged stone walls, along with dark Windsor chairs. It's easy to find, right in the center of the marketplace, with a blue facade and red café curtains. It is also a handicraft center, displaying various articles made locally. Ample parking is available in front of the tea shop.

For appetizers, try either the homemade chicken and cheese terrine, served with granary bread, or the prawn and smoked salmon terrine. The owner has widened the range of homemade main dishes to include such offerings as breast of chicken stuffed with homemade mushroom pâté, a traditional Lancashire hot-pot served with red cabbage, and pot roast brisket with Yorkshire pudding. Tempting desserts include syrup and orange sponge served with either cream or custard as are the assorted fruit pies. Expect to spend from £4 ($7), plus the price of your drink.

The place has a full table license between 11:30 a.m. and 3 p.m., and carries a fine selection of wines which are only available to those ordering meals. The owner, James Moffat, is constantly improving the standards around here, and for this I commend him.

BEAMISH: At Stanley, just a few miles south of Newcastle upon Tyne, is Beamish, the **North of England Open Air Museum** (tel. Stanley 31811), which shows the past way of life of the people of northeastern England in a living way. Buildings from the region have been rebuilt at Beamish to form a complete railway area with station and steam locomotive, a complete colliery with a "drift" mine and furnished pit cottages, and a farm with animals and exhibitions. There's a full-scale working replica of George Stephenson's *Locomotion No. 1* and tram rides, as well as a Victorian pub and a tea room open in summer only. Beamish is open from April through September daily from 10 a.m. to 6 p.m. (last admission at 5 p.m.). From October through March, hours are daily except Monday from 10 a.m. to 5 p.m. (last admission at 4 p.m.). It's best to allow four hours for your visit.

5. Tyne and Wear

In the county of Tyne and Wear, industrial Newcastle upon Tyne is the dominant focus, yet outside the city there is much natural beauty. Cattle graze on many a grassed-over mining shaft. There is such scenic beauty as moors and hills of purple-blue. The rugged coastline is beautiful. Americans like to pass through because of their interest in the ancestral home of George Washington (see below), and Newcastle also merits a stopover, particularly from motorists heading to Scotland.

The National Trust administers two sights in the region surrounding Newcastle:

Gibside Chapel, built in the classical style of James Paine in 1760, is an outstanding example of Georgian church architecture. A stately oak-lined avenue leads to the door of the chapel, which is the mausoleum of the Bowes family. The interior is decorated in delicate plasterwork and is furnished with paneled pews of cherrywood and a rare mahogany three-tiered pulpit. Gibside is open to the public daily, except Tuesday, April through September from 2 to 6 p.m. During March and October, it is open Wednesday, Saturday, and Sunday only. It is closed from November 1 until April 1. There is no charge for admission, but you'll pay 50p (88¢) to leave your car at the car park. For more information, telephone Rowlands Gill 2255. The location is 6 miles southwest of Gateshead and 20 miles northwest of Durham between Rowlands Gill and Burnopfield.

Washington Old Hall is the ancestral home of the first president of the United States, and the place from which the family took its name. Former President Carter visited the manor house in 1977. The interior of the house, whose origins date back to 1183, is furnished with period antiques and a collection of Delft ware. Relics of the Washingtons are also on display. The hall is open from March to October daily except Tuesday from noon to 5 p.m., and November to February it is open only on Saturday and Sunday from 2 to 4 p.m., charging an admission of 70p ($1.23) for adults, 35p (61¢) for children. For information, telephone Washington 466879. The location is in Washington on the east side of the A182, five miles west of Sunderland (two miles from the A1). South of Tyne Tunnel, follow signs for Washington New Town District 4 and then Washington Village.

NEWCASTLE UPON TYNE: An industrial city, Newcastle is graced with some fine streets and parks, as well as many old buildings. After crossing its best-known landmark, the Tyne Bridge, you enter a steep city which sweeps down to the Tyne, usually on narrow lanes called "chares." Once wealthy merchants built their town houses right on the quayside, and some of them remain.

For years Newcastle has been known as a shipbuilding and coal-exporting center, and gave rise to the expression of suggesting the absurdity of shipping coals to Newcastle.

Dominating the skyline, the **Cathedral of Newcastle** rises to a beautiful Scottish crown spire. It is England's most northerly cathedral, lying on a downward sweep between the Central Station and the quay. Its provost says that "the cathedral is one of the gems among the glorious churches of Northumberland." The cathedral's date of construction is unknown, but its recorded history predates 1122. The church was rebuilt in the 14th century, and John Knox preached from its pulpit.

The keep of the so-called New Castle, built by Henry II in 1170, contains the **Keep Museum,** on St. Nicholas Street, with an interpretation of the history of the castle site. It's open April to September, on Monday from 2 to 5 p.m.; Tuesday to Saturday, 10 a.m. to 5 p.m. From October to March, its Monday hours are from 2 to 4 p.m.; Tuesday to Saturday, 10 a.m. to 4 p.m.

Where to Stay

Chirton House Hotel, 46 Clifton Rd. (tel. Newcastle 730407), is a substantial hotel, owned and managed by Mr. and Mrs. Hunton who have set reasonable rates. They charge £11 ($19.25) per person for B&B. Four rooms contain private showers and toilets, and these cost an extra £3 ($5.25) per room. The rooms are well maintained and comfortable. If requested in advance, an evening meal can be prepared at an additional cost of £7 ($12.25). All tariffs are subject to VAT. Chirton House is nicely located on a quiet street, yet close to the city. In all, a dozen rooms are rented, each with hot and cold running water. In the lounge is a color TV, and there's a tiny bar for residents.

Dene Hotel, 40–42 Grosvenor Rd. Jesmond, near Newcastle upon Tyne (tel. Newcastle 811502), is a family-run hotel, off the Osborne road, managed by Mrs. H. M. Lawson. She welcomes children, as she has two of her own. The fully licensed hotel charges £9 ($15.75) daily in a single and from £16 ($28) in a double, including a full breakfast. The hotel is centrally heated, and each pleasantly furnished bedroom contains hot and cold running water. There's even music and an intercom throughout, plus cozy lounges with TV. Dinner is an extra £4.50 ($7.88). You can walk or take a bus to the city center.

Food and Drink

Dennhofer's Blackgate Restaurant, The Side, off Dean Street (tel. Newcastle 617356), seems like a little corner of the Black Forest, with its menu of German and Swiss cuisine. The menu is conveniently translated into English. In addition, a number of daily specialties and vegetarian dishes are posted on the blackboard. An inexpensive array of luncheon items is offered, including a salad made of diced chicken marinated in a brandy and orange sauce, costing from £3.20 ($5.60). Sandwiches such as rare roast beef with horseradish cream or rollmop herring with onions and gherkins go for around £1.25 ($2.19). Dinner is more elaborate, and more expensive. Perhaps you'll select the pheasant pâté with apple salad and cumberland sauce, followed by fresh grilled salmon with mussels and artichoke hearts in garlic butter, topped by a rich dessert, all for £7.65 ($13.25). The chef will gladly simplify any recipe for clients who prefer food less richly seasoned and sauced. Reservations are necessary for dinner and for lunch on crowded Thursday and Friday. Lunch hours are Monday through Friday from noon to 2:30 p.m., and dinner is served only Thursday through Saturday from 7 to 10:30 p.m.

Ristorante Roma, 22 Collingwood St. (tel. Newscastle 320612), helps you remember that holiday in Italy or your favorite little restaurant in Roma. Food is authentically Italian, prepared with care and thoughtfulness by Chef Pasquale, while the resident guitarist, Eusebio, plays enough live music to make you think you're being serenaded in Naples. A three-course meal, beginning with spaghetti al tonno (with tomatoes and tuna) and followed by saltimbocca alla romana, topped by zabaglione, would come to £7.85 ($13.74). A less expensive meal, and almost as good, could be ordered by choosing a pasta as a main course. In that event, the portion will be doubled. Try spaghetti alla pescatora (in a seafood and tomato sauce). There is dancing in the bar downstairs, and hours are daily except Sunday from noon to 3 p.m. and from 7 to 11:30 p.m.

The Falcon, Prudhoe (tel. Prudhoe 32324), is ideal when you want to drink and dine outside of town, in a contemporary pub with windows opening onto views of the country. At lunch a real bargain is offered for just £2.50 ($4.38), including, for example, soup, chicken-and-mushroom pie, with fried potatoes, vegetables, and finally, ice cream. On the à la carte lunch menu you can have a choice of salads at £1.30 ($2.28) or sandwiches for around 50p (88¢) apiece. Dinner is à la carte, and you might begin, for example, with a prawn cocktail, follow with grilled sirloin steak, and top it off with a peach Melba for

£5.45 ($9.55). Hours are noon to 2 p.m. and 6:30 to 10 p.m. Monday to Saturday, from noon to 1:30 p.m. and 7 to 10 p.m. on Sunday.

6. Northumberland

Most motorists zip through this far-northern county on their way to Scotland. Because it lies so close to Scotland, Northumberland was the scene of many a skirmish. The county now displays a number of fortified castles which saw action in those battles. Inland are the valleys of the Cheviot Hills, lying mostly within the Northumberland National Park and the remainder of the Border Forest Park, Europe's largest man-made forest.

Northumberland's coast is one of Britain's best-kept secrets. Here are islands, castles, tiny fishing villages, miles of sands, along with golf and fishing among the dunes, birdwatching in the Farne Islands—in all, an area of outstanding natural beauty.

Wallington, at Cambo, 12 miles west of Morpeth (take the A696 north from Newcastle), dates from 1688, but the present building reflects the great changes brought about in the 1740s when Daniel Garrett completely refashioned the exterior of the house. The interior is decorated with rococo plasterwork and furnished with fine porcelains, furniture, and paintings. Visitors may also visit the museum and enjoy an extensive display of dollhouses. The West Coach House contains an exhibit of ornate carriages. The main building is surrounded by 100 acres of woodlands and lakes, including a beautifully terraced garden and a conservatory. The grounds are open all year, the house from April 1 to the end of September, daily except Tuesday, from 1 to 6 p.m. Admission to the grounds is 80p ($1.40). Separate admission to the house is £1.20 ($2.10). For more information, telephone Scots Gap 283.

The **Farne Islands** are a group of small islands off the Northumbria coast, which provide a summer house for at least 20 species of sea birds as well as for one of the largest British colonies of gray seals. St. Cuthbert died here in 687, and a chapel built in the 14th century is thought to be on the site of his original cell. Only Inner Farne and Staple Island are open to the public. Visiting season extends from April through September, but access is more controlled during the breeding season, from mid-May to the end of July. Admission is £1 ($1.75), going up to £1.60 ($2.80) during the breeding season.

The best way to get to this most famous bird and animal sanctuary in the British Isles is to telephone or write Billy Shiel, the Farne Islands boatman, at 4 Southfield Ave., Seahouses, Northumberland (tel. Seahouses 720308). He has been taking people in his licensed boat for the past 40 years, so he knows the tides and the best places to film seals, puffins, and guillemots. He runs 2½-hour trips in his 40-passenger craft at a cost of £3 ($5.25) per person.

Incidentally, these are the islands where Grace Darling and her father made their famous rescue of men from a foundered ship.

HOLY ISLAND: The site of the Lindisfarne religious community during the Dark Ages, Holy Island is only accessible for ten hours of the day, high tides covering the causeway at other times. For crossing times, check with the local information centers.

Lindisfarne Castle was built on the island about 1550. It is open to the public every day, April 1 to September 30, from 11 a.m. to 5 p.m. (closed on Friday). It is open only weekends in October (Saturday and Sunday) from 11 a.m. to 5 p.m. Adults are charged £1.30 ($2.28), and children are admitted for 65p ($1.14). For more information, telephone Berioick 89244.

At Lindisfarne on Holy Island, you can stay at the **Lindisfarne Private Hotel** (tel. Holy Island 89273). This is a fine, substantial frame building with a trio of tall chimneys. It's run by members of the Massey family, who conduct it more like a private home than a hotel. Centrally heated bedrooms contain hot and cold running water and are decorated with personality, providing homelike comfort. The charge is £16 ($28) to £18 ($31.50) per person daily for half board. Boating excursions can be arranged to the Farnes.

READERS' SIGHTSEEING TIPS: "**Bamburgh Castle** guards the British shore along the North Sea. Legend has it that Lancelot and Guinevere fled here. It's open from Easter to October daily including Sunday, from 1 p.m. Admission is £1 ($1.75) for adults, 55p (96¢) for children" (Paul W. Ware, New Providence, Pa.).

"**Seaton Delaval,** the enormous country house off Whitley Bay, Northumberland, represents the architecture of Sir John Vanbrugh at its most forbidding. It looks like the stage settings for 14 Roman tragedies piled one on top of another. Walk over and look through a window in the east wing. Knights and wenches are feasting at long tables and drinking mead. You will find the guests assembled in the Presence Chamber, waiting to be summoned to the banquet. Stewards show the guests to their places at great refectory tables, which are laid with pewter plates and goblets, fresh rough bread, and dishes of butter and salt. Small daggers are the only cutlery provided. The drink is mead, the potent honey wine invented by Norsemen. This costs extra. The first remove is Delaval broth, a steaming soup drunk from the bowl and helped down with torn chunks of brown bread. The second remove is a great dish of Northumbrian spare ribbes, succulent pieces of roast lamb. The third and most substantial remove is chikeyn in browet with salumgundy. This means half a chicken, basted in honey until it is so tender that daggers are hardly needed to help it fall apart. The fourth remove, for those with any room left, is rastons, or fruit tarts, fat and swimming in cream. By the time you have been feasting for three hours, your soul may cry out for some 20th-century coffee. The price of a medieval banquet is about £8.50 ($14.88). It's best to inquire locally, as banquets are not staged every day, or even every week" (Andrew L. Glaze, New York, N.Y.).[*Author's Note:* The house may be visited on just a sightseeing expedition from May to September on Wednesday, Sunday, and bank holiday Mondays from 2 to 6 p.m. Admission is 50p (88¢) for adults, 30p (53¢) for children. Telephone Seaton Delaval 371759 for bookings.]

HADRIAN'S WALL: This wall, which extends across the north of England for 73 miles, from the North Sea to the Irish Sea, is particularly interesting for a stretch of 3½ miles west of Housesteads. Only the lower courses of the wall are preserved intact; the rest were reconstructed in the 19th century with the original stones. From several vantage points along the wall, you have incomparable views north to the Cheviot Hills along the Scottish border, and south to the Durham moors.

The wall was built following a visit of the Emperor Hadrian in A.D. 122. He wanted to see the far frontier of the Roman Empire, and he also sought to build a dramatic line between the so-called civilized world and the barbarians. Legionnaries were ordered to build a wall across the length of the island of Britain, stretching for 73½ miles, going over hills and plains, beginning at the North Sea and ending at the Irish Sea.

The wall is the premier Roman attraction in Europe, ranking with many people up with Rome's Colosseum. The western end can be reached from Carlisle, with a good museum of Roman artifacts, and the eastern end from Newcastle-upon-Tyne (some remains on the city outskirts and a good museum at the university). South Shields, Chesters, Corbridge, and Vindolanda are all good forts to visit in the area.

At Housesteads you can visit a **Roman fort** (tel. Bardon Mill 363), built about A.D. 130 to house an infantry of 1000 men. Called Vercovicium in Latin, the fort housed a full-scale military encampment, the remains of which can be seen today. The fort is open from March 15 to October 15 on weekdays from

9:30 a.m. to 6:30 p.m., on Sunday from 2 to 6:30 p.m. From October 16 to March 14, hours are from 9:30 a.m. to 4 p.m. on weekdays, from 2 to 4 p.m. on Sunday. Between April and September, the fort is also open on Sunday from 9:30 a.m. Price of admission in summer is 80p ($1.40) for adults, 40p (70¢) for children, and in winter it costs 40p (70¢) for adults and 20p (35¢) for children.

Just west of Housesteads is **Vindolanda,** another fort south of the wall at Chesterholm. The building is very well preserved, and there is also a recently excavated civilian settlement outside the fort with an interesting museum of artifacts of everyday Roman life. Admission is 80p ($1.40) for adults and 40p (70¢) for children.

HALTWHISTLE: About 20 miles east of Carlisle lies the town of Haltwhistle. There the **Grey Bull Hotel** (tel. Haltwhistle 20298) would be a good base of operations for seeing the best sections of Hadrian's Wall and its Roman garrisons. These include Housesteads, Vindolanda (the largest site in Europe), the Chesters, and Carvorum (Roman Military Museum)—all within 15 minutes' drive from the hotel. The Grey Bull has been modernized and reequipped. There are 11 bedrooms, each with its own wash basin with hot and cold running water and tea- and coffee-making facilities. The inclusive price is £8 ($14) per person for B&B. The bar at the hotel is a lively gathering place for the local people, and "pub grub" is available.

The **Milecastle Inn & Game Restaurant,** Route B6318 off Main, Newcastle to Carlisle A69 (tel. Haltwhistle 20682), is run by Jennie and Barrie W. Smith, and features such unusual specialties as hunters casserole, venison, jugged hare, grouse, quail, partridge, homemade venison sausages marinated in port, and Pickwick puddings (steak, mushroom, and oyster). The cooks also serve a few grills and fish. Meals start at £7 ($12.25). The food is prepared with pride and imagination, and the countryside is reminiscent of the days one hunted for his dinner, and with such fare to choose from you could almost believe the Smiths did just that!

White Craig, Shield Hill (tel. Haltwhistle 20565), is a farmhouse just a mile up the hill north of Haltwhistle, and about a mile from the major attraction, Hadrian's Wall. Mrs. J. W. Laidlow, a pleasant, accommodating person, rents room in a contemporary ranch-style house with a good hillside view. Two of her units have hot and cold running water with a twin and double bed. Her other twin contains a private shower. Charges are from £8 ($14) per person in one of the bathless rooms, rising to £9.50 ($16.63) per person with a private shower. She also rents a self-catering cottage sleeping four guests. It is well equipped, rented on weekly terms that range from £40 ($70) to £100 ($175), depending on the season.

READERS' GUEST HOUSE SELECTIONS: "In Haltwhistle we stayed with **Mr. and Mrs. Isaac Bell,** 3 East Lyndale (tel. Haltwhistle 20280), the most enjoyable B&B experience we had in all our travels. Their home is difficult to find, but Mr. Bell will meet you in the center of town. They invited us into their private quarters and shared evening tea with us, and we spent hours in conversation. Breakfast was cooked to order with a minimum of grease, and the cost is £6.50 ($11.38) per person per night, the lowest we found anywhere in Great Britain. The Bells have a double, a triple, and a single room available" (Mr. and Mrs. Lawrence W. Lipman, Union City, N.J.). . . . "**Ashcroft** (tel. Haltwhistle 20213) is run by Marlene and Brian Henderson, who have renovated an elegant old manor house to include 11 spacious and comfortable rooms for guests. B&B costs £7 ($12.25) per person, and we had an excellent evening meal for £3 ($5.25) each. The Hendersons will gladly give expert advice on touring" (Edmund and Carver Farrar, Mt. Pleasant, S.C.).

READER'S GUEST HOUSE SELECTION (SLAGGYFORD): "Lake House, The Island, Slaggyford, (tel. Alston 81422), is a charming 300-year-old shooting lodge in the Pennines, five miles north of Alston. It's managed by Mrs. C. Horseman, who charges £7.50 ($13.13) per person nightly which includes breakfast and evening tea. On extensive tree-covered grounds on an island by the River South Tyne complete with swimming hole and trout fishing, it is beautifully decorated and immaculately maintained. There is also space for caravan parking and an outline diesel-powered train for children or adults. The area is extremely beautiful and offers excellent hiking and fishing" (John L. Franklin, Grosse Pointe Park, Mich.).

ALLENDALE: In the southwestern sector of the shire, this unspoiled country village is the geographic center of Great Britain. It is well known for its ancient Fire Festival on New Year's Eve in the Market Place. From a base here, some of the finest scenery of Northumbria—heather-clad hills, moor, and woodland—unfolds.

For accommodations, the **Dale Hotel,** Allendale, near Hexham (tel. Allendale 212), is a village hotel built in 1870 and covered with green vines. Mr. and Mrs. W. A. Thompson have provided many facilities and considerations for their guests, including electric blankets and stoves in addition to oil-fired central heating throughout. The daily B&B rate is £7.50 ($13.13) per person, and half board is £10 ($17.50) per person daily. There are two large lounges and two dining rooms on the ground floor. In back is a large garden with a putting green and a summer house overlooking the Allen River. Guests are welcome to visit the grounds of the owners' private residence, a short distance from the village. Called Heathcote, the home is set in a three-acre garden with a lily pond.

HEXHAM: Above the Tyne River, this historic old market town is characterized by its narrow streets, old Market Square, a fine abbey church, and its Moot Hall. It makes a good base for exploring Hadrian's Wall and the Roman supply base of Corstopitum at Corbridge-on-Tyne, the ancient capital of Northumberland. The Tourist Office has masses of information on the wall for walkers, drivers, campers, and picnickers.

The Abbey Church of St. Wilfred is full of ancient relics. The Saxon font, the misericord carvings on the choir stalls, Acca's Cross, and St. Wilfred's chair are well worth seeing.

For a place to stay, try the **Beaumont Hotel,** Beaumont Street (tel. Hexham 602331), a family-run place across from the village park. It offers excellent facilities, including handsomely furnished and pleasantly decorated bedrooms, which are in the modern style, the effect livened by bright colors. Nearly all 22 bedrooms have private baths or shower units tucked in. The tariff for B&B is £16.50 ($28.88) daily in a single, rising to £26 ($45.50) in a double. Tariffs include VAT and service. Guests have a choice of two bars. Lunch is from £5.50 ($9.63), and dinner is à la carte.

Royal Hotel, Priestpopple (tel. Hexham 602270), stands just off the Market Place with its "Shambles" and Moot Hall. Two buildings are linked together by a central square tower and dome, and the car park is entered through the original coaching arch. Bar meals cost from £2 ($3.50), and dinner in the restaurant goes from £7 ($12.25). A salad buffet is presented each day in the lounge bar. Bedrooms are comfortable and well appointed, many with private bath and shower and tea- and coffee-making facilities. All have TV. Daily rates include a full English breakfast and VAT, and run from £14.50 ($25.38) in a single without bath to £29 ($50.75) in a double with bath.

The **Abbey Flags,** 19 Market Pl. (tel. Hexham 603252), is a little bistro-style restaurant overlooking the Market Square standing in the shadow of Hexham Abbey. Its owners, John Walton and Ron Hall, have a regular local following but also welcome overseas visitors. A five-course inclusive dinner is served for £10 ($17.50) featuring such dishes as Lebanese cucumber-and-yogurt soup, homemade pâté, and main dishes including Greek moussaka or traditional steak-and-kidney pie. Normal open hours are from 7 to 10 p.m. except when it closes on Sunday and Tuesday.

The **Hadrian Hotel,** Wall, near Hexham (tel. Humshaugh 232), is the ideal place to stay when visiting the Roman Wall. It's an ivy-covered inn built 350 years ago of stones taken from the wall. The lounge has a collection of antiques and curios, excellent for after-dinner coffee in front of a blazing fire. The dining room with three window walls has red tablecloths with white lace overcloths. You can look across the meadow toward the wall. The lounge has many curiosities, including a flower-filled cradle and collection of silver button hooks, old china, ancient clocks, copperware, ivory, and an Indian tray table for coffee. There are eight bedrooms, all with hot and cold running water, innerspring mattresses, and electric blankets. The daily tariff in a single is £12.75 ($22.31); in doubles, from £21 ($42). From June until September these rates increase to £13.50 ($23.63) and £22 ($38.50). Lunches are table d'hôte, costing £5 ($8.75), and dinners go for £7 ($12.25). Here you are within an hour's drive of Boston, New York, Philadelphia, and Washington (the original ones).

READER'S GUEST HOUSE SELECTION (BELLINGHAM): "One B&B facility that greatly impressed us was **Westfield House,** Bellingham, 17 miles north of Hexham (tel. Bellingham 20340), the home of Eric and Isabel Lewis. The residence is approached along a tree-lined roadway and is surrounded by spacious grounds with attractive flower gardens and terraced lawn. The rooms are much larger than most we found elsewhere, a true plus if you like to spread out your belongings and repack your suitcases occasionally. But the most significant feature of this particular stop was the warm, cordial manner of the Lewises. On entry, we were ushered into a sitting room with a welcome fire burning in the grate. When we retired we found that hot-water bottles had been placed in each bed. We were asked when we would like breakfast, rather than being told when it would be served. The Lewises simply reflect a pronounced friendly attitude that is most impressive. The charge is £8 ($14) per person nightly" (Payne Karr, Seattle, Wash.).

As a luncheon stopover, I'd suggest **The Country Kitchen,** 23 Market Pl. (tel. Hexham 603835), where you can order a good-tasting homemade soup, followed by, perhaps, sugar-baked ham with a salad or vegetables or smoked-haddock flan. Desserts include the likes of baked banana sponge pudding. Expect to pay from £3 ($5.25), plus the cost of your drink. The kitchen is open daily except Sunday and Monday from 10:30 to 11:30 a.m. for coffee, then from noon to 2:15 p.m. for lunch.

Next door is an intriguing shop, selling all sorts of local crafts, exotic food, and souvenirs.

CORBRIDGE-ON-TYNE: This is the ancient capital of Northumberland and a good base for exploring the eastern section of Hadrian's Wall. To the west of the historic village is Corstopitum, which was the Roman supply base for the wall.

For accommodations, try **The Hayes,** Newcastle Road (tel. Corbridge 2010), set in 7½ acres of flower gardens, neat lawns, and fenced-in pastureland, all owned by Mr. and Mrs. F. J. Matthews. You can stay here on B&B terms at £7.50 ($13.13) per person, or on half board for £9.50 ($16.63) per person.

Children are granted reductions according to age. On any arrangement, a cup of hot tea and cookies are provided at 10 p.m. In addition, families may want to inquire about two apartments for rent, a self-contained apartment sleeping four persons and a comfortable caravan housing five.

OTTERBURN: This mellowed old village on the Rede River was the scene of the famous Battle of Otterburn in 1388. It makes a good base for touring the Cheviot Hills.

Otterburn Tower Hotel (tel. Otterburn 20673) stands in a quiet, tree-edged hollow in the hills. It's reached by crossing over a tiny bridge, past the Otterburn Mill. Once Sir Walter Scott was a guest at the tower in 1812, and the hotel still retains many fine architectural details, including 16th-century paneling in the dining room as well as stained-glass family crests. Guests dine while seated on Windsor chairs, and in the dining lounge is an Italian marble fireplace. The bedrooms are large and traditionally furnished. A single rents for £15 ($26.25), rising to £24 ($42) in a double or twin. All tariffs include VAT and a full English breakfast. A dinner costs from £8 ($14), and substantial bar snacks are available from £1 ($1.75) to £3 ($5.25).

READER'S GUEST HOUSE SELECTION: "Anyone in the Newscastle upon Tyne area should drive to **Otterburn,** which is in the Northumberland National Park, and stay with **Mrs. Henderson** at 10 Otterburn Green, Byrnes Village (tel. Otterburn 20604). Mrs. Henderson is that rare, warm person you keep wanting to meet. Her B&B rooms are £7.50 ($13.13) per person, richly furnished and quiet. If given sufficient notice, she'll also prepare an evening meal for £5 ($8.75) per person, including tea and coffee" (John G. Sindorf, Palmer, Alaska).

ALNMOUTH: A seaside resort on the Aln estuary, Alnmouth attracts sporting people who fish for salmon and trout in the Coquet River or play on its good golf course.

The **Schooner Hotel,** Northumberland Street (tel. Alnmouth 830216), is a well-preserved Georgian inn, only a few minutes' walk to the water. The hotel is adjacent to the nine-hole Village Golf Course, the second-oldest in the country. A room with breakfast is £14 ($24.50) per person, including VAT. Guests count on the meals prepared and served at moderate prices. Set luncheons are £4 ($7); dinners, £7 ($12.25); or you can also stay here on the full-board rate of £20 ($35) per person daily, which includes either a packed picnic or bar luncheon. There are 24 bedrooms, a grill room, dining room, the Sea Hunter bar, the Chase Bar, and the Long Bar as well as a resident's lounge with color TV. Resident hostess is Christine Smith who keeps the Schooner in good and tidy form.

Alnwick Castle

In the town of Alnwick, 35 miles north of Newcastle, Alnwick Castle (tel. 0665/602722) is the seat of the Duke of Northumberland. This border fortress dates from the 11th century, when the earliest parts of the present castle were constructed by Yvo de Vescy, the first Norman Baron of Alnwick. A major restoration was undertaken by the fourth duke in the mid-19th century, and Alnwick remains relatively unchanged to this day. The rugged medieval outer walls do not prepare the first-time visitor for the richness of the interior, decorated mainly in the style of the Italian Renaissance.

Most of the castle is open to the public during visiting hours. You can tour the principal apartments, including the Armory, Guard Chamber, and Library, where you can view portraits and landscapes painted by such masters as Titian, Canaletto, and Van Dyck. You may also visit the dungeons and the Museum of Early British and Roman Relics. From the terraces within the castle's outer walls, you can look across the broad landscape stretching over the River Aln.

Alnwick is open to the public daily, except Saturday, from 1 to 5 p.m. from May to September. Admission is £1.20 ($2.10) for adults and 60p ($2.80) for children. For an additional 15p (26¢) you can also visit the Regimental Museum of the Royal Northumberland Fusiliers, within the castle grounds.

Cragside

Designed in the late 19th century by architect Richard Norman Shaw for the first Lord Armstrong, Cragside is a grand estate stretching across 900 acres on the southern edge of the Alnwick Moor. Here groves of magnificent trees and fields of rhododendrons frequently give way to peaceful ponds and lakes. Cragside is 13 miles southwest of Alnwick, the entrance being 3 miles northeast of Rothbury on the B6341 Alnwick–Rothbury road. The grounds are open April to September daily from 10:30 a.m. to 6 p.m. In October hours are daily from 10:30 a.m. to 5 p.m., and from November to March Cragside is open only Saturday and Sunday from 10:30 a.m. to 4 p.m. Admission is 60p ($1.05). The house is open April until the end of September daily except Monday from 2 to 5 p.m. To visit both the house and park costs £1.60 ($2.80). For more information, telephone Rothbury 20333.

Dunstanburgh Castle

On the coast nine miles northeast of Alnwick, this castle was begun in 1316 by Thomas, Earl of Lancaster, and enlarged in the 14th century by John of Gaunt. The dramatic ruins of the gatehouse, towers, and curtain wall stand on a promontory high above the sea. You can reach the castle on foot only, either walking from Craster in the south or across the Dunstanburgh Golf Course from Embleton and Dunstan Steads in the north. The castle is open daily from 9 a.m. to 6:30 p.m. except Sunday. Admission is 60p ($1.05).

Food and Lodging

The **Hotspur Hotel,** Bondgate Without (tel. Alnwick 602924), started in the 16th century as a coaching inn and was well known as the favorite local rendezvous for the musicians when "Billy Bones," a famed piper to the Duchess of Northumberland, was host. Now it has been extensively modernized, providing much comfort. Percy's restaurant, decorated in the William and Mary style of dark oak, has a fine cuisine. The Cocktail Bar, also in the William and Mary style, is intimate and excellent for a predinner drink. The Billy Bones Buttery also has its own character, decorated in elm with Jacobean screens. It is both informal and intimate. You can drink or dine here as well as enjoy the music of Northumbrian folksingers. There are 28 comfortable and stylish bedrooms fitted with oak furniture, radios, and telephone. Eighteen have private baths. Singles are £11 ($19.25) to £14 ($24.50) daily; doubles or twins are £21 ($36.75) to £24 ($42). Tariffs include an English breakfast, service, and VAT. The cuisine includes such dishes as kippers for breakfast, roast local beef, and poached Bulmer salmon. A luncheon goes for £5.50 ($9.63), a dinner for £6.50 ($11.38).

Part Two

SCOTLAND

Chapter XVI

SOUTHERN SCOTLAND

1. The Border Country
2. Ayr, Prestwick, and District
3. Dumfries and Galloway

IN SCOTLAND, a land of bagpipes and clans, you'll find some of the most dramatic scenery in Europe. Stretching before you will be the Lowlands, but in the far distance, the fabled Highlands loom.

If you traverse all the country, you'll discover lochs and glens, heather-covered moors, twirling kilts and tam o'shanters, pastel-bathed houses and gray-stone cottages, mountains, rivers, and sea monsters, as well as the sound of Gaelic, Shetland ponies, and misty blue hills, to name only some of its attractions.

Many visitors think of Scotland as Edinburgh and search no farther. Travel farther north and you'll find the real Scotland, along with overwhelming hospitality and a sense of exploration.

Scotland has its own legal system and issues its own currency, although English and Scottish banknotes have equal value and are readily accepted in both countries. The Church of Scotland is separate from that of England. The language of the Scot is said to be nearer to the original English than what is spoken these days, although even an English person will find it hard to understand the speech of a true and gentle Highlander.

You will hardly be aware of crossing out of England into Scotland, either by road or rail, for the two countries have been joined constitutionally since 1707. But it has not always been that way. Although the border is just a line on the map, Scotland is still very much its own country. In the sixth century a tribe of Gaels sailed across from Ireland, the Scoti by name. They settled and it is from this original tribe that the country gets its name of Scotland.

For many centuries, there were a number of tribes who effectively held Scotland in divisions until, in A.D. 563, an Irish missionary, St. Columba, landed on the island of Iona, a small rock of land to the west of Mull. He built an abbey and proceeded to preach Christianity to the heathen tribes.

Under various kings, Scotland gradually became more stable, and by the time that William the Conqueror headed north from England in the 11th century, all the land was ruled by one king, Malcolm III. From then on, battles great and small were waged between England and Scotland. When they weren't fighting the English, the Scots were fighting among themselves. The first Irish invaders had started new families who had split from the original homesteads and had resettled forming clans. "Clans" is a Gaelic word meaning "family" or "children of." This allowed them to trace their origins although they had moved far afield.

There was a strong hierarchy within each clan with a chief as its head, followed by lesser chieftains, gentlemen, and then plain clansmen. The various families warred among themselves for territory, rights, and honor. The fighting among the clans was abated in 1609 when, on the island of Iona, the statutes of Iona were signed by most of the clan chiefs. However, sporadic fighting continued for years. The last real clan battle took place in 1688 at Keppoch near Glen Roy between the Macdonalds and the Macintoshes.

Today the clans, the ancient families, and those who enjoy common ancestry are identified mainly by their tartans, the word first recorded in 1471 to describe the previously named "chequered garment" or "mantle." The kilt has a much older history as a style of dress. It was recorded in Bronze Age frescoes in Crete and worn by soldiers such as the Romans. Highland gatherings or games have their origins in the fairs organized by the tribes or clans for the exchange of goods. At these gatherings there were often trials of strength among the men, and the strongest were selected for the chief's army. The most famous gathering nowadays is that at Braemar, held in early September of each year and patronized by the royal family.

GARB O' THE GODS: Few people know that anywhere from seven to ten yards of wool tartan goes into the average kilt, and even fewer non-Scotsmen know what is actually worn beneath the voluminous folds strapped onto the muscular thighs of a parading Scotsman.

For a Highlander purist, the answer is nothing. That answer is true for any defender of the ancient tradition that only a Stewart can wear a Stewart tartan, that only a MacPherson can wear a MacPherson tartan, and that only a Scotsman looks good in a kilt. Of course any true Scotsman would wager his claymore (sword) that only a foreigner would stoop to wearing "unmentionables" (that's shorts to us) under his kilt.

Alas, commercialism has reared its ugly head with the introduction of undergarments to match the swirling folds of the bagpipe players. Nevertheless, salesmen in stores specializing in Highland garb still tell the story of a colonel, the 11th Earl of Airlie, who'd heard that the soldiers of his elite Highland Light Infantry were mollycoddling themselves with undershorts. The next day, his eyebrows bristling, he ordered the entire regiment to undress. To his horror, he found that half a dozen of his soldiers had disgraced the regiment by wearing "what only an Englishman would wear." He publicly ordered the offending garments removed. When he gave the orders to "drop your kilts" the next day, not a soldier in the regiment wore "trews" (shorts).

Naturally, years passed before a similar level of indiscretion manifested itself among the Highland infantry. Even with the general decline of standards today, the mark of a man in the Highlands is still whether he can stand drafts up against his legs and the feel of rough cloth against tender parts.

If you're not fortunate enough to be of Scottish extraction, or if you're distantly Scottish and can't trace which clan you specifically came from, there is still hope. Long ago Queen Victoria authorized two "Lowland" designs as suitable garb for Sassenachs (Saxons, Englishmen, and, more remotely, Americans). So if, during your jaunts in the Highlands, you decide to wear a kilt, and a true Scotsman sees you in a Sassenach tartan, he probably will assume that your unmentionables are appropriately covered with "unmentionables."

GETTING THERE: From Newcastle upon Tyne, the A68 heading northwest takes you to where Scotland meets England, an area long known as "Carter Bar." At this point, all of Scotland lies before you, and an unforgettable land it is.

I'd recommend to many visitors that they approach the Border Country after a stopover in the York area of England. That way, they can start exploring Scotland in the east with Edinburgh as their goal, then go up through Royal Deeside and on to Inverness, crossing over and down the west side of Glasgow, emerging at Gretna Green, near Carlisle in England's Lake District.

The Border Country is a fit introduction to Scotland, as it contains many reminders of the country's historic and literary past. A highlight of the tour is a visit to Abbotsford, the house Sir Walter Scott built on the banks of the salmon river, the Tweed.

However, if you're approaching Scotland from the west of England, you'll travel through Ayrshire—the Land of Burns. This is the former home of Scotland's most famous novelist and her national poet, Robert Burns.

Burns knew so well the southwestern corner of Scotland, which is bounded by an indented coastline of charm which attracts many artists who prefer the quiet, secluded life that prevails there. Distances aren't long, but many motorists have taken two or three days to cover some 100 miles.

The southwestern Lowlands are often called Galloway, their ancient title, and they contain some of the most impressive scenery in all the country.

At Ayr, Troon, and Prestwick (with its international airport), you'll find sandy beaches and golf courses; and you'll also find that the fishing is good in southern Scotland, as is pony-trekking.

1. The Border Country

Castles in romantic ruins and Gothic skeletons of abbeys stand as reminders, in this ballad-rich land of plunder and destruction, of interminable battles that raged between England and the proud Scots. For a long time, the so-called Border Country was a no-man's land. And this is also the land of Sir Walter Scott, that master of romantic adventure in a panoramic setting, who died in 1832. Today he is remembered for such works as *Rob Roy, Kenilworth, Ivanhoe,* and *The Bride of Lammermoor.*

Southeast Scotland contains the remains of four great abbeys built by David I in the mid-12th century: Dryburgh (where Scott was buried), Melrose, Jedburgh, and Kelso. "The Borders" are also the home of the famous "Common Ridings" gatherings celebrating major events in the past.

JEDBURGH: Jedburgh lies 325 miles from London, 48 from Edinburgh. This royal burgh and border town is famous for its ruined **Jedburgh Abbey,** founded by King David in 1147, and considered one of the finest abbeys in Scotland. Inside is a small museum, containing fragments of medieval works. Admission is 30p (53¢) for adults, 15p (26¢) for children. The abbey is open daily April through September from 9:30 a.m. to 7 p.m. (on Sunday from 2 to 7 p.m.); October through March from 9:30 a.m. to 4 p.m. (on Sunday from 2 to 4 p.m.); closed Thursday afternoon and Friday. The town lies on the River Jed.

On Queen Street, you can visit the **Mary Queen of Scots House,** where she stayed and almost died after a tiring ride visiting her beloved Bothwell at Hermitage Castle in 1566. The house, containing articles dealing with her life, paintings, and engravings, is open from March to October only, from 10 a.m. to 5:30 p.m. Admission is 30p (53¢) for adults, 20p (35¢) for children.

Food and Lodging

The accommodations offered by **Mrs. A. Richardson,** 124 Bongate (tel. Jedburgh 62480), are more like a private home than a guest house—in fact, it's an apartment in a block of buildings. The Richardsons have two bedrooms, one with double bed, the other with a double and single, which is classified as a family room. The per-person cost for an adult is £7.50 ($13.13) nightly. Mrs. Richardson gives you a hot beverage and cookies before you go to bed, and in the morning, a big breakfast. She'll also cook an evening meal, if asked beforehand, which she serves at 6:30 ("so I can go for a walk afterward").

The Carters' Restaurant (tel. Jedburgh 3414) is a pub with a downstairs dining room built of old abbey stones. The building has had a colorful history—a local grammar school from 1779, before finding its present role. This is the favorite gathering place of the people of Jedburgh who know that its owner, Michael Wares, serves good food and drink. Soups, bar snacks, and coffee are served daily in the lounge bar. The restaurant offers either British or continental dishes daily from £5 ($8.75). Lunches are served all week from noon to 2 p.m. Dinners are more elaborate, served Monday to Thursday from 6 to 9 p.m. (till 10 on Friday and Saturday). The place is also open Sunday from Easter till October. The fixed price menu of £6 ($10.50) allows for a choice of main course, coffee, and a glass of wine. There is also a full à la carte menu.

READERS' B&B SELECTION: "The beautiful Victorian home of **Mrs. Muriel McLay,** Normanie, The Friars (no phone), is matched by her thoughtfulness for the comfort of her guests. Tea and cakes on arrival and again before bedtime and freshly made scones to accompany an already huge breakfast are just an indication of her hospitality. All this for £6.50 ($11.38) per person in an attractive twin-bedded room cannot be topped" (Mr. and Mrs. Thaine W. Reynolds, Fairview Park, Ohio).

If you follow the A698 northeast of Jedburgh, the road will lead to:

KELSO: Another typical historic border town, Kelso lies at the point where the Teviot meets the Tweed. **Kelso Abbey,** now in ruins, was the earliest and probably the largest of the border abbeys. In the town's marketplace, the "Old Pretender," James Stewart, was proclaimed king, designated James VIII.

Kelso is also the home of the Duke of Roxburghe, who lives at **Floors Castle,** built in 1721 by William Adam. Part of the castle, which is open to the public, contains superb French and English furniture, porcelain, tapestries, and paintings by such artists as Gainsborough, Reynolds, and Canaletto. There are a licensed restaurant, coffeeshop, and gift shop as well as a magnificent walled garden and garden center. Floors is open daily except Friday and Saturday from the beginning of May to the end of September. The house is open at 11 a.m., the last guests shown through at 4:45 p.m. The grounds and gardens may be visited from 11 a.m. to 5:30 p.m.

Food and Lodging

Bellevue Guest House, Bowmont Street (tel. Kelso 24588), is an inexpensive stopover in the Border Country. Jean and Tom Hill, who own this simple guest house, ask £8 ($14) per person nightly for B&B. If you speak to Jean the morning before, she'll fix a tasty Scottish dinner for £4 ($7). Each of the rooms is nicely fixed up for guests and contains hot and cold water. Central heating has been installed, and the Hills have a residential liquor license.

The Quarterdeck, Bridge Street, stands near Queen's Head Hotel and Ednam Hotel. It has a simple but bright decor, and a menu which includes

This map is taken from *Historic Houses, Castles & Gardens* with permission of ABC Historic Publications, a Division of ABC Travel Guides Ltd., Oldhill London Road, Dunstable LU6 3EB

everything from a full lunch to a burger roll. Each day the cook prepares a different roast. The traditional Scottish dish, haggis, goes for only £1.70 ($2.98) here. Soups are rich tasting, and the restaurant offers freshly baked scones and homemade cakes with fresh cream. A meal of two courses, including the traditional roast, goes for £3.50 ($6.13).

From Kelso, it is only a short drive on the A699 to—

DRYBURGH: Scott is buried at Dryburgh Abbey. These Gothic ruins are surrounded by gnarled yew trees and cedars of Lebanon, said to have been planted there by knights returning from the Holy Land during the years of the Crusades. Near Dryburgh is "Scott's View," over the Tweed to his beloved Eildon Hills, considered one of the most beautiful views in the region.

The adjoining town is St. Boswells. This old village, 40 miles from Edinburgh, stands on the Selkirk–Kelso road, near Dryburgh Abbey. It lies 4 miles from Melrose and 14 miles from Kelso.

Four miles from Dryburgh Abbey is—

MELROSE: Lying 37 miles from Edinburgh, Melrose enjoys many associations with Scott. This border town, as mentioned, is also known for its ruined **Melrose Abbey,** in the Valley of the Tweed. You can visit the ruins of the abbey in which the heart of Robert Bruce is said to have been buried. Look for the beautiful carvings and the tombs of other famous Scotsmen buried in the chancel. In Scott's *The Lay of the Last Minstrel,* the abbey's east window received rhapsodic treatment, and in *The Abbot* and *The Monastery,* Melrose appears as "Kennaquhair."

The abbey is open April through September daily from 9:30 a.m. to 7 p.m. (on Sunday from 2 to 7 p.m.); October through March from 9:30 a.m. to 4 p.m. (on Sunday from 2 to 4 p.m.), charging an admission of 50p (88¢) for adults, 25p (44¢) for children.

Accommodations

The **King's Arms Hotel,** High Street (tel. Melrose 2143), is a rather simple Georgian stone building in the heart of the village, with a white portico, ideal for the Tweed River area. It has been a coaching inn for a long, long time, the oldest in Scotland possibly, but today cars, not carriages, are parked in its adjoining car park. Owners Mr. and Mrs. Martin provide comfortable and attractive bedrooms at fair prices. While you can enjoy bar snacks at noontime, an evening meal in the dining room costs from £8.50 ($14.88). The rate per person is £12 ($21) in a unit without bath, rising to £14 ($24.50) with bath. VAT is extra although there is no service charge.

Burts Hotel, Market Square (tel. Melrose 2285), standing on the market square, was built in 1722, and has been marked by the government as having historical and architectural interest. It's all white with a jet-black trim, plus an entry under an off-balance gable. The central lounge has retained its original open fireplace, and the dining room has its exposed beams. In the cocktail bar, with its old oak furniture and beams, you can have your predinner drink in front of a wood fire. A few of the bedrooms have a private bath, but all have hot and cold water. Depending on the plumbing, rates range from £12.50 ($21.88) to £14 ($24.50) per person for B&B. Reductions are granted for children, however. Lunch costs from £5 ($8.75), and dinner is from £8 ($14). VAT is included in the tariffs. Resident owners are Graham and Anne Henderson.

ABBOTSFORD: This was the home of Sir Walter Scott that he built and lived in from 1812 until he died. It contains many relics collected by the famous author, including one hall filled with spoils he collected from the battlefield at Waterloo. Other exhibits include clothes worn by Scott, as well as his death mask. Especially interesting is his study, with his writing desk and chair. In 1935 two secret drawers were found in the desk. One of them contained 57 letters, part of the correspondence between Sir Walter and his wife-to-be. The Scott home, still inhabited by his relatives, is open from March 23 to October 31, weekdays from 10 a.m. to 5 p.m. (Sunday, 2 to 5 p.m.), charging £1 ($1.75) for adults, 50p (88¢) for children.

After leaving Scott's house, you can continue along the Tweed to—

TRAQUAIR HOUSE: At Innerleithen, a few miles east of Peebles, Traquair is considered the oldest inhabited and most romantic house in Scotland. Dating back to the tenth century, it is rich in associations with Mary Queen of Scots and the Jacobite risings. Its treasures include glass, embroideries, silver, manuscripts, and paintings. Of particular interest is a brewhouse equipped as it was two centuries ago and still used regularly. The great house is lived in by the Stuarts of Traquair. There are craft workshops to be seen in the grounds with working artisans creating pottery, woodwork, candlemaking, painting, and silk-screen printing. The house and grounds are open from Easter Saturday until the fourth Sunday of October, daily from 1:30 to 5:30 p.m. During July and August, hours are from 10:30 a.m. to 5:30 p.m., with last admittance at 5 p.m. Rates are £1.40 ($2.45) for adults, 70p ($1.23) for children. To make inquiries, telephone Innerleithen 830323. Special events, such as an antique fair or a beer festival, are held in summer in the walled garden. There are also special exhibitions held in the Malt Loft Gallery.

Innerleithen is a modest little mill town, but the unmarred beauty of the River Tweed valley as seen from the town's surrounding hillsides remains constant. The Ballantyne cashmeres are manufactured here, and annual games and a Cleikum ceremony take place here in July. Scott's novel, *St. Ronan's Well,* is identified with the town.

Accommodations

The **Traquair Arms Hotel** (tel. Innerleithen 830229) is set in this small border town among beautiful scenery, close to the River Tweed where trout and salmon fishing can be arranged by the hotel's owners. What you don't expect in such a place is a warm and friendly Texas welcome. The hotel is owned and run by Capt. and Mrs. Alistair M. Macnab. Although he is a native of Innerleithen, having served for many years in the merchant marine and Royal Navy, she is Brooklyn-Irish. They purchased the hotel after having lived for several years in Houston, Texas.

There they developed a love for Texas cookery, and their restaurant, which serves from 11 a.m. until 9 p.m. daily, is known as the Texas Country Kitchen. Specialties include chicken fried steak, Mexican tacos, and jambalaya done in the Louisiana manner. A Sunday buffet costs from £4 ($7) per person, and their beefburgers begin at £2.50 ($4.38). Main-course specialties start at £2.75 ($4.81). Captain and Mrs. Macnab are among the most hospitable people you are likely to meet.

Bedrooms are comfortably furnished and range from simple singles through twin-bedded rooms to a double with bathroom en suite. Rates for a bed and a full Scottish breakfast are £15 ($26.25) per person, including tax and service charge, in a double with private bath and TV; and £12.50 ($21.88) per person, including tax and service, in a single or twin room without bath.

Caddon View, 14 Pirn Rd. (tel. Innerleithen 830208), is a spacious Victorian house of character and comfort in this friendly little town which nestles in the Tweed Valley surrounded by border hills. You are assured of a warm welcome by Mrs. Isobel Henderson, who offers her home as a high-standard B&B establishment from April to mid-November. A double or twin room with breakfast costs from £11 ($19.25) to £14 ($24.50), depending on the breakfast chosen. Singles range from £6 ($10.50) to £7.50 ($13.13). Mrs. Henderson offers a large and varied choice of breakfast fare, including a special "Taste of Scotland" menu where you can try national and regional dishes. A great favorite is the guest kitchen where you can make a bedtime drink and get together with fellow guests in the comfortable Victorian sitting room surrounded by pictures and photographs of Lang Syne.

Mrs. C. P. Alder, 8 Leithen Road (tel. Innerleithen 830360), uses a part of her home to accommodate guests, a most economical place to stay. She charges just £5.50 ($9.63) nightly, per person, and what's more you can have an evening meal for only £4 ($7). Knowing that her home is not geared for the usual demanding guest, Mrs. Alder is most considerate, and will help plan your day trips.

Tighnuilt House Hotel (tel. Innerleithen 830491) is a large country-house hotel overlooking the Tweed. Opening onto beautiful scenery with some spectacular views, the hotel is known for its cookery, ranging from simple home style to Cordon Bleu. A four-course dinner costs from £4.50 ($7.88), and a bed and a full English breakfast go for £8.50 ($14.88) per person daily. Rooms are immaculate, huge, and graciously decorated, with flannel sheets and down comforters. The sitting room provided for the guests is particularly impressive. There are three large family rooms. The hotel is surrounded by well-laid-out gardens, rockeries, and woodland, with a large variety of trees, shrubs, and hedges. Trout and salmon fishing are available to hotel guests only. Your hosts are G. D. and I. M. Buchan.

PEEBLES: This royal burgh and county town, 23 miles from Edinburgh, is a market center in the Valley of the Tweed. Scottish kings used to come here when they went to hunt in Ettrick Forest. The town is noted for its large woolen mills. Peebles is also known as a "writer's town." John Buchan Tweedsmuir, the Scottish author and statesman who died in 1940 and is remembered chiefly for writing the Stevensonian adventure story *Prester John* in 1910, lived here. He was also the author of *The Thirty-Nine Steps* (1915), the first of a highly successful series of secret-service thrillers. In 1935 he was appointed governor-general of Canada. Robert Louis Stevenson once lived at Peebles, and drew upon the surrounding countryside in *Kidnapped,* which was published first in 1886.

On the north bank of the Tweed stands **Neidpath Castle,** its peel (tower) dating from the 13th century. Cromwell besieged and took it in 1650.

Nine miles east of Peebles, you can visit the **Scottish Textile Museum** at Walkerburn. Here you can see how tartans and fine woolens are dyed and spun. You can also purchase lengths of cloth and garments to take home.

Accommodations

The **Cross Keys Hotel,** Northgate (tel. Peebles 20748), lays claim to being one of the oldest inns in Scotland, having been built in 1693. Originally it was erected as a town house for William Williamson of Cardrona (his initials can be seen in the roof tiles), and after its conversion it became an important link in the Edinburgh–London stagecoach route. It'll be known to lovers of the novels of Sir Walter Scott, who stayed here and wrote about it in his books. Much of the original character remains in the interior. There are two excellent bars, with trestle tables, Windsor chairs, and open fireplaces. The dining room has a rounded bay opening onto the garden. There are nine comfortable bedrooms with hot and cold water. B&B costs £17 ($29.75) in a double room, £10.50 ($18.38) in a single, including service and VAT. Mrs. Meg Bone, the owner, cooks most of the food, even doing the baking. A dinner costs from £6 ($10.50), and bar lunches and snacks are available.

The **Green Tree Hotel,** East End (tel. Peebles 20582), is an old-style country-town inn. It has enough room to provide a good stopover accommodation, adjacent to the public car park and the bus station. Its rear windows open onto a garden, with lawns, gravel paths, and flowering shrubbery. Bedrooms have hot and cold water, and are neat and pleasantly equipped. For cooler months there are electric blankets, although the hotel has central heating. There are two ways of staying here, aside from the usual B&B, which costs £10 ($17.50) per person nightly. It is suggested to have high tea as well as breakfast, and this goes for £12.50 ($21.88). If you want a full evening meal, then the rate would be £15 ($26.25) per person nightly. VAT and service are included in these rates.

READERS' GUEST HOUSE SELECTION: "Hope Park Lodge, Chambers Terrace (tel. Peebles 21264), is a lovely house. On a rainy afternoon, we were served tea in front of a warm, glowing fire by the owner, Mrs. J. Haydock. The cost is £6.50 ($11.38) per person for B&B. In Peebles, turn left at the church on High Street, then take the first right as you pass over the bridge onto Caledonian Road, then the first left up a hill called Frankscroft. The house is on the corner of Chambers Terrace" (Charles and Glenys Cromar, Royal Oak, Mich.).

MELLERSTAIN: The seat of Lord Binning, Mellerstain lies in "the Borders," although it is most often visited on a day trip from Edinburgh, 37 miles away. One of Scotland's famous Adam mansions, it lies near Gordon, nine miles northeast of Melrose and seven miles northwest of Kelso. It's open from May to September daily, except Saturday, from 12:30 to 5 p.m. and charges £1.50 ($2.63) for admission.

Mellerstain enjoys associations with Lady Grisel Baillie, the Scottish heroine, and Lord Binning is her descendant. William Adam built two wings of the house in 1725. The main building was designed by his more famous son, Robert, some 40 years later.

You're shown through the interior, with its decorations and ceilings designed by Robert Adam, and are allowed to view the impressive library as well as paintings by old masters and antique furniture. Later, from the garden terrace you can look south to the lake, with the Cheviot Hills in the distance, a panoramic view. Afternoon tea is served, and tweeds and souvenir gifts are on sale.

2. Ayr, Prestwick, and District

As Sir Walter Scott dominates the Borders, so does Robert Burns the country around Ayr and Prestwick. There are, in addition, a string of famous seaside resorts stretching from Girvan to Largs. Some of the greatest golf courses in Britain, including Turnberry, are found here, and Prestwick, of course, is one of the major airports of Europe.

AYR: Ayr is the most popular resort on Scotland's west coast. A busy market town, it offers 2½ miles of sands and makes for a good center for touring the Burns Country. This royal burgh is also noted for its manufacture of fabrics and carpets, so you may want to allow time to browse through its shops. With its steamer cruises, fishing, golf, and racing, it faces the Isle of Arran and the Firth of Clyde.

Ayr is full of Burns associations. The 13th-century **Auld Brig o' Ayr,** the poet's "poor narrow footpath of a street, / Where two wheelbarrows tremble when they meet," was renovated in 1910. A Burns museum is housed in the thatched **Tam o' Shanter Inn** in Ayr High Street, an alehouse in Rabbie's day.

The **Auld Kirk** of Ayr dates from 1654 when it replaced the 12th-century Church of St. John. Burns was baptized in the kirk.

Ayr is also the birthplace of the road builder John L. MacAdam, whose name was immortalized in road surfacing.

In Tarbolton village, 7½ miles northeast of Ayr, is the **Bachelors' Club,** a 17th-century house where in 1780 Burns and his friends founded a literary and debating society, now a property of the National Trust of Scotland. In 1779 Burns attended dancing lessons there, against the wishes of his father. There also, in 1781, he was initiated as a Freemason in the Lodge St. David. Eleven months later he became a member of Lodge St. James, which continues today in the village. Samuel Hay, 7 Croft St. (tel. Tarbolton 424), says the Bachelors' Club is open for visitors any time of day from April until the end of October, and he will arrange to show it at other times if you telephone. Admission is 50p (88¢) for adults, 25p (44¢) for children. Tarbolton is six miles from Prestwick Airport.

For centuries, Ayr has been associated with horse racing, and it now has the top racecourse in Scotland. One of the main streets of the town is named Racecourse Road for a stretch near the town center.

For more information on this popular area, write to the Tourist Officer, 30 Miller Rd., Ayr, Ayrshire, Scotland.

Where to Stay

The **Meteor Hotel,** 5 Racecourse Rd. (tel. Ayr 263891), is a sandstone structure with two Doric columns at the entrance where parking is available in the courtyard. The hotel offers good value in an area of more expensive lodgings—£9 ($15.75) per night per person for B&B, VAT included. There are rooms on the ground floor suitable for disabled persons. In all, the hotel has 22 bedrooms, most of them doubles. Only seven bedrooms have private baths, but all units have hot and cold water basins, and many have showers. The hotel is centrally heated, and rooms have tea- and coffee-making facilities. Proprietors Miss Logan and Mr. Logan invite their guests to enjoy the pleasant residents' lounge and bar. The hotel, a long block from the waters of the Firth of Clyde, is central for shops and entertainment. It is open all year.

Elms Court Hotel, Miller Road (tel. Ayr 64191), is opposite the Tourist Information Office and within a few minutes' walk of the city center. The hotel has 19 bedrooms, 10 of which have private baths. Color TV has been installed in all units. There are a comfortable lounge and a well-appointed bar lounge. The dining room was recently redecorated, and the food served here is good. The charge is £13.50 ($23.63) per person in a room with bath, the cost dropping to £12.50 ($21.88) per person without bath. Dinner begins at £6 ($10.50). You can recognize the Elms Court by the two stone lions couchant which guard the entrance. There is ample parking. The fully licensed hotel is open all year.

At **Chalmers Court Hotel,** Charlotte Street (tel. Ayr 265458), a two-minute walk from the Esplanade which skirts the Firth, and a five-minute walk from the seafront, Miss Hood receives paying guests in her immaculate hostelry, charging them £8.50 ($14.88) per person per night for B&B. All bedrooms have water basins and electric fires. Guests relax in the spacious lounge with a view of the Firth of Clyde. Ample parking is available, and the hotel is open all year.

For a change of pace, why not try a stay at a farmhouse where you can see the actual workings of a Strathclyde farm? **Trees Farm,** four miles east of Ayr on an unclassified road between the A70 on the north and the A713 on the south (tel. Joppa 570270), is a 120-acre farm, where Mrs. Stevenson has three bedrooms which she rents to visitors. The rates are £7 ($12.25) per person for bed and a full Scottish farm breakfast or £11 ($19.25) for half board. I recommend the latter so that you can enjoy a cuisine using fresh farm produce. The ground-floor bedrooms make this a comfortable place to stay for handicapped or elderly people. Mrs. Stevenson has color TV in the guest lounge, where she shares conversation with you. The farm receives guests from Easter until the end of September.

READERS' GUEST HOUSE SELECTION: "We were fortunate to happen upon a delightful guest house, **Clifton,** 91 Whitletts Rd. (tel. Ayr 96086), run by Alec and Margaret Walker. They are directly across the street from the race track and close to the center of town. The Walkers have two bedrooms with hot and cold running water, and meals are served in the front living room, which also doubles as the TV lounge. The charge is £7.50 ($13.13) per night per person, which is a real bargain when you see the hearty breakfast they serve. Every evening around 9:30, Mrs. Walker serves tea along with homemade cookies and cakes. The beds all have electric blankets which the Walkers turn on before bedtime. They are a friendly couple and treated us as part of their family" (Mary Train and Karen McDonald, Denver, Colo.).

Where to Eat

The **Tudor Restaurant,** 8 Beresford Terrace (tel. Ayr 61404), is a good family-style restaurant. It doesn't offer alcoholic drinks, but serves one of the best table d'hôte menus in town daily from noon to 2 p.m. For only £2 ($3.50) you are given a meal that might include a cream of tomato soup, roast beef with Yorkshire pudding and vegetables, followed by a dessert such as peach upside-down pudding. A children's lunch menu costs only £1.30 ($2.28). The traditional à la carte Scottish "high tea" is served from 3:15 to 8 p.m., and makes a substantial meal in itself. For example, you can order not only tea, bread, a scone, jam, and a piece of cake, but a selection of fish, meat, and egg dishes. For example, a ham steak or sauteed liver with bacon and tomato will cost £2.35 ($4.11).

Plough Inn, 231 High St. (tel. Ayr 62578), decorated in red, is a Stakis' chain steakhouse. You vaguely feel you might be back in Kansas City. Popular with families (there's a children's menu), the inn serves the typical fare you'd expect from a steakhouse. An appetizer, such as a healthy-looking salad, is included in the price of the main course. That is likely to be a choice-cut club steak at £6.95 ($12). If one of your party doesn't want beef that night, there is always the turkey Cordon Bleu, sauteed breast of turkey stuffed with ham and melted cheese, at £4.95 ($8.66). A limited selection of desserts is presented, or you can ask for the cheeseboard at 75p ($1.31) extra. Hours are from noon to 2 p.m. every day and evenings from 5 to 9 p.m., Monday through Friday (from 5 to 10 p.m. on Saturday and 6 to 9 p.m. on Sunday).

The Local Pub

Rabbie's Bar, Burns Statue Square (tel. Ayr 69200), right in the heart of town, is still there. It's dedicated to the memory of the poet, and on the walls you'll find a selection of some of his most famous lines, The good drink Burns himself enjoyed is still served, but I don't think the author would recognize the place. Certainly not the disco music. A good cleanup would help too.

ALLOWAY: Some three miles from the center of Ayr is where Robert Burns, Scotland's national poet, was born on January 25, 1759, in the gardener's cottage—the "auld clay biggin"—his father, William Burns, built in 1757. More than 100,000 people visit the **Burns Cottage** annually, and it still retains some of its original furniture, including the bed in which the poet was born. Chairs displayed here were said to have been used by Tam o' Shanter and Souter Johnnie. Beside the cottage in which the poet lived is a museum, open April to September on weekdays, 9 a.m. to 7 p.m.; Sunday, 2 to 7 p.m. From November to March the hours are weekdays from 10 a.m. to dusk; closed Sunday. Admission to the cottage and the Burns Monument is 70p ($1.23) for adults, 35p (61¢) for children.

The Auld Brig over the Ayr, mentioned in *Tam o' Shanter,* still spans the river, and Alloway Auld Kirk, also mentioned in the poem, stands roofless and "haunted" not far away. The poet's father is buried in the graveyard of the kirk.

The **Land o' Burns Centre** (tel. Alloway 41321) near the monument is a good place to stop. You can watch a multiscreen presentation of highlights of Burns's life, his friends, and his poetry. Information is available from the friendly personnel, and a well-stocked gift shop is there. The Russians are particularly fond of Burns and his poetry, and many come annually to visit the cottage and pore over his original manuscripts. Admission to the theater is 20p (35¢) for adults and 10p (18¢) for children.

Where to Stay

The **Burns Monument Hotel** (tel. Alloway 42466), is a 185-year-old inn which looks out onto the Doon River and the bridge, *Brig o' Doon,* immortalized in *Tam o' Shanter.* The inn is an attractive, historical place, with riverside gardens and a whitewashed bar. The rooms are pleasantly and attractively decorated, bright and cheerful, opening onto river views. All bedrooms have private baths. B&B averages around £14 ($24.50) to £20 ($35) in a single, £24 ($42) to £28 ($49) in a double. Add another £8 ($14) for dinner.

The **Balgarth Hotel,** Dunure Road, at Doonfoot (tel. Alloway 43418), lies two miles south of Ayr on the A719, a coastal road at the estuary of the Doon River, about half a mile from the village of Alloway. The hotel stands on its own grounds of pleasant gardens and woods, opening onto views of the Firth of Clyde and the Carrick Hills. Many motorists stop here en route to Ireland from the ferry station at Stranraer. Rooms are comfortably and pleasantly furnished—13 in all, most of which contain private baths. Singles rent for £14 ($24.50), going up to £15 ($26.25) with bath; doubles, £26 ($45.50) to £28 ($49). These tariffs include a full Scottish breakfast. Residents can order dinner for another £6 ($10.50). The hotel is open all year.

CULZEAN CASTLE: One of Robert Adam's most notable creations, although built around an ancient tower of the Kennedys, Culzean (pronounced Cullane), 12 miles south-southwest of Ayr, dates mainly from 1777 and is considered one of the finest Adam houses in Scotland. The castle, with a view of Ailsa Craig to the south and overlooking the Firth of Clyde, is well worth a visit and is of special interest to Americans because of General Eisenhower's connection with it and its National Guest Flat. In 1946 the guest apartment was given to the general for his lifetime in gratitude for his services as Supreme Commander of Allied Forces in World War II. Culzean stands near the famous golf courses of Turnberry and Troon, a fact which particularly pleased the golf-loving Eisenhower.

An exhibition of Eisenhower memorabilia includes sound and audio-visual spectacles, and is seen by more than 100,000 people a year. The exhibition is sponsored by the Scottish Heritage U.S.A., Inc., and Mobil Oil. To illustrate his career, there is a capsule history of World War II demonstrated with wall maps. Mementos of Eisenhower include his North African campaign desk and a replica of the Steuben glass bowl given him by his cabinet when he retired from the presidency.

The castle is open April 1 through September daily, 10 a.m. to 6 p.m. (last admission one-half hour before closing time); October 1 through October 31 daily, 10 a.m. to 4 p.m. Admission is £1.40 ($2.45) for adults, 70p ($1.23) for children.

In the castle grounds is **Culzean Country Park,** which in 1969 became the first such park in Scotland. It has an exhibition center in farm buildings by Adam. The 565-acre grounds include a walled garden, an aviary, a swan park, a camellia house, and an orangery. For information, telephone Kirkoswald 269.

After leaving Culzean Castle, you might want to take a short drive to **Kirkoswald** near Maybole. In the village is **Souter Johnnie's Cottage** (tel. 06556/603) which was the home of the village cobbler, John Davidson (Souter Johnnie), at the end of the 18th century. Davidson and his friend Douglas Graham of Shanter Farm were immortalized by Burns in his poem *Tam o' Shanter.* The cottage contains Burnsiana and contemporary cobblers' tools. In the churchyard are the graves of Tam o' Shanter and Souter Johnnie, two of his best-known characters. The cottage is open from April to September on Sunday, Thursday, and Saturday, noon to 5 p.m. Other times it is shown only by appointment. Admission is 40p (70¢) for adults and 20p (35¢) for children.

GIRVAN: About eight miles south of Culzean Castle on the A77, Girvan is the leading coastal resort of southwest Scotland, with sandy beaches and good fishing. A whisky distillery offers guided tours (and samples) for visitors.

In summer, entertainment is offered at the **Beach Pavilion,** on Knockcushan Street (tel. Girvan 2056), featuring music, dancing, children's shows, variety shows, and concerts. The local Tourist and Entertainments Committee organizes the popular Civic Week and Harbour Gala events in June and July. The many outdoor facilities include an 18-hole golf course, tennis courts, boating lake, bowling greens, putting greens, and Fantasy Land amusement park. For further information, write to the Tourist Officer, Bridge Street, Girvan, Ayrshire, Scotland.

Ailsa Craig, a 1110-foot-high, rounded rock ten miles offshore is a nesting ground and sanctuary for seabirds and formerly provided granite for stones used in the Scottish game of curling. You can sail out to the rock for a modest charge.

Three miles northeast of Girvan is the 16th-century **Kilochan Castle,** stronghold of the Cathcarts of Carleton in the valley of the Water of Girvan.

Six miles north of Girvan are the scant remains of **Turnberry Castle,** where many historians believe Robert the Bruce was born in 1274.

The **Westcliffe Hotel,** Louisa Drive (tel. Girvan 2128), is on the seafront and overlooks the Promenade, putting greens, and a children's boating lake. This is a family hotel, and the resident proprietors, Mr. and Mrs. Robert Jardine, have carried out extensive alterations, adding six ground-floor bedrooms, all with private bathrooms, at the back. Some bedrooms in the original building have showers. All bedrooms have hot and cold water and electric shaving points, and are carpeted. Rooms without bath rent for £8 ($15.75) per person for B&B. With bath, the rent is £10 ($17.50). The Westcliffe is licensed, with a cocktail bar, which looks out over the seafront and Ailsa Craig. Mrs. Jardine personally supervises preparation of the food, which is very good. Dinner is £5 ($8.75). There are tea- and coffee-making facilities in the reception area.

PRESTWICK: Prestwick is the oldest recorded baronial burgh in Scotland. But most visitors today aren't concerned with that ancient fact—rather, they fly in, landing at Prestwick's International Airport, which is in itself a popular sightseeing attraction, as spectators gather to watch planes take off and land from all over the world.

Behind St. Ninian's Episcopal Church is **Bruce's Well,** the water from which is reputed to have cured Robert the Bruce of leprosy. The **Mercat Cross** still stands outside what used to be the Registry Office and marks the center of the oldest part of Prestwick, whose existence goes back to at least 983. Prestwick is a popular holiday town, and is considered one of Scotland's most attractive resorts, with its splendid sands and golf courses. Prestwick opens onto views of Ayr Bay and the Isle of Arran.

Where to Stay

St. Nicholas Hotel, 41 Ayr Rd. (tel. Prestwick 79568), is a comfortable and spotless hotel, with ample space for parking cars at the side and tennis courts at the back. Hugh and Margaret Preston are congenial hosts who go out of their way to make guests feel welcome. The bedrooms, some with complete baths and some with showers, are immaculate, as are all the public rooms. Mrs. Preston says she's a tyrant about cleanliness. The light-olive walls and white trim in the hallways are set off by the floral-patterned carpeting throughout. Tariffs are £12 ($21) per night per person for B&B, with toilet or shower, service, and VAT included. The residents' lounge has color TV. In the dining room, good food and friendly service prevail, and you can have lunch, high tea, and dinner there. The cocktail lounge has handsome copper-topped tables and copper lampshades. The St. Nicholas is open all year.

You also won't go wrong staying at **Kincraig,** next door at 39 Ayr Rd. (tel. Prestwick 79480), an attractive Victorian-Georgian house where Mrs. Vannin rents large, comfortable bedrooms for £8 ($14) per person per night for B&B. She also serves dinner for £5 ($8.75). The solidly built house has wide carpeted stairs with a beautiful carved banister. In the residents' lounge Mrs. Vannin uses cream naugahyde-covered furniture, which makes a comfortable and attractive room. Oak woodwork is used throughout the house, and an old-fashioned antique sideboard graces the dining room. The house has a restricted license. It's open all year.

Moreland's Hotel, 45 Marina Rd. (tel. Prestwick 77590), has six double rooms and one family room. Four of the rooms have private baths. The single rate ranges from £8.50 ($14.88) to £9.50 ($16.63), and the double room tariff is from £15 ($26.25) to £19 ($33.25). Try the home-baked ham and salad with a jacket potato or the fish pie made from the local catch. A three-course meal will cost around £4 ($7). The historic structure has a garden in which guests may relax on warm evenings. Mrs. Moreland personally supervises operation of the hotel and makes every effort to see that her guests are well looked after. The all-year hotel is fully licensed, and it's two minutes from the beach and the town center.

READER'S GUEST HOUSE SELECTION: "No B&B accommodation I had rivaled that of **Saint Catherine,** 28 Seabank Rd. (tel. Prestwick 78217), operated by Mrs. Moira White. It's a block from the sea, a block from the great Prestwick golf course, and two blocks from downtown Prestwick. The neighborhood is quiet and charming. The house is a big, old red stone home of fine appearance. I found the rooms to be very large, extremely neat, and provided with their own washbowls and (most important) firm beds. The four bedrooms are on the second floor and are serviced by a large bathroom, impeccably clean, with shower and bath facilities. The breakfasts are also good. The cost is £8 ($14) per person for B&B. The accommodations were made nearly perfect by the treatment given by Mrs. White, her husband James, and their three boys. They were helpful in all ways and as friendly as could be without being intrusive" (Joseph Amato, Marshall, Minn.).

TROON: This holiday resort looks out across the Firth of Clyde to the Isle of Arran. It offers several golf links, including the "Old Troon" course. Bathers in summer find plenty of room on its two miles of sandy beaches, stretching from both sides of its harbor. The broad sands and shallow waters make it a safe haven also. From here you can take steamer trips to Arran and the Kyles of Bute.

Troon is mostly a 20th-century town, its earlier history having gone unrecorded. It takes its name from the curiously shaped promontory that juts out into the Clyde estuary on which the old town and the harbor stand. The promontory was called "Trwyn," the Cymric word for nose, and later this became the Trone and then Troon.

Fullarton Estate, on the edge of Troon beyond the municipal golf course, is the ancestral seat of the Dukes of Portland.

A massive statue of **Britannia** stands on the seafront as a memorial to the dead of the two World Wars. On her breastplate is the lion of Scotland emerging from the sea.

For accommodations, I suggest the following:

Glenside Guest House, 2 Darley Pl. off Bentinck Drive (tel. Troon 313677), is where Mrs. Chalmers makes guests feel welcome. Her corner house has hot and cold water in all the bedrooms, a dining room with separate tables, a private car park, a lounge with color TV, and central heating in the public rooms. She charges £7.50 ($13.13) per person for B&B. The house is opposite the Episcopal church on Bentinck Drive, but be sure to go around the corner to Darley Place to find Glenside.

3. Dumfries and Galloway

Southwestern Scotland is often overlooked by motorists rushing north. But this country of Burns is filled with many rewarding targets, a land of unspoiled countryside, fishing harbors, artists' colonies of color-washed houses, and romantically ruined abbeys and castles dating from the days of the border wars.

It's a fine touring country, and the hotels are generally small, of the Scottish provincial variety, but that usually means a friendly reception from a smiling staff and good traditional Scottish cookery, using the local produce.

I've documented the most important centers below, but have included some offbeat places for those seeking a more esoteric trip.

LOCKERBIE: A border market town, Lockerbie lies in the valley of Annandale, offering much fishing and golf. It's a good center for exploring some sightseeing attractions in its environs.

Lockerbie was the scene in 1593 of a battle which ended one of the last great Border family feuds. The Johnstones routed the Maxwells, killing Lord Maxwell and 700 of his men. Many of the victims had their ears cut off with a cleaver—a method of mutilation which became known throughout the Border Country as the "Lockerbie Nick."

Of interest are the remains of **Lochmaben Castle,** 3½ miles west of Lockerbie, said to have been the boyhood home (some historians say the birthplace) of Robert the Bruce. This castle, on the south shore of Castle Loch, was captured and recaptured 12 times and also withstood six attacks and sieges. James IV was a frequent visitor, and Mary Queen of Scots was here in 1565. The ruin of the early 14th-century castle is on the site of a castle of the de Brus family, ancestors of Robert the Bruce. However, the charming little hamlet of Lochmaben, with its five lochs, is reason enough to visit, regardless of who was or was not born there.

Rammerscales (tel. 038781/361) lies five miles west of Locherbie and 2½ miles south of Lochmaben on the B7020. It can easily be visited on your tour of Lochmaben and its lakes. Rammerscales is a Georgian manor house, dating from 1760. Set on high ground, it offers beautiful views of the Valley of Annandale. You can visit a walled garden of the period. It is open from June 29 to September 2 on Tuesday, Wednesday, and Thursday (2 to 5 p.m.) and on alternate Sundays beginning July 4. Admission charges are 60p ($1.05) for adults, 30p (53¢) for children. There are no teas offered, but the car park is free and there are picnic areas around the house.

If you're heading north to Lockerbie on the A74, I'd suggest a stop in the village of Ecclefechan. There you can visit **Carlyle's Birthplace,** five miles southeast of Lockerbie on the Lockerbie–Carlisle road. Even though the historian, critic, and essayist Thomas Carlyle isn't much read these days, the "arched house" in which he was born in 1795 is interesting, containing mementos and manuscripts of the author. It's open from Easter to October 31 daily, except Sunday, from 10 a.m. to 6 p.m., charging adults 40p (70¢); children, 20p (35¢).

In Lockerbie you'll find excellent accommodations at **Somerton House Hotel,** Carlisle Road (tel. Lockerbie 2583), a fully licensed hostelry where your amiable hosts will be E. and L. Gracie. On the south side of the town, standing in its acre of ground, the hotel has a beautiful garden and parking for scores of cars. The bedrooms and public rooms are comfortable, and the staff and townspeople who come to the public lounge are friendly and hospitable. The late Victorian structure has elegant arch and oak woodwork and plaster rosette friezes. One of the bathrooms has facilities which would have pleased Queen Victoria. The charge is from £13 ($22.75) in a single room, £24 ($42) in a double, including breakfast, VAT, and service. Meals in the high-ceilinged dining room include dinner from £7 ($12.25). The cuisine is excellent, using local farm produce.

MOFFAT: An Annandale town, Moffat thrives as a center of a sheep-farming area, symbolized by a statue of a ram in the wide High Street, and has been a holiday resort since the mid-17th century, because of the curative properties of its water. It was here that Robert Burns composed the drinking song "O Willie Brew'd a Peck o' Maut." Today people visit this border town on the banks of the Annan River for its good fishing and golf.

North of Moffat is spectacular hill scenery. Five miles northwest is a huge, sheer-sided 500-foot-deep hollow in the hills called the **Devil's Beef Tub,** where border cattle thieves, called reivers, hid cattle lifted in their raids.

Northeast along Moffat Water, past White Coomb, which stands 2696 feet high, is the **Grey Mare's Tail,** a 200-foot hanging waterfall formed by the Tail Burn dropping from Loch Skene. It is under the National Trust of Scotland.

Where to Stay

The **Star Hotel** (tel. Moffat 20156) is a comfortable hotel on the High Street, right in the center of the town. The proprietors, Charles Bell and Sam Beattie, extend a welcome to guests who choose this tall (four-story), narrow, interesting-looking place for their stay in Moffat. The hotel has eight bedrooms, which rent for £8 ($14) per person in a double, £8.50 ($14.88) in a single, for B&B, VAT included. All the bedrooms are comfortably furnished, and each contains a wash basin with hot and cold water. There is a residents' lounge with TV and a pleasant cocktail bar, as well as a public bar, where hotel guests may mingle with the local residents. The dining room has a high standard for food and service. For three courses, you pay £3.50 ($6.05). The Star is open all year.

The **Atlanta House Hotel,** 21–22 High St. (tel. Moffat 20343), is made up of two old houses which have been neatly joined to make a comfortable nine-bedroom hotel under the ownership of George Proudfoot. Bright carpets line the halls and stairs, and because of the age of the buildings and the original family house concept, there are numerous little stairs leading to various parts of the hotel. Each bedroom has tea- and coffee-making facilities. Mr. Proudfoot charges £6.50 ($11.38) per person for B&B. Dinner can be served in the pleasant dining room. There's a lounge bar and a lounge for guests. The hotel is open all year. Half board costs £9.25 ($16.19).

Away from the heart of town on Hartfell Crescent is **Hartfell House** (tel. Moffat 20153), an early Victorian house built in the days when Moffat was a thriving spa town attracting health-seekers from Edinburgh and Glasgow. The two-story building has a delightful garden facing the house, with a nine-hole putting green, and its inside attractions include crystal chandeliers, armoires, a window seat with the original parquet, and a bow window. Kay and Martyn West charge £9 ($15.75) in their comfortable, immaculate bedrooms for B&B per person, including VAT; £15 ($26.25) per person for half board. Otherwise, dinner costs from £6.50 ($11.38) per person. There is ample parking across from the house. The house is open March to November. To find Hartfell Crescent, turn off High Street at the Clock Tower, then go straight up the hill. Hartfell Crescent is on the right off Old Well Road.

READERS' GUEST HOUSE SELECTIONS: "**Ram Lodge Guest House,** High Street (tel. Moffat 20594), operated by Bill and Veronica Guerin, was our favorite B&B place during our tour. A few yards east of the Ram statue which dominates Moffat's main street, this is a recently established guest house in what was formerly a home above a store. There are five guest rooms, each with hot and cold running water. A shower is available. Parking was the most convenient of our entire trip. Mrs. Guerin's breakfast is tasty. B&B costs from £7 ($12.25) to £8 ($14) per person, and dinner, at a cost of £4 ($7), is available on request. We enjoyed conversation with our hosts" (Hugh Wamble, Kansas City, Mo.). . . . "**Buchan House,** Beechgrove (tel. Moffat 20378), is most enjoyable. The gracious Mrs. J. McClelland owns and operates the place, offering hot and cold running water in all bedrooms. Tea and cookies are served at 10 p.m. in the TV lounge. The beds are comfortable, and the full breakfast is outstanding. The charge is £6 ($10.50) per night per person. We also had an evening meal for which Mrs. McClelland was preparing lamb. As we did not care for lamb, she fixed us pork chops. The meal started with soup and ended with cheese, crackers, and wine, and the price was £4 ($7) each" (Dottie Farrell).

READER'S SHOPPING RECOMMENDATION: We visited the Moffat weavers at **Ladyknowe Mill,** a perfect place to purchase the least expensive tweeds, tartans, kilts, and knitwear that can be found in Britain. Wool kilts can be found for as little as £15 ($26.25). At the mill you can also watch the kiltmakers busy at work" (Anita T. Taylor, Hartsdale, N.Y.).

Where to Eat

If you're not having lunch or tea at a hotel or guest house, try the **Coffee and Cream** in the High Street, where you can range from Scottish pancakes to pizza. Try a tasty shepherd's pie at £1.50 ($2.63), and finish your meal off with a fresh cream cake. A pancake with butter and syrup costs 75p ($1.31); a beefburger roll, 70p ($1.23); and a pizza, £1.50 ($2.63). Hours are from 9:30 a.m. to 5 p.m. on weekdays, 2 to 5 p.m. on Sunday. In winter the coffeeshop closes on Wednesday and Sunday. It's also closed Christmas Day, Boxing Day, and New Year's Day.

DUMFRIES: A county town and royal burgh, this Scottish Lowland center enjoys associations with Robert Burns and James Barrie. In a sense it rivals Ayr as a mecca for admirers of Burns. He lived in Dumfries from 1791 until his death in 1796, and it was here that he wrote some of his most best-known songs, including "Auld Lang Syne" and "Ye Banks and Braes of Bonnie Doon."

The Sights

In **St. Michael's Churchyard,** a burial place for at least 900 years, stands the **Burns Mausoleum.** The poet was buried there along with his wife, Jean Armour, as well as five of their children. Burns died in 1796, but his remains weren't removed to the tomb until 1815. In the 18th-century Church of St. Michael you can still see the pew used by the Burns family.

The poet died at what is now called the **Robert Burns House** (tel. Dumfries 5297), a simple, unpretentious stone structure, which can be visited by the public as it contains personal relics and mementoes relating to Burns. His death may have been hastened by icy dips in well water which his doctor prescribed. The house is on Burns Street (formerly Mill Vennel). It is open all year from 10 a.m. to 5 p.m. (closes earlier in winter) charging adults 30p (53¢) and children 15p (26¢).

The **Town Museum,** the **Globe Inn,** and the **Hole in the Wa' Tavern** all contain Burns relics, and a statue of him stands in the High Street. You can stroll along **Burns Walk** on the banks of the River Nith.

St. Michael's is the original parish church of Dumfries and its founding is of great antiquity. The site was probably sacred before the advent of Christianity. It appears that a Christian church has stood there for more than 1300 years. The earliest written records date from the reign of William the Lion

(1165–1214). The church and the churchyard are interesting to visit because of all its connections with Scottish history, continuing through World War II.

From St. Michael's, it's a short walk to the Whitesands, where four bridges span the Nith. The earliest of these was built by Devorgilla Balliol, widow of John Balliol, father of a Scottish king. The bridge originally had nine arches but now has six and is still in constant use as a footbridge.

The Tourist Information Office is near the bridge. The wide esplanade was once the scene of horse and hiring fairs and now is a fine place to park your car and explore the town. Tour buses park here.

The **Mid Steeple** was built in 1707 as municipal buildings, courthouse, and prison. The old Scots "ell" measure of 37 inches is carved on the front of the building. A table of distances on the building includes the mileage to Huntingdon, England, which in the 18th century was the destination for Scottish cattle drovers driving their beasts south for the markets of London.

At the **Academy,** Barrie was a pupil, and he later wrote that he got the idea for *Peter Pan* from his games in the nearby garden.

Where to Stay

Newall House, 22 Newall Terrace (tel. Dumfries 2676), is run by Sheila and Charlie Cowie. Together they keep a very friendly place and do so cheerfully and well. Their rooms are clean and comfortable and include tea- and coffee-making facilities, costing £7.50 ($13.13) for a single and £7 ($12.25) per person based on double occupancy. These tariffs include a well-cooked breakfast. Mrs. Cowie will also prepare an appetizing dinner, if given fair warning, for £3.50 ($6.13).

Fulwood Private Hotel, 30 Lovers Walk (tel. Dumfries 2262), is run by congenial, friendly hosts, Mr. and Mrs. J. B. Rowland, who believe in giving wayfarers pleasure, cleanliness, and comfort in their tiny home, containing only five bedrooms (the bath must be shared). They have a wealth of information about touring in the area. Their rate is £12.50 ($21.88) for a double, including a full breakfast for two.

Aberdour Hotel, Newall Terrace (tel. Dumfries 4825), is competently operated by Mr. and Mrs. F. Bogie, who rent ten comfortable rooms—three singles, one double, and six family rooms—for £7 ($12.25) per person per night for B&B, £9.50 ($16.63) for half board. The fully licensed hotel has an attractive cocktail bar with black banquettes and a bright plaid rug, a comfortable lounge for guests with low couches, convenient tables, and color TV. The whole place is clean and bright. It's open all year.

Huntingdon Hotel, 32 Lovers Walk (tel. Dumfries 4001), opposite the railway station, is more than handily placed. It's a good choice for budget-minded guests. Mr. and Mrs. Dirom formerly had a two-star hotel in the Dumfries area, and are experienced at receiving foreign guests. They offer good service with a full English breakfast, charging £7.50 ($13.13) per person nightly. Electric blankets are provided when needed, and they have a license to serve drinks. The hotel is in an old, well-preserved building with a stone staircase and wrought-iron banisters.

Saughtree Guest House, 79 Annan Rd. (tel. Dumfries 2358), owned by Peter and Marjory Bruce, has new beds in the comfortable bedrooms, with radiators to take the chill off the rooms. For B&B, they charge £7 ($12.25) per night per person, or £11 ($19.25) for half board. At 10 p.m. Mrs. Bruce serves tea in the lounge and encourages her guests to get acquainted. Saughtree is open all year.

At the **Ben Guest House,** 29 Newall Terrace (tel. Dumfries 62950), the friendliness and wealth of information which the hosts, Mr. and Mrs. Kerr, impart are of primary importance. The charge is £11 ($19.25) per person per night for B&B and a three-course dinner in the small ground-floor dining room overlooking the back garden. At the end of the garden is an ancient cemetery surrounding St. Mary's Presbyterian Church. Tea is served in the residents' lounge at 10 p.m., while guests are enjoying TV or chatting. In fact, you can have tea at any time. As Mr. Kerr says, "The kettle is always on the stove." The proprietor is a taxidermist, and many examples of his work decorate the house. You'll learn a lot of Dumfries and Scottish history here. Mr. Kerr and his sons sometimes take guests on what he calls "hysterical" tours, acquainting them with the fact and fiction connected with historic spots.

Where to Eat

Bruno's, 5 Balmoral Rd. (tel. Dumfries 5757). It may seem ironic to recommend an Italian restaurant in the seat of Rabbie Burns, but Bruno's serves some of the best food in town. It is most unassuming, but that is part of its charm. Its minestrone is first rate, and its pastas such as lasagne are homemade. The chef doesn't serve the most imaginative Italian dishes ever sampled—in fact, the repertoire is most familiar, such as saltimbocca alla romana and pollo alla diavola, but it's done with flair. The veal is particularly tender, and the tomato sauce well spiced and blended. Steak au poivre is also excellent. The waiters are friendly and skillful and offer good advice. Bruno's serves only dinner, from 6:30 to 10 p.m., nightly except Tuesday, and it will cost you from £10 ($17.50) per person, and it's worth it. Very popular with customers is a special menu for £6.50 ($11.38) which consists of three courses.

Opus Salad Bar, 95 Queensberry St. (tel. Dumfries 55752). Don't let the obscure location of this attractive and informal unlicensed restaurant prevent you from visiting it (it's on the third floor of a shop selling fabrics in the heart of Dumfries). It is open Monday through Saturday from 9 a.m. to 5 p.m. (with an early closing on Thursday at 2:30 p.m.). The cheerful owner, Ann Halliday, serves hot meals at lunch, including, for example, lasagne at £1.45 ($2.54) or quiche and pizza at 90p ($1.58) a serving. A large selection of salads is offered at 40p (70¢) a portion. Tea is convenient to take here, a selection of cakes, tarts, and scones costing around 40p (70¢) each.

If you're looking for a place to have lunch or tea, go to **The Restaurant,** Barbour's Department Store, Buccleuch Street, where you can get tasty dishes in the dining room on the second floor, for prices ranging from 50p (88¢) for a bowl of soup to 75p ($1.31) for a meat pie. A cold table lunch is £3 ($5.25). The dining room is licensed, and there's an elevator to take you up. It's open only during store hours.

Several carry-out delicatessens are along the street across from the Tourist Information Office. The **Merry Chef,** for one, has a variety of goodies if you're in a hurry.

The Local Pub

The **Globe Inn** was a favorite haunt of Burns. It was one of the "howffs" (taverns) where he imbibed. The location is on a little side street, so ask at your hotel for directions before heading out. Cooked bar lunches beginning at £2.50 ($4.38) are offered every day except Sunday.

Excursions from Dumfries

Based in Dumfries, you can set out on treks in all directions to some of the most intriguing sightseeing goals in the Scottish lowlands.

South on the 710 leads to the village of New Abbey, dominated by the red sandstone ruins of the Cistercian abbey founded in 1273 by Devorgilla, mother of John Balliol, the "vassal King." When her husband, John Balliol the Elder, died, she became one of the richest women in Europe. Most of Galloway, with estates and castles in England and land in Normandy, belonged to her. Devorgilla founded Balliol College, Oxford, in her husband's memory. She kept his embalmed heart in a silver and ivory casket by her side for 21 years until her death in 1289 at the age of 80, when she and the casket were buried beside Balliol in front of the abbey altar. So the abbey gained the name of "Dulce Cor," Latin for "sweet heart," which has since become a part of the English language.

Built into a wall of a cottage in the village is a rough piece of sculpture showing three women rowing a boat—an allusion to the bringing of sandstone across the Nith to build the abbey.

Directly south from New Abbey on the 710 to Southerness leads to the **Arbigland Gardens and Cottage** at Kirkbean, 15 miles southwest of Dumfries. This is where John Paul Jones, one of the founders of the American navy, was born. You can visit the woodland with its water gardens arranged around a secluded bay, walking in the pathways where the great admiral once worked as a boy. The gardens are open, May to September, on Tuesday, Thursday, and Sunday from 2 to 6 p.m., charging adults 60p ($1.05); children, 30p (53¢).

Or, alternatively, you can head south from Dumfries on the 725 to **Caerlaverock Castle,** near the mouth of the River Nith, two miles south from Glencaple. Once the seat of the Maxwell family, this impressive ruined fortress dates back to the 1270s. In 1300 Edward I laid siege to it. In 1640 it yielded to Covenanters after a 13-week siege. The castle is triangular with round towers. The interior was reconstructed in the 17th century as a Renaissance mansion, with fine carving. The castle is open April to September from 9:30 a.m. to 7 p.m. (on Sunday from 2 to 7 p.m.); October to March, from 9:30 a.m. to 4 p.m. (on Sunday from 2 to 4 p.m.). Admission is 40p (70¢) for adults; 20p (35¢) for children.

Near the castle is the **Caerlaverock National Nature Reserve** between the River Nith and Lochar Water. It is a noted winter haunt of wildfowl, including barnacle geese.

After leaving the castle, continue east along the 725 to the village of **Ruthwell,** about ten miles southeast of Dumfries. There, at the early 19th-century Ruthwell Church, you'll see one of the most outstanding crosses of the Dark Ages. Standing 18 feet high, the cross is believed to date from the eighth century. Engraved with carvings, it bears the earliest known specimen of written English (a Christian poem in Runic characters).

North from Dumfries on the A76 takes you to **Lincluden College,** two miles away. This is the richly decorated remains of a 15th-century collegiate church.

Four miles away, still following the A76, leads to **Ellisland Farm,** where Robert Burns made his last attempt at farming, renting the spread from 1788 to 1791. The present occupants of the house will show you through the Burns Room. It was at this farm that Burns wrote *Tam o' Shanter.*

Continuing north, still on the A76, you reach **Thornhill,** a country resort —familiar to Burns—overlooking the River Nith. From here, it's possible to branch out for excursions in many directions.

The main target is **Drumlanrig Castle** (tel. 0848/30248), the seat of the Dukes of Buccleuch and Queensberry, built between 1679 and 1689. It lies three miles north of Thornhill, off the A76. This exquisite pink castle contains some celebrated paintings, including a famous Rembrandt and a Holbein. In addition, it is further enriched by Louis XIV antiques, silver, porcelain, and relics related to Bonnie Prince Charlie. The castle stands in a parkland ringed by wild hills, and there's even an "Adventure Woodland Playground." The gardens are gradually being restored to their 1720 magnificence. Teas are served in the old kitchen hung with gleaming copper. It is open Easter, then May and June on Monday to Thursday and Saturday from 12:30 to 5 p.m. (on Sunday from 2 to 6 p.m.). From July to the last Monday in August, it's open Monday through Thursday and again on Saturday from 11 a.m. to 5 p.m. (on Sunday from 2 to 6 p.m.). Admission is £1.20 ($2.10) for adults and 50p (88¢) for children.

Of almost equal interest, **Maxwelton House** lies three miles south of Moniaive and 13 miles north of Dumfries on the B729. It was the stronghold of the Earls of Glencairn in the 14th and 15th centuries. But it is more remembered today as the birthplace (1682) of Annie Laurie of the famous Scottish ballad. From Maxwelton you can see that the braes are just as bonnie as ever. The braes, of course, refer to the neighboring hills. The house, garden, chapel, and an agricultural museum can be visited from May to September on Wednesday and Thursday from 2 to 5 p.m. Admission is £1.40 ($2.45) for adults, 20p (35¢) for children. Telephone Moniaive 385 for more information.

Back on the A76, you can branch northwest on the B797, heading in the direction of Mennock Pass. There, at **Wanlockhead,** you'll be in the highest village in Scotland. Once this village was a gold-mining center and known as "God's Treasure House." Gold was mined here for the Scottish crown jewels.

CASTLE DOUGLAS: A cattle and sheep market town, Castle Douglas makes a good touring center for Galloway. It lies about eight miles southwest of Dumfries, at the northern tip of Carlingwark Loch. On one of the islets in the loch is an ancient lake dwelling known as a "crannog."

The favorite excursion is to **Threave Castle,** 1½ miles west on an islet in the River Dee west of town, the ruined 14th-century stronghold of the Black Douglases. The four-story tower was built between 1639 and 1690 by Archibald the Grim, Lord of Galloway. In 1455 Threave Castle was the last Douglas stronghold to surrender to James II, who employed "Mons Meg" (the famous cannon now in Edinburgh Castle) in its subjection. Over the doorway projects the "gallows knob" from which the Douglases hanged their enemies. The castle was captured by the Covenanters in 1640 and dismantled. Owned by the National Trust, the site must be reached by a *lengthy* walk through farmlands and then by small boat across the Dee. A ferry charge of 30p (53¢) is the only alternative to that very long walk. The castle is open April to September, Monday to Saturday, from 9:30 a.m. to 7 p.m. and on Sunday from 2 to 7 p.m.

Threave Gardens (tel. 0556/2575) lie one mile west of the castle. The gardens are built around Threave House, a Scottish baronial mansion 1½ miles west of Castle Douglas, off the A75. It is under the protection of the National Trust of Scotland which uses it as a school for gardening and a wildfowl refuge. In spring more than 300 varieties of daffodils burst into bloom. There is also a walled garden. The gardens are open daily from 9 a.m. to dusk, charging adults an admission of £1 ($1.75) and children, 50p (88¢).

KIRKCUDBRIGHT: Stewartry's most ancient burgh, Kirkcudbright (pronounced Kir-coo-bree) lies at the head of Kirkcudbright Bay on the Dee Estuary. This intriguing old town contains color-washed houses inhabited, in part, by artists. In fact, Kirkcudbright has been called the "St. Ives (Cornwall) of Scotland."

The Sights

In the old town graveyard are memorials to Covenanters and to Billy Marshall, the tinker king who died in 1792 at the age of 120, reportedly having fathered four children after the age of 100.

Maclellan's Castle, built in 1582 for the town's provost, Sir Thomas Maclellan, easily dominates the center of town. Kirkcudbright is an attractive town which is the center of a lively group of weavers, potters, and painters who work in the 18th-century streets and lanes.

The **Tolbooth,** a large building, dates back to the 16th and 17th centuries, and in front of it is a **Mercat Cross** of 1610. The Tolbooth is a memorial to John Paul Jones (1747–1792), the gardener's son from Kirkbean who became a slave trader, a privateer, and in due course one of the founders of the American navy. For a time, before his emigration, he was imprisoned for murder in the Tolbooth.

Art exhibitions are regularly sponsored at **Broughton House,** a 17th-century mansion which once belonged to E. A. Hornel, the artist. The house contains a large reference library with a valuable Burns collection, along with pictures by Hornel and other artists, plus antiques and other works of art. You can stroll through its beautiful garden. Broughton House is open every day in summer and Tuesday and Thursday afternoons in winter. Admission is 50p (88¢) for adults, 20p (35¢) for children.

In addition, the **Stewartry Museum in Kirkcudbright** contains a fascinating collection of antiquities, depicting the history and culture of Galloway. It is open daily, except Sunday, from 10 a.m. to 5 p.m., charging adults 40p (70¢); children, 20p (44¢). It is open from Easter to October.

North of town is the ruined **Tongland Abbey,** one of whose abbots, John Damian, once tried to fly from the battlements of Stirling Castle wearing wings of bird feathers, in the presence of James IV. He landed in a manure pile.

Dundrennan Abbey, seven miles southeast of Kirkcudbright, the ruins of a rich Cistercian house founded in 1142, include much late Norman and Transitional work. Dundrennan is a daughter abbey of Rievaulx Abbey in Yorkshire and the mother abbey of Glenluce and Sweetheart Abbeys. The small village is partly built of stones "quarried" from the abbey. Mary Queen of Scots, after escaping from Loch Leven and being defeated at the Battle of Langside, spent her last night in Scotland at the abbey in May 1568. She went to England to seek help from Elizabeth who imprisoned her instead. The transept and choir, a unique example of the Early Pointed style, remain.

Where to Stay

In accommodations, I'd suggest the **Selkirk Arms,** Old High Street (tel. Kirkcudbright 30402), where Robert Burns stayed when he composed the celebrated Selkirk Grace. (The grace was actually given on St. Mary's isle, the seat of the Douglases, Earls of Selkirk, and, in part, it went as follows: "But we ha'e meat, and we can eat, And sae the Lord be thankit.") The hotel is fairly small, 27 bedrooms, and its appointments are simple, yet it is colorful staying in such charming surroundings. The neighborhood evokes memories of John

Paul Jones, and there are little art galleries displaying the works of local painters. In all, it's a restful, tranquil atmosphere. You have a choice of rooms in the main building or in the annex. B&B is from £12.50 ($21.88) per person, and half board is £20 ($35). The hotel is open all year. It has both a TV lounge and a cocktail bar, and there is ample parking.

The font of Dundrennan Abbey (with a date on it of 1492) stands in the garden of the hotel. The Selkirk Arms also has a photostat of John Paul Jones's original commission as captain in the American navy, as well as a grandfather clock which used to belong to him and was made by the husband of Jones's sister, Janet (William Taylor of Dumfries).

Gordon House, 116 High St. (tel. Kirkcudbright 30670), is a small hotel in a Georgian building listed as of historical and architectural interest. The ten bedrooms are light and fresh, and have hot and cold water basins. Owner George Munn has kept a good Scottish tone by using plaid carpeting wherever needed. Rooms cost about £13 ($22.75) for half board, £9 ($15.75) for B&B, per person, plus VAT and service charge. There is a comfortable lounge for hotel guests, complete with color TV, and a pleasant dining room. Bar lunches are available in the pub from 12:30 to 1:30 p.m., if you're just dropping by. Every second Wednesday night a musical evening is held from 8 to 11 p.m. All the paintings in the halls and public rooms are originals.

If you'd like a smaller, quiet place to stay, looking out on the River Dee and the bridge, **Beaconsfield,** Bridge Street (tel. Kirkcudbright 30488), is ideal. Mrs. Fisher rents rooms for £12 ($21) per night based on double occupancy, for B&B. She serves dinner if you request it, except in July and August. Guests can enjoy color TV in the lounge. Mrs. Fisher has a wealth of antique objets d'art. Beaconsfield is open all year.

GATEHOUSE-OF-FLEET: This sleepy former cotton town, on the Water of Fleet, was the **Kippletringan** in Sir Walter Scott's *Guy Mannering,* and Burns composed "Scots Wha Hae wi' Wallace Bled" on the moors nearby and wrote it down in the Murray Arms Hotel there.

The town's name probably dates from 1642 when the English government opened the first military road through Galloway to assist the passage of troops to Ireland. In 1661 Richard Murray of Cally was authorized by Parliament to widen the bridge and to erect beside it an inn which was to serve as a tollhouse, with the innkeeper responsible for the maintenance of a 12-mile stretch of road. This is believed to have been the original house on the "gait," or road, which later became known as the "gait house of Fleet," and by 1790 it was being written in its present form and spelling. This ancient "gait house" is now part of the Murray Arms Hotel, used as a coffeeroom, and is therefore probably the oldest building still in existence in the town.

West of Gatehouse, on the road to Creetown, is the well-preserved 15th-century tower of the McCullochs, with its sinister "murder hole" over the entrance passage. Through this trapdoor, boiling pitch was poured onto attackers. **Cardoness Castle** was originally the seat of the McCulloch family, one of whom, Sir Godfrey McCulloch, was the last person in Scotland to be executed, at Edinburgh in 1697, by the "Maiden," the Scots version of the guillotine.

For accommodations, I recommend the following:

The **Angel Hotel,** toward the bottom of the High Street (tel. Gatehouse 204), is a three-story stone building painted white with black trim. Clean and comfortable, the bedrooms cost £10.50 ($18.38) per person including breakfast, served in an attractive dining room on the second floor. There is a lounge bar on the ground floor and a residents' lounge with TV. There is live music and a late license on Friday and Saturday night. The all-year hotel has an open parking lot.

The **Bank of Fleet Hotel,** 47 High St. (tel. Gatehouse 302), is housed, as its name implies, in an old bank building. Owner Mrs. Jean Walker charges £9 ($15.75) per person for B&B, £12 ($21) for half board. The bedrooms are cheerfully decorated with bright colors. A small residents' lounge has color TV. Comfortable brown banquette seats make the lounge bar inviting, and bar lunches are a specialty at noon. In a stone building, the hotel has a chimney at either end, with six chimney pots each. It's open all year.

NEWTON STEWART: Sometimes called "the gateway to Galloway" and the "heart of Galloway," this small town on the River Cree was made a burgh or barony in 1677 after a son of the second Earl of Galloway built some houses beside the ford across the river and gave the hamlet its present name. When the estate was later purchased by William Douglas, he changed the name to Newton Douglas, but it didn't stick. The town has a livestock market and woolen mills. Cree Bridge, built of granite in 1813 to replace one swept away by a flood, links the town with **Minnigaff** where there is an old church with interesting carved stones and some ancient memorials.

Newton Stewart is associated with Scott, Stevenson, and Burns. Today it is chiefly a center for touring, especially north for nine miles to the beauty spot of **Loch Troolin** in the Glen Trool Forest Park, 200 square miles of magnificently preserved splendor. On the way to Loch Trool, you go through the village of Glentrool where you'll find the first car park for those wanting to take the Stroan Bridge walk, a distance of 3½ miles. The hearty Scots, of course, walk the entire loch, all 4½ miles of it.

The **Crown Hotel,** on Queen Street opposite the Auction Mart (tel. Newton Stewart 2772), is a handsome old gray stone building with dormers and massive chimneys topped by many chimney pots. The manager, Mr. Smaila, rents rooms for £13 ($22.75) per person per night. It costs another £2 ($3.50) with bath. Some units contain color TV sets. There are four singles and nine doubles. Probably one of the most attractive residents' lounges in Scotland is on the second floor—large and well furnished, with a parquet floor and an expanse of windows overlooking the garden. Octagonal rugs in rose and brown and a grand piano add to the beauty of the room. There's an adjoining TV lounge with a cocktail bar at the end. On the first floor are the public bar and the Log Cabin cocktail bar, both open to nonresidents. A spacious dining room has plaid carpeting and a piano. There a lunch goes for £3.80 ($6.65), a dinner beginning at £7.50 ($13.13).

The **Galloway Arms Hotel,** on Victoria Street in the heart of town (tel. Newton Stewart 2282), displays the armorial bearings of the Earls of Galloway, original owners of the buildings which make up the hotel. The modern hotel has spacious and comfortable public rooms with large log fires. Bedrooms are centrally heated and most have private bathrooms. The price for a full Scottish breakfast and a bed in high season is £15 ($26.25) in a single, £28 ($49) in a double. In the dining room you can select from a varied à la carte menu which lives up to the best traditions of Scottish cooking and makes use of the local produce, a complete meal averaging £8 ($14). The main building dates from the 13th century. The Galloway Arms will enfold you all year.

WIGTOWN: This former county town of the district is still a center for fishing and wildfowling even if its harbor is silted up. Two market crosses, an 18th-century one topped by a sundial and another which was erected in 1816, stand in the town's central square. In 1685 two women, Margaret Maclauchlan and Margaret Wilson, Covenanters who were accused of attending meetings of their sect, were tied to stakes at the mouth of the River Bladnoch and drowned by the rising tide after refusing to give up their beliefs. An obelisk marks the traditional site of their martyrdom. A monument to all Covenanters stands on Windy Hill back of the town.

Three miles northwest of Wigtown, near Torhouskie Farm, are the **Bronze Age Stones of Torhouse,** 19 standing stones in a circle with three in the center.

The remains of **Baldoon Castle** are one mile from Wigtown. This was the setting for Sir Walter Scott's *The Bride of Lammermoor.* It was the home of David Dunbar and his wife, supposed to be the principal characters of the *Bride.* The castle was captured by Wallace in 1297.

If you wish to stay over in this clean little town, there's the **Galloway Hotel** (tel. Wigtown 2218), originally one of the oldest coaching inns in the south of Scotland, around which the town was built. It has been completely renovated, modernized, and extended. Fully licensed, the hotel has comfortable lounges and a cocktail bar, and will serve you a dinner for £5 ($8.75). Mr. and Mrs. Carleton charge £7 ($12.25) for B&B in a single bedroom, £15 ($26.25) in a double. Some more expensive rooms have private baths, and all have hot and cold running water. On the left wall as you enter the hotel, there's a four-foot by six-foot needlepoint tapestry of Bobby Burns scenes with a tartan border. The Galloway is 300 years old.

WHITHORN: Ten miles south of Wigtown, you come upon Whithorn, a modern town with a museum containing ancient crosses and tombstones, including the fifth-century **Latinus Stone,** the earliest Christian memorial in Scotland. St. Ninian, the son of a local chieftain, founded a monastery here in A.D. 397 and built his "Candida Casa" or "White House," probably the first Christian church in Scotland. In the 12th century, Fergus, Lord of Galloway, built a priory. The church and monastery were destroyed in the 16th century. Excavations in the ruins have revealed fragments of wall covered in pale plaster believed to be from Ninian's Candida Casa. The ruins are entered through the Pend, a 17th-century arch on which are carved the Royal Arms of Scotland.

A moorland walk to the west coast 2½ miles away leads to **St. Ninian's Cave** in Port Castle Bay, used by the missionary as a retreat.

The **Isle of Whithorn,** three miles southeast of the town, is where St. Ninian landed about A.D. 395 on his return from studying in Rome, to bring Christianity to Scotland. The ruins of a plain 13th-century chapel are here but no signs of any earlier church. On the point of the promontory are the remains of an Iron Age fort and a late-17th-century tower.

Chapel Finian, near the shore road on the way from Whithorn to Glenluce, is a small chapel or oratory probably dating from the 10th or 11th century, in an enclosure about 50 feet wide.

PORT WILLIAM: On Luce Bay, this little holiday resort is a center for tennis, golf, and swimming.

By taking the 714 west, you'll reach **Drumtrodden Stones,** a cluster of ring and cup markings from the Bronze Age on a rock face. Just 400 yards to the south is an alignment of three adjacent surviving stones. It's hardly Stonehenge, but interesting nevertheless.

While still on an antiquity search, you can drive directly south of Port William a short distance to **Barsalloch Fort,** the remains of a fort dating from the Iron Age.

In the pleasant village, you can stay at the **Monreith Arms Hotel** (tel. Port William 206), a big stone building at the roundabout where you will find immaculate bedrooms, comfortable public rooms, and a pleasant dining room serving good food. Mr. and Mrs. A. R. Jardine, in their fully licensed hostelry, offer B&B from £10.25 ($17.94) per night per person, and dinner from £5.50 ($9.63). The hotel is open all year.

GLENLUCE: Lying on the Water of Luce near its estuary in Luce Bay, Glenluce is another attractive village. **Glenluce Abbey,** one mile northwest, is a ruined Cistercian house founded about 1190, which has intact a 15th-century vaulted chapter house of architectural interest. The border "wizard," Michael Scott, is said to have lured the plague to the abbey in the 13th century and shut it in a vault. **Castle of Park,** a 16th-century mansion, overlooks the village from the brow of a hill across the river.

A convenient and pleasant place to stay in Glenluce is the **Judge's Keep,** in the center of town (tel. Glenluce 203), where the Atkinson family receive guests in the fully licensed hotel for £8.50 ($14.88) per person for B&B. Dinner, prepared under Mrs. Atkinson's close supervision in the immaculate kitchen on the ground floor, costs £6.50 ($11.38), and it's well worth it. Bar meals are available throughout the day, with hot dishes beginning at £2.40 ($4.20), ranging upward to £4.60 ($8.05) for a big sirloin steak with vegetables. There is a TV lounge for guests, as well as public and lounge bars and ample car parking. The hotel is open all year. The hotel offers salmon and trout fishing and can arrange for you to play golf at the local club at a cost of £2.50 ($4.38) per day.

PORTPATRICK: Until 1849 steamers sailed the 21 miles from Donaghdee in Northern Ireland to Portpatrick, which became a "Gretna Green" for the Irish. Couples would land on Saturday, have the banns called on Sunday, and marry on Monday. When the harbor became silted up, Portpatrick was replaced by Stranraer as a port.

Commanding a clifftop to the south are the ruins of **Dunskey Castle,** a grim keep built in 1510 by John Adair.

Ten miles south of Portpatrick is the quiet little hamlet of **Port Logan.** In the vicinity is **Logan House** (not open to the public), the seat of the McDouall family, which could trace their ancestry so far back that it was claimed they were as "old as the sun itself." This family laid out the world-famous gardens at Logan which are visited by people from all over the world. **Logan Botanic Garden,** an annex of the Royal Botanic Garden, Edinburgh, contains a wide range of plants from the temperate regions of the world. Cordylines, palms, tree ferns, and tender rhododendrons grow well in the mild climate of southwest Scotland. The garden is open from 10 a.m. to 5 p.m. April to September. Admission is around 50p (88¢). There is a pleasant refreshment room at the entrance. The site is 14 miles south of Stranraer off the B7065 road.

The ancient church site of **Kirkmadrine** lies in the parish of Stoneykirk, south of Portpatrick. The site now has a modern church but there is an old graveyard and early inscribed stones and crosses, including three of the earliest Christian monuments in Britain, showing the chi-rho symbol and inscriptions dating from the fifth or early sixth century.

Instead of going north to the larger town, Stranraer, you might stay at the **Carlton Guest House** in Portpatrick on the South Crescent (tel. Portpatrick 253). In their gray stone house with a green door, looking out over the Irish Sea, Mr. and Mrs. Davis rent rooms for £8.25 ($14.44) per night per person for B&B, plus VAT. Half board costs from £12.50 ($21.88) per person, including VAT. They have one single room and seven doubles, all with heaters for nights when the wind blows across from Ireland. The Davises take in guests from March to November.

If you'd like to dine in Portpatrick, I recommend the **Old Mill House** (tel. Portpatrick 358), an attractive bar and restaurant at the top of the village as you head toward Stranraer. It is owned and operated by Pat and Judy Ann Auld. The lovely gardens with a trout stream and swimming pool are worth stopping to enjoy even if you only have tea or a drink. Meals are priced from £7 ($12.25).

STRANRAER: The largest town in Wigtownshire, Stranraer is the terminal of the 35-mile ferry crossing from Larne, Northern Ireland. An early chapel, built by a member of the Adair family near the 16th-century **Castle of St. John** in the heart of town, gave the settlement its original name of Chapel, later changed to Chapel of Stranrawer and then shortened to Stranraer. The name is supposed to have referred to the row or "raw" of original houses on the "strand" or burn, now largely buried beneath the town's streets. The Castle of St. John became the town jail and in the late 17th century held Covenanters during Graham of Claverhouse's campaigns of religious persecution.

To the east is **Castle Kennedy Gardens** and **Lochinch Castle** (tel. 0776/2024), a late-19th-century Scots baronial mansion. In the grounds are White and Black Lochs and the ruins of Castle Kennedy, built during the reign of James IV, but burned down in 1716. Restored in the middle of the 19th century, the gardens contain the finest pinetum in Scotland. Go in the right season and you can wander among rhododendrons, azaleas, and magnolias. The castle is not open to the public, but the gardens are, anytime daily from 10 a.m. to dusk, April to September. They are closed over Easter, May Day, and on August bank holidays. Admission is £1 ($1.75) for adults and 50p (88¢) for children.

For accommodations, try the **North West Castle,** Royal Crescent (tel. Stranraer 4413), overlooking Loch Ryan and the departure quay for Northern Ireland. The oldest part of the house was built in 1820 by Capt. Sir John Ross, R.N., the Arctic explorer. Of course, to honor the brave man, your bedroom window should face northwest, an allusion to his search for the "North West Passage." The hotel owners will give you a brochure which relates the exploits and disappointments of the explorer. The original building has been altered and extended to meet the hotel's increasing popularity. At last count, a total of 82 rooms was offered, all of which contain private baths. Singles go from £16 ($28) to £20 ($35), doubles from £24 ($42) to £32 ($56) per person per day for B&B.

The lounges are cozy and pleasantly furnished, and the dining room is impressive, serving mainly continental fare with Scottish overtones. Fresh local ingredients are used. The bars downstairs are well stocked—I prefer the Explorers' Lounge with its views of the harbor. Further amenities include a garden, a sauna, and a solarium, plus a curling rink, games room, indoor swimming pool, and dancing to a live band on Saturday night.

Chapter XVII

EDINBURGH AND CENTRAL SCOTLAND

1. Edinburgh
2. Day Trips from Edinburgh
3. The Kingdom of Fife
4. Glasgow and the Clyde
5. The Trossachs and Loch Lomond

SCOTLAND HAS OFTEN been compared to a sandwich in that the central belt is considered the meatier part. Within a relatively small compass of land, you can not only visit the capital at Edinburgh but also enjoy such beauty as the Trossachs (the Scottish Lake District), the silver waters of Loch Lomond, or take in the cragginess of Stirling Castle. Central Scotland should be treated as far more than just a gateway to the Highlands.

Edinburgh, often called the fairest city in Europe, is our first stopover. While based there, you can take many day trips, such as to the seaside and golfing resort of North Berwick. The Scots suggest you take a "look aboot ye."

From Edinburgh, on the opposite shore of the Firth of Forth, reached by a bridge, the Kingdom of Fife is rich in treasures, Falkland Palace, the hunting retreat of the Stuart kings, and the unspoiled fishing villages along the coast, collectively known as "East Neuk," among them.

To the west of Edinburgh, a distance of some 40 miles, the industrial city of Glasgow is a target for some, although to me at least it has none of the charm of the capital. However, from Glasgow you can set out on a tour in many directions, including the glens and hills associated with the outlaw, Rob Roy. Also on Glasgow's doorstep is the scenic estuary of the Firth of Clyde. You can cruise down the Clyde on a paddle-steamer.

But assuming you're still back in the Lowlands, you can begin your descent upon—

1. Edinburgh

Scotland's capital city is Edinburgh, off the beaten path for those doing the mad whirlwind tour of Europe, as it lies 373 miles north of London.

The city is associated with John Knox, Mary Queen of Scots, Robert Louis Stevenson, Sir Arthur Conan Doyle (creator of Sherlock Holmes), David Hume, Alexander Graham Bell, Sir Walter Scott, and Bonnie Prince Charlie—to name-drop only a bit.

From the elegant Georgian crescents of the New Town, to the dark medieval "wynds" of the Old Town, down the wide, magnificent Princes Street (Stevenson's "liveliest and brightest thoroughfare"), Edinburgh lives up to its reputation as one of the fairest cities in Europe. Of course, it's not as sophisticated as Paris, nor as fast-paced as London. And it's banal to call it the Athens of the North, although the Greek Revival movement of the 19th century made many of the buildings look like pagan temples.

What Edinburgh has to offer is unique. It's Scottish (scotch is a drink—so play it safe and refer to the hearty, ruddy-faced people as Scots)—and that means it's different from English. It wasn't sameness that made these two countries fight many a bloody border skirmish.

Most travelers know that since World War II Edinburgh has been the scene of an ever-growing International Festival, with its action-packed list of cultural events. But that shouldn't be your only reason for visiting the ancient seat of Scottish royalty. Its treasures are available all year. In fact, the pace the rest of the time, when the festival-hoppers have gone south, is more relaxed. The prices are lowered, and the people themselves, under less pressure as hosts, return to their traditional hospitable nature.

GETTING THERE: Edinburgh is two hours by bus or rail from the major international airport of Scotland, Prestwick, and it lies in the center of most of the rail and bus lines leading from Scotland to England. Edinburgh's only recently improved airport, connected by frequent 30-minute bus rides to midtown, receives flights only from within the British Isles, Dublin, and Amsterdam. Fares to London, 75 minutes away by air, begin at around $115 round trip.

BritRail Passes are valid on all lines of the British Rail system, which includes the corridor between London and Edinburgh. BritRail Passes, however, are not valid on all lines of the Scottish railroad system. A Travelpass for Scotland is available to fill in the gaps (see the ABCs of Britain under "Travel by Rail").

Regardless of the kind of ticket you hold, Edinburgh is well connected by rail and bus to all other points in Britain. Standard second-class round-trip rail fare from London is $105, but substantial amounts of money can be saved by booking a special InterCity Saver ticket in advance. The round-trip fare from London to Edinburgh is a surprisingly low £32 ($56), with special conditions attached; for more information, again refer to the "Travel by Rail" section of the ABCs of Britain.

GETTING AROUND: Edinburgh doesn't benefit from a modern underground (subway to Americans) system, so you'll find that **buses** will probably be your chief method of transport in the Scottish capital. The fare you pay is determined by the distance you ride. The minimum fare is 12p (21¢) for three stops or fewer, and the maximum fare is 40p (70¢) for 20 or more stops. Children up to 10 years of age pay 15p (26¢) regardless of the number of stops.

The Edinburgh city fathers (or mothers, as the case may be) have devised several types of term bus passes for extended tourist visits to their city. The **Edinburgh Freedom Ticket** allows one day of unlimited travel on city buses at £1 ($1.75) for adults and 50p (88¢) for children. Another form of extended ticket is a **TouristCard,** allowing unlimited travel on all city buses for a specified number of days, and special discounts at certain restaurants and for tours of selected historical sites. A two-day TouristCard costs £6.60 ($11.38) for adults and £4.25 ($7.44) for children, and a 13-day TouristCard goes for £14.85 ($25.86) for adults and £8.65 ($15.31) for children.

Finally, for daily commuters or for diehard Scottish enthusiasts, a RidaCard season ticket allow unlimited travel on all buses at £6.50 ($11.38) for two weeks and £11 ($19.25) for four weeks. Travel must begin on a Sunday.

These tickets and further information may be obtained at the **Waverley Bridge Transport Office,** Waverley Bridge in Edinburgh (tel. 226-4696), or the Lothian Region Transport Office, 14 Queen St., Edinburgh EHZ 1JL (tel. 554-4494).

As a last resort, try hailing a cab or waiting at a taxi stand. The rates are set at 85p ($1.50) for the first mile and 42p (70¢) for each additional mile, not including tip.

WHERE TO STAY: Searching for a suitable hotel isn't too difficult in Edinburgh, as the city offers a full range of accommodations at different price levels throughout the year. However, during the three-week period of the festival, the establishments fill up with international visitors, so it's prudent to reserve in advance. To take care of emergency lodging all year, the **Edinburgh Tourist Information & Accommodation Service,** at 5 Waverley Bridge (tel. 226-6591), compiles a well-investigated and lengthy list of small hotels and guest houses that provide B&B for as little as £6.50 ($11.38) per person. Guest houses in this latter category may have only one to three bedrooms per household to rent. The bureau's hours during the peak season, May 1 to September 30, are from 8:30 a.m. to 8 p.m. Monday through Saturday, and from 11 a.m. to 8 p.m. on Sunday (open till 9 p.m. during July and August). A 50p (88¢) booking fee is charged.

Assuming you arrive in Edinburgh when the hotels aren't fully booked or that you will reserve a room in advance, I've prepared a representative sampling of the leading candidates in the $25-a-day budget range.

East of Princes Street

Greenside Hotel, 9 Royal Terrace (tel. 557-0022), owned by Dorothy and David Simpson, is a substantial Georgian town house with quite a few antiques to give it the right spirit. They have singles, doubles, twins, and a family room, 13 spacious units in all, each centrally heated, with hot and cold running water. Not including VAT, the per-person rate nightly is £9.50 ($16.63). The Simpsons have provided a color TV set in their lounge. Most guests approve with enthusiasm of the full breakfast. The terrace is quiet, and the hotel lies only a five-minute walk from the city center. The Simpsons are proud that their building has been described as being of "historical architectural interest." Overnight parking is available.

Halcyon Hotel, 8 Royal Terrace (tel. 556-1033), is a stately former town house, lying about a ten-minute walk from Waverley Station and only a short stroll from Princes Street. Although not furnished in an opulent style, it is nevertheless clean and comfortable, a suitable recommendation. Its 16 bedrooms are divided among singles, doubles, and family units, costing from £9 ($15.75) per person for B&B. Rooms are equipped with shaver outlets, intercom, radio, tea- and coffee-making facilities, and hot and cold running water. Children sharing a parent's room are granted reductions. Breakfast is served in a dining room looking out onto the gardens of the Royal Terrace. Guests can use a big private car park near the Halcyon. The proprietor, Mr. Miller, is most friendly and helpful. He often recommends an excellent restaurant a

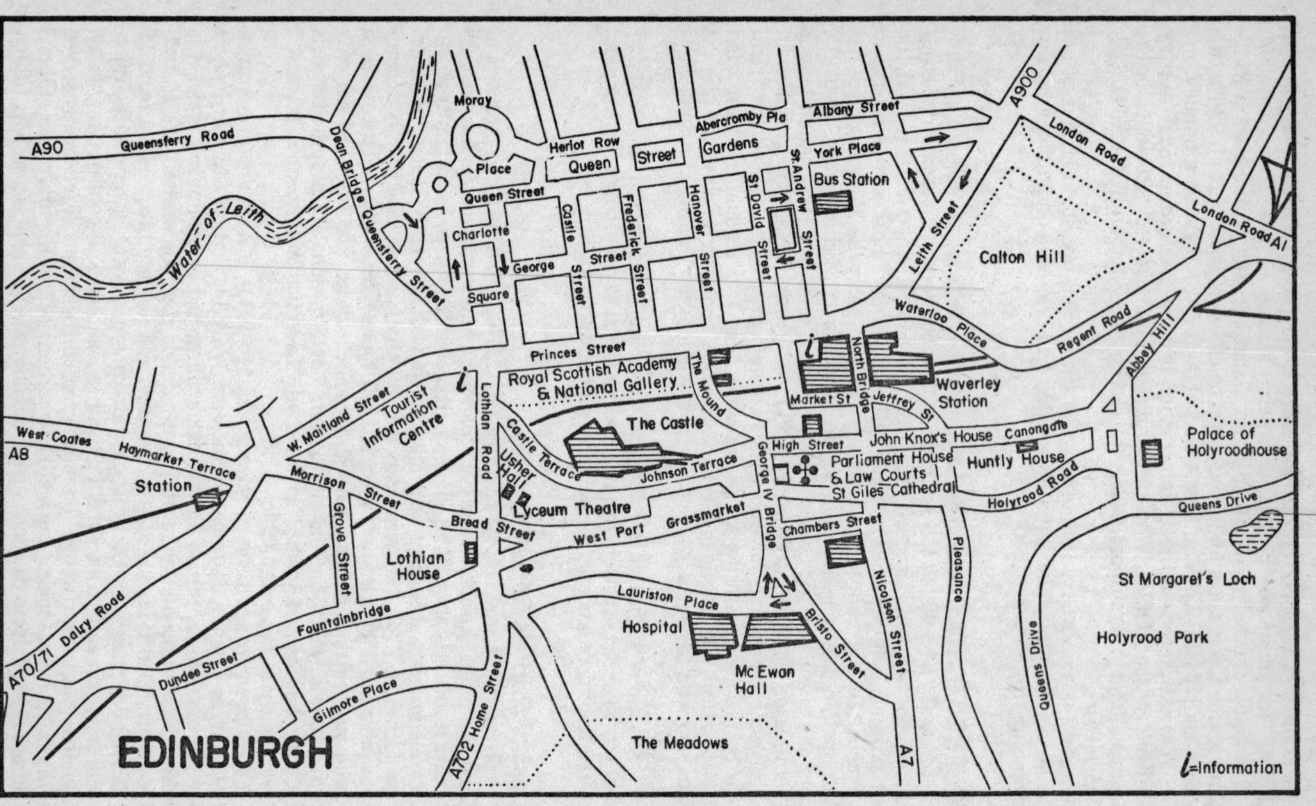
EDINBURGH
i=Information
A90
Queensferry Road
Dean Bridge
Queensferry Street
Water-of-Leith
Moray
Place
Heriot Row
Queen
Street
Abercromby Pla
Gardens
Albany Street
York Place
Bus Station
A900
London Road
London Road A1
Queen Street
Charlotte
Castle
Frederick
Hanover
St David
St.Andrew
Street
George
Street
Square
Leith Street
Calton Hill
Waterloo Place
Regent Road
Abbey Hill
Princes Street
Royal Scottish Academy
& National Gallery
The Mound
North Bridge
Market St
Jeffrey St
Waverley
Station
Tourist
Information
Centre
W. Maitland Street
Lothian Road
The Castle
Castle Terrace
Johnson Terrace
Usher Hall
Lyceum Theatre
High Street
John Knox's House
Canongate
Huntly House
Parliament House
& Law Courts
St Giles Cathedral
Palace of
Holyroodhouse
Holyrood Road
Queens Drive
West Coates
A8
Haymarket Terrace
Station
Morrison Street
Grove Street
Bread Street
West Port
Grassmarket
George IV Bridge
Chambers Street
Lothian
House
Lauriston Place
Hospital
Bristo Street
Nicolson Street
Pleasance
St Margaret's Loch
Holyrood Park
Dalry Road
A70/71
Fountainbridge
Dundee Street
Gilmore Place
A702 Home Street
McEwan
Hall
The Meadows
A7

short distance from the Halcyon. It's the **Jolly,** 9 Elm Row, and it's open daily except Sunday. The menu is varied, ranging from homemade pizza to fresh fish, and the portions are large.

Regent Terrace Hotel, 6 Regent Terrace (tel. 556-3578), is of declared architectural interest, with its Greek Doric porch and cast-iron balcony. Built in 1819, it has distinguished neighbors: on one side is the American Consulate, on the other the Royal Norwegian and Greek Consulates. There's also an unmarred view of the Palace of Holyroodhouse, the Queen's official residence, Arthur's Seat, and the Salisbury Crags. This warm, yet formal stone building has housed many famous persons—the fugitive Dauphin of France, the uncle of Robert Louis Stevenson, David Masson, biographer of Milter and friend of Dickens, Thackeray, and Carlyle. All bedrooms have central heating, basins with hot and cold water, bed lights, and innerspring mattresses. On the ground floor is color TV in the lounge. The per-person rate, including breakfast, is £11 ($19.25) per night. The hotel often has groups, and personal callers are accepted on a space-available basis. The hotel is about a ten-minute walk from the Waverley Station and St. Andrew Square Bus Station, and just two bus stops from the east end of Princes Street.

The **Arden Hotel,** 17–20 Royal Terrace (tel. 556-8688), enjoys a view across the Firth of Forth to the coast of the Kingdom of Fife. It's an excellent example of Georgian architecture. Mr. and Mrs. Komorowski have transformed it into one of the finer small hotels of Edinburgh, charging from £11 ($19.25) to £15 ($26.25) per person, plus tax, for B&B. They have double- or twin-bedded rooms—many of them large enough to be used as triple-bedded quarters—and five singles. Of these, 31 now have private baths or showers and toilets; two others have showers (no toilets). Full central heating has been installed (along with modern fire escape facilities and an elevator). There is a comfortable cocktail bar and two residents' lounges.

If you wish, you can have a fine evening meal for £7 ($12.25) per person. Polish-born Mr. Komorowski is a naturalized British subject. He came to Britain with the remnants of the Polish army who survived the evacuation of Dunkirk. Mrs. Komorowski was born in Edinburgh, however. Their family assists them in running the hotel. The Arden is most central, within a few minutes' walk of Princes Street, and only 150 yards from a bus stop. The hotel faces a public park and has its own private gardens in the back.

Belmont Hotel, 10 Carlton Terrace (tel. 556-6146), is right in the midst of a row of classic town houses, dating from the 18th and 19th centuries. A 15-minute walk from the center of Edinburgh, with views of the parks and rooftops from most of the windows, it is two houses joined together by Mr. and Mrs. Stanley, who accept paying guests all year, charging them £10 ($17.50) per person in a double, £11 ($19.25) in a single in high season, plus VAT. The price includes breakfast. Your bed will be soft, the sheets freshly laundered, the furnishings comfortable. The dining room is as old-fashioned as the rest of the place, in typical Georgian style. The hotel was awarded a commendation prize by the Edinburgh New Town Conservation Committee for the extensive renovations to the dining room, restoring it to its natural Georgian decor.

Claymore Hotel, 6 Royal Terrace (tel. 556-2693), is owned and run by Andrew and Dorothea Johnston, who welcome guests to their house on one of the most beautiful terraces in Edinburgh. Their well-run B&B is a few minutes' walk from Princes Street, Waverley Station, the post office, and bus station. Comfortably decorated rooms do not contain private baths, but there are adequate baths and showers available in the corridors. Prices are only £10 ($17.50) per person, including a full Scottish breakfast. There is also a cocktail bar as well as a color TV lounge. Units contain radio and intercom as well as tea- and coffee-making facilities.

Near the Haymarket

The **Adam Hotel,** 19 Landsdown Crescent (tel. 337-1148), is pleasantly perched in a quiet crescent within a few minutes of Princes Street. Its Georgian style is intact, a gracious place for an Edinburgh stay. Mr. and Mrs. Morley own and manage it, and have provided many comforts. All the nine bedrooms have radios, innerspring mattresses, electric blankets, and plentiful hot water, and they are quite nicely decorated. Mrs. Morley cooks good breakfasts and will prepare an evening meal as well, if requested. She charges £5 ($8.75) for a table d'hôte dinner, and will also provide beverages early in the morning and before you retire. The rate is £10.50 ($18.38) per person for B&B.

Grosvenor Guest House, 1 Grosvenor Gardens (tel. 337-4143), is a handsomely kept, well-taken-care-of Edwardian town house that is suitable for those who like to be within walking distance of most of the attractions in the heart of Edinburgh, including Princes Street. Despite its heartbeat location, the house is in a tranquil area. Only seven rooms are rented by John Gray, and they are comfortably furnished and beautifully maintained, costing from £10.50 ($18.38) in a single and from £17 ($29.75) in a double. Only two of these chambers contain private plumbing, and these are likely to be grabbed up first. There is also a trio of family rooms where children sharing with their parents are granted a reduction. On cool nights (and there are a lot of them in Edinburgh) electric blankets are provided. A full Scottish breakfast served in the communal dining room is included in the rate, and guests can also relax and read in a large lounge.

West End Hotel, 35 Palmerston Pl. (tel. 225-3656), is so Scottish you may feel you are in the Highlands. Gaelic is often spoken and sung by the clientele, and the music of the pipes, fiddles, and accordions is played in the traditional manner. Every Wednesday evening, the renowned Eagle Pipers meet for solo piping recitals. The hotel is privately owned and offers a relaxed, friendly atmosphere. The bedrooms are comfortably furnished, and all have hot and cold running water, electric heaters and kettles, radios, and TVs. The B&B rate is £12 ($21) inclusive, and lunches and dinners are available.

Thistle Hotel, 59 Manor Pl. (tel. 225-6144), was a fairly large town house when it was built in the last century, and its architectural stature prevails until this day. Now a hotel, it offers large rooms, with their original fireplaces, modern beds, and wall-to-wall carpeting. The rate for B&B is £10 ($17.50) per person nightly, including VAT. All ten bedrooms have hot and cold running water, as well as heaters. Breakfast is served on the ground floor. A cocktail lounge and dining room are on the premises. A bar lunch goes for around £1.50 ($2.63), and there's a choice of about six main hot dishes. Manor Place is about a five-minute walk from the West End.

Clifton Private Hotel, 1 Clifton Terrace (tel. 337-1002), lies near Haymarket Station, just opposite the Hearts Memorial on Clifton Terrace, a westward extension of Princes Street. But it isn't proximity to major sights that makes this such a top-notch hotel. It's the friendliness and home-cooking you'll be treated to here. The proprietors, Mr. and Mrs. Aitchison, accept B&B guests for around £9 ($15.75) nightly, plus VAT. All rooms have hot and cold running water, and there are free baths or showers, plus plenty of towels daily. A vending machine is available for hot drinks. Biscuits are also on sale. In addition, there is an inexpensive evening meal at 5:30 p.m., a high tea for £3 ($5.25), plus VAT; that means a main meat course, followed by home baking—

fruit-pie goodie and Scottish scones. You'll see how clean Scottish homes can be, if you stay here.

On the Main A7 Route South

Newington Road/Mayfield Gardens/Minto Street form the continuation of the North Bridge from Princes Street, being the main A7 route to the south. If you find yourself on Dalkeith Road, running parallel to Minto Street, this is a secondary road, forming the A68 route to the south.

Suffolk Hall Hotel, 10 Creigmillar Park (tel. 667-4810), is an impressive yellow-brick Victorian mansion standing on a corner with a rear and quiet garden. The owners, George and Mary Robertson, take a sincere interest in the comfort of their guests. They've decorated the entire house so it will be convenient. There is a cocktail lounge as well as a living room lounge with color TV. In the dining room you can have breakfast, lunch, or dinner. All bedrooms have a radio, intercom, baby-listening device, central heating, and a few have private bath. Rates here include VAT, the service charge, and a complete breakfast. Bathless singles are £15 ($26.25); bathless doubles, £22 ($38.50). Twins with bath or shower go for £30 ($52.50) nightly. The three-bedded family room costs £34 ($59.50).

Kirtle House, 8 Minto St. (tel. 667-2813), is run by Mr. and Mrs. McGlashan, a friendly and pleasant couple, who welcome you to their address a short bus ride from Princes Street. The rooms are comfortable, have adequate heat, a shower, and are very clean. B&B costs £8.50 ($14.88) per day, per person, including VAT. The McGlashans will even have your breakfast (which is abundantly satisfying) served in your room if you have an early trip to make. There is a lounge with television where tea and cookies are served in the evening on request.

Craigewan Guest House, 48 Minto St. (tel. 667-2615), is an attractive Georgian house, ten minutes from Princes Street. It is owned and run by Mrs. Jaye Levey, who charges £8 ($14) per person nightly for B&B. Winter charges are £1 ($1.75) less per person. Several rooms have private showers, costing £1 ($1.75) more, and one unit has a private toilet en suite. There are color TVs in all rooms, and the price includes a large Scottish breakfast and VAT.

Golf View Hotel, 2 Marchhall Rd. (tel. 667-4812), lies along Dalkeith Road, first left, just past the Commonwealth swimming pool and the University Halls of Residence at Marchhall Place. There Joseph and Margaret d'Ambrosio run a spotlessly kept, comfortable guest house. Most of their bedrooms have private baths or showers, and some have views over the golf course. The accommodations are well furnished, and there is a lounge with TV for a peaceful evening. Their breakfast is large and well cooked. They also provide a door key so that you can come and go at will. They offer singles, twins, and doubles, and all their twins have both a double bed and a single bed, making them ideal as family rooms. The charge is £8 ($14) per person nightly, including breakfast. There is no service charge. The hotel has a residents' lounge for the sale of alcoholic drinks.

Sonas Guest House, 3 East Mayfield (tel. 667-2781), lies one mile from Princes Street, set back from a main road so there is no traffic noise. Several buses take you to the heart of town. The guest house, run by Mr. and Mrs. D. R. Robins, was built in 1876 for the directors of the railway, so it has a lot of character. It has recently been redecorated, and full central heating has been installed along with shower facilities. All units have hot and cold running water and tea- or coffee-making facilities. A full Scottish breakfast is included in the rates, which are £8.50 ($14.88) per person in high season, dropping to £7.50 ($13.13) in low season.

South of Union Canal

Tors Hotel, 55 Leamington Terrace (tel. 229-2630), is a hotel which has great Victorian character, as does its adjoining buildings. There are 15 bedrooms—singles, twins, doubles, and family rooms. Each chamber has hot and cold water and electric or gas heat. Included in the daily fees is use of the showers. The charge in a single is £8 ($14), and £15 ($26.25) in a double, including a large breakfast. There's a TV lounge for guests, and the hotel's only a few minutes from the Meadows, perhaps a ten-minute walk from Princes Street. Alex Drummond is your helpful host.

Orwell Lodge Hotel, 29 Polwarth Terrace (tel. 229-1044), is an elegant converted Victorian house standing in its own grounds and providing ample parking space. It is serviced by regular public transport with bus stops to and from the city at the entrance to the grounds. It is also conveniently situated for visits to places of historical interest in the city and is within easy reach of theaters, cinemas, sports grounds, and golf courses. The hotel is centrally heated and presents a choice of single, double, and twin-bedded rooms. Each unit has its own tea- and coffee-making facilities and is fitted with intercom, radio, and color TV. Showers are installed in twin and double rooms. Under the personal supervision of Moira Glendinning, the hotel provides a friendly family atmosphere, good traditional Scottish home cooking, and a well-trained and attentive staff. The charge of £11 ($19.25) per person per night includes a full Scottish breakfast. All other meals and snacks (morning coffee, lunch, afternoon tea, high tea, dinner, and packed meals) are available at reasonable prices. The hotel offers a small but select wine list. Service and VAT are included in the prices quoted.

Kingsview Guest House, 28 Gilmore Pl. (tel. 229-8004), run by Marion Gibson, is a fine choice, and some of her units are suitable for families. A quick bus ride takes you into the heart of Edinburgh. The price for a double room is £16 ($28), including a good breakfast (often with hot oatcakes). In addition, afternoon tea is offered, including home-baked scones and cakes as well as shortbread. Marion Gibson also prepares an evening meal, including, for example, scotch broth, haggis, tatties, and neeps, and a sweet sherry trifle.

Newington

The following guest house recommendations lie within the central belt of Edinburgh, and most of them are only 1½ miles from Princes Street. Newington is by far the most densely populated hotel and guest house area in the city, originally having been built as large detached residences some 140 years ago.

Ashdene Guest House, 23 Fountainhall Rd. (tel. 667-6026), is a Victorian house on three floors, in a quiet place, ten minutes by bus from the city center. All rooms are furnished to a high standard and have hot and cold running water, central heating, and electric fires too. Free tea- and coffee-making facilities are provided in each room, along with electric shaver points. Ironing facilities are also available. Guests can use the showers at any time. The price, including a substantial Scottish breakfast, starts at £8 ($14) per person nightly (reductions for family rooms), and dinner can be arranged for guests making advance bookings. Mr. and Mrs. Daulby take pleasure in welcoming their visitors and will help plan trips to other parts of Scotland for anyone requesting assistance. Help with accommodations in other parts of Scotland can also be arranged.

Newington Guest House, 18 Mayfield Rd. (tel. 667-3356), takes you into the world of Mr. and Mrs. Bouchet. It's one of the special little B&B guest house establishments of Edinburgh, and deserves to be better known. Jeanne Bouchet, whose husband is French, has traveled far and wide, and their house reflects their interest. From Japan and the South Pacific, they returned with souvenirs and mementos of their journey. The house is warmed by their collection. Each of their eight bedrooms is attractively decorated, often using cane and wickerwork, along with flowery wallpaper and fabrics. Some rooms are big enough for families to rent. Rates are £11 ($19.25) in a single and from £20 ($35) in a double, including a generous Scottish breakfast (and that means porridge).

International Guest House, 37 Mayfield Gardens (tel. 667-2511), in the Newington sector, is a Victorian guest house that is a "secret address" to many Scots themselves who live in those drafty manor houses and occasionally come into the capital for a visit. Canadian-born Norton Wyse and his wife Joyce have converted the town house into one of the most recommendable guest houses in the city. Their living room, for example, is very much like that in a private home. You're invited to lounge and read there, or socialize with your fellow guests. Only seven bedrooms are offered, two with private bath, and each is comfortably and attractively furnished. Mr. and Mrs. Wyse charge from £10.25 ($17.94) in a single and from £20 ($35) in a double, including a full Scottish breakfast. Tea or coffee along with crackers are provided before you retire. Your hosts are most gracious and very concerned with the welfare of their guests.

Thrums Private Hotel, 14 Minto St., Newington (tel. 667-5545), takes the fictional name of J. M. Barrie's designation of his hometown of Kirriemuir. Mrs. Doig, the pleasant, hospitable landlady, comes from Kirriemuir, so it makes a fit designation for her little hotel which is more like a guest house. She runs an exceptionally friendly establishment, where the comfort of a guest is most important to her. She rents out only seven bedrooms, and only one of those has a private bath. Her overnight charges are £10 ($17.50) in a single and from £16 ($28) in a double. The house has many amenities, including a beautifully maintained little garden out front and a pleasant lounge. She uses good, fresh produce in the large Scottish breakfasts she prepares and includes in the room price.

Murrayfield

Ross Private Hotel, 2 Murrayfield Ave. (tel. 337-4060), in the West End residential section, is a large Victorian house with bay windows, gables, and chimneys, the domain of the cheerful and friendly owner, Jean Tulloch. Informality prevails here. Each of her nicely furnished bedrooms has hot and cold water, and there's a bathroom on each floor. All is centrally heated, and there are tea- and coffee-making facilities in each unit. Including breakfast, the daily rate ranges from £7 ($12.25) to £8 ($14) per person. Mrs. Tulloch's guests like to congregate in the television lounge nightly, although during the day they enjoy the open view south to the Pentland Hills. Car parking is available in front of the hotel.

North of Holyrood Park

Alexander Hotel, 21 Spring Gardens (tel. 661-1157), is a good bet for a family. The location is outside the center of Edinburgh, but still convenient to public transportation. The B&B house lies north of Holyrood Park, with its famous Arthur's Seat. Mr. and Mrs. Spence (or if you get to know them better, George and Terry), have children of their own and don't object to housing others in their similar circumstance. They have only seven bedrooms, which are immaculately kept and comfortable, costing from £9 ($15.75) in a single and from £15 ($26.25) in a double. Their Scottish breakfast is hearty fare which will fortify you for the day, and at night, before you go to bed, tea and crackers (they call them "biscuits") are served.

Near Prestonfield

Dorstan Private Hotel, 7 Priestfield Rd. (tel. 667-6721), is a good hotel that should appeal to families. The location is near the famous old Prestonfield House where nonresidents are invited to drop in for dinner, and the Prestonfield Golf Course. Away from the rush of traffic, Dorstan is ideal for those who want the peace and solitude found away from the center of town. In fact, it's quite near one of the largest open-air green spaces in Edinburgh, Holyrood Park, containing Arthur's Seat. Mr. and Mrs. Bradford welcome you here, housing you in one of their pleasantly and comfortably furnished rooms, for which they charge £11 ($19.25) in a single and from £20 ($35) in a double. They will provide babysitting if you want to go out for a night on the town. Children under 12 who share a room with their parents are charged from £5 ($8.75) a night. A simple evening dinner will be provided around 6 p.m. at the cost of another £5 ($8.75) per person.

Joppa

Stra'ven Guest House, 3 Brunstane Rd. North, Joppa (tel. 669-5580), belongs to a charming and able couple, Mr. and Mrs. Grant. They pride themselves on their Scottish hospitality and enjoy receiving guests in their attractive, stone home, now a century old. Their guest house lies only 15 minutes by bus from the center of the city (nos. 15, 26, and 49). If you catch the 86 bus on Princes Street, it will take you to Joppa Road, which connects with the block-long Brunstane Road, a cul-de-sac leading to the water. In season, the B&B rate is £7 ($12.25) per person based on double occupancy, £8 ($14) in a single. The Grants are proud of the view from their windows: the neighboring stone-gabled houses, the cut-flower garden against a stone wall—and best of all, the nearby beach. They have been known to go on picnics with their guests or to take them for 18 holes of golf. But they can't stay away too long, as they do their own cooking, preparing those tasty dishes for which Scotland is so well known. Meals are not skimpy here, and second helpings are quickly provided.

Seaview Guest House, 17 Seaview Terrace (tel. 669-8146), is run by Mary Hogan, who was once the head caterer to the High Court in Edinburgh. The meals she serves here in a dining room overlooking the Firth of Forth indicate her experienced culinary background. A congenial host, generous and flexible with her meals, she accepts B&B guests at a cost of from £8 ($14) nightly. A small guest house, Seaview has been redecorated, and its rooms are spacious and well appointed, the housekeeping spotless. The location is in a quiet residential area, yet it is convenient to the city center by public transportation. Miss Hogan is filled with a wealth of information about Edinburgh, and on occasions she may be able to pull a few strings and get certain guests in to watch the High Court in action.

Stay at the "Y"

The Edinburgh branch of the **Y.W.C.A.** of Great Britain, 7 Randolph Pl. (tel. 225-4379), provides self-catering accommodation for short- or long-term stays in several residences in the city. Charges for single, double, or dormitory rooms range from £16 ($28) to £21 ($36.75) per week. Inquiries can be made to the reception desk from 9 a.m. to 8 p.m. daily.

READERS' GUEST HOUSE SELECTIONS (NEWINGTON AREA): "A real find was **Cree Guest House,** 77 Mayfield Rd. (tel. 667-3177). All rooms are spotless. The breakfast is enormous and plenty of hot water is provided at no extra charge. All this costs from £8.50 ($14.88) per person per night. Mr. and Mrs. Walker are most helpful. Also, the bus stop to Princes Street is right across the street. The location is less than two miles from the city center" (Kitty Maher, Arlington, Va.). . . . The **Gifford Guest House,** 103 Dalkeith Rd. (tel. 667-4688)—the first stop after Pollack Halls of Edinburgh University. The bus to take is 33 or 21 from the stop on Princes Street, opposite the railway station. The rates per person are from £7 ($12.25) per night for B&B. The rooms are centrally heated, and each unit has a TV and tea-maker. Mrs. McBride is the owner, and the accommodations and meals are superb" (Dorothy and Ted Toporeck, Santa Barbara, Calif.). . . . "Of the many guest houses, I was lucky enough to find one suiting my taste, individual comfort, and, most of all, budget—the **Rosedene Guest House,** 4 Queen's Crescent (tel. 667-5806), owned by Mr. and Mrs. Gallo. For £7.50 ($13.13) per night, you get a beautifully decorated and clean room with the peacefulness and solitude you need after a rough day of sightseeing and shopping. This also includes breakfast, in a dining area, which consists of grapefruit juice, cereal, bacon and eggs, toast, tea/coffee, and the pleasantness of the person serving you. The house is just a few minutes from the center of town, and can be reached by bus, either no. 31 or 3 on Princes Street or no. 7, 8, or 37 on North Bridge" (Miss Louise Fionda, Roseville, Mich.).

"At **42 Mayfield Rd.** (tel. 667-3117) there is a pretty, quaint house covered with roses, the property of Mrs. Morris. She is a fine, pleasant woman who keeps her guest house immaculate. Not only are the rooms clean, but they are large and nicely decorated. The bath is on the same floor. I woke up to a fantastic breakfast and a warm, friendly smile, and I found it very easy to strike up conversation with Mrs. Morris. In the evening I asked her for a place where I could have tea, and before I knew it there were tea and biscuits waiting for me downstairs. All this costs £8 ($14), and it's truly worth it. Mrs. Morris was a memorable part of my trip." (Pamela Laskin, New York, N.Y.). . . . "We enjoyed a comfortable room and breakfast for £7 ($12.25) each per night at **Rimswell House,** 33–35 Mayfield Gardens (tel. 667-5851). Mr. Downing is a courteous host and very helpful. Breakfast was the three-course meal we found most places, but the tea and coffee were abundant. Fresh bread was served, as well as toast. Meals are served in the dining room" (Mr. and Mrs. L. E. Brown, Olympia, Wash.).

"Clarin Guest House, 4 East Mayfield (tel. 667-2433), is an impeccably clean place a short bus ride from Princes Street on four bus lines. Mrs. R. M. Stephens and her mother made us most welcome. My wife had left her overcoat at a previous place, and Mrs. Stephens's mother, without further ado, lent one of her coats for three days. Also, our laundry was washed and brought back to the room for 50p (88¢). A bed and a plentiful breakfast is £14 ($24.50) for a large double room with tea- and coffee-making facilities and hot and cold running water" (Henry A. Leigh, Cullowhee, N.C.). . . . "I had a large, very clean room with a duvet on the comfortable bed on the second floor of the **Rowan Guest House,** 13 Glenorchy Terrace (tel. 668-2191). This Georgian house is in a residential area, a few minutes' walk from an excellent bus service about a mile from Princes Street. It is just off the main route into the city from the south, and the Olympic pool is close by. There are both central heating (which runs 24 hours when needed) and metered heaters. The resident proprietor, Ian Turnbull, is also a certified chef, serving full breakfasts. Dinner is also available if requested. B&B and dinner cost from £12 ($21), including VAT. The breakfast room–TV lounge is tastefully furnished, a comfortable place for guests to gather in the evening" (Helen H. Webster, Ottawa, Ont., Canada).

READERS' GUEST HOUSE SELECTIONS (SOUTH OF UNION CANAL): "The **Granville Guest House,** 13 Granville Terrace (tel. 229-1676). In 11 months of traveling, I found no place I enjoyed more at any price. Mrs. Archibald, the charming and friendly proprietor, serves huge breakfasts in an immaculately clean and comfortable family-like setting. The bedrooms also are immaculate and comfortable, costing £8.50 ($14.88) per person per night. The guest house is on bus lines 9, 10, and 27, about five minutes from Princes Street and within easy walking distance of the King's Theatre" (Richard Wheeler, Story City, Iowa). . . . "**Robertson Guest House,** 5 Hartington Gardens (tel. 229-3862), is run as a nice-type operation by Thomas R. Sewall. His rooms are quiet; there's good bus service, and excellent breakfast menus. At this homey and wholesome place the charge is £8 ($14) per person for B&B" (John G. Sindorf, Palmer, Alaska).

"I enthusiastically recommend the **Lindsay Guest House,** 108 Polwarth Terrace (tel. 337-1580). I shared a spacious twin-bedded room with television for from £8 ($14) per person per night including a bountiful and tasty breakfast made to order from a menu offering several choices. There is a bathroom on each floor (one with tub, one with shower, one with tub and stall shower). The house is on a street served by three bus routes to the Princes Street area, a 10- to 15-minute ride away. The proprietor, Mrs. Lindsay, was helpful and generous and provided her guests with atmosphere and extras" (Miss Ronnie Maibaum, Far Rockaway, N.Y.).

READERS' GUEST HOUSE SELECTIONS (NEAR HAYMARKET): "We found a home away from home at the **Lairg Private Hotel,** 11 Coates Gardens (tel. 337-1050), with spotless quiet rooms, each with a radio, for £9 ($15.75) per person in a double room. Each unit has a shower. Breakfast was truly wonderful. Our host, Umberto Salucci, was ready, willing, and able to provide dinner on request. He is a three-year graduate of a school for chefs in Italy and presently chef at one of Edinburgh's excellent hotels. Fine food was served in a friendly, homey atmosphere" (L. V. W. Hammond, Portland, Ore.). . . . "**St. Valery Guest House,** 36 Coates Gardens (tel. 337-1893), charges £8 ($14) per person. Mr. and Mrs. Shannon are gracious and keep a lovely, quiet home, which has two flights of rooms, maybe ten in all. Breakfast is fantastic: juice or cereal, eggs, ham, sausage, three kinds of breads, marmalade, and plenty of tea or coffee. Everything is served by the hostess in a charming, cozy, front breakfast room. Our room was amply furnished, spotless, quiet, and even had a sink with hot and cold water. Do we sound enthusiastic? Definitely!" (Linda Brughelli Bolton, Davis, Calif.). . . . "We were delighted with the B&B accommodations we found with **Mrs. Margaret B. Bostock,** 12 Clifton Terrace (tel. 337-5785). For £8 ($14) per person per night you can rent a charming room in a 19th-century house. Decorated with a green-and-ivory Adam ceiling and coordinated wallpaper, our room contained lovely old mahogany furniture consisting of a large armoire, dressing table, and comfortable twin beds, along with two whimsical wicker chairs and a coffee table in front of a marble fireplace. The linens are pretty, complete with matching down comforters. Mrs. Bostock serves a complete breakfast and provides a cup of tea and a delightful assortment of cakes and cookies whenever you come in from your touring activities, always using lovely china. The convenient location of Mrs. Bostock's is across the street from the old Haymarket Station, on the bus line and a five-minute walk west to Princes Street" (Anne McKay, Macon, Ga.).

WHERE TO DINE: The Scots are hearty eaters, and you'll like the sizes of their portions as well as the quality of their fare, with choices from river, sea, and loch. You can dine on a cock-a-leekie soup, fresh Tay salmon, haggis, neeps, tatties, and whisky, Aberdeen Angus filet steak, potted hough, poacher's soup, and good old stovies and rumbledethumps. If none of the above tempts you, you'll find that the French cuisine has made an inroad as well.

The Gazebo, Caledonian Hotel, Princes Street and Lothian Road (tel. 225-2433), is housed in Edinburgh's finest hotel. The Gazebo offers a three-course luncheon and dinner from £7 ($12.25), including traditional Scottish dishes such as Auld Reekie and haggis, neeps, and champit tatties. I've also enjoyed such dishes as filet of sole in a white wine sauce and prime sirloin steak. It is also open for breakfast. Lunch is served from noon and dinner from 6:30 p.m.

Casa Espanola, 61–65 Rose St. (tel. 225-5979), is a Spanish restaurant, the best of its type in Edinburgh. Its owner, Mr. Pascual, specializes in paella, a savory offering, costing £11 ($19.25) for two persons. Or perhaps you'd have the fish stew, zarzuela, going for £9.50 ($16.63) for two persons. The gazpacho is very tasty and strongly flavored, £1.20 ($2.10). A shrimp cocktail with garlic at £2.25 ($3.94) is another appetizing opener. The best bargain is a three-course luncheon offered for £4.50 ($7.88). Matador capes, bullfight posters, and wine bottles enliven the decor. Lunch is served until 2 p.m., and dinner is from 7 to 11 p.m. Closed Sunday.

Denzler's, 80 Queen St. (tel. 226-5467), offers appetizing Swiss dishes, skillfully prepared, using high-quality ingredients. Portions are generous, and service is efficient, although informal, the waiters contributing to the relaxed atmosphere. Air-dried Swiss ham with melon is a most enticing opener. For a main course, choose from slices of venison in a piquant sauce, or else the pièce de résistance, fondue bourguignonne for two persons. For dessert, I'd endorse the apfelstrudel. Dinner is served nightly, except Sunday, from 6:30 to 10:30 p.m. At lunch, offered from noon to 2 p.m., the average charge is £7 ($12.25) per person, inclusive, and dinner goes for around £12 ($21).

Cosmo Ristorante, 58A North Castle St. (tel. 226-6743), is one of the most heavily patronized Italian restaurants in the Scottish capital. Courtesy, efficiency, and good cookery are featured here. Cosmo Tamburro is your host. In season you can ask for mussels as an appetizer, costing £2.25 ($3.94). Pastas and soups are always homemade. If you order pasta as a main course, it's served in a double portion, and you're charged accordingly. I've found the veal dishes the best cooked, and good value at that, although you may be attracted to the fritto misto (fried seafood). The cassata siciliana is well made. Main courses range in price from £5.50 ($9.63) to £8 ($14). The restaurant serves lunch until 2:15 p.m. and dinner until 10:30 p.m. It's closed for Saturday lunch, as well as on Sunday and Monday.

Madogs, 38a George St. (tel. 225-3408), provides a flair to the Scottish capital with its American and Mexican cuisine. With its menu and movie posters, it suggests someplace in California. It offers an excellent selection of American canned beers, exotic cocktails, or if preferred, pitchers of draft beer, sangría, and Margaritas, plus a good selection of French and American wines. Sopa de frijoles negros (hot black bean soup) is served with sherry and sour cream. The hot and cold sandwiches at lunchtime prove to be very popular. Chili is another favorite. Eggs Benedict and eggs ranchero are also served. The dinner menu has a continental and Mexican range: teriyaki steak, tequila pepper steak, duck with mole sauce, paella, tostados, and enchiladas. The split-level restaurant is graced with hanging baskets and potted plants. The waitresses at lunchtime and the waiters in the evening prove to be efficient. Expect to spend from £7 ($12.25). Lunch is until 3 p.m., and dinner is from 6 p.m. to midnight, from 6 to 11 p.m. on Sunday. The bar and restaurant are both licensed until 1 a.m. Madogs is closed on Sunday.

Circles Coffee House, 324 Lawnmarket (tel. 225-9505), lies along the Royal Mile, near Deacon Brodie's Tavern. A stone structure, it makes a good luncheon stopover if you're sightseeing in the area. The atmosphere suggests a coffeehouse, and at the self-service counter you make your selection of freshly made quiches, costing from £1.20 ($2.10), and dollops of salads at 60p ($1.05) per portion. I'd also suggest the pâté with freshly baked bread at £1.20 ($2.10). Hours are from 9:30 a.m. (drop in for coffee) until 5 p.m. seven days a week. However, during the festival it remains open until 9 p.m.

Luckpenny Salad Restaurant, 30 Grassmarket (tel. 225-1752). Pamela Fowler, the owner, welcomes you to her very well-run little restaurant which specializes in homebaking and freshly made salads using crisp ingredients. University students, musicians, and actors, all on limited budgets, are attracted to her precincts, enjoying rich, nutritious soups at 60p ($1.05) a serving. Vol-au-vents, stuffed with everything from seafood to poultry, are featured occasionally, costing from £2.25 ($3.94). The quiches are good too, going for £1.25 ($2.19). For dessert, I'd suggest you finish with a homemade cheesecake at £1 ($1.75). The restaurant is open from 9 a.m. (you can drop in for breakfast) until 6 p.m. (later during the festival). It is closed on Sunday.

Henderson's Salad Table, 94 Hanover St. (tel. 225-3400), is a Shangri-La for health-food faddists, as well as those who want an array of rich, nutritious salads—some of the most imaginative and original I've known. It's self-service, and you can pick and choose at 55p (96¢) per mammoth dollop. The ingredients are combined ingeniously—eggs, carrots, grapes, nuts, yogurt, cheese, potatoes, cabbage, watercress, you name it. A Scottish chef reigns in the kitchen. Reflecting his background, a variety of hot Scottish dishes are served on request. You can have a number of hot plates, such as peppers stuffed with rice and pimiento at prices ranging from 80p ($1.40) for a small portion to £1.60 ($2.80) for a large serving. The soups are well prepared, costing 50p (88¢).

Desserts are homemade, so rich and pure you'll strain trying to choose between them. Settle for a fresh fruit salad or a cake with double whipped cream and chocolate sauce. Average price is 80p ($1.40). Henderson's is open regularly from 8 a.m. to 10:45 p.m. The scene takes place in a semi-basement, and the furnishings are appropriate: pinewood tables (often shared) and crude box-stools. The Vegetarian Society raises a provocative question: "Have you ever thought that killing for food is not necessary?" At Henderson's it certainly isn't. The Sherry Bar serves "tapas." The wine cellar provides a choice of 50 wines, some 20 of which may be had by the glass. Live classical music is played most evenings. The bar may be reached by the same entrance as the Salad Table.

The restaurant is near the Tourist Information Centre, one long block from Princes Street. From The High, near St. Giles, you can walk down the seemingly endless steps leading in the direction of Princes Street.

Cleikum (tel. 556-2414) is under the North British Hotel on Princes Street, with a separate entrance down into the restaurant. It serves good food at low prices and specializes in typically Scottish fare. Hours are noon to 2:30 p.m. and 6 to 10:30 p.m. Monday to Saturday, and from noon to 2 p.m. and 6 to 9 p.m. on Sunday. At lunch there is a carvery and buffet, with fresh roast joints of meat and a chef's special, along with cold meats and salads, priced at only £5.25 ($9.19), including an appetizer and dessert. In the evening you can eat here from around £6.50 ($11.38) per person, ordering, say, a soup, followed by a main course, then a dessert and coffee. Two local specialties are "haggis and neeps" and "mince and tatties."

Café Cappuccino, 15 Salisbury Pl. (tel. 667-4265), offers, besides an aromatic cup of cappuccino, an à la carte menu of fish, grills, omelets, salads, and desserts, along with fancy ice-cream dishes. A filling meal would cost around £4 ($7). However, a more selective choice, such as a cheese omelet with a side order of grilled tomatoes, would cost only £1.80 ($3.15). The café is open daily except Sunday from 9 a.m. to 8:30 p.m.

Mr. Boni's Ice Cream Parlour, 4 Lochrin Buildings (tel. 229-5319), is well known as the maker of homemade ice cream in Edinburgh, but you can get more than that delectable dessert at this establishment. They have a good range of sandwiches, including a tasty sardine and tomato, costing £1.50 ($2.63). Jumbo hot dogs are also served, beginning at £1.95 ($3.41) if fries are included. Various versions of banana splits are featured, along with double-thick shakes and frappes. However, a double scoop of any flavor of your choice costs only 75p ($1.31). The choice is vast: you're faced with everything from heather honey lemon to black currant and bilberry. Hours are Monday, Tuesday, and Wednesday from 10:30 a.m. to 10:30 p.m., Thursday to 11:30 p.m., Friday and Saturday to midnight, and Sunday from 12:30 a.m. to 9:30 p.m. There's actually a Mr. Boni, incidentally.

Bar Italia, 100 Lothian Rd. (tel. 288-6379), stresses in its oversize menu that culture stems as much from the stomach as from the brain. If that's so, then the owners of this Italian restaurant could be included among the most civilized people in Edinburgh, as the variety and scope of their menu show. A filling bowl of pasta in a mushroom-and-cream sauce, along with a green salad, goes for £3.65 ($6.39). You might be tempted to try one of Bar Italia's imaginative pizzas, such as the Napletana (black olives, anchovies, mozzarella, tomatoes, and herbs), costing £2.30 ($4.03). If your appetite justifies a more elaborate meal, the restaurant offers a repertoire of meat and chicken main courses. A three-course regalia of prosciutto and melon as an appetizer, followed by veal scallopini with mushrooms in a cream sauce, then a dessert of pear Melba and coffee, will cost £9.90 ($17.25). Hours are from 11 a.m. to 3 a.m. daily.

Bar Roma, 39A Queensferry St. (tel. 226-2977), offers the same menu as its sister restaurant, Bar Italia, in a different section of Edinburgh (see above). More spacious than Bar Italia, it offers the same menu and culinary philosophy of its sister. Hours are from 11 a.m. to 2:30 a.m. daily.

The Pancake Place, 130 High St. (Royal Mile) (tel. 229-2658). Pancakes need not always be sweet, nor always eaten with breakfast either. Franchises of this restaurant have recently sprouted up like thistles throughout Scotland. The menu features pancakes, of course, in all their varieties. Both lunch and dinner pancakes come with a wide scope of fish, chicken, or meat fillings. Try a Rocky Mountain burger—two pancakes layered with two beefburgers and topped with a tangy cheese sauce. This, along with an appetizer of homemade soup and dessert (what else but pancakes again?), would come to £3.65 ($6.39). Hours vary slightly, but the place is generally open every day from 10 a.m. to 6 p.m. in winter and from 10 a.m. to 8 p.m., July to September.

Dining on the Outskirts

At least once you should get out into the countryside surrounding Edinburgh. One way to do this is to take bus 41 for about five miles from the West End to the little Scottish village of Cramond. Few visible traces remain today of its Roman occupation.

Quietly nestling on a sloping street is the **Cramond Inn,** on Cramond Glebe Road, which has been serving food and drinks to wayfarers for 300 years (it was known to Robert Louis Stevenson). Picture upholstered booths, opera-red carpeting, some beer-barrel upholstered chairs, a collection of local watercolors, a low ceiling, large foot-square old beams, dark oak and creamy-colored walls, recessed windows, a small stone fireplace—and you'll begin to get the feel of the inn. The manager is Sam Proudfoot, who took over this task from his father.

The restaurant can serve many diners, but you'd better call in advance (tel. 336-2035), as it's most popular. The prices are quite reasonable, considering the quality of food—some of the finest of Scottish dishes. The steak-and-kidney pie is a taste treat, costing £3.50 ($6.13), but I'm drawn to the haggis, the famed dish of Scotland, made with an assortment of chopped meats, oatmeal, and spices—going for £3.25 ($5.69) for an individual serving. For an appetizer, the

Scottish broth at £1 ($1.75) is a favorite, although the game soup for £1.50 ($2.63) is the gourmet's choice. A specialty of the house is roast duck for £5 ($8.75). Desserts average around £1 ($1.75). The inn serves lunch from noon to 2:30 p.m., dinner till 10:30 p.m. Cramond Inn is closed Sunday. Bar lunches are served in the lounge bar Monday to Saturday from noon to 2 p.m. The average price for these ranges from £2.50 ($4.38) to £3 ($5.25).

READER'S RESTAURANT SUGGESTION: "On an excursion to seek out Chinese food, we came across the fully licensed **Dragon's Castle Restaurant,** 21 Castle St. (tel. 225-7327). We tried Mr. Wan-Lie Lim's suggestion: his £3 ($5.25) Dragon Special. What the owner offers for this price beats any special we tried elsewhere in quality and quantity. In addition, he serves a three-course luncheon special for £2.40 ($4.20)" (F. E. Jaspers, Utrecht, Holland).

The Best of the Pubs

Deacon Brodie's Tavern, 435 Lawnmarket, is the neighborhood pub along the Royal Mile. It perpetuates the memory of Deacon Brodie, good citizen by day, robber by night. Mr. Brodie, it is believed, was the inspiration for Robert Louis Stevenson's *The Strange Case of Dr. Jekyll and Mr. Hyde.* Brodie ended up on the gallows on October 1, 1788. The tavern and wine cellars contain a cocktail and lounge bar decked out in Jacobean and tartan decor. It offers a traditional pub setting and lots of atmosphere, making it popular with visitors and locals alike. The tavern provides inexpensive snacks between 11 a.m. and 2:30 p.m. (every day except Sunday), with prices averaging around £1.50 ($2.63). Among the selection: cottage pie, Scotch eggs, cheese, and the ploughman's special.

Ma Scott's, 202 Rose St. (tel. 225-7401), is a corner pub with tufted settles placed back to back. It still has its Victorian water fountains on the bar. After a revamp, the pub, formerly known as Scott's, was named after its hearty empress who once commanded authority over the rugby players drawn to its precincts. Today, in a totally unpretentious atmosphere, right off Princes Street, you can enjoy good drink and bar snacks such as hamburgers at 70p ($1.23) and meat pies at £1.90 ($3.33).

The **Guildford Arms,** West Register Street (tel. 556-1053), dates back to the "mauve era" of the 1890s. This Victorian-Italianesque corner pub, still harboring its oldtime memories, has one of the most intriguing decors of any pub in Edinburgh—or Scotland for that matter. Next door to the world-famed Café Royal, it lies near the King James Hotel. It still has seven arched windows with etched glass, plus an ornate ceiling, as well as a central bar and around-the-wall seating. It's large, bustling, and at times can be a bit rough, but it's got plenty of character.

THE TOP SIGHTS: Before leaving the Scottish capital, you'll want to take a look at both the Old Town and the New Town. Both have their different attractions—the Old Town's largely medieval; the New Town, Georgian. We'll begin our exploration on the Royal Mile of the Old Town, a collective term for Canongate, Lawnmarket, and the High.

At one end on Castle Rock sits—

Edinburgh Castle

It is believed that the ancient city grew up on the seat of the dead volcano, Castle Rock. History is vague on possible settlements, although it is known that in the 11th century Malcolm III (Canmore), and his Saxon queen, Margaret, founded a castle on this spot. The good Margaret was later venerated as a saint. The only fragment left of their original castle, in fact the oldest structure in Edinburgh, was established by her. It is St. Margaret's Chapel, built in the Norman style, the present oblong structure dating principally from the 12th century. The five-ton Mons Meg, a 15th-century cannon, is situated in the French Prisons and on view to the public.

Inside the castle you can visit the State Apartments—particularly Queen Mary's Bedroom—where Mary Queen of Scots gave birth to James VI of Scotland (later James I of England). The Great Hall with its hammer-beam ceiling, was built by James IV. It displays armaments and armor, although Scottish Parliaments used to convene in this hall.

The highlight, however, is the Crown Chamber, which houses the Honours of Scotland, used at the coronation of James VI, along with the sceptre and the sword of state of Scotland. Unseen by the public for 15 years, the French Prisons have been reopened. Turned into a prison in the 18th century, these great storerooms housed hundreds of Napoleonic soldiers during the early 19th century. Many of them made wall carvings which you can see today. The castle may be visited weekdays from 9:30 a.m. to 5:05 p.m. (on Sunday from 12:30 to 4:20 p.m.) November through April. From May 1 to October 31, hours are 9:30 a.m. to 6 p.m. weekdays (11 a.m. to 6 p.m. on Sunday). The last admission tickets are sold 45 minutes before closing times. Admission November through April is 70p ($1.23) for adults, 35p (61¢) for children; May to October, it's £1.30 ($2.28) for adults, 65p ($1.14) for children.

Your ticket to the State Apartments also includes a visit to the **Scottish United Services Museum,** Crown Square, The Castle (tel. 226-6907). This is a national museum, dealing with the history of the navy, army, and air force at all periods. It is considered unique and comprehensive, the longest established collections of British armed forces historical material in the United Kingdom. The exhibitions alone are the largest single part of the areas in the castle open to the public (both sides of Crown Square).

In the case of the army, Scottish elements predominate, of course—that is, the Scottish regiments of the British army from 1660 to the present day of all arms, infantry, cavalry, artillery, whatever. Some 30,000 uniforms, associated accoutrements, and weapons are shown. The naval and air force sections concentrate on Scottish factors in the history of these services.

Along the Royal Mile

Ideally, if you have the time, walk from the castle down the hill the full length of the Royal Mile, all the way to the Palace of Holyroodhouse at the opposite end. Along the way, you'll see some of the most interesting old structures in Edinburgh, with their turrets, gables, and towering chimneys. Of all the buildings that may intrigue you, the most visited are **John Knox's House** and **St. Giles Cathedral.**

The cathedral is known as the High Kirk. Inside, one outstanding feature is its Thistle Chapel, designed by Sir Robert Lorimer and housing beautiful stalls and notable heraldic stained-glass windows. The chapel is open from 10 a.m. to 5 p.m. and may be visited for 20p (35¢). John Knox, the leader of the Reformation in Scotland, was minister of St. Giles from 1560 to 1572.

Lady Stair's House lies in a close of the same name off Lawnmarket. It was built in 1622 by a prominent merchant burgess. It takes its name from a former owner, Elizabeth, the Dowager-Countess of Stair. Today it is a treasure-house of portraits, relics, and manuscripts relating to three of Scotland's greatest men of letters—Robert Burns, Sir Walter Scott, and Robert Louis

Stevenson. It is open Monday to Saturday from 10 a.m. to 5 p.m. (until 6 p.m. from June to September).

Farther down the street at 45 High St. is **John Knox's House,** whose history goes back to the late 15th century. Even if you're not interested in the reformer who founded the Scottish Presbyterian church, you may want to visit his house, as it is characteristic of the "lands" that used to flank the Royal Mile. All of them are gone now, except Knox's house, with its timbered gallery. Inside, you'll see the tempera ceiling in the Oak Room, along with exhibitions of Knox memorabilia. The house may be visited daily (except Sunday) from 10 a.m. to 5 p.m. for 70p ($1.23) for adults, 50p (88¢) for children.

After leaving John Knox's House, continue along Canongate in the direction of the Palace of Holyroodhouse. At 163 Canongate stands one of the handsomest buildings along the Royal Mile. The **Canongate Tolbooth** was constructed in 1591 and was once the courthouse, prison, and center of municipal affairs for the burgh of Canongate. It contains the **Scottish Stone & Brass Rubbing Centre** which is open Monday to Saturday from 10 a.m. to 5 p.m. (from June to September until 6 p.m.). Telephone 225-1131 for information. You can visit the center's collection of replicas molded from ancient Pictish stones, rare Scottish brasses, and medieval church brasses. No experience is needed to make a rubbing. The center will show you how and supply materials. These rubbings make beautiful wall hangings and gifts. You can also purchase ready-made rubbings on the spot.

Across the street is **Huntly House,** an example of a restored 16th-century mansion. Now it is Edinburgh's principal museum of local history. You can stroll through period rooms and reconstructions Monday to Saturday from 10 a.m. to 5 p.m. (until 6 p.m. from June to September). During the festival it is also open on Sunday from 2 to 5 p.m.

READERS' SIGHTSEEING TIPS: "An unusual attraction is the **Museum of Childhood,** Hyndford's Close, 38 High St. (tel. 225-2424), on the Royal Mile, opposite John Knox's House. Three floors are devoted to many facets of childhood, ranging from antique toys and games to children's clothes, juvenile 'arsenals,' and many other items representing the childhood experience of different nationalities and periods" (Ralph M. Stein, Flushing, N.Y.). [*Author's Note:* The museum is open weekdays from 10 a.m. to 5 p.m. (to 6 p.m. from June through September), charging 40p (70¢) for adults, 10p (18¢) for children. During the festival, it is open on Sunday from 2 to 5 p.m.] . . . "I'd like to recommend the **Scottish Craft Centre,** 140 Canongate (tel. 556-8136), in the Acheson House on the Royal Mile. There's no pressure to buy anything—you can browse to your heart's content. The items displayed represent selected craftspeople producing high-quality work. Pieces can be purchased and assistance will be given to commission special items if required" (Hazel Blumberg, Utica, N.Y.).

The Palace of Holyroodhouse

At the eastern end of the Royal Mile, the palace was built adjacent to an Augustinian abbey established by David I in the 12th century. The nave, now in ruins, remains today. James IV founded the palace nearby in the early part of the 16th century, but of his palace only the north tower is left. Much of what you see today was ordered built by Charles II.

In the old wing occurred the most epic moments in the history of Holyroodhouse, when Mary Queen of Scots was in residence. Mary, who had been Queen of France and widowed while still a teenager, decided to return to her native Scotland. She eventually entered into an unsuccessful marriage with Lord Darnley but spent more time and settled affairs of state with her secretary, David Rizzio. Darnley plotted to kill the Italian, and he and his accomplices marched into Mary's supper room, grabbed Rizzio over her protests, then carried him to the Audience Chamber, where he was murdered by 56 stab wounds. A plaque marks the spot of his death on March 9, 1566.

Darnley was to live less than a year after, dying mysteriously in a gunpowder explosion. Mary, of course, was eventually executed on the order of her cousin, Elizabeth I. One of the most curious exhibits in Holyroodhouse is a piece of needlework by Mary, depicting a cat-and-mouse scene (Elizabeth's the cat!).

The State Apartments also contain some fine 18th-century Flemish tapestries, especially a whole series devoted to Diana, and a recently restored 17th-century state bed. In the Great Gallery are more than 100 portraits, depicting Scottish kings, including Macbeth, painted by a Dutchman, de Wet.

The palace suffered long periods of neglect, although it basked in glory at the ball in the mid-18th century thrown by Bonnie Prince Charlie. The present Queen and Prince Philip live at Holyroodhouse whenever they visit Edinburgh. When they're not in residence, you can visit the palace weekdays from 9:30 a.m. to 5:15 p.m. (Sunday from 11 a.m. to 4:30 p.m.) in high season. Winter hours are 9:30 a.m. to 3:45 p.m. weekdays (closed on Sunday). The admission is £1.20 ($2.10) for adults and 60p ($1.05) for children. When the Historical Apartments only are open, admission is 60p ($1.05) for adults and 30p (53¢) for children.

The New Town

At some point, the Old Town became too small. The burghers decided to build a whole new town across the valley, so the marsh was drained and eventually turned into public gardens. Princes Street is the most striking boulevard. Architecturally, the most interesting district of the New Town is the north side of Charlotte Square, designed by Robert Adam. It was young architect James Craig, who shaped much of the Georgian style of the New Town, with its crescents and squares.

At 7 Charlotte Square, a part of the northern facade, is the restored building known simply as the **Georgian House** (tel. 225-2160). It is a prime example of Scottish architecture and interior design in the zenith of the New Town. Originally the home of John Lamont XVII, known as "the last of the patriarchs and the first of the moderns," the house has recently been refurbished and reopened to the public by Scotland's National Trust. The furniture in this Robert Adam house is mainly Hepplewhite, Chippendale, and Sheraton, all dating from the 18th century. In a ground-floor bedroom is a sturdy old four-poster with an original 18th-century canopy. The dining room table is set for a dinner on fine Wedgwood china, and the kitchen is stocked with gleaming copper pots and pans. It is open April to October from 10 a.m. to 5 p.m. (on Sunday from 2 to 5 p.m.). In winter it is open from November 1 to mid-December on Saturday from 10 a.m. to 4:30 p.m. and on Sunday from 2 to 4:30 p.m. Last visitors are admitted 30 minutes before closing time. Admission (including audio-visual) is £1.20 ($2.10) for adults, 60p ($1.05) for children.

Note: As an Old Town complement to the New Town Georgian House, the National Trust has opened in a 1620 tenement in the Royal Mile, **Gladstone's Land,** an upstairs apartment of four rooms furnished as it might have been in the 17th century. On the ground floor, reconstructed shop booths display replicas of goods of the period. It is open April through October, Monday through Saturday, from 10 a.m. to 5 p.m. (on Sunday from 2 to 5 p.m.). Admission is 80p ($1.40) for adults, 40p (70¢) for children.

The Gothic-inspired **Scott Monument** lies in the **East Princes Street Gardens.** It is the most famous landmark of Edinburgh, completed in the mid-19th century. Sir Walter Scott's heroes are honored by small figures in the monument. You can climb the tower weekdays in summer from 9 a.m. to 6 p.m. for 40p (70¢). Off-season, you must scale the monument before 3 p.m. **West Princes Street Gardens** has the first ever **Floral Clock,** which was constructed in 1904.

Art Treasures

For the art lover, Edinburgh has a number of masterpieces, and many visitors come here just to look at the galleries. Of course, the principal museum is the **National Gallery of Scotland,** on The Mound, in the center of Princes Street Gardens. Although the gallery is small as national galleries go, the collection came about with great care and was expanded considerably by bequests, gifts, and loans. A short chronology of the collection's history and a display of catalogues is incorporated in *The Eye-Opener,* a lively introduction to the gallery, featuring an informative and entertaining slide-tape show. Watch out for the clever effects!

Recent major acquisitions include Giulio Romano's *Vièrge à la Legende.* Other Italian paintings are Verrocchio's *Ruskin Madonna,* Andrea del Sarto's *Portrait of a Man,* and Domenichino's *Adoration of the Shepherds.* However, the most acclaimed among them is Tiepolo's *Finding of Moses.*

A renowned feature of the gallery is the Duke of Sutherland loan of some 40 paintings which include two Raphaels, *Holy Family with a Palm Tree* and the *Bridgewater Madonna;* Titian's two Diana canvases, as well as his favorite subject, Venus, this time rising from the sea; and the *Seven Sacraments,* painted by the great 17th-century Frenchman Nicolas Poussin, for Fréart de Chantelou.

The Spanish masters are less well represented but shine forth in El Greco's *Saviour* and the mysterious *Fabula* (on loan), Velázquez's *Old Woman Cooking Eggs,* an early work by that great master, and *Immaculate Conception* by Zurbarán, his friend and contemporary.

The northern schools are impressively represented by fine but not numerous examples. An early Netherlandish masterpiece, historically linked to Edinburgh, is Hugo van der Goes's Trinity Altarpiece, loaned by the Queen. The Flemish school emerges notably in Rubens's *The Feast of Herod* and *The Reconciliation of Jacob and Esau.* The Dutch excel with Rembrandt's *Woman in Bed,* superb landscapes by Cuyp, Ruisdael, and Hobbema, and in one of the gallery's most recent acquisitions, *Interior of St. Bavo's Church, Haarlem,* by Pieter Saenredam, his largest and arguably finest painting, bought in 1982.

The most valuable gift to the gallery since its foundation, the Maitland Collection, includes Cézanne's *Mont St.-Victoire,* as well as works by Degas, Van Gogh, Renoir, Gauguin, and Seurat, among others. A rare early Monet, *Shipping Scene—Night Effects,* was bought in 1980. In the same year, for the first time in living memory, a stunning landscape, *Niagara Falls, from the American Side,* by the 19th-century American painter Frederic Church, went on show.

The greatest English painters are represented by excellent examples—Gainsborough's *The Hon. Mrs. Graham,* Constable's *Dedham Vale,* along with works by Turner, Reynolds, and Hogarth. Naturally, the work of Scottish painters decks the walls (in the new wing, opened in 1978), none finer than Henry Raeburn, at his best in the whimsical *The Rev. Robert Walker Skating on Duddingston Loch.*

The gallery is open from 10 a.m. to 5 p.m. weekdays (2 to 5 p.m. on Sunday). During the festival, hours are from 10 a.m. to 6 p.m. weekdays and from 11 a.m. to 6 p.m. on Sunday. Admission is free. This is one of the three National Galleries of Scotland.

It may be typical of Edinburgh that it houses the only museum collection in Britain solely of 20th-century art, the **Scottish National Gallery of Modern Art,** in the former John Watson's School. In the garden outside the gallery are major sculptures by Bourdelle, Epstein, Marini, Moore, Hepworth, Reg Butler, and William Turnbull, and a sundial by Ian Hamilton Finlay. The galleries contain works by Picasso, Matisse, Braque, Léger, Rouault, Derain, Miro, Magritte, Kirchner, Nolde, Kokoschka, Giacometti, Arp, Schwitters, Popova, and many others of the major creators of the 20th century, with a sound representation of English and, particularly, Scottish modern art. Hours are from 10 a.m. to 6 p.m. (or dusk if earlier) on weekdays, and 2 to 6 p.m. (or dusk if earlier; opening at 11 a.m. during the Edinburgh Festival) on Sunday.

Lauriston Castle

This fine country mansion standing in extensive grounds overlooking the Firth of Forth lies on the outskirts of Edinburgh about 3¼ miles northwest of Princes Street. If going by car, take the Queensferry Road (A90) as if heading for the Forth Road Bridge but turn off to the right at the Quality Street junction (look for directional signs pointing to Lauriston Castle). Then proceed down Cramond Road South until you come to the entrance on the right to the castle. If using public transport, take the Lothian Region bus no. 41 from the Mound, Hanover Street, or George Street.

The house is associated with John Law (1671–1729), the founder of the first bank in France, and its collections are strong in English Georgian and French Louis styles of furniture. The house gives one a good picture of the leisure lifestyle of the upper classes prior to World War I. Look for the Derbyshire Blue John ornaments and the Crossley wool "mosaics." The grounds are open from 9 a.m. to dusk, and each visitor to the castle is given a guided tour of about 40 minutes' duration from April to October (daily except Friday) at 11 a.m. and 1, 2, and 5 p.m. (the last tour begins at 4:20 p.m.). From November to March, tours are only on Saturday and Sunday at 1:20 and 3:20 p.m. Admission is 80p ($1.40) for adults and 40p (70¢) for children. For more information, telephone Edinburgh 336-2060.

THE FESTIVAL: The highlight of Edinburgh's year—some would say the only time when the real Edinburgh emerges—comes during the three weeks of the **Edinburgh International Festival,** from mid-August to early September. Since 1947 the festival has brought to Edinburgh artists and companies of the highest international standard in all fields of the arts, including music, opera, dance, theater, exhibition, poetry and prose, and "Auld Reekie" takes on a cosmopolitan air.

During the period of the festival, one of the most exciting spectacles is the **Military Tattoo** on the floodlit esplanade in front of Edinburgh Castle, high on its rock above the city. Vast audiences thrill to the delicate maneuvers of the famous Scottish regiments, the precision marching of military units from all parts of the world, and, of course, the stirring skirl of the bagpipes and the swirl of the kilt.

Less predictable in quality but infinitely greater in quantity is the **Edinburgh Festival Fringe,** an opportunity for anybody, whether an individual, a group of friends, or a whole company of performers, to put on their own show wherever they can find an empty stage or street corner. Late-night reviews, outrageous and irreverent contemporary drama, university theater presentations, maybe even a full-length opera—Edinburgh gives them all free rein. As if that were not enough, Edinburgh has a **Film Festival** at the same time.

Ticket prices vary from £1 ($1.75) up to about £15 ($26.25) a seat, but if you move fast enough, there are not many events which you cannot see for £2 ($3.50).

Information can be obtained at the following places: **Edinburgh Festival Society,** 21 Market St., Edinburgh EH1 1BW (tel. 226-4001); **Edinburgh Festival Fringe,** 170 High St., Edinburgh EH1 (tel. 226-5257); **Edinburgh Military Tattoo,** The Tattoo Office, 1 Cockburn St., Edinburgh EH1 1BR (tel. 225-1188); **Edinburgh Film Festival,** Department M, Edinburgh International Film Festival, The Filmhouse, 88 Lothian Rd., Edinburgh EH3 9BX (tel. 228-6382); and **Edinburgh Accommodation Bureau,** Tourist Accommodation Service, 9 Cockburn St., Edinburgh EH1 1BP.

TOURS: If you want a quick introduction to the principal attractions in and around the capital, then consider one or more of the tours offered by the **Lothian Region Transport,** whose offices are at 14 Queen St. You won't find a cheaper way to hit the highlights, and later you can go back on your own if you want a deeper experience. The luxury-type coaches leave from Waverley Bridge, near the Scott Monument. The tours start in April and run through late October. A curtailed winter program is also offered. A half-day coach tour (which takes about 4 hours) leaves daily at 9:30 a.m. and 1:30 p.m. (Sunday at 1:30 p.m. only), costing £6 ($10.50) and visiting the castle, the Palace of Holyroodhouse, and St. Giles Cathedral. Operating throughout the day are half a dozen smaller tours that show you some of the environs—such as Scott and Stevenson Country. These tours are priced from £2 ($3.50) to £3 ($5.25). For more information, telephone 226-4696. From June to September, day-and-a-half tours are offered to many parts of Scotland.

NIGHTLIFE: Unless you arrive in Edinburgh at festival time, the old city doesn't have a very advanced nightlife. Many Scots go to bed early. However, after touring during the day, you can still find some amusements.

Forrest Hill Bar, 25 Forrest Rd. (tel. 225-1156), is also known as Sandy Bell's. It is the folk music center of Edinburgh. Informal music and singing sessions happen there, and for anyone visiting Edinburgh it's a good place to start off and get the feel of the folk scene.

Folk music sessions can also be heard in **The Fiddler's Arms,** The Grassmarket, on Monday night. On Tuesday you are almost guaranteed a session in **Sandy Bell's Bar.** On Wednesday the **Edinburgh Folk Club** meets at the Carlton Hotel, charging an admission of £1.50 ($2.63). On Thursday there is invariably a folk session in the **Southsider Pub,** West Richmond Street, and on Friday the **Crown Folk Club** meets in Drummond Street, also charging about £1.50 ($2.63) for admission. Sometimes there will be a session in **The Quill,** George IV Bridge, on Saturday night. Finally, on Sunday there is usually a session in the **Glenelg Hotel,** Leamington Terrace, or the **Thistle Hotel** on Manor Place.

2. Day Trips from Edinburgh

Within easy reach of Edinburgh lie some of the most interesting castles and mansions in Scotland, the most important of which follow.

STIRLING: Almost equidistant from Glasgow and Edinburgh, Stirling is dominated by its impressive castle, perched on a 250-foot basalt rock. From Edinburgh, a bus takes about an hour and a half, traveling a distance of 37 miles.

This ancient town, with its turbulent history, was the scene of several battles, including the Battle of Bannockburn in 1314, in which the Scots routed the army of Edward II. On the right bank of the Forth, the castle dates from an unknown age, although its main gateway was built by James IV. At one time the castle was considered the "key to the Highlands."

The castle is open January to April, weekdays from 9:30 a.m. to 5:05 p.m. (on Sunday from 12:30 p.m. to 4:20 p.m.); in May from 9:30 a.m. to 6 p.m. (on Sunday from 11 a.m. to 6 p.m.); June through August from 9:30 a.m. to 7 p.m. (on Sunday from 11 a.m. to 6 p.m.); September and October, 9:30 a.m. to 6 p.m. (on Sunday from 11 a.m. to 6 p.m.); and November and December from 9:30 a.m. to 5:05 p.m. (on Sunday from 12:30 p.m. to 4:20 p.m.). Admission charges, January through April, are 25p (44¢) for adults and 10p (18¢) for children and senior citizens; May to October, 50p (88¢) for adults and 25p (44¢) for children; and November and December, 25p (44¢) for adults and 10p (18¢) for children.

Other places of interest to visit in Stirling include the 15th-century **Church of the Holy Rude,** in which Mary Queen of Scots was crowned in 1543 at the age of nine months; the **Auld Brig** over the Forth, dating from the 14th century; and the **palace** built by James V in the 16th century.

Just outside the town is the **Robert Bruce Memorial and Museum.** Admission is 20p (35¢) for a continual audio-visual presentation of stories of Bruce's times and history.

Food and Lodging

For food and lodging, I offer the following:

Portcullis Hotel, Castle Wynd (tel. Stirling 2290), is my favorite place to stay in the area. It's a tall, 14th-century, rugged stone building hugging the walls of the castle. You enter through a lower courtyard of shrubbery and trees, protected by a high old stone wall. The inviting bar, which is colorful, is on the ground floor. You ascend to the second-floor lounge with stone walls, a cathedral ceiling, and a fireplace at one end. It's furnished with a mixture of antiques and comfortable chairs. The dining room has encircling windows offering a view. The finest Scottish china is used for meals. The hotel serves the finest quality Scottish meat, fresh fish, and poultry, and whenever possible fresh vegetables and fruit are included. The chef has had many years of experience and was trained at one of Scotland's best hotels and in Paris. He doesn't approve of prepackaged and frozen foods. The bedrooms are personalized, each furnished informally and comfortably. The per-person rate for B&B is £15 ($26.25), including VAT and service. There is also a coffeeshop on the premises.

Lime Grove Hotel, 9 Clifford Rd. (tel. Stirling 4373), which is in the best residential area of Stirling, is but a short walk from the center. It's owned by Frederick Gaskin, who outdoes himself to make his guests feel at home. Although his house is small he does have a cozy sitting room with color TV. He'll serve you drinks before and after dinner. He charges £11 ($19.25) per person for B&B and around £9 ($15.75) for an à la carte dinner, including VAT. If you ask ahead, he'll prepare special Scottish dishes. His rooms are centrally heated, although you'll find an electric blanket on your bed. There is also a car park.

Dalglennan Guest House, 4 Allan Park (tel. Stirling 3432), is a B&B establishment owned by Mrs. J. Brodie. She charges £7.50 ($13.13) in a single room, £7 ($12.25) per person in a double or twin. Her rooms are clean; there is individual room heating, hot and cold water, and if you are in the mood, a lounge for watching TV. The guest house is in the residential section of Stirling, near tennis courts and swimming baths, and it's walkable from the bus and train stations.

The **Riverway Restaurant,** Kildean, outside Stirling (tel. Stirling 5734), is a fully licensed restaurant run by W. H. Bell, who enjoys an outstanding local reputation for good food at moderate tariffs. The restaurant is only half a mile from the center of Stirling, just off the M9 on the road to the Trossachs. There is an attractive view of the Forth River, and plenty of locals to look at, especially at the Saturday night dinner/dance which costs £6.75 ($11.81) per person. On workdays, the Riverway becomes a popular restaurant with a goodly array of well-prepared foods, such as grilled pork chops with apple sauce and parsley potatoes, or rainbow trout meunière. Prices of these main dishes begin at £2.65 ($4.64). At lunch you can order a real Scottish menu, say, lentil broth, Scottish haggis and turnip, then a rhubarb sponge and custard, all costing only £3.50 ($6.13). The high tea menu, really a filling early supper, costs £3.50 ($6.13) and has such rib-sticking fare as grilled hamburgers and sirloin steaks. Wine of the house is 70p ($1.23) by the glass. Hours are seven days a week from 10:30 a.m. until the last orders are taken at 6:30 p.m.

DOUNE CASTLE: At Doune, on the banks of the Teith River, four miles west of Dunblane, stands this 14th-century castle, once a royal palace. Now owned by the Earl of Moray, it was restored in 1883, making it one of the best-preserved of the medieval castles of Scotland. The castle is open daily from April to October, charging adults 60p ($1.05) for admission; children pay 40p (70¢). It is closed on Thursday in April, May, September, and October. However, its famous gardens are no longer open to the public.

After visiting the castle, guests can drive 1½ miles to the **Doune Motor Museum** (tel. 078684/203), which charges £1 ($1.75) for adults, 40p (70¢) for children. The motor museum contains about 40 vintage and postvintage motor cars, including the second-oldest Rolls-Royce in the world. It is open daily from April 1 to October 31. In April and May, the last admissions are at 4:30 p.m. From June to August, the hours are from 10 a.m. to 5:30 p.m., and in September and October, the last admissions are again at 4:30 p.m.

South of Doune is the highly popular **Blair Drummond Safari Park.** It's open every day of the year from 10 a.m. (tel. Doune 456). Apart from the cheetahs, you are likely to meet the typical safari-park cast of lions, giraffes, elephants, and performing dolphins, and there's even a pet's corner. Admission for a car is £3.80 ($6.65). If you want to use the safari bus, the charge is £1.15 ($2.01) for adults and 80p ($1.40) for children. Meals are offered in the Safari Restaurant, and free picnic areas are provided.

LINLITHGOW: In this royal burgh, a county town in West Lothian, 18 miles west of Edinburgh, Mary Queen of Scots was born. The roofless **Palace of Linlithgow,** site of her birth in 1542, can still be viewed here today, even if it is but a shell of its former self. Once a favorite residence of Scottish kings, the palace was built square-shaped. In the center are the remains of a royal fountain erected by James V. The queen's suite was in the north quarter, but this was rebuilt for the homecoming of James VI in 1620. The Great Hall is on the first floor. The palace was burned in 1746, destroying one of the gems in the Scottish architectural crown. The palace is open April through September from 9:30 a.m. to 7 p.m. (on Sunday from 2 to 7 p.m.); October through March from 9:30 a.m. to 4 p.m. (on Sunday from 2 to 4 p.m.). Admission is 40p (70¢) for adults, 20p (35¢) for children.

South of the palace stands the medieval kirk of **St. Michael the Archangel.**

From Linlithgow, it is but a 3½-mile drive east on the Queensferry road (A904) to the **House of the Binns** (tel. Philipstoun 4255), the historic home of the Dalyells. The mansion, with its fine Jacobean plaster ceilings, portraits, and panoramic vistas, receives visitors Easter Week and then from May 1 to September 30—daily, except Friday, from 2 to 5:30 p.m. The parkland is open from 10 a.m. to 7 p.m. Admission is £1.20 ($2.10) for adults, 60p ($1.05) for children and students.

In accommodations, **Woodcockdale Farm,** Lanark Road (tel. Linlithgow 2088), is a farmhouse with guest accommodations on the A706, 1½ miles from Linlithgow. Mrs. W. Erskine has rooms to rent which fit many needs. She offers three double rooms, one family room with a double and twin beds, and another two rooms with double and bunk beds. The bathroom adjoins the first-floor rooms, a toilet and shower adjoins the ground-floor rooms. The daily rate for B&B is £8 ($14) per person. A preferable way to stay here and enjoy Mrs. Erskine's cooking is to include evening dinner plus B&B, which is £10 ($17.50) per person daily. Children are welcome at reduced rates. Included are tea, cookies, or cake at 10 p.m. before you retire. The living room has color TV and a piano. The house is centrally heated.

HOPETOUN HOUSE: This is Scotland's greatest Adam mansion, and a fine example of 18th-century architecture. It is the seat of the Marquéss of Linlithgow, whose grandfather and father were respectively the governor-general of Australia and the viceroy of India. Set in the midst of beautifully landscaped grounds laid out along the lines of Versailles, the mansion (tel. 331-2451) lies near the Forth Road Bridge at South Queensferry, off the A904. On a tour you're shown through splendid reception rooms filled with 18th-century furniture, paintings, statuary, and other works of art. From a rooftop viewing platform, you look out over a panoramic view of the Firth of Forth. Even more enjoyable, perhaps, is to take the nature trail, explore the deer parks, investigate the Stables Museum, or stroll through the formal gardens, all on the grounds. Near the Ballroom Suite is a licensed restaurant which serves coffee, lunch, afternoon tea, and high tea. Hopetoun is open Easter Week and from April 30 to September 14, daily from 11 a.m. to 5:30 p.m. Last entry to the house is at 5 p.m. For £1.70 ($2.98) for adults, 80p ($1.40) for children, visitors can view the house (including the museum and rooftop viewing platform), the deer parks, nature trail, and Stables Museum.

NORTH BERWICK: This royal burgh, created in the 14th century, was once an important Scottish port. In East Lothian, 24 miles east from Edinburgh, it is today a holiday resort popular with the Scots and an increasing horde of foreigners just discovering the place. Visitors are drawn to its golf courses, beach sands, and colorful harbor life on the Firth of Forth. You can climb the rocky shoreline or else enjoy the heated outdoor swimming pool in July and August.

At the Information Centre (tel. Berwick 2197), you can pick up data on how to take boat trips to the offshore islands, including **Bass Rock,** a breeding ground inhabited by about 10,000 gannets and one or two crusty lighthouse keepers. The volcanic island is one mile in circumference. It's possible to see the rock from the harbor. The viewing is even better at **Berwick Law,** a volcanic lookout point surmounted by the jawbones of a whale.

Some three miles east of the resort stand the dramatic ruins of the 14th-century diked and rose-colored **Tantallon Castle,** rising magnificently on cliffs. This was the ancient stronghold of the Douglasses.

DIRLETON: Another popular excursion from Edinburgh is to the rose-tinted **Dirleton Castle,** with its surrounding gardens, at Dirleton on the Edinburgh–North Berwick road (A198). This 13th-century castle is well preserved, receiving visitors from April to September, weekdays from 9:30 a.m. to 7 p.m. (on Sunday from 2 to 7 p.m.); October to March, weekdays from 9:30 a.m. to 4 p.m. (on Sunday from 2 to 4 p.m.). Admission to the castle and gardens is £1 ($1.75) for adults and 50p (88¢) for children.

Dirleton vies for the title of "the prettiest village in Scotland."

The **Castle Inn** (tel. Dirleton 085221) has been unspoiled by required modernizations, and is a most satisfactory village inn for the individual traveler or family who wants an accommodation with a personal touch. It's directly opposite the village green and the castle, a long, low building in the center, with ten dormer windows, a pair of entrances, and a modest front garden. The proprietor, Douglas Stewart, has five bedrooms and another four in an annex, each pleasantly furnished and containing hot and cold water. The charge here for B&B (including all the famed Scottish dishes) is £10.50 ($18.38) and an evening meal is from £6 ($10.50). During the day it's possible to obtain light snacks. Guests have a lounge with a free-standing stone fireplace, decorated with copper pots. Against rugged stone walls are settles and trestle tables. Behind the bar the decoration is Victorian mahogany.

DUNBAR: In East Lothian, southeast of North Berwick, Dunbar, another royal burgh, is a popular seaside resort at the foot of the Lammermuir Hills. On a rock above the harbor are the remains of **Dunbar Castle,** built on the site of an earlier castle that dated from 856. Mary Queen of Scots fled there with Darnley in 1566, immediately after the murder of her secretary, Rizzio. Today the kittiwakes live where once the "Black Agnes of Dunbar," the Countess of March, held off the English. The Battle of Dunbar was fought in 1650 between Cromwell's army and the Scots led by David Leslie. The Scots, fighting valiantly, lost and nearly 3000 were killed in one day.

The **Battleblent Hotel** (tel. Dunbar 62234) lies just outside Dunbar on the road to Edinburgh, 26 miles away. Jim and Faye Ferguson own the castle-like home set on a hill surrounded by three acres of their own land overlooking Balhaven Bay on the Firth of Forth. The bedrooms are large, high-ceilinged, and comfortable, with electric heaters and facilities for making tea and coffee. Assisted by their sons Martin and Kevin, the Fergusons have a disco and lounge bar downstairs, and a small, charming, bright dining room on the first floor. The bar and disco are popular with the people of Dunbar, so you can get acquainted with the local affairs of the day. Get Mr. Ferguson to show you his collection of international coins in the downstairs lounge bar. The tariff is £13.50 ($23.63) per person for bed and a continental breakfast, or £15.50 ($27.13) per person for bed and a big Scottish breakfast.

DALKEITH: This small burgh in Midlothian, seven miles southeast of Edinburgh, is the site of **Dalkeith Palace,** rebuilt and redesigned by Sir John Vanbrugh, circa 1700. Such monarchs as George IV, Victoria, and Edward VII have stayed here during visits to Edinburgh.

Visitors flock here for **Dalkeith Park,** to explore the woodland and riverside walks in and around the extensive grounds of the palace. Luring guests are natural trails and an adventure woodland play area, a tunnel walk, and an Adam bridge. The park is open daily from 11 a.m. to 6 p.m., April 2 to October 1. To reach the park, go seven miles south of Edinburgh on the A68.

County Hotel, 152 High St. (tel. Edinburgh 663-3495), is a 16-room family hotel, owned by Mr. Philip Coppola and sons, just seven miles from Edinburgh. All rooms have private toilet and shower, and the charge is £16 ($28) in a single, rising to £25 ($43.75) in a double, these tariffs including VAT and breakfast. Facilities include a restaurant, lounge bar, TV lounge, and elevator to all floors.

HADDINGTON: Created as a royal burgh by David I, this small town of East Lothian lies on the Tyne River, about 17 miles east of Edinburgh. In the 15th century it was Scotland's largest town, but its fortunes declined thereafter.

On the right bank of the river, in the industrial suburb of Giffordgate, the Scottish reformer, John Knox, was believed to have been born in 1505. Much to the chagrin of the Catholic Mary Queen of Scots, he rose from these dire origins to found the Scottish Presbyterian church.

St. Mary's Church, built in the 14th century, in red and gray sandstone, contains the tomb of Jane Welsh, who was born in the town. She married the historian, Thomas Carlyle.

3. The Kingdom of Fife

North of Forth from Edinburgh, the county of Fife still likes to call itself a "kingdom." Its name, even today, suggests the romantic episodes and pageantry during the reign of the early Stuart kings. Fourteen of Scotland's 66 royal burghs lay within this shire. Many of the former royal palaces and castles, either restored or in colorful ruins, can be visited today, and I've previewed the most important ones coming up.

As Edinburgh is so near, the temptation is to set up headquarters in one of that city's many elegant hotels or B&B houses and explore Fife from that base. However, serious golfers may want to stay at one of the hotels in St. Andrews.

DUNFERMLINE: This ancient town was once the capital of Scotland. It is easily reached by ferry or by the railway crossing the Forth Bridge. Dunfermline lies five miles northwest of the Forth Bridge, a distance of 14 miles northwest of Edinburgh.

Dunfermline Abbey (tel. Dunfermline 422858) has been the site of a building of Christian worship for some time. Culdee Church dated back to the fifth and sixth centuries until it was rebuilt in 1072. Traces of both buildings are visible beneath gratings in the floor of the old nave. In 1150 it was replaced with a large abbey, the nave of which remains, an example of Norman architecture. Later St. Margaret's shrine, the northwest baptismal porch, the spire on the northwest tower, and the flying buttresses were added. When Dunfermline was the capital of Scotland, 22 royal persons were buried within the abbey. Except for Queen Margaret and King Robert the Bruce, no visible memorial or burial place is known. Robert the Bruce's tomb lies beneath the pulpit. The abbey church is open daily from 9:30 a.m. to 5 p.m. from April to September (on Sunday from 2 to 5 p.m.). From October to March it closes at 4 p.m.

The **Royal Palace** witnessed the birth of Kings Charles I and James I. Only the southwest wall remains of this once-gargantuan edifice. The last king to reside here was Charles II in 1651.

Andrew Carnegie, the American industrialist and philanthropist, was born here in 1835. The **Andrew Carnegie Birthplace,** a former weaver's cottage, lies at the junction of Priory Lane and Moodie Street and may be visited, free, on weekdays May to August from 11 a.m. to 1 p.m. and 2 to 4 p.m. From September to April, it is open from 11 a.m. to 1 p.m. and 2 to 4 p.m. On Sunday, hours are 2 to 5 p.m. all year.

From the fortune he made in steel, Mr. Carnegie became a great benefactor, giving away more than $400 million before his death in 1919. Dunfermline, as his birthplace, received the first of all the 2811 free libraries he provided throughout Britain and the United States. It also received public baths and **Pittencrieff Park and Glen,** so rich in history and natural charm. A statue in the park honors the hometown boy who made good, who once worked as a bobbin boy in a cotton factory.

In accommodations, **Brucefield Hotel,** 1 Woodmill Rd. (tel. Dunfermline 722199), offers rooms with or without private baths. With a private bath and shower, a double or twin goes for £26 ($45.50) a single for £15 ($26.25). If bathless (but with hot and cold running water), the charge is £20 ($35) in a double or twin, £12 ($21) in a single. Of course, this includes a three-course breakfast, and Mrs. McCleod, the hostess, can also offer other meals according to your needs.

From Dunfermline, you can take an excursion six miles west to—

Culross

This old royal burgh has been renovated by the Scottish National Trust, and is one of the most beautiful in the country. As you walk its cobbled streets, admiring its charming whitewashed houses, you'll feel you're taking a stroll back into the 17th century. Many of the cottages have crow-stepped gables and red pantiled roofs.

Set in tranquil walled gardens, **Culross Palace** was built in the village between 1597 and 1611, containing a most beautiful series of paintings on its wooden walls and ceilings. It has been handsomely restored and may be visited, April to September, daily from 9:30 a.m. to 7 p.m. (on Sunday from 2 to 7 p.m.). From October to March, it's open daily from 9:30 a.m. to 4 p.m. (on Sunday from 2 to 4 p.m.). Admission is 30p (53¢) for adults, 15p (26¢) for children.

For food and lodging, the **Red Lion Inn** (tel. Newmills 880225) stands on the north side of the Forth River midway between Forth Road Bridge and Kincardine Road Bridge. Both ancient and modern, the little pub has a few rooms which the owners, Mr. Steel and Mr. McLeary, rent for £12 ($21) per person, including a full Scottish breakfast and VAT. There is a pine-paneled pub and a lounge with a fireplace, where you can have bar snacks. You can enjoy an evening meal in the bar. Food is available from 11 a.m. to 10 p.m. As Mr. McLeary says, you can have anything from a snack at 80p ($1.40) to a three-course meal at £5 ($8.75). A plate of cold roast Highland beef and a fresh crisp salad will cost £1.70 ($2.98). The pub is easy to spot, a blue and stucco building with a slate roof in the center of the village. There's parking in the rear—next to the stone wall, overlooking the river. A mixed crowd frequents the Red Lion, the rich, the poor, locals blending with tourists. The cooking is above average, and you'll have a wide choice of whiskies, including Royal Culross.

FALKLAND: Now owned by Queen Elizabeth, Falkland was once the hunting palace of the Stuart kings. This royal burgh of cobbled streets and crooked houses lies at the northern base of the hill of East Lomond, 21 miles north of Edinburgh.

Since the 12th century, it has been connected with Scottish kings. Originally a castle stood on the site of today's palace, but it was replaced in the 16th century. Falkland then became a favorite seat of the Scottish court. A grief-stricken James V died here. Mary Queen of Scots used to come to Falkland for "hunting and hawking." It was also here that James Stewart, Earl of Bothwell, came with his men and tried to seize his cousin, James VI, son of Mary Queen of Scots. Bullet marks may be seen on the front of the towers of the gatehouse (1592). Cromwell's forces occupied Falkland in 1654.

The royal chapel and apartments are open from April 1 to October 31, weekdays from 10 a.m. to 6 p.m. and Sunday from 2 to 6 p.m. The gardens, incidentally, have been laid out to the original royal plans. At Falkland is the only royal tennis court left in Scotland. For a ticket to both the palace and gardens, adults pay £1.20 ($2.10); children, 60p ($1.05). Or else you can be admitted to the gardens for only 75p ($1.31) for adults and 35p (61¢) for children. For more information, telephone Falkland 397.

For food and lodging, I suggest the following:

Covenanter Hotel (tel. Falkland 224) has been a popular inn since the early 18th century. With modest modernization, it offers a good standard of accommodation. It's built ruggedly of local stone, with high chimneys, wooden shutters, and a modest Georgian entry. The location is on a tiny plaza, opposite the church and castle. You enter a gleaming white entry hall with a circular staircase leading to the lounges and bedrooms. The dining room is strictly "old style" and for the predinner drinks there is an intimate pub, the Covenanter Cocktail Bar. The inn is owned by George Menzies, who charges from £10 ($17.50) in a single and from £16 ($28) in a double, including a full breakfast and VAT. Lunches are served between noon and 2 p.m., three courses going for £3.85 ($6.74). Dinner is both table d'hôte at £6.95 ($12.16) or à la carte at around £10 ($17.50).

Kind Kyttock's Kitchen, Cross Wynd (tel. Falkland 477), stands right near the palace and welcomes you most of the year with a stone fireplace where logs burn brightly. The "kitchen" is also an art gallery, displaying local crafts and paintings. A specialty is four homemade oatcakes with cheese at £1.40 ($2.45). The bread is always homemade, very fresh tasting, as you'll discover if you order an open sandwich at £1.70 ($2.98). For a tea, I suggest the homemade pancake with fruit and fresh cream at 75p ($1.31). Even better, however, are the homemade tarts with fresh cream, costing 60p ($1.05). Salads are fresh and good tasting, costing from £1.80 ($3.15) a plate. A cup of Scotch broth, served with a slice of home-baked wholemeal bread, goes for 47p (82¢). Freda and Richard Lewis, who run the place, serve from 10:30 a.m. to 5:30 p.m. Off-season, it is open only on weekends.

Back at Dunfermline you can connect with the coastal road, heading east to:

Largo

Alexander Selkirk, the original Robinson Crusoe, was born here in 1676. This Scottish sailor, son of a shoemaker and tanner, was once charged with "indecent behavior in church," but he never had to pay the penalty, whatever it was, as he was away at sea. He disappeared in the South Seas, but was discovered in 1709. He returned to Largo in 1712. A statue in the village honors this hometown boy, who was clearly the inspiration for the Daniel Defoe classic. A house Selkirk purchased for his father is still standing.

THE EAST NEUK: Within a half hour's drive of St. Andrews are some of the most beautiful and unspoiled fishing villages of eastern Scotland.

Pittenweem

If you're here in the morning, try to get caught up in the action at the fish auction held under a large shed (except Sunday). The actual time depends on the tides. Afterward you can go for a walk through the village, taking in the sturdy stone homes, some of which have been preserved by Scotland's National Trust people.

At the **Anchor Inn** (tel. Anstruther 311326) you can enjoy locally caught seafood which is featured on all menus. Bob and Carol Henry specialize in bar lunches at £3.50 ($6.13) and bar suppers at £4.50 ($7.88). These menus most often feature not only fresh local fish but prawns and scampi. Children, incidentally, are welcome at lunchtime. In addition, set lunches go for around £5.50 ($9.63) and à la carte dinners, often with local lobster, for about £11 ($19.25) including wine. The Anchor, circa 1828, is an architecturally listed building with a black-and-white Georgian facade and a cozy atmosphere inside. The inn doesn't offer any accommodations, however.

Anstruther

This was once an important herring-fishing port and is now a summer resort, with a **Scottish Fisheries Museum** (tel. Anstruther 310628), down by the harbor. Tracing the history of the fishing industry in Scotland, it charges 75p ($1.31) admission for adults, 25p (44¢) for children. The museum is open from April to October from 10 a.m. to 5:30 p.m. and from November to March from 2 to 5 p.m. daily except Tuesday. From the museum, you can walk to the tiny hamlet of Cellardyke adjoining Anstruther, with many charming stone houses and its own ancient harbor.

Smuggler's Inn, High Street (tel. Anstruther 310506), stands in the heart of town, a warmly inviting inn that evokes memories of smuggling days around here. The original inn that stood on this spot dates back to 1300. In Queen Anne's day it was a well-known tavern. The ceilings are low, the floors uneven, and, of course, the stairways are winding. Overlooking the harbor, rooms are rented for £17 ($29.75) per person if bathless, rising to £18.50 ($32.38) with bath. Again, depending on the plumbing, the half-board rate ranges from £21 ($36.75) to £23.50 ($41.13) per person. If featured, ask for the local Pittenweem prawns. Mr. and Mrs. McSharry offer a set lunch for £4.50 ($7.88) and an à la carte dinner, served from 7 to 9:30 p.m., from £9 ($15.75).

The Haven, at Cellardyke Harbour (tel. Anstruther 310574), is an old-style licensed restaurant and lounge bar serving good food. Noted for comfort and service, it offers simple but well-prepared lunches that might include steak pie, local crab salad, and Aberdeen Angus steaks. A soup of the day is home-made, and roast chicken is invariably featured. At supper the menu is more elaborate and is likely to include smoked salmon or lobster bisque. Main dishes offered are fried filet of haddock, very popular in this region, although you can also order duck à l'orange. Owned and run by Graham Guthrie and David Barnett, the Haven has a set lunch for £3 ($5.35). In the evening an à la carte dinner will cost from £4.50 ($7.88). Bar snacks are offered for both lunch and dinner as well, including a choice of about eight fish, meat, and poultry dishes, plus cold meats and salads, priced from £2 ($3.50) to £2.50 ($4.38). There is also a garden bar where on a good day you can sip and sup while enjoying the view.

The Cellar, 22–24 East Green (tel. Anstruther 310378), serves good, old-fashioned Scottish food, including smoked salmon, local fish, and laird's pie. The restaurant was installed in the cellar of two old stone houses which lie near the harbor. Service is friendly and polite, and hours of business are from 12:30 to 2 p.m. and 7:30 to 9 p.m. The Cellar shuts down on Sunday and Monday. Expect to spend around £5 ($8.75) for a complete meal.

Elie

With its step-gabled houses and little harbor, this is my favorite village along the coast. Nearby is a good golf course, and there are rock-ribbed sands for bathing.

If you're passing this way, I suggest you drop in at the **Ship Inn** on the Toft, there to enjoy a pint of lager. In summer you can sit out in fair weather, overlooking the water. In colder months, a fireplace burns brightly. The pub has a nautical atmosphere, and doesn't do much in the way of food, but the friendly woman who runs it will prepare a sandwich if you're hungry.

Mrs. Barbara Walker, Dalmore, The Toft (tel. Elie 330583), is the village librarian. She wisely began to accept guests so she could afford to keep her bayfront home. Since then, she's won all sorts of new friends, especially among North Americans, and she feels she's expanded her own horizons. "We feel less isolated—now we are a part of the world," Mrs. Walker told me. Her Tudoresque, tall and stylish 19th-century villa is on a grassy terrace, just 20 steps up from the harbor. It's still a private-seeming home, with many antiques in the sitting-breakfast room, the entry, and bedrooms. She charges £7 ($12.25) per person nightly and also serves a beverage and cookies around 9 p.m. If you ask, she'll serve an evening meal for £4 ($7). It's possible to phone ahead for directions on the location of the house. In July and August, Mrs. Walker is often fully booked, so it's wise to make reservations. She receives B&B guests from May until the end of September.

The Golf Hotel, Elie (tel. Elie 330209), is a hotel for the golfer on a budget. Not only do you have the local course, but St. Andrews, Carnoustie, and Gleneagles are all within easy reach. The mansion lies between the sea and the Elie golf course, and all rooms are equipped with radio and phone. Some contain private baths as well. In high season the cost is £15 ($26.25) per person for B&B, going up to £23 ($40.25) for half board. You pay a supplement of £1.50 ($2.63) should you desire a private bath. They also do inclusive packages for golfers throughout the year, except in July and August. Mr. and Mrs. Blackhall and their family own and run the hotel. The dining room serves good nourishing dishes, with an emphasis on Scottish regional cookery.

Crail

Considered the pearl of the East Neuk of Fife, Crail is an artists' colony, and many painters live in cottages around this little harbor. Natural bathing facilities are found at Roome Bay, and there are many beaches nearby. The Balcomie Golf Course, in good condition, is one of the oldest in the world.

Croma Hotel (tel. Crail 239) is a guest house near the harbor with ten bedrooms. It's the home base of all-American ball player Jack Healy and his attractive wife Rosemarie, originally from Ireland. Brooklyn-born Jack is a strapping, handsome former Pan Am executive. From Samoa he brought handicrafts and trinkets, and has hung them against the wall-size geographic maps from Pan Am. This, the Chart Room, is fully licensed, and it's Jack's domain. Rosemarie has decorated the dining room in green and white and used Windsor chairs set in front of the bay window. Many of the artists who live in this little fishing village come here for drinks and evening meals. The Healys charge £8.50 ($14.88) per person for B&B. They serve a table d'hôte lunch for £3 ($5.25), and an evening meal for £5.50 ($9.63). You can also have a bar meal in the Chart Room for as little as £1.70 ($2.98).

ST. ANDREWS: On a bay of the North Sea, St. Andrews is sometimes known as the "Oxford of Scotland." Founded in 1411, the **University of St. Andrews** is the oldest in Scotland and the third oldest in Britain. At term time you can see the students in their characteristic red gowns.

The university's most interesting buildings include the tower and church of St. Salvator's College and the courtyard of St. Mary's College, dating from 1538. An ancient thorn tree, said to have been planted by Mary Queen of Scots, stands near the college's chapel. The church of St. Leonard's College is also from medieval days. The Scottish Parliament in 1645 met in what was once the University Library and is now a students' reading room. A modern University Library, containing more than three-quarters of a million books and many rare and ancient volumes, was opened in 1976.

The historic sea town in northeast Fife is also known as the home of golf in Britain. The world's leading golf club, the **Royal & Ancient,** was founded here in 1754. All of St. Andrews's four golf courses—the Old, the New, the Jubilee, and the Eden—are open to the public, charging modest fees. Of course, the hallowed turf of the Old Course is the sentimental favorite.

The old gray royal burgh of St. Andrews is filled with many monastic ruins and ancient houses; regrettably, they represent but a few mere skeletons of medieval St. Andrews.

The **St. Andrews Cathedral and Priory** (tel. St. Andrews 72563) was begun in 1127, although in 1160 a much bigger cathedral was launched, finally consecrated in 1318. Built in both the Norman and Gothic styles, it was the largest church in Scotland, establishing St. Andrews as the ecclesiastical capital of the country. Today the ruins can only suggest the former beauty and importance of the cathedral. The east and west gables and a part of the south wall remain, and standing still is "the Pends," part of the old main gateway of the priory.

There is a collection of early Christian and medieval monuments, as well as artifacts discovered on the cathedral site. It is open April to September daily from 9:30 a.m. to 7 p.m. (Sunday, 2 to 7 p.m.). From October to March, hours are daily from 9:30 a.m. to 4 p.m. (Sunday, 2 to 4 p.m.). Admission is 40p (70¢) for adults, 20p (35¢) for children.

The **Holy Trinity Church** ("the Town Kirk"), a beautifully restored medieval church, stood originally in the grounds of the now-ruined cathedral, near the 12th-century St. Regulus Tower with its 108-foot accessible stairway to the top and a fine view of the city. It was removed to the present site in 1410 and considerably altered after the Reformation of 1560. It was restored to its present condition in the early 20th century, with much fine stained glass and carvings.

Also of great interest is the ruined 13th-century **Castle of St. Andrews,** with its bottle dungeon and secret passages.

Food and Lodging

Argyle House Hotel, 127 North St. (tel. St. Andrews 73387), is a substantial renovated hotel in the center of town. While it has the rates of a simpler guest house, it offers many of the amenities of a larger hotel. There are three lounges—one for watching color TV, another where you can have a predinner drink, and the third for games such as chess, "snakes and ladders," backgammon, and bridge. Owners Tom and Joan Dowie and their courteous staff can make this an excellent stay. Their rooms have hot and cold water, good firm beds, and if you waken early you'll find each room has an electric kettle for making your own coffee. The rate per person, including VAT, for B&B is £9 ($15.75) to £10 ($17.50). Evening meals are offered for £5.50 ($9.63).

Number Ten, 10 Hope St. (tel. St. Andrews 74601), is run by Maureen and Ken Featherstone, who have set reasonable rates per person for B&B—£9 ($15.75). With an evening meal, which I strongly recommend, it's £13.50 ($23.63). They invite parents to bring their children along, as they charge half price for them, providing they share their parents' room and are under 12. Prices include VAT and service charge. Every room has hot and cold running water as well as tea- and coffee-making facilities. Some units also have their own shower. There is an elegant lounge with color TV. The building, sheltered behind a classic Georgian facade, is fully centrally heated and has ample free bath and shower facilities. Number Ten lies only a two-minute walk from the first tee of the Old Course.

Peover House, Murray Park (tel. St. Andrews 75787), belongs to Gladys Neill, who has a few nicely furnished, centrally heated rooms to rent. She asks from £8.50 ($14.88) to £11.50 ($20.13) per person for overnight guests. The prices include tea-making facilities in all the rooms and a full Scottish breakfast in the morning. One room has a private bath and TV. The rooms are comfortable, each bed with an electric blanket, and there's plenty of hot water. Mrs. Neill will cater to your wishes, and will get you started on a tour of historic St. Andrews. You are welcomed in the lounge which has a color TV. Her house is only a few minutes' walk from the sea, golf courses, and shopping center.

Cleveden House, 3 Murray Pl. (tel. St. Andrews 74212), belongs to John and Nan Moran, who love sharing their knowledge of St. Andrews. They'll guide you to reasonable restaurants, give you a map for a walk throughout the town, and fix a good Scottish breakfast. They charge £8 ($14) per person for B&B from April through October, lowering that for the rest of the year. Each of their homey rooms has hot and cold water.

Craigmore Guest House, 3 Murray Park (tel. St. Andrews 72142), is a row of Scottish stone cottages three stories high, now turned into a guest house. It's just a three-minute walk from the heart of town, and only two minutes from the sea. Mrs. Jean Thom, the energetic owner, has every kind of bedroom, each having electric blankets, hot and cold water, and central heating. Mrs. Thom offers down-to-earth Scottish hospitality. The charge for B&B ranges from £7 ($12.25) to £8.50 ($14.88) per person, the difference in cost depending on whether you occupy a double or a family room. There are no singles. Dinner is another £5 ($8.75). VAT is included, but not service.

Pepita's Restaurant, 11 Crail's Lane (tel. St. Andrews 74084), is tucked away in a narrow alleyway, a favorite with students. If you visit during the day, you serve yourself, selecting from bowls of salad and one or two hot dishes as well. Dinners are by candlelight, and there is waiter service. Evening hours are from 7 to 9:30 Tuesday, Wednesday, Thursday, and Sunday. On Friday and Saturday nights, service is until 10 p.m. It's open on Monday, but only from 10 a.m. to 5 p.m.

The menu changes frequently; however, I'll suggest some typical offerings. The food is continental, with many French-inspired and international dishes, such as roast beef in the Provençal style, Mexican chicken, or roast venison with a sauce of black peppers. Try also beef in paprika with a red wine cream sauce served on a bed of rice. Desserts are a special feature of the chef, ranging from baked custard with bananas to a soufflé Drambuie. Dishes are priced from £1.70 ($2.98) and a three-course meal is under £5 ($8.75). Call for a reservation in the evening.

The Pancake Place, 177–179 South St. (tel. St. Andrews 75671), offers a rustic atmosphere, and good, inexpensively priced, rib-sticking food. Don't go here if you're on a diet. Pancakes, naturally, are featured in this franchise restaurant, and they often come in unusual combinations—that is, smoked haddock in a Mornay sauce or chicken curry. Prices start at £1.65 ($2.89) for this filling main dish. To begin, you might order a bowl of homemade soup at 35p (61¢). If you don't want a pancake, try one of their crisp salads, made with ham, chicken, or cheddar cheese, costing from £1.60 ($2.80). A wide selection of sweet pancakes are offered for dessert, ranging from Alaska to the Caribbean and back to Tahiti, costing from £1.35 ($2.36). The Pancake Place is open seven days a week from 10 a.m. to 5:30 p.m. In summer, from June to September, they are likely to be open in the evening, but telephone first to make sure.

4. Glasgow and the Clyde

Forty miles west of Edinburgh, Scotland's largest city stands on the banks of the River Clyde, which was the birthplace of the *Queen Mary* and *Queen Elizabeth,* plus many other ocean-going liners. Here is housed half of Scotland's population. The Firth of Clyde is one of the loveliest waterways in the world, with its long sea lochs, islands, and hills.

The commercial capital of Scotland, and Britain's third-largest city, Glasgow is very ancient, making Edinburgh, for all its wealth of history, seem comparatively young. The village that became the city grew up beside a ford 20 miles from the mouth of the River Clyde, which is famous for its shipbuilding, iron and steelworks. Glasgow was a medieval ecclesiastical center and seat of learning. The ancient city is buried beneath 19th-century Glasgow, which is now undergoing vast urban renewal. Glasgow was founded by St. Kentigern, also called St. Mungo, who selected the site 1400 years ago for his church.

In 1136 a cathedral was erected over his remains; in 1451 the university was started, the second established in Scotland. Commercial prosperity began in the 17th century when its merchants set out to dominate the trade of the western seas. The Clyde was widened and deepened, and the city's expansion engulfed the smaller towns of Ardrie, Renfrew, Rutherglen, and Paisley, whose roots are deep in the Middle Ages.

The smoking industrial city of Glasgow is blighted in parts by the "Gorbals," some of the worst slums in Europe which are now giving way to urban development schemes.

Glasgow does contain some sightseeing attractions, enough to make the city a worthy goal for many visitors. But mainly it's a good center for touring central Scotland. For example, you can sail on Loch Lomond and Loch Katrine on the same day, and the resorts along the Ayrshire coast are only an hour away

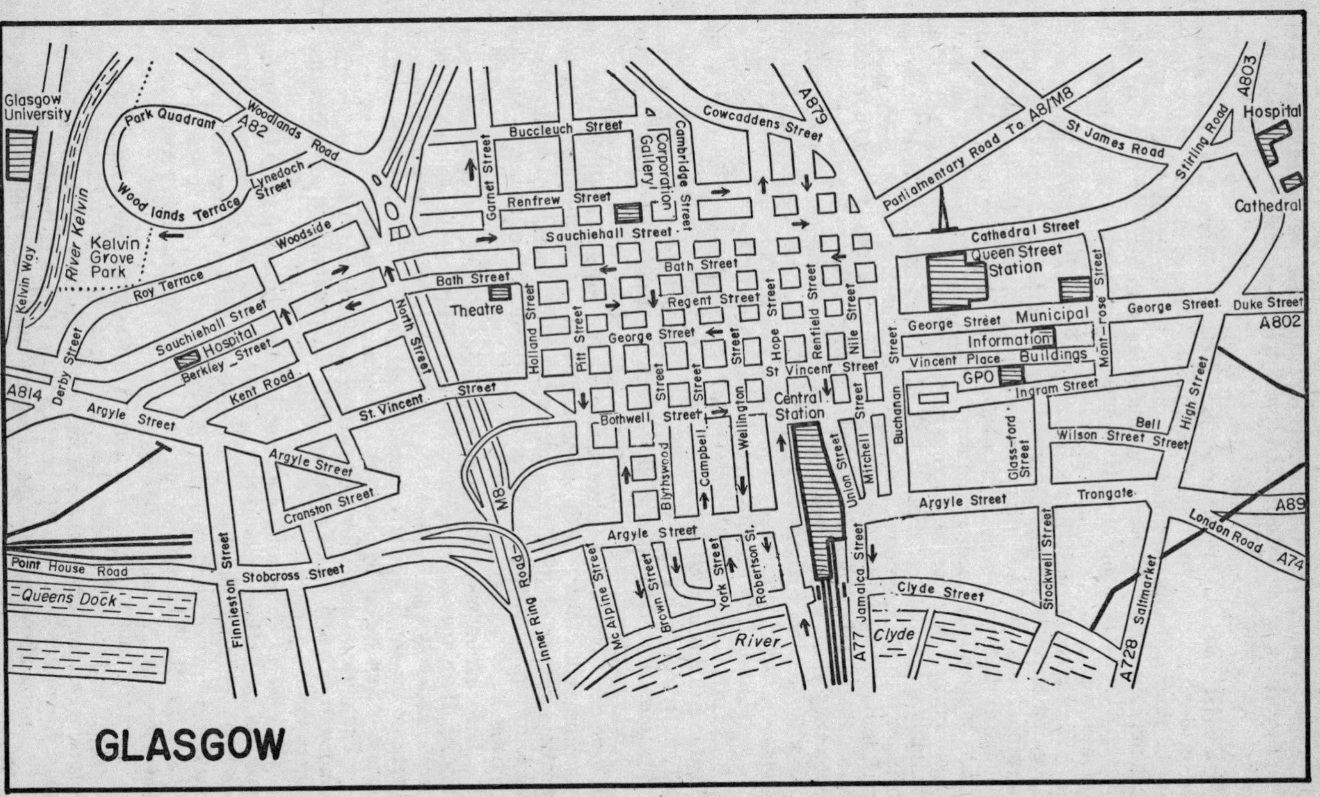
GLASGOW
Glasgow University
Park Quadrant
A82
Woodlands Road
Lynedoch Street
Wood lands Terrace
River Kelvin
Kelvin Way
Kelvin Grove Park
Woodside
Roy Terrace
Sauchiehall Street
Hospital
Berkley Street
Derby Street
A814
Argyle Street
Kent Road
North Street
St. Vincent Street
Theatre
Bath Street
Garnet Street
Buccleuch Street
Renfrew Street
Sauchiehall Street
Corporation Gallery
Cambridge Street
Cowcaddens Street
A879
Parliamentary Road To A8/M8
St James Road
Stirling Road
A803
Hospital
Cathedral
Cathedral Street
Queen Street Station
Holland Street
Pitt Street
George Street
Regent Street
Bath Street
Hope Street
Renfield Street
Nile Street
St Vincent Street
Bothwell Street
Blythswood Street
Campbell Street
Wellington Street
Central Station
Union Street
Mitchell Street
Buchanan Street
George Street
Municipal Buildings
Information
Vincent Place
GPO
Ingram Street
Mont-rose Street
George Street
Duke Street
A802
High Street
Bell Street
Wilson Street
Glass-ford Street
Argyle Street
Trongate
A89
London Road
A74
Saltmarket
A728
Stockwell Street
Clyde Street
Clyde
River
A77 Jamaica Street
Robertson St.
York Street
Brown Street
Mc Alpine Street
Argyle Street
Inner Ring Road
M8
Argyle Street
Cranston Street
Stobcross Street
Finnieston Street
Point House Road
Queens Dock

by frequent train service. From Glasgow you can also explore the Burns Country, the Stirling area, Culzean Castle, and the Trossachs.

THE SIGHTS: In Glasgow, the center of the city is **George Square,** dominated by the City Chambers which Queen Victoria opened in 1888. Of the statues in the square, the most imposing is that of Sir Walter Scott on an 80-foot column. Naturally, you'll find Victoria along with her beloved Albert, plus Robert Burns. The Banqueting Hall, lavishly decorated, is open to the public on most weekdays.

The **Cathedral of St. Kentigern,** first built in 1136, was burned down in 1192. It was rebuilt soon after, and the Laigh Kirk (Lower Church), the vaulted crypt said to be the finest in Europe, remains to this day. Visit the tomb of St. Mungo in the crypt where a light always burns. The edifice is mainland Scotland's only complete medieval cathedral, dating from the 12th and 13th centuries. Formerly a place of pilgrimage, 16th-century zeal purged it of all "monuments of idolatry." For the best view of the cathedral, cross the Bridge of Sighs into the necropolis, the graveyard containing almost every type of architecture in the world. The graveyard is built on a rocky hill and dominated by a statue of John Knox. It was first opened in 1832, and the first person to be buried there was a Jew, typical of the mixing of all races in this cosmopolitan city where tolerance reigns until the rival local football teams meet. The necropolis is full of monuments to Glasgow merchants, among them William Miller (1810–1872) who wrote the children's poem "Wee Willie Winkie."

The **Art Gallery and Museum,** at Kelvingrove Park (tel. 334-1134), is the finest in Britain outside London. The gallery contains such a fine collection of old masters, including Dutch and French painters, that one first-time woman visitor questioned their authenticity—she could not believe her eyes. Displayed are works by Giorgione *(Adulteress Brought before Christ),* Rembrandt *(Man in Armour),* Rubens, and Bellini, including four galleries of British paintings from the 16th century to the present. The gallery of 19th-century French paintings includes all the famous names. Salvador Dali gets in on the act with his *Christ of St. John of the Cross.* Scottish painting, of course, is also well represented.

The museum has an outstanding collection of European arms and armor, displays from the ethnography collections featuring the Eskimo peoples, Africa, and Polynesia, as well as a large section devoted to natural history. There are also small, regularly changing displays from the decorative art collections of silver (especially Scottish), ceramics, glass, and jewelry.

The museum and gallery are open weekdays from 10 a.m. to 5 p.m., on Sunday from 2 to 5 p.m. On the premises is a restaurant, a coffee bar, and a gallery shop.

In 1944 Sir William Burrell presented a splendid collection of paintings, tapestries, and other objets d'art. The Burrell collection is housed separately in a new gallery in Pollok Park. One highlight of the Burrell bequest are nearly two dozen drawings and paintings by Degas.

St. Enoch Exhibition Centre is a gallery for temporary exhibitions of contemporary film and decorative arts.

If time remains, **Provands Lordship,** 3 Castle St., is the oldest house in Glasgow, built in 1471. Mary Queen of Scots is said to have written the notorious "Casket letters" there. However, one has to be content to look at the house from outside, as it is not open to the public as of this writing.

Glasgow also offers a number of branch museums, including the **Museum of Transport,** 25 Albert Dr. (tel. 423-8000). Once Glasgow's trams were famous. You can see seven displayed here, dating from 1894. Many Scottish-built vintage cars are also exhibited, along with railway locomotives. The most recent extensions house a magnificent display of nearly 200 ship models and a reconstruction of the old Glasgow underground. Hours are weekdays from 10 a.m. to 5 p.m., on Sunday from 2 to 5 p.m. There is a shop and a tea room.

Pollok House, Pollok Park, was built circa 1750 and has additions from 1890 to 1908 designed by Sir Robert Rowand Anderson. It houses the Stirling Maxwell collection of Spanish and other European paintings, and it also has displays of furniture, ceramics, glass, and silver, mostly 18th century. The house may be visited weekdays from 10 a.m. to 5 p.m.; Sunday from 2 to 5 p.m.

People's Palace, Glasgow Green (tel. Glasgow 554-0223), provides a visual record of the rise of Glasgow. The palace was built originally as a cultural center for the people of the East End of Glasgow, and it was constructed between 1895 and 1897. Exhibitions trace the foundation of the city in 1175–1178. Such turbulent interludes as the reign of Mary Queen of Scots are represented by the personal relics of the queen herself. The bulk of the collections are from the 19th century, representing Victorian Glasgow, including posters, programs, and props from the music hall era. The city museum may be visited weekdays from 10 a.m. to 5 p.m., on Sunday from 2 to 5 p.m. Admission is free.

The park in which the palace is situated, **Glasgow Green,** is the oldest public park in the city. Once a common pasture for the early town, it has witnessed much history. Seek out, in particular, Nelson's monument, the first of its kind in Britain; the Saracen Fountain, opposite the palace; and Templeton's Carpet Factory, modeled on the Doge's Palace in Venice.

The **Haggs Castle Museum and Gardens** are in southwest Glasgow on St. Andrews Drive at Terregles Avenue (tel. 427-2725), and can be visited Monday to Saturday from 10 a.m. to 5:15 p.m. (Sunday, 2 to 5 p.m.). It has a series of displays showing how life has changed over the past four centuries. There's an original kitchen from 1585, a room which shows how an inhabitant lived in the 17th century, and a Victorian nursery. Children who visit can take part in activity sessions such as weaving, archery, buttermaking, and sampler sewing. You can get in touch with the museum for details of current sessions before visiting.

The principal shopping district is **Sauchiehall Street,** Glasgow's fashion center, containing many shops and department stores where you'll often find quite good bargains, particularly in woolen goods. The major shopping area, about three blocks long, has been made into a pedestrian mall.

Although it's blighted by much industry and stark commercial areas, Glasgow contains many gardens and open spaces.

Chief among these is **Bellahouston Park,** Paisley Road West, 171 acres of beauty with a sunken wall and rock gardens as well as wildlife. It's open all year daily from 8 a.m. to dusk.

Glasgow's **Botanic Gardens,** Great Western Road, covers 40 acres—an extensive collection of tropical plants and herb gardens. It, too, is open all year, daily, including Sunday, from 7 a.m. to dusk.

Linn Park, on Clarkston Road, is 212 acres of pine and woodland, with many lovely walks along the river. There's also a nature trail. The park is open all year, daily from 8 a.m. to dusk.

Greenock is an important industrial and shipbuilding town on the Clyde Estuary a few miles west of the center of Glasgow. It was the birthplace in 1736 of James Watt, inventor of the steam engine. A huge Cross of Lorraine on Lyle Hill above the town commemorates Free French sailors who died in the Battle of the Atlantic during World War II.

Past Greenock, sea lochs strike into the Strathclyde hills—Gareloch, Loch Long, and Loch Goil—with Holy Loch pointing more to the west. This was once a holiday region, but that was changed by the World War. Holy Loch has its Polaris base, and British atomic subs are stationed in these waters. There are new seaports on Loch Long and the Gareloch. Loch Long is long, but its name derives from the Gaelic word meaning "a ship," and the name really means the "loch of the ships." Long before the Clyde was world famous for shipbuilding, the galleys of the old chieftains sheltered in these waters. Vikings hauled their boats overland from Loch Long to raid the country around Loch Lomond.

Gourock, three miles west of Greenock, is a resort and yachting center. On the cliff side of Gourock is **"Granny Kempock,"** a six-foot high stone of gray schist which was probably significant in prehistoric times. In past centuries it was used by fishermen in rites to ensure fair weather. Couples planning marriage used to circle Granny to get her blessing and to ensure fertility in their marriage.

From Gourock, car-ferries take travelers to Dunoon on the Cowal peninsula.

WHERE TO STAY: One place giving a fine bargain for weekend stays is the **Newlands Hotel,** 290 Kilmarnock Rd. (tel. Glasgow 632-9171). All the bedrooms have private baths, and breakfast and VAT are included in the price of the room. Daily terms are £18 ($31.50) in a single, £36 ($63) in a twin-bedded room, and all units come with bath. Most units have color TV. The Newlands has modern features including a residents' lounge with handsome brown and gold furniture, attractively wallpapered hallways, and the Captain's Cabin, a quiet little bar for diners and residents. The Windjammer Restaurant offers both table d'hôte and à la carte menus, with lunch costing from £6 ($10.50), dinner from £7.50 ($13.13). Bar lunches are available also.

If you're going to Glasgow from either Prestwick or Glasgow Airport, the Newlands makes a convenient stopover before you get into the bustle of the heart of the city. It's also adjacent to a commuter station with regular fast trains into town.

The **Dalmeny Hotel,** 62 St. Andrew's Dr. (tel. 427-1106), stands in the center of a huge Victorian estate of stone villas and mansions, all built when Glasgow was the second-largest city in the Empire next to London. Five minutes from the center of the city, the hotel is more than 100 years old, built of light-colored sandstone with thick walls. The location is in the Pollokshields section, south of the River Clyde. Pollokshields is a Victorian conservation area and highly residential. Your hosts are Bill and Betty Burns, who take great pride in the running of their establishment. They conceive of their bedrooms as an "alternative home" for their clientele, charging from £16.50 ($28.86) in a single, from £28 ($49) in a double or twin. All units have color television and either private baths or showers. Rates quoted include VAT and a full Scottish breakfast. Parents traveling with children can ask about the family room.

Kelvin Hotel, 15 Buckingham Terrace (tel. 339-7143), stands at the west end of Glasgow, off Great Western Road on the road to Loch Lomond, about a ten-minute drive from the heart of Glasgow. Near the university, it is also convenient to the Botanic Gardens and the BBC. The rooms are comfortable, although simply furnished—14 in all, ranging in price from £10 ($17.50) in a single, to £18 ($31.50) to £20 ($35) in a double, including breakfast. No room has a private bath.

Apsley Hotel, 903 Sauchiehall St. (tel. 339-4999), unlike some of its neighbors, is a *real* hotel, with a nice lobby and pleasantly and comfortably furnished bedrooms, costing from £20 ($35) for two persons in a double unit. This tariff includes breakfast, served with a choice of menu. This same dining room also offers a good lunch, "high tea," and a well-prepared dinner, all at reasonable prices. A warm, friendly bar, where it's easy to meet and talk with people, is open until midnight. The staff is very warm and cooperative as well. In the hallways you'll find a scattering of antiques.

READERS' GUEST HOUSE SELECTIONS: "In one of Glasgow's nicest residential areas is the **Linwood House,** a guest house run by Mrs. M. D. Bienkowski, 356 Albert Dr., Pollokshields (tel. 427-3646). It is conveniently situated for sightseeing in the city and its environs. The rooms are unusually large, exceptionally clean, and some even have TV. Breakfast, which is usually served by Mr. Bienkowski, is good, wholesome, and the servings are large enough to make you consider skipping lunch. The price is £10.50 ($18.38) per person, including breakfast" (Charles E. McCabe, McLean, Va.). . . . "We found **Mrs. Snell's,** 24 Dowanside Rd. (take the excellent underground called the Circle to Hillhead exit, take a left, and walk one block to Dowanside). The charge is £7 ($12.25) per night per person in an exotic four-story Georgian House. Breakfast consists of cereal or juice, one egg, meat, toast, and coffee or tea. We liked it so much we stayed for six days" (Jan and Lisa Hubbard, Fort Worth, Texas). . . . "We enjoyed the friendliness of Scots, especially at the **Westbank Hotel,** 8 Bank St. (tel. 334-4324). For £8 ($14), we had a comfortable room, juice, cereal, bacon, egg, and as much toast or coffee as we liked. The water from the lake is great to drink and soft to bathe in. There's no extra cost for the use of the bath and plenty of hot water. The hotel is two blocks from the Kelvinbridge underground station" (Claudette and Gerald Hinsperger, Lahr, West Germany).

WHERE TO DINE: **Moussaka House,** 36 Kelvingrove St. (tel. 332-2510). In a crowded city, it's good to find reasonable parking close to this restaurant which makes a justifiable claim to offering the best value in the city. Service is Monday to Saturday from noon to 2:30 p.m. and 6 p.m. to midnight (on Sunday from 6:30 to 11 p.m.). Moussaka, as would be expected, is the house specialty, but stuffed peppers, kebabs, and soups are also featured on the menu. A pâté, followed by a moussaka and a dessert, will come to £4.50 ($7.88). Tapes of Greek music add more atmosphere. It's very clean but somewhat plastic. However, for the price, it's hard to beat.

Danish Food Centre, 56 St. Vincent St. (tel. 221-0518), offers what you'd expect, the famous Danish cold table and those delectable open-face sandwiches known as smørrebrød. You are rarely disappointed here. The smoked fish, in particular, is fresh and most reliable—so good, in fact, I've often made an entire meal of it. The restaurant serves three plats du jour every day, and for the evening in particular there is a full à la carte menu. A meal costs about £9 ($15.75), yet it is also possible to order a three-course meal for as little as £6 ($10.50). The cold table in the evening is £9.50 ($16.63). The service is friendly and efficient. Arrive between noon and 2:30 p.m. and between 6 and 10:30 p.m. Here you can enjoy a really filling menu and a change of pace from typically Scottish fare. The center is closed on Sunday and bank holidays.

Daly's Restaurant, 199 Sauchiehall St. (tel. 332-6833), is a self-service restaurant in Glasgow's most up-to-date shopping center. If you don't mind the department store shoppers and a somewhat impersonal coffeeshop atmosphere, you'll find good value in the Scottish beef and lamb served in the restaurant carvery. Hours are daily except Sunday from 9 a.m. to 5:30 p.m., and the cost is around £6 ($10.50) for a most satisfying luncheon. No alcohol is served, however.

Fraser's Restaurant, 45 Buchanan St. (tel. 221-3880), is another unlicensed self-service restaurant, with a carvery. It's a city-center department store selection, and connected to the main restaurant is a coffeeshop which is also self-service. At the carvery table, a selection of Scottish meats is always presented, and there is a salad table as well. Expect to spend from £6 ($10.50). If you drop in for "high tea" in the afternoon, many Scottish fish dishes, including the smoked variety, are presented. Hours are daily except Sunday from 11 a.m. to 5:30 p.m.

Kensington's Restaurant, 164 Darnley St. (tel. 424-3662), is a licensed table-service restaurant which is open from noon to 2 p.m. for lunch and for dinner from 7 to 10:30 p.m. Small and intimate, it is handsomely decorated. The location may be a bit hard to find, as it's tucked away in a quiet backwater on the south side of Glasgow. The chef offers seafood plucked from the west coast, along with home-killed venison. A specialty is the selection of Scottish desserts. Expect to spend around £6.50 ($11.38) for lunch, perhaps another £2 ($3.50) or so for dinner.

Potter's Wheel Restaurant, 67–77 Glassford St. (tel. 552-0523), is a tiny restaurant in a store specializing in crystal and china. It's unlicensed and self-service, presenting a standard repertoire of typically Scottish dishes, including haggis, neeps, and tatties, along with herring in oatmeal. There is a salad bar, and fresh vegetables are also regularly featured. Go here for lunch only, anytime between 11:30 a.m. and 3:30 p.m. Expect to spend from £5 ($8.75) per person.

Ubiquitous Chip, 12 Ashton Lane (tel. 334-5007), is a little whitewashed restaurant with a courtyard paved with cobblestones. It lies in a lane off Byres Road. Original batiks and murals, along with much greenery, make this restaurant an inviting little choice. It is licensed and offers table service any day except Sunday. For £6 ($10.50), you'll be served a very good lunch between noon and 2 p.m. Dinner, from 5:30 to 11 p.m., is more expensive, costing from £9 ($15.75). The menu has a tempting selection of Scottish lamb and beef, along with fish and (in season) game. Fresh produce is always featured.

Adriano's, 46 West George St. (tel. 332-0121), stands just off George's Square, a well-known landmark. It is affiliated with La Buca Pizzeria at 191 Hope St. However, Adriano's also has an adjacent lounge bar and a disco upstairs. The Italian-style restaurant, open from noon to 11 p.m. daily except Sunday, brings a Mediterranean warmth to a cool Glasgow evening. A meal could be made from one of the pizza or pasta courses, each adequate for a moderate appetite. For example, cannelloni with a salad and a glass of wine costs £3.05 ($5.34). If you prefer a more robust meal, try the cream of potato soup, followed by pollo buongustaia (breast of chicken sauteed with mortadella and parsley). This, along with a salad and dessert, would bring your tab up to £5.50 ($9.63).

La Buca, 191 Hope St. (tel. 332-7120), has brought an infusion of Latin charm to foggy Glasgow. Italian waiters serve freshly made pizzas and an assortment of pastas—each a small meal in itself—for from £1.60 ($2.80) to £2 ($3.50). More expensive dishes include grilled lamb or trout as well as Italian-style chicken dishes such as pollo Messicana (half spring chicken cooked in tomato and red wine sauce). This, plus a steamy minestrone and dessert, would bring the tab to about £5 ($8.75). Desserts, incidentally, include homemade ice creams. Extras, such as drinks and coffee, would add to this, but the most budget conscious can have a good meal of pizza (or pasta), a salad, and a light dessert for around £3 ($5.25). The restaurant is open Monday to Saturday from noon to 11 p.m.; closed Sunday.

Delta Restaurant, 283 Sauchiehall St. (tel. 332-3661), is a cellar restaurant known for its fine food and real Scottish hospitality. The house is owned by a group of bakers who have been in business since 1858. A special two-course lunch costs only £1.85 ($3.24), including, for example, a homemade lentil soup and Loch Fyne herring fried in oatmeal. The chef's special is a roast Ayrshire chicken with bacon and a choice of vegetables at £2.10 ($3.68). Service is from 9 a.m. to 7:30 p.m.

Massino's, 465 Clarkston Rd. in Muirend (tel. 637-8568), in the southern part of the city, is named after its friendly proprietor, Massino, who runs this little place with his wife Helen. Tables are pine-topped with benches. Many guests come here to order one of Massino's pizzas, costing from £1.30 ($2.28) and featuring the usual combinations. You can also order a full meal, beginning with a bowl of minestrone and following with chicken cacciatora, topped by an apple tart, all for a cost of £3.75 ($6.56). The restaurant is licensed and serves food beginning at 10:30 a.m. Monday to Saturday, with the last orders taken at 8 p.m.

Ad-Lib, 111 Hope St. (tel. 248-7102), is an American-style diner, with movie posters and a stainless-steel floor, standing opposite Glasgow's Central Station. It's one of the more popular dining spots in Glasgow, especially among young people. Ad-Lib is operated by Romano Wines. Service is Monday to Saturday from noon to 2 a.m. (yes, that late), and on Sunday from 6 p.m. to 1 a.m. Finding a place in Scotland that serves food on Sunday until 1 a.m. is still a bit of a rarity. The menu includes a wide range of all-beef hamburgers which are served with a choice of fries or baked potato, along with a selection of relishes. Expect to spend from £2 ($3.50) to £3 ($5.25) for these. If you aren't into burgers, try one of the main kebab courses, or perhaps a "vegetarian crêpe." They also cook a pretty fair southern fried chicken and Angus beef steaks, at prices ranging from £3 ($5.25) to £6 ($10.50). Desserts include pancakes with fudge sauce and fresh Scottish cream or apple pie à la mode. Try also the cheesecake with fruit and fresh cream topping. There is also a good range of salads and full bar service.

Favorite Pubs

Archie's Bar, 27 Waterloo St. (tel. 221-3210). I don't know if Scotland has an Archie Bunker or even why it's called Archie's Place. The man in charge is Bill Tindall, and he presides over the exuberant modern bar. There's a self-service area, offering cold meats and salads, along with four or five hot dishes, including steak pie, ham, fruit pies, and a trifle. Expect to spend from £2.50 ($4.38). Beer is 71p ($1.25) a pint. Archie's is open from noon to 10 p.m. daily but closed on Sunday.

The **Potstill,** Hope Street (tel. 333-0980), is the best place to go in Glasgow to sample malt whisky. A selection of more than 100 single-malt (unblended) whiskies, many at a variety of different strengths, can be tasted (hopefully not on the same night). You can also order malt whiskies at a variety of maturities—that is, years spent in casks. Many prefer the malt whisky that has been aged in a sherry cask. On one shelf is displayed a Dalmore and a Springbank whisky, each bottled more than half a century ago. They are to be looked at—never sampled.

READERS' PUB SUGGESTION: "There are the normal pub lunches in Glasgow, and one of the best we found was at **Lauder's Bar,** 76 Sauchiehall St., in the city center. You can get steak pie, beans or peas, and fries for £1.75 ($3.06). It's a great break from the rigors of shopping" (Jan and Lisa Hubbard, Fort Worth, Texas).

5. The Trossachs and Loch Lomond

"The Trossachs" is the collective name given that wild Highland area lying east and northeast of Loch Lomond. Both the Trossachs and Loch Lomond are said to contain Scotland's finest scenery in moor, mountain, and loch. The area is famed in history and romance ever since Sir Walter Scott included vivid descriptive passages in *The Lady of the Lake* and *Rob Roy.*

In Gaelic, the Trossachs means "the bristled country," an allusion to its luxuriant vegetation. The thickly wooded valley contains three lochs—Vennachar, Achray, and Katrine. The best centers for exploring are the village of the Trossachs and the "gateways" of Callander and Aberfoyle.

Legendary Loch Lomond, the largest and most beautiful of Scottish lakes, is famed for its "bonnie banks." Lying within easy reach of Glasgow, the loch is about 24 miles long. At its widest point, it stretches for five miles. At Balloch in the south the lake is a Lowland loch of gentle hills and islands. But as it moves north, the loch changes to a narrow lake of Highland character, with moody cloud formations and rugged steep hillsides.

CALLANDER: For many, this small burgh, 16 miles northwest of Stirling by road, makes the best base for exploring the Trossachs and Loch Katrine, Loch Achray, and Loch Vernachar. For years, motorists—and before them passengers traveling by bumpy coach—stopped here to rest up on the once-difficult journey between Edinburgh and Oban.

Callander stands at the entrance to the **Pass of Leny** in the shadow of the Callander Crags. The Rivers Teith and Leny meet to the west of the town.

Four miles beyond the Pass of Leny, with its beautiful falls, lies **Loch Lubnaig** ("the crooked lake"), divided into two reaches by a rock and considered fine fishing waters. Nearby is **Little Leny,** the ancestral burial ground of the Buchanans.

More falls are found at **Bracklinn,** 1½ miles northeast of Callander. In a gorge above the town, Bracklinn is considered one of the most scenic of the local beauty spots. Other places of interest include the **Roman Camp,** the **Caledonian Fort,** and the **Foundations of St. Bride's Chapel.** The tourist office will give you a map pinpointing the above-recommended sights. While there, you can also get directions for one of the most interesting excursions from Callander, to **Balquhidder Church,** 13 miles to the northwest, the burial place of Rob Roy.

Food and Lodging

Lubnaig Hotel, Leny Feus (tel. Callander 30376), is a stone country estate with its own acre garden which has been adapted to receive guests by Mr. and Mrs. Dalziel. It has plenty of character, with its many gables and bay windows. The drawing room has an attractive crystal chandelier, shaped sofas, Victorian chairs, and a beamed sunroom overlooking the garden. The intimate dining room with its stone fireplace and beams has pine trestle tables and ladderback chairs. For half board, including a private shower and toilet, the tariff is £22.30 ($39.03) per person nightly. A single person pays a £2 ($3.50) supplement. The cocktail bar has been altered to provide draft beers and light lunches. Nonresidents are served drinks only when having a meal. Drinks and coffee are served in the cocktail lounge. The view from the sunroom includes an aviary of native and foreign birds set among pine trees. Breakfast is fully Scottish, with traditional dishes. Fishing for salmon and trout, bowling, pony trekking, and canoeing are possible in the area.

Highland House Hotel, South Church Street (tel. Callander 30269), is an enchanting small stone Georgian house in a quiet tree-lined street half a block from the river. The resident owners, Eslyn and David Craven, provide a warm and friendly atmosphere with the stress on personal service. Eslyn is a Cordon Bleu cook who specializes in personally prepared food with a Scottish flavor, made from fresh local produce. David prides himself on his choice of wines and malt whiskies. All bedrooms have hot and cold water, continental quilts, and electric blankets. Some have private bathrooms with shower. The B&B rate is from £9.50 ($16.63) to £10.75 ($18.81) per person for rooms with private facilities. Dinner, with a choice of dishes, is £7 ($12.25).

Eastmains House, Bridgend (tel. Callander 30080), is a handsome 19th-century Scottish stone mansion set in two acres of garden and woods. You can see the Teith River a block away near the village. Mrs. Bowmer has furnished her home with many appropriate pieces. The drawing room has wing chairs and teakwood tables from the Far East. All is centrally heated, the bedrooms have hot and cold water, and the per-person rate, including VAT, is £8 ($14).

Dalgair Guest House, 113–115 Main St. (tel. Callander 30283), is a family-run hotel that offers modern comfortable surroundings, personal service, and excellent food. The facilities include hot and cold running water, continental quilts, shaver points, and heating in all bedrooms. Some rooms contain their own private showers and toilets. For B&B you pay £9.50 ($16.63) nightly. For half board, the cost is £16 ($28) per person nightly. Food is served at the Dalgair's restaurant, adjacent to the guest house. Fresh Scottish produce is used whenever available, and there is a good wine list. Typical dishes include cock-a-leekie soup, trout Rob Roy, and pork oaties. Mr. and Mrs. Ian M. Brown, who run both the guest house and restaurant, will serve you tea and hot homemade scones at 10 p.m. Mr. Brown has involved his three sons in the operation, teaching them all phases of the business. The cocktail lounge is one of the most attractive in Perthshire, serving both as a restaurant and coffee lounge, offering food, drink, and the piano music of your host, Mr. Brown.

White Shutters Guest House, South Church Street (tel. Callander 30442), is spotless and charming. To reach it, head down the main artery of Callander, turning into South Church Street. Run as a B&B, the house is some two centuries old. The owners, Isabel and Jack Dickinson, make you feel you are their treasured personal guest. In this friendly, congenial atmosphere, you have a country house feeling. For a single room, their rate is £8.50 ($14.88), rising to £16 ($28) in a double, including a full Scottish breakfast and a 10 p.m. supper of scones, cake, biscuits, and tea. A walk down the road will bring you to a footbridge over the Teith River, taking you into open countryside and scenic walks. Reader Mary J. Foley, Daton, Va., wrote: "Ask for the nearest pub and you'll be shown a footpath alongside the river to a door in a stone wall. You have to give the door a little kick, as it's sticky, and you find yourself in the beautiful garden of an old hotel, where a piper is playing."

Pips Coffee House and Gallery, 23 Ancaster Square (tel. Callander 30470), is visually striking from both inside and out. Janet and John Holt are your friendly hosts. Behind the striped canopies and brasswork of the facade is an interior decor made inviting by white wooden furniture and tartan carpeting. Many of the pictures and prints on the walls are for sale, and there is also a display of Limoges porcelain. Fresh, crisp salads, home-baking, sandwiches, and homemade soups are the specialties of the house. Naturally, you can order well-brewed coffee along with freshly whipped Scottish cream. There's a good-value fixed-price menu served from 6 to 9 p.m. Monday to Saturday. Clients can choose either two courses or three (with coffee included) for £3.45 ($6.04) and £3.95 ($6.91), respectively. A main dish might be rainbow trout or coq au vin. At lunch Pips offers an à la carte menu, including, for example, a smoked Scottish salmon and cucumber salad, costing £3.75 ($6.56). The restaurant is not licensed, but clients are welcome to bring their own wine. Pips is open daily from 9 a.m. to 9 p.m. (Sunday, from 11 a.m. to 7 p.m.) from May until September. After that, they open at 10 a.m., closing at 5 p.m. daily (on Sunday, 11 a.m. to 5 p.m.).

Motorists seeking "A Taste of Scotland" may want to drive out to the **Lade Inn,** which lies outside Callander on the Trossachs Road at Kilmahog (tel. Callander 30152). Here you get real Scottish hospitality and good, hearty food in a small country inn which has much character. In season local trout and salmon are prepared in the kitchen, and the homemade soups are always rich in flavor, as is the locally made pâté, which often uses game. The licensed hotel is open from noon to 2:30 p.m. when it serves a lunch for about £4 ($7). Dinner is served from 5 to 9:30 p.m. and is likely to cost from £6 ($10.50) to £8 ($14). The Lade is open only from March to November.

ABERFOYLE: Looking like an Alpine village, in the heart of the Rob Roy country, this small holiday resort is the gateway to the Trossachs, near Loch Ard. A large crafts center contains a wealth of gift items related to the Highlands.

Inverard Hotel, Loch Ard Road (tel. Aberfoyle 229), is an old stone Scottish country home, erected during Edwardian days. It stands on its own grounds and has a sunroom overlooking country scenery. The additions done in an alpine fashion add warmth. The dining room, with its pine trestle tables, Windsor chairs, rugged stone walls, and the lounge with its tartan carpeting, stone and wood paneling, make for intimacy and charm. Scottish dishes are featured, and there's a cocktail lounge for premeal drinks. All this is the concept of its enterprising owners, Mr. and Mrs. R. Williamson. They offer riding lessons, pony trekking, and deer stalking. Trout and salmon fishing are available, and packed lunches for £2.50 ($4.38) are quickly prepared for picnics and excursions. While guests usually stay at least a week, there are daily per-person terms for B&B—£9 ($15.75). In a room with private bath, the charge is £11 ($19.25) per person nightly. Meals, ordered separately, cost £7 ($12.25) at dinner, only £4 ($7) at lunch, including VAT.

The **Rob Roy Highland Motel** (tel. Aberfoyle 245), one mile from the village, is an ideal base for touring the Trossachs and the Perthshire Highlands. It is at the intersection where the A81 from Glasgow turns eastward toward Callander and Stirling. The motel is a long, one-story building of stone and stucco with a large parking lot and a gift shop on the premises. The accommodations consist of twin-bedded chalets with toilets and electric heaters, costing £12 ($21) per person for B&B, plus VAT. The attractive dining room serves breakfast, morning coffee, luncheon at £2.50 ($4.38), afternoon tea, high tea, and dinner at £6 ($10.50), with an à la carte menu available at most times. The motel is open all year.

In the heart of Aberfoyle, **Trossachs Kitchen,** serves coffee from 11 a.m. to noon, main dishes from noon, and cream teas between 3 and 5 p.m., in summer only.

THE TROSSACHS: The Duke's Road (A821) north from Aberfoyle climbs through the Achray Forest, past the **David Marshall Lodge** information center, operated by the Forestry Commission, where you can stop for snacks and a breathtaking view of the Forth Valley. The road runs to the Trossachs—the "bristly country"—between Lochs Achray and Katrine.

Loch Katrine, at the head of which Rob Roy was born, owes its fame to Sir Walter Scott who set his poem *The Lady of the Lake* there. The loch is the principal reservoir of the city of Glasgow. A small steamer, S.S. *Sir Walter Scott,* plies the waters of the loch which has submerged the Silver Strand of the romantic poet.

Sailings are between May 14 and September 24, between Trossachs Pier and Stronachlachar at a round-trip fare of £1.75 ($3.06) for adults, £1 ($1.75) for children. Complete information as to the sailing schedules is available from the Strathclyde Water Department, Lower Clyde Division, 419 Balmore Rd., Glasgow, Scotland G22 6NU (tel. Glasgow 336-5333). Light refreshments are available at Trossachs Pier.

On Loch Achray, lying between Lochs Venachar and Katrine, stands the **Loch Achray Hotel,** Trossachs (tel. Trossachs 229), a pleasant place from which to tour the Trossachs between Loch Achray and Loch Katrine. Achray Burn flows through the hotel garden. Simple bedrooms go for £10.75 ($18.81) in a single, increasing to £20 ($35) in a double, including a good Scottish breakfast. Set dinners for residents work out at £6.50 ($11.38) per person. Food is served from 11 a.m. to 9 p.m., with such standard fare offered as eggs mayonnaise and fresh fish dishes. You can eat drop in here for a good meal, paying from £4 ($7) to £6 ($10.50) for the privilege. A nice, friendly atmosphere exists, and near the hotel is some of the most spectacular scenery in the country.

LOCH LOMOND: This largest of Scotland's lochs was the center of the ancient district of Lennox, in the possession of the branch of the Stewart family from which sprang Lord Darnley, second husband of Mary Queen of Scots and father of James VI of Scotland, who was also James I of England. The ruins of Lennox Castle are on Inchmurrin, one of the 30 islands of the loch—one having ecclesiastical ruins, one noted for its yew trees planted by King Robert the Bruce to ensure a suitable supply of wood for the bows of his archers. The loch is fed by at least ten rivers from west, east, and north. On the eastern side is Ben Lomond, rising to a height of 3192 feet.

The song, "Loch Lomond," is supposed to have been composed by one of Bonnie Prince Charlie's captured followers on the eve of his execution in Carlisle Jail. The "low road" of the song is the path through the underworld which his spirit will follow to his native land after death, more quickly than his friends can travel to Scotland by the ordinary high road.

The road from Dumbarton to Crianlarich runs along the western shore of the loch, but the paddle steamer *Maid of the Loch* is an interesting, if slower, way to see the "banks and braes." It sails daily during the summer from Balloch Pier which is reached by the railway. There is a large car park serving the pier.

Traveling around Loch Lomond from the east, you'll find:

GARTOCHARN: Here, on the bank of the loch, is Ross Priory where Sir Walter Scott stayed. The summit of Duncryne, near the village, is an excellent place to get a panoramic view of the loch.

The **Gartocharn Village Hotel** (tel. Gartocharn 204) makes a good base for exploring the eastern side of Loch Lomond. It's a small white stucco building with comfortable, clean rooms with hot and cold running water, and a residents' lounge where a log fire blazes on cool days and nights. The owners,

John and Jill McKittrick, charge from £10 ($17.50) in a single and from £18 ($31.50) in a double. From noon to 9 p.m., bar snacks are served, including basket meals. High teas, a very Scottish custom, feature homemade scones, freshly made bread, and butter, along with jam and cakes, even a plate of haddock or bacon and eggs, freshly cooked and sizzling hot as a main course. If you order what is really tantamount to a supper, you'll pay £2.95 ($5.16), and that includes tea, of course. If you stay for dinner, four courses go for £7.50 ($13.13). Ample parking is provided behind the hotel, which is open all year.

LUSS: This village on the western side of Loch Lomond is the traditional home of the Colquhouns. Among its stone cottages, on the water's edge, is a branch of the Highland Arts Studios of Seil. Cruises on the loch or boat rentals may be arranged at the nearby jetty.

For a stopover in this attractive area, try **Rose Cottage** (tel. Luss 656), a small stone house on a hill overlooking the loch, at Aldlochlay, one mile outside Luss on the A82. Drive or walk up to the second house on the hill. Young, friendly Mrs. Carol Gallagher will rent you either a family room, sleeping four, or a double-bedded room for £7.50 ($13.13) per person for bed and a full Scottish breakfast.

CAIRNDOW: Barely visible from the main highway, the A83, the little town nestles between a hill and Loch Fyne, on the loch's eastern shore. It is a peaceful haven with a view of the loch and the high mountains. **Strone Woodland Garden** is open from April to September, containing unusual tree shrubs and the tallest tree in the United Kingdom.

Cairndow Stagecoach Inn & Stables Restaurant (tel. Cairndow 286) is one of the oldest coaching inns in the Highlands, having entertained such illustrious guests as Dorothy Wordsworth in 1803. Even Queen Victoria had her horses changed here in 1875. Nowadays, Douglas and Catherine Fraser welcome you in the best tradition of Scottish hospitality. Their inn lies just off the A83 on the upper reaches of Loch Fyne. In a relaxed country atmosphere, comfortably furnished rooms are rented, including two family rooms, at a rate of £9.50 ($16.63) per person for B&B. All units have hot and cold running water, and half a dozen have baths en suite. Many of the units open onto a view of the loch.

In the public bar and lounge you can sample many malt whiskies while chatting with the locals. In summer there is occasional entertainment at the inn, and once a month, a barn dance.

The stables from coaching days have been converted into the Stables Restaurant, with a beamed ceiling, candlelight, and views over the loch. A table d'hôte dinner is offered for £6.50 ($11.38), and you can also order à la carte, enjoying such local dishes as sauté haunch of venison in red wine sauce and Loch Fyne salmon steaks. Children's meals are also served, and "pub grub" is available in the bar during the day. The inn makes a good center for touring, or you can relax in the lochside garden.

Chapter XVIII

NORTHEAST SCOTLAND

1. Exploring Tayside
2. Aberdeen and Royal Deeside

COVERING THE REGIONS of Tayside and Grampian, Northeast Scotland beckons the visitor with much scenic grandeur, although some come just to hit the Whisky Trail.

Three of Scotland's most important cities—Dundee, Aberdeen, and Perth—are tucked away in this corner, and the section also contains three of the country's best-known salmon rivers: the Dee, the Spey, and the Tay.

The land is riddled with historic castles and will give you a view of Highland majesty—imposing, grand, tumultuous, including Queen Victoria's favorite view. The best known of the traditional Highland gatherings takes place at Braemar.

1. Exploring Tayside

The trouble with exploring Tayside is you may find it so fascinating in scenery you'll never make it on to the Highlands. Carved out of the old counties of Perth and Angus, Tayside is named for its major river, the 119-mile-long Tay. Its tributaries and dozens of lochans and highland streams are some of the best salmon and trout waters in Europe. One of the loveliest regions of Scotland, Tayside is filled with heather-clad Highland hills, long blue lochs under tree-clad banks, and miles and miles of walking trails.

It is a region dear to the Scots, a symbol of their desire for independence, as exemplified by the Declaration of Arbroath and the ancient coronation ritual of the "Stone of Destiny" at Scone. In cities, Perth and Dundee are among the leading six centers of Scotland.

Tayside also provided the backdrop for many novels by Sir Walter Scott, including *The Fair Maid of Perth, Waverley,* and *The Abbot.*

Its golf courses are world famous, ranging from the trio of 18-hole courses at Gleneagles to the open championships links at Carnoustie.

We'll begin our trip in an offshoot southern pocket of the county at Loch Leven, then take in Perth and its environs, heading east to Dundee, and later along the fishing villages of the North Sea, cutting west again to visit Glamis Castle, and, finally, ending our journey of exploration even further west in the lochs and glens of the Perthshire Highlands.

LOCH LEVEN: "Those never got luck who came to Loch Leven." This proverbial saying sums up the history of the **Loch Leven Castle,** on Castle Island, dating from the late 14th century. Among its more ill-fated prisoners, none was more notable than Mary Queen of Scots. Within its forbidding walls she signed her abdication on July 24, 1567. However, she effected her escape from Loch Leven on May 2, 1568. Thomas Percy, seventh Earl of Northumberland, supported her cause. For his efforts, he too was imprisoned and lodged in the castle for three years until he was handed over to the English, who beheaded him at York.

Lying to the north of Dunfermline (head toward Kinross), the loch has seven islands. Loch Leven Castle, of course, is in ruins. So is the **Priory of Loch Leven,** built on the site of one of the oldest Culdee establishments in Scotland, and lying on St. Serf's, the largest of the islands in the loch.

In Kinross, 25 miles north of Edinburgh, you can make arrangements to visit Loch Leven Castle by boat, the only means of access. Or you can overnight there at one of the following selections:

Hawthorn Vale (tel. Kinross 63117) has a picture-postcard look to it, a small stone house set in a garden, with a stone wall along the road, overlooking Loch Leven. It's the private home of Mrs. Pat Warder, who has three double rooms, one with twin beds, which she rents reasonably at £7 ($12.25) per person. Each of her rooms is acceptably attractive and comfortable, with hot and cold running water. Along the hall is a separate toilet. In Mrs. Warder's guest lounge is a TV set and a radio at your disposal. Two of her rooms overlook her garden (and she's rightly proud of how well kept it is). Her breakfasts are filling and done as you like them, and although she doesn't provide dinners (snacks are quite possible), she'll guide you to nearby restaurants.

Kirklands Hotel, High Street (tel. Kinross 63313), is a village hotel, all glistening white with bright shutters and a modernized interior. It has Georgian touches in its entry, and the pillars in the residents' lounge. Warm colors have been used throughout; even the bedrooms carry out the autumnal theme. Each bedroom is pleasant, with hot and cold water. The owners, Bill and Diana Kerr, charge from £11 ($19.25) in a single and from £22 ($38.50) in a double, including a full breakfast, VAT, and service. Bar lunches offer such items as baked avocado with a seafood and cream filling at £2.75 ($4.81), or a homemade soup with bread and butter at 55p (96¢). A set dinner costs £10.50 ($18.38), but if a resident wants only two courses, the price is reduced to just £7 ($12.25).

PERTH: From its majestic position on the Tay, the ancient city of Perth was the capital of Scotland until the middle of the 15th century. Here the Highland meets the Lowland. Sir Walter Scott immortalized the royal burgh in *The Fair Maid of Perth.* On Curfew Road you can still see the house of Catherine Glover, the fair maid herself.

The main sightseeing attraction of "the fair city" is the **Kirk of St. John the Baptist,** of which the original foundation, it is believed, dates from Pictish times. However, the present choir dates from 1440 and the nave from 1490. In 1559 John Knox preached his famous sermon here attacking idolatry, and it caused a turbulent wave of iconoclasm to sweep across the land. The church was restored as a World War I memorial in the mid-1920s. In the church is the tombstone of James I, who was murdered by Sir Robert Graham.

Food and Lodging

The **Two-O-Eight Hotel,** 208 Crieff Rd. (tel. Perth 28936), was built by its present owners, Norman and Dorothy Doris, in the mid-'70s. It's on the main road in a suburban setting on the west boundary of the city, yet just a 20-minute walk to the center of Perth. A regular bus service stops at the hotel every 20 minutes. There are 16 bedrooms, each with hot and cold running water, and innerspring mattresses. There is a fully licensed bar where you can order drinks and watch TV. The per-person rate nightly for B&B is £9 ($15.75), plus VAT. Add another £1.75 ($3.06) per person for a private bath. Mrs. Doris can fix a tasty Scottish dinner for £5 ($8.75).

Pitcullen Guest House, 17 Pitcullen Crescent, on the A94 road (tel. Perth 26506), stands in a residential district, a short walk from the city center. It's a turn-of-the-century stone building, with dormers and a crescent-shaped bay window. The owner, Mrs. Grainger, keeps her B&B rate at a minimum, asking £8 ($14) per person nightly. Most of their guests also ask for an evening meal for £4 ($7). There's central heating, hot and cold water, and tea- and coffee-making facilities in the rooms, and if you are in the mood, a color TV in the residents' lounge.

Corinna Hotel, 44 Atholl St. (tel. Perth 24623), is owned by the Davies family. It's quite simple and inexpensive. The cost of a room only is just £5 ($8.75); however, a bed and a continental breakfast served in your bedroom is £6.50 ($11.38) per person. Bed and a full Scottish breakfast costs £8 ($14) per person. Evening bar suppers are served from 7:30 to 9:30 p.m., offering a choice of eight main courses priced from 90p ($1.58) to £4.20 ($7.35), the latter price for an eight-ounce sirloin steak.

The **Miller's Table,** at City Mills Hotel, West Mill Street (tel. Perth 28281), serves one of the biggest buffet spreads in the city. From noon to 2:30 p.m., you help yourself from a table of hot and cold dishes. Homemade soups begin at 55p (96¢), and a choice of home-cooked meats is from £1.50 ($2.63) per portion. Fresh salads cost from 45p (79¢) per dollop. Finally, there's a choice of desserts from 85p ($1.49) per serving. The hotel takes its name from a millstream which flows under the structure. You can view the running water through panels of glass. The table is empty on Sunday. But there is a **Steakhouse** on the premises, if you'd like to visit at night. Including an appetizer and vegetable, it offers a half-pound Angus steak for £6.50 ($11.38). Or if you're saving money, you can order a haddock dinner, again with appetizer and vegetable, for only £4 ($7). Hours are from noon to 2:30 p.m. and from 5 to 10:30 p.m.

Hunters Lodge, at Bankfoot (tel. Perth 87325), lies six miles north of Perth (turn off the A9 at Bankfoot services) on the road to Inverness. Bruce and Jeudi Hunter, the owners, are winners of the BBC "best pub grub in Scotland" award. Naturally, they specialize in bar snacks. The Hunters are noted for their Scottish specialties. For an appetizer, your selection might be their own special pâté or smoked mackerel filet. The best fish dish is Scottish salmon which they poach to perfection and serve in a white wine sauce. For dessert, why not the Drambuie cheesecake? Expect to spend from £7.50 ($13.13) for all that, plus the cost of your drink. Children's portions are also available. The restaurant hours are from 11 a.m. to 2:30 p.m. and 5 to 9 p.m. Derivations of the dining room cuisine are served in the bar in generous portions for less expensive rates. Hunters Lodge also offers a traditional Scottish high tea at £3.80 ($6.65), big enough for a good supper. It's served daily from 5 to 7 p.m. Self-catering cabins and lodges are situated on the grounds of the hotel.

READERS' B&B SELECTION: "We were especially impressed with **Cintra,** 90 Dundee Rd. (tel. Perth 22172), owned by Ann and Archie Gilmour. The rooms are beautiful, clean, and cheerful. Ann and Archie are fantastic and served one of the best breakfasts we have ever eaten. We even had pancakes and bakery fresh rolls" (Ava and Joe Beard, Santa Fe, N.M.).

SCONE: On the River Tay, Old Scone was the ancient capital of the Picts. On a lump of granite, the "Stone of Destiny," the monarchs of the Dark Ages were enthroned. The British sovereign to this day is still crowned on the stone, but in Westminster Abbey. Edward I removed the stone there in 1296. Charles II was the last king crowned at Scone; the year: 1651.

Scone Palace (tel. Scone 52300), the seat of the Earl of Mansfield, was largely rebuilt in 1803, incorporating parts of the palace erected in 1580. Inside is an impressive collection of French antiques, furniture, china, ivories, and 16th-century needlework, including some bed hangings executed by Mary Queen of Scots. A fine collection of rare conifers is found on the grounds in the Pinetum. Rhododendrons and azaleas grow profusely in the gardens and woodlands around the palace. To reach the palace, head north of Perth on the A93. It lies two miles from the city center. The site is open from Good Friday until the second Monday in October on weekdays from 10 a.m. to 6 p.m. (on Sunday from 2 to 6 p.m.), charging an admission of £1.50 ($2.63) for adults, 90p ($1.58) for children, including entrance to both the house and grounds.

CRIEFF: At the edge of the Perthshire Highlands, Crieff makes a pleasant stopover, what with its possibilities for fishing and golf. This small burgh, 18 miles from Perth, was the seat of the court of the Earls of Strathearn until 1747. Once gallows in its marketplace were used to execute Highland cattle rustlers.

You can take a "day trail" into Strathearn, the valley of the River Earn, the very center of Scotland. Highland mountains meet gentle Lowland slopes, and moorland mingles with rich green pastures. North of Crieff the road to Aberfeldy passes through the narrow pass of the Sma' Glen with hills rising on either side to 2000 feet. The Glen is a famous beauty spot.

In addition you can explore a distillery, glassworks, a pottery center, and an aircraft museum.

Glenturret Distillery Ltd. (tel. Crieff 2424) is Scotland's oldest distillery, established in 1775. On the banks of the River Turret, it is reached from Crieff by taking the A85 toward Comrie. At a point three-quarters of a mile from Crieff, turn right at the crossroads; the distillery is a quarter mile up the road. It is all signposted. Visitors can see the milling of malt, mashing, fermentation, distillation, and cask filling, followed by a free "wee dram" dispensed at the end of the tour. Visitors are welcome, March to October, Monday to Friday from 10 a.m. to 12:30 p.m. and 1:30 to 3:45 p.m. The last morning tour is at 12:15 p.m., the last afternoon tour at 3:45 p.m. Tours leave every ten minutes. In July and August tours are Monday to Saturday from 10 a.m. to 4 p.m. The Glenturret Heritage Centre incorporates a 100-seat audio-visual theater and an exhibition display museum. Glenturret whiskies of 8, 12, and 15 years of age are available at the distillery shop.

Stuart Strathearn, Muthill Road (tel. Crieff 2942), is a factory welcoming visitors wanting to see how handmade crystal is produced. June to September it is open Monday to Saturday from 9 a.m. to 5 p.m.; on Sunday, noon to 5 p.m. You can see the traditional craftsman's skill on the Stuart Crystal film and demonstrated by factory glassworkers. The shop on the premises has a large selection of Stuart Crystal seconds and its own engraved crystal giftware. In the grounds of the factory is a picnic area, plus a children's playground.

A. W. Buchan & Co. Ltd., also on Muthill Road (tel. Crieff 3515), is a pottery shop where you can see the thistle decoration applied. The thistle, one of Scotland's best-known blooms, is applied entirely by hand, as are such other blooms as heather and bluebell. The pottery shop is open from 9:30 a.m. to 5 p.m., Monday to Friday, and from 10 a.m. to 5 p.m. on Saturday and Sunday. The Sunday opening is only from April to mid-December. Conducted tours of the pottery are given at 10:15 a.m., 11:30 a.m., and again at 1:30 p.m. and 4 p.m. Monday to Thursday. On Friday tours are at 10:15 and 11:30 a.m. There are no conducted tours on Saturday and Sunday.

The **Strathallan Aircraft Collection** is at Strathallan Airfield, near Auchterarder (tel. Auchterarder 2545). From Auchterarder, follow the B8062 for Crieff and then the signs for the museum. From Crieff, take the A822 to Muthill and follow the signs. The collection is open daily, April 1 to October 31, from 10 a.m. to 5 p.m. (later in July and August). Aircraft on display include a Lancaster bomber, a Hurricane fighter, and a Westland Lysander. There are also displays of aero engines and many other items of a nostalgic nature. Wet weather need not deter a visitor, as most exhibits are indoors. Flying weekends are held every summer.

Three miles south of Crieff, you can visit the gardens of **Drummond Castle,** the seat of the Earl of Ancaster. The second Earl of Perth laid out these ten-acre gardens in 1662 along continental lines. The grounds are open from April 1 to October 31 on Wednesday and Sunday from 2 to 6 p.m. Admission is 70p ($1.23) for adults, 30p (53¢) for children.

Food and Lodging

In accommodations, I recommend the following:

The **Birches Hotel,** Comrie Road (tel. Crieff 3172), does have birch trees in its own garden on the west end of Crieff, directly opposite McRosty Park. It's owned by Mr. and Mrs. Philip, who charge £8 ($14) per person daily for B&B. Each bedroom is attractive and tidy, with hot and cold water, a gas heater, and electric blankets for the chillier periods. The hotel is fully licensed, so you can have wine or lager with your home-cooked meals.

Gwydyr, Comrie Road (tel. Crieff 3277), now a century old, is a fine house about a five-minute walk from the center of the burgh. Ian and Christine Gillies, along with their warm and hospitable staff, welcome you to this friendly and gracious hotel. The B&B charge is £10 ($17.50) in a single, £18 ($31.50) in a double, and all of their accommodations contain hot and cold running water. The beds are comfortable, and as an added convenience, you're given facilities for making tea or coffee. The dining room serves well-prepared food, using local ingredients whenever possible. They offer a selection of dishes, all reasonably priced. The dining room is open from 7 to 8 p.m. A three-course dinner goes for £5.75 ($10.06), including coffee. If you're at the place for lunch, you can take it in the bar, enjoying soups, pâté, fried haddock, or ham steaks, a two-course meal going for about £2.50 ($4.38). The cellar is well stocked with wines, beers, and liquors. In the residents' lounge, guests gather around a color television. Gwydyr stands on its own grounds, a large garden overlooking MacRosty Park. You'll have an uninterrupted view of Ben Vorlich and Glen Artney to the south.

The **Star Hotel,** East High Street (tel. Crieff 2632), is one of the best little hotels in town, right on the main street. Owners Allan and Catherine Hendry not only have some good rooms to rent, but they offer one of the better menus in Crieff. They give you a real Scottish welcome, sheltering you in one of their pleasant and comfortable units at a cost of £9 ($15.75) in a single and from £16 ($28) in a double. With a private shower, you pay an extra £1.50 ($2.63) nightly. Some family rooms rent for £21 ($36.75) a night, including VAT.

Lunch is served daily from noon to 2 p.m., with specials featured at £1.50 ($2.63). High tea is served from 5 to 6:45 p.m., and an à la carte dinner menu is presented from 7 to 9:15 p.m. Dinner is from £5.50 ($9.63) and is likely to include such specialties as salmon from the Tay. There is both a well-stocked bar and a lounge bar.

In food, try the **Highlandman Restaurant,** East High Street (tel. Crieff 4866). This former garage has been converted into a well-run restaurant and tea room, attracting both visitors and the local trade. It is open from 10 a.m. to 7 p.m. daily except Sunday when its hours are from noon to 7 p.m. Diners can enjoy a variety of hot and cold dishes, sandwiches, desserts, and children's specials. A homemade soup followed by a Highlandman mixed grill with a cup of tea would cost only £2.30 ($4.03), with a sandwich going for around 70p ($1.23). The restaurant is fully licensed.

READER'S GUEST HOUSE SELECTION: "A splendid B&B in Crieff is owned by **Miss B. A. Sim,** 1 Addison Crescent (tel. Crieff 2434), on a quiet little cul-de-sac within minutes' walk of good shopping, Miss Sim charges £7 ($12.25) each for B&B or £9 ($15.75) with dinner. The house is cozy and comfortable, and Miss Sim is the nicest, most gracious hostess we encountered in eight weeks of travel" (W. A. Sargent, Ottawa, Ontario, Canada).

COMRIE: An attractive little village in Strathearn, 25 miles from Perth, Comrie stands at the confluence of the Earn, Ruchill, and Lednock Rivers. The A85 runs through the village to Lochearnhead, Crianlarich, Oban, and the Hebrides in the west. It's convenient as an overnight stop for travelers crossing Scotland. Waterskiing, boating, and sailing are available on Loch Earn.

The **Royal Hotel,** Melville Square (tel. Comrie 70200), was awarded the "royal" after the visit of Her Majesty, Queen Victoria. It's not, as you might imagine, a Victorian hotel, but rather an L-shaped stone inn dating back to 1765, with white trim and six bedroom dormers. Its drinking lounge, with walls and chairs in Gordon tartan, has an intriguing collection of photos, sketches, and prints of famous people who have stayed here, everybody from Madame Sarah Bernhardt to Lloyd George. The dining room is equally attractive with a fireplace and autumnal colors. The bedrooms are most comfortable, some with private bath and toilet, all with electric blankets and telephone. The charge per person nightly for B&B is £13.50 ($23.63), rising to £15 ($26.25) per person with a private bath. Dinner prices start at £8.25 ($14.44), although you can also choose à la carte.

On the A85 road, the **Museum of Scottish Tartans** contains the world's largest collection of tartans and Highland dress portrayed in pictures, models, and prints. It is open from April to October on weekdays from 9 a.m. to 5 p.m. and on Sunday from 2 to 4 p.m. In winter, hours are Monday to Friday from 10 a.m. to 4 p.m. and on Saturday from 10 a.m. to 1 p.m. They will open on Sunday in winter by appointment (telephone Comrie 70779).

There is a reconstruction of a weaver's cottage with demonstrations of hand-spinning and dyeing of cloth, as well as a special exhibition of a typical parlor of Balmoral where Queen Victoria started the great trend toward all things tartan.

DUNDEE: This royal burgh and old seaport is an industrial city, one of the largest in Scotland, lying on the north shore of the Firth of Tay. It's noted for its flax, jute, and marmalade. Spanning the Firth, the Tay Railway Bridge was opened in 1888. It's nearly two miles long, one of the longest in Europe.

In the suburbs, at **Broughty Ferry,** 3½ miles from Dundee, the castle dates from 1498. For a spectacular view, go to **Dundee Law,** a 572-foot hill just a mile north of the city.

Most visitors pass through Dundee en route to Glamis Castle, 12 miles north. However, if you'd like to stop for the night, there is the—

Carlton House Hotel, 2 Dalgleish Rd. (tel. Dundee 43456), a 19th-century building beside the roadway, with a mansard roof and adjoining modern wing, all in harmonious colors of beige nut brown, white, and curtains of tangerine. Every room has color TV, a radio, a room call system, and a private shower. B&B in a single is £13 ($22.75), and for two, £19 ($33.25). VAT is extra. You can have dinners in the pleasantly decorated Tudor dining room or a drink in the bar lounge. A three-course evening meal ranges in price from £3 ($5.25) to £4.25 ($7.44). There's also a private car park.

For a dining choice, try **Gunga-Din Restaurant,** 99c-101 Perth Rd. (tel. Dundee 65672), which lies to the west of the city in the university sector. Nearly everything is prepared to order, so don't come here seeking fast food if you're rushed. The university students and others who patronize Gunga-Din know that the meats and vegetables are seasonally fresh, and care is taken to follow original Indian recipes. You could begin a savory meal with the prawn soup, followed by a wide variety of meat or fish dishes (don't hesitate to ask the waiter for assistance). Among these, try chicken biriyani cooked with pilaf nuts, raisins, herbs, pepper, and tomatoes in clarified butter. Dessert might be a homemade mango ice cream. All this would cost about £6.50 ($11.38). You can dine for much less if you stick to the vegetable curries. The restaurant is open from noon to 2:30 p.m. and 6 to 11:30 p.m. Monday through Saturday, from 6 to 10:30 p.m. on Sunday. On weekends, you should reserve a table for dinner by calling in the morning.

The Pizza Gallery, 3–7 Peter St. (tel. Dundee 21422), is a two-level modern establishment off a shoppers' street. It is open daily except Sunday from 10 a.m. to 11 p.m., offering a choice of some 13 pizzas at a top price of £2.20 ($3.85). For reasons known only to themselves, the pizzas are named after famous artists. The Picasso is uncharacteristically basic (cheese and tomato), but the Goya is more inspired with anchovies, green pepper, and olives. For eaters wanting a more complete meal, soup followed by a large chef's salad, a heaping plate of spaghetti, and finally a strawberry cheesecake would cost £3.05 ($5.34). The restaurant is licensed to sell wine by the glass or the carafe, and it enjoys much popularity among the denizens of Dundee.

CARNOUSTIE: This seaside resort, 61 miles northeast of Edinburgh, is celebrated for its championship golf course. Lying between Dundee and Arbroath (eight miles away), Carnoustie opens onto the North Sea. In summer its five miles of sand give plenty of beach space to its visitors.

For food and lodging, I suggest:

Glencoe Hotel, Links Parade (tel. Carnoustie 53273), is not only a good place to stay, but it serves some of the best and most reasonably priced food in town. Nonresidents are welcome to drop in. This privately owned hotel, the domain of Mrs. C. B. Leslie, is fully licensed, lying in a spot overlooking the Tay estuary. Only ten bedrooms, each centrally heated, are offered. All doubles come with private bath and shower, costing £13.75 ($24.06) per person. A full Scottish breakfast is included in that tariff, along with VAT and service. The Glencoe is the hotel nearest the championship golf course, being directly opposite the first tee and the last green and adjacent to the Burnside Course. There is a resident lounge with TV, plus contemporary sun parlors with unobstructed views of the golf course. In the modern cocktail lounge you can order your favorite scotch malt whisky. A fixed-price dinner menu in the dining room goes for £5.80 ($10.15) and includes four courses of well-prepared food. First, you get the appetizer, then a main course such as roast leg of lamb with mint sauce, followed by an apple tart with fresh Scottish cream. Some of the specialties, such as Scottish salmon, cost more when chosen from the table d'hôte. Dinner is served daily from 7:30 to 9 p.m. A slightly cheaper and simplified version of the dinner menu is offered at lunch from noon to 2 p.m. daily.

Villa Rosa Hotel, 13 Philip St. (tel. Carnoustie 52182), is an 1812 house, which seemingly at one time was a large family home, with gardens and interesting architectural features. It's in the center of town, just off the High Street, a few minutes' walk from the seafront, the beach, and the first tee of the championship golf course. The interior, with its classic hallway and open staircase, has a reception lounge, a cocktail bar, another lounge with color TV, and a dining room with a bay window. Owners Mr. and Mrs. Cook charge £7.50 ($13.13) nightly per person for B&B including VAT. The dinner costs £5 ($8.75) for three courses.

Earlston Hotel, Church Street (tel. Carnoustie 52352), which has a village-cottage look to it, is quite professionally adapted to a hotel, offering all the required comforts and niceties. It stands in a long row of attached brick buildings, with white trim, a pair of bays, and four dormers. The interior is harmoniously decorated, the dining room spacious, yet cozy. The bedrooms are color coordinated, usually with a neat use of furnishings, using wood and autumnal colors. Many rooms have a private shower as well. The daily rate, not including VAT and service, is £14.50 ($25.38) per person in a bathless room. With shower it's £17 ($29.75) per person. The hotel is fully licensed, and provides set as well as à la carte meals. For evening relaxation, there is the residents' lounge with TV, plus two drinking bars.

Braemore Guest House, 24 Dundee St. (tel. Carnoustie 52076), provides budget accommodations under the care and hospitality of its owner, Margaret Warhurst. She charges only £6.50 ($11.38) per person for an overnight stay and will cook one of her well-prepared dinners for £3.50 ($6.13). Her home is centrally located, within a few minutes' walk of the golf courses, putting greens, the shops, and public transport. She has become the favorite guest house for many Americans. One San Francisco couple recently returned for their seventh visit. The bedrooms have basic necessities and are neat, with hot and cold running water.

Almondbank Hotel, 29 Ireland St. (tel. Carnoustie 59510), owned by Mr. and Mrs. A. Dunbar, is homelike and comfortable. Mrs. Dunbar likes to cook breakfasts that please, and charges £7 ($12.25) per person for this meal and your bed. She'll also prepare a lunch or dinner, charging from £3.50 ($6.13) to £4.25 ($7.44) per person for three courses, including coffee. The bedrooms are simply furnished but clean, and have hot and cold running water. The guest lounge is large, overlooking the garden with its putting green. Almondbank is within walking distance of the beach area.

ARBROATH: Samuel Johnson wasn't that much impressed with Scotland on his jaunt there, but he did say that the view of Arbroath repaid him for some of the hardships suffered in his journey. Arbroath is a popular coastal resort with a colorful fishing harbor and rugged, red sandstone cliffs weathered into grotesque shapes. Smugglers once used the sandstone caves along the coast. Arbroath "smokies" (smoked haddock) are one of the fish delicacies along the east coast of Scotland.

The "Fairport" of Sir Walter Scott's *The Antiquary,* the royal burgh of Arbroath lies 17 miles northeast of Dundee. On its High Street are the ruins of a red sandstone abbey, once the richest in Scotland. It was founded by William the Lion in 1178, and the king was buried in its precincts in 1214. The Scottish Parliament met there in 1320 and sent the pope a famous letter asserting the independence of their country. In the abbey a historical pageant is presented every year.

Two miles to the west stands **Kellie Castle,** Arbroath (tel. Arncroach 271), built in 1170 and restored in 1679. Of pink sandstone, the castle is noted for its unique courtyard and left-handed spiral stairway. Robert the Bruce once came into possession of it, during the "Black Parliament." It is open from mid-April until the end of September, daily except Friday from 2 to 6 p.m., charging adults 90p ($1.58) for admission to both the castle and grounds, although children pay only 40p (70¢).

For food and lodging, you might try—

Towerbank Hotel, James Street (tel. Arbroath 75987), is not unlike a country village inn in southern France, where there is an excellent restaurant which also rents out bedrooms for overnight guests. It's been taken over by Michael and Patricia Taddei, and their menu plans are ambitious. Their little 100-year-old hotel has a courtyard entrance and parking area. Many of their bedrooms overlook the 800-year-old abbey. There are no private baths, but all rooms have hot and cold running water and are simple, yet pleasant. The daily per-person charge is £13 ($22.75) in a single, £9 ($15.75) in a double. Lunch can be taken in either the bar or the dining room where there's a display of nine hot and nine cold dishes, a plate averaging about £2.50 ($4.38). Dinner is served between 7:30 and 11 p.m. The "starters" are good, including a smoked mackerel filet with parsley butter, followed by such main courses as a roast haunch of venison in a rich game sauce with a dash of Drambuie. Desserts are rich tasting and good, including ginger meringue cream. Dinners run about £9 ($15.75), or you can order a set three courses for £7.50 ($13.13).

Royal Hotel, High Street (tel. Arbroath 72237), is an excellent link in the Welcome Inn chain. The tab, including a big breakfast and VAT, for a single is £12 ($21); a double room goes for £22 ($38.50). Lunches in the bar start at £2.50 ($4.38), and the famed Scottish high teas, served in summer only, in the evening begin as low as £2.75 ($4.81). But if you want a pint of lager and a light noontime snack, you can get a hot or cold quick meal in the pub. The hotel is convenient, right in the center of town.

Sandhutton Guest House, 16 Addison Pl. (tel. Arbroath 72007), is a friendly oasis, and it's economical. Mary and Peter Pert make it all personal, and their little courtesies and assistance can mean all the difference. They ask £8 ($14) per person for B&B, and they serve a full cooked meal—eggs and bacon as you want them. And as a bonus in the evening, they offer tea and cookies before you retire. They have a separate dining room, and for £4 ($7) they'll prepare a tasty evening meal, but not in July and August—they're too busy then. However, they'll recommend budget restaurants nearby. There's a lounge with color TV for their guests. All their bedrooms are decorated in a homelike manner, have wash basins with hot and cold water, and electric blankets. As Mary says, "Cleanliness and comfort we can guarantee." They have no singles, but if possible they'll offer a lone guest a double if they are not crowded and can spare the room.

Anderson Hotel, Bank Street (tel. Arbroath 73378), is owned by a colorful and gracious host, Denis Mackintosh, who offers excellent bedrooms which he rents nightly for £9.50 ($16.63) per person, including a substantial breakfast. The units are comfortably furnished and well maintained. Many people in

Arbroath come here just to sample the food. During both lunch and dinner, very good meals are available in the bar. You might try, as I did, a bowl of soup, a plate of roast meat with a vegetable, then a dessert, all for only £2.20 ($3.85). If you don't want beef, pork, or lamb, try the fresh haddock in a cream sauce. Everything is freshly cooked on the premises. Denis has no passion for the frozen foods of today. "I like my meat, fish, and vegetables fresh every day," he says. "Why shouldn't my customers want the same?"

MONTROSE: Instead of heading immediately for Glamis Castle, I suggest you continue along the coastal road from Arbroath toward Montrose. Along the way you'll pass stretches of rugged beauty. Sandstone cliffs rise sharply out of the water, and little slate-roofed cottages house the families who make their living from the often turbulent sea.

Montrose stands on a bottleneck of Montrose Basin, a broad estuary inhabited by hundreds of wild birds, notably pink-footed geese. This harbor town, with its well-known golf links, is a North Sea coastal resort for holiday-makers. Its spired church and town hall date from the 18th century. David I granted Montrose its charter, and in 1352 it became one of Scotland's many royal burghs. Montrose lies 30 miles northeast of Dundee by road.

Central Hotel, High Street (tel. Montrose 2152), is one of the Welcome Inn chain which gives one assurance of a well-run hostelry. It's in the heart of town, where you can get all the necessities and sleep in peace. A bathless single with breakfast is £13.50 ($23.63), and a double or twin is £26 ($45.50) nightly. If you want a private bath, the tariff rises to £28 ($49) in a twin. In the Steakhouse, lunch starts at £4 ($7), high tea from £2.25 ($3.94), and dinners from £6 ($10.50). When in the bar, you can have a simple lunch at a low tab. All prices include VAT.

Corner House, High Street (tel. Montrose 3126), is a pub hotel directly on the High, and adjacent to a church with a clock tower. It places heavy emphasis on its street-level bar lounge. On the second floor is a dining room for residents as well as transients. In a single, the B&B cost is £16 ($28) if bathless, £20 ($35) with bath; a double the rate is £25 ($43.75) without bath, £29 ($50.75) with bath. You can get a "proper sitdown" lunch and an evening meal for about £7 ($12.25). Mrs. Reid, wife of the owner, oversees the meals, and the cooking is good. On the à la carte menu you can order an Angus filet, venison cooked in red wine, and homemade soup of the day.

KIRRIEMUIR: This town of narrow streets is the birthplace of Sir James Barrie, the "Thrums" of his novels. The Scottish dramatist and novelist, whose best-loved play is *Peter Pan,* was born here in 1860, the son of a father who was employed as a hand-loom weaver of linen. **Barrie's Birthplace,** 9 Brechin Rd. (tel. 05752/2646), a property of the National Trust of Scotland, contains manuscripts and mementos of the writer, and is open May 1 to September 30 on weekdays from 10 a.m. to 12:30 p.m. and from 2 to 6 p.m. (just afternoons on Sunday), charging 50p (88¢) for admission for adults, 25p (44¢) for children.

If you'd like to spend the night, **Thrums Hotel,** Bank Street (tel. Kirriemuir 2758), is the best bet. Providing a warm, friendly welcome, May and Alastair Simpson will give you a good bed and a traditional Scottish breakfast for £9.50 ($16.63) per person nightly. Their hotel is like an inn, standing in the heart of town. Their rooms are pleasantly kept, and everything about the hotel is well maintained. You might like the place so much you'll use it as a center for touring Tayside.

Should you be just passing through, Thrums is also ideal for lunch. It suitably honors J. M. Barrie by offering some very old-fashioned and traditional Scottish cookery, including Tayside salmon, Angus steaks, cloutie dumpling, and of course, Peter Pan porridge. For dessert, why not the Kirriemuir gingerbread? Lunch, served from noon to 2 p.m., is inexpensive: you'll rarely spend more than £5 ($8.75). Should you stay for dinner, which is served from 6:30 to 9 p.m., expect to spend around £9 ($15.55), especially if you order the Angus steak or Tayside salmon.

READER'S B&B SELECTION: "I suggest a B&B, **Torrydean,** 16 Kinnordy Rd. (tel. Kirriemuir 2343), which is owned by Mrs. H. Allen. It has a helpful, friendly, and homey atmosphere. Mrs. Allen has two spotless bedrooms for rent at £8 ($14) per person. She is able to house five guests and is located just minutes from the town center. At her suggestion we drove to nearby Clova for dinner at the **Jubilee Arms,** where we had liver and haddock dinners with a bill totaling £9 ($15.75) for two" (Diane Caldwell, El Cajon, Calif.).

GLAMIS CASTLE: After Balmoral Castle, most visitors to Scotland want to see Glamis Castle at Glamis (pronounced Glaams), for its architecture and its link with the crown. For ten centuries it has been connected to British royalty. Her Majesty, Queen Elizabeth, the Queen Mother, was brought up here; her daughter, now Queen Elizabeth II, spent a good deal of her childhood here; and Princess Margaret, the Queen's sister, was born here, becoming the first royal princess born in Scotland in three centuries. The existing castle dates in part from the middle of the 15th century, but there are records of a castle's having been in existence in the 11th century, at which time it was one of the hunting lodges of the Kings of Scotland. King Malcolm II was carried there mortally wounded in 1034 after having been attacked by his enemies while hunting in a nearby forest.

Glamis Castle has been in the possession of the Lyon family since 1372, when it formed part of the dowry of Princess Joanna, daughter of King Robert II, when she married John Lyon, secretary to the king. The castle was altered in the 16th century and restored and enlarged in the 17th, 18th, and 19th centuries. It contains some fine plaster ceilings, furniture, and paintings.

The present owner, the Queen's cousin, is the 17th Earl of Strathmore and Kinghorne. He lives at the castle with his wife and three children. He is the direct descendant of the first earl.

The castle is open to the public, who have access to the Royal Apartments and many other rooms, and also to the fine gardens, May to September, Sunday through Friday, at £1.50 ($2.63) for adults, 75p ($1.31) for children. If you wish to visit only the grounds, laid out by Capability Brown, you pay only half price. For further details of the castle opening, get in touch with the Administrator, Estates Office (tel. Glamis 242).

Also in Glamis, you may want to visit the **Angus Folk Museum,** Kirkwynd Cottages, run by the National Trust of Scotland. From the former county of Angus, rich in folklore, were collected domestic utensils, agricultural implements, furniture, and clothing. The museum is open from May 1 to September 30 from noon to 5 p.m. (last entry at 4:30 p.m.), charging adults 75p ($1.31); children, 35p (61¢).

DUNKELD: A cathedral town, Dunkeld lies in a thickly wooded valley of the Tay River, at the edge of the Perthshire Highlands. Once a major ecclesiastical center, it is one of the seats of ancient Scottish history. It was an important center of the Celtic church, for example.

The National Trust of Scotland has been effective in restoring many of the old houses and shops around the marketplace and cathedral that had fallen into decay.

The **Cathedral of Dunkeld** was founded in 815. David I converted the church into a cathedral in 1127. The 14th and 15th centuries witnessed subsequent additions. The cathedral was first restored in 1815, and at that time traces of the 12th-century structure clearly remained, as they do to this day.

Finally, Shakespeare fans may want to seek out the oak and sycamore in front of the destroyed **Birnam House,** a mile to the south. This was believed to be a remnant of the Birnam wood to which the Bard gave everlasting literary fame in *Macbeth.* In Shakespeare's drama, you may recall, the "woods of Birnam came to Dunsinane."

The **Atholl Arms Hotel** (tel. Dunkeld 219), a white, prim corner hotel, stands in the center of the village. Inside it has the aura and furnishings of a gracious country home. The lounge is all in white, with a fireplace, brightly covered armchairs, and a row of antique platters. There are 27 bedrooms, each having its own heating and hot and cold water. In the morning a cup of hot coffee can be brought to your bedside. The terms, including VAT, are £11.50 ($20.13) nightly per person, with a country-style breakfast. An evening meal is priced at £7.50 ($13.13), VAT included. Snack lunches and afternoon tea are also available.

The **Taybank Hotel** (tel. Dunkeld 340), just off the main road, is almost on the Tay River—very quiet for a good night's rest. The hotel is listed as a building of historical interest. Owned by Mr. and Mrs. Reid, the hotel has an atmosphere that is intimate and comfortable. They charge £10 ($17.50) in a single and from £20 ($35) in a double. Dinner is à la carte, but the half-board rate is an extra £6 ($10.50) per person, which is a very good value.

PITLOCHRY: After leaving Edinburgh, many motorists stop here for the night before continuing on the Highland road to Inverness. However, once they discover the charms of Pitlochry, they want to linger. This popular holiday resort center is a touring headquarters for the Valley of the Tummel.

It is particularly renowned for its **Pitlochry Festival Theatre,** Scotland's "theatre in the hills." Telephone Pitlochry 2680 for information. Founded in 1951, the festival theater draws people from all over the world to its repertoire of plays, Sunday concerts, and changing art exhibitions, presented from sometime in May until the end of September. A new theater opened in 1981 on the banks of the River Tummel near the dam and fish ladder, with a car park, a restaurant serving coffee, lunch, and dinner, and other facilities for visitors.

The **Pitlochry Dam** was created because a power station was needed, but in effect the engineers created a new loch. The famous "Salmon Ladder" was built to help the struggling salmon upstream. An underwater portion of the ladder—a salmon observation chamber—has been enclosed in glass to give fascinated sightseers a look.

Pitlochry doesn't just entertain tourists, although it would appear that way in summer. It also produces scotch whisky and tweeds.

Food and Lodging

Acarsaid, 8 Atholl Rd. (tel. Pitlochry 2389), is a combination of the old and very new. A stone Edwardian house with three decorative gables is sandwiched between two modern extensions made of stone, natural wood, and glass. Delft-blue trim bonds it together harmoniously. Eighteen of the 20 bedrooms have private baths or showers; all have hot and cold water, and electric stoves. In a bathless room, the half-board rate is £20.50 ($35.88) per person nightly, rising to £22.50 ($39.38) in a unit with private bath. B&B is £13.50 ($23.63) per person. Prices include VAT but not service. The owners, Peter and Joyce McLaren, are hoteliers of long standing, and they'll tell you about the most scenic spots in the Perthshire area.

Airdaniar Hotel, 160 Atholl Rd. (tel. Pitlochry 2266), was a private home when built originally at the turn of the century. It has distinction, and its stone walls in all shades of beige and brown, its extended sunroom, its three acres of tidy and well-planted garden, make it instantly likable. Andrew and Sue Mathieson provide good basic Scottish cooking and well-kept bedchambers. All rooms have electric blankets, individual heaters, radio, intercom, and hot and cold water. There is a children's play area, and family rooms are available with reductions for children on request. For a bed and a full Scottish breakfast, they charge £12.50 ($21.88) per person nightly. This tariff goes up to £19 ($33.25) per person for half board.

Balrobin Private Hotel, Higher Oakfield (tel. Pitlochry 2901), is a traditional Scottish country house, standing on its own grounds only a few minutes from the town center, commanding views of the Tummel Valley. The owner, H. H. D. Hohman, was a manager for ten years of three- and four-star hotels, and he maintains a very high standard, providing an enjoyable stay for clients. His hotel is centrally heated throughout, although electric blankets are also provided. There are some private bathrooms, along with a large comfortable lounge. The hotel also has a residential license, and it specializes in home-cooking with a daily choice of menus. Rates are £16 ($28) per person for dinner, bed, and breakfast.

The **Green Park Hotel** in Pitlochry (tel. Pitlochry 2537) is not only one of the finest hotels in the area, but it offers some of the best food, good-tasting, reasonably priced fare. On the grounds of Loch Faskally, this country-house hotel lies at the northwest end of Pitlochry, about a five-minute walk from the center. Anne and Graham Brown are well spoken of locally for the care and attention they devote to their restaurant. A rather large choice of food items is available at the bar lunch, including golden pea soup with ham and grilled rainbow trout almondine, followed by a steamed marmalade sponge and custard sauce, costing £3.50 ($6.13). A fixed-price dinner goes for £8 ($14) and is likely to feature a good selection of Scottish salmon and ox tongue salads, along with Tay salmon and lamb sweetbreads. For dessert, perhaps you'll be there on the night the chef does a specialty, "Dream of Rob Roy." You help yourself to the coffee in the lounge. The dining room is open March through October daily from 12:30 to 2 p.m. and 6:30 to 8 p.m.

The **Luggie Restaurant,** Rie-Achan Road (tel. Pitlochry 2085), is adapted from the grange of a farm outside Pitlochry. It still retains a rustic country-life look. Owners Ian and Diana Russell offer morning coffee with home-baked pastries every day from 10 a.m. to noon. Lunch is served from noon to 2:30 p.m., at which time a cold table of 17 different kinds of salads is presented, along with homemade soups, fresh river salmon and trout, cold meats, fresh fruit tarts with cream, and more. Expect to spend from £3.50 ($6.13). Dinner, offered only from mid-May to September, is à la carte, emphasizing Scottish specialties such as beef, lamb, and game dishes. The cost begins at £6.50 ($11.38), going up. Dinner hours are from 6:30 to 9 p.m. daily.

Excursions from Pitlochry

From the town you can take excursions in almost any direction. Heading northwest for four miles, you come to the **Pass of Killiecrankie,** where "Bonnie Dundee" and his Jacobites won their famous victory over the armies of General Mackay fighting for King William in 1689. This is one of the scenic highlights of the area. A **Visitors Centre** (tel. 0796/3233) stands near the sight of the famous battle. It presents an interesting exhibition and is also a center for rangers and naturalists. Dedicated Scots will answer questions on walks, whatever, which are possible in the area. The center is open April to October daily from 10 a.m. to 6 p.m., charging an admission of 20p (35¢).

If time remains, try to see another attraction, **Queen's View,** where Victoria herself picnicked. The view is reached by taking the road alongside Loch Tummel. At the eastern end, Victoria looked down the length of the loch toward Schiehallion.

BLAIR ATHOLL: Eight miles to the northwest of Pitlochry stands the gleaming white **Blair Castle** (tel. Blair Atholl 355), the home of the Duke of Atholl, on the A9. Built in the Scottish baronial style, and dating from 1269, the castle allows you to view more than 30 rooms. Inside is an impressive collection of Jacobite relics, furniture, china, lace, and armor, along with many family portraits. It is open Easter weekend, then Sunday and Monday in April, and then again daily from the first Sunday in May until the second Sunday in October. Hours are weekdays from 10 a.m. to 5 p.m. (Sunday from 2 to 5 p.m.).

Atholl Arms Hotel (tel. Blair Atholl 205). Once lords and ladies who couldn't find room at Blair Castle stayed here, and some of the grand balls of old Perthshire were held at the hotel. Now the Atholl Arms is a stately stone-gabled roadside inn, attracting motorists en route to Inverness. A cocktail lounge has been created, and there's a public bar to attract locals. The grandiose ballroom has been turned into a dinner and dance restaurant, complete with a minstrels' gallery. There's also a more intimate dining room with a collection of antique mahogany chairs. The menu offers substantial choices. The bedrooms are individually styled and well fitted; each one I inspected had a completely different character. Each has hot and cold water and central heating. The B&B price is £11.50 ($20.13) per person. For an additional charge of £2 ($3.50) per person, you can enjoy the comforts of a private bath en suite. Including VAT, a set luncheon goes for £4 ($7) and an evening dinner for £7.50 ($13.13). A wide variety of bar meals is also available.

Bruar Falls Hotel (tel. Calvine 243) is a two-level cottage-style building, with a roadside stone wall and surrounding gardens. It was built around 1700 and used as a billet by some of the Highlanders in the 1745 Rebellion. It has the charm of an oldtime inn, but with contemporary necessities. Three miles from the nearest village, it is a ten-minute walk from the Falls of Bruar, where 200 feet of water falls in three levels. These falls were immortalized by Robert Burns in verse when he visited them in 1778. On summer evenings it's still light enough for nearby walks, to be climaxed by dinner in the old farmhouse restaurant. You are welcomed by George and Moira Proudfoot. There's a clan museum next to the motel, and you may locate your family tartan. B&B is £8.35 ($14.61) per person nightly. Dinner, if ordered separately, is another £ 6.60 ($11.55). Bar snacks are also available, including soups, pâtés, salads, minute steaks, sausages, and farmers' pie. A three-course meal in the bar will cost around £2.90 ($5.08).

ABERFELDY: The "Birks o' Aberfeldy" are among the beauty spots made famous by Robert Burns. Once a Pictish center, this small town makes a fine base for touring Perthshire's glens and lochs. Loch Tay lies 6 miles to the west; Glen Lyon, 15 miles west; and Kinloch Rannoch, 18 miles northwest.

In Aberfeldy, General Wade in 1733 built the bridge spanning the Tay. In the town's shops you'll find good buys in tweeds and tartans, plus other items of Highland dress.

For food and lodging, I recommend the following:

Breadalbane Arms Hotel, Bridgend (tel. Aberfeldy 20364), is enthusiastically recommended for several reasons—its appearance first, and second, its character. It's a 200-year-old stone coaching inn, with tall chimneys and a row of small dormers. Its rear bedrooms overlook beautiful countryside. George and Mary Stewart rent 26 bedrooms, a few with private baths "en suite," all with hot and cold water and central heating. The daily per-person rate for a bed and a bountiful breakfast is £8 ($14). However, it is closed from November to March. A packed lunch for a picnic is £1.50 ($2.63); a set dinner costs £4 ($7).

Crown Hotel, Bank Street (tel. Aberfeldy 20448), is a long, low inn, with many years of innkeeping behind it. It stands directly on the roadway, with a rear garden. It's an all-purpose hotel, equipped with good-size public rooms, a cocktail as well as a public bar, a resident's TV lounge, a sitting room with comfortable chairs drawn around a fireplace, and a dining room. Each bedroom has a hot and cold running water basin, and there are adequate corridor bathrooms. B&B is economical here, costing £8.50 ($14.88) per person without VAT. I also recommend the dinner at £5.25 ($9.19). It's a lively inn, and during the summer season there's entertainment.

Nessbank Private Hotel, Crieff Road (tel. Aberfeldy 20214), is small and homey, a stone house built more than a century ago. At the edge of Aberfeldy, it has a large, attractive garden running alongside the "Birks." From the garden a private gate leads into the Den of Moness, a deep wooded glen along the course of a mountain stream. The hotel is run by John and Margaret Holroyd, who accept guests who enjoy their breakfasts and evening meals. Their daily terms including these two meals range from £16.50 ($28.86) to £17.50 ($30.63) per person. The food is freshly cooked, and whenever possible, eggs, fruit, and vegetables from their own poultry and kitchen garden are used. Bedrooms have views and are equipped with tea- and coffee-making facilities, along with electric blankets, water basins, and razor points. The house has been refurbished, and there is a welcoming log fire in the lounge. The hotel also has a restricted liquor license and maintains a modest cellar.

Crossroads Guest House, Kenmore Street (tel. Aberfeldy 20293), is owned by the very considerate Mrs. Duncan, who does much to aid her house guests. Not only is her establishment well maintained and attractive, it's very economical. The daily rate here of £7 ($12.25) per person includes a big Scottish breakfast with oatmeal. Even tea and cookies are served before you retire.

The **Weem Hotel** (tel. Aberfeldy 20381) is a pleasant country inn with two floors of comfortable bedrooms, many with private bathrooms. This 17th-century inn stands one mile from Aberfeldy on the B846 Loch Rannoch road and has a sweeping view of the Tay Valley. The inn has its own attractive gardens and lawns. The old wood-paneled bar with its open log fire is welcoming. The B&B rate is £11 ($19.25) per person. Half board costs £18 ($31.50) per person per night. The hotel owns nearly two miles on the left bank of the River Tay, and fishing is free to guests. There are 22 golf courses within 35 miles of the hotel, including the Taymouth Castle 18-hole course some three miles away.

The **Cruachan Hotel,** Kenmore Street (tel. Aberfeldy 545), stands at the edge of town in about three acres of flowery gardens and greenery. The hotel is small and immaculately kept, renting out only three singles, six doubles, and one family room, each containing hot and cold running water. The single rate is £11.50 ($20.13), from £22 ($38.50) in a double, including breakfast. Dinner is an optional £5 ($8.75) and is served to residents only. The centrally heated private hotel is closed from December to February. On the grounds is a nine-hole putting green for the use of guests.

KILLIN: Just over the border from Tayside, Killin is a village on the Dochart at the lower end of Loch Tay, in the geographical center of Scotland. Lying 45 miles west of Perth by road, Killin is both a summer holiday resort and a winter sports center. The **Falls of Dochart** are world famous, but the town itself is noted for beauty spots, and there are sights of historical interest as well.

Killin Church contains a font more than 1000 years old. Less than a quarter of a mile from the church stands an upright stone said to mark the grave of Fingal. An island in the Dochart was the ancient burial place of the MacNab Clan.

The ruins of **Finlarig Castle** contain a beheading pit near the castle gate which was written about in Scott's *The Fair Maid of Perth.* Perched a thousand feet above the loch, the castle was the seat of "Black Duncan of the Cowl," a notoriously ruthless chieftain of the Campbell Clan.

For food and lodging, why not try the following recommendations?

Dall Lodge Hotel (tel. Killin 217) is a 19th-century stone house overlooking the River Lochay on the outskirts of the village. For B&B, the tariff including VAT is £10.25 ($17.94) per person, and the five-course dinners are £8 ($14). All bedrooms have hot and cold running water and tea- and coffee-making facilities. Some units have private bathrooms. The hotel specializes in serving as many traditional Scottish dishes as possible, including salmon, trout, venison, haggis, Aberdeen Angus beef, Scottish hill lamb, and cloutie dumpling. There are also a wide range of fine wines and Scottish malt whiskies.

Falls of Dochart Hotel (tel. Killin 237), under the guidance of Mr. and Mrs. Peter George, offers real value. In a dining room of character, a Scottish-continental cuisine is served. Some rooms have shower units at no extra charge, and all of them have hot and cold running water. The daily rate for half board is from £14.50 ($25.38) per person, rising another £2 ($3.50) for those desiring a private bath. You can have a premeal drink in the cocktail lounge. Tariffs include service and VAT, and children are granted a 30% reduction if they share a room with their parents.

Craigard Hotel (tel. Killin 285) is a small country hotel in the heart of the village, handy for many points of interest. The owners, Geoff and Kate Sheridan, make their hotel homelike. Their residents' lounge overlooks Loch Tay and the surrounding hills. Guests gather in the Finlarig cocktail bar for a lager. Its traditional Scottish decor portrays much of the history and legend of local clans. The dining room is inviting, and here you can order a high tea or a four-course dinner at about £5.50 ($9.63). The B&B rate is from £9.50 ($16.63) per person. They have a fishing boat complete with outboard motor available with a ghillie for salmon and trout fishing on Loch Tay.

2. Aberdeen and Royal Deeside

Traveling north from the lochs, heading toward Royal Deeside, you pass through Glen Shee and Glen Clunie, a most spectacular route which will give you your first taste of Highland scenery.

As you journey across uncrowded roads into Scotland's northeast, you'll pass heather-covered moorland and peaty lochs, wood glens and salmon-filled rivers, granite-stone villages and fishing harbors, as well as North Sea beach resorts.

This is the Grampian region, with such centers as Aberdeen and Braemar, and such sights as Balmoral Castle and the "Whisky Trail." Even the Queen herself comes here for holidays.

BRAEMAR: This little Deeside resort is the site of the **Royal Highland Gathering,** which takes place there annually, either in late August or early September. It is usually attended by Queen Elizabeth. The royal "link" dates from the 1840s when Queen Victoria first attended the games.

The capital of the Deeside Highlands, Braemar is overrun with foreign visitors, as well as the British themselves, during the gathering. Anyone thinking of attending would be wise to make application for accommodation anywhere within a 20-mile radius of Braemar not later than early April.

The gathering in Braemar is the most famous of the many Highland games. The spectacular occasion is held in the **Princess Royal and Duke of Fife Memorial Park.** Competitions include tossing the caber, throwing the hammer, sprinting, vaulting, a tug-o'-war, the long leap, Highland dancing, putting a 16-pound ball, sword dancing, relay races, and, naturally, a bagpiping contest. At a vast refreshment tent, Scottish lassies serve tea, coffee, buns, and other refreshments.

The romantic 17th-century **Braemar Castle** (tel. Braemar 219) lies half a mile northeast of Braemar on the A93. A fully furnished private residence of architectural grace, scenic charm, and historical interest, it is the seat of Capt. A. A. Farquharson of Invercauld. Opening onto the Dee River, it was built in 1628 by the Earl of Mar. However, the so-called "Black Colonel" attacked and burned it in 1689. The castle is built in the shape of an L, with a spiral stairway and a circular main tower. Inside it has barrel vaulted ceilings and an underground prison, and is known for its remarkable star-shaped defensive curtain wall. It can be visited from May 1 until the first Monday in October, daily from 10 a.m. to 6 p.m., costing adults 90p ($1.58); children under 13 pay 45p (79¢).

Food and Lodging

Braemar Lodge Hotel (tel. Braemar 617) is run by the delightful Mrs. McKay, who is frightfully apologetic that on bookings in advance she must insist on a £5 ($8.75) deposit. The house is an old hunting lodge but has been converted into a friendly hotel with a small lounge for guests. The bedrooms are warm and neat, and there are adequate bathroom facilities. B&B costs £11 ($19.25). Dinner, served at 7 p.m. (and don't be late), costs from £7.50 ($13.13). You can sit afterward in the lounge, ordering coffee and Drambuie if you wish. Local information is willingly given, and the small staff will go out of their way to make you feel at home. Mrs. McKay spends a lot of time in the kitchen, and the food is plain and excellent, served by attractive young women. When booking, say whether you plan to be there for dinner, as that helps Mrs. McKay plan the meals. Close to the hotel is the cottage where Robert Louis Stevenson wrote *Treasure Island.*

Callater Lodge (tel. Braemar 275) has rural charm, off the side of the road, in its own garden. It's an added-to stone farmhouse with bay and dormer windows, used a great deal by sportsmen. Owners Mr. and Mrs. William Rose can accommodate 18 guests, charging £18 ($31.50) per person for dinner and B&B. Mrs. Rose will prepare a picnic lunch for you for £1.80 ($3.15) and afternoon tea, served in the residents' lounge, for £1.78 ($3.11). Their beds are comfortable, and in cold months hot-water bottles are provided. All rooms have hot and cold water and an electric heater.

Moorfield Hotel, Chapel Brae (tel. Braemar 244), occupies an imposing position overlooking the famed Braemar games park. The Moorfield has three acres of well-planted garden, offering seclusion and good views. Owners Bobby and Nan Campbell have a few bedrooms with private bath, and this costs £2 ($3.50) extra per person. B&B in one of their bathless rooms is £11.50 ($20.13) per person. With dinner it's £19 ($33.25). If you want a bar lunch (bowl of soup, meat, potatoes, and vegetables), it's obtainable for £3 ($5.25), VAT included. The bedrooms are cozy and nicely appointed, with hot and cold water.

Cranford (tel. Braemar 675) is a modest guest house set up from the roadway, with its own garden. Mrs. McKellar keeps her small house tidy, and her bedrooms are homey and snug. During the colder months she provides electric blankets, and all the rooms are centrally heated and contain hot and cold running water. She charges £8 ($14) per person for B&B daily. If you request dinner in the evening, you're treated to home-cooking at a cost of £4.50 ($7.88) per person. In the winter months Mrs. McKellar also caters to skiers, as the Glenshee ski slopes are only eight miles away on the main Perth–Aberdeen road. There is bus service every day to the slopes. Also there's an 18-hole golf course open to visitors for about £4 ($7) per day.

Bellevue, Chapel Brae (tel. Braemar 633), is a B&B accommodation run by Mrs. G. J. Beech, whose rooms and visitors' lounge are all furnished in excellent taste. Most of the rooms look out at the mountains. The cost per person is £6.50 ($11.38) nightly. You can get directions to Bellevue from the local tourist office. Mrs. Beech will prepare one of the finest meals in town for £6 ($10.50), by prior arrangement. She enjoys getting fresh ingredients, preparing them, cooking them, and serving the meal herself. She has very high standards.

THE WHISKY TRAIL: Extending north from Braemar, from Grantown and Dufftown to Elgin, are many distilleries of scotch whisky. Many are open for visits only by appointment—collect the list of telephone numbers from the local tourist office at Braemar. However, **Grant's Glenfiddich Distillery in Dufftown** (tel. 0340/20373) is open Monday through Friday from 10:30 a.m. to 12:30 p.m. and from 2 to 4:30 p.m. Visitors are shown around the plant, and the process of distilling is explained by charming young women in tartans. A film of the history of distilling is also shown. At the finish of the tour, you're given a free dram of malt whisky, and the whole tour is free. There is a souvenir shop where you can buy glasses, tankards, and hip flasks, plus other tokens of your visit to what is, perhaps, the only malt distillery left in Scotland which is still owned by the founding family and not by a combine.

If you'd like to stay in Dufftown, try the **Fife Arms Hotel,** The Square (tel. 0340/20220), a small, 40-year-old hotel built to replace an ancient predecessor. Today the Murray family is in charge. Mrs. Murray used to take guests in her house, The Elms, and she still offers the same warm, friendly hospitality she provided there. The charge is £8 ($14) per person for a bed and a large

Scottish breakfast. Meals are served in the lounge bar of the hotel, a three-course evening meal presented from 5:30 to 7:30 p.m., which Mrs. Murray assures me, are "the real high tea tours." You'll pay around £3 ($5.25), or you can order a large plate of fresh fried fish and chips at £1.75 ($3.06).

BALLATER: On the Dee River, with the Grampian mountains in the background, Ballater is a holiday resort center where visitors flock to attend one of Scotland's most popular sightseeing attractions, Balmoral Castle (see below).

The town still centers around its **Station Square,** where the royal family used to be photographed as they arrived to spend holidays. The railway has since been closed.

From Ballater you can drive west to view the magnificent scenery of **Glen Muick and Lochnagar,** where you'll see herds of deer.

Food and Lodging

Moorside, Braemar Road (tel. Ballater 55492), a stone building with twin bay windows flanking the main entry, is 90 years old, the former manse of the Free Church of Scotland. It stands only 200 yards from the center of the village on the main road leading out of Ballater toward Braemar on the A93. Open all year, it charges £9 ($15.75) per person for B&B. Half board is £13 ($22.75) per person. There are eight double bedrooms, four with private bathrooms (one of which is on the ground floor), and two public baths. All rooms are centrally heated and have electric blankets, hot and cold water, and tea- and coffee-making facilities. There is an attractive dining room and lounge with color TV. Ample parking is available.

Coyles Hotel, Golf Road (tel. Ballater 212), stands in its own attractive garden, near the local golf course and tennis courts. From nearly every window there are pleasant views. Coyles is owned by Maureen and Ian Todd, and kept open all year. In addition to the rooms in the main house, there's a pleasant garden chalet with one double and one twin with shower and toilet, and this costs no more. It's rented out on a first-come, first-served basis. All rooms in the main house have hot and cold water, unmetered heating, and electric blankets. Guests can use the sun lounge and another living room as well. There's a view dining room where bountiful breakfasts and dinners are served. B&B costs £6.50 ($11.38) per person daily, increasing to £10 ($17.50) on the half-board arrangement.

Pannanich Wells Hotel, on the outskirts (tel. Ballater 55279), is lovely enough to photograph with its double row of village cottages beside the Dee. It's the oldest established hotel on Royal Deeside, two miles from Ballater on the South Deeside road (A973). It was built in 1760 after the discovery of its healing waters (rich in iron, calcium, and magnesium). Queen Victoria visited here to drink the healing waters. Guests help themselves at the original well on the hotel grounds. Owner Stan Roberts runs a nicely decorated place with clean bedrooms. From the kitchen emerge well-prepared Scottish meals. He charges £10 ($17.50) per person in a single or double, including breakfast. Depending on your choice, meals begin as low as £2 ($3.05), going up to £7 ($12.25).

Westbank Hotel (tel. Ballater 55305), is a substantial flintstone village house, neatly kept and immaculate. It's just one block from the Dee River and the shops, and it overlooks the first tee of an 18-hole golf course. The atmosphere is warm and friendly, and the hotel is run by owners Alex and Hazel Clark. They have eight bedrooms, each well proportioned and clean, with central heating, hot and cold water, and bed lights. The B&B charge is £9 ($15.75) per person, including VAT and evening tea. An evening meal is available. Reductions are granted for longer stays.

Dee Valley, 26 Viewfield Rd. (tel. Ballater 408), may charm you, mainly because of its owner, Evelyn Gray, who never fails to be helpful and friendly. Her very simple place was once a private nursing home, used by the Duke of Kent and his brother. She has four double or twin rooms, each with hot and cold water, all on the second floor. The charge per person for B&B is £6.50 ($11.38) and with an evening meal (half board) £10 ($17.50). There is a surcharge of £1.50 ($2.63) for a double rented as a single. Showers are included, as are VAT and service charges. On the ground floor is the neat dining and sitting room. Mrs. Gray will tell you of the special Scottish events that you can enjoy, including the Ballater donkey derby.

Glen Lui (tel. Ballater 55402) stands on two acres of private grounds overlooking the golf course at Ballater (access from the grounds). An ideal center for a holiday in Royal Deeside, Glen Lui is run by Mr. and Mrs. M. G. Fraser. Their hotel is small, with only one single and nine double rooms, some with shower and toilet. Their welcome is big. Careful consideration has gone into the planning of the bedrooms, with such touches as razor points.

What sets Glen Lui above the standard small hotel along the Deeside is their cuisine, reinforced by a good wine cellar. Mr. and Mrs. Fraser are recommended by hoteliers in the area who might be full. However, it's important to reserve, as Glen Lui, owing to its size, can fill up quickly. The B&B rate is £11.50 ($20.13). For half board, the charge is around £18 ($31.50) per person. The hotel is open only from March to November.

Morvada Guest House, Braemar Road (tel. Ballater 55501), is run by John and Freda Nimmo, who offer only six bedrooms, along with adequate bath and shower facilities in the corridors. Their rooms are comfortable, their lounge nicely furnished, and their food good. The welcome is very friendly, and the Nimmos believe in heat when it's cold. Even in June, if it's nippy they've been known to turn on the lounge fire and nonmetered electric heaters in the bedrooms when guests walk in. They charge from £7.50 ($13.13) per person for B&B, but it's better to take the half-board rate of £12 ($21) per person, as their dinners are varied and well cooked.

READER'S HOTEL SELECTION: "The **Aspen Hotel** (tel. Ballater 55486) can boast a real bargain in accommodations £13 ($22.75) for half board. The B&B rate is £8.50 ($14.88) per person. You dine royally here, as the proprietors are the owners of the local bakery (by appointment to Her Majesty the Queen), and supply the hotel's baked goods. Indeed, they made Princess Anne's wedding cake. Apart from this, the kind, attentive service is a treasure in itself. Try to book in advance, however, as others guard this find jealously" (Mrs. D. Clee, King City, Ontario, Canada).

Balmoral Castle

"This dear paradise" is how Queen Victoria described this castle, rebuilt in the Scottish baronial style by her beloved Albert. It was completed in 1855. Today Balmoral, eight miles west of Ballater, is still a private residence of the British sovereign. Albert, the prince consort, leased the property in 1848, and bought it in 1852. As the small castle left by the Farquharsons proved too small, the present castle was rebuilt 1855. Its principal feature is a 100-foot tower. On the grounds are many memorials to the royal family. The grounds can be visited daily, except Sunday, in May, June, and July from 10 a.m. to 5 p.m. Only the castle ballroom is open to the public, where facilities include an exhibition of pictures, porcelain, and works of art. In addition to the gardens, there are souvenir shops and a refreshment room. Admission is £1 ($1.75) for adults, 50p (88¢) for children.

BANCHORY: On lower Deeside, this pleasant resort is rich in woodland and river scenery. From this base, you can take excursions to two of the most popular castles in the Grampian region.

Crathes Castle and Gardens lies two miles to the east of Banchory (tel. Crathes 525), a fine early Jacobean building which is celebrated for its gardens, its sculptured yews dating from 1702. Just north of the A93 on the north bank of the Dee, this baronial castle contains remarkable painted ceilings. The castle is open from April 1 through 4 and then May 1 to September 30 from 11 a.m. to 6 p.m. (on Sunday from 2 to 6 p.m.). Last admission to the castle is at 5:15 p.m. Admission to the castle and grounds is £1.55 ($2.71) for adults and 80p ($1.40) for children, including parking.

Structurally unchanged since its completion in 1626, **Craigievar Castle** (tel. Lumphanan 635) is an exceptional tower house where Scottish baronial architecture reached its pinnacle of achievement. It has magnificent contemporary plaster ceilings in nearly all its rooms. It had been continuously lived in by the descendents of the builder, William Forbes, until it came under the care of the National Trust of Scotland in 1963. The family collection of furnishings is complete. It is open daily except Friday, from 2 to 6 p.m., from May 1 to September 30. Admission is £1.20 ($2.10) for adults, 60p ($1.05) for children. The grounds are open throughout the year, and admission is by donation. Craigievar is 26 miles west of Aberdeen, 5 miles north of Lumphanan.

A mile from the castle is **Macbeth's Cairn,** where, according to legend, Macduff put an end to Macbeth.

Food and Lodging

The **Burnett Arms Hotel,** The High (tel. Banchory 2545), is a large country inn in the heart of the Banchory, a coaching stop dating back before 1840. There are 17 bedrooms, each nicely appointed and furnished. Eleven contain private baths. All have hot and cold water, central heating, electric blankets, a radio, baby-listening service, and, if you ask for it, color TV. B&B costs £18 ($31.50) per person daily, including VAT. The dining room is fully licensed, as are the lounge bar and cocktail bar.

Douglas Arms Hotel, High Street (tel. Banchory 2547), is a village inn right in the heart of everything. It's very casual, and the warmth of its staff and its good meals make it worthwhile. There is a dining room as well as a traditional public bar where you can get excellent malt whisky. Stay here only if you like to retire late, certainly after midnight. The inn is the scene several nights a week of disco and jazz bands, bagpipe playing, whatever, usually beginning at 8 p.m. The walls of this old building are likely to vibrate with the noise. It can be fun for the young at heart but a disaster to those who like to go to bed early with a good book. The cost for a single with breakfast is £9.50 ($16.63), and a double goes for £17 ($29.75). High tea costs £2.75 ($4.81), and you get all you can eat.

STONEHAVEN: South of Aberdeen, this is a seaside resort with a colorful fishing harbor and many old stone structures, including a Tolbooth from the 15th century. It has a number of accommodations and might be a good place to search for a room if Aberdeen is overcrowded, as it often is in its oil-rich days.

Mill Inn (tel. Stonehaven 62324) is a soft brown regional stone pub-hotel at the southern entrance to town, set back behind a BH petrol station. There are 12 traditional bedrooms for rent, each with electric blankets for wintertime, as well as heating kettles for odd-hours tea or coffee. B&B is £9.50 ($16.63) in a single, £17 ($29.75) for two. Each room has its own hot and cold water basin. The lounge bar is inviting and a good place to get to know fellow guests. You can have a bar lunch, and a traditional high tea is served until 7:30 p.m., costing £3 ($5.25) to £4 ($7).

ABERDEEN: The harbor in this seaport in the northeast of Scotland is one of the largest fishing ports in the country, literally infested with kipper and deep-sea trawlers. The **Fish Market** is well worth a visit, as it's the liveliest in Britain.

Bordered by fine sandy beaches (delightful if you're a polar bear), Scotland's third city is often called "the granite city," as its buildings are constructed largely of granite, in pink or gray, hewn from the Rubislaw quarries.

Aberdeen has become the capital of the oil workers pouring into northeast Scotland to help harvest the riches from six North Sea oilfields. The city lies on the banks of the salmon- and trout-filled Don and Dee Rivers. Spanning the Don is the **Brig o' Balgownie,** a steep Gothic arch, begun in 1285.

In Castlegate is the **Mercat Cross,** a hexagonally shaped structure, built in 1686, and considered the most handsome of the old crosses in Scotland.

Aberdeen University is a fusion of two separate colleges. King's College is older, dating from 1483, and it contains the oldest school of medicine in Great Britain. The chapel of King's College is crowned by a stately tower from 1505. Marischal College, founded in 1593, is recognized as one of the finest granite buildings in the world.

The university is in Old Aberdeen, as is the **Cathedral of St. Machar,** founded in 1131, although the present structure dates from the 15th century. Its splendid heraldic ceiling contains three rows of shields representing the kings and princes of Europe along with the Scottish ecclesiastical and aristocratic hierarchy. The modern stained-glass windows are magnificent, the work of Douglas Strachan. The cathedral is open daily from 9 a.m. to 5 p.m.

Provost Skene's House, 45 Guestrow (tel. Aberdeen 50086), is named for a rich merchant who was Lord Provost of Aberdeen during 1676-1685. Off Broad Street, it is now a museum with period rooms and artifacts of domestic life. Admission is free, and the house can be visited Monday to Saturday from 10 a.m. to 5 p.m.

Provost Ross's House, in Shiprow, is the oldest house in Aberdeen, built in 1593 and recently restored. It is open to the public, Monday and Friday, from 2:30 to 4:30 p.m.

Where to Stay

Because of the increasing numbers of tourists and business visitors to the Granite City, now established as Europe's Offshore Oil Capital, hotels are likely to be heavily booked any time of year, so that you may find yourself in the position of Dr. Johnson and Boswell in 1773, who "found the inn so full that we had some difficulty in obtaining admission." In that case, it's best to go to the **Tourist Bureau,** St. Nicholas House, Broad Street (tel. Aberdeen 23456). A member of the staff there will assist with hotel or guest house reservations. If you're calling on a Saturday, use a different telephone number (tel. Aberdeen 24890).

Guild Hotel, Guild Street (tel. Aberdeen 29411), is part of the Welcome Inn chain, which has good standards and moderate prices. The resident manager, Kevin Lawrie, takes care of his guests. Refreshment service is available 24 hours a day, and local information is given at the reception desk. The daily terms, including VAT, are £18 ($31.50) in a single room, £35 ($61.25) in a twin. Each unit has its own toilet and bath/shower, and is centrally heated. The restaurant serves lunches and high teas daily, from £2 ($3.50), and bar lunches and suppers are offered from £1.25 ($2.19).

Albert & Victoria Guest House, 1-2 Albert Terrace (tel. Aberdeen 641717), are two adjoining Victorian-style houses (almost cottages) in a quiet residential part of the town. Yet they are only minutes away from the west end of Union Street. The owners, Mr. and Mrs. Canale, will prepare very filling three-course breakfasts, and their rooms are centrally heated. As a bonus, there's a TV in every room. The daily price for a single is £11 ($19.25), or for a double, £18 ($31.50), and a room for three rents for £21 ($36.75). As a typical nicety Mrs. Canale will provide hot drinks 24 hours a day (well, almost). There's street parking for your car.

Craig Rossie Guest House, 293 Great Western Rd. (tel. Aberdeen 21548), may well be the most desirable guest house in the area. It's set back from the roadway, with an exquisitely kept garden. It's the end home of a row of fine stone houses, this one having a bay tower. The hostess is Mrs. E. Robertson, who lives there with her husband and two children. A night here is like being in a true Scottish home, where gentle manners and hospitality are important. The living room is filled with attractive home-style furnishings, and there is a color TV. The bedrooms are centrally heated, and you'll have hot and cold water in your sunny room. The inclusive charge is £9 ($15.75) per person nightly, and that includes one of Mrs. Robertson's excellent, filling breakfasts. Buses 23 and 24 stop nearby.

Klibreck, 410 Great Western Rd. (tel. Aberdeen 36115), belongs to Dorothy Ramsay, who is known for her friendly good nature. Her two-story guest house is built of granite, part of a flank of "row houses," with front bay windows and a third-floor dormer. Klibreck is in a quiet residential area in the west end of the city, and the center is just ten minutes away by bus. Every room is centrally heated; there's color TV in the guests' lounge, and each room has hot and cold running water. It costs £10.50 ($18.38) per person nightly in a single, £18 ($31.50) in a double. If you ask early enough you can have a homemade dinner for £4.50 ($7.88) per person.

Kittybrewster Hotel, 75 Powis Terrace (tel. Aberdeen 46574), is owned by the forthright Kathleen E. Slatter, who is the first to tell you the shortcomings of her simple, small hotel. It's only five minutes by bus from the center of town, but is on a busy main road. There is no garden, but there are plenty of parks and places to see in the city. There are no ground-floor rooms, and no car-parking facilities. However, the little hotel is cozy, and you'll enjoy the cleanliness, the care taken with the rooms. There are no private baths, although each room has its hot and cold water. You'll be welcomed to the lounge for TV viewing. There's no liquor license, but next door stands a local pub. The rate, including B&B and VAT, is £9.50 ($16.63) per person in a double, £10.50 ($11.83) in a single. If you wish, you can have a tasty, Scottish lunch for £2.50 ($4.38), and dinner costs £5 ($8.75).

READERS' B&B SELECTIONS: "The B&B accommodations of **Mr. and Mrs. Anderson,** Queen Street, Woodside (tel. Aberdeen 493974), made our stay in Aberdeen one to remember. On our arrival we were greeted with a pot of tea and a plate of assorted cakes and biscuits. This generous treatment continued throughout our stay. Besides ample showers and comfortable rooms, complete with tea-making facilities and radio, there is a family lounge room where guests may relax. Breakfast is more than satisfying, and tasty evening meals are available for a mere £2.50 ($4.38). The Andersons' house is easily accessible from the town center by either bus or car. The charge per person is £6.50 ($11.38)" (Helen Broadhurst and Karen Coleman, Maribyrnong, Victoria, Australia). . . . "Although the tempo of life in the famous fishing port of Aberdeen has increased in recent years due to its proximity to the North Sea oil fields, it has still retained its traditional Scottish charm. We found **Mrs. Leslie's Guest House,** 75 Dee St. (tel. Aberdeen 22517), to be very conveniently situated, comfortable, and reasonably priced, with singles at £8 ($14), doubles at £14 ($24.50). The usual cooked breakfast was one of the tastiest we experienced, and prior to one very early morning departure, we were served a specially prepared breakfast in our room" (Peter and Michelle Scully, West Enendon, Victoria, Australia).

Dining in Aberdeen

What's Cookin', 18 Holborn St. (tel. Aberdeen 575685), is a bright, sophisticated, bistro-style restaurant, offering some imaginative dishes, a refreshing change of pace from the standard Aberdeen cuisine repertoire. For example, you might get your repast started by ordering either the Catalan seafood soup or a tasty duck and orange pâté. Continental specialties are prepared with flair—pork with fruits or seafood vol-au-vent. At its cheapest a meal will cost from around £10 ($17.50), and your fellow diners are likely to be newly prosperous oilmen. A cheerful little place, it offers friendly service.

Kardomah, 1 Union Bridge (tel. Aberdeen 50459), lies in the center of a main shopping street, having both a self-service coffeeshop at street level and a restaurant with waitress service on the second landing. A property of Trust Houses Forte, the restaurant offers good value with a tempting array of omelets, hamburgers, salads, sandwiches, grilled meats, and especially desserts for which it is noted. There's always a hot soup of the day, followed by good hamburgers which begin at £1.80 ($3.15). Fish dishes, costing around £2 ($3.50), are limited mainly to plaice and haddock. There is the usual selection of grills, such as liver and bacon and sirloin steak (seven ounces), plus some toasted club sandwiches. From the continent comes quiche lorraine and lasagne verde. A children's menu serves as a coloring book for your favorite nephew back home. In addition to the restaurant, Kardomah operates the coffeeshop, with sandwiches averaging £1 ($1.75) and hot meals costing from £1.30 ($2.28) to £2 ($3.50). Both establishments are open from 9 a.m. until 6:30 p.m. every day.

Oliver's Bar and Diner, Caledonian Thistle Hotel, Union Terrace (tel. Aberdeen 640233), is one of an increasing number of restaurants in Scotland featuring American themes. Ollie's Diner turns toward the movies, with a striking decor of black and white, just like those vintage silent-screen reels. Food items are often named after the stars. My only objection is the Mae West temptation. The legendary silent-screen star is listed under appetizers, when she should have been elevated—at least—to a main course. Most diners come here for one of the charcoal-grilled hamburgers, costing from £2.75 ($4.81). Toppings range from a coating of pâté to a Mexican chili sauce. Steaks, costing from £5.40 ($9.45) and made from Angus beef, are also featured. Along with the meat you get the usual salads, soups, and desserts. Wines, including some good California selections, are also served. You can even order an American beer. The bar is open from 11 a.m. to 2:30 p.m. and 5 to 11 p.m. (till 1 a.m. on Friday and till midnight on Saturday). On Sunday hours are only from 6:30 to 11 p.m. The diner is open from noon to 2:30 p.m. and 6 to 11:30 p.m., except on Friday when it stays open until 12:30 a.m. (on Sunday from 6:30 to 11 p.m.).

If you're really hungry at lunch, I suggest a visit to **Ferryhill House Hotel,** 169 Bon Accord St. (tel. Aberdeen 50867), a Georgian house only five minutes from the city center. Business people are especially attracted to its open buffet, served between noon and 2 p.m. at a cost of £2.50 ($4.38) to £6 ($10.50). Tender roast beef and home-baked ham are invariably featured, along with some excellent fish dishes and crisp salads. A daily hot dish is served along with the cold meat and salad platters. On its own grounds, with plenty of parking space, the hotel stands between Fonthill Road and Springbank Terrace.

On the outskirts, if you're heading for Royal Deeside, try a dining stopover at **Marycutler House** (tel. Aberdeen 732124), about six miles from Aberdeen on the South Deeside road. World traveler Jennifer Martin purchased this 17th-century house beside the river, imaginatively decorating the dining rooms with treasures brought back from her trips. The baronial bar has an eclectic collection—an African mask, an Early English settle, a Victorian sofa, and Adam bar. In addition to the bar are two handsome dining rooms as well as one with a glass roof, evoking memories of Marrakesh. The menu is likely to change by the time of your visit, but it's international in scope—soupe au pistou, oxtail stew, chicken cardamon, with a side helping of ratatouille, turkey pie, real Scottish salmon with hollandaise sauce, along with fresh vegetables cooked to perfection. If you order à la carte, expect a splurge price of £15 ($26.25). However, you can enjoy a set dinner at £9.50 ($16.63). Lunch is until 2 p.m., and dinner (make a reservation) is from 7:30 to 9:30 p.m. If you're stopping in for lunch, you can only order a light pub meal in front of the fireplace. A dish costs around £2 ($3.50), and you're given a choice of hot or cold, always with a roll, butter, and salad. The house is closed on Sunday.

EXCURSIONS IN "CASTLE COUNTRY": Aberdeen is the center of "castle country," as 40 inhabited castles lie within a 40-mile radius. Two of the most popular castle excursions are previewed below. For others, refer above to Banchory.

Drum Castle: The handsome mansion (tel. Drumoak 204) was added in 1619, but the great square tower dates from the late 13th century, making it one of the three oldest tower houses in the country. Historic Drum lies ten miles west of Aberdeen, off the A93. It is open from May 1 to September 30 from 2 to 6 p.m. The gardens are open daily from 9:30 a.m. to dusk. Admission to the house and gardens is 90p ($1.58) for adults, 45p (79¢) for children.

Muchalls Castle: Built by the Burnetts of Leys in 1619, this castle is now lived in by Mrs. Maurice A. Simpson. It is noted for its elaborate plasterwork ceilings and fireplaces. The castle itself lies five miles north of Stonehaven, nine miles south of Aberdeen. It is open May to September on Tuesday and Sunday from 3 to 5 p.m. charging 30p (53¢) for adults, 10p (18¢) for children.

Chapter XIX

HIGHLANDS AND ISLANDS

1. Aviemore, Speyside, and Elgin
2. Inverness and Loch Ness
3. Fort William and Lochaber
4. Kyle of Lochalsh and Skye
5. Oban and District
6. The Inner Hebrides
7. Kintyre, Arran and Islay

FROM ITS ROMANTIC GLENS and its rugged mountainous landscapes, the Highlands suggest a timeless antiquity. Off the coast, mysterious islands, such as Skye with its jagged peaks, rise from the sea, inviting further exploration. These lands are sparsely inhabited even today, and much wildlife, such as the red deer, still flourishes.

As the unofficial capital of the Highlands, Inverness is the terminus of that rail journey from London, a distance of some 570 miles. As such, many visitors use it as a base for Highland adventures.

From Inverness, you can journey along Loch Ness (especially if you're a monster watcher) to Fort William, dominated by Ben Nevis, the highest mountain in Britain. Oban is the main resort on Scotland's West Highland coastline. It is also one of the major ports for journeying to the Hebridean islands.

If at all possible, try to explore some of these islands, the largest of which is Lewis, where the Standing Stones of Callanish, a prehistoric monument, evoke Stonehenge. Numerous interisland air services allow you to go "island-hopping."

Many pleasure trips are possible to the islands in the Firth of Clyde, Scotland's greatest yachting center. Dominated by the peak of Goat Fell, Arran is the largest of these Clyde islands.

1. Aviemore, Speyside, and Elgin

Aviemore is the winter sports capital of Britain, but it also enjoys mass popularity in summer, too. Aviemore Centre, previewed below, is Scotland's most modern holiday resort, an all-year, all-weather center, endowed with a multitude of outdoor pursuits, such as golfing, angling, skiing, or ice skating.

Those seeking a more traditional Scottish ambience will gravitate to one of the many Speyside villages, each with its own attractions and atmosphere. Ranking next to Aviemore, Grantown-on-Spey is another major center.

The Spey itself is the fastest flowing river in the British Isles, known not only for its scenery, but its salmon and ski slopes.

Finally, on your way to Inverness, you might care to stop off at the old cathedral city of Elgin.

Our first stop up the Spey follows.

NEWTONMORE: This Highland resort on Speyside is a good center for the Grampian and Monadhliath mountains, and it offers excellent fishing, golf, pony trekking, and hill walking. Most motorists zip through it on the way to Aviemore, but sightseers may want to stop off and visit the **Clan MacPherson House & Museum** (tel. 0540/3332), at the south end of the village. Displayed are clan relics and memorials, including the Black Chanter and Green Banner as well as a "charmed sword," and the broken fiddle of the freebooter, James MacPherson—a Scottish Robin Hood. Sentenced to death in 1700, he is said to have played the dirge "MacPherson's Rant" on his fiddle as he stood on the gallows at Banff. He then offered the instrument to anyone who would think well of him. There were no takers, so he smashed it. The museum is open from May to September on weekdays from 10 a.m. to noon and from 2 to 6 p.m.

A track from the village climbs past the Calder River to Loch Dubh and the massive Carn Ban (3087) feet, where eagles fly. Castle Cluny, ancient seat of the MacPherson chiefs, is six miles west of Newtonmore.

A good place to stay is the **Pines Hotel,** Station Road (tel. Newtonmore 271), on a hill overlooking the Spey Valley, with the Cairngorms, the Grampians, and the Monadhliath mountains all in view. The resident proprietors, John and Fran Raw, offer six bedrooms of different combinations—family, double, twin, and single rooms—all with heating and hot and cold running water. There are also two bathrooms offering both baths and showers. The restaurant features all home-cooked food, such as trout, salmon, venison, chicken, beef, and lamb, all freshly supplied locally and complemented by a substantial wine list, while fine malt whisky and liqueurs can be sampled from the pine bar in front of an open log fire in the TV lounge. The proprietors will personally see to it that your stay is made as relaxing and pleasant as possible. The charges are £9 ($15.75) for B&B in low season and £9.50 ($16.63) from mid-June to mid-September. Half board is recommended, at £13.50 ($23.63) per person in low season and £14 ($24.50) in high. As its name implies, the hotel is in the middle of its own pine-wooded grounds of more than 1½ acres.

KINGUSSIE: Your next stop along the Spey might be at this little summer holiday resort and winter ski center (it's pronounced King-youcie), the so-called capital of Badenoch, a district known as "the drowned land" because the Spey can flood the valley when the snows of a severe winter melt in the spring. There you can visit the six-acre **Highland Folk Museum,** on Duke Street (tel. Kingussie 307), just off High Street, with its comprehensive collection of artifacts, including weaponry, bagpipes, and fiddles illustrating more than two centuries of Highland customs, plus the work of craftspeople. Naturally, there are tartans. A furnished cottage with a mill and a farming shed stand on the museum grounds. There is a new attraction in the open-air section of the museum, a reproduction of an 18th-century cruck-framed house with turf walls from Badenoch. Hours are April to October on weekdays, 10 a.m. to 6 p.m. (on Sunday from 2 to 6 p.m.). From November to March, the museum is open 10 a.m. to 3 p.m. weekdays. It is owned and maintained by the Highland

Regional Council. Admission is 70p ($1.23) for adults and 30p (53¢) for children.

The **Highland Wildlife Park** at Kincraig, near Kingussie (tel. Kingussie 270), is a natural area of parkland with a collection of Highland wildlife, herds of bison, deer, wolves, and foxes, along with many animals now extinct in Scotland, including the lynx and sea-eagles. There is a children's park along with a souvenir shop, a café, and a picnic site. The park is open from 10 a.m. daily from March until the end of October. Admission is £3 ($5.25) per car.

If you'd like to stop here instead of at Aviemore, I recommend the following establishments.

The **Osprey Hotel,** Ruthven Road (tel. Kingussie 510), is a convenient place to stay, with nine comfortable bedrooms, all with hot and cold running water, central heating, electric blankets, electric fires, and heated towel rounds. The proprietors, Duncan and Pauline Reeves, charge £13.50 ($23.63) per person for B&B. All food served is 100% whole and homemade, from the whole-meal bread on. A dinner costs from £8.50 ($14.88), and their banner is pure fresh food. Fresh vegetables are used exclusively (in summer a large number are compost-grown). They are noted for their fresh, prime Scottish meats, including local venison, beef, lamb, pork, and "free-range" chickens. In summer they also offer fish from local rivers, including the Spey. The salmon and trout offered, either fresh or peat-smoked, is superb. Breakfast often features oak-smoked haddock and kippers and local "heather honey." More than 120 wines in their list cover the majority of the wine-producing areas of Europe. The coffee is outstanding, and in every way this small, homey hotel is a good experience. Comfort is its watchword, not pseudo-luxury. A licensed bar, residents' lounge, and TV lounge are housed in the hotel, and babysitter/listening service is provided. The Reeves will offer information and assistance in arranging for pony trekking or horseback riding. Laundry and ironing facilities are available. It's closed mid-April to mid-May.

Friendly Mrs. Jean Filshie accommodates guests at **Arden House,** Newtonmore Road (tel. Kingussie 369), at a charge of £6.50 ($11.38) per person for B&B, including VAT and service. She has four doubles and two family rooms, all with hot and cold running water. The house is centrally heated, and guests can relax in the residents' lounge or, in summer, in the garden. You'll be greeted in a pleasant reception area with blue wallpaper. Ample parking is available, and the house is open all year.

If Arden House is full, you might try **Dunmore House,** 67 High St. (tel. Kingussie 529), where Mrs. Leask takes guests for £6.50 ($11.38) per person for B&B. She has a cozy residents' lounge and a pleasant dining room. However, her house is closed November through March.

If you're not dining at a hotel, try the **Wood'n Spoon,** 3 High St. (tel. Kingussie 488), on the A9, run by Mr. and Mrs. David Russell. Luncheon from noon till 2:30 p.m. features simple fare such as grills, homemade pies, quiches, and especially salads. But dinners, from 5:30 to 9:30 p.m. (Highland dining is early), offers some of the fish caught in the Spey. Most often it is presented with butter, its natural flavors preserved and not hidden by sauces. Try the traditional stovie potatoes, £1 ($1.75), and the Spey Valley trout, £4.50 ($7.88). Venison burgers and homemade smoked fish pâté are also specialties. Expect to pay about £8 ($14) for a complete meal. The restaurant is open seven days a week.

Adjoining the Wood'n Spoon is an interesting pub called the **Creel Bar.** This is a homey pub featuring a real fishing boat.

AVIEMORE CENTRE: This year-round holiday complex on the Spey was opened in 1966 in the heart of the Highlands, at the foot of the historic rock of Craigellachie. This rock was the rallying place for Clan Grant.

In winter, ski runs are available for both beginners and experts (four chair lifts and seven T-bar tows). Après-ski activities include swimming in a heated indoor pool 82 feet long, folk singing, table tennis, or just relaxing and drinking in one of the many bars in the complex.

The ice rink is the second-largest indoor ice rink in Britain, with seven curling lanes and ice skating on a separate 4000-square-foot pad. At night younger people are attracted to the discos, although others seek out one of the Scottish nights, country dancing, supper dances, or dancing in the large Osprey Ballroom with a sprung maple floor.

In summer, sailing, canoeing, pony trekking, hill walking, and mountain climbing, as well as golf and fishing, are just some of the many activities. The **Speyside Theatre,** seating 720, changes its film programs three times a week, and often is host to live shows and concerts. The center's shopping precincts cover a wide range of services, ranging from banking to hairdressing to car-rental offices. The center's activities are suitable for everyone and include ice skating, swimming, saunas, solarium, squash, table tennis, snooker, discos, putting, go-karting, and much more.

Children always like to visit **Santa Claus Land,** set on a six-acre site, with a log cabin, toy factory, doll's house, and a permanently frozen "North Pole" in peppermint colors. It also includes pony rides, cowboy trail, veteran cars, and a gingerbread house. Since it's Scotland, there is also Santa Shortbread.

Adjacent to Santa Claus Land is the **Highland Craft Centre,** where woodcarvers, potters, jewelers, glass makers, artists, and engravers maintain the ancient skills and crafts of the Highlands. Their products are offered for sale.

Later, you can visit **Alan Keegan's Craft Shop,** where you can see 135 different kinds of scotch whisky from 65 different distilleries. He doesn't sell drinks. Collecting scotch whisky is his hobby. He's good at it too, as his collection is considered the largest in Scotland. The most expensive is a Sprinkbank whisky. Only one cask was ever produced.

Food and Lodging

Aviemore Chalets Motel, Aviemore Centre (tel. Aviemore 810619), is best for the budget, offering comfortable, centrally heated, chalet accommodation. Each chalet, named after a Highland clan, has two double-tiered bunks with foam mattresses and continental quilts, individual reading lamps, built-in clothes storage, two wash basins, a shower, and a heated drying cupboard. Based on four persons in a room, the rate is £6.50 ($11.38) per person. Also rented are twin-bedded rooms with color TV, complimentary tea and coffee, a private shower, and toilet, going for £13 ($22.75) per person. Self-catering suites sleeping up to six persons—ideal for families—cost from £31 ($54.25) per suite. The reception chalet offers a large lounge, TV, and a comfortable lounge bar. In the Pinewood, it's cafeteria style (self-service), but in Das Strubel, an Austrian-style grillroom, friendly waitresses serve your meals. The motel is open all year.

Ravenscraig Guest House (tel. Aviemore 810278) is on the main highway near the edge of town after you pass Aviemore Centre going toward Inverness. Robert and Christine Thompson have four double-bedded rooms, four with twin beds, and two family rooms. All rooms have hot and cold running water. There's a comfortable residents' lounge with color TV and tea- and coffee-making facilities, plus a garden where guests may relax in warm weather. The guest house has central heating and clothes-drying facilities. The tariff is £9 ($15.75) for B&B. It's open all year, and you can arrange for skiing through the Thompsons.

Mrs. F. McKenzie rents rooms at **Balavoulin** (tel. Aviemore 810672), in the same vicinity as Ravenscraig. She has one double and four family rooms, with hot and cold running water in all rooms. She charges £8 ($14) per person. There's a pleasant garden behind the house. An evening meal is optional at £3.50 ($6.13) per person. It's open all year.

At **Feithlinn** on Dalfaber Road (tel. Aviemore 810839), Mr. Mark Van Twest accommodates guests for B&B or for full board. The B&B charge is £6.50 ($11.38) per person, plus another £3.75 ($6.56) if you have the optional three-course evening meal, with coffee. There's a pleasant residents' lounge and a garden. The house is centrally heated.

At the **Happy Haggis Chip Shop,** Grampian Road (tel. Aviemore 810430), you can get fish and chips to take out, with prices beginning at £2.50 ($4.38). Visitors from North America are also delighted to discover the selection of beefburgers and Stateside-style thickshakes available in the north of Scotland. But, to honor its namesake, you can also sample haggis, of course.

GRANTOWN-ON-SPEY: This holiday resort, with its gray granite buildings, stands in a wooded valley and commands splendid views of the Cairngorm mountains. It is a key center of winter sports in Scotland. Fishermen are also attracted to its setting, because the Spey is renowned for its salmon. Lying 34 miles southeast of Inverness by road, it was one of Scotland's many 18th-century planned towns, founded on a heather-covered moor in 1765 by Sir James Grant of Grant, becoming the seat of that ancient family. Grantown became famous in the 19th century as a Highland tourist center, enticing visitors with its planned concept, the beauty of surrounding pine forests, the Spey River, and the mountains around it.

From a base here you can explore the valleys of the Don and Dee, the already-mentioned Cairngorms, and Culloden Moor, scene of the historic battle in 1746.

In accommodations, the leading recommendations follow:

The **Strathspey Hotel,** High Street (tel. Grantown-on-Spey 2002), has been renovated by its resident hosts, Scott and Margaret Martin, who give you a warm welcome. Their hotel has seven bedrooms—one family room, three double-bedded rooms, and three with twin beds. Two of the doubles and two of the twins have private baths; the other rooms have hot and cold water basins. The Martins charge £8.50 ($14.88) per person for B&B, £12.50 ($21.88) for half board. Rooms with private bath cost £1 ($1.75) more per person. Guests can enjoy a dram in the Strath Corner lounge bar or mingle with the locals in the public bar. There's also a residents' lounge, and a separate lounge off the public bar where families can be served bar lunches for about £2.20 ($3.85). Bedrooms are color coordinated, with electric wall heaters, and baths done in light-blue and white tiles. The building housing the Strathspey Hotel was erected in 1803. It's the second-oldest licensed premises in Grantown and is open all year.

Willowbank Guest House, High Street (tel. Grantown-on-Spey 2089), catches the eye of the passerby with its cheery sun porch done in light blue and white on the front of a gray stone building. Mrs. MacLean has eight rooms for rent, charging £6 ($10.50) for B&B. Every room has hot and cold running water and an electric heater. There's a color TV lounge and ample parking in front. At 10 p.m., Mrs. MacLean serves tea and crackers to her guests and an evening meal by arrangement.

Riversdale Guest House, Grant Road (tel. Grantown-on-Spey 2648), is a lovely old residence owned by Helen and Jim Shedden, who accept paying guests. Its many dormers and gables, its bay windows, its surrounding stone wall and flower garden make it an attractive place for your stay. Their area attracts nature lovers, those who like to swim, skate, go sailing, pony trekking, or canoeing, and it's ideal for birdwatchers, who try to spot ospreys, crested tits, and less exotic birds. All bedrooms have much comfort, central heating, and hot and cold water. The rate per person is £8.50 ($14.88). If you want an evening meal, it's best to let the owners know when reserving your room. You're given a hearty, filling meal, perhaps roast beef and Yorkshire pudding, followed by dessert and coffee, at a cost of £5 ($8.75). All prices are inclusive of VAT, and there is no service charge.

Umaria Guest House, Woodlands Terrace (tel. Grantown-on-Spey 2104), is a former private home now turned into an attractive guest house, owned by Rosemary and Alan Fisher. It's built of rugged stone, with twin gables and bay windows facing the street. It's pleasantly situated on the edge of this country town, only a few minutes' walk from the riverside and center. The owners are keen on Scottish cooking, and you'll get traditional dishes for breakfast and dinner. The B&B rate per person is £7 ($12.25); with dinner, £11 ($19.25). Children get a reduction. Each bedroom has personalized decorating, individual tea-making equipment, and electric blankets on the beds.

Dar-Il-Hena, Grant Road (tel. Grantown-on-Spey 2929), is run by Jack and Ann Barstow. Reader Donald E. Bishop, Tacoma, Wash., writes, "This guest house has to be the all-time favorite as well as the 'best value' in all of Great Britain." Quite a recommendation. Its rooms are very spacious, the woodwork attractive, and the food and service outstanding. It is a good place at which to center during your tour of "The Whisky Trail." The cost for B&B is from £9 ($15.75) per person, plus another £5.50 ($9.63) for an excellent evening meal.

Craggan Mill, Grantown-on-Spey (tel. Grantown 2288), is a licensed restaurant and lounge bar run by Bruno and Ann Belleni. Look for a white stucco country-style building, with a warmly rustic interior. Assuming that you and a companion differ in your preference for a British or Italian cuisine, the owners offer both cuisines at attractive prices. Therefore your appetizer might be smoked trout in deference to Scotland, or ravioli, inspired by sunny Italy. For a main course the selection might be breast of chicken with cream or chicken cacciatore, followed by a dessert of either rum-raisin ice cream or peach Melba. A choice of one of the course courses just mentioned would cost about £5.50 ($9.63). Hours are from noon to 2 p.m. and 6 to 10 p.m. A good selection of Italian wines is also offered.

FOCHABERS: This village, on the Inverness–Aberdeen road, dates from 1776 and was created as one of the early planned towns by John Baxter, for the fourth Duke of Gordon. Most of the buildings along High Street are protected and have not been changed much in 200 years. On the Spey, Fochabers is distinguished by its **Market Cross** and **Tower of Gordon Castle.**

If you're stopping over, try the **Grant Arms Hotel,** High Street (tel. Fochabers 820202), which has one single room, three doubles, three twin-bedded, and one family room. The tariff is £10 ($17.50) per person for B&B. There's a residents' lounge with color TV and a cocktail bar, where you can get a good bar lunch if you're just passing through. Bar snacks begin at 40p

(70¢) for the homemade soup, going up to £1.60 ($2.80) for the hot dish of the day. High teas, served between 5 and 6:30 p.m., begin at £2.20 ($3.85). The proprietors, Mr. and Mrs. Jefferies, provide central heating, and there's ample parking. The hotel is open all year.

ELGIN: The center of local government in the Moray district, an ancient royal burgh, this cathedral city lies on the Lossie River, 38 miles from Inverness by road. Once called the "lantern of the north," the **Cathedral of Moray** is now in ruins. It was founded in 1224 but almost destroyed in 1390 by the "wolf of Badenoch," the natural son of Robert II. After its destruction, the citizens of Elgin rebuilt their beloved cathedral, turning it into one of the most attractive and graceful buildings in Scotland. The architect's plan was that of a Jerusalem cross. However, when the central tower fell in 1711, the cathedral was allowed to fall into decay. But a faithful cobbler still respected its grandeur, and he became its caretaker. At his death, in 1841, he had removed most of the debris that had fallen. Today tourists wander among its ruins, snapping pictures. Best preserved is the 15th-century chapter house.

On the outskirts, you can visit **Glenfarcias** at Ballindalloch (tel. 080/72245), one of the last of the malt distilleries that is still independent of the big giants. Founded in 1836, it is open Monday to Friday from 9 a.m. to 4:30 p.m. An exhibition center displays not only mementos of the whisky industry, but smuggling and illicit distilling gear, along with a craft shop.

Samuel Johnson and Boswell came this way on their Highland tour, reporting a "vile dinner" at the Red Lion Inn in 1773.

Today, you should fare better at the **Pinegrove Hotel,** Pinefield Crescent (tel. Elgin 44268), where Bill Mutch rents out two double-bedded and four twin-bedded rooms for £25 ($43.75) for two persons for B&B, plus VAT and service. Singles rent for £14 ($24.50). Some units contain color TV. Dinners are à la carte, with main dishes beginning at £4.50 ($7.88). The licensed hotel has a good restaurant with a table d'hôte and an à la carte menu. Regular entertainment is offered, and you can enjoy the game room with its full-size billiard table and three pool tables.

You may prefer the **Royal Hotel,** corner of Station Road and Moss Street (tel. Elgin 2320), a pleasant, privately owned hotel standing on its own grounds about four minutes from the center of Elgin. It lies in the vicinity of the railway station and in close proximity to golf and tennis courts. A pleasant, privately owned hotel, it offers B&B for £11 ($19.25) in a single, £20 ($35) in a double or twin room. Bar lunches and the evening meal range from £3 ($5.25) to £5 ($8.75), and steak dinners go for £5 ($8.25) to £6 ($10.50). You may relax in traditional style, in the lovely cocktail bar with a peat fire burning on cooler days. A separate games room is available for children, and there is a comfortable TV lounge for children's use. This grand old house with its beautiful double staircase with wrought-iron banisters and a mahogany rail boasts many other features of architectural interest. It was built in 1865 by James Grant, the founder of the Glen Grant Distillery, who also built all the railways in northwest Scotland north to Wick. The hotel is open all year, and the owners, Mr. and Mrs. I. G. McAllister, try to make your stay pleasant.

South Bank Guest House, 36 Academy St. (tel. Elgin 7132), has 11 bedrooms for which the charge is £8 ($14) per night per person for B&B. Two of the rooms are small singles. There are no private baths, but the public facilities are conveniently placed. Electric heaters are in all the rooms. Mr. and Mrs. Allan Smith, the proprietors, serve an evening meal for £4 ($7). Guests can enjoy TV in an attractive lounge, and the Smiths have a residents' license to serve alcohol.

For a lunch or dinner stop, **Enrico's Restaurant,** 15 Greyfriars St. (tel. Elgin 2849), is a good choice. The food is tasty and varied, with a number of Scottish dishes included in the menu, particularly trout and salmon, and game in season. Prices begin at £7 ($12.25) for a complete meal, although the chef prepares a business luncheon of three courses for £3 ($5.25).

LOSSIEMOUTH: Almost due north of Elgin on the North Sea coast, this popular holiday resort, at the mouth of the Lossie River, with long stretches of sandy beaches, is also a busy fishing port. Golfing, sea and river fishing, sailing, and surfing are enjoyed.

Eastcliff, Stotfield Road (tel. Lossiemouth 2183), adjoins the golf course and has a superb view over Moray Firth. It's only one minute from the beach. Mrs. Pickering has only one family room and two double bedrooms which she rents for £6.50 ($11.38) per person per night. Ample parking is available. It is open from Easter until October.

FINDHORN: As you travel westward from Elgin to Forres, a turn to the right and then to the left will bring you to Findhorn, a tiny village whose name has become internationally known through its connection with the University of Light in Forres and as a gathering spot for persons seeking a place where communal living and creativity have burgeoned. Actually, a caravan park just before you arrive in Findhorn is the center of these activities. Findhorn is on a unique tidal bay at the mouth of the River Findhorn, which makes it ideal for yacht racing, sailing, and waterskiing. Across the bay from Findhorn is the Culbin Sands, under which lies a buried village.

In Findhorn, a good place to stay is the **Culbin Sands Hotel** (tel. Findhorn 252), which has panoramic views of Moray Firth, Findhorn Bay, and Culbin Forest, and is within two minutes' walk of sandy beaches which stretch for eight miles. The hotel has 14 bedrooms, all with hot and cold running water, renting for £12 ($21) in a single, £21 ($36.75) in a double, for B&B, VAT included. Extra cots can be supplied in rooms, and half price is charged for children under 12. The hotel boasts three well-stocked bars, a pleasant dining room, and a color TV lounge. Bar lunches are served in both the cocktail and public bars seven days a week. Throughout the season there is both disco action along with live entertainment, and fishing, pony trekking, and waterskiing are within easy reach of the place. Ample parking facilities are offered. It's best to reserve well in advance if you plan to visit Findhorn in the high season.

If you don't want to drive on to Inverness for the night, you might stop over in the following town.

FORRES: This ancient burgh, mainly residential in character, stands on the Aberdeen–Inverness road, between Elgin and Nairn (ten miles to the east). Near the mouth of the Findhorn, it is one of Scotland's oldest towns. Once a castle associated with Duncan and Macbeth stood here. Nearby is **Sueno's Stone,** a 23-foot sandstone monolith containing 10th- and 11th-century Celtic carvings with intricate figures of men. The **Witches' Stone,** in the same vicinity, marks the site of the burnings of persons accused of witchcraft.

The best hotels include the **Ramnee,** Victoria Road (tel. Forres 72410), a charming house set back from the road and entered through well-kept gardens. Mrs. Jill Martini personally supervises the day-to-day running of the place, keeping it spotless. There are two lounges plus a pleasant dining room with wood panels and gleaming napery where meals are served. A full breakfast is included in the overnight cost, and dinner consists of a four-course table d'hôte menu featuring grilled steak, fish, or poultry. There is as well a bar for the use of residents. The bedrooms are large and, where bathrooms have been added, the workmanship has been professional—you don't feel that your toilet has been carved out of a corner of your room. The charge is £12 ($21) per person, £1.75 ($3.06) extra for a room with bath, plus VAT. A set dinner costs from £7.50 ($13.13).

Nearby, the **Park Hotel,** Victoria Road (tel. Forres 72328), is very much the same sort of house. Set on spacious, well-kept grounds, it overlooks Findhorn Bay and the Moray Firth. The bedrooms are comfortable and well appointed, containing hot and cold running water. In season fresh fruit and vegetables come from the garden, the produce used in the hotel's kitchen. Mr. and Mrs. Leslie welcome guests, charging them £11 ($19.25) to £14 ($24.50), the higher price for a room with a private bath, plus VAT and service, for B&B. Bar lunches are served. An evening meal goes for £5.50 ($9.63). The hotel also has a cocktail bar, drawing room, and television lounge.

For dining in the area, the best choice is **The Elizabethan Inn,** Mundole, near Forres (tel. Forres 72737). You can see the Findhorn River from the windows of this stone house, about 1½ miles west of Forres. The furnishings are country Victorian, and the food is home-cooked and very popular with the local residents. Margaret le Philip and her sister are partners in this little venture. A three-course lunch from a fixed-price menu, costing £3.45 ($6.04), is served daily from 12:30 to 1:30 p.m. It could consist of an egg-salad appetizer, then hot roast sirloin with a horseradish sauce, topped off by a homemade dessert or cheese and crackers. Because the food is good, the atmosphere relaxed, and the prices moderate, it's wise to phone ahead for a table. A three-course dinner, served every evening except Wednesday from 7:30 to 8:30 p.m., costs £8 ($14) on the table d'hôte menu. I recently enjoyed a turkey pâté salad, followed by venison goulash with roast potatoes and two fresh vegetables, then a homemade dessert and cheese.

2. Inverness and Loch Ness

After Glasgow, most motorists wanting to explore the Highlands head for Inverness, its ancient capital. From its doorstep, you can explore a romantic land of hills, lochs, and lots of myths.

Of course, the most popular excursion is to Loch Ness, where you can set up an observation point to await the appearance of "Nessie," the Loch Ness monster. But even if the monster doesn't put in an appearance, the loch itself has splendid scenery. I have a scattering of recommendations around the loch for those wanting to base there.

Finally, visitors going east may want to explore the old town of Nairn, and those adventurous readers wanting to venture into the forlorn and relatively uninhabited section of northwest Scotland may want to do so from a base at the old spa of Strathpeffer.

INVERNESS: The capital of the Highlands, Inverness is a royal burgh and seaport, at the north end of Great Glen, lying on both sides of the Ness River. It is considered the best base for touring the north. At the Highland Games, with their festive balls, the season in Inverness reaches its social peak.

The city has a luxurious theater complex on the bank of the River Ness, the **Eden Court Theatre,** Bishops Road (tel. Inverness 221718), which has a superb restaurant, bars, and an art gallery. Included in the repertoire are variety shows, drama, ballet, pop music, movies, opera, rock and folk concerts, and a summer-season traditional Scottish show with top stars. The theater, which opened in 1976, was constructed with an ingenious use of hexagonal shapes and has a horseshoe-shaped auditorium. Programs are advertised in most hotels and guest houses. The box office is open 10:30 a.m. to 8 p.m., Monday through Saturday.

Inverness is one of the oldest inhabited localities in Scotland.

On **Craig Phadrig** are the remains of a vitrified fort, believed to date from the fourth century B.C., where the Pictish King Brude is said to have been visited by St. Columba in A.D. 565. The old castle of Inverness stood to the east of the present Castlehill, the site still retaining the name **Auld Castlehill.** Because of the somewhat shaky geography of Shakespeare in dramatizing the crime of Macbeth by murdering King Duncan, some scholars claim that the deed was done in the old castle of Inverness while others say it happened at Cawdor Castle, 4½ miles to the south where Macbeth held forth as Thane of Cawdor. However, a spokesman for Cawdor Castle says that historically King Duncan was killed in combat by his cousin Macbeth on August 14, 1040, at Pitgaveny near Elgin, which is about 40 miles from the castle.

King David built the first stone castle in Inverness around 1141. **The Clock Tower** is all that remains of a fort erected by Cromwell's army between 1652 and 1657. The 16th-century **Abertarff House** is now the headquarters of An Comunn Gaidhealach, the Highland association which preserves the Gaelic language and culture.

Inverness today has a castle, but it's a "modern" one—that is, dating from 1835. Crowning a low cliff of the east bank of the Ness, the **Castle of Inverness** occupies the site of an ancient fortress blown up by the Jacobites in 1746. Today the castle houses county offices and law courts. Mary Queen of Scots was denied admission to the castle in 1562, and she subsequently occupied a house on Bridge Street. From the window of this house, she witnessed the execution of her cousin, Sir John Gordon. For not gaining admission to the castle, she took reprisals, taking the fortress and hanging the governor.

Opposite the town hall is the **Old Mercat Cross,** with its **Stone of the Tubs,** an Inverness landmark said to be where women rested their washtubs as they ascended from the river. Known as "Clachnacudainn," the lozenge-shaped stone was the spot where the early kings were crowned.

Inverness Museum and Art Gallery, Castle Wynd (tel. Inverness 237114), has on display collections representing the social and natural history, archeology, art, and culture of the Scottish Highlands, with special emphasis on the Inverness district. There is an important collection of Highland silver, with a reconstructed silversmith's workshop; displays on the "Life of the Clans"; a reconstruction of a local taxidermist's workshop; a reconstructed Inverness kitchen of the 1920s; displays of Highland weapons; and an art gallery. Open from 1982 is a permanent exhibition on the story of the Inverness district, from local geology and archeology to the present day. This includes extensive natural history displays. Other facilities include a public cloakroom and toilets, a souvenir shop, a coffeeshop for meals and refreshments, a regular program of temporary exhibitions and events, and an information service. The museum is open all year Monday to Saturday from 9 a.m. to 5 p.m. (closed on Sunday). Admission is free.

West of the river rises the wooded hill of **Tomnahurich,** known as "the hill of the fairies." It is now a cemetery, and from here the views are magnificent.

In the Ness are wooded islands, linked to Inverness by suspension bridges and turned into parks.

From Inverness, you can visit **Culloden Battlefield,** six miles to the east. This is the spot where Bonnie Prince Charlie and the Jacobite army were finally crushed at the battle on April 16, 1746. A cairn marks the site on Drummossie Moor where the battle raged. **Leanach Cottage,** around which the battle took place, still stands and was inhabited until 1912. A path from the cottage leads through the Field of the English, where 76 men of the Duke of Cumberland's forces who died during the battle are said to be buried. Features of interest include the **Graves of the Clans,** communal burial places with simple stones bearing individual clan names alongside the main road and through the woodland; the great memorial cairn, erected in 1881; the **Well of the Dead,** a single stone with the inscription: "The English Were Buried Here"; and the huge **Cumberland Stone** from which the victorious "Butcher" Cumberland is said to have reviewed the scene. The battle lasted only 40 minutes; the prince's army lost some 1200 men out of 5000, and the king's army 310. A visitors' center and museum are open all year.

Between Inverness and Nairn, also about six miles to the east of Inverness, are the **Stones of Clava,** one of the most important prehistoric monuments in the north. These cairns and standing stones are from the Bronze Age.

Back in Inverness, we'll investigate—

Where to Stay

Redcliffe, 1 Gordon Terrace (tel. Inverness 32767), is a small hotel set on its own grounds, commanding a peaceful perch above the Ness and the castle, yet lying within a three-minute walk of the main shopping district. Your hosts, Mr. and Mrs. West, have completely modernized the interior, but have kept the traditional stone facade intact. The bedrooms are pleasantly decorated and have hot and cold running water. Singles rent for £12.90 ($22.58), rising to £25.80 ($45.15) in a double, these tariffs including breakfast. In a spacious, comfortable lounge, guests gather to watch TV. At the hotel is a permanent exhibition of the work of local artists, with all works for sale. The hotel also serves excellent Highland dinners with pheasant, haggis, venison, and salmon (the latter should be requested in advance when making a reservation). An à la carte meal, including coffee later in the lounge, costs about £9.50 ($16.63) per person.

On the east side of the River Ness, which flows from Loch Ness to the sea, a short street hugging the riverside, Ness Bank, has a number of guest houses and private hotels in varying price ranges but all with a delightful view of the river and the Eden Court Theatre on the other side.

Riverside House, 8 Ness Bank (tel. Inverness 31052), is an immaculate place run by Jean and Dougie Robertson. Occupying perhaps the most scenic spot on the river, it stands opposite St. Andrews Cathedral and Eden Court Theatre, only three minutes' walk from the town center. All year, they have nine rooms to rent, including three singles, for which the charge is £9.50 ($16.63) per person for B&B or £14.50 ($25.38) per person for half board. Good home-cooking with a choice of menu is featured. The residents' lounge, which is open all day, is tastefully decorated and has a color TV. Tea and biscuits are served here at 9:30 p.m. All rooms have hot and cold running water, and there are two large bathrooms, one with a shower. Full heating is found in all areas, and there are electric blankets on all beds.

Brae Ness, Ness Bank (tel. Inverness 231732), is run by four resident owners, Margaret and John Hill and Jean and Tony Gatcombe. These two friendly couples are eager to help visitors enjoy Inverness. Brae Ness is a Georgian house, built in 1830, that has been upgraded to incorporate modern comforts while still retaining much of its original character. Some of the 14 bedrooms have private baths. For B&B expect to pay from £10.25 ($17.94) per person, plus another £1.50 ($2.63) if you get a room with private plumbing. In the dining room home-cooking and baking are served, and traditional Scottish fare such as salmon, venison, and other local produce in season is offered, a dinner costing from £6 ($10.50). The hotel isn't licensed, but you are invited to bring in your own wine. Brae Ness has a TV lounge, plus a separate drawing room with a log fire, and all units are centrally heated. Ten of the rooms overlook the river. The owners urge that reservations be made in advance, as this is a popular area with travelers.

In other sections of the city: **Villa Fontana Guest House,** 13 Bishops Rd. (tel. Inverness 32999), is a large stone house which was formerly a private home. Mrs. Gander has transformed it into a pleasant guest house, with the original handsome entry hall and frosted, etched glass doors setting the tone. The house is centrally heated, and the two family rooms, two doubles, and one single bedroom are large, attractive, and immaculate. The tariff is £7.50 ($13.13) per night per person for B&B, except in July and August when it is £8.50 ($14.88). A reduction is granted for children sharing a family room with their parents. All rooms have hot and cold running water, and there are two large, spotless bathrooms. No evening meal is served. A guest lounge has a color TV and facilities for making tea and coffee. It is open all year.

If Mrs. Gander cannot accommodate you, you might try **Whitelodge,** 15 Bishops Rd. (tel. Inverness 230693). Young Mrs. Dodds rents two twin-bedded rooms at £7 ($12.25) per night for B&B. The red sandstone, two-story house is attractive, and the rooms are large and comfortable, with tea- and coffee-making facilities. There's a lounge with color TV for residents. Her place is open all year.

Across the street, approaching Glenurquhart Road, Mrs. Margaret Charlesworth takes in guests at **Amapola,** 12 Bishops Rd. (tel. Inverness 234028), charging £7.50 ($13.13) per person for B&B to lodgers in her two doubles and two family rooms. TV and tea- and coffee-making facilities, plus heaters, are in all bedrooms, as well as hot and cold running water. There is a clean and convenient bathroom and another room with shower and toilet. Central heating has been installed in the house.

Moraine, 5 Porterfield Rd. (tel. Inverness 40436), is the domain of Mr. and Mrs. Telford. Margaret Telford is a most hospitable hostess, often meeting late arrivals with hot tea and cookies. Their home is beautifully kept and most comfortable, and the Scottish breakfast is hearty. Yet the charge is only from £6.50 ($11.38) per person nightly.

READERS' GUEST HOUSE SELECTIONS: "Rossmount, 32 Argyle St. (tel. Inverness 40525), a ten-minute walk from the train station, is operated by Mrs. Elspeth Morrow. The Morrows are wonderful hosts. We arrived in the early evening, and they suggested some very reasonable cafés where we could have an evening meal. At 9:30 p.m., we were served tea and biscuits in the sitting room. They visited with us until midnight, much to our pleasure. The following morning, we were served orange juice, cornflakes, bacon, sausage, a fried egg, toast, butter, marmalade, and tea or coffee. Again tea and biscuits were served to us after we arrived home from attending the Highland Fling. In addition, Mrs. Morrow insisted that she serve us breakfast before our train departed at 6:15 a.m.

The hospitality we received from this family gave us a very favorable opinion of the people of Scotland. They charge £7.50 ($13.13) per person per night for B&B" (Betty Hansen, New Hampton, Texas). . . . "We had a pleasant stay at the guest house of **Mrs. Galleitch,** 7 Porterfield Road (tel. Inverness 233901). The bed was excellent (the best we had in Europe), the house sparkling clean, the breakfast very good, and the proprietor friendly and helpful. We enjoyed all this for £5.50 ($9.63) per person for B&B" (Mr. and Mrs. Carel M. van Vliet, Montreal, Canada).

"**Abertarff Guest House,** 12 Crown Ave. (tel. Inverness 30896), is run by Mrs. MacDonald, an outstanding host. The house is about 175 years old, in immaculate condition. She serves excellent full breakfasts, also tea with cookies, cake, or crackers in the afternoon and again in the evening. The guest house opens onto a beautiful view of the city, as it is on a hill. This place costs £7 ($12.25) per person per night" (Mr. and Mrs. P. W. Smith). . . . "We stayed at **MacDonald House Hotel,** 1 Ardoss Terrace, on the west bank of the River Ness, across from the castle. For £7 ($12.25) each per night, we had a large double room, plenty of hot water, central heating, color TV, a lounge in which tea and biscuits were served before bedtime, and a hearty breakfast of juice, porridge, bacon, sausage, eggs, toast, and tea. The proprietor, Mrs. Allan, was friendly, and the house was carpeted with tartan throughout" (Mrs. Lois Ashton, Dorval, Quebec, Canada). . . . "The home of Flora Ross, **Glencairn,** 30 Argyle St. (tel. Inverness 31857), is beautiful, enhanced by her hospitality. We enjoyed a comfortable double room with a basin (hot and cold water), as well as the hot shower and bath. The evenings proved pleasant, with Mrs. Ross and the excellent color TV in the lounge. We were served a tasty breakfast in the morning. The charge is £7.50 ($13.13) per person" (Mr. and Mrs. Don McGilvray, Oakland, Calif.). . . . "The **Blair-Ord Guest House,** 10 Ballifeary Rd. (tel. Inverness 34472), is well located, about ten minutes' walk from the city center along the River Ness. It is a large single house with gate and garden in front. The rooms are light and comfortable, and there is a basin in each, with toilets, bath, and shower not far from the rooms. The breakfast room is large and airy. Single and double rooms are available at £8.50 ($14.88) per person per night. The proprietors are Mr. and Mrs. Joyce" (Raymond and Edith Hebb, Elmira, N.Y.).

"I came across **Cambeth Lodge,** 49 Fairfield Rd., a ten-minute walk from the city center, where Mrs. Carson has a lovely old home with several large bedrooms. The comfortable beds have pretty eiderdowns. The bathroom has a great, hot, high-pressure shower. Mrs. Carson sets a charming breakfast table with bone china and roses from her garden. The food is abundant and well cooked. Most impressive is Mrs. Carson's willingness to please her guests. On our first morning we were offered cereal or juice as a first course. When we asked for porridge, she apologized profusely for not having any, and for the rest of our stay she made a special pot of porridge just for us. All of this costs only £6.50 ($11.38) per person per night" (Lynne Widli, New York, N.Y.). . . . "**Whinpark Guest House,** 17 Ardross St. (tel. Inverness 32549), is within walking distance from theaters and downtown. Mr. and Mrs. Nicoll welcomed us with tea and cookies on our arrival and also served them at bedtime. There is a nice lounge for guests. The charge is £9 ($15.75) per person for a double with toilet and shower, breakfast included. An ample and good dinner is put on the table for £5.50 ($9.63) per person, and the desserts are just great. You could not wish for friendlier hosts" (Henry A. Leigh, Cullowhee, N.C.).

Where to Eat

The restaurant at the Eden Court Theatre complex is called the **Bishops Table,** Bishops Road (tel. Inverness 39841), after Bishop Eden who was in charge of the adjacent cathedral in the 19th century and lived in the Bishops Palace, now used as offices and dressing rooms for the theater. The restaurant offers a superb value buffet with freshly prepared hot and cold food, at prices starting at less than £1.50 ($2.63) at lunchtime. Full evening meals commence at around £4 ($7). The restaurant offers expertly prepared salmon and venison in season, the best Scottish beefsteaks, and of course, haggis is regularly on the menu. Morning coffee is served from 10:30 a.m. to noon, lunch from noon to 2 p.m., afternoon tea from 3:30 to 4:30 p.m. Dinner is served, except on nonperformance Monday, from 6 to 8:30 p.m. April to September, 6 to 8 p.m. October to March.

St. Andrews Cathedral, adjacent to the Eden Court Theatre, complex, operates a **Tea Garden** from around Easter until the first week of September. Indoors when wet or cold, the Tea Garden offers homemade broth, filled rolls, home baking, tea, çoffee, and soft drinks. To sample something of everything costs less than £1 ($1.75). The women of the cathedral give their services voluntarily and do all the baking themselves, the proceeds going to cathedral funds. Hours are from 10:30 a.m. to 4 p.m. Flasks will be filled, and rolls and cakes may be taken away.

The cathedral is open to visitors from 9 a.m. to 9 p.m., and this northernmost diocese of the Episcopal Church of Scotland boasts a fine example of this form of architecture. For information, get in touch with the Provost, 15 Ardross St.

Pizzaland, 7–9 Lombard St. (tel. Inverness 234328). Pizza in Inverness? It's enough to stir up a Highland uprising. Actually, the modern Scots don't survive entirely these days on haggis and neeps. Increasingly continental in their tastes, shoppers along this mall come here for pizzas in many combinations, all for under £2 ($3.50). If you don't want pizza, you can order homemade lasagne at £1.75 ($3.06), and help yourself from the salad bar, a wide selection costing from 95p ($1.66). Some of the pizza combinations are unusual. I suggest you skip the ham and pineapple and turn to more traditional selections, such as pepperoni and onion. Desserts average 95p ($1.66). The pizzeria serves Monday to Saturday from 10 a.m. to 11 p.m. (from noon to 6 p.m. only on Sunday). On summer Sundays they remain open until 8 p.m.

In the Environs

North of Inverness is a fertile peninsula known as the **Black Isle** because it is seldom whitened by snow. Here tropical plants flourish, and **Cromarty,** at the northeast tip, has fine sandy beaches. The cottage there where Hugh Miller, noted geologist, was born in 1802 is now a geological museum. **Fortrose,** an ancient town facing the Moray Firth, has a sheltered bay for yachting.

Dingwall is a town in Easter Ross district near the mouth of the River Conon. The town arms, a starfish, are displayed on the tolbooth (originally a booth for collecting tolls), dating from 1730. In front of this is the shaft of a former Mercat Cross, and beside it is an iron gate of the old town jail.

Strathpeffer, about six miles west of Dingwall, is a good center for touring Easter Ross, where the countryside is dominated by the 3433-foot summit of Ben Wyvis.

Heading back toward Inverness, an interesting stop is at **Beauly,** 12 miles west of the city, where you can visit the ruins of a Valliscaulian priory built in 1230. On the south bank of the River Beauly southwest of the town is **Beaufort Castle,** a 19th-century baronial mansion which is the seat of the Frasers of Lovat whose ancestor was the "Lovat of the Forty-five." The original seat of the Lovats was Castle Dounie, built about 1400, but it was destroyed by "Butcher" Cumberland after his victory at Culloden.

NAIRN: A favorite family seaside resort on the sheltered Moray Firth, Nairn is a royal burgh, lying at the mouth of the Nairn River. Its fishing harbor was constructed in 1820, and golf has been played here since 1672, as it still is today. A large uncrowded beach, tennis, and angling draw a horde of vacationers in summer.

At **Cawdor Castle** (tel. Cawdor 615), to the south of Nairn, you encounter 600 years of Highland history. Since the early 14th century it's been the home of the Thanes of Cawdor. The castle has all the architectural ingredients you associate with the medieval: a drawbridge, an ancient tower (this one built around a tree), and fortified walls. The severity is softened by the handsome gardens, flowers, trees, and rolling lawns. As I mentioned earlier, even the Scots can't agree as to where Macbeth, who actually was made Thane of Cawdor by King Duncan, committed his foul deed of murdering the king—at Cawdor or in the castle which once stood on Auld Castlehill in Inverness, if at all. In fact, recent historic discoveries indicate that the king was indeed killed by his cousin, Macbeth, but that the slaying was in combat at Pitgaveny near Elgin. The castle is open to the public from 10 a.m. to 5:30 p.m. every day from May 1 to October 2. Admission is £1.60 ($2.80) for adults, 80p ($1.40) for children. Last admission is at 5 p.m.

If you're staying in Nairn, I'd recommend:

The **Windsor Hotel,** Albert Street (tel. Nairn 53108), a fine sandstone building which has been renovated and refurbished to good effect. The resident proprietors, Mr. and Mrs. Charles Woolley, see to it that the hotel provides a comfortable family atmosphere and first-class cuisine. The hotel is centrally heated, and each bedroom contains its own basin with hot and cold running water. There are numerous bathrooms, showers, and toilets throughout the hotel. The color TV lounge, residents' lounge, and fully licensed cocktail bar add to the guests' enjoyment. Daily rates for B&B are £15 ($26.25) to £18 ($31.50) per person in high season, slightly lower in low season. Special rates are allowed for children. Dinner costs £7 ($12.25). The hotel is close to centers of transportation and sports facilities, and is open all year.

Greenlawns Private Hotel, Seafield Street (tel. Nairn 52738), a good center for touring northern Scotland, is within easy reach of beaches, a bowling green, golf courses, tennis courts, an indoor swimming pool, and a shopping center. Guests relax in a pleasant sun lounge. Parking is available on the grounds. All bedrooms have hot and cold running water, electric blankets, heating, TV, and coffee- and tea-making facilities. Mr. and Mrs. Caldwell do much to see that their guests have a comfortable stay, charging them from £10.50 ($18.38) per person for B&B.

DRUMNADROCHIT: This pleasant little hamlet lies about a mile from Loch Ness at the entrance to Glen Urquhart. The ruined **Urquhart Castle,** one of Scotland's largest castles, is a mile and a half southeast on a promontory overlooking Loch Ness. The chief of Clan Grant owned the castle in 1509, and most of the existing building dates from that period. In 1692, the castle was blown up by the Grants to prevent its becoming a Jacobite stronghold. It is here at Urquhart Castle that sightings of the Loch Ness monster are most often reported.

In 1980 a **Loch Ness Monster Exhibition** opened in the village, and it's been packing them in ever since. You can view fuzzy pictures and movies of the so-called monster, and learn about serious attempts by scientists to get to the heart of the age-old mystery (for example, submarines have been lowered into the murky water, as have cameras and diving bells). Talk to Curator Tony Harmsworth. He makes a convincing case for the existence of the creature (or creatures).

Capt. and Mrs. A. D. MacDonald-Haig run **Borlum Farm** (tel. Drumnadrochit 220), about 1½ miles from the village. The Highland farmhouse is fully centrally heated and has two bedrooms and a bathroom on the ground floor and two family rooms and a twin, all with hot and cold running water, and a bathroom upstairs. The charge is £7.50 ($13.13) per night per person for bed and a full Scottish breakfast. Borlum, a 300-acre farm, offers a place where you can view shaggy Highland cattle grazing in the hills overlooking Loch Ness and see foals playing in fields bordering the loch shore. You can watch the blacksmith at work shoeing horses and ponies for the use of guests interested in pony trekking or riding into the hills. When you return from a day of Highland activity, you can relax in the large sitting room with a blazing log fire or in the dining room with its incredible view far down the loch with hills bordering either side. It is advisable that reservations be made at least a month ahead, especially for August, and a deposit of £3 ($5.25) per person per night is required.

FORT AUGUSTUS: This Highland touring center stands at the head (the southernmost end) of Loch Ness. The town took its name from a fort named for the Duke of Cumberland. Built after the 1715 Rising, the present Benedictine Abbey stands on its site.

In accommodations, it offers the **Brae Hotel** (tel. Fort Augustus 6289). Set on two acres of ground, the hotel has a view of Fort Augustus and the Caledonian Canal from its perch on a hill. The resident proprietor, Dileas Leslie, rents eight bedrooms, two with private bathrooms and two with showers. Tariffs for B&B are £10.50 ($18.38) per person in a bathless room, £13 ($22.75) with bath. The hotel is centrally heated, and there are a cocktail bar and an attractive dining room. The lounge and the sun porch afford panoramic views. You can enjoy bar snacks from 60p ($1.05); lunch, either eaten at the hotel or packed to take on excursions, is from £2 ($3.50); and dinner is £6.50 ($11.38). You can board a bus to Inverness or to the center of Drumnadrochit right at the foot of the hill.

INVERGARRY: A Highland center for fishing and deer stalking, Invergarry is noted for its fine scenery. It, too, is a good center for exploring Glen More and Loch Ness. At Invergarry is the beginning of the road through the West Highland Glens and mountains, forming one of the famous "Road to the Isles" that terminates at Kyle of Lochalsh.

Near Invergarry, you can visit the **Well of the Heads,** on the west side of Loch Oich near its southern tip, erected in 1812 by MacDonnell of Glengarry to commemorate the decapitation by the family bard of seven brothers who had murdered the two sons of a 17th-century chief of Clan Keppoch, a branch of the MacDonnell Clan. The seven heads were washed in the well before being presented to the chief of the MacDonnells at Glengarry.

Lundie View Guest House, Aberchalder (tel. Invergarry 291), sits in a pleasant garden, accommodating guests in one of its three double rooms or three family rooms for £7 ($12.25) per person per night for B&B, or £10.50 ($18.38) per person for half board. Mr. and Mrs. Peter Upstone have a pleasant residents' lounge in their centrally heated house, and babysitter/listening service is provided. Open all year, the guest house lies 3½ miles northeast of Invergarry on the A82. Surrounded by beautiful scenery, the house stands in the Great Glen. Pony trekking, fishing, walking, and touring are convenient, and just four miles away you can take your chance at spotting the Loch Ness monster.

SPEAN BRIDGE: This village is a busy intersection of the Fort William–Perth and Fort William–Inverness roads, as well as having daily train service to Fort William, Glasgow, and London, and bus service to Inverness and Fort

William. Two miles outside the town, in Glen Spean, is the striking **Commando Memorial** by Scott Sutherland which the Queen Mother unveiled in 1952. In this area many commandos were trained during World War II. Numerous war movies have been filmed here.

On the outskirts of the village on the A86 going toward Newtonmore and Perth is **Coire Glas** (tel. Spean Bridge 272), a motel-style guest house with 15 bedrooms. Mr. and Mrs. MacFarlane have added onto the back of their one-story home, to come up with an attractive and convenient place for visitors to stay overnight or for long periods. All the rooms are equipped with hot and cold running water, and ample bathroom facilities are provided. The MacFarlanes charge £7 ($12.25) per person per night for B&B. If you book a room with private toilet and shower, a supplement of £1.50 ($2.62) per person nightly is assessed. Dinner is £5.50 ($9.63). A lunch will be packed for you upon request for £2 ($3.50). Spean Bridge is a central area for touring the loch country, and from Coire Glas, looking across a wide, grassy lawn, you can see Ben Gurry, which is a part of the Ben Nevis range.

Letterfinlay Lodge (tel. Invergloy 222) is the "Forsyth Family" hotel, a comfortable, well-appointed establishment on the A82 near Spean Bridge, about halfway between Fort Augustus and Fort William. Between the highway and Loch Lochy, against a backdrop of rugged scenery, it operates all year, and is known both for its personal service and level of cuisine, mostly plain Highland dishes that use high-quality ingredients, such as fresh salmon and sea trout, Aberdeen Angus beef, and Scottish hill lamb. Your bedroom window is likely to look out upon Loch Lochy. All units, including some family rooms, are tastefully furnished, with hot and cold running water. In the corridors are ample toilets and baths. Some units contain private baths or showers as well. Depending on the plumbing, charges are from £11 ($19.25) to £15.50 ($27.13) per person, these tariffs including a full Scottish breakfast. Dinner, including coffee, is about £8 ($14). The hotel also offers a sun lounge and a cocktail bar. Trout fishing is available at the doorstep.

3. Fort William and Lochaber

Fort William, the capital of Lochaber, is the major touring center for the western Highlands. Wildly beautiful Lochaber, the area around Fort William, has been called "the land of bens, glens, and heroes."

Dominating the area is **Ben Nevis,** Britain's highest mountain, rising 4418 feet. In summer when it's clear of snow, there's a safe path to the summit. Fort William stands on the site of a fort built by General Monk in 1655, which was pulled down to make way for the railroad. This district is the western end of what is known as Glen Mor—the Great Glen, geologically a fissure which divides the northwest of Scotland from the southeast and contains Loch Lochy, Loch Oich, and Loch Ness. The Caledonian Canal, opened in 1847, linked these lochs, the River Ness, and Moray Firth. It provided sailing boats a safe alternative to the stormy route around the north of Scotland. Larger steamships made the canal out of date commercially, but fishing boats and pleasure steamers still use it. Good roads run the length of the Great Glen, partly following the line of General Wade's military road. From Fort William you can take steamer trips to Staffa and Iona.

The ruins of **Old Inverlochy Castle,** scene of the famous battle in 1645, can be reached by driving on the A82 two miles north of Fort William. At a point just one mile north of Fort William is **Glen Nevis,** one of the most beautiful in Scotland.

About 15 miles west of Fort William, on the A830 toward Mallaig, at Glenfinnan at the head of Loch Shiel is the **Glenfinnan Monument,** which marks the spot where Bonnie Prince Charlie unfurled his proud red-and-white silk banner on August 19, 1745, in the ill-fated attempt to restore the Stuarts to the British throne. The monument is topped by the figure of a kilted Highlander. At a Visitors' Centre you can learn of the prince's campaign from Glenfinnan to Derby and back to the final defeat at Culloden.

FORT WILLIAM: The town, on the shores of Loch Linnhe, is most often used as a touring center. While there, you can visit the **West Highland Museum,** on Cameron Square (tel. Fort William 2169), containing all aspects of local history, including a large Jacobite and tartan section. A special exhibition is devoted to Prince Charles Edward and the '45 Rising. The museum is open Monday to Saturday, September to June, from 9:30 a.m. to 1 p.m. and from 2 to 5 p.m.; in July and August its hours are from 9:30 a.m. to 9 p.m. Admission costs 30p (53¢) for adults, 10p (18¢) for children under 16.

Where to Stay

There is no shortage of B&B accommodations in Fort William, most with a good view of Loch Linnhe. The Tourist Information Office at the train-bus station can supply you with a list. My recommendations are:

Ben View Guest House (tel. Fort William 2966), in the midst of the cluster of hotels and guest houses fronting on the loch in the heart of the city, is a two-story red stone building with central heating and comfortable rooms. Tariffs in high season are £9.20 ($16.10) per person for B&B. The Ben View has 2 single rooms, 11 doubles, and 2 family rooms, and seven of the double rooms have private baths. Guests can relax in a pleasant residents' lounge, or dine overlooking the loch, a dinner costing £5.50 ($9.63). The house is closed December through February.

Mrs. Sillars rents rooms in **Torosay,** Cameron Road (tel. Fort William 3299). Her attractive house is on a quiet road on a hill overlooking the busy town and the loch. The charge in her well-furnished, modern rooms is £8.50 ($14.88) per person for bed and a full Scottish breakfast, which is served in a pleasant dining room with a loch view. The two double bedrooms and one family room have hot and cold running water, and the bathrooms are immaculate. A roomy residents' lounge has color TV. A good three-course dinner costs only £2.50 ($4.38). Mrs. Sillars will direct you to the town's main street, a short walk, and to places of interest in the area. Torosay is open all year.

Innseagan Guest House, Achintore Road (tel. Fort William 2452), is about 1½ miles south of Fort William on the A82. The original building is more than 100 years old, but extensive modernization has created a pleasant combination of old and new. The guest house is licensed and offers some rooms with private baths. The tariff for half board is from £13 ($22.75) per person. Ample parking space is available, as the house sits in its own extensive grounds. It is open April to October.

READERS' GUEST HOUSE SELECTIONS: "We found the excellent **Stronchreggan View Guest House,** Achintore Road (tel. Fort William 4644), owned by Mr. and Mrs. McQueen who are ably assisted by their sons and grandmother. This is a spacious modern home, overlooking Loch Linnhe, about 1½ miles from the center of Fort William on the A82. The charge is £12.50 ($21.88) per person for bed, breakfast, and dinner, VAT included. Each day the tasty meals vary and are served in a sunny dining room. Our carpeted bedroom was huge, with the most comfortable twin beds of our trip, plenty of cupboard and drawer space, and excellent lighting. The house can accommodate 18 visitors and has three toilets, two showers, and one tub available exclusively for guests. The McQueens make every effort to please, including providing a huge living room in which you can select a book from the shelf, admire the view of Loch Linnhe, or get acquainted with other guests. Mr. McQueen has provided high-quality protection for his guests, including fire doors and alarms. The McQueens' Scottish hospitality was one of the high points of our trip" (Christopher Mitchell, Wiarton, Ont., Canada). . . . "The most elegant B&B we found on our entire trip was in Fort William, **Crolinnke,** a large private home in a quiet residential area on Grange Road (tel. Fort William 2709), only five minutes' walk to the town center. The beautifully decorated house is set in a half acre of gardens with views of the hills and the loch. The facilities are outstanding, and a surprise evening tea is placed in each room. A 10% discount is offered to guests using other family businesses in the town, i.e., a fine restaurant and a tweed and tartan shop. The friendly proprietors are Kenneth and Flora MacKenzie, and the cost is £7 ($12.25) per person" (Marian C. Jackson, Oxford, Ohio).

Where to Dine

Like its counterpart in Oban, **McTavish's Kitchen** and the **Tweeddale Restaurant** (tel. Fort William 2406), under the same management, are at either end of Fort William High Street. The restaurants are open from mid-May until the end of October. The self-service at McTavish's Kitchens and the Tweeddale Restaurant caters for meals and refreshments throughout the day, and the menu includes such Scottish specialties as haggis and fresh filet of haddock. You can lunch or dine well for around £4 ($7).

If you prefer waitress service, the licensed restaurant at McTavish's Kitchens on the second floor provides a reasonably priced à la carte menu. Items include haggis at £3 ($5.25), smoked salmon at £5 ($8.75), kippers (smoked herring) for £3 ($5.25), and a set lunch for £3.50 ($6.13). Should you wish a drink before your meal, the adjoining Lairds Bar provides a snug tavern with photographs of an old Scottish laird.

A feature of the licensed restaurant is Scottish cabaret, with singers, a piper, and a Highland dancer. Show times are at 8:30 and 10:30 p.m. each evening from mid-May to the end of September. There is also a small dance floor. Admission is £1.25 ($2.19) for adults and 60p ($1.05) for children.

The Angus, 66 High St. (tel. Fort William 2654). If red is indeed the color that makes bulls go crazy, then there are plenty of agitated steers here. Red is the decor theme in this licensed 60-seat second-floor restaurant (there's a bar lounge on the ground level). Mary Lamont welcomes you to the premises which serve in season daily except Sunday from 10 a.m. to 10 p.m. The tempting sirloin steak is a meal in itself at £4.65 ($8.14). A filling soup of the day followed by grilled Lochry trout, plus a cream cake for dessert, would cost £4.85 ($8.49). If you've been in Scotland for a while and haven't ordered the famous haggis and neeps, you can here for £2.10 ($3.68).

At Ballachulish, the **Ballachulish Hotel** (tel. Ballachulish 239), does excellent snack lunches to satisfy the traveler. A large and filling bowl of potato soup, followed by steak-and-kidney pie, potatoes, and peas, will cost about £3 ($5.25). There are also quiches, hamburgers, and homemade pizza, going for about £1.75 ($3.06) a portion.

GLENCOE: On the shores of Loch Leven, near where it joins Loch Linnhe, the Ballachulish Bridge now links the villages of North and South Ballachulish, at the entrance to Glencoe. The bridge saves a long drive to the head of the loch if you are coming from the north, but many visitors enjoy the scenic drive to Kinlochleven to come upon the wild and celebrated Glencoe from the east.

Glencoe runs from Rannoch Moor to Loch Leven between some magnificent mountains, including 3766-foot Bidean nam Bian. Known as the "Glen of Weeping," Glencoe is where, on February 13, 1692, Campbells massacred MacDonalds—men, women, and children—who had been their hosts for 12 days. Although massacres were not uncommon in those times, this one shocked even the Highlanders because of the breach of hospitality. When the killing was done, the crime of "murder under trust" was regarded by law as an aggravated form of murder, and carried the same penalties as treason.

The glen, much of which now belongs to the Scottish National Trust, is full of history and legend. A tiny lochan is known as "the pool of blood" because by its side some men are said to have quarreled over a piece of cheese, and all were killed.

This is an area of massive splendor, with towering peaks and mysterious glens where you can well imagine the fierce battle among the kilted Highlanders to the skirl of the pipes and the beat of the drums.

Splurge into History

Almost where Glen Etive joins Glencoe, under the jagged peak of Buchaille Etive Mor dominating the road (A82), lies the **King's House Hotel** (tel. King's House 259), several miles from the village of Glencoe. A building has stood here since the time of the Jacobite Rising of 1745, when it was required to accommodate troops on their way south from Fort William. It is now a center for skiing and attracts thousands from far and near.

Believed to be the oldest licensed inn in Scotland, King's House Hotel has now been enlarged and modernized by its present laird, Robin Fleming of Black Mount. Warm, well-furnished rooms, many with private baths, are provided, and of course views of the majestic scenery. The lounge, too, has views, and the dining room relies on a lot of good fresh produce for its appetizing meals. There is a fine wine cellar, plus a bar. Such pleasant amenities as a drying room are provided for those who want to walk, fish, or go climbing. At £13.25 ($23.19) per night per person for B&B, the tariff may be too high for the budget traveler, but it's worth a stop just to have tea. Some double rooms contain private baths, and these cost an extra £2.75 ($4.81) per person nightly. A set dinner is featured for £8 ($14).

A ski lift is almost opposite the hotel. The Buachaille Etive Mor guards Glencoe's eastern end. This mountain provides a challenge for climbers and was the training ground for Sir John Hunt and the party he took to the top of Everest in Coronation year.

Besides access from the Glasgow–Inverness highway, guests at the King's House Hotel can be met at the Bridge of Orchy railway station by arrangement. **Glen Orchy,** to the south, is well worth a visit too, with the wild river and mountain scenery being beautiful and photogenic. It was the birthplace of the Gaelic bard Duncan Ban MacIntyre, whose song, "In Praise of Ben Doran," is considered a masterpiece.

In Glencoe Village

As you turn away from Loch Leven to enter the historic glen, you will find a number of accommodations available in the village of Glencoe.

Glencoe Hotel (tel. Ballachulish 245) is a spruce and stucco building with a slate mansard roof, dominating its area. In the hotel are 14 rooms, including one with a double bed and a private bathroom and one twin-bedded with a private bath, while the other doubles, twins, family, and singles have hot and cold running water. The hotel is fully heated and has a large restaurant and three bars. The charge is from £10.50 ($18.38) per person for B&B. Dinner costs from £5.50 ($9.63), and snacks are served all day. VAT is included in all charges, and the hotel is open all year.

For a less expensive accommodation, turn off the A82 directly into the little village and go to the Bridge of Coe on the edge of the town. You'll see a sign, **The Ridges,** to your right, which is Mrs. Carmichael's immaculate, homey B&B house (tel. Ballachulish 331). She has two double bedrooms and one family room which she rents for £7 ($12.25) per person, including breakfast and a cup of tea at bedtime. Guests are invited to relax and chat with Mrs. Carmichael in her pleasant living room. Rooms are equipped with electric blankets and hot and cold running water, and the house is centrally heated.

4. Kyle of Lochalsh and Skye

From the Kyle of Lochalsh you can take a ferry to the mystical Isle of Skye, off the northwest coast of Scotland. The island has inspired many of the best-loved and best-known of Scottish ballads such as "Over the Sea to Skye" and "Will Ye Not Come Back Again." On the 48-mile-long island, you can explore castle ruins, duns, and brochs, enjoying a Highland welcome. For the Scots, the island will forever evoke images of Flora MacDonald, who conducted Bonnie Prince Charlie to Skye. She disguised him as Betty Burke after the Culloden defeat.

Once on Skye, you'll find ferry service back to Kyle or to Mallaig from Armadale. The Armadale ferry transports cars, but the service is less frequent than the one to Kyle. If you're planning to take your car, reservations are recommended.

Caledonian MacBrayne, the Pier, Gourock, near Glasgow (tel. Gourock 33755), runs ferry services to Skye, as well as to Mull and the Outer Hebrides. The company also offers inclusive tours for people and cars to "island-hop," using their services between islands. This is an ideal opportunity to visit places well away from the beaten track. The information office at Gourock is most helpful, and someone there will assist you in planning a trip if you wish to make up your own journey.

The largest island of the Inner Hebrides, Skye is separated from the mainland by the Sound of Sleat on its southeastern side. At Kyleakin, on the eastern end, the channel is only a quarter of a mile wide and thus the ferry docks there. Dominating the land of summer seas, streams, woodland glens, mountain passes, cliffs, and waterfalls are the Cuillin Hills, a range of jagged black mountains. The Peninsula of Sleat, the island's southernmost arm, is known as "The Garden of Skye."

DORNIE: This small crofting village on the road to the Isle of Skye is the meeting place of three lochs—Duich, Long, and Alsh. On a rocky islet stands **Eilean Donan Castle,** Wester Ross at Dornie, eight miles east of Kyle of Lochalsh on the A87. This romantic castle was built in 1220 as a defense against the Danes. In 1719 it was shelled by the British frigate *Worcester.* In ruins for 200 years, it was restored by Colonel MacRae of Clan MacRae in 1932 and is now a clan war memorial and museum, containing Jacobite relics, mostly with clan connections. It is open April to September 30—daily, including Sunday, from 10 a.m. to 12:30 p.m. and from 2 to 6 p.m., charging 50p (88¢) for admission.

South of Dornie and Eilean Donan Castle is Shiel Bridge. From here, an "unclassified road" leads to **Glenelg,** after a twisting climb over Ratagan Pass with a fine view of the mountain range known as the **Five Sisters of Kintail,** which is dominated by Sgurr Fhuaran, 3505 feet high. In summer a car ferry crosses the Sound of Sleat to Skye. It was from Glenelg that Dr. Johnson and James Boswell crossed to Skye in 1773. In Gleann Beag, two miles to the southeast, stand two of the best-preserved Iron Age brochs on the Scottish mainland—**Dun Telve** and **Dun Troddan.** Brochs are stone towers with double walls, probably built more than 2000 years ago by the Picts for protection against raiders. The walls of the two brochs are more than 30 feet high.

Just outside Dornie, across Loch Long and at the end of Loch Duich, is the **Loch Duich Hotel,** Ardelve, near Kyle of Lochalsh (tel. Dornie 213). A long white house, it is set back from the road overlooking fields and then down Loch Duich to Eilean Donan Castle, surely one of the most attractive vistas in the country. In the other direction you'll see the Cuillins on Skye. The hosts will greet you warmly and show you to your pretty, simply furnished room. Some of the accommodations are tiny and under the eaves. Many have wonderful views of the already-mentioned castle.

The hotel is owned by Rod and Geraldine Stenson, a young couple who have brought energy and enthusiasm to the place. They lived for two years on the island of Rhum, running a castle and a guest house, and there they learned to be self-sufficient. Geraldine cooks—really cooks! She turns out bread, oatcakes, pâtés, broth, scones, and shortbread, and even makes yogurt from their own goats' milk and cream cheese from the same herd. She offers breakfast, lunch, tea, and dinner daily. For her good honest fare, a three-course meal with coffee will cost £7 ($12.25). B&B is another £11.50 ($20.13) per person, with a proper porridge in the morning. At lunch light snacks are available for around £1.50 ($2.63), and they are served in the bar or on the patio. They also have a boat, and you can rent it for fishing. Geraldine will cook your catch for supper.

From Dornie, it is a short drive to the—

KYLE OF LOCHALSH: This popular center for touring the western Highlands is also a good jumping-off point to the islands. A car ferry leaves for Kyleakin on the Isle of Skye. There is no need to book in advance. The journey is only ten minutes. The ferry shuttles back and forth all day, and you will have plenty of time to drive the length of Skye in a day, returning to the mainland by night if you want to. If that is your intent, you might register at:

Fernbank, Pladaig Road (tel. Kyle 4247), where Miss MacKay receives paying guests in her house, set in a pleasant garden. For B&B, she charges £9 ($15.75) per person per night. After your day on Skye, you can relax in the small lounge and watch the neighboring island fade into the dusk.

ISLE OF SKYE: Skye is the largest of the Inner Hebrides, 48 miles long and between 3 and 25 miles wide. It is separated from the mainland by the Sound of Sleat (pronounced Slate). There are many stories as to the origin of the name, Skye. Some believe it is from the Norse "ski," meaning a cloud, while others say it is from the Gaelic word for winged. There are Norse names on the island, however, as the Norsemen held sway for four centuries before 1263. Overlooking the Kyle is the ruined Castle Maol, once the home of a Norwegian princess.

For those who want to overnight or else spend a longer holiday on the Isle of Skye itself, I offer the following suggestions, scattered in the island's various hamlets. However, in summer be sure to reserve in advance, as accommodations are extremely limited.

Getting There: The easiest way to get there is on a ferry service from the Kyle of Lochalsh to Kyleakin. The boat leaves every half hour daily, charging passengers about 75¢ and car owners $6.50 for the round-trip voyage. Another way to go is on the Mallaig–Armadale ferry, with about five weekday crossings. On this one, passengers pay about $5 for a one-way trip, and cars, depending on their size, anywhere from $20 to $33.

Kyleakin

The ferry from Kyle of Lochalsh docks at this tiny waterfront village. For those seeking a quiet, well-kept place to stay, I recommend:

Dunringell Hotel (tel. Kyle 4180) sits in 4½ acres of extensive lawns in which rhododendrons, azaleas, and other flowering shrubs provide a riot of color from March to July. Dunringell is a spacious structure, built in 1912, with large bedrooms and public rooms. The cost of B&B is from £10.35 ($18.11) per person nightly, rising to £16.10 ($28.18) should you desire half board. For a private shower, the charge is an additional £1.75 ($3.06) per person. VAT is included. Both a smoking and nonsmoking lounge are maintained for guests. For those who wish to participate, the proprietors, Mr. and Mrs. MacPherson, hold a short worship service in one of the lounges each evening.

Portree

Skye's capital, Portree, is the port for steamers making trips around the island and linking Skye with the 15-mile-long island of Raasay. Sligachan, nine miles south, and Glenbrittle, seven miles farther southwest, are centers for climbing the Cuillin (Coolin) Hills.

The **Isles Hotel,** on the town square just across from the Bank of Scotland (tel. Portree 2129), is, appropriately, owned and managed by John and Meg Isles, who live on the premises. The white stone building has a slate roof and three dormers overlooking the square. Cost per night per person for staying in one of the 12 bedrooms is £12.50 ($21.88) in high season, £11 ($19.25) in low. All of the bedrooms are bathless, with hot and cold running water, but there are four bathrooms and seven toilets. The hotel has a restricted license and a residents' lounge with television. Dinner with a good choice of dishes is à la carte, and the hotel is open only from April to October.

The **Rosedale Hotel,** Beaumont Crescent (tel. Portree 2531), lying in a secluded part of Portree, has been owned and managed by the Andrew family since 1950. They have an enviable reputation for their good rooms, Scottish hospitality, and tasty cuisine. The bedrooms are modern, 20 in all, opening onto views of the harbor and Portree Bay. The units have private baths as well. Guests are received from May to October at a cost of £14 ($24.50) in a single, from £25 ($43.75) in a double, including a Scottish breakfast. In addition to two modern lounges, a cocktail bar carries a wide range of Highland malt whiskies. The location is in the midst of fishermen's cottages that flank a rock-strewn path along the water, right near the steamer pier. A festive holiday atmosphere pervades.

READERS' GUEST HOUSE SELECTIONS: "We didn't want to bother searching for a restaurant for dinner on the Isle of Skye, and happily chose to stay with **Mrs. F. Macleod,** 6 Fisherfield (tel. Portree 2250). The charge of £11 ($19.25) includes B&B and dinner. Breakfast is not the standard, but rather includes kippers and scrambled eggs if you desire them. A lovely three-course home-cooked turkey dinner was served, and our room had a view of the bay" (Shirley Horowitz, North Bergen, N.J.) . . . "The B&B of **Mr. and Mrs. Myles MacDonald,** 1 Woodpark, Dunvegan Road (tel. Portree 2358), is just outside of Portree, near the entrance to the Skye Woollen Mill. We enjoyed a huge, homey bedroom, and there was a spotless bathroom next door. It was like being at home or at a friend's as a guest. In the morning, we were served a huge breakfast. The charge is £ 7 ($12.25) per person for B&B" (Karen Ackerman, Springfield, Ill.).

Uig

This village is on Trotternish, the largest Skye peninsula, and ferry port for Harris and Uist in the Outer Hebrides. It is 15 miles north of Portree and 49 miles from Kyle of Lochalsh. **Monkstadt House,** a mile and a half north, is where Flora MacDonald brought Prince Charles, in the guise of a girl named Betty Burke, after their the escape flight from Benbecula. In **Kilmuir** churchyard, five miles north, Flora was buried, wrapped in a sheet used by the prince. Her grave is marked by a Celtic cross.

The **Ferry Inn** (tel. Uig 242) has been recently recarpeted and refurbished by its owners, John and Betty Campbell, who rent out six bedrooms, one with private bath, at a charge of £11 ($19.25) per night per person for B&B, or £13 ($22.75) with private bath. These tariffs include VAT and service. The inn has central heating, a cozy cocktail bar, a public bar, and a lounge.

READER'S GUEST HOUSE SELECTION: "Woodbine Guesthouse (tel. Uig 243) is nicely placed about Uig Bay, a few minutes from ferries to the Outer Hebrides. The white walls are freshly painted, with contrasting bright colors in the furnishings. The door to each room is pine, made by Mr. Raper, the owner, and each is varnished beautifully and gives a contemporary appearance to the house. Mrs. Raper will serve tea at 9 p.m. downstairs, always accompanied by something tasty. The Rapers try to help with local information and personally attend to all visitors. Raper's parents, and they altogether are personal and personable. The cost is £8 ($14) per person per night" (Kathleen Hinton-Braaten, Arlington, Va.).

Dunvegan

The village of Dunvegan grew up around **Dunvegan Castle,** the principal man-made sight on the Isle of Skye, seat of the chiefs of Clan MacLeod who have lived there for 700 years. The castle, which stands on a rocky promontory, was once accessible only by boat, but now the moat is bridged and the castle open to the public. It holds many fascinating relics, including a "fairy flag." It is reputed to be the oldest inhabited castle in Britain. It is open in April and May (and through October) from 2 to 5 p.m. From May through September, it is open from 10:30 a.m. to 5 p.m. daily except Sunday. Admission is £1.40 ($2.45) for adults, 70p ($1.23) for children.

The **Skye Water Mill and Black House Folk Museum,** four miles from Dunvegan on the Glendale Road (tel. Glendale 291), contains implements and furniture of bygone days and has a peat fire burning throughout the day. A replica of an illicit whisky still can be seen behind the museum. The museum is open from Easter to the end of September from 10 a.m. to 7 p.m., charging adults 40p (70¢) and children 20p (35¢). Still in working order, the water mill is two miles down the road, costing adults 25p (44¢) and children 10p (18¢).

At **Trumpan,** nine miles north of Dunvegan, are the remains of a church which was set afire in 1597 by MacDonald raiders while the congregation, all MacLeods, were inside at worship. Only one woman survived. The MacLeods of Dunvegan rushed to the defense, and only two MacDonalds escaped death.

Atholl House Hotel (tel. Dunvegan 219) lies right in the village of Dunvegan, only half a mile from Skye's most popular sightseeing attraction, Dunvegan Castle. The owner of Atholl House, Ena McPhie, a Gaelic singer, welcomes guests seeking a B&B accommodation from April to October. She charges from £8 ($14) per person, including a hearty Scottish breakfast that will fortify you for the day. She offers only 12 rooms, including a trio rented to families. The rooms themselves are clean and pleasantly furnished. There is a spacious lounge which adds to the comfort of Atholl House.

Three Chimneys Restaurant, Colbost, near Dunvegan (tel. Glendale 258), is installed in an old-fashioned Skye croft house on the shores of Loch Dunvegan. Its atmosphere is definitely "olde worlde," with stone walls, beamed ceilings, and open fires. The chef-owner prepares not only a "modern" cuisine, but a traditional Scottish one as well. Local salmon, shellfish, and trout appear regularly on the menu. He also bakes granary bread and does the celebrated "cloutie dumpling." Lunch is from 12:30 to 2 p.m., costing from £7 ($12.25), and dinner is from 6:30 to 8:30 p.m., when your tab is likely to run about £10 ($17.50). The restaurant is closed on Sunday except in the peak tourist months of July and August.

Skeabost Bridge

Eastward from Dunvegan is Skeabost Bridge, with an island cemetery of great antiquity. The graves of four Crusaders are here.

Nearby is the **Skeabost House Hotel** (tel. Skeabost Bridge 202), one of the most comfortable, refreshing, and inviting country homes of Skye, receiving paying guests from mid-April to mid-October. Thoroughly modernized, it is interesting architecturally with its dormers, chimneys, tower, and gables, everything a weather-worn beige. Inside the taste level is high, with wood paneling and carpets. Once a private estate, it has been converted into a lochside hotel, standing on beautiful grounds that in summer are studded with flowering bushes. The location is 35 miles from Kyle of Lochalsh and 5 miles from Portree.

Sports people are attracted to the hotel, gathering in the firelit lounge for a mellow scotch whisky. The atmosphere is of hardy tweeds with the distinctive aroma of a good cigar. The loch outside is well stocked with salmon and trout.

Of the 27 handsomely furnished rooms, 11 contain private baths. Singles are accepted at a rate of £17.50 ($30.63), doubles from £14 ($24.50) to £20 ($35) per person, including a full Scottish breakfast, a view, and a private bath. The Scottish fare, featuring smoked salmon, is served on fine china and elegant silver. A bar buffet lunch goes for £3 ($5.25), a four-course dinner for £8.50 ($14.88).

RAASAY: For an offbeat adventure, I'd suggest a side trip to this 14-mile-long island, which has a great panoramic view over the Isle of Skye.

A car ferry, leaving from Sconsar on Skye, is in service about three times a day (check at the tourist office in Skye for exact times of departure). From June 25 to around mid-August the service is increased to four times a day. Each passenger must pay $1.75 (U.S.) for a one-way fare or about $15 per car.

On a recent visit, I didn't find the gaiety and laughter Johnson and Boswell did. The local school is rapidly dwindling in population, and there are only about 100 people who still inhabit the island. Most of them seemed to be hovering around 65. The island's young people have mostly gone on to such cities as Glasgow, returning only for the Christmas holidays, and sometimes not even then.

But it is this very remoteness that attracts many to Raasay, visitors who like to wander around a depopulated countryside, enjoying the quiet of a country lane, the uncrowded feeling everywhere, and the beautiful, but remote, scenery, with an eye out for birdlife.

You can find lodging and food on the island at the **Raasay Hotel** (tel. Raasay 222), which is run by Alistair Nicolson, a man who has long ago grown accustomed to rugged winter weather. He is also the captain of that ferry boat that took you over from Skye. His is the only guesthouse on the island, and he has many stories—often sad—to relate about the depopulation of his island. However, he has hopes for the future, especially tourism, as he has made enlargements and improvements in his Edwardian house. He has a dozen rooms, each with private plumbing, renting for about $35 per person daily on a half-board arrangment. Scottish breakfasts are hearty here. You'll need one to fortify you for the day.

5. Oban and District

Oban (meaning "small bay") is the great port for the Western Isles and a center of Gaelic culture.

A number of colorful sites are near the port town, including Port Appin and Inveraray, where visitors can soak up the atmosphere of the district away from the major towns.

OBAN: One of Scotland's leading coastal resorts, the bustling port town of Oban is set in a sheltered bay that is almost landlocked by the island of Kerrera. A yachting center and small burgh, it lies about 50 miles south of Fort William.

From Pulpit Hill in Oban there is a fine view across the Firth of Lorn and the Sound of Mull. Overlooking the town is an unfinished replica of the Colosseum of Rome, built by a banker, John Stuart McCaig, in 1897-1900 as a memorial to his family and to try to curb local unemployment during a slump. Its walls are two feet thick and from 37 to 40 feet high. The courtyard within is landscaped and the tower is floodlit at night. It is known locally as **McCaig's Folly.**

In September the Oban Highland Games are held, with massed pipe bands marching through the streets. The Oban Pipe Band plays regularly throughout the summer, parading up and down main street. Paul W. Ware, New Providence, Pennsylvania, writes: "During evening, the promenade is traversed by little dogs pulling their masters who are wearing tweed jackets and smoking pipes. But the town also attracts young people."

On the island of Kerrera stands **Gylen Castle,** home of the MacDougalls, dating back to 1587.

Near the little granite **Cathedral of the Isles,** one mile north of the end of the bay, is the ruin of the 13th-century **Dunollie Castle,** seat of the Lords of Lorn who once owned a third of Scotland.

You can visit **Dunstaffnage Castle,** 3½ miles to the north, which was believed to have been the royal seat of the Dalriadic monarchy in the eighth century. The present castle was probably built in 1263. "The Stone of Destiny," now in Westminster Abbey, was kept here before its removal to Scone. The castle is open April to September from 9:30 a.m. to 7 p.m. (on Sunday from 2 to 7 p.m.); October to March, from 9:30 a.m. to 4 p.m. (on Sunday from 2 to 4 p.m.). It is closed on Thursday and Friday. Admission is 30p (53¢) for adults, 15p (26¢) for children.

In Oban, Gaelic is taught in schools as a "leaving certificate subject."

Where to Stay

As a holiday resort, Oban has a number of good hotels and guest houses within easy reach of the seafront and the piers from which cruises to the offshore islands can be booked.

Queens Hotel, Esplanade (tel. Oban 2505), is close to the town center, commanding a magnificent view of Oban Bay, Kerrera, Lismore, Mull, and Marvern, as well as the scenic views in Oban and down the Firth of Lorn. The hotel, completely modernized, is fully licensed, with a number of inviting public rooms. Open from April 1 to the end of October, the hotel charges from £18 ($31.50) in a single and from £34 ($59.50) in a double. The half-board rate ranges from £16 ($28) to £23 ($40.25) per person. All 46 bedrooms have private bathrooms. Ample car parking is available.

Lancaster, Esplanade (tel. Oban 62587), is distinguished by its attractive pseudo-Tudor facade. On the crescent of the bay, it commands views from its public rooms of the islands of Lismore and Kerrera, including the more distant peaks of Mull. Open all year, the hotel is managed by its resident owners, Mr. and Mrs. J. T. Ramage and family, who welcome you to one of their well-furnished bedrooms, charging from £20 ($35) per person, including breakfast. A number of rooms offer central heating, and a few have private baths or showers. The Lancaster is the only hotel in Oban featuring a heated indoor swimming pool, a sauna bath, a spa bath, and a solarium.

Wellpark Hotel (tel. Oban 62948) is a substantial stone house with a gabled bay window, positioned on the seafront and commanding views of the bay and the islands of Kerrera, Mull, and Lismore. It's also one of the best bargains in Oban. Mr. and Mrs. R. B. Dickison welcome you, charging £9.50 ($16.63) per person for B&B. It is quiet at night and has parking for cars in the grounds. Their rooms are simple but pleasantly comfortable, contain hot and cold running water and are equipped with electric blankets. The hotel receives guests from April to October.

Where to Dine

McTavish's Kitchens, 34 George St. (tel. Oban 63064), like its cousin in Fort William, is dedicated to preserving the local cuisine. Downstairs is a self-service restaurant which is open in summer from 9 a.m. till 9 p.m., serving breakfast, main meals, haggis, cakes, snacks, teas, and coffees. The two bars are the upstairs Lairds Bar and, around the corner from the self-service, the Mantrap Bar with a "real mantrap."

The licensed second-floor restaurant has a more ambitious Scottish and continental menu with higher prices, but there are also budget lunches for £2.50 ($4.38) and high teas for £2.75 ($4.81). The à la carte menu includes haggis, Loch Fyne kippers (smoked herring), prime Scottish steaks, smoked salmon, salmon steak, and venison, and there is a special four-course "Taste of Scotland" menu at approximately £8 ($14).

A feature of the restaurant is the entertainment with music by local artists, Scottish dance music, singing, piping, and Highland dancing from 8:30 to 10:30 every evening while the upstairs restaurant is open, from mid-May until the end of September. Admission is £1.25 ($2.19) for adults and 60p ($1.05) for children. The bagpipes provide haunting melodies, new and old.

The Gallery, Gibraltar Street (tel. Oban 64647), is another good possibility. Right in the heart of town, the Gallery is presided over by the friendly and welcoming Iain Reid. A dining companion and I recently paid £6 ($10.50) each for scampi, a veal T-bone, along with wine and coffee which we considered very good value. Arrive for dinner after 6:30 p.m. when the atmosphere is cozy and pleasant. You can also order a lunch here for about £2.50 ($4.38) and up. The restaurant takes its last orders about 9:30 p.m. and receives visitors, both foreign and domestic, from April to October.

PORT APPIN: To the north of Oban lies a beautiful lochside district, including Lismore Island. On an islet nearby is a famous landmark, **Castle Stalker,** the ancient seat of the Stewarts of Appin, built in the 15th century by Duncan Stewart, son of the first chief of Appin. Dugald, the ninth chief, was forced to sell the estate in 1765, and the castle slowly fell into ruin. It was recently restored and is once again inhabited. According to myth, there's a subterranean undersea passage at Port Appin where a piper supposedly entered with his dog. Only the dog returned, and he was hairless. Port Appin is a small hamlet of stone cottages.

If you'd like to spend the night there, **Linnhe House** (tel. Appin 245), gives you the Highland hospitality of Mr. and Mrs. Alasdair M. Seton-Winton, who invite you to take your holiday in this private country-house atmosphere. Since you're located here in a remote and unspoiled village in the West Highlands, most guests will want to take the half-board tariff of £15 ($26.25) nightly. A few of the pleasantly furnished rooms have private showers, for which there is no extra charge. Beds are soft and comfortable, and the food is good and hearty. Guests can also enjoy an attractive lounge with TV. There are only four double rooms, one family, and one single, so reservations are necessary. Guests are accepted from March 1 until October 15. The house overlooks the sea, and the hosts will explain the attractions of the area to you, including boating, fishing, golf, and pony trekking.

For the super-splurge in Port Appin, the **Airds Hotel** (tel. Appin 236), is one of the most outstanding hotels of Scotland. For food, comfort, and service, it's a gem. Eric and Betty Allen make it so. Theirs is an old ferry inn in one of the most beautiful spots in the historic district of Appin. Many of the rooms look out onto the island of Lismore, the mountains of Morvern, and Loch Linnhe. Everything is immaculately maintained, handsomely decorated, and the setting is tranquil, good as a headquarters for either boat excursions or walking tours. There is also an annex in the hotel garden which is furnished in the same high standard of the parent building, consisting of one double bedded room, one twin-bedded room, a bath and a toilet. The Airds takes in guests from April until the end of October, charging them from £25 ($43.75) to £29 ($50.75) per person for half board. Rates are always cheaper in the annex, of course. With a private bath, the tariff in the main hotel rises to £31 ($54.25) per person.

It is the food that makes the Airds such an outstanding place to visit. Mrs. Allen is one of the great cooks of Scotland, and a meal here will cost from £15 ($26.25), plus the cost of your drink. (Snacks are available at lunch if you're just dropping in.) In her repertoire of fine Scottish cuisine, home-baking is a specialty, and fresh produce is used in making up the menus. Specialties include Loch Fyne kippers, smoked mackerel salad, and an exceptional kidney soup. Sole is often served stuffed with crab mousse, or perhaps you'll sample the roast haunch of venison with rowan jelly if featured. Desserts are mouthwatering concoctions, including the likes of walnut fudge tart. Reservations for dinner are absolutely necessary.

DUROR: Just ten minutes' drive north from Castle Stalker, on the A828, the tiny village of Duror sits at the mouth of Glen Duror, near enough to Ballachulish to make it a good base for visiting Glencoe and surrounding attractions.

Duror Hotel (tel. Duror 219) is personally operated by the resident owner, Mr. Evan McD. Cameron, who has 12 bedrooms and three chalets for rent. The bedrooms have hot and cold running water, and the tiny, cozy chalets contain private baths and double beds. Mr. Cameron charges £8 ($14) per person per night for B&B. Meals are served in a glassed-in porch looking out over a vista of the Highlands. Adjoining is the Kidnapped Bar, with black furniture and a bright plaid carpet. Good cooking is a feature of the hotel, with dinners costing £6 ($10.50). All the soups are homemade and tasty. The hotel is open all year, and there's ample parking.

SEIL: Those seeking a hidden oasis in the district south of Oban can leave town on the 816, turning west at Kilninver on the 844 until Clachan Bridge is reached. The locals claim, somewhat whimsically, that this is "the only bridge across the Atlantic Ocean." Easdale is an attractive, tiny slate village, nestling under the cliffs of Seil Island, with a view of Mull. Here you have complete serenity.

LOCH AWE: Twenty-two miles long and in most places only about a mile wide, Loch Awe for years acted as a natural moat protecting the Campbells of Inveraray from their enemies to the north. Along its banks and on its islands are many reminders of its fortified past. There is a ruined castle at Fincharn, at the southern end of the loch, and another on the island of Fraoch Eilean. The **Isle of Inishail** has an ancient chapel and burial ground, and at the northern end of the loch are the ruins of **Kilchurn Castle,** built by Sir Colin Campbell in 1440. The bulk of Ben Cruachan, 3689 feet, dominates Loch Awe at its northern end and attracts climbers. On the ben is the world's second-largest hydro-electric power station, which pumps water from Loch Awe to a reservoir high up the mountain. Below the mountain are the **Falls of Cruachan** and the wild **Pass of Brander,** where Robert the Bruce routed the Clan MacDougall in 1308.

In this area, the Forestry Commission has vast forests, and a new road now makes it possible to travel around Loch Awe, so that it is more than ever a popular angling center. Sharp-eyed James Bond fans may even recognize some scenes which appeared in one of the films.

The Pass of Brander where Loch Awe narrows was the scene of many a fierce battle in bygone times, and something of that bloody past seems to brood over the narrow defile. Through it the waters of the Awe flow on their way to Loch Etive. This winding sea loch is 19 miles long, stretching from Dun Dunstaffnage Bay at Oban to Glen Etive, reaching into the Moor of Rannoch at the foot of the 3000-foot Buachaille Etive (the Shepherd of Etive), into which Glencoe also reaches.

THE CRINAN CANAL: The nine-mile long canal, constructed during 1793-1801, was designed to provide water communication between the Firth of Clyde, Argyll, the western Highlands, and the islands. It runs roughly north from Ardrishaig and curves gradually to the west before reaching Loch Crinan on the Sound of Jura. Four miles north of **Cairnbaan** which is on the canal is the ruined hill-fort of **Dunadd,** once capital of Dalriada, kingdom of the Scots. There are numerous Bronze Age stone circles in the vicinity, and **Kil-**

martin churchyard, five miles north of Cairnbaan, has a carved cross dating from the 16th century. **Carnasserie Castle,** also to the north of the canal, built in the late 16th century, was the home of John Carswell, the first post-Reformation bishop of the isles, whose translation of John Knox's liturgy into Gaelic was the first book to be published in that language.

Crinan, a yachtsman's haven on the Sound of Jura, is overlooked by the early 11th-century **Duntrune Castle,** one of the oldest castles in Scotland, and still inhabited by the descendants of the original owners, the Clan Malcolm. Crinan is a charming little village.

Lochgilphead, a pleasant little town sitting just where the canal turns westward, is the address of my recommendation for a stopover in this area:

The **Cairnbaan Motor Inn** (tel. Lochgilphead 2488). Formerly an old coach inn and now a privately owned hotel open all year, this is an excellent base for touring Argyll and the islands. Nearby are safe beaches, and for the sports person there are loch fishing, sea angling, and salmon fishing on the River Add. The motor inn has comfortable, modern bedrooms, some with private bath and verandas. All bedrooms have built-in wardrobes, wash basins, razor sockets, radios, intercoms, and baby-listening service. The tariff in a twin-bedded room without bath is £11 ($19.25) per person, £15 ($26.25) with bath, the same charges holding in a single room.

The Grill Room has a good view southward down the busy canal. Emphasis for the cuisine is on Scottish dishes. There are a handsome cocktail bar and a comfortable sun lounge with a patio beyond.

Crinan Hotel (tel. Crinan 235), off the B841, seven miles northwest of Lochgilphead, is a splurge inn with a bright, attractive decor and modern comforts and conveniences. Because of its location on a canal and yacht basin, it is naturally a favorite with yachtsmen, who book its 22 rooms with private bath in July and August, the peak sailing months. If you're reserving (and I highly recommend that you do), ask for one of the rooms with private balconies opening onto mountains and lochside sunsets.

The hotel is managed by Nicolas Ryan, who once worked as a bellboy on the old *Queen Mary,* later rising rapidly within the Cunard organization. Bedrooms rent for £26 ($45.50) in a single, from £21 ($36.75) to £23.50 ($41.13) in a double, including a breakfast that often features oatcakes and hot croissants.

Open from mid-March to mid-October, the hotel serves exceptionally good food—dishes such as fresh salmon, Crinan clams mornay, roast duckling in black cherry sauce, and Scottish sirloin. Meals are served noon to 2 p.m. and from 7 to 9 p.m. A table d'hôte luncheon goes for £5 ($8.75), a set dinner for £11 ($19.25), although you are likely to pay £15 ($26.25) if you order from the à la carte menu. Luncheon in fair weather is served al fresco. The hotel is one of the best run in the area. As efficient as Mr. Ryan's staff is, they never overlook Scottish hospitality and friendliness.

INVERARAY: This small resort and royal burgh occupies a splendid Highland setting on the upper shores of Loch Fyne. The hereditary seat of the Dukes of Argyll, **Inveraray Castle** has been headquarters of the Clan Campbell since the early 15th century. In 1644, the original village was burned by the Royalist Marquess of Montrose. The third Duke of Argyll built a new town and castle between 1744 and 1788. The castle was badly damaged by fire in 1975, but it has been restored. The present laird, the 12th Duke of Argyll and 26th MacCailein Mor, chief of the Clan Campbell, has opened the castle to the public, with a special welcome for anyone who is related to Clan Campbell. The castle is among the earliest examples of Gothic revival in Britain, and offers a fine collection of pictures and 18th-century French furniture, old English and continental porcelain, and a magnificent Armoury Hall, which alone contains 1300 pieces. There is a castle shop for souvenirs and a tea room where homemade cakes and scones are served. The castle is open daily from the first Saturday in April until the second Sunday in October, charging £1.50 ($2.63) for adults and 75p ($1.31) for children. It is closed on Friday except in July and August.

At one end of the main street of the town is a Celtic burial cross from Iona. The parish church is divided by a wall enabling services to be held in Gaelic and English at the same time.

The **Auchindrain Museum of Country Life** (tel. Furnace 235), six miles southwest of Inveraray, is an open-air museum of traditional Highland farming life. It is a unique survival of the past, whose origins are so far back as to be a subject for archeology. The farming township stands more or less as it was in the 1800s, but studies are now revealing at least four centuries before that. At present, Auchindrain consists of 20-odd acres of the "infield," about which stand 21 houses and barns of the 18th and 19th centuries. Some are furnished to their appropriate period, and others contain displays. There is also a display center and a museum shop. The land is being brought back into use, and it is already growing traditional crops and supporting livestock. Open daily during the summer, it charges adults £1 ($1.75) and children 60p ($1.05). There is no charge for children 7 years old and under. The museum is closed Saturday during April, May, and September. Auchindrain and mid-Argyll are in an area crammed with things and places of interest for historians, antiquarians, and archeologists.

A fine woodland garden may be visited at **Crarae Lodge,** four miles southwest of the village.

For food and accommodations in Inveraray, I suggest the **George, Main** Street (tel. Inveraray 2111), which is a small inn, open year round, offering singles at the rate of £9 ($15.75) to £11 ($19.25), doubles from £17 ($29.75) to £20 ($35), including breakfast. The rooms are simply furnished, with a minimum of plumbing, decidedly old-fashioned. The dining room, however, is attractively modern with bright furnishings. Downstairs there's a public bar with stone walls and a flagstone floor, a part of which was connected with the stables when the George was a stagecoach inn. Here you can order snacks at lunch, costing from £1 ($1.75) to £2.75 ($4.81), along with your lager. A three-course dinner goes for £5 ($8.75).

6. The Inner Hebrides

Geologists wandering through bog and bracken used to mingle with painters and birdwatchers, and stumble across an occasional sea-angler or mountain climber. But that was some time ago. These special-interest groups still frequent the islands of the Hebrides, but so do more and more general tourists.

Most everybody's heard of Mull and Iona, but what about Rhum, Aigg, and Muck? Sounds like a goblin Christmas recipe. Visitors can meet crofters (small farmers), fisher folk, and join in a real island ceilidh (singing party).

(Arran, Islay, that most southerly of the Hebridean islands, and the Isle of Jura, along with romantic Skye, are covered in other sections.)

Mull, featured in R. L. Stevenson's *Kidnapped,* has wild scenery, golf courses, and a treasure-trove tradition. Iona played a major part in the spread of Christianity in Britain, and a trip there usually includes a visit to Staffa, a tiny uninhabited volcanic island where Fingal's Cave inspired Mendelssohn.

These places are on the regular tourist circuit. However, more adventurous readers will also seek out Coll and Tyree, along with Rhum, Eigg, Muck, and Canna.

This chain of islands lies just off the west coast of the Scottish mainland. To visit them, you'll be following a worthy tradition in the footsteps of Samuel Johnson and his faithful Boswell.

Caledonian MacBrayne (tel. 0475/33755) provides the main link for boat transportation around the Inner Hebrides. Call them for information about departures.

MULL: The largest island in the Inner Hebrides, Mull is rich in legend and folklore, a land of ghosts, monsters, and the wee folk. Over log fires that burn on cold winter evenings, the talk is of myths and ancient times. The island is wild and mountainous, characterized by sea lochs and sandy bays.

The capital is **Tobermory,** lying on a bay guarded by **Duart Castle,** restored in 1912 and still the seat of the once-fiery MacLeans, who shed much blood in and around the castle during their battles with the Lords of the Isles. In the bay—somewhere—lies the *Florencia,* a Spanish galleon that went down laden with treasure. Many attempts have been made to bring it up, but so far all of them have failed.

To the southeast, near Salen, are the ruins of **Aros Castle,** once the stronghold of the Lords of the Isles.

On the far south coast at Lochbuie, **Moy Castle** has a water-filled dungeon. The wild countryside of Mull was the scene of many of David Balfour's adventures in *Kidnapped* by Robert Louis Stevenson.

Roads on Mull are few and can be quite rough. If you're taking a bus tour, the driver often has to stop to let sheep and cattle cross.

From Oban you can take one of the car-ferry services to Mull, operated by **Caledonian MacBrayne,** The Pier, Gourock (tel. Gourock 33755). In Tobermory, on Mull, you can reach the steamer office by telephoning 2017.

Always make a reservation if you're planning to spend the night on Mull.

Salen

After exploring the ruins of Aros Castle, a good luncheon stopover is **The Puffer Aground Restaurant,** Salen (tel. Aros 389). It provides home-style typically Scottish cooking, and whenever possible, Mull produce is used. The atmosphere is friendly, and the decor reflects a maritime theme. In summer exhibitions of marine paintings are presented. This is a licensed table-service restaurant, offering lunch from 12:30 to 2:30 p.m., costing from £5 ($8.75). Dinner is served from 6:30 to 9 p.m., at a price beginning at £8 ($14). The restaurant is closed Sunday and Monday until mid-May.

Tobermory

Carnaberg Hotel, 55 Main St. (tel. Tobermory 2479), lies right on the quay, overlooking the harbor and the Sound of Mull. The house has been pleasantly redecorated, and the rooms are comfortable. Ian MacLean charges £7.50 ($13.13) per person nightly—small reductions for children—this tariff including a Scottish breakfast. If you're there on a cold night, you might be given a hot-water bottle to take to bed with you.

Suidhe Hotel, 59 Main St. (tel. Tobermory 2209). Suidhe is Gaelic for "sit, rest, or a break in a journey," and that's exactly what this place is. Jim and Christine Scott, delightful people, run this clean, friendly little hotel charging

£17 ($29.75) per person nightly, for half board. The meals are well prepared and most filling. All rooms have hot and cold water. Trout fishing, sea angling, and pony trekking are available locally. Suidhe is in a village off the western coast, right on the harbor, facing mountains covered with all shades of rhododendron in spring. In the village is a craft shop in a former church.

Craignure

Pennygate Lodge (tel. Craignure 333) is a former Georgian manse now run as a family guest house. The property which overlooks the Sound of Mull is centrally heated and offers a total of nine rooms, including two family apartments. All are spacious and well furnished. Prices, which include a full Scottish breakfast, range from £9 ($15.75) for single occupancy to £16 ($28) for doubles, with reductions for children. Pennygate Lodge is open all year.

Dervaig

Bellachroy (tel. Dervaig 225) is a small hotel, consisting of eight double rooms. It remains open all year, welcoming visitors and charging them £16 ($28) per person nightly for a comfortable bed, a hearty Scottish breakfast the next morning, and a big dinner that evening. The Ballachroy is run by Mr. and Mrs. Andrew Arnold and is situated in one of the most beautiful parts of the Western Isles. Salmon and trout loch and river fishing are available nearby. Calgary Sands is five miles away and a golf course is eight miles distant at Tobermory.

The **Old Byre Heritage Centre,** near Dervaig, houses one of the most charming museums you could hope to find. A series of tableaux with life-size figures recapture the atmosphere of life on Mull during the second half of the 19th century. The scenes become alive with an audio dramatization featuring the voices of local people, many of whom helped in the original construction of the tableaux. The performance which takes half an hour tells the story of the harsh existence of the crofters evicted from their land in the Land Clearances. The museum is open from 10:20 a.m. to 5 p.m. from Easter to October from Monday to Saturday and on Sunday from 1:50 to 5 p.m. Admission is £1 ($1.75) for adults, 50p (88¢) for children. There is a gift shop where you can buy home-baked bread and cakes, and a café on the premises does light lunches. For more information, telephone Dervaig 229.

IONA: Someone once said, "When Edinburgh was but a barren rock and Oxford but a swamp, Iona was famous." It has been known as a place of spiritual power and pilgrimage for centuries. It was the site of the first Christian settlement in Scotland. A remote, low-lying, and treeless island, Iona lies off the southwestern coast of Mull and is only 1 mile by 3½ miles in size. It is accessible only by passenger ferry from the Isle of Mull (cars must remain on Mull). The ferry to Iona is run by local fishermen, and it's very informal in service, depending in large part on the weather.

Since 1695 the island was owned by the Dukes of Argyll, but the 12th duke was forced to sell to pay $1 million in real estate taxes owed since 1949. The island was purchased by Sir Hugh Fraser, the former owner of Harrods and other stores. He secured Iona's future and made it possible for money raised by the National Trust for Scotland to be turned over to the trustees of the restored abbey.

Iona is known for its **"Graves of the Kings."** A total of 48 Scottish kings, including Macbeth and his victim, Duncan, were buried on Iona, as were four Irish kings and eight Norwegian kings.

Today the island attracts nearly 1000 visitors a week in high season. Most of them come here mainly to see the **Abbey of Iona,** part of which dates back to the 13th century. But they also visit relics of the settlement founded there by St. Columba in 563, from which Celtic Christianity spread through Scotland. The abbey has been restored by an ecumenical group called the Iona Community, which conducts workshops on Christianity, sponsors a youth camp, offers tours of the abbey, and leads a seven-mile hike to the various holy and historic spots on the island each Wednesday. It is possible to stay at the abbey.

Although there are many visitors to the abbey, the atmosphere on the island remains very rare, peaceful, and spiritual. It's possible to walk off among the sheep that wander freely everywhere to the top of Dun-I, a small mountain, and contemplate the ocean and the landscape as if you were the only person on earth.

One reader, Capt. Robert Haggart, Laguna, California, described his experience this way: "I was enchanted by the place. It really has a mystic atmosphere—one *feels* something ancient here, something spiritual, sacred, long struggles and wonderment about the strength of religion."

Most of the islanders live by crofting and fishing. In addition, they supplement their income by taking in paying guests in season, charging usually very low or at least fair prices. You can, of course, check into the hotel recommended below, but a stay here in a private home may be an altogether rewarding travel adventure. If you don't stay on Iona, you must catch one of the ferries back to Mull, and they rarely leave after 5 p.m.

Accommodations are extremely limited, although there is the **St. Columba Hotel** (tel. Iona 304), which stands right outside the village, in the vicinity of the cathedral. It offers a total of 29 simply furnished rooms which cost from £15 ($26.25) in a single, from £23 ($40.25) in one of the bathless doubles. However, if you want a double room with private bath, and there are only two in this category, you'll be charged from £19 ($33.25). These tariffs include a full Scottish breakfast. The half-board rate ranges from £18 ($31.50) to £23 ($40.25) per person. The food is good, especially the fish dishes, but, remember, the last order for dinner is taken at 7 p.m. People turn in early on Iona. Try to get a room overlooking the sea, but know that it's virtually impossible to secure an accommodation here in August without a reservation made well in advance.

STAFFA: **Fingal's Cave,** on Staffa, a 75-acre island in the Hebrides off Scotland's west coast, has been attracting visitors for more than 200 years. It has been the inspiration for music, poetry, paintings, and prose. No less a personage than Queen Victoria visited the cave in the 19th century and wrote: "The effect is splendid, like a great entrance into a vaulted hall. The sea is immensely deep in the cave. The rocks under water were all colors—pink, blue and green." The sound of the crashing waves and swirling waters caused Mendelssohn to write the "Fingal's Cave Overture." Turner painted the cave on canvas, and Keats, Wordsworth, and Tennyson all praised it in their poetry.

The cave is unique in that it is the only known cave in the world formed of basalt columns. Over the centuries, the sea has carved a huge cavern in the basalt, leaving massive hexagonal columns to create the "vaulted hall" effect which enchanted Queen Victoria.

The Gaelic name of the cave is An Uamh Ehinn or the "musical cave."

Although the island of Staffa has not been inhabited for more than 160 years, visitors can still explore the cave, thanks to the Laird of Staffa, Alastair de Watteville. In his hydrojet-equipped boat, *Fulmar,* the laird makes three trips a day from the quay at Ulva Ferry on the Isle of Mull to the rocky shores of Staffa. After docking, visitors are led along the basalt path and into Fingal's Cave. Inside, the noise of the pounding sea is deafening.

Another cave, **Clamshell Cave,** can also be visited, but only at low tide. Appropriately named, **Boat Cave** is accessible only by water.

Kenway Travel operates a range of excursions, cruises, and tours from Oban, Argyll, and the nearby Isle of Mull. There are daily sailings in summer (May 23 to September 26) to Staffa, Iona, Mull, and a variety of beauty spots on the Argyll coast. Visits to Staffa include opportunities to land on this unique island, explore Fingal's Cave, and study the remarkable sea caves formed in the hexagonal basalt. All trips present views of dramatic, beautiful scenery and sights of varied marine and seabird life. Puffins, cormorants, gannets, kittiwakes, fulmars, and many kinds of gull are frequently seen, as are seals and porpoises.

Prices are from £15 ($26.25) for day excursions to Mull, Staffa, and Iona. Kenway Travel is at 13 Stafford St., Oban (tel. Oban 64747).

RHUM: This enticingly named island lies about nine miles southwest of the previously explored Isle of Skye. There are those who will tell you not to go. "If you like a barren desert, where it rains all the time, you'll love Rhum," a skipper in Mallaig recently told me.

It's stark all right. And very wet. In fact, with more than 90 inches of rainfall recorded annually, it is said to be the "wettest" island of the Inner Hebrides.

Since the mid-'50s Rhum has been owned by the Nature Conservation Board, and they have wisely selected a considerate, conscientious warden, Laughton Johnston, to preside over the little "kingdom," which is only about eight by eight miles long. Obviously, conservation is of paramount importance on the island, and attempts are being made to bring back the sea-eagle, which used to live on the island in Victoria's day.

On this storm-tossed outpost, mountain climbers appear in summer to meet challenging peaks, and anglers are also attracted to the oceanic island by reports (which are accurate) of its good trout fishing. Bird-lovers seek out the Manx shearwaters which live on the island in great numbers. Red deer and ponies add color, along with the wildflowers of summer, to an otherwise bleak landscape.

Quite astonishingly, in such a foreboding place you come upon a hotel, **Kinloch Castle** (tel. Mallaig 2037), which is a mansion of imposing stature and grandeur, built by a wealthy British industrialist, Sir George Bullogh at the turn of the century. He wanted a retreat from the world, and in this monument to the opulence of the Edwardian era, he found it on Rhum. The location is at the top of a loch on the eastern coast of the island.

From around March until September, guests are accommodated at the castle, paying about $45 a day for a room and all meals, served on a dining table rescued from a yacht. The food is quite good, and in season, you are likely to be served Scottish salmon and venison. Only one bedroom has a private bath, as no one has seen fit to alter the original house plans (and who would want to?). Otherwise, the shared baths are quite grand.

The decor is exactly what you'd expect life in a castle to be: monumental paintings and lots of stuffed animals. Here you can experience what the lifestyle of a wealthy laird was all about.

To reach Rhum, you can take a passenger ferry from Mallaig, on the western coast of Scotland. It leaves about four times a week, and no cars are carried. A one-way passenger fare from Mallaig to Rhum is about $5.

EIGG: "Egg Island," as it is called, is reached by passenger ferry from Mallaig at a cost of $3.25 per person. Boats sail infrequently, so it's best to check with Caledonian MacBrayne (tel. 0475/33755).

The tiny island, about 4½ miles by 3, lies some four miles southeast of the just-explored Rhum. The laird of the island, Keith Schellenberg, an Englishman, purchased Eigg in 1975 at a reported cost of half a million dollars.

He welcomes visitors who come here to see the Sgurr of Eigg, a tall column of lava, said to be the biggest such pitchstone mass in the United Kingdom. Climbers on its north side try to reach its impressive height of 1300 feet.

After your arrival at Galmisdale, the principal hamlet and pier, you can take an antique omnibus to Cleadale. Once there, you walk across moors to Camas Sgiotaig, with its well-known beach of the Singing Sands (its black-and-white quartz grains are decidedly off-key). The cost of a ride across the green glen to the Singing Sands is only $2 for a one-way ticket.

If you want lunch or dinner, call **Mrs. Margaret Alderson** (tel. 0687/82428), who will provide something suitable for about £6 ($10.50). She'll also put you up overnight in a B&B-type establishment, charging from £10 ($17.50) per person, including a Scottish breakfast.

MUCK: Directly to the southwest of Eigg, Muck, unlike Rhum, has such an unappetizing name that visitors may turn away and not want to explore it. This little 2½ square miles is misnamed. Muck is not used in the sense we know it, but is based on a Gaelic word, *muic,* meaning the island of the sow. That, too, doesn't make it appealing, but it is much more attractive than its name, and many seabirds find it a suitable place for nesting.

Often storm-tossed by the ocean, Muck is actually a farm run by its resident laird, Lawrence MacEwen. There are hardly more than two dozen people on Muck, and all of them are concerned in some way with the running of the island farm.

Laird MacEwen runs the one hotel, **Port Mhor House** (tel. Mallaig 2362), which is actually a cottage skillfully converted to receive guests. The food often uses produce from the farm's garden, and the fare here is hearty. You can call ahead and reserve space in the dining room, even if you aren't a resident. Expect to spend from £8 ($14) for a meal. Later you can enjoy a malt whisky around an open log fire. A double bedroom rents for about £18 ($31.50) nightly. For reservations, write to the laird at Gallanach, Isle of Muck, Inverness.

Naturalists come here looking for everything from rare butterflies to otters. Visitors are allowed to visit the farm.

A one-way ferry ride from Mallaig (passengers only) costs $4.50.

CANNA: Some three miles northwest of Rhum, Canna is another of the so-called "Small Isles," and is really one of the hardest to reach. A one-way ferry from Mallaig is infrequent and unreliable, costing about $7 per passenger. Canna is not really in the tourist business, like Muck, and only the most persistent may want to seek it out.

The laird of the island, John Lorne Campbell, is concerned with farming, including the raising of Cheviot sheep and Highland cattle. He married a native of Pennsylvania, Margaret Shaw, and they have owned the island since before World War II. They are traditionalists, and believe mightily in the preservation of the Gaelic language and culture. In 1981 the laird willed the island to the National Trust of Scotland.

COLL AND TYREE: If you like your scenery stark and tranquil, try Coll and Tyree, tiny islands that attract those visitors seeking remoteness. On Tyree (also Tiree), the shell-sand machair increases the cultivable area, differentiating it from the inner isles.

A lot of British pensioners live on Coll and Tyree, and they seem to like to keep the place pretty much to themselves.

But the outside world intrudes when the ferry arrives. Sometimes that ferry doesn't come in, as gales often cause cancellations. The ferry stops at Mull and then, if conditions are right, goes on to Coll and Tyree.

If you go at the wrong time of year (and nobody knows when the wrong time is), you could easily be stranded for a while waiting for the next departure. By car ferry from Oban (via Mull), passengers are charged about $15 for the trip, and cars, depending on their size, are assessed at a rate ranging from $75 to $100. These are round-trip tariffs. Loganair also flies directly to Tyree from Glasgow, with about six scheduled flights weekly, an excursion fare costing $65.

On Tyree, try **Tyree Lodge Hotel** (tel. Scarinish 368), which has about eight rooms, but is comfortable and immaculately kept, charging around $25 per person nightly for a good Inner Hebrides breakfast and a hearty dinner.

Also on Tyree, **Balephetrish House** (tel. Scarinish 549) welcomes visitors to one of its small rooms, only five in all. Again, everything is kept spic and span, and your fellow guest at dinner that night is likely to be a geologist or a pensioner. Rates are cheaper than at the previously recommended lodge: about $20 daily per person for a good breakfast and a filling dinner, along with your room of course.

Coll offers the appropriately named **Isle of Coll Hotel** (tel. Coll 334), which to some looks a little rundown, but in this part of the world you welcome whatever comfort you find. Rates are from $32 to $38 per person nightly on the half-board arrangement.

7. Kintyre, Arran, and Islay

For many foreign visitors, the Atlantic seaboard of the old county of Argyll will represent a journey into the unknown. For those who want to sample a bygone age, this is one of the most rewarding trips off the coastline of western Scotland. My recommendations lie on islands, easily reached by ferries, except the Kintyre Peninsula which is a virtual island in itself. You'll soon discover that the Gaelic traditions of the islands endure. Peace and tranquility prevail.

ISLE OF ARRAN: At the mouth of the Firth of Clyde, this island is often described as Scotland in miniature, because of its wild and varied scenery, containing an assortment of glens, moors, lochs, sandy bays, and rocky coasts that have made the country famous. Ferry services making the 50-minute crossing operate from Ardrossan to Brodick, the major village of Arran, lying on the eastern shore. There are also ferry connections linking the northern part of Arran with the Kintyre Peninsula and the Highlands. Once on Arran, you'll find buses take you to the various villages, each with its own character. A coast road, 60 miles long, runs the length of the island.

Arran contains some splendid mountain scenery, notably the conical peak of **Goatfell** in the north, reaching a height of 2866 feet. It's called "the mountain of the winds."

Students of geology flock to Arran to study igneous rocks of the Tertiary Age. Cairns and standing stones at **Tormore** intrigue archeologists as well.

Arran is also filled with beautiful glens, especially **Glen Sannox** in the northeast and **Glen Rosa,** directly north of Brodick. In one day you can see a lot, as the island is only 25 miles long, 10 miles wide.

After the ferry docks at Brodick, you may want to head for Arran's major sight—**Brodick Castle** (tel. Brodick 2202), 1½ miles north of the Brodick pierhead. The historic home of the Dukes of Hamilton, the castle dates from the 13th century and contains antiques, portraits, and objets d'art. It is open on Easter weekend, then on Monday, Wednesday, and Saturday from 1 to 5 p.m. until May. From May 1 to September 30, hours are daily from 1 to 5 p.m. (last entry at 4:40 p.m.). The gardens are open all year, daily from 10 a.m. to 5 p.m. Admission to both the castle and gardens is £1.20 ($2.10) for adults, 65p ($1.14) for children.

Brodick

Altanna Hotel (tel. Brodick 2232) is less than half a mile from the village center with a sweeping view of the valley and high hills of Arran. There's an 18-hole golf course across from the hotel, and the beach is only 300 yards away. Within half a mile there is tennis as well as boating, fishing, and pony trekking. Owners Ian and Jill Waller welcome guests, usually for at least a week, but when possible one can stay by the day. The rate is £13.50 ($23.63) per person daily for half board. This includes VAT, and children are accepted at half the rate.

Hotel Ormidale (tel. Brodick 2293), across from the Brodick golf course, stands in seven acres of its own garden and woodlands. It's just a five-minute walk to the beach and shops, and 15 minutes from the ferry. Golfers will find the hotel is literally yards from the first tee. The hotel is fully licensed, offering 30 malt whiskies in the Tartan Lounge. There's a sun lounge and fisherman's bar for local color. The hotel is centrally heated, and the bedrooms have hot and cold water. B&B per person is £9.50 ($16.63) nightly, and you can have a full dinner starting at £5 ($8.75). Children up to 12 pay half this rate.

Kilmichael House Hotel (tel. Brodick 2219) is an oblong, neatly designed historic mansion house, surrounded by its own gardens, just one mile from the village, as well as golf, tennis, and the beach. If you wish, a picnic lunch can be prepared. In the evenings, before guests go to bed, tea and cookies are served in the living room. Each bedroom has hot and cold water and electric blankets. B&B is £7 ($12.25) per person, plus another £4 ($7) for dinner. Children are given reductions.

Whiting Bay

Burlington Private Hotel (tel. Whiting Bay 255) is a twin-gabled suburban home with bay windows and small surrounding garden. The proprietors have been accepting guests for quite a while, and many clients are repeat customers. Burlington stands on a stretch of sandy shore, convenient for golf, fishing, bathing, bowling, and dancing. The family-style lounge has color TV. For half board, the tariff per person is £11 ($19.25).

Stanford Guest House (tel. Whiting Bay 313), owned by Mr. and Mrs. J. Ritchie, is a small family-run guest house directly on the seafront. It's convenient for fishing, pony trekking, walks, or bowling. Catherine Ritchie prepares good-tasting breakfasts, and I'd advise arranging for an evening meal as well. The B&B rate is £8 ($14) per person including VAT. With dinner the tab rises to £12 ($21) per person. Bikes can be rented, as well as a 14-foot boat with engine, and fishing rods as well. Mrs. Ritchie will pack a picnic lunch for you. For evening there's a TV set in the guest lounge and always an enjoyable view from the bay windows. Children are welcomed at reduced rates. It's a friendly, congenial home.

Invermay Hotel (tel. Whiting Bay 431) is a neat, three-story suburban-style house right on the roadway, with a half-stone facade and bay windows. It faces the seafront across from an attractive bathing beach, with good scenic views. Run by Jill and Bobby Shand, who are thoughtful, considerate hosts, the guest home is kept immaculate. Rooms contain hot and cold running water and razor sockets, and all beds have electric blankets. The charge is £7 ($12.25) per person nightly for B&B. However, I recommend the half-board rate of £13 ($22.75) per person. The Shands specialize in good, Scottish slanted home-cookery such as porridge, haggis, cock-a-leekie soup, and other dishes. However, for those not desiring such dishes, there are other selections. Activities nearby include golf, fishing, climbing, pony trekking, and, of course, walking.

Kildonan

Breadalbane Hotel/Apartments (tel. Kildonan 284), a long, low white country hotel, has a dramatic location, directly on the water. Once a farmhouse, it has been extended and altered to make it a comfortable but unsophisticated place to stay. Each unit has a private bath, lounge, kitchen, electric blanket, and heating. The charge, not including VAT, is £8 ($14) to £16 ($28) for a unit which can sleep four or five persons. There is no service charge. Buffet lunches are served as well as light snacks at noon. There's color TV in the lounge, a room for games, plus an 18-hole putting course.

Lamlash

Glenisle Hotel (tel. Lamlash 258) is a whitewashed country place with well-kept gardens and a view across the bay to the Holy Isle. Its gardens, including a putting course, have flower beds and tall old trees. The public rooms are brightly treated, with a reception lounge, water-view dining room, plus a TV lounge. Each bedroom has its hot and cold water, a radio, electric blankets, tea and coffee makers, and room call. Daily cost for B&B is £8.50 ($14.88) per person, increasing to £11.75 ($20.56) per person in a unit with a private bath or shower. Dinner is an extra £6 ($10.50) per person. It's open from March to October.

The **Bay Hotel** (tel. Lamlash 224), opposite the yacht club, was once a fine country home, standing in its own garden, 100 yards back from the main road. Now converted into a hotel, it attracts guests who enjoy its home-cooking and comfortable bedrooms. Each chamber has innerspring mattresses and hot and cold water. Mrs. Isobel Shaw, the wife of the owner, sets the pace of friendliness and consideration. For half board, her terms are £12 ($21) per person nightly, only £9 ($15.75) for B&B. It's open in mid-May, closing in September.

KINTYRE PENINSULA: The longest peninsula in Scotland, Kintyre is more than 60 miles in length, containing much beautiful scenery, pleasant villages, and magnificent gardens on the Isle of Gigha, which lies off its western shores. The largest center on Kintyre is Campbeltown, and Tarbert in the north is also popular. In the evening you just might hear the music of the "ceilidhs" in hotels and village halls.

The major sight is an excursion to Gigha's famous gardens. They're called **Achamore** and are located a quarter of a mile from Ardminish on the Isle of Gigha. The island is reached by ferry boat which picks up passengers at the Tayinloan jetty on Kintyre. Weather permitting, sailings are about every 20 minutes.

These extensive gardens contain roses, hydrangeas, rhododendrons, camellias, and azaleas. They are open March to October from 10 a.m. to dusk, charging adults 50p (88¢); children, 30p (53¢).

Tarbert

A sheltered harbor protects this fishing port and yachting center which lies on a narrow neck of the northern tip of the Kintyre Peninsula, between West Loch Tarbert and the head of herring-filled Loch Fyne.

Campbeltown

This is a fishing port and resort with a shingle beach at the southern tip of the Kintyre peninsula. A mile to the southeast stands the ruins of Kilkerran Castle. You can ask in town about excursions to St. Kieran's Cave and the Islands of Davaar, which lie in the Campbeltown Loch.

Argyll Arms (tel. Campbeltown 3431) is the largest hotel in town, containing 32 bedrooms, some of which offer a private bath. Centrally heated throughout, the hotel has plain but adequate accommodations that go for £13 ($22.75) per person, including breakfast. Open all year, the hotel is fully licensed, containing a garage and a TV lounge. An evening meal is offered for £6 ($10.50). It's near golf and sandy beaches at Machrihanish (five miles away) and Southend (ten miles). Arrangements can be made for loch and river fishing.

ISLE OF ISLAY: The southernmost island of the Inner Hebrides, Islay lies 16 miles west of the Kintyre Peninsula and less than a mile southwest of Jura, from which it is separated only by a narrow sound. At its maximum breadth, Islay is only 15 miles wide (25 miles long).

Called "the Queen of the Hebrides," it is a peaceful unspoiled island of moors, salmon-filled lochs, sandy bays, and wild rocky cliffs. Islay was the ancient seat of the Lords of the Isles, and today you'll see the ruins of two castles and several Celtic crosses.

Near Port Charlotte are the graves of the U.S. seamen and army troops who lost their lives in 1918 when their carriers, the *Tuscania* and *Otranto*, were torpedoed off the shores of Islay. There's a memorial tower on the Mull of Oa, eight miles from Port Ellen.

The island is noted for its distilleries producing single-malt Highland whiskies by the antiquated pot-still method. Of these, **Laphroaig** at Port Ellen (tel. 0496/2418), allows guided tours on Tuesday and Thursday at 11 a.m. and 3 p.m. You should call first for an appointment.

Port Askaig

Port Askaig Hotel (tel. Port Askaig 245) is a genuine old island inn, dating from the 18th century, built on the site of an even older inn. It stands on the Sound of Islay overlooking the pier where a MacBrayne steamer berths daily. The hotel is quite charming, offering island hospitality and Scottish fare, including broiled trout, cock-a-leekie soup, roast pheasant, smoked Scottish salmon, and, of course, haggis. The hotel is a major destination for anglers on Islay, and the bar at the inn is popular with local fishermen. All year the friendly staff welcomes you to one of its modestly furnished bedrooms, costing from £16.75 ($29.31) in a single and from £27 ($47.25) in a double, including breakfast, service, and VAT. Children are granted reduced rates. Dinner is an extra £6.50 ($11.38). The hotel, incidentally, offers only nine rooms, half of which contain private baths.

Bridgend

Bridgend Hotel (tel. Bowmore 212) is a good base if you're crossing Islay, making your headquarters around the capital at Bowmore. All year the resident owners of this hotel will welcome you to their quiet retreat, opening onto Loch Indaal. The hotel is plainly furnished. The Bridgend offers only nine rooms, none of which contain private baths. For these, you pay from £14 ($24.50) per person, including breakfast. The half-board tariff is £22 ($38.50) per person. Meals—good, simple, unassuming cookery—are served between 7 and 7:30 p.m. The hotel also has a fully licensed cocktail bar.

ISLE OF JURA: This is the fourth-largest island in the Inner Hebrides. It perhaps takes its name from the Norse "Jura," meaning "deer island." The red deer on Jura outnumber the people by about 20 to 1. At four feet high, the deer are the largest wild animals roaming Scotland. The hearty islanders number only about 250 brave souls, and most of them live along the east coast. The west coast is virtually uninhabited.

The capital, **Craighouse,** is hardly more than a hamlet. It is connected by steamer to West Loch Tarbert on the Kintyre Peninsula. If you're already on Islay, you can journey to Jura by taking a five-minute ferry ride from Port Askaig, docking at the Feolin Ferry berth.

The breadth of Jura varies from two to eight miles, and at its maximum length it is 27 miles long. The island's landscape is dominated by the **Paps of Jura,** reaching a peak of 2571 feet at Beinn-an-Oir. An arm of the sea, **Loch Tarbert** nearly divides the island, cutting into it for nearly six miles.

The square tower of **Claig Castle,** now in ruins, was the stronghold of the MacDonalds until they were subdued by the Campbells in the 17th century.

Literary historians may be interested to know that George Orwell in the bitter postwar winters of 1946 and 1947 lived at Jura.

In splurge accommodations, the **Jura Hotel** (tel. Jura 243) at Craighouse is the only licensed premises on the island. Overlooking the sea, it actually has palms growing on its grounds, thanks to the benevolence of the Gulf Stream. All year it rents 18 bedrooms, four of which contain private baths. The tariff is £16 ($28) per person, including breakfast. The half-board terms are from £24 ($42) per person daily. Rooms are simply although agreeably furnished. However, bring along some mosquito repellant to combat the pest of the islands. Your host will dispense the local single-malt in a cozy little bar opening onto the bay. The peaty whisky is distilled right near the hotel.